Image Processing, Analysis, and Machine Vision

Image Processing, Analysis, and Machine Vision

Fourth Edition

Milan Sonka
The University of Iowa, Iowa City

Vaclav Hlavac
Czech Technical University, Prague

Roger Boyle
Prifysgol Aberystwyth, Aberystwyth

CENGAGE
Learning·

Australia • Brazil • Japan • Mexico • Singapore • United Kingdom • United States

10 0731R642

Image Processing, Analysis, and Machine Vision, Fourth Edition, International Edition
Milan Sonka, Vaclav Hlavac, and Roger Boyle

Publisher: Timothy L. Anderson

Senior Development Editor: Hilda Gowans

Senior Editorial Assistant: Tanya Altieri

Art and Cover Direction, Production Management: PreMediaGlobal

Compositor: Hrvoje Bugonovic

Rights Acquisition Director: Audrey Pettengill

Rights Acquisition Specialist, Text and Image: Amber Hosea

Text & Image Permissions Researcher: Kristiina Paul

Senior Manufacturing Planner: Doug Wilke

Cover Image: © Milan Sonka, Vaclav Hlavac, and Roger Boyle

International Edition:

ISBN–13: 978-1-133-59369-0

ISBN–10: 1-133-59369-0

Cengage Learning International Offices

Asia
www.cengageasia.com
tel: (65) 6410 1200

Australia/New Zealand
www.cengage.com.au
tel: (61) 3 9685 4111

Brazil
www.cengage.com.br
tel: (55) 11 3665 9900

India
www.cengage.co.in
tel: (91) 11 4364 1111

Latin America
www.cengage.com.mx
tel: (52) 55 1500 6000

UK/Europe/Middle East/Africa
www.cengage.co.uk
tel: (44) 0 1264 332 424

Represented in Canada by Nelson Education, Ltd.
www.nelson.com
tel: (416) 752 9100 / (800) 668 0671

Cengage Learning is a leading provider of customized learning solutions with office locations around the globe, including Singapore, the United Kingdom, Australia, Mexico, Brazil, and Japan. Locate your local office at: **www.cengage.com/global**

For product information and free companion resources:
www.cengage.com/international
Visit your local office: **www.cengage.com/global**
Visit our corporate website: **www.cengage.com**

AVAILABILITY OF RESOURCES MAY DIFFER BY REGION. Check with your local Cengage Learning representative for details.

Printed in the United States of America
1 2 3 4 5 6 7 17 16 15 14 13

Abbreviations

1D	one dimension(al)
2D, 3D, ...	two dimension(al), three dimension(al), ...
AAM	active appearance model
AGC	automatic gain control
AI	artificial intelligence
ART	adaptive resonance theory
ASM	active shape model
BBF	best bin first
BBN	Bayesian belief network
BRDF	bi-directional reflectance distribution function
B-rep	boundary representation
CAD	computer-aided design
CCD	charge-coupled device
CHMM	coupled HMM
CIE	International Commission on Illumination
CMOS	complementary metal-oxide semiconductor
CMY	cyan, magenta, yellow
CONDENSATION	CONditional DENSity propagATION
CRT	cathode ray tube
CSF	cerebro-spinal fluid
CSG	constructive solid geometry
CT	computed tomography
dB	decibel, 20 times the decimal logarithm of a ratio
DCT	discrete cosine transform
DFT	discrete Fourier transform
dof	degrees of freedom
DPCM	differential PCM
DWF	discrete wavelet frame
ECG	electro-cardiogram
EEG	electro-encephalogram
EM	expectation-maximization
FFT	fast Fourier transform
FLANN	fast library for approximate nearest neighbors
FOE	focus of expansion
GA	genetic algorithm

GB	Giga byte $= 2^{30}$ bytes $= 1,073,741,824$ bytes
GIS	geographic information system
GMM	Gaussian mixture model
GRBF	Gaussian radial basis function
GVF	gradient vector flow
HDTV	high definition TV
HLS	as HSI
HMM	hidden Markov model
HOG	histogram of oriented gradients
HSI	hue, saturation, intensity
HSL	as HSI
HSV	hue, saturation, value
ICA	independent component analysis
ICP	iterative closest point algorithm
ICRP	iterative closest reciprocal point algorithm
IHS	intensity, hue, saturation
JPEG	Joint Photographic Experts Group
Kb	Kilo bit $= 2^{10}$ bits $= 1,024$ bits
KB	Kilo byte $= 2^{10}$ bytes $= 1,024$ bytes
KLT	Kanade-Lucas-Tomasi (tracker)
LBP	local binary pattern
LCD	liquid crystal display
MAP	maximum a posteriori
Mb	Mega bit $= 2^{20}$ bits $= 1,048,576$ bits
MB	Mega byte $= 2^{20}$ bytes $= 1,048,576$ bytes
MB, MB2	Manzanera–Bernard skeletonization
MCMC	Monte Carlo Markov chain
MDL	minimum description length
MJPEG	motion JPEG
MPEG	moving picture experts group
MRF	Markov random field
MRI	magnetic resonance imaging
MR	magnetic resonance
MSE	mean-square error
MSER	maximally stable extremal region
ms	millisecond

μs	microsecond
OCR	optical character recognition
OS	order statistics
PCA	principal component analysis
PDE	partial differential equation
p.d.f.	probability density function
PDM	point distribution model
PET	positron emission tomography
PMF	Pollard-Mayhew-Frisby (correspondence algorithm)
PTZ	pan-tilt-zoom
RANSAC	RANdom SAmple Consensus
RBF	radial basis function
RCT	reversible component transform
RGB	red, green, blue
RMS	root mean square
SIFT	scale invariant feature transform
SKIZ	skeleton by inference zones
SLR	single lens reflex‘
SNR	signal-to-noise ratio
STFT	short term Fourier transform
SVD	singular value decomposition
SVM	support vector machine
TLD	tracking-learning-detection
TV	television
USB	universal serial bus

Symbols

$\arg(x, y)$	angle (in radians) from x axis to the point (x, y)
$\underset{i}{\mathrm{argmax}}\big(\mathrm{expr}(i)\big)$	the value of i that causes $\mathrm{expr}(i)$ to be maximal
$\underset{i}{\mathrm{argmin}}\big(\mathrm{expr}(i)\big)$	the value of i that causes $\mathrm{expr}(i)$ to be minimal
div	integer division or divergence
mod	remainder after integer division
$\mathrm{round}(x)$	largest integer which is not bigger than $x + 0.5$
$\emptyset$	empty set
A^c	complement of set A
$A \subset B,\ B \supset A$	set A is included in set B
$A \cap B$	intersection between sets A and B
$A \cup B$	union of sets A and B
$A \setminus B$	difference between sets A and B
$\mathbf{A}$	(uppercase bold) matrices
$\mathbf{x}$	(lowercase bold) vectors
$\|\mathbf{x}\|$	magnitude (or modulus) of vector $\mathbf{x}$
$\mathbf{x} \cdot \mathbf{y}$	scalar product between vectors $\mathbf{x}$ and $\mathbf{y}$
$\tilde{x}$	estimate of the value x
$|x|$	absolute value of a scalar
$\delta(x)$	Dirac function
Δx	small finite interval of x, difference
$\partial f / \partial x$	partial derivative of the function f with respect to x
$\nabla \mathbf{f}$, grad $\mathbf{f}$	gradient of $\mathbf{f}$
$\nabla^2 \mathbf{f}$	Laplace operator applied to $\mathbf{f}$
$f * g$	convolution between functions f and g
$F .* G$	element-by-element multiplication of matrices F, G
D_E	Euclidean distance
D_4	city block distance
D_8	chessboard distance
F^*	complex conjugate of the complex function F
$\mathrm{rank}(A)$	rank of a matrix A
T^*	transformation dual to transformation T, also complex conjugate of T
$\mathcal{E}$	mean value operator
$\mathcal{L}$	linear operator
$\mathcal{O}$	origin of the coordinate system

#	number of (e.g., pixels)
$\check{B}$	point set symmetrical to point set B
$\oplus$	morphological dilation
$\ominus$	morphological erosion
$\circ$	morphological opening
$\bullet$	morphological closing
$\otimes$	morphological hit-or-miss transformation
$\oslash$	morphological thinning
$\odot$	morphological thickening
$\wedge$	logical and
$\vee$	logical or
trace	sum of elements on the matrix main diagonal
cov	covariance matrix
sec	secant, $\sec \alpha = 1/\cos \alpha$

Contents

List of algorithms   xxi

Preface   xxv

Possible course outlines   xxxi

1 Introduction   1

     1.1   Motivation   1
     1.2   Why is computer vision difficult?   3
     1.3   Image representation and image analysis tasks   5
     1.4   Summary   9
     1.5   Exercises   10
     1.6   References   10

2 The image, its representations and properties   11

     2.1   Image representations, a few concepts   11
     2.2   Image digitization   14
         2.2.1   Sampling   14
         2.2.2   Quantization   15
     2.3   Digital image properties   16
         2.3.1   Metric and topological properties of digital images   16
         2.3.2   Histograms   23
         2.3.3   Entropy   24
         2.3.4   Visual perception of the image   25
         2.3.5   Image quality   27
         2.3.6   Noise in images   28
     2.4   Color images   30
         2.4.1   Physics of color   30
         2.4.2   Color perceived by humans   32
         2.4.3   Color spaces   36
         2.4.4   Palette images   38
         2.4.5   Color constancy   39
     2.5   Cameras: An overview   40
         2.5.1   Photosensitive sensors   40
         2.5.2   A monochromatic camera   42
         2.5.3   A color camera   44
     2.6   Summary   45

	2.7	Exercises	46
	2.8	References	48

3 The image, its mathematical and physical background   **50**

	3.1	Overview	50
		3.1.1 Linearity	50
		3.1.2 The Dirac distribution and convolution	51
	3.2	Linear integral transforms	52
		3.2.1 Images as linear systems	53
		3.2.2 Introduction to linear integral transforms	53
		3.2.3 1D Fourier transform	54
		3.2.4 2D Fourier transform	59
		3.2.5 Sampling and the Shannon constraint	62
		3.2.6 Discrete cosine transform	65
		3.2.7 Wavelet transform	66
		3.2.8 Eigen-analysis	72
		3.2.9 Singular value decomposition	73
		3.2.10 Principal component analysis	74
		3.2.11 Radon transform	77
		3.2.12 Other orthogonal image transforms	78
	3.3	Images as stochastic processes	79
	3.4	Image formation physics	82
		3.4.1 Images as radiometric measurements	82
		3.4.2 Image capture and geometric optics	83
		3.4.3 Lens aberrations and radial distortion	86
		3.4.4 Image capture from a radiometric point of view	89
		3.4.5 Surface reflectance	92
	3.5	Summary	95
	3.6	Exercises	97
	3.7	References	98

4 Data structures for image analysis   **100**

	4.1	Levels of image data representation	100
	4.2	Traditional image data structures	101
		4.2.1 Matrices	101
		4.2.2 Chains	104
		4.2.3 Topological data structures	106
		4.2.4 Relational structures	107
	4.3	Hierarchical data structures	108
		4.3.1 Pyramids	108
		4.3.2 Quadtrees	109
		4.3.3 Other pyramidal structures	111
	4.4	Summary	112
	4.5	Exercises	113
	4.6	References	115

5 Image pre-processing   **116**

	5.1	Pixel brightness transformations	117

	5.1.1	Position-dependent brightness correction	117
	5.1.2	Gray-scale transformation	117
5.2		Geometric transformations	120
	5.2.1	Pixel co-ordinate transformations	121
	5.2.2	Brightness interpolation	123
5.3		Local pre-processing	125
	5.3.1	Image smoothing	125
	5.3.2	Edge detectors	133
	5.3.3	Zero-crossings of the second derivative	139
	5.3.4	Scale in image processing	143
	5.3.5	Canny edge detection	144
	5.3.6	Parametric edge models	147
	5.3.7	Edges in multi-spectral images	148
	5.3.8	Local pre-processing in the frequency domain	148
	5.3.9	Line detection by local pre-processing operators	155
	5.3.10	Detection of corners (interest points)	156
	5.3.11	Detection of maximally stable extremal regions	160
5.4		Image restoration	162
	5.4.1	Degradations that are easy to restore	163
	5.4.2	Inverse filtering	163
	5.4.3	Wiener filtering	164
5.5		Summary	165
5.6		Exercises	167
5.7		References	174
6		**Segmentation I**	**178**
6.1		Thresholding	179
	6.1.1	Threshold detection methods	181
	6.1.2	Optimal thresholding	183
	6.1.3	Multi-spectral thresholding	186
6.2		Edge-based segmentation	187
	6.2.1	Edge image thresholding	188
	6.2.2	Edge relaxation	190
	6.2.3	Border tracing	191
	6.2.4	Border detection as graph searching	196
	6.2.5	Border detection as dynamic programming	206
	6.2.6	Hough transforms	210
	6.2.7	Border detection using border location information	217
	6.2.8	Region construction from borders	218
6.3		Region-based segmentation	220
	6.3.1	Region merging	221
	6.3.2	Region splitting	224
	6.3.3	Splitting and merging	225
	6.3.4	Watershed segmentation	229
	6.3.5	Region growing post-processing	232
6.4		Matching	232
	6.4.1	Template matching	233
	6.4.2	Control strategies of templating	235

6.5		Evaluation issues in segmentation	236
	6.5.1	Supervised evaluation	237
	6.5.2	Unsupervised evaluation	240
6.6		Summary	241
6.7		Exercises	245
6.8		References	248

7   Segmentation II   **255**

7.1		Mean shift segmentation	255
7.2		Active contour models—snakes	263
	7.2.1	Traditional snakes and balloons	264
	7.2.2	Extensions	267
	7.2.3	Gradient vector flow snakes	268
7.3		Geometric deformable models—level sets and geodesic active contours	273
7.4		Fuzzy connectivity	280
7.5		Towards 3D graph-based image segmentation	288
	7.5.1	Simultaneous detection of border pairs	289
	7.5.2	Suboptimal surface detection	293
7.6		Graph cut segmentation	295
7.7		Optimal single and multiple surface segmentation— LOGISMOS	303
7.8		Summary	317
7.9		Exercises	319
7.10		References	321

8   Shape representation and description   **329**

8.1		Region identification	333
8.2		Contour-based shape representation and description	335
	8.2.1	Chain codes	336
	8.2.2	Simple geometric border representation	337
	8.2.3	Fourier transforms of boundaries	341
	8.2.4	Boundary description using segment sequences	343
	8.2.5	B-spline representation	346
	8.2.6	Other contour-based shape description approaches	348
	8.2.7	Shape invariants	349
8.3		Region-based shape representation and description	353
	8.3.1	Simple scalar region descriptors	353
	8.3.2	Moments	358
	8.3.3	Convex hull	360
	8.3.4	Graph representation based on region skeleton	365
	8.3.5	Region decomposition	370
	8.3.6	Region neighborhood graphs	372
8.4		Shape classes	373
8.5		Summary	373
8.6		Exercises	375
8.7		References	379

9   Object recognition   **385**

| 9.1 | | Knowledge representation | 386 |

9.2	Statistical pattern recognition	390
	9.2.1 Classification principles	392
	9.2.2 Nearest neighbors	393
	9.2.3 Classifier setting	395
	9.2.4 Classifier learning	398
	9.2.5 Support vector machines	400
	9.2.6 Cluster analysis	406
9.3	Neural nets	407
	9.3.1 Feed-forward networks	409
	9.3.2 Unsupervised learning	411
	9.3.3 Hopfield neural nets	412
9.4	Syntactic pattern recognition	413
	9.4.1 Grammars and languages	415
	9.4.2 Syntactic analysis, syntactic classifier	417
	9.4.3 Syntactic classifier learning, grammar inference	420
9.5	Recognition as graph matching	421
	9.5.1 Isomorphism of graphs and subgraphs	421
	9.5.2 Similarity of graphs	425
9.6	Optimization techniques in recognition	426
	9.6.1 Genetic algorithms	427
	9.6.2 Simulated annealing	430
9.7	Fuzzy systems	432
	9.7.1 Fuzzy sets and fuzzy membership functions	432
	9.7.2 Fuzzy set operators	434
	9.7.3 Fuzzy reasoning	435
	9.7.4 Fuzzy system design and training	438
9.8	Boosting in pattern recognition	439
9.9	Random forests	442
	9.9.1 Random forest training	444
	9.9.2 Random forest decision making	446
	9.9.3 Random forest extensions	448
9.10	Summary	448
9.11	Exercises	452
9.12	References	459
10	**Image understanding**	**464**
10.1	Image understanding control strategies	466
	10.1.1 Parallel and serial processing control	466
	10.1.2 Hierarchical control	466
	10.1.3 Bottom-up control	467
	10.1.4 Model-based control	468
	10.1.5 Combined control	469
	10.1.6 Non-hierarchical control	472
10.2	SIFT: Scale invariant feature transform	474
10.3	RANSAC: Fitting via random sample consensus	477
10.4	Point distribution models	481
10.5	Active appearance models	492
10.6	Pattern recognition methods in image understanding	503

	10.6.1	Classification-based segmentation	503
	10.6.2	Contextual image classification	505
	10.6.3	Histograms of oriented gradients—HOG	509
10.7	Boosted cascades of classifiers	513
10.8	Image understanding using random forests	517
10.9	Scene labeling and constraint propagation	524
	10.9.1	Discrete relaxation	525
	10.9.2	Probabilistic relaxation	527
	10.9.3	Searching interpretation trees	530
10.10	Semantic image segmentation and understanding	531
	10.10.1	Semantic region growing	532
	10.10.2	Genetic image interpretation	534
10.11	Hidden Markov models	543
	10.11.1	Applications	548
	10.11.2	Coupled HMMs	549
	10.11.3	Bayesian belief networks	551
10.12	Markov random fields	553
	10.12.1	Applications to images and vision	555
10.13	Gaussian mixture models and expectation–maximization	556
10.14	Summary	564
10.15	Exercises	568
10.16	References	572

11 3D geometry, correspondence, 3D from intensities   **582**

11.1	3D vision tasks	583
	11.1.1	Marr's theory	585
	11.1.2	Other vision paradigms: Active and purposive vision	587
11.2	Basics of projective geometry	589
	11.2.1	Points and hyperplanes in projective space	590
	11.2.2	Homography	592
	11.2.3	Estimating homography from point correspondences	594
11.3	A single perspective camera	598
	11.3.1	Camera model	598
	11.3.2	Projection and back-projection in homogeneous coordinates	601
	11.3.3	Camera calibration from a known scene	602
11.4	Scene reconstruction from multiple views	602
	11.4.1	Triangulation	603
	11.4.2	Projective reconstruction	604
	11.4.3	Matching constraints	605
	11.4.4	Bundle adjustment	607
	11.4.5	Upgrading the projective reconstruction, self-calibration	608
11.5	Two cameras, stereopsis	609
	11.5.1	Epipolar geometry; fundamental matrix	610
	11.5.2	Relative motion of the camera; essential matrix	612
	11.5.3	Decomposing the fundamental matrix to camera matrices	613
	11.5.4	Estimating the fundamental matrix from point correspondences	614
	11.5.5	Rectified configuration of two cameras	615
	11.5.6	Computing rectification	617

11.6	Three cameras and trifocal tensor	619
	11.6.1 Stereo correspondence algorithms	621
	11.6.2 Active acquisition of range images	627
11.7	3D information from radiometric measurements	630
	11.7.1 Shape from shading	631
	11.7.2 Photometric stereo	635
11.8	Summary	636
11.9	Exercises	637
11.10	References	639

12 Use of 3D vision — **644**

12.1	Shape from X	644
	12.1.1 Shape from motion	644
	12.1.2 Shape from texture	651
	12.1.3 Other shape from X techniques	652
12.2	Full 3D objects	655
	12.2.1 3D objects, models, and related issues	655
	12.2.2 Line labeling	656
	12.2.3 Volumetric representation, direct measurements	658
	12.2.4 Volumetric modeling strategies	660
	12.2.5 Surface modeling strategies	662
	12.2.6 Registering surface patches and their fusion to get a full 3D model	663
12.3	2D view-based representations of a 3D scene	670
	12.3.1 Viewing space	670
	12.3.2 Multi-view representations and aspect graphs	670
12.4	3D reconstruction from an unorganized set of 2D views, and Structure from Motion	671
12.5	Reconstructing scene geometry	674
12.6	Summary	677
12.7	Exercises	678
12.8	References	680

13 Mathematical morphology — **684**

13.1	Basic morphological concepts	684
13.2	Four morphological principles	686
13.3	Binary dilation and erosion	687
	13.3.1 Dilation	688
	13.3.2 Erosion	689
	13.3.3 Hit-or-miss transformation	692
	13.3.4 Opening and closing	692
13.4	Gray-scale dilation and erosion	694
	13.4.1 Top surface, umbra, and gray-scale dilation and erosion	694
	13.4.2 Umbra homeomorphism theorem, properties of erosion and dilation, opening and closing	697
	13.4.3 Top hat transformation	698
13.5	Skeletons and object marking	699
	13.5.1 Homotopic transformations	699

13.5.2   Skeleton, medial axis, maximal ball   699
13.5.3   Thinning, thickening, and homotopic skeleton   701
13.5.4   Quench function, ultimate erosion   704
13.5.5   Ultimate erosion and distance functions   706
13.5.6   Geodesic transformations   707
13.5.7   Morphological reconstruction   709
13.6   Granulometry   711
13.7   Morphological segmentation and watersheds   713
13.7.1   Particle segmentation, marking, and watersheds   713
13.7.2   Binary morphological segmentation   714
13.7.3   Gray-scale segmentation, watersheds   716
13.8   Summary   717
13.9   Exercises   718
13.10 References   720

14 Image data compression   **722**

14.1   Image data properties   723
14.2   Discrete image transforms in image data compression   724
14.3   Predictive compression methods   727
14.4   Vector quantization   730
14.5   Hierarchical and progressive compression methods   730
14.6   Comparison of compression methods   732
14.7   Other techniques   733
14.8   Coding   733
14.9   JPEG and MPEG image compression   734
14.9.1   JPEG—still image compression   734
14.9.2   JPEG–2000 compression   736
14.9.3   MPEG—full-motion video compression   738
14.10 Summary   740
14.11 Exercises   742
14.12 References   744

15 Texture   **747**

15.1   Statistical texture description   750
15.1.1   Methods based on spatial frequencies   750
15.1.2   Co-occurrence matrices   752
15.1.3   Edge frequency   754
15.1.4   Primitive length (run length)   755
15.1.5   Laws' texture energy measures   757
15.1.6   Local binary patterns—LBPs   757
15.1.7   Fractal texture description   762
15.1.8   Multiscale texture description—wavelet domain approaches   764
15.1.9   Other statistical methods of texture description   768
15.2   Syntactic texture description methods   769
15.2.1   Shape chain grammars   770
15.2.2   Graph grammars   772
15.2.3   Primitive grouping in hierarchical textures   773

15.3 Hybrid texture description methods   775
15.4 Texture recognition method applications   776
15.5 Summary   777
15.6 Exercises   779
15.7 References   782

16 Motion analysis   **787**

16.1 Differential motion analysis methods   790
16.2 Optical flow   794
      16.2.1 Optical flow computation   794
      16.2.2 Global and local optical flow estimation   797
      16.2.3 Combined local–global optical flow estimation   800
      16.2.4 Optical flow in motion analysis   801
16.3 Analysis based on correspondence of interest points   804
      16.3.1 Detection of interest points   805
      16.3.2 Lucas–Kanade point tracking   805
      16.3.3 Correspondence of interest points   807
16.4 Detection of specific motion patterns   810
16.5 Video tracking   814
      16.5.1 Background modeling   815
      16.5.2 Kernel-based tracking   820
      16.5.3 Object path analysis   826
16.6 Motion models to aid tracking   831
      16.6.1 Kalman filters   831
      16.6.2 Particle filters   837
      16.6.3 Semi-supervised tracking—TLD   840
16.7 Summary   843
16.8 Exercises   846
16.9 References   848

Index   **853**

List of algorithms

2.1	Distance transform	20
2.2	Computing the brightness histogram	23
2.3	Generation of additive, zero mean Gaussian noise	28
4.1	Co-occurrence matrix $C_r(z, y)$ for the relation r	102
4.2	Integral image construction	103
5.1	Histogram equalization	119
5.2	Smoothing using a rotating mask	130
5.3	Efficient median filtering	131
5.4	Canny edge detector	146
5.5	Harris corner detector	159
5.6	Enumeration of extremal regions.	161
6.1	Basic thresholding	179
6.2	Otsu's threshold detection	184
6.3	Recursive multi-spectral thresholding	186
6.4	Non-maximal suppression of directional edge data	188
6.5	Hysteresis to filter output of an edge detector	189
6.6	Inner boundary tracing	191
6.7	Outer boundary tracing	193
6.8	Extended boundary tracing	195
6.9	Border tracing in gray-level images	196
6.10	A-algorithm graph search	198
6.11	Heuristic search for image borders	205
6.12	Boundary tracing as dynamic programming	208
6.13	Curve detection using the Hough transform	212
6.14	Generalized Hough transform	217
6.15	Region forming from partial borders	219
6.16	Region merging (outline)	221
6.17	Region merging via boundary melting	223
6.18	Split and merge	226
6.19	Split and link to the segmentation tree	227
6.20	Single-pass split-and-merge	228
6.21	Efficient watershed segmentation	230
6.22	Removal of small image regions	232
7.1	Mean shift mode detection	259
7.2	Mean shift discontinuity-preserving filtering	261
7.3	Mean shift image segmentation	262
7.4	Absolute fuzzy connectivity segmentation	282

7.5	Fuzzy object extraction	284
7.6	Fuzzy object extraction with preset connectedness	285
7.7	Graph cut segmentation	300
7.8	Optimal surface segmentation	304
7.9	Multiple optimal surface segmentation	311
8.1	4-neighborhood and 8-neighborhood region labeling	333
8.2	Region identification in run length encoded data	335
8.3	Quadtree region identification	335
8.4	Curvature estimation – HK2003 algorithm	338
8.5	Calculating area in quadtrees	354
8.6	Region area calculation from Freeman 4-connectivity chain code representation	354
8.7	Region convex hull construction	361
8.8	Simple polygon convex hull detection	363
8.9	Fully parallel skeleton by thinning – MB algorithm	366
8.10	Fully parallel skeleton by thinning – MB2 algorithm	367
8.11	Region graph construction from skeleton	370
9.1	Minimum distance classifier learning and classification	393
9.2	Nearest neighbor search with K-D trees	394
9.3	Learning and classification by estimating normal distribution probability densities	400
9.4	Support vector machine learning and classification	404
9.5	K-means cluster analysis	406
9.6	Back-propagation learning	410
9.7	Unsupervised learning of the Kohonen feature map	411
9.8	Recognition using a Hopfield net	413
9.9	Syntactic recognition	414
9.10	Graph isomorphism	424
9.11	Maximal clique location	425
9.12	Genetic algorithm	429
9.13	Simulated annealing optimization	431
9.14	Fuzzy system design	438
9.15	AdaBoost	440
9.16	AdaBoost-MH	441
10.1	Bottom-up control	467
10.2	Coronary border detection—a combined control strategy	471
10.3	Non-hierarchical control	472
10.4	Scale Invariant Feature Transform—SIFT	476
10.5	Random sample consensus for model fitting—RANSAC	478
10.6	Approximate alignment of similar training shapes	482
10.7	Fitting an ASM	487
10.8	AAM construction	492
10.9	Active appearance model matching	495
10.10	Contextual image classification	507
10.11	Recursive contextual image classification	508
10.12	HOG object detection and localization	510
10.13	Classifier generation for Viola-Jones face detection	514
10.14	Discrete relaxation	527

10.15	Probabilistic relaxation	529
10.16	Updating a region adjacency graph and dual to merge two regions	532
10.17	Semantic region merging	533
10.18	Genetic image segmentation and interpretation	537
10.19	Gaussian mixture parameters via expectation-maximization	559
10.20	Expectation-maximization (a generalization of Algorithm 10.19)	562
10.21	Baum-Welch training for HMMs (the forward-backward algorithm)	564
11.1	Image rectification	618
11.2	PMF stereo correspondence	626
11.3	Reconstructing shape from shading	633
12.1	Line labeling	657
12.2	Iterative closest reciprocal points	668
15.1	Auto-correlation texture description	750
15.2	Co-occurrence method of texture description	753
15.3	Edge-frequency texture description	754
15.4	Primitive-length texture description	756
15.5	Shape chain grammar texture synthesis	770
15.6	Texture primitive grouping	774
16.1	Relaxation computation of optical flow from dynamic image pairs	796
16.2	Optical flow computation from an image sequence	796
16.3	General Lucas–Kanade tracking	806
16.4	Velocity field computation from two consecutive images	808
16.5	Background maintenance by median filtering	816
16.6	Background maintenance by Gaussian mixtures	818
16.7	Kernel-based object tracking	823
16.8	Condensation (particle filtering)	837
16.9	Tracking-Learning-Detection—TLD	842

Preface

Image processing, analysis, and machine vision are an exciting and dynamic part of cognitive and computer science. Following an explosion of interest during the 1970s and 1980s, subsequent decades were characterized by a maturing of the field and significant growth of active applications; remote sensing, technical diagnostics, autonomous vehicle guidance, biomedical imaging (2D, 3D, and 4D) and automatic surveillance are the most rapidly developing areas. This progress can be seen in an increasing number of software and hardware products on the market—as a single example of many, the omnipresence of consumer-level digital cameras, each of which depends on a sophisticated chain of embedded consumer-invisible image processing steps performed in real time, is striking. Reflecting this continuing development, the number of digital image processing and machine vision courses offered at universities worldwide continues to increase rapidly.

There are many texts available in the areas we cover—a lot of them are referenced in this book. The subject suffers, however, from a shortage of texts which are 'complete' in the sense that they are accessible to the novice, of use to the educated, and up to date. Here we present the fourth edition of a text first published in 1993. We include many of the very rapid developments that have taken and are still taking place, which quickly age some of the very good textbooks produced in the recent past.

Our target audience spans the range from the undergraduate with negligible experience in the area through to the Master's, Ph.D., and research student seeking an advanced springboard in a particular topic. The entire text has been updated since the third version (particularly with respect to most recent development and associated references). We retain the same Chapter structure, but many sections have been rewritten or introduced as new. Among the new topics are the Radon transform, a unified approach to image/template matching, efficient object skeletonization (MB and MB2 algorithms), nearest neighbor classification including BBF/FLANN, histogram-of-oriented-Gaussian (HOG) approach to object detection, random forests, Markov random fields, Bayesian belief networks, scale invariant feature transform (SIFT), recent 3D image analysis/vision development, texture description using local binary patterns, and several point tracking approaches for motion analysis. Approaches to 3D vision evolve especially quickly and we have revised this material and added new comprehensive examples. In addition, several sections have been rewritten or expanded in response to reader and reviewer comments. All in all, about 15% of this edition consists of newly written material presenting state-of-the-art methods and techniques that already have proven their importance in the field; additionally, the whole text has been edited for currency and to correct a small number of oversights detected in the previous edition.

In response to demand, we have re-incorporated exercises (both short-form questions, and longer problems frequently requiring practical usage of computer tools and/or development of application programs) into this text. These re-use the valuable practical companion text to the third edition [Svoboda et al., 2008], but also cover material that was not present in earlier editions. The companion text provides Matlab-based implementations, introduces additional problems, explains steps leading to solutions, and provides many useful linkages to allow practical use: a Solution Manual is available via the Cengage secure server to registered instructors. In preparing this edition, we gratefully acknowledge the help and support of many people, in particular our reviewers Saeid Belkasim, Georgia State University, Thomas C. Henderson, University of Utah, William Hoff, Colorado School of Mines, Lina Karam, Arizona State University, Peter D. Scott, the University at Buffalo, SUNY and Jane Zhang, California Polytechnic State University. Richard W. Penney, Worcestershire, UK gave close attention to our third edition which has permitted the correction of many shortcomings. At our own institutions, Reinhard Beichel, Gary Christensen, Hannah Dee, Mona Garvin, Ian Hales, Sam Johnson, Derek Magee, Ipek Oguz, Kalman Palagyi, Andrew Rawlins, Joe Reinhardt, Punam Saha, and Xiaodong Wu have been a constant source of feedback, inspiration and encouragement.

This book reflects the authors' experience in teaching one- and two-semester undergraduate and graduate courses in Digital Image Processing, Digital Image Analysis, Image Understanding, Medical Imaging, Machine Vision, Pattern Recognition, and Intelligent Robotics at their respective institutions. We hope that this combined experience will give a thorough grounding to the beginner and provide material that is advanced enough to allow the more mature student to understand fully the relevant areas of the subject. We acknowledge that in a very short time the more active areas will have moved beyond this text.

This book could have been arranged in many ways. It begins with low-level processing and works its way up to higher levels of image interpretation; the authors have chosen this framework because they believe that image understanding originates from a common database of information. The book is formally divided into 16 chapters, beginning with low-level processing and working toward higher-level image representation, although this structure will be less apparent after Chapter 12, when we present mathematical morphology, image compression, texture, and motion analysis which are very useful but often special-purpose approaches that may not always be included in the processing chain.

Decimal section numbering is used, and equations and figures are numbered within each chapter. Each chapter is supported by an extensive list of references and exercises. A selection of algorithms is summarized formally in a manner that should aid implementation. Not all the algorithms discussed are presented in this way (this might have doubled the length of the book); we have chosen what we regard as the key, or most useful or illustrative, examples for this treatment. Each chapter further includes a concise Summary section, Short-answer questions, and Problems/Exercises.

Chapters present material from an introductory level through to an overview of current work; as such, it is unlikely that the beginner will, at the first reading, expect to absorb all of a given topic. Often it has been necessary to make reference to material in later chapters and sections, but when this is done an understanding of material in hand will not depend on an understanding of that which comes later. It is expected that the more advanced student will use the book as a reference text and signpost to current activity in the field—we believe at the time of going to press that the reference list is full in its indication of current directions, but record here our apologies to any work we have overlooked. The serious reader will note that the reference list contains citations of both the classic material that has survived the test of time as well as references that are very recent and represent what the authors consider promising new directions. Of course, before long, more relevant work will have been published that is not listed here.

This is a long book and therefore contains material sufficient for much more than one course. Clearly, there are many ways of using it, but for guidance we suggest an ordering that would generate five distinct modules:

Digital Image Processing I, an undergraduate course.

Digital Image Processing II, an undergraduate/graduate course, for which Digital Image Processing I may be regarded as prerequisite.

Computer Vision I, an undergraduate/graduate course, for which Digital Image Processing I may be regarded as prerequisite.

Computer Vision II, a graduate course, for which Computer Vision I may be regarded as prerequisite.

Image Analysis and Understanding, a graduate course, for which Computer Vision I may be regarded as prerequisite.

The important parts of a course, and necessary prerequisites, will naturally be specified locally; a suggestion for partitioning the contents follows this Preface.

Assignments should wherever possible make use of existing software; it is our experience that courses of this nature should not be seen as 'programming courses', but it is the case that the more direct practical experience the students have of the material discussed, the better is their understanding. Since the first edition was published, an explosion of web-based material has become available, permitting many of the exercises we present to be conducted without the necessity of implementing from scratch. We do not present explicit pointers to Web material, since they evolve so quickly; however, pointers to specific support materials for this book and others may be located via the designated book web page, http://www.cengage.com/engineering .

In addition to the print version, this textbook is also available online through **MindTap**, a personalized learning program. If you purchase the *MindTap* version of this book, you will obtain access to the book's *MindTap Reader* and will be able to complete assignments online. If your class is using a *Learning Management System* (such as *Blackboard, Moodle,* or *Angel*) for tracking course content, assignments, and grading, you can seamlessly access the *MindTap* suite of content and assessments for this course. In *MindTap*, instructors can:

- Personalize the learning path to match the course syllabus by rearranging content, hiding sections, or appending original material to the textbook content.

- Connect a *Learning Management System* portal to the online course and Reader.

- Customize online assessments and assignments.

- Track student progress and comprehension with the Progress application.

- Promote student engagement through interactivity and exercises.

Additionally, students can listen to the text through *ReadSpeaker*, take notes and highlight content for easy reference, as well as self-check their understanding of the material.

The book has been prepared using the LaTeX text processing system. Its completion would have been impossible without extensive usage of the Internet computer network and electronic mail. We would like to acknowledge the University of Iowa, the Czech Technical University, the Department of Computer Science at Prifysgol Aberystwyth, and the School of Computing at the University of Leeds for providing the environment in which this book was born and re-born.

Milan Sonka is Director of the Iowa Institute for Biomedical Imaging, Professor/Chair of Electrical & Computer Engineering, and Professor of Ophthalmology & Visual Sciences and Radiation Oncology at the University of Iowa, Iowa City, Iowa, USA. His research interests include medical image analysis, computer-aided diagnosis, and machine vision. Václav Hlaváč is Professor of Cybernetics at the Czech Technical University, Prague. His research interests are knowledge-based image analysis, 3D model-based vision and relations between statistical and structural pattern recognition. Roger Boyle very recently retired from the School of Computing at the University of Leeds, England, where he had been Head. His research interests are in low-level vision and pattern recognition, and he now works within the UK National Phenomics Centre at Prifysgol Aberystwyth, Cymru.

All authors have contributed throughout—the ordering on the cover corresponds to the weight of individual contribution. Any errors of fact are the joint responsibility of all.

Final typesetting has been the responsibility of Hrvoje Bogunović at the University of Iowa. This fourth collaboration has once more jeopardized domestic harmony by consuming long periods of time; we remain very happy to invest more work in this text in response to readers' comments.

References

Svoboda T., Kybic J., and Hlavac V. *Image Processing, Analysis, and Machine Vision: A MATLAB Companion.* Thomson Engineering, 2008.

Milan Sonka

The University of Iowa
Iowa City, Iowa, USA

milan-sonka@uiowa.edu
http://www.engineering.uiowa.edu/~sonka

Václav Hlaváč

Czech Technical University
Prague, Czech Republic

hlavac@cmp.felk.cvut.cz
http://cmp.felk.cvut.cz/~hlavac

Roger Boyle

Prifysgol Aberystwyth
United Kingdom

rogerdboyle@gmail.com
http://users.aber.ac.uk/rob21/

Possible course outlines

Here, one possible ordering of the material covered in the five courses proposed in the Preface is given. This should not, of course, be considered the only option—on the contrary, the possibilities for organizing Image Processing and Analysis courses are practically endless. Therefore, what follows shall only be regarded as suggestions, and instructors shall tailor content to fit the assumed knowledge, abilities, and needs of the students enrolled.

Figure 1 shows course pre-requisite dependencies of the proposed ordering. Figure 2 shows the mapping between the proposed course outlines and the material covered in the individual chapters and sections.

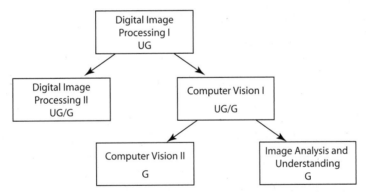

Figure 1: Pre-requisite dependencies of the proposed five courses. UG = undergraduate course, G = graduate course. © *Cengage Learning 2015.*

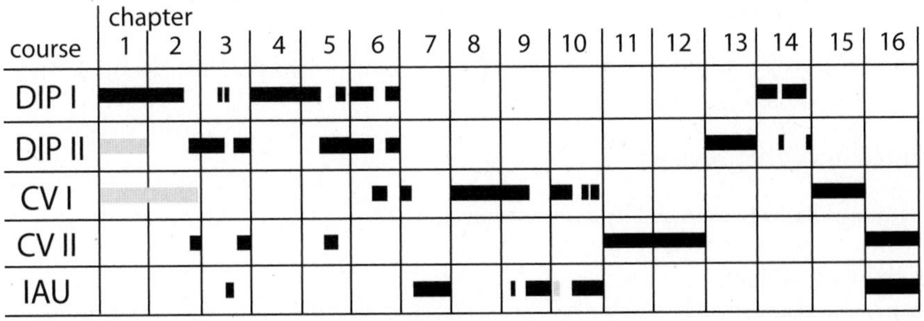

Figure 2: Mapping between the proposed course outlines and material covered in individual chapters and sections. See course outlines for details. © *Cengage Learning 2015.*

Digital Image Processing I (DIP I)

An undergraduate course.

1 Introduction

2 The image, its representation and properties

      2.1 Image representations

      2.2 Image digitization

      2.3 Digital image properties

4 Data structures for image analysis

5 Image pre-processing

      5.1 Pixel brightness transformations

      5.2 Geometric transformations

      5.3 Local pre-processing (except 5.3.6–5.3.7, 5.3.9–5.3.11, limited coverage of 5.3.4, 5.3.5)

      5.4 Image restoration (except 5.4.3)

6 Segmentation I

      6.1 Thresholding (except 6.1.3)

      6.2 Edge-based segmentation (except 6.2.4, 6.2.5, 6.2.7, 6.2.8)

      6.3 Region growing segmentation (except 6.3.4)

      6.4 Matching

      6.5 Evaluation issues in segmentation

3 The image, its mathematical and physical background

      3.2 Linear integral transforms (3.2.1–3.2.4, 3.2.6 only)

14 Image data compression (except wavelet compression, except 14.9)

   Practical image processing projects

Digital Image Processing II (DIP II)

An undergraduate/graduate course, for which Digital Image Processing I may be regarded as prerequisite.

1 Introduction (brief review)

2 The image, its representation and properties

      2.4 Color images

      2.5 Cameras

3 The image, its mathematical and physical background (except 3.2.8–3.2.10)

5   Image pre-processing

     5.3.4   Scale in image processing

     5.3.5   Canny edge detection

     5.3.6   Parametric edge models

     5.3.7   Edges in multi-spectral images

     5.3.8   Pre-processing in frequency domain

     5.3.9   Line detection

     5.3.10   Corner detection

     5.3.11   Maximally stable extremal regions

       5.4   Image restoration

6   Segmentation I

       6.1   Thresholding – considering color image data

     6.2.1   Edge image thresholding – considering color image data

  6.3.1–3   Region-based segmentation – considering color image data

       6.4   Matching – considering color image data

14   Image compression

      14.2   Discrete image transforms in image compression

      14.9   JPEG and MPEG

13   Mathematical morphology

  Practical image processing projects

Computer Vision I (CV I)

An undergraduate/graduate course, for which Digital Image Processing I may be regarded as prerequisite.

1   Introduction (brief review)

2   The image, its representation and properties (brief review)

6   Segmentation I

     6.2.4   Border detection as graph searching

     6.2.5   Border detection as dynamic programming

     6.2.7   Border detection using border location information

     6.2.8   Region construction from borders

     6.3.4   Watershed segmentation

7   Segmentation II

7.1 Mean shift segmentation

7.2 Active contour models

8 Shape representation and description

9 Object recognition

9.1 Knowledge representation

9.2 Statistical pattern recognition (except 9.2.5)

9.3 Neural networks

9.4 Syntactic pattern recognition

10 Image understanding

10.1 Image understanding control strategies

10.2 SIFT

10.3 RANSAC

10.6 Pattern recognition methods in image understanding

10.9 Scene labeling

10.10 Semantic image segmentation and understanding

15 Texture

Practical computer vision projects

Computer Vision II (CV II)

A graduate course, for which Computer Vision I may be regarded as prerequisite.

2 The image, its representation and properties

2.4 Color images

2.5 Cameras

3 The image, its mathematical and physical background

3.4 Image formation physics

5 Image pre-processing

5.3.4 Scale in image processing

5.3.5 Canny edge detection

5.3.6 Parametric edge models

5.3.7 Edges in multi-spectral images

5.3.9 Line detection

5.3.10 Corner detection

5.3.11 Maximally stable extremal regions

11 3D Vision, geometry and radiometry

12 Use of 3D vision

16 Motion analysis

Practical 3D vision projects

Image Analysis and Understanding (IAU)

A graduate course, for which Computer Vision I may be regarded as prerequisite.

7 Segmentation II (except 7.1, 7.2)

9 Object recognition

  9.2.5 Support vector machines

  9.5 Recognition as graph matching

  9.6 Optimization techniques in recognition

  9.7 Fuzzy systems

  9.8 Boosting in pattern recognition

  9.9 Random forests

3 The image, its mathematical and physical background

  3.2.8 Eigen analysis

  3.2.9 Singular value decomposition

  3.2.10 Principal component analysis

10 Image understanding

  10.1 Image understanding control strategies

  10.4 Point distribution models

  10.5 Active appearance models

  10.7 Boosted cascade of classifiers

  10.8 Image understanding using random forests

  10.11 Hidden Markov models

  10.12 Markov random fields

  10.13 Gaussian mixture models and expectation maximization

16 Motion analysis

Practical image understanding projects

Chapter 1

Introduction

1.1 Motivation

Vision allows humans to perceive and understand the world surrounding them, while computer vision aims to duplicate the effect of human vision by electronically perceiving and understanding an image. Books other than this one would dwell at length on this sentence and the meaning of the word 'duplicate'—whether computer vision is *simulating* or *mimicking* human systems is philosophical territory, and very fertile territory too.

Giving computers the ability to see is not an easy task—we live in a three-dimensional (3D) world, and when computers try to analyze objects in 3D space, the visual sensors available (e.g., TV cameras) usually give two-dimensional (2D) images, and this projection to a lower number of dimensions incurs an enormous loss of information. Sometimes, equipment will deliver images that are 3D but this may be of questionable value: analyzing such datasets is clearly more complicated than 2D, and sometimes the 'three-dimensionality' is less than intuitive to us ... terahertz scans are an example of this. Dynamic scenes such as those to which we are accustomed, with moving objects or a moving camera, are increasingly common and represent another way of making computer vision more complicated.

Figure 1.1 could be witnessed in thousands of farmyards in many countries, and serves to illustrate just some of the problems that we will face.

Figure 1.1: A frame from a video of a typical farmyard scene: the cow is one of a number walking naturally from right to left. *Courtesy of D. R. Magee, University of Leeds.*

There are many reasons why we might wish to study scenes such as this, which are attractively simple *to us*. The beast is moving slowly, it is clearly black and white, its movement is rhythmic, etc.; however, automated analysis is very fraught—in fact, the animal's boundary is often very difficult to distinguish clearly from the background, the motion of the legs is self-occluding and (subtly) the concept of 'cow-shaped' is not something easily encoded. The application from which this picture was taken[1] made use of many of the algorithms presented in this book: starting at a low level, moving features were identified and grouped. A 'training phase' taught the system what a cow might look like in various poses (see Figure 1.2), from which a model of a 'moving' cow could be derived (see Figure 1.3).

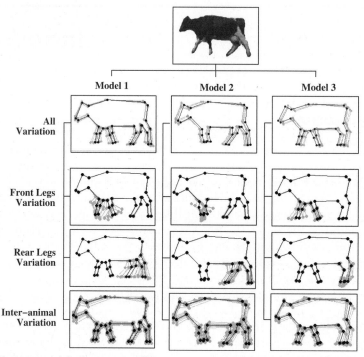

Figure 1.2: Various models for a cow silhouette: a straight-line boundary approximation has been learned from training data and is able to adapt to different animals and different forms of occlusion. *Courtesy of D. R. Magee, University of Leeds.*

These models could then be fitted to new ('unseen') video sequences. Crudely, at this stage anomalous behavior such as lameness could be detected by the model failing to fit properly, or well.

Thus we see a sequence of operations—image capture, early processing, segmentation, model fitting, motion prediction, qualitative/quantitative conclusion—that is characteristic of image understanding and computer vision problems. Each of these phases (which may not occur sequentially!) may be addressed by a number of algorithms which we shall cover in due course.

---

[1] The application was serious; there is a growing need in modern agriculture for automatic monitoring of animal health, for example to spot lameness. A limping cow is trivial for a human to identify, but it is very challenging to do this automatically.

Figure 1.3: Three frames from a cow sequence: notice the model can cope with partial occlusion as the animal enters the scene, and the different poses exhibited. *Courtesy of D. R. Magee, University of Leeds.*

This example is relatively simple to explain, but serves to illustrate that many computer vision techniques use the results and methods of mathematics, pattern recognition, artificial intelligence (AI), psycho-physiology, computer science, electronics, and other scientific disciplines.

Why is computer vision hard? As an exercise, consider a single gray-scale (monochromatic) image: put the book down and before proceeding write down a few reasons why you feel automatic inspection and analysis of it may be difficult.

1.2 Why is computer vision difficult?

This philosophical question provides some insight into the complex landscape of computer vision. It can be answered in many ways: we briefly offer six—most of them will be discussed in more detail later in the book.

Loss of information in 3D → 2D is a phenomenon which occurs in typical image capture devices such as a camera or an eye. Their geometric properties have been approximated by a pinhole model for centuries (a box with a small hole in it—a 'camera obscura' in Latin). This physical model corresponds to a mathematical model of perspective projection; Figure 1.4 summarizes the principle. The projective transformation maps points along rays but does not preserve angles and collinearity.

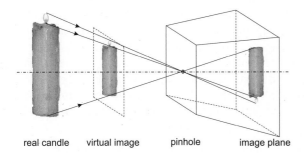

real candle   virtual image   pinhole   image plane

Figure 1.4: The pinhole model of imaging geometry does not distinguish size of objects. © *Cengage Learning 2015.*

The main trouble with the pinhole model and a single available view is that the projective transformation sees a small object close to the camera in the same way as a big object remote from the camera. In this case, a human needs a 'yardstick' to guess the actual size of the object which the computer does not have.

Interpretation of image(s) is a problem humans solve unwittingly that is the principal tool of computer vision. When a human tries to understand an image then previous knowledge and experience is brought to the current observation. Human ability to reason allows representation of long-gathered knowledge, and its use to solve new problems. Artificial intelligence has worked for decades to endow computers with the capability to understand observations; while progress has been tremendous, the practical ability of a machine to understand observations remains very limited.

From the mathematical logic and/or linguistics point of view, image interpretation can be seen as a mapping

$$interpretation: image\ data \longrightarrow model.$$

The (logical) model means some specific world in which the observed objects make sense. Examples might be nuclei of cells in a biological sample, rivers in a satellite image, or parts in an industrial process being checked for quality. There may be several interpretations of the same image(s). Introducing interpretation to computer vision allows us to use concepts from mathematical logic, linguistics as syntax (rules describing correctly formed expressions), and semantics (study of meaning). Considering observations (images) as an instance of formal expressions, semantics studies relations between expressions and their meanings. The interpretation of image(s) in computer vision can be understood as an instance of semantics.

Practically, if the image understanding algorithms know into which particular domain the observed world is constrained, then automatic analysis can be used for complicated problems.

Noise is inherently present in each measurement in the real world. Its existence calls for mathematical tools which are able to cope with uncertainty; an example is probability theory. Of course, more complex tools make the image analysis much more complicated compared to standard (deterministic) methods.

Too much data. Images are big, and video—increasingly the subject of vision applications–correspondingly bigger. Technical advances make processor and memory requirements much less of a problem than they once were, and much can be achieved with consumer level products. Nevertheless, efficiency in problem solutions is still important and many applications remain short of real-time performance.

Brightness measured in images is given by complicated image formation physics. The radiance ($\approx$ brightness, image intensity) depends on the irradiance (light source type, intensity and position), the observer's position, the surface local geometry, and the surface reflectance properties. The inverse tasks are ill-posed—for example, to reconstruct local surface orientation from intensity variations. For this reason, image-capture physics is usually avoided in practical attempts at image understanding. Instead, a direct link between the appearance of objects in scenes and their interpretation is sought.

Local window vs. need for global view. Commonly, image analysis algorithms analyze a particular storage bin in an operational memory (e.g., a pixel in the image) and its local neighborhood; the computer sees the image through a keyhole; this makes it very difficult to understand more global context. This problem has a long tradition in artificial intelligence: in the 1980s McCarthy argued that formalizing context was a crucial step toward the solution of the problem of generality. It is often very difficult to interpret an image if it is seen only locally or if only a few local keyholes are available. Figure 1.5 illustrates this pictorially. How context is taken into account is an important facet of image analysis.

Figure 1.5: Illustration of the world seen through several keyholes providing only a local context. It is very difficult to guess what object is depicted; the complete image is shown in Figure 1.6. © *Cengage Learning 2015.*

1.3 Image representation and image analysis tasks

Image understanding by a machine can be seen as an attempt to find a relation between input image(s) and previously established models of the observed world. Transition from the input image(s) to the model reduces the information contained in the image to relevant information for the application domain. This process is usually divided into several steps and several levels representing the image are used. The bottom layer contains raw image data and the higher levels interpret the data. Computer vision designs these intermediate representations and algorithms serving to establish and maintain relations between entities within and between layers.

Image representation can be roughly divided according to data organization into four levels, see Figure 1.7. The boundaries between individual levels are inexact, and more detailed divisions are also proposed in the literature. Figure 1.7 suggests a bottom up approach, from signals with almost no abstraction, to the highly abstract description needed for image understanding. Note that the flow of information does not need to be unidirectional; often feedback loops are introduced which allow the modification of algorithms according to intermediate results.

This hierarchy of image representation and related algorithms is frequently categorized in an even simpler way—*low-level* image processing and *high-level* image understanding.

Low-level processing methods usually use very little knowledge about the content of images. In the case of the computer knowing image content, it is usually provided by high-level algorithms or directly by a human who understands the problem domain. Low-level methods may include image compression, pre-processing methods for noise filtering, edge extraction, and image sharpening, all of which we shall discuss in this book. Low-level image processing uses data which resemble the input image; for example, an input image captured by a TV camera is 2D in nature, being described by an image function $f(x, y)$ whose value, at simplest, is usually brightness depending on the co-ordinates x, y of the location in the image.

If the image is to be processed using a computer it will be digitized first, after which it may be represented by a rectangular matrix with elements corresponding to the brightness at appropriate image locations. More probably, it will be presented in color, implying (usually) three channels: red, green and blue. Very often, such a data set will

Figure 1.6: It is easy for humans to interpret an image if it is seen globally: compare to Figure 1.5. © *Cengage Learning 2015.*

be part of a video stream with an associated frame rate. Nevertheless, the raw material will be a set or sequence of matrices which represent the inputs and outputs of low-level image processing.

High-level processing is based on knowledge, goals, and plans of how to achieve those goals, and artificial intelligence methods are widely applicable. High-level computer vision tries to imitate human cognition (although be mindful of the health warning given in the very first paragraph of this chapter) and the ability to make decisions according to the information contained in the image. In the example described, high-level knowledge would be related to the 'shape' of a cow and the subtle interrelationships between the different parts of that shape, and their (inter-)dynamics.

High-level vision begins with some form of formal model of the world, and then the 'reality' perceived in the form of digitized images is compared to the model. A match is attempted, and when differences emerge, partial matches (or subgoals) are sought that overcome them; the computer switches to low-level image processing to find information needed to update the model. This process is then repeated iteratively, and 'understanding' an image thereby becomes a co-operation between top-down and bottom-up processes. A feedback loop is introduced in which high-level partial results create tasks for low-level image processing, and the iterative image understanding process should eventually converge to the global goal.

Computer vision is expected to solve very complex tasks, the goal being to obtain similar results to those provided by biological systems. To illustrate the complexity of these tasks, consider Figure 1.8 in which a particular image representation is presented—

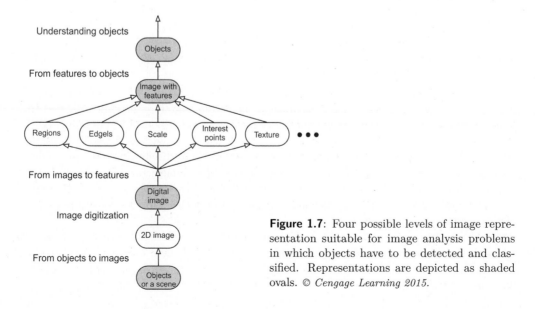

Figure 1.7: Four possible levels of image representation suitable for image analysis problems in which objects have to be detected and classified. Representations are depicted as shaded ovals. © *Cengage Learning 2015.*

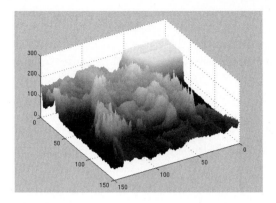

Figure 1.8: An unusual image representation. © *R.D. Boyle 2015.*

the value on the vertical axis gives the brightness of its corresponding location in the [gray-scale] image. Consider what this image might be before looking at Figure 1.9, which is a rather more common representation of the same image.

Both representations contain exactly the same information, but for a human observer it is very difficult to find a correspondence between them, and without the second, it is unlikely that one would recognize the face of a child. The point is that a lot of a priori knowledge is used by humans to interpret the images; the machine only begins with an array of numbers and so will be attempting to make identifications and draw conclusions from data that to us are more like Figure 1.8 than Figure 1.9. Increasingly, data capture equipment is providing very large data sets that do *not* lend themselves to straightforward interpretation by humans—we have already mentioned terahertz imaging as an example. Internal image representations are not directly understandable—while the computer is able to process local parts of the image, it is difficult for it to locate global knowledge. General knowledge, domain-specific knowledge, and information extracted from the image will be essential in attempting to 'understand' these arrays of numbers.

Low-level computer vision techniques overlap almost completely with digital image processing, which has been practiced for decades. The following sequence of processing steps is commonly seen: An image is captured by a sensor (such as a camera) and digitized; then the computer suppresses noise (image pre-processing) and maybe enhances some object features which are relevant to understanding the image. Edge extraction is an example of processing carried out at this stage.

Image segmentation is the next step, in which the computer tries to separate objects from the image background and from each other. Total and partial segmentation may be distinguished; total segmentation is possible only for very simple tasks, an example being the recognition of dark non-touching objects from a light background. For example, in analyzing images of printed text (an early step in optical character recognition, OCR) even this superficially simple problem is very hard to solve without error. In more complicated problems (the general case), low-level image processing techniques handle the partial segmentation tasks, in which only the cues which will aid further high-level processing are extracted. Often, finding parts of object boundaries is an example of low-level partial segmentation.

Object description and classification in a totally segmented image are also understood as part of low-level image processing. Other low-level operations are image compression, and techniques to extract information from (but not *understand*) moving scenes.

Figure 1.9: Another representation of Figure 1.8.
© R.D. Boyle 2015.

Low-level image processing and high-level computer vision differ in the data used. Low-level data are comprised of original images represented by matrices composed of brightness (or similar) values, while high-level data originate in images as well, but only those data which are relevant to high-level goals are extracted, reducing the data quantity considerably. High-level data represent knowledge about the image content—for example, object size, shape, and mutual relations between objects in the image. High-level data are usually expressed in symbolic form.

Many low-level image processing methods were proposed in the 1970s or earlier: research is trying to find more efficient and more general algorithms and is implementing them on more technologically sophisticated equipment, in particular, parallel machines (including GPU's) are being used to ease the computational load. The requirement for better and faster algorithms is fuelled by technology delivering larger images (better spatial or temporal resolution), and color.

A complicated and so far unsolved problem is how to order low-level steps to solve a specific task, and the aim of automating this problem has not yet been achieved. It is usually still a human operator who finds a sequence of relevant operations, and domain-specific knowledge and uncertainty cause much to depend on this operator's intuition and previous experience.

High-level vision tries to extract and order image processing steps using all available knowledge—image understanding is the heart of the method, in which feedback from high-level to low-level is used. Unsurprisingly this task is very complicated and computationally intensive. David Marr's book [Marr, 1982], discussed in Section 11.1.1, influenced computer vision considerably throughout the 1980s; it described a new methodology and computational theory inspired by biological vision systems. Developments in the 1990s moved away from dependence on this paradigm, but interest in properly understanding and then modeling human visual (and other perceptual) systems persists—it remains the case that the only known solution to the 'vision problem' is our own brain!

Consider *3D vision problems* for a moment. We adopt the user's view, i.e., what tasks performed routinely by humans would be good to accomplish by machines. What is the relation of these 3D vision tasks to low-level (image processing) and high-level (image analysis) algorithmic methods? There is no widely accepted view in the academic community. Links between (algorithmic) components and representation levels are tailored to the specific application solved, e.g., navigation of an autonomous vehicle. These applications have to employ specific knowledge about the problem solved to be competitive with tasks which humans solve. Many researchers in different fields work on related problems and research in 'cognitive systems' could be the key which may disentangle the complicated world of perception which includes also computer vision.

Figure 1.10 depicts several 3D vision tasks and algorithmic components expressed on different abstraction levels. In most cases, the bottom-up and top-down approach is adopted to fulfill the task.

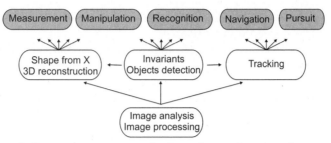

Figure 1.10: Several 3D computer vision tasks from the user's point of view are on the upper line (filled). Algorithmic components on different hierarchical levels support it in a bottom-up fashion. © *Cengage Learning 2015.*

1.4 Summary

- Human vision is natural and seems easy; computer mimicry of this is difficult.

- We might hope to examine pictures, or sequences of pictures, for quantitative and qualitative analysis.

- Many standard and advanced AI techniques are relevant.

- 'High' and 'low' levels of computer vision can be identified.

- Processing moves from digital manipulation, through pre-processing, segmentation, and recognition to understanding—but these processes may be simultaneous and co-operative.

- An understanding of the notions of heuristics, a priori knowledge, syntax, and semantics is necessary.

- The vision literature is large and growing; books may be specialized, elementary, or advanced.

- A knowledge of the research literature is necessary to stay up to date with the topic.

- Developments in electronic publishing and the Internet are making access to vision simpler.

1.5   Exercises

Short-answer questions

S1.1 In your own, or a local, university, determine how long image processing, image analysis, or computer vision have been taught. Try to determine the major syllabus or course offering changes over the last 1, 5, and (if possible) 10 years.

S1.2 What is the difference between image analysis (or computer vision) on one side and computer graphics on the other side?

S1.3 Walking around your local town, locate five instances in which digital images are now publicly visible or in use where they would not have been 10–15 years ago.

S1.4 Determine the current cost of domestic video cameras and storage, and image-capture hardware for home computers. Try to determine the cost of comparable equipment 1, 5, and 10 years ago. Make some predictions about the power and price of comparable equipment in 1, 5, and 10-year time.

S1.5 For some or all of the instances identified in Exercise S1.3, estimate the economics of the application—the size of market implied and the cost of the unit.

S1.6 Locate a topic area of computer science outside vision in which *a priori information* is commonly used.

S1.7 Locate a topic area of computer science outside vision in which *semantics* are commonly used.

S1.8 Locate a topic area of computer science outside vision in which *heuristics* are commonly used.

S1.9 Locate a topic area of computer science outside vision in which *syntax* is commonly used.

S1.10 Locate in a library some of the references selected in Exercise S1.12; study the publication dates of references listed there, and draw another histogram of years. What do this exercise and Exercise S1.12 tell you about the development of computer vision?

S1.11 In a technical or academic library, locate the section on computer vision. Examine the texts there, noting the date of publication and chapter titles; compare them with those of this text. Draw some conclusions about the topics (or, at least, their titles) that are static, and those which have developed recently.

S1.12 Select *at random* some journal references from the listings at the end of each chapter in this book. Construct a histogram of publication year.

S1.13 Make yourself familiar with solved problems and **Matlab** implementations of selected algorithms provided in the corresponding chapter of the **Matlab Companion** to this text [Svoboda et al., 2008]. The **Matlab Companion** homepage http://visionbook.felk.cvut.cz offers images used in the problems, and well-commented **Matlab** code is provided for educational purposes.

S1.14 Use the **Matlab Companion** [Svoboda et al., 2008] to develop solutions to additional exercises and practical problems provided there. Implement your solutions using **Matlab** or other suitable programming languages.

1.6   References

Marr D. *Vision—A Computational Investigation into the Human Representation and Processing of Visual Information.* Freeman, San Francisco, 1982.

Svoboda T., Kybic J., and Hlavac V. *Image Processing, Analysis, and Machine Vision: A MATLAB Companion.* Thomson Engineering, 2008.

Chapter 2

The image, its representations and properties

This chapter and the next introduce concepts and mathematical tools which are widely used in image analysis, and will be used throughout this book. We have separated this material into essential basics (this chapter) and more intense mathematical theory (the next). This division is intended to help the reader to start practical work immediately; mathematical details may be skipped in favor of concentrating on the intuitive meaning of the basic concepts while the next chapter provides a thorough anchoring to a mathematical background. Such a division can never be perfect, and this chapter contains some forward references and dependencies on its successor.

2.1 Image representations, a few concepts

Mathematical models are often used to describe images and other signals. A signal is a function depending on some variable with physical meaning; it can be one-dimensional (e.g., dependent on time), two-dimensional (e.g., an image dependent on two co-ordinates in a plane), three-dimensional (e.g., describing a volumetric object in space), or higher-dimensional. A scalar function might be sufficient to describe a monochromatic image, while vector functions may be used to represent, for example, color images consisting of three component colors.

Functions we shall work with may be categorized as **continuous**, **discrete**, or **digital**. A continuous function has continuous domain and range; if the domain set is discrete, then we have a discrete function; if the range set is also discrete, then we have a digital function. Many of these functions will be linear, and correspondingly simple to deal with.

We shall take the usual intuitive definition of **image**—an example might be the image on the human retina, or captured by a video camera. This can be modeled by a continuous (image) function of two variables $f(x, y)$ where (x, y) are co-ordinates in a plane, or perhaps three variables $f(x, y, t)$, where t is time. This model is reasonable in the great majority of applications that we encounter, and which are presented in this book. Nevertheless, it is worth realizing that an 'image' may be acquired in many ways. We shall note often that color is the norm, even when algorithms are presented for monochromatic images, but we do not need to constrain ourselves to the visible spectrum. Infra-red cameras are now very common (for example, for night-time surveillance). Other parts of the electro-magnetic [EM] spectrum may also be used; microwave imaging, for example, is becoming widely available. Further, image acquisition outside the EM spectrum is also common: in the medical domain, datasets are generated via magnetic resonance (MR), X-ray computed tomography (CT), ultrasound etc. All of these approaches generate large arrays of data requiring analysis and understanding and with increasing frequency these arrays are of 3 or more dimensions. We imply a study of all these modalities in the title of this book.

The continuous image function

The (gray-scale) image function values correspond to brightness at image points. The function value can express other physical quantities as well (temperature, pressure distribution, distance from the observer, etc.). **Brightness** integrates different optical quantities—using brightness as a basic quantity allows us to avoid the complicated process of image formation which will be discussed in Section 3.4.

The image on the retina or on a camera sensor is intrinsically two-dimensional (2D). We shall call such an image bearing information about brightness points an **intensity image**. The 2D image on the imaging sensor is commonly the result of projection of a three-dimensional (3D) scene. The simplest mathematical model for this is a pin-hole camera (see Figure 1.4).

The 2D intensity image is the result of a **perspective projection** of the 3D scene, which is modeled by the image captured by a pin-hole camera illustrated in Figure 2.1. In this figure, the image plane has been reflected with respect to the XY plane in order

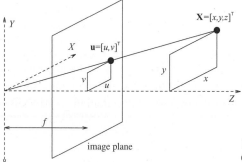

Figure 2.1: Perspective projection geometry.
© *Cengage Learning 2015.*

not to get a mirrored image with negative co-ordinates. The quantities x, y, and z are co-ordinates of the point $\mathbf{X}$ in a 3D scene, and f is the distance from the pinhole to the image plane. f is commonly called the focal length because in lenses it has a similar meaning. The projected point $\mathbf{u}$ has co-ordinates (u, v) in the 2D image plane, which can easily be derived from similar triangles

$$u = \frac{x\,f}{z}\,, \qquad v = \frac{y\,f}{z}\,. \tag{2.1}$$

A non-linear perspective projection is often approximated by a linear **parallel** (or **orthographic) projection**, where $f \to \infty$. Implicitly, $z \to \infty$ says that the orthographic projection is a limiting case of the perspective projection for faraway objects.

When 3D objects are mapped into the camera plane by perspective projection, a lot of information disappears because such a transform is not one-to-one. Recognizing or reconstructing objects in a 3D scene from one image is an ill-posed problem. In Chapter 11, we shall consider more elaborate representations that attempt to recapture information about the original scene that an image depicts. As may be expected, this is not a simple task and involves intermediate representations that try to establish the **depth** of points in the image. The aim is to recover a full 3D representation such as may be used in computer graphics—that is, a representation independent of the viewpoint, and expressed in the co-ordinate system of the object rather than of the viewer. If such a representation can be recovered, then any intensity image view of the object(s) may be synthesized by standard graphics techniques.

Recovering information lost by perspective projection is only one, mainly geometric, problem of computer vision—another is understanding image brightness. The only information available in an intensity image is the brightness of the appropriate pixel, which is dependent on a number of independent factors such as object surface reflectance properties (given by the surface material, microstructure, and marking), illumination properties, and object surface orientation with respect to viewer and light source—see Section 3.4. It is a non-trivial and again ill-posed problem to separate these components when trying to recover the 3D geometry of an object from the intensity image.

Some applications work with 2D images directly—for example, an image of a flat specimen viewed by a microscope with transparent illumination, a character drawn on a sheet of paper, the image of a fingerprint, etc. Many basic and useful methods used in digital image analysis do not therefore depend on whether the object was originally 2D or 3D. Much of the material in this book restricts itself to the study of such methods—the problem of 3D understanding is addressed explicitly in Chapters 11 and 12.

Image processing often deals with **static** images, in which time is constant. A monochromatic static image is represented by a continuous image function $f(x, y)$ whose arguments are co-ordinates in the plane. Most images considered in this book will be presented as monochromatic and static, but we will frequently note that they are taken from color or dynamic applications, and extensions of the techniques we develop will be obvious.

Computerized image processing uses digital image functions which are usually represented by matrices, so co-ordinates are natural numbers. The domain of the image function is a region R in the plane

$$R = \left\{ (x, y),\ 1 \le x \le x_m,\ 1 \le y \le y_n \right\}, \tag{2.2}$$

where x_m, y_n represent the maximal co-ordinates. The function has a limited domain—infinite summation or integration limits can be used, as the image function value is zero outside the domain R. The customary orientation of co-ordinates in an image is in the normal Cartesian fashion (horizontal x-axis, vertical y-axis, origin bottom-left), although the (*row, column*, origin top-left) orientation used in matrices is also often used.

The range of image function values is also limited; by convention, in monochromatic images the lowest value corresponds to black and the highest to white. Brightness values bounded by these limits are **gray-levels**.

The quality of a digital image grows in proportion to the spatial, spectral, radiometric, and time resolutions. The **spatial resolution** is given by the proximity of image samples in the image plane; **spectral resolution** is given by the bandwidth of the light frequencies captured by the sensor; **radiometric resolution** corresponds to the number of distinguishable gray-levels; and **time resolution** is given by the interval between time samples at which images are captured. The question of time resolution is important in dynamic image analysis, where time sequences of images are processed.

Images $f(x, y)$ can be treated as deterministic functions or as realizations of stochastic processes. Mathematical tools used in image description have roots in linear system theory, integral transforms, discrete mathematics, and the theory of stochastic processes. Mathematical transforms usually assume that the image function $f(x, y)$ is 'well-behaved', meaning that the function is integrable, has an invertible Fourier transform, etc. A comprehensive explanation of the mathematical background useful for representing and treating image functions is given in [Bracewell, 2004; Barrett and Myers, 2004].

2.2 Image digitization

An image to be processed by computer must be represented using an appropriate discrete data structure, for example, a matrix. An image captured by a sensor is expressed as a continuous function $f(x, y)$ of two co-ordinates in the plane. Image digitization means that the function $f(x, y)$ is **sampled** into a matrix with M rows and N columns. Image **quantization** assigns to each continuous sample an integer value—the continuous range of the image function $f(x, y)$ is split into K intervals. The finer the sampling (i.e., the larger M and N) and quantization (the larger K), the better the approximation of the continuous image function $f(x, y)$ achieved.

Image function sampling poses two questions. First, the sampling period should be determined—this is the distance between two neighboring sampling points in the image. Second, the geometric arrangement of sampling points (sampling grid) should be set.

2.2.1 Sampling

Clearly, there is a relationship between the density of digital sampling and the detail that the image will contain; the theoretical aspects of this (in particular, Shannon's theorem) are given in Section 3.2.5—the reader is strongly encouraged to understand at least the implications of this important result. It is worth glancing ahead to Figure 3.11 to see a clear illustration of this intuitive issue.

For now, it is sufficient to appreciate that if quality comparable to an ordinary (standard) television image is required, sampling into a 512×512 grid is used (768×576 for PAL format and 640×480 for NTSC format using a rectangular capture window); this is the reason many image digitizers use this (or higher) resolution. Resolution of high-definition television (HDTV) is up to 1920×1080 pixels. Such a resolution turns out to be adequate for a very wide range of practically useful tasks. Yet, much higher image resolutions are routinely available – for example provided by digital cameras or smartphones – with $10,000 \times 7,096$ pixels being the highest resolution available from a CMOS chip in 2013 (79 Megapixels, see also Section 2.5.1).

A continuous image is digitized at **sampling points**. These sampling points are ordered in the plane, and their geometric relation is called the **grid**. The digital image is then a data structure, usually a matrix. Grids used in practice are usually square (Figure 2.2a) or hexagonal (Figure 2.2b). It is important to distinguish the grid from the raster; the **raster** is the grid on which a neighborhood relation between points is defined.[1]

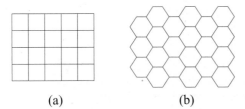

(a)   (b)

Figure 2.2: (a) Square grid. (b) Hexagonal grid. © *Cengage Learning 2015.*

One infinitely small sampling point in the grid corresponds to one picture element also called a **pixel** or **image element** in the digital image; in a three-dimensional image, an image element is called a **voxel** (volume element). The set of pixels together covers the entire image; however, the pixel captured by a real digitization device has finite size (since the sampling function is not a collection of ideal Dirac impulses but a collection of limited impulses—see Section 3.2.5). The pixel is a unit which is not further divisible[2] from the image analysis point of view. We shall often refer to a pixel as a 'point'.

2.2.2   Quantization

A value of the sampled image $f_s(j\,\Delta x, k\,\Delta y)$ is expressed as a digital value in image processing. The transition between continuous values of the image function (brightness) and its digital equivalent is called **quantization**. The number of quantization levels should be high enough to permit human perception of fine shading details in the image. Most digital image processing devices use quantization into k equal intervals. If b bits are used to express the values of the pixel brightness then the number of brightness levels is $k = 2^b$. Eight bits per pixel per channel (one each for red, green, blue) are commonly used although systems using other numbers (e.g., 16) can be found. An efficient computer representation of brightness values in digital images requires that eight bits, four bits, or one bit are used per pixel, meaning that one, two, or eight pixel brightnesses can be stored in one byte.

The main problem in images quantized with insufficient brightness levels is the occurrence of false contours which effect arises when the number of brightness levels is lower than that which humans can easily distinguish. This number is dependent on many factors—for example, the average local brightness—but displays which avoid this effect will normally provide a range of at least 100 intensity levels. This problem can be reduced when quantization into intervals of unequal length is used; the size of intervals corresponding to less probable brightnesses in the image is enlarged. These gray-scale transformation techniques are considered in Section 5.1.2.

Figures 3.11a and 2.3a-d demonstrate the effect of reducing the number of brightness levels in an image. An original image with 256 brightness levels (Figure 3.11a) has its

---

[1]E.g., if 4-neighborhoods are used on the square grid, the square raster is obtained. Similarly, if 8-neighborhoods are used on the same square grid, then the octagonal raster is obtained. These 4-neighborhood and 8-neighborhood concepts are introduced in Section 2.3.1.

[2]In some case, the properties of an image at subpixel resolution can be computed. This is achieved by approximating the image function by a continuous function.

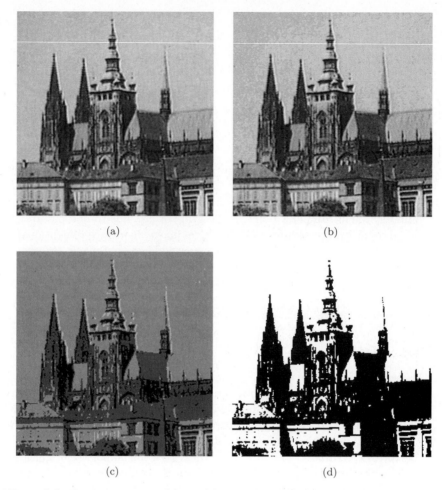

Figure 2.3: Brightness levels. (a) 64. (b) 16. (c) 4. (d) 2. © *Cengage Learning 2015*.

number of brightness levels reduced to 64 (Figure 2.3a), and no degradation is perceived. Figure 2.3b uses 16 brightness levels and false contours begin to emerge, and this becomes clearer in Figure 2.3c with four brightnesses and in Figure 2.3d with only two.

2.3 Digital image properties

A digital image has several properties, both metric and topological, which are somewhat different from those of continuous two-dimensional functions. Human perception of digital images is a frequent aspect, since judgment of image quality is also important.

2.3.1 Metric and topological properties of digital images

A digital image consists of picture elements with finite size—these pixels carry information about the brightness of a particular location in the image. Usually (and we assume this hereafter) pixels are arranged into a rectangular sampling grid. Such a digital image is represented by a two-dimensional matrix whose elements are natural numbers corresponding to the quantization levels in the brightness scale.

Some intuitively clear properties of continuous images have no straightforward analogy in the domain of digital images. **Distance** is an important example. Any function D holding the following three condition is a 'distance' (or a *metric*)

$$D(\mathbf{p}, \mathbf{q}) \geq 0 \,; D(\mathbf{p}, \mathbf{q}) = 0 \text{ if and only if } \mathbf{p} = \mathbf{q}\,, \quad identity,$$
$$D(\mathbf{p}, \mathbf{q}) = D(\mathbf{q}, \mathbf{p})\,, \quad\quad\quad\quad\quad\quad symmetry,$$
$$D(\mathbf{p}, \mathbf{r}) \leq D(\mathbf{p}, \mathbf{q}) + D(\mathbf{q}, \mathbf{r})\,, \quad\quad triangular\ inequality.$$

The distance between points with co-ordinates (i, j) and (h, k) may be defined in several different ways.

The **Euclidean distance** D_E known from classical geometry and everyday experience is defined by

$$D_E\big((i, j), (h, k)\big) = \sqrt{(i - h)^2 + (j - k)^2}\,. \tag{2.3}$$

The advantage of Euclidean distance is that it is intuitively obvious. The disadvantages are costly calculation due to the square root, and its non-integral value.

The distance between two points can also be expressed as the minimum number of elementary steps in the digital grid which are needed to move from the starting point to the end point. If only horizontal and vertical moves are allowed, the **'city block' distance** distance D_4 is obtained (also called the L_1 metric or Manhattan distance, because of the analogy with the distance between two locations in a city with a rectangular grid of streets):

$$D_4\big((i, j), (h, k)\big) = \mid i - h \mid + \mid j - k \mid\,. \tag{2.4}$$

If moves in diagonal directions are allowed in the digitization grid, we obtain the distance D_8, or **'chessboard' distance**. D_8 is equal to the minimal number of king-moves on the chessboard from one part to another:

$$D_8\big((i, j), (h, k)\big) = \max\big\{\mid i - h \mid, \mid j - k \mid\big\}\,. \tag{2.5}$$

These distance definitions are illustrated in Figure 2.4.

Figure 2.4: Distance metrics D_e, D_4, and D_8. © *Cengage Learning 2015.*

Pixel **adjacency** is another important concept in digital images. Two pixels $(\mathbf{p}, \mathbf{q})$ are called **4-neighbors** if they have distance $D_4(\mathbf{p}, \mathbf{q}) = 1$. Analogously, **8-neighbors** have $D_8(\mathbf{p}, \mathbf{q}) = 1$—see Figure 2.5.

It will become necessary to consider important sets consisting of several adjacent pixels—**regions** (in set theory, a region is a connected set). More descriptively, we can define a **path** from pixel P to pixel Q as a sequence of points A_1, A_2, ..., A_n, where $A_1 = P$, $A_n = Q$, and A_{i+1} is a neighbor of A_i, $i = 1, \dots, n - 1$; then a region is a set of pixels in which there is a path between any pair of its pixels, all of whose pixels also belong to the set.

If there is a path between two pixels in the set of pixels in the image, these pixels are called **contiguous**. Alternatively, we can say that a region is a set of pixels in which

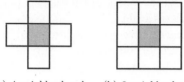

(a) 4-neighborhood   (b) 8-neighborhood

Figure 2.5: Neighborhood of the representative pixel (gray filled pixel in the middle). © *Cengage Learning 2015.*

each pair of pixels is contiguous. The relation 'to be contiguous' is reflexive, symmetric, and transitive and therefore defines a decomposition of the set (the image in our case) into equivalence classes (regions). Figure 2.6 illustrates a binary image decomposed by the relation 'contiguous' into three regions.

Figure 2.6: The relation 'to be contiguous' decomposes an image into individual regions. The Japanese Kanji character meaning 'near from here' decomposes into 3 regions. © *Cengage Learning 2015.*

Assume that R_i are disjoint regions in the image which were created by the relation 'to be contiguous', and further assume (to avoid special cases) that these regions do not touch the image bounds. Let R be the union of all regions R_i; R^C be the set complement of R with respect to the image. The subset of R^C which is contiguous with the image bounds is called the **background**, and the remainder of the complement R^C is called **holes**.[3] A region is called **simple contiguous** if it has no holes. Equivalently, the complement of a simply contiguous region is contiguous. A region with holes is called **multiple contiguous**.

Note that the concept of region uses only the property 'to be contiguous'. Secondary properties can be attached to regions which originate in image data interpretation. It is common to call some regions in the image **objects**; a process which determines which regions in an image correspond to objects in the world is a part of image **segmentation** and is discussed in Chapters 6 and 7.

The brightness of a pixel is a very simple property which can be used to find objects in some images; if, for example, a pixel is darker than some predefined value (threshold), then it belongs to the object. All such points which are also contiguous constitute one object. A hole consists of points which do not belong to the object and are surrounded by the object, and all other points constitute the background. An example is the black printed text on this white sheet of paper, in which individual letters are objects. White areas surrounded by the letter are holes, for example, the area inside the letter 'o'. Other white parts of the paper are the background.

These neighborhood and contiguity definitions on the square grid create interesting paradoxes. Figure 2.7a shows two digital line segments with 45° slope. If 4-connectivity is used, the lines are not contiguous at each of their points. An even worse conflict with intuitive understanding of line properties is also illustrated; two perpendicular lines do intersect in one case (upper right intersection) and do not intersect in another case (lower left), as they do not have any common point (i.e., their set intersection is empty).

---

[3]Some literature does not distinguish holes and background, and calls both of them background.

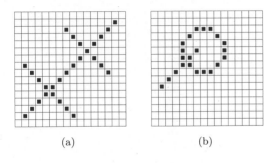

      (a)   (b)

Figure 2.7: Paradoxes of crossing lines. © *Cengage Learning 2015.*

It is known from Euclidean geometry that each closed curve (e.g., a circle) divides the plane into two non-contiguous regions. If images are digitized in a square grid using 8-connectivity, we can draw a line from the inner part of a closed curve into the outer part which does not intersect the curve (Figure 2.7b). This implies that the inner and outer parts of the curve constitute only one region because all pixels of the line belong to only one region, giving another paradox. One possible solution to contiguity paradoxes is to treat objects using 4-neighborhoods and background using 8-neighborhoods (or vice versa). A more exact treatment of digital images paradoxes and their solution for binary and other images can be found in [Klette and Rosenfeld, 2004].

These problems are typical on square grids—a hexagonal grid (see Figure 2.2), however, solves many of them. Any point in the hexagonal raster has the same distance to all its six neighbors. There are some problems peculiar to the hexagonal raster as well (for example, it is difficult to express a Fourier transform on it). For reasons of simplicity and ease of processing, most digitizing devices use a square grid despite the known drawbacks.

An alternative approach to the connectivity problems is to use discrete topology based on cellular complexes [Kovalevsky, 1989]. This approach develops a complete strand of image encoding and segmentation that deals with many issues we shall come to later, such as the representation of boundaries and regions. The idea, first proposed by the German mathematician Riemann in the nineteenth century, considers families of sets of different dimensions; points, which are 0-dimensional sets, may then be assigned to sets containing higher-dimensional structures (such as pixel arrays). This approach permits the removal of the paradoxes we have seen.

The **distance transform**—also called the **distance function** or **chamfering algorithm** or simply **chamfering**—is a simple application of the concept of distance. The idea is important as it provides the basis of several fast algorithms that will be seen multiple times in this book. The distance transform provides the distance of pixels from some image subset (perhaps describing objects or some features). The resulting 'image' has pixel values of 0 for elements of the relevant subset, low values for close pixels, and then high values for pixels remote from it—the appearance of this array gives the name to the technique.

For illustration, consider a binary image, in which ones represent the objects and zeros the background. The input image is shown in Figure 2.8 and the result of the D_4 distance transform is illustrated in Figure 2.9.

To calculate the transform, a two-pass algorithm has been suggested [Rosenfeld and Pfaltz, 1966, 1968] for distances D_4 and D_8. The idea is to traverse the image by a small local mask. The first pass starts from the top-left of the image and moves horizontally

0	0	0	0	0	0	1	0
0	0	0	0	0	1	0	0
0	0	0	0	0	1	0	0
0	0	0	0	0	1	0	0
0	1	1	0	0	0	1	0
0	1	0	0	0	0	0	1
0	1	0	0	0	0	0	0
0	1	0	0	0	0	0	0

5	4	4	3	2	1	0	1
4	3	3	2	1	0	1	2
3	2	2	2	1	0	1	2
2	1	1	2	1	0	1	2
1	0	0	1	2	1	0	1
1	0	1	2	3	2	1	0
1	0	1	2	3	3	2	1
1	0	1	2	3	4	3	2

Figure 2.8: Input image: gray pixels correspond to objects and white to background. © *Cengage Learning 2015.*

Figure 2.9: Result of the $[D_4]$ distance transform. © *Cengage Learning 2015.*

left to right until it reaches the bounds of the image and then returns to the beginning of the next row. The second pass goes from the bottom-right corner in the opposite bottom-up, right to left direction using a different local mask. The effectiveness of the algorithm comes from propagating the values of the previous image investigation in a 'wave-like' manner. The masks used in calculations are shown in Figure 2.10.

Figure 2.10: Pixel neighborhoods used in distance transform calculations—**p** is the central one. The neighborhood on the left is used in the first pass (top-down, left to right); that on the right is used in the second (bottom-up, right to left). © *Cengage Learning 2015.*

Algorithm 2.1: Distance transform

1. Choose a distance N_{max} that exceeds the image dimension with respect to the chosen distance metric (D_4 or D_8). Initialize an image F of the same dimension as the input: set pixels corresponding to the subset(s) to be chamfered to 0, and all others to N_{max}.

2. (*Refer to Figure 2.10.*) Pass through image pixels from top to bottom and left to right. For a given pixel, consider neighbors above and to the left and set

$$F(\mathbf{p}) = \min_{\mathbf{q} \in AL} \left(F(\mathbf{p}), D(\mathbf{p}, \mathbf{q}) + F(\mathbf{q}) \right).$$

3. (*Refer to Figure 2.10.*) Pass through image pixels from bottom to top and right to left. For a given pixel, consider neighbors above and to the left and set

$$F(\mathbf{p}) = \min_{\mathbf{q} \in BR} \left(F(\mathbf{p}), D(\mathbf{p}, \mathbf{q}) + F(\mathbf{q}) \right).$$

4. If any pixels remain still set at N_{max}, go to (2).

5. The array F now holds a chamfer of the chosen subset(s).

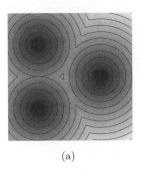 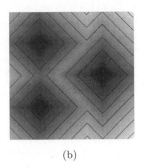 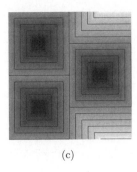

(a)   (b)   (c)

Figure 2.11: Three distances used often in distance transform calculations—the input consists of three isolated 'ones'. Output distance is visualized as intensity; lighter values denote higher distances. Contour plots are superimposed for better visualization. (a) Euclidean distance D_E. (b) City block distance D_4. (c) Chessboard distance D_8. © *Cengage Learning 2015*.

This algorithm needs obvious adjustments at image boundaries, where the sets AL and BR are truncated. It is open to various improvements by using different distance calculations [Montanari, 1968; Barrow et al., 1977; Borgefors, 1986; Breu et al., 1995; Maurer et al., 2003]. Distance transform performance for D_E, D_4, D_8 on an input consisting only of three distinct 'ones' is shown in Figure 2.11.

The distance transform has many applications, e.g., in discrete geometry, path planning and obstacle avoidance in mobile robotics, finding the closest feature in the image, and skeletonization (discussed with mathematical morphology methods in Section 13.5.5).

An **edge** is a further important concept used in image analysis. This is a local property of a pixel and its immediate neighborhood—it is a vector given by a magnitude and direction which tells us how fast the image intensity varies in a small neighborhood of a pixel. Images with many brightness levels are used for edge computation, and the gradient of the image function is used to compute edges. The edge direction is perpendicular to the gradient direction which points in the direction of the fastest image function growth. Edges are considered in detail in Section 5.3.2.

The related concept of the **crack edge** creates a structure between pixels in a similar manner to that of cellular complexes. However, it is more pragmatic and less mathematically rigorous. Four crack edges are attached to each pixel, which are defined by its relation to its 4-neighbors. The direction of the crack edge is that of increasing brightness, and is a multiple of 90°, while its magnitude is the absolute difference between the brightness of the relevant pair of pixels. Crack edges are illustrated in Figure 2.12 and may be be used in considering image segmentation (Chapter 6).

The **border** (boundary) of a region is another important concept in image analysis. The border of a region R is the set of pixels within the region that have one or more neighbors outside R. The definition corresponds to an intuitive understanding of the border as a set of points at the bound of the region. This definition is sometimes referred to as the **inner border** to distinguish it from the **outer border**, that is, the border of the background (i.e., its complement) of the region. Inner and outer borders are illustrated in Figure 2.13. Due to the discrete nature of the image, some inner border elements which would be distinct in the continuous case coincide in the discrete case, as can be seen with the one-pixel-wide line at the right of Figure 2.13.

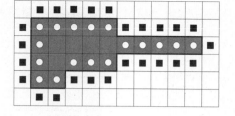

Figure 2.12: Crack edges. © *Cengage Learning 2015.*

Figure 2.13: Region inner borders shown as white circles and outer borders shown as black squares (using 4-neighborhoods). © *Cengage Learning 2015.*

While edges and borders are related, they are not the same thing. 'Border' is a global concept related to a region, while 'edge' expresses local properties of an image function. One possibility for finding boundaries is chaining the significant edges (points with high gradient of the image function). Methods of this kind are described in Section 6.2.

A region is described as **convex** if any two points within it are connected by a straight line segment, and the whole line lies within the region—see Figure 2.14. The property of convexity decomposes all regions into two equivalence classes: convex and non-convex.

 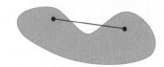

Figure 2.14: A convex region (left) and non-convex region (right). © *Cengage Learning 2015.*

A **convex hull** of a region is the smallest convex region containing the input (possibly non-convex) region. Consider an object whose shape resembles the letter 'R' (see Figure 2.15). Imagine a thin rubber band pulled around the object; the shape of the rubber band provides the convex hull of the object. Convex hull calculation is described in Section 8.3.3.

Region   Convex   ■ Lakes
          hull   ▨ Bays

Figure 2.15: Description using topological components: An 'R' object, its convex hull, and the associated lakes and bays. © *Cengage Learning 2015.*

Topological properties are not based on the distance concept. Instead, they are invariant to *homeomorphic* transforms which can be illustrated for images as **rubber sheet transforms**. Imagine a small rubber balloon with an object painted on it; topological properties of the object are those which are invariant to arbitrary stretching of the rubber sheet. Stretching does not change contiguity of the object parts and does not change the number of holes in regions. We use the term 'topological properties' of the region to describe its qualitative properties invariant to small changes (e.g., the property of being convex), even though an arbitrary homeomorphic transformation can change a convex region to a non-convex one and vice versa. Considering the rubber sheet analogy, we mean that the stretching of the sheet is only gentle. Further properties of regions that are not rubber sheet invariant are described in Section 8.3.1.

An object with non-regular shape can be represented by a collection of its topological components, Figure 2.15. The set inside the convex hull which does not belong to an object is called the **deficit of convexity**. This can be split into two subsets: **lakes** (dark gray) are fully surrounded by the object; and **bays** (light gray) are contiguous with the border of the convex hull of the object.

The convex hull, lakes, and bays are sometimes used for object description; these features are used in Chapter 8 (object description) and in Chapter 13 (mathematical morphology).

2.3.2   Histograms

The **brightness histogram** $h_f(z)$ of an image provides the frequency of the brightness value z in the image—the histogram of an image with L gray-levels is represented by a one-dimensional array with L elements.

Algorithm 2.2: Computing the brightness histogram

1. Assign zero values to all elements of the array h_f.

2. For all pixels (x, y) of the image f, increment $h_f\big(f(x,y)\big)$ by 1.

The histogram provides a natural bridge between images and a probabilistic description. We might want to find a first-order probability function $p_1(z; x, y)$ to indicate the probability that pixel (x, y) has brightness z. Dependence on the position of the pixel is not of interest in the histogram; the function $p_1(z)$ is of interest and the brightness histogram is its estimate. The histogram is often displayed as a bar graph, see Figure 2.16.

The histogram is usually the only global information about the image which is available. It is used when finding optimal illumination conditions for capturing an image, gray-scale transformations, and image segmentation to objects and background. Note

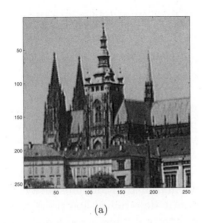

(a)

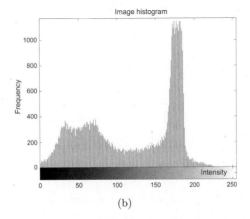

(b)

Figure 2.16: Original image (a) and its brightness histogram (b). © *Cengage Learning 2015*.

that one histogram may correspond to several images; for instance, a change of the object position on a constant background does not affect it.

The histogram of a digital image typically has many local minima and maxima, which may complicate its further processing. This problem can be avoided by local smoothing of the histogram; this may be done, for example, using local averaging of neighboring histogram elements as the base, so that a new histogram $h'_f(z)$ is calculated according to

$$ h'_f(z) = \frac{1}{2K+1} \sum_{j=-K}^{K} h_f(z+j) \,, \qquad (2.6) $$

where K is a constant representing the size of the neighborhood used for smoothing. This algorithm would need some boundary adjustment, and carries no guarantee of removing all local minima. Other techniques for smoothing exist, notably Gaussian blurring; in the case of a histogram, this would be a one-dimensional simplification of the 2D Gaussian blur, equation (5.47), which will be introduced in Section 5.3.3.

2.3.3   Entropy

If a probability density p is known then image information content can be estimated regardless of its interpretation using **entropy** H. The concept of entropy has roots in thermodynamics and statistical mechanics but it took many years before it was related to information. The information-theoretic formulation comes from Shannon [Shannon, 1948] and is often called **information entropy**.

An intuitive understanding of information entropy relates to the amount of uncertainty about an event associated with a given probability distribution. The entropy can serve as an measure of 'disorder'. As the level of disorder rises, entropy increases and events are less predictable.

Entropy is formally defined assuming a discrete random variable X with possible outcomes (called also states) $x_1, \ldots, x_n$. Let $p(x_k)$ be the probability of the outcome x_k, $k = 1, \ldots n$. Then the entropy is defined as

$$ H(X) \equiv \sum_{k=1}^{n} p(x_k) \log_2 \left(\frac{1}{p(x_k)} \right) = -\sum_{k=1}^{n} p(x_k) \log_2 p(x_k) \,. \qquad (2.7) $$

The entropy of the random variable X is the sum, over all possible outcomes k of X, of the product of the probability of outcome x_k with the logarithm of the inverse of the probability of x_k.

The base of the logarithm in this formula determines the unit in which entropy is measured. If this base is two then the entropy is given in bits. Recall that the probability density $p(x_k)$ needed to calculate the entropy is often estimated using a gray-level histogram in image analysis, Section 2.3.2.

Entropy measures the uncertainty about the realization of a random variable. For Shannon, it served as a proxy capturing the concept of information contained in a message as opposed to the portion of the message that is strictly determined and predictable by inherent structures. For example, we shall explore entropy to assess redundancy in an image for image compression (Chapter 14).

2.3.4 Visual perception of the image

Anyone who creates or uses algorithms or devices for digital image processing should take into account the principles of human image perception. If an image is to be analyzed by a human the information should be expressed using variables which are easy to perceive; these are psycho-physical parameters such as contrast, border, shape, texture, color, etc. Humans will find objects in images only if they may be distinguished effortlessly from the background. A detailed description of the principles of human visual perception can be found in [Bruce et al., 1996; Palmer, 1999]. Human perception of images provokes many illusions, the understanding of which provides valuable clues about visual mechanisms. Some of the better-known illusions will be mentioned here—the topic is covered exhaustively from the point of view of computer vision in [Frisby, 1979].

The situation would be relatively easy if the human visual system had a linear response to composite input stimuli—i.e., a simple sum of individual stimuli. A decrease of some stimulus, e.g., area of the object in the image, could be compensated by its intensity, contrast, or duration. In fact, the sensitivity of human senses is roughly logarithmically proportional to the intensity of an input signal. In this case, after an initial logarithmic transformation, response to composite stimuli can be treated as linear.

Contrast

Contrast is the local change in brightness and is defined as the ratio between average brightness of an object and the background. Strictly speaking, we should talk about luminance[4] instead of brightness if our aim is to be physically precise. The human eye is logarithmically sensitive to brightness, implying that for the same perception, higher brightness requires higher contrast.

Apparent brightness depends very much on the brightness of the local surroundings; this effect is called conditional contrast. Figure 2.17 illustrates this with five circles of the same size surrounded by squares of different brightness. Humans perceive the brightness of the small circles as different.

Figure 2.17: Conditional contrast effect. Circles inside squares have the same brightness and are perceived as having different brightness values. © *Cengage Learning 2015*.

Acuity

Acuity is the ability to detect details in an image. The human eye is less sensitive to slow and fast changes in brightness in the image plane but is more sensitive to intermediate changes. Acuity also decreases with increasing distance from the optical axis.

Resolution in an image is firmly bounded by the resolution ability of the human eye; there is no sense in representing visual information with higher resolution than that of

---

[4]Luminance describes the amount of light that passes through or is emitted from a particular area, and falls within a given solid angle. Luminance is given candela per square meter [cd/m^2].

the viewer. Resolution in optics is defined as the inverse value of a maximum viewing angle between the viewer and two proximate points which humans cannot distinguish, and so fuse together.

Human vision has the best resolution for objects which are at a distance of about 250 mm from an eye under illumination of about 500 lux; this illumination is provided by a 60 W bulb from a distance of 400 mm. Under these conditions the distance between two distinguishable points is approximately 0.16 mm.

Some visual illusions

Human perception of images is prone to many illusions. For a comprehensive treatment of the subject, see [Palmer, 1999].

Object borders carry a lot of information for humans. Boundaries of objects and simple patterns such as blobs or lines enable adaptation effects similar to conditional contrast, mentioned above. The Ebbinghaus illusion is a well-known example—two circles of the same diameter in the center of images appear to have different diameters (Figure 2.18).

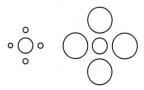

Figure 2.18: The Ebbinghaus illusion. © *Cengage Learning 2015.*

Perception of one dominant shape can be fooled by nearby shapes. Figure 2.19 shows parallel diagonal line segments which are not perceived as parallel. Figure 2.20 contains rows of black and white squares which are all parallel. However, the vertical zigzag squares disrupt our horizontal perception.

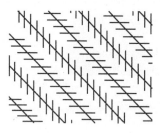

Figure 2.19: Disrupted parallel diagonal lines. © *Cengage Learning 2015.*

Figure 2.20: Horizontal lines are parallel, although not perceived as such. © *Cengage Learning 2015.*

Perceptual grouping

Perceptual grouping [Palmer, 1999] is a principle used in computer vision to aggregate elements provided by low-level operations such as edgels, which are small blobs to bigger chunks having some meaning. Its roots are in Gestalt psychology first postulated by

Wertheimer in 1912 [Brett King and Wertheimer, 2005]. Gestalt psychology proposes that the operational principle of the mind and brain is holistic, parallel, and with self-organizing tendencies.

Gestalt theory was meant to have general applicability; its main tenets, however, were induced almost exclusively from observations on visual perception. The overriding theme of the theory is that stimulation is perceived in organized or configuration terms. Gestalt in German means configuration, structure or pattern of physical, biological, or psychological phenomena so integrated to constitute a functional unit with properties not derivable by summation of its parts. Patterns take precedence over elements and have properties that are not inherent in the elements themselves.

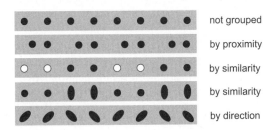

Figure 2.21: Grouping according to properties of elements. © *Cengage Learning 2015.*

The human ability to group items according to various properties is illustrated in Figure 2.21. Perceived properties help people to connect elements together based on strongly perceived properties as parallelism, symmetry, continuity and closure taken in a loose sense as illustrated in Figure 2.22.

Figure 2.22: Illustration of properties perceived in images which allow humans to group together elements in cluttered scenes. © *Cengage Learning 2015.*

It has been demonstrated that mimicking perceptual grouping in machine vision system is a plausible technique. It permits the creation of more meaningful chunks of information from meaningless outcomes of low-level operations such as edge detection. Such grouping is useful in image understanding. This principle will be used in this book mainly for image segmentation.

2.3.5   Image quality

An image might be degraded during capture, transmission, or processing, and measures of image quality can be used to assess the degree of degradation. The quality required naturally depends on the purpose for which an image is used.

Methods for assessing **image quality** can be divided into two categories: subjective and objective. Subjective methods are often used in television technology, where the ultimate criterion is the perception of a selected group of professional and lay viewers. They appraise an image according to a list of criteria and give appropriate marks. Details about subjective methods may be found in [Pratt, 1978].

Objective quantitative methods measuring image quality are more interesting for our purposes. Ideally such a method also provides a good subjective test, and is easy to apply; we might then use it as a criterion in parameter optimization. The quality of an image $f(x, y)$ is usually estimated by comparison with a known reference image $g(x, y)$ [Rosenfeld and Kak, 1982], and a synthesized image is often used for this purpose. One class of methods uses simple measures such as the mean quadratic difference $\sum(g - f)^2$, but this does not distinguish a few big differences from many small differences. Instead of the mean quadratic difference, the mean absolute difference or simply maximal absolute difference may be used. Correlation between images f and g is another alternative.

Another class measures the resolution of small or proximate objects in the image. An image consisting of parallel black and white stripes is used for this purpose; then the number of black and white pairs per millimeter gives the resolution.

2.3.6   Noise in images

Real images are often degraded by some random errors—this degradation is usually called **noise**. Noise can occur during image capture, transmission, or processing, and may be dependent on, or independent of, the image content.

Noise is usually described by its probabilistic characteristics. Idealized noise, called **white noise** is often used. White noise has a constant power spectrum (explained in Section 3.2.3), meaning that all noise frequencies are present and have the same intensity. For example, the intensity of white noise does not decrease with increasing frequency as is typical in real-world signals. White noise is frequently employed to model the worst approximation of degradation, the advantage being that its use simplifies calculations.

A special case of white noise is **Gaussian noise**. A random variable with a Gaussian (normal) distribution has its probability density function given by the Gaussian curve. In the 1D case the density function is

$$p(x) = \frac{1}{\sigma\sqrt{2\pi}} \, e^{\frac{-(x-\mu)^2}{2\sigma^2}} \,, \tag{2.8}$$

where μ is the mean and σ the standard deviation of the random variable. Gaussian noise is a very good approximation to noise that occurs in many practical cases.

When an image is transmitted through some channel, noise which is usually independent of the image signal occurs. This signal-independent degradation is called **additive noise** and can be described by the model

$$f(x, y) = g(x, y) + \nu(x, y) \,, \tag{2.9}$$

where the noise ν and the input image g are independent variables. Algorithm 2.3 will generate zero mean additive Gaussian noise in an image—this can often be of use in testing or demonstrating many algorithms in this book which are designed to remove noise, or to be noise resistant.

Algorithm 2.3: Generation of additive, zero mean Gaussian noise

1. Suppose an image has gray-level range $[0, G - 1]$. Select $\sigma > 0$; low values generate less noise.

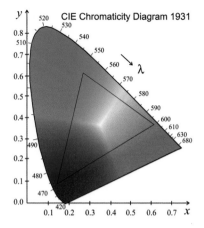

Plate 1: © *Cengage Learning 2015. Page 35, Figure 2.30.*

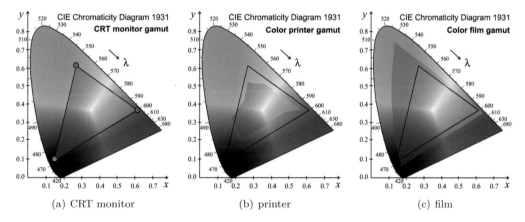

(a) CRT monitor   (b) printer   (c) film

Plate 2: © *Cengage Learning 2015. Page 35, Figure 2.31.*

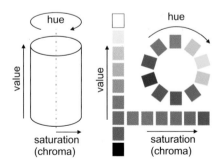

Plate 3: © *Cengage Learning 2015. Page 37, Figure 2.33.*

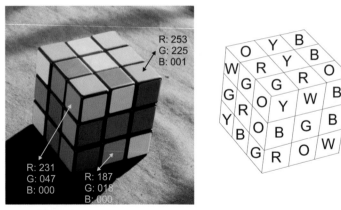

Plate 4: © *Cengage Learning 2015. Page 39, Figure 2.34.*

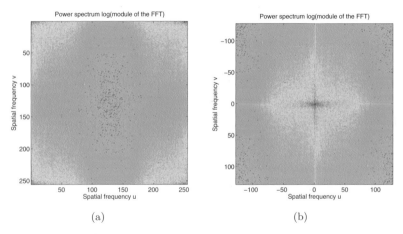

(a)   (b)

Plate 5: © *Cengage Learning 2015. Page 61, Figure 3.7.*

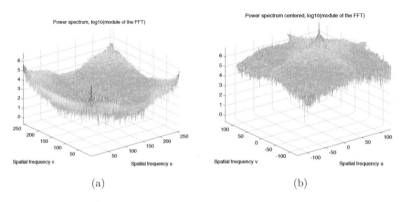

(a)   (b)

Plate 6: © *Cengage Learning 2015. Page 62, Figure 3.9.*

Plate 7: *Courtesy of M. Urban, Czech Technical University, Prague. Page 159, Figure 5.34.*

Plate 8: *Courtesy of J. Matas, Czech Technical University, Prague. Page 160, Figure 5.35.*

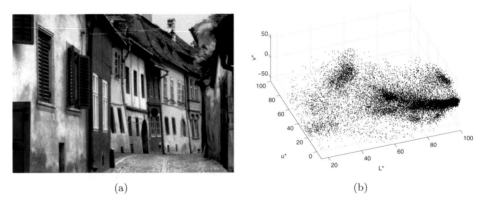

(a)   (b)

Plate 9: © 2002 IEEE. Reprinted, with permission, from D. Comaniciu, P. Meer, "Mean shift: A robust approach toward feature space analysis," IEEE Trans. Pattern Anal. Machine Intell., vol. 24, pp. 603-619, 2002. Page 259, Figure 7.2.

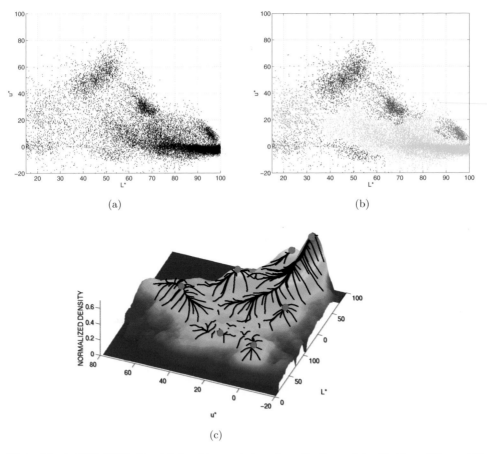

Plate 10: © 2002 IEEE. Reprinted, with permission, from D. Comaniciu, P. Meer, "Mean shift: A robust approach toward feature space analysis," IEEE Trans. Pattern Anal. Machine Intell, vol. 24, pp. 603-619, 2002. Page 260, Figure 7.3.

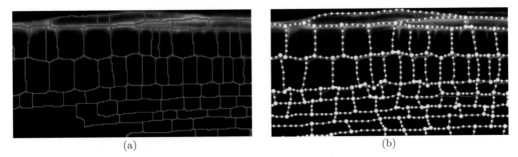

(a)   (b)

Plate 11: *Republished with permission of American Society of Plant Biologists, from The Plant Cell, Pound et al., "CellSeT: Novel Software to Extract and Analyze Structured Networks of Plant Cells from Confocal Images," 1989; permission conveyed through Copyright Clearance Center, Inc. Page 268, Figure 7.11.*

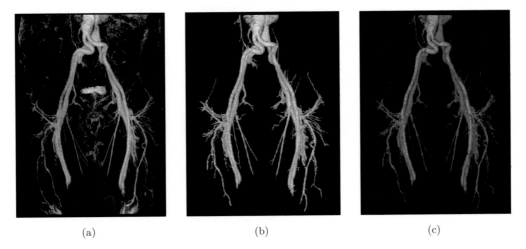

(a)   (b)   (c)

Plate 12: *Courtesy of J. K. Udupa, University of Pennsylvania. Page 287, Figure 7.28.*

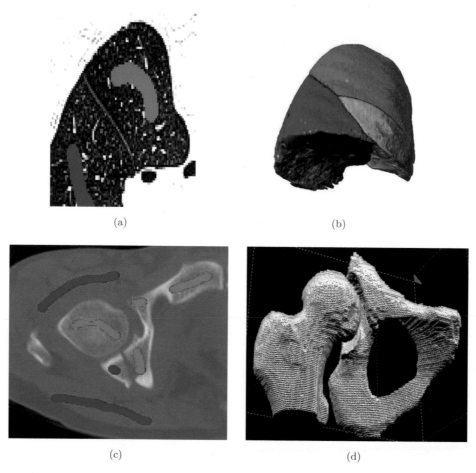

(a)

(b)

(c)

(d)

Plate 13: *Courtesy of Y. Boykov, University of Western Ontario and B. Geiger, Siemens Research. Page 302, Figure 7.38.*

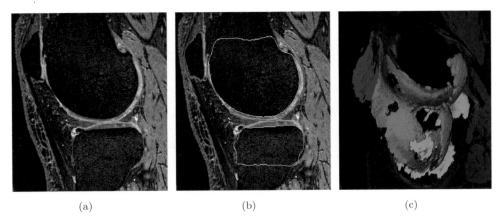

(a)   (b)   (c)

Plate 14: *Yin, Y., Zhang, X., Williams, R., Wu, X., Anderson, D.D., Sonka, M., "LOGISMOS-Layered Optimal Graph Image Segmentation of Multiple Objects and Surfaces: Cartilage Segmentation in the Knee Joint," Medical Imaging, IEEE Transactions, Volume: 29, Issue: 12, Digital Object Identifier: 10.1109/TMI.2010.2058861, Publication Year: 2010, Page(s): 2023-2037. Page 316, Figure 7.48.*

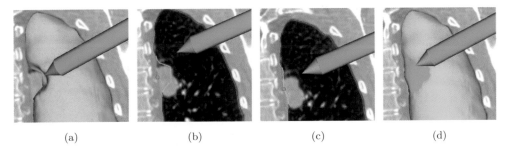

(a)   (b)   (c)   (d)

Plate 15: *Sun S., Sonka M., and Beichel R., "Lung segmentation refinement based on optimal surface finding utilizing a hybrid desktop/virtual reality user interface," Computerized Medical Imaging and Graphics, 37(1):15-27, 2013b. Page 316, Figure 7.49.*

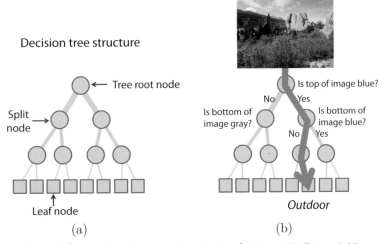

Plate 16: *Based on [Criminisi et al., 2011]. Page 443, Figure 9.35.*

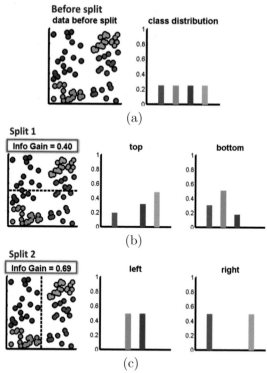

Plate 17: *Based on [Criminisi et al., 2011]. Page 444, Figure 9.36.*

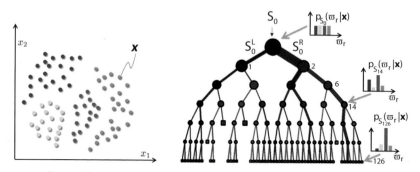

Plate 18: *Based on [Criminisi et al., 2011]. Page 445, Figure 9.37.*

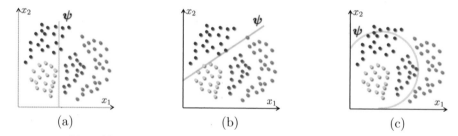

Plate 19: *Based on [Criminisi et al., 2011]. Page 446, Figure 9.38.*

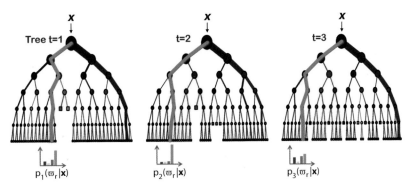

Plate 20: *Based on [Criminisi et al., 2011]. Page 447, Figure 9.39.*

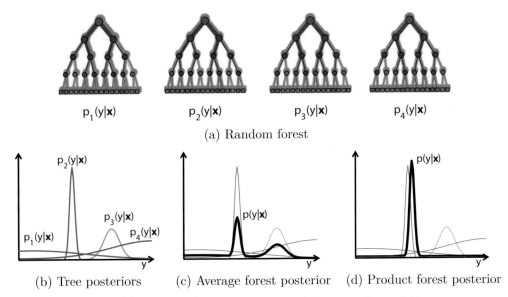

(a) Random forest

(b) Tree posteriors   (c) Average forest posterior   (d) Product forest posterior

Plate 21: *Based on [Criminisi et al., 2011]. Page 447, Figure 9.40.*

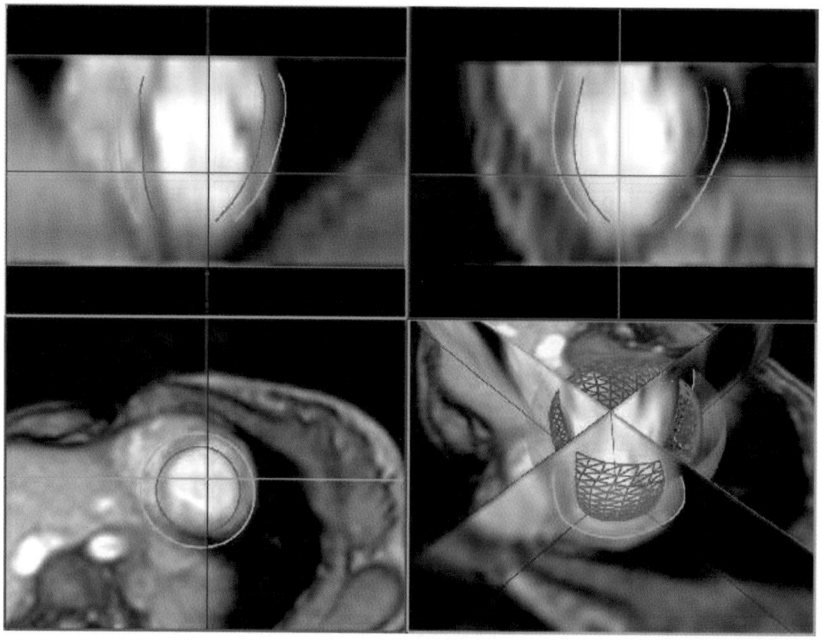

(a)

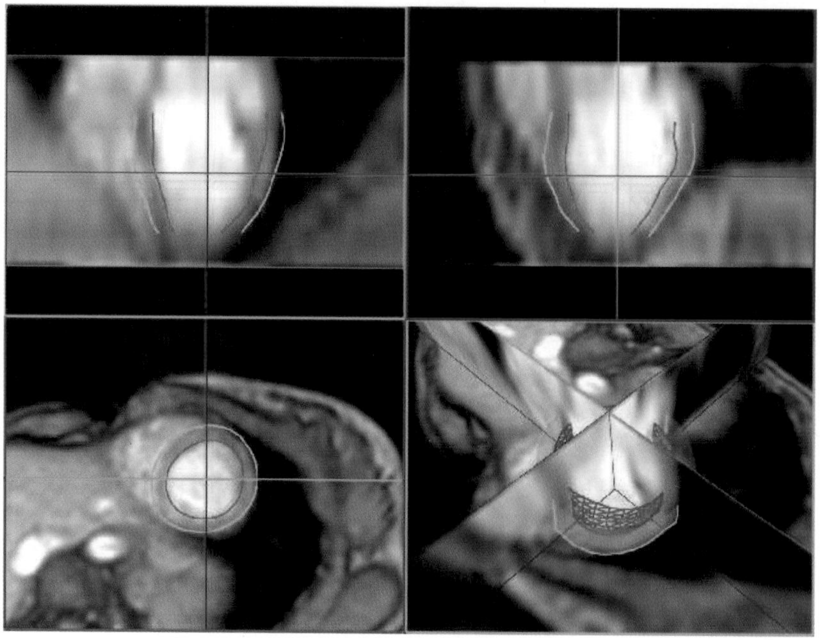

(b)

Plate 22: *Handbook of Mathematical Models in Computer Vision, "3D active shape and appearance models in cardiac image analysis," 2006, pp. 471-486, B. Lelieveldt, A. Frangi, S. Mitchell, H. van Assen, S. Ordas, J. Reiber, and M. Sonka. Page 499, Figure 10.20.*

Plate 23: © 2005 IEEE. Reprinted, with permission, from N. Dalal and B. Triggs, "Histograms of oriented gradients for human detection," Conference on Computer Vision and Pattern Recognition, pp. 886-893, 2005. Page 512, Figure 10.31.

(a)   (b)   (c)   (d)   (e)   (f)   (g)

Plate 24: © 2005 IEEE. Reprinted, with permission, from N. Dalal and B. Triggs, "Histograms of oriented gradients for human detection," Conference on Computer Vision and Pattern Recognition, pp. 886-893, 2005. Page 513, Figure 10.32.

Plate 25: With kind permission from Springer Science+Business Media: Outdoor and Large-Scale Real-World Scene Analysis, "An introduction to random forests for multi-class object detection," 2012, pp. 243-263, J. Gall, N. Razavi, and L. Gool. Page 518, Figure 10.37.

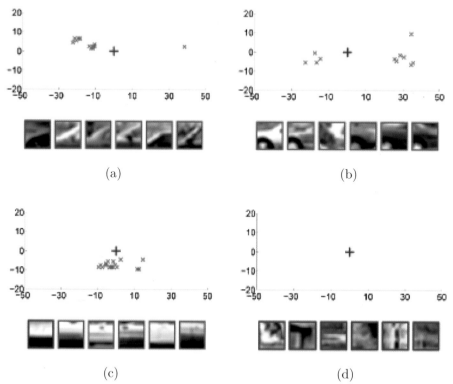

(a)

(b)

(c)

(d)

Plate 26: © 2011 IEEE. Reprinted, with permission, from Gall, J., Yao, A., Razavi, N., Van Gool, L., Lempitsky, V., "Hough forests for object detection, tracking, and action recognition," IEEE Trans. Pattern Anal. Machine Intell, vol. 33, pp. 2188-2202, IEEE, 2011. Page 519, Figure 10.38.

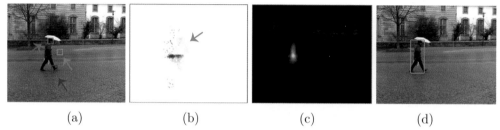

(a)   (b)   (c)   (d)

Plate 27: © 2011 IEEE. Reprinted, with permission, from Gall, J., Yao, A., Razavi, N., Van Gool, L., Lempitsky, V., "Hough forests for object detection, tracking, and action recognition," IEEE Trans. Pattern Anal. Machine Intell, vol. 33, pp. 2188-2202, IEEE, 2011. Page 521, Figure 10.39.

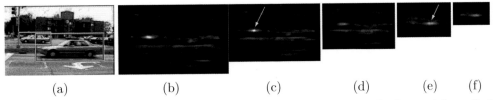

(a) (b) (c) (d) (e) (f)

Plate 28: *With kind permission from Springer Science+Business Media: Outdoor and Large-Scale Real-World Scene Analysis, "An introduction to random forests for multi-class object detection," 2012, pp. 243-263, J. Gall, N. Razavi, and L. Gool. Page 521, Figure 10.40.*

Plate 29: *A. Criminisi, J. Shotton, and E. Konukoglu, Decision Forests for Classfication, Regression, Density Estimation, Manifold Learning and Semi-Supervised Learning. Microsoft Research technical report TR-2011-114. © 2012 Microsoft Corporation. All rights reserved. Page 522, Figure 10.41.*

(a)

(b)

Plate 30: *© 2011 IEEE. Reprinted, with permission, from Shotton J., Fitzgibbon A., Cook M., Sharp T., Finocchio M., Moore R., Kipman A., and Blake A., "Real-time human pose recognition in parts from single depth images," Computer Vision and Pattern Recognition (CVPR), 2011 IEEE Conference, pp. 1297-1304, 2011. Page 522, Figure 10.42.*

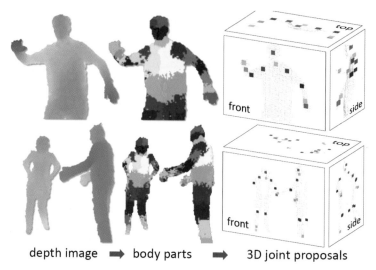

depth image ➡ body parts ➡ 3D joint proposals

Plate 31: © 2011 IEEE. Reprinted, with permission, from Shotton J., Fitzgibbon A., Cook M., Sharp T., Finocchio M., Moore R., Kipman A., and Blake A., "Real-time human pose recognition in parts from single depth images," Computer Vision and Pattern Recognition (CVPR), 2011 IEEE Conference, pp. 1297-1304, 2011. Page 523, Figure 10.44.

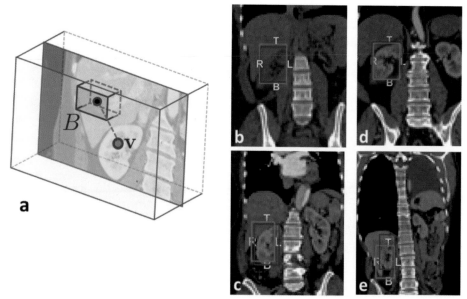

Plate 32: A. Criminisi, J. Shotton, and E. Konukoglu, Decision Forests for Classfication, Regression, Density Estimation, Manifold Learning and Semi-Supervised Learning. Microsoft Research technical report TR-2011-114. © 2012 Microsoft Corporation. All rights reserved. Page 523, Figure 10.44.

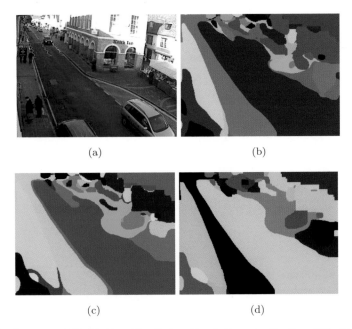

(a)   (b)

(c)   (d)

Plate 33: *Courtesy of H. M. Dee, The University of Aberystwyth. Page 556, Figure 10.61.*

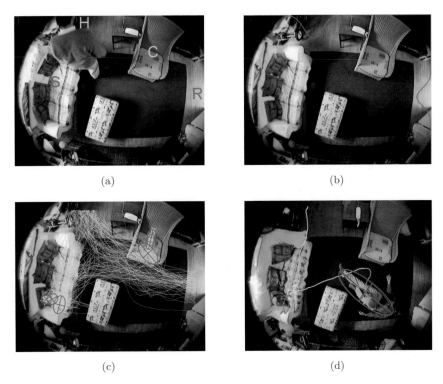

(a)   (b)

(c)   (d)

Plate 34: *With kind permission from Springer Science+Business Media: Pattern Analysis and Applications, Volume 7, Issue 4, 2004, pp 386-401, Stephen J. McKenna, figures 1, 12, 6 and 13, Copyright © 2005, Springer-Verlag London Limited. Page 557, Figure 10.62.*

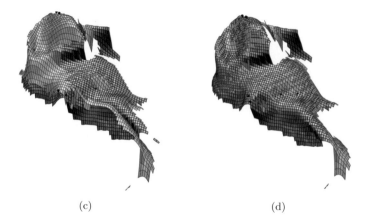

(c)   (d)

Plate 35: *Courtesy of T. Pajdla, D. Večerka, Czech Technical University. Page 668, Figure 12.22.*

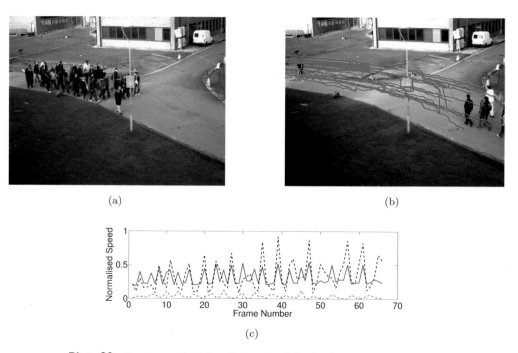

(a)   (b)

(c)

Plate 36: *Courtesy of I. Hales, University of Leeds. Page 677, Figure 12.34.*

Plate 37: *Courtesy of H. M. Dee, The University of Aberystwyth. Page 807, Figure 16.11.*

2. For each pair of horizontally neighboring pixels (x, y), $(x, y+1)$ generate a pair of independent random numbers r, ϕ in the range $[0, 1]$.

3. Calculate

$$z_1 = \sigma \cos(2\pi\phi)\sqrt{-2 \ln r} \,,$$
$$z_2 = \sigma \sin(2\pi\phi)\sqrt{-2 \ln r} \,. \tag{2.10}$$

(This is the Box-Muller transform which assumes that z_1, z_2 are independently normally distributed with zero mean and variance σ^2.)

4. Set $f'(x, y) = g(x, y) + z_1$ and $f'(x, y+1) = g(x, y+1) + z_2$, where g is the input image.

5. Set

$$f(x, y) = \begin{cases} 0 & \text{if } f'(x, y) < 0 \,, \\ G-1 & \text{if } f'(x, y) > G-1 \,, \\ f'(x, y) & \text{otherwise,} \end{cases} \tag{2.11}$$

$$f(x, y+1) = \begin{cases} 0 & \text{if } f'(x, y+1) < 0 \,, \\ G-1 & \text{if } f'(x, y+1) > G-1 \,, \\ f'(x, y+1) & \text{otherwise.} \end{cases} \tag{2.12}$$

6. Go to 3 until all pixels have been scanned.

The truncation performed by equations (2.11) and (2.12) will attenuate the Gaussian nature of the noise; this will become more marked for values of σ that are high relative to G. Other algorithms for noise generation may be found in [Pitas, 1993].

Equation (2.9) leads to a definition of **signal-to-noise ratio** (SNR); computing the total square value of the noise contribution

$$E = \sum_{(x,y)} \nu^2(x, y) \,,$$

which we compare this with the total square value of the observed signal

$$F = \sum_{(x,y)} f^2(x, y) \,.$$

The *signal-to-noise ratio* is then

$$\text{SNR} = \frac{F}{E} \tag{2.13}$$

(strictly, we are comparing the mean observation with the mean error—the computation is obviously the same). SNR represents a measure of image quality, with high values being 'good'. It is often expressed in the logarithmic scale, in decibels

$$\text{SNR}_{\text{dB}} = 10 \log_{10} \text{SNR} \,. \tag{2.14}$$

The noise magnitude depends in many cases on the signal magnitude itself

$$f = g\nu.$$
(2.15)

This model describes **multiplicative noise**. An example of multiplicative noise is television raster degradation, which depends on TV lines; in the area of a line this noise is maximal, and between two lines it is minimal.

Quantization noise occurs when insufficient quantization levels are used, for example, 50 levels for a monochromatic image. In this case false contours appear. Quantization noise can be eliminated simply, see Section 2.2.2.

Impulse noise means that an image is corrupted with individual noisy pixels whose brightness differs significantly from that of the neighborhood. The term **salt-and-pepper noise** is used to describe saturated impulsive noise—an image corrupted with white and/or black pixels is an example. Salt-and-pepper noise can corrupt binary images.

The problem of suppressing noise in images is addressed in Chapter 5. If nothing is known a priori about noise properties, local pre-processing methods are appropriate (Section 5.3). If the noise parameters are known in advance, image restoration techniques can be used (Section 5.4).

2.4 Color images

Human color perception adds a subjective layer on top of underlying objective physical properties—the wavelength of electromagnetic radiation. Consequently, **color** may be considered a psycho-physical phenomenon.

Color has long been used in painting, photography and films to display the surrounding world to humans in a similar way to that in which it is perceived in reality. There is considerable literature on the variants in the naming of colors across languages, which is a very subtle affair [Kay, 2005]. The human visual system is not very precise in perceiving color in absolute terms; if we wish to express our notion of color precisely we would describe it relative to some widely used color which is used as a standard: recall, e.g., the red of a British pillar box. There are whole industries which present images to humans—the press, films, displays, and hence a desire for color constancy. In computer vision, we have the advantage of using a camera as a measuring device, which yields measurements in absolute quantities.

Newton reported in the 17th century that white light from the sun is a spectral mixture, and used the optical prism to perform decomposition. This was a radical idea to propose at time; over 100 years later influential scientists and philosophers such as Goethe refused to believe it.

2.4.1 Physics of color

The electromagnetic spectrum is illustrated in Figure 2.23.

Only a narrow section of the electromagnetic spectrum is visible to a human, with wavelength from approximately 380 nm to 740 nm. Visible colors with the wavelengths shown in Figure 2.24 are called **spectral colors** and are those which humans see when white light is decomposed using a Newtonian prism, or which are observed in a rainbow on the sky. Colors can be represented as combinations of the **primary colors**, e.g., red,

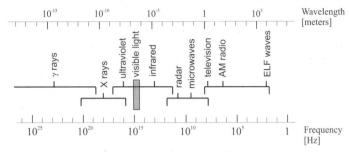

Figure 2.23: Division of the electromagnetic spectrum (ELF is Extremely Low Frequencies). © *Cengage Learning 2015*.

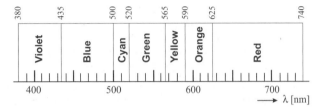

Figure 2.24: Wavelength λ of the spectrum visible to humans. © *Cengage Learning 2015*.

green, and blue, which for the purposes of standardization have been defined as 700 nm, 546.1 nm, and 435.8 nm, respectively [Pratt, 1978], although this standardization does not imply that all colors can be synthesized as combinations of these three.

The intensity of irradiation for different wavelengths λ usually changes. This variation is expressed by a **power spectrum** (called also power spectrum distribution) $S(\lambda)$.

Why do we see the world in color? There are two predominant physical mechanisms describing what happens when a surface is irradiated. First, the **surface reflection** rebounds incoming energy in a similar way to a mirror. The spectrum of the reflected light remains the same as that of the illuminant and it is independent of the surface—recall that shiny metals 'do not have a color'. Second, the energy diffuses into the material and reflects randomly from the internal pigment in the matter. This mechanism is called **body reflection** and is predominant in dielectrics such as plastic or paints. Figure 2.25 illustrates both surface reflection (mirroring along surface normal **n**) and body reflection. Colors are caused by the properties of pigment particles which absorb certain wavelengths from the incoming illuminant wavelength spectrum.

Most sensors used for color capture, e.g., in cameras, do not have direct access to color; the exception is a **spectrophotometer** which in principle resembles Newton's prism. Incoming irradiation is decomposed into spectral colors and intensity along the

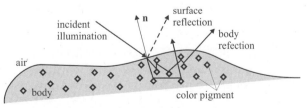

Figure 2.25: Observed color of objects is caused by certain wavelength absorptions by pigment particles in dielectrics. © *Cengage Learning 2015*.

spectrum with changing wavelength λ is measured in a narrow wavelength band, for instance, by a mechanically moved point sensor. Actual spectrophotometers use diffraction gratings instead of a glass prism.

Sometimes, intensities measured in several narrow bands of wavelengths are collected in a vector describing each pixel. Each spectral band is digitized independently and is represented by an individual digital image function as if it were a monochromatic image. In this way, **multispectral images** are created. Multispectral images are commonly used in remote sensing from satellites, airborne sensors and in industry. Wavelength usually span from ultraviolet through the visible section to infrared. For instance, the LAND-SAT 7 satellite transmits digitized images in eight spectral bands from near-ultraviolet to infrared.

2.4.2   Color perceived by humans

Evolution has developed a mechanism of indirect color sensing in humans and some animals. Three types of sensors receptive to the wavelength of incoming irradiation have been established in humans, thus the term **trichromacy**. Color sensitive receptors on the human retina are the **cones**. The other light sensitive receptors on the retina are the **rods** which are dedicated to sensing monochromatically in low ambient light conditions. Cones are categorized into three types based on the sensed wavelength range: S (short) with maximum sensitivity at $\approx 430\,\text{nm}$, M (medium) at $\approx 560\,\text{nm}$, and L (long) at $\approx 610\,\text{nm}$. Cones S, M, L are occasionally called cones B, G and R, respectively, but that is slightly misleading. We do not see red solely because an L cone is activated. Light with equally distributed wavelength spectrum looks white to a human, and an unbalanced spectrum appears as some shade of color.

The reaction of a photoreceptor or output from a sensor in a camera can be modeled mathematically. Let i be the specific type of sensor, $i = 1, 2, 3$, (the retinal cone type S, M, L in the human case). Let $R_i(\lambda)$ be the spectral sensitivity of the sensor, $I(\lambda)$ be the spectral density of the illumination, and $S(\lambda)$ describe how the surface patch reflects each wavelength of the illuminating light. The spectral response q_i of the i-th sensor, can be modeled by integration over a certain range of wavelengths

$$q_i = \int_{\lambda_1}^{\lambda_2} I(\lambda)\, R_i(\lambda)\, S(\lambda)\, d\lambda \,. \tag{2.16}$$

Consider the cone types S, M, L. How does the vector (q_S, q_M, q_L) represent the color of the surface patch? It does not according to equation (2.16) since the output from the photosensors depends on the three factors $I(\lambda)$, $S(\lambda)$ and $R(\lambda)$. Only the factor $S(\lambda)$ is related to the surface patch. Only in the ideal case, when the illumination is perfectly white, i.e., $I(\lambda) = 1$, can we consider (q_S, q_M, q_L) as an estimate of the color of the surface.

Figure 2.26 illustrates qualitatively the relative sensitivities of S, M, L cones. Measurements were taken with the white light source at the cornea so that absorption of wavelength in cornea, lens and inner pigments of the eye is taken into account [Wandell, 1995].

A phenomenon called **color metamer** is relevant. A metamer, in general, means two things that are physically different but perceived as the same. Red and green adding

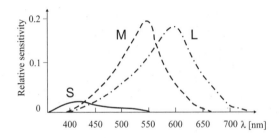

Figure 2.26: Relative sensitivity of S, M, L cones of the human eye to wavelength. © *Cengage Learning 2015.*

to produce yellow is a color metamer, because yellow could have also been produced by a spectral color. The human visual system is fooled into perceiving that red and green is the same as yellow.

Consider a color matching experiment in which someone is shown a pattern consisting of two adjacent color patches. The first patch displays a test light—a spectral color of certain wavelength. The second patch is created as an additive combination of three selected primary lights, e.g., colors red=645.2 nm, green=525.3 nm and blue=444.4 nm. The observer is asked to control the red, green and blue intensities until both patches look identical. This color matching experiment is possible because of the color metamer. The result of measurements (redrawn from [Wandell, 1995]) is in Figure 2.27. Negative lobes can be seen on the curves for red and green in this figure. This would seem to be impossible. For wavelengths exhibiting negative values the three additive lights do not perceptually match the spectral color because it is darker. If the perceptual match has to be obtained then the observer has to add the intensity to the patch corresponding to the spectral color. This increase of this intensity is depicted as a decrease in the color matching function. Hence the negative values.

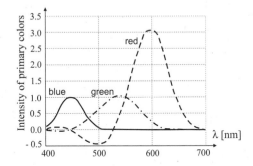

Figure 2.27: Color matching functions obtained in the color matching experiment. Intensities of the selected primary colors which perceptually match spectral color of given wavelength λ. *Based on [Wandell, 1995].*

Human vision is prone to various illusions. Perceived color is influenced, besides the spectrum of the illuminant, by the colors and scene interpretation surrounding the observed color. In addition, eye adaptation to changing light conditions is not very fast and perception is influenced by adaptation. Nevertheless, we assume for simplicity that the spectrum of light coming to a point on the retina fully determines the color.

Since color can be defined by almost any set of primaries, the world community agreed on primaries and color matching functions which are widely used. The **color model** was introduced as a mathematical abstraction allowing us to express colors as tuples of numbers, typically as three or four values of color components. Being motivated by the press and the development of color film, in 1931, CIE (International Commission on Illumination, still acting in Lausanne, Switzerland) issued a technical standard called **XYZ color space**.

The standard is given by the three imaginary lights X=700.0 nm, Y=546.1 nm, Z=435.8 nm and by the color matching functions $X(\lambda)$, $Y(\lambda)$ and $Z(\lambda)$ corresponding to the perceptual ability of an average human viewing a screen through an aperture providing a 2° field of view. The standard is artificial because there is no set of physically realizable primary lights that would yield the color matching functions in the experiment. Nevertheless, if we wanted to characterize the imaginary lights then, roughly speaking, $X \approx$ red, $Y \approx$ green and $Z \approx$ blue. The CIE standard is an example of an absolute standard, i.e., defining unambiguous representation of color which does not depend on other external factors. There are more recent and more precise absolute standards: CIELAB 1976 (ISO 13665) and HunterLab (http://www.hunterlab.com). Later, we will also discuss relative color standards such as RGB color space: there are several RGB color spaces used—two computer devices may display the same RGB image differently.

The XYZ color standard fulfills three requirements:

- Unlike the color matching experiment yielding negative lobes of color matching functions, the matching functions of XYZ space are required to be non-negative.

- The value of $Y(\lambda)$ should coincide with the brightness (luminance).

- Normalization is performed to assure that the power corresponding to the three color matching functions is equal (i.e., the area under all three curves is equal).

The resulting color matching functions are shown in Figure 2.28. The actual color is a mixture (more precisely a convex combination) of

$$c_X\, X + c_Y\, Y + c_Z\, Z\,, \tag{2.17}$$

where $0 \le c_X,\, c_Y,\, c_Z \le 1$ are weights (intensities) in the mixture. The subspace of colors perceivable by humans is called the color gamut and is demonstrated in Figure 2.29.

3D figures are difficult to represent, and so a planar view of a 3D color space is used. The projection plane is given by the plane passing through extremal points on all three

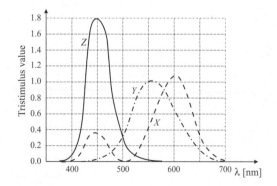

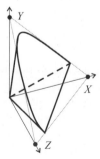

Figure 2.28: Color matching functions for the CIE standard from 1931. $X(\lambda)$, $Y(\lambda)$, $Z(\lambda)$ are color matching functions. *Based on [Wandell, 1995].*

Figure 2.29: Color gamut - a subspace of the X, Y, Z color space showing all colors perceivable by humans. © *Cengage Learning 2015.*

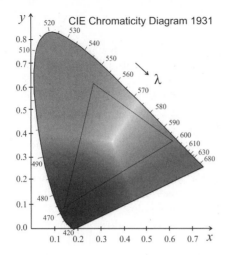

Figure 2.30: CIE chromaticity diagram is a projection of XYZ color space into a plane. The triangle depicts a subset of colors spanned by red, green, and blue. These are TV colors, i.e., all possible colors, which can be seen on a CRT display. © *Cengage Learning 2015. A color version of this figure may be seen in the color inset—Plate 1.*

axes, i.e., points X, Y, Z. The new 2D coordinates x, y are obtained as

$$x = \frac{X}{X + Y + Z}\,, \qquad y = \frac{Y}{X + Y + Z}\,, \qquad z = 1 - x - y\,.$$

The result of this plane projection is the CIE chromaticity diagram, see Figure 2.30. The horseshoe like subspace contains colors which people are able to see. All monochromatic spectra visible to humans map into the curved part of the horseshoe—their wavelengths are shown in Figure 2.30.

Display and printing devices use three selected real primary colors (as opposed to three synthetic primary colors of XYZ color space). All possible mixtures of these primary colors fail to cover the whole interior of the horseshoe in CIE chromaticity diagram. This situation is demonstrated qualitatively for three particular devices in Figure 2.31.

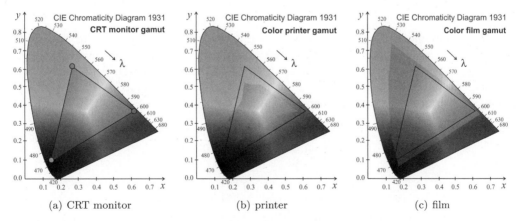

(a) CRT monitor (b) printer (c) film

Figure 2.31: Gamuts which can be displayed using three typical display devices. © *Cengage Learning 2015. A color version of this figure may be seen in the color inset—Plate 2.*

2.4.3   Color spaces

Several different primary colors and corresponding color spaces are used in practice, and these spaces can be transformed into each other. If the absolute color space is used then the transformation is the one-to-one mapping and does not lose information (except for rounding errors). Because color spaces have their own gamuts, information is lost if the transformed value appears out of the gamut. See [Burger and Burge, 2008] for a full explanation and for algorithms; here, we list several frequently used color spaces.

The **RGB** color space has its origin in color television where Cathode Ray Tubes (CRT) were used. RGB color space is an example of a relative color standard (as opposed to the absolute one, e.g., CIE 1931). The primary colors (R–red, G–green and B–blue) mimicked phosphor in CRT luminophore. The model uses additive color mixing to inform what kind of light needs to be emitted to produce a given color. The value of a particular color is expressed as a vector of three elements—intensities of three primary colors, and a transformation to a different color space is expressed by a 3×3 matrix. Assume that values for each primary are quantized to $m = 2^n$ values; let the highest intensity value be $k = m - 1$; then $(0,0,0)$ is black, (k,k,k) is (television) white, $(k,0,0)$ is 'pure' red, and so on. The value $k = 255 = 2^8 - 1$ is common, i.e., 8 bits per color channel. There are $256^3 = 2^{24} = 16,777,216$ possible colors in such a discretized space.

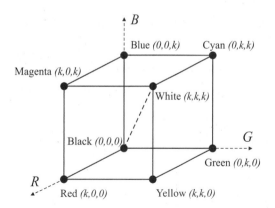

Figure 2.32: RGB color space with primary colors red, green, blue and secondary colors yellow, cyan, magenta. Gray-scale images with all intensities lie along the dashed line connecting black and white in RGB color space. © *Cengage Learning 2015.*

The RGB model may be thought of as a 3D co-ordinatization of color space (see Figure 2.32); note the secondary colors which are combinations of two pure primaries. There are specific instances of the RGB color model such as sRGB, Adobe RGB and Adobe Wide Gamut RGB, which differ slightly in transformation matrices and the gamut. One of the transformations between RGB and XYZ color spaces is

$$\begin{bmatrix} R \\ G \\ B \end{bmatrix} = \begin{bmatrix} 3.24 & -1.54 & -0.50 \\ -0.98 & 1.88 & 0.04 \\ 0.06 & -0.20 & 1.06 \end{bmatrix} \begin{bmatrix} X \\ Y \\ Z \end{bmatrix},$$

$$\begin{bmatrix} X \\ Y \\ Z \end{bmatrix} = \begin{bmatrix} 0.41 & 0.36 & 0.18 \\ 0.21 & 0.72 & 0.07 \\ 0.02 & 0.12 & 0.95 \end{bmatrix} \begin{bmatrix} R \\ G \\ B \end{bmatrix}. \tag{2.18}$$

The US and Japanese color television formerly used **YIQ** color space. The Y component describes intensity and I, Q represent color. YIQ is another example of additive color mixing. This system stores a luminance value with two chrominance values, corresponding approximately to the amounts of blue and red in the color. This color space corresponds closely to the YUV color model in the PAL television norm (Australia, Europe, except France, which uses SECAM). YIQ color space is rotated 33° with respect to the YUV color space. The YIQ color model is useful since the Y component provides all that is necessary for a monochrome display; further, it exploits advantageous properties of the human visual system, in particular our sensitivity to **luminance**, the perceived energy of a light source.

The **CMY**—for Cyan, Magenta, Yellow—color model uses subtractive color mixing which is used in printing processes. It describes what kind of inks need to be applied so the light reflected from the white substrate (paper, painter's canvas) and passing through the inks produces a given color. CMYK stores ink values for black in addition. Black can be generated from C, M and Y components but as it is abundant in printed documents, it is of advantage to have a special black ink. Many CMYK colors spaces are used for different sets of inks, substrates, and press characteristics (which change the color transfer function for each ink and thus change the appearance).

HSV – Hue, Saturation, and Value (also known as HSB, hue, saturation, brightness) is often used by painters because it is closer to their thinking and technique. Artists commonly use three to four dozen colors (characterized by the hue; technically, the dominant wavelength). If another color is to be obtained then it is mixed from the given ones, for example, 'purple' or 'orange'. The painter also wants colors of different saturation, e.g., to change 'fire brigade red' to pink. She will mix the 'fire brigade red' with white (and/or black) to obtain the desired lower saturation. The HSV color model is illustrated in Figure 2.33.

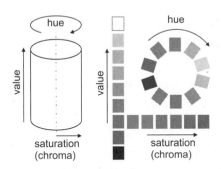

Figure 2.33: HSV color model illustrated as a cylinder and unfolded cylinder. © *Cengage Learning 2015. A color version of this figure may be seen in the color inset—Plate 3.*

HSV decouples intensity information from color, while hue and saturation correspond to human perception, thus making this representation very useful for developing image processing algorithms. This will become clearer as we proceed to describe image enhancement algorithms (for example, equalization Algorithm 5.1), which if applied to each component of an RGB model would corrupt the human sense of color, but which would work more or less as expected if applied to the intensity component of HSV (leaving the color information unaffected). HSL (hue, saturation, lightness/luminance), also known as HLS or HSI (hue, saturation, intensity) is similar to HSV. 'Lightness' replaces 'brightness'. The difference is that the brightness of a pure color is equal to the brightness of white, while the lightness of a pure color is equal to the lightness of a medium gray.

Models	Color spaces	Applications
Colorimetric	XYZ	Colorimetric calculations
Device oriented, nonuniform spaces	RGB, UIQ	Storage, processing, coding, color TV
Device oriented, Uniform spaces	LAB, LUV	Color difference, analysis
User oriented	HSL, HSI	Color perception, computer graphics

2.4.4 Palette images

Palette images (also called **indexed images**) provide a simple way to reduce the amount of data needed to represent an image. The pixel values constitute a link to a **lookup table** (also called a color table, color map, **palette**). The table contains as many entries as the range of possible values in the pixel, which is typically 8 bits $\equiv$ 256 values. Each entry of the table maps the pixel value to the color, so there are three values, one for each of three color components. In the typical case of the RGB color model, values for red, green and blue are provided. It is easy to see that this approach would reduce data consumption to one-third if each of the RGB channels had originally been using 8 bits (plus size of the look up table). Many widely used image formats for raster images such as TIFF, PNG and GIF can store palette images.

If the number of colors in the input image is less than or equal to the number of entries in the lookup table then all colors can be selected and no loss of information occurs. Such images may be cartoon movies, or program outputs. In the more common case, the number of colors in the image exceeds the number of entries in the lookup table, a subset of colors has to be chosen, and a loss of information occurs.

This color selection may be done many ways. The simplest is to quantize color space regularly into cubes of the same size. In the 8 bit example, there would be $8 \times 8 \times 8 = 512$ such cubes. If there is, e.g., a green frog in green grass in the picture then there will not be enough shades of green available in the lookup table to display the image well. In such a case, it is better to check which colors appear in the image by creating histograms for all three color components and quantize them to provide more shades for colors which occur in the image frequently. If an image is converted to a palette representation then the nearest color (in some metric sense) in the lookup table is used to represent the original color. This is an instance of **vector quantization** (see Section 14.4) which is widely used in analyzing large multi-dimensional datasets. It is also possible to view the occupation by the pixels of RGB space as a **cluster analysis** problem (see Section 9.2.6), susceptible to algorithms such as k-means (Algorithm 9.5).

The term **pseudo-color** is usually used when an original image is gray-level and is displayed in color; this is often done to exploit the color discriminatory power of human vision. The same palette machinery as described above is used for this purpose; a palette is loaded into the lookup table which visualizes the particular gray-scale image the best. It could either enhance local changes, or might provide various views of the image. Which palette to choose depends on the semantics of the image and cannot be derived from image statistics alone. This selection is an interactive process.

Almost all computer graphics cards work with palette images directly in hardware. The content of the lookup table will be filled by the programmer.

2.4.5 Color constancy

Consider the situation in which the same surface is seen under different illumination, e.g., for a Rubik's cube in Figure 2.34. The same surface colors are shown fully illuminated and in shadow. The human vision system is able to abstract to a certain degree from the illumination changes and perceive several instances of a particular color as the same. This phenomenon is called color constancy. Of course, it would be desirable to equip artificial perception systems based on photosensors with this ability too, but this is very challenging.

 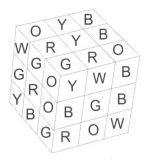

Figure 2.34: Color constancy: The Rubik cube is captured in sunlight, and two of three visible sides of the cube are in shadow. The white balance was set in the shadow area. There are six colors on the cube: R-red, G-green, B-blue, O-orange, W-white, and Y-yellow. The assignment of the six available colors to 3×9 visible color patches is shown on the right. Notice how different the same color patch can be: see *RGB* values for the three instances of orange. © *Cengage Learning 2015. A color version of this figure may be seen in the color inset—Plate 4.*

Recall equation (2.16) which models the spectral response q_i of the i-th sensor by integration over a range of wavelengths as a multiplication of three factors: spectral sensitivity $R_i(\lambda)$ of the sensor $i = 1, 2, 3$, spectral density of the illumination $I(\lambda)$, and surface reflectance $S(\lambda)$. A color vision system has to calculate the vector q_i for each pixel as if $I(\lambda) = 1$. Unfortunately, the spectrum of the illuminant $I(\lambda)$ is usually unknown.

Assume for a while the ideal case in which the spectrum $I(\lambda)$ of the illuminant is known. Color constancy could be obtained by dividing the output of each sensor with its sensitivity to the illumination. Let q_i' be the spectral response after compensation for the illuminant (called von Kries coefficients), $q_i' = \rho_i q_i$, where

$$\rho_i = 1 \Big/ \int_{\lambda_1}^{\lambda_2} I(\lambda) R_i(\lambda) \, d\lambda \,. \tag{2.19}$$

Partial color constancy can be obtained by multiplying color responses of the three photosensors with von Kries coefficients ρ_i.

In practice, there are several obstacles that make this procedure intractable. First, the illuminant spectrum $I(\lambda)$ is not known; it can only be guessed indirectly from reflections in surfaces. Second, only the approximate spectrum is expressed by the spectral response q_i of the i-th sensor. Clearly the color constancy problem is ill-posed and cannot be solved without making additional assumptions about the scene.

Several such assumptions have been suggested in the literature. It can be assumed that the average color of the image is gray. In such a case, it is possible to scale the sensitivity of each sensor type until the assumption becomes true. This will result in an insensitivity to the color of the illumination. This type of color compensation is often used in automatic white balancing in video cameras. Another common assumption is that the brightest point in the image has the color of the illumination. This is true when the scene contains specular reflections which have the property that the illuminant is reflected without being transformed by the surface patch.

The problem of color constancy is further complicated by the perceptual abilities of the human visual system. Humans have quite poor quantitative color memory, and also perform color adaptation. The same color is sensed differently in different local contexts.

2.5   Cameras: An overview

2.5.1   Photosensitive sensors

Photosensitive sensors most commonly found in cameras can be divided into two groups:

Sensors based on photo-emission principles exploit the photoelectric effect. An external photon carried in incoming radiation brings enough energy to provoke the emission of a free electron. This phenomenon is exhibited most strongly in metals. In image analysis related applications, it has been used in photomultipliers and vacuum tube TV cameras.

Sensors based on photovoltaic principles became widely used with the development of semiconductors. The energy of a photon causes an electron to leave its valence band and changes to a conduction band. The quantity of incoming photons affects macroscopic conductivity. The excited electron is a source of electric voltage which manifests as electric current; the current is directly proportional to the amount of incoming energy (photons). This phenomenon is exploited in several technological elements as a photodiode, an avalanche photodiode (an amplifier of light which has similar behavior from the user's point of view as the photomultiplier; it also amplifies noise and is used, e.g., in night vision cameras), a photoresistor, and Schottky photodiode.

There are two types of semiconductor photoresistive sensors used widely in cameras: CCDs (charge-coupled devices) and CMOS (complementary metal oxide semiconductor), both developed in the 1960s and 1970s. CCDs initially became technologically mature in the 1970s and became the most widely used photosensors in cameras. CMOS technology started being technologically mastered from about the 1990s.

In a CCD sensor, every pixel's charge is transferred through just one output node to be converted to voltage, buffered, and sent off-chip as an analog signal. All of the pixel area can be devoted to light capture. In a CMOS sensor, each pixel has its own charge-to-voltage conversion, and the sensor often includes amplifiers, noise-correction, and digitization circuits, so that the chip outputs (digital) bits. These other functions increase the design complexity and reduce the area available for light capture. The chip can be built to require less off-chip circuitry for basic operation.

The basic CCD sensor element includes a Schottky photodiode and a field-effect transistor. A photon falling on the junction of the photodiode liberates electrons from the crystal lattice and creates holes, resulting in the electric charge that accumulates in a capacitor. The collected charge is directly proportional to the light intensity and duration of its falling on the diode. The sensor elements are arranged into a matrix-like grid of pixels—a CCD chip. The charges accumulated by the sensor elements are transferred to a horizontal register one row at a time by a vertical shift register. The charges are shifted out in a bucket brigade fashion to form the video signal.

There are three inherent problems with CCD chips.

- The blooming effect is the mutual influence of charges in neighboring pixels.

- It is impossible to address directly individual pixels in the CCD chip because read out through shift registers is needed.

- Individual CCD sensor elements are able to accumulate approximately 30-200 thousands electrons. The usual level of inherent noise of the CCD sensor is on the level of 20 electrons. The signal-to-noise ratio (SNR) in the case of a cooled CCD chip is SNR $= 20 \log(200000/20)$, i.e., the logarithmic noise is approximately 80 dB at best. This means that the sensor is able to cope with four orders of magnitude of intensity in the best case. This range drops to approximately two orders of magnitude with common uncooled CCD cameras. The range of incoming light intensity variations is usually higher.

Here, current technology does not beat the human eye. Evolution equipped us with the ability to perceive intensity (brightness) in a remarkable range of nine orders of magnitude (if time for adaptation is provided). This range is achieved because the eye response to intensity is proportional logarithmically to the incoming intensity. Nevertheless, among the sensors available, CCD cameras have high sensitivity (are able to see in darkness) and low levels of noise. CCD elements are abundant, also due to widely used digital photo cameras.

The development of semiconductor technology permits the production of matrix-like sensors based on CMOS technology. This technology is used in mass production in the semiconductor industry because processors and memories are manufactured using the same technology. This yields two advantages. The first is that mass production leads to low prices; because of the same CMOS technology, the photosensitive matrix-like element can be integrated to the same chip as the processor and/or operational memory. This opens the door to 'smart cameras' in which image capture and basic image processing is performed on the same chip.

The advantage of CMOS cameras (as opposed to CCD) is a higher range of sensed intensities (about 4 orders of magnitude), high speed of read-out (about 100 ns) and random access to individual pixels. The disadvantage is a higher level of noise by approximately one degree of magnitude.

2.5.2 A monochromatic camera

The camera consists of the optical system (lens), the photosensitive sensor(s) and electronics which enables the processing of a captured image, and transfer to further processing.

While image acquisition increasingly uses fully digital cameras, the earlier generation analog cameras are briefly described for completeness. Analog cameras generate a complete TV signal which contains information about light intensity, and horizontal and vertical synchronization pulses allowing row by row display. The frame scan can be with interlaced lines as in ordinary analog TV, which was introduced to reduce image flickering on cathode-ray tube (CRT) screens. A rate of 60 half-frames per second is used in the USA and Japan, and 50 half-frames per second in Europe and elsewhere. The whole image has 525 lines in the USA and Japan, 625 lines in Europe and elsewhere. Analog cameras require a digitizer card (a frame grabber) to be incorporated in the image acquisition chain.

Analog cameras have problems with jitter which means that two neighboring lines are not aligned properly and 'float' in a statistical manner one against the other. The human eye is insensitive to jitter because it is able to smooth out the statistical variation. However, jitter causes problems when the camera is used for measurement purposes such as gauging. Non-interlaced analog cameras with an appropriate frame grabber suppress this problem. Non-interlaced cameras do not need to conform to TV norms, and usually provide higher resolution such as 1024×720 pixels. Nowadays, the preferred solution is to use digital cameras offering much higher resolution in measurement applications—with CMOS camera chip resolution reaching $10,000 \times 7,096$ at the time this edition was prepared (2013).

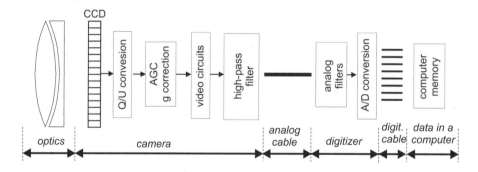

Figure 2.35: Analog CCD camera. © *Cengage Learning 2015.*

A block diagram of an analog camera with a CCD chip is in Figure 2.35. The block AGC (Automatic Gain Control) automatically changes the gain of the camera according to the amount of light in the scene. The gain is set as a compromise between necessary sensitivity in low illuminated areas and the attempt to avoid saturation of bright areas.

Cameras usually contain another block named γ correction which performs nonlinear transformation of the intensity scale. The necessity for this in the display chain originates in television technology with cathode-ray tubes (CRT). The dependency between the grid bias voltage U and the resulting irradiance L ($\sim$ brightness) of the luminophore follows a power law, $L = U^\beta$—the typical value of β is 2.2. The shape of the transfer curve is roughly parabolic. Note that the intensity of modern flat Liquid Crystal Displays (LCD) depends linearly on the input voltage.

In order to maintain a linear transfer function of the whole display chain with CRT, there is a need to compensate the non-linear transfer function by an inverse curve. It was easier and cheaper to include compensation circuitry into a few cameras at the beginning of the television era than to put it into a mass produced TV set. Due to the need for backward compatibility, there is a module in cameras which modifies the dependency of the output voltage of the camera U_k on the input radiation E, $U_k = E^{1/\beta} = E^\gamma$. The typical value is thus $\gamma = 1/2.2 \approx 0.45$. Some cameras allow the γ-value to be set in the range [0,1]. The value $\gamma=1$ corresponds to the correction being switched off.

Sometimes, it is necessary to use the camera as an absolute measuring device of incoming intensities. The image capturing chain has to be radiometrically calibrated before the actual measurement starts. In such a case, there is a need to switch off AGC and γ-correction. Higher quality cameras allow both AGC and γ-correction to be switched on or off. In cheaper cameras, it may be possible to switch off AGC and γ correction by intervening into the camera electronics.

Analog cameras are equipped with video circuitry which adds frame synchronization pulses to the signal. The high-pass filter in the camera compensates for a decrease of high frequencies in the optical part. The TV signal is usually conducted by a coaxial cable to a digitizer (frame grabber) in a computer. At the input of the digitizer, there are sometimes equalization filters to compensate for the loss of high frequencies in the cable.

A block diagram of a digital camera is in Figure 2.36. The conversion from photon energy to voltage is the same as in analog cameras including potential AGC and/or γ-correction. The analog-to-digital (A/D) converter provides a number proportional to the input intensity. These numbers have to be transferred to the computer for further processing—the connection can be done using either parallel or serial hardware. Serial connections usually exploit widely used technology standardized in the IEEE 1394 (FireWire) or USB (Universal Serial Bus) protocols. In the case of parallel connection, only short cables of length about 1 meter can be used.

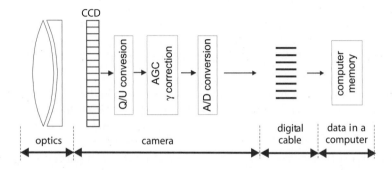

Figure 2.36: Digital CCD camera. © *Cengage Learning 2015.*

Analog cameras		Digital cameras	
+	Cheap.	+	Cheap webcams. Dropping price for others.
+	Long cable possible (up to 300 m).	−	Shorter cable ($\approx$ 10 m for Firewire). Kilometers after conversion to optical cable. Any length for Internet cameras.
−	Multiple sampling of a signal.	+	Single sampling.
−	Noisy due to analog transmission.	+	No transmission noise.
−	Line jitter.	+	Lines are vertically aligned.

2.5.3   A color camera

Electronic photosensitive sensors are monochromatic. Three strategies are usually employed to capture color images:

- Record three different images in succession by employing color filters in front of monochromatic cameras. This approach is used only in precise laboratory measurements because it is impractical and impossible for any image capture involving motion.

- Using a color filter array on a single sensor.

- The incoming light is split into several color channels using a prism-like device.

A color filter array mosaic is often combined with a single photosensitive sensor to create a color camera. Each pixel is covered with an individual filter which can be implemented either on a cover glass on the chip package (hybrid filter) or directly on the silicon (monolithic filter). Each pixel captures only one color. Consequently, the color resolution is about one third of the geometric resolution which would correspond to a monochromatic camera with same number of pixels. The full color values for each pixel can be interpolated from pixel values of the same color in local neighborhood.

The human eye is most sensitive to green, less to red, and least to blue. This property is used by the most common color filter for single chip cameras called the Bayer filter mosaic or pattern (Bryce Bayer, US patent 3971065, 1976), see Figure 2.37. It can be seen that the number of green-sensitive pixels is equal to the combined number of pixels sensitive to red and blue.

G	B	G	B	G	B	G	B
R	G	R	G	R	G	R	G
G	B	G	B	G	B	G	B
R	G	R	G	R	G	R	G

Figure 2.37: Bayer filter mosaic for single chip color cameras. © *Cengage Learning 2015.*

A great advantage of a mosaic filter is its optical simplicity. It provides the single focal plane necessary for the use of standard film lenses. Good mosaic filters provide excellent band-pass transmission. Many professional digital SLR and studio cameras use mosaic filters.

Multiple-chip cameras use color filters to split incoming light into separate color channels. Photosensors are simple and preserve the spatial resolution. Aligning and registering the sensors to the color splitter to the prism requires high precision. For pixels of the same size, color splitter systems should allow higher sensitivity in low light conditions, since they should lose less light in the filters. In practice, this advantage is not always available. Color splitting devices often include absorption filters because simple refraction may not provide sufficiently precise color separation. The beam splitter approach complicates the optical system and limits lens selection significantly. The additional optical path of the prism increases both lateral and longitudinal aberration for each color's image. The longitudinal aberration causes different focal lengths for each color; the photosensor could be moved independently to each color's focal point, but then the lateral aberration would produce different magnification for each color. These aberrations can be overcome with a lens specifically designed for use with the prism, but such camera-specific lenses would be rare, inflexible, and expensive.

2.6   Summary

- **Basic concepts**

  - A 2D image gray-scale image is represented by a scalar function $f(x, y)$ of two variables which give coordinates in a plane.

  - In many cases, a 2D image is formed as the result of a projection of a 3D scene into 2D.

  - The domain of the digitized image is a limited discrete grid the coordinates of which are natural numbers. The range of the digitized image is a limited discrete set of gray values (brightnesses). A pixel is the elemental part of an image.

- **Image digitization**

  - Digitization (sampling) of an image can be seen as a product of a sampling function and a continuous image function.

  - Usually the grid consists of regular polygons (squares or hexagons). The second aspect of sampling is setting the distance between the sampling points (the smaller sampling distance the higher the resolution of the image).

  - Gray level quantization governs the appearance of shading and false contour. A human is able to recognize about 60 gray levels at most. Images containing only black and white pixels are called the binary.

- **Digital image properties**

  - The neighborhood relation of a pixel has to be defined to be able to represent discrete geometry.

  - A function providing distance between two pixels has to be established. The most commonly used are 'city block', 'chessboard', and everyday Euclidean distance. If the neighborhood relation is set for a grid then a raster is obtained.

  - Given a raster, topological properties are induced. These properties are based on the relation 'being contiguous' and lead to concepts of region, background, hole, and region border. The convex hull of a region is the minimal convex subset containing it.

- 4-neighborhoods and 8-neighborhoods lead to 'crossing line' paradoxes which complicate basic discrete geometry algorithms. However, there exist solutions to these paradoxes for both binary and gray-level images.

- The distance transform of a binary image gives the distance from each pixel to the nearest non-zero pixel. A two-pass algorithm can compute this, the complexity of which depends linearly on the number of pixels.

- The brightness histogram is a global descriptor of the image giving the estimate of the probability density that a pixel has a given brightness.

- Human visual perception is vulnerable to various illusions. Some of the properties of human perception of images as perceptual grouping are inspirations for computer vision methods.

- Live images as any other measurements or observations are always prone to noise. Noise can be quantitatively assessed using, e.g., signal-to-noise ratio.

- White, Gaussian, impulse, and salt-and-pepper noise are common models.

- **Color images**

  - Human color perception is a subjective psycho-physical layer on top of underlying objective physical properties—the wavelength of electromagnetic radiation.

  - Humans have three types of sensors receptive to the wavelength of incoming irradiation. Color sensitive receptors on the human retina are cones. The retina also has rods which are dedicated to sensing monochromatically in low ambient light conditions. Cones are categorized into three types based on the sensed wavelength range, approximately corresponding to red, green and blue.

- **Cameras**

  - Most cameras use either CCD or CMOS photosensitive elements, both using photovoltaic principles. They capture brightness of a monochromatic image.

  - Cameras are equipped with necessary electronics to provide digitized images. Color cameras are similar to monochromatic ones and contain color filters.

2.7 Exercises

Short-answer questions

S2.1 Why the analog television norms as NTSC, PAL (which are several decades old) use interlaced image lines?

S2.2 Define:

- Spatial resolution
- Spectral resolution
- Radiometric resolution
- Time resolution

S2.3 Define:

- Additive noise
- Multiplicative noise
- Gaussian noise
- Impulsive noise
- Salt-and-pepper noise

S2.4 Define, with diagrams, *perspective projection* and *orthographic projection*.

S2.5 A photoreceptor or camera sensor can be modeled by the following equation:

$$q_i = \int_{\lambda_1}^{\lambda_2} I(\lambda)\, R_i(\lambda)\, S(\lambda)\, d\lambda \tag{2.20}$$

- Name/describe the individual variables.
- What is q_i?

S2.6 Use Matlab or similar software to generate images of very low contrast: determine what contrast is detectable by humans.

S2.7 Explain the concept of color constancy. Why is it important for color image processing and/or analysis?

S2.8 Briefly describe the relationship between the color gamut perceivable by humans and available in a typical CRT or LCD display.
Provide a rough sketch of each of these two gamuts in a single CIE chromaticity diagram.

Problems

P2.1 An interlaced television signal of 50 half-frames per second is sampled into the discrete image (matrix) of 500×500 pixels in 256 gray levels. Calculate the minimal sampling frequency in kHz (kiloHertz) which has to be used in the framegrabber performing analog to digital conversion?

P2.2 Acquire some RGB images. Develop software to convert them into YIQ and HSI representations. Subject them to various degrees of noise (by, for example, Algorithm 2.3) and convert back to RGB for display.

P2.3 Using software of your choice (Matlab or its equivalents are ideal) extract some 'interesting' subimages and plot them in the manner of Figure 1.8. Observe for yourself the difficulty in 'translating' between the visual sense and pixels.

P2.4 Develop a program that reads an input image and manipulates its resolution in the spatial and gray domains; for a range of images (synthetic, of man-made objects, of natural scenes ...) conduct experiments on the minimum resolution that leaves the image recognizable. Conduct such experiments on a range of subjects.

P2.5 Discuss the various factors that influence the *brightness* of a pixel in an image.

P2.6 For each uppercase printed letter of the alphabet, determine the number of lakes and bays it has. Derive a look-up table that lists the candidate letters, given the number of lakes and bays. Comment on this quality of this *feature* as an identifier of letters.

P2.7 For a range of images and a range of noise corruption, compute the signal-to-noise ratio (equation 2.13). Draw some subjective conclusions about what 'bad' noise is.

P2.8 Implement Algorithm 2.3. For a range of images, plot the distribution of $f(x,y)-g(x,y)$ for various values of σ. Measure the deviation of this distribution from a 'perfect' zero mean Gaussian.

P2.9 Write a program that computes an image histogram; plot the histogram of a range of images. Plot also the histogram of the three components of a color image when represented as

- RGB
- YIQ
- HSI

P2.10 Implement histogram smoothing; determine how much smoothing is necessary to suppress turning points in the histogram due to what you consider to be noise, or small-scale image effects.

P2.11 Implement chamfering on a rectangular grid, and test it on a synthetic image consisting of a (black) subset of specified shape on a (white) background. Display the results for a range of shapes, basing the chamfering on:

- The Euclidean metric
- The city block metric
- The chessboard metric

P2.12 Implement chamfering on a hexagonal grid and display the results.

P2.13 Using gray level frequencies (from the histogram) as an estimate of p in Equation 2.7, compute the entropy of a range of images/subimages. What causes it to increase/decrease?

P2.14 One solution to digitization paradoxes is to mix connectivities. Using 8-neighborhoods for foreground and 4-neighborhoods for background, examine the paradoxes cited in the text (Figure 2.7). Do new paradoxes occur? What might be the disadvantages of such an approach?

P2.15 Make yourself familiar with solved problems and **Matlab** implementations of selected algorithms provided in the corresponding chapter of the **Matlab Companion** to this text [Svoboda et al., 2008]. The **Matlab Companion** homepage http://visionbook.felk.cvut.cz offers images used in the problems, and well-commented **Matlab** code is provided for educational purposes.

P2.16 Use the **Matlab Companion** [Svoboda et al., 2008] to develop solutions to additional exercises and practical problems provided there. Implement your solutions using **Matlab** or other suitable programming languages.

2.8 References

Barrett H. H. and Myers K. J. *Foundation of Image Science*. Willey Series in Pure and Applied Optics. Wiley & Sons, Hoboken, New Jersey, USA, 2004.

Barrow H. G., Tenenbaum J. M., Bolles R. C., and Wolf H. C. Parametric correspondence and chamfer matching: Two new techniques for image matching. In *5th International Joint Conference on Artificial Intelligence*, Cambridge, CA, pages 659–663. Carnegie-Mellon University, 1977.

Borgefors G. Distance transformations in digital images. *Computer Vision Graphics and Image Processing*, 34(3):344–371, 1986.

Bracewell R. N. *Fourier Analysis and Imaging.* Springer-Verlag, 1st edition, 2004.

Brett King D. and Wertheimer M. *Max Wertheimer and Gestalt Theory.* New Brunswick, 2005.

Breu H., Gil J., Kirkpatrick D., and Werman M. Linear time euclidean distance transform algorithms. *IEEE Transactions on Pattern Analysis and Machine Intelligence*, 17(5):529–533, 1995.

Bruce V., Green P. R., and Georgeson M. A. *Visual Perception: Physiology, Psychology, and Ecology.* Psychology Press, Boston, 3rd edition, 1996.

Burger W. and Burge M. J. *Digital Image Processing: An Algorithmic Introduction Using Java.* Springer-Verlag, 2008.

Frisby J. P. *Seeing—Illusion, Brain and Mind.* Oxford University Press, Oxford, 1979.

Kay P. Color categories are not arbitrary. *Cross-cultural Research*, 39(1):39–55, 2005.

Klette R. and Rosenfeld A. *Digital Geometry, Geometric Methods for Digital Picture Analysis.* Morgan Kaufmann, San Francisco, CA, 2004.

Kovalevsky V. A. Finite topology as applied to image analysis. *Computer Vision, Graphics, and Image Processing*, 46:141–161, 1989.

Maurer C. R., Qi R., and Raghavan V. A linear time algorithm for computing exact Euclidean distance transforms of binary images in arbitrary dimensions. *IEEE Transactions on Pattern Analysis and Machine Intelligence*, 25(2):265–270, 2003.

Montanari U. A method for obtaining skeletons using a quasi-euclidean distance. *Journal of the Association for Computing Machinery*, 15(4):600–624, 1968.

Palmer S. E. *Vision Science : Photons to Phenomenology.* The MIT Press, Cambridge, MA, USA, 1999.

Pitas I. *Digital Image Processing Algorithms.* Prentice-Hall, Hemel Hempstead, UK, 1993.

Pratt W. K. *Digital Image Processing.* Wiley, New York, 1978.

Rosenfeld A. and Kak A. C. *Digital Picture Processing.* Academic Press, New York, 2nd edition, 1982.

Rosenfeld A. and Pfaltz J. L. Distance functions on digital pictures. *Pattern Recognition*, 1(1):33–62, 1968.

Rosenfeld A. and Pfaltz J. L. Sequential operations in digital picture processing. *Journal of the Association for Computing Machinery*, 13(4):471–494, 1966.

Shannon C. E. A mathematical theory of communication. *Bell System Technical Journal*, 27:379–423, 623–656, 1948.

Svoboda T., Kybic J., and Hlavac V. *Image Processing, Analysis, and Machine Vision: A MATLAB Companion.* Thomson Engineering, 2008.

Wandell B. *Foundation of Vision.* Sinauer Associates, 1995.

Chapter 3

The image, its mathematical and physical background

3.1 Overview

This chapter considers various aspects of digital images in greater theoretical depth than the last; we do not present all the necessary mathematics and physics since they are considered in thorough detail in many more relevant places. Readers unfamiliar with this background are recommended to consider the descriptive textual presentation only; this chapter may be omitted without detriment to an understanding of the algorithms that appear later in the book.

The chapter is divided into three parts: Section 3.2 is devoted to linear integral transforms which provide a different insight into an image and are often used in analysis. This material is usually taught in university mathematics or signal processing courses.

Section 3.3 overviews probabilistic methods necessary if images cannot be represented deterministically. In this case, a more complicated approach is often needed in which images are understood as a realization of stochastic processes.

Section 3.4 is an introduction to image formation physics—it is of advantage to understand how an image is created before its computer analysis. The section begins with basic geometric optics which illustrate how to realize an optical system which mimics the pin-hole camera. Then radiometric and photometric concepts which explain image formation from the point of view of physics are presented. In many practical cases, image formation physics is not directly explored because it is too complicated to determine all the parameters which describe a particular capture setting, and some related tasks are ill-posed. Nevertheless, it is recommended the reader browse this material to understand how physical knowledge of the image capturing process can contribute to analysis.

3.1.1 Linearity

The notion of **linearity** will occur frequently in this book: this relates to **vector (linear) spaces** where commonly matrix algebra is used. Linearity also concerns more general elements of vector spaces, for instance, functions. The **linear combination** is a key concept in linear mathematics, permitting the expression of a new element of a vector space as a sum of known elements multiplied by coefficients (scalars, usually real numbers). A general linear combination of two vectors x, y can be written as $ax + by$, where a, b are scalars.

Consider a mapping $\mathcal{L}$ between two linear spaces. It is called **additive** if $\mathcal{L}(x+y) = \mathcal{L}x + \mathcal{L}y$ and **homogeneous** if $\mathcal{L}(ax) = a\mathcal{L}x$ for any scalar a. From a practical point of view, this means that the sum of inputs (respectively, multiple) results in the sum of the respective outputs (respectively, multiple). This property is also called a **superposition principle**. We call the mapping $\mathcal{L}$ *linear* if it is additive and homogeneous (i.e., satisfies the superposition principle). Equivalently, a linear mapping satisfies $\mathcal{L}(ax+by) = a\mathcal{L}x + b\mathcal{L}y$ for all vectors x, y and scalars a, b, i.e., it preserves linear combinations.

3.1.2 The Dirac distribution and convolution

Some formal background on moving from the continuous to discrete domains will be of help, as will a definition of convolution. These are fundamental motivators for appreciating the use of linear algebra An ideal impulse is an important input signal; the ideal impulse in the image plane is defined using the **Dirac distribution** $\delta(x, y)$,

$$\int_{-\infty}^{\infty} \int_{-\infty}^{\infty} \delta(x, y) \, dx \, dy = 1 \,, \tag{3.1}$$

and $\delta(x, y) = 0$ for all $(x, y) \neq 0$.

Equation (3.2) is called the 'sifting property' of the Dirac distribution; it provides the value of the function $f(x, y)$ at the point (λ, μ)

$$\int_{-\infty}^{\infty} \int_{-\infty}^{\infty} f(x, y) \, \delta(x - \lambda, y - \mu) \, dx \, dy = f(\lambda, \mu) \,. \tag{3.2}$$

This 'sifting' equation can be used to describe the sampling process of a continuous image function $f(x, y)$. We may express the image function as a linear combination of Dirac pulses located at the points a, b that cover the whole image plane; samples are weighted by the image function $f(x, y)$

$$\int_{-\infty}^{\infty} \int_{-\infty}^{\infty} f(a, b) \, \delta(a - x, b - y) \, da \, db = f(x, y) \,. \tag{3.3}$$

Convolution is an important operation in the linear approach to image analysis. It is an integral which expresses the amount of overlap of one function $f(t)$ as it is shifted over another $h(t)$. A 1D convolution $f * h$ of functions f, h over a finite range $[0, t]$ is given by

$$(f * h)(t) \equiv \int_{0}^{t} f(\tau) \, h(t - \tau) \, d\tau \,. \tag{3.4}$$

To be precise, the convolution integral has bounds $-\infty, \infty$. Here we can restrict to the interval $[0, t]$, because we assume zero values for negative co-ordinates

$$(f * h)(t) \equiv \int_{-\infty}^{\infty} f(\tau) \, h(t - \tau) \, d\tau = \int_{-\infty}^{\infty} f(t - \tau) \, h(\tau) \, d\tau \,. \tag{3.5}$$

Let f, g, h be functions and a a scalar constant. Convolution satisfies the following properties

$$f * h = h * f \,, \tag{3.6}$$
$$f * (g * h) = (f * g) * h \,, \tag{3.7}$$
$$f * (g + h) = (f * g) + (f * h) \,, \tag{3.8}$$
$$a\,(f * g) = (a\,f) * g = f * (a\,g) \,. \tag{3.9}$$

Taking the derivative of a convolution gives

$$\frac{\mathrm{d}}{\mathrm{d}x}\,(f * h) = \frac{\mathrm{d}f}{\mathrm{d}x} * h = f * \frac{\mathrm{d}h}{\mathrm{d}x} \,. \tag{3.10}$$

This equation will later prove useful, e.g., in edge detection of images.

Convolution can be generalized to higher dimensions. Convolution of 2D functions f and h is denoted by $f * h$, and is defined by the integral

$$
\begin{aligned}
(f * h)(x, y) &= \int_{-\infty}^{\infty} \int_{-\infty}^{\infty} f(a, b)\, h(x - a, y - b)\, \mathrm{d}a\, \mathrm{d}b \\
&= \int_{-\infty}^{\infty} \int_{-\infty}^{\infty} f(x - a, y - b)\, h(a, b)\, \mathrm{d}a\, \mathrm{d}b \\
&= (h * f)(x, y) \,.
\end{aligned}
\tag{3.11}
$$

In digital image analysis, the **discrete convolution** is expressed using sums instead of integrals. A digital image has a limited domain on the image plane. However, the limited domain does not prevent us from using convolutions as their results outside the image domain are zero. The convolution expresses a linear filtering process using the filter h; linear filtering is often used in local image pre-processing and image restoration.

Linear operations calculate the resulting value in the output image pixel $g(i, j)$ as a linear combination of image intensities in a local neighborhood $\mathcal{O}$ of the pixel $f(i, j)$ in the input image. The contribution of the pixels in the neighborhood $\mathcal{O}$ is weighted by coefficients h

$$f(i, j) = \sum_{(m,n) \in \mathcal{O}} h(i - m, j - n)\, g(m, n) \,. \tag{3.12}$$

Equation (3.12) is equivalent to discrete convolution with the kernel h, which is called a **convolution mask**. Rectangular neighborhoods $\mathcal{O}$ are often used with an odd number of pixels in rows and columns, enabling specification of the neighborhood's central pixel.

3.2   Linear integral transforms

Linear integral transforms are frequently employed in image processing. Using such transforms, images are treated as linear (vector) spaces. As when dealing with 1D signals, there are two basic and commonly used **representations** of image functions: the **spatial domain** (pixels) and the **frequency domain** (frequency spectra). In the latter case, the image is expressed as a linear combination of some basis functions of some linear integral transform. For instance, the Fourier transform uses sines and cosines as basis functions. If linear operations are involved in the spatial domain (an important example of such linear operation is convolution) then there is a one-to-one mapping between the spatial and frequency representations of the image. Advanced signal/image processing goes beyond linear operations, and these non-linear image processing techniques are mainly used in the spatial domain.

3.2.1 Images as linear systems

Images and their processing can be modeled as superposition of point spread functions which are represented by Dirac pulses δ (equation 3.1). If this image representation is used, well-developed linear system theory can be employed.

An operator is a mapping from one vector space to another. A linear operator $\mathcal{L}$ (also called linear system) has the property

$$\mathcal{L}\{af_1 + bf_2\} = a\,\mathcal{L}\{f_1\} + b\,\mathcal{L}\{f_2\}\,. \tag{3.13}$$

An image f can be expressed as a linear combination of point spread functions represented by Dirac pulses δ. Assume that the input image f is given by equation (3.3). The response g of the linear system $\mathcal{L}$ to the input image f is given by

$$
\begin{aligned}
g(x,y) = \mathcal{L}\{f(x,y)\} &= \int_{-\infty}^{\infty}\int_{-\infty}^{\infty} f(a,b)\,\mathcal{L}\{\delta(x-a,y-b)\}\,\mathrm{d}a\,\mathrm{d}b \\
&= \int_{-\infty}^{\infty}\int_{-\infty}^{\infty} f(a,b)\,h(x-a,y-b)\,\mathrm{d}a\,\mathrm{d}b = (f*h)(x,y)\,,
\end{aligned}
\tag{3.14}
$$

where h is the impulse response of the linear system $\mathcal{L}$. In other words the output of the linear system $\mathcal{L}$ is expressed as the convolution of the input image f with an impulse response h of the linear system $\mathcal{L}$. If the Fourier transform (explained in Sections 3.2.3 and 3.2.4) is applied to equation (3.14) and the Fourier images are denoted by the respective capital letters then the following equation is obtained

$$G(u,v) = F(u,v)\,H(u,v)\,. \tag{3.15}$$

Equation (3.15) is often used in image pre-processing to express the behavior of smoothing or sharpening operations, and is considered further in Chapter 5.

It is important to remember that operations on real images are not in fact linear—both the image co-ordinates and values of the image function (brightness) are limited. Real images always have limited size, and the number of brightness levels is also finite. Nevertheless, image processing can be approximated by linear systems in many cases.

3.2.2 Introduction to linear integral transforms

Linear integral transforms provide a tool which permits representations of signals and images in a more suitable domain, where information is better visible and the solution of related problems is easier. Specifically, we are interested in the 'frequency domain', and where the inverse transform exists. In such a case, there is a one-to-one mapping between the spatial and frequency domains. The most commonly used linear integral transforms in image analysis are the Fourier, cosine, and wavelet transforms.

The usual application of a linear integral transform in image processing is image filtering, a term which comes from signal processing—the input image is processed by some filter to get the output image. Filtering can be performed in either the spatial or frequency domains, as illustrated in Figure 3.1. In the frequency domain, filtering can be seen as boosting or attenuating specific frequencies.

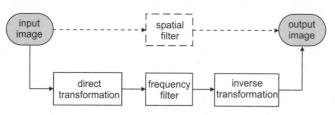

Figure 3.1: The image can be processed in either spatial or frequency domains. For linear operations, these two ways should provide equivalent results. © *Cengage Learning 2015.*

We begin by reviewing the simpler 1D Fourier transform [Karu, 1999], and will then proceed to the 2D Fourier transform, and mention briefly cosine and wavelet transforms.

3.2.3   1D Fourier transform

Developed by the French mathematician Joseph Fourier, the 1D Fourier transform $\mathcal{F}$ transforms a function $f(t)$ (e.g., dependent on time) into a frequency domain representation, $\mathcal{F}\{f(t)\} = F(\xi)$, where ξ [Hz=s^{-1}] is a frequency and $2\pi\xi$ [s^{-1}] is an angular frequency. The complex function F is called the (complex) frequency spectrum in which it is easy to visualize relative proportions of different frequencies. For instance, the sine wave has a simple spectrum consisting of a double spike, symmetric around 0, for positive frequencies, indicating that only a single frequency is present.

Let i be the usual imaginary unit. The continuous Fourier transform $\mathcal{F}$ is given by

$$\mathcal{F}\{f(t)\} = F(\xi) = \int_{-\infty}^{\infty} f(t)\, e^{-2\pi i \xi t}\, \mathrm{d}t\,. \tag{3.16}$$

The inverse Fourier transform $\mathcal{F}^{-1}$ is then

$$\mathcal{F}^{-1}\{F(\xi)\} = f(t) = \int_{-\infty}^{\infty} F(\xi)\, e^{2\pi i \xi t}\, \mathrm{d}\xi\,. \tag{3.17}$$

The conditions for the existence of the Fourier spectrum of a function f are:

- $\int_{-\infty}^{\infty} |f(t)|\, \mathrm{d}t < \infty$.

- f can have only a finite number of discontinuities in any finite interval.

The Fourier transform always exists for digital signals (including images) as they are bounded and have a finite number of discontinuities. We will see later that if we use the Fourier transform for images we have to adopt the assumption that they are periodic. The fact that they typically are not presents problems which will be discussed later.

Attempting to understand what equation (3.16) means, it is useful to express the inverse Fourier transform as a Riemannian sum

$$f(t) \doteq \left(\ldots + F(\xi_0)\, e^{2\pi i \xi_0 t} + F(\xi_1)\, e^{2\pi i \xi_1 t} + \ldots \right) \Delta\xi\,, \tag{3.18}$$

where $\Delta\xi = \xi_{k+1} - \xi_k$ for all k. The inverse formula shows that any 1D function can be decomposed as a weighted sum (integral) of many different complex exponentials. These exponentials can be decomposed into sines and cosines (also called harmonic functions) because $e^{i\omega} = \cos\omega + i\sin\omega$. The decomposition of $f(t)$ into sines and cosines starts with some basic frequency ξ_0. Other sines and cosines have frequencies obtained by multiplying ξ_0 by increasing natural numbers. The coefficients $F(\xi_k)$ are complex numbers in general and give both magnitude and phase of the elementary waves.

The Fourier transform exhibits predictable symmetries. Recall the notion of even, odd, and conjugate symmetric function, illustrated in Table 3.1.

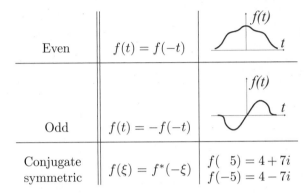

Even	$f(t) = f(-t)$	
Odd	$f(t) = -f(-t)$	
Conjugate symmetric	$f(\xi) = f^*(-\xi)$	$f(\ \ 5) = 4 + 7i$ $f(-5) = 4 - 7i$

Table 3.1: Concepts of even, odd and conjugate symmetric functions (denoted by a superscript *). © *Cengage Learning 2015.*

Note that any 1D function $f(t)$ shape can always be decomposed into its even and odd parts $f_e(t)$ and $f_o(t)$

$$f_e(t) = \frac{f(t) + f(-t)}{2} \ , \qquad f_o(t) = \frac{f(t) - f(-t)}{2} \ . \tag{3.19}$$

The ability to form a function from its even and odd parts is illustrated in Figure 3.2.

Figure 3.2: Any 1D function can be decomposed into its even and odd parts. © *Cengage Learning 2015.*

The symmetries of the Fourier transform and its values are summarized (without proof) in Table 3.2.

real $f(t)$	values of $F(\xi)$	symmetry of $F(\xi)$
general	complex	conjugate symmetric
even	only real	even
odd	only imaginary	odd

Table 3.2: Fourier transform symmetries if $f(t)$ is a real function. © *Cengage Learning 2015.*

Table 3.3 summarizes some elementary properties of the transform, all easily obtained by manipulation with the definitions of equation (3.16).

Some other properties are related to areas under the function f or its Fourier representation F. The DC offset (DC from Direct Current[1]) is $F(0)$ and is given by the area

---

[1] The 1D Fourier transform was first widely used in electrical engineering.

Property	$f(t)$	$F(\xi)$
Linearity	$af_1(t) + bf_2(t)$	$a\,F_1(\xi) + b\,F_2(\xi)$
Duality	$F(t)$	$f(-\xi)$
Convolution	$(f * g)(t)$	$F(\xi)\,G(\xi)$
Product	$f(t)\,g(t)$	$(F * G)(\xi)$
Time shift	$f(t - t_0)$	$e^{-2\pi i \xi t_0}\,F(\xi)$
Frequency shift	$e^{2\pi i \xi_0 t}\,f(t)$	$F(\xi - \xi_0)$
Differentiation	$\frac{df(t)}{dt}$	$2\pi i \xi F(\xi)$
Multiplication by t	$t\,f(t)$	$\frac{i}{2\pi}\frac{dF(\xi)}{d\xi}$
Time scaling	$f(a\,t)$	$\frac{1}{|a|}F(\xi/a)$

Table 3.3: Properties of the Fourier transform. © *Cengage Learning 2015.*

under the function f

$$F(0) = \int_{-\infty}^{\infty} f(t)\,dt\,, \tag{3.20}$$

and a symmetric property holds for the inverse formula. The value of $f(0)$ is the area under the frequency spectrum $F(\xi)$,

$$f(0) = \int_{-\infty}^{\infty} F(\xi)\,d\xi\,. \tag{3.21}$$

Parceval's theorem equates the area under the squared magnitude of the frequency spectrum and squared function $f(t)$. It can be interpreted as saying that the signal 'energy' in the time domain is equal to the 'energy' in the frequency domain. The theorem states (for a real function f, which is our case for images, the absolute value can be omitted)

$$\int_{-\infty}^{\infty} |f(t)|^2\,dt = \int_{-\infty}^{\infty} |F(\xi)|^2\,d\xi\,. \tag{3.22}$$

Figures 3.3, 3.4 and 3.5 show some properties of transforms of simple signals.

Let $\mathrm{Re}(c)$ denote the real part of a complex number c and $\mathrm{Im}(c)$ its imaginary part. The formulas describing four function-spectrum definitions are as follows:

Complex spectrum $\qquad F(\xi) = \mathrm{Re}\left(F(\xi)\right) + i\,\mathrm{Im}\left(F(\xi)\right),$

Amplitude spectrum $\qquad |F(\xi)| = \sqrt{\mathrm{Re}\left(F^2(\xi)\right) + \mathrm{Im}\left(F^2(\xi)\right)},$

Phase spectrum $\qquad \phi(\xi) = \arctan\left(\mathrm{Im}\left(F(\xi)\right)/\mathrm{Re}\left(F(\xi)\right)\right),\quad$ if defined,

Power spectrum $\qquad P(\xi) = |F(\xi)|^2 = \mathrm{Re}(F(\xi))^2 + \mathrm{Im}(F(\xi))^2\,. \tag{3.23}$

It can be seen from Figures 3.4 and 3.5 that time signals of short duration or quick changes have wide frequency spectra and vice versa. This is a manifestation of the

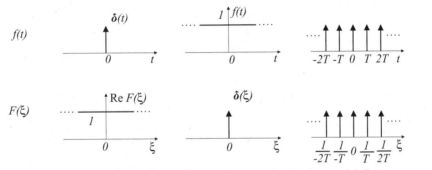

Figure 3.3: 1D Fourier transform of the Dirac pulse, constant value and infinite sequence of Dirac pulses. © *Cengage Learning 2015.*

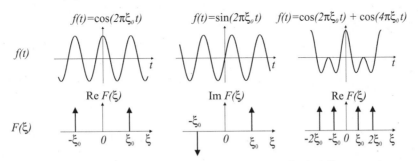

Figure 3.4: 1D Fourier transform of the sine, cosine, and sum of two different cosines. © *Cengage Learning 2015.*

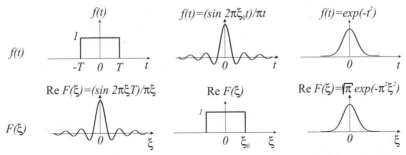

Figure 3.5: 1D Fourier transform of the idealized rectangular pulse of length $2T$ in the time domain gives the spectrum $(2\cos 2\pi\xi T)/\xi$. Symmetrically, the idealized rectangular spectrum corresponds to an input signal of the form $(2\cos 2\pi\xi_0 t)/t$. The right column shows that a Gaussian pulse has the same form as its Fourier spectrum. © *Cengage Learning 2015.*

uncertainty principle which states that it is impossible to have a signal which is arbitrarily narrow in both time and frequency domains. If the duration of the signal in the time domain and the bandwidth in the frequency domain were expressed as statistical moments, then the following compact uncertainty principle can be proved,

$$\text{'signal duration'} \cdot \text{'frequency bandwidth'} \geq \frac{1}{\pi}. \tag{3.24}$$

The uncertainty principle is also of theoretical importance, and has a relation to the Heisenberg uncertainty principle from quantum mechanics [Barrett and Myers, 2004].

There is also a related question of interest for practitioners: which function f has the smallest duration-bandwidth product? It can be shown that such a function is Gaussian in the form $f(t) = \exp(-t^2)$. The uncertainty principle allows for qualitative questions, such as which signal has the higher bandwidth in the frequency domain: $\sin(t)/t$ or $\sin(3t)/3t$? The answer is the latter, because it is narrower.

If we need to process a **non-stationary signal**, one option is to divide it into smaller pieces (called often windows), and assume that outside these windows the signal is periodic. This approach is called the **short time Fourier transformation**—STFT— and was first introduced by Gabor in 1946. The STFT has been used in many disciplines, such as speech recognition. Unfortunately, mere cutting of the signal by non-overlapping rectangular windows is not good as it introduces discontinuities which induce wide bandwidth in the frequency domain. This is why the signal at the bounds of the local window is smoothly damped to zero by, e.g., a Gaussian or Hamming window. Any signal processing textbook will provide a more detailed explanation of windowing.

The Fourier spectrum expresses global properties of the signal (as information of the speed of signal changes) but it does not reveal in which time instant such a change appears. On the other hand, the time domain represents precisely what happens at certain instants but does not represent global properties of the signal. There are two ways to step towards having a little of both—global frequency properties and localization. The first is the STFT, and the second is the use of different basis functions in the linear integral transformation which are less regular than sines and cosines. The wavelet transformation is one example, see Section 3.2.7.

Computers deal with discrete signals: the discrete signal $f(n)$, $n = 0 \ldots N - 1$, is obtained by equally spaced samples from a continuous function f. The Discrete Fourier Transform (DFT) is defined as

$$F(k) = \frac{1}{N} \sum_{n=0}^{N-1} f(n) \exp\left(-2\pi i\,\frac{nk}{N}\right) \tag{3.25}$$

and its inverse is defined as

$$f(n) = \sum_{k=0}^{N-1} F(k) \exp\left(2\pi i\,\frac{nk}{N}\right) . \tag{3.26}$$

The spectrum $F(k)$ is periodically extended with period N.

Computational complexity is an issue with the Discrete Fourier Transform. We will be interested in the time complexity as opposed to memory complexity—we would like to know how many steps it takes to calculate the Fourier spectrum as a function of the size of the input. The Discrete Fourier Transform (DFT), if computed from its definition for the samples discretized into n samples, see equations (3.25), (3.26), has time complexity $\mathcal{O}(n^2)$. The result can be calculated much faster if the Fast Fourier Transformation (FFT) algorithm is used. This algorithm depends on the number of samples used to represent a signal being a power of two. The basic trick is that a DFT of length N can be expressed as a sum of two DFTs of length $N/2$ consisting of odd or even samples. This scheme permits the calculation of intermediate results in a clever way. The time complexity of the FFT is $\mathcal{O}(n \log n)$; any signal processing textbook will provide details. The FFT is implemented in many software tools and libraries.

3.2.4   2D Fourier transform

The 1D Fourier transform can be easily generalized to 2D [Bracewell, 2004]. An image f is a function of two coordinates (x, y) in a plane. The **2D Fourier transform** also uses harmonic functions for spectral decomposition. The 2D Fourier transform for the continuous image f is defined by the integral

$$F(u, v) = \int_{-\infty}^{\infty} \int_{-\infty}^{\infty} f(x, y) \, e^{-2\pi i(xu + yv)} \, dx \, dy \tag{3.27}$$

and its inverse transform is defined by

$$f(x, y) = \int_{-\infty}^{\infty} \int_{-\infty}^{\infty} F(u, v) \, e^{2\pi i(xu + yv)} \, du \, dv \,. \tag{3.28}$$

Parameters (u, v) are called **spatial frequencies**. The function f on the left-hand side of equation (3.28) can be interpreted analogously to the 1D case $\big($see equation (3.18)$\big)$, i.e., as a linear combination of simple periodic patterns $e^{2\pi i(xu + yv)}$. The real and imaginary components of the pattern are cosine and sine functions. The complex spectrum $F(u, v)$ is a weight function which represents the influence of the elementary patterns.

Equation (3.27) can be abbreviated to

$$\mathcal{F}\{f(x, y)\} = F(u, v) \,.$$

From the image processing point of view, the following properties (corresponding to the 1D case) are easily derived:

- Linearity:
$$\mathcal{F}\{a \, f_1(x, y) + b \, f_2(x, y)\} = a \, F_1(u, v) + b \, F_2(u, v) \,. \tag{3.29}$$

- Shift of the origin in the image domain:
$$\mathcal{F}\{f(x - a, y - b)\} = F(u, v) \, e^{-2\pi i(au + bv)} \,. \tag{3.30}$$

- Shift of the origin in the frequency domain:
$$\mathcal{F}\{f(x, y) \, e^{2\pi i(u_0 x + v_0 y)}\} = F(u - u_0, v - v_0) \,. \tag{3.31}$$

- If $f(x, y)$ is real-valued then
$$F(-u, -v) = F^*(u, v) \,. \tag{3.32}$$

  The image function is always real-valued and we can thus use the results of its Fourier transform in the first quadrant, i.e., $u \geq 0$, $v \geq 0$, without loss of generality. If in addition the image function has the property $f(x, y) = f(-x, -y)$ then the result of the Fourier transform $F(u, v)$ is a real function.

- Duality of the convolution: Convolution, equation (3.11), and its Fourier transform are related by

$$\begin{aligned} \mathcal{F}\{(f * h)(x, y)\} &= F(u, v) \, H(u, v) \,, \\ \mathcal{F}\{f(x, y) \, h(x, y)\} &= (F * H)(u, v) \,. \end{aligned} \tag{3.33}$$

  This is the **convolution theorem**.

The 2D Fourier transform can be used for discrete images too: integration is changed to summation in the respective equations. The discrete 2D Fourier transform is defined as

$$F(u,v) = \frac{1}{MN} \sum_{m=0}^{M-1} \sum_{n=0}^{N-1} f(m,n) \exp\left[-2\pi i\left(\frac{mu}{M} + \frac{nv}{N}\right)\right],$$

$$u = 0, 1, \ldots, M-1, \qquad v = 0, 1, \ldots, N-1,$$

(3.34)

and the inverse Fourier transform is given by

$$f(m,n) = \sum_{u=0}^{M-1} \sum_{v=0}^{N-1} F(u,v) \exp\left[2\pi i\left(\frac{mu}{M} + \frac{nv}{N}\right)\right],$$

$$m = 0, 1, \ldots, M-1, \qquad n = 0, 1, \ldots, N-1.$$

(3.35)

Considering implementation of the discrete Fourier transform, note that equation (3.34) can be modified to

$$F(u,v) = \frac{1}{M} \sum_{m=0}^{M-1} \left[\frac{1}{N} \sum_{n=0}^{N-1} \exp\left(\frac{-2\pi i n v}{N}\right) f(m,n)\right] \exp\left(\frac{-2\pi i m u}{M}\right),$$

$$u = 0, 1, \ldots, M-1, \qquad v = 0, 1, \ldots, N-1.$$

(3.36)

The term in square brackets corresponds to the one-dimensional Fourier transform of the mth line and can be computed using standard fast Fourier transform (FFT) procedures if N is a power of two. Each line is substituted with its Fourier transform, and the one-dimensional discrete Fourier transform of each column is computed.

Periodicity is an important property of the discrete Fourier transform. A periodic transform F is derived and a periodic function f defined

$$\begin{aligned} F(u,-v) &= F(u, N-v), & f(-m,n) &= f(M-m,n), \\ F(-u,v) &= F(M-u,v), & f(m,-n) &= f(m, N-n), \end{aligned}$$

(3.37)

and

$$F(aM+u, bN+v) = F(u,v), \qquad f(aM+m, bN+n) = f(m,n), \qquad (3.38)$$

where a and b are integers.

The outcome of the 2D Fourier transform is a complex-valued 2D spectrum. Consider the input gray-level image (before the 2D Fourier transform was applied) with intensity values in the range, say, $[0, \ldots, 255]$. The 2D spectrum has the same spatial resolution. However, the values in both real and imaginary part of the spectrum usually span a bigger range, perhaps millions—this makes the spectrum difficult to visualize and also to represent precisely in memory because too many bits are needed for it. For easier visualization, the range of values is usually decreased by applying a monotonic function, e.g., $\sqrt{|F(u,v)|}$ or $\log|F(u,v)|$.

It is also useful to visualize a centered spectrum, i.e., with the origin of the coordinate system $(0,0)$ in the middle of the spectrum. This is because centering has the effect of placing the low frequency information in the center and the high frequencies near the corners—consider the definition given in equation (3.34).

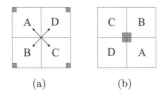

(a)   (b)

Figure 3.6: Centering of the 2D Fourier spectrum places the low frequencies around the coordinates origin. (a) Original spectrum. (b) Centered spectrum with the low frequencies in the middle. © *Cengage Learning 2015.*

Assume the original spectrum is divided into four quadrants, see Figure 3.6a. The small gray-filled squares in the corners represent positions of low frequencies. Due to the symmetries of the spectrum the quadrant positions can be swapped diagonally and the low frequencies locations appear in the middle of the image, see Figure 3.6b.

Figure 3.7 illustrates the spectrum of Figure 3.8. The left image demonstrates the non-centered power spectrum and the right image the centered spectrum. The latter option is used more often. The range of spectrum values has to be decreased to allow an observer to perceive it better; $\log P(u, v)$ is used here. For illustration of the particular range of this power spectrum, the pair of (minimum, maximum) for $P(u, v)$ is $(2.4 \cdot 10^{-1}, 8.3 \cdot 10^{6})$ and the (minimum, maximum) for $\log P(u, v)$ is $(-0.62, 6.9)$. A quite distinct light cross can be seen in the centered power spectrum on the right of Figure 3.9. This is caused by discontinuities on the limits of the image while assuming periodicity. These abrupt changes are easily visible in Figure 3.8.

The use of the Fourier transform in image analysis is pervasive. We will see in Chapter 5 how it can assist in noise filtering; in the detection of edges by locating high frequencies (sharp changes) in the image function; it also has applications in restoring images from corruption (Section 5.4.2), fast matching using the convolution theorem (Section 6.4.2), boundary characterization (Section 8.2.3), image compression (Chapter 14), and several other areas.

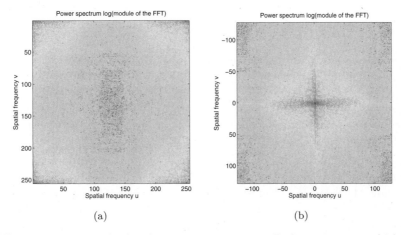

(a)   (b)

Figure 3.7: Power spectrum displayed as an intensity image. Lighter tones mean higher values. (a) Non-centered. (b) Centered. © *Cengage Learning 2015. A color version of this figure may be seen in the color inset—Plate 5.*

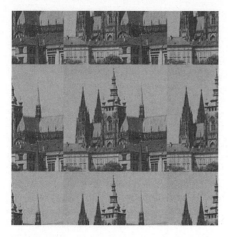

Figure 3.8: Input image in the spatial domain is assumed periodic. Notice induced discontinuities on the borders of the image which manifests badly in the Fourier spectrum. The image is the Saint Vitus Cathedral, part of the Prague Castle—the original is 256×256 pixels in 256 gray levels. © *Cengage Learning 2015.*

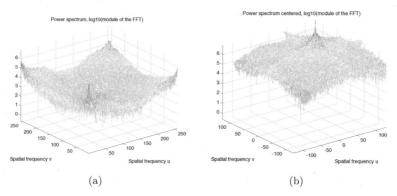

(a)   (b)

Figure 3.9: Power spectrum displayed as height in a 3D mesh; lighter tones mean higher values. (a) Non-centered. (b) Centered. © *Cengage Learning 2015. A color version of this figure may be seen in the color inset—Plate 6.*

3.2.5   Sampling and the Shannon constraint

Equipped with understanding of the Fourier transform, we can now discuss more fully the issues surrounding sampling. A continuous image function $f(x, y)$ can be sampled using a discrete grid of sampling points in the plane, but a second possibility is to expand the image function using some orthonormal functions as a basis—the Fourier transform is an example—and the coefficients of this expansion then represent the digitized image.

The image is sampled at points $x = j \, \Delta x$, $y = k \, \Delta y$, for $j = 1, \ldots, M$ and $k = 1, \ldots, N$. Two neighboring sampling points are separated by distance Δx along the x axis and Δy along the y axis. Distances $\Delta x, \Delta y$ are called **sampling intervals** (on the x, y axes), and the matrix of samples $f(j \, \Delta x, k \, \Delta y)$ constitutes the discrete image. The ideal sampling $s(x, y)$ in the regular grid can be represented using a collection of Dirac distributions δ

$$s(x, y) = \sum_{j=1}^{M} \sum_{k=1}^{N} \delta(x - j \, \Delta x, \, y - k \, \Delta y) \, . \tag{3.39}$$

The sampled image $f_s(x, y)$ is the product of the continuous image $f(x, y)$ and the sampling function $s(x, y)$

$$f_s(x, y) = f(x, y)\, s(x, y)$$

$$= f(x, y) \sum_{j=1}^{M} \sum_{k=1}^{N} \delta(x - j\,\Delta x, y - k\,\Delta y)\,. \tag{3.40}$$

We may consider an infinite sampling grid which is periodic with periods Δx, Δy and expand the sampling into a Fourier series. We obtain (see [Oppenheim et al., 1997])

$$\mathcal{F}\left\{ \sum_{j=-\infty}^{\infty} \sum_{k=-\infty}^{\infty} \delta(x - j\,\Delta x, y - k\,\Delta y) \right\} = \frac{1}{\Delta x\,\Delta y} \sum_{m=-\infty}^{\infty} \sum_{n=-\infty}^{\infty} \delta\left(u - \frac{m}{\Delta x}, v - \frac{n}{\Delta y} \right)\,. \tag{3.41}$$

Equation (3.40) can be expressed in the frequency domain using equation (3.41):

$$F_s(u, v) = \frac{1}{\Delta x\,\Delta y} \sum_{m=-\infty}^{\infty} \sum_{n=-\infty}^{\infty} F\left(u - \frac{m}{\Delta x}, v - \frac{n}{\Delta y} \right)\,. \tag{3.42}$$

Thus the Fourier transform of the sampled image is the sum of periodically repeated Fourier transforms $F(u, v)$ of the image. We can demonstrate this effect in the 1D case: assume that the maximal frequency of the signal is f_m, so the signal is **band-limited** (so its Fourier transform F is zero outside a certain interval, $|f| > f_m$). The spectra will be repeated as a consequence of discretization—see Figure 3.10. In the case of 2D images, band-limited means that the spectrum $F(u, v) = 0$ for $|u| > U$, $|v| > V$, where U, V are maximal frequencies.

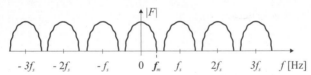

Figure 3.10: Repeated spectra of the 1D signal due to sampling. Non-overlapped case when $f_s \geq 2f_m$. © *Cengage Learning 2015.*

Periodic repetition of the Fourier transform result $F(u, v)$ may under certain conditions cause distortion of the image, which is called **aliasing**; this happens when individual digitized components $F(u, v)$ overlap. Overlapping of the periodically repeated results of the Fourier transform $F(u, v)$ of an image with band-limited spectrum can be prevented if the sampling interval is chosen such that

$$\Delta x < \frac{1}{2U}\,, \qquad \Delta y < \frac{1}{2V}\,. \tag{3.43}$$

This is **Shannon's sampling theorem**, known from signal processing theory. It has a simple physical interpretation in image analysis: The sampling interval should be chosen such that it is less than *half* of the smallest interesting detail in the image.

The sampling function is not the Dirac distribution in real digitizers—limited impulses (quite narrow ones with limited amplitude) are used instead. Assume a rectangular sampling grid which consists of $M \times N$ such equal and non-overlapping impulses $h_s(x, y)$ with sampling period Δx, Δy; this function realistically simulates real image sensors. Outside the sensitive area of the sensor, $h_s(x, y) = 0$. Values of image samples are obtained by integration of the product fh_s—in reality this integration is done on the sensitive surface of the sensor element. The sampled image is then given by

$$f_s(x, y) = \sum_{j=1}^{M} \sum_{k=1}^{N} f(x, y) \, h_s(x - j\,\Delta x, y - k\,\Delta y) \,. \tag{3.44}$$

The sampled image f_s is distorted by the convolution of the original image f and the limited impulse h_s. The distortion of the frequency spectrum of the function F_s can be expressed using the Fourier transform

$$F_s(u, v) = \frac{1}{\Delta x \, \Delta y} \sum_{m=-\infty}^{\infty} \sum_{n=-\infty}^{\infty} F\left(u - \frac{m}{\Delta x}, v - \frac{n}{\Delta y}\right) H_s\left(\frac{m}{\Delta x}, \frac{n}{\Delta y}\right), \tag{3.45}$$

where $H_s = \mathcal{F}\{h_s\}$.

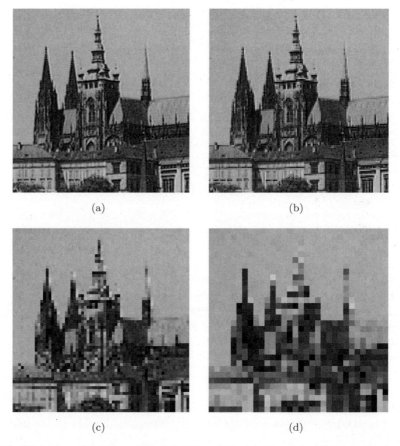

Figure 3.11: Digitizing. (a) 256 × 256. (b) 128 × 128. (c) 64 × 64. (d) 32 × 32. Images have been enlarged to the same size to illustrate the loss of detail. © *Cengage Learning 2015*.

In real image digitizers, a sampling interval about ten times smaller than that indicated by the Shannon sampling theorem is used—this is because algorithms which reconstruct the continuous image on a display from the digitized image function use only a step function, i.e., a line in the image is created from pixels represented by individual squares.

A demonstration with an image of 256 gray-levels will illustrate the effect of sparse sampling. Figure 3.11a shows a monochromatic image with 256×256 pixels; Figure 3.11b shows the same scene digitized into a reduced grid of 128×128 pixels, Figure 3.11c into 64×64 pixels, and Figure 3.11d into 32×32 pixels. Decline in image quality is clear in these. Quality may be improved by viewing from a distance and with screwed-up eyes, implying that the under-sampled images still hold substantial information. Much of this visual degradation is caused by aliasing in the reconstruction of the continuous image function for display. This can be improved by the reconstruction algorithm interpolating brightness values in neighboring pixels and this technique is called **anti-aliasing**, often used in computer graphics [Rogers, 1985]. If anti-aliasing is used, the sampling interval can be brought near to the theoretical value of Shannon's theorem. In real image processing devices, anti-aliasing is rarely used because of its computational requirements.

3.2.6 Discrete cosine transform

The **discrete cosine transform** (DCT) is a linear integral transformation similar to the discrete Fourier transform (DFT) [Rao and Yip, 1990]. In 1D, cosines with growing frequencies constitute the basis functions used for function expansion: the expansion is a linear combination of these basis cosines, and real numbers suffice for such an expansion (the Fourier transform required complex numbers). The DCT expansion corresponds to a DFT of approximately double length operating on a function with even symmetry.

Similarly to the DFT, the DCT operates on function samples of finite length, and a periodic extension of this function is needed to be able to perform DCT (or DFT) expansion. The DCT requires a stricter periodic extension (a more strict boundary condition) than the DFT—it requires that the extension is an even function.

Two options arise in relation to boundary conditions for a discrete finite sequence. The first one is whether the function is even or odd at both the left and right boundaries of the domain, and the second is about which point the function is even or odd. As illustration, consider an example sequence $wxyz$. If the data are even about sample w, the even extension is $zyxwxyz$. If the sequence is even about the point halfway between w and the previous point, the extension sequence is $zyxwwxyz$.

Consider the general case which covers both the discrete cosine transform (with even symmetry) and the discrete sine transform (with odd symmetry). The first choice has to be made about the symmetry at both left and right bounds of the signal, i.e., $2\times2=4$ possible options. The second choice is about which point the extension is performed, also at both left and right bounds of the signal, i.e., an additional $2\times2=4$ possible options. Altogether $4\times4=16$ possibilities are obtained. If we do not allow odd periodic extensions then the sine transforms are ruled out and 8 possible choices remain yielding 8 different types of DCT. If the same type of point is used for extension at left and right bounds then only half the options remain, i.e., $8/2=4$. This yields four basic types of DCT—they are usually denoted by suffixing Roman numbers as DCT-I, DCT-II, DCT-III, DCT-IV.

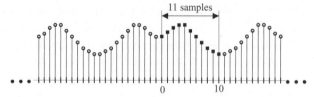

Figure 3.12: Illustration of the periodic extension used in DCT-II. The input signal of length 11 is denoted by squares. Its periodic extension is shown as circles. © *Cengage Learning 2015*.

The most commonly used variant of DCT in image processing, mainly in image compression (Chapter 14) is DCT-II. The periodic extension is even at both left and right bounds of the input sequence. The sequence is even about the point halfway between the bound and the previous point: the periodic extension for the input sequence is illustrated in Figure 3.12. The figure demonstrates the advantage of periodic extension used in DCT-II—mirroring involved in periodic extension yields a smooth periodic function, which means that fewer cosines are needed to approximate the signal.

The DCT can easily be generalized to two dimensions which is shown here for the square image, $M = N$. The 2D DCT-II is [Rao and Yip, 1990]

$$F(u, v) = \frac{2\, c(u)\, c(v)}{N} \sum_{m=0}^{N-1} \sum_{n=0}^{N-1} f(m, n) \cos\left(\frac{2m+1}{2N} u\pi\right) \cos\left(\frac{2n+1}{2N} v\pi\right) , \qquad (3.46)$$

where $u = 0, 1, \ldots, N-1$, $v = 0, 1, \ldots, N-1$ and the normalization constant $c(k)$ is

$$c(k) = \begin{cases} \frac{1}{\sqrt{2}} & \text{for } k = 0, \\ 1 & \text{otherwise.} \end{cases}$$

The inverse cosine transform is

$$f(m, n) = \frac{2}{N} \sum_{u=0}^{N-1} \sum_{v=0}^{N-1} c(u)\, c(v)\, F(u, v) \cos\left(\frac{2m+1}{2N} u\pi\right) \cos\left(\frac{2n+1}{2N} v\pi\right) , \qquad (3.47)$$

where $m = 0, 1, \ldots, N-1$ and $n = 0, 1, \ldots, N-1$.

There is a computational approach analogous to the FFT which yields computational complexity in the 1D case of $\mathcal{O}(N \log N)$, where N is the length of the sequence.

Efficacy of an integral transformation can be evaluated by its ability to compress input data into as few coefficients as possible. The DCT exhibits excellent energy compaction for highly correlated images. This and other properties of the DCT have led to its widespread deployment in many image/video processing standards, for example, JPEG (classical), MPEG-4, MPEG-4 FGS, H.261, H.263 and JVT (H.26L).

3.2.7 Wavelet transform

The Fourier transform (Section 3.2.3) expands a signal as a possibly infinite linear combination of sines and cosines. The disadvantage is that only information about the frequency spectrum is provided, and no information is available on the *time* at which events occur. In another words, the Fourier spectrum provides all the frequencies present in an image but does not tell where they are present. We also know that the relation between the frequency and spatial resolutions is given by the uncertainty principle, equation (3.24).

One solution to the problem of localizing changes in the signal (image) is to use the short time Fourier transform, where the signal is divided into small windows and treated locally as it were periodic (see Section 3.2.3). The uncertainty principle provides guidance on how to select the windows to minimize negative effects, i.e., windows have to join neighboring windows smoothly. The window dilemma remains—a narrow window yields poor frequency resolution, while a wide window provides poor localization.

The wavelet transform goes further than the short time Fourier transform. It also analyzes the signal (image) by multiplying it by a window function and performing an orthogonal expansion, analogously to other linear integral transformations. There are two directions in which the analysis is extended.

In the first direction, the basis functions (called **wavelets**, meaning a small wave) are more complicated than sines and cosines. They provide localization in space to a certain degree, not entire localization due to the uncertainty principle. Five commonly used 'mother' wavelets are illustrated in Figure 3.13 in a qualitative manner and in a single of many scales.

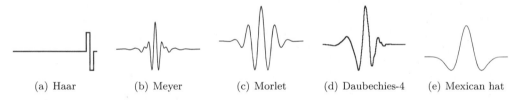

(a) Haar   (b) Meyer   (c) Morlet   (d) Daubechies-4   (e) Mexican hat

Figure 3.13: Examples of mother wavelets. © *Cengage Learning 2015.*

In the second direction, the analysis is performed at **multiple scales**. To understand this, note that modeling a spike in a function (a noise dot, for example) with a sum of a huge number of functions will be hard because of the spike's strict locality. Functions that are already local will be better suited to the task. This means that such functions lend themselves to more compact representation via wavelets—sharp spikes and discontinuities normally take fewer wavelet bases to represent compared to sine-cosine basis functions. Localization in the spatial domain together with the wavelet's localization in frequency yields a sparse representation of many practical signals. This sparseness opens the door to successful applications in data/image compression, noise filtering and detecting features in images.

We will start from the 1D, continuous case—the 1D **continuous wavelet transform**. A function $f(t)$ is decomposed into a set of basis functions Ψ—wavelets

$$c(s, \tau) = \int_R f(t)\, \Psi^*_{s,\tau}(t)\, \mathrm{d}t\,, \quad s \in R^+ - \{0\}\,, \quad \tau \in R \tag{3.48}$$

(complex conjugation is denoted by *). The new variables after transformation are s (scale) and τ (translation).

Wavelets are generated from the single **mother wavelet** $\Psi(t)$ by scaling s and translation τ

$$\Psi_{s,\tau}(t) = \frac{1}{\sqrt{s}}\, \Psi\left(\frac{t - \tau}{s}\right)\,. \tag{3.49}$$

The factor $1/\sqrt{s}$ is applied to normalize energy across different scales.

The inverse continuous wavelet transform serves to synthesize the 1D signal $f(t)$ of finite energy from wavelet coefficients $c(s, \tau)$

$$f(t) = \int_{R+} \int_{R} c(s, \tau) \, \Psi_{s,\tau}(t) \, ds \, d\tau \, . \tag{3.50}$$

Equations (3.48)–(3.49) do not specify a mother wavelet: the user can select or design the basis of the expansion according to application needs.

There are constraints which a function $\Psi_{s,\tau}$ must obey to be a wavelet, of which the most important are *admissibility* and *regularity*. Admissibility requires that the wavelet has a band-pass spectrum; consequently, the wavelet must be oscillatory—a wave. The wavelet transform of a 1D signal is two dimensional as can be seen from equation (3.48), and similarly, the transform of a 2D image is four dimensional. This is complex to deal with, and the solution is to impose an additional constraint on the wavelet function which secures fast decrease with decreasing scale. This is achieved by the regularity, which states that the wavelet function should have some smoothness and concentration in both time and frequency domains. A more detailed explanation can be found in, e.g., [Daubechies, 1992].

We illustrate scaling and shifting on the oldest and the simplest mother, the Haar wavelet, which is a special case of the Daubechies wavelet. Scaling functions are denoted by Φ. Simple scaling functions used for Haar wavelets are given by the set of scaled and translated 'box' functions

$$\Phi_{ji}(x) = 2^{j/2} \, \Phi(2^j x - i) \, , \quad i = 0, \ldots, 2^j - 1 \, , \text{ where} \tag{3.51}$$

$$\Phi(x) = \begin{cases} 1 & \text{for } 0 \le x < 1 \, , \\ 0 & \text{otherwise.} \end{cases} \tag{3.52}$$

and $2^{j/2}$ is a normalization factor. An example of four instances of scaling function which constitute a basis of the appropriate vector space are shown in Figure 3.14. Wavelets corresponding to the box basis are called the **Haar wavelets** and are given by

$$\Psi_{ji}(x) = 2^{j/2} \, \Psi(2^j x - i) \, , \quad i = 0, \ldots, 2^j - 1 \, , \text{ where} \tag{3.53}$$

$$\Psi(x) = \begin{cases} 1 & \text{for } 0 \le x < \frac{1}{2} \, , \\ -1 & \text{for } \frac{1}{2} \le x < 1 \, , \\ 0 & \text{otherwise,} \end{cases} \tag{3.54}$$

An example of Haar wavelets Ψ_{11}, Ψ_{12} is given in Figure 3.15. The transform which uses Haar wavelets is called the Haar transform.

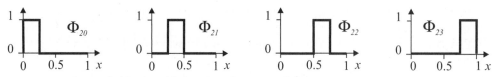

Figure 3.14: 'Box-like' scaling functions Φ. © *Cengage Learning 2015.*

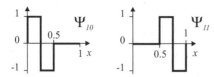

Figure 3.15: Haar wavelets Ψ_{11}, Ψ_{12}.
© *Cengage Learning 2015.*

It is not practical to use equation (3.48) in the general case for three reasons:

- There is much redundancy because the calculation is performed by continuously scaling the mother wavelet, shifting it and correlating it with the analyzed signal.

- The intention is to reduce the infinite number of wavelets taking part in calculations.

- The final result of the transform cannot be calculated analytically: further an efficient numerical solution is needed of comparable complexity to, e.g., the FFT.

The solution is the **discrete wavelet transform**. If the scales and positions are based on a power of two (dyadic scales and positions) then the wavelet analysis becomes much more computationally efficient and just as accurate.

Mallat [Mallat, 1989] developed an efficient way to calculate the discrete wavelet transform and its inverse. The scheme is actually a variant of the classical scheme—a two-channel subband coder—known in signal processing. This method yields a **fast wavelet transform** which can be imagined as a box into which a signal (an image) enters and the wavelet coefficients c appear quickly at its output.

Consider a discrete 1D signal s of length N which has to be decomposed into wavelet coefficients c. The fast wavelet transform consists of $\log_2 N$ steps at most. The first decomposition step takes the input and provides two sets of coefficients at level 1: approximation coefficients cA_1 and detail coefficients cD_1. The vector s is convolved with a low-pass filter for approximation and with a high-pass filter for detail. Dyadic decimation follows which down-samples the vector by keeping only its even elements. Such down-sampling will be denoted by ($\downarrow 2$) in block diagrams. The coefficients at level $j+1$ are calculated from the coefficients at level j analogously, see Figure 3.16. This procedure is repeated recursively to obtain approximation and detail coefficients at further levels. The structure of coefficients for level $j=3$ is illustrated in Figure 3.17.

The inverse discrete wavelet transform takes as input the approximation and detail coefficients cA_j, cD_j and inverts the decomposition step. Vectors are extended (up-

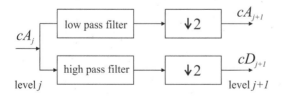

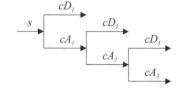

Figure 3.16: A single decomposition step of the 1D discrete wavelet transform consists of the convolution of coefficients from previous level j by a low/high pass filter and down-sampling by dyadic decimation. Approximation and detail coefficients at level $j+1$ are obtained. © *Cengage Learning 2015.*

Figure 3.17: Example illustrating the structure of approximation and detail coefficients for levels up to a level $j=3$. © *Cengage Learning 2015.*

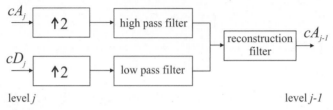

Figure 3.18: 1D discrete inverse wavelet transformation. © *Cengage Learning 2015.*

sampled) to double length by inserting zeros at odd-indexed elements and convolving the result with the reconstruction filters. Analogously to down-sampling, up-sampling is denoted ($\uparrow$ 2) in Figure 3.18, which illustrates the 1D inverse discrete wavelets transformation.

Similar wavelet decomposition and reconstruction algorithms were developed for 2D signals (images). The 2D discrete wavelet transformation decomposes a single approximation coefficient at level j into four components at level $j + 1$: the approximation coefficient cA_{j+1} and detail coefficients at three orientations—horizontal cD^h_{j+1}, vertical cD^v_{j+1} and diagonal cD^d_{j+1}—Figures 3.19 and 3.20 illustrate this. The symbol (col $\downarrow$ 2) represents down-sampling columns by keeping only even indexed columns. Similarly,

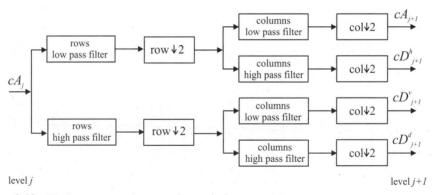

Figure 3.19: 2D discrete wavelet transform. A decomposition step. © *Cengage Learning 2015.*

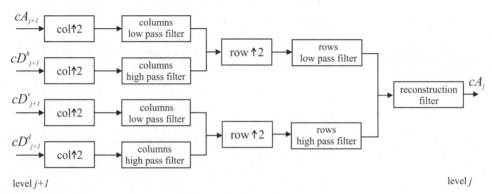

Figure 3.20: 2D inverse discrete wavelet transform. A reconstruction step. © *Cengage Learning 2015.*

(row $\downarrow$ 2) means down-sampling rows by keeping only evenly indexed rows. (col $\uparrow$ 2) represents up-sampling columns by inserting zeros at odd-indexed columns. Similarly, (row $\uparrow$ 2) means up-sampling rows by inserting zeros at odd-indexed rows.

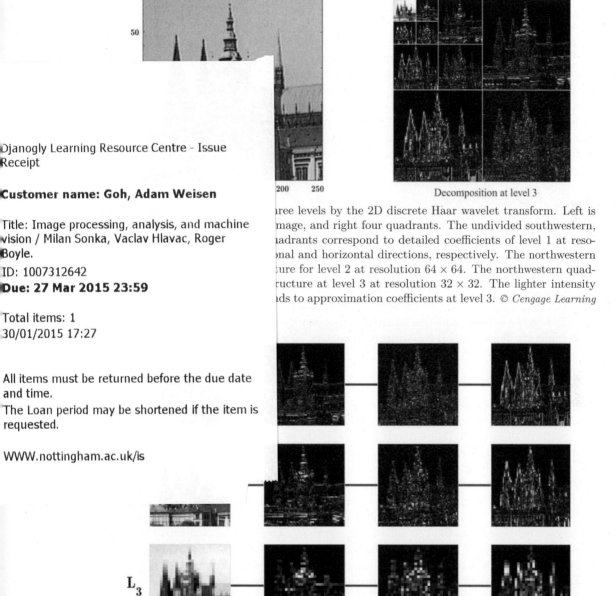

Decomposition at level 3

...ree levels by the 2D discrete Haar wavelet transform. Left is ...mage, and right four quadrants. The undivided southwestern, ...adrants correspond to detailed coefficients of level 1 at reso-...nal and horizontal directions, respectively. The northwestern ...ture for level 2 at resolution 64 × 64. The northwestern quad-...ructure at level 3 at resolution 32 × 32. The lighter intensity ...ds to approximation coefficients at level 3. © *Cengage Learning*

Approximations   **Horizontal Details**   **Diagonal Details**   **Vertical Details**

Figure 3.22: 2D wavelet decomposition; another view of the same data as Figure 3.21. © *Cengage Learning 2015.*

Figure 3.21 illustrates the decomposition of the previous example. The resolution of levels 2 and 3 is insufficient qualitatively to see the character of wavelet coefficients. Figure 3.22 shows the same data for all three levels in a different form.

The wavelet transform discussed thus far is a special case of a more versatile **wavelet packet** transform. Wavelet packets are particular linear combinations of wavelets which retain many of the localization, smoothness and orthogonality properties of their parent wavelets. Linear combinations of coefficients are again calculated in a recursive way. Using discrete wavelets, only the detail branch of the decomposition tree is split, but both detail and approximation branches can be split in wavelet packet analysis.

Applications have proved the value of the approach. Wavelets have been used with enormous success in data compression, feature detection and in image noise suppression— it is possible to erase to zero the contribution of wavelet components that are 'small' and correspond to noise without erasing the important small detail in the underlying image. The interested reader is referred to specialized texts for a fuller exposition on this topic [Chui, 1992; Daubechies, 1992; Meyer, 1993; Chui et al., 1994; Castleman, 1996].

3.2.8   Eigen-analysis

Many disciplines, including image analysis, seek to represent observations, signals, images and general data in a form that enhances the mutual independence of contributory components. Linear algebra provides very good tools for such representations. One observation or measurement is assumed to be a point in a linear space; this space will have some 'natural' basis vectors which allow data to be expressed as a linear combination in a new coordinate system consisting of *orthogonal* basis vectors. These basis vectors are the **eigen-vectors**, and the inherent orthogonality of eigen-vectors secures mutual independence. For an $n \times n$ square regular matrix A, eigen-vectors are solutions of the equation

$$A\mathbf{x} = \lambda \mathbf{x}, \qquad (3.55)$$

where λ is called an **eigen-value** (which may be complex).

A system of linear equations can be expressed in a matrix form as $A\mathbf{x} = \mathbf{b}$, where A is the matrix of the system. The extended matrix of the system is created by concatenating a column vector $\mathbf{b}$ to the matrix A, i.e., $[A|\mathbf{b}]$. Frobenius' theorem says that this system has a unique solution if and only if the rank of the matrix A is equal to the rank of the extended matrix $[A|\mathbf{b}]$.

If the system of equations is not degenerate then it has as many equations as unknown variables $\mathbf{x} = (x_1, \ldots, x_n)^\top$ and the system has a unique solution. Gaussian elimination is the commonly used method to solve such a system. The method performs equivalent transformations of $[A|\mathbf{b}]$ which do not change the solution of the system of equations, and the extended matrix is finally expressed in upper triangular form. When the elimination is finished, the last row of the matrix provides the solution value of x_n. This solution allows the stepwise calculation of $x_{n-1}, \ldots, x_1$.

There is another class of matrix transformation called *similar* transformations. If A is a regular matrix, matrices A and B with real or complex entries are called similar if there exists an invertible square matrix P such that $P^{-1}AP = B$. Similar matrices share many useful properties—they have the same rank, determinant, trace, characteristic polynomial, minimal polynomial and eigen-values (but not necessarily the same eigen-vectors). Similarity transformations allow us to express regular matrices in several useful forms.

Let I be the unit matrix (with 1's on the main diagonal and zeros elsewhere). The polynomial of degree n given by $\det(A - \lambda I)$ is called the *characteristic polynomial*. Then the eigen-equation (3.55) has nontrivial solutions if $\det(A - \lambda I) = 0$ and the characteristic polynomial's roots are the eigen-values λ. Consequently, A has n eigen-values which are not necessarily distinct—multiple eigen-values arise from multiple roots of the polynomial.

Here we will be interested in the *Jordan canonical form*. Any Hermitian (in particular, symmetric) matrix is similar to a matrix in the Jordan canonical form

$$
\begin{bmatrix} J_1 & & 0 \\ & \ddots & \\ 0 & & J_p \end{bmatrix} , \text{ where } J_i \text{ are Jordan blocks } \begin{bmatrix} \lambda_i & 1 & & 0 \\ 0 & \lambda_i & \ddots & 0 \\ 0 & 0 & \ddots & 1 \\ 0 & 0 & & \lambda_i \end{bmatrix} , \tag{3.56}
$$

and λ_i are the multiple eigen-values. The multiplicity of the eigen-value gives the size of the *Jordan block*. If the eigen-value is not multiple then the Jordan block degenerates to the eigen-value itself. This happens very often in practice.

Consider the case when the linear system is over-constrained, meaning that there are more equations than variables to be determined; this case is very common in practice, when abundant data comes from many observations or measurements. Strictly speaking, the observations are likely to be in contradiction with respect to the system of linear equations. In the deterministic world, the conclusion would be that the system of linear equations has no solution, but the practical need is different. There is an interest in finding the solution to the system which is in some sense 'closest' to the observations, perhaps compensating for noise in observations. We will usually adopt a statistical approach by minimizing the least square error. This leads to the principal component analysis method, explained in Section 3.2.10.

Seeking roots of the characteristic polynomial is usually rather poor computationally, and more effective methods such as singular value decomposition are used.

3.2.9   Singular value decomposition

Eigen-values and eigen-vectors are defined on square matrices; a generalization—*singular values*—operates on rectangular matrices, and is approached via **singular value decomposition** (SVD). A non-negative real number σ is a *singular value* of a matrix A (not necessarily square) if and only if there exist unit-length vectors u and v such that

$$
A v = \sigma u \quad \text{and} \quad A^* u = \sigma v .
$$

Note the similarity to the eigen-equation (3.55). The vectors u and v are called *left-singular* and *right-singular vectors* for σ, respectively.

SVD is a powerful linear algebra factorization technique of a rectangular real or complex matrix; it works even for singular or numerically near-singular matrices. It is used with many applications for solving linear equations in the least-square sense, e.g., in signal processing and statistics. It can be viewed as a generalization of the transformation to the Jordan canonical form to arbitrary, not necessarily square, matrices. Basic information necessary to use SVD can be found in many texts: for example, [Press et al., 1992], and a rigorous mathematical treatment is given in [Golub and Loan, 1989]. Most software packages for numerical calculations such as Matlab contain SVD.

SVD proceeds by noting that any $m \times n$ matrix A, $m \geq n$, (with real or complex entries) can be decomposed into a product of three matrices,

$$A = U\,D\,V^* \,, \tag{3.57}$$

where U is $m \times m$ with orthonormal columns and rows, D is a non-negative diagonal matrix, and V^* has orthonormal rows.

SVD can be understood as decoupling input of size m into output of size n. The matrix V contains a set of orthonormal 'input' or basis vector directions (left-singular vectors) for the matrix A, and U contains a set of orthonormal 'output' basis vector directions (right-singular vectors) for A. D contains the singular values, which can be understood as scalar 'gains' by which each corresponding input is multiplied to give the corresponding output.

It is conventional to reorder the input and output values to have the diagonal entries of the diagonal matrix D non-increasing, making D unique for any given A. The matrices U and V are not unique in general.

There is a relation between singular values and vectors, and eigen-values and vectors. In the special case, when A is Hermitian (also self-adjoint, $A = A^*$), all eigen-values of A are real and non-negative. In this case, the singular values and singular vectors coincide with the eigen-values and eigen-vectors, $A = V\,D\,V^*$.

SVD can be used to find a solution of a set of linear equations corresponding to a singular matrix that has no exact solution—it locates the closest possible solution in the least-square sense. Sometimes it is required to find the 'closest' singular matrix to the original matrix A—this decreases the rank from n to $n-1$ or less. This is done by replacing the smallest diagonal element of D by zero—this new matrix is closest to the old one with respect to the Frobenius norm (calculated as a sum of the squared values of all matrix elements). SVD is also very popular because of its numerical stability and precision [Press et al., 1992].

3.2.10 Principal component analysis

Principal component analysis (PCA) is a powerful and widely used linear technique in statistics, signal processing, image processing, and elsewhere. It appears under several names: it is also called the (discrete) *Karhunen-Loève transform* (after Kari Karhunen and Michael Loève) or the *Hotelling transform* (after Harold Hotelling).

In statistics, PCA is a method for simplifying a multidimensional dataset to lower dimensions for analysis or visualization. It is a linear transform that represents the data in a new coordinate system in which basis vectors follow modes of greatest variance in the data: it is the optimal linear transformation which divides an observed space into orthogonal subspaces with the largest variance. Thus, new basis vectors are calculated for the particular data set. One price to be paid for PCA's flexibility is in higher computational requirements as compared to, e.g., the fast Fourier transform.

As it reduces dimensionality, PCA can be used for lossy data compression while retaining those characteristics of the dataset which contribute most to its variance. PCA transforms a number of possibly correlated variables into the same number of uncorrelated variables called *principal components*. The first principal component accounts for as much of the variability in the data as possible, and each succeeding component accounts for as much of the remaining variability as possible. If the dataset has to be approximated in a lower dimension then lower-order principal components are considered and higher-order ones are omitted.

Suppose a data set comprises N observations, each of M variables (dimensions). Usually $N \gg M$. The intention is to reduce the dimensionality of the data so that each observation can be usefully represented with only L variables, $1 \leq L < M$. Data are arranged as a set of N column data vectors, each representing a single observation of M variables: the n-th observations is a column vector $\mathbf{x}_n = (x_1, \ldots, x_M)^\top$, $n = 1, \ldots, N$. We thus have an $M \times N$ data matrix X. Such matrices are often huge because N may be very large: this is in fact good, since many observations imply better statistics.

This procedure is not applied to the raw data R but to **normalized data** X as follows. The raw observed data is arranged in a matrix R and the empirical mean is calculated along each row of R to give a vector $\mathbf{u}$, the elements of which are scalars

$$u(m) = \frac{1}{N} \sum_{n=1}^{N} R(m, n), \quad \text{where } m = 1, \ldots, M. \tag{3.58}$$

The empirical mean is subtracted from each column of R: if $\mathbf{e}$ is a vector of size N consisting of ones only, we will write

$$X = R - \mathbf{u}\,\mathbf{e}.$$

If we approximate X in a lower dimensional space of dimension M by the lower dimensional matrix Y (of dimension L), then the mean square error ε^2 of this approximation is given by

$$\varepsilon^2 = \frac{1}{N} \sum_{n=1}^{N} |\mathbf{x}_n|^2 - \sum_{i=1}^{L} \mathbf{b}_i^\top \left(\frac{1}{N} \sum_{n=1}^{N} \mathbf{x}_n \mathbf{x}_n^\top \right) \mathbf{b}_i, \tag{3.59}$$

where $\mathbf{b}_i$, $i = 1, \ldots, L$ are basis vector of the linear space of dimension L. If ε^2 is to be minimized then the following term has to be maximized

$$\sum_{i=1}^{L} \mathbf{b}_i^\top \, \text{cov}(\mathbf{x}) \, \mathbf{b}_i, \quad \text{where } \text{cov}(\mathbf{x}) = \sum_{n=1}^{N} \mathbf{x}_n \mathbf{x}_n^\top$$

is the covariance matrix.

The covariance matrix $\text{cov}(\mathbf{x})$ has special properties: it is real, symmetric and positive semi-definite and so can be guaranteed to have real eigen-values. Matrix theory tells us that these may be sorted (largest to smallest) and the associated eigen-vectors taken as the basis vectors that provide the maximum we seek. In the data approximation, dimensions corresponding to the smallest eigen-values are omitted. The mean square error ε^2 of equation (3.59) is given by

$$\varepsilon^2 = \text{trace}\left(\text{cov}(\mathbf{x}) \right) - \sum_{i=1}^{L} \lambda_i = \sum_{i=L+1}^{M} \lambda_i,$$

where trace(A) is the *trace*—sum of the diagonal elements—of the matrix A. The trace equals the sum of all eigenvalues.

As an example, consider the use of PCA on images—this approach was popularized by its application to face recognition [Turk and Pentland, 1991]. The image is considered as a very long 1D vector by concatenating image pixels column by column (or alternatively row by row). Figure 3.23 is an example where the image is $321 \times 261 = 83781$ pixels 'long'. In this example, we have just 32 examples of this vector (contrary to the discussion above in which the number of examples is expected to exceed the dimensionality).

If we have fewer observations than unknowns, the system of linear equations is not over-constrained but PCA is still applicable. The number of principal components is less than or equal to the number of observations available; this is because the (square) covariance matrix has a size corresponding to the number of observations (number of observations minus one when doing PCA on centered data, which is usual). The eigen-vectors we derive are called **eigen-images**, after rearranging back from the 1D vector to a rectangular image.

One image is treated as a single point (a single observation) in a high-dimensional feature space. The set of images analyzed populates only a tiny fraction of the feature space. Considering Figure 3.23, note that the images were geometrically aligned; this was done manually by cropping to 321×261 and approximately positioning the nose tip to the same pixel. The reconstruction from four basis vectors is shown in Figure 3.24. Note that basis vectors are images.

PCA applied to images has also drawbacks. By rearranging pixels column by column to a 1D vector, relations of a given pixel to pixels in neighboring rows are not taken into account. Another disadvantage is in the global nature of the representation; small change or error in the input images influences the whole eigen-representation. However, this property is inherent in all linear integral transforms. Section 10.4 illustrates a widespread application of PCA, and a more detailed treatment of PCA applied to images can be found in [Leonardis and Bischof, 2000].

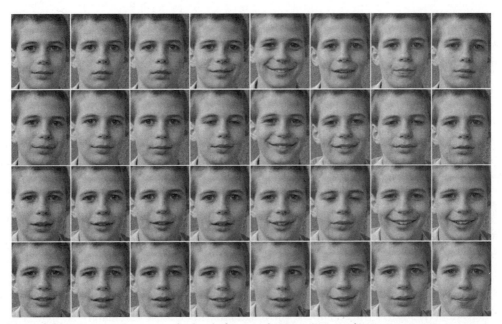

Figure 3.23: 32 original images of a boy's face, each 321×261 pixels. © *Cengage Learning 2015*.

Figure 3.24: Reconstruction of the image from four basis vectors $\mathbf{b}_i$, $i = 1, \ldots, 4$ which can be displayed as images. The linear combination was computed as $q_1\mathbf{b}_1 + q_2\mathbf{b}_2 + q_3\mathbf{b}_3 + q_4\mathbf{b}_4 = 0.078\,\mathbf{b}_1 + 0.062\,\mathbf{b}_2 - 0.182\,\mathbf{b}_3 + 0.179\,\mathbf{b}_4$. © *Cengage Learning 2015*.

3.2.11 Radon transform

Projections of images prove to reveal many important properties, and can also be realized by a number of physical processes. A complete (continuous) set of projections contains the same amount of information as the original image, and is known as the **Radon transform** [Barrett and Myers, 2004].

Formally, if $f(x, y)$ is a 2D function that vanishes outside some disk, we consider the set of lines L in 2D and define the Radon transform $\mathcal{R}_f$ as

$$\mathcal{R}_f(L) = \int_L f(\mathbf{x})|d\mathbf{X}| \,.$$

It is common to parameterize lines by their distance from the origin and angle to the Cartesian axes (see Figure 3.25)

$$((x(t), y(t)) = ((t \sin\alpha + s \cos\alpha), (-t \cos\alpha + s \sin\alpha)) \,.$$

Then

$$\begin{aligned}
\mathcal{R}_f(\alpha, s) &= \int_{-\infty}^{\infty} f(x(t), y(t))dt \\
&= \int_{-\infty}^{\infty} f(t \sin\alpha + s \cos\alpha, -t \cos\alpha + s \sin\alpha)dt \,.
\end{aligned} \qquad (3.60)$$

Conceptually, we are integrating the image function over every ray passed through the image, at every angle; this is what CT image acquisition does with X-rays.

The inverse of the Radon transform is accessible via the Fourier techniques we have seen, specifically the *Fourier Slice Theorem*. Informally, the 1D Fourier transform of

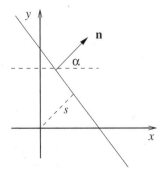

Figure 3.25: A straight line parameterized by its distance from the origin s and angle α. © *Cengage Learning 2015*.

(a)   (b)

Figure 3.26: (a) The iconic Chamberlin-Powell-Bon Computing building of the University of Leeds. (b) Edge detection (see Section 5.3.2)—the straight lines are very evident. © *R.D. Boyle 2015.*

Figure 3.27: The Radon transform of Figure 3.26. The horizontal axis is 180 wide (measured in degrees); the vertical is 751, being the 'diameter' of the original 394 × 640 image. The image has been contrast-stretched for display. With the origin at the image center in Figure 3.26, the primary peaks are evident at $(1, 196)$, columns at the image left; $(-18, 48)$, the oblique from upper left to center right, above a line of windows; $(-25, 95)$, similarly, the floor above. © *Cengage Learning 2015.*

the Radon transform with respect to angle α delivers one line (slice) of the 2D Fourier transform of f. Thus computing the set of 2D Fourier transforms of $\mathcal{R}_f(\alpha, s)$ generates the 2D Fourier transform of f, which may then be inverted using established techniques. This is how 'body slice' images are derived from the raw output of a CT scanner.

In digital images, the transform is realized by summing across a set of rays cast through an image; the dimensions of the transform depend on the maximal image diameter and the granularity of the angle between rays. Figures 3.26 and 3.27 illustrate the Radon transform of a Sobel edge detection (see Section 5.3.2) of an image with a number of pronounced lines; the peaks locate these lines successfully. It will become clear that the Radon transform has relationships with the Hough transform (see Section 6.2.6).

3.2.12   Other orthogonal image transforms

Many other orthogonal image transforms exist. The **Hadamard-Haar** transform is a combination of the Haar and Hadamard transforms, and a modified Hadamard-Haar transform is similar. The **Slant** transform and its modification the **Slant-Haar** transform represent another transform containing sawtooth waveforms or *slant* base vectors; a fast computational algorithm is also available. The **discrete sine transform** is very similar to the discrete cosine transform. The **Paley** and **Walsh** transforms are both very similar to the Hadamard transform, using matrices consisting of ±1 elements only. All transforms mentioned here are discussed in detail in [Gonzalez and Woods, 1992; Barrett and Myers, 2004], where references for computational algorithms can also be found.

3.3 Images as stochastic processes

Images are statistical in nature due to random changes and noise, and it is sometimes of advantage to treat image functions as realizations of a stochastic process [Papoulis, 1991; Barrett and Myers, 2004]. In such an approach, questions regarding image information content and redundancy can be answered using probability distributions, and simplifying probabilistic characterizations as the mean, dispersion, correlation functions, etc.

A **stochastic process** (random process, random field) is a generalization of the random variable concept. We will constrain ourselves to stochastic processes of with two variables x, y which are the coordinates in the image. We denote a stochastic process by ϕ and $\phi(x, y)$ is a random variable representing the gray-level at pixel (x, y). A specific image is obtained as a **realization** of the stochastic process ϕ and is a real deterministic function f which provides the gray-level values which the image finally has.

An example will illustrate: the original input is the image of Prague Castle, Figure 3.11(a). Figure 3.28 gives three of many possible realizations of a stochastic process ϕ. In this example, the realizations were generated artificially from the input image by corrupting images with Gaussian noise with zero mean and standard deviation 0.1 in the scale of $[0, 1]$. The noise at each pixel is statistically independent of noise at other pixels. After realizations are created, each image is deterministic. However, the corre-

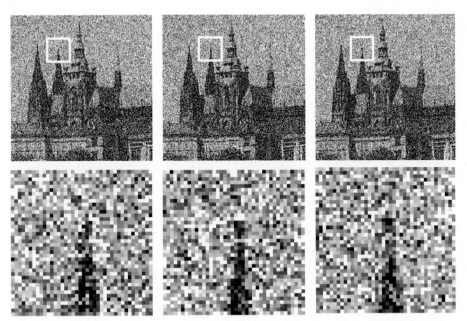

Figure 3.28: Above: three 256×256 images are shown as realizations of a stochastic process ϕ. The crop windows are marked by white squares in the images. Below: the content of these windows is enlarged. Notice that pixels really differ in the same locations in three realizations.
© *Cengage Learning 2015.*

sponding pixels in images are three different realizations of the same stochastic process. There are dependencies among gray-level values of pixels in the same image. The exact description of these dependencies would require a finite and extremely large number of joint distribution functions.

A stochastic process ϕ is entirely described by a collection of k-dimensional *distribution functions* P_k, $k = 1, 2, \ldots$. The distribution function of k arguments $z_1, \ldots, z_k$ is

$$P_k(z_1, \ldots, z_k; x_1, y_1, \ldots, x_k, y_k) = \mathcal{P}\left\{\phi(x_1, y_1) < z_1, \phi(x_2, y_2) < z_2, \ldots, \phi(x_k, y_k) < z_k\right\},$$
$$(3.61)$$

where $\mathcal{P}$ denotes the probability of the conjunction of events listed in the brackets. This equation expresses the dependence of k pixels $(x_1, y_1), \ldots, (x_k, y_k)$. For a complete probabilistic description, we would need these joint distribution functions for k equal to the number of pixels in the image.

The probability distributions of order k are not used in practice. They express a complex relation among many events. These descriptors are of theoretical importance and would need very many realizations (experiments) to be estimated. Most often, not more than a pair of events is related.

The *second-order distribution function* is used to relate pairs of events. Even simpler characterization of the stochastic process is the *first-order distribution function* which expresses probabilistic properties of the gray-level value of a single pixel independently of the others.

The probabilistic relations described by the distribution function $P_1(z; x, y)$ can be equivalently expressed using the probability density defined as

$$p_1(z; x, y) = \frac{\partial P_1(z; x, y)}{\partial z}.$$
$$(3.62)$$

The distribution is often roughly represented by simple characteristics. The mean of the stochastic process ϕ is defined using the first-order probability density by the equation

$$\mu_\phi(x, y) = E\left\{\phi(x, y)\right\} = \int_{-\infty}^{\infty} z\, p_1(z; x, y)\, \mathrm{d}z,$$
$$(3.63)$$

where E is the mathematical expectation operator.

The *autocorrelation* and *cross correlation* functions [Papoulis, 1991] are often used in searching for similarities in images or image parts. The autocorrelation function $R_{\phi\phi}$ of the random process ϕ is defined as a mean of the product of the random variables $\phi(x_1, y_1)$ and $\phi(x_2, y_2)$

$$R_{\phi\phi}(x_1, y_1, x_2, y_2) = E\left\{\phi(x_1, y_1)\,\phi(x_2, y_2)\right\}.$$
$$(3.64)$$

The *autocovariance* function $C_{\phi\phi}$ is defined as

$$C_{\phi\phi}(x_1, y_1, x_2, y_2) = R_{\phi\phi}(x_1, y_1, x_2, y_2) - \mu_\phi(x_1, y_1)\,\mu_\phi(x_2, y_2).$$
$$(3.65)$$

The *cross correlation* function $R_{\phi\gamma}$ and *cross covariance* function $C_{\phi\gamma}$ use similar definitions to equations (3.64) and (3.65). The only difference is that a point from one image (process) $\phi(x_1, y_1)$ is related to a point from another image (process) $\gamma(x_2, y_2)$. Two stochastic processes are *uncorrelated* if their cross covariance function is zero for any two points (x_1, y_1), (x_2, y_2).

A **stationary process** is a special stochastic process; its properties are independent of absolute position in the image plane. The mean μ_f of a stationary process is a constant.

The autocorrelation function $R_{\phi\phi}$ of a stationary stochastic process is translation invariant and depends only on the difference between co-ordinates $a = x_1 - x_2$, $b = y_1 - y_2$:

$$R_{\phi\phi}(x_1, y_1, x_2, y_2) = R_{\phi\phi}(a, b, 0, 0) \equiv R_{\phi\phi}(a, b),$$

$$R_{\phi\phi}(a, b) = \int_{-\infty}^{\infty} \int_{-\infty}^{\infty} \phi(x + a, y + b)\, \phi(x, y)\, dx\, dy. \tag{3.66}$$

Similarly, the cross correlation function between samples of stationary processes $\phi(x_1, y_1)$ and $\gamma(x_2, y_2)$ is defined as

$$R_{\phi\gamma}(x_1, y_1, x_2, y_2) = R_{\phi\gamma}(a, b, 0, 0) \equiv R_{\phi\gamma}(a, b),$$

$$R_{\phi\gamma}(a, b) = \int_{-\infty}^{\infty} \int_{-\infty}^{\infty} \phi(x + a, y + b)\, \gamma(x, y)\, dx\, dy. \tag{3.67}$$

Note that infinitely many functions have the same correlation function and therefore the same power spectrum as well. If an image is shifted then its power spectrum remains unchanged.

Let $\gamma(x, y)$ be the result of the convolution of the functions $\phi(x, y)$ and $\eta(x, y)$, Equation (3.11). Assume that $\phi(x, y)$, $\gamma(x, y)$ are stationary stochastic processes and $S_{\phi\phi}$, $S_{\gamma\gamma}$ are their corresponding power spectral densities. If the mean of the process $\phi(x, y)$ is zero, then

$$S_{\gamma\gamma}(u, v) = S_{\phi\phi}(u, v)\, S_{\eta\eta}(u, v), \tag{3.68}$$

where $S_{\eta\eta}(u, v)$ is the power spectrum of the stochastic process $\eta(x, y)$. Equation (3.68) is used to describe spectral properties of a linear image filter η.

The properties of correlation functions of stationary processes are interesting after a transform into the frequency domain. The Fourier transform of the cross correlation function of a stationary stochastic process can be expressed as the product of the Fourier transforms of involved processes (images in image analysis),

$$\mathcal{F}\{R_{\phi\gamma}(a, b)\} = F^*(u, v)\, G(u, v). \tag{3.69}$$

Similarly, the autocorrelation function can be written as

$$\mathcal{F}\{R_{\phi\phi}(a, b)\} = F^*(u, v)\, F(u, v) = |F(u, v)|^2. \tag{3.70}$$

The Fourier transform of the autocorrelation function, equation (3.66)—also called the *power spectrum*[2] or *spectral density*— is given by

$$S_{\phi\phi}(u, v) = \int_{-\infty}^{\infty} \int_{-\infty}^{\infty} R_{\phi\phi}(a, b)\, e^{-2\pi i(au + bv)}\, da\, db, \tag{3.71}$$

where u, v are spatial frequencies. The power spectral density communicates how much power the corresponding spatial frequency of the signal has.

---

[2]The concept of power spectrum can also be defined for functions for which the Fourier transform is not defined.

3.4   Image formation physics

Humans, using their eyes, comprehend intensities and colors in a relative sense, but the camera can be used as a measuring device which is able to provide absolute measurements. If we want to understand the quantities measured, then we have to look at the physical principles of image formation. We will survey some basic principles to understand how an image is created. These are straightforward and easy to explain; they are widely used in computer graphics to create visually appealing 2D images from 3D models.

Unfortunately, the inverse task is under-constrained; having as input the observed image intensities and aiming at determination of physical quantities such as light sources (their types, radiance, direction), shapes of surfaces in the scene, surface reflectance, and direction to the viewer is difficult. This inverse task is of prime interest in computer vision. Because of its complexity, practitioners often try to avoid its solution by finding a shortcut in segmenting objects corresponding to some semantically appealing entities in the scene, but the price to pay for this approach is a loss of generality. The segmentation usually works only in their application domain, image capturing setting, etc.

There are special cases, in which the inverse task to image formation is of practical use. These application domains are mainly 'shape from shading' and 'photometric stereo', which we will explain in Chapter 11. Direct measurement of radiance-like quantities is also used in quality control checks in industrial production, medical imaging, etc.

3.4.1   Images as radiometric measurements

Three types of emitted energy can be used to image objects:

1. **Electromagnetic radiation** including γ rays, X-ray, ultraviolet radiation, visible light, infrared radiation, microwaves, and radio waves. Radiation propagates in vacuum at the speed of light, and through matter at lower speeds which also depends on wavelength. In this book, we concentrate on the visible spectrum unless said otherwise.

2. **Radiation of particles**, e.g., electrons or neutrons.

3. **Acoustic waves** in gases, liquids and solids. Only longitudinal waves are spread in gases and liquids, and transverse waves may be evident in solids. The speed at which such waves propagate is directly related to the elastic properties of the medium which they traverse.

Radiation integrates with matter on the surface of objects or in its volume. The energy (radiation) is sent out from objects either because of thermal motion of molecules (hot radiant body) or because of external stimulation (e.g, reflected radiance, luminescence). Radiation is accompanied by information which can be used to identify observed objects and to assist in measurement of some of their properties. Examples are:

1. **Frequency** of radiation expressed by wavelength.

2. **Amplitude**, i.e., intensity of the radiation.

3. **Polarization mode** for transverse waves.

4. **Phase** which is accessible only if coherent imaging techniques are used, as in interferometry or holography.

We will consider an explanation of image formation in the case of reflection of radiation from the surface of nontransparent objects in the visible spectrum.

3.4.2 Image capture and geometric optics

We begin with a simple model of image capture in which geometric optics play a key role. We consider a photographic or video camera—a device for capturing intensity images. The camera consists of a lens, a photosensitive image sensor converting photons to electrical signals, and electronics that will provide image data for further processing.

The lens concentrates incoming light to the image sensor. The physical quantity measured is irradiance, often informally called brightness or intensity. We wish the lens to mimic ideal perspective projection (a pin-hole model, see Figure 2.1), and will use geometric optics which match the pin-hole model. The key concept of the pin-hole model is that of a **ray** which is a straight line segment mapping a point on a scene to a point on the image plane (or a photosensitive sensor of a camera). More complicated phenomena, which require more sophisticated mathematical models of wave or quantum optics, are not considered. Wave optics permit the explanation of phenomena such as light diffraction, interference, and polarization—many texts will explain these topics in depth to the interested reader (e.g., [Hecht, 1998] is recommended if the reader). Here, we will follow conventions used in optical literature; light propagates from left to right.

The **pin-hole model** (camera obscura) is an unrealistic idealization because a very small hole prevents energy passing through it. Wave properties of light cause another deviation from the pin-hole model—**diffraction**. The direction of light propagation is bent if the obstacles are of a size comparable to the wavelength. Strictly speaking, only planar mirrors comply with the geometric optics model.

The ideal geometric pin-hole model is more or less valid for the ideal **thin lens**, see Figure 3.29. A ray passing through the center of the lens (called the **principal point**) does not change its direction. If the lens is focused, then incoming rays which are not coincident with the optical axis refract. Incoming rays parallel with the optical axis intersect the optical axis in a single point called the **focal point**. This process is described by the thin lens equation which can be derived using similar triangles in Figure 3.29. The lens equation in Newtonian form says

$$\frac{1}{z' + f} = \frac{1}{f} - \frac{1}{f + z} \quad \text{or in a simpler form} \quad z\,z' = f^2 \,, \tag{3.72}$$

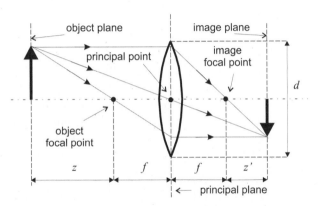

Figure 3.29: The thin lens.
© *Cengage Learning 2015.*

where f is the **focal length**, the distance between the principal point and the (object, image) focal point, z is the distance between the object plane and the object focal point, and z' is the distance between the object plane and the image focal point. Let X be the size of the object (the length of the arrow in the object plane in Figure 3.29) and x be the size of this object in the image plane. The **magnification** m of the optical system is

$$m = \frac{x}{X} = \frac{f}{z} = \frac{z'}{f} .$$

The disadvantage of the thin lens is that the only rays it maps sharply are those starting from points in a plane perpendicular to the optical axis within a distance z of the principal point.

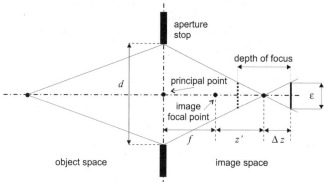

Figure 3.30: Depth of focus in an optical system. © *Cengage Learning 2015.*

Consider what happens if the image plane is shifted off the focal point [Jähne, 1997]; imagine a bundle of rays intersecting in the image focal point. The point will be displayed as a small circle (the circle of permitted defocus) with diameter ε, see Figure 3.30. Δz is the distance between the shifted image plane and the image focal point, d is the diameter of the aperture stop, f if the focal length of the lens, and $f+z'$ is the distance between the principal point and the image focal point. The diameter ε of the circle can be calculated using similar triangles

$$\frac{d}{f+z'} = \frac{\varepsilon}{\Delta z} \quad \Longrightarrow \quad \varepsilon = \frac{d\,\Delta z}{f+z'} .$$

$n_f = f/d$ is called the *f-number* of the lens-see Section 3.4.4.

The previous equation can be rewritten as

$$\varepsilon = \frac{\Delta z\, f}{n_f(f+z')} = \frac{\Delta z}{n_f(1+z/f)} .$$

The concepts **depth of focus** and **depth of field** are based on the understanding that it is of advantage if the image is a little off-focus, as then the range of depth in the scene which will be focused will be effectively bigger. It does not make sense to require ε to be zero—it is reasonable to be the size of a pixel. The smaller the pixels are, the smaller the effect this improvement has. The depth of focus is the interval of permitted shifts of the image plane $[-\Delta z, \Delta z]$ for which the diameter of the circle ε is smaller than a predefined value corresponding to pixel size. Δz is calculated from the previous equation

$$\Delta z = n_f \left(1+\frac{z'}{f}\right) \varepsilon = n_f \left(1+m\right) \varepsilon , \tag{3.73}$$

where m is the magnification of the lens. Equation (3.73) demonstrates an important role played by the f-number. The smaller the diameter of the aperture stop, the bigger the depth of focus is.

A more important concept from the user's point of view is the **depth of field** on the object side of the lens. This governs the permitted range of positions of observed objects in the scene which will be effectively in focus; i.e., with allowed defocus of maximal ε. Depth of field is illustrated in Figure 3.31.

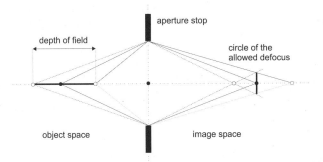

Figure 3.31: Depth of field on the object side of the lens. © *Cengage Learning 2015.*

Real lenses (objectives) are composed of several individual lenses and their model in geometric optics is called a **thick lens**. It has two parallel principal axes and two principal points, one on each side. The ray coming to the lens through the object principal point, which passes the system of lenses, and leaves it from the image principal point under the same angle. The distance between the object and the image principal points gives the effective length of the thick lens. Otherwise, mathematical expressions for the ray passing the lens remain almost the same.

In optical gauging, it is often difficult to guarantee that the measured object lies in the object plane. If it comes closer to the lens it looks bigger and if it recedes then it appears smaller. There is a practically useful optical trick which makes gauging easier—a **telecentric lens**. A small aperture stop is positioned into the image focal point; in a normal lens the aperture stop is in the principal point (Figure 3.32a). In a telecentric lens the image is formed only by rays which are approximately collinear to the optical axis; this is illustrated in Figure 3.32b. Only part of the rays and irradiation is passed through the telecentric lens to its image side, and this energy reduction is the reason why observed scenes have to be illuminated more strongly, which in industrial gauging setting is usually not difficult to provide. The disadvantage of telecentric lenses is that their diameter has to be greater than the measured distances. Telecentric lenses of larger diameters ($> 50\,\text{mm}$, say) are expensive because they typically use the Fresnel lens principle, used in lighthouses since the 1820s.

If the aperture stop is positioned between the image focal point and the image plane then a **hypercentric lens** is obtained, Figure 3.32c.

The properties of normal, telecentric, and hypercentric lenses are illustrated by considering a tube viewed along its axis (Figure 3.33). A normal lens sees the cross section of the tube and its inner surface due to divergent rays. The telecentric lens sees only the cross section because only rays approximately parallel to the optical axis are selected. The hypercentric lens sees the cross section and the outer surface of the tube, and not the inner surface.

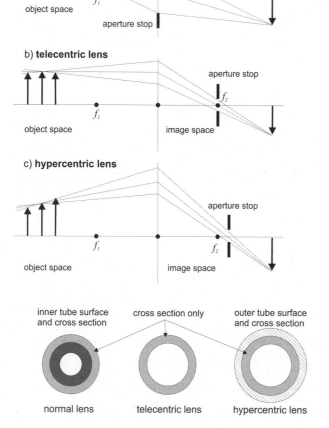

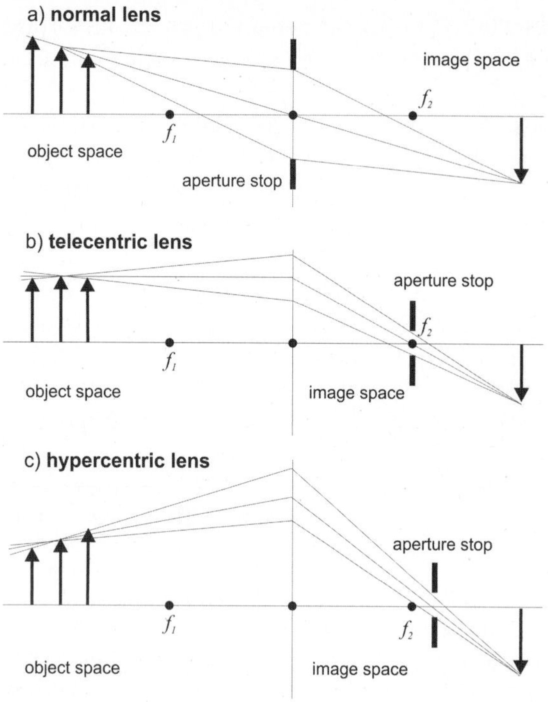

Figure 3.32: Normal, telecentric and hypercentric lens. The focal point on the object side of the lens is denoted f_1 and the focal point on the image side is denoted f_2. © *Cengage Learning 2015.*

Figure 3.33: Axial view of a tube by a normal, a telecentric and a hypercentric lens. The cross section is shown in light gray, the inner surface in dark gray and the outer surface is hatched. © *Cengage Learning 2015.*

3.4.3   Lens aberrations and radial distortion

Lenses and other optical systems such as mirrors or prisms have defects which lead to blur, color changes, geometric distortion from the ideal ray, etc. These errors are usually called **aberrations** in optics. Rays have to pass through some medium, such as air, which also causes blur. Sometimes, blur can be roughly modeled as a drop of high frequencies in the Fourier spectrum, which can be approximately compensated by a high-pass frequency filter.

In an ideal optical system, every point on the object will focus to a single point of zero size on the image. In reality, a point on the object side is not a point in the image plane. The result is a distribution of intensities in the volume which is not symmetrical in shape. Blurring occurs because a lens is not a perfect image producer. The output is close to the ideal mathematical model given by equation (3.72) for lenses having spherical surfaces and for rays passing through its principal point and rays making only small angles with the optical axis. Six main groups of aberrations can be distinguished: (1) spherical aberration, (2) coma, (3) astigmatism, (4) curvature of field, (5) geometric distortion (especially radial distortion), and (6) color aberration occurring for light mixed from many wavelengths. The first five aberrations also occur for light of a single wavelength.

Spherical aberration prevents rays from meeting at the same image point. Rays passing through the lens close to its center are focused farther away than rays passing its rim.

Coma is produced when rays from an off-axis object point are imaged by different zones of the lens. The name arises because a point on the object side of the lens is blurred into a comet shape. In spherical aberration, images of an on-axis object point that fall on a plane at right angles to the optical axis are circular in shape, of varying size, and superimposed about a common center. In coma, images of an off-axis object point are circular in shape, of varying size, but displaced with respect to each other. Coma is usually reduced by a diaphragm which eliminates the outer cones of rays.

Astigmatism occurs when an optical system has different foci for rays that propagate in two perpendicular planes. If such a system is used to form an image of a cross, the vertical and horizontal lines will be in sharp focus at two different distances.

Curvature of field (which manifests in **geometric distortion**, both radial and tangential) refers to the location of image points with respect to one another. Geometric distortion usually remains after the first three aberrations have been corrected by lens designers. Curvature of field describes the phenomenon whereby the image of a plane object perpendicular to the optical axis on the object side of the lens projects to a paraboloidal surface called a *Petzval* surface[3]. Geometric distortion refers to deformation of an image. If the object on the object side is a flat grid consisting of squares then it is projected either as a barrel or pincushion, see Figure 3.34. In barrel distortion, magnification decreases with distance from the axis. In pincushion distortion, magnification increases with distance from the axis.

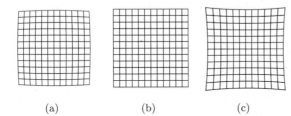

(a)   (b)   (c)

Figure 3.34: Radial distortion illustrated on a 12 × 12 square grid. (a) Barrel distortion. (b) Undistorted. (c) Pincushion distortion. © *Cengage Learning 2015.*

Chromatic aberration expresses the failure of a lens to focus all colors in the same plane. Because the refractive index is least at the red end of the spectrum, the focal length of a lens in air will be greater for red than blue.

Computer vision users of optical systems do not usually have any influence on aberrations beyond the right lens. The exception is radial distortion, which often has to be estimated and corrected in computer vision applications, and which we will explain in more detail. A typical lens performs distortion of several pixels which a human observer does not notice while looking at a natural scene. However, when an image is used for measurements, compensation for the distortion is necessary.

---

[3]Petzval surface—after Slovak mathematician Jozef Petzval, 1807-1891.

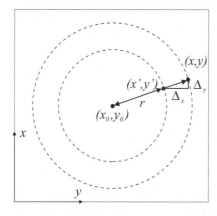

Figure 3.35: Radial distortion model; (x', y') are pixel coordinates measured in the image (uncorrected); (x, y) are pixel coordinates after correction; (x_0, y_0) are coordinates of the principal point, and (Δ_x, Δ_y) are components of the necessary correction; r is the distance between pixel (x_0, y_0) and pixel (x', y'). © *Cengage Learning 2015*.

(a)   (b)   (c)

Figure 3.36: Radial distortion illustrated on an image of a book shelf. (a) Barrel distortion. (b) Undistorted. (c) Pincushion distortion. © *Cengage Learning 2015*.

The practical model of lens geometric aberration includes two distortion components. The first is **radial distortion** which is caused because the lens bends a ray more or less than in the ideal case. The second is the **shift of the principal point** with respect to the image midpoint. We will discuss the second component in Section 11.3.1 where the intrinsic parameters of a single 3D camera will be explained.

It can be seen that the pincushion and barrel distortions in Figure 3.34 are centrally (radially) symmetric. A simple mathematical model is used which approximates the necessary correction by a low order polynomial depending on the distance r of the observed point (x', y') from the principal point (x_0, y_0) of the image. The variables involved are introduced in Figure 3.35. The coordinates of a pixel after the correction are $x = x' + \Delta_x$ and $y = y' + \Delta_y$.

Radial distortion is approximated as a rotationally symmetric function with respect to the principal point and dependent on the distance r of the measured pixel (x', y') from the principal point (x_0, y_0)

$$r = \sqrt{(x - x_0)^2 + (y - y_0)^2} \,. \tag{3.74}$$

Low order polynomials (usually with order at most six) with even order dependent only on r are used to assure rotational symmetry. The approximation is

$$\begin{aligned}
\Delta_x &= (x' - x_0)\left(\kappa_1 r^2 + \kappa_2 r^4 + \kappa_3 r^6\right), \\
\Delta_y &= (y' - y_0)\left(\kappa_1 r^2 + \kappa_2 r^4 + \kappa_3 r^6\right).
\end{aligned} \tag{3.75}$$

The distortion is represented by the coefficients κ_1, κ_2, κ_3 which are obtained experimentally for a particular lens by observing a known calibration image, e.g., covered with some regular pattern of blobs or lines. Often it is sufficient to use only one nonzero coefficient κ_1 in the approximation.

The effect of the radial distortion model applied to a real image is illustrated in Figure 3.36. More complicated lens models cover tangential distortions that model such effects as lens de-centering. Full and alternative details may be found in [Tsai, 1987; Jain et al., 1995; Prescott and McLean, 1997].

3.4.4 Image capture from a radiometric point of view

A TV camera and most other artificial vision sensors measure the amount of received light energy in individual pixels as the result of interaction among various materials and light source(s); the value measured is informally called a gray-level (or brightness). **Radiometry** is a branch of physics that deals with the measurement of the flow and transfer of radiant energy, and is the appropriate tool to consider the mechanism of image creation. The gray-level corresponding to a point on a 3D surface depends informally on the shape of the object, its reflectance properties, the position of the viewer, and properties and position of the illuminants.

The radiometric approach to understanding gray-levels is very often avoided in practical applications because of its complexity and numerical instability. The gray-level measured typically does not provide a precise quantitative measurement (one reason is that commonly used cameras are much more precise geometrically than radiometrically; another, more serious, reason is that the relation between the gray-level and shape is too complex). One way to circumvent this is to use task-specific illumination that allows the location of objects of interest on a qualitative level, and their separation from the background. If this attempt is successful then an object/background separation task is solved which is usually much simpler than a complete inversion of the image formation task from a radiometric point of view. Of course, some information is lost which could be provided by radiometric analysis of intensity changes.

Photometry is a discipline closely related to radiometry that studies the sensation of radiant light energy in the human eye; both disciplines describe similar phenomena using similar quantities.

Herein, we shall describe physical units using square brackets; when there is a danger of confusion we shall denote photometric quantities using the subscript ph, and leave radiometric ones with no subscript.

The basic radiometric quantity is **radiant flux** $\Phi[\mathrm{W}]$, and its photometric counterpart is **luminous flux** Φ_{ph} [lm (= lumen)]. For light of wavelength $\lambda = 555\,\mu\mathrm{m}$ and daylight vision, we can convert between these quantities with the relation $1\,\mathrm{W} = 680\,\mathrm{lm}$. Different people have different abilities to perceive light, and photometric quantities depend on the spectral characteristic of the radiation source and on the sensitivity of the photoreceptive cells of a human retina. For this reason, the international standardization body Commission International de l'Éclairage (CIE) defined a 'standard observer' corresponding to average abilities. Let $K(\lambda)$ be the **luminous efficacy** [$\mathrm{lm\,W^{-1}}$], $S(\lambda)$ [W] the spectral power of the light source, and λ [m], the wavelength. Then luminous flux

Φ_{ph} is proportional to the intensity of perception and is given by

$$\Phi_{ph} = \int_\lambda K(\lambda)\, S(\lambda)\, d\lambda\,. \tag{3.76}$$

Since photometric quantities are also observer dependent, we shall consider radiometric ones.

From a viewer's point of view, the surface of an object can reflect energy into a half-sphere, differently into different directions. The **spatial angle** is given by the area on the surface of the unit sphere that is bounded by a cone with an apex in the center of the sphere, so an entire half-sphere corresponds to a spatial angle of 2π [sr (= steradians)]. A small area A at distance R from the origin (i.e., $R^2 \gg A$) and with angle Θ between the normal vector to the area and the radius vector between the origin and the area corresponds to the spatial angle Ω [sr] (see Figure 3.37)

$$\Omega = \frac{A \cos \Theta}{R^2}\,. \tag{3.77}$$

Irradiance E [$\mathrm{W\,m^{-2}}$] describes the power of the light energy that falls onto a unit area of the object surface, $E = \delta\Phi/\delta A$, where δA is an infinitesimal element of the surface area; the corresponding photometric quantity is **illumination** [$\mathrm{lm\,m^{-2}}$]. **Radiance** L [$\mathrm{W\,m^{-2}\,sr^{-1}}$] is the power of light that is emitted from a unit surface area into some spatial angle, and the corresponding photometric quantity is called **brightness** L_{ph} [$\mathrm{lm\,m^{-2}\,sr^{-1}}$]. Brightness is used informally in image analysis to describe the quantity that the camera measures.

Irradiance is given by the amount of energy that an image-capturing device gets per unit of an efficient sensitive area of the camera [Horn, 1986]—then gray-levels of image pixels are quantized estimates of image irradiance. The efficient area copes with foreshortening that is caused by the mutual rotation between the elementary patch on the emitting surface and the elementary surface patch of the sensor. We shall consider the relationship between the irradiance E measured in the image and the radiance L produced by a small patch on the object surface. Only part of this radiance is captured by the lens of the camera.

The geometry of the setup is given in Figure 3.38. The optical axis is aligned with the horizontal axis Z, and a lens with focal length f is placed at the co-ordinate origin

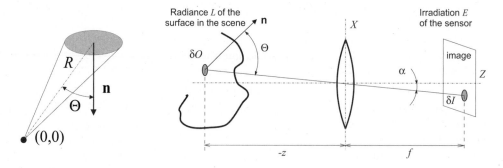

Figure 3.37: Spatial angle for an elementary surface area. © *Cengage Learning 2015.*

Figure 3.38: The relation between irradiance E and radiance L. © *Cengage Learning 2015.*

(the optical center). The elementary object surface patch δO is at distance z. We are interested in how much light energy reaches an elementary patch of the sensor surface δI. The off-axis angle α spans between the axis Z and the line connecting δO with δI; as we are considering a perspective projection, this line must pass through the origin. The elementary object surface patch δO is tilted by the angle Θ measured between the object surface normal $\mathbf{n}$ at the patch and a line between δO and δI.

Light rays passing through the lens origin are not refracted; thus the spatial angle attached to the elementary surface patch in the scene is equal to the spatial angle corresponding to the elementary patch in the image. The foreshortened elementary image patch as seen from the optical center is $\delta I \cos \alpha$, and its distance from the optical center is $f/\cos \alpha$. The corresponding spatial angle is

$$\frac{\delta I \cos \alpha}{(f/\cos \alpha)^2} .$$

Analogously, the spatial angle corresponding to the elementary patch δO on the object surface is

$$\frac{\delta O \cos \Theta}{(z/\cos \alpha)^2} .$$

As the spatial angles are equal,

$$\frac{\delta O}{\delta I} = \frac{\cos \alpha}{\cos \Theta} \frac{z^2}{f^2} . \tag{3.78}$$

Consider how much light energy passes through the lens if its aperture has diameter d; the spatial angle Ω_L that sees the lens from the elementary patch on the object is

$$\Omega_L = \frac{\pi}{4} \frac{d^2 \cos \alpha}{(z/\cos \alpha)^2} = \frac{\pi}{4} \left(\frac{d}{z}\right)^2 \cos^3 \alpha . \tag{3.79}$$

Let L be the radiance of the object surface patch that is oriented towards the lens. Then the elementary contribution to the radiant flux Φ falling at the lens is

$$\delta \Phi = L \, \delta O \, \Omega_L \cos \Theta = \pi L \, \delta O \left(\frac{d}{z}\right)^2 \frac{\cos^3 \alpha \cos \Theta}{4} . \tag{3.80}$$

The lens concentrates the light energy into the image. If energy losses in the lens are neglected and no other light falls on the image element, we can express the irradiation E of the elementary image patch as

$$E = \frac{\delta \Phi}{\delta I} = L \frac{\delta O}{\delta I} \frac{\pi}{4} \left(\frac{d}{z}\right)^2 \cos^3 \alpha \cos \Theta . \tag{3.81}$$

If we substitute for $\delta O / \delta I$ from equation (3.78), we obtain an important equation that explains how scene radiance influences irradiance in the image:

$$E = L \frac{\pi}{4} \left(\frac{d}{f}\right)^2 \cos^4 \alpha . \tag{3.82}$$

The term $\cos^4 \alpha$ describes a systematic lens optical defect called **vignetting**[4], which implies that optical rays with larger span-off angle α are attenuated more; this means

---

[4]One of the meanings of **vignette** is a photograph or drawing with edges that are shaded off.

that pixels closer to image borders are darker. This effect is more severe with wide-angle lenses than with tele-lenses. Since vignetting is a systematic error, it can be compensated for with a radiometrically calibrated lens. The term d/f is called the f-number of the lens and describes by how much the lens differs from a pinhole model.

3.4.5   Surface reflectance

In many applications, pixel gray-level is constructed as an estimate of image irradiance as a result of light reflection from scene objects. Consequently, it is necessary to understand different mechanisms involved in reflection. We will give a brief overview sufficient to underpin the idea behind shape from shading, Section 11.7.1.

The radiance of an opaque object that does not emit its own energy depends on irradiance caused by other energy sources. The illumination that the viewer perceives depends on the strength, position, orientation, type (point or diffuse) of the light sources, and ability of the object surface to reflect energy and the local surface orientation (given by its normal vector).

An important concept is **gradient space** which describes surface orientations. Let $z(x,y)$ be the surface height; at nearly every point a surface has a unique normal **n**. The components of the surface gradient

$$p = \frac{\partial z}{\partial x} \quad \text{and} \quad q = \frac{\partial z}{\partial y} \tag{3.83}$$

can be used to specify the surface orientation. We shall express the unit surface normal using surface gradient components; if we move a small distance δx in the x direction, the change of height is $\delta z = p\,\delta x$. Thus the vector $[1,0,p]^\top$ is the tangent to the surface, and analogously $[0,1,q]^\top$ is too. The surface normal is perpendicular to all its tangents, and may be computed using the vector product as

$$\begin{bmatrix} 1 \\ 0 \\ p \end{bmatrix} \times \begin{bmatrix} 0 \\ 1 \\ q \end{bmatrix} = \begin{bmatrix} -p \\ -q \\ 1 \end{bmatrix}. \tag{3.84}$$

The unit surface normal **n** can be written as

$$\mathbf{n} = \frac{1}{\sqrt{1 + p^2 + q^2}} \begin{bmatrix} -p \\ -q \\ 1 \end{bmatrix}. \tag{3.85}$$

Here we suppose that the z component of the surface normal is positive.

Consider now spherical co-ordinates used to express the geometry of an infinitesimal surface patch—see Figure 3.39. The **polar angle** (also called zenith angle) is Θ and the **azimuth** is φ.

We wish to describe the ability of different materials to reflect light. The direction towards the incident light is denoted by subscript i (i.e., Θ_i and φ_i), while subscript v identifies the direction toward the viewer (Θ_v and φ_v)—see Figure 3.40. The irradiance of the elementary surface patch from the light source is $dE(\Theta_i, \varphi_i)$, and the elementary contribution of the radiance in the direction towards the viewer is $dL(\Theta_v, \varphi_v)$. In general, the ability of the body to reflect light is described using a **bi-directional reflectance**

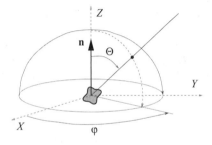

Figure 3.39: Spherical angles used to describe orientation of a surface patch. © *Cengage Learning 2015.*

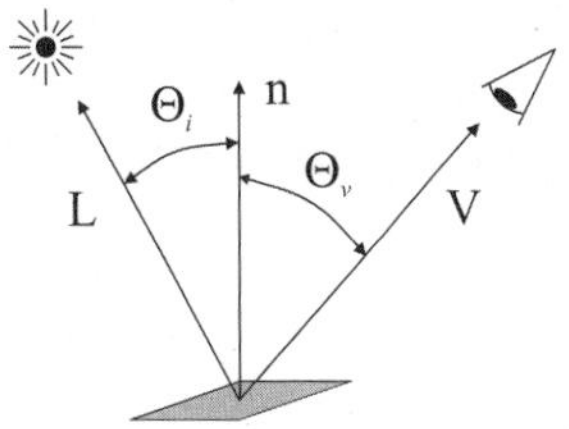

Figure 3.40: Directions towards the viewer and the light source. © *Cengage Learning 2015.*

distribution function f_r [sr^{-1}], abbreviated BRDF [Nicodemus et al., 1977]

$$f_r(\Theta_i, \varphi_i; \Theta_v, \varphi_v) = \frac{\mathrm{d}L(\Theta_v, \varphi_v)}{\mathrm{d}E(\Theta_i, \varphi_i)} \ . \tag{3.86}$$

The BRDF f_r describes the brightness of an elementary surface patch for a specific material, light source, and viewer direction. The domain of the BRDF is the Cartesian product of all incident and reflected directions which are traditionally represented in spherical coordinates.

Modeling of the BRDF is also important for realistic rendering in computer graphics [Foley et al., 1990]. The BRDF in its full complexity (equation (3.86)) is used for modeling reflection properties of materials with oriented microstructure (e.g., tiger's eye—a semi-precious golden-brown stone, a peacock's feather, a rough cut of aluminum).

The extension of BRDF to color is straightforward. All quantities are expressed 'per unit wavelength' and the adjective 'spectral' is added. Radiance becomes *spectral radiance* and is expressed in 'watts per square meter, per steradian, per unit wavelength'. Irradiance becomes *spectral irradiance* expressed in 'watts per square meter, per unit wavelength'. Dependence on wavelength λ is introduced into *spectral BRDF*

$$BRDF = f(\Theta_i, \Phi_i, \Theta_e, \Phi_e, \lambda) = \frac{\mathrm{d}L(\Theta_i, \Phi_i, \lambda)}{\mathrm{d}E(\Theta_e, \Phi_e, \lambda)} \ . \tag{3.87}$$

The observed color depends on the power spectrum of the illuminant and reflectance and/or transparency properties of objects in the scene. There is often more interest in the relative spectral composition than in the absolute spectral radiation or spectral irradiation. Instead of spectral BRDF, the reflectance or transparency properties are modeled by wavelength-by-wavelength multiplication of the corresponding relative energies (intensities) in each surface point manifested in each pixel of the image.

Fortunately, for most practically applicable surfaces, the BRDF remains constant if the elementary surface patch rotates along the normal vector to the surface. In this case it is simplified and depends on $\varphi_i - \varphi_v$, i.e., $f_r(\Theta_i, \Theta_v, (\varphi_i - \varphi_v))$. This simplification holds for both ideal diffuse (Lambertian) surfaces and for ideal mirrors.

Let $E_i(\lambda)$ denote the irradiance caused by the illumination of the surface element, and $E_r(\lambda)$ the energy flux per unit area scattered by the surface element back to the whole half-space. The ratio

$$\rho(\lambda) = \frac{E_r(\lambda)}{E_i(\lambda)} \tag{3.88}$$

is called the *reflectance coefficient* or *albedo*: this is the proportion of incident energy reflected back to the half-space. For simplicity, assume that we may neglect color properties of the surface, and that albedo does not depend on wavelength λ. This proportion is then an integral of the surface radiance L over the solid angle Ω representing the half-space

$$E_r = \int_\Omega L(\Omega)\,d\Omega\,. \tag{3.89}$$

Now define a *reflectance function* $R(\Omega)$ that models the influence of the local surface geometry onto the spatial spread of the reflected energy. Angle $d\Omega$ is an infinitesimal solid angle around the viewing direction

$$\int_\Omega R(\Omega)\,d\Omega = 1\,. \tag{3.90}$$

In general, surface reflectance properties depend on three angles between the direction to the light source $\mathbf{L}$, the direction towards the viewer $\mathbf{V}$, and the local surface orientation given by the surface normal $\mathbf{n}$ (recall Figure 3.40). The cosines of these angles can be expressed as scalar products of vectors; thus the reflectance function is a scalar function of the following three dot products

$$R = R(\mathbf{n}\cdot\mathbf{L}, \mathbf{n}\cdot\mathbf{V}, \mathbf{V}\cdot\mathbf{L})\,. \tag{3.91}$$

A **Lambertian surface** (also ideally opaque, with ideal diffusion) reflects light energy in all directions, and thus the radiance is constant in all directions. The BRDF f_{Lambert} is constant:

$$f_{\text{Lambert}}(\Theta_i, \Theta_v, \varphi_i - \varphi_v) = \frac{\rho(\lambda)}{\pi}\,. \tag{3.92}$$

If albedo $\rho(\lambda)$ is assumed constant and unitary then the Lambertian surface reflectance can be expressed as

$$R(\mathbf{n}, \mathbf{L}, \mathbf{V}) = \frac{1}{\pi}\mathbf{n}\,\mathbf{L} = \frac{1}{\pi}\cos\Theta_i\,. \tag{3.93}$$

Because of its simplicity, the Lambertian reflectance function has been widely accepted as a reasonable reflectance model for shape from shading (Section 11.7.1). Notice that the reflectance function for a Lambertian surface is independent of viewing direction $\mathbf{V}$.

The dependence of the surface radiance on local surface orientation can be expressed in gradient space, and the *reflectance map* $R(p,q)$ is used for this purpose. The reflectance map $R(p,q)$ can be visualized in the gradient space as nested iso-contours corresponding to the same observed irradiance.

Values of the reflectance map may be:

1. Measured experimentally on a device called a goniometer stage that is able to set angles Θ and φ mechanically. A sample of the surface is attached to the goniometer and its reflectance measured for different orientations of viewer and light sources.

2. Set experimentally if a calibration object is used. Typically a half-sphere is used for this purpose.

3. Derived from a mathematical model describing surface reflecting properties.

The best-known surface reflectance models are the Lambertian model for ideal opaque surfaces, the *Phong* model which models reflection from dielectric materials, the *Torrance-Sparrow* model which describes surfaces as a collection of planar mirror-like micro-facets with normally distributed normals, and the wave theory-based *Beckmann-Spizzichino* model. A survey of surface reflection models from the point of view of computer vision can be found in [Ikeuchi, 1994].

The irradiance $E(x, y)$ of an infinitely small light sensor located at position x, y in the image plane is equal to the surface radiance at a corresponding surface patch given by its surface parameters u, v if the light is not attenuated in the optical medium between the surface and the sensor. This important relation between surface orientation and perceived image intensity is called the **image irradiance equation**

$$E(x, y) = \rho(u, v)\, R\big(\mathbf{N}(u, v)\mathbf{L}, \mathbf{N}(u, v)\mathbf{V}, \mathbf{V}\mathbf{L}\big) \,. \tag{3.94}$$

In an attempt to reduce complexity, several simplifying assumptions [Horn, 1990] are usually made to ease the shape from shading task. It is assumed that:

- The object has uniform reflecting properties, i.e. $\rho(u, v)$ is constant.

- Light sources are distant; then both irradiation in different places in the scene and direction towards the light sources are approximately the same.

- The viewer is very distant. Then the radiance emitted by scene surfaces does not depend on position but only on orientation. The perspective projection is simplified to an orthographic one.

We present the simplified version of the image irradiance equation for the Lambertian surface, constant albedo, single distant illuminant, distant viewer in the same direction as illuminant, and the reflectance function R expressed in gradient space (p, q)

$$E(x, y) = \beta R\big(p(x, y), q(x, y)\big) \,. \tag{3.95}$$

$R(p, q)$ gives the radiance of the corresponding point in the scene; the proportionality constant β comes from equation (3.82) and depends on the f-number of the lens. The vignetting degradation of the lens is negligible as the viewer is aligned to the illuminant. The measured irradiance E can be normalized and the factor β omitted; this permits us to write the **image irradiance equation** in the simplest form as

$$E(x, y) = R\big(p(x, y), q(x, y)\big) = R\left(\frac{\partial z}{\partial x}, \frac{\partial z}{\partial y}\right) \,. \tag{3.96}$$

The image irradiance equation in its simplest form is a first-order differential equation. It is typically nonlinear as the reflectance function R in most cases depends non-linearly on the surface gradient. This is the basic equation that is used to recover surface orientation from intensity images.

3.5 Summary

- The Dirac impulse is an idealized infinitely narrow impulse of a finite area. In image processing, it helps to express image digitization in an elegant way.

- Convolution is a linear operation often used in image processing. Convolution expresses the relation between two overlapped images.

- **Linear integral transforms**

  - Linear integral transforms provide a rich representations of signals in a frequency domain, in which some application tasks are easier. The inverse transforms permit the conversion of data back to signals or images.

  - Commonly used transforms in image analysis are Fourier, cosine, wavelet, Radon and PCA.

  - The Fourier transform expands a periodic 1D or 2D function as a possibly infinite linear combination of sines and cosines. The basis of the expansion are waves with a basic frequency ω_0, and waves with growing frequencies ω_0, $2\omega_0$, $2\omega_0$, $3\omega_0$, etc. The complex frequency spectrum $F(\omega)$ gives both magnitude and phase of the elementary waves.

  - The Shannon sampling theorem states that the necessary distance between sampling points is at most half the smallest detail to be seen in the image.

  - If the Shannon sampling theorem is violated then aliasing occurs.

  - The wavelet transform analyzes a signal by multiplying it by a window function and performing an orthogonal expansion with more complex basis functions, allowing localization of events not only in frequency but also in time. The expansion is performed at multiple scales.

  - Principal Component Analysis (PCA) is the optimal linear transformation which divides an observed space into orthogonal subspaces with the largest variance. The new basis vectors are calculated for the particular data set. PCA is used for dimensionality reduction of data.

- **Images as a stochastic processes**

  - Images are statistical in nature due to random changes and noise. It is sometimes of advantage to treat image functions as realizations of a stochastic process.

  - Such analysis is performed using statistical descriptors as the mean, dispersion, covariance function or correlation function.

- **Image formation physics**

  - Image formation is well understood in radiometry. Observed irradiation from a surface patch depends on light sources, surface reflectance, and mutual relation between directions towards observer, towards the illuminator(s), the surface patch normal and its reflectance. Computer vision is interested in the inverse task which is ill-posed in many cases.

  - Image formation physics is not directly explored in many applications because it is too complicated to get all the parameters which describe the particular image formation process. Instead, objects are segmented based on semantic knowledge about a specific application.

  - Geometric optics models lens systems used commonly in computer vision.

3.6   Exercises

Short-answer questions

S3.1   Explain how the Fourier transform can be used to remove periodic image noise.

S3.2   Define *photometry*.

S3.3   Determine the Fourier transform of the Dirac $\delta(x, y)$ function.

S3.4   Give a definition of: frequency spectrum, phase spectrum, power spectrum.

S3.5   What do you understand by *aliasing*?

S3.6   Give the formulae for the Fourier transform and its inverse.

S3.7   Why are wavelets better suited to analyze image data in multiple scales than the Fourier transform?

S3.8   State the convolution theorem.

Problems

P3.1   Suppose a convolution of two finite digital functions is to be performed; determine how many elemental operations (additions and multiplications) are required for given sized domains. How many operations are required if the convolution theorem is exploited (excluding the cost of the Fourier transform).

P3.2   Implement the 1D Fourier transform for yourself and study its output for some sample digital functions.

P3.3   Why might high frequencies of an image function be of interest? Why would the Fourier transform be of use in their analysis?

P3.4   Many very efficient implementations of the Fourier transform can be freely found: seek and download one if you do not already have one to hand. Run it on a range of deliberately simple images and study its output. Given the transform of an image, can you guess some features of the original?

P3.5   Explain the aliasing effect in terms of Fourier frequency overlaps.

P3.6   Employing the two-dimensional Fourier transform, develop a program for high-pass, low-pass, and band-pass image filtering.

P3.7   Locate an implementation of the Radon transform and run it on some images with pronounced straight lines (such as Figure 3.26). Extract the directional maxima it suggests and compare them to the lines in the original.

P3.8   Locate a package that finds the eigen-system of a matrix (there are many freely available). For some matrices of your choice, look at the eigen-values and how they change when you perturb a matrix, or one column of it, or just one term of it.

P3.9   Better quality digital cameras permit manual setting of focus, aperture and exposure time: if you can, experiment with these to see the effects of depth of focus on image quality.

P3.10 Make yourself familiar with solved problems and **Matlab** implementations of selected algorithms provided in the corresponding chapter of the **Matlab Companion** to this text [Svoboda et al., 2008]. The **Matlab Companion** homepage http://visionbook.felk.cvut.cz offers images used in the problems, and well-commented **Matlab** code is provided for educational purposes.

P3.11 Use the **Matlab Companion** [Svoboda et al., 2008] to develop solutions to additional exercises and practical problems provided there. Implement your solutions using **Matlab** or other suitable programming languages.

3.7   References

Barrett H. H. and Myers K. J. *Foundation of Image Science*. Willey Series in Pure and Applied Optics. Wiley & Sons, Hoboken, New Jersey, USA, 2004.

Bracewell R. N. *Fourier Analysis and Imaging*. Springer-Verlag, 1st edition, 2004.

Castleman K. R. *Digital Image Processing*. Prentice-Hall, Englewood Cliffs, NJ, 1996.

Chui C. K. *An Introduction to Wavelets*. Academic Press, New York, 1992.

Chui C. K., Montefusco L., and Puccio L. *Wavelets: Theory, Algorithms, and Applications*. Academic Press, San Diego, CA, 1994.

Daubechies I. *Ten Lectures on Wavelets*. SIAM, Philadelphia, USA, 2nd edition, 1992.

Foley J. D., van Dam A., Feiner S. K., and Hughes J. F. *Computer Graphics—Principles and Practice*. Addison-Wesley, Reading, MA, 2nd edition, 1990.

Golub G. H. and Loan C. F. V. *Matrix Computations*. Johns Hopkins University Press, Baltimore, MD, 2nd edition, 1989.

Gonzalez R. C. and Woods R. E. *Digital Image Processing*. Addison-Wesley, Reading, MA, 1992.

Hecht E. *Optics*. Addison-Wesley, Reading, Massachusetts, 3rd edition, 1998.

Horn B. K. P. *Robot Vision*. MIT Press, Cambridge, MA, 1986.

Horn B. K. P. Height and gradient from shading. *International Journal of Computer Vision*, 5 (1):37–75, 1990.

Ikeuchi K. Surface reflection mechanism. In Young T. Y., editor, *Handbook of Pattern Recognition and Image Processing: Computer Vision*, pages 131–160, San Diego, 1994. Academic Press.

Jähne B. *Practical Handbook on Image Processing for Scientific Applications*. CRC Press, Boca Raton, Florida, 1997.

Jain R., Kasturi R., and Schunk B. G. *Machine Vision*. McGraw-Hill, New York, 1995.

Karu Z. Z. *Signals and Systems, Made Ridiculously Simple*. ZiZi Press, Cambridge, MA, USA, 3rd edition, 1999.

Leonardis A. and Bischof H. Robust recognition using eigenimages. *Computer Vision and Image Understanding*, 78(1):99–118, 2000.

Mallat S. G. A theory of multiresolution signal decomposition: The wavelet representation. *IEEE Transactions on Pattern Analysis and Machine Intelligence*, 11(7):674–693, 1989.

Meyer Y. *Wavelets: Algorithms and Applications*. Society for Industrial and Applied Mathematics, Philadelphia, 1993.

Nicodemus F. E., Richmond J. C., Hsia J. J., Ginsberg I. W., and Limperis T. Geometrical considerations and nomenclature for reflectance. US Department of Commerce, National Bureau of Standards, Washington DC, 1977.

Oppenheim A. V., Willsky A. S., and Nawab S. *Signal and Systems*. Prentice Hall, Upper Saddle River, NJ, USA, 2 edition, 1997.

Papoulis A. *Probability, Random Variables, and Stochastic Processes*. McGraw-Hill International Editions, 3rd edition, 1991.

Prescott B. and McLean G. F. Line-based correction of radial lens distortion. *Graphical Models and Image Processing*, 59(1):39–77, 1997.

Press W. H., , Teukolsky S. A., Vetterling W. T., and Flannery B. P. *Numerical Recipes in C*. Cambridge University Press, Cambridge, England, 2nd edition, 1992.

Rao K. R. and Yip P. *Discrete Cosine Transform, Algorithms, Advantages, Applications.* Academic Press, Boston, 1990.

Rogers D. F. *Procedural Elements of Computer Graphics.* McGraw-Hill, New York, 1985.

Svoboda T., Kybic J., and Hlavac V. *Image Processing, Analysis, and Machine Vision: A MATLAB Companion.* Thomson Engineering, 2008.

Tsai R. Y. A versatile camera calibration technique for high-accuracy 3D machine vision metrology using off-the-shelf cameras and lenses. *IEEE Journal of Robotics and Automation*, RA-3 (4):323—344, 1987.

Turk M. and Pentland A. Eigenfaces for recognition. *Journal of Cognitive Neuroscience*, 3(1): 71–86, 1991.

Chapter **4**

Data structures for image analysis

Data and an algorithm are the two essentials of any program. Data organization often considerably affects the simplicity of the selection and the implementation of an algorithm, and the choice of data structures is therefore a fundamental question when writing a program [Wirth, 1976]. Representations of image data, and the data which can be deduced from them, will be introduced here before explaining different image processing methods. Relations between different types of representations of image data will then be clearer.

First we shall deal with basic levels of representation of information in image analysis tasks; then with traditional data structures such as matrices, chains, and relational structures. Lastly we consider hierarchical data structures such as pyramids and quadtrees.

4.1 Levels of image data representation

The aim of computer visual perception is to find a relation between an input image and models of the real world. During the transition from the raw input image to the model, image information becomes denser and semantic knowledge about the interpretation of image data is used more. Several levels of visual information representation are defined on the way between the input image and the model; computer vision then comprises a design of the:

- **Intermediate representations** (data structures).

- **Algorithms** used for the creation of representations and introduction of relations between them.

The representations can be stratified in four levels [Ballard and Brown, 1982]—however, there are no strict borders between them and a more detailed classification of the representational levels is used in some applications. These four representational levels are ordered from signals at a low level of abstraction to the description that a human can perceive. The information flow between the levels may be bi-directional, and for some specific uses, some representations can be omitted.

The lowest representational level—**iconic images**—consists of images containing original data: integer matrices with data about pixel brightness. Images of this kind are also outputs of pre-processing operations used for highlighting some aspects of the image important for further treatment.

The second level is **segmented images**. Parts of the image are joined into groups that probably belong to the same objects. For instance, the output of the segmentation of a scene with polyhedra is either line segments coinciding with borders or two-dimensional regions corresponding to faces of bodies. It is useful to know something about the application domain while doing image segmentation; it is then easier to deal with noise and other problems associated with erroneous image data.

The third level is **geometric representations** holding knowledge about 2D and 3D shapes. Quantification of a shape is very difficult but also very important. Geometric representations are useful while doing general and complex simulations of the influence of illumination and motion in real objects. We also need them for the transition between natural raster images acquired by a camera) and data used in computer graphics (CAD—computer-aided design, DTP—desktop publishing).

The fourth representational level is **relational models**. They give us the ability to treat data more efficiently and at a higher level of abstraction. A priori knowledge about the case being solved is usually used in processing of this kind. Artificial intelligence (AI) techniques are often explored; the information gained from the image may be represented by semantic nets or frames [Nilsson, 1982].

An example will illustrate a priori knowledge. Imagine a satellite image of a piece of land, and the task of counting planes standing at an airport; the a priori knowledge is the position of the airport, which can be deduced, for instance, from a map. Relations to other objects in the image may help as well, e.g., to roads, lakes, or urban areas. Additional a priori knowledge is given by geometric models of planes for which we are searching. Segmentation will attempt to identify meaningful regions such as runways, planes and other vehicles, while third-level reasoning will try to make these identifications more definite. Fourth-level reasoning may, for example, determine whether the plane is arriving, departing or undergoing maintenance, etc.

4.2 Traditional image data structures

Traditional image data structures such as matrices, chains, graphs, lists of object properties, and relational databases are important not only for the direct representation of image information, but also as a basis for more complex hierarchical methods of image representation.

4.2.1 Matrices

A **matrix** is the most common data structure for low-level representation of an image. Elements of the matrix are integer numbers corresponding to brightness, or to another property of the corresponding pixel of the sampling grid. Image data of this kind are usually the direct output of the image-capturing device. Pixels of both rectangular and hexagonal sampling grids can be represented by a matrix. The correspondence between data and matrix elements is obvious for a rectangular grid; with a hexagonal grid every even row in the image is shifted half a pixel to the right.

Image information in the matrix is accessible through the co-ordinates of a pixel that correspond with row and column indices. The matrix is a full representation of the image, independent of the contents of image data—it implicitly contains **spatial relations** among semantically important parts of the image. The space is two-dimensional in the case of an image. One very natural spatial relation is the **neighborhood relation**.

Some special images that are represented by matrices are:

- A **binary image** (an image with two brightness levels only) is represented by a matrix containing only zeros and ones.

- Several matrices can contain information about one **multispectral image**. Each single matrix contains one image corresponding to one spectral band.

- Matrices of different resolution are used to obtain **hierarchical image data structures**. Such hierarchical representations can be very convenient for parallel computers with the 'processor array' architecture.

Most programming languages use a standard array data structure to represent a matrix. Historically, memory limitations were a significant obstacle to image applications, but this is no longer the case.

There is much image data in the matrix. Algorithms can be sped up if global information is derived from the original image matrix first—global information is more concise and occupies less memory. We have already mentioned the most popular example of global information—the histogram—in Section 2.3.2. Looking at the image from a probabilistic point of view, the normalized histogram is an estimate of the probability density of a phenomenon: that an image pixel has a certain brightness.

Another example of global information is the **co-occurrence matrix** [Pavlidis, 1982], which represents an estimate of the probability of two pixels appearing in a spatial relationship in which a pixel (i_1, j_1) has intensity z and a pixel (i_2, j_2) has intensity y. Suppose that the probability depends only on a certain spatial relation r between a pixel of brightness z and a pixel of brightness y; then information about the relation r is recorded in the square co-occurrence matrix C_r, whose dimensions correspond to the number of brightness levels of the image. To reduce the number of matrices C_r, introduce some simplifying assumptions; first consider only direct neighbors, and then treat relations as symmetrical (without orientation). The following algorithm calculates the co-occurrence matrix C_r from the image $f(i, j)$.

Algorithm 4.1: Co-occurrence matrix $C_r(z, y)$ for the relation r

1. Set $C_r(z, y) = 0$ for all $z, y \in [0, L]$, where L is the maximum brightness.

2. For all pixels (i_1, j_1) in the image, determine all (i_2, j_2) which have the relation r with the pixel (i_1, j_1), and perform

$$C_r\big[f(i_1, j_1), f(i_2, j_2)\big] = C_r\big[f(i_1, j_1), f(i_2, j_2)\big] + 1.$$

If the relation r is *to be a southern or eastern 4-neighbor of the pixel* (i_1, j_1), *or identity*[1], elements of the co-occurrence matrix have some interesting properties. Diagonal elements of the matrix $C_r(k, k)$ are equal to the area of the regions in the image with brightness k, and so correspond to the histogram. Off-diagonal elements $C_r(k, j)$ are equal to the length of the border dividing regions with brightnesses k and j, $k \neq j$. For instance, in an image with low contrast, the elements of the co-occurrence matrix that are far from the diagonal are equal to zero or are very small. For high-contrast images the opposite is true.

The main reason for considering co-occurrence matrices is their ability to describe texture: this approach is introduced in Chapter 15.

The **integral image** is another matrix representation that holds global image information [Viola and Jones, 2001]. It is constructed so that its values $ii(i, j)$ in the location (i, j) represent the sums of all the original image pixel-values left of and above (i, j):

$$ii(i, j) = \sum_{k \leq i, l \leq j} f(k, l) , \qquad (4.1)$$

where f is the original image. The integral image can be efficiently computed in a single image pass using recurrences:

Algorithm 4.2: Integral image construction

1. Let $s(i, j)$ denote a cumulative row sum, and set $s(i, -1) = 0$.

2. Let $ii(i, j)$ be an integral image, and set $ii(-1, j) = 0$.

3. Make a single row-by-row pass through the image. For each pixel (i, j) calculate the cumulative row sums $s(i, j)$ and the integral image value $ii(i, j)$ using

$$s(i, j) = s(i, j - 1) + f(i, j) , \qquad (4.2)$$
$$ii(i, j) = ii(i - 1, j) + s(i, j) . \qquad (4.3)$$

4. After completing a single pass through the image, the integral image ii is constructed.

The main use of integral image data structures is in rapid calculation of simple rectangle image features at multiple scales. This kind of features is used for rapid object identification (Section 10.7) and for object tracking (Section 16.5).

Figure 4.1 illustrates that any rectangular sum can be computed using four array references, and so a feature reflecting a difference between two rectangles requires eight references. Considering the rectangle features shown in Figure 4.2a,b, the two-rectangle features require only six array references since the rectangles are adjacent. Similarly, the three- and four-rectangle features of Figure 4.2c,d can be calculated using eight and nine references to the integral image values, respectively. Such features can be computed extremely efficiently and in constant time once the integral image is formed.

---

[1] For the purpose of co-occurrence matrix creation we need to consider the identity relation $(i_1, j_1) = (i_2, j_2)$, or individual pixels would not contribute to the histogram.

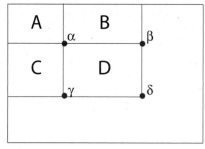

Figure 4.1: Calculation of rectangle features from an integral image. The sum of pixels within rectangle D can be obtained using four array references. $D_{sum} = ii(\delta) + ii(\alpha) - (ii(\beta) + ii(\gamma))$, where $ii(\alpha)$ is the value of the integral image at point α (and similarly for β, γ, δ). © *Cengage Learning 2015.*

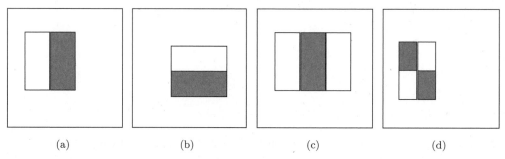

(a)	(b)	(c)	(d)

Figure 4.2: Rectangle-based features may be calculated from an integral image by subtraction of the sum of the shaded rectangle(s) from the non-shaded rectangle(s). The figure shows (a,b) two-rectangle, (c) three-rectangle, and (d) four-rectangle features. Sizes of the individual rectangles can be varied to yield different features as well as features at different scales. Contributions from the regions may be normalized to account for possibly unequal region sizes. © *Cengage Learning 2015.*

4.2.2   Chains

Chains are used for the description of object borders in computer vision. One element of the chain is a basic symbol; this approach permits the application of formal language theory for computer vision tasks. Chains are appropriate for data that can be arranged as a sequence of symbols, and the neighboring symbols in a chain usually correspond to the neighborhood of primitives in the image. The primitive is the basic descriptive element that is used in syntactic pattern recognition (see Chapter 9).

This rule of proximity (neighborhood) of symbols and primitives has exceptions—for example, the first and the last symbol of the chain describing a closed border are not neighbors, but the corresponding primitives in the image are. Similar inconsistencies are typical of image description languages [Shaw, 1969], too. Chains are linear structures, which is why they cannot describe spatial relations in the image on the basis of neighborhood or proximity.

Chain codes (and Freeman codes) [Freeman, 1961] are often used for the description of object borders, or other one-pixel-wide lines in images. The border is defined by the co-ordinates of its reference pixel and the sequence of symbols corresponding to the line of the unit length in several pre-defined orientations. Notice that a chain code is of a relative nature; data are expressed with respect to some reference point. Figure 4.3 shows an example of a chain code in which where 8-neighborhoods are used—4-neighborhoods can be used as well. An algorithm to extract a chain code may be implemented as an obvious simplification of Algorithm 6.6; chain codes and their properties are described in more detail in Chapter 8.

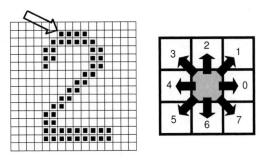

Figure 4.3: An example chain code; the reference pixel starting the chain is marked by an arrow: 00077665555556600000000644444444222111111234445652211. © *Cengage Learning 2015.*

If local information is needed from the chain code, then it is necessary to search through the whole chain systematically. For instance, if we want to know whether the border turns somewhere to the left by 90°, we must just find a sample pair of symbols in the chain—it is simple. On the other hand, a question about the shape of the border near the pixel (i_0, j_0) is not trivial. It is necessary to investigate all chain elements until the pixel (i_0, j_0) is found and only then we can start to analyze a short part of the border that is close to the pixel (i_0, j_0).

The description of an image by chains is appropriate for syntactic pattern recognition based on formal language theory methods. When working with real images, the problem of how to deal with uncertainty caused by noise arises, which is why several syntactic analysis techniques with deformation correction have arisen [Lu and Fu, 1978]. Another way to deal with noise is to smooth the border or to approximate it by another curve. This new border curve is then described by chain codes [Pavlidis, 1977].

Run length coding has been used for some time to represent strings of symbols in an image matrix. For simplicity, consider a binary image first. Run length coding records only areas that belong to objects in the image; the area is then represented as a list of lists. Various schemes exist which differ in detail—a representative one describes each row of the image by a sublist, the first element of which is the row number. Subsequent terms are co-ordinate pairs; the first element of a pair is the beginning of a run and the second is the end (the beginning and the end are described by column coordinates). There can be several such sequences in the row. Run length coding is illustrated in Figure 4.4. The main advantage of run length coding is the existence of simple algorithms for intersections and unions of regions in the image.

Run length coding can be used for an image with multiple brightness levels as well—in this case sequences of neighboring pixels in a row that has constant brightness are considered. In the sublist we must record not only the beginning and the end of the sequence, but its brightness, too.

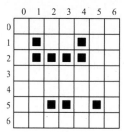

Figure 4.4: Run length coding; the code is $((11144)(214)(52355))$.
© *Cengage Learning 2015*.

4.2.3   Topological data structures

Topological data structures describe the image as a set of elements and their relations; these relations are often represented using graphs. A **graph** $G = (V, E)$ is an algebraic structure which consists of a set of nodes $V = \{v_1, v_2, \ldots, v_n\}$ and a set of arcs $E = \{e_1, e_2, \ldots, e_m\}$. Each arc e_k is incident to an unordered (or ordered) pair of nodes $\{v_i, v_j\}$ which are not necessarily distinct. The *degree* of a node is equal to the number of incident arcs of the node.

A **weighted graph** is a graph in which values are assigned to arcs, to nodes, or to both—these values may, for example, represent weights, or costs.

The **region adjacency graph** is typical of this class of data structures, in which nodes correspond to regions and neighboring regions are connected by an arc. The segmented image (see Chapter 6) consists of regions with similar properties (brightness, texture, color, ...) that correspond to some entities in the scene, and the neighborhood relation is fulfilled when the regions have some common border. An example of an image with areas labeled by numbers and the corresponding region adjacency graph is shown in Figure 4.5; the label 0 denotes pixels out of the image. This label is used to indicate regions that touch borders of the image in the region adjacency graph.

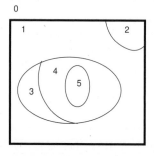

Figure 4.5: An example region adjacency graph.
© *Cengage Learning 2015*.

The region adjacency graph has several attractive features. If a region encloses other regions, then the part of the graph corresponding with the areas inside can be separated by a cut in the graph. Nodes of degree 1 represent simple holes.

Arcs of the graph can include a description of relations between neighboring regions—the relations *to be to the left* or *to be inside* are common. It can be used for matching with a stored pattern for recognition purposes.

The region adjacency graph is usually created from the **region map**, which is a matrix of the same dimensions as the original image matrix whose elements are identification labels of the regions. To create the region adjacency graph, borders of all regions in the image are traced, and labels of all neighboring regions are stored. The region adjacency graph can also easily be created from an image represented by a quadtree (Section 4.3.2).

The region adjacency graph stores information about the neighbors of all regions in the image explicitly. The region map contains this information as well, but it is much more difficult to recall from there. If we want to relate the region adjacency graph to the region map quickly, it is sufficient for a node in the region adjacency graph to be marked by the identification label of the region and some representative pixel (e.g., the top left pixel of the region).

Construction of the boundary data structures that represent regions is not trivial, and is considered in Section 6.2.3. Region adjacency graphs can be used to approach region merging (where, for instance, neighboring regions thought to have the same image interpretation are merged into one region)—this topic is considered in Section 10.10. In particular, note that merging representations of regions that may border each other more than once can be intricate, for example, with the creation of 'holes' not present before the merge—see Figure 4.6.

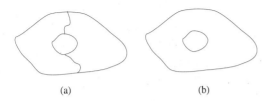

(a) (b)

Figure 4.6: Region merging may create holes: (a) Before a merge. (b) After. © *Cengage Learning 2015.*

4.2.4 Relational structures

Relational databases [Kunii et al., 1974] can also be used for representation of information from an image; all the information is then concentrated in relations between semantically important parts of the image—objects—that are the result of segmentation (Chapter 6). Relations are recorded in the form of tables. An example of such a representation is shown in Figure 4.7 and Table 4.1, where individual objects are associated with their names and other features, e.g., the top-left pixel of the corresponding region in the image. Relations between objects are expressed in the relational table. Here, such a relation is *to be inside*; for example, the object 7 (pond) is situated inside the object 6 (hill).

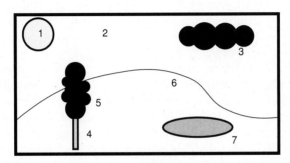

Figure 4.7: Description of objects using relational structure. © *Cengage Learning 2015.*

No.	Object name	Color	Min. row	Min. col.	Inside
1	sun	white	5	40	2
2	sky	blue	0	0	–
3	cloud	gray	20	180	2
4	tree trunk	brown	95	75	6
5	tree crown	green	53	63	–
6	hill	light green	97	0	–
7	pond	blue	100	160	6

Table 4.1: Relational table. © *Cengage Learning 2015.*

Description by means of relational structures is appropriate for higher levels of image understanding. In this case searches using keys, similar to database searches, can be used to speed up the whole process.

4.3   Hierarchical data structures

Computer vision is by its nature very computationally expensive, if for no other reason than the large amount of data to be processed. Usually a very quick response is expected because video real-time or interactive systems are desirable. One of the solutions is to use parallel computers (in other words brute force). Unfortunately there are many computer vision problems that are very difficult to divide among processors, or decompose in any way. Hierarchical data structures make it possible to use algorithms which decide a strategy for processing on the basis of relatively small quantities of data. They work at the finest resolution only with those parts of the image for which it is essential, using knowledge instead of brute force to ease and speed up the processing. We are going to introduce two typical hierarchical structures, pyramids and quadtrees.

4.3.1   Pyramids

Pyramids are among the simplest hierarchical data structures. We distinguish between **M-pyramids** (matrix-pyramids) and **T-pyramids** (tree-pyramids).

A **Matrix-pyramid** (M-pyramid) is a sequence $\{M_L, M_{L-1}, \ldots, M_0\}$ of images, where M_L has the same dimensions and elements as the original image, and M_{i-1} is derived from the M_i by reducing the resolution by one-half. When creating pyramids, it is customary to work with square matrices having dimensions equal to powers of 2—then M_0 corresponds to one pixel only.

M-pyramids are used when it is necessary to work with an image at different resolutions simultaneously. An image having one degree smaller resolution in a pyramid contains four times less data, so it is processed approximately four times as quickly.

Often it is advantageous to use several resolutions simultaneously rather than choose just one image from the M-pyramid. For such algorithms we prefer to use **tree-pyramids**, a tree structure. Let 2^L be the size of an original image (the highest resolution). A tree-pyramid (T-pyramid) is defined by:

1. A set of nodes $P = \{p = (k, i, j) \text{ such that level } k \in [0, L]; \, i, j \in [0, 2^k - 1]\}$.

2. A mapping F between subsequent nodes P_{k-1}, P_k of the pyramid

$$F(k, i, j) = (k - 1, \text{floor}(i/2), \text{floor}(j/2)).$$

3. A function V that maps a node of the pyramid P to Z, where Z is the subset of the whole numbers corresponding to the number of brightness levels, for example, $Z = \{0, 1, 2, \ldots, 255\}$.

Nodes of a T-pyramid correspond for a given k with image points of an M-pyramid; elements of the set of nodes $P = \{(k, i, j)\}$ correspond with individual matrices in the M-pyramid—k is called the level of the pyramid. An image $P = \{(k, i, j)\}$ for a specific k constitutes an image at the kth level of the pyramid. F is the so-called parent mapping, which is defined for all nodes P_k of the T-pyramid except its root $(0, 0, 0)$. Every node of the T-pyramid has four child nodes except leaf nodes, which are nodes of level L that correspond to the individual pixels in the image.

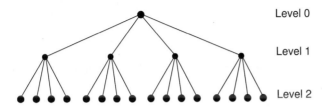

Level 0

Level 1

Level 2

Figure 4.8: T-pyramid.
© *Cengage Learning 2015.*

Values of individual nodes of the T-pyramid are defined by the function V. Values of leaf nodes are the same as values of the image function (brightness) in the original image at the finest resolution; the image size is 2^L. Values of nodes in other levels of the tree are either an arithmetic mean of four child nodes or they are defined by coarser sampling, meaning that the value of one child (e.g., top left) is used. Figure 4.8 shows the structure of a simple T-pyramid.

The number of image pixels used by an M-pyramid for storing all matrices is given by

$$N^2 \left(1 + \frac{1}{4} + \frac{1}{16} + \ldots\right) \approx 1.33\, N^2, \tag{4.4}$$

where N is the dimension of the original matrix (the image of finest resolution)—usually a power of two, 2^L.

The T-pyramid is represented in memory similarly. Arcs of the tree need not be recorded because addresses of the both child and parent nodes are easy to compute due to the regularity of the structure. An algorithm for the effective creation and storing of a T-pyramid is given in [Pavlidis, 1982].

4.3.2 Quadtrees

Quadtrees are modifications of T-pyramids. Every node of the tree except the leaves has four children (NW, north-western; NE, north-eastern; SW, south-western; SE, south-eastern). Similarly to T-pyramids, the image is divided into four quadrants at each hierarchical level; however, it is not necessary to keep nodes at all levels. If a parent node has four children of the same value (e.g., brightness), it is not necessary to record

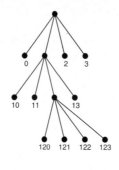

Figure 4.9: Quadtree. © *Cengage Learning 2015.*

them. This representation is less expensive for an image with large homogeneous regions; Figure 4.9 is an example of a simple quadtree.

An advantage of image representation by means of quadtrees is the existence of simple algorithms for addition of images, computing object areas, and statistical moments. The main disadvantage of quadtrees and pyramid hierarchical representations is their dependence on the position, orientation, and relative size of objects. Two similar images with just very small differences can have very different pyramid or quadtree representations. Even two images depicting the same, slightly shifted scene, can have entirely different representations.

These disadvantages can be overcome using a normalized shape of quadtree in which we do not create the quadtree for the whole image, but for its individual objects. Geometric features of objects such as the center of gravity and principal axis are used (see Chapter 8); the center of gravity and principal axis of every object are derived first and then the smallest enclosing square centered at the center of gravity having sides parallel with the principal axes is located. The square is then represented by a quadtree. An object described by a normalized quadtree and several additional items of data (coordinates of the center of gravity, angle of main axes) is invariant to shifting, rotation, and scale.

Quadtrees are usually represented by recording the whole tree as a list of its individual nodes, every node being a record with several items characterizing it. An example is given in Figure 4.10. In the item *Node type* there is information about whether the node is a leaf or inside the tree. Other data can be the level of the node in the tree, position in the picture, code of the node, etc. This kind of representation is expensive in memory. Its advantage is easy access to any node because of pointers between parents and children.

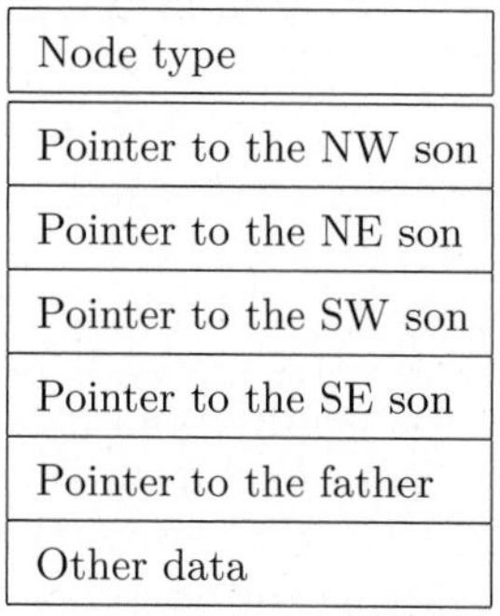

Node type
Pointer to the NW son
Pointer to the NE son
Pointer to the SW son
Pointer to the SE son
Pointer to the father
Other data

Figure 4.10: Record describing a quadtree node. © *Cengage Learning 2015.*

It is possible to represent a quadtree with less demand on memory by means of a **leaf code**. Any point of the picture is coded by a sequence of digits reflecting successive divisions of the quadtree; zero means the NW (north-west) quadrant, and likewise for other quadrants: 1-NE, 2-SW, 3-SE. The most important digit of the code (on the left) corresponds to the division at the highest level, the least important one (on the right) with the last division. The number of digits in the code is the same as the number of levels of the quadtree. The whole tree is then described by a sequence of pairs—the leaf code and the brightness of the region. Programs creating quadtrees can use recursive procedures to advantage.

T-pyramids are very similar to quadtrees, but differ in two basic respects. A T-pyramid is a balanced structure, meaning that the corresponding tree divides the image regardless of the contents, which is why it is regular and symmetric. A quadtree is not balanced. The other difference is in the interpretation of values of the individual nodes.

Quadtrees have seen widespread application, particularly in the area of Geographic Information Systems (GIS) where, along with their three-dimensional generalization *octrees*, they have proved very useful in hierarchical representation of layered data [Samet, 1989, 1990].

4.3.3   Other pyramidal structures

The pyramidal structure is widely used, and has seen several extensions and modifications. Recalling that a (simple) M-pyramid was defined as a sequence of images $\{M_L, M_{L-1}, \ldots, M_0\}$ in which M_i is a 2×2 reduction of M_{i+1}, we can define the notion of a **reduction window**; for every cell c of M_i, the reduction window is its set of children in M_{i+1}, $w(c)$. Here, a *cell* is any single element of the image M_i at the corresponding level of pyramidal resolution. If the images are constructed such that all interior cells have the same number of neighbors (e.g., a square grid, as is customary), and they all have the same number of children, the pyramid is called **regular**.

A taxonomy of regular pyramids may be constructed by considering the reduction window together with the **reduction factor** λ, which defines the rate at which the image area decreases between levels;

$$\lambda \leq \frac{|M_{i+1}|}{|M_i|}, i = 0, 1, \ldots, L - 1 .$$

In the simple case, in which reduction windows do not overlap and are 2×2, we have $\lambda = 4$; if we choose to let the reduction windows overlap, the factor will reduce. The notation used to describe this characterization of regular pyramids is (*reduction window*)/(*reduction factor*). Figure 4.11 illustrates some simple examples.

The reduction window of a given cell at level i may be propagated down to higher resolution than level $i + 1$. For a cell c_i at level i, we can write $w^0(c_i) = w(c_i)$, and then recursively define

$$w^{k+1}(c_i) = \bigcup_{q \in w(c_i)} w^k(q) , \tag{4.5}$$

$w^k(c_i)$ is the **equivalent window** that covers all cells at level $i+k+1$ that link to the cell c_i. Note that the shape of this window is going to depend on the type of pyramid—for example, an $n \times n/2$ pyramid will generate octagonal equivalent windows, while for an

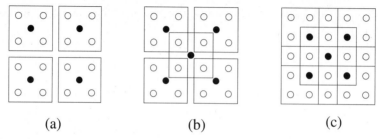

Figure 4.11: Several regular pyramid definitions. (a) $2 \times 2/4$. (b) $2 \times 2/2$. (c) $3 \times 3/2$. (Solid dots are at the higher level, i.e., the lower-resolution level.) © *Cengage Learning 2015.*

$n \times n/4$ pyramid they will be square. Use of non-square windows prevents domination of square features, as is the case for simple $2 \times 2/4$ pyramids.

The $2 \times 2/4$ pyramid is widely used and is what is usually called an 'image pyramid'; the $2 \times 2/2$ structure is often referred to as an 'overlap pyramid'. $5 \times 5/2$ pyramids have been used [Burt and Adelson, 1983] in compact image coding, where the image pyramid is augmented by a **Laplacian** pyramid of differences. Here, the Laplacian at a given level is computed as the per-pixel difference between the image at that level, and the image derived by 'expanding' the image at the next lower resolution. The Laplacian may be expected to have zero (or close) values in areas of low contrast, and therefore be amenable to compression.

Irregular pyramids are derived from contractions of graphical representations of images (for example, region adjacency graphs). Here, a graph may be reduced to a smaller one by selective removal of arcs and nodes. Depending on how these selections are made, important structures in the parent graph may be retained while reducing its overall complexity [Kropatsch, 1995]. The pyramid approach is quite general and lends itself to many developments—for example, the reduction algorithms need not be deterministic [Meer, 1989].

4.4 Summary

- **Level of image data representation**

    - Data structures together with algorithms are used to devise solutions to computational tasks.

    - Data structures for vision may be loosely classified as

        * Iconic
        * Segmented
        * Geometric
        * Relational

    Boundaries between these layers may not be well defined.

- **Traditional image data structures**

    - The matrix (2D array) is the most common data structure used for low-level representations, implemented as an array.

- Matrices hold image data explicitly. Spatial characteristics are implicitly available.

- Binary images are represented by binary matrices; multispectral images are represented by vectors of matrices; Hierarchical image structures are represented by matrices of different dimensions;

- The *co-occurrence matrix* is an example of global information derived from an image matrix; it is useful in describing texture.

- Chains may be used to describe pixel paths, especially borders.

- Chain codes are useful for recognition based on syntactic approaches.

- Run length codes are useful for simple image compression.

- Graph structures may be used to describe regions and their adjacency. These may be derived from a region map, a matrix of the same size as the image.

- Relational structures may be used to describe semantic relationships between image regions.

- **Hierarchical data structures**

  - Hierarchical structures can be used to extract large-scale features, which may be used to initialize analysis. They can provide significant computational efficiency.

  - M-pyramids and T-pyramids provide data structures to describe multiple image resolutions.

  - Quadtrees are a variety of T-pyramid in which selected areas of an image are stored at higher resolution than others, permitting selective extraction of detail.

  - Many algorithms for manipulation of quadtrees are available. Quadtrees are prone to great variation from small image differences.

  - Leaf codes provide a more efficient form of quadtree.

  - Many ways of deriving pyramids exist, dependent on choice of reduction window.

4.5 Exercises

Short-answer questions

S4.1 Determine the 4- and 8-neighborhood chain codes of the regions shown in Figure 4.12.

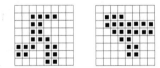

Figure 4.12: © *Cengage Learning 2015.*

S4.2 Define *M-pyramid.*

S4.3 Define *T-pyramid*.

S4.4 Define *run length encoding*.

S4.5 Determine the run length encoding of the images shown in Figure 4.12.

S4.6 Define a *region adjacency graph*.

S4.7 Draw the region adjacency graph for the image depicted in Figure 4.13.

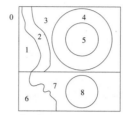

Figure 4.13: © *Cengage Learning 2015*.

S4.8 Integral image

(a) What is an integral image?

(b) Describe a simple and efficient algorithm to construct an integral image.

Problems

P4.1 Write a program that derives the quadtree representation of an image using the homogeneity criterion of equal intensity.

P4.2 Write a program that computes the T-pyramid of an image.

P4.3 Implement Algorithm 4.1. Run it on a variety of images for a variety of neighborhood relations.

P4.4 Implement Algorithm 4.2. Run it on a range of inputs and plot/visualize the output integral image. What relationships can you detect between input and output?

P4.5 Implement run length encoding, as described in Section 4.2.2. Run it on a range of binary images and determine the compression ratio achieved (this is most usefully done with the most compact possible representation of the run length code).

P4.6 Adapt the program written for Problem P4.5 to work for images which are not binary. Test it on a range of synthetic and real images, computing each time the compression ratio it provides.

P4.7 Make yourself familiar with solved problems and **Matlab** implementations of selected algorithms provided in the corresponding chapter of the **Matlab Companion** to this text [Svoboda et al., 2008]. The **Matlab Companion** homepage http://visionbook.felk.cvut.cz offers images used in the problems, and well-commented **Matlab** code is provided for educational purposes.

P4.8 Use the **Matlab Companion** [Svoboda et al., 2008] to develop solutions to additional exercises and practical problems provided there. Implement your solutions using **Matlab** or other suitable programming languages.

4.6   References

Ballard D. H. and Brown C. M. *Computer Vision.* Prentice-Hall, Englewood Cliffs, NJ, 1982.

Burt P. J. and Adelson E. H. The Laplacian pyramid as a compact image code. *IEEE Transactions on Computers,* COM-31(4):532–540, 1983.

Freeman H. On the encoding of arbitrary geometric configuration. *IRE Transactions on Electronic Computers,* EC–10(2):260–268, 1961.

Kropatsch W. G. Building irregular pyramids by dual graph contraction. *IEE Proceedings: Vision, Image and Signal Processing,* 142(6):366–374, 1995.

Kunii T. L., Weyl S., and Tenenbaum I. M. A relation database schema for describing complex scenes with color and texture. In *Proceedings of the 2nd International Joint Conference on Pattern Recognition,* pages 310–316, Copenhagen, Denmark, 1974.

Lu S. Y. and Fu K. S. A syntactic approach to texture analysis. *Computer Graphics and Image Processing,* 7:303–330, 1978.

Meer P. Stochastic image pyramids. *Computer Vision, Graphics, and Image Processing,* 45(3): 269–294, 1989.

Nilsson N. J. *Principles of Artificial Intelligence.* Springer Verlag, Berlin, 1982.

Pavlidis T. *Structural Pattern Recognition.* Springer Verlag, Berlin, 1977.

Pavlidis T. *Algorithms for Graphics and Image Processing.* Computer Science Press, New York, 1982.

Samet H. *The Design and Analysis of Spatial Data Structures.* Addison-Wesley, Reading, MA, 1989.

Samet H. *Applications of Spatial Data Structures.* Addison-Wesley, Reading, MA, 1990.

Shaw A. C. A formal picture description schema as a basis for picture processing systems. *Information and Control,* 14:9–52, 1969.

Svoboda T., Kybic J., and Hlavac V. *Image Processing, Analysis, and Machine Vision: A MATLAB Companion.* Thomson Engineering, 2008.

Viola P. and Jones M. Rapid object detection using a boosted cascade of simple features. In *Proceedings IEEE Conf. on Computer Vision and Pattern Recognition,* pages 511–518, Kauai, Hawaii, 2001. IEEE.

Wirth N. *Algorithms + Data Structures = Programs.* Prentice-Hall, Englewood Cliffs, NJ, 1976.

Chapter 5

Image pre-processing

Pre-processing is the name used for operations on images at the lowest level of abstraction —both input and output are intensity images. Such images are usually of the same kind as the original data captured by the sensor, with an intensity image usually represented by a matrix or matrices of brightness values.

Pre-processing does not increase image information content. If information is measured using entropy (Section 2.3.3), pre-processing typically decreases it. Thus from the information-theoretic viewpoint the best pre-processing is no pre-processing: without question, the best way to avoid (elaborate) pre-processing is to concentrate on high-quality image acquisition. Nevertheless, pre-processing is very useful in a variety of situations since it helps to suppress information irrelevant to the specific image processing or analysis task. Therefore, the aim of pre-processing is an improvement of the image data that suppresses undesired distortions or enhances some image features important for further processing. Geometric transformations of images (e.g., rotation, scaling, translation) are also classified as pre-processing methods here since similar techniques are used.

Here we classify image pre-processing methods into four categories according to the size of the pixel neighborhood used for the calculation of a new pixel brightness. Section 5.1 deals with pixel brightness transformations, Section 5.2 describes geometric transformations, Section 5.3 considers methods that use a local neighborhood, and Section 5.4 introduces image restoration that requires knowledge about the entire image.

Considerable redundancy of information in most images allows image pre-processing methods to explore data to learn image characteristics in a statistical sense. These characteristics are used either to suppress unintended degradations such as noise or to enhance the image. Neighboring pixels corresponding to objects in real images usually have the same or similar brightness value, so if a distorted pixel can be picked out from the image, it may be restored as an average value of neighboring pixels.

If pre-processing aims to correct some degradation in the image, the nature of a priori information is important:

- Some methods uses little or no knowledge about the nature of the degradation.

- Other methods assume knowledge of properties of the image acquisition device, and conditions under which the image was obtained. The nature of noise (usually its spectral characteristics) is sometimes known.

- A third approach uses knowledge about objects that are sought in the image. If knowledge about objects is not available in advance, it can be estimated during the processing.

5.1 Pixel brightness transformations

A brightness transformation modifies pixel brightness—the transformation depends on the properties of a pixel itself. There are two classes of pixel brightness transformations: **brightness corrections** and **gray-scale transformations**. Brightness correction modifies the pixel brightness taking into account its original brightness and its position in the image. Gray-scale transformations change brightness without regard to position in the image.

5.1.1 Position-dependent brightness correction

Ideally, the sensitivity of image acquisition and digitization devices should not depend on position in the image, but this assumption is not valid in many practical cases. A lens attenuates light more if it passes farther from the optical axis, and the photosensitive part of the sensor is not of uniform sensitivity. Uneven object illumination is also a source of degradation.

If degradation is systematic, it can be suppressed by brightness correction. A multiplicative error coefficient $e(i, j)$ describes the change from the ideal. Assume $g(i, j)$ is the original undegraded image and $f(i, j)$ is the degraded version. Then

$$f(i, j) = e(i, j) \, g(i, j) \,. \tag{5.1}$$

The error coefficient $e(i, j)$ can be obtained if a reference image $g(i, j)$ with known brightnesses is captured, the simplest being an image of constant brightness c. The degraded result is the image $f_c(i, j)$. Then systematic brightness errors can be suppressed by

$$g(i, j) = \frac{f(i, j)}{e(i, j)} = \frac{c \, f(i, j)}{f_c(i, j)} \,. \tag{5.2}$$

This method can be used only if the image degradation process is stable.

This method implicitly assumes linearity of the transformation, which is not true in reality because the brightness scale is limited to some interval. Equation (5.1) can overflow, and the limits of the brightness scale are used instead, implying that the best reference image has brightness that is far enough from both limits. If the gray-scale has 256 brightness levels, the ideal image has constant brightness values of 128.

5.1.2 Gray-scale transformation

Gray-scale transformations do not depend on the position of the pixel in the image. A transformation $\mathcal{T}$ of the original brightness p from scale $[p_0, p_k]$ into brightness q from a new scale $[q_0, q_k]$ is given by

$$q = \mathcal{T}(p) \,. \tag{5.3}$$

The most common gray-scale transformations are shown in Figure 5.1; the piecewise linear function a enhances the image contrast between brightness values p_1 and p_2. The function b is called **brightness thresholding** and results in a black-and-white image; the straight line c denotes the negative transformation.

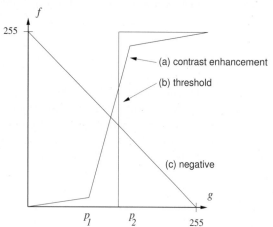

Figure 5.1: Some gray-scale transformations. © *Cengage Learning 2015.*

Digital images have a limited number of gray-levels, so gray-scale transformations are easy to realize both in hardware and software via a **look-up table**. Image signals usually pass through a look-up table in image displays, enabling simple gray-scale transformation in real time. The same principle can be used for color displays. A color signal consists of three components—red, green, and blue; three look-up tables provide all possible color scale transformations. (See Section 2.4 for more detail on color representation).

Gray-scale transformations are used mainly when an image is viewed by a human observer, and contrast enhancement may be beneficial. A transformation for contrast enhancement is usually found automatically using **histogram equalization**. The aim is to create an image with equally distributed brightness levels over the whole brightness scale (see Figure 5.2). Histogram equalization enhances contrast for brightness values close to histogram maxima, and decreases contrast near minima.

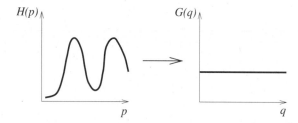

Figure 5.2: Histogram equalization. © *Cengage Learning 2015.*

Denote the input histogram by $H(p)$ and recall that the input gray-scale is $[p_0, p_k]$. The intention is to find a monotonic pixel brightness transformation $q = \mathcal{T}(p)$ such that the desired output histogram $G(q)$ is uniform over the whole output brightness scale $[q_0, q_k]$.

The monotonic property of the transform $\mathcal{T}$ implies

$$\sum_{i=0}^{k} G(q_i) = \sum_{i=0}^{k} H(p_i) \,. \tag{5.4}$$

The equalized histogram $G(q)$ corresponds to the uniform probability density function f whose function value is a constant

$$f = \frac{N^2}{q_k - q_0} \,. \tag{5.5}$$

for an $N \times N$ image. For the 'idealized' continuous probability density, we can substitute equation (5.5) into equation (5.4) and derive

$$N^2 \int_{q_0}^{q} \frac{1}{q_k - q_0} \, \mathrm{d}s = \frac{N^2(q - q_0)}{q_k - q_0} = \int_{p_0}^{p} H(s) \, \mathrm{d}s \tag{5.6}$$

from which $\mathcal{T}$ can be derived as

$$q = \mathcal{T}(p) = \frac{q_k - q_0}{N^2} \int_{p_0}^{p} H(s) \, \mathrm{d}s + q_0 \,. \tag{5.7}$$

The integral in equation (5.7) is called the **cumulative histogram**, which is approximated by a sum in digital images, so the resulting histogram is not equalized ideally.

Of course, we are dealing with a discrete approximation, and seek a realization of equation (5.7) that exploits as much of the available gray range as possible, and that generates a distribution invariant to reapplication of the procedure. Formally, the algorithm is:

Algorithm 5.1: Histogram equalization

1. For an $N \times M$ image of G gray-levels, initialize an array H of length G to 0.

2. Form the image histogram: Scan every pixel p—if it has intensity g_p, perform

$$H[g_p] = H[g_p] + 1 \,.$$

   Then let g_{min} be the minimum g for which $H[g] > 0$ (the lowest occurring gray level in the image).

3. Form the cumulative image histogram H_c:

$$H_c[0] = H[0] \,,$$
$$H_c[g] = H_c[g-1] + H[g] \,, \quad g = 1, 2, \ldots, G-1 \,.$$

   Let $H_{min} = H_c[g_{min}]$.

4. Set

$$T[g] = \mathrm{round}\left(\frac{H_c[g] - H_{min}}{MN - H_{min}} (G - 1) \right) \,.$$

5. Rescan the image and write an output image with gray-levels g_q, setting

$$g_q = T[g_p] \,.$$

These results can be demonstrated on an X-ray CT image of a lung. An input image and its equalization are shown in Figure 5.3; their respective histograms are shown in Figure 5.4.

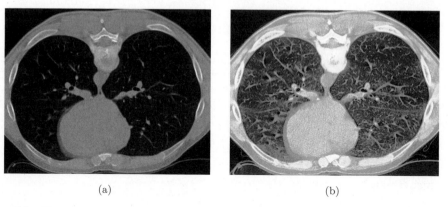

(a)   (b)

Figure 5.3: Histogram equalization. (a) Original image. (b) Equalized image. © *Cengage Learning 2015.*

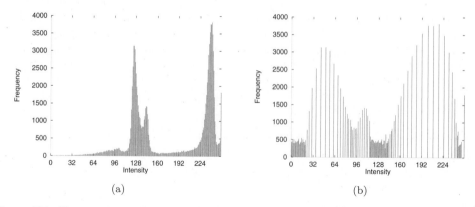

(a)   (b)

Figure 5.4: Histogram equalization: Original and equalized histograms corresponding to Figure 5.3a,b. © *Cengage Learning 2015.*

The **logarithmic** gray-scale transformation function is another frequently used technique. It is also used to compensate for exponential γ-correction used in cameras (see Section 2.5.2).

Pseudo-color is another kind of gray-scale transform. where individual brightnesses in the input monochromatic image are coded to some color. Since the human eye is very sensitive to change in color, much more detail can be perceived in pseudo-colored images.

5.2   Geometric transformations

Geometric transforms permit elimination of the geometric distortion that occurs when an image is captured, for example in an attempt to match remotely sensed images of the

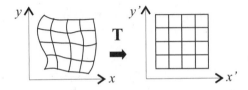

Figure 5.5: Geometric transform on a plane. © *Cengage Learning 2015.*

same area taken a different times but from different positions: we will execute a geometric transformation, and then subtract one image from the other. We consider geometric transformations only in 2D, as this is sufficient for most digital images.

A geometric transform is a vector function **T** that maps the pixel (x, y) to a new position (x', y')—an illustration of the whole region transformed on a point-to-point basis is in Figure 5.5. **T** is defined by its two component equations

$$x' = T_x(x, y), \qquad y' = T_y(x, y).$$
(5.8)

The transformation functions T_x and T_y are either known in advance—for example, in the case of rotation, translation, scaling—or can be determined from known original and transformed images. Several pixels in both images with known correspondences are used to derive the unknown transformation.

A geometric transform consists of two basic steps. First is the **pixel co-ordinate transformation**, which maps the co-ordinates of the input image pixel to the point in the output image. Output point co-ordinates will be continuous values (real numbers), as position are unlikely to match the digital grid after the transform. The second step finds the point in the digital raster which best matches the transformed point and determines its brightness value. This is usually computed as an **interpolation** of the brightnesses of several points in the neighborhood.

5.2.1 Pixel co-ordinate transformations

Equation (5.8) shows the general case of finding the co-ordinates of a point in the output image after a geometric transform. It is usually approximated by a polynomial equation

$$x' = \sum_{r=0}^{m} \sum_{k=0}^{m-r} a_{rk} \, x^r \, y^k, \qquad y' = \sum_{r=0}^{m} \sum_{k=0}^{m-r} b_{rk} \, x^r \, y^k.$$
(5.9)

This transform is linear with respect to the coefficients a_{rk}, b_{rk} and so if pairs of corresponding points (x, y), (x', y') in both images are known, it is possible to determine a_{rk}, b_{rk} by solving a set of linear equations.

In the case where the geometric transform does not change rapidly depending on position in the image, low-order polynomials, $m = 2$ or $m = 3$, are used, needing at least 6 or 10 pairs of corresponding points. Corresponding points should be distributed in the image in a way that can express the geometric transformation—usually they are spread uniformly.

Equation (5.8) is in practice approximated by a **bilinear transform** for which four pairs of corresponding points are sufficient to find the transformation coefficients

$$\begin{aligned} x' &= a_0 + a_1 \, x + a_2 \, y + a_3 \, x \, y, \\ y' &= b_0 + b_1 \, x + b_2 \, y + b_3 \, x \, y. \end{aligned}$$
(5.10)

Even simpler is the **affine transformation**, for which three pairs of corresponding points are sufficient to find the coefficients

$$x' = a_0 + a_1\, x + a_2\, y\,,$$
$$y' = b_0 + b_1\, x + b_2\, y\,. \tag{5.11}$$

The affine transformation includes typical geometric transformations such as rotation, translation, scaling, and skewing.

A geometric transform applied to the whole image may change the co-ordinate system, and a **Jacobian determinant** J provides information about how the co-ordinate system changes

$$J = \left| \frac{\partial(x', y')}{\partial(x, y)} \right| = \left| \begin{array}{cc} \partial x'/\partial x & \partial x'/\partial y \\ \partial y'/\partial x & \partial y'/\partial y \end{array} \right|\,. \tag{5.12}$$

If the transformation is singular (has no inverse), then $J = 0$. If the area of the image is invariant under the transformation, then $|J| = 1$.

The Jacobian determinant for the bilinear transform (5.10) is

$$J = a_1\, b_2 - a_2\, b_1 + (a_1\, b_3 - a_3\, b_1)\, x + (a_3\, b_2 - a_2\, b_3)\, y \tag{5.13}$$

and for the affine transformation (5.11) it is

$$J = a_1\, b_2 - a_2\, b_1\,. \tag{5.14}$$

Some important geometric transformations are:

- **Rotation** by the angle ϕ about the origin:

$$x' = x\, \cos\phi + y\, \sin\phi\,,$$
$$y' = -x\, \sin\phi + y\, \cos\phi\,,$$
$$J = 1\,. \tag{5.15}$$

- **Change of scale** a in the x axis and b in the y axis:

$$x' = a\, x\,,$$
$$y' = b\, x\,,$$
$$J = a\, b\,. \tag{5.16}$$

- **Skewing by the angle** ϕ, given by:

$$x' = x + y\, \tan\phi\,,$$
$$y' = y\,,$$
$$J = 1\,. \tag{5.17}$$

It is possible to approximate complex geometric transformations (distortion) by partitioning an image into smaller rectangular subimages; for each subimage, a simple geometric transformation is estimated using pairs of corresponding pixels. The geometric transformation (distortion) is then repaired separately in each subimage.

5.2.2   Brightness interpolation

Equation (5.8) provides new point co-ordinates (x', y') that do not in general fit the discrete raster of the output image. Values on the integer grid are needed; each pixel value in the output image raster can be obtained by **brightness interpolation** of some neighboring non-integer samples [Moik, 1980].

The simpler the interpolation, the greater the loss in geometric and photometric accuracy, but interpolation neighborhoods are often reasonably small due to computational load. The three most common interpolation methods are nearest neighbor, linear, and bi-cubic.

The interpolation problem is usually expressed in a *dual* way by determining the brightness of the original point in the input image that corresponds to a point in the output image lying on the raster. Assume we wish to compute the brightness value of the pixel (x', y') in the output image (integer numbers, illustrated by solid lines in figures). The co-ordinates of the point (x, y) in the original image can be obtained by inverting the planar transformation in equation (5.8):

$$(x, y) = \mathbf{T}^{-1}(x', y') . \tag{5.18}$$

In general, the real co-ordinates after inverse transformation (dashed lines in figures) do not fit the discrete raster (solid lines), and so the brightness is not known. The only information available about the originally continuous image function $f(x, y)$ is its sampled version $g_s(l \Delta x, k \Delta y)$. To get the brightness value of (x, y), the input image is resampled.

Denote the result of the brightness interpolation by $f_n(x, y)$, where n distinguishes different interpolation methods. The brightness can be expressed by the convolution equation

$$f_n(x, y) = \sum_{l=-\infty}^{\infty} \sum_{k=-\infty}^{\infty} g_s(l \Delta x, k \Delta y) \, h_n(x - l \Delta x, y - k \Delta y) . \tag{5.19}$$

The function h_n is called the **interpolation kernel**. Usually, only a small neighborhood is used, outside which h_n is zero. Three examples of interpolation will illustrate this: for clarity, the common simplification $\Delta x = \Delta y = 1$ is adopted.

Nearest-neighborhood interpolation assigns to the point (x, y) the brightness value of the nearest point g in the discrete raster, see Figure 5.6. On the right side is the interpolation kernel h_1 in the 1D case. The left side of Figure 5.6 shows how the new brightness is assigned. Dashed lines show how the inverse planar transformation maps the raster of the output image into the input image; full lines show the raster of the input

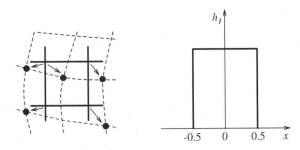

Figure 5.6: Nearest-neighborhood interpolation. The discrete raster of the original image is depicted by the solid line. © *Cengage Learning 2015.*

image. Nearest-neighborhood interpolation is given by

$$f_1(x, y) = g_s\big(\text{round}(x), \text{round}(y)\big) \,. \tag{5.20}$$

The position error of nearest-neighborhood interpolation is at most half a pixel. This error is perceptible on objects with straight-line boundaries that may appear step-like after the transformation.

Linear interpolation explores four points neighboring the point (x, y), and assumes that the brightness function is linear in this neighborhood. Linear interpolation is demonstrated in Figure 5.7, the left-hand side of which shows which points are used for interpolation. Linear interpolation is given by the equation

$$\begin{aligned}
f_2(x, y) &= (1 - a)(1 - b)\, g_s(l, k) \\
&\quad + a\,(1 - b)\, g_s(l + 1, k) + b\,(1 - a)\, g_s(l, k + 1) + a\,b\,g_s(l + 1, k + 1)\,, \\
&\quad l = \text{floor}(x)\,, \quad a = x - l\,, \quad k = \text{floor}(y)\,, \quad b = y - k\,.
\end{aligned} \tag{5.21}$$

This can cause a small decrease in resolution and blurring due to its averaging nature but the problem of step-like straight boundaries is reduced.

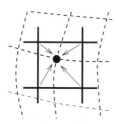 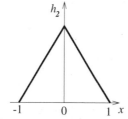

Figure 5.7: Linear interpolation. The discrete raster of the original image is depicted by the solid line. © *Cengage Learning 2015.*

Bi-cubic interpolation improves the model of the brightness function by approximating it locally by a bi-cubic polynomial surface; 16 neighboring points are used for interpolation. The one-dimensional interpolation kernel ('Mexican hat') is shown in Figure 5.8 and is given by

$$h_3 = \begin{cases} 1 - 2\,|x|^2 + |x|^3 & \text{for } 0 \le |x| < 1\,, \\ 4 - 8\,|x| + 5\,|x|^2 - |x|^3 & \text{for } 1 \le |x| < 2\,, \\ 0 & \text{otherwise.} \end{cases} \tag{5.22}$$

Bi-cubic interpolation does not suffer from the step-like boundary problem of nearest-neighborhood interpolation, and copes with linear interpolation blurring as well. Bi-cubic interpolation is often used in raster displays that enable zooming with respect to an arbitrary point. If the nearest-neighborhood method were used, areas of the same brightness would increase. Bi-cubic interpolation preserves fine details in the image very well.

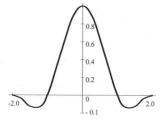

Figure 5.8: Bi-cubic interpolation kernel. © *Cengage Learning 2015.*

5.3   Local pre-processing

Local pre-processing methods are divided into two groups according to the goal of the processing. **Smoothing** aims to suppress noise or other small fluctuations in the image; it is equivalent to the suppression of high frequencies in the Fourier transform domain. Unfortunately, smoothing also blurs all sharp edges that bear important information about the image. **Gradient operators** are based on local derivatives of the image function. Derivatives are bigger at locations of the image where the image function undergoes rapid changes, and the aim of gradient operators is to indicate such locations in the image. Gradient operators have a similar effect to suppressing low frequencies in the Fourier transform domain. Noise is often high frequency in nature; unfortunately, if a gradient operator is applied to an image, the noise level increases simultaneously. Clearly, smoothing and gradient operators have conflicting aims. Some pre-processing algorithms solve this problem and permit smoothing and edge enhancement simultaneously.

Another classification of local pre-processing methods is according to the transformation properties; **linear** and **non-linear** transformations can be distinguished. Linear operations calculate the resulting value in the output image pixel $f(i, j)$ as a linear combination of brightnesses in a local neighborhood $\mathcal{O}$ of the pixel $g(i, j)$ in the input image. The contribution of the pixels in the neighborhood $\mathcal{O}$ is weighted by coefficients h:

$$f(i, j) = \sum\sum_{(m,n)\in\mathcal{O}} h(i - m, j - n)\, g(m, n)\,. \qquad (5.23)$$

Equation (5.23) is equivalent to discrete convolution with the kernel h, which is called a **convolution mask**. Rectangular neighborhoods $\mathcal{O}$ are often used with an odd number of pixels in rows and columns, enabling specification of the central pixel of the neighborhood.

The choice of the local transformation, size, and shape of the neighborhood $\mathcal{O}$ depends strongly on the size of objects in the processed image. If objects are rather large, an image can be enhanced by smoothing of small degradations.

5.3.1   Image smoothing

Image smoothing uses redundancy in image data to suppress noise, usually by some form of averaging of brightness values in some neighborhood $\mathcal{O}$. Smoothing poses the problem of blurring sharp edges, and so we shall consider smoothing methods which are **edge preserving** here, the average is computed only from points in the neighborhood which have similar properties to the point being processed.

Local image smoothing can effectively eliminate impulse noise or degradations appearing as thin stripes, but does not work if degradations are large blobs or thick stripes. Such problems may be addressed by image restoration techniques, described in Section 5.4.

Averaging, statistical principles of noise suppression

Assume that the noise value ν at each pixel is an independent random variable with zero mean and standard deviation σ. We might capture the same static scene under the same conditions n times. From each captured image a particular pixel value g_i, $i = 1, \ldots, n$ is selected. An estimate of the correct value can be obtained as an average of these values, with corresponding noise values $\nu_1, \ldots, \nu_n$

$$\frac{g_1 + \ldots + g_n}{n} + \frac{\nu_1 + \ldots + \nu_n}{n} . \tag{5.24}$$

The second term here describes the noise, which is again a random value with zero mean and standard deviation $\sigma/\sqrt{n}$. Thus, if n images of the same scene are available, smoothing can be accomplished without blurring the image by

$$f(i, j) = \frac{1}{n} \sum_{k=1}^{n} g_k(i, j) . \tag{5.25}$$

This reasoning is a well-known statistical result: a random sample is taken from a population and the corresponding sample mean value is calculated. If random samples are repeatedly selected and their sample mean values calculated, we would obtain a distribution of sample mean values. This distribution of sample means has some useful properties:

- The mean value of the distribution of sample mean values is equal to the population mean.

- The distribution of sample mean values has variance $\sigma/\sqrt{n}$, which is clearly smaller than that of than the original population.

- If the original distribution is normal (Gaussian) then the distribution of sample mean values is also normal. Better, the distribution of sample means converges to normal whatever the original distribution. This is the **central limit theorem**.

- From the practical point of view, it is important that not too many random selections have to be made. The central limit theorem tell us the distribution of sample mean values without the need to create them. In statistics, usually about 30 samples are considered the lowest limit of the necessary number of observations.

Usually, only one noise corrupted is available, and averaging is then performed in a local neighborhood. Results are acceptable if the noise is smaller in size than the smallest objects of interest in the image, but blurring of edges is a serious disadvantage. Averaging is a special case of discrete convolution [equation (5.23)]. For a 3×3 neighborhood, the convolution mask h is

$$h = \frac{1}{9} \begin{bmatrix} 1 & 1 & 1 \\ 1 & 1 & 1 \\ 1 & 1 & 1 \end{bmatrix} . \tag{5.26}$$

The significance of the pixel in the center of the convolution mask h or its 4-neighbors is sometimes increased, as it better approximates the properties of noise with a Gaussian probability distribution (Gaussian noise, see Section 2.3.6)

$$h = \frac{1}{10} \begin{bmatrix} 1 & 1 & 1 \\ 1 & 2 & 1 \\ 1 & 1 & 1 \end{bmatrix} , \qquad h = \frac{1}{16} \begin{bmatrix} 1 & 2 & 1 \\ 2 & 4 & 2 \\ 1 & 2 & 1 \end{bmatrix} . \tag{5.27}$$

There are two commonly used smoothing filters whose coefficients gradually decrease to have near-zero values at the window edges. This is the best way to minimize spurious

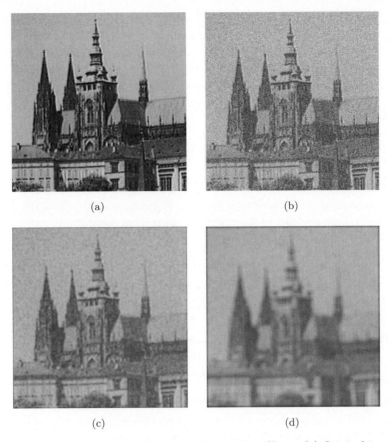

(a) (b)

(c) (d)

Figure 5.9: Noise with Gaussian distribution and averaging filters. (a) Original image. (b) Superimposed noise (random Gaussian noise characterized by zero mean and standard deviation equal to one-half of the gray-level standard deviation of the original image). (c) 3×3 averaging. (d) 7×7 averaging. © *Cengage Learning 2015.*

oscillations in the frequency spectrum (see the discussion of the uncertainty principle, equation 3.24). These are the Gaussian and the Butterworth filters. Larger convolution masks for averaging by Gaussian filter are created according to the Gaussian distribution formula (equation 5.47) and the mask coefficients are normalized to have a unit sum. The Butterworth filter will be explained in Section 5.3.8 dealing with local pre-processing in the frequency domain.

An example will illustrate the effect of this noise suppression (low resolution images, 256×256, were chosen deliberately to show the discrete nature of the process). Figure 5.9a shows an original image of Prague castle; Figure 5.9b shows the same image with superimposed additive noise with Gaussian distribution; Figure 5.9c shows the result of averaging with a 3×3 convolution mask (equation 5.27)—noise is significantly reduced and the image is slightly blurred. Averaging with a larger mask (7×7) is demonstrated in Figure 5.9d, where the blurring is much more serious.

Such filters can be very computationally costly, but this is considerably reduced in the important special case of **separable filters**. Separability in 2D means that the convolution kernel can be factorized as a product of two one-dimensional vectors, and theory provides a clue as to which convolution masks are separable.

As an example, consider a binomic filter. Its elements are binomic numbers which are created as a sum of the corresponding two numbers in Pascal's triangle. Consider such a filter of size 5×5—it can be decomposed into a product of two 1D vectors, h_1, h_2.

$$
\begin{bmatrix}
1 & 4 & 6 & 4 & 1 \\
4 & 16 & 24 & 16 & 4 \\
6 & 24 & 36 & 24 & 6 \\
4 & 16 & 24 & 16 & 4 \\
1 & 4 & 6 & 4 & 1
\end{bmatrix}
= \begin{bmatrix} h_1 \end{bmatrix} \begin{bmatrix} h_2 \end{bmatrix}
= \begin{bmatrix} 1 \\ 4 \\ 6 \\ 4 \\ 1 \end{bmatrix}
\begin{bmatrix} 1 & 4 & 6 & 4 & 1 \end{bmatrix} .
$$

Suppose a convolution kernel is of size $2N + 1$. Equation (5.23) allows the convolution to be rewritten taking account of the special properties of separability

$$
g(x,y) = \sum_{m=-N}^{N} \sum_{n=-N}^{N} h(m,n)\, f(x+m, y+n) = \sum_{m=-N}^{N} h_1(m) \sum_{n=-N}^{N} h_2(n)\, f(x+m, y+n).
$$

The direct calculation of the convolution according to equation (5.23) would need, in our case of 5×5 convolution kernel, 25 multiplications and 24 additions for each pixel. If the separable filter is used then only 10 multiplications and 8 additions suffice.

Averaging with limited data validity

Methods that average with limited data validity [McDonnell, 1981] try to avoid blurring by averaging only those pixels which satisfy some criterion, the aim being to prevent involving pixels that are part of a separate feature.

A very simple criterion is to define a brightness interval of *invalid* data [min, max] (typically corresponding to noise of known image faults), and apply image averaging only to pixels in that interval. For a point (m, n), the convolution mask is calculated in the neighborhood $\mathcal{O}$ by the non-linear formula

$$
h(i,j) = \begin{cases} 1 & \text{for } g(m+i, n+j) \notin [\text{min,max}] \\ 0 & \text{otherwise} \end{cases} , \tag{5.28}
$$

where (i, j) specify the mask element. Therefore, only values of pixels with invalid gray-levels are replaced with an average of their neighborhoods, and only valid data contribute to the averages. The power of this approach is illustrated in Figure 5.10—with the exception of slight local blurring of the towers, the method successfully removes significant image corruption.

A second method performs averaging only if the computed brightness change of a pixel is in some pre-defined interval; this permits repair to large-area errors resulting from slowly changing brightness of the background without affecting the rest of the image.

A third method uses edge strength (i.e., gradient magnitude) as a criterion. The magnitude of some gradient operator (Section 5.3.2) is first computed for the entire image, and only pixels with a small gradient are used in averaging. This method effectively rejects averaging at edges and therefore suppresses blurring, but setting of the threshold is laborious.

(a)   (b)

Figure 5.10: Averaging with limited data validity. (a) Original corrupted image. (b) Result of corruption removal. © *Cengage Learning 2015.*

Averaging according to inverse gradient

Within a convolution mask of odd size, the *inverse gradient* δ of a point (i, j) with respect to the central pixel (m, n) is defined as [Wang and Vagnucci, 1981]

$$\delta(i, j) = \frac{1}{|g(m, n) - g(i, j)|} . \tag{5.29}$$

If $g(m, n) = g(i, j)$, then we define $\delta(i, j) = 2$, so δ is in the interval $(0, 2]$, and is smaller at the edge than in the interior of a homogeneous region. Weight coefficients in the convolution mask h are normalized by the inverse gradient, and the whole term is multiplied by 0.5 to keep brightness values in the original range: the mask coefficient corresponding to the central pixel is defined as $h(i, j) = 0.5$. The constant 0.5 has the effect of assigning half the weight to the central pixel (m, n), and the other half to its neighborhood

$$h(i, j) = 0.5 \frac{\delta(i, j)}{\sum_{(m,n) \in \mathcal{O}} \delta(i, j)} . \tag{5.30}$$

This method assumes sharp edges. When the convolution mask is close to an edge, pixels from the region have larger coefficients than pixels near the edge, and it is not blurred. Isolated noise points within homogeneous regions have small values of the inverse gradient; points from the neighborhood take part in averaging and the noise is removed.

Averaging using a rotating mask

The smoothing discussed thus far was linear, which has the disadvantage that edges in the image are inevitably blurred. Alternative non-linear methods exist which reduce this. The neighborhood of the current pixel is inspected and divided into two subsets by a homogeneity criterion of the user's choice. One set consists of all pixels neighboring the current pixel or any pixel already included in this set, which satisfy the homogeneity criterion. The second set is the complement. This selection operation is non-linear and causes the whole filter to be non-linear. Having selected the homogeneous subset containing the current pixel, the most probable value is sought in it by a linear or non-linear technique.

Averaging using a rotating mask is such a non-linear method that avoids edge blurring, and the resulting image is in fact sharpened [Nagao and Matsuyama, 1980]. The brightness average is calculated only within this region; a brightness dispersion σ^2 is used as the region homogeneity measure. Let n be the number of pixels in a region R and g be the input image. Dispersion σ^2 is calculated as

$$\sigma^2 = \frac{1}{n} \sum_{(i,j)\in R} \left(g(i,j) - \frac{1}{n} \sum_{(i,j)\in R} g(i,j) \right)^2. \tag{5.31}$$

Having computed region homogeneity, we consider its shape and size. The eight possible 3×3 masks that cover a 5×5 neighborhood of a current pixel (marked by the small cross) are shown in Figure 5.11. The ninth mask is the 3×3 neighborhood of the current pixel itself. Other mask shapes—larger or smaller—can also be used.

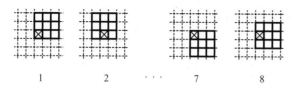

1   2 $\cdots$ 7   8

Figure 5.11: Eight possible rotated 3×3 masks. © *Cengage Learning 2015.*

Algorithm 5.2: Smoothing using a rotating mask

1. Consider each image pixel (i, j).

2. Calculate dispersion for all possible mask rotations about pixel (i, j) according to equation (5.31).

3. Choose the mask with minimum dispersion.

4. Assign to the pixel $f(i, j)$ in the output image f the average brightness in the chosen mask.

Algorithm 5.2 can be used iteratively and the process converges quite quickly to a stable state. The size and shape of masks influence the convergence—the smaller the mask, the smaller are the changes and more iterations are needed. A larger mask suppresses noise faster and the sharpening effect is stronger. On the other hand, information about details smaller than the mask may be lost. The number of iterations is also influenced by the shape of regions in the image and noise properties.

Median filtering

In probability theory, the **median** divides the higher half of a probability distribution from the lower half. For a random variable x, the median M is the value for which the probability of the outcome $x < M$ is 0.5. The median of a finite list of real numbers is simply found by ordering the list and selecting the middle member. Lists are often constructed to be odd in length to secure uniqueness.

Median filtering is a non-linear smoothing method that reduces the blurring of edges [Tyan, 1981], in which the idea is to replace the current point in the image by the median of the brightnesses in its neighborhood. The median in the neighborhood is not affected by individual noise spikes and so median smoothing eliminates impulse noise quite well. Further, as median filtering does not blur edges much, it can be applied iteratively. Clearly, performing a sort on pixels within a (possibly large) rectangular window at every pixel position may become very expensive. A more efficient approach [Huang et al., 1979; Pitas and Venetsanopoulos, 1990] is to notice that as the window moves across a row by one column, the only change to its contents is to lose the leftmost column and replace it with a new right column—for a median window of m rows and n columns, $mn - 2m$ pixels are unchanged and do not need re-sorting. The algorithm is as follows:

Algorithm 5.3: Efficient median filtering

1. Set
$$t = \frac{m\,n}{2}\,.$$

   (We would always avoid unnecessary floating point operations: if m and n are both odd, round t.)

2. Position the window at the beginning of a new row, and sort its contents. Construct a histogram H of the window pixels, determine the median m, and record n_m, the number of pixels with intensity less than or equal to m.

3. For each pixel p in the leftmost column of intensity p_g, perform

$$H[p_g] = H[p_g] - 1\,.$$

   Further, if $p_g \leq m$, set
$$n_m = n_m - 1\,.$$

4. Move the window one column right. For each pixel p in the rightmost column of intensity p_g, perform
$$H[p_g] = H[p_g] + 1\,.$$

   If $p_g \leq m$, set
$$n_m = n_m + 1\,.$$

5. If $n_m = t$ then go to (8).

6. If $n_m > t$ then go to (7).
   Repeat

$$m = m + 1\,,$$
$$n_m = n_m + H[m]\,,$$

   until $n_m \geq t$. Go to (8).

---

7. (We have $n_m > t$, if here). Repeat

$$n_m = n_m - H[m]\,,$$
$$m = m - 1\,,$$

until $n_m \le t$.

8. If the right-hand column of the window is not at the right-hand edge of the image, go to (3).

9. If the bottom row of the window is not at the bottom of the image, go to (2).

Median filtering is illustrated in Figure 5.12. The main disadvantage of median filtering in a rectangular neighborhood is its damaging of thin lines and sharp corners—this can be avoided if another shape of neighborhood is used. For instance, if horizontal/vertical lines need preserving, a neighborhood such as that in Figure 5.13 can be used.

Median smoothing is a special instance of more general **rank filtering** techniques [Rosenfeld and Kak, 1982; Yaroslavskii, 1987], the idea of which is to order pixels in some neighborhood into a sequence. The results of pre-processing are some statistics over this sequence, of which the median is one possibility. Another variant is the maximum or the minimum values of the sequence. This defines generalizations of dilation and erosion operators (Chapter 13) in images with more brightness values.

A similar generalization of median techniques is given in [Borik et al., 1983]. Their method is called **order statistics** (OS) filtering. Values in the neighborhood are again ordered into sequence, and a new value is given as a linear combination of the values of this sequence.

(a)

(b)

Figure 5.12: Median filtering. (a) Image corrupted with impulse noise (14% of image area covered with bright and dark dots). (b) Result of 3×3 median filtering. © *Cengage Learning 2015.*

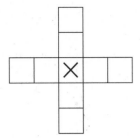

Figure 5.13: Horizontal/vertical line preserving neighborhood for median filtering. © *Cengage Learning 2015*.

Non-linear mean filter

The non-linear mean filter is another generalization of averaging techniques [Pitas and Venetsanopulos, 1986]; it is defined by

$$f(m,n) = u^{-1}\left(\frac{\sum_{(i,j)\in\mathcal{O}} a(i,j)\, u\big(g(i,j)\big)}{\sum_{(i,j)\in\mathcal{O}} a(i,j)}\right), \tag{5.32}$$

where $f(m,n)$ is the result of the filtering, $g(i,j)$ is the pixel in the input image, and $\mathcal{O}$ is a local neighborhood of the current pixel (m,n). The function u of one variable has an inverse function u^{-1}; the $a(i,j)$ are weight coefficients.

If the weights $a(i,j)$ are constant, the filter is called **homomorphic**. Some homomorphic filters used in image processing are:

- Arithmetic mean, $u(g) = g$.

- Harmonic mean, $u(g) = 1/g$.

- Geometric mean, $u(g) = \log g$.

5.3.2 Edge detectors

Edge detectors are a collection of very important local image pre-processing methods used to locate changes in the intensity function; edges are pixels where this function (brightness) changes abruptly.

Neurological and psychophysical research suggests that locations in the image in which the function value changes abruptly are important for image perception. Edges are to a certain degree invariant to changes of illumination and viewpoint. If only edge elements with strong magnitude (edgels) are considered, such information often suffices for image understanding. The positive effect of such a process is that it leads to significant reduction of image data. Nevertheless such data reduction does not undermine understanding the content of the image (interpretation) in many cases. Edge detection provides appropriate generalization of the image data; for instance, line drawings perform such a generalization, see the example by the German painter Albrecht Dürer in Figure 5.14.

We shall consider which physical phenomena in the image formation process lead to abrupt changes in image values—see Figure 5.15. Calculus describes changes of continuous functions using derivatives; an image function depends on two variables—co-ordinates in the image plane—and so operators describing edges are expressed using partial derivatives. A change of the image function can be described by a gradient that points in the direction of the largest growth of the image function.

Figure 5.14: Artist's mother, year 1514.
Albrecht Dürer (1471-1528).

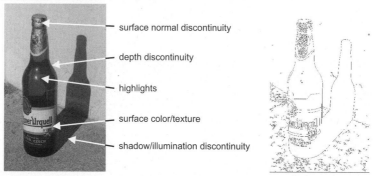

— surface normal discontinuity

— depth discontinuity

— highlights

— surface color/texture

— shadow/illumination discontinuity

Figure 5.15: Origin of edges, i.e., physical phenomena in image formation process which lead to edges in images. At right, a Canny edge detection (see Section 5.3.5). © *Cengage Learning 2015*.

An edge is a property attached to an individual pixel and is calculated from the image function behavior in a neighborhood of that pixel. It is a **vector variable** with two components, **magnitude** and **direction**. The edge magnitude is the magnitude of the gradient, and the edge direction ϕ is rotated with respect to the gradient direction ψ by $-90°$. The gradient direction gives the direction of maximum growth of the function, e.g., from black $f(i,j) = 0$ to white $f(i,j) = 255$. This is illustrated in Figure 5.16, in which closed lines are lines of equal brightness. The orientation $0°$ points east.

Edges are often used in image analysis for finding region boundaries. Provided that the region has homogeneous brightness, its boundary is at the pixels where the image function varies and so in the ideal case without noise consists of pixels with high edge

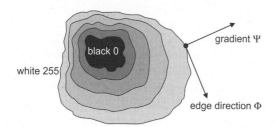

gradient Ψ

black 0

white 255

edge direction Φ

Figure 5.16: Gradient direction and edge direction. © *Cengage Learning 2015*.

magnitude. It can be seen that the boundary and its parts (edges) are perpendicular to the direction of the gradient. Figure 5.17 shows examples of several standard edge profiles. Edge detectors are usually tuned for some type of edge profile.

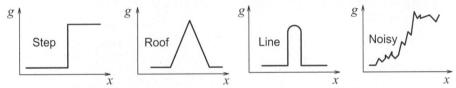

Figure 5.17: Typical edge profiles. © *Cengage Learning 2015.*

The gradient magnitude $|\text{grad } g(x, y)|$ and gradient direction ψ are continuous image functions calculated as

$$|\text{grad } g(x,y)| = \sqrt{\left(\frac{\partial g}{\partial x}\right)^2 + \left(\frac{\partial g}{\partial y}\right)^2},\tag{5.33}$$

$$\psi = \arg\left(\frac{\partial g}{\partial x}, \frac{\partial g}{\partial y}\right),\tag{5.34}$$

where $\arg(x, y)$ is the angle (in radians) from the x axis to (x, y). Sometimes we are interested only in edge magnitudes without regard to their orientations—a linear differential operator called the **Laplacian** may then be used. The Laplacian has the same properties in all directions and is therefore invariant to rotation. It is defined as

$$\nabla^2 g(x,y) = \frac{\partial^2 g(x,y)}{\partial x^2} + \frac{\partial^2 g(x,y)}{\partial y^2}.\tag{5.35}$$

Image **sharpening** [Rosenfeld and Kak, 1982] has the objective of making edges steeper—the sharpened image is intended to be observed by a human. The sharpened output image f is obtained from the input image g as

$$f(i,j) = g(i,j) - C\,S(i,j),\tag{5.36}$$

where C is a positive coefficient which gives the strength of sharpening and $S(i, j)$ is a measure of the image function sheerness, calculated using a gradient operator. The Laplacian is very often used for this purpose. Figure 5.18 gives an example of image sharpening using a Laplacian.

Image sharpening can be interpreted in the frequency domain as well. We know that the result of the Fourier transform is a combination of harmonic functions. The derivative of the harmonic function $\sin(nx)$ is $n\cos(nx)$; thus the higher the frequency, the higher the magnitude of its derivative.

A similar image sharpening technique to that of equation (5.36), called **unsharp masking**, is often used in printing industry applications [Jain, 1989]. A signal proportional to an unsharp (e.g., heavily blurred by a smoothing operator) image is subtracted from the original image. A digital image is discrete in nature and so equations (5.33) and (5.34), containing derivatives, must be approximated by **differences**. The first differences of the image g in the vertical direction (for fixed i) and in the horizontal direction (for fixed j) are given by

$$\Delta_i\, g(i,j) = g(i,j) - g(i - n, j),$$
$$\Delta_j\, g(i,j) = g(i,j) - g(i, j - n),\tag{5.37}$$

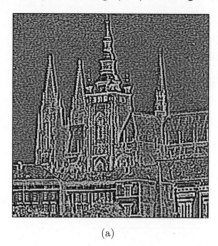

(a)   (b)

Figure 5.18: Laplace gradient operator. (a) Laplace edge image using the 8-connectivity mask. (b) Sharpening using the Laplace operator (equation 5.36, $C = 0.7$). Compare the sharpening effect with the original image in Figure 5.9a. © *Cengage Learning 2015*.

where n is a small integer, usually 1. The value n should be chosen small enough to provide a good approximation to the derivative, but large enough to neglect unimportant changes in the image function. Symmetric expressions for the differences,

$$\Delta_i\, g(i,j) = g(i+n, j) - g(i-n, j)\,,$$
$$\Delta_j\, g(i,j) = g(i, j+n) - g(i, j-n)\,,$$

(5.38)

are not usually used because they neglect the impact of the pixel (i, j) itself.

Gradient operators as a measure of edge sheerness can be divided into three categories:

1. Operators approximating derivatives of the image function using differences. Some are rotationally invariant (e.g., Laplacian) and thus are computed from one convolution mask only. Others, which approximate first derivatives, use several masks. The orientation is estimated on the basis of the best matching of several simple patterns.

2. Operators based on zero-crossings of the image function second derivative (e.g., Marr-Hildreth or Canny edge detectors).

3. Operators which attempt to match an image function to a parametric model of edges.

The remainder of this section will consider some of the many operators which fall into the first category, and the next section will consider the second. The last category is briefly outlined in Section 5.3.6.

Edge detection is an extremely important step facilitating higher-level image analysis and remains an area of active research. Examples of the variety of approaches found in current literature are fuzzy logic, neural networks, or wavelets. It may be difficult to select the most appropriate edge detection strategy; some comparisons of edge detection approaches and an assessment of their performance may be found in [Ramesh and Haralick, 1994; Demigny et al., 1995; Senthilkumaran and Rajesh, 2009].

Individual gradient operators that examine small local neighborhoods are in fact convolutions (cf. equation 5.23), and can be expressed by convolution masks. Operators which are able to detect edge direction are represented by a collection of masks, each corresponding to a certain direction.

Roberts operator

The Roberts operator is one of the oldest [Roberts, 1965], and is very easy to compute as it uses only a 2×2 neighborhood of the current pixel. Its masks are

$$h_1 = \begin{bmatrix} 1 & 0 \\ 0 & -1 \end{bmatrix}, \qquad h_2 = \begin{bmatrix} 0 & 1 \\ -1 & 0 \end{bmatrix}, \tag{5.39}$$

so the magnitude of the edge is computed as

$$\left| g(i, j) - g(i + 1, j + 1) \right| + \left| g(i, j + 1) - g(i + 1, j) \right|. \tag{5.40}$$

The primary disadvantage of the Roberts operator is its high sensitivity to noise, because very few pixels are used to approximate the gradient.

Laplace operator

The Laplace operator ∇^2 is a very popular operator approximating the second derivative which gives the edge magnitude only. The Laplacian, equation (5.35), is approximated in digital images by a convolution sum. A 3×3 mask h is often used; for 4-neighborhoods and 8-neighborhoods it is defined as

$$h = \begin{bmatrix} 0 & 1 & 0 \\ 1 & -4 & 1 \\ 0 & 1 & 0 \end{bmatrix}, \qquad h = \begin{bmatrix} 1 & 1 & 1 \\ 1 & -8 & 1 \\ 1 & 1 & 1 \end{bmatrix}. \tag{5.41}$$

A Laplacian operator with stressed significance of the central pixel or its neighborhood is sometimes used. In this approximation it loses invariance to rotation

$$h = \begin{bmatrix} 2 & -1 & 2 \\ -1 & -4 & -1 \\ 2 & -1 & 2 \end{bmatrix}, \qquad h = \begin{bmatrix} -1 & 2 & -1 \\ 2 & -4 & 2 \\ -1 & 2 & -1 \end{bmatrix}. \tag{5.42}$$

The Laplacian operator has a disadvantage—it responds doubly to some edges in the image.

Prewitt operator

The Prewitt operator, similarly to the Sobel, Kirsch, and some other operators, approximates the first derivative. The gradient is estimated in eight (for a 3×3 convolution mask) possible directions, and the convolution result of greatest magnitude indicates the gradient direction. Larger masks are possible. We present only the first three 3×3 masks for each operator; the others can be created by simple rotation.

$$h_1 = \begin{bmatrix} 1 & 1 & 1 \\ 0 & 0 & 0 \\ -1 & -1 & -1 \end{bmatrix}, \quad h_2 = \begin{bmatrix} 0 & 1 & 1 \\ -1 & 0 & 1 \\ -1 & -1 & 0 \end{bmatrix}, \quad h_3 = \begin{bmatrix} -1 & 0 & 1 \\ -1 & 0 & 1 \\ -1 & 0 & 1 \end{bmatrix}, \quad \ldots \tag{5.43}$$

The direction of the gradient is given by the mask giving maximal response. This is also the case for all the following operators approximating the first derivative.

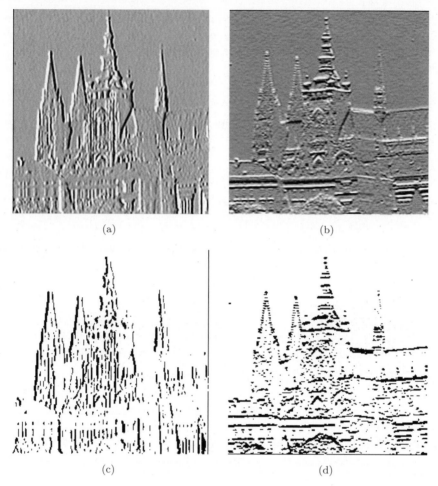

Figure 5.19: First-derivative edge detection using Prewitt operators. (a) North direction (the brighter the pixel value, the stronger the edge). (b) East direction. (c) Strong edges from (a). (d) Strong edges from (b). © *Cengage Learning 2015.*

Sobel operator

$$h_1 = \begin{bmatrix} 1 & 2 & 1 \\ 0 & 0 & 0 \\ -1 & -2 & -1 \end{bmatrix}, \quad h_2 = \begin{bmatrix} 0 & 1 & 2 \\ -1 & 0 & 1 \\ -2 & -1 & 0 \end{bmatrix}, \quad h_3 = \begin{bmatrix} -1 & 0 & 1 \\ -2 & 0 & 2 \\ -1 & 0 & 1 \end{bmatrix}, \quad \dots \quad (5.44)$$

The Sobel operator is often used as a simple detector of horizontality and verticality of edges, in which case only masks h_1 and h_3 are used. If the h_1 response is y and the h_3 response x, we might then derive edge strength (magnitude) as

$$\sqrt{x^2 + y^2} \qquad \text{or} \qquad |x| + |y| \qquad (5.45)$$

and direction as $\arctan(y/x)$.

Kirsch operator

$$h_1 = \begin{bmatrix} 3 & 3 & 3 \\ 3 & 0 & 3 \\ -5 & -5 & -5 \end{bmatrix}, \quad h_2 = \begin{bmatrix} 3 & 3 & 3 \\ -5 & 0 & 3 \\ -5 & -5 & 3 \end{bmatrix}, \quad h_3 = \begin{bmatrix} -5 & 3 & 3 \\ -5 & 0 & 3 \\ -5 & 3 & 3 \end{bmatrix}, \quad \ldots \quad (5.46)$$

To illustrate the application of gradient operators on real images, consider again the image given in Figure 5.9a. The Laplace edge image calculated is shown in Figure 5.18a; the value of the operator has been histogram equalized to enhance its visibility.

The properties of an operator approximating the first derivative are demonstrated using the Prewitt operator—results of others are similar. The original image is again given in Figure 5.9a; Prewitt approximations to the directional gradients are in Figures 5.19a,b, in which north and east directions are shown. Significant edges (those with above-threshold magnitude) in the two directions are given in Figures 5.19c,d.

5.3.3   Zero-crossings of the second derivative

In the 1970s, Marr's theory (see Section 11.1.1) concluded from neurophysiological experiments that object boundaries are the most important cues that link an intensity image with its interpretation. Edge detection techniques existing at that time (e.g., the Kirsch, Sobel, and Pratt operators) were based on convolution in very small neighborhoods and worked well only for specific images. The main disadvantage of these edge detectors is their dependence on the size of the object and sensitivity to noise.

An edge detection technique based on the **zero-crossings** of the second derivative (in its original form, the **Marr-Hildreth** edge detector [Marr and Hildreth, 1980, 1991] explores the fact that a step edge corresponds to an abrupt change in the image function. The first derivative of the image function should have an extremum at the position corresponding to the edge in the image, and so the second derivative should be zero at the same position; however, it is much easier and more precise to find a zero-crossing position than an extremum. In Figure 5.20 this principle is illustrated in 1D for the sake of simplicity. Figure 5.20a shows step edge profiles of the original image function with two different slopes, Figure 5.20b depicts the first derivative of the image function, and Figure 5.20c illustrates the second derivative; notice that this crosses the zero level at the same position as the edge.

Considering a step-like edge in 2D, the 1D profile of Figure 5.20a corresponds to a cross section through the 2D step. The steepness of the profile will change if the

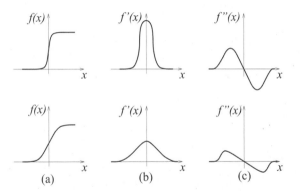

Figure 5.20: 1D edge profile of the zero-crossing. © *Cengage Learning 2015.*

orientation of the cutting plane changes—the maximum steepness is observed when the plane is perpendicular to the edge direction.

The crucial question is how to compute the second derivative robustly. One possibility is to smooth an image first (to reduce noise) and then compute second derivatives. When choosing a smoothing filter, there are two criteria that should be fulfilled [Marr and Hildreth, 1980]. First, the filter should be smooth and roughly band limited in the frequency domain to reduce the possible number of frequencies at which function changes can take place. Second, the constraint of spatial localization requires the response of a filter to be from nearby points in the image. These two criteria are conflicting, but they can be optimized simultaneously using a Gaussian distribution. In practice, one has to be more precise about what is meant by the localization performance of an operator, and the Gaussian may turn out to be suboptimal. We shall consider this in the next section.

The 2D Gaussian smoothing operator $G(x, y)$ (also called a Gaussian filter, or simply a Gaussian) is given by

$$G(x, y) = e^{-(x^2+y^2)/2\sigma^2} , \tag{5.47}$$

where x, y are the image co-ordinates and σ is a standard deviation of the associated probability distribution. Sometimes this is presented with a normalizing factor

$$G(x, y) = \frac{1}{2\pi\sigma^2} e^{-(x^2+y^2)/2\sigma^2} \quad \text{or} \quad G(x, y) = \frac{1}{\sqrt{2\pi}\,\sigma} e^{-(x^2+y^2)/2\sigma^2} .$$

The standard deviation σ is the only parameter of the Gaussian filter—it is proportional to the size of the neighborhood on which the filter operates. Pixels more distant from the center of the operator have smaller influence, and pixels farther than 3σ from the center have negligible influence.

Our goal is to obtain a second derivative of a smoothed 2D function $f(x, y)$. We have already seen that the Laplace operator ∇^2 gives the second derivative, and is non-directional (isotropic). Consider then the Laplacian of an image $f(x, y)$ smoothed by a Gaussian (expressed using a convolution $*$). The operation is often abbreviated as **LoG**, from **Laplacian of Gaussian**

$$\nabla^2 \big[G(x, y, \sigma) * f(x, y)\big] . \tag{5.48}$$

The order of performing differentiation and convolution can be interchanged because of the linearity of the operators involved

$$\big[\nabla^2 G(x, y, \sigma)\big] * f(x, y) . \tag{5.49}$$

The derivative of the Gaussian filter $\nabla^2 G$ can be pre-computed analytically, since it is independent of the image under consideration, and so the complexity of the composite operation is reduced. From equation (5.47), we see

$$\frac{\partial G}{\partial x} = -\left(\frac{x}{\sigma^2}\right) e^{-(x^2+y^2)/2\sigma^2} ,$$

and similarly for y. Hence

$$\frac{\partial^2 G}{\partial x^2} = \frac{1}{\sigma^2}\left(\frac{x^2}{\sigma^2} - 1\right) e^{-(x^2+y^2)/2\sigma^2} , \quad \frac{\partial^2 G}{\partial y^2} = \frac{1}{\sigma^2}\left(\frac{y^2}{\sigma^2} - 1\right) e^{-(x^2+y^2)/2\sigma^2}$$

and so

$$\nabla^2 G(x, y, \sigma) = \frac{1}{\sigma^2} \left(\frac{x^2 + y^2}{\sigma^2} - 2 \right) e^{-(x^2+y^2)/2\sigma^2} .$$

After introducing a normalizing multiplicative coefficient c, we get a convolution mask of a LoG operator:

$$h(x, y) = c \left(\frac{x^2 + y^2 - 2\sigma^2}{\sigma^4} \right) e^{-(x^2+y^2)/2\sigma^2} , \qquad (5.50)$$

where c normalizes the sum of mask elements to zero. Because of its shape, the inverted LoG operator is commonly called a **Mexican hat**. An example of a 5×5 discrete approximation [Jain et al., 1995] (wherein a 17×17 mask is also given) is

$$\begin{bmatrix} 0 & 0 & -1 & 0 & 0 \\ 0 & -1 & -2 & -1 & 0 \\ -1 & -2 & 16 & -2 & -1 \\ 0 & -1 & -2 & -1 & 0 \\ 0 & 0 & -1 & 0 & 0 \end{bmatrix} .$$

Of course, these masks represent truncated and discrete representations of infinite continuous functions, and care should be taken in avoiding errors in moving to this representation [Gunn, 1999].

Finding second derivatives in this way is very robust. Gaussian smoothing effectively suppresses the influence of the pixels that are more than a distance 3σ from the current pixel; then the Laplace operator is an efficient and stable measure of changes in the image.

After image convolution with $\nabla^2 G$, the locations in the convolved image where the zero level is crossed correspond to the positions of edges. The advantage of this approach compared to classical edge operators of small size is that a larger area surrounding the current pixel is taken into account; the influence of more distant points decreases according to the σ of the Gaussian. In the ideal case of an isolated step edge, the σ variation does not affect the location of the zero-crossing.

Convolution masks become large for larger σ; for example, $\sigma = 4$ needs a mask about 40 pixels wide. Fortunately, there is a separable decomposition of the $\nabla^2 G$ operator [Huertas and Medioni, 1986] that can speed up computation considerably.

The practical implication of Gaussian smoothing is that edges are found reliably. If only globally significant edges are required, the standard deviation σ of the Gaussian smoothing filter may be increased, having the effect of suppressing less significant evidence.

The $\nabla^2 G$ operator can be very effectively approximated by convolution with a mask that is the difference of two Gaussian averaging masks with substantially different σ—this method is called the **difference of Gaussians**, abbreviated as **DoG**. The correct ratio of the standard deviations σ of the Gaussian filters is discussed in [Marr, 1982].

When implementing a zero-crossing edge detector, trying to detect *zeros* in the LoG or DoG image will inevitably fail, while naive approaches of thresholding the LoG/DoG image and defining the zero-crossings in some interval of values close to zero give piecewise disconnected edges at best. To create a well-functioning second-derivative edge detector, it is necessary to implement a true zero-crossing detector. A simple detector may identify a zero-crossing in a moving 2×2 window, assigning an edge label to any one corner pixel, say the upper left, if LoG/DoG image values of both polarities occur in the 2×2 window; no edge label would be given if values within the window are either all positive or all negative. Another post-processing step to avoid detection of zero-crossings corresponding to non-significant edges in regions of almost constant gray-level would admit only those zero-crossings for which there is sufficient edge evidence from a first-derivative edge detector. Figure 5.21 provides several examples of edge detection using zero crossings of the second derivative.

Many other approaches improving zero-crossing performance can be found in the literature [Qian and Huang, 1994; Mehrotra and Shiming, 1996]; some of them are used in pre-processing [Hardie and Boncelet, 1995] or post-processing steps [Alparone et al., 1996]. The traditional second-derivative zero-crossing technique has disadvantages as

(a)   (b)

(c)   (d)

Figure 5.21: Zero-crossings of the second derivative, see Figure 5.9a for the original image. (a) DoG image ($\sigma_1 = 0.10, \sigma_2 = 0.09$), dark pixels correspond to negative values, bright pixels to positive. (b) Zero-crossings of the DoG image. (c) DoG zero-crossing edges after removing edges lacking first-derivative support. (d) LoG zero-crossing edges ($\sigma = 0.20$) after removing edges lacking first-derivative support—note different scale of edges due to different Gaussian smoothing parameters. © *Cengage Learning 2015*.

well. First, it smooths the shape too much; for example, sharp corners are lost. Second, it tends to create closed loops of edges (nicknamed the 'plate of spaghetti' effect).

Neurophysiological experiments [Marr, 1982; Ullman, 1981] provide evidence that the human eye retina in the form of the **ganglion cells** performs operations very similar to the $\nabla^2 G$ operations. Each such cell responds to light stimuli in a local neighborhood called the **receptive field**, which has a center-surround organization of two complementary types, off-center and on-center. When a light stimulus occurs, activity of on-center cells increases and that of off-center cells is inhibited. The retinal operation on the image can be described analytically as the convolution of the image with the $\nabla^2 G$ operator.

5.3.4   Scale in image processing

Many image processing techniques work locally, theoretically at the level of individual pixels—edge detection methods are an example. The essential problem in such computation is **scale**. Edges correspond to the gradient of the image function, which is computed as a difference between pixels in some neighborhood. There is seldom a sound reason for choosing a particular size of neighborhood, since the 'right' size depends on the size of the objects under investigation. To know what the objects are assumes that it is clear how to interpret an image, and this is not in general known at the pre-processing stage. The solution to the problem formulated above is a special case of a general paradigm called the **system approach**. This methodology is common in cybernetics or general system theory to study complex phenomena.

The phenomenon under investigation is expressed at different resolutions of the description, and a formal model is created at each resolution. Then the qualitative behavior of the model is studied under changing resolution of the description. Such a methodology enables the deduction of meta-knowledge about the phenomenon that is not seen at the individual description levels.

Different description levels are easily interpreted as different scales in the domain of digital images. The idea of scale is fundamental to Marr's edge detection technique, introduced in Section 5.3.3, where different scales are provided by different sizes of Gaussian filter masks. The aim was not only to eliminate fine scale noise but also to separate events at different scales arising from distinct physical processes [Marr, 1982].

Assume that a signal has been smoothed with several masks of variable sizes. Every setting of the scale parameters implies a different description, but it is not known which one is correct; for many tasks, no one scale is categorically correct. If the ambiguity introduced by the scale is inescapable, the goal of scale-independent description is to reduce this ambiguity as much as possible. Here we shall consider just three examples of the application of multiple scale description to image analysis.

The first approach [Lowe, 1989] aims to process planar noisy curves at a range of scales—the segment of curve that represents the underlying structure of the scene needs to be found. The problem is illustrated by an example of two noisy curves; see Figure 5.22. One of these may be interpreted as a closed (perhaps circular) curve, while the other could be described as two intersecting straight lines.

Local tangent direction and curvature of the curve are significant only with some idea of scale after the curve is smoothed by a Gaussian filter with varying standard deviations.

A second approach [Witkin, 1983], called **scale-space filtering**, tries to describe signals qualitatively with respect to scale. The problem was formulated for 1D signals $f(x)$, but it can easily be generalized for 2D functions as images. The original 1D signal

Figure 5.22: Curves that may be analyzed at multiple scales. © *Cengage Learning 2015.*

$f(x)$ is smoothed by convolution with a 1D Gaussian

$$G(x, \sigma) = e^{-x^2/2\sigma^2} \ . \tag{5.51}$$

If the standard deviation σ is slowly changed, the function

$$F(x, \sigma) = f(x) * G(x, \sigma) \tag{5.52}$$

represents a surface on the (x, σ) plane that is called the **scale-space image**. Inflexion points of the curve $F(x, \sigma_0)$ for a distinct value σ_0

$$\frac{\partial^2 F(x, \sigma_0)}{\partial x^2} = 0 \quad \text{and} \quad \frac{\partial^3 F(x, \sigma_0)}{\partial x^3} \neq 0 \tag{5.53}$$

describe the curve $f(x)$ qualitatively. The positions of inflexion points can be drawn as a set of curves in (x, σ) co-ordinates (see Figure 8.16). Coarse to fine analysis of the curves corresponding to inflexion points, i.e., in the direction of decreasing value of the σ, localizes large-scale events.

The qualitative information contained in the scale-space image can be transformed into a simple **interval tree** that expresses the structure of the signal $f(x)$ over all observed scales. The interval tree is built from the root that corresponds to the largest scale $(\sigma_{\max})$, and then the scale-space image is searched in the direction of decreasing σ. The interval tree branches at those points where new curves corresponding to inflexion points appear (see Chapter 8 and Section 8.2.4).

The third example of the application of scale is that used by the popular **Canny edge detector**. Since the Canny detector is a significant and widely used contribution to edge detection techniques, its principles will be explained in detail.

5.3.5   Canny edge detection

Canny proposed an approach to edge detection [Canny, 1986] that is optimal for step edges corrupted by white noise. The optimality of the detector is related to three criteria.

- The **detection** criterion expresses the fact that important edges should not be missed and that there should be no spurious responses.

- The **localization** criterion says that the distance between the actual and located position of the edge should be minimal.

- The **one response** criterion minimizes multiple responses to a single edge. This is partly covered by the first criterion, since when there are two responses to a single edge, one of them should be considered as false. This third criterion solves the problem of an edge corrupted by noise and works against non-smooth edge operators [Rosenfeld and Thurston, 1971].

Canny's derivation is based on several ideas.

1. The edge detector was expressed for a 1D signal and the first two optimality criteria. A closed-form solution was found using the calculus of variations.

2. If the third criterion (multiple responses) is added, the best solution may be found by numerical optimization. The resulting filter can be approximated effectively with error less than 20% by the first derivative of a Gaussian smoothing filter with standard deviation σ [Canny, 1986]; the reason for doing this is the existence of an effective implementation. There is a strong similarity here to the LoG based Marr-Hildreth edge detector [Marr and Hildreth, 1980], see Section 5.3.3.

3. The detector is then generalized to two dimensions. A step edge is given by its position, orientation, and possibly magnitude (strength). It can be shown that convolving an image with a symmetric 2D Gaussian and then differentiating in the direction of the gradient (perpendicular to the edge direction) forms a simple and effective directional operator (recall that the Marr-Hildreth zero-crossing operator does not give information about edge direction, as it uses a Laplacian filter).

Suppose G is a 2D Gaussian [equation (5.47)] and assume we wish to convolve the image with an operator G_n which is a first derivative of G in some direction $\mathbf{n}$

$$G_n = \frac{\partial G}{\partial \mathbf{n}} = \mathbf{n}\,\nabla G\,. \tag{5.54}$$

We would like $\mathbf{n}$ to be perpendicular to the edge: this direction is not known in advance, but a robust estimate of it based on the smoothed gradient direction is available. If f is the image, the normal to the edge $\mathbf{n}$ is estimated as

$$\mathbf{n} = \frac{\nabla(G * f)}{\left|\nabla(G * f)\right|}\,. \tag{5.55}$$

The edge location is then at the local maximum of the image f convolved with the operator G_n in the direction $\mathbf{n}$

$$\frac{\partial}{\partial \mathbf{n}}\,G_n * f = 0\,. \tag{5.56}$$

Substituting in equation (5.56) for G_n from equation (5.54), we get

$$\frac{\partial^2}{\partial \mathbf{n}^2}\,G * f = 0\,. \tag{5.57}$$

This equation (5.57) illustrates how to find local maxima in the direction perpendicular to the edge; this operation is often referred to as **non-maximal suppression** (see also Algorithm 6.4).

As the convolution and derivative are associative operations in equation (5.57), we can first convolve an image f with a symmetric Gaussian G and then compute the directional second-derivative using an estimate of the direction $\mathbf{n}$ computed according to equation (5.55). The strength of the edge (magnitude of the gradient of the image intensity function f) is measured as

$$\left|G_n * f\right| = \left|\nabla(G * f)\right|\,. \tag{5.58}$$

4. Spurious responses to a single edge caused by noise usually create a 'streaking' problem that is very common in edge detection in general. The output of an edge detector is usually thresholded to decide which edges are significant, and streaking may break up edge contours as the operator fluctuates above and below the threshold. Streaking can be eliminated by **thresholding with hysteresis**, employing a hard (high) threshold and a soft (lower) threshold—see Algorithm 6.5. The low and high thresholds are set according to an estimated signal-to-noise ratio [Canny, 1986].

5. The correct scale for the operator depends on the objects contained in the image. The solution to this unknown is to use multiple scales and aggregate information from them. Different scales for the Canny detector are represented by different standard deviations σ of the Gaussians. There may be several scales of operators that give significant responses to edges (i.e., signal-to-noise ratio above the threshold); in this case the operator with the smallest scale is chosen, as it gives the best localization of the edge.

Canny proposed a **feature synthesis** approach. All significant edges from the operator with the smallest scale are marked first, and the edges of a hypothetical operator with larger σ are synthesized from them (i.e., a prediction is made of how the large σ should perform on the evidence gleaned from the smaller σ—see also Section 5.3.4 and Figure 8.16). Then the synthesized edge response is compared with the actual edge response for larger σ. Additional edges are marked only if they have a significantly stronger response than that predicted from synthetic output.

This procedure may be repeated for a sequence of scales, a cumulative edge map being built by adding those edges that were not identified at smaller scales.

Algorithm 5.4: Canny edge detector

1. Convolve an image f with a Gaussian of scale σ.

2. Estimate local edge normal directions $\mathbf{n}$ using equation (5.55) for each pixel in the image.

3. Find the location of the edges using equation (5.57) (non-maximal suppression).

4. Compute the magnitude of the edge using equation (5.58).

5. Threshold edges in the image with hysteresis (Algorithm 6.5) to eliminate spurious responses.

6. Repeat steps (1) through (5) for ascending values of the standard deviation σ.

7. Aggregate the final information about edges at multiple scale using the 'feature synthesis' approach.

Figure 5.23a shows the edges of Figure 5.9a detected by a Canny operator with $\sigma = 1.0$. Figure 5.23b shows the edge detector response for $\sigma = 2.8$ (feature synthesis has not been applied here).

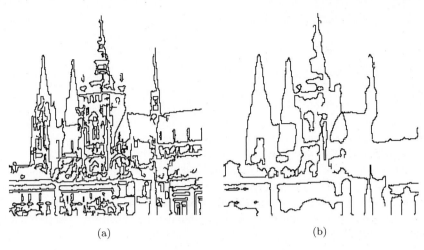

(a)   (b)

Figure 5.23: Canny edge detection at two different scales. © *Cengage Learning 2015*.

Canny's detector represents a complicated but major contribution to edge detection. Its full implementation is unusual, it being common to find implementations that omit feature synthesis—that is, just steps 1–5 of Algorithm 5.4.

5.3.6 Parametric edge models

Parametric models are based on the idea that the discrete image intensity function can be considered a sampled and noisy approximation of an underlying continuous or piecewise continuous image intensity function [Nevatia, 1977]. While this function is not known, it can be estimated from the available discrete image intensity function and image properties can be determined from this continuous estimate, possibly with subpixel precision. It is usually impossible to represent image intensities using a single continuous function since a single function leads to high-order intensity functions in x and y. Instead, piecewise continuous function estimates called **facets** are used to represent (a neighborhood of) each image pixel. Such an image representation is called a **facet model** [Haralick and Watson, 1981; Haralick, 1984; Haralick and Shapiro, 1992].

The intensity function in a neighborhood can be estimated using models of different complexity. The simplest one is the flat facet model that uses piecewise constants and each pixel neighborhood is represented by a flat function of constant intensity. The sloped model uses piecewise linear functions forming a sloped plane fitted to local image intensities. Quadratic and bi-cubic facet models employ correspondingly more complex functions.

Once the facet model parameters are available for each image pixel, edges can be detected as extrema of the first directional derivative and/or zero-crossings of the second directional derivative of the local continuous facet model functions.

A thorough treatment of facet models and their modifications for peak noise removal, segmentation into constant-gray-level regions, determination of statistically significant edges, gradient edge detection, directional second-derivative zero-crossing edge detection, and line and corner detection is given in [Haralick and Shapiro, 1992]. Importantly, techniques for facet model parameter estimation are given there.

An example will illustrate: consider a bi-cubic facet model

$$g(i,j) = c_1 + c_2\, x + c_3\, y + c_4\, x^2 + c_5\, x\, y + c_6\, y^2 + c_7\, x^3 + c_8\, x^2\, y + c_9\, x\, y^2 + c_{10}\, y^3 , \quad (5.59)$$

whose parameters are estimated from a pixel neighborhood (the co-ordinates of the central pixel are $(0,0)$). This may be performed by, e.g., a least-squares method with SVD (Section 3.2.9); alternatively, coefficients c_i can be computed directly using a set of ten 5×5 kernels that are provided in [Haralick and Shapiro, 1992]. Once parameters are available at each pixel, edges may be located as extrema of the first directional derivative, or zero crossings of the second derivative, of the local facet model functions.

Edge detectors based on parametric models describe edges more precisely than convolution-based edge detectors. Additionally, they carry the potential for subpixel edge localization. However, their computational requirements are much higher. Promising extensions combine facet models with Canny's edge detection criteria (Section 5.3.5) and relaxation labeling (Section 6.2.2) [Matalas et al., 1997].

5.3.7   Edges in multi-spectral images

One pixel in a multi-spectral image is described by an n-dimensional vector, and brightness values in n spectral bands are the vector components. There are several possibilities for the detection of edges in multi-spectral images [Faugeras, 1993].

Trivially, we might detect edges separately in individual image spectral components using the ordinary local gradient operators mentioned in Section 5.3.2. Individual images of edges can be combined to get the resulting image, with the value corresponding to edge magnitude and direction being a selection or combination of the individual edge spectral components [Nagao and Matsuyama, 1980].

Alternatively, we may create a multi-spectral edge detector which uses brightness information from all n spectral bands; this approach is also applicable to multi-dimensional images forming three- or higher-dimensional data volumes. An edge detector of this kind was proposed in [Cervenka and Charvat, 1987]. The neighborhood used has size $2 \times 2 \times n$ pixels, where the 2×2 neighborhood is similar to that of the Roberts gradient, equation (5.39). The coefficients weighting the influence of the component pixels are similar to the correlation coefficients. Let $\overline{f}(i,j)$ denote the arithmetic mean of the brightnesses corresponding to the pixels with the same co-ordinates (i,j) in all n spectral component images, and f_r be the brightness of the rth spectral component. The edge detector result in pixel (i,j) is given as the minimum of the following expression:

$$\frac{\sum_{r=1}^{n} \left[d(i,j) \right] \left[d(i+1,j+1) \right]}{\sqrt{\sum_{r=1}^{n} \left[d(i,j) \right]^2 \sum_{r=1}^{n} \left[d(i+1,j+1) \right]^2}} \quad \frac{\sum_{r=1}^{n} \left[d(i+1,j) \right] \left[d(i,j+1) \right]}{\sqrt{\sum_{r=1}^{n} \left[d(i+1,j) \right]^2 \sum_{r=1}^{n} \left[d(i,j+1) \right]^2}} ,$$

where $\quad d(k,l) = f_r(k,l) - \overline{f}(k,l) .$

$$(5.60)$$

5.3.8   Local pre-processing in the frequency domain

Section 3.2.4 noted that the Fourier transform makes convolution of two images in the frequency domain very easy, and it is natural to consider applying many of the filters of Sections 5.3 in the frequency domain. Such operations are usually called **spatial frequency filtering**.

Assume that f is an input image and F is its Fourier transform. A convolution filter h can be represented by its Fourier transform H; h may be called the unit pulse response of the filter and H the frequency transfer function, and either of the representations h or H can be used to describe the filter. The Fourier transform of the filter output after an image f has been convolved with the filter h can be computed in the frequency domain

$$G = F .* ,\qquad(5.61)$$

where $.*$ represents an element-by-element multiplication of matrices F and H (not matrix multiplication). The filtered image g can be obtained by applying the inverse Fourier transform to $\mathbf{G}$—equation (3.28).

Some basic examples of spatial filtering are linear **low-pass**, **high-pass**, and **band-pass** frequency filters.

- A low-pass filter is defined by a frequency transfer function $H(u, v)$ with small values at points located far from the co-ordinate origin in the frequency domain (that is, small transfer values for high spatial frequencies) and large values at points close to the origin (large transfer values for low spatial frequencies)—see Figure 5.24a. It preserves low spatial frequencies and suppresses high spatial frequencies, and has behavior similar to smoothing by standard averaging—it blurs sharp edges.

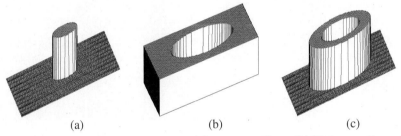

(a) (b) (c)

Figure 5.24: Frequency filters displayed in 3D. (a) Low-pass filter. (b) High-pass filter. (c) Band-pass filter. © *Cengage Learning 2015.*

- A high-pass filter is defined by small transfer function values located around the frequency co-ordinate system origin, and larger values outside this area—larger transfer coefficients for higher frequencies (Figure 5.24b).

- Band-pass filters, which select frequencies in a certain range for enhancement, are constructed in a similar way, and also filters with directional response, etc. (Figure 5.24c).

The most common image enhancement problems include noise suppression, edge enhancement, and removal of noise which is structured in the frequency spectrum. Noise represents a high-frequency image component, and it may be suppressed applying a low-pass filter as shown in Figure 5.25, which demonstrates the principles of frequency filtering on Fourier image spectra; the original image spectrum is multiplied by the filter spectrum and a low-frequency image spectrum results. Unfortunately, all high-frequency phenomena are suppressed, including high frequencies that are not related to noise (sharp edges, lines, etc.). Low-pass filtering results in a blurred image.

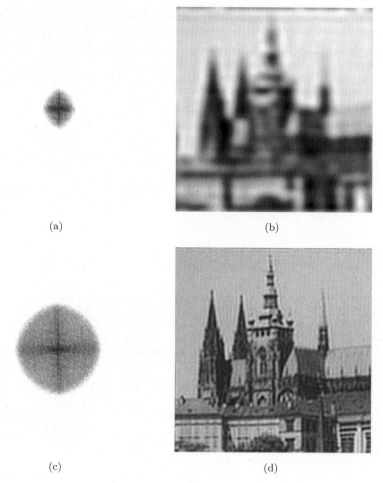

(a)

(b)

(c)

(d)

Figure 5.25: Low-pass frequency-domain filtering—for the original image and its spectrum see Figure 3.7. (a) Spectrum of a low-pass filtered image, all higher frequencies filtered out. (b) Image resulting from the inverse Fourier transform applied to spectrum (a). (c) Spectrum of a low-pass filtered image, only very high frequencies filtered out. (d) Inverse Fourier transform applied to spectrum (c). © *Cengage Learning 2015*.

Again, edges represent a high-frequency image phenomenon. Therefore, to enhance them, low-frequency components of the image spectrum must be suppressed—to achieve this, a high-frequency filter must be applied.

To remove noise which is structured in the frequency domain, the filter design must include a priori knowledge about the noise properties. This knowledge may be acquired either from the image data or from the corrupted image Fourier spectrum, where the structured noise usually causes notable peaks.

Some examples of frequency domain image filtering are shown in Figures 5.25–5.28. The original image was shown in Figure 3.8 and its frequency spectrum in Figure 3.7. Figure 5.26 shows results after application of a high-pass filter followed by an inverse Fourier transform. It can be seen that edges represent high-frequency phenomena in the image. Results of band-pass filtering can be seen in Figure 5.27. Figure 5.28 gives

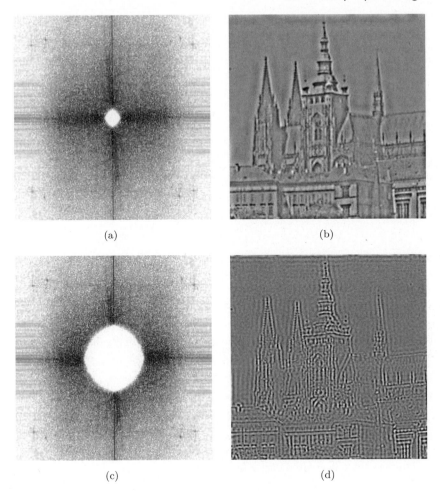

(a)

(b)

(c)

(d)

Figure 5.26: High-pass frequency domain filtering. (a) Spectrum of a high-pass filtered image, only very low frequencies filtered out. (b) Image resulting from the inverse Fourier transform applied to spectrum (a). (c) Spectrum of a high-pass filtered image, all lower frequencies filtered out. (d) Inverse Fourier transform applied to spectrum (c). © *Cengage Learning 2015*.

an even more powerful example of frequency filtering—removal of periodic noise. The vertical noise lines in the original image are transformed into frequency spectrum peaks after the transform. To remove these frequencies, a filter was designed which suppresses the periodic noise in the image, which is visible as white circular areas.

There are several filters which prove useful for filtering in the frequency domain: two important representatives of them are the Gaussian and Butterworth filters. Choose an isotropic filter for simplicity, $D(u, v) = D(r) = \sqrt{u^2 + v^2}$, and let D_0 be a parameter of the filter called the cut-off frequency. For the Gaussian, D_0 coincides with the dispersion σ. The Fourier spectrum of a low-pass Gaussian filter G_{low} is

$$G_{\text{low}}(u, v) = \exp\left(-\frac{1}{2}\left(\frac{D(u, v)}{D_0}\right)^2\right). \tag{5.62}$$

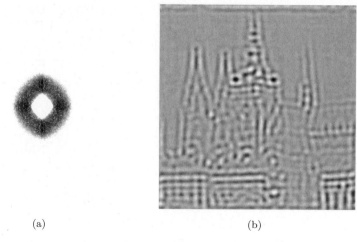

(a)   (b)

Figure 5.27: Band-pass frequency domain filtering. (a) Spectrum of a band-pass-filtered image, low and high frequencies filtered out. (b) Image resulting from the inverse Fourier transform applied to spectrum (a). © *Cengage Learning 2015*.

The Butterworth filter [Butterworth, 1930] is specified to have maximally flat frequency response over a spectrum band, and is also called a 'maximally flat magnitude filter'. The frequency response of the 2D low-pass Butterworth filter B_{low} of degree n is

$$B_{\text{low}} = \frac{1}{1 + \left(\frac{D(u,v)}{D_0}\right)^n} \,. \tag{5.63}$$

The usual Butterworth filter degree is $n = 2$, which will be used here. Figure 5.29 illustrates the shape of the Gaussian and Butterworth filters for $D_0 = 3$ in 1D plots.

The high-pass filter is created easily from the low-pass filter. If the Fourier frequency spectrum of a low-pass filter is H_{low}, the high-pass filter can be created by just flipping it vertically, $H_{\text{high}} = 1 - H_{\text{low}}$.

Another useful pre-processing technique operating in the frequency domain is an instance of **homomorphic filtering**, discussed at the end of Section 5.3.1. Homomorphic filtering is used to remove multiplicative noise. The aim of the particular homomorphic filtering to be discussed here is to simultaneously increase contrast and normalize image intensity across the image.

The assumption is that the image function $f(x,y)$ can be factorized as a product of two independent multiplicative components in each pixel: illumination $i(x,y)$ and the reflectance $r(x,y)$ at the point in the observed scene, $f(x,y) = i(x,y)\,r(x,y)$. These two components can be separated in some images because the illumination component tends to vary slowly and the reflectance component varies more quickly.

The idea of the separation is to apply a logarithmic transform to the input image

$$z(x,y) = \log f(x,y) = \log i(x,y) + \log r(x,y) \,. \tag{5.64}$$

If the image $z(x,y)$ is converted to Fourier space (denoted by capital letters) then its additive components remain additive due to the linearity of the Fourier transform

$$Z(u,v) = I(u,v) + R(u,v) \,. \tag{5.65}$$

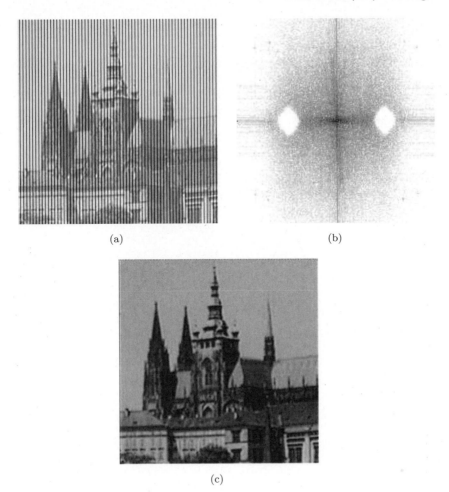

(a)

(b)

(c)

Figure 5.28: Periodic noise removal. (a) Noisy image. (b) Image spectrum used for image reconstruction—note that the areas of frequencies corresponding with periodic vertical lines are filtered out. (c) Filtered image. © *Cengage Learning 2015.*

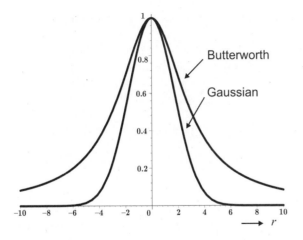

Figure 5.29: Gaussian and Butterworth low-pass filters. © *Cengage Learning 2015.*

Assume that the Fourier spectrum $Z(u,v)$ is filtered by the filter $H(u,v)$ and the spectrum $S(u,v)$ is the result

$$S = H .* Z = H .* I + H .* R . \tag{5.66}$$

Usually a high-pass filter is used for this purpose; assuming a high-pass Butterworth filter, it has to be damped in order not to suppress low frequencies entirely as they bear needed information too. The Butterworth filter modified by damping coefficient 0.5 is shown in Figure 5.30.

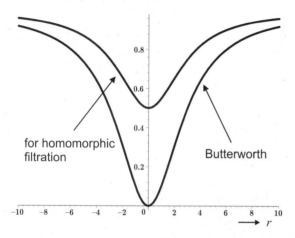

Figure 5.30: High-pass filter used in homomorphic filtering. It is a Butterworth filter damped by a 0.5 coefficients to retain some low frequencies. © *Cengage Learning 2015.*

Having the filtered spectrum $S(u,v)$, we can return to spatial coordinates using the inverse Fourier transform, $s(x,y) = \mathcal{F}^{-1}S(u,v)$. Recall that the logarithm was first applied to the input image $f(x,y)$ in equation (5.64). Now the image has to be transformed by the logarithm inverse function; this inverse function is the exponential. The result—the image $g(x,y)$ filtered by the homomorphic filter—is given by $g(x,y) = \exp\big(s(x,y)\big)$.

An illustration of the effect of homomorphic filtering is in Figure 5.31, an image of a person in a dark tunnel with strong illumination at the entrance. Detail of the tunnel surface on the top and right side are not visible because the surface is too dark. The result of homomorphic filtering is in Figure 5.31b. More details can be seen in this image.

(a)   (b)

Figure 5.31: Illustration of homomorphic filtering. (a) Original image. (b) Homomorphic filtering. *Courtesy of T. Svoboda, Czech Technical University, Prague.*

5.3 Local pre-processing   **155**

5.3.9   Line detection by local pre-processing operators

Several other local operations exist which do not belong to the taxonomy given in Section 5.3, as they are used for different purposes such as line finding, line thinning, and line filling operators. Another group of operators finds 'interest points' or 'locations of interest' in the image. Yet another class of local nonlinear operators are mathematical morphology techniques, described in Chapter 13.

It is interesting to seek features richer than edges which can be reliably detected in the image and which can outperform simple edge detectors in some classes of applications. Line detectors and corner detectors are some such. Line detectors are used to detect linear objects such as dimension lines in engineering drawings or railways or roads in satellite images. Corner detectors and other interest point-like detectors are used mainly to register two or more images one to the other (e.g, in stereo vision, motion analysis, panorama stitching, object recognition from images) or to index the image or dominant objects in it to an image database.

Line finding operators aim to find very thin curves in the image; it is assumed that curves do not bend sharply. Such curves and straight lines are called **lines** for the purpose of describing this technique. If a cross section perpendicular in direction to the tangent of a line is examined, we get a roof profile (see Figure 5.17) when examining edges. We assume that the width of the lines is approximately one or two pixels.

The presence of a line may be detected by local convolution of the image with convolution kernels which serve as line patterns [Vernon, 1991; Petrou, 1993]. The simplest collection of four such patterns of size 3×3 is able to detect lines rotated modulo the angle 45°. Three of four such convolution kernels are

$$h_1 = \begin{bmatrix} -1 & -1 & -1 \\ 2 & 2 & 2 \\ -1 & -1 & -1 \end{bmatrix} , \quad h_2 = \begin{bmatrix} 2 & -1 & -1 \\ -1 & 2 & -1 \\ -1 & -1 & 2 \end{bmatrix} , \quad h_3 = \begin{bmatrix} -1 & 2 & -1 \\ -1 & 2 & -1 \\ -1 & 2 & -1 \end{bmatrix} , \quad \dots \quad (5.67)$$

A similar principle can be applied to bigger masks. The case of 5×5 masks is common.

Such line detectors sometimes produce more lines than needed, and other non-linear constraints may be added to reduce this number. More sophisticated approaches determine lines in images as ridges and ravines using the facet model [Haralick and Shapiro, 1992]. Line detection is frequently used in remote sensing and in document processing; examples include [Venkateswar and Chellappa, 1992; Tang et al., 1997].

Local information about edges is the basis of a class of image segmentation techniques that are discussed in Chapter 6. Edges which are likely to belong to object boundaries are usually found by simple thresholding of the edge magnitude—such edge thresholding does not provide ideal contiguous boundaries that are one pixel wide. Sophisticated segmentation techniques that are dealt with in the next chapter serve this purpose. Here, much simpler edge thinning and filling methods are described. These techniques are based on knowledge of small local neighborhoods and are very similar to other local pre-processing techniques.

Thresholded edges are usually wider than one pixel, and **line thinning** techniques may give a better result. One line thinning method uses knowledge about edge orientation and in this case edges are thinned before thresholding. Edge magnitudes and directions provided by some gradient operator are used as input, and the edge magnitudes of two neighboring pixels perpendicular to the edge direction are examined for each pixel in the image. If at least one of these pixels has edge magnitude higher than the edge magnitude of the examined pixel, then the edge magnitude of the examined pixel is assigned a zero value—see Algorithm 6.4.

There are many other line thinning methods. In most cases the best results are achieved using mathematical morphology methods, explained in Chapter 13.

5.3.10   Detection of corners (interest points)

The location of points (rather than edges) in images is frequently useful, particularly when seeking correspondence—or registration—between two views of the same scene. We came across this fact in Section 5.2 when considering geometric transforms. Knowing point correspondences enables the estimation of parameters describing geometric transforms from live data. We shall see later on that finding corresponding points is also a core problem in the analysis of moving images (Chapter 16), and for recovering depth information from pairs of stereo images (Section 11.5).

In general, all possible pairs of pixels should be examined to solve this **correspondence problem**, and this is very computationally expensive. If two images have n pixels each, the complexity is $\mathcal{O}(n^2)$. This process might be simplified if the correspondence is examined among a much smaller number of points, called **interest points**. An interest point will have some local property [Ballard and Brown, 1982]. For example, if square objects are present in the image, then **corners** are very good interest points.

Corners in images can be located using local detectors; input to the corner detector is the gray-level image, and output is an image in which values are proportional to the likelihood that the pixel is a corner. **Interest points** are obtained by thresholding the result of the corner detector.

Corners serve better than lines when the correspondence problem is to be solved. This is due to the **aperture problem**. If a moving line is seen through a small aperture, only the motion vector perpendicular to the line can be observed, and the component collinear with the line remains invisible. The situation is better with corners, which provide ground for unique matching.

Edge detectors themselves are not stable at corners. This is natural as the gradient at the tip of the corner is ambiguous. This is illustrated in Figure 5.32 in which a triangle with a sharp corner is shown. Near the corner there is a discontinuity in the gradient direction, and this observation is used in corner detectors.

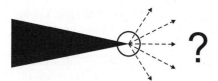

Figure 5.32: Ambiguity of edge detector at the corner tip. © *Cengage Learning 2015.*

A **corner** in an image can be defined as a pixel in whose immediate neighborhood there are two dominant, different edge directions. This definition is not precise as an isolated point of local intensity maximum or minimum, line endings, or an abrupt change in the curvature of a curve gives a response similar to a corner. Nevertheless, such detectors are named corner detectors in the literature and are widely used. If corners have to be detected then some additional constraints have to be applied.

Corner detectors are not usually very robust. This deficiency is overcome either by manual expert supervision or large redundancies introduced to prevent the effect of individual errors from dominating the task. This means that many more corners are detected in two or more images than are necessary for estimating a transformation sought between these images.

The simplest corner detector is the **Moravec detector** [Moravec, 1977] which is maximal in pixels with high contrast, which are on corners and sharp edges. The Moravec operator MO is given by

$$\text{MO}(i,j) = \frac{1}{8} \sum_{k=i-1}^{i+1} \sum_{l=j-1}^{j+1} \left| f(k,l) - f(i,j) \right|. \tag{5.68}$$

Better results are produced by computationally more expensive corner operators such as those proposed by Zuniga–Haralick [Zuniga and Haralick, 1983; Haralick and Shapiro, 1992] or Kitchen–Rosenfeld [Huang, 1983] which are based on the facet model (Section 5.3.6). The image function f is approximated in the neighborhood of the pixel (i,j) by a cubic polynomial with coefficients c_k:

$$f(i,j) = c_1 + c_2\,x + c_3\,y + c_4\,x^2 + c_5\,x\,y + c_6\,y^2 + c_7\,x^3 + c_8\,x^2\,y + c_9\,x\,y^2 + c_{10}\,y^3. \tag{5.69}$$

The Zuniga–Haralick operator ZH is given by

$$\text{ZH}(i,j) = \frac{-2\left(c_2^2\,c_6 - c_2\,c_3\,c_5 + c_3^2\,c_4\right)}{\left(c_2^2 + c_3^2\right)^{3/2}}. \tag{5.70}$$

The Kitchen-Rosenfeld KR operator has the same numerator as equation (5.70), but the denominator is $(c_2^2 + c_3^2)$.

The **Harris corner detector** [Harris and Stephen, 1988] improved upon Moravec's by considering the differential of the corner score (sum of square differences). Consider a 2D gray-scale image f. An image patch $W \in f$ is taken and is shifted by $\Delta x, \Delta y$. The sum of square differences S between values of the image f given by the patch W and its shifted variant by $\Delta x, \Delta y$ is given by:

$$S_W(\Delta x, \Delta y) = \sum_{x_i \in W} \sum_{y_i \in W} \left(f(x_i, y_i) - f(x_i - \Delta x, y_i - \Delta y) \right)^2. \tag{5.71}$$

A corner point not suffering from the aperture problem must have a high response of $S_W(\Delta x, \Delta y)$ for all $\Delta x, \Delta y$. If the shifted image patch is approximated by the first-order Taylor expansion

$$f(x_i - \Delta x, y_i - \Delta y) \approx f(x_i, y_i) + \left[\frac{\partial f(x_i, y_i)}{\partial x}, \frac{\partial f(x_i, y_i)}{\partial y} \right] \begin{bmatrix} \Delta x \\ \Delta y \end{bmatrix}, \tag{5.72}$$

then the minimum of $S_W(\Delta x, \Delta y)$ can be obtained analytically. Substitute this approximation given by equation (5.72) into equation (5.71)

$$
\begin{aligned}
S(x,y) &= \sum_{x_i \in W} \sum_{y_i \in W} \left(f(x_i, y_i) - f(x_i, y_i) - \left[\frac{\partial f(x_i, y_i)}{\partial x}, \frac{\partial f(x_i, y_i)}{\partial y} \right] \begin{bmatrix} \Delta x \\ \Delta y \end{bmatrix} \right)^2 \\
&= \sum_{x_i \in W} \sum_{y_i \in W} \left(- \left[\frac{\partial f(x_i, y_i)}{\partial x}, \frac{\partial f(x_i, y_i)}{\partial y} \right] \begin{bmatrix} \Delta x \\ \Delta y \end{bmatrix} \right)^2 \\
&= \sum_{x_i \in W} \sum_{y_i \in W} \left(\left[\frac{\partial f(x_i, y_i)}{\partial x}, \frac{\partial f(x_i, y_i)}{\partial y} \right] \begin{bmatrix} \Delta x \\ \Delta y \end{bmatrix} \right)^2
\end{aligned}
$$

having in mind that $\mathbf{u}^2 = \mathbf{u}^\top \mathbf{u}$

$$
\begin{aligned}
&= \sum_{x_i \in W} \sum_{y_i \in W} [\Delta x, \Delta y] \left(\begin{bmatrix} \frac{\partial f}{\partial x} \\ \frac{\partial f}{\partial y} \end{bmatrix} \begin{bmatrix} \frac{\partial f}{\partial x} & \frac{\partial f}{\partial y} \end{bmatrix} \right) \begin{bmatrix} \Delta x \\ \Delta y \end{bmatrix} \\
&= [\Delta x, \Delta y] \left(\sum_{x_i \in W} \sum_{y_i \in W} \begin{bmatrix} \frac{\partial f}{\partial x} \\ \frac{\partial f}{\partial y} \end{bmatrix} \begin{bmatrix} \frac{\partial f}{\partial x} & \frac{\partial f}{\partial y} \end{bmatrix} \right) \begin{bmatrix} \Delta x \\ \Delta y \end{bmatrix} \\
&= [\Delta x, \Delta y] \, A_W(x,y) \begin{bmatrix} \Delta x \\ \Delta y \end{bmatrix} ,
\end{aligned}
$$

where the Harris matrix $A_W(x,y)$ represents one half the second derivative of the image patch W around the point $(x,y) = (0,0)$. A is

$$
A(x,y) = 2 \cdot \begin{bmatrix} \sum_{x_i \in W} \sum_{y_i \in W} \left(\frac{\partial f(x_i, y_i)}{\partial x} \right)^2 & \sum_{x_i \in W} \sum_{y_i \in W} \frac{\partial f(x_i, y_i)}{\partial x} \frac{\partial f(x_i, y_i)}{\partial y} \\ \sum_{x_i \in W} \sum_{y_i \in W} \frac{\partial f(x_i, y_i)}{\partial x} \frac{\partial f(x_i, y_i)}{\partial y} & \sum_{x_i \in W} \sum_{y_i \in W} \left(\frac{\partial f(x_i, y_i)}{\partial y} \right)^2 \end{bmatrix} . \quad (5.73)
$$

Usually an isotropic window is used, such as a Gaussian. The response will be isotropic too.

The local structure matrix A represents the neighborhood—this Harris matrix is symmetric and positive semi-definite. Its main modes of variation correspond to partial derivatives in orthogonal directions and are reflected in its eigenvalues λ_1, λ_2. Three distinct cases can occur:

1. Both eigenvalues are small. This means that image f is flat at the examined pixel—there are no edges or corners in this location.

2. One eigenvalue is small and the second large. The local neighborhood is ridge-shaped. Significant change of f occurs if a small movement is made perpendicularly to the ridge.

3. Both eigenvalues are rather large. A small shift in any direction causes significant change of image f. A corner has been found.

Cases 2 and 3 are illustrated in Figure 5.33. An example of Harris corner detection applied to a real scene is in Figure 5.34.

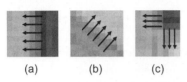

(a)   (b)   (c)

Figure 5.33: The Harris corner detector according to eigenvalues of the local structure matrix. (a), (b) Ridge detected, no corner at this position. (c) Corner detected. © *Cengage Learning 2015.*

Figure 5.34: Red crosses mark Harris corners. *Courtesy of M. Urban, Czech Technical University, Prague. A color version of this figure may be seen in the color inset—Plate 7.*

Harris suggested that exact eigenvalue computation can be avoided by calculating the response function $R(A) = \det(A) - \kappa \operatorname{trace}^2(A)$, where κ is a tunable parameter; values from 0.04 to 0.15 were reported in literature as appropriate.

Algorithm 5.5: Harris corner detector

1. Filter the image with a Gaussian.

2. Estimate intensity gradient in two perpendicular directions for each pixel, $\frac{\partial f(x,y)}{\partial x}$, $\frac{\partial f(x,y)}{\partial y}$. This is performed by twice using a 1D convolution with the kernel approximating the derivative.

3. For each pixel and a given neighborhood window:

   - Calculate the local structure matrix A.
   - Evaluate the response function $R(A)$.

4. Choose the best candidates for corners by selecting a threshold on the response function $R(A)$ and perform non-maximal suppression.

The Harris corner detector has proved very popular: it is insensitive to 2D shift and rotation, to small illumination variations, to small viewpoint change, and has low computational requirements. On the other hand, it is not invariant to larger scale change, viewpoint changes and significant changes in contrast.

Many more corner-like detectors exist, and the reader is referred to the overview papers [Mikolajczyk and Schmid, 2004; Mikolajczyk et al., 2005].

5.3.11   Detection of maximally stable extremal regions

When effects of noise and discretization are negligible, the output of a Harris detector on a rotated and/or translated image is a rotated and/or translated set of points. However, if the image is rescaled or transformed projectively, the output of a Harris detector changes rapidly. **Maximally Stable Extremal Regions** (MSERs) [Matas et al., 2004] are an example of an image structure that can be repeatably detected not only after translations and rotations, but also after similarity and affine transforms.

Figure 5.35: MSERs: Red bordered regions are results of the algorithm on the increasingly ordered list of intensities. Green bordered regions come from the list with decreasing ordering. *Courtesy of J. Matas, Czech Technical University, Prague. A color version of this figure may be seen in the color inset—Plate 8.*

Informally, MSERs can be explained by imagining all possible thresholdings of an input gray-level image I. We will refer to the pixels below a threshold as 'black' and to those above or equal as 'white'. If we were shown a movie of thresholded images I_t, with frame t corresponding to threshold t, we would see first a white image; black spots corresponding to local intensity minima will appear and grow, and at some points regions corresponding to two local minima will merge. Finally, the last image will be black. The connected components in these frames are the set of *maximal regions*; *minimal regions* can be obtained by inverting the intensity of I and running the same process. In many images one observes this local binarization is stable over a large range of thresholds in certain regions. Such *maximally stable extremal regions* are of interest since they have the following properties:

- Invariance to monotonic transformations. The set of extremal regions is unchanged after transformation M, $I(p) < I(q) \rightarrow M\big(I(p)\big) = I'(p) < I'(q) = M\big(I(q)\big)$ since M does not affect adjacency (and thus contiguity). The intensity ordering is preserved.

- Invariance to adjacency preserving (continuous) transformations.

- Stability, since only extremal regions whose support is virtually unchanged over a range of thresholds are selected.

- Multi-scale detection. Since no smoothing is involved, both very fine and very large structure is detected.

- The set of all extremal regions can be enumerated in $\mathcal{O}(n \log \log n)$, i.e., almost in linear time for 8 bit images.

The algorithm is illustrated in Figure 5.35.

Algorithm 5.6: Enumeration of extremal regions.

1. Sort image pixels by intensity: this can be done efficiently by, e.g., binsort, in $\mathcal{O}(n)$ time.

2. Starting at the minimum intensity g_{min}, iterate upward.

3. Consider pixels of the current intensity g; introduce the pixel and update the connected component structure. This may be done using the efficient union-find algorithm [Sedgewick, 1998].

4. If two regions merge, this is viewed as the death of the smaller component.

5. When all intensities have been processed, we have a data structure holding the area of each connected component as a function of a threshold. If $Q_1, \ldots Q_i$ are a sequence of nested extremal regions, so $Q_g \subset Q_{g+1}$, then extremal region $Q_{\hat{g}}$ is maximally stable iff $q(g) = |Q_{g+\Delta} \setminus Q_{g-\Delta}|/|Q_g|$ has a local minimum at $\hat{g}$, where $|.|$ denotes cardinality and Δ is a parameter of the method.

Algorithm 5.6 and an efficient watershed algorithm (Sections 6.3.4 and 13.7.3) are essentially identical. However, the structure of output of the two algorithms is different. In watershed computation, the focus is on thresholds where regions merge and watershed basins touch. Such thresholds are highly unstable—after a merge, the region area changes abruptly. In MSER detection, a range of thresholds is sought that leaves the watershed basin effectively unchanged.

Detection of MSERs is also related to thresholding. Every extremal region is a connected component of a thresholded image. However, no global or 'optimal' threshold is needed, all thresholds are tested and the stability of the connected components evaluated.

In empirical studies [Mikolajczyk et al., 2005; Frauendorfer and Bischof, 2005], the MSER has shown the highest repeatability of affine-invariant detectors in a number of experiments. MSER has been used successfully for challenging wide baseline matching problems [Matas et al., 2004] and in state-of-the-art object recognition systems [Obdrza-lek and Matas, 2002; Sivic and Zisserman, 2004].

5.4   Image restoration

Pre-processing methods that aim to suppress degradation using knowledge about its nature are called **image restoration**. Most image restoration methods are based on convolution applied globally to the whole image. There is a wide literature on restoration and only the basic principles and some simple degradations are considered here.

Image degradation can have many causes: defects of optical lenses, non-linearity of the electro-optical sensor, graininess of the film material, relative motion between an object and camera, wrong focus, atmospheric turbulence in remote sensing or astronomy, scanning of photographs, etc. The objective of image restoration is to reconstruct the original image from its degraded version.

Image restoration techniques can be classified as **deterministic** or **stochastic**. Deterministic methods are applicable to images with little noise and a known degradation function. The original image is obtained by applying the function inverse to the degraded one. Stochastic techniques try to find the best restoration according to a particular statistical criterion, e.g., a least-squares method. There are three typical degradations with a simple function: relative constant speed movement of the object with respect to the camera, wrong lens focus, and atmospheric turbulence.

In most practical cases, there is insufficient knowledge about the degradation, and it must be estimated and modeled. This may be done on an a priori or a posteriori basis:

- A priori knowledge about degradation is either known in advance or can be obtained before restoration. For example, if it is known that the image was degraded by relative motion of an object with respect to the sensor, then the modeling determines only the speed and direction of the motion. Alternatively, we may seek to to estimate parameters of a device such as a TV camera or digitizer, whose degradation remains unchanged over a period of time and can be modeled by studying a known sample image and its degraded version.

- A posteriori knowledge is that obtained by analyzing the degraded image. A typical example is to find some interest points in the image (e.g., corners, straight lines) and guess how they looked before degradation. Another possibility is to use spectral characteristics of the regions in the image that are relatively homogeneous.

A degraded image g can arise from the original image f by a process which can be expressed as

$$g(i,j) = s \left(\int \int_{(a,b) \in \mathcal{O}} f(a,b) \, h(a,b,i,j) \, \mathrm{d}a \, \mathrm{d}b \right) + \nu(i,j) \,, \tag{5.74}$$

where s is some non-linear function and ν describes the noise. This is often simplified by neglecting the non-linearity and assuming that the function h is invariant with respect to position in the image, giving

$$g(i,j) = (f * h)(i,j) + \nu(i,j) \,. \tag{5.75}$$

If the noise is not significant in this equation, then restoration equates to inverse convolution (also called deconvolution). If noise is not negligible, then the inverse convolution is solved as an overdetermined system of linear equations. Methods based on minimization of least square error such as Wiener filtering (off-line) or Kalman filtering (recursive, on-line; see Section 16.6.1) are examples [Bates and McDonnell, 1986].

5.4.1 Degradations that are easy to restore

In the Fourier domain, we can express equation (5.75) as

$$G = H\,F\,. \tag{5.76}$$

Therefore, overlooking image noise ν, knowledge of the degradation function fully facilitates image restoration by inverse convolution (Section 5.4.2).

Relative motion of camera and object

Relative motion of a camera with a mechanical shutter and the photographed object during the shutter open time T causes smoothing of the object in the image. Suppose V is the constant speed in the direction of the x axis; the Fourier transform $H(u,v)$ of the degradation caused in time T is given by [Rosenfeld and Kak, 1982]

$$H(u,v) = \frac{\sin(\pi\,V\,T\,u)}{\pi\,V\,u}\,. \tag{5.77}$$

Wrong lens focus

Image smoothing caused by imperfect focus of a thin lens can be described by the function [Born and Wolf, 1969]

$$H(u,v) = \frac{J_1(a\,r)}{a\,r}\,, \tag{5.78}$$

where J_1 is the Bessel function of the first order, $r^2 = u^2 + v^2$, and a is the displacement—the model is not space invariant.

Atmospheric turbulence

Atmospheric turbulence is degradation that needs to be restored in remote sensing and astronomy. It is caused by temperature non-homogeneity in the atmosphere that deviates passing light rays. One mathematical model [Hufnagel and Stanley, 1964] is

$$H(u,v) = e^{-c(u^2+v^2)^{5/6}}\,, \tag{5.79}$$

where c is a constant that depends on the type of turbulence which is usually found experimentally. The exponent $5/6$ is sometimes replaced by 1.

5.4.2 Inverse filtering

Inverse filtering assumes that degradation was caused by a linear function $h(i,j)$ (cf. equation 5.75) and considers the additive noise ν as another source of degradation. It is further assumed that ν is independent of the signal. After applying the Fourier transform to equation (5.75), we get

$$G(u,v) = F(u,v)\,H(u,v) + N(u,v)\,. \tag{5.80}$$

The degradation can be eliminated using the restoration filter with a transfer function that is inverse to the degradation h. We derive the original image F (its Fourier transform to be exact) from its degraded version G (equation 5.80), as

$$F(u,v) = G(u,v)\,H^{-1}(u,v) - N(u,v)\,H^{-1}(u,v)\,. \tag{5.81}$$

This shows that inverse filtering works well for images that are not corrupted by noise [not considering possible computational problems if $H(u,v)$ gets close to zero at some location of the u,v space—fortunately, such locations can be neglected without perceivable effect on the restoration result]. However, if noise is present, two problems arise. First, the noise influence may become significant for frequencies where $H(u,v)$ has small magnitude. This situation usually corresponds to high frequencies u,v. In reality, $H(u,v)$ usually decreases in magnitude much more rapidly than $N(u,v)$ and thus the noise effect may dominate the entire restoration result. Limiting the restoration to a small neighborhood of the u,v origin in which $H(u,v)$ is sufficiently large overcomes this problem, and the results are usually quite acceptable. Secondly, we usually do not have enough information about the noise to determine $N(u,v)$ sufficiently.

5.4.3   Wiener filtering

Wiener (least mean square) filtering [Wiener, 1942; Gonzalez and Woods, 1992; Castleman, 1996] attempts to take account of noise properties by incorporating a priori knowledge in the image restoration formula. Restoration by the **Wiener filter** gives an estimate $\hat{f}$ of the original uncorrupted image f with minimal mean square error

$$e^2 = \mathcal{E}\left\{ \left(f(i,j) - \hat{f}(i,j) \right)^2 \right\},$$ (5.82)

where $\mathcal{E}$ denotes the mean operator. If no constraints are applied to the solution of equation (5.82), then an optimal estimate $\hat{f}$ is the conditional mean value of the ideal image f under the condition g. This approach is complicated from the computational point of view. Moreover, the conditional probability density between the optimal image f and the corrupted image g is not usually known. The optimal estimate is in general a non-linear function of the image g.

Minimization of equation (5.82) is easy if the estimate $\hat{f}$ is a linear combination of the values in image g; the estimate $\hat{f}$ is then close (but not necessarily equal) to the theoretical optimum. The estimate is equal to the theoretical optimum only if the stochastic processes describing images f, g, and the noise ν are homogeneous, and their probability density is Gaussian [Andrews and Hunt, 1977]. These conditions are not usually fulfilled for typical images.

Denote the Fourier transform of the Wiener filter by H_W. Then, the estimate $\hat{F}$ of the Fourier transform F of the original image f can be obtained as

$$\hat{F}(u,v) = H_W(u,v)\, G(u,v).$$ (5.83)

H_W is not derived here, but may be found elsewhere [Gonzalez and Woods, 1992] as

$$H_W(u,v) = \frac{H^*(u,v)}{\left|H(u,v)\right|^2 + \left[S_{\nu\nu}(u,v)/S_{ff}(u,v)\right]},$$ (5.84)

where H is the transform function of the degradation, $*$ denotes complex conjugate, $S_{\nu\nu}$ is the spectral density of the noise, and S_{ff} is the spectral density of the undegraded image.

If Wiener filtering is used, the nature of degradation H and statistical parameters of the noise need to be known. Wiener filtering theory solves the problem of optimal a posteriori linear mean square estimates—all statistics (for example, power spectrum) should be available in advance. Note the term $S_{ff}(u,v)$ in equation (5.84), which represents the spectrum of the undegraded image, which may be difficult to obtain with no foreknowledge of the undegraded image.

Restoration is illustrated in Figure 5.36 where an image that was degraded by 5 pixels motion in the direction of the x axis: Figure 5.36b shows the result of restoration by Wiener filtering.

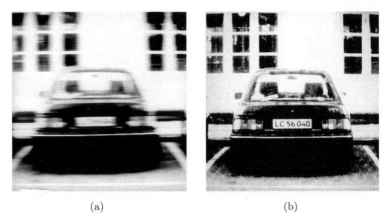

(a)   (b)

Figure 5.36: Restoration of motion blur using Wiener filtering. *Courtesy of P. Kohout, Criminalistic Institute, Prague.*

Despite its unquestionable power, Wiener filtering suffers several substantial limitations. First, the criterion of optimality is based on minimum mean square error and weights all errors equally, a mathematically fully acceptable criterion that unfortunately does not perform well if an image is restored for human viewing. The reason is that humans perceive the restoration errors more seriously in constant-gray-level areas and in bright regions, while they are much less sensitive to errors located in dark regions and in high-gradient areas. Second, spatially variant degradations cannot be restored using the standard Wiener filtering approach, and these degradations are common. Third, most images are highly non-stationary, containing large homogeneous areas separated by high-contrast edges. Wiener filtering cannot handle non-stationary signals and noise. To deal with real-life image degradations, more sophisticated approaches may be needed. Examples include **power spectrum equalization** and **geometric mean filtering**. These and other specialized restoration techniques can be found in higher-level texts devoted to this topic; [Castleman, 1996] is well suited for such a purpose.

5.5 Summary

- **Image pre-processing**

    - Operations with images at the lowest level of abstraction are called *pre-processing*. Both input and output are intensity images.

    - Pre-processing aims to suppress unwanted distortions, or enhance some image features important for further processing.

    - Four basic types of pre-processing methods exist:

- ∗ Brightness transformations
- ∗ Geometric transformations
- ∗ Local neighborhood pre-processing
- ∗ Image restoration

- **Pixel brightness transformations**

  - There are two classes of pixel brightness transformations:
    - ∗ Brightness corrections
    - ∗ Gray-scale transformations
  - Brightness corrections modify pixel brightness taking into account its original brightness and its position in the image.
  - Gray-scale transformations change brightness without regard to position.
  - Frequently used brightness transformations include:
    - ∗ Brightness thresholding
    - ∗ Histogram equalization
    - ∗ Logarithmic gray-scale transforms
    - ∗ Look-up table transforms
    - ∗ Pseudo-color transforms
  - The goal of histogram equalization is to create an image with equally distributed brightness levels over the whole brightness scale.

- **Geometric transformations**

  - Geometric transforms permit the elimination of the geometric distortions that occur when an image is captured.
  - A geometric transform typically consists of two basic steps:
    - ∗ Pixel co-ordinate transformation
    - ∗ Brightness interpolation
  - Pixel co-ordinate transformations map the co-ordinates of the input image pixel to a point in the output image; *affine* and *bilinear* transforms are frequently used.
  - Output point co-ordinates usually do not match the digital grid after the transform; interpolation is employed to determine brightnesses of output pixels. *Nearest-neighbor*, *linear*, and *bi-cubic* interpolations are frequently used.

- **Local pre-processing**

  - Local pre-processing methods use a small neighborhood of a pixel in an input image to produce a new brightness value in the output image.
  - Two groups are common in pre-processing: *smoothing* and *edge detection*.
  - Smoothing aims to suppress noise or other small fluctuations in the image; it is equivalent to suppressing high frequencies in the Fourier domain.
  - Smoothing approaches based on direct averaging blur image edges. Improved approaches reduce blurring by averaging in homogeneous local neighborhoods.

- *Median* smoothing is a non-linear operation; it reduces blurring by replacing the current point in the image by the median of the brightnesses in its neighborhood.

- *Gradient operators* determine *edges*—locations in which the image function undergoes rapid changes. Their effect is similar to suppressing low frequencies in the Fourier domain.

- *Edge* is a property attached to a pixel and has *magnitude* and *direction*.

- Most gradient operators can be expressed using *convolution masks*; examples include Roberts, Laplace, Prewitt, Sobel, and Kirsch operators.

- The main disadvantage of convolution edge detectors is scale dependence and noise sensitivity. Choice of best size of a local operator is not easy to determine.

- *Zero-crossings* of the second derivative are more robust than small-size gradient detectors and can be calculated as a Laplacian of Gaussians (LoG) or as a difference of Gaussians (DoG).

- The *Canny* edge detector is optimal for step edges corrupted by white noise. The optimality criterion is based on requirements of *detecting* important edges, small *localization* error, and *single-edge response*. It convolves an image with a symmetric 2D Gaussian and then differentiates in the direction of the gradient; further steps include *non-maximal edge suppression*, *hysteresis thresholding*, and *feature synthesis*.

- Edges can also be detected in multi-spectral images.

- Other local pre-processing operations include *line finding*, *line thinning*, *line filling*, and *interest point detection*.

- Structures in an image such as corners and maximally stable extremal regions are more information rich and more stable to detect than edges. They are often used in image matching.

- **Image restoration**

  - Image restoration methods aim to suppress degradation using knowledge about its nature. Most image restoration methods are based on *deconvolution* applied globally to the entire image.

  - Relative-constant-speed movement of the object with respect to the camera, wrong lens focus, and atmospheric turbulence are three typical image degradations with simple degradation functions.

  - *Inverse filtering* assumes that degradation was caused by a linear function.

  - *Wiener filtering* gives an estimate of the original uncorrupted image with minimal mean square error; it is in general a non-linear function of the corrupted image.

5.6 Exercises

Short-answer questions

S5.1 Explain the rationale of histogram equalization.

S5.2 Explain why the histogram of a discrete image is not flat after histogram equalization.

S5.3 Consider the image given in Figure 5.3a. After histogram equalization (Figure 5.3b), much more detail is visible. Does histogram equalization increase the amount of information contained in image data? Explain.

S5.4 Give examples of situations in which brightness transformations, geometric transformations, smoothing, edge detection, and/or image restorations are typically applied.

S5.5 What is the main aim of image pre-processing?

S5.6 What is the main difference between brightness correction and gray-scale transformation?

S5.7 What are the two main steps of geometric transforms?

S5.8 Give a geometric transformation equation for

(a) Rotation

(b) Change of scale

(c) Skewing by an angle

S5.9 What is the minimum number of corresponding pixel pairs that must be determined if the following transforms are used to perform a geometric correction?

(a) Bilinear transform

(b) Affine transform

S5.10 Explain why smoothing typically blurs image edges.

S5.11 Explain why Gaussian filtering is often the preferred averaging method.

S5.12 Explain why smoothing and edge detection have conflicting aims.

S5.13 Name several smoothing methods that try to avoid image blurring. Explain their main principles.

S5.14 Give convolution masks for the following edge detectors:

(a) Roberts

(b) Laplace

(c) Prewitt

(d) Sobel

(e) Kirsch

Which ones can serve as compass operators? List several applications in which determining edge direction is important.

S5.15 Explain why median filtering performs well in images corrupted by impulse noise.

S5.16 Consider brightness interpolation—explain why it is better to perform brightness interpolation using brightness values of neighboring points in the input image than interpolating in the output image.

S5.17 Explain the principles of nearest-neighbor interpolation, linear interpolation, and bicubic interpolation.

S5.18 Explain why subtraction of a second derivative of the image function from the original image results in the visual effect of image sharpening.

S5.19 Propose a robust way of detecting significant image edges using zero-crossings.

S5.20 What are LoG and DoG? How do you compute them? How are they used?

S5.21 Explain why LoG is a better edge detector than Laplace edge detector.

S5.22 Explain the importance of hysteresis thresholding and non-maximal suppression in the Canny edge detection process. How do these two concepts influence the resulting edge image?

S5.23 Give image distortion functions for

(a) Relative camera motion

(b) Out-of-focus lens

(c) Atmospheric turbulence

S5.24 Explain the principles of noise suppression, histogram modification, and contrast enhancement performed in adaptive neighborhoods.

S5.25 Explain the notion of scale in image processing.

S5.26 Explain the principles of image restoration based on

(a) Inverse convolution

(b) Inverse filtration

(c) Wiener filtration

List the main differences among the above methods.

S5.27 What is the aperture problem? How does it affect finding correspondence for line features and corner features? Add a simple sketch to your answer demonstrating the concept of aperture and the consequences for correspondence of lines and corners.

Problems

P5.1 Implement histogram equalization as described in Algorithm 5.1. Select several images with a variety of gray-level histograms to test the method's performance, include over- and under-exposed images, low-contrast images, and images with large dark or bright background regions. Compare the results.

P5.2 Write a program that performs histogram equalization on HSI images (see Section 2.4). Verify visually that equalizing the I component alone has the desired effect, while equalizing the others does not.

P5.3 Apply histogram equalization to an already equalized image; compare and explain the results of 1-step and 2-step histogram equalization.

P5.4 Determine a gray-scale transformation that maps the darkest 5% of image pixels to black (0), the brightest 10% of pixels to white (255), and linearly transforms the gray-levels of all remaining pixels between black and white.

P5.5 Develop programs for the three gray-scale image transforms given in Figure 5.1. Apply them to several images and make a subjective judgment about the usefulness of the transforms.

P5.6 Develop a program for gray-scale transformations as described in Problem P5.4. Develop it in such a way that the percentages of dark and bright pixels mapped to pure black and white are program parameters and can be modified by the operator.

P5.7 Consider calibrating a TV camera for non-homogeneous lighting. Develop a program that determines camera calibration coefficients after an image of a constant-gray-level surface is acquired with this camera. After calibration, the program should perform appropriate brightness correction to remove the effects of non-homogeneous lighting on other images acquired using the same camera under the same lighting conditions. Test the program's functionality under several non-homogeneous lighting conditions.

P5.8 Develop a program for image convolution using a rectangular convolution mask of any odd size. The mask should be input as an ASCII text file. Test your program using the following convolution kernels:

(a) 3×3 averaging

(b) 7×7 averaging

(c) 11×11 averaging

(d) 5×5 Gaussian filtering (modification of equation 5.27)

P5.9 Develop programs for the following geometric transforms:

(a) Rotation

(b) Change of scale

(c) Skewing

(d) Affine transform calculated from three pairs of corresponding points

(e) Bilinear transform calculated from four pairs of corresponding points

To avoid writing code for solving systems of linear equations, use a mathematical software package (such as Matlab) to determine transformation coefficients for the affine and bilinear transforms (d) and (e). For each of the above transforms, implement the following three brightness interpolation approaches:

- Nearest-neighbor interpolation
- Linear interpolation
- Bi-cubic interpolation

To implement all possible combinations efficiently, design your programs in a modular fashion with substantial code reuse. Compare the subjective image quality resulting from the three brightness interpolation approaches.

P5.10 Implement image averaging using a rotating mask as described in Algorithm 5.2. Use the masks specified in Figure 5.11. Assess the amount of image blurring and sharpening in comparison to standard image averaging.

P5.11 An imperfect camera is used to capture an image of a static scene:

(a) The camera is producing random noise with zero mean. Single images look quite noisy.

(b) The camera has a dark spot in the middle of the image—the image is visible there, but it is darker than the rest of the image.

What approaches would you choose to obtain the best possible image quality? You can capture as many frames of the static scene as you wish; you may capture an image of a constant gray-level; you may capture any other image with known gray-level properties. Give complete step-by-step procedures including the associated mathematics for both cases.

P5.12 As an extension of Problem P5.10, consider iterative application of averaging using a rotating mask until convergence. Assess the smoothing/sharpening effect of the iterative approach in comparison to the single-step approach developed in Problem P5.10.

P5.13 Demonstrate the linear character of Gaussian averaging and the non-linear character of median filtering: that is, show that $\mathrm{med}[f_1(x) + f_2(x)] \neq \mathrm{med}[f_1(x)] + \mathrm{med}[f_2(x)]$ for an arbitrary region of pixels x and two image brightness functions f_1 and f_2.

P5.14 Develop a program performing averaging with limited data validity, as described by equation (5.28). The program must allow averaging with square masks from 3×3 to 15×15 (odd sizes), the convolution kernel coefficients must be calculated in the program, not listed as kernel values for each filter size. Averaging should only be done for pixels (i, j) with gray values $g(i, j)$ from the interval of invalid data ($\min\{invalid\} \leq g(i, j) \leq \max\{invalid\}$) and only valid data should contribute to the average calculated. Test your program on images corrupted by impulse noise and images corrupted by narrow (several pixels wide) elongated objects of gray-levels from a narrow gray-level interval. How does the effectiveness of your method compare to that of simple averaging and median filtering?

P5.15 Implement efficient median filtering as described in Algorithm 5.3. Compare the processing efficiency in comparison with a 'naive' median filtering implementation. Use median filter sizes ranging from 3×3 to 15×15 (odd sizes) for comparison.

P5.16 Consider the binary image given in Figure 5.37. Show the result of 3×3 median filtering if the following masks are used (a 'zero' in a mask position means that the corresponding pixel is not used for median calculation):

$$(a) \begin{bmatrix} 1 & 1 & 1 \\ 1 & 1 & 1 \\ 1 & 1 & 1 \end{bmatrix} \quad (b) \begin{bmatrix} 0 & 1 & 0 \\ 1 & 1 & 1 \\ 0 & 1 & 0 \end{bmatrix} \quad (c) \begin{bmatrix} 0 & 0 & 0 \\ 1 & 1 & 1 \\ 0 & 0 & 0 \end{bmatrix} \quad (d) \begin{bmatrix} 1 & 1 & 1 \\ 0 & 0 & 0 \\ 0 & 0 & 0 \end{bmatrix}$$

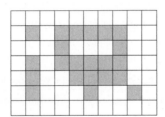

Figure 5.37: © *Cengage Learning 2015.*

P5.17 Median filtering that uses a 3×3 mask,

$$\begin{bmatrix} 1 & 1 & 1 \\ 1 & 1 & 1 \\ 1 & 1 & 1 \end{bmatrix}$$

is damaging to thin lines and sharp corners. Give a 3×3 mask that can be used for median filtering and does not exhibit this behavior.

P5.18 Continuing Problem P5.17, develop a program performing median filtering in neighborhoods of any size and shape. To test the behavior of different sizes and shapes of the median mask, corrupt input images with:

(a) Impulse noise of varying severity

(b) Horizontal lines of different width

(c) Vertical lines of different width

(d) Combinations of lines of different width and different direction

For each of these, determine the mask providing the subjectively best performance.

P5.19 Continuing Problem P5.18, consider the option of iteratively repeating median filtering several times in a sequence. For each of the situations given in Problem P5.18, assess the performance of the mask considered the best in Problem P5.18 in comparison to some other mask applied iteratively several times. Determine the mask and the number of iterations providing the subjectively best pre-processing performance. Consider the extent of removing the image corruption as well as the amount of image blurring introduced.

P5.20 Consider the binary image given in Figure 5.38. Show the resulting edge images (magnitude and direction images where applicable) if the following edge detectors are used:

(a) Laplace in 4-neighborhood

(b) Prewitt

(c) Sobel

(d) Kirsch

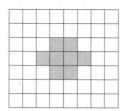

Figure 5.38: © *Cengage Learning 2015.*

P5.21 Create a set of noisy images by corrupting an image with

(a) Additive Gaussian noise of five different severity levels

(b) Multiplicative Gaussian noise of five different severity levels

(c) Impulse noise of five different severity levels

Apply

- Averaging filters of different sizes (equation 5.26)
- Gaussian filters of different standard deviations
- Median filters of different sizes and/or numbers of iterations
- Averaging with limited data validity
- Averaging according to inverse gradient
- Rotating mask averaging

to remove the superimposed noise as much as possible. Quantitatively compare the efficiency of individual approaches by calculating a mean square error between the original and pre-processed images. Formulate a general recommendation about applicability of pre-processing techniques for removing specific types of noise.

P5.22 Using the program developed in Problem P5.8, implement the following edge detectors:

(a) Laplace in 4-neighborhood

(b) Laplace in 8-neighborhood

P5.23 Design a simple 5×5 detector (convolution mask) that is responsive to thin (1–3 pixel wide) straight lines. How do you detect lines of all directions with such an operator?

P5.24 Develop a program for image sharpening as specified by equation (5.36). Use

(a) A non-directional Laplacian to approximate $S(i, j)$

(b) Unsharp masking

Experiment with the value of the parameter C for both approaches and with the extent of smoothing for unsharp masking. Compare the sharpening effects of the two approaches.

P5.25 Consider the double-step edge shown in Figure 5.39. Show that the locations of the zero-crossing of the second derivative depend on σ. Discuss the behavior of the zero-crossings as σ increases.

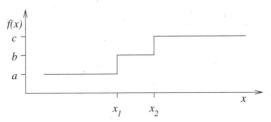

Figure 5.39: © *Cengage Learning 2015.*

P5.26 Develop programs for determining magnitude and direction edge image pairs using each of the *Prewitt*, *Sobel* and *Kirsch* compass edge detectors. The programs must display:

- Magnitude edge image
- Direction edge image
- Magnitude edge image for edges of a specified direction

Use an image of a circle to demonstrate that your programs give correct results.

P5.27 Develop a program determining zero-crossing of the second derivative. Use the

(a) LoG definition

(b) DoG definition

Explain why borders are disconnected if only zero pixels are used for zero-crossing definition. Propose and implement a modification providing contiguous borders. Is it possible to use zero crossings to determine edge positions with subpixel accuracy? If yes, how?

P5.28 Apply the LoG edge detector developed in Problem P5.27 with several values of the smoothing parameter σ. Explain the relationship between σ and the scale of the resulting edge image.

P5.29 Implement the Canny edge detector as described by steps 1-5 of Algorithm 5.4 (implementing feature synthesis is hard, therefore we recommend skipping step 7).

P5.30 Based on your theoretical understanding of Canny edge detector parameters of non-maximal suppression and hysteresis thresholding, generate hypotheses of how changes of these parameters will influence resulting edge images. Using the Canny detector developed in Problem P5.29 (or one of many freely downloadable versions) prove the validity of your hypotheses by experimenting.

P5.31 Develop a program for image restoration using inverse convolution. Use the program to restore images after the following degradations:

      (a) Relative motion of the camera

      (b) Wrong camera focus

Assume that the degradation parameters are known. Test the programs on artificially degraded images. (Although not corresponding exactly to equation (5.77), camera motion distortion can be modeled using a simple sinusoidal filter. Create a sinusoidal image of the same size as your input image and use it as a sinusoidal filter in the frequency domain. By changing the numbers of waves along width and height, you can create a 'double exposure' image that may have resulted from abrupt camera motion.)

P5.32 Design and implement at least one operator (different from those given in text) for each of the following tasks:

      (a) Line finding

      (b) Line thinning

      (c) Line filling

      (d) Corner detection

Test your operators in artificially generated images using the program developed in Problem P5.8

P5.33 Make yourself familiar with solved problems and Matlab implementations of selected algorithms provided in the corresponding chapter of the Matlab Companion to this text [Svoboda et al., 2008]. The Matlab Companion homepage http://visionbook.felk.cvut.cz offers images used in the problems, and well-commented Matlab code is provided for educational purposes.

P5.34 Use the Matlab Companion [Svoboda et al., 2008] to develop solutions to additional exercises and practical problems provided there. Implement your solutions using Matlab or other suitable programming languages.

5.7   References

Alparone L., Baronti S., and Casini A. A novel approach to the suppression of false contours. In *International Conference on Image Processing*, pages 825–828, Los Alamitos, CA, 1996. IEEE.

Andrews H. C. and Hunt B. R. *Digital Image Restoration*. Prentice-Hall, Englewood Cliffs, NJ, 1977.

Ballard D. H. and Brown C. M. *Computer Vision*. Prentice-Hall, Englewood Cliffs, NJ, 1982.

Bates R. H. T. and McDonnell M. J. *Image Restoration and Reconstruction*. Clarendon Press, Oxford, 1986.

Borik A. C., Huang T. S., and Munson D. C. A generalization of median filtering using combination of order statistics. *IEEE Proceedings*, 71(31):1342–1350, 1983.

Born M. and Wolf E. *Principles of Optics*. Pergamon Press, New York, 1969.

Butterworth S. On the theory of filter amplifiers. *Experimental Wireless and the Radio Engineer*, 7:536–541, 1930.

Canny J. F. A computational approach to edge detection. *IEEE Transactions on Pattern Analysis and Machine Intelligence*, 8(6):679–698, 1986.

Castleman K. R. *Digital Image Processing*. Prentice-Hall, Englewood Cliffs, NJ, 1996.

Cervenka V. and Charvat K. Survey of the image processing research applicable to the thematic mapping based on aerocosmic data (in Czech). Technical Report A 12–346–811, Geodetic and Carthographic Institute, Prague, Czechoslovakia, 1987.

Demigny D., Lorca F. G., and Kessal L. Evaluation of edge detectors performances with a discrete expression of Canny's criteria. In *International Conference on Image Processing*, pages 169–172, Los Alamitos, CA, 1995. IEEE.

Faugeras O. D. *Three-Dimensional Computer Vision: A Geometric Viewpoint*. MIT Press, Cambridge, MA, 1993.

Frauendorfer F. and Bischof H. A novel performance evaluation method of local detectors on non-planar scenes. In *Proceedings of the Workshop Empirical Evaluation Methods in Computer Vision adjoint to the conference Computer Vision and Pattern Recognition*, San Diego, USA, 2005. IEEE Computer Society.

Gonzalez R. C. and Woods R. E. *Digital Image Processing*. Addison-Wesley, Reading, MA, 1992.

Gunn S. R. On the discrete representation of the Laplacian of Gaussian. *Pattern Recognition*, 32(8):1463–1472, 1999.

Haralick R. M. Digital step edges from zero crossing of second directional derivatives. *IEEE Transactions on Pattern Analysis and Machine Intelligence*, 6:58–68, 1984.

Haralick R. M. and Shapiro L. G. *Computer and Robot Vision, Volume I*. Addison-Wesley, Reading, MA, 1992.

Haralick R. M. and Watson L. A facet model for image data. *Computer Graphics and Image Processing*, 15:113–129, 1981.

Hardie R. C. and Boncelet C. G. Gradient-based edge detection using nonlinear edge enhancing prefilters. *IEEE Transactions on Image Processing*, 4:1572–1577, 1995.

Harris C. and Stephen M. A combined corner and edge detection. In Matthews M. M., editor, *Proceedings of the 4th ALVEY vision conference*, pages 147–151, University of Manchaster, England, 1988.

Huang T. S., editor. *Image Sequence Processing and Dynamic Scene Analysis*. Springer Verlag, Berlin, 1983.

Huang T. S., Yang G. J., and Tang G. Y. A fast two-dimensional median filtering algorithm. *IEEE Transactions on Acoustics, Speech and Signal Processing*, ASSP-27(1):13–18, 1979.

Huertas A. and Medioni G. Detection of intensity changes with subpixel accuracy using Laplacian-Gaussian masks. *IEEE Transactions on Pattern Analysis and Machine Intelligence*, 8:651–664, 1986.

Hufnagel R. E. and Stanley N. R. Modulation transfer function associated with image transmission through turbulent media. *Journal of the Optical Society of America*, 54:52–61, 1964.

Jain A. K. *Fundamentals of Digital Image Processing*. Prentice-Hall, Englewood Cliffs, NJ, 1989.

Jain R., Kasturi R., and Schunck B. G. *Machine Vision*. McGraw-Hill, New York, 1995.

Lowe D. G. Organization of smooth image curves at multiple scales. *International Journal of Computer Vision*, 1:119–130, 1989.

Marr D. *Vision—A Computational Investigation into the Human Representation and Processing of Visual Information*. Freeman, San Francisco, 1982.

Marr D. and Hildreth E. Theory of edge detection. *Proceedings of the Royal Society*, B 207: 187–217, 1980.

Marr D. and Hildreth E. Theory of edge detection. In Kasturi R. and Jain R. C., editors, *Computer Vision*, pages 77–107. IEEE, Los Alamitos, CA, 1991.

Matalas L., Benjamin R., and Kitney R. An edge detection technique using the facet model and parameterized relaxation labeling. *IEEE Transactions on Pattern Analysis and Machine Intelligence*, 19:328–341, 1997.

Matas J., Chum O., Urban M., and Pajdla T. Robust wide-baseline stereo from maximally stable extremal regions. *Image and Vision Computing*, 22(10):761–767, 2004.

McDonnell M. J. Box filtering techniques. *Computer Graphics and Image Processing*, 17(3): 65–70, 1981.

Mehrotra R. and Shiming Z. A computational approach to zero-crossing-based two-dimensional edge detection. *Graphical Models and Image Processing*, 58:1–17, 1996.

Mikolajczyk K. and Schmid C. Scale and affine invariant interest point detectors. *International Journal of Computer Vision*, 60(1):63 – 86, 2004.

Mikolajczyk K., Tuytelaars T., Schmid C., Zisserman A., Matas J., Schaffalitzky F., Kadir T., and Gool L. v. A comparison of affine region detectors. *International Journal of Computer Vision*, 65(7):43 – 72, 2005. ISSN 0920-5691.

Moik J. G. *Digital Processing of Remotely Sensed Images*. NASA SP–431, Washington, DC, 1980.

Moravec H. P. Towards automatic visual obstacle avoidance. In *Proceedings of the 5th International Joint Conference on Artificial Intelligence*, Pittsburgh, PA, 1977. Carnegie-Mellon University.

Nagao M. and Matsuyama T. *A Structural Analysis of Complex Aerial Photographs*. Plenum Press, New York, 1980.

Nevatia R. Evaluation of simplified Hueckel edge-line detector. *Computer Graphics and Image Processing*, 6(6):582–588, 1977.

Obdrzalek S. and Matas J. Object recognition using local affine frames on distinguished regions. In Rosin P. L. and Marshall D., editors, *Proceedings of the British Machine Vision Conference*, volume 1, pages 113–122, London, UK, 2002. BMVA.

Petrou M. Optimal convolution filters and an algorithm for the detection of wide linear features. *IEE Proceedings*, I: 140(5):331–339, 1993.

Pitas I. and Venetsanopoulos A. N. *Nonlinear Digital Filters: Principles and Applications*. Kluwer, Boston, 1990.

Pitas I. and Venetsanopulos A. N. Nonlinear order statistic filters for image filtering and edge detection. *Signal Processing*, 10(10):573–584, 1986.

Qian R. J. and Huang T. S. Optimal edge detection in two-dimensional images. In *ARPA Image Understanding Workshop*, Monterey, CA, pages 1581–1588, Los Altos, CA, 1994. ARPA.

Ramesh V. and Haralick R. M. An integrated gradient edge detector. Theory and performance evaluation. In *ARPA Image Understanding Workshop*, Monterey, CA, pages 689–702, Los Altos, CA, 1994. ARPA.

Roberts L. G. Machine perception of three-dimensional solids. In Tippett J. T., editor, *Optical and Electro-Optical Information Processing*, pages 159–197. MIT Press, Cambridge, MA, 1965.

Rosenfeld A. and Kak A. C. *Digital Picture Processing*. Academic Press, New York, 2nd edition, 1982.

Rosenfeld A. and Thurston M. Edge and curve detection for visual scene analysis. *IEEE Transactions on Computers*, 20(5):562–569, 1971.

Sedgewick R. *Algorithms in C : Parts 1-4 : Fundamentals ; Data Structures ; Sorting ; Searching.* Addison-Wesley, Reading, Massachusetts, 3rd edition, 1998.

Senthilkumaran N. and Rajesh R. Edge detection techniques for image segmentation—a survey of soft computing approaches. *International Journal of Recent Trends in Engineering*, 1(2): 250–254, 2009.

Sivic J. and Zisserman A. Video data mining using configurations of viewpoint invariant regions. In *Proceedings of the IEEE Conference on Computer Vision and Pattern Recognition, Washington, DC*, volume 1, pages 488–495, 2004.

Svoboda T., Kybic J., and Hlavac V. *Image Processing, Analysis, and Machine Vision: A MATLAB Companion.* Thomson Engineering, 2008.

Tang Y. Y., Li B. F., and Xi D. Multiresolution analysis in extraction of reference lines from documents with gray level background. *IEEE Transactions on Pattern Analysis and Machine Intelligence*, 19:921–926, 1997.

Tyan S. G. Median filtering, deterministic properties. In Huang T. S., editor, *Two–Dimensional Digital Signal Processing*, volume II. Springer Verlag, Berlin, 1981.

Ullman S. Analysis of visual motion by biological and computer systems. *IEEE Computer*, 14 (8):57–69, 1981.

Venkateswar V. and Chellappa R. Extraction of straight lines in aerial images. *IEEE Transactions on Pattern Analysis and Machine Intelligence*, 14:1111–1114, 1992.

Vernon D. *Machine vision.* Prentice-Hall, Englewood Cliffs, New Jersey, USA, 1991.

Wang D. C. C. and Vagnucci A. H. Gradient inverse weighting smoothing schema and the evaluation of its performace. *Computer Graphics and Image Processing*, 15, 1981.

Wiener N. *Extrapolation, Interpolation and Smoothing of Stationary Time Series.* MIT Press, Cambridge, MA, 1942.

Witkin A. P. Scale-space filtering. In *Proceedings of the 8th Joint Conference on Artificial Intelligence*, pages 1019–1022, Karlsruhe, Germany, 1983. W Kaufmann.

Yaroslavskii L. P. *Digital Signal Processing in Optics and Holography* (in Russian). Radio i svjaz, Moscow, 1987.

Zuniga O. and Haralick R. M. Corner detection using the facet model. In *Computer Vision and Pattern Recognition*, pages 30–37, Los Alamitos, CA, 1983. IEEE.

Chapter **6**

Segmentation I

Image segmentation is one of the most important steps leading to the analysis of processed image data—its main goal is to divide an image into parts that have a strong correlation with objects or areas of the real world contained in the image. We may aim for **complete segmentation**, which results in a set of disjoint regions corresponding uniquely with objects in the input image, or for **partial segmentation**, in which regions do not correspond directly with image objects. A complete segmentation of an image R is a finite set of regions $R_1, \ldots, R_S$,

$$R = \bigcup_{i=1}^{S} R_i \,, \quad R_i \cap R_j = \emptyset \,, \quad i \neq j \,. \tag{6.1}$$

To achieve this, cooperation with higher processing levels which use specific knowledge of the problem domain is usually necessary. However, there is a whole class of segmentation problems that can be solved successfully using lower-level processing only. In this case, the image commonly consists of contrasted objects located on a uniform background— simple assembly tasks, blood cells, printed characters, etc. Here, a simple global approach can be used and the complete segmentation of an image into objects and background can be obtained. Such processing is context independent; no object-related model is used, and no knowledge about expected segmentation results contributes to the final segmentation.

If partial segmentation is the goal, an image is divided into separate regions that are homogeneous with respect to a chosen property such as brightness, color, reflectivity, texture, etc. If an image of a complex scene is processed, for example, an aerial photograph of an urban scene, a set of possibly overlapping homogeneous regions may result. The partially segmented image must then be subjected to further processing, and the final image segmentation may be found with the help of higher-level information.

Totally correct and complete segmentation of complex scenes usually cannot be achieved in this processing phase, although an immediate gain is a substantial reduction in data volume. A reasonable aim is to use partial segmentation as an input to higher-level processing.

Image data ambiguity is one of the main segmentation problems, often accompanied by information noise. Segmentation methods can be divided into three groups according to the dominant features they employ: First is **global knowledge** about an image or its part; this is usually represented by a histogram of image features. **Edge-based** segmentations form the second group, and **region-based** segmentations the third—many different characteristics may be used in edge detection or region growing, for example, brightness, texture, velocity field, etc. The second and the third groups solve a dual problem. Each region can be represented by its closed boundary, and each closed boundary describes a region. Because of the different natures of the various edge- and region-based algorithms, they may be expected to give somewhat different results and consequently different information. The segmentation results of these two approaches can therefore be combined. A common example of this is a region adjacency graph, in which regions are represented by nodes and graph arcs represent adjacency relations based on detected region borders (Section 4.2.3).

6.1 Thresholding

Gray-level thresholding is the simplest segmentation process. Many objects or image regions are characterized by constant reflectivity or light absorption of their surfaces; then a brightness constant or *threshold* can be determined to segment objects and background. Thresholding is computationally inexpensive and fast—it is the oldest segmentation method and is still widely used in simple applications; it can easily be performed in real time.

Thresholding is the transformation of an input image f to an output (segmented) binary image g:

$$
\begin{aligned}
g(i,j) &= 1 \quad \text{for } f(i,j) > T\,, \\
&= 0 \quad \text{for } f(i,j) \leq T\,,
\end{aligned}
\tag{6.2}
$$

where T is the threshold, $g(i,j) = 1$ for image elements of objects, and $g(i,j) = 0$ for image elements of the background (or vice versa).

Algorithm 6.1: Basic thresholding

1. Search all pixels $f(i,j)$ of the image f. A pixel $g(i,j)$ of the segmented image is an object pixel if $f(i,j) \geq T$, and is a background pixel otherwise.

Complete segmentation can result from thresholding in simple scenes. If objects do not touch each other, and if their gray-levels are clearly distinct from background gray-levels, thresholding is a suitable segmentation method. Such an example is illustrated in Figure 6.1.

Correct threshold selection is crucial for successful segmentation; this selection can be determined interactively or it can be the result of some threshold detection method that will be discussed in the next section. Only under very unusual circumstances will a single threshold for the whole image—*global thresholding*—be successful: even in very simple images there are likely to be gray-level variations in objects and background; this variation may be due to non-uniform lighting, non-uniform input device parameters or a number of other factors. Segmentation using variable thresholds—*adaptive thresholding*—in which

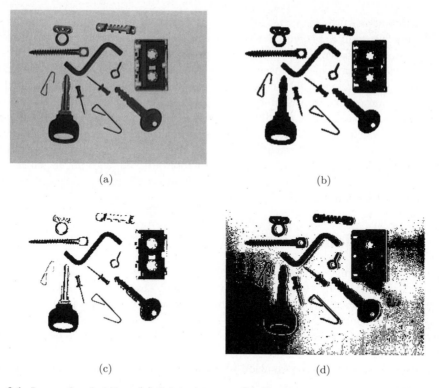

(a)   (b)

(c)   (d)

Figure 6.1: Image thresholding. (a) Original image. (b) Threshold segmentation. (c) Threshold too low. (d) Threshold too high. © *Cengage Learning 2015.*

threshold values vary over the image as a function of local image characteristics, can sometimes produce the solution in these cases.

A global threshold is determined from the whole image f:

$$T = T(f) \tag{6.3}$$

while local thresholds are position dependent

$$T = T(f, f_c), \tag{6.4}$$

where f_c is that image part in which the threshold is determined. One option is to divide the image into subimages and determine a threshold independently in each one; then if a threshold cannot be determined in some subimage, it can be interpolated from neighboring subimages. Each subimage is then processed with respect to its local threshold.

Basic thresholding as defined by equation (6.2) has many modifications. One possibility is to segment an image into regions of pixels with gray-levels from a set D and into background otherwise (band thresholding):

$$\begin{aligned} g(i,j) &= 1 \quad \text{for } f(i,j) \in D, \\ &= 0 \quad \text{otherwise.} \end{aligned} \tag{6.5}$$

This thresholding can be useful, for instance, in microscopic blood cell segmentations, where a particular gray-level interval represents cytoplasma, the background is lighter,

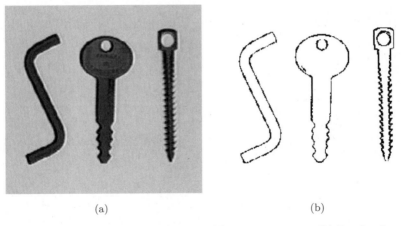

(a)   (b)

Figure 6.2: Image thresholding modification. (a) Original image. (b) Border detection using band-thresholding. © *Cengage Learning 2015*.

and the cell kernel darker. This approach can work as a border detector as well; assuming dark objects on a light background, some gray-levels between those of objects and background will only be found in the object borders. If the gray-level set D is chosen to contain just these object-border gray-levels, and if thresholding according to equation (6.5) is used, object borders result as shown in Figure 6.2.

There are many modifications that use multiple thresholds, after which the resulting image is no longer binary, but rather consists of a limited set of gray-levels:

$$
\begin{aligned}
g(i,j) &= 1 \quad \text{for } f(i,j) \in D_1\,, \\
&= 2 \quad \text{for } f(i,j) \in D_2\,, \\
&= 3 \quad \text{for } f(i,j) \in D_3\,, \\
&\cdots \\
&= n \quad \text{for } f(i,j) \in D_n\,, \\
&= 0 \quad \text{otherwise},
\end{aligned}
\tag{6.6}
$$

where each D_i is a specified subset of mutually distinct gray-levels.

Thresholding can be applied to arrays other than gray-level images; such an array may represent gradient, a local texture property (Chapter 15), or the value of any other image decomposition criterion.

6.1.1 Threshold detection methods

If some property of an image segmentation is known a priori, the task of threshold selection is simplified, since it is chosen to ensure that this property is satisfied. For example, we may know that on a page of printed text the characters cover $1/p$ of the sheet area. Using this prior information, it is very easy to choose a threshold T (based on the image histogram) such that $1/p$ of the image area has gray values less than T (and the rest larger than T). This method is called p-*tile thresholding*. Unfortunately, we do not usually have such definite prior information about area ratios.

More complex methods of threshold detection are based on histogram shape analysis. If an image consists of objects of approximately the same gray-level that differ from the

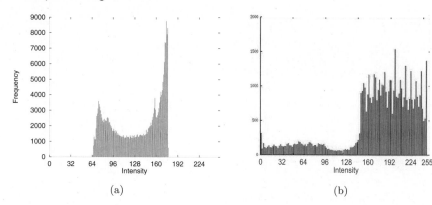

(a)   (b)

Figure 6.3: Bimodal histograms. (a) In cases with well-separable objects from the background, the shown histogram is clearly bimodal. (b) An example of a more shallow bimodal histogram (see top-left of Figure 6.5 for original image, in which the distinction between foreground and background has been deliberately perturbed). Note a wide, shallow peak whose distribution reaches from 0 to approximately 140, and a higher one more easily visible to the right. The distributions overlap in the gray-levels 100–160. © *Cengage Learning 2015*.

gray-level of the background, the resulting histogram is bimodal. Pixels of objects form one of its peaks, while pixels of the background form the second peak—Figure 6.3 shows typical examples. The histogram shape illustrates the fact that gray values between the two peaks are uncommon in the image, and probably result from border pixels between objects and background. The threshold should meet minimum segmentation error requirements—it makes intuitive sense to determine the threshold as the gray-level that has a minimum histogram value between the two maxima. If the histogram is multi-modal, more thresholds may be determined at minima between any two maxima: each threshold gives different segmentation results, of course. Multi-thresholding as given in equation (6.6) is another option.

To decide if a histogram is bimodal or multi-modal may not be simple, it often being impossible to interpret the significance of histogram local maxima. A two-part image with one half white and the second half black actually has the same histogram as an image with randomly spread white and black pixels (i.e., a salt-and-pepper noise image, see Section 2.3.6). Further, bimodality itself does not guarantee correct threshold segmentation—correct segmentation may not occur if objects are on a background of varying gray-levels.

A more general approach takes gray-level occurrences inside a local neighborhood into consideration when constructing a histogram, the goal being to build a histogram with a better peak-to-valley ratio. One option is to weight histogram contributions to suppress the influence of pixels with a high image gradient. This means that a histogram will consist mostly of the gray values of objects and background, and that border gray-levels (with higher gradient) will not contribute. This will produce a deeper histogram valley and allow an easier determination of the threshold. Another, similar, method uses only high-gradient pixels to form the gray-level histogram, meaning that the histogram will consist mostly of border gray-levels and should be unimodal, in which the peak corresponds to the gray-level of borders between objects and background. The segmentation threshold can be determined as the gray value of this peak, or as a mean of a substantial part of the peak. Many modifications of *histogram transformation* methods can be found in literature.

Thresholding is a very popular segmentation tool, and a large variety of threshold detection techniques exist in addition to those which have been discussed. The survey [Sezgin and Sankur, 2004] gives a good overview of existing methods with an extensive list of references. High processing speed is typical for threshold segmentations, and images can easily be thresholded in real time.

6.1.2 Optimal thresholding

An alternative approach called *optimal thresholding* seeks to model the histogram of an image using a weighted sum of two or more probability densities with normal distribution. The threshold is set as the gray-level closest to the minimum probability between the maxima of the normal distributions, which results in minimum error segmentation (the smallest number of pixels is mis-segmented) [Rosenfeld and Kak, 1982; Gonzalez and Wintz, 1987]; see Figure 6.4 (and also compare maximum-likelihood classification methods, Section 9.2.3 and expectation-maximization, Section 10.13). The difficulty with these methods is in estimating normal distribution parameters together with the uncertainty that the distribution may be considered normal. These difficulties may be overcome if an optimal threshold is sought that maximizes gray-level variance between objects and background. Note that this approach can be applied even if more than one threshold is needed [Otsu, 1979; Kittler and Illingworth, 1986; Cho et al., 1989]. Many approaches to this attractively simple idea exist—overviews may be found in [Glasbey, 1993; Sezgin and Sankur, 2004]. Section 10.13 is also relevant.

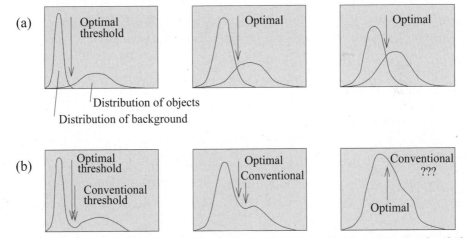

Figure 6.4: Gray-level histograms approximated by two normal distributions—the threshold is set to give minimum probability of segmentation error. (a) Probability distributions of background and objects. (b) Corresponding histograms and optimal threshold. © *Cengage Learning 2015.*

The prevalent approach to automatic threshold detection is *Otsu's algorithm*, summarized in Algorithm 6.2 [Otsu, 1979]. The underlying idea here is to test each possible threshold, and to compute the gray-level variances of both foreground and background each one implies. When a weighted sum of these variances is minimal we can deduce

THE ABERYSTWYTH FUNICULAR DISASTER   THE ABERYSTWYTH FUNICULAR DISASTER

DISASTER   DISASTER   DISASTER

Figure 6.5: Top left, an image with artificially stretched white background—the image has also been showered with random noise. Top right, thresholded with Otsu's method: the histogram is shown in Figure 6.3, and the algorithm delivers $t = 130$. At bottom, the results of $t = 115, 130, 145$ on the trickiest part of the image; segmentation quality degrades very quickly. © *Cengage Learning 2015.*

that the threshold is separating the histogram in some 'best' sense as both background and foreground distributions are at their 'tightest'. The weights will pertain to the probability of pixels coming from foreground or background with respect to the threshold in question.

Algorithm 6.2: Otsu's threshold detection

1. For an image I on G gray levels, compute the gray-level histogram $H(0), H(1), \ldots, H(G-1)$. Normalize the histogram by dividing through by the number of pixels in I—the histogram now represents the probability of each gray-level.

2. For each possible threshold $t = 0, \ldots, G-2$ partition the histogram into background B (gray-levels less than or equal to t), and foreground F (gray-levels more than t).

3. Compute $\sigma_B(t), \sigma_F(t)$, the variance of the background and foreground gray-levels. Compute the probability of a pixel being background

$$\omega_B(t) = \sum_{j=0}^{t} H(j)$$

and $\omega_F(t)$ similarly.

Set

$$\sigma(t) = \omega_B(t)\sigma_B(t) + \omega_F(t)\sigma_F(t)$$

and select as threshold $\hat{t} = \min_t(\sigma(t))$.

Figure 6.5 illustrates an application of this algorithm, which is very widely implemented (for example, in Matlab) with downloadable codes. Step 3 of the algorithm is at first sight computationally costly, but various widely documented shortcuts allow very efficient implementation.

An example of a combination of optimal and adaptive thresholding (equation 6.4) is illustrated by brain image segmentation from MR image data. [Frank et al., 1995]. Optimal gray-level segmentation parameters are determined within local subregions. Gray-level distributions corresponding to n individual (possibly non-contiguous) regions are fitted to each local histogram h_{region} which is modeled as a sum h_{model} of n Gaussian distributions so that the difference between the modeled and the actual histograms is minimized

$$h_{\text{model}}(g) = \sum_{i=1}^{n} a_i\, e^{-(g-\mu_i)^2/(2\sigma_i^2)} ,$$

$$F = \sum_{g \in G} \left(h_{\text{model}}(g) - h_{\text{region}}(g) \right)^2 . \tag{6.7}$$

Here, g represents values from the set G of image gray-levels, a_i; μ_i and σ_i denote parameters of the Gaussian distribution for the region i. The optimal parameters of the Gaussian distributions are determined by minimizing the *fit function F*.

Levenberg-Marquardt [Marquardt, 1963; Press et al., 1992] minimization was successfully used for segmentation of three-dimensional T1-weighted images from a magnetic resonance scanner into regions of white matter (WM), gray matter (GM), and cerebrospinal fluid (CSF) (see Section 10.6.1 for a description of a different approach to the same problem using multi-band image data). A nine-parameter model ($n = 3$) was first fitted to the entire volume histogram, and the problem simplified by choosing parameters σ_i and μ_{CSF} from the global histogram. (μ_{CSF} can be chosen globally since CSF regions are relatively small and localized.) An example of a global histogram, fitted Gaussian distributions, and the three distributions corresponding to WM, GM, and CSF is shown in Figure 6.6. The remaining five parameters are determined locally by minimizing F in each of the overlapping $45 \times 45 \times 45$ voxel 3D subregions located 10 voxels apart in all three dimensions. Then, Gaussian distribution parameters are tri-linearly interpolated for voxels between the minimized fit locations. Thus, the optimal thresholds can be determined for each voxel and used for segmentation. Figure 6.7 gives an example of such a segmentation. The brighter the voxel location in individual segmented images, the higher the volume percentage of the GM, WM, or CSF in that particular voxel. In each voxel, the sum of partial volume percentages is 100%.

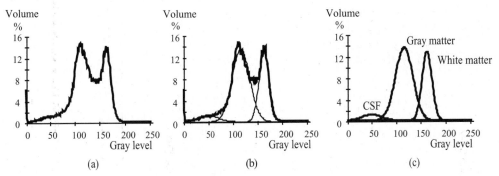

Figure 6.6: Segmentation of 3D T1-weighted MR brain image data using optimal thresholding. (a) Local gray-level histogram. (b) Fitted Gaussian distributions, global 3D image fit. (c) Gaussian distributions corresponding to WM, GM, and CSF. *Courtesy of R. J. Frank, T. J. Grabowski, The University of Iowa.*

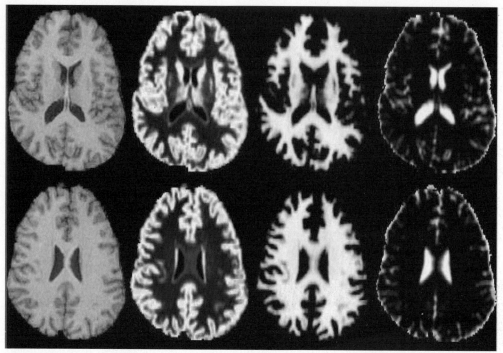

Figure 6.7: Optimal MR brain image segmentation. Left column: original T1-weighted MR images, two of 120 slices of the 3D volume. Middle left: Partial-volume maps of gray matter. The brighter the voxel, the higher is the partial volume percentage of gray matter in the voxel. Middle right: Partial-volume maps of white matter. Right column: Partial-volume maps of cerebro-spinal fluid. *Courtesy of R. J. Frank, T. J. Grabowski, The University of Iowa.*

6.1.3   Multi-spectral thresholding

Many practical segmentation problems need more information than is contained in one spectral band. Color images are a natural example, in which information is usually presented in red, green, and blue bands; multi-spectral remote sensing images or meteorological satellite images often have many more spectral bands. One segmentation approach determines thresholds independently in each spectral band and combines them into a single segmented image.

Algorithm 6.3: Recursive multi-spectral thresholding

1. Initialize the whole image as a single region.

2. Compute a smoothed histogram (see Section 2.3.2) for each spectral band. Find the most significant peak in each histogram and determine two thresholds as local minima on either side of this maximum. Segment each region in each spectral band into subregions according to these thresholds. Each segmentation in each spectral band is projected into a multi-spectral segmentation—see Figure 6.8. Regions for the next processing steps are those in the multi-spectral image.

3. Repeat step 2 for each region of the image until each region's histogram contains only one significant peak.

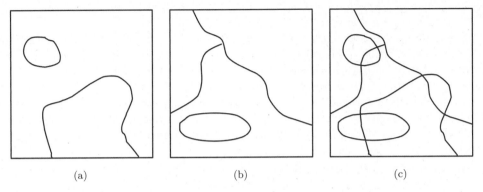

(a)   (b)   (c)

Figure 6.8: Recursive multi-spectral thresholding. (a) Band 1 thresholding. (b) Band 2 thresholding. (c) Multi-spectral segmentation. © *Cengage Learning 2015*.

Multi-spectral segmentations are often based on n-dimensional vectors of gray-levels in n spectral bands for each pixel or small pixel neighborhood. This segmentation approach, widely used in remote sensing, results from a classification process which is applied to these n-dimensional vectors. Generally speaking, regions are formed from pixels with similar properties in all spectral bands, with similar n-dimensional description vectors; see Chapter 9. Segmentation and region labeling based on supervised, unsupervised, and contextual classification is discussed in more detail in Section 10.6.1.

6.2   Edge-based segmentation

A large group of methods perform segmentation based on information about edges in the image; it is one of the earliest segmentation approaches and remains very important. Edge-based segmentations rely on edge detecting operators—these edges mark image locations of discontinuities in gray-level, color, texture, etc. A variety of edge detecting operators was described in Section 5.3.2, but the image resulting from edge detection cannot be used as a segmentation result. Supplementary processing steps must follow to combine edges into edge chains that correspond better with borders in the image. The final aim is to reach at least a partial segmentation—that is, to group local edges into an image where only edge chains with a correspondence to existing objects or image parts are present.

We will discuss several edge-based segmentation strategies leading to final border construction, and how differing amounts of prior information that can be incorporated into the method. The more prior information that is available to the segmentation process, the better the segmentation results that can be obtained. Prior knowledge can be included in the confidence evaluation of the resulting segmentation as well. Prior information affects segmentation algorithms; if a large amount is available, the boundary shape and relations with other image structures are specified very strictly and the segmentation must satisfy all these specifications. If little information about the boundary is known, the segmentation method must take more local information about the image into consideration and combine it with specific knowledge that is general for an application area. Similarly, if little prior information is available, it cannot be used to evaluate the confidence of segmentation results, and therefore no basis for feedback corrections of segmentation results is available.

The most common problems of edge-based segmentation, caused by image noise or unsuitable information in an image, are an edge presence in locations where there is no border, and no edge presence where a real border exists. Clearly both these cases have a negative influence on segmentation results.

First, we will discuss simple edge-based methods requiring minimum prior information, and the necessity for prior knowledge will increase during the section. Construction of regions from edge-based partial segmentations is discussed later

6.2.1 Edge image thresholding

Almost no zero-value pixels are present in an edge image—small edge values correspond to non-significant gray-level changes resulting from quantization noise, small lighting irregularities, etc. Simple thresholding of an edge image can be applied to remove these small values. The approach is based on an image of edge magnitudes [Kundu and Mitra, 1987] processed by an appropriate threshold. Figure 6.9 shows an original image, an edge image [as produced by a non-directional Sobel edge detector, see Section 5.3.2, equation (5.45)], an 'over-thresholded' image and an 'under-thresholded' image. Selection of an appropriate global threshold is often difficult and sometimes impossible; p-tile thresholding can be applied to define a threshold, and a more exact approach using orthogonal basis functions is described in [Flynn, 1972] which, if the original data has good contrast and is not noisy, gives good results.

A problem with simple detectors is the thickening that is evident in Figure 6.9b where there should only be a simple boundary. This can be partially rectified if edges carry directional information (as they do with the Sobel) by performing some form of non-maximal suppression (see also Section 5.3.5, in which this is performed automatically) to suppress multiple responses in the neighborhood of single boundaries. The following algorithm generates Figure 6.11a from Figure 6.9b.

Algorithm 6.4: Non-maximal suppression of directional edge data

1. Quantize edge directions eight ways according to 8-connectivity (cf. Figures 2.5 and 4.3).

2. For each pixel with non-zero edge magnitude, inspect the two adjacent pixels indicated by the direction of its edge (see Figure 6.10).

3. If the edge magnitude of either of these two exceeds that of the pixel under inspection, mark it for deletion.

4. When all pixels have been inspected, re-scan the image and erase to zero all edge data marked for deletion.

This algorithm is based on 8-connectivity and may be simplified for 4-connectivity; it is also open to more sophisticated measurement of edge direction.

It is probable that such data will still be cluttered by noise (as in this case). The hysteresis approach outlined in Section 5.3.5 is also generally applicable if suitable thresholds can be determined. Supposing that edge magnitudes exceeding t_1 can be taken as

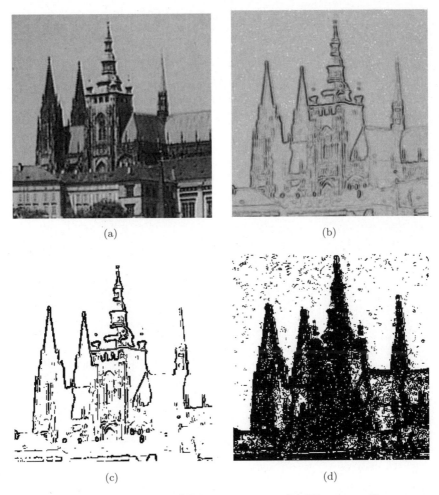

Figure 6.9: Edge image thresholding. (a) Original image. (b) Edge image (low contrast edges enhanced for display). (c) Edge image thresholded at 30. (d) Edge image thresholded at 10. © *Cengage Learning 2015.*

certain (i.e., not due to noise), and that edge magnitudes less than t_0 may be assumed to be noise induced, the following algorithm may be defined.

Algorithm 6.5: Hysteresis to filter output of an edge detector

1. Mark all edges with magnitude greater than t_1 as correct.

2. Scan all pixels with edge magnitude in the range $[t_0, t_1]$.

3. If such a pixel borders another already marked as an edge, then mark it too. 'Bordering' may be defined by 4- or 8-connectivity.

4. Repeat from step 2 until stability.

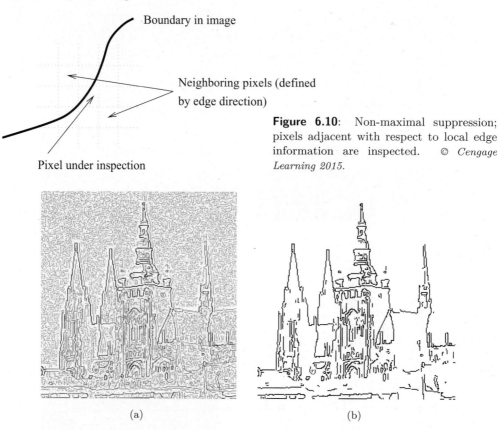

Boundary in image

Neighboring pixels (defined
by edge direction)

Pixel under inspection

Figure 6.10: Non-maximal suppression; pixels adjacent with respect to local edge information are inspected. © *Cengage Learning 2015.*

(a)   (b)

Figure 6.11: (a) Non-maximal suppression of the data in Figure 6.9b. (b) Hysteresis applied to (a); high threshold 70, low threshold 10. © *Cengage Learning 2015.*

Canny [Canny, 1986] reports choosing t_1/t_0 to be in the range 2 to 3; clearly, if a p-tile approach is available, this would guide the choice of t_1, as would any plausible model of image noise in choosing t_2. Figure 6.11b illustrates the application of this algorithm. Hysteresis is a generally applicable technique that may be deployed when evidence is generated with 'strength' that is not susceptible to simple thresholding.

6.2.2   Edge relaxation

Relaxation is a well-known approach to improving estimates of some property by paying regard to estimated values of that property in an immediate neighborhood—thus, some understanding of *local*, probably with an associated metric, is necessary. We shall encounter relaxation elsewhere in connection with region labeling (Section 10.9), 'Shape from X' computation (Chapter 11) and optical flow (Section 16.2) but its early uses in computer vision were in connection with extracting boundaries from edge maps.

There have been many application of relaxation to the boundary extraction problem: most of those have been superseded by more recent techniques (in particular the theoretically well-grounded Markov Random Field, 10.12). Relaxation is often heuristic in approach but remains appealing as it is often effective, and is simple to comprehend.

Crudely, the output of an edge detector is considered as an initialization; iteratively, pixels connected (that is, local) to strong edge responses are viewed as 'likely' to be edges themselves, while strong responses isolated from any others are viewed as less likely. This idea updates edge responses, and is iterated until some convergence is reached—it is improved by incorporating edge direction information. Edge responses are often usefully interpreted as probabilities. The principle is illustrated in Figure 6.12.

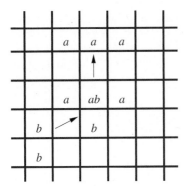

Figure 6.12: The principle of edge relaxation: two directed strong edges—oriented upwards (compass N) and up-right (compass ENE)—are indicated by arrows. Pixels marked *a* receive 'encouragement' for edges directed N; pixels marked *b* receive encouragement for edges directed ENE. Note one pixel receives encouragement to join the marked edges. © *Cengage Learning 2015*.

In practice, relaxation normally accomplishes most in very few iterations. It can be computationally very expensive, but (because it considers local information only) is very amenable to parallel implementation. An early and popular implementation considered crack-edges between pixels [Hanson and Riseman, 1978; Prager, 1980], and this was successfully parallelized [Clark, 1991]. A method to determine probabilistic distribution of possible edge neighborhoods is given in [Sher, 1992]. In [Kim and Cho, 1994], fuzzy logic is used to assess neighborhood edge patterns; neural networks are employed as a means for fuzzy rule training.

6.2.3 Border tracing

If a region border is not known but regions have been defined in the image, borders can be detected uniquely. Initially, assume that the image with regions is either binary or that regions have been labeled (see Section 8.1). The first goal is to determine **inner** region borders. As defined earlier, an inner region border is a subset of the region—conversely, the **outer** border is not a subset of the region. The following algorithm provides inner boundary tracing in both 4-connectivity and 8-connectivity.

Algorithm 6.6: Inner boundary tracing

1. Search the image from top left until a pixel P_0 of a new region is found; this has the minimum column value of all pixels of that region having the minimum row value. P_0 is a starting pixel of the region border. Define a variable *dir* which stores the direction of the previous move along the border from the previous border element to the current border element. Assign

    (a) *dir* = 3 if the border is detected in 4-connectivity (Figure 6.13a),

    (b) *dir* = 7 if the border is detected in 8-connectivity (Figure 6.13b).

2. Search the 3×3 neighborhood of the current pixel in an anti-clockwise direction, beginning the neighborhood search in the pixel positioned in the direction

   (a) $(dir + 3) \bmod 4$ (Figure 6.13c),
   (b) $(dir + 7) \bmod 8$ if dir is *even* (Figure 6.13d),
       $(dir + 6) \bmod 8$ if dir is *odd* (Figure 6.13e).

   The first pixel found with the same value as the current pixel is a new boundary element P_n. Update the dir value.

3. If the current boundary element P_n is equal to the second border element P_1, and if the previous border element P_{n-1} is equal to P_0, stop. Otherwise repeat step 2.

4. Pixels $P_0 \ldots P_{n-2}$ are now the detected inner border.

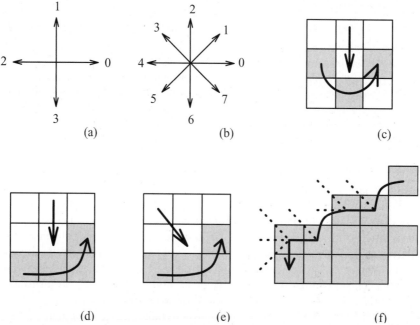

Figure 6.13: Inner boundary tracing. (a) Direction notation, 4-connectivity. (b) 8-connectivity. (c) Pixel neighborhood search sequence in 4-connectivity. (d), (e) Search sequence in 8-connectivity. (f) Boundary tracing in 8-connectivity (dotted lines show pixels tested during the border tracing). © *Cengage Learning 2015*.

Algorithm 6.6 works for all regions larger than one pixel. It is able to find region borders but does not find borders of region holes, which may be located by identifying border elements unallocated thus far to borders. The search for border elements always starts after a traced border is closed, and the search for 'unused' border elements can continue in the same way as the search for the first border element. Note that if objects are of unit width, more conditions must be added.

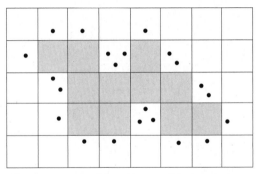

Figure 6.14: Outer boundary tracing; • denotes outer border elements. Note that some pixels may be listed several times. © *Cengage Learning 2015.*

This algorithm, under 4-connectivity, can be adapted to deliver an outer region border.

Algorithm 6.7: Outer boundary tracing

1. Trace the inner region boundary in 4-connectivity until done.

2. The outer boundary consists of all non-region pixels that were tested during the search process; if some pixels were tested more than once, they are listed more than once in the outer boundary list.

Note that some border elements may be repeated in the outer border up to three times—see Figure 6.14. The outer region border is useful for deriving properties such as perimeter, compactness, etc., and is consequently often used (see Chapter 8).

The inner border is always part of a region but the outer border never is. Therefore, if two regions are adjacent, they never have a common border, which causes difficulties in higher processing levels with region description, region merging, etc. The inter-pixel boundary extracted, for instance, from crack edges is common to adjacent regions; nevertheless, its position cannot be specified in single pairs of pixel co-ordinates (compare the supergrid data structure in Figure 6.39). **Extended** borders provide properties that are preferable to both inner and outer borders [Pavlidis, 1977]: their main advantage is that they define a single common border between adjacent regions which may be specified using standard pixel co-ordinates (see Figure 6.15). All the useful properties of the outer border remain; in addition, the boundary shape is exactly equal to the inter-pixel shape but is shifted one half-pixel down and one half-pixel right. The existence of a common border between regions makes it possible to incorporate into tracing a boundary description process. A weighted graph consisting of border segments and vertices may be derived directly from the boundary tracing process; also, the border between adjacent regions may be traced only once and not twice as in conventional approaches.

The extended boundary is defined using 8-neighborhoods, and the pixels are coded according to Figure 6.16a, e.g., $P_4(P)$ denotes the pixel immediately to the left of pixel P. Four kinds of inner boundary pixels of a region R are defined; if Q denotes pixels

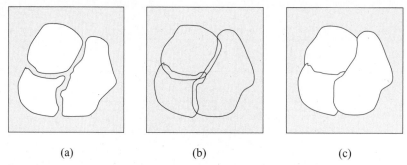

(a)   (b)   (c)

Figure 6.15: Boundary locations for inner, outer, and extended boundary definition. (a) Inner. (b) Outer. (c) Extended. © *Cengage Learning 2015.*

outside the region R, then a pixel $P \in R$ is

$$
\begin{aligned}
&\text{a LEFT pixel of } R &&\text{if } P_4(P) \in Q \,, \\
&\text{a RIGHT pixel of } R &&\text{if } P_0(P) \in Q \,, \\
&\text{an UPPER pixel of } R &&\text{if } P_2(P) \in Q \,, \\
&\text{a LOWER pixel of } R &&\text{if } P_6(P) \in Q \,.
\end{aligned}
$$

Let LEFT(R), RIGHT(R), UPPER(R), LOWER(R) represent the corresponding subsets of R. The extended boundary EB is defined as a set of points P, P_0, P_6, P_7 satisfying the following conditions [Pavlidis, 1977; Liow, 1991]:

$$
\begin{aligned}
\text{EB} =& \big\{P : P \in \text{LEFT}(R)\big\} \cup \big\{P : P \in \text{UPPER}(R)\big\} \\
& \cup \big\{P_6(P) : P \in \text{LOWER}(R)\big\} \cup \big\{P_0(P) : P \in \text{RIGHT}(R)\big\} \\
& \cup \big\{P_7(P) : P \in \text{RIGHT}(R)\big\} \,.
\end{aligned}
\tag{6.8}
$$

Figure 6.16 illustrates the definition.

The extended boundary can easily be constructed from the outer boundary. Using an intuitive definition of RIGHT, LEFT, UPPER, and LOWER outer boundary points, EB

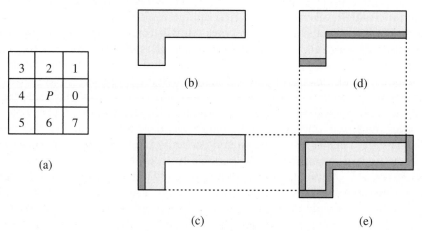

(a)   (c)   (e)

Figure 6.16: Extended boundary definition. (a) Pixel coding scheme. (b) Region R. (c) LEFT(R). (d) LOWER(R). (e) Extended boundary. © *Cengage Learning 2015.*

may be obtained by shifting all the UPPER outer boundary points one pixel down and right, shifting all the LEFT outer boundary points one pixel to the right, and shifting all the RIGHT outer boundary points one pixel down. The LOWER outer boundary point positions remain unchanged; see Figure 6.17.

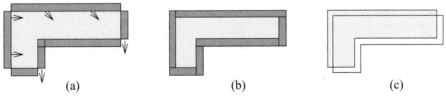

(a)   (b)   (c)

Figure 6.17: Constructing the extended boundary from outer boundary. (a) Outer boundary. (b) Extended boundary construction. (c) Extended boundary has the same shape and size as the natural object boundary. © *Cengage Learning 2015*.

A more sophisticated method and efficient algorithm for extended boundary extraction was introduced in [Liow, 1991]. The approach is based on detecting common boundary segments between adjacent regions and vertex points in boundary segment connections. The detection process is based on a look-up table, which defines all 12 possible situations of the local configuration of 2×2 pixel windows, depending on the previous detected direction of boundary, and on the status of window pixels which can be inside or outside a region.

Algorithm 6.8: Extended boundary tracing

1. Define a starting pixel of an extended boundary in some standard way.

2. The first move along the traced boundary from the starting pixel is in direction $dir = 6$ (down), corresponding to the situation (i) in Figure 6.18.

3. Trace the extended boundary using the look-up table in Figure 6.18 until a closed extended border results.

Note that no hole-border tracing is included in the algorithm. Holes are considered separate regions so borders between a region and a hole are traced as a border of the hole.

The look-up table approach makes tracing more efficient than conventional methods and makes parallel implementation possible. A pseudo-code description of algorithmic details is given in [Liow, 1991], where a solution to the problems of tracing all the borders in an image in an efficient way is given. In addition to extended boundary tracing, it provides a description of each boundary segment in chain code form together with information about vertices. This method is very suitable for representing borders in higher-level segmentation approaches including methods that integrate edge-based and region-based segmentation results.

A more difficult situation is encountered if borders are traced in gray-level images where regions have not yet been defined [Dudani, 1976]. Then, the border is represented by a *simple path* of high-gradient pixels in the image (see Section 2.3.1). Border tracing is initialized at a pixel with a high probability of being a border element, and then

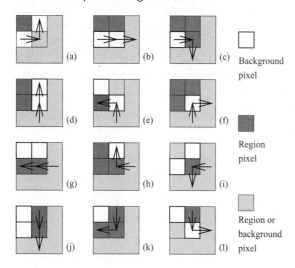

Figure 6.18: Look-up table defining all possibilities that appear during extended border tracing. Current position is the central pixel; direction of the next move depends on local configuration of background and region points, and on direction of approach to the current pixel. *Based on [Liow, 1991].*

border construction proceeds by adding the next elements which are in the most probable direction. To find the following border elements, edge gradient magnitudes and directions are usually computed in pixels of probable border continuation.

Algorithm 6.9: Border tracing in gray-level images

1. Suppose the border has been determined up to the border element $\mathbf{x}_i$.

2. Define an element $\mathbf{x}_j$ as a pixel adjacent to $\mathbf{x}_i$ in the direction $\phi(\mathbf{x}_i)$. If the gradient magnitude in $\mathbf{x}_j$ is larger than a preset threshold, $\mathbf{x}_j$ is considered a border element; return to step 1.

3. Compute the average gray-level value in the 3×3 neighborhood of the pixel $\mathbf{x}_j$. Compare the result with some preset gray-level value and decide whether $\mathbf{x}_j$ is positioned inside or outside the region.

4. Try to continue tracing at pixel $\mathbf{x}_k$, adjacent to $\mathbf{x}_i$ in direction $[\phi(\mathbf{x}_i) \pm \pi/4]$, the sign being determined by the result of step 3. If a continuation is found, $\mathbf{x}_k$ is a new border element, and return to step 1. If $\mathbf{x}_k$ is not a border element, start tracing at another promising pixel.

This algorithm can be applied to multi-spectral or dynamic images (temporal image sequences) as well, based on multi-dimensional gradients.

6.2.4 Border detection as graph searching

Whenever additional knowledge is available for boundary detection, it should be used. One example of prior knowledge is a known starting point and a known ending point of the border, even if the precise border location is not known. Even relatively weak additional requirements such as smoothness or low curvature may be included as prior knowledge. If this kind of supporting information is available, general AI problem-solving methods can be applied.

A graph is a general structure consisting of a set of nodes n_i and arcs between the nodes (n_i, n_j) (see Section 4.2.3). We consider oriented and numerically weighted arcs, these weights being called **costs**. The border detection process is transformed into a search for the optimal path in a weighted graph, the aim being to find the best path that connects two specified nodes, the start and end nodes.

Assume that both edge magnitude $s(\mathbf{x})$ and edge direction $\phi(\mathbf{x})$ information is available in an edge image. Each image pixel corresponds to a graph node weighted by a value $s(\mathbf{x})$. We can construct a graph as follows: to connect a node n_i representing the pixel $\mathbf{x}_i$ with a node n_j representing the pixel $\mathbf{x}_j$, pixel $\mathbf{x}_j$ must be one of three existing neighbors of $\mathbf{x}_i$ in the direction $d \in [\phi(\mathbf{x}_i) - \pi/4, \phi(\mathbf{x}_i) + \pi/4]$. Further, $s(\mathbf{x}_i)$ and $s(\mathbf{x}_j)$ must be greater than some preset threshold of edge significance T, These conditions can be modified in specific edge detection problems.

Figure 6.19a shows an image of edge directions, with only significant edges listed. Figure 6.19b shows an oriented graph constructed from these edges.

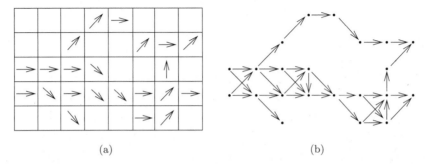

(a)   (b)

Figure 6.19: Graph representation of an edge image. (a) Edge directions of pixels with above-threshold edge magnitudes. (b) Corresponding graph. © *Cengage Learning 2015.*

The application of graph search to edge detection was first published in [Martelli, 1972], in which Nilsson's A-algorithm [Nilsson, 1982] was used. Let $\mathbf{x}_A$ be the starting border element, and $\mathbf{x}_B$ be the end border element. To use graph search for region border detection, a method of oriented weighted-graph expansion must first be defined (one possible method was described earlier). A cost function $f(\mathbf{x}_i)$ must also be defined that is a cost estimate of the path between nodes n_A and n_B (pixels $\mathbf{x}_A$ and $\mathbf{x}_B$) which goes through an intermediate node n_i (pixel $\mathbf{x}_i$). The cost function $f(\mathbf{x}_i)$ typically consists of two components; an estimate $\tilde{g}(\mathbf{x}_i)$ of the minimum path cost between the starting border element $\mathbf{x}_A$ and $\mathbf{x}_i$, and an estimate $\tilde{h}(\mathbf{x}_i)$ of the minimum path cost between $\mathbf{x}_i$ and the end border element $\mathbf{x}_B$. The cost $\tilde{g}(\mathbf{x}_i)$ of the path from the starting point to the node n_i is usually a sum of costs associated with the arcs or nodes that are in the path. The cost function must be separable and monotonic with respect to the path length, and therefore the local costs associated with arcs are required to be non-negative. A simple example of $\tilde{g}(\mathbf{x}_i)$ satisfying the given conditions is to consider the path length from $\mathbf{x}_A$ to $\mathbf{x}_i$. An estimate $\tilde{h}(\mathbf{x}_i)$ may be the length of the border from $\mathbf{x}_i$ to $\mathbf{x}_B$, it making sense to prefer shorter borders between $\mathbf{x}_A$ and $\mathbf{x}_B$ as the path with lower cost. This implies that the following graph search algorithm (Nilsson's A-algorithm) can be applied to the border detection.

Algorithm 6.10: A-algorithm graph search

1. Expand the starting node n_A and put all its successors into an OPEN list with pointers back to the starting node n_A. Evaluate the cost function f for each expanded node.

2. If the OPEN list is empty, fail. Determine the node n_i from the OPEN list with the lowest associated cost $f(n_i)$ and remove it. If $n_i = n_B$, then trace back through the pointers to find the optimum path and stop.

3. If the option to stop was not taken in step 2, expand the specified node n_i, and put its successors on the OPEN list with pointers back to n_i. Compute their costs f. Go to step 2.

An example of this algorithm is given in Figure 6.20. Here, nodes currently on the OPEN list are shaded and the minimum-cost node on the OPEN list is shaded and outlined. In Figure 6.20c, note that the node with a cumulative cost of 7 is also expanded; however no successors are found. In Figure 6.20e, since an expansion of a node in the final graph layer was attempted, the search is over.

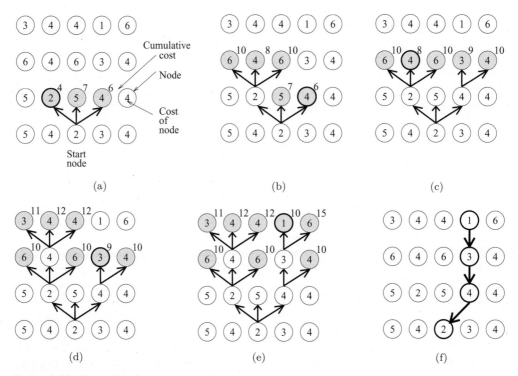

Figure 6.20: Example of a graph searching sequence using the A-algorithm (see text for description of progress of algorithm). (a) Step 1, expansion of the start node. (b) Step 2. (c) Steps 3 and 4. (d) Step 5. (e) Step 6. (f) The optimal path is defined by back-tracking. © *Cengage Learning 2015.*

If no additional requirements are set on the graph construction and search, this process can easily result in an infinite loop (see Figure 6.21). To prevent this behavior,

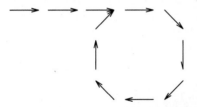

Figure 6.21: Following a closed loop in image data. © *Cengage Learning 2015.*

no node expansion is allowed that puts a node on the OPEN list if this node has already been visited and put on the OPEN list in the past. A simple solution to the *loop* problem is not to allow searching in a backward direction. This approach can be used if a priori information about the boundary location and its local direction is available. In this case, it may be possible to straighten the processed image (and the corresponding graph) as shown in Figure 6.22. The edge image is geometrically warped by re-sampling the image along profile lines perpendicular to the approximate position of the sought border. The pre-processing step that straightens the image data provides a substantial computational convenience. No backward searches may be allowed to trace boundaries represented this way. This approach can be extremely useful if the borders of thin, elongated objects such as roads, rivers, vessels, etc., are to be detected. On the other hand, prohibiting backward search may limit the shapes of borders that can be successfully identified. In [van der Zwet and Reiber, 1994], a graph-search based method called the **gradient field transform** is introduced that allows searching to proceed successfully in any direction.

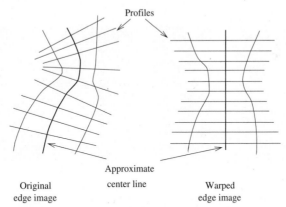

Figure 6.22: Geometric warping produces a straightened image: The graph constructed requires searches in one main direction only (e.g., top-down). *Based on [Fleagle et al., 1989].*

The estimate of the cost of the path from the current node n_i to the end node n_B has a substantial influence on the search behavior. If this estimate $\tilde{h}(n_i)$ of the true cost $h(n_i)$ is not considered, so $\tilde{h}(n_i) = 0$, no heuristic is included in the algorithm and a breadth-first search is done. Because of this, the detected path will always be optimal according to the criterion used, and thus the minimum-cost path will always be found. Heuristics may lead to suboptimal solutions, but can often be much faster.

Given natural conditions for estimates $\tilde{g}$, the minimum-cost path result can be guaranteed if $\tilde{h}(n_i) \leq h(n_i)$ and if the true cost of any part of the path $c(n_p, n_q)$ is larger than the estimated cost of this part $\tilde{c}(n_p, n_q)$. The closer the estimate $\tilde{h}(n_i)$ is to $h(n_i)$, the lower the number of nodes expanded in the search. The problem is that the exact cost of the path from the node n_i to the end node n_B is not known beforehand. In some applications, it may be more important to get a quick rather than an optimal solution. Choosing $\tilde{h}(n_i) > h(n_i)$, optimality is not guaranteed but the number of expanded nodes will typically be smaller because the search can be stopped before the optimum is found.

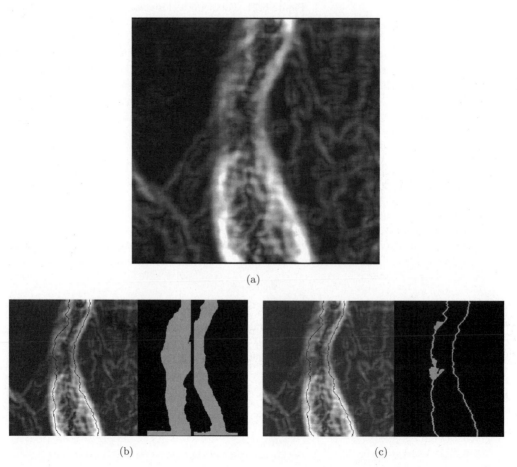

Figure 6.23: Comparison of optimal and heuristic graph search performance. (a) Raw cost function (inverted edge image of a vessel). (b) Optimal graph search, resulting vessel borders are shown adjacent to the cost function, expanded nodes shown (38%). (c) Heuristic graph search, resulting borders and expanded nodes (2%). © *Cengage Learning 2015.*

A comparison of optimal and heuristic graph search border detection is shown in Figure 6.23. The raw cost function—the inverted edge image— is in Figure 6.23a; Figure 6.23b shows the optimal borders resulting from graph search when $\tilde{h}(n_i) = 0$; 38% of nodes were expanded during the search, and expanded nodes are shown as white regions. When a heuristic search was applied [$\tilde{h}(n_i)$ was about 20% overestimated], only 2% of graph nodes were expanded during the search and the border detection was 15 times faster

(Figure 6.23c). Comparing resulting borders in Figures 6.23b and 6.23c, it can be seen that despite a very substantial speedup, the resulting borders do not differ significantly.

In summary:

- If $\tilde{h}(n_i) = 0$, the algorithm produces a minimum-cost search.

- If $\tilde{h}(n_i) > h(n_i)$, the algorithm may run faster, but the minimum-cost result is not guaranteed.

- If $\tilde{h}(n_i) \leq h(n_i)$, the search will produce the minimum-cost path if and only if

$$c(n_p, n_q) \geq \tilde{h}(n_p) - \tilde{h}(n_q)$$

for any p, q, where $c(n_p, n_q)$ is the true minimum cost of getting from n_p to n_q, which is not easy to fulfill for a specific $f(x)$.

- If $h(n_i) = \tilde{h}(n_i)$, the search will always produce the minimum-cost path with a minimum number of expanded nodes.

- The better the estimate of $h(n)$, the smaller the number of nodes that must be expanded.

In image segmentation applications, the existence of a path between a start pixel x_A and an end pixel x_B is not guaranteed because of possible discontinuities in the edge image, and so more heuristics must often be applied to overcome these problems. For example, if there is no node in the OPEN list which can be expanded, it may be possible to expand nodes with non-significant edge-valued successors—this can build a bridge to pass these small discontinuities in border representations.

A crucial question is how to choose the evaluation cost functions for graph-search border detection. A good cost function should have elements common to most edge detection problems and also specific terms related to the particular application. Some generally applicable cost functions are:

- Strength of edges forming a border: The heuristic 'the stronger the edges that form the border, the higher the probability of the border' is very natural and almost always gives good results. Note that if a border consists of strong edges, the cost of that border is small. The cost of adding another node to the border will be

$$\left(\max_{\text{image}} s(\mathbf{x}_k) \right) - s(\mathbf{x}_i) , \tag{6.9}$$

where the maximum edge strength is obtained from all pixels in the image.

- Border curvature: Sometimes, borders with small curvature are preferred. Then, total border curvature can be evaluated as a monotonic function of local curvature increments:

$$\text{diff}\big(\phi(\mathbf{x}_i) - \phi(\mathbf{x}_j)\big) , \tag{6.10}$$

where *diff* is some suitable function evaluating the difference in edge directions in two consecutive border elements.

- Proximity to an approximate border location: If an approximate boundary location is known, it is natural to support paths that are closer to the known approximation than others. A border element value can be weighted by the distance '*dist*' from the approximate boundary, the distance having either additive or multiplicative influence on the cost

$$\text{dist}(\mathbf{x}_i, \text{approximate\_boundary}) . \tag{6.11}$$

- Estimates of the distance to the goal (end point): If a border is reasonably straight, it is natural to support expansion of those nodes that are located closer to the goal node than other nodes

$$\tilde{h}(\mathbf{x}_i) = \text{dist}(\mathbf{x}_i, \mathbf{x}_B) . \tag{6.12}$$

Since the range of border detection applications is wide, cost functions may need some modification to be relevant to a particular task. For example, if the aim is to determine a region that exhibits a border of a moderate strength, a closely adjacent border of high strength may incorrectly attract the search if the cost given in equation (6.9) is used. Clearly, functions may have to be modified to reflect the appropriateness of individual costs properly. In the given example, a Gaussian cost transform may be used with the mean of the Gaussian distribution representing the desired edge strength and the standard deviation reflecting the interval of acceptable edge strengths. Thus, edge strengths close to the expected value will be preferred in comparison to edges of lower or higher edge strength. A variety of such transforms may be developed; a set of generally useful cost transforms can be found in [Falcao et al., 1995].

Graph-based border detection methods very often suffer from large numbers of expanded nodes stored in the OPEN list, these nodes with pointers back to their predecessors representing the searched part of the graph. The cost associated with each node in the OPEN list is a result of all the cost increases on the path from the starting node to that node. This implies that even a good path can generate a higher cost in the current node than costs of the nodes on worse paths which did not get so far from the starting node. This results in expansion of these 'bad' nodes representing shorter paths with lower total costs, even with the general view that their probabilities are low. An excellent way to solve this problem is to incorporate a heuristic estimate $\tilde{h}(\mathbf{x}_i)$ into the cost evaluation, but unfortunately, a good estimate of the path cost from the current node to the goal is not usually available. Some modifications which make the method more practically useful, even if some of them no longer guarantee the minimum-cost path, are available:

- **Pruning the solution tree:** The set of nodes in the OPEN list can be reduced during the search. Deleting those paths that have high average cost per unit length, or deleting paths that are too short whenever the total number of nodes in the OPEN list exceeds a defined limit, usually gives good results (see also Section 9.4.2).

- **Least maximum cost:** The strength of a chain may be given by the strength of the weakest element—this idea is included in cost function computations. The cost of the current path is then set as the cost of the most expensive arc in the path from the starting node to the current node, whatever the sum of costs along the path. The path cost does not therefore necessarily grow with each step, and this is what favors expansion of good paths for a longer time.

- **Branch and bound:** This modification is based on maximum allowed cost of a path, no path being allowed to exceed this cost. This maximum path cost is either known beforehand or is computed and updated during the graph search. All paths that exceed the allowed maximum path cost are deleted from the OPEN list.

- **Lower bound:** Another way to increase search speed is to reduce the number of poor edge candidate expansions. Poor edge candidates are always expanded if the cost of the best current path exceeds that of any worse but shorter path in the graph. If the cost of the best successor is set to zero, the total cost of the path does not grow after the node expansion and the good path will be expanded again. The method reported in [Sonka et al., 1993] assumes that the path is searched in a straightened graph resulting from a warped image as discussed earlier. The cost of the minimum-cost node on each profile is subtracted from each node on the profile (lower bound). In effect, this shifts the range of costs from

$$\min(\text{profile\_node\_costs}) \leq \text{node\_cost} \leq \max(\text{profile\_node\_costs})$$

to

$$0 \leq \text{new\_node\_cost} \leq$$
$$\leq \big(\max(\text{profile\_node\_costs}) - \min(\text{profile\_node\_cost})\big).$$

Note that the range of the costs on a given profile remains the same, but the range is translated such that at least one node for each profile is assigned a zero cost. Because the costs of the nodes for each profile are translated by different amounts, the graph is expanded in an order that supports expansion of good paths. For graph searching in the straightened image, the lower bound can be considered heuristic information when expanding nodes and assigning costs to subpaths in the graph. By summing the minimum value for each profile, the total is an estimate of the minimum-cost path through the graph. Obviously, the minimum cost nodes for each profile may not form a valid path, i.e., they may not be neighbors as required. However, the total cost will be the lower limit of the cost of any path through the graph. This result allows the heuristic to be admissible, thus guaranteeing the success of the algorithm in finding the optimal path. The assignment of a heuristic cost for a given node is implemented in a pre-processing step through the use of the lower bound.

- **Multi-resolution processing:** The number of expanded nodes can be decreased if a sequence of two graph search processes is applied. The first search is done in lower resolution and detects an approximate boundary: a smaller number of graph nodes is involved in the search and a smaller number is expanded, compared to full resolution. The second search is done in full resolution using the low-resolution results as a model, and the full-resolution costs are weighted by a factor representing the distance from the approximate boundary acquired in low resolution (equation 6.11). This approach assumes that the approximate boundary location can be detected from the low-resolution image [Sonka et al., 1993, 1994].

- **Incorporation of higher-level knowledge:** Including higher-level knowledge into the graph search may significantly decrease the number of expanded nodes. The search may be directly guided by a priori knowledge of approximate boundary

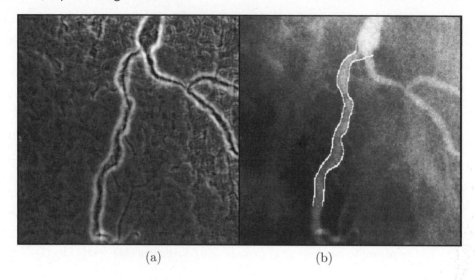

(a)   (b)

Figure 6.24: Graph search applied to coronary vessel border detection. (a) Edge image. (b) Determined vessel borders. © *Cengage Learning 2015*.

position. Another possibility is to incorporate a boundary shape model into the cost function computation. Both these approaches together with additional specific knowledge and the multi-resolution approach applied to coronary border detection are discussed in detail in Chapter 10 (see Figure 6.24 and Section 10.1.5).

Graph searching techniques offer a convenient way to ensure global optimality of detected contours, and have often been applied to the detection of approximately straight contours. The detection of closed structure contours would involve geometrically transforming the image using a polar-to-rectangular co-ordinate transformation in order to 'straighten' the contour, but this may prevent the algorithm from detecting the non-convex parts of the contour. To overcome this, the image may be divided into two segments (iteratively, if necessary) and separate, simultaneous searches can be conducted in each segment. The searches are independent and proceed in opposite directions from a start point until they meet at the dividing line between the two image segments.

Searching for borders in the image without knowledge of the start and end points is more complex. In an approach based on magnitudes and directions of edges in the image, edges are merged into edge chains (i.e., partial borders). Edge chains are constructed by applying a bi-directional heuristic search in which half of each 8-neighborhood expanded node is considered as lying in front of the edge, the second half as lying behind the edge (see Figure 6.25). Partial borders are grouped together using other heuristics which

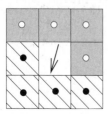

Figure 6.25: Bidirectional heuristic search: Edge predecessors (marked ∘) and successors (marked •). © *Cengage Learning 2015*.

may be similar to edge relaxation (Section 6.2.2), and final region borders result. The following algorithm describes these ideas in more detail and is an example of applying a bottom-up control strategy (see Chapter 10).

Algorithm 6.11: Heuristic search for image borders

1. Search for the strongest unconsidered/unmarked edge in the image, and mark it. If the edge magnitude is less than the preset threshold or if no image edge was found, go to step 5.

2. Expand all the image edges positioned in front of the specified starting edge until no new successors can be found.

3. Expand all the image edges positioned behind the specified starting edge until no new predecessors can be found. In steps 2 and 3 do not include edges that are already part of any existing edge chain.

4. If the resulting edge chain consists of at least three edges, it is stored in the chain list, otherwise it is deleted. Proceed to step 1.

5. Modify edge chains according to the rules given in Figure 6.26.

6. Repeat step 5 until resulting borders do not change substantially from step to step.

The rules given in Figure 6.26 (used in step 5 of Algorithm 6.11) solve three standard situations. First, thinner edge responses to a single border are obtained. Second, edge responses resulting from changes of lighting, where no real border exists, are removed.

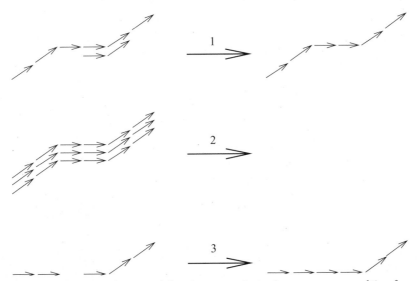

Figure 6.26: Rules for edge chain modification; note that edge responses resulting from continuous changes of illumination are removed (case 2). © *Cengage Learning 2015*.

Third, small gaps in boundary-element chains are bridged. Detailed behavior given by these general rules can be modified according to the particular problem.

A good overview of border detection and edge linking methods can be found in [v. d Heijden, 1995]. An approach to border detection that uses enhancements of corners and junctions can be found in [Demi, 1996].

6.2.5   Border detection as dynamic programming

Dynamic programming is an optimization method based on the **principle of optimality** [Bellmann, 1957; Pontriagin, 1962]. It searches for optima of functions in which not all variables are simultaneously interrelated. (Dynamic programming underlies the very important Viterbi algorithm, introduced in Section 10.11.)

Consider the following simple boundary-tracing problem (Figure 6.27). The aim is to find the best (minimum cost) 8-connected path between one of the possible start points A, B, C and one of the possible ending points G, H, I. The graph representing the problem, together with assigned partial costs, is shown in Figure 6.27a,b. There are three ways to get to the node E: connecting A–E gives the cost $g(A, E) = 2$; connecting B–E, cost $g(B, E) = 6$; connecting C–E, cost $g(C, E) = 3$.

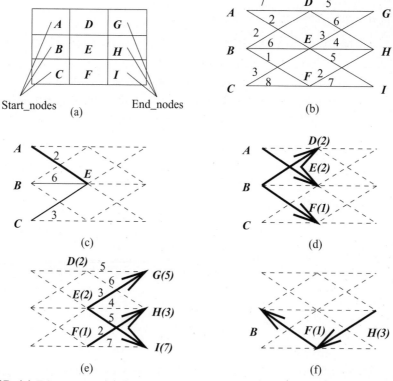

Figure 6.27: (a) Edge image. (b) Corresponding graph, partial costs assigned. (c) Possible paths from any start point to E, $A-E$ is optimal. (d) Optimal partial paths to nodes D, E, F. (e) Optimal partial paths to nodes G, H, I. (f) Back-tracking from H defines the optimal boundary.
© *Cengage Learning 2015.*

The main idea of the principle of optimality is: *Whatever the path to the node E was, there exists an optimal path between E and the end point.* In other words, *if the optimal path start point–endpoint goes through E, then both its parts start point–E and E–end point, are also optimal.*

In our case, the optimal path between the start point and E is the partial path A–E (see Figure 6.27c). Only the following information need be stored for future use; to get to E, the optimal path is A-E, cost $C(E) = 2$. Using the same approach, to get to D the optimal path is B–D, cost $C(D) = 2$; the best path to F is B–F, cost $C(F) = 1$ (see Figure 6.27d). The path may get to node G from either D or E. The cost of the path through the node D is a sum of the cumulative cost $C(D)$ of the node D and the partial path cost $g(D, G)$. This cost $C(G_D) = 7$ represents the path B–D–G because the best path to D is from B. The cost to get to G from E is $C(G_E) = 5$, representing the path A–E–G. It is obvious that the path going through node E is better, the optimal path to G is the path A–E–G with cost $C(G) = 5$ (see Figure 6.27e). Similarly, cost $C(H) = 3$ (B–F–H) and cost $C(I) = 7$ (A–E–I). Now, the end point with the minimum path cost represents the optimum path; node H is therefore the optimal boundary end point, and the optimal boundary is B–F–H (see Figure 6.27f). Figure 6.28 gives an example in which node costs are used (not arc costs as in Figure 6.27). Note that the graph, the cost function, and the resulting path are identical to those used in Figure 6.20.

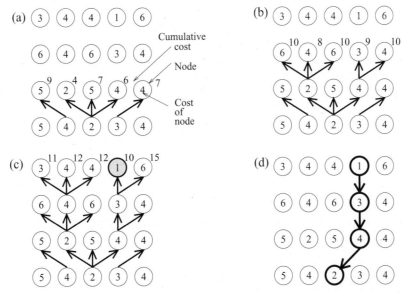

Figure 6.28: Example of a graph searching sequence using dynamic programming. (a) Step 1, expansion of the first graph layer. (b) Step 2. (c) Step 3—the minimum-cost node in the last layer marked. (d) The optimal path is defined by back-tracking. © *Cengage Learning 2015.*

If the graph has more than three layers, the process is repeated until one of the end points is reached. Each repetition consists of a simpler optimization as shown in Figure 6.29a

$$C\left(x_k^{m+1}\right) = \min_i \left(C(x_i^m) + g^m(i, k)\right), \tag{6.13}$$

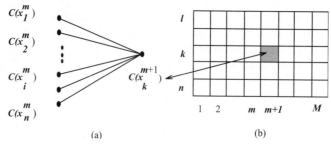

(a)   (b)

Figure 6.29: Dynamic programming. (a) One step of the cost calculation. (b) Graph layers, node notation. © *Cengage Learning 2015*.

where $C(x_k^{m+1})$ is the new cost assigned to the node x_k^{m+1}, and $g^m(i,k)$ is the partial path cost between nodes x_i^m and x_k^{m+1}. For the complete optimization problem,

$$\min\left(C(x^1, x^2, \ldots, x^M)\right) = \min_{k=1,\ldots,n}\left(C(x_k^M)\right), \tag{6.14}$$

where x_k^M are the end point nodes, M is the number of graph layers between start and end points (see Figure 6.29b), and $C(x^1, x^2, \ldots, x^M)$ denotes the cost of a path between the first and last (M^{th}) graph layer. Requiring an 8-connected border and assuming n nodes x_i^m in each graph layer m, $3n$ cost combinations must be computed for each layer, $3n(M-1) + n$ being the total number of cost combination computations. Compared to the brute-force enumerative search, where $n(3^{M-1})$ combinations must be computed, the improvement is obvious. The final optimal path results from back-tracking through the searched graph. Note that the number of neighbors depends on the definition of contiguity and definition of the searched graph, and is not limited to three.

The complete graph must be constructed to apply dynamic programming, and this may follow general rules given in the previous section, from which evaluation functions may also be appropriate. Figure 6.30 shows the result of dynamic programming applied to detection of pulmonary fissures from X-ray CT images. Since the fissures are visualized as bright pixels, the cost function simply reflects inverted pixel gray values. Despite the fact that vessels are substantially brighter (their pixels correspond to locally lower costs), the path of the lowest overall cost reflects the continuous character of the fissure.

Algorithm 6.12: Boundary tracing as dynamic programming

1. Specify initial costs $C(x_i^1)$ of all nodes in the first graph layer, $i = 1, \ldots, n$ and partial path costs $g^m(i,k)$, $m = 1, \ldots, M-1$.

2. Repeat step 3 for all $m = 1, \ldots, M-1$.

3. Repeat step 4 for all nodes $k = 1, \ldots, n$ in the graph layer m.

4. Let

$$C\left(x_k^{m+1}\right) = \min_{i=-1,0,1}\left(C(x_{k+i}^m) + g^m(i,k)\right). \tag{6.15}$$

Set pointer from node x_k^{m+1} back to node x_i^{m*}; where $*$ denotes the optimal predecessor.

5. Find an optimal node x_k^{M*} in the last graph layer M and obtain an optimal path by back-tracking through the pointers from x_k^{M*} to x_i^{1*}.

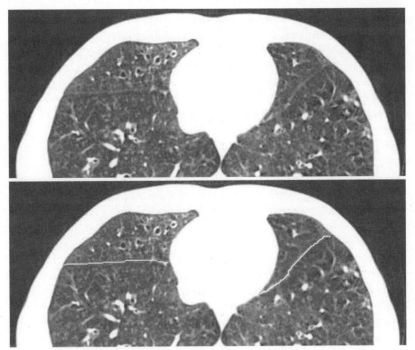

Figure 6.30: Detection of pulmonary fissures using dynamic programming. Top: Subregion of an original cross-sectional X-ray CT image of a human lung. Bottom: Detected fissures shown in white. © *Cengage Learning 2015*.

It has been shown that heuristic search may be more efficient than dynamic programming for finding a path between two nodes in a graph [Martelli, 1976]. Further, an A-algorithm-based graph search does not require explicit definition of the graph. However, dynamic programming presents an efficient way of simultaneously searching for optimal paths from multiple starting and ending points. If these points are not known, dynamic programming is probably a better choice, especially if computation of the partial costs $g^m(i, k)$ is simple. Nevertheless, which approach is more efficient for a particular problem depends on evaluation functions and on the quality of heuristics for an A-algorithm. A comparison between dynamic programming and heuristic search efficiency can be found in [Ney, 1992]; dynamic programming was found to be faster and less memory demanding for a word recognition problem. Tracing borders of elongated objects such as roads and rivers in aerial photographs, and vessels in medical images, represents typical applications of dynamic programming in image segmentation.

Practical border detection using two-dimensional dynamic programming was developed by Barrett et al. and Udupa et al. [Mortensen et al., 1992; Udupa et al., 1992; Falcao et al., 1995; Barrett and Mortensen, 1996]. An interactive real-time border detection method called the *live wire* and/or *intelligent scissors* combines automated border detection with manual definition of the boundary start point and interactive positioning of the end point. In dynamic programming, the graph that is searched is always completely constructed at the beginning of the search process; therefore, interactive positioning of the end point invokes no time-consuming recreation of the graph as would be the case in heuristic graph searching (Section 6.2.4). Thus, after construction of the complete graph and associated node costs, optimal borders connecting the fixed start point and the interactively changing end point can be determined in real time. In the case of large or more complicated regions, the complete region border is usually constructed from several border segments. After definition of the initial start point, the operator interactively steers the end point so that the calculated optimal border is visually correct. If the operator is satisfied with the current border, and if further movement of the end point causes the border to diverge from the desired location, the end point is fixed and becomes a new start point for the next border segment detection. A new complete graph is calculated and the operator interactively defines the next end point. In many cases, a closed region contour can be formed from just two segments. While the border detection in response to the interactive modification of the end point is very fast, the initial construction of a complete graph needed for each optimal border segment search is computationally demanding, since the graph is of the size of the entire image.

To overcome the computational needs of the live wire method, a modification called the *live lane* was developed [Falcao et al., 1995]. In this approach, an operator defines a region of interest by approximately tracing the border by moving a square window. The size of the window is either pre-selected or is adaptively defined from the speed and acceleration of the manual tracing. When the border is of high quality, the manual tracing is fast and the live lane method is essentially identical to the live wire method applied to a sequence of rectangular windows. If the border is less obvious, manual tracing is usually slower and the window size adaptively decreases. If the window size reduces to a single pixel, the method degenerates to manual tracing. A flexible method results that combines the speed of automated border detection with the robustness of manual border detection whenever needed. Since the graph is constructed using an image portion comparable in size to the size of the moving window, the computational demands of the live lane method are much less than those of the live wire method.

Several additional features of the two *live* methods are worth mentioning. As was stressed earlier, design of border-detection cost functions often requires substantial experience and experimentation. To facilitate the method's use by non-experts, an automated approach has been developed that determines optimal border features from examples of the correct borders. Another automated step is available to specify optimal parameters of cost transforms to create a powerful cost function (Section 6.2.4). Consequently, the resultant optimal cost function is specifically designed for a particular application and can be conveniently obtained by presenting a small number of example border segments during the method's training stage. Additionally, the method can easily be applied to three-dimensional image data by incorporation of a cost element comparing the border positions in adjacent image slices.

6.2.6   Hough transforms

If an image consists of objects with known shape and size, segmentation can be viewed as a problem of finding this object within it. Typical tasks are to locate circular pads in printed circuit boards, or to find objects of specific shapes in aerial or satellite data, etc. One of many possible ways to solve these problems is to move a mask with an appropriate shape and size along the image and look for correlation between the image and the mask, as discussed in Section 6.4. Unfortunately, the specified mask often differs too much from the object's representation in the processed data, because of shape distortions, rotation, zoom, etc. One very effective method that can solve this problem is the **Hough**

transform, which can even be used successfully in segmentation of overlapping or semi-occluded objects.

The Hough transform was designed to detect straight lines (for which see also the Radon transform, Section 3.2.11, which has similarities to the following) and curves [Hough, 1962], and this original method can be used if analytic equations of object border lines are known—no prior knowledge of region position is necessary. A big advantage of this approach is robustness of segmentation results; that is, segmentation is not too sensitive to imperfect data or noise. We shall present the idea of the transform for such analytic curves and illustrate with examples of circles and straight lines; later the case of shapes that may not be represented analytically will be considered.

Suppose we seek instances of curves satisfying the equation $f(\mathbf{x}, \mathbf{a}) = 0$, where $\mathbf{a}$ is an n-dimensional vector of curve parameters. We suppose an edge detector has been passed over the image and thresholded to determine all likely edge pixels—each of these may, a priori, lie at any point of a suitable curve. There is an infinite number of these,

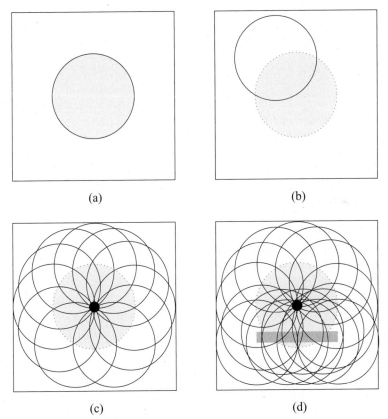

(a)   (b)

(c)   (d)

Figure 6.31: Hough transform—example of circle detection. (a) Image of a dark circle, of known radius r, on a bright background. (b) For each dark pixel, a potential circle-center locus is defined by a circle with radius r and center at that pixel. (c) The frequency with which image pixels occur 0n circle-center loci is determined—the highest-frequency pixel represents the center of the circle (marked by ●). (d) The Hough transform correctly detects the circle (marked by ●) in the presence of incomplete circle information and overlapping structures. (See Figure 6.32 for a real-life example.) © *Cengage Learning 2015*.

but we will quantize the vector $\mathbf{a}$ in some manner to make it finite—we shall associate an n-dimensional **accumulator array** A with it, initialized to zeroes. Now for each edge pixel $\mathbf{x}$ we increment $A(\mathbf{a})$ for each value of $\mathbf{a}$ that satisfies $f(\mathbf{x}, \mathbf{a}) = 0$. This will develop into a voting mechanism—an instance of the curve in the image will generate a local maximum in A at the appropriate value of $\mathbf{a}$. Formally:

Algorithm 6.13: Curve detection using the Hough transform

1. Quantize parameter space within the limits of parameters $\mathbf{a}$.

2. Form an n-dimensional accumulator array $A(\mathbf{a})$ with structure matching the quantization of parameter space; set all elements to zero.

3. For each image point (x_1, x_2) in the appropriately thresholded gradient image, increase all accumulator cells $A(\mathbf{a})$ if $f(\mathbf{x}, \mathbf{a}) = 0$

$$A(\mathbf{a}) = A(\mathbf{a}) + \Delta A$$

for all $\mathbf{a}$ inside the limits used in step 1.

4. Local maxima in the accumulator array $A(\mathbf{a})$ correspond to realizations of curves $f(\mathbf{x}, \mathbf{a})$ that are present in the original image.

An important property of the Hough transform is its insensitivity to missing parts of lines, to image noise, and to other structures co-existing in the image. This is caused by the robustness of transformation from the image space into the accumulator space—a missing part of the line will cause only a lower local maximum because a smaller number of edge pixels contributes to the corresponding accumulator cell. A noisy or only approximate curve will not be transformed into a point in the parameter space, but rather will result in a cluster of points, and the cluster center of gravity can be considered the curve representation.

To be specific, if we are looking for circles, the analytic expression $f(\mathbf{x}, \mathbf{a})$ of the desired curve is

$$(x_1 - a)^2 + (x_2 - b)^2 = r^2 \, , \tag{6.16}$$

where the circle has center (a, b) and radius r so the accumulator data structure must be three-dimensional. For each pixel $\mathbf{x}$ whose edge magnitude exceeds a given threshold, all accumulator cells corresponding to potential circle centers (a, b) are incremented in step 3 of the algorithm. The accumulator cell $A(a, b, r)$ is incremented if the point (a, b) is at distance r from point $\mathbf{x}$, and this condition is valid for all triplets (a, b, r) satisfying equation (6.16). If some potential center (a, b) of a circle of radius r is frequently found in the parameter space, it is highly probable that a circle with radius r and center (a, b) really exists in the processed data. This procedure is illustrated in Figure 6.31.

Figure 6.32 demonstrates circle detection when circular objects of known radius overlap and the image contains many additional structures causing the edge image to be very noisy. Note that the parameter space with three local maxima corresponding to centers of three circular objects.

Similarly, if a straight line is sought we would look for solutions of the equation

$$x_2 = k x_1 + q \, . \tag{6.17}$$

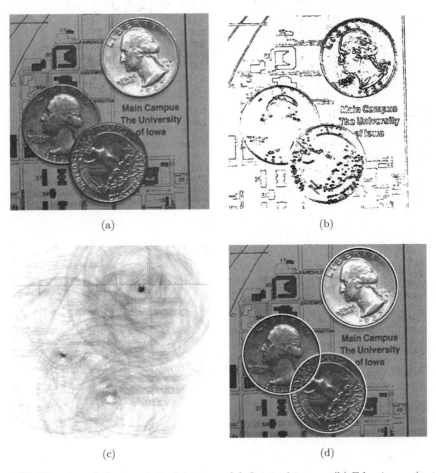

Figure 6.32: Hough transform—circle detection. (a) Original image. (b) Edge image (note that the edge information is far from perfect). (c) Parameter space. (d) Detected circles. © *Cengage Learning 2015*.

Now the parameter space is given by (k, q) and is two-dimensional. However, when we try to quantize this there is a problem as the gradient k is unbounded (vertical lines having infinite gradient). In this case we reformulate the equation as

$$s = x_1 \cos \theta + x_2 \sin \theta , \qquad (6.18)$$

and seek solutions in (s, θ) space (cf. Figure 3.25)—while this is less intuitive, both parameters are bounded and easily quantized. This is illustrated in Figure 6.33. A practical example showing the segmentation of an MR image of the brain into the left and right hemispheres is given in Figure 6.34. The Hough-transform was used to independently detect a line depicting the brain fissure in each 2D MR slice from the 3D brain image consisting of about 100 slices.

Discretization of the parameter space is an important part of this approach [Yuen and Hlavac, 1991]; also, detecting local maxima in the accumulator array is a non-trivial problem. In reality, the resulting discrete parameter space usually has more than one

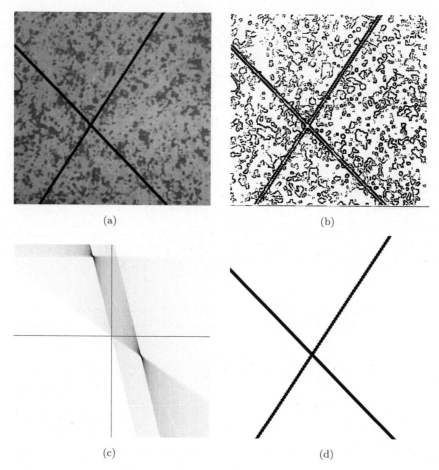

Figure 6.33: Hough transform—line detection. (a) Original image. (b) Edge image (note many edges, which do not belong to the line). (c) Parameter space. (d) Detected lines. © *Cengage Learning 2015.*

local maximum per line existing in the image, and smoothing the discrete parameter space may be a solution.

Even though the Hough transform is a very powerful technique for curve detection, exponential growth of the accumulator data structure with the increase of the number of curve parameters restricts its practical usability to curves with few parameters. If prior information about edge directions is used, computational demands can be decreased significantly. Suppose we are seeking a circular boundary of a dark region, letting the circle have a constant radius $r = R$ for simplicity. Without using edge direction information, all accumulator cells $A(a, b)$ are incremented in the parameter space if the corresponding point (a, b) is on a circle with center $\mathbf{x}$. With knowledge of direction, only a small number of the accumulator cells need be incremented. For example, if edge directions are quantized into eight possible values, only one-eighth of the circle need take part in incrementing of accumulator cells. Of course, estimates of edge direction are unlikely to be precise—if we anticipate edge direction errors of $\pi/4$, three-eighths of the circle will require accumulator cell incrementing. Using edge directions, candidates for parameters

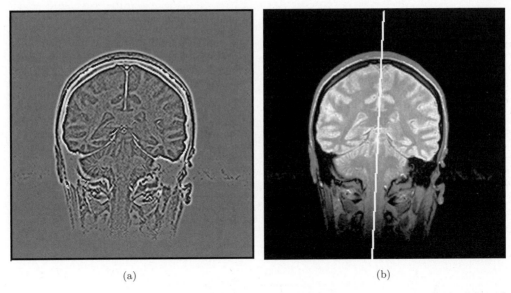

(a)   (b)

Figure 6.34: Hough transform line detection used for MRI brain segmentation to the left and right hemispheres. (a) Edge image. (b) Segmentation line in original image data. © *Cengage Learning 2015.*

a and b can be identified from the following formulae:

$$a = x_1 - R\cos\left(\psi(\mathbf{x})\right),$$
$$b = x_2 - R\sin\left(\psi(\mathbf{x})\right), \qquad \psi(\mathbf{x}) \in \left[\phi(\mathbf{x}) - \Delta\phi, \phi(\mathbf{x}) + \Delta\phi\right], \tag{6.19}$$

where $\phi(\mathbf{x})$ refers to the edge direction in pixel $\mathbf{x}$ and $\Delta\phi$ is the maximum anticipated edge direction error. Accumulator cells in the parameter space are then incremented only if (a, b) satisfy equation (6.19).

Further heuristics that have a beneficial influence on curve search are:

- To weight the contributions to accumulator cells $A(\mathbf{a})$ by the edge magnitude in pixel $\mathbf{x}$; thus the increment ΔA in step 3 of Algorithm 6.13 $[A(\mathbf{a}) = A(\mathbf{a}) + \Delta A]$ will be greater if it results from the processing of a pixel with larger edge magnitude.

- A two-pass technique to reduce noise in the accumulator array. A 'back projection' step identifies the accumulator cell of highest score associated with each edge pixel, and other votes associated with that pixel are deleted [Gerig and Klein, 1986]. This has the effect of sharpening responses significantly, since most votes in accumulator space are noise.

The randomized Hough transform provides a different, more efficient, approach [Xu and Oja, 1993]; it randomly and repeatedly selects n pixels from the edge image and determines n parameters of the detected curve followed by incrementing a single accumulator cell only. There are some similarities in this approach to the RANSAC algorithm, Section 10.3.

Frequently, a boundary is sought for which a parametric representations does not exist; in this case, a generalized Hough transform [Ballard, 1981; Davis, 1982; Illingworth and Kittler, 1987] can provide the solution. This method constructs a parametric curve (region border) description based on sample situations detected in the learning stage. Assume that shape, size, and orientation of the sought region are known: a reference point $\mathbf{x}^R$ is chosen at any location inside the sample region, then an arbitrary line can be constructed starting at this reference point aiming in the direction of the region border (see Figure 6.35). The border direction (edge direction) is found at the intersection of the line and the region border. A reference table (referred to as the R-table in [Ballard, 1981]) is constructed, and intersection parameters are stored as a function of the border direction at the intersection point; using different lines aimed from the reference point, all the distances of the reference point to region borders and the border directions at the intersections can be found. The resulting table can be ordered according to the border directions at the intersection points. As Figure 6.35 makes clear, different points $\mathbf{x}$ of the region border can have the same border direction, $\phi(\mathbf{x}) = \phi(\mathbf{x}')$. This implies that there may be more than one (r, α) pair for each ϕ that can determine the co-ordinates of a potential reference point.

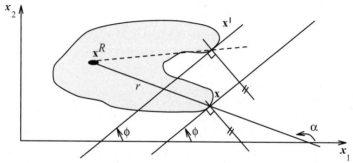

Figure 6.35: Principles of the generalized Hough transform: geometry of R-table construction. © *Cengage Learning 2015.*

An example of an R-table is given in Table 6.1. Assuming no rotation and known size, remaining description parameters required are the co-ordinates of the reference point (x_1^R, x_2^R). If scale and orientation of the region may vary, the number of parameters increases to four. Each pixel $\mathbf{x}$ with a significant edge in the direction $\phi(\mathbf{x})$ has co-ordinates of potential reference points $\{x_1 + r(\phi)\cos\left(\alpha(\phi)\right), x_2 + r(\phi)\sin\left(\alpha(\phi)\right)\}$. These must be computed for all possible values of r and α according to the border direction $\phi(\mathbf{x})$ given in the R-table. Algorithm 6.14 presents the generalized Hough transform in the case in which orientation (τ) and scale (S) may both change.

$$
\begin{array}{ll}
\phi_1 & (r_1^1, \alpha_1^1), (r_1^2, \alpha_1^2), \ldots, (r_1^{n_1}, \alpha_1^{n_1}) \\
\phi_2 & (r_2^1, \alpha_2^1), (r_2^2, \alpha_2^2), \ldots, (r_2^{n_2}, \alpha_2^{n_2}) \\
\phi_3 & (r_3^1, \alpha_3^1), (r_3^2, \alpha_3^2), \ldots, (r_3^{n_3}, \alpha_3^{n_3}) \\
\cdots & \qquad\qquad \cdots \\
\phi_k & (r_k^1, \alpha_k^1), (r_k^2, \alpha_k^2), \ldots, (r_k^{n_k}, \alpha_k^{n_k})
\end{array}
$$

Table 6.1: R-table © *Cengage Learning 2015.*

Algorithm 6.14: Generalized Hough transform

1. Construct an R-table description of the desired object.

2. Form a data structure $A(x_1, x_2, S, \tau)$ that represents the potential reference points and erase it to zeroes.

3. For each pixel (x_1, x_2) in a thresholded gradient image, determine the edge direction $\Phi(\mathbf{x})$; find all potential reference points $\mathbf{x}^R$ and increase all

$$A(\mathbf{x}^R, S, \tau) = A(\mathbf{x}^R, S, \tau) + \Delta A$$

for all possible values of rotation and size change

$$x_1^R = x_1 + r(\phi + \tau) S \cos\left(\alpha(\phi + \tau)\right),$$
$$x_2^R = x_2 + r(\phi + \tau) S \sin\left(\alpha(\phi + \tau)\right).$$

4. The location of suitable regions is given by local maxima in A.

The generalized Hough transform can be used to detect arbitrary shapes, but requires the complete specification of the exact shape of the target object to achieve precise segmentation. Therefore, it allows detection of objects with complex but pre-determined, shapes. Other varieties exist that allow detection of objects whose exact shape is unknown, assuming a priori knowledge can be used to form an approximate model of the object.

The Hough transform has many desirable features [Illingworth and Kittler, 1988]. It recognizes partial or slightly deformed shapes, therefore behaving extremely well in recognition of occluded objects. It may be also used to measure similarity between a model and a detected object on the basis of size and spatial location of peaks in the parameter space. It is very robust in the presence of additional structures in the image (other lines, curves, or objects) as well as being insensitive to image noise. Moreover, it may search for several occurrences of a shape during the same processing pass. Unfortunately, the conventional sequential approach requires a lot of storage and extensive computation. However, its inherent parallel character gives the potential for real-time implementations.

The Hough transform has a distinguished history and is widely applied. While we have not discussed in depth many issues surrounding it (curve parameterization, maxima location, computational efficiency ...), it remains in the forefront of use. The general approach of devising a voting mechanism to locate good parameter sets is even more widely used. There is an extensive literature on the transform—thorough coverage and a good bibliography are given in [Davies, 2005].

6.2.7 Border detection using border location information

If any information about boundary location or shape is known, it is of benefit to use it. The information may, for instance, be based on some higher-level knowledge, or can result from segmentation applied to a lower-resolution image. Various heuristics take this approach, but have been superseded by better founded techniques such as *snakes* [Kass et al., 1987]—see Section 7.2.

If the approximate location of a boundary is known (see Figure 6.36), we might seek border pixels as significant edges with the correct direction along profiles perpendicular to the assumed border. If a large number satisfying the given conditions is found, an approximate curve is computed based on these pixels, and a new, more accurate, border results.

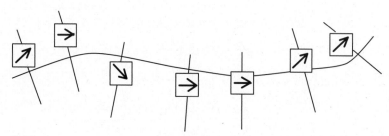

Figure 6.36: A priori information about boundary location. © *Cengage Learning 2015.*

Alternatively, if there is prior knowledge of end points we can iteratively partition the border and search for the strongest edge located on perpendiculars to the line connecting end points of each partition; perpendiculars are located at the center of the connecting straight line (see Figure 6.37). This procedure can be iterated.

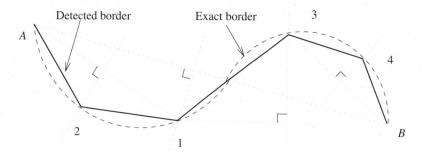

Figure 6.37: Divide-and-conquer iterative border detection; numbers show the sequence of division steps. © *Cengage Learning 2015.*

6.2.8   Region construction from borders

If a complete segmentation has been achieved, the borders segment an image into regions; but if only a partial segmentation is available, regions are not defined uniquely. Methods exist that are able to construct regions from partial borders which do not form closed boundaries; these methods do not always find acceptable regions, but they are useful in many practical situations.

One such is a method described in [Hong et al., 1980] based on the existence of partial borders in the processed image. Region construction is based on probabilities that pixels are located inside a region closed by the partial borders. The border pixels are described by their positions and by pixel edge directions $\phi(\mathbf{x})$. The closest 'opposite' edge pixel is sought along a perpendicular to each significant image edge, and then closed borders are constructed from pairs of opposite edge pixels. A pixel is a potential region member if it is on a straight line connecting two opposite edge pixels. The final decision on which of the potential region pixels will form a region is probabilistic.

Algorithm 6.15: Region forming from partial borders

1. For each border pixel $\mathbf{x}$, search for an opposite edge pixel within a distance not exceeding a given maximum M. If an opposite edge pixel is not found, process the next border pixel in the image. If an opposite edge pixel is found, mark each pixel on the connecting straight line as a potential region member.

2. Compute the number of markers for each pixel in the image (the number of markers tells how often a pixel was on a connecting line between opposite edge pixels). Let $b(\mathbf{x})$ be the number of markers for the pixel $\mathbf{x}$.

3. The weighted number of markers $B(\mathbf{x})$ is then determined as follows:

$$
\begin{aligned}
B(\mathbf{x}) = 0.0 &\quad \text{for } b(\mathbf{x}) = 0\,, \\
= 0.1 &\quad \text{for } b(\mathbf{x}) = 1\,, \\
= 0.2 &\quad \text{for } b(\mathbf{x}) = 2\,, \\
= 0.5 &\quad \text{for } b(\mathbf{x}) = 3\,, \\
= 1.0 &\quad \text{for } b(\mathbf{x}) > 3\,.
\end{aligned}
\tag{6.20}
$$

The confidence that a pixel $\mathbf{x}$ is a member of a region is given as the sum $\sum_i B(\mathbf{x_i})$ in a 3×3 neighborhood of the pixel $\mathbf{x}$. If the confidence that a pixel $\mathbf{x}$ is a region member is one or larger, then pixel $\mathbf{x}$ is marked as a region pixel, otherwise it is marked as a background pixel.

Note that this method allows the construction of bright regions on a dark background as well as dark regions on a bright background by taking either of the two options in the search for opposite edge pixels—step 1. Search orientation depends on whether relatively dark or bright regions are constructed. If $\phi(\mathbf{x})$ and $\phi(\mathbf{y})$ are directions of edges, the condition that must be satisfied for $\mathbf{x}$ and $\mathbf{y}$ to be opposite is

$$
\frac{\pi}{2} < \left| (\phi(\mathbf{x}) - \phi(\mathbf{y})) \bmod (2\pi) \right| < \frac{3\pi}{2}\,.
\tag{6.21}
$$

Note that it is possible to take advantage of prior knowledge of maximum region sizes—this information defines the value of M in step 1 of the algorithm, the maximum search length for the opposite edge pixel.

This method was applied to form texture primitives (Chapter 15, [Hong et al., 1980]) as shown in Figure 6.38. The differences between the results of this region detection method and those obtained by thresholding applied to the same data are clearly visible if Figures 6.38b and 6.38c are compared.

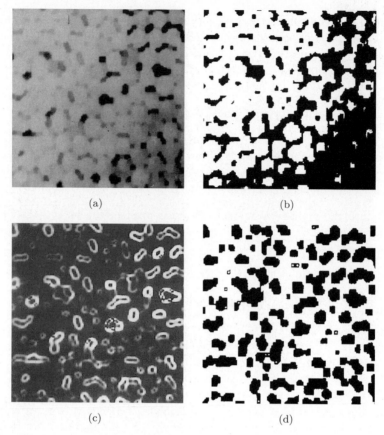

(a)   (b)

(c)   (d)

Figure 6.38: Region forming from partial borders. (a) Original image. (b) Thresholding. (c) Edge image. (d) Regions formed from partial borders. © *Cengage Learning 2015.*

6.3 Region-based segmentation

It is easy to construct regions from their borders, and to detect borders of existing regions. However, segmentations resulting from edge-based methods and region-growing methods are not usually the same, and a combination of results may often be an improvement on both. *Region growing* techniques are generally better in noisy images, where borders are extremely difficult to detect. Homogeneity is an important property of regions and is used as the main segmentation criterion in region growing, whose basic idea is to divide an image into zones of maximum homogeneity. The criteria for homogeneity can be based on gray-level, color, texture, shape, model (using semantic information), etc. Properties chosen to describe regions influence the form, complexity, and amount of prior information in the specific region-growing segmentation method. Methods that address region-growing segmentation of color images are reported in [Schettini, 1993; Vlachos and Constantinides, 1993; Gauch and Hsia, 1992; Priese and Rehrmann, 1993].

Regions were discussed earlier and equation (6.1) stated the basic requirements of segmentation into regions. Further assumptions needed here are that regions must satisfy the conditions:

$$H(R_i) = \text{TRUE}\,, \quad i = 1, 2, \ldots, S\,, \tag{6.22}$$

$$H(R_i \cup R_j) = \text{FALSE}\,, \quad i \neq j\,, \quad R_i \text{ adjacent to } R_j\,, \tag{6.23}$$

where S is the total number of regions in an image and $H(R_i)$ is a binary homogeneity evaluation of the region R_i. Resulting regions of the segmented image must be both homogeneous and maximal, where by 'maximal' we mean that the homogeneity criterion would not be true after merging a region with any adjacent region.

The simplest homogeneity criterion uses an average gray-level of the region, its color properties, simple texture properties, or an m-dimensional vector of average gray values for multi-spectral images. While the region growing methods discussed below consider two-dimensional images, three-dimensional implementations are often possible. Considering three-dimensional connectivity constraints, homogeneous regions (volumes) of a three-dimensional image can be determined using three-dimensional region growing. Three-dimensional filling represents its simplest form and can be described as a three-dimensional connectivity-preserving variant of thresholding.

6.3.1 Region merging

The most natural method of region growing is to begin the growth in the raw image data, each pixel representing a single region. These regions almost certainly do not satisfy the condition of equation (6.23), and so regions will be merged as long as equation (6.22) remains satisfied.

Algorithm 6.16: Region merging (outline)

1. Define some initialization to segment the image into many small regions satisfying condition (6.22).

2. Define a criterion for merging two adjacent regions.

3. Merge all adjacent regions satisfying the criterion. If no two regions can be merged maintaining condition (6.22), stop.

This algorithm represents a general approach to region merging segmentation. Specific methods differ in the definition of the starting segmentation and in the criterion for merging. In the descriptions that follow, regions are those parts of the image that can be sequentially merged into larger regions satisfying equations (6.22) and (6.23). The result of region merging usually depends on the order in which regions are merged (so results may differ if segmentation begins in the upper left or lower right corner). This is because the merging order can cause two similar adjacent regions R_1 and R_2 not to be merged, since an earlier merge used R_1 and its new characteristics no longer allow it to be merged with region R_2, while if the process used a different order, this merge may have been realized.

The simplest methods begin merging by starting the segmentation using regions of 2×2, 4×4, or 8×8 pixels. Region descriptions are then based on their statistical gray-level properties—a regional gray-level histogram is a good example. A region description is compared with the description of an adjacent region; if they match, they are merged into a larger region and a new description is computed. Otherwise, regions are marked as non-matching. Merging of adjacent regions continues between all neighbors, including newly formed ones. If a region cannot be merged with any of its neighbors, it is marked 'final'; the merging process stops when all image regions are so marked.

State space search is an essential principle of problem solving in AI, which was applied early to image segmentation [Brice and Fennema, 1970]. According to this approach, pixels of the raw image are considered the starting state, each pixel being a separate region. A change of state can result from the merging of two regions or the splitting of a region into subregions. The problem can be described as looking for permissible changes of state while producing the best image segmentation. This state space approach brings two advantages; first, well-known methods of state space search can be applied which also include heuristic knowledge; second, higher-level data structures can be used which allow the possibility of working directly with regions and their borders, and no longer require the marking of each image element according to its region marking. Starting regions are formed by pixels of the same gray-level—these regions are small in real images. The first state changes are based on crack edge computations (Section 2.3.1), where local boundaries between regions are evaluated by the strength of crack edges along their common border. The data structure used in this approach (the so-called **supergrid**) carries all the necessary information (see Figure 6.39); this allows for easy region merging in 4-adjacency when crack edge values are stored in the 'o' elements. Region merging uses the following two heuristics:

- Two adjacent regions are merged if a significant part of their common boundary consists of weak edges (*significance* can be based on the region with the shorter perimeter; the ratio of the number of *weak* common edges to the total length of the region perimeter may be used).

- Two adjacent regions are also merged if a significant part of their common boundary consists of weak edges, but in this case not considering the total length of the region borders.

Of the two given heuristics, the first is more general and the second cannot be used alone because it does not consider the influence of different region sizes.

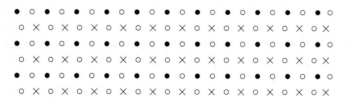

Figure 6.39: Supergrid data structure: ×, image data; ○, crack edges; ●, unused. © *Cengage Learning 2015.*

Edge significance can be evaluated according to the formula

$$v_{ij} = 0 \quad \text{if } s_{ij} < T_1 \,,$$
$$= 1 \quad \text{otherwise,} \tag{6.24}$$

where $v_{ij} = 1$ indicates a significant edge, $v_{ij} = 0$ a weak edge, T_1 is a preset threshold, and s_{ij} is the crack edge value $s_{ij} = \left| f(\mathbf{x_i}) - f(\mathbf{x_j}) \right|$.

Algorithm 6.17: Region merging via boundary melting

1. Define a starting image segmentation into regions of constant gray-level. Construct a supergrid edge data structure in which to store the crack edge information.

2. Remove all weak crack edges from the edge data structure (using equation 6.24 and threshold T_1).

3. Recursively remove common boundaries of adjacent regions R_i, R_j, if

$$\frac{W}{\min(l_i, l_j)} \geq T_2 \, ,$$

where W is the number of weak edges on the common boundary, l_i, l_j are the perimeter lengths of regions R_i, R_j, and T_2 is another preset threshold.

4. Recursively remove common boundaries of adjacent regions R_i, R_j if

$$\frac{W}{l} \geq T_3 \tag{6.25}$$

or, using a weaker criterion [Ballard and Brown, 1982]

$$W \geq T_3 \, , \tag{6.26}$$

where l is the length of the common boundary and T_3 is a third threshold.

Note that although we have described a region growing method, the merging criterion is based on border properties and so the merging does not necessarily keep the condition given in equation (6.22) true. The supergrid data structure allows precise work with edges and borders, but a big disadvantage of this data structure is that it is not suitable for the representation of regions—it is necessary to refer to each region as a part of the image, especially if semantic information about regions and neighboring regions is included. This problem can be solved by the construction and updating of a data structure describing region adjacencies and their boundaries, and for this purpose a good data structure to use can be a planar-region adjacency graph and a dual-region boundary graph [Pavlidis, 1977], (see Section 10.10).

Figure 6.40 gives a comparison of region merging methods. An original image and its pseudo-color representation (to see the small gray-level differences) are given in Figures 6.40a,b. The original image cannot be segmented by thresholding because of the significant and continuous gray-level gradient in all regions. Results of a recursive region merging method, which uses a simple merging criterion that allows pixels to be merged in the row-first fashion as long as they do not differ by more than a pre-specified parameter from the seed pixel is shown in Figure 6.40c; note the resulting horizontally elongated regions corresponding to vertical changes of image gray-levels. If region merging via boundary melting is applied, the segmentation results improve dramatically; see Figure 6.40d.

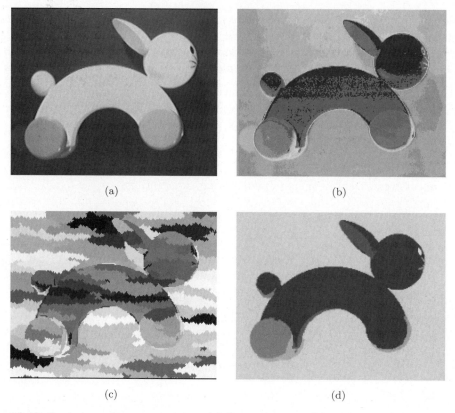

(a) (b)

(c) (d)

Figure 6.40: Region merging segmentation. (a) Original image. (b) Pseudo-color representation of the original image (in grayscale). (c) Recursive region merging. (d) Region merging via boundary melting. *Courtesy of R. Marik, Czech Technical University.*

6.3.2 Region splitting

Region splitting is the opposite of region merging—it begins with the whole image represented as a single region which does not usually satisfy condition specified by equation (6.22). Existing image regions are sequentially split to satisfy conditions (6.1), (6.22) and (6.23). Even if this approach seems to be dual to region merging, region splitting does not result in the same segmentation even if the same homogeneity criteria are used. Some regions may be homogeneous during the splitting process and therefore are not split anymore; considering the homogeneous regions created by region merging procedures, some may not be constructed because of the impossibility of merging smaller subregions earlier in the process. A fine black-and-white chessboard is an example: a homogeneity criterion may be based on variance of average gray-levels in the quadrants of the evaluated region in the next lower pyramid level—if the segmentation process is based on region splitting, the image will not be split into subregions because its quadrants would have the same value of the measure as the starting region consisting of the whole image. The region merging approach, on the other hand, will merge single pixel regions into larger regions, and this process will stop when they match the chessboard squares.

Region splitting methods generally use similar homogeneity criteria as region merging methods, and differ only in the direction of their application. The multi-spectral segmentation discussed in considering thresholding (Section 6.1.3) can be seen as an example of a region splitting method. As mentioned there, other criteria can be used to split regions (e.g., cluster analysis, pixel classification, etc.).

6.3.3   Splitting and merging

A combination of splitting and merging may result in a method with the advantages of both. Split-and-merge approaches work using pyramid image representations; regions are square shaped and correspond to elements of the appropriate pyramid level.

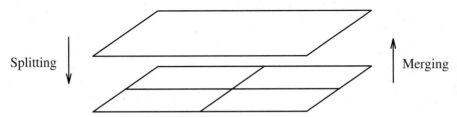

Figure 6.41: Split-and-merge in a hierarchical data structure. © *Cengage Learning 2015*.

If any region in any pyramid level is not homogeneous (excluding the lowest level), it is split into four subregions—these are elements of higher resolution at the level below. If four regions exist at any pyramid level with approximately the same value of homogeneity measure, they are merged into a single region in an upper pyramid level (see Figure 6.41). The segmentation process can be understood as the construction of a segmentation quadtree where each leaf node represents a homogeneous region—that is, an element of some pyramid level. Splitting and merging corresponds to removing or building parts of the segmentation quadtree—the number of leaf nodes of the tree corresponds to the number of segmented regions after the segmentation process is over. Split-and-merge methods usually store the adjacency information in region adjacency graphs (or similar data structures). Using segmentation trees, in which regions do not have to be contiguous, is both implementationally and computationally easier. An unpleasant drawback of segmentation quadtrees is the square-region shape assumption (see Figure 6.42), and it is therefore advantageous to add more processing steps that permit the merging of regions which are not part of the same branch of the segmentation tree. Starting image regions can either be chosen arbitrarily or can be based on prior knowledge. Because both split-and-merge processing options are available, the starting segmentation does not have to satisfy either condition (6.22) or (6.23).

The homogeneity criterion plays a major role in split-and-merge algorithms, just as it does in all other region growing methods. See [Chen et al., 1991] for an adaptive split-and-merge algorithm and a review of region homogeneity analysis. For simple images, a split-and-merge approach can be based on local image properties, but if the image is complex, even elaborate criteria including semantic information may not give acceptable results.

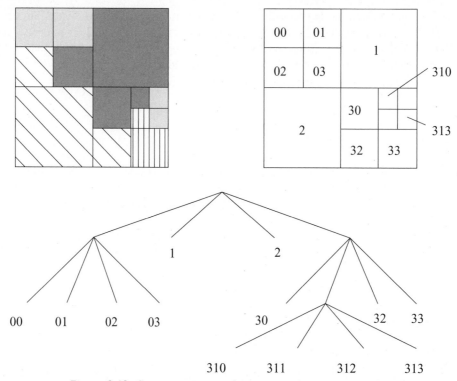

Figure 6.42: Segmentation quadtree. © *Cengage Learning 2015.*

Algorithm 6.18: Split and merge

1. Define an initial segmentation into regions, a homogeneity criterion, and a pyramid data structure.

2. If any region R in the pyramid data structure is not homogeneous [$H(R) =$ FALSE], split it into four child-regions; if any four regions with the same parent can be merged into a single homogeneous region, merge them. If no region can be split or merged, go to step 3.

3. If any two adjacent regions R_i, R_j (even if they are in different pyramid levels or do not have the same parent) can be merged into a homogeneous region, merge them.

4. Merge small regions with the most similar adjacent region if it is necessary to remove small-size regions.

A pyramid data structure with overlapping regions (Section 4.3.3) is an interesting modification of this method [Pietikainen et al., 1982]. Each region has four potential parent elements in the upper pyramid level and 16 possible child elements in the lower pyramid level. Segmentation tree generation begins in the lowest level. Properties of each region are compared with properties of each of its potential parents and the segmentation branch is linked to the most similar of them. After construction of the tree is complete, all the homogeneity values of all the elements in the pyramid data structure are recomputed to be based on child-region properties only. This recomputed pyramid data structure is used to generate a new segmentation tree, beginning again at the lowest level. The pyramid updating process and new segmentation tree generation is repeated until no significant segmentation changes can be detected between steps. Assume that the segmented image has a maximum of 2^n (non-contiguous) regions. Any of these regions must link to at least one element in the highest allowed pyramid level—let this pyramid level consist of 2^n elements. Each element of the highest pyramid level corresponds to one branch of the segmentation tree, and all the leaf nodes of this branch construct one region of the segmented image. The highest level of the segmentation tree must correspond to the expected number of image regions, and the pyramid height defines the maximum number of segmentation branches. If the number of regions in an image is less than 2^n, some regions can be represented by more than one element in the highest pyramid level. If this is the case, some specific processing steps can either allow merging of some elements in the highest pyramid level or can restrict some of these elements to be segmentation branch roots. If the number of image regions is larger than 2^n, the most similar regions will be merged into a single tree branch, and the method will not be able to give acceptable results.

Algorithm 6.19: Split and link to the segmentation tree

1. Define a pyramid data structure with overlapping regions. Evaluate the starting region description.

2. Build a segmentation tree starting with leaves. Link each node of the tree to that one of the four possible parents to which it has the most similar region properties. Build the whole segmentation tree. If there is no link to an element in the higher pyramid level, assign the value zero to this element.

3. Update the pyramid data structure; each element must be assigned the average of the values of all its existing children.

4. Repeat steps 2 and 3 until no significant segmentation changes appear between iterations (a small number of iterations is usually sufficient).

Considerably lower memory requirements can be found in a single-pass split-and-merge segmentation. A local 'splitting pattern' is detected in each 2×2 pixel image block and regions are merged in overlapping blocks of the same size [Suk and Chung, 1983]. In contrast to previous approaches, a single pass is sufficient here, although a second pass may be necessary for region identification (see Section 8.1). The computation is more efficient and the data structure implemented is very simple; the 12 possible splitting patterns for a 2×2 block are given in a list, starting with a homogeneous block up to a block consisting of four different pixels (see Figure 6.43). Pixel similarity can be evaluated adaptively according to the mean and variance of gray-levels of blocks throughout the image.

Algorithm 6.20: Single-pass split-and-merge

1. Search an entire image line by line except the last column and last line. Perform the following steps for each pixel.

2. Find a splitting pattern for a 2×2 pixel block.

3. If a mismatch between assigned labels and splitting patterns in overlapping blocks is found, try to change the assigned labels of these blocks to remove the mismatch (discussed below).

4. Assign labels to unassigned pixels to match a splitting pattern of the block.

5. Remove small regions if necessary.

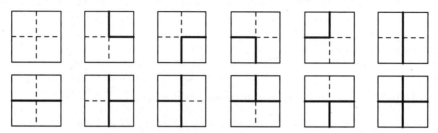

Figure 6.43: Splitting of 2×2 image blocks, all 12 possible cases. © *Cengage Learning 2015*.

The image blocks overlap during the image search. Except at image borders, three of the four pixels have been assigned a label in previous search locations, but these labels do not necessarily match the splitting pattern found in the processed block. If a mismatch is detected in step 3 of the algorithm, it is necessary to resolve possibilities of merging regions that were considered separate so far—to assign the same label to two regions previously labeled differently. Two regions R_1 and R_2 are merged if

$$H(R_1 \cup R_2) = \text{TRUE}, \qquad (6.27)$$

$$|m_1 - m_2| < T, \qquad (6.28)$$

where m_1 and m_2 are the mean gray-level values in regions R_1 and R_2, and T is some appropriate threshold. If region merging is not allowed, regions keep their previous labels. To get a final segmentation, information about region merging must be stored and the merged-region characteristics must be updated after each merging operation. The assignment of labels to non-labeled pixels in the processed block is based on the block splitting pattern and on the labels of adjacent regions (step 4). If a match between a splitting pattern and the assigned labels was found in step 3, then it is easy to assign a label to the remaining pixel(s) to keep the label assignment and splitting pattern matched. Conversely, if a match was not found in step 3, an unassigned pixel is either merged with an adjacent region (the same label is assigned) or a new region is started. If a 2×2 block size is used, the only applicable pixel property is gray-level. If larger blocks are used, more complex image properties can be included in the homogeneity criteria (even if these larger blocks are divided into 2×2 subblocks to determine the splitting pattern).

Parallelization of this approach is clearly attractive and has been widely applied [Willebeek-Lemair and Reeves, 1990; Chang and Li, 1995]. Additional sections describing more sophisticated methods of semantic region growing segmentation can be found in Chapter 10.

6.3.4 Watershed segmentation

The concepts of **watersheds** and **catchment basins** are well known in topography. Watershed lines divide individual catchment basins. The North American Continental Divide is a textbook example of a watershed line with catchment basins formed by the Atlantic and Pacific Oceans. Working with gradient images and following the concept introduced in Chapter 1, Figures 1.8 and 1.9, image data may be interpreted as a topographic surface where the gradient image gray-levels represent altitudes. Thus, region edges correspond to high watersheds and low-gradient region interiors correspond to catchment basins. According to equation (6.22), the goal of region growing segmentation is to create homogeneous regions; in watershed segmentation, catchment basins of the topographic surface are homogeneous in the sense that all pixels belonging to the same catchment basin are connected with the basin's region of minimum altitude (gray-level) by a *simple path* of pixels (Section 2.3.1) that have monotonically decreasing altitude (gray-level) along the path. Such catchment basins then represent the regions of the segmented image (Figure 6.44). While the concept of watersheds and catchment basins is quite straightforward, development of algorithms for watershed segmentation is a complex task.

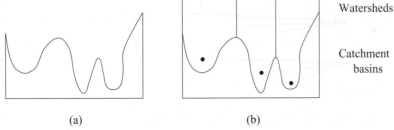

Figure 6.44: One-dimensional example of watershed segmentation. (a) Gray-level profile of image data. (b) Watershed segmentation—local minima of gray-level (altitude) yield catchment basins, local maxima define the watershed lines. © *Cengage Learning 2015*.

The first algorithms for watershed segmentation were developed for topographic digital elevation models [Collins, 1975; Soille and Ansoult, 1990]. Most of the existing algorithms start with extraction of potential watershed line pixels using a local 3 × 3 operation, which are then connected into geomorphological networks in subsequent steps. Due to the local character of the first step, these approaches are often inaccurate [Soille and Ansoult, 1990].

Early approaches were not efficient because of their extreme computational demands and inaccuracy, but a seminal paper [Vincent and Soille, 1991] makes the idea practical. Considering the gradient image, catchment basins fill from the bottom—as explained earlier, each minimum represents one catchment basin, and the strategy is to start at the

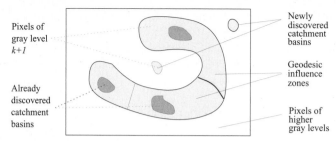

Figure 6.45: Geodesic influence zones of catchment basins. © *Cengage Learning 2015*.

altitude minima. Imagine there is a hole in each local minimum, and that the topographic surface is immersed in water. As a result, the water starts filling all catchment basins, minima of which are under the water level. If two catchment basins would merge as a result of further immersion, a dam is built all the way to the highest surface altitude and the dam represents the watershed line. An efficient algorithm for such watershed segmentation was presented in [Vincent and Soille, 1991]: It is based on *sorting* the pixels in increasing order of their gray values, followed by a *flooding* step consisting of a fast breadth-first scanning of all pixels in the order of their gray-levels.

Algorithm 6.21: Efficient watershed segmentation

1. Construct a histogram of the gradient image: from it, construct a list of pointers to pixels of intensity h to permit direct access. This can be done very efficiently—in linear time.

2. Suppose flooding has been conducted up to level k so every pixel having gray-level less than or equal to k has already been assigned a unique catchment basin or watershed label.

3. Consider pixels of intensity $k+1$: construct a FIFO queue of all such candidates.

4. Construct a *geodesic influence zone* for all hitherto determined catchment basins: for basin l_i this is the locus of non-labeled image pixels of gray-level $k+1$ that are contiguous (via pixels of intensity $\leq k+1$) with the basin l_i, for which their distance to l_i is smaller than their distance to any other basin l_j (Figure 6.45).

5. Pixels from the queue are processed sequentially: those that belong to the influence zone of catchment basin l are also labeled as l, causing the basin to grow. Those that are on the boundary of influence zones become marked as watershed. Pixels that cannot be assigned an existing label or watershed represent newly discovered catchment basins and are marked with new and unique labels.

The original reference includes a useful pseudo-C coding of this algorithm [Vincent and Soille, 1991].

Figure 6.46 shows an example of watershed segmentation. Note that the raw watershed segmentation produces a severely oversegmented image with hundreds or thousands of catchment basins (Figure 6.46c). To overcome this problem, region markers and other approaches have been suggested to generate better segmentation (Figure 6.46d) [Meyer and Beucher, 1990; Vincent and Soille, 1991; Higgins and Ojard, 1993].

While this method works well in a continuous space with the watershed lines accurately dividing the adjacent catchment basins, watersheds in images with large plateaus may be quite thick in discrete spaces. Figure 6.47 illustrates such a situation, consisting of pixels equidistant to two catchment basins in 4-connectivity. To avoid such behavior, detailed rules using successively ordered distances stored during the breadth-search process were developed that yield exact watershed lines. Full details, and pseudo-code for a fast watershed algorithm, are in found in [Vincent and Soille, 1991]. Further improvements of the watershed segmentation based on immersion simulations are given in [Dobrin et al., 1994].

The watershed transformation can also be presented in the context of mathematical morphology (see Chapter 13). Unfortunately, without special hardware, watershed transformations based on mathematical morphology are computationally demanding and time consuming.

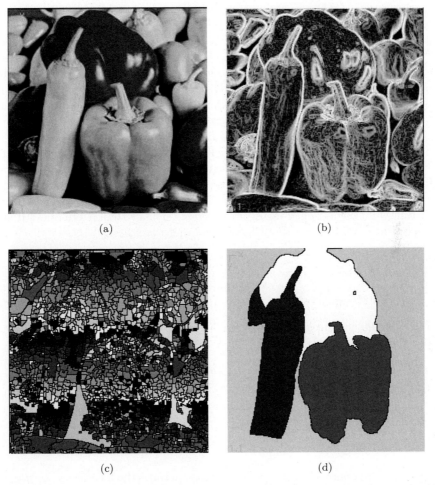

(a)   (b)

(c)   (d)

Figure 6.46: Watershed segmentation. (a) Original;. (b) Gradient image, 3×3 Sobel edge detection, histogram equalized. (c) Raw watershed segmentation. (d) Watershed segmentation using region markers to control oversegmentation. *Courtesy of W. Higgins, Penn State University.*

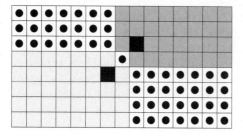

Figure 6.47: Thick watershed lines may result in gray-level plateaus. Earlier identified catchment basins are marked as black pixels, and new catchment basin additions resulting from this processing step are shown in the two levels of gray. The thick watersheds are marked with ●. To avoid thick watersheds, specialized rules must be developed. © *Cengage Learning 2015.*

6.3.5 Region growing post-processing

Images segmented by region growing methods often contain either too many regions (under-growing) or too few regions (over-growing) as a result of non-optimal parameter setting. To improve classification results, a variety of post-processors has been developed. Some of them combine segmentation information obtained from region growing and edge-based segmentation. An approach introduced in [Pavlidis and Liow, 1990] solves several quadtree-related region growing problems and incorporates two post-processing steps. First, boundary elimination removes some borders between adjacent regions according to their contrast properties and direction changes along the border, taking resulting topology into consideration. Second, contours from the previous step are modified to be located precisely on appropriate image edges. A combination of independent region growing and edge-based detected borders is described in [Koivunen and Pietikainen, 1990]. Other approaches combining region growing and edge detection can be found in [Manos et al., 1993; Gambotto, 1993; Wu, 1993; Chu and Aggarwal, 1993].

Simpler post-processors are based on general heuristics and decrease the number of small regions in a segmented image that cannot be merged with any adjacent region according to the originally applied homogeneity criteria. These small regions are usually not significant in further processing and can be considered as segmentation noise. Such an algorithm will execute much faster if all regions smaller than a pre-selected size are merged with their neighbors without having to order them first.

Algorithm 6.22: Removal of small image regions

1. Search for the smallest image region $R_{\min}$.

2. Find the adjacent region R most similar to $R_{\min}$, according to the homogeneity criteria, and merge them.

3. Repeat until all regions smaller than a pre-selected size are removed.

6.4 Matching

Matching is a basic approach to segmentation that permits the location of known objects in an image, search for specific patterns, etc. The issue of *matching* pervades artificial intelligence and computer vision in particular. It is easy to understand why: most applications have at their heart a known model that is sought, and an image or some derivation of an image in which the seeking is done—we wish to match the model to the data. Of course, this very general problem may manifest in a number of ways; for example:

- At simplest, known binary patterns representing characters of a font may be sought in properly aligned scans of text—this is template matching (see Section 6.4.1) applied to OCR.

- More generally, font-independent OCR demands recognition of characters of unknown font and size, perhaps with skew—this requires the matching of the *pattern* of characters.

- More generally still, face recognition requires the matching of the *pattern of a face* into a picture of a 3D scene: pose, alignment, scale, beards, spectacles, color will all be unknowns.

- At the most abstract, perhaps a pedestrian has been matched in a video sequence, and we seek to match the individual's *behavior* to some known model—is the pedestrian crossing a road? Queuing? Acting suspiciously?

Each of these examples implies matching a model pattern M to some observation from the image(s) X, and the algorithm used may be elementary when the problem is straightforward, or at the limit of computer vision research in the case of applications such as behavior modeling [Valera and Velastin, 2005]. Matching algorithms appear throughout this book and will usually be based on some criterion of optimality: principal examples are the Hough transform (Section 6.2.6), shape invariants (Section 8.2.7), snakes (Section 7.2), graph matching (Section 9.5), PDMs/AAMs (Sections 10.4, 10.5), correspondence (Chapter 11), hypothesize and verify (Section 10.1.4), SIFT (Section 10.2), etc. In this section, we cover some key approaches to this important issue.

It is worth noting that image registration, a significant area of image processing that we do not cover in this book, naturally belongs to the broad field of image matching. The general form of the registration problem takes two independent views of a scene and derives a correspondence between them—we shall see some aspects of this in considering stereo correspondence (Section 11.5). Registration is a large area, in particular in the medical domain where, for example, large datasets may be acquired by different modalities (CT, MR, ...) that require matching. Thorough texts of comparable length are devoted to this topic: for example [Fitzpatrick et al., 2000; Yoo, 2004; Goshtasby, 2005; Hajnal and Hill, 2010].

6.4.1 Template matching

The simplest approach to locating a known object in an image is to seek its pixel-perfect copy. This implies no variation in scale or rotation and is accordingly an artificially simple task. In this simplified form we are seeking to match a *template*—the known image.

Given a template T of dimension $r_T \times c_T$ and an image I, we will hold it at offsets $\mathbf{x} = (x_a, x_b)$. If the template fits perfectly we will have

$$E(\mathbf{x}) = \sum_{i=1}^{r_T} \sum_{j=1}^{c_T} (T_{i,j} - I_{x_a+i,x_b+j})^2 = 0 \,, \tag{6.29}$$

(where E measures the error of the fit). Further, local minima of $E(\mathbf{x})$ will give some indication of quality of template fit. In fact, we have

$$
\begin{aligned}
E(\mathbf{x}) &= \sum_{i=1}^{r_T}\sum_{j=1}^{c_T}(T_{i,j} - I_{x_a+i,x_b+j})^2 \\
&= \sum_{i=1}^{r_T}\sum_{j=1}^{c_T}(T_{i,j})^2 - 2\sum_{i=1}^{r_T}\sum_{j=1}^{c_T}(T_{i,j}I_{x_a+i,x_b+j}) + \sum_{i=1}^{r_T}\sum_{j=1}^{c_T}(I_{x_a+i,x_b+j})^2 \,, \quad (6.30)
\end{aligned}
$$

in which the first term is constant and the third is in most circumstances slowly varying with $\mathbf{x}$. Template matching may thus be performed by maximizing the correlation expression

$$
Corr_T(\mathbf{x}) = \sum_{i=1}^{r_T}\sum_{j=1}^{c_T}(T_{i,j}I_{x_a+i,x_b+j}) \,. \quad (6.31)
$$

Note that the summation is sensitive both to intensity range and size of the region T, and use of a spatial and/or intensity scaling parameters may be in order. Whether partial pattern positions, crossing the image borders, and similar special cases are considered depends on the implementation.

In practical use, this is severely limited—very small rotations of the template or changes in scale can cause radical jumps in the 'error' measure E. Section 16.3.2 presents a more sophisticated approach to minimizing E when the template may be subject to affine (or more complex) transformation. Figure 6.48 illustrates simple template matching in use.

Figure 6.48: Template matching: A template of the letter **R** is sought in an image that has itself, a slightly rotated version, and a smaller version. The correlation response (contrast stretched for display) illustrates the diffuse response seen for even small adjustments to the original. © *Cengage Learning 2015.*

An alternative criterion for the same idea to minimize E in equation (6.29) might be to maximize

$$
C(\mathbf{x}) = \frac{1}{1 + E(\mathbf{x})} \,. \quad (6.32)
$$

Figure 6.49 gives an example of the use of this criterion—the best matched position is in the upper left corner. In Figure 6.50, an X-shaped correlation mask was used to detect positions of magnetic resonance markers [Fisher et al., 1991].

The Fourier convolution theorem (see Section 3.2.4) provides an efficient way of computing the correlation of a template and an image—to compute the product of two Fourier transforms, they must be of the same size; a template may have zero-valued lines and columns added to inflate it to the appropriate size. Sometimes, it may be better to add non-zero numbers, for example, the average gray-level of processed images.

$$
\begin{vmatrix}
1 & 1 & 0 & 0 & 0 \\
1 & 1 & 1 & 0 & 0 \\
1 & 0 & 1 & 0 & 0 \\
0 & 0 & 0 & 0 & 0 \\
0 & 0 & 0 & 0 & 8
\end{vmatrix}
\qquad
\begin{vmatrix}
1 & 1 & 1 \\
1 & 1 & 1 \\
1 & 1 & 1
\end{vmatrix}
\qquad
\begin{vmatrix}
\underline{1/3} & 1/6 & 1/8 & \times & \times \\
1/5 & 1/7 & 1/8 & \times & \times \\
1/8 & 1/9 & 1/57 & \times & \times \\
\times & \times & \times & \times & \times \\
\times & \times & \times & \times & \times
\end{vmatrix}
$$

$$
\text{(a)} \qquad\qquad\qquad \text{(b)} \qquad\qquad\qquad \text{(c)}
$$

Figure 6.49: Optimality matching criterion evaluation. (a) Image data. (b) Matched pattern. (c) Values of the optimality criterion C (the best match underlined). © *Cengage Learning 2015.*

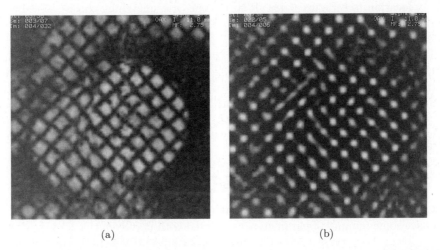

(a)   (b)

Figure 6.50: X-shaped mask matching. (a) Original image (see also Figure 16.22). (b) Correlation image; the better the local correlation with the X-shaped mask, the brighter the correlation image. (Figures 16.22, 16.23 show how the identified matches are used for motion analysis.) *Courtesy of D. Fisher, S. M. Collins, The University of Iowa.*

A related approach uses the chamfer image (which computes distances from image subsets, see Algorithm 2.1) to locate features such as known boundaries in edge maps. If we construct a chamfer image from an edge detection of the image under inspection, then any position of a required boundary can be judged for fit by summing the corresponding pixel values under each of its component edges in a positioning over the image—low values will be good and high poor. Since the chamfering will permit gradual changes in this measure with changes in position, standard optimization techniques (see Section 9.6) can be applied to its movement in search of a best match.

6.4.2 Control strategies of templating

While it is unusual for a known object to appear 'pixel perfect' in an image, it is often the case that *components* of it—which may be quite small—will do. If we imagine the larger pattern as being composed of these components connected by elastic links, then the match of the larger pattern will require stretching or contraction of these links to accord with identification of the smaller components. A good strategy is to look for the best partial matches first, followed by a heuristic graph construction of the best combination of these partial matches in which graph nodes represent pattern parts.

Template-based segmentation is time consuming even in the simplest cases, but the process can often be accelerated. The sequence of match tests must be data driven. Fast testing of image locations with a high probability of match may be the first step; then it is not necessary to test all possible pattern locations. Another speed improvement can be derived if a mismatch can be detected before all the corresponding pixels have been tested.

If a pattern is highly correlated with image data in some specific image location, then typically the correlation of the pattern with image data in some neighborhood of this location is also good. In other words, correlation changes slowly around the best matching location (see Figure 6.48). If this is the case, matching can be tested at lower resolution first, looking for an exact match in the neighborhood of good low-resolution matches only.

Mismatches should be detected as early as possible since they are found much more often than matches. Thus in equation (6.32), testing in a specified position must stop when the value in the denominator (measure of mismatch) exceeds some preset threshold. This implies that it is better to begin the correlation test in pixels with a high probability of mismatch in order to get a steep growth in the mismatch criterion. This criterion growth will be faster than that produced by an arbitrary pixel order computation.

6.5   Evaluation issues in segmentation

The range of segmentation techniques available is large and will grow. Each algorithm has or will have some number of parameters associated with it. Given this large toolbox, and a new problem, how might we decide which algorithm and which parameters are best? Or, less challenging, given two choices, which is better than the other? Such questions require us to evaluate performance in some objective manner. Meanwhile, evaluation of a single algorithm on different datasets provides information about robustness, and ability to handle data acquired under different conditions and by different modalities.

The issue of evaluation in computer vision applies in almost all areas as the science matures: where once researchers would devise and publish algorithms, it is now expected that they also provide some evidence of their improved performance–often this is done with respect to accepted databases of images or videos to ensure comparability, a process begun informally many years ago with the widespread use of the 'Lena' [Rosenberg, 2001] image to benchmark compression algorithms. The increasing formalization of these activities is leading to respected workshops and conferences dedicated to evaluation. Segmentation evaluation is no exception to these developments; for example [Chabrier et al., 2006; Forbes and Draper, 2000; Hoover et al., 1996; Wang et al., 2006; Zhang, 1996].

Evaluating segmentations raises two problems;

- How do we determine what is 'right', in order to compare a segmentation with reality?

- What do we measure? And how do we measure it?

The answer to the second here is dependent on our answer to the first, as there are currently two independent ways of considering evaluation.

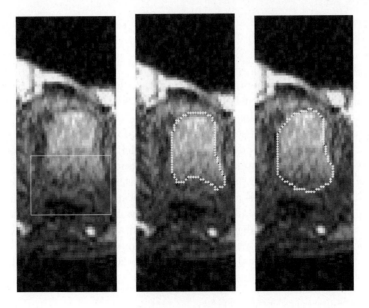

Figure 6.51: A region from a dynamically enhanced MRI study with partly ambiguous boundary. Two different experts have overlaid their judgments. *Courtesy of O. Kubassova, S. Tanner, University of Leeds.*

6.5.1 Supervised evaluation

Supervised evaluation proceeds on an assumption that the 'right' answer is known–normally this implies the defining of ground truth, perhaps by interactive drawing of correct boundaries on the image(s) via a suitable interface [Chalana and Kim, 1997; Heath et al., 1997; Shin et al., 2001]. Obviously, this is a labor intensive task if a dataset of sufficient size is to be compiled, but it is also the case that 'truth' is often far from clear. Many segmentation problems are fraught by low contrast, blur, and other ambiguities, and issues surrounding uncertainty in human opinion are beginning to attract interest [Dee and Velastin, 2008; Needham and Boyle, 2003]. This issue is well illustrated in Figure 6.51. Clearly, it is simple (if costly) to take the judgments of several experts and somehow average them [Williams, 1976; Alberola-Lopez et al., 2004; Chalana and Kim, 1997], but the elusiveness of 'truth' remains an issue. As a consequence, the need for a metric which accounts for possible inconsistencies has been identified by many researchers.

Nearly all supervised evaluation techniques are based on one of two (very well established) approaches [Beauchemin and Thomson, 1997; Zhang, 1996]: misclassified area [Dice, 1945], or assessment of border positioning errors [Yasnoff et al., 1977].

6.5.1.1 Misclassified area–mutual overlap

The *mutual overlap* approach, best known as Dice evaluation, is based on computing the area of overlap between ground truth and a segmented region [Bowyer, 2000; Dice, 1945; Hoover et al., 1996]. This is illustrated in Figure 6.52. The area is normalized to the total area of the two defining regions; if A_1 is the area of the segmented region, A_2 is the area of ground truth, MO is the area of their mutual overlap, then the mutual overlap metric is defined as

$$M_{\mathrm{MO}} = \frac{2\,\mathrm{MO}}{A_1 + A_2}.$$

It is customary to measure acceptable quality with respect to this metric by setting a percentage threshold for M_{MO}, usually greater than 50% [Bowyer, 2000], but this will vary to reflect the strictness of the definition.

This approach is popular and seen to work well on, for example, binary, RGB or some satellite data, but is not always adequate. The simplicity of the measure often conceals quality differences between different segmentations, and gives little if any information about boundaries which may be partially correct; further it assumes a closed contour, which is not always available. It is at its best when distances from a segmented boundary to ground truth are distributed unimodally with low variance, but it is poor at handling uncertainty in ground truth definition. Despite these drawbacks, this metric is attractive because of its simplicity, and is widely used for evaluation of segmentation algorithms executed on, for example, medical imagery [Bowyer, 2000; Campadelli and Casirahgi, 2005; Chrastek et al., 2005; Prastawa et al., 2005].

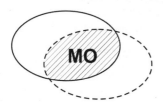

Figure 6.52: Mutual overlap: machine segmented region in solid, ground truth in dashed. © *Cengage Learning 2015.*

6.5.1.2   Border positioning errors

Some time ago, an approach considering Euclidean distance between segmented and ground truth pixels was devised [Yasnoff et al., 1977]. This is related to the Hausdorff measure between the sets [Rote, 1991]; the *Hausdorff distance* between two sets A and B is computed by finding the minimum distance from each element of one to some element of the other, and then finding the maximum such.

$$h(A, B) = \max_{a \in A} \left(\min_{b \in B} d(a, b) \right), \tag{6.33}$$

where $d(a, b)$ is some suitable distance metric, commonly the Euclidean metric. The Hausdorff distance is oriented (asymmetric); usually $h(A, B) \neq h(B, A)$. A general definition of the Hausdorff distance between two sets is [Rote, 1991]:

$$H(A, B) = \max \left(h(A, B), h(B, A) \right). \tag{6.34}$$

This defines a measure of the sets' mutual proximity, indicating how far (at most) two sets of points are from each other.

$H(A, B)$ has been adapted by some authors [Chalana and Kim, 1997] as an evaluation measure for the quality of segmentation results, where A is the pixels of a ground truth region, and B the pixels of a segmented region. Again, this does not afford an application-adaptable threshold for a degree of tolerance in segmentation error and does not permit quality measurement of partial boundaries.

This idea has been adapted to consider only boundary pixels–measuring the distance between boundaries of the regions instead of the regions themselves permits evaluation of open boundaries. Local border positioning errors are determined for each point of the segmented borders as a directional distance between pairs of points, the first being on the computer-determined border and a the second on the ground truth. Clearly, the direction of measurement is still relevant, as Figure 6.53 demonstrates.

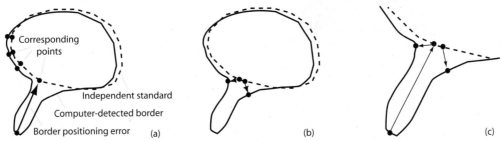

Figure 6.53: Border positioning errors. (a) Border positioning errors are computed as directed distances between the computer-determined and correct borders. (b) If errors are calculated in the opposite direction (from ground truth to the computer-determined border), a substantially different answer may result. (c) Zoomed area showing the difference in calculating directional errors. © *Cengage Learning 2015.*

Border positioning errors are usually averaged for the entire length of the segmented border and reported as mean ± standard deviation. Other statistics might assist in assessing different aspects of the segmentation performance; for example, signed and/or unsigned mean border positioning errors, maximum border positioning errors, and/or root-mean-square surface positioning errors are typically computed. For signed border positioning errors, an arbitrary convention must be followed in which a computer-border point located on one side of ground truth has a positive sign, and on the other side of the border a negative sign. Then, the mean signed border positioning error represents a global bias of the computer segmentation, and its standard deviation describes a degree of departure from the independent standard along the entire length of the border. Using the mean error distributions for the entire test set of multiple segmented objects, border positioning errors can be summarized as test-set mean ± test-set standard deviation.

This approach has been enhanced to consider tolerance issues. Let N_A be the number of pixels in boundary A, and $A_t(B)$ be the pixels of A within a distance t of a pixel of B. If N_{A_t} is the cardinality of $A_t(B)$, and N_B and N_{B_t} are defined similarly,

$$H_t(A, B) = \frac{1}{2}\left(\frac{N_{A_t}}{N_A} + \frac{N_{B_t}}{N_B}\right) \tag{6.35}$$

provides a metric that will increase monotonically with t, and converge to 1.

The parameter t is an interval of tolerance, within which pixels from one boundary are considered as being 'close enough' to the other. This reflects the acceptable error of segmentation which may be acquired from width of ambiguous boundary sections, or the opinion of experts. As the tolerance can be extracted from the domain, it can reflect an application-dependent acceptable segmentation error.

Figure 6.54 illustrates the use of this metric, which has been shown to be of use in algorithm comparison [Kubassova et al., 2006].

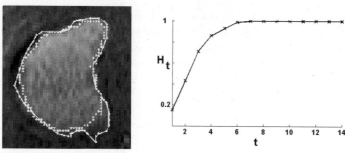

Figure 6.54: Use of the H_t metric on a segmentation from dynamically enhanced MRI; ground truth is dotted and a sample segmentation is solid. *Courtesy of O. Kubassova, University of Leeds.*

6.5.2   Unsupervised evaluation

Difficulties in acquiring ground truth such as imprecise definition, paucity of information, and time consumption make unsupervised approaches attractive: these quantify quality by considering different statistics derived from the properties of an image and segmentation, without knowledge of ground truth.

Of course, this is trying to answer a poorly defined question; in many images the nature of a 'good segmentation' will depend upon the application–for example, in a picture of traffic we may seek to segment out cars if monitoring congestion, or parts of cars if counting the number of Morgans driving past. Unsupervised evaluation metrics bypass such issues completely, and will be based on the location, shape, size, contrast, or intensity of segmented regions [Peters and Strickland, 1992]. They depend on either global image statistics, which can be derived from the pixels in the image, or regional statistics, which characterize the regions segmented. Characteristically, certain assumptions are made about a 'good segmentation' and these are either verified or not from the presented data.

A simple example is the inter-region dissimilarity criterion [Levine and Nazif, 1985] which assumes that a good segmentation produces regions of uniform intensity with high contrast along borders. If a gray-scale image contains an object with average intensity level f_0, and the average intensity of the local background is f_b, the measure M at its most straightforward is defined as

$$M = \frac{|f_0 - f_b|}{f_0 + f_b} \, . \tag{6.36}$$

This early metric is very simple: successors include the intra-region uniformity criterion [Nazif and Levine, 1984; Weszka and Rosenfeld, 1978] (which assumes that an adequate segmentation should produce images with high intra-region uniformity), the Borsotti criterion [Borsotti et al., 1998; Lui and Yang, 1994; Chabrier et al., 2005] (which assumes that an image should be segmented into homogeneous regions, of simple shape), and the Zeboudj criterion [Jourlin et al., 1989] (which assumes a good segmentation delivers regions of high contrast). All of these have advantages and disadvantages, but the more sophisticated they are, the more complex and less intuitive their definitions become.

All unsupervised metrics have their merits and can be demonstrated to be of value: this can be done, for example, by correlating their performance with a trusted supervised metric (or ground truth) on a large database [Chabrier et al., 2006]. Frequently, the results of such exercises are inconclusive and sometime contradictory as a result of definitions being very limiting and inapplicable to challenging domains.

One approach gaining wide acceptance (especially in medical image segmentation assessment) is an expectation-maximization algorithm for simultaneous truth and performance level estimation, or **STAPLE** [Warfield et al., 2004]. STAPLE starts with a collection of segmentations and the true segmentation is determined as a probabilistic estimate taking performance-weighted segmentations by experts or automated algorithms in consideration. The weights given to individual segmentations are determined according to the estimated performance levels of individual contributors, segmentation priors, and spatial homogeneity constraints. Its development is continuing with a **MAP STAPLE** being the latest contribution that was shown to outperform the original STAPLE algorithm [Commowick et al., 2012].

Evaluation of segmentation algorithms is clearly important, but there does not currently exist a consensus on approach. Existing supervised approaches are labor intensive and of limited performance, while unsupervised approaches are often demonstrated on synthetic data sets and put constraints on image properties which often cannot be satisfied in real world applications.

For practical purposes, one must typically answer three questions:

1. How frequently a method fails to provide a meaningful segmentation: the answer is typically task-dependent and is often left to human experts to identify.

2. How accurate the method is: segmentation accuracy can be assessed by the methods described, or some other performance assessment index.

3. How reproducible is the segmentation in successful cases: even if not absolutely accurate, segmentation reproducibility (precision) is valuable in many applications. For example, if changes of some object property are followed over time, reproducibility may be more important than absolute accuracy. Since many segmentation techniques are dependent on a number of parameters and/or on initialization, such sensitivity can be assessed by determination of reproducibility. The Bland-Altman statistical approach is frequently used for this purpose [Bland and Altman, 1986, 1999].

To evaluate segmentation performance, the reader has access to a number of approaches to this important, if unglamorous, phase. A comparative review, with pointers to benchmark databases, is at [Chabrier et al., 2008].

6.6 Summary

- **Image segmentation**

    - The main goal of image segmentation is to divide an image into parts that have a strong correlation with objects or areas of the real world depicted in the image.

- Segmentation methods may be categorized as: **thresholding**, **edge-based** and **region-based**.

- Each region can be represented by its closed boundary, and each closed boundary describes a region.

- The primary segmentation problems are image data ambiguity and information noise.

- The more a priori information is available to the segmentation process, the better the segmentation results that can be obtained.

- **Thresholding**

  - Thresholding is simplest image segmentation process; it is computationally inexpensive and fast. A constant **threshold** segments objects and background.

  - Thresholds may be applied to the entire image (**global threshold**) or may vary in image parts (**local threshold**). It is rare for a single threshold to be successful for a whole image.

  - Many modifications of thresholding exist: **local thresholding**, **band thresholding**, **multi-thresholding**, etc.

  - **Threshold detection** methods determine thresholds automatically. If some post-segmentation image property is known a priori, threshold detection is simplified, since the threshold can be selected to satisfy this property. Threshold detection can use p-**tile thresholding**, **histogram shape analysis**, **optimal thresholding**, etc.

  - In **bimodal histograms**, the threshold can be determined as a minimum between the two highest local maxima.

  - **Optimal thresholding** determines the threshold as the closest gray-level corresponding to the minimum probability between the maxima of two or more normal distributions. Such thresholding results in minimum error segmentation.

  - **Multi-spectral thresholding** is appropriate for color or multi-band images.

- **Edge-based image segmentation**

  - Edge-based segmentation relies on edge detecting operators; *edges* mark image locations of discontinuities in gray-level, color, texture, etc.

  - Image noise or unsuitable information may often cause an edge presence in locations where there is no border, and no edge presence where a real border exists.

  - **Edge image thresholding** is based on construction of an edge image that is processed by an appropriate threshold.

  - **Edge relaxation** considers edges in the context of neighboring edges. If sufficient evidence of border presence exists, local edge strength increases and vice versa. A global relaxation (optimization) process constructs borders.

- **Inner**, **outer**, and **extended** border may be defined. The inner border is always part of a region; the outer border never is. Thus using inner or outer borders, two adjacent regions never have a common border. Extended borders are defined as single common borders between adjacent regions still being specified by standard pixel co-ordinates.

- If an optimality criterion is defined, globally optimal borders can be determined using **(heuristic) graph searching** or **dynamic programming**. Graph-search-based border detection are an extremely powerful segmentation approach—the border detection process is transformed into a search for an optimal path in the weighted graph. Costs are associated with graph nodes that reflect the likelihood that the border passes through a particular node (pixel). The optimal path (optimal border, with respect to some objective function) that connects two specified nodes or sets of nodes that represent the border's beginning and end is determined.

- **Cost definition** (evaluation functions) is the key to successful border detection. Cost calculation complexity may range from simple inverted edge strength to complex representation of a priori knowledge about the sought borders, segmentation task, image data, etc.

- Graph searching uses Nilsson's **A-algorithm** and guarantees optimality. **Heuristic graph search** may substantially increase search speed, although the heuristics must satisfy additional constraints to guarantee optimality.

- **Dynamic programming** is based on the principle of optimality and presents an efficient way of simultaneously searching for optimal paths from multiple starting and ending points.

- Using the A-algorithm to search a graph, it is not necessary to construct the entire graph since the costs associated with expanded nodes are calculated only if needed. In dynamic programming, a complete graph must be constructed.

- If calculation of the local cost functions is computationally inexpensive, dynamic programming may represent a computationally less demanding choice. However, which of the two graph searching approaches (A-algorithm, dynamic programming) is more efficient for a particular problem depends on the evaluation functions and on the quality of heuristics for an A-algorithm.

- **Hough transform** segmentation is applicable if objects of known shape are to be detected within an image. The Hough transform can detect straight lines and curves (object borders) if their analytic equations are known. It is robust in recognition of occluded and noisy objects.

- The generalized Hough transform can be used if the analytic equations of the searched shapes are not available; the parametric curve (region border) description is based on sample situations and is determined in the learning stage.

- While forming the regions from complete borders is trivial, **region determination from partial borders** may be a very complex task. Region construction may be based on probabilities that pixels are located inside a region closed by the partial borders. Such methods do not always find acceptable regions but they are useful in many practical situations.

- **Region-based image segmentation**

  - **Region growing** should satisfy the condition of complete segmentation—equation (6.1)— and the maximum region homogeneity conditions—equations (6.22), (6.23).

  - Three basic approaches to region growing exist: **region merging**, **region splitting**, and **split-and-merge** region growing.

  - **Region merging** starts with an oversegmented image in which regions satisfy equation (6.22). Regions are merged to satisfy condition given by equation (6.23) as long as equation (6.22) remains satisfied.

  - **Region splitting** is the opposite of region merging. Region splitting begins with an undersegmented image which does not satisfy condition given by equation (6.22). Existing image regions are sequentially split to satisfy conditions (6.1), (6.22), and (6.23).

  - A combination of **splitting and merging** may result in a method with the advantages of both. Split-and-merge approaches typically use pyramid image representations. Because both options are available, the starting segmentation does not have to satisfy either condition given by equations (6.22) or (6.23).

  - In **watershed** segmentation, catchment basins represent the regions of the segmented image. The first watershed segmentation approach starts with finding a downstream path from each pixel of the image to local minima of image surface altitude. A catchment basin is then defined as the set of pixels for which their respective downstream paths all end up in the same altitude minimum. In the second approach, each gray-level minimum represents one catchment basin and the strategy is to start filling the catchment basins from the bottom.

  - Images segmented by region growing methods often contain either too many regions (under-growing) or too few regions (over-growing) as a result of non-optimal parameter setting. Many **post-processors** has been developed to improve classification. Simpler post-processors decrease the number of small regions in the segmented image. More complex post-processing may combine segmentation information obtained from region growing and edge-based segmentation.

- **Matching**

  - Template matching can be used to locate objects of known appearance in an image, to search for specific patterns, etc. The best match is based on some criterion of optimality which depends on object properties and object relations.

  - Matching criteria can be defined in many ways; in particular, correlation between a pattern and the searched image data is often used as a general matching criterion.

  - Chamfer matching may be used to locate one-dimensional features that might otherwise defeat cost-based optimality approaches.

  - Template-based segmentation is time consuming but the process can be accelerated by employing appropriate control strategies of templating.

- **Evaluation**

  - Evaluation of segmentation is useful in deciding between algorithms, or parameter choice for a given algorithm.
  - *Supervised* evaluation compares algorithm output to ground truth.
  - Supervised approaches usually compare area overlap, or distance between boundaries—there are several ways of doing this.
  - Ground truth is often poorly defined or expensive to extract. *Unsupervised* approaches judge segmentations in ignorance of it.
  - Many unsupervised approaches exist but they are usually constrained by assumptions about image regions.

6.7   Exercises

Short-answer questions

S6.1 If an image histogram is bimodal, under what circumstances can a threshold be found that segments it perfectly?

S6.2 What are the advantages and disadvantages of edge-based segmentation?

S6.3 Explain the main concept of border detection using edge relaxation.

S6.4 List the main advantages and disadvantages of inner, outer, and extended border definitions.

S6.5 Mark all pixels forming the

(a) Outer

(b) Extended

border for the object given in Figure 6.55. If any pixel occurs more than once in the border, mark it more than once.

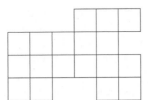

Figure 6.55: Determine the borders of this object. (Later: Problem S6.15) Construct an R-table for this object, using the third pixel from the left in the second row as reference. © *Cengage Learning 2015*.

S6.6 Explain why the lower-bound method for modification of node costs increases the A-algorithm graph search speed.

S6.7 Consider a heuristic graph searching algorithm; explain how the accuracy of the estimate $\tilde{h}(\mathbf{x}_i)$ of the path cost from the current node $\mathbf{x}_i$ to the end node influences the search behavior. Specify under which conditions the optimality of the search is guaranteed.

S6.8 What is the main idea of the principle of optimality? How is it used in dynamic programming?

S6.9 What is the complexity of an optimal path search in a general graph? Give examples of how this complexity can be reduced for more constrained cases.

S6.10 What are the main differences between A-algorithm graph searching and dynamic programming. Explain why dynamic programming is often faster than the A-algorithm.

S6.11 Using a polar representation, explain the main concept of the Hough transform for line detection. Draw several lines in the image space and sketch the corresponding Hough transforms in the parameter space. Label all important points, lines, and axes.

S6.12 Explain why the polar co-ordinate representation of lines $s = x \cos \theta + y \sin \theta$ is more suitable for line detection using the Hough transform than the standard line representation $y = kx + q$.

S6.13 What is the dimensionality of a Hough accumulator array if circles of all sizes are to be determined in a two-dimensional image? List all necessary accumulator array variables.

S6.14 Explain how a priori information about edge directions may increase the speed of Hough transform-based image segmentation.

S6.15 Construct an R-table for the object given in Figure 6.55; use the third pixel from the left in the second row from the top as the reference point. It is enough to consider angles which are multiples of $90°$.

S6.16 Explain the main conceptual differences in edge-based and region-based approaches to image segmentation. Are these two approaches dual?

S6.17 Specify mathematically the goal of region-based segmentation using the criterion of region homogeneity.

S6.18 Explain the principles of and differences among the three basic approaches to region growing—merging, splitting, and split-and-merge.

S6.19 Explain the main principles of watershed segmentation. Discuss why filling the catchment basins from the bottom is several orders of magnitude faster than the approaches using mathematical morphology.

S6.20 Explain why watershed segmentation tends to over-segment images.

S6.21 Explain why a strategy of fast determination of a mismatch can typically speed up the process of image matching more than a strategy of increasing the efficiency of proving a match.

Problems

P6.1 In preparation, using Matlab or a similar environment, develop some known test images with a mixture of straight, curved and more complex borders, enclosing regions of uniform and variable intensity. Record their area and boundary positions. Create more images by superimposing additive Gaussian noise with a given standard deviation, and random impulse noise of a given severity.

P6.2 Implement the various methods for threshold-based segmentation described in the text and apply to your test images (Problem P6.1). Determine the thresholds manually by trial and error, and compare segmentation accuracy for individual methods.

P6.3 Implement adaptive thresholding and apply it to your test images (Problem P6.1). Use the Otsu's optimal method for threshold selection. Assess each method qualitatively.

P6.4 Implement recursive multi-spectral thresholding and apply it to color images represented by three RGB bands.

P6.5 Implement Algorithms 6.4 and 6.5, and run them on your test images (Problem P6.1) for a range of values of hysteresis thresholds t_0 and t_1. Make a subjective judgment about the best values, then try to relate these to properties of the distribution of edge magnitudes in the image (for example, does it help to select either threshold such that a given percentage of edges have higher or lower magnitudes?).

P6.6 Using 4- and/or 8-connectivity, develop a program for inner border tracing that finds borders of objects as well as borders of object holes. Test the program on a variety of binary images and on the segmentation results obtained in the previous problems. Make sure the program works well for single pixel objects and single-pixel-wide objects.

P6.7 Develop a program for extended border tracing. Test in the same images as were used in Problem P6.6.

P6.8 Using A-algorithm graph search, find the optimal path through the graph given in Figure 6.56, numbers within the circles specify node costs; consider three possible node successors. Show all steps of your graph searching, including the status of all associated data structures during each step.

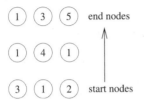

Figure 6.56: Use the A-algorithm to find an optimal path through this graph. © *Cengage Learning 2015*.

P6.9 Assume that an optimal border is detected using the A-algorithm in a rectangular graph, with costs associated with each node. The optimal border corresponds to the minimum-cost path through the graph. Discuss how the following changes in node costs influence the resulting border and the number of graph nodes expanded during the graph search.

(a) The costs of all nodes are increased by a constant.

(b) The costs of all nodes are decreased by a constant but no cost becomes negative.

(c) The costs of all nodes are decreased by a constant and some costs become negative.

(d) The costs of one or more (but not all) graph profiles are increased by a constant.

(e) The costs of one or more (but not all) graph profiles are decreased by a constant but no cost becomes negative.

(f) The costs of one or more (but not all) graph profiles are decreased by a constant and some costs become negative.

P6.10 Using dynamic programming, find the optimal path through the graph given in Figure 6.56 (numbers within the circles specify node costs); consider three possible node successors. Show all steps of your graph searching, including the status of all associated data structures during each step.

P6.11 Implement watershed segmentation and apply it to your test images (Problem P6.1). Design a strategy to avoid severe over-segmentation of noisy images.

P6.12 Using template matching, detect all locations of a specific printed character on a scanned printed page.

1. Search for characters of the same font and size.

2. Search for characters of the same font across different sizes.

3. Search for the same characters across different fonts and sizes.

4. Employ different levels of image quality in the above tasks.

5. Employ different strategies of matching and compare achieved processing times.

P6.13 Using template matching, detect all locations of a specific image template on a set of images. Consider situations, in which a specific template does not appear in the processed image. Employ different levels of image quality.

P6.14 Implement the following approaches to region growing and apply to your test images (Problem P6.1). Compare segmentation accuracy for individual methods.

    (a) Region merging

    (b) Region splitting

    (c) Split-and-merge

    (d) Region merging via boundary melting

    (e) Split and link to the segmentation tree

    (f) Single pass split-and-merge

P6.15 Select some of the segmentations you have implemented, and measure their quality quantitatively with the Dice (mutual overlap) metric.

P6.16 Select some of the segmentations you have implemented, and measure their quality quantitatively with the Hausdorff based (border mis-positioning) metric. How do these two metrics compare?

P6.17 Make yourself familiar with solved problems and **Matlab** implementations of selected algorithms provided in the corresponding chapter of the **Matlab Companion** to this text [Svoboda et al., 2008]. The **Matlab Companion** homepage http://visionbook.felk.cvut.cz offers images used in the problems, and well-commented **Matlab** code is provided for educational purposes.

P6.18 Use the **Matlab Companion** [Svoboda et al., 2008] to develop solutions to additional exercises and practical problems provided there. Implement your solutions using **Matlab** or other suitable programming languages.

6.8 References

Alberola-Lopez C., Martin-Fernandez M., and Ruiz-Alzola J. Comments on: A methodology for evaluation of boundary detection algorithms on medical images. *IEEE Transactions on Medical Imaging*, 23(5):658–660, 2004.

Ballard D. H. Generalizing the Hough transform to detect arbitrary shapes. *Pattern Recognition*, 13:111–122, 1981.

Ballard D. H. and Brown C. M. *Computer Vision*. Prentice-Hall, Englewood Cliffs, NJ, 1982.

Barrett W. A. and Mortensen E. N. Fast, accurate, and reproducible live-wire boundary extraction. In *Visualization in Biomedical Computing*, pages 183–192, Berlin, Heidelberg, 1996. Springer Verlag.

Beauchemin M. and Thomson K. P. B. The evaluation of segmentation results and the overlapping area matrix. *Remote Sensing*, 18:3895–3899, 1997.

Bellmann R. *Dynamic Programming*. Princeton University Press, Princeton, NJ, 1957.

Bland J. M. and Altman D. G. Statistical methods for assessing agreement between two methods of clinical measurement. *Lancet*, 1(8476):307–310, 1986.

Bland J. M. and Altman D. G. Measuring agreement in method comparison studies. *Stat Methods Med Res*, 8:135–160, 1999.

Borsotti M., Campadelli P., and Schettini R. Quantitative evaluation of colour image segmentation results. *Pattern Recognition Letters*, 19(8):741–747, 1998.

Bowyer K. W. Validation of medical image analysis techniques. In Sonka M. and Fitzpatrick J. M., editors, *Handbook of Medical Imaging*, volume 2, pages 567–607. Press Monograph, Bellingham, WA, 1 edition, 2000. ISBN 0-8194-3622-4.

Brice C. R. and Fennema C. L. Scene analysis using regions. *Artificial Intelligence*, 1:205–226, 1970.

Campadelli P. and Casirahgi E. Lung field segmentation in digital posterior-anterior chest radiographs. *3rd International Conference on Advances in Pattern Recognition,* Bath, UK, 3687:736–745, 2005.

Canny J. F. A computational approach to edge detection. *IEEE Transactions on Pattern Analysis and Machine Intelligence*, 8(6):679–698, 1986.

Chabrier S., Rosenberger C., Laurent H., and Rakotomamonjy A. Segmentation evaluation using a support vector machine. *3rd International Conference on Advances in Pattern Recognition,* Bath, UK, 2:889–896, 2005.

Chabrier S., Emile B., Rosenberger C., and Laurent H. Unsupervised performance evaluation of image segmentation. *EURASIP Journal on Applied Signal Processing*, 2006:1–12, 2006.

Chabrier S., Laurent H., Rosenberger C., and Emile B. Comparative study of contour detection evaluation criteria based on dissimilarity measures. *EURASIP Journal on Image and Video Processing*, 2008, 2008.

Chalana V. and Kim Y. A methodology for evaluation of boundary detection algorithms on medical images. *IEEE Transactions on Medical Imaging*, 16(5):642–652, 1997.

Chang Y. L. and Li X. Fast image region growing. *Image and Vision Computing*, 13:559–571, 1995.

Chen S. Y., Lin W. C., and Chen C. T. Split-and-merge image segmentation based on localized feature analysis and statistical tests. *CVGIP – Graphical Models and Image Processing*, 53 (5):457–475, 1991.

Cho S., Haralick R., and Yi S. Improvement of Kittler and Illingworth's minimum error thresholding. *Pattern Recognition*, 22(5):609–617, 1989.

Chrastek R., Wolf M., Donath K., Niemann H., Paulus D., Hothorn T., Lausen B., Lammer R., Mardin C. Y., and Michelson G. Automated segmentation of the optic nerve head for diagnosis of glaucoma. *Medical Image Analysis*, 9(4):297–314, 2005.

Chu C. C. and Aggarwal J. K. The integration of image segmentation maps using region and edge information. *IEEE Transactions on Pattern Analysis and Machine Intelligence*, 15: 1241–1252, 1993.

Clark D. Image edge relaxation on a hypercube. Technical Report Project 55:295, University of Iowa, 1991.

Collins S. H. Terrain parameters directly from a digital terrain model. *Canadian Surveyor*, 29 (5):507–518, 1975.

Commowick O., Akhondi-Asl A., and Warfield S. Estimating a reference standard segmentation with spatially varying performance parameters: Local MAP STAPLE. *Medical Imaging, IEEE Transactions on*, 31:1593–1606, 2012.

Davies E. R. *Machine vision - theory, algorithms, practicalities*. Morgan Kaufman, 3 edition, 2005.

Davis L. S. Hierarchical generalized Hough transforms and line segment based generalized Hough transforms. *Pattern Recognition*, 15(4):277–285, 1982.

Dee H. M. and Velastin S. How close are we to solving the problem of automated visual surveillance? *Machine Vision and Applications*, 19(5-6):329–343, 2008.

Demi M. Contour tracking by enhancing corners and junctions. *Computer Vision and Image Understanding*, 63:118–134, 1996.

Dice L. R. Measures of the amount of ecologic association between species. *Ecology*, 26(3): 297–302, 1945.

Dobrin B. P., Viero T., and Gabbouj M. Fast watershed algorithms: Analysis and extensions. In *Proceedings of the SPIE Vol. 2180*, pages 209–220, Bellingham, WA, 1994. SPIE.

Dudani S. A. Region extraction using boundary following. In Chen C. H., editor, *Pattern Recognition and Artificial Intelligence*, pages 216–232. Academic Press, New York, 1976.

Falcao A. X., Udupa J. K., Samarasekera S., Sharma S., Hirsch B. E., and Lotufo R. A. User-steered image segmentation paradigms: Live wire and live lane. Technical Report MIPG213, Deptartment of Radiology, University of Pennsylvania., 1995.

Fisher D. J., Ehrhardt J. C., and Collins S. M. Automated detection of noninvasive magnetic resonance markers. In *Computers in Cardiology,* Chicago, IL, pages 493–496, Los Alamitos, CA, 1991. IEEE.

Fitzpatrick J. M., Hill D. L. G., and Maurer, Jr. C. R. Image registration. In Sonka M. and Fitzpatrick J. M., editors, *Medical Image Processing, Volume II of the Handbook of Medical Imaging*, pages 447–513. SPIE Press, Bellingham, WA, 2000.

Fleagle S. R., Johnson M. R., Wilbricht C. J., Skorton D. J., Wilson R. F., White C. W., Marcus M. L., and Collins S. M. Automated analysis of coronary arterial morphology in cineangiograms: Geometric and physiologic validation in humans. *IEEE Transactions on Medical Imaging*, 8(4):387–400, 1989.

Flynn M. J. Some computer organizations and their effectivness. *IEEE Transactions on Computers*, 21(9):948–960, 1972.

Forbes L. A. and Draper B. A. Inconsistencies in edge detector evaluation. *Computer Vision and Pattern Recognition*, 2(5):398–404, 2000.

Frank R. J., Grabowski T. J., and Damasio H. Voxelvise percentage tissue segmentation of human brain magnetic resonance images (abstract). In *Abstracts, 25th Annual Meeting, Society for Neuroscience*, page 694, Washington, DC, 1995. Society for Neuroscience.

Gambotto J. P. A new approach to combining region growing and edge detection. *Pattern Recognition Letters*, 14:869–875, 1993.

Gauch J. and Hsia C. W. A comparison of three color image segmentation algorithms in four color spaces. In *Proceedings of the SPIE Vol. 1818*, pages 1168–1181, Bellingham, WA, 1992. SPIE.

Gerig G. and Klein F. Fast contour identification through efficient hough transform and simplified interpretation strategy. In *Proceedings of the 8th International Joint Conference on Pattern Recognition*, pages 498–500, Paris, France, 1986.

Glasbey C. A. An analysis of histogram-based thresholding algorithms. *CVGIP – Graphical Models and Image Processing*, 55:532–537, 1993.

Gonzalez R. C. and Wintz P. *Digital Image Processing*. Addison-Wesley, Reading, MA, 2nd edition, 1987.

Goshtasby A. A. *2-D and 3-D Image Registration: for Medical, Remote Sensing, and Industrial Applications*. Wiley-Interscience, 2005.

Hajnal J. and Hill D. *Medical Image Registration*. Biomedical Engineering. Taylor & Francis, 2010. ISBN 9781420042474. URL http://books.google.co.uk/books?id=2dtQNsk-qBQC.

Hanson A. R. and Riseman E. M., editors. *Computer Vision Systems*. Academic Press, New York, 1978.

Heath M., Sarkar S., Sanocki T., and Bowyer K. W. A robust visual method for assessing the relative performance of edge detection algorithms. *IEEE Transactions on Pattern Analysis and Machine Intelligence*, 19(12):1338–1359, 1997.

Higgins W. E. and Ojard E. J. 3D images and use of markers and other topological information to reduce oversegmentations. *Computers in Medical Imaging and Graphics*, 17:387–395, 1993.

Hong T. H., Dyer C. R., and Rosenfeld A. Texture primitive extraction using an edge-based approach. *IEEE Transactions on Systems, Man and Cybernetics*, 10(10):659–675, 1980.

Hoover A., Jean-Baptiste G., Jiang X., Flynn P. J., Bunke H., Goldof D. B., Bowyer K., Eggert D. W., Fitzgibbon A., and Fisher R. B. An experimental comparison of range segmentation algorithms. *IEEE Transactions on Pattern Analysis and Machine Intelligence*, 18(7):673–689, 1996.

Hough P. V. C. *A Method and Means for Recognizing Complex Patterns*. US Patent 3,069,654, 1962.

Illingworth J. and Kittler J. The adaptive Hough transform. *IEEE Transactions on Pattern Analysis and Machine Intelligence*, 9(5):690–698, 1987.

Illingworth J. and Kittler J. Survey of the Hough transform. *Computer Vision, Graphics, and Image Processing*, 44(1):87–116, 1988.

Jourlin M., Pinoli J. C., and Zeboudj R. Contrast definition and contour detection for logarithmic images. *Journal of Microscopy*, 156:33–40, 1989.

Kass M., Witkin A., and Terzopoulos D. Snakes: Active contour models. In *1st International Conference on Computer Vision*, London, England, pages 259–268, Piscataway, NJ, 1987. IEEE.

Kim J. S. and Cho H. S. A fuzzy logic and neural network approach to boundary detection for noisy imagery. *Fuzzy Sets and Systems*, 65:141–159, 1994.

Kittler J. and Illingworth J. Minimum error thresholding. *Pattern Recognition*, 19:41–47, 1986.

Koivunen V. and Pietikainen M. Combined edge and region-based method for range image segmentation. In *Proceedings of SPIE—The International Society for Optical Engineering*, volume 1381, pages 501–512, Bellingham, WA, 1990. Society for Optical Engineering.

Kubassova O., Boyle R. D., and Radjenovic A. A novel method for quantitative evaluation of segmentation outputs for dynamic contrast-enhanced MRI data in RA studies. In *Proceedings of the Joint Disease Workshop, 9th International Conference on Medical Image Computing and Computer Assisted Intervention*, volume 1, pages 72–79, 2006.

Kundu A. and Mitra S. K. A new algorithm for image edge extraction using a statistical classifier approach. *IEEE Transactions on Pattern Analysis and Machine Intelligence*, 9(4):569–577, 1987.

Levine M. D. and Nazif A. M. Dynamic measurement of computer generated image segmentations. *IEEE Transactions on Pattern Analysis and Machine Intelligence*, 7(2):155–164, 1985.

Liow Y. T. A contour tracing algorithm that preserves common boundaries between regions. *CVGIP – Image Understanding*, 53(3):313–321, 1991.

Lui J. and Yang Y. H. Multiresolution color image segmentation. *IEEE Transactions on Pattern Analysis and Machine Intelligence*, 16(7):689–700, 1994.

Manos G., Cairns A. Y., Ricketts I. W., and Sinclair D. Automatic segmentation of hand-wrist radiographs. *Image and Vision Computing*, 11:100–111, 1993.

Marquardt D. W. An algorithm for least squares estimation of non-linear parameters. *Journal of the Society for Industrial and Applied Mathematics*, 11:431–444, 1963.

Martelli A. Edge detection using heuristic search methods. *Computer Graphics and Image Processing*, 1:169–182, 1972.

Martelli A. An application of heuristic search methods to edge and contour detection. *Communications of the ACM*, 19(2):73–83, 1976.

Meyer F. and Beucher S. Morphological segmentation. *Journal of Visual Communication and Image Representation*, 1:21–46, 1990.

Mortensen E., Morse B., Barrett W., and Udupa J. Adaptive boundary detection using 'live-wire' two-dimensional dynamic programming. In *Computers in Cardiology*, pages 635–638, Los Alamitos, CA, 1992. IEEE Computer Society Press.

Nazif A. M. and Levine M. D. Low level image segmentation: an expert system. *IEEE Transactions on Pattern Analysis and Machine Intelligence*, 6(5):555–577, 1984.

Needham C. J. and Boyle R. D. Performance evaluation metrics and statistics for positional tracker evaluation. In Crowley J., Piater J., Vincze M., and Paletta L., editors, *Proc. Intl. Conference on Computer Vision Systems*, number 2626 in LNCS, pages 278–289, Graz, Austria, 2003. Springer Verlag.

Ney H. A comparative study of two search strategies for connected word recognition: Dynamic programming and heuristic search. *IEEE Transactions on Pattern Analysis and Machine Intelligence*, 14(5):586–595, 1992.

Nilsson N. J. *Principles of Artificial Intelligence*. Springer Verlag, Berlin, 1982.

Otsu N. A threshold selection method from gray–level histograms. *IEEE Transactions on Systems, Man and Cybernetics*, 9(1):62–66, 1979.

Pavlidis T. *Structural Pattern Recognition*. Springer Verlag, Berlin, 1977.

Pavlidis T. and Liow Y. Integrating region growing and edge detection. *IEEE Transactions on Pattern Analysis and Machine Intelligence*, 12(3):225–233, 1990.

Peters R. A. and Strickland R. N. A review of image complexity metrics for automatic target recognizers. *8th Meeting of Optical Engineering*, 1992. http://www.vuse.vanderbilt.edu/~rap2/resume.html.

Pietikainen M., Rosenfeld A., and Walter I. Split–and–link algorithms for image segmentation. *Pattern Recognition*, 15(4):287–298, 1982.

Pontriagin L. S. *The Mathematical Theory of Optimal Processes*. Interscience, New York, 1962.

Prager J. M. Extracting and labeling boundary segments in natural scenes. *IEEE Transactions on Pattern Analysis and Machine Intelligence*, 2(1):16–27, 1980.

Prastawa M., Gilmore J. H., Lin W., and Gerig G. Automatic segmentation of MR images of the developing newborn brain. *Medical Image Analysis*, 5(9):457–466, 2005.

Press W. H., Teukolsky S. A., Vetterling W. T., and Flannery B. P. *Numerical Recipes in C: The Art of Scientific Computing*. Cambridge University Press, Cambridge, 2nd edition, 1992.

Priese L. and Rehrmann V. On hierarchical color segmentation and applications. In *Computer Vision and Pattern Recognition (Proceedings)*, pages 633–634, Los Alamitos, CA, 1993. IEEE.

Rosenberg C. The Lenna Story, 2001. http://www.cs.cmu.edu/~chuck/lennapg/.

Rosenfeld A. and Kak A. C. *Digital Picture Processing*. Academic Press, New York, 2nd edition, 1982.

Rote G. Computing the minimum Hausdorff distance between two point sets on a line under translation. *Information Processing Letters*, 38(3):123–127, 1991.

Schettini R. A segmentation algorithm for color images. *Pattern Recognition Letters*, 14:499–506, 1993.

Sezgin M. and Sankur B. Survey over image thresholding techniques and quantitative performance evaluation. *Journal of Electronic Imaging*, 13(1):146–168, January 2004.

Sher D. B. A technique for deriving the distribution of edge neighborhoods from a library of occluding objects. In *Proceedings of the 6th International Conference on Image Analysis and Processing. Progress in Image Analysis and Processing II*, pages 422–429, Singapore, 1992. World Scientific.

Shin M. C., Goldgof D. B., and Bowyer K. W. Comparison of edge detector performance through use in an object recognition task. *Computer Vision and Image Understanding*, 84 (1):160–178, 2001.

Soille P. and Ansoult M. Automated basin delineation from DEMs using mathematical morphology. *Signal Processing*, 20:171–182, 1990.

Sonka M., Wilbricht C. J., Fleagle S. R., Tadikonda S. K., Winniford M. D., and Collins S. M. Simultaneous detection of both coronary borders. *IEEE Transactions on Medical Imaging*, 12(3):588–599, 1993.

Sonka M., Winniford M. D., Zhang X., and Collins S. M. Lumen centerline detection in complex coronary angiograms. *IEEE Transactions on Biomedical Engineering*, 41:520–528, 1994.

Suk M. and Chung S. M. A new image segmentation technique based on partition mode test. *Pattern Recognition*, 16(5):469–480, 1983.

Svoboda T., Kybic J., and Hlavac V. *Image Processing, Analysis, and Machine Vision: A MATLAB Companion*. Thomson Engineering, 2008.

Udupa J. K., Samarasekera S., and Barrett W. A. Boundary detection via dynamic programming. In *Visualization in Biomedical Computing, Proc. SPIE Vol. 1808*, pages 33–39, Bellingham, WA, 1992. SPIE.

Valera M. and Velastin S. A. Intelligent distributed surveillance systems: A review. In *IEE Proceedings - Vision, Image and Signal Processing*, 2005.

Heijden F. v. d. Edge and line feature extraction based on covariance models. *IEEE Transactions on Pattern Analysis and Machine Intelligence*, 17:69–77, 1995.

van der Zwet P. M. J. and Reiber J. H. C. A new approach for the quantification of complex lesion morphology: The gradient field transform; basic principles and validation results. *Journal of the Amercian College of Cardiologists*, 82:216–224, 1994.

Vincent L. and Soille P. Watersheds in digital spaces: An efficient algorithm based on immersion simulations. *IEEE Transactions on Pattern Analysis and Machine Intelligence*, 13(6):583–598, 1991.

Vlachos T. and Constantinides A. G. Graph-theoretical approach to colour picture segmentation and contour classification. *IEE Proceedings Communication, Speech and Vision*, 140:36–45, 1993.

Wang S., Ge F., and Liu T. Evaluating edge detection through boundary detection. *EURASIP Journal on Applied Signal Processing*, 2006:1–15, 2006.

Warfield S., Zou K., and Wells W. Simultaneous truth and performance level estimation (STAPLE): An algorithm for the validation of image segmentation. *Medical Imaging, IEEE Transactions on*, 23:903–921, 2004.

Weszka J. S. and Rosenfeld A. Threshold evaluation techniques. *IEEE Transactions on Systems, Man and Cybernetics*, 8(8):622–629, 1978.

Willebeek-Lemair M. and Reeves A. Solving nonuniform problems on SIMD computers—case study on region growing. *Journal of Parallel and Distributed Computing*, 8:135–149, 1990.

Williams G. W. Comparing the joint agreement of several raters with another rater. *Biometrics*, 32(3):619–627, 1976.

Wu X. Adaptive split-and-merge segmentation based on piecewise least-square approximation. *IEEE Transactions on Pattern Analysis and Machine Intelligence*, 15:808–815, 1993.

Xu L. and Oja E. Randomized Hough transform (RHT): Basic mechanisms, algorithms, and computational complexities. *CVGIP – Image Understanding*, 57:131–154, 1993.

Yasnoff W. A., Mui J. K., and Bacus J. W. Error measures for scene segmentation. *Pattern Recognition Letters*, 9:217–231, 1977.

Yoo T. S. *Insight into Images: Principles and Practice for Segmentation, Registration, and Image Analysis*. AK Peters Ltd, 2004. ISBN 1568812175.

Yuen S. Y. K. and Hlavac V. An approach to quantization of the Hough space. In *Proceedings of the 7th Scandinavian Conference on Image Analysis*, Aalborg, Denmark, pages 733–740, Copenhagen, Denmark, 1991. Pattern Recognition Society of Denmark, Copenhagen.

Zhang Y. J. A survey on evaluation methods for image segmentation. *Pattern Recognition*, 29 (8):1335–1346, 1996.

Chapter **7**

Segmentation II

Chapter 6 introduced a range of standard image segmentation methods, where we stressed the important and paramount role of segmentation in almost all aspects of image analysis. Unsurprisingly, image segmentation methods are rapidly developing as novel and more powerful approaches continue to appear. New approaches will aim to cater for datasets of increasing size, as well as with increasing dimensionality.

This chapter contains more advanced material on segmentation, and focuses on techniques with three-dimensional or higher-dimensional capabilities. The methods presented have several other features in common—each called for a paradigm shift when introduced, and they have all proved valuable, flexible, and highly applicable.

Of a variety of segmentation techniques reported in the literature, we have selected techniques using *mean shift segmentation*, *fuzzy connectivity*, *deformable models*, *gradient vector flow*, *graph search*, *graph cuts*, and *optimal single and multiple surface detection* for inclusion. These methods bring a number of new concepts, clearly demonstrating the departure of more recent segmentation methods from 2D to 3D (and higher dimensionality), with their multi-dimensional capabilities inherently present rather than appearing as an afterthought.

7.1 Mean shift segmentation

In Section 6.1.2, an optimal thresholding method was introduced in which gray-level statistics of individual objects and background were estimated to yield a set of segmentation thresholds by assuming that the gray level distributions were Gaussian. In this and other similar approaches, the main problem is to identify a number of parameters of a pre-determined probability density function—for example, equation (6.7) requires that three parameters be determined. Unfortunately, the assumptions of specific statistical distributions (which are rarely Gaussian) as well as the need to estimate a number of their parameters complicate this otherwise elegant approach.

Mean shift image segmentation avoids estimation of the probability density function and consists of 2 main steps—*discontinuity-preserving filtering* and *mean shift clustering*. A non-parametric technique for the analysis of a complex multi-modal feature space and identification of feature clusters called the *mean shift* procedure was originally introduced in [Fukunaga and Hostetler, 1975], and re-introduced after 20 years neglect in [Cheng, 1995]. Use of the mean shift approach in a number of image processing and vision tasks appeared in [Comaniciu and Meer, 1997, 2002; Comaniciu et al., 2000] (see also Section 16.5.2). In image processing, the feature space consists of quantitative image properties, which are mapped into a point in a multi-dimensional space of image description parameters. Once the mapping of all image points is completed, the feature space is more densely populated in locations corresponding to significant image features. These denser regions of the feature space form clusters, which in the image segmentation context may correspond to the individual image objects and background. More generally, the goal of the feature space analysis is delineation of the underlying clusters (compare Section 9.2.6). An intuitive description of the mean shift procedure is given in Figure 7.1.

Note that the only free parameters of this process are the size and shape of the region of interest—or more precisely identification of the *multivariate density kernel estimator*. For all practical purposes, radially symmetric kernels $K(\mathbf{x})$ are used satisfying

$$K(\mathbf{x}) = c\,k\big(\|\mathbf{x}\|^2\big)\,, \tag{7.1}$$

where c is a strictly positive constant that makes $K(\mathbf{x})$ to integrate to one. Two typical such kernels include the *normal* $K_N(\mathbf{x})$ and *Epanechnikov* $K_E(\mathbf{x})$ kernels. The normal

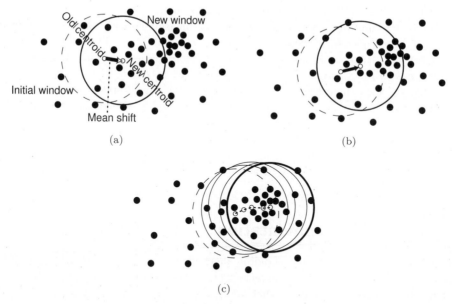

Figure 7.1: Principle of the mean shift procedure—the most dense region of data is identified in an iterative process. (a) The initial region of interest is randomly positioned over data and its centroid is determined; the region is moved to the location of the identified centroid. The vector determining the region's positional change is the mean shift. (b) Next step—a new mean shift vector is determined and the region is moved accordingly. (c) The mean shift vectors are determined in the remaining steps of the procedure until convergence. The final location identifies the local density maximum, or the local *mode*, of the probability density function. © *Cengage Learning 2015.*

kernel is defined by

$$K_N(\mathbf{x}) = c \exp\left(-\frac{1}{2}\|\mathbf{x}\|^2\right), \tag{7.2}$$

the kernel profile $k_N(x)$ of which is

$$k_N(x) = \exp\left(-\frac{x}{2}\right) \quad \text{for } x \geq 0. \tag{7.3}$$

$K_N(\mathbf{x})$ is often symmetrically truncated to obtain a kernel with finite support.

The Epanechnikov kernel is defined as

$$K_E(\mathbf{x}) = \begin{cases} c\left(1 - \|\mathbf{x}\|^2\right) & \text{if } \|\mathbf{x}\| \leq 1, \\ 0 & \text{otherwise}, \end{cases} \tag{7.4}$$

the kernel profile $k_E(x)$ of which is given by

$$k_E(x) = \begin{cases} 1 - x & \text{for } 0 \leq x \leq 1, \\ 0 & \text{for } x > 1, \end{cases} \tag{7.5}$$

and is not differentiable at the boundary.

Given n data points $\mathbf{x}_i$ in d-dimensional space R^d, the multivariate kernel density estimator $\widetilde{f}_{h,K}(\mathbf{x})$ computed at point $\mathbf{x}$ is

$$\widetilde{f}_{h,K}(\mathbf{x}) = \frac{1}{n\,h^d} \sum_{i=1}^{n} K\left(\frac{\mathbf{x} - \mathbf{x}_i}{h}\right), \tag{7.6}$$

where h represents the kernel size, also called kernel *bandwidth*.

As Figure 7.1 illustrates, we are interested in locating zeros of the gradient of $f_{h,K}(\mathbf{x})$, i.e., identifying $\mathbf{x}$ for which $\nabla f_{h,K}(\mathbf{x}) = 0$. The mean shift procedure is an elegant way of identifying these locations *without* estimating the underlying probability density function. In other words, from estimating the *density*, the problem becomes one of estimating the *density gradient*

$$\nabla \widetilde{f}_{h,K}(\mathbf{x}) = \frac{1}{n\,h^d} \sum_{i=1}^{n} \nabla K\left(\frac{\mathbf{x} - \mathbf{x}_i}{h}\right). \tag{7.7}$$

Using the kernel form in which $k(x)$ is the kernel's profile, and assuming that its derivative exists $-k'(x) = g(x)$ for all $x \in [0, \infty)$ except for a finite set of points,

$$K\left(\frac{\mathbf{x} - \mathbf{x}_i}{h}\right) = c_k\, k\left(\left\|\frac{\mathbf{x} - \mathbf{x}_i}{h}\right\|^2\right), \tag{7.8}$$

where c_k is a normalizing constant, h represents the kernel size. (Note that the profile $g_E(x)$ is uniform if $K(\mathbf{x}) = K_E(\mathbf{x})$; for $K(\mathbf{x}) = K_N(\mathbf{x})$, the profile of $g_N(x)$ is defined by the same exponential expression as $k_N(x)$.) Using $g(x)$ for a profile-defining kernel

$G(\mathbf{x}) = c_g\, g(\|\mathbf{x}\|^2)$, equation (7.7) changes to

$$
\begin{aligned}
\nabla \widetilde{f}_{h,K}(\mathbf{x}) &= \frac{2\,c_k}{n\,h^{(d+2)}} \sum_{i=1}^{n} (\mathbf{x} - \mathbf{x}_i)\, k'\!\left(\left\|\frac{\mathbf{x} - \mathbf{x}_i}{h}\right\|^2\right) \\
&= \frac{2\,c_k}{n\,h^{(d+2)}} \sum_{i=1}^{n} (\mathbf{x}_i - \mathbf{x})\, g\!\left(\left\|\frac{\mathbf{x} - \mathbf{x}_i}{h}\right\|^2\right) \\
&= \frac{2\,c_k}{n\,h^{(d+2)}} \left(\sum_{i=1}^{n} g_i\right)\left(\frac{\sum_{i=1}^{n} \mathbf{x}_i\, g_i}{\sum_{i=1}^{n} g_i} - \mathbf{x}\right) ,
\end{aligned}
\tag{7.9}
$$

where $\sum_{i=1}^{n} g_i$ is designed to be positive; $g_i = g\big(\|(\mathbf{x} - \mathbf{x}_i)/h\|^2\big)$.

The first term of equation (7.9) $2c_k/nh^{(d+2)} \sum_{i=1}^{n} g_i$ is proportional to a density estimator $\widetilde{f}_{h,G}$ computed with the kernel G:

$$
\widetilde{f}_{h,G}(\mathbf{x}) = \frac{c_g}{n\,h^{(d)}} \sum_{i=1}^{n} g\!\left(\left\|\frac{\mathbf{x} - \mathbf{x}_i}{h}\right\|^2\right) .
\tag{7.10}
$$

The remaining bracketed term represents the mean shift vector $m_{h,G}(\mathbf{x})$

$$
m_{h,G}(\mathbf{x}) = \frac{\sum_{i=1}^{n} \mathbf{x}_i\, g\!\left(\left\|\frac{\mathbf{x}-\mathbf{x}_i}{h}\right\|^2\right)}{\sum_{i=1}^{n} g\!\left(\left\|\frac{\mathbf{x}-\mathbf{x}_i}{h}\right\|^2\right)} - \mathbf{x} .
\tag{7.11}
$$

The successive locations $\{\mathbf{y}_j\}_{j=1,2,\dots}$ of the kernel G are then

$$
\mathbf{y}_{j+1} = \sum_{i=1}^{n} \mathbf{x}_i\, g\!\left(\left\|\frac{\mathbf{y}_j - \mathbf{x}_i}{h}\right\|^2\right) \Big/ \sum_{i=1}^{n} g\!\left(\left\|\frac{\mathbf{y}_j - \mathbf{x}_i}{h}\right\|^2\right) ,
\tag{7.12}
$$

where $\mathbf{y}_1$ is the initial position of the kernel G.

The corresponding sequence of density estimates computed with kernel K is therefore

$$
\widetilde{f}_{h,K}(j) = \widetilde{f}_{h,K}(\mathbf{y}_j) .
\tag{7.13}
$$

If the kernel K has a convex and monotonically decreasing profile, the sequences $\{\mathbf{y}_j\}_{j=1,2,\dots}$ and $\{\widetilde{f}_{h,K}(j)\}_{j=1,2,\dots}$ converge while $\{\widetilde{f}_{h,K}(j)\}_{j=1,2,\dots}$ increases monotonically (this is proved in [Comaniciu and Meer, 2002]). The guaranteed convergence of the algorithm to a local maximum of a probability density function, or the *density mode*, is obtained due to the adaptive magnitude of the mean shift vector (the mean shift vector magnitude converges to zero). The convergence speed depends on the kernel employed. When using the Epanechnikov kernel on discrete data, convergence is achieved in a finite number of steps. When data point weighting is involved, such as when using the normal kernel, the mean shift procedure is infinitely convergent. Clearly, a small lower bound value of change between steps may be used to stop the convergence process.

The set of all locations that converge to the same mode $\mathbf{y}_{\text{con}}$ defines the *basin of attraction* associated with this mode. Note that convergence may also stop at a local plateau or a saddle point. To avoid such behavior, each presumed point of convergence is perturbed by a small random vector and the mean shift procedure process restarted.

If the process converges to the same location within some tolerance, the point is a local maximum and identifies the density mode. A general algorithm for density function mode detection is:

Algorithm 7.1: Mean shift mode detection

1. Using multiple initializations covering the entire feature space, employ the mean shift procedure to identify the stationary points of $\widetilde{f}_{h,K}$.

2. Prune these points to retain only local maxima corresponding to the density modes.

The mean shift procedure has a number of advantages and some disadvantages, both connected to the global nature of its data representation. Among the advantages, the generality of the tool is one of the strongest. Due to substantial noise robustness, the approach is well suited to real-world applications. It can handle arbitrary cluster shapes and feature spaces. The only parameter to choose—the kernel size h–actually has a physical and understandable meaning. However, behavior in response to the choice of h is an important limitation since defining an appropriate value is not always trivial. Its importance is further strengthened by the fact that too large a value of h may cause modes to be merged, while too small a value may introduce insignificant additional modes and thus cause artificial cluster splitting. Methods for locally adaptive data-driven identification of h exist although they are more computationally expensive [Comaniciu et al., 2001; Georgescu et al., 2003].

The figures in this section were generated using the EDISON software [Christoudias et al., 2002]. Figure 7.2 shows a color image represented in an L, u, v perceived color feature space [Connolly, 1996; Wyszecki and Stiles, 1982]. L corresponds to the lightness

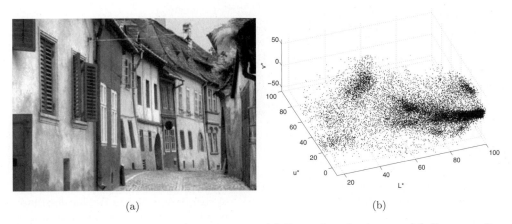

| (a) | (b) |

Figure 7.2: Color image L, u, v feature space. (a) Example color image. (b) Corresponding L, u, v feature space. *Courtesy of P. Meer, Rutgers University. © 2002 IEEE. Reprinted, with permission, from D. Comaniciu, P. Meer, "Mean shift: A robust approach toward feature space analysis," IEEE Trans. Pattern Anal. Machine Intell., vol. 24, pp. 603-619, 2002. A color version of this figure may be seen in the color inset—Plate 9.*

or relative pixel brightness, u and v are chromaticity features. Figure 7.3 gives an example of a 2D space analysis initialized from 159 distinct starting points.

A d-dimensional image is represented by a d-dimensional grid (spatial domain) of p-dimensional pixels (voxels), where p represents the number of spectral bands associated with the image (range domain); $p = 1$ for grayscale images, $p = 3$ for color images, etc. Assuming a Euclidean metric for both domains, the spatial and range vectors representing the complete information about the pixel's location and image properties can be concatenated to form a joint spatial–range domain. The resulting joint-domain kernel $K_{h_s,h_r}(\mathbf{x})$ consists of two radially symmetric kernels with parameters h_s and h_r repre-

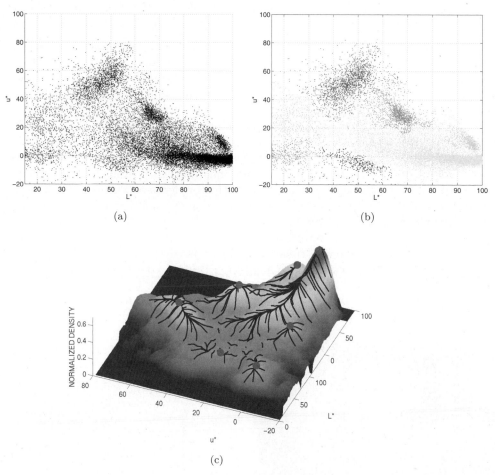

(a)   (b)

(c)

Figure 7.3: 2D feature space analysis using the mean shift procedure. (a) Feature space consisting of over 110,000 points representing the first two components of L, u, v color descriptors (see Figure 7.2). (b) Clustering of the feature space resulting from 159 separate initializations. (c) Mean shift procedure trajectories (using the Epanechnikov kernel). Some paths were pruned and stopped prematurely due to plateau presence. *Courtesy of P. Meer, Rutgers University. © 2002 IEEE. Reprinted, with permission, from D. Comaniciu, P. Meer, "Mean shift: A robust approach toward feature space analysis," IEEE Trans. Pattern Anal. Machine Intell, vol. 24, pp. 603-619, 2002. A color version of this figure may be seen in the color inset—Plate 10.*

senting spatial- and range-domain kernel sizes, respectively;

$$K_{h_s,h_r}(\mathbf{x}) = \frac{c}{h_s^d, h_r^p} \, k \left(\left\| \frac{\mathbf{x}^s}{h_s} \right\|^2 \right) k \left(\left\| \frac{\mathbf{x}^r}{h_r} \right\|^2 \right), \tag{7.14}$$

where $\mathbf{x}^s$ and $\mathbf{x}^r$ are the spatial and range parts of a feature vector, $k(x)$ is the common profile used in both domains, and c is a normalization constant—both Epanechnikov and normal kernels were shown to provide good performance. Therefore, setting the resolution level of the mode detection is obtained by two parameters of a single vector $h = (h_s, h_r)$.

For *mean shift image segmentation*, a 2-step sequence of discontinuity-preserving filtering and mean shift clustering is employed. Let pixels in the original d-dimensional image be denoted by $\mathbf{x}_i$ and pixels of the filtered image by $\mathbf{z}_i$, both being represented in the joint spatial–range domain.

Algorithm 7.2: Mean shift discontinuity-preserving filtering

1. For each image pixel $\mathbf{x}_i$, initialize step $j = 1$ and $\mathbf{y}_{i,1} = \mathbf{x}_i$.

2. Compute $\mathbf{y}_{i,j+1}$ as given in equation (7.12) until convergence $\mathbf{y}_{i,\text{con}}$.

3. Define filtered pixel values $\mathbf{z}_i = (\mathbf{x}_i^s, \mathbf{y}_{i,\text{con}}^r)$, i.e., the value of the filtered pixel at the location $\mathbf{x}_i^s$ is assigned the image value of the pixel of convergence $\mathbf{y}_{i,\text{con}}^r$.

Once the image is filtered, mean shift image segmentation takes advantage of the association between each filtered image pixel $\mathbf{z}_i$ and a significant mode of the joint domain density located in this pixel's neighborhood after pruning nearby less significant modes. Let pixels $\mathbf{x}_i$ and $\mathbf{z}_i$ be defined in the joint spatial–range domain as above, and let L_i be the segmentation label associated with pixel i in the segmented image.

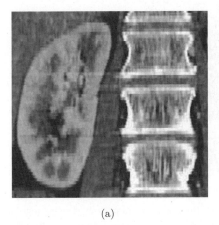 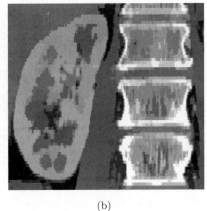

(a)   (b)

Figure 7.4: Mean shift filtering. (a) Original X-ray computed tomography image of human kidney and spine. (b) Filtered image. *Courtesy of R. Beichel, The University of Iowa.*

Algorithm 7.3: Mean shift image segmentation

1. Employ Algorithm 7.2 and store information about the d-dimensional convergence points $\mathbf{y}_{i,\text{con}}$.

2. Determine clusters $\{C_p\}_{p=1,\ldots,m}$ by grouping all $\mathbf{z}_i$, which are closer than h_s in the spatial domain and h_r in the range domain: that is, merge the *basins of attraction* of these convergence points.

3. Assign $L_i = \{p \mid \mathbf{z}_i \in \mathbf{C}_p\}$ for each pixel $i = 1, \ldots, n$.

4. If desired, eliminate regions smaller than P pixels as described in Algorithm 6.22.

Figure 7.4 shows an example of a mean shift filtering process, and Figure 7.5 an example of a mean shift segmentation.

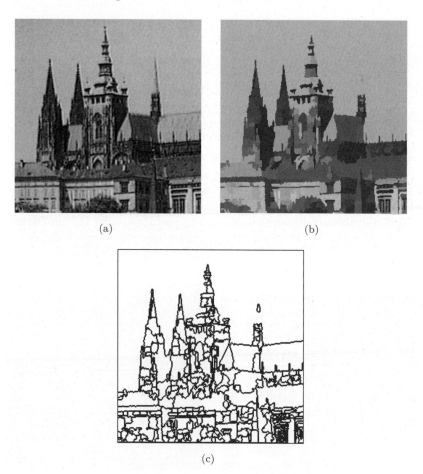

(a)　　　　　(b)

(c)

Figure 7.5: Mean shift-based image segmentation. (a) Original image. (b) Image segmentation obtained with $h_s = 5, h_r = 10, P = 20$. Note the meaningful segmentation of regions with slowly varying brightness, e.g., the sky or roofs. (c) Segmentation boundaries. Segmentation generated using EDISON software [Christoudias et al., 2002]. © *Cengage Learning 2015.*

7.2   Active contour models—snakes

Active contour models were developed in the 1980s by Kass, Witkin, and Terzopoulos [Kass et al., 1987; Witkin et al., 1987; Terzopoulos et al., 1987], and offer a solution to a variety of tasks in image analysis and machine vision. This section is based on the energy-minimization approach of [Kass et al., 1987]; the original notation is used.

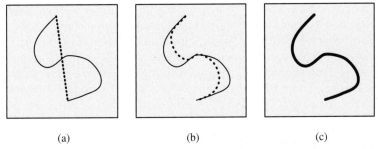

(a)   (b)   (c)

Figure 7.6: Active contour model—snake. (a) Initial snake position (dotted) defined interactively near the true contour. (b), (c) Iteration steps of snake energy minimization: the snake is pulled toward the true contour. © *Cengage Learning 2015.*

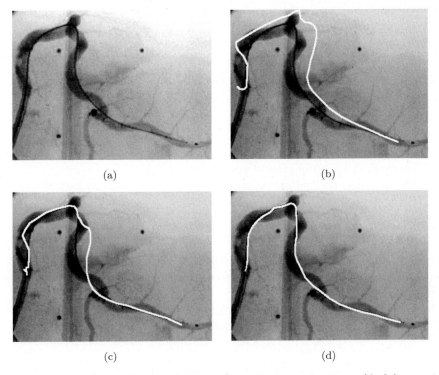

(a)   (b)

(c)   (d)

Figure 7.7: Snake-based detection of the intravascular ultrasound catheter (dark line positioned inside the coronary artery lumen) in an angiographic X-ray image of a pig heart. (a) Original angiogram. (b) Initial position of the snake. (c) Snake deformation after 4 iterations. (d) Final position of the snake after 10 iterations. © *Cengage Learning 2015.*

Active contour models may be used in image segmentation and understanding, and are also suitable for analysis of dynamic image data or 3D image data. The active contour model, or **snake**, is defined as an energy-minimizing spline (see Section 8.2.5)—the snake's energy depends on its shape and location within the image. Local minima of this energy then correspond to desired image properties. Snakes may be understood as a special case of a more general technique of matching a deformable model to an image by means of energy minimization. Snakes do not solve the entire problem of finding contours in images; rather, they depend on other mechanisms such as interaction with a user, interaction with some higher-level image understanding process, or information from image data adjacent in time or space. This interaction must specify an approximate shape and starting position for the snake somewhere near the desired contour. A priori as well as image-based information are then used to push the snake toward an appropriate solution—see Figures 7.6 and 7.7. Unlike most other image models, the snake is *active*, always minimizing its energy functional, therefore exhibiting dynamic behavior.

7.2.1   Traditional snakes and balloons

The energy functional which is minimized is a weighted combination of internal and external forces. The internal forces emanate from the shape of the snake, while the external forces come from the image and/or from higher-level image understanding processes. The snake is defined parametrically as $\mathbf{v}(s) = [x(s), y(s)]$, where $x(s), y(s)$ are x, y co-ordinates along the contour and $s \in [0, 1]$ (see Figure 8.12a). The energy functional to be minimized may be written as

$$
\begin{aligned}
E^*_{\text{snake}} &= \int_0^1 E_{\text{snake}}\big(\mathbf{v}(s)\big)\, \mathrm{d}s \\
&= \int_0^1 \Big(E_{\text{int}}\big(\mathbf{v}(s)\big) + E_{\text{image}}\big(\mathbf{v}(s)\big) + E_{\text{con}}\big(\mathbf{v}(s)\big) \Big)\, \mathrm{d}s\,,
\end{aligned}
\tag{7.15}
$$

where E_{int} represents the internal energy of the spline due to bending, E_{image} denotes image forces, and E_{con} external constraint forces. Usually, $\mathbf{v}(s)$ is approximated as a spline to ensure desirable properties of continuity.

The internal spline energy can be written

$$
E_{\text{int}} = \alpha(s) \left| \frac{\mathrm{d}\mathbf{v}}{\mathrm{d}s} \right|^2 + \beta(s) \left| \frac{\mathrm{d}^2\mathbf{v}}{\mathrm{d}s^2} \right|^2,
\tag{7.16}
$$

where $\alpha(s), \beta(s)$ specify the *elasticity* and *stiffness* of the snake. Note that setting $\beta(s_k) = 0$ at a point s_k allows the snake to become second-order discontinuous at that point, and develop a corner.

The second term of the energy integral (equation 7.15) is derived from the image data over which the snake lies. As an example, a weighted combination of three different functionals is presented which attracts the snake to lines, edges, and terminations:

$$
E_{\text{image}} = w_{\text{line}}\, E_{\text{line}} + w_{\text{edge}}\, E_{\text{edge}} + w_{\text{term}}\, E_{\text{term}}\,.
\tag{7.17}
$$

The line-based functional may be very simple

$$
E_{\text{line}} = f(x, y)\,,
\tag{7.18}
$$

where $f(x, y)$ denotes image gray-levels at image location (x, y). The sign of w_{line} specifies whether the snake is attracted to light or dark lines. The edge-based functional

$$E_{\text{edge}} = -\left|\nabla f(x, y)\right|^2 \tag{7.19}$$

attracts the snake to contours with large image gradients—that is, to locations of strong edges. Line terminations and corners may influence the snake using a weighted energy functional E_{term}: let g be a slightly smoothed version of the image f, let $\psi(x, y)$ denote the gradient directions along the spline in the smoothed image g, and let

$$\mathbf{n}(x, y) = \big(\cos\psi(x, y), \sin\psi(x, y)\big), \qquad \mathbf{n}_R(x, y) = \big(-\sin\psi(x, y), \cos\psi(x, y)\big)$$

be unit vectors along and perpendicular to the gradient directions $\psi(x, y)$. Then the curvature of constant-gray-level contours in the smoothed image can be written as [Kass et al., 1987]

$$
\begin{aligned}
E_{\text{term}} &= \frac{\partial\psi}{\partial\mathbf{n}_R} = \frac{\partial^2 g/\partial\mathbf{n}_R^2}{\partial g/\partial\mathbf{n}} \\
&= \frac{(\partial^2 g/\partial y^2)(\partial g/\partial x)^2 - 2\,(\partial^2 g/\partial x\partial y)(\partial g/\partial x)(\partial g/\partial y) + (\partial^2 g/\partial x^2)(\partial g/\partial y)^2}{\big((\partial g/\partial x)^2 + (\partial g/\partial y)^2\big)^{3/2}} \,.
\end{aligned}
\tag{7.20}
$$

The snake behavior may be controlled by adjusting the weights w_{line}, w_{edge}, w_{term}. A snake attracted to edges and terminations is shown in Figure 7.8.

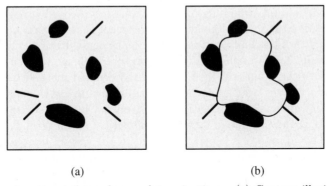

(a)   (b)

Figure 7.8: A snake attracted to edges and terminations. (a) Contour illusion. (b) A snake attracted to the subjective contour. *Based on [Kass et al., 1987].*

The third term of the integral (equation 7.15) comes from external constraints imposed either by a user or some other higher-level process which may force the snake toward or away from particular features. If the snake is near to some desirable feature, energy minimization will pull the snake the rest of the way. However, if the snake settles in a local energy minimum that a higher-level process determines as incorrect, an area of energy peak may be made at this location to force it away to a different local minimum. A contour is defined to lie in the position in which the snake reaches a local energy minimum. From equation (7.15), the functional to be minimized is

$$E_{\text{snake}}^* = \int_0^1 E_{\text{snake}}\big(\mathbf{v}(s)\big)\mathrm{d}s \,.$$

Then, from the calculus of variations, the Euler-Lagrange condition states that the spline $\mathbf{v}(s)$ which minimizes E^*_{snake} must (neglecting higher-order effects) satisfy

$$\frac{\mathrm{d}}{\mathrm{d}s} E_{\mathbf{v}_s} - E_{\mathbf{v}} = 0 \,, \tag{7.21}$$

where $E_{\mathbf{v}_s}$ is the partial derivative of E with respect to $\mathrm{d}\mathbf{v}/\mathrm{d}s$ and $E_{\mathbf{v}}$ is the partial derivative of E with respect to $\mathbf{v}$. Using equation (7.16) and denoting $E_{\text{ext}} = E_{\text{image}} + E_{\text{con}}$, the previous equation reduces to

$$-\frac{\mathrm{d}}{\mathrm{d}s}\left(\alpha(s)\frac{\mathrm{d}\mathbf{v}}{\mathrm{d}s}\right) + \frac{\mathrm{d}^2}{\mathrm{d}s^2}\left(\beta(s)\frac{\mathrm{d}^2\mathbf{v}}{\mathrm{d}s^2}\right) + \nabla E_{\text{ext}}\big(\mathbf{v}(s)\big) = 0 \,. \tag{7.22}$$

To solve the Euler-Lagrange equation, suppose an initial estimate of the solution is available. An evolution equation is formed:

$$\frac{\partial \mathbf{v}(s,t)}{\partial t} - \frac{\partial}{\partial s}\left(\alpha(s)\frac{\partial \mathbf{v}(s,t)}{\partial s}\right) + \frac{\partial^2}{\partial s^2}\left(\beta(s)\frac{\partial^2 \mathbf{v}(s,t)}{\partial s^2}\right) + \nabla E_{\text{ext}}\big(\mathbf{v}(s,t)\big) = 0 \,. \tag{7.23}$$

The solution is found if $\partial \mathbf{v}(s,t)/\partial t = 0$. Nevertheless, minimization of the snake energy integral is still problematic; numerous parameters must be designed (weighting factors, iteration steps, etc.), a reasonable initialization must be available, and, moreover, the solution of the Euler-Lagrange equation suffers from numerical instability.

Originally, a resolution minimization method was proposed [Kass et al., 1987]; partial derivatives in s and t were estimated by the finite-differences method. Later [Amini et al., 1988, 1990], a dynamic programming approach was proposed which allows 'hard' constraints to be added to the snake. Further, a requirement that internal snake energy must be continuous may thus be eliminated and some snake configurations may be prohibited (that is, have infinite energy), allowing more a priori knowledge to be incorporated.

Difficulties with the numerical instability of the original method were overcome by Berger [Berger and Mohr, 1990] by incorporating an idea of *snake growing*. A different approach to energy integral minimization based on a Galerkin solution of the finite-element method has the advantage of greater numerical stability and better efficiency [Cohen, 1991]. This approach is especially useful in the case of closed or nearly closed contours. An additional pressure force is added to the contour interior by considering the

(a)   (b)

Figure 7.9: Active contour model—balloon. (a) Initial contour. (b) Final contour after inflation and energy minimization. *Based on [Cohen and Cohen, 1992].*

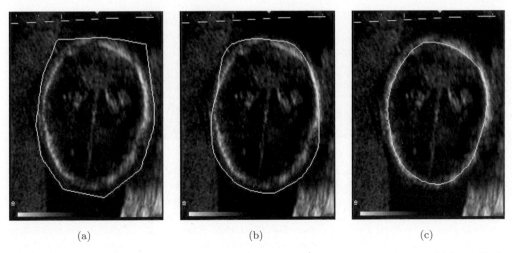

(a)   (b)   (c)

Figure 7.10: Balloon-based image segmentation of a fetal head ultrasound image. (a) Initial balloon position. (b) Deformation after 10 iterations. (c) Final balloon position after 25 iterations. *Courtesy of V. Chalana.*

curve as a **balloon** which is inflated. This allows the snake to overcome isolated energy valleys resulting from spurious edge points, giving better results all over (see Figures 7.9 and 7.10). Another approach using a finite-element method [Karaolani et al., 1992] also significantly improves the solution's efficiency; forces are scaled by the size of an element, preventing very small contributions (which may be noise) from contributing to the global solution as much as longer elements.

7.2.2   Extensions

Snakes are now a mature part of the segmentation armory with a wide literature and a number of generalizations. Examples would be generalization to three dimensions [Terzopoulos et al., 1987, 1988; McInerney and Terzopoulos, 1993], fast algorithms for active contour models [Williams and Shah, 1992; Olstad and Tysdahl, 1993; Lam and Yan, 1994], approaches to assist with initialization and problems of spurious edges [Etoh et al., 1993; Neuenschwander et al., 1994; Etoh et al., 1993; Ronfard, 1994; McInerney and Terzopoulos, 1995; Figueiredo et al., 1997].

A particular limitation of the snake approach is that the segmentation delivers a closed contour which is unsatisfactory in many applications: road networks, aerial views of field boundaries, microscopic cell networks all present segmentation problems that snakes were designed to solve, but exhibit nodes of degree more than 2 (and sometimes of degree 1). This presents difficulty in the computation of E_{edge} (equation 7.19). This issue has been addressed in the development of *network snakes* [Butenuth and Heipke, 2012] where the definition of E_{image} (equation 7.17) is adjusted to take account of the local topology: then, an initialization of the [network] snake with the correct topology can converge to a good solution. Figure 7.11 shows an example of this algorithm in action, segmenting cell structures [Pound et al., 2012].

Several variants of active contour models have emerged: These variants aimed at an increase of robustness against noise, decrease of initialization sensitivity, improved

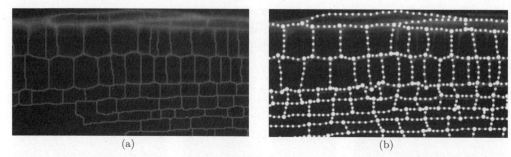

(a)   (b)

Figure 7.11: Use of network snakes [Butenuth and Heipke, 2012]. (a) An initial, inaccurate, segmentation of a cell image—here, watershed segmentation (Section 13.7.3) was used. (b) After the application of the network snake algorithm. Sometimes, a short interactive phase will ensure the correct starting topology. *Courtesy of M. P. Pound et al.   Republished with permission of American Society of Plant Biologists, from The Plant Cell, Pound et al., "CellSeT: Novel Software to Extract and Analyze Structured Networks of Plant Cells from Confocal Images," 1989; permission conveyed through Copyright Clearance Center, Inc. A color version of this figure may be seen in the color inset—Plate 11.*

selectivity for certain classes of objects, etc. Notable among these are *finite element snakes* [Cohen and Cohen, 1993], *B-snakes* [Menet et al., 1990; Blake and Isard, 1998], and *Fourier deformable models* [Staib and Duncan, 1992]. *United snakes* combine several snake variants—namely the finite difference, B-spline, and *Hermite polynomial* snakes in a comprehensive finite element formulation [Liang et al., 1999]. United snakes also include unification with live wire and intelligent scissor methods for interactive contour-based segmentation (Section 6.2.5) [Liang et al., 2006].

7.2.3   Gradient vector flow snakes

Two main limitations common to these approaches are the requirement of initialization to be close to the desired solution, and difficulties in segmenting concave boundary portions. *Gradient vector flow* (GVF) fields have been used to overcome these problems [Xu and Prince, 1998].

A GVF field is a non-irrotational external force field that points toward the boundaries when in their proximity and varies smoothly over homogeneous image regions all the way to image borders. Consequently, it can drive a snake toward a border from a large distance and can segment object concavities. In comparison to the classical snake approach it does not suffer from edge localization problems caused by edge distortion from their smoothing, and does not require careful fine-tuning of balloon pressure forces to overcome noise but not overcome salient image features, and can attract the snake when initialized at either side of the boundary.

The field is derived from an image by minimization of an energy functional by solving decoupled linear partial differential equations via diffusing the gradient vectors of the edge image. The GVF is then used as an external force in the snake equations (7.15), (7.22) forming a *GVF snake*—insensitivity to initialization and ability to segment concave boundaries result. The GVF field $\mathbf{g}(x,y) = \big(u(x,y), v(x,y)\big)$ minimizes the energy functional

$$E = \iint \mu \left(u_x^2 + u_y^2 + v_x^2 + v_y^2 \right) + |\nabla f|^2 \, |\mathbf{g} - \nabla f|^2 \, \mathrm{d}x \, \mathrm{d}y \,, \tag{7.24}$$

where μ is a regularization parameter balancing the weight of the first and second terms (increasing μ with increased noise), the subscripts denote directional partial derivatives. The GVF can be obtained by solving the Euler equations

$$\mu\,\nabla^2 u - \left(u - f_x\right)\left(f_x^2 + f_y^2\right) = 0\,, \tag{7.25}$$

$$\mu\,\nabla^2 v - \left(v - f_y\right)\left(f_x^2 + f_y^2\right) = 0\,, \tag{7.26}$$

where ∇^2 is a Laplacian operator [Xu and Prince, 1998]. The second term in these equations is zero in homogeneous regions since the directional gradients f_x, f_y are zero. Consequently, the GVF behavior in the homogeneous regions is fully defined by the Laplace equation effectively diffusing the information from the boundaries to the homogeneous parts of the image. Solutions to equations (7.25), (7.26) can be found by treating u and v as functions of time and solving the following two decoupled equations for $t \to \infty$:

$$u_t(x,y,t) = \mu\,\nabla^2 u(x,y,t) - \left(u(x,y,t) - f_x(x,y)\right)\left(f_x(x,y)^2 + f_y(x,y)^2\right)\,, \tag{7.27}$$

$$v_t(x,y,t) = \mu\,\nabla^2 v(x,y,t) - \left(v(x,y,t) - f_y(x,y)\right)\left(f_x(x,y)^2 + f_y(x,y)^2\right)\,. \tag{7.28}$$

These *generalized diffusion equations* can be solved as separate scalar partial differential equations in u and v and are used in heat conduction, fluid flow, etc. [Charles and Porsching, 1990].

Once $\mathbf{g}(x,y)$ is computed, equation (7.22) is modified using the GVF external force $E_{\text{ext}} = \mathbf{g}(x,y)$ yielding the GVF snake equation

$$\mathbf{v}_t(s,t) = \alpha\,\mathbf{v}''(s,t) - \beta\,\mathbf{v}''''(s,t) + \mathbf{g}\,, \tag{7.29}$$

which can be solved as before by an iterative process following discretization.

Figure 7.12 shows a convergence process and snake-attracting forces of a classic snake. It can be seen that there is no force that would pull the snake towards the concave portion

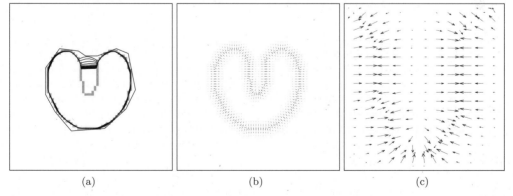

(a)   (b)   (c)

Figure 7.12: Classic snake convergence. (a) Convergent sequence of snake locations. Note that the snake fails to segment the concave boundary. (b) Classic external forces. (c) Close-up of the concave object region. No forces exist capable of pulling the snake inside the bay. *Courtesy of J. L. Prince and C. Xu, Johns Hopkins University. © 1998 IEEE. Reprinted, with permission, from C. Xu and J. L. Prince, "Snakes, Shapes, and Gradient Vector Flow," IEEE Trans. on Image Processing, vol. 7, pp. 359-369, 1998.*

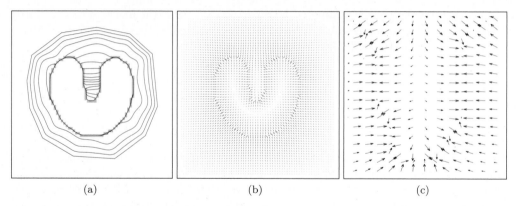

(a)   (b)   (c)

Figure 7.13: GVF snake convergence. (a) Convergent sequence of snake locations. Note that the snake succeeded in segmenting the concave boundary. (b) GVF external forces. (c) Close-up of the concave object region. Forces exist capable of pulling the snake inside the bay. *Courtesy of J. L. Prince and C. Xu, Johns Hopkins University. © 1998 IEEE. Reprinted, with permission, from C. Xu and J. L. Prince, "Snakes, Shapes, and Gradient Vector Flow," IEEE Trans. on Image Processing, vol. 7, pp. 359-369, 1998.*

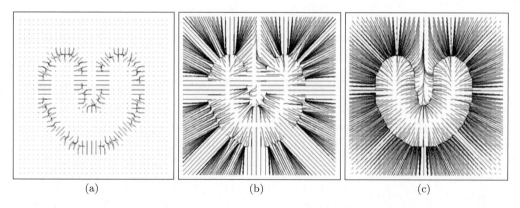

(a)   (b)   (c)

Figure 7.14: Streamlines originating in a regular 32×32 grid of points. (a) Classic potential force field–only locations very close to the border can be attracted to the object. (b) Distance-based external force field. Note that there is insufficient pull of the locations inside the bay to correctly segment the concave region. However, the snake can be initialized at a distance from the object. (c) GVF force field demonstrating the ability to correctly segment the concave region and maintaining the ability of a large-distance initialization. *Courtesy of J. L. Prince and C. Xu, Johns Hopkins University. © 1998 IEEE. Reprinted, with permission, from C. Xu and J. L. Prince, "Snakes, Shapes, and Gradient Vector Flow," IEEE Trans. on Image Processing, vol. 7, pp. 359-369, 1998.*

of the boundary and so the segmentation fails in that area. When adding distance-based forces, the segmentation fails in a similar fashion. In comparison, the GVF snake successfully segments the object as demonstrated in Figure 7.13. Figure 7.14 shows the attraction force coverage of an entire image using the classic, distance-based, and GVF field forces clearly demonstrating the advantages of the GVF approach. Figure 7.15 compares the segmentation of an object with incomplete, concave, and convex boundary

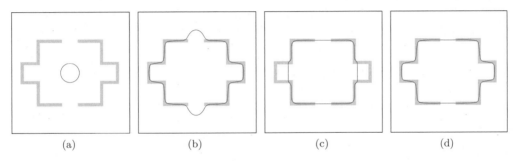

Figure 7.15: Balloon, distance potential and GVF snake behavior. (a) Initialization. (b) Balloon with an outward pressure force. (c) Distance potential force snake. (d) GVF snake. *Courtesy of J. L. Prince and C. Xu, Johns Hopkins University. © 1998 IEEE. Reprinted, with permission, from C. Xu and J. L. Prince, "Snakes, Shapes, and Gradient Vector Flow," IEEE Trans. on Image Processing, vol. 7, pp. 359-369, 1998.*

segments when initialized from within the object. Importantly, the GVF snake gives virtually the same segmentation if initialized from the outside with no change of parameters. Figure 7.16 shows an application of a GVF snake to cardiac MR segmentation.

The GVF can be generalized to higher dimensions defining the d-dimensional GVF field $\mathbf{g}(\mathbf{x})$ as minimizing the energy functional (cf. equation 7.24).

$$E = \int_{\mathcal{R}^d} \mu \, |\nabla \mathbf{g}|^2 + |\nabla f|^2 \, |\mathbf{g} - \nabla f|^2 \mathrm{d}\mathbf{x} \,, \tag{7.30}$$

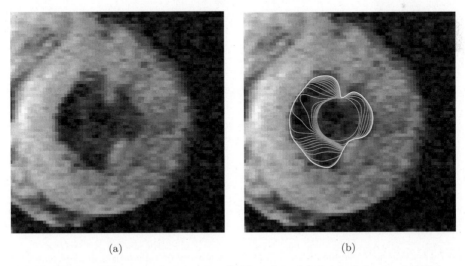

Figure 7.16: Cardiac MR segmentation using GVF snakes. (a) Original short axis MR image of the left cardiac ventricle. (b) GVF snake segmentation showing the convergence process. *Courtesy of J. L. Prince and C. Xu, Johns Hopkins University. © 1998 IEEE. Reprinted, with permission, from C. Xu and J. L. Prince, "Snakes, Shapes, and Gradient Vector Flow," IEEE Trans. on Image Processing, vol. 7, pp. 359-369, 1998.*

where the gradient operator is applied to each component of **g** separately. The GVF field must then satisfy the Euler equation (compare equations 7.25, 7.26).

$$\mu \nabla^2 \mathbf{g} - (\mathbf{g} - \nabla f)\, |\nabla f|^2 = 0 \,, \tag{7.31}$$

where again ∇^2 is applied to each component of **g** separately. Introducing a time variable t as before allows finding a solution for $t \to \infty$ of (compare equations 7.27, 7.28).

$$\mathbf{g}_t = \mu \nabla^2 \mathbf{g} - (\mathbf{g} - \nabla f)\, |\nabla f|^2 \,, \tag{7.32}$$

where $\mathbf{g}_t$ denotes a partial derivative with respect to t. Similarly to the 2D case, equation (7.32) contains d decoupled scalar linear second order parabolic partial differential equations in each element of **g** and can be solved iteratively. Figure 7.17 demonstrates a GVF snake segmentation of a star-shaped object in 3D. Figure 7.18 shows an application of a 3D GVF snake in brain segmentation [Tosun et al., 2004].

Active contour models differ substantially from classical approaches, where features are extracted from an image and higher-level processes try to interpolate sparse data to find a representation that matches the original data. They start from an initial estimate based on higher-level knowledge, and an optimization method is used to refine this.

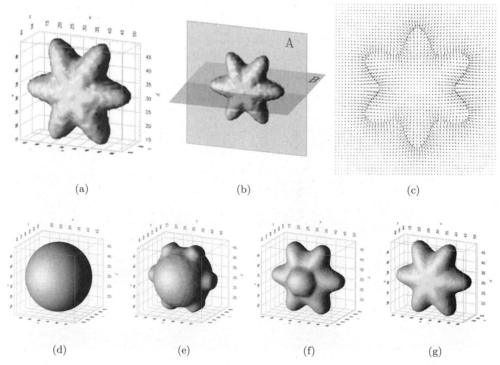

(a)   (b)   (c)

(d)   (e)   (f)   (g)

Figure 7.17: GVF snake segmentation in 3D. (a) Isosurface of a 3D object defined on a 64^3 grid. (b) Position of plane A on which 3D GVF vectors are depicted in (c). (d) Initial configuration of a deformable surface using GVF and its positions after (e) 10, (f) 40, and (g) 100 iterations. *Courtesy of J. L. Prince and C. Xu, Johns Hopkins University. © 1998 IEEE. Reprinted, with permission, from C. Xu and J. L. Prince, "Snakes, Shapes, and Gradient Vector Flow," IEEE Trans. on Image Processing, vol. 7, pp. 359-369, 1998.*

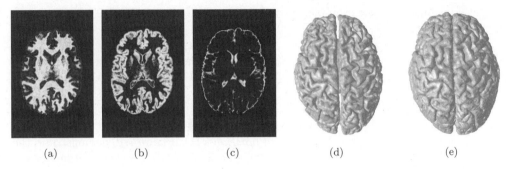

(a)   (b)   (c)   (d)   (e)

Figure 7.18: 3D segmentation of the MR brain image using GVF snakes. (a-c) Fuzzy classification of the white matter (a), gray matter (b), and cerebrospinal fluid (c) in the cerebrum. A fuzzy classification yielded three membership functions, cross sections of which are shown. (d,e) GVF snake segmentation was used to obtain anatomically feasible surfaces representing the central (d), and pial (e) surfaces bounding the cortex. *Courtesy of J. L. Prince, Johns Hopkins University.*

During the optimization, image data, an initial estimate, desired contour properties, and knowledge-based constraints are considered. Feature extraction and knowledge-based constrained grouping of these features are integrated into a single process, which seems to be the biggest advantage. Active contour models, however, search for *local* energy minima not attempting to achieve globally optimal solutions. Applications can be found in many areas of machine vision and medical image analysis.

7.3 Geometric deformable models—level sets and geodesic active contours

There are two main groups of deformable contour/surface models: the snakes discussed in the previous section belong to the *parametric model* family as borders are represented in a parametric form. While appropriate for many segmentation tasks, they may yield cusps or intersecting boundaries in some situations. The second family of deformable surfaces— *geometric deformable models*—overcome this problem by representing developing surfaces by partial differential equations. There is an extensive literature on geometric deformable models, reporting a variety of applications in which deformable model based segmentation can be used. An excellent treatment can be found in [Xu et al., 2000], which also provided conceptual guidance to this section.

Geometric deformable models were introduced independently by Malladi et al. and Caselles et al. and named *level set front propagation* and *geodesic active contour* segmentation approaches [Caselles et al., 1993; Malladi et al., 1993, 1995]. The main feature separating geometric deformable models from parametric ones is that curves are evolved using only geometric computations, independent of any parameterization: the process is *implicit*. Consequently, the curves and/or surfaces can be represented as *level sets* of higher dimensional functions yielding seamless treatment of topological changes. Hence, without resorting to dedicated contour tracking, unknown numbers of multiple objects can be detected simultaneously. There is a wide literature on curve evolution theory and level set methods—for example, [Sethian, 1999; Osher and Fedkiw, 2002; Osher and Paragios, 2003].

Let a closed curve moving in time t be $\mathbf{X}(s,t) = [X(s,t), Y(s,t)]$, where s is curve parameterization. Let $\mathbf{N}$ be the moving curve's inward normal, and c curvature, and let the curve develop along its normal direction according to the partial differential equation

$$\frac{\partial \mathbf{X}}{\partial t} = V(c)\,\mathbf{N} \,. \tag{7.33}$$

Here, curve evolution is defined by the *speed function* $V(c)$: Figure 7.19 demonstrates the concept of front evolution. As the curve is moving, it may need to be reparameterized to satisfy equation (7.33).

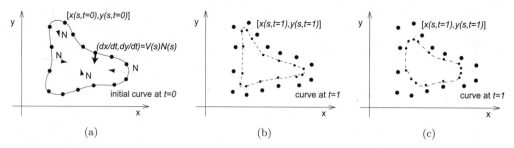

(a)   (b)   (c)

Figure 7.19: Concept of front evolution. (a) Initial curve at $t = 0$. (b) Curve at $t = 1$. Note that each curve point moved in direction $\mathbf{N}$ by distance given by velocity V. (c) Curve at $t = 1$ assuming the velocity $V(c)$ is a function of curvature. © *Cengage Learning 2015*.

If the curve evolution is driven by a *curvature deformation* equation, the partial differential equation describes a curve smoothing process which removes potential singularities and eventually shrinks the curve to a point

$$\frac{\partial \mathbf{X}}{\partial t} = \alpha\, c\, \mathbf{N} \,, \tag{7.34}$$

where α is a constant similar to elastic internal forces used in snakes (Section 7.2). Figure 7.20 shows deformation behavior using positive ($\alpha > 0$) and negative ($\alpha < 0$) curvature.

Curve deformation driven by the *constant deformation* equation (7.35) is complementary, and is similar to the inflation balloon force discussed in Section 7.2 and may introduce singularities like sharp corners

$$\frac{\partial \mathbf{X}}{\partial t} = V_0\, \mathbf{N} \,, \tag{7.35}$$

where V_0 determines constant speed of deformation.

Geometric deformable models perform image segmentation by starting with an initial curve and evolving its shape using the speed equation (7.33). During the evolution process, curvature deformation and/or constant deformation are used and the speed of curve evolution is locally dependent on the image data— this represents the motivation for the approach. The ultimate goal of curve evolution is to yield desirable image segmentation for $t \to \infty$: in other words, curve evolution should stop at object boundaries. This evolution can be implemented using *level sets* and—similar to many general techniques—the

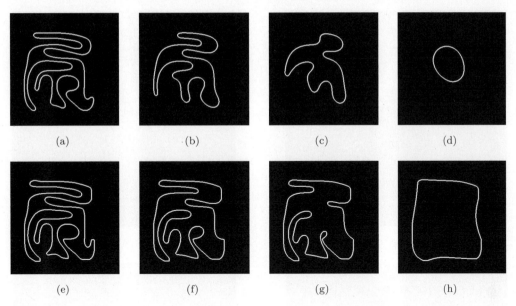

Figure 7.20: Evolution of a closed 2D curve using curvature deformation. (a–d) Using positive curvature, iterations 100, 2000, 4000, 17000. (e–h) Using negative curvature, iterations 100, 2000, 4000, 17000. © *Cengage Learning 2015*.

exact behavior depends on the segmentation parameters. In this case, the segmentation behavior depends on the design of the speed function (equation 7.33).

A basic version of the speed function that combines curvature and constant deformation is of the form [Caselles et al., 1993; Malladi et al., 1995]

$$\frac{\partial \phi}{\partial t} = k \left(c + V_0 \right) \left| \nabla \phi \right|, \tag{7.36}$$

where

$$k = \frac{1}{1 + \left| \nabla (G_\sigma * I) \right|} . \tag{7.37}$$

Here, ϕ represents the propagating curve front (and denotes a level set function, see below). The term $\nabla(G_\sigma * I)$ denotes gradient of a Gaussian-smoothed image, where σ is a smoothing parameter. As can be seen, a positive value of V_0 expands the curve while k serves as a stopping term, with $k \to 0$ for image locations exhibiting a large image gradient, i.e., image edges. Clearly, the edges must be strong for the curve evolution to stop (or rather, almost stop; a simple edge-strength threshold may be used to force a slow-moving front to halt). An obvious problem with this speed function is that it will not slow down sufficiently at weaker or indistinct boundaries, and once the curve passes the boundary location, it will continue moving with no force pulling it back. Figure 7.21 gives an example of segmentation sensitivity to the stopping criterion.

An energy minimization approach to overcome this behavior was introduced in [Caselles et al., 1997; Yezzi et al., 1997]

$$\frac{\partial \phi}{\partial t} = k \left(c + V_0 \right) \left| \nabla \phi \right| + \nabla k \, \nabla \phi . \tag{7.38}$$

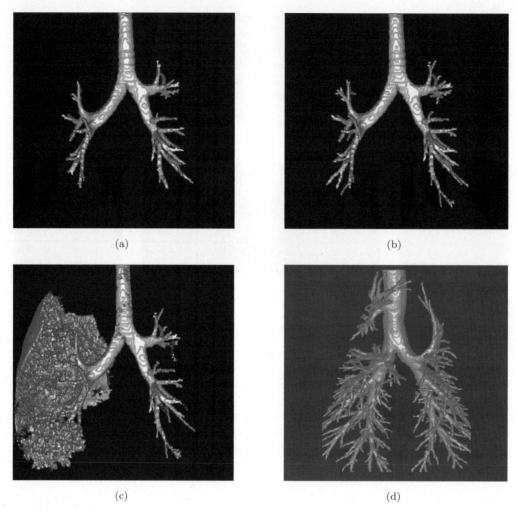

(a)   (b)

(c)   (d)

Figure 7.21: Pulmonary airway tree segmentation using a 3D fast marching level set approach applied to X-ray computed tomography data. The speed function was defined as $V = 1/intensity$; the segmentation front moves faster in dark regions corresponding to air in CT images and slower in bright regions corresponding to airway walls. The stopping criterion uses a combination of gradient threshold value T_g and local image intensity threshold T_i—increasing gradient and image intensity slow down and stop the front propagation. (a) Human airway tree segmentation result employing $T_i=6$. (b) $T_i=11$. (c) $T_i=13$—a segmentation leak occurs. (d) Sheep airway tree segmentation—obtaining a larger number of airways is due to a higher X-ray dose yielding better quality image data. © *Cengage Learning 2015*.

The stopping term $\nabla k \nabla \phi$ acts to pull the boundary back to the object border once the curve evolution passes it. Other speed functions can be found in [Siddiqi et al., 1998].

An important question remains: how to efficiently execute the curve evolution process. The idea that made geometric deformable models feasible is to represent the segmentation boundary/surface implicitly as a level set of a higher-dimensional function— the *level set function ϕ*—defined on the same image domain [Osher and Sethian, 1988;

Sethian, 1985, 1989]. Using the level set representation of the curve permits evolution by updating the level set function $\phi(t)$ at fixed time points. Instances of curve evolution are obtained by determination of the zero-level set for individual time points ($\phi(t) = 0$). In other words, the evolving curve at time t is found as a set of points on the image domain for which the function value (height) of the level set function at time t is equal to zero, and the final solution is given by the zero-level set $\phi(t \to \infty) = 0$. Importantly, the level set function remains a valid function during the updating process even if the embedded level set curve changes topology, develops singularities, etc. Figures 7.22 and 7.23 illustrate the level set concept of curve embedding, evolution, and topology change.

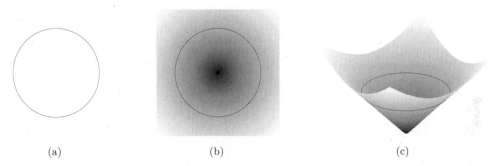

(a)   (b)   (c)

Figure 7.22: Example of embedding a curve as a level set. (a) A single curve. (b) The level set function where the curve is embedded as the zero level set $\phi[\mathbf{X}(s,t), t] = 0$ (in black). (c) The height map of the level set function with its zero level set depicted in black. *Courtesy of J. L. Prince, Johns Hopkins University. Xu C., Pham D. L., and Prince J. L., "Image segmentation using deformable models." In Sonka M. and Fitzpatrick J. M., editors, Handbook of Medical Imaging, Volume 2: Medical Image Processing and Analysis, pp. 129-174. SPIE, Bellingham, WA, 2000.*

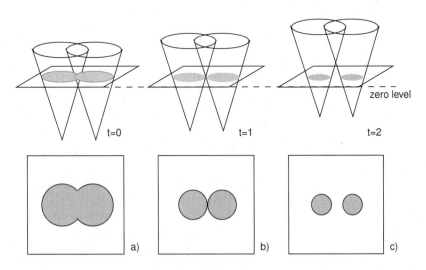

Figure 7.23: Topology change using level sets. As the level set function is updated for $t = 1, 2, 3$, the zero-level set changes topology, eventually providing a 2-object boundary. © *Cengage Learning 2015.*

A more formal treatment to define a level set embedding of the curve evolution equation (7.33) is now appropriate. Having a level set function $\phi(x, y, t)$ with the contour $\mathbf{X}(s, t)$ as its zero-level set, the situation is described by

$$\phi\big(\mathbf{X}(s, t), t\big) = 0 . \tag{7.39}$$

Differentiating with respect to t applying the chain rule,

$$\frac{\partial \phi}{\partial t} + \nabla \phi \cdot \frac{\partial \mathbf{X}}{\partial t} = 0 . \tag{7.40}$$

Now assuming that ϕ is negative inside the zero-level set and positive outside, the inward unit normal to the level set curve is

$$\mathbf{N} = -\frac{\nabla \phi}{|\nabla \phi|}$$

and so from the speed equation (7.33)

$$\frac{\partial \mathbf{X}}{\partial t} = -\frac{V(c)\, \nabla \phi}{|\nabla \phi|} \tag{7.41}$$

and hence

$$\frac{\partial \phi}{\partial t} - \nabla \phi \, \frac{V(c)\, \nabla \phi}{|\nabla \phi|} = 0 \tag{7.42}$$

and so

$$\frac{\partial \phi}{\partial t} = V(c)\, |\nabla \phi| . \tag{7.43}$$

The curvature c at the zero-level set is

$$c = \nabla \frac{\nabla \phi}{|\nabla \phi|} = \frac{\phi_{xx}\, \phi_y^2 - 2\, \phi_x\, \phi_y\, \phi_{xy} + \phi_{yy}\, \phi_x^2}{\big(\phi_x^2 + \phi_y^2\big)^{3/2}} . \tag{7.44}$$

Equation (7.43) shows how to perform curve evolution specified by equation (7.33) using the level set method.

To implement geometric deformable contours, an initial level set function $\phi(x, y, t = 0)$ must be defined, the speed function must be derived for the entire image domain, and evolution must be defined for locations in which normals do not exist due to the development of singularities. The initial level set function is frequently based on the signed distance $D(x, y)$ from each grid point to the zero-level set, $\phi(x, y, 0) = D(x, y)$. An efficient algorithm for construction of the signed distance function is called a *fast marching method* [Sethian, 1999].

Note that the evolution equation (7.43) is only derived for the zero-level set. Consequently, the speed function $V(c)$ is needs to be extended to all level sets. A number of extension approaches, including the frequently used *narrow band* extension, can be found in [Malladi et al., 1995; Sethian, 1999]. Although the equations for $\mathbf{N}$ and c hold for all level sets, the distance function property may become invalid over the course of curve evolution causing inaccuracies in curvature and normal vector computations. Consequently, reinitialization of the level set function to a signed distance function is often required. Another method [Adalsteinsson and Sethian, 1999] does not suffer from this problem.

As described above, using the *constant deformation* approach may cause sharp corners of the zero-level set resulting in an ambiguous normal direction. In that case, the deformation can be continued using an *entropy condition* [Sethian, 1982].

The speed function given in equation (7.36) uses image gradient to stop the curve evolution. To overcome the inherent problems of edge-based stopping criteria, considering the region properties of the segmented objects is frequently helpful. For example, a piecewise constant minimal variance criterion based on the Mumford-Shah functional [Mumford and Shah, 1989] was proposed [Chan and Vese, 2001] to deal with such situations. Considering a 2D image consisting of pixels $I(x, y)$ and the segmentation defined by an evolving closed zero-level set curve ϕ, the *Chan–Vese energy functional* is

$$C(\phi, a_1, a_2) = C_1(\phi, a_1, a_2) + C_2(\phi, a_1, a_2) \tag{7.45}$$

$$= \int_{inside(\phi)} \Big(I(x, y) - a_1 \Big)^2 \, \mathrm{d}x \, \mathrm{d}y + \int_{outside(\phi)} \Big(I(x, y) - a_2 \Big)^2 \, \mathrm{d}x \, \mathrm{d}y \, .$$

Constants a_1, a_2 represent the mean intensities of the interior and exterior of the segmented object(s). The energy $C(\phi, a_1, a_2)$ is minimized when the zero-level set ϕ coincides with the object boundary and best separates object and background with respect to their mean intensities. Of course, properties other than image intensities can be used.

If the curve ϕ is outside the object, then $C_1(\phi) > 0$ and $C_2(\phi) \approx 0$. If it is inside the object, then $C_1(\phi) \approx 0$ and $C_2(\phi) > 0$. If it is both inside and outside the object, then $C_1(\phi) > 0$ and $C_2(\phi) > 0$ as shown in Figure 7.24.

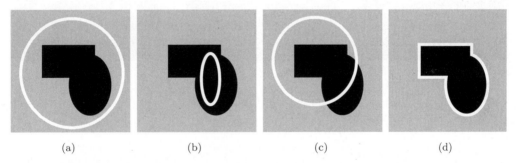

(a)	(b)	(c)	(d)

Figure 7.24: Chan–Vese energy functional. (a) $C_1(\phi) > 0$, $C_2(\phi) \approx 0$. (b) $C_1(\phi) \approx 0$, $C_2(\phi) > 0$. (c) $C_1(\phi) > 0$, $C_2(\phi) > 0$. (d) $C_1(\phi) \approx 0$, $C_2(\phi) \approx 0$. © *Cengage Learning 2015*.

In order to solve more complicated segmentation tasks, regularizing terms like curve length ϕ or region area inside ϕ may be included, yielding an energy functional:

$$C'(\phi, a_1, a_2) = \mu \, (\text{Length of } \phi) + \nu \, (\text{Area inside } \phi) \tag{7.46}$$

$$+ \lambda_1 \int_{inside(\phi)} \Big(I(x, y) - a_1 \Big)^2 \, \mathrm{d}x \, \mathrm{d}y + \lambda_2 \int_{outside(\phi)} \Big(I(x, y) - a_2 \Big)^2 \, \mathrm{d}x \, \mathrm{d}y \, ,$$

where $\mu \geq 0$, $\nu \geq 0$, $\lambda_1, \lambda_2 \geq 0$. The *inside* ϕ portion of image I corresponds to $\phi(x, y) > 0$ and *outside* ϕ corresponds to $\phi(x, y) < 0$. Using the Heaviside function $H(z)$

$$H(z) = \begin{cases} 1, & z \geq 0 \\ 0, & z < 0 \end{cases} \quad , \qquad \delta_0 = \frac{\mathrm{d}H(z)}{\mathrm{d}z} \, , \tag{7.47}$$

the level set equation minimizing the Chan–Vese energy functional C' (equation 7.46) is

$$\frac{\partial \phi}{\partial t} = \delta(\phi) \left(\mu \, \text{div} \left(\frac{\nabla \phi}{|\nabla \phi|} \right) - \nu - \lambda_1 \big(I(x,y) - a_1 \big)^2 + \lambda_2 \big(I(x,y) - a_2 \big)^2 \right) . \qquad (7.48)$$

The level set equation can be solved iteratively using time step Δt. However, inherent time step requirements exist to ensure stability of the numerical scheme via the Courant-Friedrichs-Lewy (CFL) condition [Heath, 2002]. In Chan and Vese's approach, the following time step can be used

$$\Delta t \leq \frac{\min(\Delta x, \Delta y, \Delta z)}{\big(|\mu| + |\nu| + |\lambda_0 + \lambda_1| \big)} . \qquad (7.49)$$

An example of noisy image segmentation using the Chan–Vese energy equation (7.46) is in Figure 7.25: here, 2D curvature was taken as the approximation of div $\big(\nabla \phi / |\nabla \phi| \big)$.

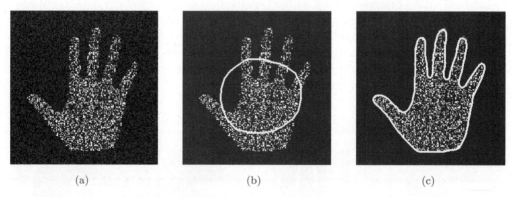

(a)   (b)   (c)

Figure 7.25: Chan-Vese level set segmentation. (a) Original image. (b) Initial contour. (c) Segmentation result. © *Cengage Learning 2015*.

A large variety of applications exist in which geometric deformable models were used for image segmentation. Examples include a level set-based cortical unfolding method [Hermosillo et al., 1999]; cell segmentation [Yang et al., 2005]; cardiac image analysis [Lin et al., 2003; Angelini et al., 2004], and many others.

The ability of geometric deformable model segmentations to allow topology changes is an important contribution to the image segmentation tool set. However, this behavior may be as detrimental as it may be useful. When applied to noisy data with boundary gaps, shapes may be generated which have topology inconsistent with that of the underlying objects. In such situations, topology constraints may be required and a choice of parametric deformable models or graph-based approaches may be more suitable.

7.4   Fuzzy connectivity

Many image segmentation methods are based on crisp (or *hard-coded*) relationships between or within the individual regions to be segmented. In many cases, however, these relationships may vary across the image due to noise, uneven illumination, limited spatial resolution, partial occlusions, etc. *Fuzzy* segmentation takes these uncertainties into consideration. Rather than defining crisp relations, it attempts to describe the segmentation task with fuzzy rules such as *if two regions have about the same gray-value and if they are relatively close to each other in space, then they likely belong to the same object.* A framework for such a reasoning approach is called *fuzzy logic*, considered in more detail in Section 9.1. While not essential for understanding the method described here, reading the fuzzy logic section may provide additional insight into this powerful concept.

Fuzzy connectivity segmentation attempts to mimic the analysis strategy of a trained human observer who is typically able to perform a segmentation task by hand, frequently considering the likelihood of whether nearby image elements belong together. If they seem to belong to the same object based on their image and spatial properties, they are assigned to the same region. In other words, the image pixels seem to *hang together* when forming an object—this property is then described using fuzzy logic. Early work in the field was reported in [Rosenfeld, 1984; Bloch, 1993; Dellepiane and Fontana, 1995]. Udupa et al. stated an important concept that voxels belonging to the same objects tend to *hang together* thus defining objects by a combination of the spatial relationship of its elements (pixels, voxels), at the same time considering local image properties [Udupa and Samarasekera, 1996a; Udupa et al., 1997; Rice and Udupa, 2000; Saha et al., 2000]. The spatial relationships should be determined for *each* pair of image elements in the entire image. To accomplish that, local and global image properties are considered.

The *local* fuzzy relation is called *fuzzy affinity*, denoted by $\psi \in [0, 1]$, and represents a strength of *hanging togetherness* of nearby image elements. Each such image element or *spatial element* is called a *spel*. (In 2D, a spel is equivalent to a pixel, in 3D a voxel.) We will use *spel* and *image element* interchangeably. *Affinity* is a function of the spatial distance between two fuzzy adjacent image elements considering their image intensities or other image-derived properties (e.g., image edges). As such, any image I can be represented by a pair $I = (C, f)$, in which C represents the image domain and f represents local image properties. Then, $f(c) \in [0, 1]$ represents a normalized image property (feature) associated with spel c. Fuzzy affinity is considered in detail below.

The *fuzzy adjacency* $\mu(c, d) \in [0, 1]$ of two elements c, d is determined by the fuzzy adjacency function. *Hard*-adjacency results in binary values–spels that share a common face (e.g., 4-connectivity in 2D, 6-connectivity in 3D) are regarded as fully adjacent (*adjacency value* = 1). Any other spel pair is considered non-adjacent (*adjacency value* = 0). When using hard six-adjacency in 3D ($n = 3$) and considering two spels c and d, the binary adjacency values can be defined as

$$\mu(c, d) = \begin{cases} 1 & \text{if } c \text{ and } d \text{ are identical } or \text{ differ in exactly one coordinate by } 1 \,, \\ 0 & \text{otherwise.} \end{cases} \tag{7.50}$$

A general n-dimensional fuzzy spel adjacency may be defined [Udupa and Samarasekera, 1996a]

$$\mu(c, d) = \begin{cases} \frac{1}{1 + k_1 \sqrt{\sum_{i=1}^{n} (c_i - d_i)^2}} & \text{if } \sum_{i=1}^{n} |c_i - d_i| \leq n \,, \\ 0 & \text{otherwise,} \end{cases} \tag{7.51}$$

where k_1 is a non-negative constant. Non-binary definitions of adjacency are possible with values ranging from 0 to 1. The affinity function $\psi(c, d)$ discussed above is only determined for spels c, d that are *fuzzy adjacent*, i.e. which have adjacency value $\mu(c, d) \neq 0$.

Fuzzy connectedness μ_ψ is a *global* fuzzy relationship that assigns every pair of image elements c and d a value in the interval [0,1] based on the affinity values ψ along all possible paths between these two image elements. The elements c and d are not expected to be nearby. They are connected by a path $\pi = \langle c^{(0)}, \ldots, c^{(N)} \rangle$ of spels, with $c = c^{(0)}$ and $d = c^{(N)}$. Each pair of consecutive spels is characterized by a fuzzy affinity $\psi(c^{(n)}, c^{(n+1)}), 0 \leq n \leq N - 1$. For each path, its strength is defined as the minimum affinity value of all pairwise consecutive elements on the path, so the strength of the entire path is defined by the strength of its weakest local connection, quantified by

$$\psi'(\pi) = \min_{0 \leq n \leq N-1} \psi\big(c^{(n)}, c^{(n+1)}\big). \tag{7.52}$$

Many different paths may connect two spels c and d. Let M denote the set of paths joining c, d. Note that M is not necessarily finite. The fuzzy connectedness is defined as

$$\mu_\psi(c, d) = \max_{\pi \in M} \psi'(\pi), \tag{7.53}$$

i.e., the value of fuzzy connectedness (global hanging togetherness) of c and d is determined as the maximum strength of all possible paths between c and d. The strength of connectedness of all possible pairs of elements defining a fuzzy connected object is determined via dynamic programming [Udupa and Samarasekera, 1996a] (Algorithm 7.5).

Starting from a seed-spel c and determining the fuzzy connectedness $\mu_\psi(c, d_i)$ to every other spel d_i in the image domain C, assigning the corresponding connectedness value to every spel, the resulting image is a fuzzy *connectedness map* representing the degree of connectedness of every spel in the image with the seed-spel c. A very strong connectedness is denoted by 1, no connectedness by 0. By thresholding the map with an appropriate value, only spels with a certain pre-determined minimum degree of connectedness to the seed-spel remain. Thresholding the connectedness map yields the segmentation result.

Algorithm 7.4: Absolute fuzzy connectivity segmentation

1. Define properties of fuzzy adjacency and fuzzy affinity.

2. Determine the affinity values for all pairs of fuzzy adjacent spels.

3. Determine the segmentation seed element c.

4. Determine all possible paths between the seed c and all other image elements d_i in the image domain C (not forming loops) considering the fuzzy adjacency relationship.

5. For each path, determine its strength according as the minimum affinity along the path (equation 7.52).

6. For each image element d_j, determine its fuzzy connectedness $\mu_\psi(c, d_j)$ to the seed point c as the maximum strength of all possible paths $\langle c, \ldots, d_j \rangle$ (equation 7.53) and form an image connectedness map.

7. Threshold the connectedness map with an appropriate threshold t to segment the image into an object containing the seed c and the background.

The fuzzy affinity concept requires additional explanation. In most real-world applications, performance of fuzzy connectivity segmentation largely depends on the appropriate design of fuzzy affinity, which is computed using local image properties. Let the *fuzzy affinity* $\psi(c,d)$ quantify the hanging-togetherness of two spels c and d; by definition, $\psi(c,d)$ has to be reflexive and symmetric; transitivity is not required. The fuzzy affinity $\psi(c,d)$ is a function of fuzzy adjacency $\mu(c,d)$, spel properties $f(c)$, $f(d)$, and—in spatially variant cases—of c and d

$$\psi(c,d) = \frac{\mu(c,d)}{1 + k_2|f(c) - f(d)|} \,, \tag{7.54}$$

where μ is the fuzzy adjacency defined by equation (7.51), k_2 is a non-negative constant.

A general affinity function can be defined as [Udupa and Samarasekera, 1996a]

$$\psi(c,d) = \begin{cases} \mu(c,d)\Big(\omega\, h_1\big(f(c), f(d)\big) + (1-\omega)\, h_2\big(f(c), f(d)\big)\Big) & c \neq d\,, \\ 1 & \text{otherwise,} \end{cases} \tag{7.55}$$

where ω is a weighting factor, h_1 and h_2 are segmentation task dependent and may be constructed from the following terms

$$g_1\big(f(c), f(d)\big) = \exp\left(-\frac{1}{2}\left(\frac{\frac{1}{2}[f(c) + f(d)] - m_1}{\sigma_1}\right)^2\right), \tag{7.56}$$

$$g_2\big(f(c), f(d)\big) = \exp\left(-\frac{1}{2}\left(\frac{|f(c) - f(d)| - m_2}{\sigma_2}\right)^2\right), \tag{7.57}$$

$$g_3\big(f(c), f(d)\big) = 1 - g_1\big(f(c), f(d)\big)\,, \tag{7.58}$$

$$g_4\big(f(c), f(d)\big) = 1 - g_2\big(f(c), f(d)\big)\,, \tag{7.59}$$

where m_1 and m_2 are mean values, and σ_1 and σ_2 standard deviations reflecting properties of the object of interest. These m and σ values can be calculated from the spels that are known a priori to belong to the object or background. Such a set of spels can either be provided by the user, or can be determined automatically using a rough presegmentation. As noted by [Udupa and Samarasekera, 1996a], $g_1(\cdot)$ and $g_2(\cdot)$ in equations (7.56) and (7.57) can also be expressed in a multivariate version.

Affinity function behavior can be influenced by the choice of the functions h_1 and h_2. For example, choosing $h_1\big(f(c), f(d)\big) = g_1\big(f(c), f(d)\big)$, $\omega = 1$ favors spels that are closer to an expected mean value μ_1. Choosing $h_1\big(f(c), f(d)\big) = g_1\big(f(c), f(d)\big)$, $h_2\big(f(c), f(d)\big) = g_4\big(f(c), f(d)\big)$, and $\omega = 0.5$ decreases the affinity $\psi(c,d)$ if the gradient between the spels is close to the mean value μ_2. A slightly different function is in [Carvalho et al., 1999], and a function in which *homogeneity-based* and *object-feature-based* components are treated separately was proposed in [Saha et al., 2000].

Finding the fuzzy connectedness $\mu_\psi(c,d)$ for every spel of the image domain $d \in C$, $c \neq d$ and assigning the respective connectedness value to every spel results in the *connectedness map* introduced above. Algorithm 7.5 generates a connectedness map that can subsequently be thresholded at any value (possibly in an interactive way) as described in Algorithm 7.4. Algorithms 7.5 and 7.6 are based on dynamic programming [Udupa and Samarasekera, 1996a]. Generally, they output an image with values f_c expressing strength of connectivity between the seed-spell c and all other spels $d \in C$.

Algorithm 7.5: Fuzzy object extraction

1. Define a seed-point c in the input image.

2. Form a temporary queue Q and a real-valued array f_c with one element $f_c(d)$ for each spel d.

3. For all spels $d \in C$, initialize array $f_c(d) := 0$ if $d \neq c$; $f_c(d) := 1$ if $d = c$.

4. For all spels $d \in C$ for which fuzzy adjacency $\mu_\psi(c,d) > 0$, add d to queue Q.

5. While the Q is not empty, remove d from Q and perform:
   $$f_{\max} := \max_{e \in C} \min\big(f_c(e), \psi(d,e)\big)$$
   if $f_{\max} > f_c(d)$ then
   $\quad f_c(d) := f_{\max}$
   $\quad$ for all spels g for which $\psi(d,g) > 0$, add g to queue Q
   endif
   endwhile

6. Once the queue Q is empty, the connectedness map (C, f_c) is obtained.

Proof of convergence can be found in [Udupa and Samarasekera, 1996a]. As described in Algorithm 7.4, the connectedness map must be thresholded so that the segmented object only contains spels with an above-threshold connectedness to the seed-point. It can be shown that the resulting object is contiguous.

A simple segmentation example associated with Algorithm 7.5 is given in Figure 7.26. Starting with a tiny 2×2 image the intensities of which are shown in Figure 7.26a and using the intensity as image features used for calculating the fuzzy affinity according to equation (7.54), Figure 7.26b gives the affinity map $\psi(c,d)$. Let the image spels (pixels) be identified with capital characters A,B,C,D–and let the seed c be located in pixel D.

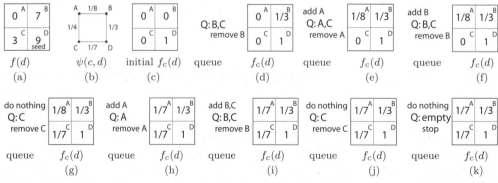

Figure 7.26: Fuzzy object extraction using Algorithm 7.5. (a) Image properties, which can be represented as image intensities. (b) Fuzzy affinity $\psi(c,d)$ calculated according to equation (7.54), $k_2 = 1$. (c) Initialized array $f_c(d)$. (d) Initial queue Q, temporary values of $f_c(d)$ after removal of spel B from queue Q. (e-j) Intermediate algorithm steps. (k) The queue Q is empty, stop. Values of array $f_c(d)$ represent the connectedness map. © Cengage Learning 2015.

The initialization of array f_c can be seen in panel (c)–step (3) of Algorithm 7.5. Panel (d) shows the initial queue content according to step 4 of Algorithm 7.5. When B is removed from the queue ($d = B$), $f_{\max}$ is calculated as given in step 5 examining all spels $e \in \{A, C, D\}$. For $e = A, C, D$

$$\min \big[f_c(A), \psi(B, A) \big] = \min[0, 1/8] = 0 \,,$$
$$\min \big[f_c(C), \psi(B, C) \big] = \min[0, 0] = 0 \,, \qquad (7.60)$$
$$\min \big[f_c(D), \psi(B, D) \big] = \min[1, 1/3] = 1/3 \,,$$

and the maximum $f_{\max} = 1/3$. Since $f_{\max} > 0$ ($> f_c(B)$), $f_c(B)$ is updated to 1/3 as shown in panel (d). As further specified in step 5 of the algorithm, $g = A$ is the only spel with non-zero affinity $\psi(d, g) = \psi(B, A)$ and is consequently added to the queue. Following the same set of operations of step 5, the intermediate states of the queue Q and array f_c are given in panels (e–j) of Figure 7.26. Note that some spels are repeatedly added to and removed from the queue. Once the queue becomes empty, the values held in array f_c represent the connectedness map that can be thresholded to obtain the segmentation result as given in step 7 of Algorithm 7.4.

If a lower bound of the connectedness map threshold is known beforehand, the slightly more efficient Algorithm 7.6 can be used. The increase in efficiency is indicated by t: the closer t is to 1, the greater the gain. Θ_t is used to denote a subinterval of $[0, 1]$ defined as

$$\Theta_t = [t, 1] \,, \quad \text{with } 0 \le t \le 1 \,. \qquad (7.61)$$

Algorithm 7.6: Fuzzy object extraction with preset connectedness

1. Define a seed-point c in the input image.

2. Form a temporary queue Q and a real-valued array f_c with one element $f_c(d)$ for each spel d.

3. For all spels $d \in C$, initialize array $f_c(d) := 0$ if $d \ne c$; $f_c(d) := 1$ if $d = c$.

4. For all spels $d \in C$ for which fuzzy spel adjacency $\mu_\psi(c, d) > t$, add spel d to queue Q.

5. While the queue Q is not empty, remove spel d from queue Q and perform the following operations:
   $f_{\max} := \max_{e \in C} \min \big(f_c(e), \psi(d, e) \big)$
   if $f_{\max} > f_c(d)$ then
      $f_c(d) := f_{\max}$
      for all spels g for which $\psi(d, g) > 0$, add g to queue Q
   endif
   endwhile

6. Once the queue Q is empty, the connectedness map (C, f_c) is obtained.

Note that in both Algorithms 7.5 and 7.6, a spel may be queued more than once. This leads to the repeated exploration of the same subpaths and suboptimal processing time.

A connectedness map generation approach based on Dijkstra's algorithm can modify Algorithm 7.5 to deliver a 6- to 8-fold speedup [Carvalho et al., 1999].

The absolute fuzzy connectivity method suffers from problems similar to traditional region growing algorithms [Jones and Metaxas, 1997] and determining the optimal threshold of the connectivity map is difficult to automate. The absolute fuzzy connectivity method is however a foundation for more powerful extensions to the basic method.

Relative fuzzy connectivity was introduced in [Udupa et al., 1999; Saha and Udupa, 2001]. The main contribution is the elimination of the connectedness map thresholding step. Instead of extracting a single object at a time as described above, two objects are extracted. During the segmentation, these two objects are competing against each other with each individual spel assigned to the object with a stronger affinity to it.

The 2-object relative fuzzy connectivity method was later refined to include **multiple objects** in [Herman and Carvalho, 2001; Saha and Udupa, 2001]. The authors prove that simply using different affinities for different objects is not possible since this would mean that fundamental properties of fuzzy connectivity are no longer guaranteed. Instead, affinities of different objects have to be combined into a single affinity—this is done by calculating the fuzzy union of the individual affinities. The extension to multiple object segmentation is a significant improvement compared to relative fuzzy connectivity.

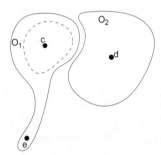

Figure 7.27: Segmentation task that can be solved by iterative fuzzy connectivity. © *Cengage Learning 2015*.

Figure 7.27 demonstrates a situation in which fuzzy connectivity will probably fail to identify objects correctly. Two objects O_1 and O_2 are located very close to each other. Due to limited resolution, the border between O_1 and O_2 may be weak causing $\mu_\psi(d, e)$ to be of similar magnitude to $\mu_\psi(c, e)$: O_1 and O_2 may thus be segmented as a single object. This problem can be overcome by considering **iterative fuzzy connectivity** [Udupa et al., 1999; Saha and Udupa, 2000]. As can be seen from the figure, the optimal path between d and e probably passes through the core of O_1, depicted by a dashed line around c. This core can be segmented first, for example with the relative fuzzy connectivity algorithm. After that, paths for the object O_2 between two spels not located in this core (like d and e) are not allowed to pass through the core of O_1. The objects are segmented in an iterative process. In this approach, the same affinity function must be used for all objects.

Scale-based fuzzy connectivity considers neighborhood properties of individual spels when calculating the fuzzy affinity functions $\psi(c, d)$ [Saha et al., 2000]. Calculating $\psi(c, d)$ is performed in two hyperballs centered at c and d, respectively. The scale of the calculation is defined by the radii of the hyperballs, which are derived from image data based on the image content. The scale is thus adaptively varying and is location specific. This approach generally leads to an improved segmentation, but with a considerable increase in computational cost.

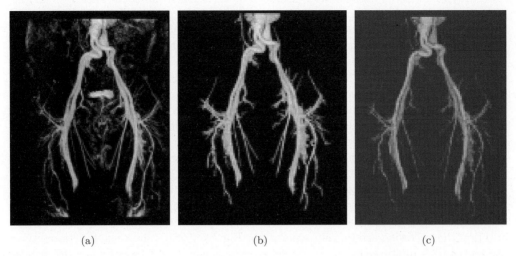

(a)   (b)   (c)

Figure 7.28: Segmentation and separation of vascular trees using fuzzy connectivity segmentation. (a) Maximum intensity projection image of the original magnetic resonance angiography data used for artery-vein segmentation in lower extremities. (b) Segmentation of the entire vessel tree using absolute fuzzy connectivity. (c) Artery–vein separation using relative fuzzy connectivity. *Courtesy of J. K. Udupa, University of Pennsylvania. A color version of this figure may be seen in the color inset—Plate 12.*

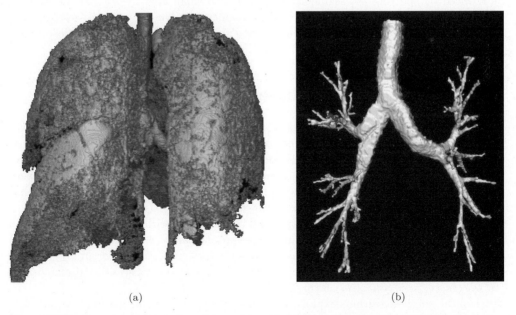

(a)   (b)

Figure 7.29: Segmentation result using multi-seeded fuzzy connectivity. (a) Region growing segmentation results in severe segmentation leak. (b) Multi-seeded fuzzy connectivity succeeded with the image segmentation using a standard setting of the method. © *Cengage Learning 2015.*

Fuzzy connectivity segmentation has been utilized in a variety of applications including interactive detection of multiple sclerosis lesions in 3D magnetic resonance images in which an improved segmentation reproducibility was achieved compared to manual segmentation [Udupa and Samarasekera, 1996a]. An approach for abdomen and lower extremities arterial and venous tree segmentation and artery–vein separation was reported in [Lei et al., 1999, 2000]. First, an entire vessel tree is segmented from MR angiography data using absolute fuzzy connectedness. Next, arteries and veins are separated using iterative relative fuzzy connectedness. For the artery–vein separation step, seed image elements are interactively determined inside an artery and inside a vein; large-aspect arteries and veins are separated, smaller-aspect separation is performed in an iterative process. To separate the arteries and veins, a distance transform image is formed from the binary image of the entire vessel structure (Figure 7.28a). Separate centerlines of arterial and venous segments between two bifurcations are determined using a cost function reflecting the distance transform values. All image elements belonging to the arterial or venous centerlines are then considered new seed elements for the fuzzy connectivity criterion thus allowing artery–vein separation. Figures 7.28b,c show the functionality of the method. A multi-seeded fuzzy connectivity segmentation was developed for robust detection of pulmonary airway trees from standard- and low-dose computed tomography images [Tschirren et al., 2005]. The airway segmentation algorithm presented here is based on *fuzzy connectivity* as proposed by Udupa et al. [Udupa and Samarasekera, 1996b] and Herman et al. [Herman and Carvalho, 2001]. During the execution of this algorithm, two regions—foreground and background—are competing against each other. This method has the great advantage that it can overcome image gradients and noise; the disadvantage is its relatively high computational complexity. Computing time can be reduced by splitting the segmentation space into small adaptive regions of interest, which follow the airway branches as they are segmented. The use of multi-seeded fuzzy connectivity significantly improved the method's performance in noisy low-dose image data, see Figure 7.29.

7.5 Towards 3D graph-based image segmentation

Graph-based approaches play an important role in image segmentation. The general theme of these approaches is the formation of a weighted graph $G = (V, E)$ with *node set V* and *arc set E*. The nodes $v \in V$ correspond to image pixels (or voxels), and arcs $\langle v_i, v_j \rangle \in E$ connect the nodes v_i, v_j according to some neighborhood system. Every node v and/or arc $\langle v_i, v_j \rangle \in E$ has a cost representing some measure of preference that the corresponding pixels belong to the object of interest.

Depending on the specific application and the graph algorithm being used, the graph may be *directed* or *undirected*. In a directed graph the arcs $\langle v_i, v_j \rangle$ and $\langle v_j, v_i \rangle$ $(i \neq j)$ are considered distinct, and may have different costs. If a directed arc $\langle v_i, v_j \rangle$ exists, the node v_j is called a *successor* of v_i. A sequence of consecutive directed arcs $\langle v_0, v_1 \rangle, \langle v_1, v_2 \rangle, \dots, \langle v_{k-1}, v_k \rangle$ form a directed path from v_0 to v_k.

Typical graph algorithms exploited for image segmentation include minimum spanning trees [Zahn, 1971; Xu et al., 1996; Felzenszwalb and Huttenlocher, 2004], shortest paths [Udupa and Samarasekera, 1996a; Falcao et al., 2000; Falcao and Udupa, 2000; Falcao et al., 2004], and graph-cuts [Wu and Leahy, 1993; Jermyn and Ishikawa, 2001; Shi and Malik, 2000; Boykov and Jolly, 2000, 2001; Wang and Siskind, 2003; Boykov and Kolmogorov, 2004; Li et al., 2004c], which have become the most powerful of graph-based mechanisms for image segmentation (see Section 10.12). They provide a clear and flexible global optimization tool with significant computational efficiency. An approach to single and multiple surface segmentation using graph transforms and graph cuts was reported in [Wu and Chen, 2002; Li et al., 2006].

Several fundamental approaches to edge-based segmentation were presented in Section 6.2. Of them, the concept of optimal border detection (Sections 6.2.4, 6.2.5) is extremely powerful and deserves more attention. In this section, two advanced graph-based border detection approaches are introduced. The first of them, *simultaneous border detection*, facilitates optimal identification of border pairs by finding a path in a three-dimensional graph. The second, *suboptimal surface detection*, uses multi-dimensional graph search for determination of optimal surfaces in three- or higher-dimensional image data. These methods pave the way to *optimal* graph-based segmentation approaches described in Sections 7.6 and 7.7.

7.5.1 Simultaneous detection of border pairs

Border detection approaches discussed in Sections 6.2.4 and 6.2.5 identified individual region borders. If the goal is to determine borders of elongated objects, it may be advantageous to search for the pair of left and right borders **simultaneously** [Sonka et al., 1993, 1995]; following a border of a road or river in a satellite image is an example. Such an approach facilitates more robust performance if the borders forming the border pair are interrelated, allowing information about one border to help identify the second. Examples include situations in which one border is locally noisy, ambiguous, or uncertain, where identifying borders individually may fail. Figure 7.30a illustrates that left and right borders, if considered individually, seem to be reasonable. However, if taken as a pair, it is unlikely that they represent left and right borders of, say, a river. Obviously, there is information contained in the position of one border that might be useful in identifying the position of the other, and more probable borders may be detected if this is considered (Figure 7.30b).

(a)   (b)

Figure 7.30: Individual and simultaneous border detection. (a) Individually identified borders may not be reasonable as a pair. (b) Simultaneously identified borders satisfy border-pair properties. © *Cengage Learning 2015.*

To search for an optimal border pair, the graph must be three-dimensional. Shown in Figure 7.31a are two adjacent but independent two-dimensional graphs, nodes in which correspond to pixels in the straightened edge image (Section 6.2.4). The column of nodes separating the left graph and the right graph corresponds to the pixels on the approximate region centerline. A row of nodes in the left graph corresponds to the resampled pixels along a line perpendicular to and left of the region centerline. If we connect nodes in the left graph as shown in Figure 7.31a, the resulting path corresponds to a possible position for the left border of the elongated region. Similarly, linking nodes together in the right graph produces a path corresponding to a possible position of the right region border. If conventional border detection methods described earlier are applied, the 2D graphs would be searched independently to identify optimal left and right region borders.

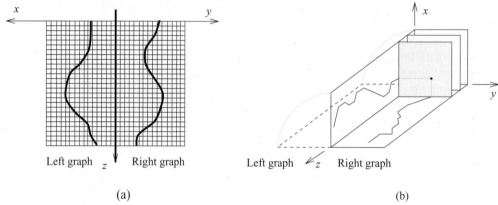

Figure 7.31: Three-dimensional graph construction. (a) Separate identification of the left and right borders by linking nodes in individual two-dimensional graphs corresponding to the left and right halves of the region segment of interest. (b) By rotating up the left graph, a three-dimensional graph results in which paths correspond to pairs of region borders. © *Cengage Learning 2015.*

The process of constructing the three-dimensional graph can be visualized as one of rotating up the 2D graph corresponding to the pixels left of the approximate region centerline (Figure 7.31b). The result is a three-dimensional array of nodes in which each node corresponds to possible positions of the left and right region borders for a given point along the length of the elongated region, and a path through the graph corresponds to a possible pair of left and right region borders. Nodes in the 3D graph are referenced by their (x, y, z) co-ordinates; for a point along the region centerline defined by the co-ordinate z, a node with co-ordinates (x_1, y_1, z) corresponds to a left border that is x_1 pixels to the left of the centerline and a right border that is y_1 pixels to the right of the centerline.

As in the 2D case, it is necessary to specify a node successor rule, that is, the rule for linking nodes into complete paths. Since the left border must be continuous, each parent node in the 2D graph corresponding to the left border has three successors as discussed earlier, corresponding to a left border whose distance from the centerline decreases, increases, or stays the same as a function of position along the centerline, with successor co-ordinates of $(x - 1, z + 1)$, $(x + 1, z + 1)$, $(x, z + 1)$ respectively. A similar statement holds for the right border. In the 3D graph, each parent node has nine successors corresponding to the possible combinations of change of positions of the left and right borders with respect to the centerline, thus forming a 3×3 successor window. With this successor rule, all paths through the 3D graph contain one and only one node from each *profile plane* in the 3D graph; that is, every path contains a single node derived from each of the left and right profile lines. This link definition ensures that region borders are continuous in the straightened image space.

Key aspects of the simultaneous approach for accurately identifying region borders are the assignment of costs to pairs of candidate borders and the identification of the optimal pair of region borders or lowest-cost path in the 3D graph. The cost function for a node in the 3D graph is derived by combining edge costs associated with the corresponding pixels on the left and right profiles in a way that allows the position of the left border to influence the position of the right border and vice versa. This strategy resembles that employed by a human observer in situations where border positions are ambiguous. In designing the cost function, the aim is to discriminate against border pairs that are unlikely to correspond to the true region borders and to identify border pairs that have the greatest overall probability of matching the actual borders. After the function is defined, methods such as heuristic graph search or dynamic programming can be used for optimal border detection.

Similarly to the 2D case, the cost of a path in the 3D graph is defined as the sum of the costs of the nodes forming the path. While many different cost functions can be designed corresponding to the recommendations of Section 6.2.4, the following one was found appropriate for description of border properties of a mutually interrelated border pair. Considering the cost minimization scheme, costs are assigned to nodes using:

$$C_{\text{total}}(x, y, z) = \left(C_s(x, y, z) + C_{pp}(x, y, z)\right) w(x, y, z) - P_L(z) + P_R(z) \,. \qquad (7.62)$$

Each of the components of the cost function depends on the edge costs associated with image pixels. The edge costs of the left and right edge candidates located at positions x and y on profile z are inversely related to effective edge strength or other appropriate local border property descriptor $E_L(x, z)$, $E_R(y, z)$ and are given by

$$
\begin{aligned}
C_L(x, z) &= \max_{x \in X, z \in Z} \left(E_L(x, z)\right) - E_L(x, z) \,, \\
C_R(y, z) &= \max_{y \in Y, z \in Z} \left(E_R(y, z)\right) - E_R(y, z) \,,
\end{aligned}
\qquad (7.63)
$$

X and Y are sets of integers ranging from 1 to the length of the left and right halves of the region profiles, and Z is the set of integers ranging from 1 to the length of the region centerline. To help avoid detection of regions adjacent to the region of interest, knowledge about the probable direction of the actual border may be incorporated into the local edge property descriptors $E_L(x, z)$, $E_R(y, z)$.

Considering the individual terms of the cost function (7.62), the term C_s is the sum of the costs for the left and right border candidates and causes the detected borders to *follow* image positions with low cost values. It is given by

$$C_s(x, y, z) = C_L(x, z) + C_R(y, z) \,. \qquad (7.64)$$

The C_{pp} term is useful in cases where one border has higher contrast (or other stronger border evidence) than the opposite border and causes the position of the low contrast border to be influenced by the position of the high-contrast border. It is given by

$$C_{pp}(x, y, z) = \left(C_L(x, z) - P_L(z)\right)\left(C_R(y, z) - P_R(z)\right) \qquad (7.65)$$

where

$$
\begin{aligned}
P_L(z) &= \max_{x \in X, z \in Z} \left(E_L(x, z)\right) - \max_{x \in X} \left(E_L(x, z)\right) \,, \\
P_R(z) &= \max_{y \in Y, z \in Z} \left(E_R(y, z)\right) - \max_{y \in Y} \left(E_R(y, z)\right) \,.
\end{aligned}
\qquad (7.66)
$$

Combining equations (7.63), (7.65), and (7.66), the C_{pp} term can also be expressed as

$$C_{pp}(x, y, z) = \left(\max_{x \in X} \left(E_L(x, z) \right) - E_L(x, z) \right) \left(\max_{y \in Y} \left(E_R(y, z) \right) - E_R(y, z) \right) \qquad (7.67)$$

The $w(x, y, z)$ component of the cost function incorporates a model of the region boundary in a way that causes the positions of the left and right borders to follow certain preferred directions relative to the model. This component has the effect of discriminating against borders that are unlikely to correspond to the actual region borders when considered as a pair. This is accomplished by including a weighting factor that depends on the direction by which a node is reached from its predecessor. For example, if the region is known to be approximately symmetric and its approximate centerline is known, the weighting factor may be given by (Figure 7.32)

$$\begin{aligned}
w(x, y, z) &= 1 \quad \text{for } (x, y) \in \left\{ (\hat{x} - 1, \hat{y} - 1), (\hat{x}, \hat{y}), (\hat{x} + 1, \hat{y} + 1) \right\}, \\
w(x, y, z) &= \alpha \quad \text{for } (x, y) \in \left\{ (\hat{x} - 1, \hat{y}), (\hat{x} + 1, \hat{y}), (\hat{x}, \hat{y} - 1), (\hat{x}, \hat{y} + 1) \right\}, \qquad (7.68) \\
w(x, y, z) &= \beta \quad \text{for } (x, y) \in \left\{ (\hat{x} - 1, \hat{y} + 1), (\hat{x} + 1, \hat{y} - 1) \right\},
\end{aligned}$$

where the node at co-ordinates (x, y, z) is the successor of the node at $(\hat{x}, \hat{y}, z-1)$. In this case, the influence of the region model is determined by the values of α and β, typically $\alpha > \beta$. In coronary border detection applications, the α ranged from 1.2 to 1.8 and β from 1.4 to 2.2 [Sonka et al., 1995]. The larger the values of α and β, the stronger is the model's influence on the detected borders.

The number of possible paths in a 3D graph is very large, and so identification of the optimal path can be computationally very demanding. Improvement in accuracy achieved

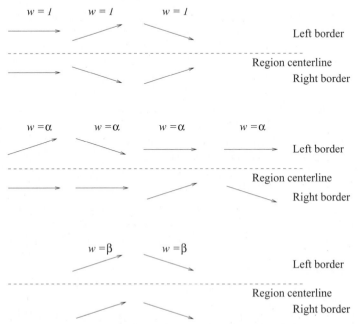

Figure 7.32: The weighting factors $w(x, y, z)$ associated with local directions of the potential border elements for a symmetric region model. © *Cengage Learning 2015*.

with simultaneous border detection is accomplished at the expense of an increase in computational complexity that is quite substantial for the heuristic graph search approach, but less so for dynamic programming (Sections 6.2.4 and 6.2.5).

Improving graph search performance is of great importance, and the $P_L(z) + P_R(z)$ term in the cost function represents the lower-bound heuristic introduced in Section 6.2.4, and does not influence the detected border; it does, however, substantially improve search efficiency if heuristic graph search is used [Sonka et al., 1993].

A second way to increase search efficiency is to use a multi-resolution approach (Section 10.1.5). First, the approximate positions of the region borders are identified in a low-resolution image; these approximate borders are used to guide the full-resolution search by limiting the portion of the full-resolution three-dimensional graph that is searched to find the precise region border positions.

To enhance border detection accuracy, a multi-stage border identification process may also be included. The goal of the first stage is to identify reliably the approximate borders of the region segment of interest while avoiding detection of other structures. Having identified the approximate positions, the second stage is designed to localize the actual region borders accurately. In the first stage, the 3D simultaneous border detection algorithm is used to identify approximate region borders in a half-resolution image. Since this first stage is designed in part to avoid detection of structures other than the region of interest, a relatively strong region model is used. Region boundaries identified in the low-resolution image are used in the second stage to guide the search for the optimal borders in the full-resolution cost image, as described in the previous paragraph. A somewhat weaker region model may be used in the second stage to allow more influence from the image data (Section 10.1.5). Further details about the cost function design can be found in [Sonka et al., 1993, 1995].

7.5.2 Suboptimal surface detection

If three-dimensional volumetric data are available, the task may be to identify 3D surfaces representing object boundaries in the 3D space. This task is common in segmentation of volumetric medical image data sets from scanners which produce 3D volumes consisting of stacked 2D image slices, such as magnetic resonance. Usually, the 2D images are more or less independently analyzed and the 2D results stacked to form the final 3D segmentation. It is intuitively obvious that a set of 2D borders detected in individual slices may be far from optimal if the entire 3D volume is considered, and concurrent analysis of the entire volume may give better results if a globally optimal surface is determined (see Section 7.7).

Consider an example of brain cortex visualization from three-dimensional magnetic resonance data sets of a human brain (Figure 7.33). Note that the internal cortex surfaces are not directly visible unless the brain is segmented into the right and left hemispheres. An example of such a segmentation applied to an individual MR slice was given earlier in Figure 6.34. If the 3D case is considered, the goal is to identify the *surface* that optimally divides the brain (Figure 7.34).

It is necessary to define a criterion of optimality for the surface. Since it must be contiguous in 3D space, it will consist of a mesh of 3D connected voxels. Consider a 3D graph that corresponds in size with the 3D image data volume; the graph nodes correspond to image voxels. If a cost is associated with each graph node, the optimal surface can be defined as that with the minimum total cost of all *legal* surfaces that can be

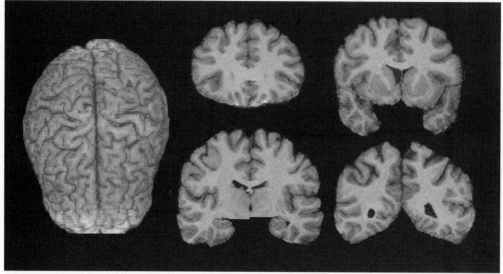

Figure 7.33: Magnetic resonance images of human brain. Left: Three-dimensional surface rendering of original MR image data after segmentation of the brain from the skull. Right: Four of 120 two-dimensional slices that form the three-dimensional image volume. *Courtesy of R. J. Frank and H. Damasio, The University of Iowa.*

defined in the 3D volume. *Legality* is defined by the 3D surface connectivity requirements that depend on the application at hand, and the total cost associated with a surface can be calculated as the sum of individual costs of all nodes forming the surface. Therefore, it should be possible to determine the optimal surface by application of optimal graph searching principles similar to those presented in Sections 6.2.4 and 6.2.5. Unfortunately, standard graph searching approaches cannot be directly extended from a search for a path to a search for a surface [Thedens et al., 1995]. Two distinct approaches can be developed to overcome this problem: New graph searching algorithms may be designed to search directly for a surface, or a surface detection task may be represented in a way that permits conventional graph searching algorithms to be used.

Compared to the search for an optimal path through a graph (even through a 3D graph as shown in Section 7.5.1), the search for an optimal surface results in combinatorial explosion of complexity, and the absence of an efficient search algorithm has represented a limiting factor on 3D surface detection. One approach based on cost minimization in a graph was given in [Thedens et al., 1990, 1995]. It used standard graph searching principles applied to a transformed graph in which standard search for a *path* was used to define a *surface*. While the method guaranteed surface optimality, it was impractical due to its enormous computational requirements. The same authors developed a heuristic approach to surface detection that was computationally feasible [Thedens et al., 1995].

A suboptimal approach to direct detection of surfaces called *surface growing* was introduced in [Thedens et al., 1995; Frank et al., 1996]. This is based on dynamic programming and avoids the problem of combinatorial explosion by introducing local conditions that must be satisfied by all legal surfaces. The graph size corresponds directly to image size, and due to the local character of surface growing, graph construction is straightforward and orderly. The entire approach is simple, elegant, computationally efficient,

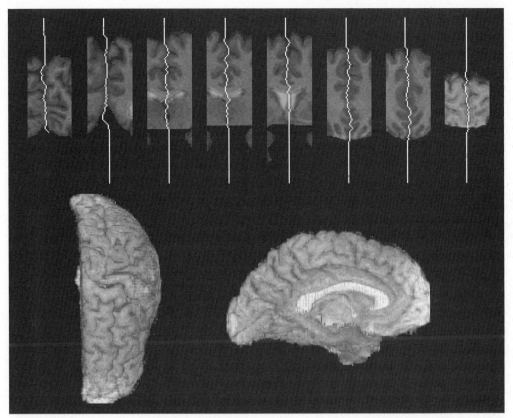

Figure 7.34: Surface detection. Top: Borders between the left and right hemispheres forming the 3D surface are shown in eight of 120 individual slices. Bottom: After the segmentation into left and right hemispheres, the internal cortex surfaces may be visualized. *Courtesy of R. J. Frank and H. Damasio, The University of Iowa.*

and fast. Additionally, it can be generalized to searching higher-dimensional spaces, e.g., time-variant three-dimensional surfaces. While the resulting surfaces typically represent good solutions, surface optimality is not guaranteed.

Figures 7.33 and 7.34 illustrate suboptimal three-dimensional graph searching applied to brain cortex segmentation. The cost function was based on inverted gray-level values of the image voxels after the ventricles were three-dimensionally filled not to represent a large low-cost region.

7.6 Graph cut segmentation

The *direct* use of minimum cut/maximum flow combinatorial optimization algorithms in image processing was first used for binary image reconstruction [Greig et al., 1989]. Using the same family of graph optimization algorithms, a technique for optimal boundary and region segmentation in n-D image data was presented in [Boykov and Jolly, 2001; Boykov and Kolmogorov, 2001; Boykov and Funka-Lea, 2006]. This approach has proved exceptionally powerful, and is usually motivated in the context of Markov Random Fields, which are presented in Section 10.12. For a broad overview of successful graph approaches in image processing and analysis, see [Lezoray and Grady, 2012].

The method is initiated by interactive or automated identification of one or more points representing the 'object' and one or more points representing the 'background'—these points are called *seeds* and serve as segmentation hard constraints. Additional soft constraints reflect boundary or region information. As with other optimal graph search techniques, the segmentation solution is globally optimal with respect to an objective function. The general version of the cost function C calculated on a segmentation f follows the *Gibbs model* [Geman and Geman, 1984]

$$C(f) = C_{\mathrm{data}}(f) + C_{\mathrm{smooth}}(f) \,. \tag{7.69}$$

—the background to this is discussed further in Section 10.12 (also, compare this with cost functions discussed in Section 10.10). To minimize $C(f)$, a special class of arc-weighted graphs $G_{\mathrm{st}} = (V \cup \{s, t\}, E)$ is employed. In addition to the set of nodes V corresponding to pixels (voxels) of the image I, the node set of G_{st} contains two special *terminal* nodes, namely the *source* s and the *sink* t. These terminals are hard-linked with the segmentation seed points (bold links in Figure 7.35) and represent the segmentation labels (object, background).

The arcs E in G_{st} can be classified into two categories: *n-links* and *t-links*. The n-links connect pairs of neighboring pixels whose costs are derived from the smoothness term $C_{\mathrm{smooth}}(f)$. The t-links connect pixels and terminals with costs derived from the data term $C_{\mathrm{data}}(f)$. An s–t cut in G_{st} is a set of arcs whose removal partitions the nodes into two disjoint subsets S and T, such that $s \in S$ (all nodes linked to source) and $t \in T$ (all nodes linked to sink) and no directed path can be established from s to t. The cost of a cut is the total cost of arcs in the cut, and a minimum s–t cut is a cut whose cost is minimal. The **minimum** s–t **cut** problem and its dual, the **maximum flow** problem, are classic combinatorial problems that can be solved by various polynomial-time algorithms [Ford and Fulkerson, 1956; Goldberg and Tarjan, 1988; Goldberg and Rao, 1998]. Figure 7.35 shows a simple example of the use of graph cut for segmentation.

Let O, B be sets of image pixels corresponding to object and background seeds, respectively; $O \subset V$, $B \subset V$, $O \cap B = \emptyset$. The seeds are used to form hard t-links in the graph. Then, the graph cut is determined to form the object(s) and background from image pixels in such a way that all object pixels are connected to the object seed terminal and all background pixels to the background seed terminal. This is accomplished by searching for a graph cut that minimizes a cost function (equation 7.69), the terms of which are a weighted combination of regional and boundary properties of the object with respect to the background.

Let the set of all image pixels be denoted by I, and let N denote a set of all directed pairs of pixels (p, q), $p, q \in I$ representing neighborhood pixel relationships. For example, 2D image pixels form a rectangular 2D grid with 4- or 8-neighborhood connectivity links contained in N. In the 3D case, image voxels form a three-dimensional grid and all their pairwise neighborhood relationships (e.g., reflecting 26-connectivity) are contained in N. This concept can be directly extended to n-D. A cost of (p, q) may differ from that of (q, p) allowing incorporation of asymmetric neighborhood relationships.

If each image pixel i_k takes a binary label $L_k \in \{obj, bgd\}$ where *obj* and *bgd* represent the object and background labels, then the labeling vector $\mathbf{L} = (L_1, L_2, ..., L_{|I|})$ defines a binary segmentation. The cost function C that is minimized to achieve optimal labeling

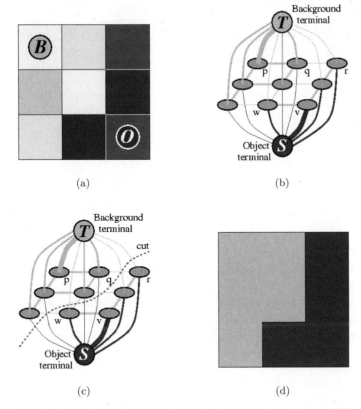

Figure 7.35: Example of graph cut segmentation: (a) Image with seeds—seed B corresponds to background and seed O to object. (b) Graph. (c) Graph cut. (d) Segmentation result. *Courtesy of Y. Boykov, University of Western Ontario. © 2001 IEEE. Reprinted, with permission, from Y. Boykov and M.-P. Jolly, "Interactive Graph Cuts for Optimal Boundary & Region Segmentation of Objects in N-D images," International Conference on Computer Vision, (ICCV), vol. I, pp. 105-112, 2001.*

may be defined as a λ-weighted combination of a regional property term $R(\mathbf{L})$ and a boundary property term $B(\mathbf{L})$ [Greig et al., 1989; Boykov and Jolly, 2001] (compare equation 7.69)

$$C(\mathbf{L}) = \lambda\, R(\mathbf{L}) + B(\mathbf{L}), \tag{7.70}$$

where

$$R(\mathbf{L}) = \sum_{p \in I} R_p(L_p), \tag{7.71}$$

$$B(\mathbf{L}) = \sum_{(p,q) \in N} B_{(p,q)}\, \delta(L_p, L_q), \tag{7.72}$$

and

$$\delta(L_p, L_q) = \begin{cases} 1 & \text{if } L_p \neq L_q, \\ 0 & \text{otherwise.} \end{cases}$$

Table 7.1: Cost terms for Graph Cut segmentation. K may be interpreted as the maximum needed flow capacity of the arc from source s to $p \in O$ (or from $p \in B$ to sink t), increased by one so that the arc gets never saturated; $K = 1 + \max_{p \in I} \Sigma_{q:(p,q) \in N} B_{(p,q)}$. © *Cengage Learning 2015.*

Graph arc	Cost	
(p, q)	$B_{(p,q)}$	for $(p, q) \in N$
(s, p)	$\lambda R_p(bgd)$	for $p \in I, p \notin (O \cup B)$
	K	for $p \in O$
	0	for $p \in B$
(p, t)	$\lambda R_p(obj)$	for $p \in I, p \notin (O \cup B)$
	0	for $p \in O$
	K	for $p \in B$

Here, $R_p(obj)$ may be understood as a pixel-specific cost associated with labeling pixel p as *object* and $R_p(bgd)$ a cost of labeling the same pixel p as *background*. For example, expecting bright objects on a dark background, the cost $R_p(obj)$ will be large in dark pixels and small in bright pixels. Similarly, $B_{(p,q)}$ is a cost associated with a local labeling discontinuity between neighboring pixels p, q. $B_{(p,q)}$ should be large for both p and q belonging to either object or background, and small if one of p, q belongs to object and the other to background, i.e., across object/background boundaries. Thus, $B_{(p,q)}$ may correspond, e.g., to the inverted image gradient magnitude between pixels p and q. As described above, the complete graph includes n-links and t-links. Weights of individual graph arcs are assigned to the graph according to Table 7.1. The minimum cost cut on the graph G can be computed in polynomial time for two-terminal graph cuts assuming the arc weights are non-negative [Ford and Fulkerson, 1962].

The minimum s–t cut problem can be solved by finding a maximum flow from the source s to the sink t, where the 'capacity' of a directed arc is given by its cost. The maximum flow from s to t saturates a set of arcs in the graph, and these saturated arcs divide the nodes into two disjoint parts S and T, corresponding to minimum cuts [Ford and Fulkerson, 1962]. The maximum flow value is equal to the cost of the minimum cut. The literature gives a wide range of algorithms that can be used to solve this combinatorial optimization task. Most existing algorithms can be categorized in two groups—**push-relabel** methods [Goldberg and Tarjan, 1988] and **augmenting path** methods [Ford and Fulkerson, 1962]; a comparison of major graph cut algorithms with applications in vision can be found in [Boykov and Kolmogorov, 2004].

Augmenting path algorithms (e.g., [Dinic, 1970]) push the flow through the graph from s to t until the maximum flow is reached. The process is initialized with zero flow and during the steps leading to saturation, the current status of the flow distribution is continuously maintained in a **residual graph** G_f, where f is the current flow. While the topology of G_f is identical to that of G_{st}, the arc values keep the remaining arc capacity considering current flow status. At each iteration step, the algorithm finds the shortest $s \rightarrow t$ path along the non-saturated arcs of the residual graph. The flow through this path is augmented by pushing the maximum possible flow so that at least one of the arcs along this path is saturated. In other words, the flow along the path is increased by Δf, the residual capacities of the path arcs are decreased by Δf, and the residual capacities of the reverse path arcs are increased by Δf. Each of these augmentation steps increases the total flow from the source to sink. Once the flow cannot be increased any more (so no new $s \rightarrow t$ path can be defined consisting exclusively of non-saturated arcs) the maximum flow is reached and the optimization process terminates. The separation of the S and T graph nodes defining the segmentation—the minimum s–t cut—is defined by the saturated graph arcs.

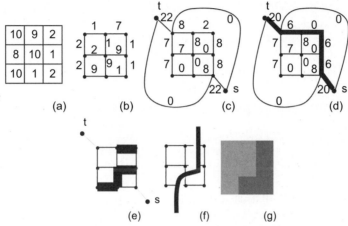

Figure 7.36: Image segmentation using graph cuts and maximum flow optimization. (a) Original image data—corresponding to Figure 7.35a. (b) Edge magnitudes calculated as image intensity differences in 4-connectivity. (c) G_{st} graph constructed according to Table 7.1; $\lambda = 0$; n-link costs calculated as in equation (6.9); reverse path residual capacities are not shown. (d) Residual graph G_f after the one and only shortest path with non-saturated $s \rightarrow t$ connection was identified and saturated. No new non-saturated $s \rightarrow t$ path can be found. (e) Saturated graph arcs identified by thick black lines. (f) Resulting minimum s–t cut separating S and T nodes. (g) Corresponding image segmentation. © *Cengage Learning 2015*.

The algorithm given in [Dinic, 1970] identifies the shortest path from s to t using a breadth-first search. Once all paths of length k are saturated, the algorithm starts with exploring $s \rightarrow t$ paths of lengths $k + 1$. The algorithm's complexity is $\mathcal{O}(mn^2)$, where n is the number of nodes and m is the number of arcs in the graph. Figure 7.36 gives an example of the steps needed for determining the minimum cut using an augmenting path maximum flow algorithm.

Push-relabel algorithms for maximum flow optimization [Goldberg and Tarjan, 1988] maintain a labeling of nodes with a lower bound estimate of its distance to the sink node along the shortest non-saturated path. The algorithm's functionality attempts to 'push' excess flow towards the nodes with shorter estimated distances to the sink. In each step, the node with the largest distance label is subjected to the push operation. Alternatively perhaps, a first-in-first-out strategy may be used. The distance estimate labels increase as more and more arcs are saturated after the push operations. As excessive flow may be pushed onto a node, this is eventually drained back to the source. Details of this approach can be found in [Cook et al., 1998].

Recall that the goal of graph-cut segmentation is to minimize the objective function given in equation (7.70) subject to the requirement of labeling all seeds according to the initial hard constraints. Algorithm 7.7 describes this optimization process.

Algorithm 7.7: Graph cut segmentation

1. Create an arc-weighted directed graph corresponding in size and dimensionality to the image to be segmented.

2. Identify object and background seeds—example points required to be part of the background or object(s) in the final segmentation. Create a source node s and a sink node t; connect all seeds with either the source or sink node based on their object or background label.

3. Associate an appropriate arc cost with each link of the graph according to Table 7.1.

4. Use a maximum flow graph optimization algorithm to determine the graph cut.

5. The minimum s–t cut solution identifies the graph nodes that correspond to the image boundaries separating the object(s) and the background.

An important feature of this approach is its ability to improve a previously obtained segmentation interactively in an efficient way. Suppose the user has identified initial seeds, the cost function is available, and the graph cut optimization yielded a segmentation that was not as good as required. It can be improved by adding supplemental object or background seeds. Suppose a new object seed is added—while it is possible to recompute the graph cut segmentation from scratch, an efficient way does not require restarting. Rather, the previous status of the graph optimization can be used to initialize the next graph cut optimization process.

Let a maximum flow algorithm be used for identifying the optimal graph s–t cut. In this case, the algorithmic solution is characterized by saturation of the graph by maximum flow. Adding a new object seed p requires forming corresponding hard t-links according to Table 7.1: weight (s, p) is set to K and weight (p, t) is set to 0. The latter may lead to appearance of negative capacities in the residual network of the current flow. This is easily compensated for by increasing values c_p of t-links as specified in Table 7.2. The new costs are consistent with the costs of pixels in O since the additional constant c_p appears at both t-links and thus does not change the optimal cut. Therefore, the new optimal cut can be efficiently obtained starting from the previous flow solution without starting from scratch. Of course, the same approach can be used if a new background seed is added. Again, the cost constants added to the new t-links should be consistent with the cost table and need to be modified by the same constant.

As is always the case with optimization techniques, cost function design influences the method's performance in real-world applications. For example, the seeds identifying the object and background exemplars may consist of small patches and may thus be used to sample the object and background image properties, e.g., calculating histograms of object and background patches. Let $P(I|O)$ and $P(I|B)$ represent probabilities of a particular gray level belonging to object or background, respectively. These probabilities

Table 7.2: Cost term $c_p = \lambda(R_p(bgd) + R_p(obj))$ modification for sequential improvement of graph cut segmentation after adding object seed p. © *Cengage Learning 2015*.

t-link	initial cost	added cost	new cost
(s,p)	$\lambda R_p(bgd)$	$K + \lambda R_p(obj)$	$K + c_p$
(p,t)	$\lambda R_p(obj)$	$\lambda R_p(bgd)$	c_p

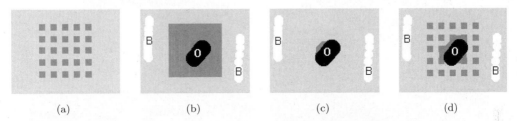

(a) (b) (c) (d)

Figure 7.37: Graph cut segmentation behavior on a synthetic image. In all cases, the segmentation was initialized using the object patch as marked in black and background patch marked in white. The resulting segmentation is shown in light gray (background) and dark gray (objects). The initialization patches are parts of the segmented object(s) or background. (a) Original image. (b) Segmentation result for $\lambda \in [7, 43]$, i.e., only using a wide weighting range of region and boundary cost terms. (c) Segmentation result for $\lambda = 0$, i.e., only using the boundary cost term. (d) Segmentation result for $\lambda = 60$, i.e., using almost solely the region cost term. Notice the ability of the method to change the topology of the segmentation result. *Courtesy of Y. Boykov, University of Western Ontario. © 2001 IEEE. Reprinted, with permission, from Y. Boykov and M.-P. Jolly, "Interactive Graph Cuts for Optimal Boundary & Region Segmentation of Objects in N-D images," International Conference on Computer Vision, (ICCV), vol. I, pp. 105-112, 2001.*

can be derived from the patch histograms (but more complex probability functions could be used instead). Then, the regional R_p and boundary $B(p,q)$ costs can be determined as [Boykov and Jolly, 2001]

$$R_p(obj) = -\ln P(I_p|O),$$
$$R_p(bgd) = -\ln P(I_p|B),$$
$$B(p,q) = \exp\left(-\frac{(I_p - I_q)^2}{2\,\sigma^2}\right)\frac{1}{\|p,q\|}, \tag{7.73}$$

where $\|p,q\|$ denotes distance between pixels p,q. Thus, $B(p,q)$ is high for small differences between image values $|I_p - I_q| < \sigma$ (within object or background). Cost $B(p,q)$ is low for boundary locations where $|I_p - I_q| > \sigma$. Here, σ represents allowed or expected intensity variation within the object and/or background.

Using the cost functions given in equation (7.73), Figure 7.37 demonstrates the method's behavior and the role of the weighting coefficient λ in equation (7.70). Graph cut applications range from stereo through multi-view image stitching, video texture synthesis, or image reconstruction, to n-dimensional image segmentation. Figure 7.38

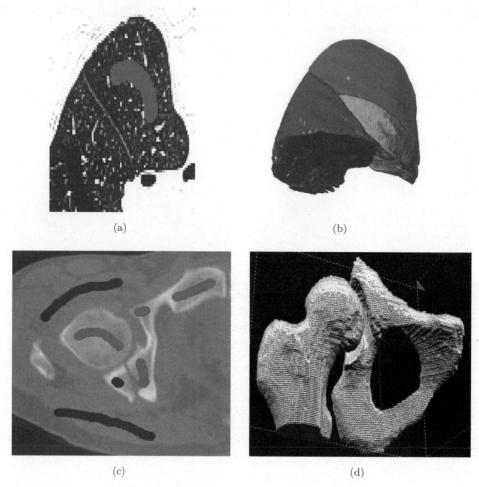

(a)

(b)

(c)

(d)

Figure 7.38: Graph cut segmentation in a 3D X-ray computed tomography image of human lungs and bones. (a) Original 3D image data with lung lobe and background initialization shown in two shades of gray—the segmentation works in a full 3D volumetric dataset. (b) Resulting lung lobe segmentation. (c) Bone and background initialization. (d) Resulting 3D segmentation. *Courtesy of Y. Boykov, University of Western Ontario and B. Geiger, Siemens Research. A color version of this figure may be seen in the color inset—Plate 13.*

demonstrates the capability of the method to segment lung lobes from X-ray computed tomography data.

Boykov and Jolly's method is flexible and shares some of the elegance of level set methods. It has been shown that that if the arcs of G_{st} are properly constructed and their costs properly assigned, a minimum s–t cut in G_{st} can be used to minimize the cost function of a more general form combining length, area, and flux terms globally in an efficient way [Kolmogorov and Boykov, 2005; Boykov et al., 2006]. In turn, if the cost function is appropriately designed, a minimum s–t cut can segment an image into objects and background as desired. Similarly to level sets, the results are topology-unconstrained and may be sensitive to initial seed point selections unless a priori shape knowledge about the objects is incorporated. While the graph cut approach provides an inherently binary segmentation, it can be extended to multi-label segmentation problems [Boykov and Veksler, 2006]. Unfortunately, the multi-way cut problem is NP–complete and an α-expansion algorithm may be used to obtain a good approximate solution [Boykov et al., 2001]. A combination of graph cuts and geodesic active contours is reported in [Boykov and Kolmogorov, 2003]. A connection between discrete graph cut algorithms and global optimization of a wide class of continuous surface functionals can be found in [Kolmogorov and Boykov, 2005]. In-depth discussion of associations between the level set and graph cut approaches can be found in [Boykov and Kolmogorov, 2003; Boykov and Funka-Lea, 2006; Boykov et al., 2006]. Experimental comparison of performance of several min-cut/max-flow algorithms for energy minimization in vision applications can be found in [Boykov et al., 2001].

7.7 Optimal single and multiple surface segmentation— LOGISMOS

The task of optimally identifying three-dimensional surfaces representing object boundaries is important in segmentation and quantitative analysis of volumetric images. In addition to single standalone surfaces, many surfaces that need to be identified appear in mutual interactions. These surfaces are *coupled* in a way that their topology and relative positions are usually known, and appear in some specific relationship. Clearly, incorporating such surface-interrelation information into the segmentation will further improve its accuracy and robustness. Simultaneous segmentation of coupled surfaces in volumetric images is an under-explored topic, especially when more than two are involved.

A polynomial time method exists for n-D ($n \geq 3$) optimal hyper-surface detection with hard smoothness constraints, making globally optimal surface segmentation in volumetric images practical [Wu and Chen, 2002; Li et al., 2004b]. By modeling the problem with a weighted *geometric graph*, the method transforms the problem into computing a minimum s–t cut in a directed graph, which simplifies the problem and consequently solves it in polynomial time. Note that the general method of graph cut optimization is used again, which accounts for a possibly confusing terminological similarity between direct graph cut segmentation (Section 7.6) and the optimal surface segmentation methods reported here. Nevertheless, the two approaches are principally different as becomes obvious below.

Optimal surface segmentation facilitates simultaneous detection of k ($k \geq 2$) interrelated surfaces by modeling the n-D problem in an $(n+1)$-D geometric graph (or simply *graph*), where the $(n+1)$-th dimension holds special arcs that control interrelations between pairs of sought surfaces [Li et al., 2004a, 2006]. The apparently daunting combinatorial explosion in computation is avoided by transforming the problems into computing minimum s–t cuts. The **Layered Optimal Graph Image Segmentation of Multiple Objects and Surfaces** is abbreviated as **LOGISMOS** [Yin et al., 2010].

Like other graph-search based segmentation methods, this approach first builds a graph that contains information about the boundaries of the target objects in the input image, and then searches the graph for a segmentation solution. However, to make this approach work effectively for segmentation problems, several key issues must be handled: (i) How to obtain relevant information about the target object boundaries; (ii) how to capture such information in a graph; and (iii) how to search the graph for the *optimal* surfaces of the target objects. The general approach consists of five main steps, which constitute a high level solution to these three key issues. Of course, in solving different segmentation problems, variations of these steps may be applied.

Algorithm 7.8: Optimal surface segmentation

1. *Pre-segmentation.* Given an input image, perform a pre-segmentation to obtain an approximation to the (unknown) surfaces for target object boundaries. This gives useful information on the topological structures of the target object(s). Several approximate surface detection methods are available, such as active appearance models, level sets, and atlas-based registration. For surfaces with a geometry that is known to be relatively simple and thus allows the unfolding process (e.g., terrain-like, cylindrical, tubular, or spherical surfaces), this first step may not be needed.

2. *Mesh Generation.* From the resulting approximate surface(s), a mesh is computed. The mesh is used to specify the structure of a graph G_B, called the *base graph*. G_B defines the neighboring relations among voxels on the sought (optimal) surfaces. Voronoi diagram and Delaunay triangulation algorithms or isosurfacing methods (e.g., marching cubes) can be used for mesh generation. For surfaces allowing an unfolding operation, this step may not be needed, since in many cases a mesh can be obtained easily.

3. *Image Resampling.* For each voxel v on the sought surfaces, a vector of voxels is created that is expected to contain v. This is done by resampling the input image along a ray intersecting every vertex u of the mesh (one ray per mesh vertex). The direction of the ray is either an approximate normal of the meshed surface at u, or is defined by a center point/line of the target object. These voxel vectors produced by the resampling form a new image.

4. *Graph Construction.* A weighted directed graph G is built on the vectors of voxels in the image that resulted from the resampling. Each voxel vector corresponds to a list of nodes in G (called a *column*). G is a *geometric* graph since it is naturally embedded in an n-D space ($n \geq 3$). Neighboring relations among voxels on the surfaces are represented by adjacency relations among the columns of G, as specified by the arcs in the base graph G_B. Each column contains exactly one voxel located on the sought surfaces. The arcs of G are used to enforce constraints on the surfaces, such as smoothness and inter-surface separation constraints. The intensity of each voxel in the vectors is related to the cost of the corresponding node in G. The node costs of G can also encode edge-based and region-based cost functions. Information on the constraints and cost functions of a target segmentation problem needs to be obtained.

5. *Graph Search.* The graph construction scheme ensures that the sought optimal surfaces correspond to an *optimal closed set* in the weighted directed graph G [Wu and Chen, 2002; Li et al., 2006]. Thus, the sought optimal surfaces are obtained by searching for an optimal closed set in G using efficient closed set algorithms in graph theory and can be achieved by using standard s–t cut algorithms.

Simple example The formal description of graph search algorithms given here is precise but not very intuitive. To reach an intuitive understanding of the underlying processes before a formal description, a simple 2D example is presented corresponding to a tiny 2×4 image. Let graph nodes correspond to image pixels with a cost associated with each node (Figure 7.39a). The goal is to find the *minimum-cost path* from left to right— the path cost is calculated as the sum of its node costs. The list of all paths in the graph includes (considering that the maximum allowed vertical distance between the two next-column nodes of the path is 1): *ae*, *af*, *be*, *bf*, *bg*, *cf*, *cg*, *ch*, *dg* and *dh*. The minimum-cost path can be easily identified as *cg* with a cost of 2.

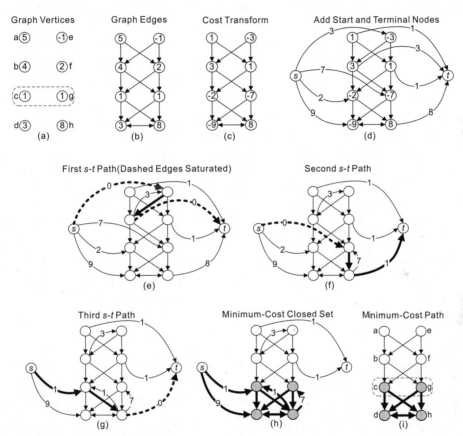

Figure 7.39: Simple example of the minimum cost graph-search detection algorithm. See text for details. © *Cengage Learning 2015*.

The arcs of the graph are constructed as shown in Figure 7.39b. Cost transformation is performed by subtracting the cost of the node immediately below from the cost of the node under consideration (Figure 7.39c). The costs of the bottommost two nodes are left unchanged, unless their cost sum is greater or equal to 0. If so, the sum of the bottom node costs is increased by one and subtracted from any single one of the bottommost nodes. In this example, the sum of the bottommost two nodes is 11; select node *d* and subtract 12 from its cost (Figure 7.39c). A closed set is a subset of the graph nodes with no arcs leaving the set. Every potential path in Figure 7.39a uniquely corresponds to a closed set in Figure 7.39c. Importantly, the *minimum-cost path* corresponds to the *minimum-cost closed set* in Figure 7.39c.

To compute the minimum-cost closed set of the graph, a transform to an arc-weighted directed graph is performed. Two new auxiliary nodes are added to the graph—a start node s with a connecting arc to every negative-cost node, and a terminal node t with an arc from every non-negative-cost node. Every arc is assigned a capacity. Arc capacities from (to) the start (terminal) node are the absolute values of the costs of the nodes they are connected to (from) (Figure 7.39d). All other arcs have infinite capacity. The node costs are no longer used and are ignored. The minimum-cost closed set of the graph in Figure 7.39c can be obtained by computing the *minimum s–t cut* or *maximum flow* from s to t in the graph.

The graph transforms described above represent the core of this approach. To solve the next step, several algorithms for computing the minimum s–t cut exist as outlined in the previous section. Following the maximum flow optimization approach (Section 7.6), the negative-cost (non-negative-cost) nodes are tunnels allowing water to flow in (out), and arcs are pipes connecting the source, tunnels and the sink. The pipes are directional, and the cumulative water flow cannot exceed pipe capacity. Due to the limited pipe capacities, the amount of water that can flow from the source to the sink will have some maximum. To achieve this maximum flow, some pipes will be saturated, meaning that the water flowing through them will equal their capacities. In Figure 7.39e, the path from s to t was found with a capacity of 3, which will saturate the path's pipes (arcs) from the source s and to the sink t. These two saturated pipes are removed and a new pipe is created in the reverse direction along the path having a capacity of 3. In Figure 7.39f, another s–t path is found with a capacity 7. Similarly, a reverse path with capacity 7 is created. Figure 7.39g identifies the third and final path that can be found—its capacity of 1 saturates the pipe to the sink that was not completely saturated in the previous step. Since this was the last path, all tunnels that can be reached from the source are identified (Figure 7.39h) as belonging to the minimum cost closed set (Figure 7.39i). The uppermost nodes of the minimum closed set form the minimum cost path thus determining the solution.

Graph construction   A key innovation of this method is its non-trivial graph construction, aiming to transform the surface segmentation problem into computing a minimum *closed set* in a node-weighted directed graph. A closed set Z in a digraph is a subset of nodes such that all successors of any nodes in Z are also contained in Z. The *cost* of a closed set is the total cost of the nodes in the set. The minimum closed set problem is to search for a closed set with the minimum cost, which can be solved in polynomial time by computing a minimum s–t cut in a derived arc-weighted digraph [Hochbaum, 2001].

Single surface graph construction   A volumetric image can be viewed as a 3D matrix $I(\mathbf{x}, \mathbf{y}, \mathbf{z})$ (Figure 7.40). Without loss of generality, a *surface* in I is considered to be terrain-like and oriented as shown in Figure 7.41. Let X, Y and Z denote the image sizes in $\mathbf{x}$, $\mathbf{y}$ and $\mathbf{z}$ directions, respectively. We utilize a *multi-column* modeling technique. A surface is defined by a function $S : (x, y) \to S(x, y)$, where $x \in \mathbf{x} = \{0, \ldots, X - 1\}$, $y \in \mathbf{y} = \{0, \ldots, Y - 1\}$ and $S(x, y) \in \mathbf{z} = \{0, \ldots, Z - 1\}$. Thus, any surface in I intersects with exactly one voxel of each *column* (of voxels) parallel to the $\mathbf{z}$-axis, and it consists of exactly $X \times Y$ voxels.

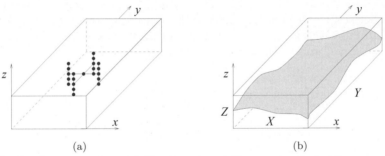

Figure 7.40: Graph construction. (a) Graph node neighbors—considering the smoothness constraint $\Delta_{\mathbf{x}} = \Delta_{\mathbf{y}} = 2$). (b) 3D graph XYZ and the 3D surface dividing the graph into upper and lower parts. © *Cengage Learning 2015*.

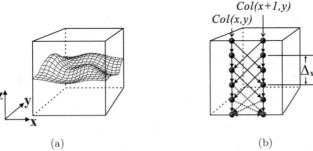

Figure 7.41: The single surface detection problem. (a) The surface orientation. (b) Two adjacent columns of the constructed directed graph. Arcs shown in dashed lines are optional. © *Cengage Learning 2015*.

A surface is regarded as *feasible* if it satisfies some application-specific *smoothness constraint*, defined by two smoothness parameters, $\Delta_{\mathbf{x}}$ and $\Delta_{\mathbf{y}}$; this constraint guarantees surface connectivity in 3D. More precisely, if $I(x, y, z)$ and $I(x + 1, y, z')$ are two voxels on a feasible surface, then $|z - z'| \leq \Delta_{\mathbf{x}}$: and if $I(x, y, z)$ and $I(x, y+1, z')$ are two voxels on a feasible surface, then $|z - z'| \leq \Delta_{\mathbf{y}}$. If $\Delta_{\mathbf{x}}$ $(\Delta_{\mathbf{y}})$ is small, any feasible surface is stiff along the $\mathbf{x}$ $(\mathbf{y})$ direction, and the stiffness decreases with larger $\Delta_{\mathbf{x}}$ $(\Delta_{\mathbf{y}})$.

By defining a cost function, a cost value is computed for each voxel $I(x, y, z)$ of I, denoted by $c(x, y, z)$. Generally, $c(x, y, z)$ is an arbitrary real value that is inversely related to the likelihood that the desired surface contains the voxel $I(x, y, z)$. The cost of a surface is the total cost of all voxels on the surface. An *optimal surface* is the surface with the minimum cost among all feasible surfaces definable in the 3D volume.

A node-weighted directed graph $G = (V, E)$ is constructed as follows. Every node $V(x, y, z) \in V$ represents one and only one voxel $I(x, y, z) \in I$, whose cost $w(x, y, z)$ is assigned according to:

$$w(x, y, z) = \begin{cases} c(x, y, z) & \text{if } z = 0 \,, \\ c(x, y, z) - c(x, y, z - 1) & \text{otherwise.} \end{cases} \tag{7.74}$$

A node $V(x, y, z)$ is *above* (resp., *below*) another node $V(x', y', z')$ if $z > z'$ (resp., $z < z'$). For each (x, y) pair with $x \in \mathbf{x}$ and $y \in \mathbf{y}$, the node subset $\{V(x, y, z)|z \in \mathbf{z}\}$ is called the (x, y)-*column* of G, denoted by $Col(x, y)$. Two (x, y)-columns are *adjacent* if their

(x, y) coordinates are neighbors under a given neighborhood system. For instance, under the 4-neighbor setting, the column $Col(x, y)$ is adjacent to $Col(x + 1, y)$, $Col(x - 1, y)$, $Col(x, y + 1)$, and $Col(x, y - 1)$. Hereafter, the 4-connectivity is assumed. The arcs of G consist of two types, *intra-column* arcs and *inter-column* arcs:

- *Intra-column arcs E^a:* Along each column $Col(x, y)$, every node $V(x, y, z)$, $z > 0$ has a directed arc to the node $V(x, y, z - 1)$, i.e.,

$$E^a = \left\{ \langle V(\mathbf{x}, \mathbf{y}, z), V(\mathbf{x}, \mathbf{y}, z - 1) \rangle \big| z > 0 \right\}. \tag{7.75}$$

- *Inter-column arcs E^r:* Consider any two adjacent columns, $Col(x, y)$ and $Col(x + 1, y)$. Along the **x**-direction and for any $x \in \mathbf{x}$, a directed arc is constructed from each node $V(x, y, z) \in Col(x, y)$ to node $V(x + 1, y, \max(0, z - \Delta_\mathbf{x})) \in Col(x + 1, y)$. Similarly, a directed arc is connected from $V(x + 1, y, z) \in Col(x + 1, y)$ to $V(x, y, \max(0, z - \Delta_\mathbf{x})) \in Col(x, y)$. The same construction is done in the **y**-direction. These arcs enforce the smoothness constraints. In summary,

$$
\begin{aligned}
E^r = &\left\{ \langle V(x, \mathbf{y}, z), V(x + 1, \mathbf{y}, \max(0, z - \Delta_\mathbf{x})) \rangle \mid x \in \{0, \ldots, X - 2\}, z \in \mathbf{z} \right\} \quad \cup \\
&\left\{ \langle V(x, \mathbf{y}, z), V(x - 1, \mathbf{y}, \max(0, z - \Delta_\mathbf{x})) \rangle \mid x \in \{1, \ldots, X - 1\}, z \in \mathbf{z} \right\} \quad \cup \\
&\left\{ \langle V(\mathbf{x}, y, z), V(\mathbf{x}, y + 1, \max(0, z - \Delta_\mathbf{y})) \rangle \mid y \in \{0, \ldots, Y - 2\}, z \in \mathbf{z} \right\} \quad \cup \\
&\left\{ \langle V(\mathbf{x}, y, z), V(\mathbf{x}, y - 1, \max(0, z - \Delta_\mathbf{y})) \rangle \mid y \in \{1, \ldots, Y - 1\}, z \in \mathbf{z} \right\} \quad .
\end{aligned}
\tag{7.76}
$$

Intuitively, the inter-column arcs guarantee that if voxel $I(x, y, z)$ is on a feasible surface S, then its neighboring voxels on S along the **x**-direction, $I(x + 1, y, z')$ and $I(x - 1, y, z'')$, must be no 'lower' than voxel $I(x, y, \max(0, z - \Delta_\mathbf{x}))$, i.e., $z', z'' \geq \max(0, z - \Delta_\mathbf{x})$. The same rule applies to the **y**-direction. The inter-column arcs make the node set $V(\mathbf{x}, \mathbf{y}, 0)$ *strongly connected*, meaning that in $V(\mathbf{x}, \mathbf{y}, 0)$, every node is reachable from every other node through some directed path. $V(\mathbf{x}, \mathbf{y}, 0)$ also forms the 'lowest' feasible surface that can be defined in G. Because of this, the node set $V(\mathbf{x}, \mathbf{y}, 0)$ is given a special name called the *base set*, denoted by V^B.

As presented, the graph search approach would only facilitate plane-like surface detection (see Figure 7.40b). However, the 3D surface to be searched often has a cylindrical shape and the method can detect circular surfaces after a straightforward extension. Assume that the desired surface is required to be *wraparound* along the **x**- (or **y**-) direction. The cylindrical surface is first unfolded into a terrain-like surface using a cylindrical coordinate transform before applying the algorithm (Figure 7.42). Then, the first and last rows along the unfolding plane shall satisfy the smoothness constraints. In the **x**-wraparound case, each node $V(0, y, z)$, resp., $V(X - 1, y, z)$, also connects to $V(X - 1, y, \max(0, z - \Delta_\mathbf{x}))$, resp., $V(0, y, \max(0, z - \Delta_\mathbf{x}))$. The same rule applies to the **y**-wraparound case.

Multiple surface graph construction   For simultaneously segmenting k ($k \geq 2$) distinct but interrelated surfaces, the optimality is not only determined by the inherent costs and smoothness properties of the individual surfaces, but also confined by their interrelations.

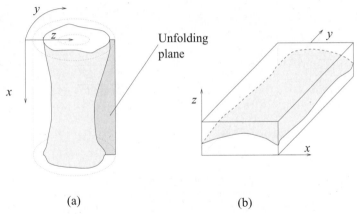

(a)   (b)

Figure 7.42: Image unfolding. (a) A tubular object in a volumetric image. (b) 'Unfolding' the tubular object in (a) to form a new 3D image. The boundary of the tubular object in the original data corresponds to the surface to be detected in the unfolded image. © *Cengage Learning 2015.*

If surface interactions are not considered, the k surfaces S_i can be detected in k separate 3D graphs $G_i = (V_i, E_i) = (V_i, E_i^a \cup E_i^r)$, $i = 1, \ldots, k$. Each G_i is constructed as presented above. The node costs are computed utilizing k cost functions (not necessarily distinct), each of which is designed for searching one surface. Taking surface interrelations into account, another set of arcs E^s is needed, forming a directed graph $G(V, E)$ in 4D space with $V = \cup_{i=1}^k V_i$ and $E = \cup_{i=1}^k E_i \cup E^s$. The arcs in E^s are called *inter-surface* arcs, which model the pairwise relations between surfaces. For each pair of the surfaces, their relations are described using two parameters, $\delta^l \geq 0$ and $\delta^u \geq 0$, representing the *surface separation constraint*.

The construction of E^s for double-surface segmentation is detailed below. The ideas can easily be generalized to handling more than two surfaces. In many practical problems, the surfaces are expected not to intersect or overlap. Suppose that for two surfaces S_1 and S_2 to be detected, prior knowledge requires S_2 being below S_1. Let the minimum distance between them be δ^l voxel units, and the maximum distance be δ^u voxel units. Let the 3D graphs used for the search of S_1 and S_2 be G_1 and G_2, respectively, and let $Col_1(x, y)$ and $Col_2(x, y)$ denote two corresponding columns in G_1 and G_2.

For any node $V_1(x, y, z)$ in $Col_1(x, y)$ with $z \geq \delta^u$, a directed arc in E^s connecting $V_1(x, y, z)$ to $V_2(x, y, z - \delta^u)$ is constructed. Also, for each node $V_2(x, y, z)$ in $Col_2(x, y)$ with $z < Z - \delta^l$, a directed arc in E^s connecting $V_2(x, y, z)$ to $V_1(x, y, z + \delta^l)$ is introduced. This construction is applied to every pair of corresponding columns of G_1 and G_2.

Because of the separation constraint (S_2 is at least δ^l voxel units below S_1), any node $V_1(x, y, z)$ with $z < \delta^l$ cannot be on surface S_1. Otherwise, no node in $Col_2(x, y)$ could be on surface S_2. Likewise, any node $V_2(x, y, z)$ with $z \geq Z - \delta^l$ cannot belong to surface S_2. These nodes that cannot appear in any feasible solution to the problem are called *deficient* nodes. Hence, for each column $Col_1(x, y) \in G_1$, it is safe to remove all nodes $V_1(x, y, z)$ with $z < \delta^l$ and their incident arcs in E_1. Similarly, for each column $Col_2(x, y) \in G_2$, all nodes $V_2(x, y, z)$ with $z \geq Z - \delta^l$ and their incident arcs in E_2 can be safely eliminated.

Due to the removal of deficient nodes, the base set of G_1 becomes $V_1(\mathbf{x}, \mathbf{y}, \delta^l)$. Correspondingly, the cost of each node $V_1(x, y, \delta^l)$ is modified as $w_1(x, y, \delta^l) = c_1(x, y, \delta^l)$,

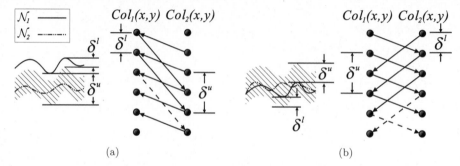

Figure 7.43: Summary of surface interrelation modeling. S_1 and S_2 are two desired surfaces. $Col_1(x, y)$ and $Col_2(x, y)$ are two corresponding columns in the constructed graphs. Arcs shown in dashed lines are optional. (a) The non-crossing case. (b) The case with crossing allowed. © Cengage Learning 2015.

where $c_1(x, y, \delta^l)$ is the original cost of voxel $I(x, y, \delta^l)$ for surface S_1. The inter-column arcs of G_1 are modified to make $V_1(\mathbf{x}, \mathbf{y}, \delta^l)$ strongly connected. The base set of G then becomes $V^B = V_1(\mathbf{x}, \mathbf{y}, \delta^l) \cup V_2(\mathbf{x}, \mathbf{y}, 0)$. The directed arcs $\langle V_1(0, 0, \delta^l), V_2(0, 0, 0) \rangle$ and $\langle V_2(0, 0, 0), V_1(0, 0, \delta^l) \rangle$ are introduced to E^s to make V_B strongly connected.

In summary, the inter-surface arc set E^s for modeling non-crossing surfaces is constructed as

$$
\begin{aligned}
E^s = &\left\{ \langle V_1(\mathbf{x}, \mathbf{y}, z), V_2(\mathbf{x}, \mathbf{y}, z - \delta^u) \rangle \,\middle|\, z \geq \delta^u \right\} \cup \left\{ \langle V_1(0, 0, \delta^l), V_2(0, 0, 0) \rangle \right\} \\
&\cup \left\{ \langle V_2(\mathbf{x}, \mathbf{y}, z), V_1(\mathbf{x}, \mathbf{y}, z + \delta^l) \rangle \,\middle|\, z < Z - \delta^l \right\} \cup \left\{ \langle V_2(0, 0, 0), V_1(0, 0, \delta^l) \rangle \right\}.
\end{aligned}
\tag{7.77}
$$

In other situations, two interacting surfaces may be allowed to cross each other. This may be encountered when tracking a moving surface over time. For these problems, instead of modeling the minimum and maximum distances between them, δ^l and δ^u specify the maximum distances that a surface can vary below and above the other surface, respectively. The inter-surface arcs for this case consist of the following: $\langle V_1(x, y, z), V_2(x, y, \max(0, z - \delta^l)) \rangle$ and $\langle V_2(x, y, z), V_1(x, y, \max(0, z - \delta^u)) \rangle$ for all $x \in \mathbf{x}$, $y \in \mathbf{y}$ and $z \in \mathbf{z}$. A summary of all cases is illustrated in Figure 7.43.

Surface detection algorithm   The segmentation of optimal surfaces is formulated as computing a minimum closed set in a geometric graph constructed from I. The time bound of the algorithm is independent of both the smoothness parameters ($\Delta_{\mathbf{x}_i}$ and $\Delta_{\mathbf{y}_i}$, $i = 1, \ldots, k$) and the surface separation parameters ($\delta^l_{i,i+1}$ and $\delta^u_{i,i+1}$, $i = 1, \ldots, k-1$). Note that improper specifications of these constraints may lead to an infeasible problem, i.e., the constraints are self-conflicting and thus no k surfaces satisfying all the constraints exist in I.

In the single-surface case, for any feasible surface S in I, the subset of nodes on or below S in G, namely $Z = \{ V(\mathbf{x}, \mathbf{y}, z) \,|\, z \leq S(x, y) \}$, forms a closed set in G. It can be observed that if $V(x, y, z)$ is in the closed set Z, then all nodes below it on $Col(x, y)$ are also in Z. Moreover, due to the node cost assignments in equation (7.74), the costs of S and Z are equal. In fact, as proven in [Wu and Chen, 2002], any feasible S in I uniquely corresponds to a nonempty closed set Z in G with the same cost. This is a key observation to transforming the optimal surface problem into seeking a minimum closed set in G.

Computation of a minimum-cost *nonempty* closed set Z^* in G is a well studied problem in graph theory. Z^* in G can be obtained by computing a minimum s–t cut in a related graph G_{st} [Hochbaum, 2001; Wu and Chen, 2002], Let V^+ and V^- denote the sets of nodes in G with non-negative and negative costs, respectively. Define a new directed graph $G_{st} = (V \cup \{s, t\}, E \cup E_{st})$. An infinite cost is assigned to each arc in E. E_{st} consists of the following arcs: The source s is connected to each node $v \in V^-$ by a directed arc of cost $-w(v)$; every node $v \in V^+$ is connected to the sink t by a directed arc of cost $w(v)$. Let (S, T) denote a finite-cost s–t cut in G_{st}, and $c(S, T)$ denote the total cost of the cut. It was shown that

$$c(S, T) = -w(V^-) + \sum_{v \in S - \{s\}} w(v), \tag{7.78}$$

where $w(V^-)$ is fixed and is the cost sum of all nodes with negative costs in G. Since $S \setminus \{s\}$ is a closed set in G [Hochbaum, 2001], the cost of a cut (S, T) in G_{st} and the cost of the corresponding closed set in G differ by a constant. Hence, the source set $S^* \setminus \{s\}$ of a minimum cut in G_{st} corresponds to a minimum closed set Z^* in G. Because the graph G_{st} has $\mathcal{O}(kn)$ nodes and $\mathcal{O}(kn)$ arcs, the minimum closed set Z^* in G can be computed in $T(kn, kn)$ time.

For the multiple surface case, the optimal k surfaces correspond to the upper envelope of the minimum closed set Z^*. For each i ($i = 1, \ldots, k$), the subgraph G_i is used to search for the target surface S_i. For every $x \in \mathbf{x}$ and $y \in \mathbf{y}$, let $V_i^B(x, y)$ be the subset of nodes in both Z^* and the (x, y)-column $Col_i(x, y)$ of G_i, i.e., $V_i^B(x, y) = Z^* \cap Col_i(x, y)$. Denote by $V_i(x, y, z^*)$ the node in $V_i^B(x, y)$ with the largest $\mathbf{z}$-coordinate. Then, voxel $I(x, y, z^*)$ is on the i-th optimal surface S_i^*. In this way, the minimum closed set Z^* of G uniquely defines the optimal k surfaces $\{S_1^*, \ldots, S_k^*\}$ in I.

Algorithm 7.9: Multiple optimal surface segmentation

1. Determine parameters representing a priori knowledge about the number of surfaces and the hard and soft segmentation constraints: k, $\Delta_{\mathbf{x}}$, $\Delta_{\mathbf{y}}$, δ^l, δ^u, cost function(s).

2. Construct graph $G_{st} = (V \cup \{s, t\}, E \cup E_{st})$.

3. Compute the minimum s–t cut (S^*, T^*) in G_{st}.

4. Recover the k optimal surfaces from $S^* \setminus \{s\}$.

Cost functions   Designing appropriate cost functions is of paramount importance for any graph-based segmentation method. In real-world problems, the cost function usually reflects either a region-based or edge-based property of the surface to be identified.

Edge-based cost functions   A typical edge-based cost function aims to position the boundary surface accurately in the volumetric image; several alternative cost functions were presented in Section 6.2.4. An advanced version of an edge-based cost function may utilize a combination of the first and second derivatives of the image intensity function [Sonka et al., 1997], and may consider preferred directions of the identified surface. The combination of the first and second derivatives permits fine-tuning of the cost function to maximize border positioning accuracy.

Let the analyzed volumetric image be $I(\mathbf{x}, \mathbf{y}, \mathbf{z})$. Then, the cost $c(x, y, z)$ assigned to the image voxel $I(x, y, z)$ can be constructed as:

$$c(x, y, z) = -e(x, y, z) \cdot p(\phi(x, y, z)) + q(x, y, z), \tag{7.79}$$

where $e(x, y, z)$ is a raw edge response derived from the first and second derivatives of the image, $\phi(x, y, z)$ denotes the edge orientation at location (x, y, z) that is reflected in the cost function via an orientation penalty $p(\phi(x, y, z))$. $0 < p < 1$ when $\phi(x, y, z)$ falls outside a specific range around the preferred edge orientation; otherwise $p = 1$. A position penalty term $q(x, y, z) > 0$ may be incorporated so that a priori knowledge about expected border position can be modeled:

$$e(x, y, z) = (1 - |\omega|) \cdot (I * \mathcal{M}_{\text{first derivative}})(x, y, z) \;\dotplus\; \omega \cdot (I * \mathcal{M}_{\text{second derivative}})(x, y, z).$$

The $\dotplus$ operator stands for a pixel-wise summation, and $*$ is a convolution operator. The weighting coefficient $-1 \leq \omega \leq 1$ controls the relative strength of the first and second derivatives, allowing accurate edge positioning. The values of ω, p, q may be determined from a desired boundary surface positioning information in a training set of images; values of ω are frequently scale dependent.

Region based cost functions   The object boundaries do not have to be defined by gradients as discussed in Section 7.3 (and shown in 2D in equation 7.45). In 3D, the Chan-Vese functional is

$$C(S, a_1, a_2) = \int_{\text{inside}(S)} (I(x, y, z) - a_1)^2 \, dx \, dy \, dz + \int_{\text{outside}(S)} (I(x, y, z) - a_2)^2 \, dx \, dy \, dz.$$

As in equation (7.45), a_1 and a_2 are the mean intensities in the interior and exterior of the surface S and the energy $C(S, a_1, a_2)$ is minimized when S coincides with the object boundary, and best separates the object and background with respect to their mean intensities.

The variance functional can be approximated using a per-voxel cost model, and in turn be minimized using a graph-based algorithm. Since the application of the Chan–Vese cost functional may not be immediately obvious, consider a single-surface segmentation example. Any feasible surface uniquely partitions the graph into two disjoint subgraphs. One subgraph consists of all nodes that are on or below the surface, and the other consists of all nodes that are above the surface. Without loss of generality, let a node on or below a feasible surface be considered as being inside the surface; otherwise let it be outside the surface. Then, if a node $V(x', y', z')$ is on a feasible surface S, then the nodes $V(x', y', z)$ in $Col(x', y')$ with $z \leq z'$ are all inside S, while the nodes $V(x', y', z)$ with $z > z'$ are all outside S. Hence, the voxel cost $c(x', y', z')$ is assigned as the sum of the inside and outside variances computed in the column $Col(x', y')$, as follows

$$c(x', y', z') = \sum_{z \leq z'} (I(x', y', z) - a_1)^2 + \sum_{z > z'} (I(x', y', z) - a_2)^2. \tag{7.80}$$

Then, the total cost of S will be equal to cost $C(S, a_1, a_2)$ (discretized on the grid $(\mathbf{x}, \mathbf{y}, \mathbf{z})$). However, the constants a_1 and a_2 are not easily obtained, since the surface is not well-defined before the global optimization is performed. Therefore, the knowledge of which part of the graph is inside and outside is unavailable. Fortunately, the graph construction guarantees that if $V(x', y', z')$ is on S, then the nodes $V(\mathbf{x}, \mathbf{y}, \mathbf{z_1})$ with $\mathbf{z_1} \equiv \{z \mid z \leq \max(0, z' - |x - x'|\Delta_\mathbf{x} - |y - y'|\Delta_\mathbf{y})\}$ are in the closed set Z corresponding to S. Accordingly, the nodes $V(\mathbf{x}, \mathbf{y}, \mathbf{z_2})$ with $\mathbf{z_2} \equiv \{z \mid z' + |x - x'|\Delta_\mathbf{x} + |y - y'|\Delta_\mathbf{y} < z < Z\}$ must not be in Z. This implies that if the node $V(x', y', z')$ is on a feasible surface S, then the nodes $V(\mathbf{x}, \mathbf{y}, \mathbf{z_1})$ are inside S, while the nodes $V(\mathbf{x}, \mathbf{y}, \mathbf{z_2})$ are outside S.

Consequently, $\hat{a}_1(x', y', z')$ and $\hat{a}_2(x', y', z')$ can be computed, that are approximations of the constants a_1 and a_2 for each voxel $I(x', y', z')$

$$\hat{a}_1(x', y', z') = \operatorname{mean}\big(I(\mathbf{x}, \mathbf{y}, \mathbf{z_1})\big),$$ (7.81)

$$\hat{a}_2(x', y', z') = \operatorname{mean}\big(I(\mathbf{x}, \mathbf{y}, \mathbf{z_2})\big).$$ (7.82)

The estimates are then used in equation (7.80) instead of a_1 and a_2.

Extensions   The LOGISMOS approach is under continuing development and a number of extensions to the original have been reported. Simultaneous segmentation of multiple surfaces belonging to multiple objects appeared in [Yin et al., 2010; Song et al., 2010a]. The graph-based image segmentation approach presented above utilizes node-based costs. To allow incorporation of surface shape-priors to influence resulting segmentations, local costs must be associated with graph arcs rather than nodes. An arc-based graph segmentation approach was introduced in [Song et al., 2010b]. One of the frequently occurring segmentation problems is simultaneous segmentation of mutually-interacting regions and surfaces: a solution to this task that combines LOGISMOS with the graph cut approach (Section 7.6) is given in [Song et al., 2011]. A surface segmentation approach simultaneously considering image data from two or more registered image sources was reported in [Han et al., 2011b]. The **Just-Enough-Interaction** (JEI) paradigm achieves image segmentation in a sequence of two main steps—automated image segmentation followed by expert-guided modifications [Sun et al., 2013b,a]. The goal of this two-step process is to achieve sufficient segmentation correctness in all analyzed cases, even if the initial automated segmentation is locally imperfect. As mentioned in Section 7.6, graph s–t cut optimization can be applied iteratively without restarting the optimization process from scratch. This property of the s–t cut graph optimization is utilized when LOGISMOS is employed in both the first and second steps of the JEI approach. Once LOGISMOS produces the initial automated segmentation, user interactions can identify desirable surface locations in areas of local inaccuracy. These interactions are used to locally modify the respective local/regional graph costs, and a new graph optimization solution can be obtained iteratively and very efficiently in close to real time after each such interaction. As a result, the two-step method uses LOGISMOS in both steps and contributes to the resulting surface detection by employing a highly efficient user-guided approach [Sun et al., 2013b,a]. In addition to image segmentation, the LOGISMOS approach can also be used for image and video resizing and multi-piece image stitching [Han et al., 2011a].

Examples   To demonstrate the method, consider first segmenting a simple but difficult to segment computer-generated volumetric image shown in Figure 7.44a. This image

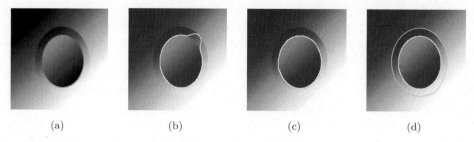

Figure 7.44: Single-surface versus coupled-surfaces. (a) Cross section of the original image. (b) Single surface detection using standard edge-based cost function. (c) Single surface detection using the algorithm and a cost function with a shape term. (d) Double-surface segmentation. © *Cengage Learning 2015*.

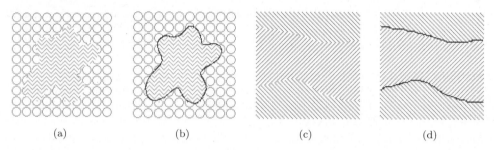

Figure 7.45: Segmentation using the minimum-variance cost function. (a,c) Original images. (b,d) The segmentation results. © *Cengage Learning 2015*.

consists of 3 identical slices stacked together to form a 3D volume—the gradual change of intensity causes the gradient strengths to locally vanish. Consequently, border detection using an edge-based cost function fails locally (Figure 7.44b). Using a cost function that includes a shape term produces a good result (Figure 7.44c). Figure 7.44d demonstrates the method's ability to segment both borders of the sample image.

Figure 7.45 presents segmentation examples obtained using the minimum-variance cost function in images with no apparent edges. The objects and background were differentiated by their respective textures. In Figure 7.45, curvature and edge orientation were used instead of original image data [Chan and Vese, 2001]. The two boundaries in Figure 7.45c,d were segmented simultaneously.

The LOGISMOS method has been used in a number of medical image analysis applications involving volumetric medical images from CT, MR, and ultrasound scanners. Figure 7.46 shows a comparison of segmentation performance in human pulmonary CT images. To demonstrate the ability of handling more than two interacting surfaces, four surfaces of excised human ilio-femoral specimens–lumen, intima-media (internal elastic lamina (IEL)), media-adventitia (external elastic lamina (EEL)), and the outer wall– were segmented in vascular MR images. The optimal multiple-surface segmentation clearly outperformed the previously used 2D approach [Yang et al., 2003] and did not require any interactive guidance (Figure 7.47). A number of successful applications of the LOGISMOS approach includes, for example, simultaneous segmentation of six surfaces belonging to three mutually interacting objects—segmentation of the bone and cartilage surfaces of the knee joint [Yin et al., 2010], Figure 7.48; segmentation of 11 reti-

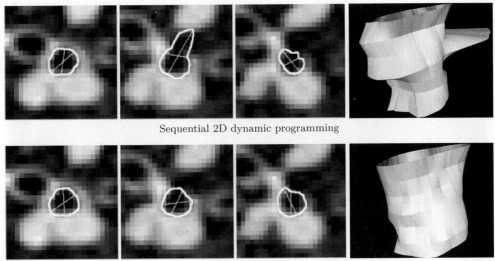

Sequential 2D dynamic programming

3D single-surface segmentation

Figure 7.46: Comparison of 2D and 3D inner airway wall segmentation results. A preliminary airway tree segmentation is shown in Figure 7.21. The three bottom and top left panels demonstrate resampling of airway segments to obtain orthogonal slices on which the border detection is performed. Results of 2D slice-by-slice dynamic programming approach in three consecutive slices together with 3D surface rendering of the entire segment (10 slices) is shown in the upper row. The bottom row shows the same segment with the luminal surface detected using the optimal 3D graph searching approach. Note the failure of the 2D approach in one of the slices. © *Cengage Learning 2015.*

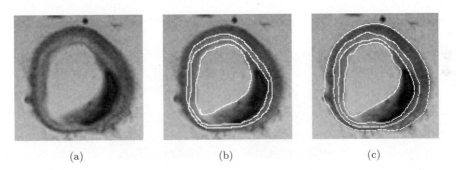

(a)   (b)   (c)

Figure 7.47: Multi-surface segmentation of arterial wall and plaque in volumetric MR images. (a) Original MR image of femoral artery cross section–the volumetric 3D image consisted of 16 cross sections. (b) Three manually identified wall layer borders. (c) Four computer-detected surfaces of plaque and wall layers. © *Cengage Learning 2015.*

nal layer surfaces from optical coherence tomography (OCT) images of human retinas [Abramoff et al., 2010]; magnetic resonance and ultrasound segmentation of cardiac chambers [Zhang et al., 2010], multi-modality segmentation of cancer tumors from Positron Emission Tomography and X-ray CT [Han et al., 2011b]; as well as motion-artifact reduction for 4D X-ray CT [Han et al., 2011a]. The *Just-Enough-Interaction* extension to the LOGISMOS method is finding applicability in 3D and 4D segmentations of pathologic medical images, see Figure 7.49 [Sun et al., 2013b,a].

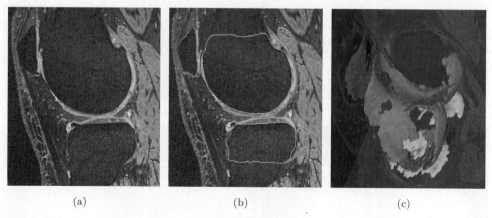

(a)   (b)   (c)

Figure 7.48: Three-dimensional segmentation of multiple surfaces in multiple objects. Six surfaces are simultaneously segmented using LOGISMOS (3 bone surfaces—femur, tibia, patella; 3 surfaces of corresponding cartilages). MR images are from a knee showing cartilage thinning and severe degeneration. (a) Original images, central slice shown from a 3D dataset. (b) The same slice with bone/cartilage segmentation. (c) Cartilage segmentation shown in 3D, note the cartilage thinning and "holes". *Yin, Y., Zhang, X., Williams, R., Wu, X., Anderson, D.D., Sonka, M,, "LOGISMOS-Layered Optimal Graph Image Segmentation of Multiple Objects and Surfaces: Cartilage Segmentation in the Knee Joint," Medical Imaging, IEEE Transactions, Volume: 29, Issue: 12, Digital Object Identifier: 10.1109/TMI.2010.2058861, Publication Year: 2010, Page(s): 2023-2037. A color version of this figure may be seen in the color inset—Plate 14.*

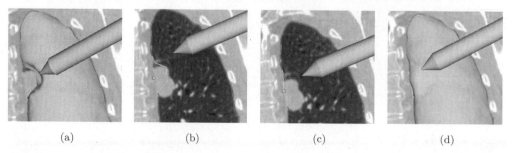

(a)   (b)   (c)   (d)

Figure 7.49: Just-Enough-Interaction paradigm. Interactive graph-based lung-surface segmentation refinement for a lung with a tumor adjacent to the boundary. (a) The user inspects the lung segmentation and locates a segmentation error. (b) In a cross section, the user selects a point on the correct boundary location (using a virtual pen). Note that the incorrect portion of the contour is highlighted in light blue and was automatically generated based on the selected point. (c,d) Refinement result after the refinement optimization step via recalculating maximum-flow with the interaction-affected costs. The corrected surface region is highlighted in green. *Sun S., Sonka M., and Beichel R., "Lung segmentation refinement based on optimal surface finding utilizing a hybrid desktop/virtual reality user interface," Computerized Medical Imaging and Graphics, 37(1):15-27, 2013b. A color version of this figure may be seen in the color inset—Plate 15.*

The optimal surface detection method remains fully compatible with conventional graph search. For example, when employed in 2D, it produces an identical result when the same objective function and hard constraints are employed. Consequently, many existing problems that were tackled using graph search in a slice-by-slice manner can be migrated to this framework with little or no change to the underlying objective function. Compared to other techniques, one of the major innovations is that the smoothness constraint can be modeled in a graph with a non-trivial arc construction. Thus, smoothness becomes a *hard constraint* that has a clear geometric meaning, as opposed to a *soft constraint* defined by a weighted energy term as discussed in Section 7.5.1. As a consequence, the objective function may become more transparent and easier to design. The smoothness thus modeled is not discontinuity-preserving, as desired by some problems in vision (e.g., stereo, multicamera scene construction). However, discontinuity-preservation is not always desirable. The presented ability to identify multiple coupled surfaces in an optimal way is a major advance in graph search-based segmentation.

7.8 Summary

- **Mean shift segmentation**

  - Mean shift segmentation is a non-parametric technique for the analysis of a complex multi-modal feature space and identification of feature clusters.

  - The only free parameters of the mean shift process are the size and shape of the region of interest, i.e., the multivariate density kernel estimator.

  - Density estimation is modified so that the density gradient is estimated.

  - For mean shift image segmentation, a 2-step sequence of discontinuity-preserving filtering and mean shift clustering is used.

- **Active contour models—snakes**

  - A snake is an energy minimizing spline—energy depends on shape and location within the image. Local energy minima correspond to desired image properties.

  - Snakes are parametric deformable models.

  - The energy functional which is minimized is a weighted combination of internal and external forces.

  - Gradient vector flow field increases the effective area of snake attraction decreasing the snake's sensitivity to initialization and allowing segmentation of concave boundaries.

- **Geometric deformable models**

  - Geometric deformable models represent developing surfaces by partial differential equations.

  - The movements of the propagating fronts are described by speed functions.

  - The evolving curves and/or surfaces are represented as level sets of higher dimensional functions yielding seamless treatment of topologic changes.

- **Fuzzy connectivity**

  - Fuzzy connectivity segmentation uses the hanging-togetherness property to identify image elements that form the same object. Rather than being crisp, the hanging togetherness is described using fuzzy logic.
  - Fuzzy affinity describes local fuzzy relationships.
  - Fuzzy connectedness is a global fuzzy relationship that assigns every pair of image elements a value based on the affinity values along all possible paths between these two image elements.

- **Simultaneous border detection**

  - Simultaneous border detection facilitates optimal identification of border pairs by finding an optimal path in a three-dimensional graph.
  - Information contained in the position of one border is used in identifying the position of the other border. After a cost function that combines edge information from the left and right borders has been defined, heuristic graph searching or dynamic programming methods can be used for optimal border detection.

- **Suboptimal surface detection**

  - Suboptimal surface detection uses multi-dimensional graph search to identify legal surfaces in three- or higher-dimensional image data.
  - Surface growing is based on dynamic programming and avoids the problem of combinatorial explosion by introducing local conditions that must be satisfied by all legal surfaces.

- **Direct graph cut segmentation**

  - Graph cuts solve a region-based segmentation problem by the use of minimum s–t cut / maximum flow combinatorial optimization algorithms.
  - Segmentation outcome is controlled by hard and soft constraints, and a cost function.
  - The minimum s–t cut problem is solved by finding a maximum flow from the source s to the sink t.

- **Optimal single and multiple surface segmentation**

  - Single and multiple interactive surfaces are identified by optimal graph searching in a transformed graph.
  - Combinatorial explosion in computation is avoided by transforming the problems into computing minimum s–t cuts.
  - Despite using graph-cut optimization, the method is different in principal from direct graph cut segmentation.
  - Multiple interacting surfaces can be identified by incorporating mutual surface-to-surface interrelationships as inter-surfaces arcs in $n+1$-dimensional graphs.

7.9   Exercises

Short-answer questions

S7.1 What is a probability density mode?

S7.2 Given a set of multidimensional samples, what is the result of the mean-shift procedure?

S7.3 Describe the principle of mean-shift segmentation.

S7.4 Give equations for the normal kernel, its profile, and its derivative.

S7.5 Give equations for the Epanechnikov kernel, its profile, and its derivative.

S7.6 What is a basin of attraction?

S7.7 Give an example of a useful internal snake energy and explain its aim and influence.

S7.8 Give an example of a useful external snake energy and explain its aim and influence.

S7.9 Design an image energy term of a snake to trace lines of gray level 128.

S7.10 Give a continuous snake evolution equation and describe its discretization in time.

S7.11 Give a continuous snake evolution equation and describe its discretization in space.

S7.12 Explain the conceptual difference between snakes and balloons.

S7.13 What is the purpose of the gradient vector flow field for active contour segmentation?

S7.14 What are the advantages and disadvantages of a level set representation?

S7.15 How should we choose the time step of a level set evolution?

S7.16 For Level Set 'speed functions'

    (a) Explain the main role the function in image segmentation.

    (b) Give a general expression for a function based on curvature and constant deformation.

    (c) Using this function, explain the behavior leading to convergence.

S7.17 Define fuzzy connectedness.

S7.18 Explain how an optimal pair of borders can be simultaneously detected using graph searching. How is the cost of a pair of border points determined from the underlying image data?

S7.19 Explain why simultaneous detection of two borders in a 2D image requires a 3D graph; sketch how such a graph may be constructed.

S7.20 Formulate binary segmentation as a problem of searching a minimum cut in a graph.

S7.21 Explain why optimal surface detection results in combinatorial explosion of the search space.

Problems

P7.1 Implement mean-shift discontinuity-preserving filtering (Algorithm 7.2) and demonstrate its image-smoothing performance on example images. Implement both gray-scale and color versions of the algorithm.

P7.2 Extend the method of Problem P7.1 to yield image segmentation (Algorithm 7.3).

P7.3 Formulate snake evolution as an energy minimization. Derive the corresponding Euler-Lagrange evolution equation.

P7.4 Design an internal energy term of a snake to facilitate closely tracing sharp corners.

P7.5 Design an image energy term of a snake to trace lines of gray-level $G = 128$.

P7.6 Develop a program for snake-based line detection; use the energy functional specified by equation (7.15). Test its behavior in

  (a) Ideal images of contrasting lines on a homogeneous background.

  (b) Images of incomplete contrasting lines on a homogeneous background.

  (c) Images with superimposed impulse noise of varying severity—can the adverse effect of noise be overcome be adjusting the parameters of the snake functional?

P7.7 Derive the relation between the level set function evolution in time and the normal speed of the isocontour.

P7.8 Explain the concept of hanging togetherness as used in fuzzy connectivity based image segmentation. Support your explanation by providing a sketch.

P7.9 Implement image segmentation based on absolute fuzzy connectivity (Algorithm 7.4). Apply to gray-scale and color images. Discuss this method's performance in comparison with other implemented approaches.

P7.10 Implement a method for object detection based on fuzzy object extraction (Algorithms 7.5 and 7.6). Apply to gray-scale and color images. Discuss this method's performance in comparison with other implemented approaches.

P7.11 Describe the main principles of an augmenting path (Ford-Fulkerson) maximum flow search algorithm.

P7.12 Using publicly available code (using the maximum flow or another approach), deploy and study Boykov's graph cut approach to image segmentation. Apply to gray-scale and color images. Discuss this method's performance in comparison with other implemented approaches.

P7.13 Explain graph construction for multi-surface image segmentation used in the LOGIS-MOS approach. Explain how the graph is, or may be, constructed for multi-object LOGISMOS segmentation. Explain the role of the electric lines of force (ELF) to construct the graph columns—what other approaches may be relevant instead of the ELF approach?

P7.14 Considering LOGISMOS, sketch a graph that can be used for simultaneous segmentation of 2 borders in a two-dimensional 3×6 image (width of 3 pixels, height of 6 pixels) for which the minimum distance of the two borders is 1 pixel and the maximum is 2 pixels. (Borders run in the left-to-right direction through the image).

P7.15 Apply implementations of algorithms in this Chapter (your own, or downloaded from the Web) to a selection of the images generated as part of the Exercises of Chapter 6 (Problem P6.1). Form a qualitative view of success for each; also, deploy the formal segmentation evaluation developed during work on Section 6.5.

P7.16 Make yourself familiar with solved problems and **Matlab** implementations of selected algorithms provided in the corresponding chapter of the **Matlab Companion** to this text [Svoboda et al., 2008]. The **Matlab Companion** homepage http://visionbook.felk.cvut.cz offers images used in the problems, and well-commented **Matlab** code is provided for educational purposes.

P7.17 Use the **Matlab Companion** [Svoboda et al., 2008] to develop solutions to additional exercises and practical problems provided there. Implement your solutions using **Matlab** or other suitable programming languages.

7.10   References

Abramoff M., Garvin M., and Sonka M. Retinal imaging and image analysis. *IEEE Reviews in Biomedical Engineering*, 3:169–208, 2010.

Adalsteinsson D. and Sethian J. A. The fast construction of extension velocities in level set methods. *J. Computational Physics*, 148:2–22, 1999.

Amini A., Tehrani S., and Weymouth T. Using dynamic programming for minimizing the energy of active contours in the presence of hard constraints. In *2nd International Conference on Computer Vision,* Tarpon Springs, FL, pages 95–99, Piscataway, NJ, 1988. IEEE.

Amini A., Weymouth T., and Jain R. Using dynamic programming for solving variational problems in vision. *IEEE Transactions on Pattern Analysis and Machine Intelligence*, 12 (9):855–867, 1990.

Angelini E., Otsuka R., Homma S., and Laine A. Comparison of ventricular geometry for two real time 3D ultrasound machines with three dimensional level set. In *Proceedings of the IEEE International Symposium on Biomedical Imaging (ISBI)*, volume 1, pages 1323–1326. IEEE, 2004.

Berger M. O. and Mohr R. Towards autonomy in active contour models. In *10th International Conference on Pattern Recognition,* Atlantic City, NJ, pages 847–851, Piscataway, NJ, 1990. IEEE.

Blake A. and Isard M. *Active Contours.* Springer, Berlin, 1998.

Bloch I. Fuzzy connectivity and mathematical morphology. *Pattern Recognition Letters*, 14: 483–488, 1993.

Boykov Y. and Funka-Lea G. Graph-cuts and efficient N-D image segmentation. *International Journal of Computer Vision*, 70:109–131, 2006.

Boykov Y. and Kolmogorov V. Computing geodesics and minimal surfaces via graph cuts. In *Proc. International Conference on Computer Vision (ICCV)*, pages 26–33, Nice, France, October 2003.

Boykov Y. and Kolmogorov V. An experimental comparison of min-cut/max-flow algorithms for energy minimization in computer vision. In *Third International Workshop on Energy Minimization Methods in Computer Vision and Pattern Recognition (EMMCVPR)*, Springer-Verlag, 2001.

Boykov Y. and Veksler O. Graph cuts in vision and graphics: Theories and applications. In Paragios N., Chen Y., and Faugeras O., editors, *Handbook of Mathematical Models in Computer Vision*, pages 79–96. Springer, New York, 2006.

Boykov Y. and Jolly M.-P. Interactive organ segmentation using graph cuts. In *Proc. Medical Image Computing and Computer-Assisted Intervention (MICCAI)*, pages 276–286, Pittsburgh, PA, USA, 2000.

Boykov Y. and Jolly M.-P. Interactive graph cuts for optimal boundary & region segmentation of objects in N-D images. In *Proc. International Conference on Computer Vision (ICCV)*, volume 1935-I, pages 105–112, July 2001.

Boykov Y. and Kolmogorov V. An experimental comparison of min-cut/max-flow algorithms for energy minimization in vision. *IEEE Transactions on Pattern Analysis and Machine Intelligence*, 26(9):1124–1137, 2004.

Boykov Y., Veksler O., and Zabih R. Fast approximate energy minimization via graph cuts. *IEEE Transactions on Pattern Analysis and Machine Intelligence*, 23(11):1222–1239, 2001.

Boykov Y., Kolmogorov V., Cremers D., and Delong A. An integral solution to surface evolution PDEs via geo-cuts. In *European Conference on Computer Vision (ECCV)*, pages 409–422, Graz, Austria, 2006. Springer.

Butenuth M. and Heipke C. Network snakes: graph-based object delineation with active contour models. *Machine Vision and Applications*, 23(1):91–109, 2012.

Carvalho B. M., Gau C. J., Herman G. T., and Kong T. Y. Algorithms for Fuzzy Segmentation. *Pattern Analysis & Applications*, 2:73–81, 1999.

Caselles V., Catte F., Coll T., and Dibos F. A geometric model for active contours in image processing. *Numer. Math.*, 66:1–31, 1993.

Caselles V., Kimmel R., and Sapiro G. Geodesic active contours. *International Journal of Computer Vision*, 22:61–79, 1997.

Chan T. F. and Vese L. A. Active contour without edges. *IEEE Trans. Image Processing*, 10 (2):266–277, 2001.

Charles A. H. and Porsching T. A. *Numerical Analysis of Partial Differential Equations*. Prentice Hall, Englewood Cliffs, NJ, 1990.

Cheng Y. Mean shift, mode seeking, and clustering. *IEEE Transactions on Pattern Analysis and Machine Intelligence*, 17:790–799, 1995.

Christoudias M., Georgescu B., and Meer P. Synergism in low level vision. In *Proc. ICPR*, pages 150–155, Quebec City, Canada, 2002. http://www.caip.rutgers.edu/riul/research/code/EDISON/index.html.

Cohen L. D. On active contour models and balloons. *CVGIP – Image Understanding*, 53(2): 211–218, 1991.

Cohen L. D. and Cohen I. Deformable models for 3D medical images using finite elements & balloons. In *Proceedings, IEEE Conference on Computer Vision and Pattern Recognition*, Champaign, IL, pages 592–598, Los Alamitos, CA, 1992. IEEE.

Cohen L. D. and Cohen I. Finite element methods for active contour models and balloons for 2D and 3D images. *IEEE Transactions on Pattern Analysis and Machine Intelligence*, 15: 1131–1147, 1993.

Comaniciu D. and Meer P. Mean shift: A robust approach toward feature space analysis. *IEEE Transactions on Pattern Analysis and Machine Intelligence*, 24:603–619, 2002.

Comaniciu D. and Meer P. Robust analysis of feature spaces: Color image segmentation. In *Proc. IEEE Conf. on Computer Vision and Pattern Recognition*, pages 750–755. IEEE, 1997.

Comaniciu D., Ramesh V., and Meer P. Real-time tracking of non-rigid objects using mean shift. In *Proc. IEEE Conf. on Computer Vision and Pattern Recognition, vol. II*, pages 142–149, Hilton Head Island, SC, 2000.

Comaniciu D., Ramesh V., and Meer P. The variable bandwidth mean shift and data-driven scale selection. In *8th Int. Conf. Computer Vision, vol. I*, pages 438–445, Vancouver, BC, Canada, 2001.

Connolly C. The relationship between colour metrics and the appearance of three-dimensional coloured objects. *Color Research and Applications*, 21:331–337, 1996.

Cook W. J., Cunningham W. H., and Pulleyblank W. R. *Combinatorial Optimization*. J Wiley, New York, 1998.

Dellepiane S. and Fontana F. Extraction of intensity connectedness for image processing. *Pattern Recognition Letters*, 16:313–324, 1995.

Dinic E. A. Algorithm for solution of a problem of maximum flow in networks with power estimation. *Soviet Math. Dokl*, 11:1277–1280, 1970.

Etoh M., Shirai Y., and Asada M. Active contour extraction based on region descriptions obtained from clustering. *Systems and Computers in Japan*, 24:55–65, 1993.

Falcao A. X., Stolfi J., Alencar d, and Lotufo R. The image foresting transform: Theory, algorithms, and applications. *IEEE Transactions on Pattern Analysis and Machine Intelligence*, 26:19–29, 2004.

Falcao A. X. and Udupa J. K. A 3D generalization of user-steered live-wire segmentation. *Medical Image Analysis*, 4:389–402, 2000.

Falcao A. X., Udupa J. K., and Miyazawa F. K. An ultra-fast user-steered image segmentation paradigm: Live wire on the fly. *IEEE Trans. Med. Imag.*, 19:55–62, 2000.

Felzenszwalb P. F. and Huttenlocher D. P. Efficient graph-based image segmentation. *Intl. Journal of Computer Vision*, 59:167–181, 2004.

Figueiredo M. A. T., Leitao J. M. N., and Jain A. K. Adaptive B-splines and boundary estimation. In *Computer Vision and Pattern Recognition*, pages 724–730, Los Alamitos, CA, 1997. IEEE Computer Society.

Ford L. R. and Fulkerson D. R. Maximal flow through a network. *Canadian Journal of Mathematics*, 8:399–404, 1956.

Ford L. R. and Fulkerson D. R. *Flows in Networks*. Princeton University Press, Princeton, NJ, 1962.

Frank R. J., McPherson D. D., Chandran K. B., and Dove E. L. Optimal surface detection in intravascular ultrasound using multi-dimensional graph search. In *Computers in Cardiology*, pages 45–48, Los Alamitos, CA, 1996. IEEE.

Fukunaga K. and Hostetler L. D. The estimation of the gradient of a density function, with applications in pattern recognition. *IEEE Transactions on Information Theory*, 21:32–40, 1975.

Geman S. and Geman D. Stochastic relaxation, Gibbs distributions, and the Bayesian restoration of images. *IEEE Transactions on Pattern Analysis and Machine Intelligence*, 6(6): 721–741, 1984.

Georgescu B., Shimshoni I., and Meer P. Mean shift based clustering in high dimensions: A texture classification example. In *9th Int. Conf. Computer Vision*, pages 456–463, Nice, France, 2003.

Goldberg A. V. and Rao S. Beyond the flow decomposition barrier. *Journal of the ACM*, 45: 783–797, 1998.

Goldberg A. V. and Tarjan R. E. A new approach to the maximum-flow problem. *Journal of the ACM*, 35:921–940, 1988.

Greig D., Porteous B., and Seheult A. Exact maximum a posteriori estimation for binary images. *J Royal Stat Soc - Series B*, 51:271–279, 1989.

Han D., Bayouth J., Song Q., Bhatia S., Sonka M., and Wu X. Feature guided motion artifact reduction with structure-awareness in 4D CT images. In *Proc. of 22nd International Conference on Information Processing in Medical Imaging (IPMI), Lecture Notes in Computer Science, Volume 6801*, pages 1057–1064, Kloster Irsee, Germany, 2011a. Springer.

Han D., Bayouth J., Song Q., Taurani A., Sonka M., Buatti J., and Wu X. Globally optimal tumor segmentation in PET-CT images: A graph-based co-segmentation method. In *Proc. of 22nd International Conference on Information Processing in Medical Imaging (IPMI), Lecture Notes in Computer Science, Volume 6801*, pages 245–256, Kloster Irsee, Germany, 2011b. Springer.

Heath M. T. *Scientific Computing, An Introductory Survey*. McGraw-Hill, New York, 2nd edition, 2002.

Herman G. T. and Carvalho B. M. Multiseeded segmentation using fuzzy connectedness. *IEEE Transactions on Pattern Analysis and Machine Intelligence*, 23(5):460–474, 2001.

Hermosillo G., Faugeras O., and Gomes J. Unfolding the cerebral cortex using level set methods. In *in Proc. 2nd Int. Conf. Scale-Space Theories Computer.*, volume 1682, page 58, 1999.

Hochbaum D. A new-old algorithm for minimum-cut and maximum-flow in closure graphs. *Networks*, 37:171–193, 2001.

Jermyn I. and Ishikawa H. Globally optimal regions and boundaries as minimum ratio cycles. *IEEE Transactions on Pattern Analysis and Machine Intelligence*, 23(10):1075–1088, 2001.

Jones T. N. and Metaxas D. N. Automated 3D Segmentation Using Deformable Models and Fuzzy Affinity. In *Information Processing in Medical Imaging Conference (IPMI)*, pages 113–126, 1997.

Karaolani P., Sullivan G. D., and Baker K. D. Active contours using finite elements to control local scale. In Hogg D. C. and Boyle R. D., editors, *Proceedings of the British Machine Vision Conference,* Leeds, UK, pages 472–480, London, 1992. Springer Verlag.

Kass M., Witkin A., and Terzopoulos D. Snakes: Active contour models. In *1st International Conference on Computer Vision,* London, England, pages 259–268, Piscataway, NJ, 1987. IEEE.

Kolmogorov V. and Boykov Y. What metrics can be approximated by geo-cuts, or global optimization of length/area and flux. In *International Conference on Computer Vision (ICCV), vol. I,* pages 564–571, Beijing, China, 2005. Springer.

Lam K. M. and Yan H. Fast greedy algorithm for active contours. *Electronics Letters*, 30:21–23, 1994.

Lei T., Udupa J. K., Saha P. K., and Odhner D. 3D MR angiographic visualization and artery-vein separation. In *Medical Imaging 1999 – Image Display, Vol. 3658*, pages 52–59. SPIE, Bellingham, WA, 1999.

Lei T., Udupa J. K., Saha P. K., and Odhner D. Separation of artery and vein in contrast-enhanced MRA images. In *Medical Imaging – Physiology and Function from Multidimensional Images*, pages 233–244. SPIE, Bellingham, WA, 2000.

Lezoray O. and Grady L. *Image Processing and Analysis With Graphs: Theory and Practice.* Digital imaging and computer vision series. Taylor & Francis, 2012.

Li K., Wu X., Chen D. Z., and Sonka M. Optimal surface segmentation in volumetric images — A graph-theoretic approach. *IEEE Transactions on Pattern Analysis and Machine Intelligence*, 28:119–134, 2006.

Li K., Wu X., Chen D. Z., and Sonka M. Globally optimal segmentation of interacting surfaces with geometric constraints. In *Proc. IEEE Conf. on Computer Vision and Pattern Recognition*, volume I, pages 394–399, June 2004a.

Li K., Wu X., Chen D. Z., and Sonka M. Efficient optimal surface detection: Theory, implementation and experimental validation. In *Proc. SPIE International Symposium on Medical Imaging: Image Processing*, volume 5370, pages 620–627, May 2004b.

Li Y., Sun J., Tang C.-K., and Shum H.-Y. Lazy snapping. *ACM Trans. Graphics (TOG), Special Issue: Proc. 2004 SIGGRAPH Conference*, 23:303–308, 2004c.

Liang J., McInerney T., and Terzopoulos D. United snakes. In *Proceedings of the Seventh IEEE International Conference on Computer Vision*, pages 933–940. IEEE, 1999.

Liang J., McInerney T., and Terzopoulos D. United snakes. *Medical Image Analysis*, 10:215–233, 2006.

Lin N., Yu W., and Duncan J. S. Combinative multi-scale level set framework for echocardiographic image segmentation. *Medical Image Analysis*, 7:529–537, 2003.

Malladi R., Sethian J. A., and Vemuri B. C. A topology-independent shape modeling scheme. In *Proc. SPIE Conference on Geometric Methods in Computer Vision II, Vol. 2031*, pages 246–258, San Diego CA, 1993. SPIE.

Malladi R., Sethian J., and Vemuri B. Shape Modeling with Front Propagation: A Level Set Approach. *IEEE Trans. on Pattern Analysis and Machine Intelligence*, 17:158–175, 1995.

McInerney T. and Terzopoulos D. A finite element based deformable model for 3D biomedical image segmentation. In *Proceedings SPIE, Vol. 1905, Biomedical Image Processing and Biomedical Visualization,* San Jose, CA, pages 254–269, Bellingham, WA, 1993. SPIE.

McInerney T. and Terzopoulos D. Topologically adaptable snakes. In *5th International Conference on Computer Vision,* Boston, USA, pages 840–845, Piscataway, NJ, 1995. IEEE.

Menet S., Saint-Marc P., and Medioni G. B-snakes: Implementation and application to stereo. In *Proceedings DARPA*, pages 720–726, 1990.

Mumford D. and Shah J. Optimal approximation by piecewise smooth functions and associated variational problems. *Commun. Pure Appl. Math*, 42:577–685, 1989.

Neuenschwander W., Fua P., Szekely G., and Kubler O. Initializing snakes (object delineation). In *Proceedings Computer Vision and Pattern Recognition*, pages 658–663, Los Alamitos, CA, 1994. IEEE.

Olstad B. and Tysdahl H. E. Improving the computational complexity of active contour algorithms. In *8th Scandinavian Conference on Image Analysis,* Tromso, pages 257–263, Oslo, 1993. International Association for Pattern Recognition.

Osher S. and Sethian J. A. Fronts propagating with curvature-dependent speed: Algorithms based on Hamilton-Jacobi Formulation. *Comput. Phys.*, 79:12–49, 1988.

Osher S. and Fedkiw R. *Level Set Methods and Dynamic Implicit Surfaces.* Springer-Verlag, first edition, 2002. 296 pages.

Osher S. and Paragios N., editors. *Geometric Level Set Methods in Imaging, Vision and Graphics.* Springer, 2003. ISBN 0-387-95488-0.

Pound M. P., French A. P., Wells D. M., Bennett J. M., and Pridmore T. P. CellSeT: Novel software to extract and analyze structured networks of plant cells from confocal images. *Plant Cell*, 2012.

Rice B. L. and Udupa J. K. Clutter-free volume rendering for magnetic resonance angiography using fuzzy connectedness. *International Journal of Imaging Systems and Technology*, 11: 62–70, 2000.

Ronfard R. Region-based strategies for active contour models. *International Journal of Computer Vision*, 13:229–251, 1994.

Rosenfeld A. The fuzzy geometry of image subsets. *Patter Recognition Letters*, 2:311–317, 1984.

Saha P. K., Udupa J. K., and Odhner D. Scale-based fuzzy connected image segmentation: Theory, algorithms, and validation. *Computer Vision and Image Understanding*, 77:145–174, 2000.

Saha P. K. and Udupa J. K. Iterative relative fuzzy connectedness and object definition: Theory, algorithms, and applications in image segmentation. In *Proceedings of the IEEE Workshop on Mathematical Methods in Biomedical Image Analysis (MMBIA'00)*, pages 254–269, 2000.

Saha P. K. and Udupa J. K. Relative fuzzy connectedness among multiple objects: Theory, algorithms, and applications in image segmentation. *Computer Vision and Image Understanding*, 82(1):42–56, 2001.

Sethian J. A. *An Analysis of Flame Propagation.* Ph.D. thesis, Dept. of Mathematics, University of California, Berkeley, CA, 1982.

Sethian J. A. Curvature and evolution of fronts. *Commun. Math. Phys.*, 101:487–499, 1985.

Sethian J. A. A review of recent numerical algorithms for hypersurfaces moving with curvature dependent speed. *J. Differential Geometry*, 31:131–161, 1989.

Sethian J. A. *Level Set Methods and Fast Marching Methods Evolving Interfaces in Computational Geometry, Fluid Mechanics, Computer Vision, and Materials Science*. Cambridge University Press, Cambridge, UK, second edition, 1999. 400 pages.

Shi J. and Malik J. Normalized cuts and image segmentation. *IEEE Transactions on Pattern Analysis and Machine Intelligence*, 22:888–905, 2000.

Siddiqi K., Lauzière Y. B., Tannenbaum A., and Zucker S. W. Area and length minimizing flows for shape segmentation. *IEEE Transactions on Image Processing*, 7:433–443, 1998.

Song Q., Liu Y., Liu Y., Saha P., Sonka M., and X.Wu. Graph search with appearance and shape information for 3-D prostate and bladder segmentation. In *Proceedings of 13th International Conference on Medical Image Computing and Computer-Assisted Intervention (MICCAI 2010), Lecture Notes in Computer Science, Volume 6363*, pages 172–180. Springer, 2010a.

Song Q., Wu X., Liu Y., Garvin M. K., and Sonka M. Simultaneous searching of globally optimal interacting surfaces with convex shape priors. In *CVPR 2010: IEEE Conference on Computer Vision and Pattern Recognition*, pages 2879–2886. IEEE, 2010b.

Song Q., Chen M., Bai J., Sonka M., and X.Wu. Surface-region context in optimal multi-object graph based segmentation: Robust delineation of pulmonary tumors. In *Proc. of 22nd International Conference on Information Processing in Medical Imaging (IPMI), Lecture Notes in Computer Science, Volume 6801*, pages 61–72, Kloster Irsee, Germany, 2011. Springer.

Sonka M., Wilbricht C. J., Fleagle S. R., Tadikonda S. K., Winniford M. D., and Collins S. M. Simultaneous detection of both coronary borders. *IEEE Transactions on Medical Imaging*, 12(3):588–599, 1993.

Sonka M., Winniford M. D., and Collins S. M. Robust simultaneous detection of coronary borders in complex images. *IEEE Transactions on Medical Imaging*, 14(1):151–161, 1995.

Sonka M., Reddy G. K., Winniford M. D., and Collins S. M. Adaptive approach to accurate analysis of small-diameter vessels in cineangiograms. *IEEE Trans. Med. Imag.*, 16:87–95, February 1997.

Staib L. H. and Duncan J. S. Boundary finding with parametrically deformable models. *IEEE Transactions on Pattern Analysis and Machine Intelligence*, 14(11):1061–1075, 1992.

Sun S., Sonka M., and Beichel R. Graph-based IVUS segmentation with efficient computer-aided refinement. *IEEE Transactions on Medical Imaging*, 32:In press, 2013a.

Sun S., Sonka M., and Beichel R. Lung segmentation refinement based on optimal surface finding utilizing a hybrid desktop/virtual reality user interface. *Computerized Medical Imaging and Graphics*, 37(1):15–27, 2013b.

Svoboda T., Kybic J., and Hlavac V. *Image Processing, Analysis, and Machine Vision: A MATLAB Companion*. Thomson Engineering, 2008.

Terzopoulos D., Witkin A., and Kass M. Symmetry-seeking models for 3D object reconstruction. In *1st International Conference on Computer Vision*, London, England, pages 269–276, Piscataway, NJ, 1987. IEEE.

Terzopoulos D., Witkin A., and Kass M. Constraints on deformable models: Recovering 3D shape and nonrigid motion. *Artificial Intelligence*, 36(1):91–123, 1988.

Thedens D. R., Skorton D. J., and Fleagle S. R. A three-dimensional graph searching technique for cardiac border detection in sequential images and its application to magnetic resonance image data. In *Computers in Cardiology*, pages 57–60, Los Alamitos, CA, 1990. IEEE.

Thedens D. R., Skorton D. J., and Fleagle S. R. Methods of graph searching for border detection in image sequences with application to cardiac magnetic resonance imaging. *IEEE Transactions on Medical Imaging*, 14:42–55, 1995.

Tosun D., Rettman M. E., Han X., Tao X., Xu C., Resnick S. N., Pham D. L., and Prince J. L. Cortical surface segmentation and mapping. *Neuroimage*, 23:S108–S118, 2004.

Tschirren J., Hoffman E. A., McLennan G., and Sonka M. Intrathoracic airway trees: segmentation and airway morphology analysis from low-dose CT scanss. *IEEE Transactions on Medical Imaging*, 24:1529–1539, 2005.

Udupa J. K. and Samarasekera S. Fuzzy connectedness and object definition: Theory, algorithms, and applications in image segmentation. *Graphical Models and Image Processing*, 58:246–261, 1996a.

Udupa J. K., Wei L., Samarasekera S., Miki Y., Buchem M. A. v, and Grossman R. I. Multiple sclerosis lesion quantification using fuzzy-connectedness principles. *IEEE Transactions on Medical Imaging*, 16:598–609, 1997.

Udupa J. K. and Samarasekera S. Fuzzy connectedness and object definition: Theory, algorithms, and applications in image segmentation. *Graphics Models and Image Processing*, 58 (3):246–261, 1996b.

Udupa J. K., Saha P. K., and Lotufo R. A. Fuzzy connected object definition in images with respect to co-objects. In *SPIE Conference on Image Processing, San Diego, California*, pages 236–245, 1999.

Wang S. and Siskind J. Image segmentation with ratio cut. *IEEE Transactions on Pattern Analysis and Machine Intelligence*, 25:675–690, June 2003.

Williams D. J. and Shah M. A fast algorithm for active contours and curvature estimation. *CVGIP – Image Understanding*, 55(1):14–26, 1992.

Witkin A., Terzopoulos D., and Kass M. Signal matching through scale space. *International Journal of Computer Vision*, 1(2):133–144, 1987.

Wu X. and Chen D. Z. Optimal net surface problems with applications. In *Proc. of the 29th International Colloquium on Automata, Languages and Programming (ICALP)*, pages 1029–1042, July 2002.

Wu Z. and Leahy R. An optimal graph theoretic approach to data clustering: Theory and its application to image segmentation. *IEEE Transactions on Pattern Analysis and Machine Intelligence*, 15:1101–1113, November 1993.

Wyszecki G. and Stiles W. S. *Color Science: Concepts and Methods, Quantitative Data and Formulae*. J Wiley, New York, 2nd edition, 1982.

Xu C. and Prince J. L. Snakes, Shapes, and Gradient Vector Flow. *IEEE Transactions on Image Processing*, Vol. 7:359 –369, 1998.

Xu C., Pham D. L., and Prince J. L. Image segmentation using deformable models. In Sonka M. and Fitzpatrick J. M., editors, *Handbook of Medical Imaging, Volume 2: Medical Image Processing and Analysis*, pages 129–174. SPIE, Bellingham, WA, 2000.

Xu Y., Olman V., and Uberbacher E. A segmentation algorithm for noisy images. In *Proc. IEEE International Joint Symposia on Intelligence and Systems*, pages 220–226, November 1996.

Yang F., Holzapfel G., Schulze-Bauer C., Stollberger R., Thedens D., Bolinger L., Stolpen A., and Sonka M. Segmentation of wall and plaque in in vitro vascular MR images. *The International Journal of Cardiac Imaging*, 19:419–428, October 2003.

Yang F., Mackey M. A., Ianzini F., Gallardo G., and Sonka M. Cell segmentation, tracking, and mitosis detection using temporal context. In Duncan J. S. and Gerig G., editors, *Medical*

Image Computing and Computer-Assisted Intervention - MICCAI 2005, 8th International Conference, Palm Springs, CA, USA, October 26-29, 2005, Proceedings, Part I, volume 3749 of *Lecture Notes in Computer Science*, pages 302–309. Springer, 2005.

Yezzi A., Kichenassamy S., Kumar A., Olver P., and Tennenbaum A. A geometric snake model for segmentation of medical imagery. *IEEE Transactions on Medical Imaging*, 16:199–209, 1997.

Yin Y., Zhang X., Williams R., Wu X., Anderson D., and Sonka M. LOGISMOS–layered optimal graph image segmentation of multiple objects and surfaces: Cartilage segmentation in the knee joint. *IEEE Transactions on Medical Imaging*, 29:2023–2037, 2010.

Zahn C. Graph-theoretic methods for detecing and describing Gestalt clusters. *IEEE Transactions on Computing*, 20:68–86, 1971.

Zhang H., Wahle A., Johnson R., Scholz T., and Sonka M. 4-D cardiac MR image analysis: Left and right ventricular morphology and function. *IEEE Transactions on Medical Imaging*, 29:350–364, 2010.

Chapter 8

Shape representation and description

The previous chapter was devoted to image segmentation methods and showed how to construct homogeneous regions of images and/or their boundaries. Recognition of image regions is an important step on the way to understanding image data, and requires an exact region description in a form suitable for a classifier (Chapter 9). This description should generate a numeric feature vector, or a non-numeric syntactic description word, which characterizes properties (for example, shape) of the region. Region description is the third of the four levels given in Chapter 4, implying that the description already comprises some abstraction—for example, 3D objects can be represented in a 2D plane and shape properties that are used for description are usually computed in two dimensions. If we are interested in a 3D object description, we have to process at least two images of the same object taken from different viewpoints (stereo vision), or derive the 3D shape from a sequence of images if the object is in motion. A 2D shape representation is sufficient in the majority of practical applications, but if 3D information is necessary—if, say, 3D object reconstruction is the goal— the object description task is much more difficult; these topics are introduced in Chapter 11. Here, we will limit our discussion to 2D shape features and proceed under the assumption that object descriptions result from the image segmentation process.

Defining the *shape* of an object is difficult. It is usually represented verbally or in figures, and people use terms such as *elongated, rounded, with sharp edges*, etc. Automatic processing requires us to describe even very complicated shapes precisely, and while many practical shape description methods exist, there is no generally accepted methodology. Further, it is not known what is important in shape. Shape description approaches have both positive and negative attributes; computer graphics [Woodwark, 1986] or mathematics [Lord and Wilson, 1984] use effective shape representations which are unusable in shape recognition [Juday, 1988] and vice versa. In spite of this, it is possible to find features common to most shape description approaches. Location and description of substantial variations in the first derivative of object boundaries often yield suitable information. Examples include alphanumeric optical character recognition (OCR), technical drawings, electro-cardiogram (ECG) curve characterization, etc.

Shape is an object property which has been carefully investigated and much may be found dealing with numerous applications—OCR, ECG analysis, electro-encephalogram (EEG) analysis, cell classification, chromosome recognition, automatic inspection, technical diagnostics, etc. Despite this variety, differences among many approaches are limited mostly to terminology. These common methods can be characterized from different points of view:

- **Input representation:** Object description can be based on boundaries (contour-based, external) or on knowledge of whole regions (region-based, internal).

- **Object reconstruction ability:** That is, whether an object's shape can or cannot be reconstructed from the description. Many varieties of shape-preserving methods exist which differ in the degree of precision with respect to object reconstruction.

- **Incomplete shape recognition:** That is, to what extent a shape can be recognized from a description if objects are occluded and only partial shape information is available.

- **Local/global description character:** Global descriptors can only be used if complete object data are available for analysis. Local descriptors describe local object properties using partial information. Thus, local descriptors can be used for description of occluded objects.

- **Mathematical/heuristic techniques:** For example, a mathematical technique is description based on the Fourier transform and a heuristic method may be 'elongatedness'.

- **Statistical or syntactic object description** (Chapter 9).

- **Robustness to translation, rotation, and scale transformations:** Shape description properties in different resolutions and poses.

The role of different description methods in image analysis and image understanding is illustrated by Figure 8.1.

Problems of scale (resolution) are common in digital images. Sensitivity to scale is even more serious if a shape description is derived, because shape may change substantially with image resolution. Contour detection may be affected by noise in high resolution, and small details may disappear in low resolution (see Figure 8.2). Therefore, shape has been studied in multiple resolutions which again causes difficulties with matching corresponding shape representations from different resolutions. Moreover, shape descriptions can change discontinuously. **Scale-space** approaches [Babaud et al., 1986; Witkin, 1986; Yuille and Poggio, 1986; Maragos, 1989] aim to obtain continuous shape descriptions if the resolution changes continuously. This approach is an extension of existing techniques, and more robust shape methods may result from developing and retaining their parameters over a range of scales.

In many tasks, it is important to represent classes of shapes properly, e.g., shape classes of apples, oranges, pears, bananas, etc. The **shape classes** should represent the generic shapes of the objects well. Obviously, shape classes should emphasize shape differences among classes, while the influence of variations within classes should not be reflected in the class description. Research challenges include development of approaches to automated learning about shape and reliable definition of shape classes (Section 8.4).

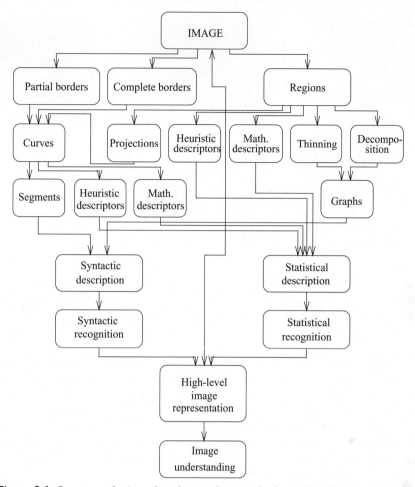

Figure 8.1: Image analysis and understanding methods. © *Cengage Learning 2015*.

Object representation and shape description methods discussed here are not an exhaustive list—we will try to introduce generally applicable methods. It is necessary to apply a problem-oriented approach to the solution of specific problems of description and recognition. This means that the following methods are appropriate for a large variety of descriptive tasks and the following ideas may be used to build a specialized, highly efficient method suitable for a particular problem description. Such a method will no longer be general since it will take advantage of a priori knowledge about the problem. This is how human beings can solve vision and recognition problems, by using highly specialized knowledge.

It should be understood that despite the fact that we are dealing with two-dimensional shape and its description, our world is three-dimensional and the same objects, if seen from different angles (or changing position/orientation in space), may form very different 2D projections (see Chapter 11). The ideal case would be to have a universal shape descriptor capable of overcoming these changes—to design projection-invariant descriptors. Consider an object with planar faces and imagine how many different 2D shapes may result from a given face if the position and 3D orientation changes with respect to an

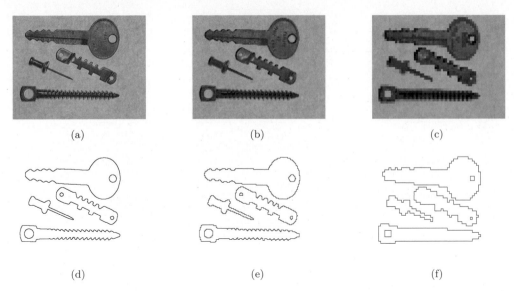

Figure 8.2: (a) Original image 640×480. (d) Contours of (a). (b) Original image 160×120. (e) Contours of (b). (c) Original image 64×48. (f) Contours of (c). © *Cengage Learning 2015*.

observer. In some special cases, such as circles which transform to ellipses, or planar polygons, projectively invariant features (called **invariants**) can be found. Unfortunately, no existing shape descriptor is perfect and in fact, most are far from it. Therefore, a careful choice of descriptors resulting from detailed analysis of the shape recognition problem should precede any implementation, and whether or not a 2D representation is capable of describing a 3D shape must also be considered. For some 3D shapes, their 2D projection may bear enough information for recognition—aircraft contours are a good example. In many other cases, objects must be seen from a specific direction to get enough descriptive information—human faces are such a case.

Object occlusion is another hard problem in shape recognition. However, the situation is easier here (if pure occlusion is considered, not combined with orientation variations yielding changes in 2D projections as discussed above), since visible parts of objects may be used for description. Here, the shape descriptor choice must be based on its ability to describe local object properties—if the descriptor gives only a global object description (e.g., object size, average boundary curvature, perimeter), such a description is useless if only a part of an object is visible. If a local descriptor is applied (e.g., description of local boundary changes), this information may be used to compare the visible part of the object to all objects which may appear in the image. Clearly, if object occlusion occurs, the local or global character of the shape descriptor must be considered first.

In Sections 8.2 and 8.3, descriptors are sorted according to whether they are based on boundary information (contour-based, external description) or whether information from regions is used (region-based, internal description). This classification of shape description methods corresponds to previously described boundary-based and region-based segmentation methods. However, both contour-based and region-based shape descriptors may be local or global and differ in sensitivity to translation, rotation, scaling, etc.

8.1   Region identification

Region identification is necessary for region description. One of the many methods for region identification is to label each region (or each boundary) with a unique integer; such identification is called **labeling** or **coloring** (also **connected component labeling**), and the largest integer label usually gives the number of regions in the image. Another method is to use a smaller number of labels (four is theoretically sufficient [Appel and Haken, 1977; Wilson and Nelson, 1990]), and ensure that no two neighboring regions have the same label; then information about some region pixel must be added to the description to provide full region reference. This information is usually stored in a separate data structure. Alternatively, mathematical morphology approaches (Chapter 13) may be used for region identification.

Assume that the segmented image R consists of m disjoint regions R_i (as in equation 6.1). The image R often consists of objects and a background

$$R_b^C = \bigcup_{i=1, i \neq b}^{m} R_i \,,$$

where R^C is set complement, R_b is considered background, and other regions are considered objects. Input to a labeling algorithm is usually either a binary or multi-level image, where background may be represented by zero pixels, and objects by non-zero values. A multi-level image is often used to represent the result, background being represented by zero values, and regions represented by their non-zero labels. A sequential approach to labeling a segmented image is:

Algorithm 8.1: 4-neighborhood and 8-neighborhood region labeling

1. First pass: Search the entire image R row by row and assign a non-zero value v to each non-zero pixel $R(i, j)$. v is chosen according to the labels of the pixel's neighbors, where the *neighboring* is defined by Figure 8.3.

   - If all neighbors are background pixels (with pixel value zero), $R(i, j)$ is assigned a new (and as yet) unused label.

   - If there is just one neighboring pixel with a non-zero label, assign this label to $R(i, j)$.

   - If there is more than one non-zero pixel among the neighbors, assign the label of any one to the labeled pixel. If the labels of any of the neighbors differ (*label collision*), store the label pair as being equivalent. Equivalence pairs are stored in a separate data structure—an equivalence table.

2. Second pass: All region pixels were labeled during the first pass, but some regions have pixels with different labels (due to label collisions). The image is scanned again, and pixels are re-labeled using the equivalence table information (for example, with the lowest value in an equivalence class).

Label collision is common—examples of image shapes experiencing this are U-shaped objects, mirrored E ($\exists$) objects, etc. (see Figure 8.3c). The equivalence table is a list of

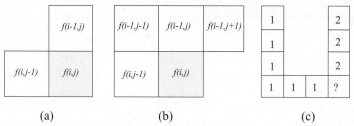

(a)   (b)   (c)

Figure 8.3: Region identification masks: (a) 4-connectivity. (b) 8-connectivity. (c) Label collision. © *Cengage Learning 2015*.

all label pairs present in an image; equivalent labels are replaced by a unique label in the second step. Since the number of label collisions is not known beforehand, it is necessary to pre-allocate or dynamically allocate sufficient memory to store the equivalence table. Further, if pointers are used for label specification, re-scanning the image during the second pass is not necessary since we can rewrite labels to which these pointers are pointing, which is much faster.

The algorithm is basically the same in 4-connectivity and 8-connectivity, the only difference being in the neighborhood mask shape (Figure 8.3b). It is useful to assign region labels incrementally to permit regions to be counted easily in the second pass. An example of partial results is given in Figure 8.4.

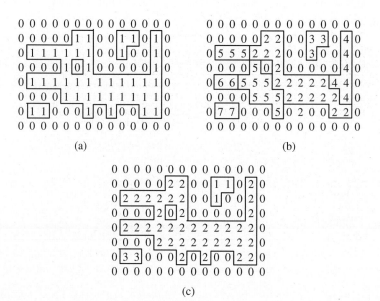

(c)

Figure 8.4: Object identification in 8-connectivity. (a), (b), (c) Algorithm steps. Equivalence table after step (b): 2-5, 5-6, 2-4. © *Cengage Learning 2015*.

While not commonly used, region identification can be performed on images that are not represented as straightforward matrices; the following algorithm [Rosenfeld and Kak, 1982] may be applied to images that are run length encoded (see Chapter 4).

Algorithm 8.2: Region identification in run length encoded data

1. First pass: Use a new label for each continuous run in the first image row that is not part of the background.

2. For the second and subsequent rows, compare positions of runs.

   - If a run in a row does not neighbor (in the 4- or 8-sense) any run in the previous row, assign a new label.

   - If a run neighbors precisely one run in the previous row, assign its label to the new run.

   - If the new run neighbors more than one run in the previous row, a label collision has occurred. Store the collision information and label the new run with the label of any one of its neighbors.

3. Second pass: Search the image row by row and re-label the image according to the equivalence table information.

If the image is represented by a quadtree, Algorithm 8.3 may be applied. (Details and the procedure for identifying neighboring leaf nodes can be found in [Rosenfeld and Kak, 1982; Samet, 1984]).

Algorithm 8.3: Quadtree region identification

1. First pass: Search quadtree nodes in a given order—e.g., beginning from the root and in NW, NE, SW, SE directions. Whenever an unlabeled non-zero leaf node is entered, a new label is assigned to it. Then search for neighboring leaf nodes in the E and S directions (plus SE in 8-connectivity). If those leaves are non-zero and have not yet been labeled, assign the label of the node from which the search started. If the neighboring leaf node has already been labeled, store the collision information.

2. Repeat step 1 until the whole tree has been searched.

3. Second pass: Re-label the leaf nodes according to the equivalence table.

The **region counting** task is closely related to the region identification problem and, as we have seen, counting can be an intermediate result of region identification. If it is only necessary to count regions a one-pass algorithm is sufficient [Rosenfeld and Kak, 1982; Atkinson et al., 1985].

8.2 Contour-based shape representation and description

Region borders are most commonly represented by mathematical form. **rectangular** pixel co-ordinates as a function of path length n. Other useful representations are (see Figure 8.5):

- **Polar** co-ordinates: border elements are represented as pairs of angle ϕ and distance r;

- **Tangential** co-ordinates: tangential directions $\theta(\mathbf{x}_n)$ of curve points are encoded as a function of path length n.

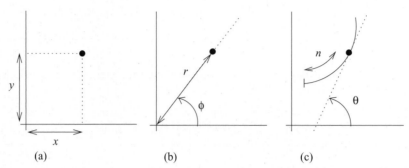

Figure 8.5: Co-ordinate systems. (a) Rectangular (Cartesian). (b) Polar. (c) Tangential. © *Cengage Learning 2015*.

8.2.1   Chain codes

Chain codes describe an object by a sequence of unit-size line segments with a given orientation (see Section 4.2.2), with the first element bearing information about its position to permit the region to be reconstructed. The process results in a sequence of numbers (see Figure 8.6); to exploit the position invariance of chain codes the first element is omitted. This definition is known as **Freeman's** code [Freeman, 1961]. Note that a chain code object description may easily be obtained as a by-product of border detection; see Section 6.2.3 for a description of border detection algorithms.

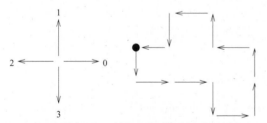

Figure 8.6: Chain code in 4-connectivity, and its derivative. Code: 3, 0, 0, 3, 0, 1, 1, 2, 1, 2, 3, 2; derivative: 1, 0, 3, 1, 1, 0, 1, 3, 1, 1, 3, 1. © *Cengage Learning 2015*.

If the chain code is used for matching, it must be independent of the choice of the first border pixel in the sequence. One possibility for normalizing the chain code is to find the pixel in the border sequence which results in the minimum integer number if the description chain is interpreted as a base 4 number—that pixel is then used as the starting pixel [Tsai and Yu, 1985]. A *mod 4* or *mod 8* difference code, called a chain code **derivative**, is another numbered sequence that represents relative directions of region boundary elements, measured as multiples of counter-clockwise 90° or 45° direction changes (Figure 8.6). Chain codes are very sensitive to noise, and arbitrary changes in scale and rotation may cause problems if used for recognition. The smoothed version of the chain code (averaged directions along a specified path length) is less noise sensitive.

8.2.2 Simple geometric border representation

These descriptors are based mostly on geometric properties of regions. Because of the discrete character of digital images, all of them are sensitive to image resolution.

Boundary length

Boundary length is an elementary region property, simply derived from a chain code representation. Vertical and horizontal steps have unit length, and the length of diagonal steps in 8-connectivity is $\sqrt{2}$. It can be shown that a boundary is longer in 4-connectivity, where a diagonal step consists of two rectangular steps with a total length of 2. A closed-boundary length (**perimeter**) can also be easily evaluated from run length or quadtree representations. Boundary length increases as the image raster resolution increases; on the other hand, region area is not affected by higher resolution and converges to some limit (see also the description of fractal dimension in Section 15.1.7). To provide continuous-space perimeter properties (area computation from the boundary length, shape features, etc.), it is better to define the region border as being the outer or extended border (see Section 6.2.3). If inner borders are used, some properties are not satisfied—e.g., the perimeter of a 1-pixel region is 4 if the outer boundary is used, and 1 if the inner is used.

Curvature

In the continuous case, curvature is defined as the rate of change of slope. In discrete space, the curvature description must be slightly modified to overcome difficulties resulting from smoothness violation.

The curvature scalar descriptor (also called boundary straightness) finds the ratio between the total number of boundary pixels (length) and the number of boundary pixels where the boundary direction changes significantly. The smaller the number of direction changes, the straighter the boundary. The algorithm is based on the detection of angles between line segments positioned b boundary pixels before and after the current pixel. The angle need not be represented numerically; rather, relative position of line segments can be used as a property. The parameter b determines sensitivity to local changes of direction (Figure 8.7). Curvature computed from chain codes can be found in [Rosenfeld, 1974], and tangential border representation is also suitable for curvature computation. Curvature values at all boundary pixels can be represented by a histogram; relative numbers then provide information on how common specific boundary direction changes are. Histograms of boundary angles, such as the β angle in Figure 8.7, can be built in a similar way—such histograms can be used for region description. If the distance b is varied, we can build three-dimensional histograms that can also be used for shape description.

There are many approaches to estimating curvature at each boundary point; see, for example, [Hermann and Klette, 2003; Kerautret et al., 2008]. The approach above depends on a fixed parameter b. Clearly, the values obtained do not always derive from the most relevant neighborhood, and it is intuitively obvious that adaptive determination of b would be desirable. When traveling sequentially around the boundary, such an adaptive specification can use different distances from predecessor (denoted bp) and successor (bs) points. Such an adaptive determination of distances bp and bs can be based, among other approaches, on approximation of digital straight segments [Coeurjolly et al., 2001; Hermann and Klette, 2003], see also Section 8.2.4.

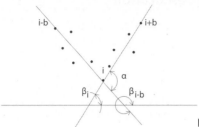

Figure 8.7: Curvature. © *Cengage Learning 2015.*

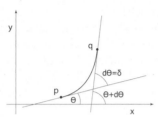

Figure 8.8: Tangent-based curvature estimation.
© *Cengage Learning 2015.*

Traveling along a planar curve, let p be a predecessor to point q and let δ be the angle between the positive tangent directions at these two points (Figure 8.8). Continuous curvature κ can then be defined as

$$\kappa(p) = \lim_{pq \to 0} \frac{\delta}{pq} \,. \tag{8.1}$$

In a discrete space, three points p_{i-bp}, p_i, p_{i+bs} are used for curvature calculation by determination of predecessor and successor digital straight segments. The algorithm can be summarized as:

Algorithm 8.4: Curvature estimation – HK2003 algorithm

1. For each point p_i of a boundary curve, determine distances bp and bs as lengths of the longest backward and/or forward digital straight segments originating at point p_i (Section 8.2.4).

2. Compute
$$l_p = ||p_{i-bp}, p_i|| \,, \ \ l_s = ||p_i, p_{i+bs}|| \,,$$

$$\Theta_p = \arctan\left(\frac{x_{i+bs} - x_i}{y_{i-bp} - y_i}\right) \,, \ \ \Theta_s = \arctan\left(\frac{x_{i+bs} - x_i}{y_{i+bs} - y_i}\right) \,,$$

$$\Theta = \frac{\Theta_p + \Theta_s}{2} \,,$$

$$\delta_p = |\Theta_p - \Theta| \,, \ \ \delta_s = |\Theta_s - \Theta| \,.$$

3. Curvature C_i at point p_i is then:

$$C_i = \frac{\delta_p}{2l_p} + \frac{\delta_s}{2l_s} \,.$$

This algorithm is a useful and simple approach yielding unsigned curvature values [Hermann and Klette, 2003, 2007]. Convexity and/or concavity can be obtained from analyzing coordinates of the points used for the calculations.

Bending energy

The bending energy (BE) of a border (curve) is the energy necessary to bend a rod to the desired shape, and is computed as a sum of squares of border curvature $c(k)$ over the border length L.

$$\text{BE} = \frac{1}{L} \sum_{k=1}^{L} c^2(k) \, . \tag{8.2}$$

Bending energy can easily be computed from Fourier descriptors using Parseval's theorem [Oppenheim et al., 1983; Papoulis, 1991]. To represent the border, Freeman's chain code or its smoothed version may be used; see Figure 8.9.

Signature

The signature of a region is obtained as a sequence of normal contour distances: The normal contour distance is calculated for each boundary element as a function of the path length. For each border point A, the shortest distance to an opposite border point B is sought in a direction perpendicular to the border tangent at point A (Figure 8.10. Note that *being opposite* is not a symmetric relation (compare Algorithm 6.15). Signatures are noise sensitive, but using smoothed signatures or signatures of smoothed contours reduces this. Signatures may be applied to the recognition of overlapping objects or whenever only partial contours are available [Vernon, 1987]. Position, rotation, and scale-invariant modifications based on gradient-perimeter and angle-perimeter plots are discussed in [Safaee-Rad et al., 1989].

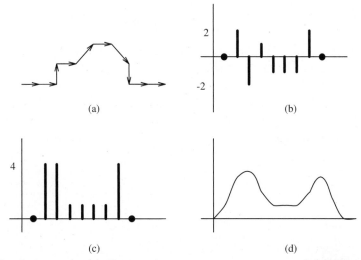

Figure 8.9: Bending energy. (a) Chain code 0, 0, 2, 0, 1, 0, 7, 6, 0, 0. (b) Curvature 0, 2, -2, 1, -1, -1, -1, 2, 0. (c) Sum of squares gives the bending energy. (d) Smoothed version. © *Cengage Learning 2015.*

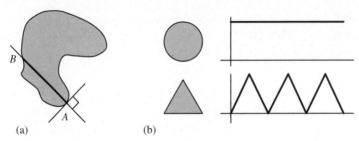

Figure 8.10: Signature. (a) Construction. (b) Signatures for a circle and a triangle. © *Cengage Learning 2015.*

Chord distribution

A line joining any two points of the region boundary is a chord, and the distribution of lengths and angles of all chords on a contour may be used for shape description. Let $b(x, y) = 1$ represent the contour points, and $b(x, y) = 0$ represent all other points. Note that for the continuous case, $b(x, y)$ must be represented by a Dirac δ function in contour point locations so that the integral in equation (8.3) is non-zero. The chord distribution can be computed (see Figure 8.11a) as

$$h(\Delta x, \Delta y) = \int \int b(x, y) \, b(x + \Delta x, y + \Delta y) \, dx \, dy \tag{8.3}$$

or in digital images as

$$h(\Delta x, \Delta y) = \sum_i \sum_j b(i, j) \, b(i + \Delta x, j + \Delta y) . \tag{8.4}$$

A rotation-independent radial distribution $h_r(r)$ is given by integrating over all angles (Figure 8.11b).

$$h_r(r) = \int_{-\pi/2}^{\pi/2} h(\Delta x, \Delta y) \, r \, d\theta , \tag{8.5}$$

where $r = \sqrt{\Delta x^2 + \Delta y^2}$, $\theta = \sin^{-1}(\Delta y / r)$. This function varies linearly with scale. The angular distribution $h_a(\theta)$ is independent of scale, while rotation causes a proportional offset.

$$h_a(\theta) = \int_0^{\max(r)} h(\Delta x, \Delta y) \, dr . \tag{8.6}$$

Combination of both distributions gives a robust shape descriptor [Cootes et al., 1992].

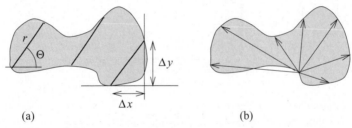

Figure 8.11: Chord distribution. © *Cengage Learning 2015.*

8.2.3   Fourier transforms of boundaries

Suppose C is a closed curve in the complex plane (Figure 8.12a). Traveling anti-clockwise along this curve keeping constant speed such that one circuit takes time 2π, a periodic complex function $z(t)$ is obtained, where t is a time variable: the function has period 2π. This permits a Fourier representation of $z(t)$ (see Section 3.2.4),

$$z(t) = \sum_n T_n \, e^{int} \, . \tag{8.7}$$

The coefficients T_n of the series are called the **Fourier descriptors** of C. It is more useful to consider the curve distance s in comparison to time

$$t = 2\pi s / L \, , \tag{8.8}$$

where L is the curve length. The Fourier descriptors T_n are given by

$$T_n = \frac{1}{L} \int_0^L z(s) \, e^{-i(2\pi/L)ns} \, \mathrm{d}s \, . \tag{8.9}$$

The descriptors are influenced by the curve shape and the initial point. Working with digital data, boundary co-ordinates are discrete and $z(s)$ is not continuous. Assume that $z(k)$ is a discrete version of $z(s)$, where 4-connectivity is used to get a constant sampling interval; the descriptors T_n can be computed from the discrete Fourier transform (Section 3.2) of $z(k)$

$$z(k) \longleftarrow \text{DFT} \longrightarrow T_n \, . \tag{8.10}$$

The Fourier descriptors can be invariant to translation and rotation if the co-ordinate system is appropriately chosen [Pavlidis, 1977; Lin and Chellappa, 1987]. In a handwritten alphanumeric character application [Shridhar and Badreldin, 1984], the character boundary was represented by co-ordinate pairs (x_m, y_m) in 4-connectivity, $(x_1, y_1) = (x_L, y_L)$. Then

$$a_n = \frac{1}{L-1} \sum_{m=1}^{L-1} x_m \, e^{-i[2\pi/(L-1)]nm} \, , \tag{8.11}$$

$$b_n = \frac{1}{L-1} \sum_{m=1}^{L-1} y_m \, e^{-i[2\pi/(L-1)]nm} \, . \tag{8.12}$$

The coefficients a_n, b_n are not invariant but after the transform

$$r_n = \left(|a_n|^2 + |b_n|^2 \right)^{1/2} \, , \tag{8.13}$$

r_n are translation and rotation invariant. To achieve a magnification invariance the descriptors w_n are used

$$w_n = r_n / r_1 \, . \tag{8.14}$$

The first 10–15 descriptors w_n are found to be sufficient for character description.

A closed boundary can be represented as a function of angle tangents versus the distance between the boundary points from which the angles were determined (Figure 8.12b). Let φ_k be the angle measured at the kth boundary point, and let l_k be the

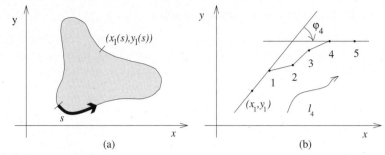

Figure 8.12: Fourier description of boundaries. (a) Descriptors T_n. (b) Descriptors S_n. © *Cengage Learning 2015.*

distance between the boundary starting point and the kth boundary point. A periodic function can be defined .

$$a(l_k) = \varphi_k + u_k \, , \qquad (8.15)$$

$$u_k = 2\pi \, l_k / L \, . \qquad (8.16)$$

The descriptor set is then

$$S_n = \frac{1}{2\pi} \int_0^{2\pi} a(u) \, e^{-inu} \, \mathrm{d}u \, . \qquad (8.17)$$

The discrete Fourier transform is used in all practical applications [Pavlidis, 1977].

The high-quality boundary shape representation obtained using only a few lower-order coefficients is a favorable property common to Fourier descriptors. The S_n descriptors have more high-frequency components present in the boundary function due to more significant changes of tangent angles, and as a result, they do not decrease as fast as the T_n descriptors. In addition, the S_n descriptors are not suitable for boundary reconstruction since they often result in a non-closed boundary. A method for obtaining a closed boundary using S_n descriptors is given in [Strackee and Nagelkerke, 1983]. The T_n descriptor values decrease quickly for higher frequencies, and their reconstruction always results in a closed boundary. Moreover, the S_n descriptors cannot be applied for squares, equilateral triangles, etc. unless the solution methods introduced in [Wallace and Wintz, 1980] are applied.

Fourier descriptors can also be used for calculation of region area, location of centroid, and computation of second-order moments [Kiryati and Maydan, 1989]. Fourier descriptors are a general technique, but problems with describing local information exist. A modified technique using a combined frequency-position space that deals better with local curve properties exists, another modification that is invariant under rotation, translation, scale, mirror reflection, and shifts in starting points is discussed in [Krzyzak et al., 1989]. Conventional Fourier descriptors cannot be used for recognition of occluded objects. Nevertheless, classification of partial shapes using Fourier descriptors is introduced in [Lin and Chellappa, 1987]. Boundary detection and description using elliptic Fourier decomposition of the boundary is described in [Staib and Duncan, 1992].

8.2.4   Boundary description using segment sequences

Boundaries (and curves) may also be described by **segments** with specified properties. If the segment type is known for all segments, the boundary can be described as a chain of segment types, a code word consisting of representatives of a type alphabet—an example is given in Figure 8.15. This sort of description is suitable for syntactic recognition (see Section 9.4). A trivial segment chain is used to obtain the Freeman code description discussed in Section 8.2.1.

A **polygonal representation** approximates a region by a polygon, the region being represented using its vertices. They are obtained as a result of a simple boundary segmentation, and boundaries can be approximated with varying precision; if a more precise description is necessary, a larger number of line segments may be employed. Any two boundary points x_1, x_2 define a line segment, and a sequence of points x_1, x_2, x_3 represents a chain of line segments—from the point x_1 to the point x_2, and from x_2 to x_3. If $x_1 = x_3$, a closed boundary results. There are many types of digital straight-segment (DSS) boundary representations [Pavlidis, 1977; Lindenbaum and Bruckstein, 1993; Debled-Rennesson and Reveillès, 1995]; the problem lies in determining the location of boundary vertices, one solution to which is to apply a split-and-merge algorithm. The merging step consists of going through a set of boundary points and adding them to a straight segment as long as a straightness criterion is satisfied. If the straightness characteristic of the segment is lost, the last connected point is marked as a vertex and construction of a new straight segment begins. This general approach has many variations [Pavlidis, 1977].

Boundary vertices can be detected as boundary points with a significant change of boundary direction using the curvature (boundary straightness) criterion (see Section 8.2.2). This approach works well for boundaries with rectilinear boundary segments.

Another (suboptimal [Tomek, 1974]) method for determining the boundary vertices is a **tolerance interval approach** based on setting a maximum allowed difference e. Assume that point x_1 is the end point of a previous segment and so by definition the first point of a new segment. Define points x_2, x_3 positioned a distance e from the point x_1 to be rectilinear—x_1, x_2, x_3 are positioned on a straight line—see Figure 8.13. The next step is to locate a segment which can fit between parallels directed from points x_2 and x_3.

These methods are single-pass algorithms of boundary segmentation using a segment-growing approach. Often they do not result in the best possible boundary segmentation because the vertex which is located often indicates that the real vertex should have been

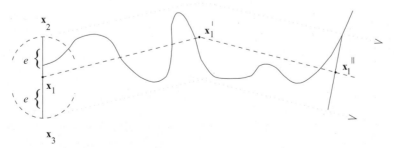

Figure 8.13: Tolerance interval. © *Cengage Learning 2015.*

located a few steps back. A splitting approach of segmenting boundaries into smaller segments can sometimes help, and the best results can be anticipated using a combination of both methods. If the splitting approach is used, segments are usually divided into two smaller segments until the new segments meet the final requirements [Duda and Hart, 1973; Pavlidis, 1977]. A simple procedure for splitting begins from end points x_1 and x_2 of a curve; these end points are connected by a line segment. The next step searches all the curve points for the curve point x_3 with the largest distance from the line segment. If the point located is within a preset distance between itself and the line segment, the segment x_1–x_2 is an end segment and all curve vertices are found, the curve being represented polygonally by vertices x_1 and x_2. Otherwise the point x_3 is set as a new vertex and the process is applied recursively to both resulting segments x_1–x_3 and x_3–x_2 (see Figure 8.14 and Section 6.2.7).

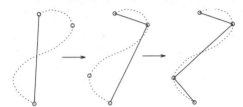

Figure 8.14: Recursive boundary splitting. © *Cengage Learning 2015.*

Boundary segmentation into segments of **constant curvature** is another possibility for boundary representation. The boundary may also be split into segments which can be represented by polynomials, usually of second order, such as circular, elliptic, or parabolic segments [Costabile et al., 1985; Rosin and West, 1989; Wuescher and Boyer, 1991]. Segments are considered as primitives for syntactic shape recognition procedures—a typical example is the syntactic description and recognition of chromosomes [Fu, 1974], where boundary segments are classified as convex segments of large curvature, concave segments of large curvature, straight segments, etc., as illustrated in Figure 8.15.

Other syntactic object recognition methods based on a contour partitioning into primitives from a specified set are described in [Jakubowski, 1990]. Partitioning of the contour using location of points with high positive curvatures (corners) is described in [Chien and Aggarwal, 1989], together with applications to occluded contours. A discrete curvature function based on a chain code representation of a boundary is used with a morphological approach to obtain segments of constant curvature in [Leymarie and Levine, 1989]. Contour partitioning using segments of constant intensity is suggested in

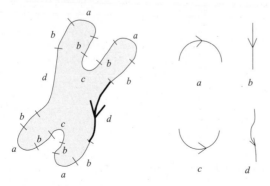

Figure 8.15: chain of boundary segments, code word: d, b, a, b, c, b, a, b, d, b, a, b, c, b, a, b. *Based on [Fu, 1974].*

[Marshall, 1989], and polygonal representation used in a *hypothesize and verify* approach to recognition of occluded objects may be found in [Koch and Kashyap, 1987].

We have noted that sensitivity of shape descriptors to scale (resolution) is an undesirable feature of many descriptors. Shape description varies with scale, and different results are achieved at different resolutions. This problem is no less important if a curve is to be divided into segments; some curve segmentation points exist in one resolution and disappear in others without any direct correspondence. Considering this, a **scale-space** approach to curve segmentation that guarantees a continuously changing position of segmentation points is a significant achievement [Babaud et al., 1986; Witkin, 1986; Yuille and Poggio, 1986; Maragos, 1989]. Here, only new segmentation points can appear at higher resolutions, and no existing segmentation points can disappear. This is in agreement with our understanding of varying resolutions; finer details can be detected in higher resolution, but significant details should not disappear if the resolution increases. This technique is based on application of a unique Gaussian smoothing kernel to a one-dimensional signal (e.g., a curvature function) over a range of sizes and the result is differentiated twice. To determine peaks of curvature, the zero-crossing of the second derivative is detected; the positions of zero-crossings give the positions of curve segmentation points. Different locations of segmentation points are obtained at varying resolution (different Gaussian kernel size). An important property of the Gaussian kernel is that the location of segmentation points changes continuously with resolution which can be seen in the **scale-space image** of the curve, Figure 8.16a. Fine details of the curve disappear in pairs with increasing size of the kernel, and two segmentation points always merge to form a closed contour, showing that any segmentation point existing in coarse resolution must also exist in finer resolution. Moreover, the position of a segmentation point is most accurate in finest resolution, and this position can be traced from coarse to fine resolution using the scale-space image. A multi-scale curve description can be represented by an **interval tree**, Figure 8.16b. Each pair of zero-crossings is represented by a rectangle, its position corresponding with segmentation point locations

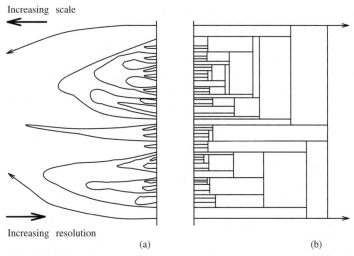

Figure 8.16: (a) Varying number and locations of curve segmentation points as a function of scale. (b) Curve representation by an interval tree. © *Cengage Learning 2015.*

on the curve, its height showing the lowest resolution at which the segmentation point can be detected. Interval trees can be used for curve decomposition in different scales, keeping the possibility of segment description using higher-resolution features.

Another scale-space approach to curve decomposition is the **curvature primal sketch** [Asada and Brady, 1986] (compare Section 11.1.1). A set of primitive curvature discontinuities is defined and convolved with first and second derivatives of a Gaussian in multiple resolutions. The curvature primal sketch is computed by matching the multi-scale convolutions of a shape. It then serves as a shape representation; shape reconstruction may be based on polygons or splines. Another multi-scale border-primitive detection technique that aggregates curve primitives at one scale into curve primitives at a coarser scale is described in [Saund, 1990]. A robust approach to multi-scale curve corner detection that uses additional information extracted from corner behavior in the whole multi-resolution pyramid is given in [Fermuller and Kropatsch, 1992].

8.2.5   B-spline representation

Representation of curves using piecewise polynomial interpolation to obtain smooth curves is widely used in computer graphics. B-splines are such curves whose shape is closely related to their control polygon—a chain of vertices giving a polygonal representation of a curve. B-splines of the third order are most common because this is the lowest order which includes the change of curvature. Splines have very good representation properties and are easy to compute: First, they change their shape less than their control polygon, and they do not oscillate between sampling points as many other representations do. Furthermore, a spline curve is always positioned inside a convex $n + 1$-polygon for a B-spline of the nth order—Figure 8.17. Second, the interpolation is local in character. If a control polygon vertex changes its position, a resulting change of the spline curve will occur in only a small neighborhood of that vertex. Third, methods of matching region boundaries represented by splines to image data are based on a direct search of original image data. These methods are similar to the segmentation methods described in Section 6.2.6. A spline direction can be derived directly from its parameters.

Let $\mathbf{x}_i$, $i = 1, \dots, n$ be points of a B-spline interpolation curve $\mathbf{x}(s)$. The s parameter changes linearly between points $\mathbf{x}_i$—that is, $\mathbf{x}_i = \mathbf{x}(i)$. Each part of a cubic B-spline curve is a third-order polynomial, meaning that it and its first and second derivatives are continuous. B-splines are given by

$$\mathbf{x}(s) = \sum_{i=0}^{n+1} \mathbf{v}_i \, B_i(s) \,, \tag{8.18}$$

where $\mathbf{v}_i$ are coefficients representing a spline curve, and $B_i(s)$ are base functions whose shape is given by the spline order. The coefficients $\mathbf{v}_i$ bear information dual to information about the spline curve points $\mathbf{x}_i$— $\{\mathbf{v}_i\}$ can be derived from $\{\mathbf{x}_i\}$ values and vice versa. The coefficients $\mathbf{v}_i$ represent vertices of the control polygon, and if there are n points $\mathbf{x}_i$, there must be $n+2$ points $\mathbf{v}_i$: two end points $\mathbf{v}_0$, $\mathbf{v}_{n+1}$ are specified by binding conditions. If the curvature of a B-spline is to be zero at the curve beginning and end,

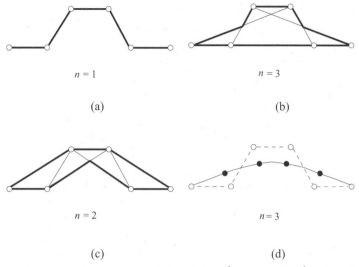

(a)   (b)

(c)   (d)

Figure 8.17: Convex $n+1$-polygon for a B-spline of the nth order. (d) 3rd-order spline. © *Cengage Learning 2015.*

then

$$\mathbf{v}_0 = 2\,\mathbf{v}_1 - \mathbf{v}_2\,,$$
$$\mathbf{v}_{n+1} = 2\,\mathbf{v}_n - \mathbf{v}_{n-1}\,. \tag{8.19}$$

If the curve is closed, then $\mathbf{v}_0 = \mathbf{v}_n$ and $\mathbf{v}_{n+1} = \mathbf{v}_1$.

The base functions are non-negative and are of local importance only. Each base function $B_i(s)$ is non-zero only for $s \in (i-2, i+2)$, meaning that for any $s \in (i, i+1)$, there are only four non-zero base functions for any i: $B_{i-1}(s)$, $B_i(s)$, $B_{i+1}(s)$, and $B_{i+2}(s)$. If the distance between the $\mathbf{x}_i$ points is constant (e.g., unit distances), all the base functions are of the same form and consist of four parts $C_j(t)$, $j = 0, \ldots, 3$.

$$C_0(t) = \frac{t^3}{6}\,,$$
$$C_1(t) = \frac{-3\,t^3 + 3\,t^2 + 3\,t + 1}{6}\,,$$
$$C_2(t) = \frac{3\,t^3 - 6\,t^2 + 4}{6}\,,$$
$$C_3(t) = \frac{-t^3 + 3\,t^2 - 3\,t + 1}{6}\,.$$

Because of equation (8.18) and zero-equal base functions for $s \notin (i-2, i+2)$, $\mathbf{x}(s)$ can be computed from the addition of only four terms for any s

$$\mathbf{x}(s) = C_{i-1,3}(s)\,\mathbf{v}_{i-1} + C_{i,2}(s)\,\mathbf{v}_i + C_{i+1,1}(s)\,\mathbf{v}_{i+1} + C_{i+2,0}(s)\,\mathbf{v}_{i+2}\,. \tag{8.20}$$

Here, $C_{i,j}(s)$ means that we use the jth part of the base function B_i (see Figure 8.18). Note that

$$C_{i,j}(s) = C_j(s-i)\,, \quad i = 0, \ldots, n+1\,, \quad j = 0, 1, 2, 3\,. \tag{8.21}$$

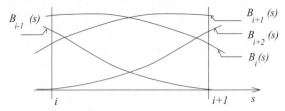

Figure 8.18: The only four non-zero base functions for $s \in (i, i+1)$. © *Cengage Learning 2015.*

To work with values inside the interval $[i, i+1)$, the interpolation curve $\mathbf{x}(s)$ can be computed as

$$\mathbf{x}(s) = C_3(s-i)\,\mathbf{v}_{i-1} + C_2(s-i)\,\mathbf{v}_i + C_1(s-i)\,\mathbf{v}_{i+1} + C_0\,\mathbf{v}_{i+2}\,. \qquad (8.22)$$

Specifically, if $s = 5$, s is positioned at the beginning of the interval $[i, i+1)$, therefore $i = 5$ and

$$\mathbf{x}(5) = C_3(0)\,\mathbf{v}_4 + C_2(0)\,\mathbf{v}_5 + C_1(0)\,\mathbf{v}_6 = \frac{1}{6}\mathbf{v}_4 + \frac{4}{6}\mathbf{v}_5 + \frac{1}{6}\mathbf{v}_6\,, \qquad (8.23)$$

or, if $s = 7.7$, then $i = 7$ and

$$\mathbf{x}(7.7) = C_3(0.7)\,\mathbf{v}_6 + C_2(0.7)\,\mathbf{v}_7 + C_1(0.7)\mathbf{v}_8 + C_0(0.7)\mathbf{v}_9\,. \qquad (8.24)$$

Other useful formulae can be found in [DeBoor, 1978; Ballard and Brown, 1982].

Splines generate curves which are usually considered pleasing. They allow a good approximation, and can easily be used for image analysis curve representation problems. A technique transforming curve samples to B-spline control polygon vertices is described in [Paglieroni and Jain, 1988] together with a method of efficient computation of boundary curvature, shape moments, and projections from control polygon vertices. Splines differ in their complexity; one of the simplest applies the B-spline formula for curve modeling as well as for curve extraction from image data [DeBoor, 1978]. Splines are used in computer vision to form exact and flexible inner model representations of complex shapes which are necessary in model-driven segmentation and in complex image understanding tasks. On the other hand, they are highly sensitive to change in scale.

8.2.6   Other contour-based shape description approaches

The **Hough transform** has excellent shape description abilities and is discussed in detail in in Section 6.2.6 (see also [McKenzie and Protheroe, 1990]). Region-based shape description using **statistical moments** is covered in Section 8.3.2 where a technique of contour-based moments computation from region borders is also included. The **fractal** approach to shape [Mandelbrot, 1982], can also be used for shape description.

Mathematical morphology can be used for shape description, typically in connection with region skeleton construction (see Section 8.3.4) [Reinhardt and Higgins, 1996]. A different approach is introduced in [Loui et al., 1990], where a **geometrical correlation function** represents two-dimensional continuous or discrete curves. This function is translation, rotation, and scale invariant and may be used to compute basic geometrical properties.

Neural networks (Section 9.3) can be used to recognize shapes in raw boundary representations directly. Contour sequences of noiseless reference shapes are used for training, and noisy data are used in later training stages to increase robustness; effective representations of closed planar shapes result [Gupta et al., 1990]. Another neural network shape representation system uses a modified Walsh-Hadamard transform (Section 3.2.2) to achieve position-invariant shape representation.

8.2.7 Shape invariants

It is clear that the shape of regions projected into an image will depend on viewpoint—this is trivially illustrated in Figure 8.19. If we are able to identify features of shape that are *invariant* under certain transforms then we may be able to use them in matching models into images: Machine vision is especially concerned with the class of projective transforms.

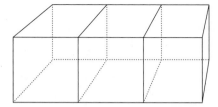

Figure 8.19: Change of shape caused by a projective transform. The same rectangular cross section is represented by different polygons in the image plane. © *Cengage Learning 2015.*

The importance of shape invariance has been known since the nineteenth century, but it was some time before it was used in machine vision [Weiss, 1988; Kanatani, 1990]. Here, we give a brief overview taken from two sources [Forsyth et al., 1991; Mundy and Zisserman, 1992] from which additional details can be found. The latter gives an overview in its Introduction, and its Appendix presents an excellent and detailed survey of projective geometry for machine vision.

Co-linearity is the simplest example of a projectively invariant image feature. Any straight line is projected as a straight line under any projective transform. Similarly, the basic idea of the projection-invariant shape description is to find such shape features that are unaffected by the transform between the object and the image plane.

A standard technique of projection-invariant description is to hypothesize the pose (position and orientation) of an object and transform this object into a specific co-ordinate system; then shape characteristics measured in this co-ordinate system yield an invariant description. However, the pose must be hypothesized for each object and each image, which makes this approach difficult and unreliable.

Another approach is to use **invariant theory**, where invariant descriptors can be computed directly from image data without the need for a particular co-ordinate system. In addition, invariant theory can determine the total number of functionally independent invariants for a given situation, therefore showing completeness of the description invariant set. Invariant theory is based on a collection of transforms that can be composed and inverted. In vision, the **plane-projective group** of transforms is considered which contains all the perspectives as a subset. The **group approach** provides a mathematical tool for generating invariants; if the transform does not satisfy the properties of a group, this machinery is not available [Mundy and Zisserman, 1992]. Therefore, the change of co-ordinates due to the plane-projective transform is generalized as a **group action**. **Lie group** theory is especially useful in designing new invariants.

Let corresponding entities in two different co-ordinate systems be distinguished by capital and lowercase letters. An invariant of a linear transformation is defined as follows:

> An invariant, $I(\mathbf{P})$, of a geometric structure described by a parameter vector $\mathbf{P}$, subject to a linear transformation $\mathbf{T}$ of the co-ordinates $\mathbf{x} = \mathbf{TX}$, is transformed according to $I(\mathbf{p}) = I(\mathbf{P})|\mathbf{T}|^w$. Here $I(\mathbf{p})$ is the function of the parameters after the linear transformation, and $|\mathbf{T}|$ is the determinant of the matrix $\mathbf{T}$.

In this definition, w is referred to as the weight of the invariant. If $w = 0$, the invariants are called **scalar invariants**. Invariant descriptors are unaffected by object pose, by perspective projection, and by the intrinsic parameters of a camera.

Three examples of invariants are:

1. **Cross ratio**: The cross ratio represents a classic invariant of a projective line. A straight line is always projected as a straight line: Any four collinear points A, B, C, D may be described by the cross-ratio invariant

$$I = \frac{(A - C)(B - D)}{(A - D)(B - C)} \,, \tag{8.25}$$

where $(A - C)$ is the distance between points A and C (see Figure 8.20). Note that the cross ratio depends on the order in which the four collinear points are labeled.

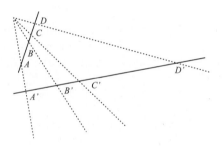

Figure 8.20: Cross ratio; four collinear points form a projective invariant. © *Cengage Learning 2015.*

2. **Systems of lines or points**: A system of four co-planar concurrent lines (meeting at the same point) is dual to a system of four collinear points and the cross ratio is its invariant; see Figure 8.20.

A system of five general co-planar lines forms two invariants

$$I_1 = \frac{|\mathbf{M}_{431}| \, |\mathbf{M}_{521}|}{|\mathbf{M}_{421}| \, |\mathbf{M}_{531}|} \,, \qquad I_2 = \frac{|\mathbf{M}_{421}| \, |\mathbf{M}_{532}|}{|\mathbf{M}_{432}| \, |\mathbf{M}_{521}|} \,, \tag{8.26}$$

where $\mathbf{M}_{ijk} = (\mathbf{l}_i, \mathbf{l}_j, \mathbf{l}_k)$. $\mathbf{l}_i = (l_i^1, l_i^2, l_i^3)^T$ is a representation of a line $l_i^1 x + l_i^2 y + l_i^3 = 0$, where $i \in [1, 5]$, and $|\mathbf{M}|$ is the determinant of $\mathbf{M}$.

If the three lines forming the matrix $\mathbf{M}_{ijk}$ are concurrent, the matrix becomes singular and the invariant is undefined.

A system of five co-planar points is dual to a system of five lines and the same two invariants are formed. These two functional invariants can also be formed as two cross ratios of two co-planar concurrent line quadruples; see Figure 8.21. Note that even though combinations other than those given in Figure 8.21 may be formed, only the two presented functionally independent invariants exist.

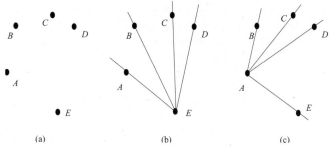

Figure 8.21: Five co-planar points form two cross-ratio invariants. (a) Co-planar points. (b) Five points form a system of four concurrent lines. (c) The same five points form another system of four co-planar lines. © *Cengage Learning 2015*.

3. **Plane conics**: A plane conic may be represented by an equation

$$a\,x^2 + b\,x\,y + c\,y^2 + d\,x + e\,y + f = 0 \tag{8.27}$$

for $\mathbf{x} = (x, y, 1)^T$. Then the conic may also be defined by a matrix $\mathbf{C}$

$$\mathbf{C} = \begin{bmatrix} a & b/2 & d/2 \\ b/2 & c & e/2 \\ d/2 & e/2 & f \end{bmatrix}$$

and

$$\mathbf{x}^T \mathbf{C} \mathbf{x} = 0. \tag{8.28}$$

For any conic represented by a matrix $\mathbf{C}$, and any two co-planar lines not tangent to the conic, one invariant may be defined

$$I = \frac{\left(\mathbf{l}_1^T \mathbf{C}^{-1} \mathbf{l}_2\right)^2}{\left(\mathbf{l}_1^T \mathbf{C}^{-1} \mathbf{l}_1\right)\left(\mathbf{l}_2^T \mathbf{C}^{-1} \mathbf{l}_2\right)}. \tag{8.29}$$

The same invariant can be formed for a conic and two co-planar points.

Two invariants can be determined for a pair of conics represented by their respective matrices $\mathbf{C}_1, \mathbf{C}_2$ normalized so that $|\mathbf{C}_i| = 1$

$$I_1 = \text{trace}\left[\mathbf{C}_1^{-1}\mathbf{C}_2\right], \qquad I_2 = \text{trace}\left[\mathbf{C}_2^{-1}\mathbf{C}_1\right]. \tag{8.30}$$

For non-normalized conics, the invariants of associated quadratic forms are

$$I_1 = \text{trace}\left[\mathbf{C}_1^{-1}\mathbf{C}_2\right]\left(\frac{|\mathbf{C}_1|}{|\mathbf{C}_2|}\right)^{\frac{1}{3}}, \qquad I_2 = \text{trace}\left[\mathbf{C}_2^{-1}\mathbf{C}_1\right]\left(\frac{|\mathbf{C}_2|}{|\mathbf{C}_1|}\right)^{\frac{1}{3}}, \tag{8.31}$$

and two true invariants of the conics are [Quan et al., 1992]

$$I_1 = \frac{\text{trace}\left[\mathbf{C}_1^{-1}\mathbf{C}_2\right]}{\text{trace}^2\left[\mathbf{C}_2^{-1}\mathbf{C}_1\right]}\frac{|\mathbf{C}_1|}{|\mathbf{C}_2|}, \qquad I_2 = \frac{\text{trace}\left[\mathbf{C}_2^{-1}\mathbf{C}_1\right]}{\text{trace}^2\left[\mathbf{C}_1^{-1}\mathbf{C}_2\right]}\frac{|\mathbf{C}_2|}{|\mathbf{C}_1|}. \tag{8.32}$$

Two plane conics uniquely determine four points of intersection, and any point that is not an intersection point may be chosen to form a five-point system together with the four intersection points. Therefore, two invariants exist for the pair of conics, as for the five-point system.

Many man-made objects consist of a combination of straight lines and conics, and these invariants may be used for their description. However, if the object has a contour which cannot be represented by an algebraic curve, the situation is much more difficult. **Differential invariants** can be formed (e.g., curvature, torsion, Gaussian curvature) which are not affected by projective transforms. These invariants are local—that is, the invariants are found for each point on the curve, which may be quite general. Unfortunately, these are extremely large and complex polynomials, requiring up to seventh derivatives of the curve, which makes them practically unusable due to image noise and acquisition errors. However, if additional information is available, higher derivatives may be avoided [Mundy and Zisserman, 1992]. Higher derivatives are traded for extra reference points which can be detected on curves in different projections, although the necessity of matching reference points in different projections brings other difficulties.

Designing new invariants is an important part of invariant theory in its application to machine vision. The easiest way is to combine primitive invariants, forming new ones from these combinations, but no new information is obtained from these combinations. Further, complete tables of invariants for systems of vectors under the action of the rotation group, the affine transform group, and the general linear transform group may be found in [Weyl, 1946]. To obtain new sets of functional invariants, several methods (eliminating transform parameters, the infinitesimal method, the symbolic method) can be found in [Forsyth et al., 1991; Mundy and Zisserman, 1992].

Stability of invariants is another crucial property which affects their applicability. The robustness of invariants to image noise and errors introduced by image sensors is of prime importance, although not much is known about this. Results of plane-projective invariant stability testing (cross ratio, five co-planar points, two co-planar conics) can be found in [Forsyth et al., 1991]. Further, different invariants have different stabilities and distinguishing powers. It was found, for example [Rothwell et al., 1992], that measuring a single conic and two lines in a scene is too computationally expensive to be worthwhile. It is recommended to combine different invariants to enable fast object recognition.

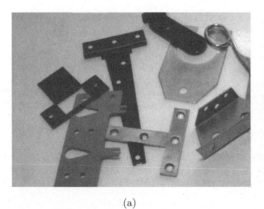

(a)   (b)

Figure 8.22: Object recognition based on shape invariants. (a) Original image of overlapping objects taken from an arbitrary viewpoint. (b) Object recognition based on line and conic invariants. *Courtesy of D. Forsyth, The University of Iowa; C. Rothwell, A. Zisserman, University of Oxford; J. Mundy, General Electric Corporate Research and Development, Schenectady, NY.*

An example of recognition of man-made objects using invariant description of four co-planar lines, a conic and two lines, and a pair of co-planar conics is given in [Rothwell et al., 1992]. The recognition system is based on a model library containing over 30 object models—a significant number at that time. Moreover, the construction of the model library is extremely easy; no special measurements are needed, the object is digitized in a standard way, and the projectively invariant description is stored as a model, and there is no need for camera calibration. The recognition accuracy is 100% for occluded objects viewed from different viewpoints if the objects are not severely disrupted by shadows and specularities. An example of such object recognition is given in Figure 8.22.

8.3 Region-based shape representation and description

We can use boundary information to describe a region, and shape can be described from the region itself. A large group of techniques is represented by heuristic approaches which yield acceptable results in description of simple shapes—region area, rectangularity, elongatedness, direction, compactness, etc., are examples. Unfortunately, they cannot be used for region reconstruction and do not work for more complex shapes. Other procedures based on region decomposition into smaller and simpler subregions must be applied to describe more complicated regions, then subregions can be described separately using heuristic approaches. Objects are represented by a planar graph with nodes representing subregions resulting from region decomposition, and region shape is then described by the graph properties [Rosenfeld, 1979; Bhanu and Faugeras, 1984; Turney et al., 1985]. There are two general approaches to acquiring a graph of subregions: The first is region thinning leading to the **region skeleton**, which can be described by a graph. The second starts with the **region decomposition** into subregions, which are then represented by nodes, while arcs represent neighborhood relations of subregions. It is common to stipulate that subregions be convex.

Graphical representation of regions has many advantages. The resulting graphs:

- Are translation and rotation invariant; position and rotation can be included in the graph definition.

- Are insensitive to small changes in shape.

- Are highly invariant with respect to region magnitude.

- Generate a representation which is understandable.

- Can easily be used to obtain the information-bearing features of the graph.

- Are suitable for syntactic recognition.

On the other hand, the shape representation can be difficult to obtain and the classifier-learning stage is not easy either (see Chapter 9).

8.3.1 Simple scalar region descriptors

A number of simple heuristic shape descriptors exist which relate to statistical feature description. These basic methods may be used for description of subregions in complex regions, and then be used to define graph node classification [Bribiesca and Guzman, 1980].

Area

The simplest and most natural property of a region is its area, given by the number of pixels within it. The *real* area of each pixel may be taken into consideration to get the *real size* of a region, noting that in many cases (e.g., satellite imagery) pixels in different positions correspond to different areas in the real world. If an image is represented as a rectangular raster, simple counting of region pixels will provide its area. If the image is represented by a quadtree, however, it may be more difficult to find the area. Assuming that regions have been identified by labeling, Algorithm 8.5 may be used.

Algorithm 8.5: Calculating area in quadtrees

1. Set all region area variables to zero, and determine the global quadtree depth H; for example, the global quadtree depth is $H = 8$ for a 256×256 image.

2. Search the tree in a systematic way. If a leaf node at a depth h has a non-zero label, proceed to step 3.

3. Compute:
$$area[region\_label] = area[region\_label] + 4^{(H-h)} .$$

4. The region areas are stored in variables $area[region\_label]$.

A region may be represented by n polygon vertices (i_k, j_k), and $(i_0, j_0) = (i_n, j_n)$: the area is then given by

$$area = \frac{1}{2} \left| \sum_{k=0}^{n-1} (i_k j_{k+1} - i_{k+1} j_k) \right| \tag{8.33}$$

—the sign of the sum represents the polygon orientation. If a smoothed boundary is used to overcome noise sensitivity problems, the region area value resulting from equation (8.33) is usually somewhat reduced. Various smoothing methods and accurate area-recovering techniques are given in [Koenderink and v Doorn, 1986].

If the region is represented by the (anti-clockwise) Freeman chain code, the following algorithm provides the area.

Algorithm 8.6: Region area calculation from Freeman 4-connectivity chain code representation

1. Set the region *area* to zero. Assign the value of the starting point i co-ordinate to the variable *vertical_position*.

2. For each element of the chain code (values 0, 1, 2, 3) do

```
switch(code) {
    case 0:
        area := area - vertical_position;
        break;
```

```
        case 1:
            vertical_position := vertical_position + 1;
            break;
        case 2:
            area := area + vertical_position;
            break;
        case 3:
            vertical_position := vertical_position - 1;
            break;
    }
```

3. If all boundary chain elements have been processed, the region area is stored in the variable *area*.

Euler Poincaré characteristic

The Euler-Poincaré characteristic ϑ (sometimes called **genus**) describes a simple, topologically invariant property of the object. It is based on S, the number of contiguous parts of an object, and N, the number of holes in the object (an object can consist of more than one region; see Section 2.3.1). Then

$$\vartheta = S - N \, . \tag{8.34}$$

Special procedures to compute Euler's number can be found in [Dyer, 1980; Rosenfeld and Kak, 1982; Pratt, 1991], and in Chapter 13.

Projections

Horizontal and vertical region projections $p_h(i)$ and $p_v(j)$ are defined as

$$p_h(i) = \sum_j f(i,j) \, , \qquad p_v(j) = \sum_i f(i,j) \, . \tag{8.35}$$

Description by projections is usually used in binary image processing. Projections can easily provide definitions of related region descriptors; for example, the width (height) of a region with no holes is given by the maximum value of the horizontal (vertical) projection of a binary image of the region. These definitions are illustrated in Figure 8.23.

In fact, $p_h(i)$ and $p_v(j)$ are vector quantities that often capture useful features of binary regions (especially if normalized)—a simple example might be in OCR where *ascenders* in letters such as 'h' or 'k' will generate recognizable peaks in the horizontal histogram, while gaps between letters will generate troughs. Of course, we do not need to constrain the projection to directions h and v, in which case we might derive the *Radon transform*—see Section 3.2.11. This proves very useful in detecting lines in noise, for example skew in handwriting, giving it an obvious relationship to the Hough transform (Section 6.2.6), although it has far wider and consequential applications. It can also be the source of further scalar measurements—for example, the number of pronounced peaks in the transform has been used as a feature in symbol identification [Terrades and Valveny, 2003] and character recognition [Miciak, 2010].

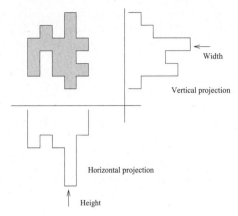

Figure 8.23: Projections.   © *Cengage Learning 2015.*

Eccentricity

The simplest eccentricity characteristic is the ratio of the length of the maximum chord A to the maximum chord B which is perpendicular to A (the ratio of major and minor axes of an object)—see Section 8.2.2, Figure 8.24. Another approximate eccentricity measure is based on a ratio of main region axes of inertia [Ballard and Brown, 1982; Jain, 1989].

Figure 8.24: Eccentricity.   © *Cengage Learning 2015.*

Elongatedness

Elongatedness is the aspect ratio of the region bounding rectangle. This is the rectangle of minimum area that bounds the shape, which is located by turning in discrete steps until a minimum is located (see Figure 8.25a). This criterion cannot succeed in curved regions (see Figure 8.25b), when elongatedness must be based on maximum region thickness. Elongatedness can be evaluated as a ratio of the region area and the square of its thickness. The maximum region thickness (holes must be filled if present) can be determined as the number of erosion steps (see Chapter 13) that may be applied before the region totally disappears. If the number of erosion steps is d, elongatedness is then

$$elongatedness = \frac{area}{(2d)^2} \ . \tag{8.36}$$

Note that the bounding rectangle can be computed efficiently from boundary points, if its direction θ is known. Defining

$$\alpha(x,y) = x\cos\theta + y\sin\theta \ , \qquad \beta(x,y) = -x\sin\theta + y\cos\theta \ , \tag{8.37}$$

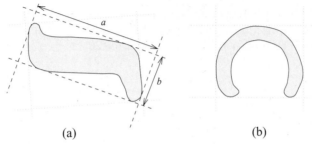

(a)   (b)

Figure 8.25: Elongatedness. (a) Bounding rectangle gives acceptable results. (b) Bounding rectangle cannot represent elongatedness. © *Cengage Learning 2015*.

search for the minimum and maximum of α and β over all boundary points (x, y). The values of $\alpha_{\min}, \alpha_{\max}, \beta_{\min}, \beta_{\max}$ then define the bounding rectangle, and $l_1 = (\alpha_{\max} - \alpha_{\min})$ and $l_2 = (\beta_{\max} - \beta_{\min})$ are its length and width.

Rectangularity

Let F_k be the ratio of region area and the area of a bounding rectangle with direction k. **Rectangularity** maximizes this ratio over discrete steps in k;

$$rectangularity = \max_k F_k \, . \tag{8.38}$$

The direction need only be turned through one quadrant. Rectangularity assumes values from the interval $(0, 1]$, with 1 representing a perfectly rectangular region. Sometimes, it may be more natural to draw a bounding triangle; a method for similarity evaluation between two triangles called **sphericity** is presented in [Ansari and Delp, 1990].

Direction

Direction is a property which makes sense in elongated regions only, and is defined as the direction of the longer side of a minimum bounding rectangle. If the shape moments are known (Section 8.3.2), the direction θ can be computed as

$$\theta = \frac{1}{2} \arctan \left(\frac{2 \mu_{11}}{\mu_{20} - \mu_{02}} \right) \, . \tag{8.39}$$

Elongatedness and rectangularity are independent of linear transformations—translation, rotation, and scaling. Direction is independent on all linear transformations which do not include rotation. Mutual direction of two rotating objects is rotation invariant.

Compactness

Compactness is a shape description characteristic independent of linear transformations:

$$compactness = \frac{(region\_border\_length)^2}{area} \, . \tag{8.40}$$

The most compact region in a Euclidean space is a circle. Compactness assumes values in the interval $[1, \infty)$ in digital images if the boundary is defined as an inner boundary (see Section 6.2.3); using the outer boundary, compactness assumes values in the interval $[16, \infty)$. Independence from linear transformations is gained only if an outer boundary representation is used. Examples are shown in Figure 8.26.

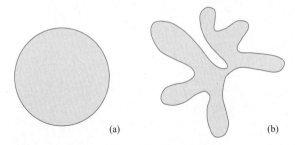

(a)   (b)

Figure 8.26: Compactness: (a) compact; (b) non-compact. © *Cengage Learning 2015.*

8.3.2   Moments

Region moment representations interpret a normalized gray-level image function as a probability density of a 2D random variable. Properties of this random variable can be described using statistical characteristics—**moments** [Papoulis, 1991]. Assuming that non-zero pixel values represent regions, moments can be used for binary or gray-level region description. A moment of order $(p + q)$ is dependent on scaling, translation, rotation, and even on gray-level transformations and is given by

$$m_{pq} = \int_{-\infty}^{\infty} \int_{-\infty}^{\infty} x^p \, y^q \, f(x, y) \, \mathrm{d}x \, \mathrm{d}y \,. \tag{8.41}$$

In digitized images we evaluate sums

$$m_{pq} = \sum_{i=-\infty}^{\infty} \sum_{j=-\infty}^{\infty} i^p \, j^q \, f(i, j) \,, \tag{8.42}$$

where x, y, i, j are the region point co-ordinates (pixel co-ordinates in digitized images). Translation invariance can be achieved if we use the central moments

$$\mu_{pq} = \sum_{i=-\infty}^{\infty} \sum_{j=-\infty}^{\infty} (i - x_c)^p \, (j - y_c)^q \, f(i, j) \,, \tag{8.43}$$

where x_c, y_c are the co-ordinates of the region's center of gravity (centroid), which can be obtained using:

$$x_c = \frac{m_{10}}{m_{00}} \,, \qquad y_c = \frac{m_{01}}{m_{00}} \,. \tag{8.44}$$

In the binary case, m_{00} represents the region area (see equations 8.41 and 8.42). Scale-invariant features can be found from scaled central moments η_{pq} (scale change $x' = \alpha x, y' = \alpha y$)

$$\eta_{pq} = \frac{\mu_{pq}}{(\mu_{00})^{(p+q)/2+1}} \tag{8.45}$$

and normalized un-scaled central moments ϑ_{pq}

$$\vartheta_{pq} = \frac{\mu_{pq}}{(\mu_{00})^\gamma} \,. \tag{8.46}$$

Rotation invariance can be achieved if the co-ordinate system is chosen such that $\mu_{11} = 0$ [Cash and Hatamian, 1987]. Many aspects of moment properties, normalization, descriptive power, sensitivity to noise, and computational cost are discussed in [Savini, 1988]. A less general form of invariance was given in [Hu, 1962] and is discussed in [Jain, 1989; Pratt, 1991], in which seven rotation-, translation-, and scale-invariant moment characteristics are used.

$$\varphi_1 = \vartheta_{20} + \vartheta_{02} \, , \tag{8.47}$$

$$\varphi_2 = (\vartheta_{20} - \vartheta_{02})^2 + 4\,\vartheta_{11}^2 \, , \tag{8.48}$$

$$\varphi_3 = (\vartheta_{30} - 3\,\vartheta_{12})^2 + (3\,\vartheta_{21} - \vartheta_{03})^2 \, , \tag{8.49}$$

$$\varphi_4 = (\vartheta_{30} + \vartheta_{12})^2 + (\vartheta_{21} + \vartheta_{03})^2 \, , \tag{8.50}$$

$$\varphi_5 = (\vartheta_{30} - 3\,\vartheta_{12})(\vartheta_{30} + \vartheta_{12})\big((\vartheta_{30} + \vartheta_{12})^2 - 3(\vartheta_{21} + \vartheta_{03})^2\big)$$
$$+ (3\,\vartheta_{21} - \vartheta_{03})(\vartheta_{21} + \vartheta_{03})\big(3(\vartheta_{30} + \vartheta_{12})^2 - (\vartheta_{21} + \vartheta_{03})^2\big) \, , \tag{8.51}$$

$$\varphi_6 = (\vartheta_{20} - \vartheta_{02})\big((\vartheta_{30} + \vartheta_{12})^2 - (\vartheta_{21} + \vartheta_{03})^2\big) + 4\,\vartheta_{11}(\vartheta_{30} + \vartheta_{12})(\vartheta_{21} + \vartheta_{03}) \, , \tag{8.52}$$

$$\varphi_7 = (3\,\vartheta_{21} - \vartheta_{03})(\vartheta_{30} + \vartheta_{12})\big((\vartheta_{30} + \vartheta_{12})^2 - 3(\vartheta_{21} + \vartheta_{03})^2\big)$$
$$- (\vartheta_{30} - 3\vartheta_{12})(\vartheta_{21} + \vartheta_{03})\big(3(\vartheta_{30} + \vartheta_{12})^2 - (\vartheta_{21} + \vartheta_{03})^2\big) \, , \tag{8.53}$$

where the ϑ_{pq} values can be computed from equation (8.46).

While these seven characteristics were shown to be useful, they are invariant only to translation, rotation, and scaling. Improved algorithms for fast computation of translation-, rotation-, and scale-invariant moments were given in [Li and Shen, 1991; Jiang and Bunke, 1991]. However, these do not yield descriptors that are invariant under general affine transforms. Details of a process for the derivation of invariants and examples of invariant moment object descriptions can be found in [Flusser and Suk, 1993], where a complete set of four affine moment invariants derived from second- and third-order moments is presented.

$$I_1 = \frac{\mu_{20}\,\mu_{02} - \mu_{11}^2}{\mu_{00}^4} \, , \tag{8.54}$$

$$I_2 = \frac{\mu_{30}^2\,\mu_{03}^2 - 6\,\mu_{30}\,\mu_{21}\,\mu_{12}\,\mu_{03} + 4\,\mu_{30}\,\mu_{12}^3 + 4\,\mu_{21}^3\,\mu_{03} - 3\,\mu_{21}^2\,\mu_{12}^2}{\mu_{00}^{10}} \, , \tag{8.55}$$

$$I_3 = \frac{\mu_{20}(\mu_{21}\,\mu_{03} - \mu_{12}^2) - \mu_{11}(\mu_{30}\,\mu_{03} - \mu_{21}\,\mu_{12}) + \mu_{02}(\mu_{30}\,\mu_{12} - \mu_{21}^2)}{\mu_{00}^7} \, , \tag{8.56}$$

$$I_4 = \Big(\mu_{20}^3\,\mu_{03}^2 - 6\,\mu_{20}^2\,\mu_{11}\,\mu_{12}\,\mu_{03} - 6\,\mu_{20}^2\,\mu_{02}\,\mu_{21}\,\mu_{03} + 9\,\mu_{20}^2\,\mu_{02}\,\mu_{12}^2$$
$$+ 12\,\mu_{20}\,\mu_{11}^2\,\mu_{21}\,\mu_{03} + 6\,\mu_{20}\,\mu_{11}\,\mu_{02}\,\mu_{30}\,\mu_{03} - 18\,\mu_{20}\,\mu_{11}\,\mu_{02}\,\mu_{21}\,\mu_{12}$$
$$- 8\,\mu_{11}^3\,\mu_{30}\,\mu_{03} - 6\,\mu_{20}\,\mu_{02}^2\,\mu_{30}\,\mu_{12} + 9\,\mu_{20}\,\mu_{02}^2\,\mu_{21}^2$$
$$+ 12\,\mu_{11}^2\,\mu_{02}\,\mu_{30}\,\mu_{12} - 6\,\mu_{11}\,\mu_{02}^2\,\mu_{30}\,\mu_{21} + \mu_{02}^3\,\mu_{30}^2\Big)\Big/\mu_{00}^{11} \, . \tag{8.57}$$

All moment characteristics are dependent on the linear gray-level transformations of regions; to describe region shape properties, we work with binary image data $\big(f(i,j) = 1$ in region pixels$\big)$ and dependence on the linear gray-level transform disappears.

Moment characteristics can be used in shape description even if the region is represented by its boundary. A closed boundary is characterized by an ordered sequence $z(i)$

that represents the Euclidean distance between the centroid and all N boundary pixels of the digitized shape. No extra processing is required for shapes having spiral or concave contours. Translation-, rotation-, and scale-invariant one-dimensional normalized contour sequence moments $\overline{m}_r, \overline{\mu}_r$ are defined in [Gupta and Srinath, 1987]. The rth contour sequence moment m_r and the rth central moment μ_r can be estimated as

$$m_r = \frac{1}{N} \sum_{i=1}^{N} \left(z(i) \right)^r , \tag{8.58}$$

$$\mu_r = \frac{1}{N} \sum_{i=1}^{N} \left(z(i) - m_1 \right)^r . \tag{8.59}$$

The rth normalized contour sequence moment $\overline{m}_r$ and normalized central contour sequence moment $\overline{\mu}_r$ are defined as

$$\overline{m}_r = \frac{m_r}{\mu_2^{r/2}} = \frac{\frac{1}{N} \sum_{i=1}^{N} \left(z(i) \right)^r}{\left(\frac{1}{N} \sum_{i=1}^{N} \left(z(i) - m_1 \right)^2 \right)^{r/2}} , \tag{8.60}$$

$$\overline{\mu}_r = \frac{\mu_r}{(\mu_2)^{r/2}} = \frac{\frac{1}{N} \sum_{i=1}^{N} \left(z(i) - m_1 \right)^r}{\left(\frac{1}{N} \sum_{i=1}^{N} \left(z(i) - m_1 \right)^2 \right)^{r/2}} . \tag{8.61}$$

While the set of invariant moments $\overline{m}_r, \overline{\mu}_r$ can be used directly for shape representation, less noise-sensitive results can be obtained from [Gupta and Srinath, 1987]

$$F_1 = \frac{(\mu_2)^{1/2}}{m_1} = \frac{\left(\frac{1}{N} \sum_{i=1}^{N} \left(z(i) - m_1 \right)^2 \right)^{1/2}}{\frac{1}{N} \sum_{i=1}^{N} z(i)} , \tag{8.62}$$

$$F_2 = \frac{\mu_3}{(\mu_2)^{3/2}} = \frac{\frac{1}{N} \sum_{i=1}^{N} \left(z(i) - m_1 \right)^3}{\left(\frac{1}{N} \sum_{i=1}^{N} \left(z(i) - m_1 \right)^2 \right)^{3/2}} , \tag{8.63}$$

$$F_3 = \frac{\mu_4}{(\mu_2)^2} = \frac{\frac{1}{N} \sum_{i=1}^{N} \left(z(i) - m_1 \right)^4}{\left(\frac{1}{N} \sum_{i=1}^{N} \left(z(i) - m_1 \right)^2 \right)^2} , \tag{8.64}$$

$$F_4 = \overline{\mu}_5 . \tag{8.65}$$

Lower probabilities of error classification were obtained using contour sequence moments than area-based moments (equations 8.47–8.53) in a shape recognition test; also, contour sequence moments are less computationally demanding.

8.3.3   Convex hull

A region R is convex if and only if for any two points $\mathbf{x}_1, \mathbf{x}_2 \in R$, the whole line segment $\mathbf{x}_1 \mathbf{x}_2$ defined by its end points $\mathbf{x}_1, \mathbf{x}_2$ is inside the region R. The convex hull of a region is the smallest convex region H which satisfies the condition $R \subseteq H$—see Figure 8.27. The convex hull has some special properties in digital data which do not exist in the continuous case. For instance, concave parts can appear and disappear in digital data

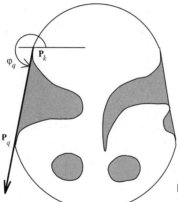

Figure 8.27: Convex hull. © *Cengage Learning 2015.*

due to rotation, and therefore the convex hull is not rotation invariant in digital space [Gross and Latecki, 1995]. The convex hull can be used to describe region shape properties and can be used to build a tree structure of region concavity.

A discrete convex hull can be defined by Algorithm 8.7 which may also be used for convex hull construction. It has complexity $\mathcal{O}(n^2)$ and is presented here as an intuitive way of detecting the convex hull. Algorithm 8.8 describes a more efficient approach.

Algorithm 8.7: Region convex hull construction

1. Find all pixels of a region R with the minimum row co-ordinate, and from them the pixel P_1 with minimum column co-ordinate. Assign $\mathbf{P}_k = \mathbf{P}_1$, $\mathbf{v} = (0, -1)$; vector $\mathbf{v}$ represents the direction of the previous line segment of the convex hull.

2. Search the region boundary in an anti-clockwise direction (Algorithm 6.6) and compute the angle orientation φ_n for every boundary point $\mathbf{P}_n$ which lies after the point $\mathbf{P}_1$ (in the direction of boundary search—see Figure 8.27). The angle orientation φ_n is the angle of vector $\mathbf{P}_k\mathbf{P}_n$. The point $\mathbf{P}_q$ satisfying the condition $\varphi_q = \min_n \varphi_n$ is an element (vertex) of the region convex hull.

3. Assign $\mathbf{v} = \mathbf{P}_k - \mathbf{P}_q$, $\mathbf{P}_k = \mathbf{P}_q$.

4. Repeat steps 2 and 3 until $\mathbf{P}_k = \mathbf{P}_1$.

The first point $\mathbf{P}_1$ need not be chosen as described, but it must be an element of a convex segment of the inner region boundary.

More efficient algorithms exist, especially if the object is defined by an ordered sequence $P = \{\mathbf{v}_1, \mathbf{v}_2, \ldots, \mathbf{v}_n\}$ of n vertices, $\mathbf{v}_i$ representing a polygonal boundary of the object. Many algorithms [Toussaint, 1985] exist for detection of the convex hull with computational complexity $\mathcal{O}(n \log n)$ in the worst case.

If the polygon P is a *simple* polygon (self-non-intersecting polygon) which is always the case in a polygonal representation of object borders, the convex hull may be found in linear time $\mathcal{O}(n)$: the algorithm of [McCallum and Avis, 1979] was the first correct one. The simplest correct convex hull algorithm, which we now discuss, was given in [Melkman, 1987].

Let $P = \{\mathbf{v}_1, \mathbf{v}_2, \ldots, \mathbf{v}_n\}$ be the simple polygon for which the convex hull is to be determined, and let the vertices be processed in this order. For any three vertices $\mathbf{x,y,z}$ in an ordered sequence, a directional function δ may be evaluated (Figure 8.28)

$$
\begin{aligned}
\delta(\mathbf{x,y,z}) &= 1 \quad \text{if } \mathbf{z} \text{ is to the right of the directed line } \mathbf{xy}, \\
&= 0 \quad \text{if } \mathbf{z} \text{ is collinear with the directed line } \mathbf{xy}, \\
&= -1 \quad \text{if } \mathbf{z} \text{ is to the left of the directed line } \mathbf{xy}.
\end{aligned}
$$

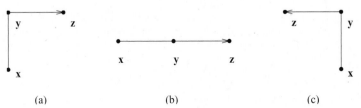

(a)   (b)   (c)

Figure 8.28: Directional function δ. (a) $\delta(\mathbf{x,y,z}) = 1$. (b) $\delta(\mathbf{x,y,z}) = 0$. (c) $\delta(\mathbf{x,y,z}) = -1$. © *Cengage Learning 2015.*

The main data structure H is a list of vertices of polygonal vertices already processed. H represents the convex hull of the currently processed part of the polygon, and after the detection is completed, provides the convex hull. Therefore, H always represents a closed polygonal curve, $H = \{d_b, \ldots, d_t\}$ where d_b points to the bottom of the list and d_t points to its top. Note that d_b and d_t always refer to the same vertex simultaneously representing, the first and the last vertex of the closed polygon.

The first three vertices A, B, C from the sequence P form a triangle (if not collinear) and this triangle represents a convex hull of the first three vertices—Figure 8.29a. The next vertex D in the sequence is then tested for being located inside or outside the current convex hull. If D is located inside, the current convex hull does not change—Figure 8.29b. If D is outside the current convex hull, it must become a new hull vertex (Figure 8.29c) and, based on the current convex hull shape, either none, one, or several vertices must be removed from the current hull—Figure 8.29c,d. This process is repeated for all remaining vertices in the sequence P.

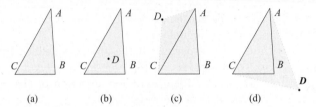

(a)   (b)   (c)   (d)

Figure 8.29: Convex hull detection. (a) First three vertices A, B, C form a triangle. (b) If the next vertex D is positioned inside the current convex hull ABC, current hull does not change. (c) If the next vertex D is outside the current convex hull, it becomes a new vertex of the new current hull $ABCDA$. (d) In this case, vertex B must be removed from the current hull and the new current hull is $ADCA$. © *Cengage Learning 2015.*

Following the terminology used in [Melkman, 1987], the variable **v** refers to the input vertex under consideration, and the following operations are defined:

$$\texttt{push } \mathbf{v}: \quad t := t+1, \quad d_t \rightarrow \mathbf{v},$$

$$\texttt{pop } d_t: \quad t := t-1,$$

$$\texttt{insert } \mathbf{v}: \; b := b-1, \quad d_b \rightarrow \mathbf{v},$$

$$\texttt{remove } d_b: \; b := b+1,$$

$$\texttt{input } \mathbf{v}: \quad \text{next vertex is entered from sequence } P, \text{ if } P \text{ is empty, stop,}$$

where $\rightarrow$ means 'points to'. The algorithm is then:

Algorithm 8.8: Simple polygon convex hull detection

1. Initialize.
   - $t := -1$;
   - $b := 0$;
   - `input` $\mathbf{v}_1$; `input` $\mathbf{v}_2$; `input` $\mathbf{v}_3$;
   - `if ` ($\delta(\mathbf{v}_1, \mathbf{v}_2, \mathbf{v}_3) > 0$)
   - `{ push ` $\mathbf{v}_1$;
   - `push ` $\mathbf{v}_2$; `}`
   - `else`
   - `{ push ` $\mathbf{v}_2$;
   - `push ` $\mathbf{v}_1$; `}`
   - `push ` $\mathbf{v}_3$;
   - `insert ` $\mathbf{v}_3$;

2. If the next vertex **v** is inside the current convex hull H, enter and check a new vertex; otherwise process steps 3 and 4;
   - `input v`;
   - `while ` ($\delta(\mathbf{v}, d_b, d_{b+1}) \geq 0$ `  AND  ` $\delta(d_{t-1}, d_t, \mathbf{v}) \geq 0$)
   - `input v`;

3. Rearrange vertices in H, top of the list.
   - `while ` ($\delta(d_{t-1}, d_t, \mathbf{v}) \leq 0$)
   - `pop ` d_t;
   - `push v`;

4. Rearrange vertices in H, bottom of the list.
   - `while ` ($\delta(\mathbf{v}, d_b, d_{b+1}) \leq 0$)
   - `remove ` d_b;
   - `insert v`;
   - `go to step 2`;

The algorithm as presented may be difficult to follow, but a less formal version would be hard to implement; a formal proof is given in [Melkman, 1987]. The following example makes it more understandable.

Let $P = \{A, B, C, D, E\}$ as shown in Figure 8.30a. The data structure H is created in the first step:

$$
\begin{array}{cccccc}
t, b \ldots & & -1 & 0 & 1 & 2 \\
H & = & C & A & B & C \\
& & d_b & & & d_t
\end{array}
$$

In the second step, vertex D is entered (Figure 8.30b):

$$
\begin{aligned}
\delta(D, d_b, d_{b+1}) &= \delta(D, C, A) = \;\; 1 > 0\,, \\
\delta(d_{t-1}, d_t, D) &= \delta(B, C, D) = -1 < 0\,.
\end{aligned}
$$

Based on the values of the directional function δ, in this case, no other vertex is entered during this step. Step 3 results in the following current convex hull H

$$
\delta(B, C, D) = -1 \longrightarrow \texttt{pop } d_t \longrightarrow
\begin{array}{cccccc}
t, b \ldots & & -1 & 0 & 1 & 2 \\
H & = & C & A & B & C \\
& & d_b & & d_t &
\end{array}\,,
$$

$$
\delta(A, B, D) = -1 \longrightarrow \texttt{pop } d_t \longrightarrow
\begin{array}{cccccc}
t, b \ldots & & -1 & 0 & 1 & 2 \\
H & = & C & A & B & C \\
& & d_b & d_t & &
\end{array}\,,
$$

$$
\delta(C, A, D) = 1 \longrightarrow \texttt{push } D \longrightarrow
\begin{array}{cccccc}
t, b \ldots & & -1 & 0 & 1 & 2 \\
H & = & C & A & D & C \\
& & d_b & & d_t &
\end{array}\,.
$$

In step 4—Figure 8.30c

$$
\delta(D, C, A) = 1 \longrightarrow \texttt{insert } D \longrightarrow
\begin{array}{ccccccc}
t, b \ldots & & -2 & -1 & 0 & 1 & 2 \\
H & = & D & C & A & D & C \\
& & d_b & & & d_t &
\end{array}\,.
$$

Go to step 2; vertex E is entered—Figure 8.30d

$$
\begin{aligned}
\delta(E, D, C) &= 1 > 0\,, \\
\delta(A, D, E) &= 1 > 0\,.
\end{aligned}
$$

A new vertex should be entered from P, but there is no unprocessed vertex and the hull generation process stops. The resulting convex hull is defined by the sequence $H = \{d_b, \ldots, d_t\} = \{D, C, A, D\}$, which represents a polygon $DCAD$, always in the clockwise direction—Figure 8.30e.

A **region concavity tree** is another shape representation option [Sklansky, 1972]. A tree is generated recursively during the construction of a convex hull. A convex hull of the whole region is constructed first, and convex hulls of concave residua are found next. The resulting convex hulls of concave residua of the regions from previous steps are searched until no concave residuum exists. The resulting tree is a shape representation of the region. Concavity tree construction can be seen in Figure 8.31.

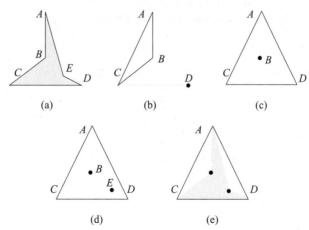

(a)   (b)   (c)

(d)   (e)

Figure 8.30: Example of convex hull detection. (a) The processed region—polygon $ABCDEA$. (b) Vertex D is entered and processed. (c) Vertex D becomes a new vertex of the current convex hull ADC. (d) Vertex E is entered and processed, E does not become a new vertex of the current convex hull. (e) The resulting convex hull $DCAD$. © *Cengage Learning 2015*.

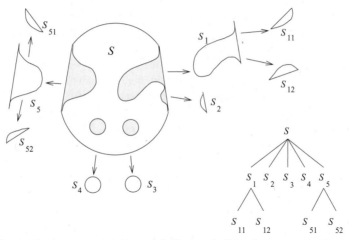

Figure 8.31: Concavity tree construction. (a) Convex hull and concave residua. (b) Concavity tree. © *Cengage Learning 2015*.

8.3.4   Graph representation based on region skeleton

This method corresponds significantly curving points of a region boundary (Section 8.2.2) to graph nodes. The main disadvantage of boundary-based description methods is that geometrically close points can be far away from one another when the boundary is described—graphical representation methods overcome this disadvantage. Shape properties are then derived from the graph properties.

    The region graph is based on the region skeleton, and the first step is the skeleton construction. There are four basic approaches to skeleton construction:

- Thinning—iterative removal of region boundary pixels.

- Wave propagation from the boundary.

- Detection of local maxima in the distance-transformed image of the region.

- Analytical methods.

Expected properties of skeletonization algorithms include [Bernard and Manzanera, 1999]:

- Homotopy – skeletons must preserve the topology of the original shapes/images.

- One-pixel thickness – skeletons should be made of one-pixel thick lines.

- Mediality – skeletons should be positioned in the middle of shapes (with all skeleton points having the same distance from two closest points on object boundary).

- Rotation invariance – in discrete spaces, this can only be satisfied for rotation angles, which are multiples of $\pi/2$, but should be approximately satisfied for other angles.

- Noise immunity – skeletons should be insensitive to shape-boundary noise.

Some of these requirements are contradictory—noise immunity and mediality cannot be satisfied simultaneously. Similarly, rotation invariance and one-pixel thickness requirements work against each other. While all five requirements contribute to the quality of resulting skeletons, satisfying homotopy, mediality, and rotation invariance is of major importance [Manzanera et al., 1999].

Most thinning procedures repeatedly remove boundary elements until a pixel set with maximum thickness of 1 or 2 is found. In general, these methods can be either sequential, iteratively directionally parallel, or iteratively fully parallel. The following MB algorithm is an iteratively fully parallel skeletonization algorithm and it constructs a skeleton of maximum thickness of 2 [Manzanera et al., 1999]. It is simple, preserves topology (i.e., no single component is deleted or split into several components, no object cavity is merged with the background or another cavity, and no new cavity is created) and it is geometrically correct (i.e., objects are shrunk uniformly in all directions and the produced skeleton lines are positioned in the middle of the objects). While it has limited rotational invariance, it is computationally fast.

Algorithm 8.9: Fully parallel skeleton by thinning – MB algorithm

1. Consider a binary image consisting of object pixels and background pixels.

2. Identify a set $\mathcal{Y}$ of object pixels, for which the thinning mask shown in Figure 8.32a matches the local image configuration while the restoring mask Figure 8.32b does not match the local image configuration. This step is performed in parallel for all object pixels of the image and all $\pi/2$ rotations of the masks.

3. Remove all object pixels $\mathcal{Y}$.

4. Repeat the two previous steps as long as $\mathcal{Y}$ is nonempty.

A refined version of the MB skeletonization algorithm—called MB2—offers substantially improved rotational invariance while maintaining all other good properties [Bernard

Figure 8.32: Masks for the MB skeletonization algorithm [Manzanera et al., 1999]. All 90-degree rotations of these two are included. Panel (a) shows the thinning mask (plus all $\pi/2$ rotations). Panel (b) shows the restoring mask (plus all $\pi/2$ rotations). The central mask pixel is marked with a diagonal cross, background pixels are white and object pixels are black. © *Cengage Learning 2015.*

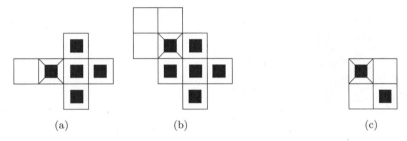

Figure 8.33: Masks for the MB2 skeletonization algorithm [Bernard and Manzanera, 1999]—all $\pi/2$ rotations are included. Panels (a) and (b) show the thinning masks (plus all $\pi/2$ rotations). Panel (c) shows the restoring mask (plus all $\pi/2$ rotations). The central mask pixel is marked with a diagonal cross, background pixels are white and object pixels are black. © *Cengage Learning 2015.*

and Manzanera, 1999]. While still computationally fast when compared to other approaches, it is somewhat slower than Algorithm 8.9.

Algorithm 8.10: Fully parallel skeleton by thinning – MB2 algorithm

1. Consider a binary image consisting of object pixels and background pixels.

2. Identify a set $\mathcal{Y}$ of object pixels, for which at least one of the thinning masks shown in Figure 8.33a,b matches the local image configuration while the restoring mask Figure 8.33c does not. This step is performed in parallel for all object pixels of the image.

3. Remove all object pixels $\mathcal{Y}$.

4. Repeat the two previous steps as long as $\mathcal{Y}$ is nonempty.

Examples of MB and MB2 skeletons and the effects on them resulting from minor changes of object shapes due to variations in segmentation threshold can be seen in Figure 8.34.

Since the MB and MB2 algorithms yield skeleton segments which may have a thickness of 1 or 2, (Figure 8.34b,e) an extra step can be added to reduce those to a thickness of one, although care must be taken not to break the skeleton connectivity. One-pixel skeleton thickness can be obtained using an asymmetric two-dimensional thinning algorithm as a post-processing step, in which simple points are removed [Rosenfeld, 1975]. While removal of a simple-point pixel will not alter topology, parallel removal of two or more of such pixels may result in a topology change. In other words, if all candidate pixels are removed in parallel, topology may be affected and the skeleton may break into pieces. The basic idea of obtaining a 1-pixel wide skeleton using this approach [Rosenfeld, 1975] is therefore to divide the thinning process in substeps and in each substep remove—in parallel—all pixels that have no neighbor belonging to the object in exactly one of the four main directions (north, south, east, west). The 4 directions are rotated in

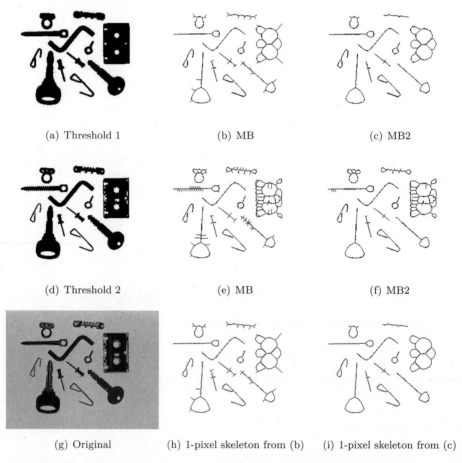

(a) Threshold 1   (b) MB   (c) MB2

(d) Threshold 2   (e) MB   (f) MB2

(g) Original   (h) 1-pixel skeleton from (b)   (i) 1-pixel skeleton from (c)

Figure 8.34: MB and MB2 skeletons from skeletonization of image in Figure 6.1a (shown here in panel (g)). These skeletonization algorithms produce 1- or 2-pixel skeletons. (a) and (d) Binary images resulting from thresholding of panel (g). (b) and (e) MB skeletons. (c) and (f) MB2 skeletons. (g) Original image. (h) 1-pixel wide MB skeleton of image in panel (a)—derived from MB skeleton of panel (b). (i) 1-pixel wide MB2 skeleton of image in panel (a)—derived from MB2 skeleton of panel (c). Note the effect of different threshold on the resulting skeleton—compare panels (a–c) and (d–f). *Courtesy of L. Zhang, The University of Iowa.*

subsequent applications of the parallel pixel removal substeps. The substeps are repeated until convergence—as long as at least one pixel can be removed during the substep. This strategy results in a one-pixel wide skeleton while preserving its topology.

A large number of thinning algorithms can be found in the literature [Hildich, 1969; Pavlidis, 1978] and a useful comparison of parallel thinning algorithms is in [Couprie, 2005]. Mathematical morphology is another powerful tool used to find region skeletons, and thinning algorithms which use morphology are given in Section 13.5; see also [Maragos and Schafer, 1986], where the morphological approach is shown to unify many other approaches to skeletonization.

Thinning procedures often use a medial axis transform (also symmetric axis transform) to construct a region skeleton [Pavlidis, 1977; Samet, 1985; Pizer et al., 1987; Lam et al., 1992; Wright and Fallside, 1993]. Under the medial axis definition, the skeleton is the set of all region points which have the same minimum distance from the region boundary for at least two separate boundary points. Examples of such skeletons are shown in Figures 8.35 and 8.36. Such a skeleton can be constructed using a distance transform which assigns a value to each region pixel representing its (minimum) distance from the region's boundary, and the skeleton is then determined as the set of pixels whose distance from the region's border is locally maximal. As a post-processing step, local maxima can be detected using operators that detect linear features and roof profiles [Wright and Fallside, 1993]. Every skeleton element can be accompanied by information about its distance from the boundary—this gives the potential to reconstruct a region as an envelope curve of circles with center points at skeleton elements and radii corresponding to the stored distance values. Shape descriptions, as discussed in Section 8.3.1 can be derived from this skeleton but, with the exception of elongatedness, the evaluation can be difficult. In addition, this skeleton construction is time-consuming, and the result is highly sensitive to boundary noise and errors. Small changes in the boundary may cause serious changes in the skeleton—see Figure 8.35. This sensitivity can be removed by first representing the region as a polygon, then constructing the skeleton. Boundary noise removal can be absorbed into the polygon construction. A multi-resolution (scale-space) approach to skeleton construction may also result in decreased sensitivity to boundary noise [Pizer et al., 1987; Maragos, 1989]. Similarly, the approach using the Marr-Hildreth edge detector with varying smoothing parameter facilitates scale-based representation of the region's skeleton [Wright and Fallside, 1993].

Skeleton construction algorithms do not result directly in graphs, but the transformation from skeletons to graphs is relatively straightforward. Consider first a 1-pixel wide skeleton—this is advantageous since any skeleton pixel A with only one neighbor corresponds to a leaf vertex (end point) of the graph, pixels with 3 or more neighbors are

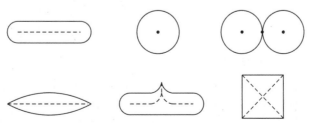

Figure 8.35: Region skeletons; small border changes can have a substantial effect on skeleton. © *Cengage Learning 2015.*

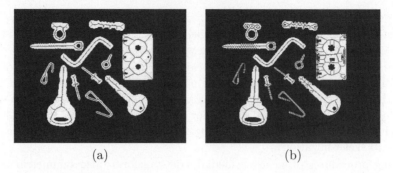

(a)   (b)

Figure 8.36: Medial axis skeletons [Pavlidis, 1981] overlaid in mid-level gray over original binary data given in Figure 8.34a,d. *Courtesy of K. Palagyi, University of Szeged, Hungary.*

associated with branching graph nodes (node points), and all remaining skeleton pixels with 2 neighbors (normal points) translate to arcs between branching and/or leaf vertices. Now consider medial axis skeletons and assume that a minimum radius circle has been drawn from each point of the skeleton which has at least one point common with a region boundary: let *contact* be each contiguous subset of the circle which is common to the circle and to the boundary. If a circle drawn from its center A has one contact only, A is a skeleton end point. If the point A has two contacts, it is a normal skeleton point. If A has three or more contacts, the point A is a skeleton node point.

Algorithm 8.11: Region graph construction from skeleton

1. Label each skeleton point as one of end point, node point, normal point.

2. Let graph node points be all end points and node points. Connect any two graph nodes by a graph arc (graph edge) if they are connected by a sequence of normal points in the region skeleton.

It can be seen that boundary points of high curvature have the main influence on the graph. They are represented by graph nodes, and therefore influence the graph structure.

If other than medial axis skeletons are used for graph construction, end points can be defined as skeleton points having just one skeleton neighbor, normal points as having two skeleton neighbors, and node points as having at least three skeleton neighbors. It is no longer true that node points are never neighbors and additional conditions must be used to decide when node points should and should not be represented as nodes in a graph.

8.3.5 Region decomposition

The decomposition approach is based on the idea that shape recognition is a hierarchical process. Shape **primitives**—the simplest elements which form the region—are defined at the lower level. A graph is constructed at the higher level—nodes result from primitives, arcs describe the mutual primitive relations. Convex sets of pixels are one example of simple shape primitives.

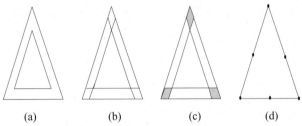

Figure 8.37: Region decomposition. (a) Region—between the triangles. (b) Primary regions—3 overlapping trapezia. (c) Primary subregions (unshaded) and kernels (shaded). (d) Decomposition graph. © *Cengage Learning 2015.*

The solution to the decomposition problem consists of two main steps: The first step is to segment a region into simpler subregions (primitives), and the second is their analysis. Primitives are simple enough to be described successfully using simple scalar shape properties (see Section 8.3.1). A detailed description of how to segment a region into primary convex subregions, methods of decomposition to concave vertices, and graph construction resulting from a polygonal description of subregions are given in [Pavlidis, 1977]. The general idea of decomposition is shown in Figure 8.37, where the original region, one possible decomposition, and the resulting graph are presented. Primary convex subregions are labeled as primary subregions or kernels. Kernels (shaded in Figure 8.37c) are subregions which belong to several primary convex subregions. If subregions are represented by polygons, graph nodes bear the following information:

1. Node type representing primary subregion or kernel.

2. Number of vertices of the subregion represented by the node.

3. Area of the subregion represented by the node.

4. Main axis direction of the subregion represented by the node.

5. Center of gravity of the subregion represented by the node.

If a graph is derived using attributes 1–4, the final description is translation invariant. If it is derived from attributes 1–3, it is translation and rotation invariant. Derivation using the first two attributes results in a description which is size invariant in addition to possessing translation and rotation invariance.

A decomposition of a region uses its structural properties, and results in a syntactic graph description. Problems of how to decompose a region and how to construct the description graph are still open; an overview of some techniques that have been investigated can be found in [Pavlidis, 1977; Shapiro, 1980; Held and Abe, 1994]. Shape decomposition into a complete set of convex parts ordered by size is described in [Cortopassi and Rearick, 1988], and a morphological approach to skeleton decomposition is used to decompose complex shapes into simple components in [Pitas and Venetsanopoulos, 1990; Wang et al., 1995; Reinhardt and Higgins, 1996]; the decomposition is shown to be invariant to translation, rotation, and scaling. Recursive subdivision of shape based on second central moments is another translation-, rotation-, scaling-, and intensity shift-invariant decomposition technique. Hierarchical decomposition and shape description that uses region and contour information, addresses issues of local versus global information, scale, shape parts, and axial symmetry is given in [Rom and Medioni, 1993]. Multi-resolution approaches to decomposition are reported in [Loncaric and Dhawan, 1993; Cinque and Lombardi, 1995].

8.3.6   Region neighborhood graphs

Any time a region decomposition into subregions or an image decomposition into regions is available, the region or image can be represented by a region neighborhood graph (the region adjacency graph described in Section 4.2.3 being a special case). This graph represents every region as a graph node, and nodes of neighboring regions are connected by edges. A region neighborhood graph can be constructed from a quadtree image representation, from run length encoded image data, etc. Binary tree shape representation is described in [Leu, 1989], where merging of boundary segments results in shape decomposition into triangles, their relations being represented by the binary tree.

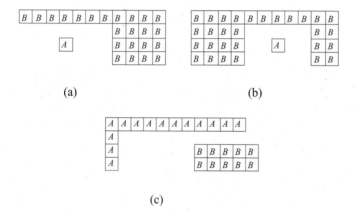

(a)   (b)

(c)

Figure 8.38: Binary relation *to be left of*; see text. © Cengage Learning 2015.

Very often, the relative position of two regions can be used in the description process—for example, a region A may be positioned to the *left of* a region B, or *above* B, or *close to* B, or a region C may lie *between* regions A and B, etc. We know the meaning of all of the given relations if A, B, C are points, but, with the exception of the relation *to be close*, they can become ambiguous if A, B, C are regions. For instance (see Figure 8.38), the relation *to be left of* can be defined in many different ways:

- All pixels of A must be positioned to the left of all pixels of B.

- At least one pixel of A must be positioned to the left of some pixel of B.

- The center of gravity of A must be to the left of the center of gravity of B.

All of these definitions seem to be satisfactory in many cases, but they can sometimes be unacceptable because they do not meet the usual meaning of *being left of*. Human observers are generally satisfied with the definition:

- The center of gravity of A must be positioned to the left of the leftmost point of B and (logical AND) the rightmost pixel of A must be left of the rightmost pixel of B [Winston, 1975].

Many other inter-regional relations are defined in [Winston, 1975], where relational descriptions are studied in detail.

An example of applying geometrical relations between simply shaped primitives to shape representation and recognition is in [Shariat, 1990], where recognition is based on a *hypothesize and verify* control strategy. Shapes are represented by region neighborhood graphs that describe geometrical relations among primitive shapes. The model-based approach increases shape recognition accuracy and makes partially occluded object recognition possible. Recognition of any new object is based on a definition of a new shape model.

8.4 Shape classes

Representation of **shape classes** is considered a challenging problem of shape description [Hogg, 1993]. The shape classes are expected to represent the generic shapes of the objects belonging to the class well and emphasize shape differences between classes, while the shape variations allowed within classes should not influence the description.

There are many ways to deal with such requirements. A widely used representation of in-class shape variations is determination of class-specific regions in the feature space. The feature space can be defined using a selection of shape features described in this chapter (for more information about feature spaces, see Chapter 9). Another approach to shape class definition is to use a single prototype shape and determine a planar warping transform that if applied to the prototype produces shapes from the particular class. The prototype shape may be derived from examples.

If a set of landmarks can be identified on the regions belonging to specific shape classes, the landmarks can characterize the classes in a simple and powerful way. Landmarks are usually selected as easily recognizable border or region points. For planar shapes, a co-ordinate system can be defined that is invariant to similarity transforms of the plane (rotation, translation, scaling) [Bookstein, 1991]. If such a landmark model uses n points per 2D object, the dimensionality of the shape space is $2n$. Clearly, only a subset of the entire shape space corresponds to each shape class and the shape class definition reduces to the definition of the shape space subsets. In [Cootes et al., 1992], principal components in the shape space are determined from training sets of shapes after the shapes are iteratively aligned. This very efficient approach is referred to as a **point distribution model** and is discussed in detail in Section 10.4.

8.5 Summary

- **Shape representation and description**

    - Region description generates a numeric feature vector or a non-numeric syntactic description word, which characterize properties (for example, shape) of the region.

    - Many practical shape description methods exist, but there is no generally accepted methodology of shape description; it is not known what is important in shape.

- Shape may change substantially and discontinuously with image resolution. A **scale-space** approach aims to obtain continuous shape descriptions for continuous resolution changes.

- **Shape classes** represent the generic shapes of the objects belonging to the same classes. Classes should emphasize shape differences among classes, while the variations within classes should not be reflected in the shape class description.

• **Region identification**

- Region identification assigns unique **labels** to image regions.

- If non-repeating ordered numerical labels are used, the largest integer label gives the number of regions in the image.

• **Contour-based shape descriptors**

- **Chain codes** describe an object by a sequence of unit-size line segments with a given orientation, called **Freeman's** code.

- **Simple geometric border representations** are based on geometric properties of described regions, e.g.:
    * Boundary length
    * Curvature
    * Bending energy
    * Signature
    * Chord distribution

- **Fourier shape descriptors** can be applied to closed curves, co-ordinates of which can be treated as periodic signals.

- Shape can be represented as a sequence of **segments** with specified properties. If the segment type is known for all segments, the boundary can be described as a chain of segment types, a code word consisting of representatives of a type alphabet.

- **B-splines** are piecewise polynomial curves whose shape is closely related to their control polygon—a chain of vertices giving a polygonal representation of a curve. Third order B-splines are most common, representing the lowest order which includes the change of curvature.

- **Shape invariants** represent properties of geometric configurations that remain unchanged under an appropriate class of transforms; machine vision is especially concerned with the class of projective transforms.

• **Region-based shape descriptors**

- Simple geometric region descriptors use geometric properties of described regions:
    * Area
    * Euler's number
    * Projections

     * Height, width

     * Eccentricity

     * Elongatedness

     * Rectangularity

     * Direction

     * Compactness

- **Statistical moments** interpret a normalized gray-level image function as a probability density of a 2D random variable. Properties of this random variable can be described using statistical characteristics—**moments**. Moment-based descriptors can be defined to be independent of scaling, translation, and rotation.

- The **convex hull** of a region is the smallest convex region H which satisfies the condition $R \subset H$.

- More complicated shapes can be described using region decomposition into smaller and simpler subregions. Objects can be represented by a planar graph with nodes representing subregions resulting from region decomposition; shape can then be described by graph properties. There are two general approaches to acquiring a graph of subregions:

     * Region thinning

     * Region decomposition

- **Region thinning** leads to the region **skeleton** that can be described by a graph. Thinning procedures often use a medial axis transform to construct a region skeleton. Under the medial axis definition, the skeleton is the set of all region points which have the same minimum distance from the region boundary for at least two separate boundary points.

- **Region decomposition** considers shape recognition to be a hierarchical process. Shape **primitives** are defined at the lower level, primitives being the simplest elements which form the region. A graph is constructed at the higher level—nodes result from primitives, arcs describe the mutual primitive relations.

- **Region neighborhood graphs** represents every region as a graph node, and nodes of neighboring regions are connected by edges. The **region adjacency graph** is a special case of the region neighborhood graph.

- **Shape classes**

  - Shape classes represent the generic shapes of the objects belonging to the class and emphasize shape differences among classes.

  - A widely used representation of in-class shape variations is determination of class-specific regions in the feature space.

8.6   Exercises

Short-answer questions

S8.1 What are the prerequisites of shape description?

S8.2 What are the main distinguishing aspects among various shape representation and shape description methods?

S8.3 Explain how high or low image resolution affects shape descriptors, their discriminability and repeatability.

S8.4 Explain the rationale behind projection-invariant shape descriptors.

S8.5 Define the three most common representations of region borders.

S8.6 Define the boundary chain code in 4- and 8-connectivity.

S8.7 Define the chain code derivative in 4- and 8-connectivity.

S8.8 Define the following border-based region descriptors:

  (a) Boundary length

  (b) Curvature

  (c) Bending energy

  (d) Signature

  (e) Chord distribution

  (f) Fourier transform of boundaries using T_n descriptors

  (g) Fourier transform of boundaries using S_n descriptors

  (h) Polygonal segment representation

  (i) Constant curvature representation

  (j) Tolerance interval representation

S8.9 An object is described by the following chain code in 4-connectivity: 10123230.

  (a) Determine the normalized version of the chain code.

  (b) Determine the derivative of the original chain code.

S8.10 What is a chord distribution for a shape?

S8.11 Explain the concept of multi-scale curve description using interval trees in the scale space.

S8.12 Describe the concept of B-spline curve interpolation.

S8.13 Define the following projection-invariant shape descriptors:

  (a) Cross ratio

  (b) System of four co-planar concurrent lines

  (c) System of five co-planar concurrent lines

  (d) System of five co-planar points

  (e) Plane conics

S8.14 Describe a subclass of boundary shapes to which the invariants listed in Question S8.13 can be applied.

S8.15 Explain the difference between local and global invariants.

S8.16 Determine the Euler number of the following characters: 0, 4, 8, A, B, C, D.

S8.17 Define the following region shape descriptors:

  (a) Area

  (b) Euler's number

(c) Horizontal and vertical projections

(d) Eccentricity

(e) Elongatedness

(f) Rectangularity

(g) Direction

(h) Compactness

(i) Statistical moments

(j) Convex hull

(k) Region concavity tree

S8.18 Describe the principles of region skeletonization by thinning.

S8.19 Describe the medial axis transform.

S8.20 Sketch the skeleton of two touching filled circles.

S8.21 Name the main desirable properties of object/region skeletons.
Which ones of them (which pairs) are mutually contradictory?

S8.22 Describe the principles of shape description using graph decomposition.

S8.23 Explain what shape classes are and why are they important.

Problems

P8.1 Write a function for region identification in 4-neighborhood connectivity.

P8.2 Write a function for region identification in 8-neighborhood connectivity.

P8.3 Develop a program for region identification and region counting that will use function(s) developed in Problems P8.1 and P8.2. Test on binary segmented images.

P8.4 Modify the program developed in Problem P8.3 to accept multi-level segmented images, assuming that the background gray-level is known.

P8.5 Develop a program for region identification and region counting in run length encoded image data. Use the program developed in Problem P4.5 to generate run length encoded image data.

P8.6 Develop a program for region identification and region counting in quadtrees. Use the program developed in Problem P4.1 to generate quadtree image data.

P8.7 Write a function for chain code generation in 4-connectivity. Test on images in which the regions have been identified using one of the programs developed in Problems P8.3–P8.6.

P8.8 Write a function for chain code generation in 8-connectivity. Test on images in which the regions have been identified using one of the programs developed in Problems P8.3–P8.6.

P8.9 Define the border-based descriptor signature. Draw signatures for a rectangle, triangle, and a circle.

P8.10 Prove the statement that the most compact region in a Euclidean space is a circle. Compare the compactness values of a square and a rectangle of any aspect ratio—what can you conclude?

P8.11 Write functions determining the following border descriptors:

(a) Boundary length

(b) Curvature

(c) Bending energy

(d) Signature

(e) Chord distribution

(f) Fourier transform of boundaries using T_n descriptors

(g) Fourier transform of boundaries using S_n descriptors

Use the functions in a program to determine shape features of binary objects.

P8.12 Write functions determining the following region shape descriptors:

(a) Area

(b) Area from chain code border representation

(c) Area from quadtree region representation

(d) Euler's number

(e) Horizontal and vertical projections

(f) Eccentricity

(g) Elongatedness

(h) Rectangularity

(i) Direction

(j) Compactness

(k) Affine transform invariant statistical moments

Use the functions in a program to determine shape features of binary objects.

P8.13 Develop a program to determine the shape features listed in Problems P8.11–P8.12 in images containing several objects simultaneously. The program should report the features in a table, and the objects should be identified by their centroid co-ordinates.

P8.14 Develop a program to determine the shape features listed in Problems P8.11–P8.12 from shapes encoded using run length code and/or quadtree image data.

P8.15 Implement moment based descriptors from equations (8.54–8.57) and verify experimentally their invariance with respect to affine transforms.

P8.16 Develop a program to generate digital images of simple shapes (rectangle, diamond, circle, etc.) in various sizes and rotations. Using the functions prepared in Problems P8.11–P8.12, compare the shape features determined by individual shape descriptors as a function of size and a function of rotation.

P8.17 Develop a program for simple polygon convex hull detection.

P8.18 Develop a program for region concavity tree construction.

P8.19 Determine a medial axis skeleton of a circle, square, rectangle, and triangle.

P8.20 Develop a program constructing a medial axis of a binary region.

(a) Apply the program to computer-generated letters and numerals.

(b) Apply the program to printed letters and numerals after their digitization using a video camera or a scanner.

(c) Explain the differences in performance of your algorithm.

(d) Develop a practically applicable thinning algorithm that constructs line shapes from scanned characters.

P8.21 Make yourself familiar with solved problems and Matlab implementations of selected algorithms provided in the corresponding chapter of the Matlab Companion to this text [Svoboda et al., 2008]. The Matlab Companion homepage http://visionbook.felk.cvut.cz offers images used in the problems, and well-commented Matlab code is provided for educational purposes.

P8.22 Use the Matlab Companion [Svoboda et al., 2008] to develop solutions to additional exercises and practical problems provided there. Implement your solutions using Matlab or other suitable programming languages.

8.7 References

Ansari N. and Delp E. J. Distribution of a deforming triangle. *Pattern Recognition*, 23(12): 1333–1341, 1990.

Appel K. and Haken W. Every planar map is four colourable: Part I: discharging. *Illinois Journal of Mathematics*, 21:429–490, 1977.

Asada H. and Brady M. The curvature primal sketch. *IEEE Transactions on Pattern Analysis and Machine Intelligence*, 8(1):2–14, 1986.

Atkinson H. H., Gargantini, I, and Walsh T. R. S. Counting regions, holes and their nesting level in time proportional to the border. *Computer Vision, Graphics, and Image Processing*, 29:196–215, 1985.

Babaud J., Witkin A. P., Baudin M., and Duda R. O. Uniqueness of the Gaussian kernel for scale-space filtering. *IEEE Transactions on Pattern Analysis and Machine Intelligence*, 8 (1):26–33, 1986.

Ballard D. H. and Brown C. M. *Computer Vision*. Prentice-Hall, Englewood Cliffs, NJ, 1982.

Bernard T. M. and Manzanera A. Improved low complexity fully parallel thinning algorithm. In *Proc. 10th International Conference on Image Analysis and Processing, ICIAP'99*, pages 215–220, 1999.

Bhanu B. and Faugeras O. D. Shape matching of two–dimensional objects. *IEEE Transactions on Pattern Analysis and Machine Intelligence*, 6(2):137–155, 1984.

Bookstein F. L. *Morphometric Tools for Landmark Data*. Cambridge University Press, Cambridge, 1991.

Bribiesca E. and Guzman A. How to describe pure form and how to measure differences in shapes using shape numbers. *Pattern Recognition*, 12(2):101–112, 1980.

Cash G. L. and Hatamian M. Optical character recognition by the method of moments. *Computer Vision, Graphics, and Image Processing*, 39:291–310, 1987.

Chien C. H. and Aggarwal J. K. Model construction and shape recognition from occluding contours. *IEEE Transactions on Pattern Analysis and Machine Intelligence*, 11(4):372–389, 1989.

Cinque L. and Lombardi L. Shape description and recognition by a multiresolution approach. *Image and Vision Computing*, 13:599–607, 1995.

Coeurjolly D., M S., and Tougne L. Discrete curvature based on osculating circle estimation. In *Proceedings of the 4th International Workshop on Visual Form*, IWVF-4, pages 303–312, London, UK, 2001. Springer-Verlag.

Cootes T. F., Cooper D. H., Taylor C. J., and Graham J. Trainable method of parametric shape description. *Image and Vision Computing*, 10(5), 1992.

Cortopassi P. P. and Rearick T. C. Computationally efficient algorithm for shape decomposition. In *CVPR '88: Computer Society Conference on Computer Vision and Pattern Recognition*, Ann Arbor, MI, pages 597–601, Los Alamitos, CA, 1988. IEEE.

Costabile M. F., Guerra C., and Pieroni G. G. Matching shapes: A case study in time-varying images. *Computer Vision, Graphics, and Image Processing*, 29:296–310, 1985.

Couprie M. Note on fifteen 2D parallel thinning algorithms. Technical Report IGM2006-01, Universite de Marne-la-Vallee, 2005.

Debled-Rennesson I. and Reveillès J. P. A linear algorithm for segmentation of digital curves. *IJPRAI*, 9:635–662, 1995.

DeBoor C. A. *A Practical Guide to Splines*. Springer Verlag, New York, 1978.

Duda R. O. and Hart P. E. *Pattern Classification and Scene Analysis*. Wiley, New York, 1973.

Dyer C. R. Computing the Euler number of an image from its quadtree. *Computer Graphics and Image Processing*, 13:270–276, 1980.

Fermuller C. and Kropatsch W. Multi-resolution shape description by corners. In *Proceedings, 1992 Computer Vision and Pattern Recognition*, Champaign, IL, pages 271–276, Los Alamitos, CA, 1992. IEEE.

Flusser J. and Suk T. Pattern recognition by affine moment invariants. *Pattern Recognition*, 26:167–174, 1993.

Forsyth D., Mundy J. L., Zisserman A., Coelho C., Heller A., and Rothwell C. Invariant descriptors for 3D object recognition and pose. *IEEE Transactions on Pattern Analysis and Machine Intelligence*, 13(10):971–991, 1991.

Freeman H. On the encoding of arbitrary geometric configuration. *IRE Transactions on Electronic Computers*, EC–10(2):260–268, 1961.

Fu K. S. *Syntactic Methods in Pattern Recognition*. Academic Press, New York, 1974.

Gross A. and Latecki L. Digital geometric invariance and shape representation. In *Proceedings of the International Symposium on Computer Vision*, pages 121–126, Los Alamitos, CA, 1995. IEEE.

Gupta L. and Srinath M. D. Contour sequence moments for the classification of closed planar shapes. *Pattern Recognition*, 20(3):267–272, 1987.

Gupta L., Sayeh M. R., and Tammana R. Neural network approach to robust shape classification. *Pattern Recognition*, 23(6):563–568, 1990.

Held A. and Abe K. On the decomposition of binary shapes into meaningful parts. *Pattern Recognition*, 27:637–647, 1994.

Hermann S. and Klette R. Multigrid analysis of curvature estimators. Technical Report CITR-TR-129, Massey University, 2003.

Hermann S. and Klette R. A comparative study on 2D curvature estimators. In *ICCTA*, pages 584–589. IEEE Computer Society, 2007.

Hildich C. J. Linear skeletons from square cupboards. In Meltzer B. and Michie D., editors, *Machine Intelligence IV*, pages 403–420. Elsevier, New York, 1969.

Hogg D. C. Shape in machine vision. *Image and Vision Computing*, 11:309–316, 1993.

Hu M. K. Visual pattern recognition by moment invariants. *IRE Transactions Information Theory*, 8(2):179–187, 1962.

Jain A. K. *Fundamentals of Digital Image Processing*. Prentice-Hall, Englewood Cliffs, NJ, 1989.

Jakubowski R. Decomposition of complex shapes for their structural recognition. *Information Sciences*, 50(1):35–71, 1990.

Jiang X. Y. and Bunke H. Simple and fast computation of moments. *Pattern Recognition*, 24: 801–806, 1991.

Juday R. D., editor. *Digital and Optical Shape Representation and Pattern Recognition,* Orlando, FL, Bellingham, WA, 1988. SPIE.

Kanatani K. *Group-Theoretical Methods in Image Understanding.* Springer Verlag, Berlin, 1990.

Kerautret B., Lachaud J. O., and Naegel B. Comparison of discrete curvature estimators and application to corner detection. In *Proceedings of the 4th International Symposium on Advances in Visual Computing*, ISVC '08, pages 710–719, Berlin, Heidelberg, 2008. Springer-Verlag.

Kiryati N. and Maydan D. Calculating geometric properties from Fourier representation. *Pattern Recognition*, 22(5):469–475, 1989.

Koch M. W. and Kashyap R. L. Using polygons to recognize and locate partially occluded objects. *IEEE Transactions on Pattern Analysis and Machine Intelligence*, 9(4):483–494, 1987.

Koenderink J. J. and Doorn A. J. v. Dynamic shape. Technical report, Department of Medical and Physiological Physics, State University, Utrecht, The Netherlands, 1986.

Krzyzak A., Leung S. Y., and Suen C. Y. Reconstruction of two-dimensional patterns from Fourier descriptors. *Machine Vision and Applications*, 2(3):123–140, 1989.

Lam L., Lee S. W., and Suen C. Y. Thinning methodologies—a comprehensive survey. *IEEE Transactions on Pattern Analysis and Machine Intelligence*, 14(9):869–885, 1992.

Leu J. G. View-independent shape representation and matching. In *IEEE International Conference on Systems Engineering*, Fairborn, OH, pages 601–604, Piscataway, NJ, 1989. IEEE.

Leymarie F. and Levine M. D. Shape features using curvature morphology. In *Visual Communications and Image Processing IV,* Philadelphia, PA, pages 390–401, Bellingham, WA, 1989. SPIE.

Li B. C. and Shen J. Fast computation of moment invariants. *Pattern Recognition*, 24:807–813, 1991.

Lin C. C. and Chellappa R. Classification of partial 2D shapes using Fourier descriptors. *IEEE Transactions on Pattern Analysis and Machine Intelligence*, 9(5):686–690, 1987.

Lindenbaum M. and Bruckstein A. On recursive, o(n) partitioning of a digitized curve into digital straight segments. *IEEE Transactions on Pattern Analysis and Machine Intelligence*, 15:949–953, 1993.

Loncaric S. and Dhawan A. P. A morphological signature transform for shape description. *Pattern Recognition*, 26:1029–1037, 1993.

Lord E. A. and Wilson C. B. *The Mathematical Description of Shape and Form.* Halsted Press, Chichester, England, 1984.

Loui A. C. P., Venetsanopoulos A. N., and Smith K. C. Two-dimensional shape representation using morphological correlation functions. In *Proceedings of the 1990 International Conference on Acoustics, Speech, and Signal Processing—ICASSP 90,* Albuquerque, NM, pages 2165–2168, Piscataway, NJ, 1990. IEEE.

Mandelbrot B. B. *The Fractal Geometry of Nature.* Freeman, New York, 1982.

Manzanera A., Bernard T. M., Preteux F., and Longuet B. Ultra-fast skeleton based on isotropic fully parallel algorithm. In *Proc. of Discrete Geometry for Computer Imagery*, 1999.

Maragos P. A. Pattern spectrum and multiscale shape representation. *IEEE Transactions on Pattern Analysis and Machine Intelligence*, 11:701–716, 1989.

Maragos P. A. and Schafer R. W. Morphological skeleton representation and coding of binary images. *IEEE Transactions on Acoustics, Speech and Signal Processing*, 34(5):1228–1244, 1986.

Marshall S. Application of image contours to three aspects of image processing; compression, shape recognition and stereopsis. In *Third International Conference on Image Processing and its Applications*, Coventry, England, pages 604–608, Stevenage, England, 1989. IEE, Michael Faraday House.

McCallum D. and Avis D. A linear algorithm for finding the convex hull of a simple polygon. *Information Processing Letters*, 9:201–206, 1979.

McKenzie D. S. and Protheroe S. R. Curve description using the inverse Hough transform. *Pattern Recognition*, 23(3–4):283–290, 1990.

Melkman A. V. On-line construction of the convex hull of a simple polyline. *Information Processing Letters*, 25(1):11–12, 1987.

Miciak M. Radon transformation and principal component analysis method applied in postal address recognition task. *IJCSA*, 7(3):33–44, 2010.

Mundy J. L. and Zisserman A. *Geometric Invariance in Computer Vision*. MIT Press, Cambridge, MA; London, 1992.

Oppenheim A. V., Willsky A. S., and Young I. T. *Signals and Systems*. Prentice-Hall, Englewood Cliffs, NJ, 1983.

Paglieroni D. W. and Jain A. K. Control point transforms for shape representation and measurement. *Computer Vision, Graphics, and Image Processing*, 42(1):87–111, 1988.

Papoulis A. *Probability, Random Variables, and Stochastic Processes*. McGraw-Hill, New York, 3rd edition, 1991.

Pavlidis T. *Structural Pattern Recognition*. Springer Verlag, Berlin, 1977.

Pavlidis T. A review of algorithms for shape analysis. *Computer Graphics and Image Processing*, 7:243–258, 1978.

Pavlidis T. A flexible parallel thinning algorithm. In *Proc. IEEE Computer Soc. Conf. Pattern Recognition, Image Processing*, pages 162–167, 1981.

Pitas I. and Venetsanopoulos A. N. Morphological shape decomposition. *IEEE Transactions on Pattern Analysis and Machine Intelligence*, 12(1):38–45, 1990.

Pizer S. M., Oliver W. R., and Bloomberg S. H. Hierarchical shape description via the multiresolution symmetric axis transform. *IEEE Transactions on Pattern Analysis and Machine Intelligence*, 9(4):505–511, 1987.

Pratt W. K. *Digital Image Processing*. Wiley, New York, 2nd edition, 1991.

Quan L., Gros P., and Mohr R. Invariants of a pair of conics revisited. *Image and Vision Computing*, 10(5):319–323, 1992.

Reinhardt J. M. and Higgins W. E. Efficient morphological shape representation. *IEEE Transactions on Image Processing*, 5:89–101, 1996.

Rom H. and Medioni G. Hierarchical decomposition and axial shape description. *IEEE Transactions on Pattern Analysis and Machine Intelligence*, 15:973–981, 1993.

Rosenfeld A. Digital straight line segments. *IEEE Transactions on Computers*, 23:1264–1269, 1974.

Rosenfeld A. A characterization of parallel thinning algorithms. *Information and Control*, 29: 286–291, 1975.

Rosenfeld A. *Picture Languages—Formal Models for Picture Recognition*. Academic Press, New York, 1979.

Rosenfeld A. and Kak A. C. *Digital Picture Processing*. Academic Press, New York, 2nd edition, 1982.

Rosin P. L. and West G. A. W. Segmentation of edges into lines and arcs. *Image and Vision Computing*, 7(2):109–114, 1989.

Rothwell C. A., Zisserman A., Forsyth D. A., and Mundy J. L. Fast recognition using algebraic invariants. In Mundy J. L. and Zisserman A., editors, *Geometric Invariance in Computer Vision*. MIT Press, Cambridge, MA; London, 1992.

Safaee-Rad R., Benhabib B., Smith K. C., and Ty K. M. Position, rotation, and scale-invariant recognition of 2 dimensional objects using a gradient coding scheme. In *IEEE Pacific RIM Conference on Communications, Computers and Signal Processing*, Victoria, BC, Canada, pages 306–311, Piscataway, NJ, 1989. IEEE.

Samet H. A tutorial on quadtree research. In Rosenfeld A., editor, *Multiresolution Image Processing and Analysis*, pages 212–223. Springer Verlag, Berlin, 1984.

Samet H. Reconstruction of quadtree medial axis transforms. *Computer Vision, Graphics, and Image Processing*, 29:311–328, 1985.

Saund E. Symbolic construction of a 2D scale-space image. *IEEE Transactions on Pattern Analysis and Machine Intelligence*, 12:817–830, 1990.

Savini M. Moments in image analysis. *Alta Frequenza*, 57(2):145–152, 1988.

Shapiro L. A structural model of shape. *IEEE Transactions on Pattern Analysis and Machine Intelligence*, 2(2):111–126, 1980.

Shariat H. A model-based method for object recognition. In *IEEE International Conference on Robotics and Automation*, Cincinnati, OH, pages 1846–1851, Los Alamitos, CA, 1990. IEEE.

Shridhar M. and Badreldin A. High accuracy character recognition algorithms using Fourier and topological descriptors. *Pattern Recognition*, 17(5):515–524, 1984.

Sklansky J. Measuring concavity on a rectangular mosaic. *IEEE Transactions on Computers*, 21(12):1355–1364, 1972.

Staib L. H. and Duncan J. S. Boundary finding with parametrically deformable models. *IEEE Transactions on Pattern Analysis and Machine Intelligence*, 14(11):1061–1075, 1992.

Strackee J. and Nagelkerke N. J. D. On closing the Fourier descriptor presentation. *IEEE Transactions on Pattern Analysis and Machine Intelligence*, 5(6):660–661, 1983.

Svoboda T., Kybic J., and Hlavac V. *Image Processing, Analysis, and Machine Vision: A MATLAB Companion*. Thomson Engineering, 2008.

Terrades O. R. and Valveny E. Radon transform for lineal symbol representation. In *Proceedings of the 7th International Conference on Document Analysis and Recognition*, pages 195–, Edinburgh, Scotland, August 2003.

Tomek I. Two algorithms for piecewise linear continuous approximation of functions of one variable. *IEEE Transactions on Computers*, 23(4):445–448, 1974.

Toussaint G. A historical note on convex hull finding algorithms. *Pattern Recognition Letters*, 3(1):21–28, 1985.

Tsai W. H. and Yu S. S. Attributed string matching with merging for shape recognition. *IEEE Transactions on Pattern Analysis and Machine Intelligence*, 7(4):453–462, 1985.

Turney J. L., Mudge T. N., and Volz R. A. Recognizing partially occluded parts. *IEEE Transactions on Pattern Analysis and Machine Intelligence*, 7(4):410–421, 1985.

Vernon D. Two-dimensional object recognition using partial contours. *Image and Vision Computing*, 5(1):21–27, 1987.

Wallace T. P. and Wintz P. A. An efficient three-dimensional aircraft recognition algorithm using normalized Fourier descriptors. *Computer Graphics and Image Processing*, 13:99–126, 1980.

Wang D., Haese-Coat V., and Ronsin J. Shape decomposition and representation using a recursive morphological operation. *Pattern Recognition*, 28:1783–1792, 1995.

Weiss I. Projective invariants of shapes. In *Proceedings of the DARPA Image Understanding Workshop,* Cambridge, MA, volume 2, pages 1125–1134. DARPA, 1988.

Weyl H. *The Classical Groups and Their Invariants.* Princeton University Press, Princeton, NJ, 1946.

Wilson R. and Nelson R. *Graph Colourings.* Longman Scientific and Technical; Wiley, Essex, England, and New York, 1990.

Winston P. H., editor. *The Psychology of Computer Vision.* McGraw-Hill, New York, 1975.

Witkin A. P. Scale-space filtering. In Pentland A. P., editor, *From Pixels to Predicates*, pages 5–19. Ablex, Norwood, NJ, 1986.

Woodwark J. *Computing Shape: An Introduction to the Representation of Component and Assembly Geometry for Computer-Aided Engineering.* Butterworths, London–Boston, 1986.

Wright M. W. and Fallside F. Skeletonisation as model-based feature detection. *IEE Proceedings Communication, Speech and Vision*, 140:7–11, 1993.

Wuescher D. M. and Boyer K. L. Robust contour decomposition using a constant curvature criterion. *IEEE Transactions on Pattern Analysis and Machine Intelligence*, 13(10):41–51, 1991.

Yuille A. L. and Poggio T. A. Scaling theorems for zero-crossings. *IEEE Transactions on Pattern Analysis and Machine Intelligence*, 8(1):15–25, 1986.

Chapter 9

Object recognition

Even the simplest machine vision tasks require the help of recognition. Basic methods of pattern recognition must be understood in order to study more complex machine vision processes leading to region and object classification. Classification of objects or regions has been mentioned several times; recognition is then the last step of the bottom-up image processing approach, and is often also used in other control strategies for image understanding.

Consider a simple recognition problem. Two different parties take place at the same hotel at the same time—the first is a celebration of a successful basketball season, and the second a yearly meeting of jockeys. The receptionist is giving directions to guests, asking which party they are to attend, but quickly learns that no questions are necessary and directs the guests to the right places, noticing that instead of questions, the obvious physical features of basketball players and jockeys can be used. Maybe just two features are used to make a decision: weight and height: All small and light men are directed to the jockey party, all tall and heavier guests are sent to the basketball party. So the early guests answered the doorman's question as to which party they are going to visit and this information, together with characteristic features of these guests, resulted in the ability to classify them based only on their features. Plotting height and weight in a two-dimensional space (see Figure 9.1), it is clear that jockeys and basketball players form two easily separable classes and that this recognition task is extremely simple. Real object recognition problems are often more difficult, and the classes do not differ so substantially, but the principles remain the same.

Pattern recognition is discussed at length in many references [Duda and Hart, 1973; Haykin, 1998; Duda et al., 2000; Bishop, 2006], and only a brief introduction will be given here. We will also introduce some other related techniques: graph matching, neural nets, genetic algorithms, simulated annealing, and fuzzy logic. Many open-source pattern recognition packages have become available; the Weka project (in Java) and pattern recognition for the **R** statistical package are perhaps the most prominent [Weka 3 Team, 2013; R Development Core Team, 2008; R Software Team, 2013]. Since many pattern recognition tasks can be efficiently solved by employing such well-developed and well-tested tools, becoming proficient with their use may be of interest.

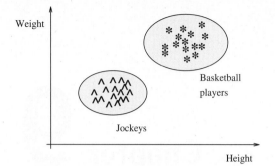

Figure 9.1: Recognition of basketball players and jockeys. © *Cengage Learning 2015.*

No recognition is possible without knowledge. Decisions about classes into which objects are classified are based on such knowledge. Both specific knowledge about the objects being processed and hierarchically higher and more general knowledge about object classes is required.

9.1 Knowledge representation

Here we present a short outline of common knowledge representation techniques and representations as they are used in AI, and an overview of some basic knowledge representations. More detailed coverage can be found in [Michalski et al., 1983; Wechsler, 1990; Reichgelt, 1991; Sowa, 1999; Brachman and Levesque, 2004].

A good knowledge representation design is the most important part of solving the understanding problem and a small number of relatively simple control strategies is often sufficient for AI systems to show complex behavior, assuming an appropriately complex knowledge base is available. In other words, given a rich, well-structured representation of a large set of a priori data and hypotheses a high degree of control sophistication is not required for intelligent behavior.

Other terms of which regular use will be made are **syntax** and **semantics** [Winston, 1984]. The **syntax** of a representation specifies the symbols that may be used and the ways that they may be arranged while the **semantics** of a representation specifies how meaning is embodied in the symbols and the symbol arrangement allowed by the syntax. A **representation** is then a set of syntactic and semantic conventions that make it possible to describe things.

The main knowledge representation techniques used in AI are formal grammars and languages, predicate logic, production rules, semantic nets, and frames. Note that knowledge representation data structures are mostly extensions of conventional data structures such as lists, trees, graphs, tables, hierarchies, sets, rings, nets, and matrices.

Descriptions, features

Descriptions and features are not pure knowledge representations but can nevertheless be used for representing knowledge as a part of a more complex structure. Descriptions usually represent some scalar properties of objects, and are called **features**. Typically, several descriptions are combined into **feature vectors**. Numerical feature vectors are inputs for statistical pattern recognition techniques (see Section 9.2).

Grammars, languages

Feature description is not adequate to describe an object's structure; a structural description is formed from existing primitives (elementary structural properties of the objects) and relations between them.

The simplest form of structure representations are chains, trees, and general graphs. A well-known example is structural description of chromosomes using border segments as primitives [Fu, 1982] (see Figure 8.15), where borders are represented by a chain of symbols, the symbols representing specific types of border primitives. Hierarchical structures can be represented by trees—the concavity tree of Figure 8.31 is an example. A more general graph representation is used in Chapter 15, where a graph grammar (Figure 15.11) is used for texture description. Many examples of syntactic object description may be found in [Fu, 1982].

One object can be described by a chain, a tree, a graph, etc., of symbols. Nevertheless, the whole class of objects cannot be described by a single chain, a single tree, etc., but a class of structurally described objects can be represented by **grammars** and **languages**. Grammars and languages provide rules defining how the chains, trees, or graphs can be constructed from a set of primitives. A more specific description of grammars and languages is given in Section 9.4.

Predicate logic

Predicate logic plays a very important role in knowledge representation—it introduces a mathematical formalism to derive new knowledge from old knowledge by applying mathematical deduction. Predicate logic works with combinations of logic variables, quantifiers ($\exists, \forall$), and logic operators (*and, or, not, implies, equivalent*). The logic variables are binary (*true, false*). The idea of proof and rules of inference such as **modus ponens** and **resolution** are the principal building blocks.

Predicate logic forms the essence of the programming language PROLOG, which is widely used if objects are described by logic variables. Requirements of 'pure truth' represent the main weakness of predicate logic in knowledge representation, since it does not allow uncertain or incomplete information.

Production rules

Production rules represent a wide variety of knowledge representations that are based on **condition action** pairs. The essential model of behavior of a system based on production rules (a production system) can be described as follows:

$$if \text{ condition } X \text{ holds } then \text{ action } Y \text{ is appropriate.}$$

Information about what action is appropriate at what time represents knowledge. The procedural character of knowledge represented by production rules is another important property—not all the information about objects must be listed as an object property. Consider a simple knowledge base where the following knowledge is presented using a production rule:

$$if \text{ ball } then \text{ circular.} \tag{9.1}$$

and suppose the knowledge base also includes the statements

$$\text{object A } \textit{is\_a} \text{ ball,}$$
$$\text{object B } \textit{is\_a} \text{ ball,}$$
$$\text{object C } \textit{is\_a} \text{ shoe,} \tag{9.2}$$
$$\text{etc.}$$

To answer the question *how many objects are circular?*, if enumerative knowledge representation is used, the knowledge must be listed as

$$\text{object A } \textit{is\_a} \text{ (ball, circular),}$$
$$\text{object B } \textit{is\_a} \text{ (ball, circular),} \tag{9.3}$$
$$\text{etc.}$$

If procedural knowledge is used, the knowledge base (equation 9.2) together with the knowledge (equation 9.1) gives the same information in a significantly more efficient manner.

Both production rule knowledge representation and production systems appear frequently in computer vision and image understanding problems. Furthermore, production systems, together with a mechanism for handling uncertainty information, form a basis of expert systems.

Fuzzy logic

Fuzzy logic was developed [Zadeh, 1965; Zimmermann et al., 1984] to overcome the obvious limitations of numerical or crisp representation of information. Consider the use of knowledge represented by production rule (equation 9.1) for recognition of balls; using the production rule, the knowledge about balls may be represented as

if circular *then* ball.

If the object in a two-dimensional image is considered circular then it may represent a ball. Our experience with balls, however, says that they are usually close to, but not perfectly, circular. Thus, it is necessary to define some circularity threshold so that all *reasonably* circular objects from our set of objects are labeled as balls. Here is the fundamental problem of crisp descriptions: how circular must an object be to be considered circular? If humans represent such knowledge, the rule for ball circularity may look like

if circularity is HIGH *then* object is a ball with HIGH confidence.

Clearly, high circularity is a preferred property of balls. Such knowledge representation is very close to common sense representation of knowledge, with no need for exact specification of the circularity/non-circularity threshold. **Fuzzy rules** are of the form

if X *is* A *then* Y *is* B,

where X and Y represent some properties and A and B are **linguistic variables**. Fuzzy logic can be used to solve object recognition and other decision-making tasks, among others; this is discussed further in Section 9.7.

Semantic nets

Semantic nets are a special variation of relational data structures (see Chapter 4). The semantics distinguish them from general nets—semantic nets consist of objects, their description, and a description of relations between objects (often just relations between neighbors). Logical forms of knowledge can be included in semantic nets, and predicate logic can be used to represent and/or evaluate the local information and local knowledge. Semantic nets can also represent common sense knowledge that is often imprecise and needs to be treated in a probabilistic way. Semantic nets have a hierarchical structure; complex representations consist of less complex representations, which can in turn be divided into simpler ones, etc. Relations between partial representations are described at all appropriate hierarchical levels.

Figure 9.2: A human face: *A face is a circular part of the human body that consists of two eyes, one nose, and one mouth; One eye is positioned left of the other eye; The nose is between and below the eyes; The mouth is below the nose; An eye is approximately circular; The nose is vertically elongated; The mouth is horizontally elongated.* © *Cengage Learning 2015.*

Semantic nets are represented by labeled graphs: nodes represent objects and arcs represent relations between them. A simple example is illustrated in Figure 9.2, and its associated semantic net is shown in Figure 9.3.

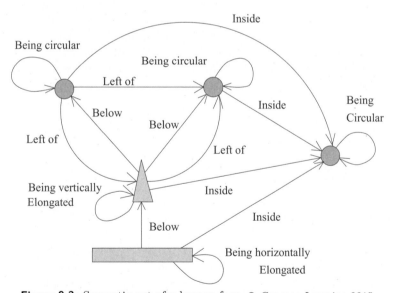

Figure 9.3: Semantic net of a human face. © *Cengage Learning 2015.*

The descriptive structures found in real images match the knowledge represented by a semantic net with varying degrees of closeness. How well such structures are represented by a semantic net is discussed in Section 9.5 and Chapter 10.

A detailed discussion of semantic nets related to image information can be found in [Niemann, 1990], and more general properties of semantic nets are described in [Michalski et al., 1983; Sharples et al., 1989].

Frames, scripts

Frames—which are considered high-level knowledge representation—provide a very general method for knowledge representation which may contain all the knowledge representation principles discussed so and is suitable for representing common sense knowledge under specific circumstances. They are sometimes called **scripts** because of their similarity to film scripts. Consider a frame called *plane_start*, which may consist of the following sequence of actions:

1. Start the engines.

2. Taxi to the runway.

3. Increase RPMs of engines to maximum.

4. Travel along runway increasing speed.

5. Fly.

Assuming this frame represents knowledge of how planes *usually* start, the situation of a plane standing on a runway with engines running causes the prediction that the plane will start in a short time. The frame can be used as a substitute for missing information which may be extremely important in vision-related problems.

Assuming that one part of the runway is not visible from the observation point, using the *plane_start* frame, a computer vision system can overcome the lack of continuous information between the plane moving at the beginning of the runway and flying when it next appears. If it is a passenger plane, the frame may have additional items such as *time of departure, time of arrival, departure city, arrival city, airline, flight number,* etc., because in a majority of cases it makes sense to be interested in this information if we identify a passenger plane.

From a formal point of view, a frame is represented by a general semantic net accompanied by a list of relevant variables, concepts, and concatenation of situations. No standard form of frame exists. Frames represent a tool for organizing knowledge in prototypical objects, and for description of mutual influences of objects using stereotypes of behavior in specific situations. Examples of frames can be found elsewhere [Michalski et al., 1983; Sharples et al., 1989].

9.2 Statistical pattern recognition

A physical object is usually represented in image analysis and computer vision by a region in a segmented image. The set of objects can be divided into disjoint subsets, that, from the classification point of view, have some common features and are called **classes**. How objects are divided into classes is imprecise and depends on the classification goal.

Object recognition assigns classes to objects, and the algorithm that does this is called a **classifier**. The number of classes is usually known beforehand, and typically can be derived from the problem specification. Nevertheless, there are approaches in which the number of classes may not be known (see Section 9.2.6).

The classifier (similarly to a human) does not decide about the class from the object itself—rather, sensed object properties serve this purpose. For example, to distinguish steel from sandstone, we do not have to determine molecular structures, even though this would describe them well. Properties such as texture, specific weight, hardness, etc., are used instead. These properties are called the **pattern**, and the classifier actually recognizes the patterns and not the objects. Object recognition and pattern recognition can be considered synonymous.

The main pattern recognition steps are shown in Figure 9.4. The block 'Construction of formal description' is based on the experience and intuition of the designer. A set of elementary properties is chosen which describe some characteristics of the object; these properties are measured in an appropriate way and form the description pattern of the object. These properties can be either quantitative or qualitative in character and their form can vary (numerical vectors, chains, etc.). The theory of recognition deals with the problem of designing the classifier for the specific (chosen) set of elementary object descriptions.

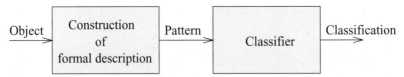

Figure 9.4: Main pattern recognition steps. © *Cengage Learning 2015.*

Statistical object description uses elementary numerical descriptions called **features**, $x_1, x_2, \ldots, x_n$; in image analysis, the features result from object description as discussed in Chapter 8. The pattern (also referred to as pattern vector, or feature vector) $\mathbf{x} = (x_1, x_2, \ldots, x_n)$ that describes an object is a vector of elementary descriptions, and the set of all possible patterns forms the **pattern space** X (also called **feature space**). If the elementary descriptions are chosen well, patterns of objects of each class are 'close' in pattern space. The classes form clusters in the feature space, which can be separated by a discrimination curve (or hyper-surface in a multi-dimensional feature space)—see Figure 9.5.

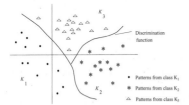

Figure 9.5: Discrimination functions between three classes. © *Cengage Learning 2015.*

If a discrimination hyper-surface exists which separates the feature space such that only objects from one class are in each separated region, the problem is called a recognition task with **separable classes**. If the discrimination hyper-surfaces are hyper-planes, it is called a **linearly separable** task. Intuitively, we may expect that separable classes can be recognized without errors.

The majority of object recognition problems do not have separable classes, in which case the locations of the discrimination hyper-surfaces in the feature space can never separate the classes correctly and some objects will always be misclassified.

9.2.1   Classification principles

A statistical classifier is a device with n inputs representing the n features $x_1, x_2, \ldots, x_n$ measured from an object to be classified, and 1 output. An R-class classifier will generate one of R symbols $\omega_1, \omega_2, \ldots, \omega_R$ as an output, and the user interprets this output as a decision about the class of the processed object. The generated symbols ω_r are the **class identifiers**.

A **decision rule** is a function $d(\mathbf{x}) = \omega_r$ which describes relations between classifier inputs and the output. The decision rule divides the feature space into R disjoint subsets K_r, $r = 1, \ldots, R$, each of which includes all the feature representation vectors $\mathbf{x}'$ of objects for which $d(\mathbf{x}') = \omega_r$. The borders between subsets K_r, $r = 1, \ldots, R$ form the discrimination hyper-surfaces. The determination of discrimination hyper-surfaces (or definition of the decision rule) is the goal of classifier design.

The discrimination hyper-surfaces can be defined by R scalar functions $g_1(\mathbf{x})$, $g_2(\mathbf{x})$, $\ldots$, $g_R(\mathbf{x})$ called **discrimination functions**. $g_r(\mathbf{x})$ is maximal for $\mathbf{x} \in K_r$:

$$g_r(\mathbf{x}) \geq g_s(\mathbf{x}) \, , s \neq r \, . \tag{9.4}$$

Then the discrimination hyper-surface between class regions K_r and K_s is defined by

$$g_r(\mathbf{x}) - g_s(\mathbf{x}) = 0 \, . \tag{9.5}$$

The decision rule results from this definition:

$$d(\mathbf{x}) = \omega_r \quad \Longleftrightarrow \quad g_r(\mathbf{x}) = \max_{s=1,\ldots,R} g_s(\mathbf{x}) \, . \tag{9.6}$$

Linear discrimination functions are the simplest and are widely used. Their general form is

$$g_r(\mathbf{x}) = q_{r_0} + q_{r_1} x_1 + \ldots + q_{r_n} x_n \tag{9.7}$$

for all $r = 1, \ldots, R$. If all the discrimination functions of the classifier are linear, it is called a **linear classifier**.

Non-linear classifiers usually transform the original feature space X^n into a new feature space X^m applying some appropriate non-linear function $\mathbf{\Phi}$, where the superscripts n, m refer to the space dimensionality

$$\mathbf{\Phi} = (\phi_1, \phi_2, \ldots, \phi_m) : X^n \to X^m \, . \tag{9.8}$$

After the transformation, a linear classifier is applied in the new feature space—the role of the function $\mathbf{\Phi}$ is to 'straighten' the non-linear discrimination hyper-surfaces of the original space into hyper-planes in the transformed space. The discrimination functions of such a classifier are

$$g_r(\mathbf{x}) = q_{r0} + q_{r1} \, \phi_1(\mathbf{x}) + \ldots + q_{rm} \, \phi_m(\mathbf{x}) \, , \tag{9.9}$$

where $r = 1, \ldots, R$. We may re-write the formula in vector representation

$$g_r(\mathbf{x}) = \mathbf{q}_r \cdot \mathbf{\Phi}(\mathbf{x}) \, , \tag{9.10}$$

where $\mathbf{q}_r$, $\mathbf{\Phi}(\mathbf{x})$ are vectors consisting of $q_{r0}, \ldots, q_{rm}$ and $\phi_0(\mathbf{x}), \ldots, \phi_m(\mathbf{x})$, respectively, $\phi_0(\mathbf{x}) \equiv 1$. Non-linear classifiers are described in detail in [Sklansky, 1981; Devijver and Kittler, 1982]. This important idea is revisited in Section 9.2.5 in considering support vector machines.

9.2.2 Nearest neighbors

We may construct classifiers based on the **minimum distance** principle; the resulting classifier is just a special case of classifiers with discrimination functions, but has computational advantages and may easily be implemented on digital computers. Assume that R points are defined in the feature space, $\mathbf{v}_1, \mathbf{v}_2, \ldots, \mathbf{v}_R$ that represent **exemplars** (sample patterns) of classes $\omega_1, \omega_2, \ldots, \omega_R$. A minimum distance classifier classifies a pattern $\mathbf{x}$ into the class to whose exemplar it is closest.

$$d(\mathbf{x}) = \omega_r \quad \Longleftrightarrow \quad |\mathbf{v}_r - \mathbf{x}| = \min_{s=1,\ldots,R} |\mathbf{v}_s - \mathbf{x}| . \tag{9.11}$$

Discrimination hyper-planes are perpendicular to and bisect line segments $\mathbf{v}_s\mathbf{v}_r$ (Figure 9.6). If each class is represented by just one exemplar, a linear classifier results; one implementation of this is:

Algorithm 9.1: Minimum distance classifier learning and classification

1. Learning: For all classes, compute class exemplars $\mathbf{v}_i$ based on the training set

$$\mathbf{v}_i(k_i + 1) = \frac{1}{k_i + 1} \Big(k_i\, \mathbf{v}_i(k_i) + \mathbf{x}_i(k_i + 1) \Big),$$

where $\mathbf{x}_i(k_i+1)$ are objects from the class i and k_i denotes the number of objects from class i used thus far for learning.

2. Classification: For an object description vector $\mathbf{x}$, determine the distance of $\mathbf{x}$ from the class exemplars $\mathbf{v}_i$. Classify the object into the class j if the distance of $\mathbf{x}$ from $\mathbf{v}_j$ is the minimum such (equation 9.11).

If more than one exemplar represents some class, the classifier gives piecewise linear discrimination hyper-planes—this is the elementary but widely applied **nearest neighbor** or NN classifier, which classifies an unseen pattern into the class of the nearest known training pattern. This simple idea is often made more resilient by allocating the new pattern to the most populous class of the k closest training patterns—this a k-NN classifier.

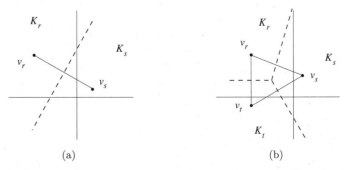

(a)   (b)

Figure 9.6: Minimum distance discrimination functions. © *Cengage Learning 2015*.

The nearest neighbor principle is very widely used in computer vision; often it is computed in some feature space as we outline here, and sometimes in connection with 2D or 3D spatial issues. It will be clear that for large data sets, especially if the dimensionality of the feature space is high—as it often is—the computation of nearest neighbor information may be very expensive. If the data come, for example, from a video stream then the expensive computation may need repeating with high frequency. The fundamental problem is that distance computation is costly and the total cost is unavoidably linear in the number of points compared. To increase the processing speed, it is possible to partition the data space and reduce this number significantly using K-D trees [Friedman et al., 1977]. If the data are in N dimensions, this data structure recursively partitions it on the co-ordinate which exhibits maximum variation: the resulting tree has leaves which are 'small' in densely occupied areas, and large in more sparse ones. The NN search is performed firstly in the leaf occupied by a test vector, and then only in neighboring leaves which contain plausible candidates.

Algorithm 9.2: Nearest neighbor search with K-D trees

1. For an N-dimensional dataset $X = \{\mathbf{x}_1, \mathbf{x}_2, \ldots, \mathbf{x}_n\}$ determine the dimension i, $1 \leq i \leq N$ which exhibits greatest variation. Cut the data with a plane at its median value along that dimension.

2. Recurse this procedure to create a balanced binary tree of depth d.

3. To locate the NN of an input vector $\mathbf{y}$, determine which leaf cell it lies within. Perform an exhaustive search within this cell.

4. Traverse neighboring cells that could contain an element closer to $\mathbf{y}$ than the current best candidate.

Since the exhaustive search is performed at a small number of leaves (perhaps only one), this algorithm will run in $\log(n)$ time and is a great improvement.

Algorithm 9.2 works well for low N, but the number of neighbors to search can become high as N increases. For these reasons, a selection of *approximate* nearest neighbor algorithms is available that most of the time generate solutions that, if imperfect, are near optimal: at simplest, we may terminate after step 3. Very often this delivers the NN but if not, it is likely to be close.

Better approximate algorithms rely on selectively applying step 4—Beis and Lowe [Beis and Lowe, 1997] have developed a Best Bin First (BBF) algorithm which prioritizes the order in which neighbors are searched. A hypersphere centered at $\mathbf{y}$ of radius the best yet NN distance is considered, and leaves with the largest intersection to it are considered first. The search is halted after some pre-determined number of neighbors E_{max} has been searched.

BBF is open to various improvements—Muja and Lowe have developed an approach which chooses a 'best' algorithm for the problem in hand [Muja and Lowe, 2009]. A software suite implementing this is publicly available at http://www.cs.ubc.ca/~mariusm/index.php/FLANN/FLANN.

9.2.3   Classifier setting

A classifier based on discrimination functions is a deterministic machine—one pattern **x** will always be classified into the same class. Note however that one pattern may represent objects from different classes, so the classifier decision may be correct for some objects and incorrect for others. The choice of *optimal* classifier will seek to minimize these incorrect judgements in some sense.

Suppose a particular classifier is characterized by a parameter vector **q**. The value of the mean loss $J(\mathbf{q})$ of this classifier depends on the decision rule that is applied: $\omega = d(\mathbf{x}, \mathbf{q})$. We will seek $\mathbf{q}^*$ that minimizes the mean loss:

$$J(\mathbf{q}^*) = \min_{\mathbf{q}} J(\mathbf{q}) \qquad d(\mathbf{x}, \mathbf{q}) \in D \,. \tag{9.12}$$

—then $\mathbf{q}^*$ is the vector of optimal parameters.

The **minimum error criterion** (Bayes criterion, maximum likelihood) uses loss functions of the form $\lambda(\omega_r|\omega_s)$, where $\lambda(.)$ describes quantitatively the loss incurred if a pattern **x** which should be classified into the class ω_s is incorrectly classified into the class ω_r

$$\omega_r = d(\mathbf{x}, \mathbf{q}) \,. \tag{9.13}$$

The mean loss is

$$J(\mathbf{q}) = \int_X \sum_{s=1}^{R} \lambda\big(d(\mathbf{x}, \mathbf{q})|\omega_s\big) p(\mathbf{x}|\omega_s) P(\omega_s) \, \mathbf{dx} \,, \tag{9.14}$$

where $P(\omega_s)$, $s = 1, \ldots, R$ are the a priori probabilities of classes, and $p(\mathbf{x}|\omega_s)$, $s = 1, \ldots, R$ are the conditional probability densities of objects **x** in the class ω_s.

A classifier that has been set according to the minimum-loss optimality criterion is easy to construct using discrimination functions; usually, unit loss functions are considered

$$\begin{aligned} \lambda(\omega_r|\omega_s) &= 0 \quad \text{for } r = s \,, \\ &= 1 \quad \text{for } r \neq s \,, \end{aligned} \tag{9.15}$$

and the discrimination functions are

$$g_r(\mathbf{x}) = p(\mathbf{x}|\omega_r) P(\omega_r) \quad r = 1, \ldots, R \,, \tag{9.16}$$

where $g_r(\mathbf{x})$ corresponds (up to a multiplicative constant) to the value of the a posteriori probability $P(\omega_r|\mathbf{x})$.

This probability describes how often a pattern **x** is from the class ω_r. Clearly, the optimal decision is to classify a pattern **x** to a class ω_r if the a posteriori probability $P(\omega_r|\mathbf{x})$ is the highest of all possible a posteriori probabilities

$$P(\omega_r|\mathbf{x}) = \max_{s=1,\ldots,R} P(\omega_s|\mathbf{x}) \,. \tag{9.17}$$

Bayes theorem tells us

$$P(\omega_s|\mathbf{x}) = \frac{p(\mathbf{x}|\omega_s) P(\omega_s)}{p(\mathbf{x})} \,, \tag{9.18}$$

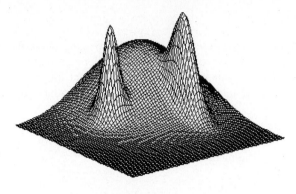

Figure 9.7: Minimum error classifier: a posteriori probabilities. © *Cengage Learning 2015.*

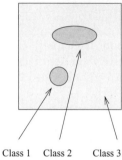

Class 1   Class 2   Class 3

Figure 9.8: Minimum error classifier: discrimination hyper-surfaces and resulting classes. © *Cengage Learning 2015.*

where $p(\mathbf{x})$ is the mixture density. An example plot of a posteriori probabilities is shown in Figure 9.7, and corresponding discrimination hyper-surfaces for a three-class classifier are in Figure 9.8.

Analytic minimization of the extrema problem is in many practical cases impossible because the multi-dimensional probability densities are not available. Criteria for loss function evaluation can be found in [Sklansky, 1981; Devijver and Kittler, 1982]. The requirements for classification correctness, and the set of objects accompanied by information about their classes, are usually available in practical applications—very often this is all the information that can be used for the classifier design and setting.

The ability to set classification parameters from a set of examples is the very important issue of **classifier learning**. Classifier learning is based on a set of objects (represented by their feature vectors), each being accompanied by knowledge of its proper classification—this set of patterns and classes is called the **training set**. Clearly, the quality of the classifier setting depends on the quality and size of this finite training set. After setting, we may expect patterns that were not used for classifier learning to enter the classifier. Classifier learning methods must be **inductive** in the sense that information obtained from the elements of the training set must be generalized to cover the whole feature space, implying that the learning should be (near) optimal for all feasible patterns, not only for those patterns that were present in the training set. The classifier should be able to recognize even those objects that it has never 'seen' before.

It may be that a solution for a given problem does not exist. The larger the training set, the better the guarantee that the classifier may be set correctly—classification correctness and the size of the training set are closely related. If the statistical properties of patterns are known, the necessary sizes of the training sets can be estimated, but in reality this is rarely the case. The training set is actually supposed to substitute this missing statistical information. Only after processing of the training set can the designer know whether it was sufficient, and whether an increase in size is necessary. Typically, training set size will be increased several times until the correct classification setting is achieved.

In practice, some proportion of the known training data will be held back to provide an objective test of performance when the classifier has been trained—this is called the test set, and will generate a measure of performance on hitherto unseen data. If just one data item is held back, this is called *leave one out testing*, and *leave K out testing* is defined similarly. If the K data items used for testing are selected randomly N times, a statistically robust testing scheme called *N-fold leave K out testing* results.

The general idea of sequential increase in training set size can be understood as presenting small portions of a large training set to the classifier, whose performance is checked after each portion—the smallest portion size is just one element. Sequential processing of information (which cannot be avoided in principle) has some substantial consequences in the classifier setting process.

All properties of classifier learning methods have analogies in the learning process of living organisms.

- **Learning** is the process of automated system optimization based on the sequential presentation of examples.

- The **goal of learning** is to minimize the optimality criterion. The criterion may be represented by the mean loss caused by incorrect decisions.

- Finite training set size requires the **inductive** character of learning. The goal of learning must be achieved by generalizing the information from examples, before all feasible examples have been presented. The examples may be chosen at random.

- The unavoidable requirements of sequential information presentation and the finite size of system memory necessitate the **sequential character of learning**. Therefore, learning is not a one-step process, but rather a step-by-step process of improvement.

The learning process searches out the optimal classifier setting from examples. The classifier system is constructed as a universal machine that becomes optimal after processing the training set examples (supervised learning), meaning that it is not necessary to repeat the difficult optimal system design if a new application appears. Learning methods do not depend on the application—it is possible to use the same learning to train a medical diagnostics classifier as an an object recognition classifier for robot vision.

The quality of classifier decisions is closely related to the quality and amount of information that is available. From this point of view, patterns should represent as complex a description as possible, but conversely, this would imply a large number of description features. Therefore, object description is always a trade-off between permissible classification error, the complexity of the classifier construction, and the time required for classification. This results in a question of how to choose the best features from a set of available features, and how to detect the features with the highest contribution to the recognition success. Methods of determination of **informativity** and **discriminativity** of measured features can be found in [Young and Calvert, 1974; Pudil et al., 1994].

9.2.4 Classifier learning

Two common learning strategies will be presented in this section:

- **Probability density estimation** estimates the probability densities $p(\mathbf{x}|\omega_r)$ and probabilities $P(\omega_r)$, $r = 1, \ldots, R$. The discrimination functions are computed according to the minimum error criterion (equation 9.16).

- **Direct loss minimization** finds the decision rule $\omega = d(\mathbf{x}, \mathbf{q}^*)$ by direct minimization of losses $J(\mathbf{q})$ without estimation of probability densities and probabilities. The criterion of the best approximation is applied.

Probability density estimation methods differ in computational difficulty according to the amount of prior information available about them. If some prior information is available, it usually describes the shape of probability density functions $p(\mathbf{x}|\omega_r)$. The parameters of the distribution are usually not known, and learning must estimate them. Therefore, this class of learning methods is sometimes called **parametric learning**.

Assume the patterns in the rth class can be described by a normal distribution, $N(\boldsymbol{\mu}_r, \boldsymbol{\Psi}_r)$. The probability density for patterns from the class ω_r can be computed as

$$p(\mathbf{x}|\omega_r) = \frac{1}{(2\pi)^{n/2} \sqrt{\det \boldsymbol{\Psi}_r}} \exp\left(-\frac{1}{2}(\mathbf{x} - \boldsymbol{\mu}_r)^T \boldsymbol{\Psi}_r^{-1} (\mathbf{x} - \boldsymbol{\mu}_r)\right) , \qquad (9.19)$$

where $\boldsymbol{\Psi}_r$ is the covariance matrix. Details about multi-variate probability density function estimation may be found in [Rao, 1965; Johnson and Wichern, 1990]. The computation process depends on additional information about $\boldsymbol{\mu}_r$ and $\boldsymbol{\Psi}_r$; three cases can be distinguished:

1. The covariance matrix $\boldsymbol{\Psi}_r$ is known, but the mean vector $\boldsymbol{\mu}_r$ is not. A feasible estimate may be the average

$$\tilde{\boldsymbol{\mu}}_r = \bar{\mathbf{x}} \qquad (9.20)$$

which can be computed recursively

$$\bar{\mathbf{x}}(k + 1) = \frac{1}{k + 1}\left(k\,\bar{\mathbf{x}}(k) + \mathbf{x}_{k+1}\right) , \qquad (9.21)$$

where $\mathbf{x}_{k+1}$ is the $(k + 1)^{\text{st}}$ pattern from the class r from the training set. This estimate is unbiased, consistent, efficient, and linear.

Alternatively, if the a priori estimate of the mean $\tilde{\boldsymbol{\mu}}_r(0)$ is available, the Bayes approach to estimation of the normal distribution parameters can be used. Then, the estimate can be computed recursively

$$\tilde{\boldsymbol{\mu}}_r(k + 1) = \frac{a + k}{a + k + 1}\tilde{\boldsymbol{\mu}}_r(k) + \frac{1}{a + k + 1}\mathbf{x}_{k+1} . \qquad (9.22)$$

The parameter a represents the confidence in the a priori estimate $\tilde{\boldsymbol{\mu}}_r(0)$. In training, a specifies the number of steps during which the designer believes more in the a priori estimate than in the mean value so far determined by training. Note that for $a = 0$, the Bayes estimate is identical to equation (9.21).

2. The covariance matrix Ψ_r is unknown, but the mean value vector μ_r is known. The estimate of the dispersion matrix Ψ_r is then usually taken as

$$\tilde{\Psi}_r = \frac{1}{K} \sum_{k=1}^{K} (\mathbf{x}_k - \mu_r)(\mathbf{x}_k - \mu_r)^T \qquad (9.23)$$

or, in recursive form

$$\tilde{\Psi}_r(k+1) = \frac{1}{k+1} \left(k\, \tilde{\Psi}_r(k) + (\mathbf{x}_{k+1} - \mu_r)(\mathbf{x}_{k+1} - \mu_r)^T \right). \qquad (9.24)$$

This estimate is unbiased and consistent.

As another option, if the a priori estimate $\tilde{\Phi}_r(0)$ of the dispersion matrix Ψ_r is known, the Bayes approach can be applied. Let K be the number of samples in the training set, and $\tilde{\Psi}_r(K)$ be calculated as in equation (9.24). Then

$$\tilde{\Phi}_r(K) = \frac{b\, \tilde{\Phi}_r(0) + K\, \tilde{\Psi}_r(K)}{b+K} \qquad (9.25)$$

and $\tilde{\Phi}_r(K)$ is considered the Bayes estimate of the dispersion matrix Ψ_r. Parameter b represents the confidence in the a priori estimate $\tilde{\Phi}_r(0)$.

3. Both the covariance matrix Ψ_r and the mean value vector μ_r are unknown. The following estimates can be used

$$\tilde{\mu}_r = \bar{\mathbf{x}}, \qquad (9.26)$$

$$\tilde{\Psi}_r = \mathbf{S} = \frac{1}{K-1} \sum_{k=1}^{K} (\mathbf{x}_k - \bar{\mathbf{x}})(\mathbf{x}_k - \bar{\mathbf{x}})^T \qquad (9.27)$$

or, in the recursive form

$$\mathbf{S}(k+1) = \frac{1}{k} \Big((k-1)\mathbf{S}(k) + \big(\mathbf{x}_{k+1} - \bar{\mathbf{x}}(k+1)\big)\big(\mathbf{x}_{k+1} - \bar{\mathbf{x}}(k+1)\big)^T$$
$$+ k\big(\bar{\mathbf{x}}(k) - \bar{\mathbf{x}}(k+1)\big)\big(\bar{\mathbf{x}}(k) - \bar{\mathbf{x}}(k+1)\big)^T \Big). \qquad (9.28)$$

Alternatively, if the a priori estimate $\tilde{\Phi}_r(0)$ of the dispersion matrix Ψ_r and the a priori estimate $\tilde{\nu}_r(0)$ of the mean vector for class r are known, the Bayes estimates can be determined as follows

$$\tilde{\nu}_r(K) = \frac{a\, \tilde{\mu}_r(0) + K\, \tilde{\mu}_r(K)}{a+K}, \qquad (9.29)$$

where K is the number of samples in the training set and $\tilde{\mu}_r(K)$ is determined using equations (9.20) and (9.21). The dispersion matrix estimate is calculated as

$$\tilde{\Phi}_r(K) = \frac{b}{b+K}\ \tilde{\Phi}_r(0) + a\, \tilde{\nu}_r(0)\, \tilde{\nu}_r(0)^T + (K-1)\, \tilde{\Psi}_r(K)$$
$$+ K\, \tilde{\mu}_r(K)\, \tilde{\mu}_r(K)^T - (a+K)\, \tilde{\nu}_r(K)\, \tilde{\nu}_r(K)^T, \qquad (9.30)$$

where $\tilde{\Psi}_r(K)$ is calculated as given in equation (9.24). Then, $\tilde{\nu}_r(K)$ and $\tilde{\Phi}_r(K)$ are considered the Bayes estimates of the mean vector and the dispersion matrix for class r, respectively. Again, parameters a, b represent the confidence in the a priori estimates of $\tilde{\Phi}_r(0)$ and $\tilde{\nu}_r(0)$.

The a priori probabilities of classes $P(\omega_r)$ are estimated as relative frequencies

$$P(\omega_r) = \frac{K_r}{K} \, , \tag{9.31}$$

where K is the total number of objects in the training set; K_r is the number of objects from the class r in the training set.

Algorithm 9.3: Learning and classification by estimating normal distribution probability densities

1. Learning: Compute estimates of the mean vector $\boldsymbol{\mu}_r$ and the covariance matrix $\boldsymbol{\Psi}_r$.

2. Compute estimates of the a priori probability densities $p(\mathbf{x}|\omega_r)$, equation (9.19).

3. Compute estimates of the a priori probabilities of classes, equation (9.31).

4. Classification: Classify all patterns into the class r if

$$\omega_r = \max_{i=1,\ldots,s} \Big(p(\mathbf{x}|\omega_i)\, P(\omega_i) \Big)$$

(equations 9.16 and 9.6).

If no prior information is available (i.e., even the distribution type is not known), the computation is more complex. In such cases, if it is not necessary to use the minimum error criterion, it is advantageous to use a direct loss minimization method.

No probability densities or probabilities are estimated in the second group of methods based on direct minimization of losses. The minimization process can be compared to gradient optimization methods, but pure gradient methods cannot be used because of unknown probability densities, so the gradient cannot be evaluated. Nevertheless, the minimum can be found using methods of **stochastic approximations** that are discussed in [Sklansky, 1981].

The most important conclusion is that the learning algorithms can be represented by recursive formulae in both groups of learning methods and it is easy to implement them.

9.2.5   Support vector machines

The support vector machine [SVM] approach has proved powerful and popular. Optimal classification of a separable two-class problem is achieved by maximizing the width of the empty area (**margin**) between the two classes—this width is defined as the distance between the discrimination hyper-surfaces in n-dimensional feature space. Vectors from each class that are closest to the discriminating surface are called **support vectors**. The support vectors thus specify the discrimination function. Usually, many discriminating hyper-surfaces exist, and the ability to identify the *optimal* discriminating surface is a major strength of this approach and assists in dealing with the problem of over-fitting during training. From the theoretical viewpoint, it can be shown that such an optimal hyper-surface has the lowest **capacity**—a requirement based on the statistical learning theory of Vapnik and Chervonenkis [Burges, 1998].

Consider first the two-class linearly separable case, with a set of n-dimensional feature vectors $\mathbf{x}$ and class identifiers ω associated with them, $\omega \in \{-1, 1\}$. For simplicity, assume that the individual feature values x_i are scaled so that $x_i \in [0, 1]$ to overcome uneven influence from features with different variance. Discrimination between the two classes is achieved by defining a separating hyper-plane

$$\mathbf{w} \cdot \mathbf{x} + b = 0 \tag{9.32}$$

(compare equation 9.7). To maximize the margin, two parallel hyper-planes are defined

$$\mathbf{w} \cdot \mathbf{x} + b = 1 \,, \qquad\qquad \mathbf{w} \cdot \mathbf{x} + b = -1 \,, \tag{9.33}$$

passing through the support vectors and having no training patterns between them. To guarantee that no training patterns are present between these two hyper-planes, for all $\mathbf{x}_i$ we must have

$$\omega_i(\mathbf{w} \cdot \mathbf{x}_i + b) \geq 1 \,. \tag{9.34}$$

Suppose $\mathbf{x}^+$ is on the positive plane, and $\mathbf{x}^-$ is the closest point on the negative plane. Then $\mathbf{x}^+ - \mathbf{x}^-$ is normal to the plane(s) and so for some λ

$$\begin{aligned} \lambda\mathbf{w} &= \mathbf{x}^+ - \mathbf{x}^- \,, \\ \lambda\|\mathbf{w}\|^2 &= \mathbf{x}^+ \cdot \mathbf{w} - \mathbf{x}^- \cdot \mathbf{w} \,, \\ \lambda\|\mathbf{w}\|^2 &= 2 \end{aligned} \tag{9.35}$$

and hence $|\mathbf{x}^+ - \mathbf{x}^-| = (2/\|\mathbf{w}\|)$. To maximize the margin, we need to minimize $\|\mathbf{w}\|$ subject to the constraint given in equation (9.34), which is a quadratic programming optimization problem. Once optimized, the discrimination hyperplane is parallel to and positioned in the middle between these two parallel hyper-planes (Figure 9.9c).

Lagrangian theory is employed to reformulate the minimization problem avoiding inequality constraints, and thereby simplifying the optimization process. The Lagrangian function is defined as

$$L\left(\mathbf{w}, b, \alpha\right) = \frac{1}{2} \parallel \mathbf{w} \parallel - \sum_{i=1}^{N} \alpha_i\, \omega_i\left(\mathbf{w}_i \cdot \mathbf{x}_i + b\right) + \sum_{i=1}^{N} \alpha_i \,, \tag{9.36}$$

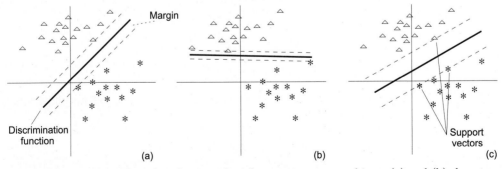

Figure 9.9: Basic two-class classification idea of support vector machines. (a) and (b) show two examples of non-optimal linear discrimination. (c) An optimal linear discriminator maximizes the margin between patterns of the two classes. The optimal hyperplane is a function of the support vectors. © *Cengage Learning 2015.*

where α_i are Lagrange multipliers. $L(\mathbf{w}, b, \alpha)$ is minimized with respect to $\mathbf{w}$ and b, while α_i are constrained to $\alpha_i \geq 0$. Taking the partial derivative of the Lagrangian function with respect to $\mathbf{w}$ and b results in

$$\frac{\partial L(\mathbf{w}, b, \alpha)}{\partial \mathbf{w}} = \mathbf{w} - \sum_{i=1}^{N} \alpha_i \, \omega_i \, \mathbf{x}_i \,, \tag{9.37}$$

$$\frac{\partial L(\mathbf{w}, b, \alpha)}{\partial b} = \sum_{i=1}^{N} \alpha_i \, \omega_i \,, \tag{9.38}$$

and setting both equations to zero creates the following relationships:

$$\mathbf{w} = \sum_{i=1}^{N} \alpha_i \, \omega_i \, \mathbf{x}_i \,, \tag{9.39}$$

$$\sum_{i=1}^{N} \alpha_i \, \omega_i = 0 \,. \tag{9.40}$$

These relations are substituted back into the original Lagrangian function, equation (9.36), to create an alternative optimization problem known as a dual formulation, taking into consideration pairwise relationships between training patterns $\mathbf{x}_i$ and $\mathbf{x}_j$ and their respective class labels ω_i, ω_j,

$$L(\mathbf{w}, b, \alpha) = \sum_{i=1}^{N} \alpha_i - \frac{1}{2} \sum_{i,j=1}^{N} \alpha_i \, \alpha_j \, \omega_i \, \omega_j (\mathbf{x}_i \cdot \mathbf{x}_j) \,, \tag{9.41}$$

where $L(\mathbf{w}, b, \alpha)$ is maximized with respect to α_i, subject to $\sum_{i=1}^{N} \omega_i \alpha_i = 0$ and $\alpha_i \geq 0$. The scalar b has dropped out, but can be easily computed from the original dataset once equation (9.41) is optimized.

The two-class classification of a pattern $\mathbf{x}$ can be accomplished according to the following discrimination function:

$$f(\mathbf{x}) = \mathbf{w} \cdot \mathbf{x}_i + b \,, \tag{9.42}$$

where

$$\begin{aligned} \omega_{\mathbf{x}} &= +1 \quad \text{if } f(\mathbf{x}) \geq 0 \,, \\ &= -1 \quad \text{if } f(\mathbf{x}) < 0 \,. \end{aligned} \tag{9.43}$$

The discrimination function is restated in terms of training vectors and multipliers by substituting $\mathbf{w}$ using equation (9.39)

$$f(\mathbf{x}) = \sum_{i \in \text{SV}} \alpha_i \, \omega_i (\mathbf{x}_i \cdot \mathbf{x}) + b \,. \tag{9.44}$$

Each of the Lagrange multipliers α_i shares a corresponding training vector $\mathbf{x}_i$. Those vectors that contribute to the maximized margin will have non-zero α_i and are the *support vectors*. The rest of the training vectors do not contribute to the final discrimination function—therefore, the summation is only performed over those values of i for which $\mathbf{x}_i$ is a support vector ($i \in$ SV).

Equation (9.43) shows that the decision as to whether a vector $\mathbf{x}$ belongs to class $\omega_{\mathbf{x}} = +1$ or $\omega_{\mathbf{x}} = -1$ depends only on the support vectors associated with the maximum margin as identified in the training phase. Therefore, the discrimination hyperplane in the feature space can be obtained from vectors in the input space and dot products in the feature space. Consequently, the training can be based on a small set of support vectors, even in large training sets, thus limiting the computational complexity of training with explicitly represented feature vectors.

If a separating hyperplane cannot be found to partition the feature space into two classes, one explanation is a linear inseparability of the training patterns. One solution is to tolerate some minimal mis-classification, but this is difficult to formulate as a quadratic programming problem. More commonly, the **kernel trick** (due to Aizerman [Aizerman et al., 1964]) is employed [Boser et al., 1992]. In the linear space, we determined the similarity of two patterns $\mathbf{x}_i$ and $\mathbf{x}_j$ with a **kernel function** $k(\mathbf{x}_i, \mathbf{x}_j) = (\mathbf{x}_i \cdot \mathbf{x}_j)$. The dot products of the linear support vector classifier can be replaced with non-linear kernel functions

$$k(\mathbf{x}_i, \mathbf{x}_j) = \Phi(\mathbf{x}_i) \cdot \Phi(\mathbf{x}_j) \,. \tag{9.45}$$

—the idea here is to transform the vectors into a space in which a linear discrimination hyperplane can be determined, corresponding to a non-linear hyper-surface in the original feature space (Figure 9.10, see also Section 9.2.1, and equations 9.8–9.10). The support vector classification algorithm is formally identical to that used for linear discrimination, while every dot product used earlier is replaced by a non-linear kernel function. Due to the kernel trick, the support vector classifier can locate the linearly separating hyperplane in the transformed space by defining an appropriate kernel function.

While calculating the right-hand side of equation (9.45) may be expensive in general, a number of simple kernels can be used to serve the purpose, for example homogeneous d^{th} order polynomials, equation (9.46); non-homogeneous d^{th} order polynomials, equation (9.47); radial basis functions, equation (9.48); Gaussian radial basis functions,

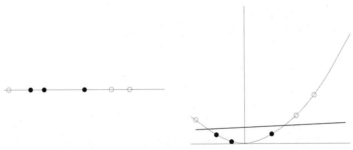

Figure 9.10: Achieving linear separability by application of a kernel function. On the left, the two classes are not linearly separable in 1D: on the right, the function $\Phi(x) = x^2$ creates a linearly separable problem. © *Cengage Learning 2015.*

equation (9.49); and other kernels:

$$k(\mathbf{x_i}, \mathbf{x_j}) = (\mathbf{x_i} \cdot \mathbf{x_j})^d \,, \tag{9.46}$$

$$k(\mathbf{x_i}, \mathbf{x_j}) = (\mathbf{x_i} \cdot \mathbf{x_j} + 1)^d \,, \tag{9.47}$$

$$k(\mathbf{x_i}, \mathbf{x_j}) = \exp\left(-\gamma \|\mathbf{x_i} - \mathbf{x_j}\|^2\right), \quad \text{for } \gamma > 0 \,, \tag{9.48}$$

$$k(\mathbf{x_i}, \mathbf{x_j}) = \exp\left(-\frac{\|\mathbf{x_i} - \mathbf{x_j}\|}{2\,\sigma^2}\right). \tag{9.49}$$

Applying the kernel technique to the dual Lagrange function yields

$$L(\mathbf{w}, b, \alpha) = \sum_{i=1}^{N} \alpha_i - \frac{1}{2} \sum_{i,j=1}^{N} \alpha_i \alpha_j \omega_i \omega_j k(\mathbf{x_i}, \mathbf{x_j}) \tag{9.50}$$

and the resulting discrimination function is

$$f(\mathbf{x}) = \sum_{i \in \text{sv}} \alpha_i\, \omega_i\, k(\mathbf{x_i}, \mathbf{x}) + b\,. \tag{9.51}$$

Linear support vector classification is identical to a classifier with linear discriminant functions if we somehow knew which training patterns constitute the support vectors, and disregard the remaining training patterns.

Algorithm 9.4 summarizes the training and classification steps using a support vector machine.

Algorithm 9.4: Support vector machine learning and classification

1. Training: Select an appropriate kernel function, $k(\mathbf{x_i}, \mathbf{x_j})$.

2. Minimize $\|\mathbf{w}\|$ subject to the constraint given in equation (9.34). This is accomplished by maximizing the kernel-modified Lagrange function, equation (9.50), with respect to α_i subject to the constraints $\sum_{i=1}^{N} \alpha_i \omega_i = 0$ and $\alpha_i \geq 0$.

3. Store only the non-zero α_i and corresponding training vectors $\mathbf{x}_i$. These are the support vectors.

4. Classification: For each pattern $\mathbf{x}$, compute the discrimination function, equation (9.51) using the support vectors $\mathbf{x}_i$ and the corresponding weights α_i. The sign of the function determines the classification of $\mathbf{x}$.

Interestingly, the choice of the kernel function is frequently not critical and classifier performance is often comparable for several of the simple kernel functions, with performance much more dependent on data preparation [Schoelkopf, 1998; Hearst, 1998; Leopold and Kindermann, 2002].

Figure 9.11 shows an example of support vector machine training for a non-linearly separable problem; here, the kernel of equation (9.49) was used.

N-class classification is accomplished by combining N 2-class classifiers, each discriminating between a specific class and the rest of the training set. During the classification stage, a pattern is assigned to the class with the largest positive distance between the classified pattern and the individual separating hyperplane for the N binary classifiers. (This approach can lead to very imbalanced classes in training, with one much more populous than the other—this issue is considered in [Li et al., 2009]). Alternatively, we might build $\frac{N(N-1)}{2}$ pairwise classifiers: classification is performed by applying them all and using a voting mechanism.

The support vector optimization problem can be solved analytically for small amounts of data, or if the support vector sets can be identified beforehand, but in most real-world cases the quadratic optimization problem must be solved numerically. For small problems, almost any general purpose quadratic optimization package will work sufficiently well. A survey of available solvers for larger-scale problems can be found in [More and Toraldo, 1993]. There is a substantial literature available discussing theoretical treatment as well as practical issues of support vector machine applications.

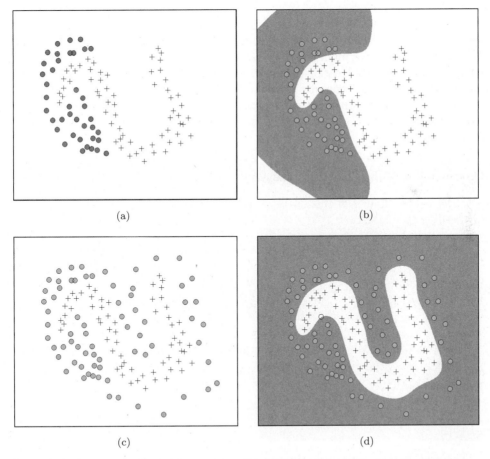

(a)　　　　　　　　　　　　　　　　(b)

(c)　　　　　　　　　　　　　　　　(d)

Figure 9.11: Support vector machine training; Gaussian radial basis function kernel used (equation 9.49). (a,c) Two-class pattern distribution in a feature space. (Note that the "+" patterns in (a) and (b) are identical while the "o" patterns in (a) are a subset of patterns in (b)). (b,d) Non-linear discrimination functions obtained after support vector machine training. © *Cengage Learning 2015.*

9.2.6 Cluster analysis

We noted earlier that unsupervised learning classification methods do not require training sets, and in particular do not need information about the class of objects in the learning stage. One such group of classification methods is called **cluster analysis**. Cluster analysis methods divide the set of patterns into subsets (clusters) based on the mutual similarity of subset elements. Objects that are dissimilar reside in different clusters.

Cluster analysis methods are *hierarchical* or *non-hierarchical*. Hierarchical methods construct a clustering tree; the set of patterns is divided into the two most dissimilar subsets, and subsets are recursively divided into smaller subsets. Non-hierarchical methods sequentially assign each pattern to one cluster. Methods and algorithms for cluster analysis can be found in [Duda et al., 2000; Everitt et al., 2001; Romesburg, 2004]

Non-hierarchical cluster analysis methods are either parametric or non-parametric. Parametric approaches are based on known class-conditioned distributions and require distribution parameter estimation similar to that used in minimum error classification described in Section 9.2.4.

Non-parametric cluster analysis is a popular, simple, and practically useful non-hierarchical approach to cluster analysis: the k-means algorithm is very well known and widely applied. It takes as input N n-dimensional data points and assumes the number of clusters K is known. The location of cluster *exemplars* is initialized, perhaps at random, or exploiting known data structure if available. Iteratively, data points are allocated to their closest exemplar, and then the exemplars are recomputed as the centroid of their associated data points. The algorithm terminates when the exemplars' positions have stabilized.

Algorithm 9.5: K-means cluster analysis

1. Define the number of clusters K to be sought in a set $X = \{\mathbf{x}_1, \mathbf{x}_2, \ldots, \mathbf{x}_N\}$ of n-dimensional data.

2. Initialize the cluster starting points (exemplars, initial guesses) $\mathbf{v}_1, \mathbf{v}_2, \ldots, \mathbf{v}_k, \ldots, \mathbf{v}_K$. This may be random, or from K data points, or from other prior knowledge.

3. Allocate data points to the closest $\mathbf{v}_i$ using some distance metric d (Euclidean is obvious and common).

4. Recompute the $\mathbf{v}_i$ as centroids of their associated data, V_i

$$V_i = \{\mathbf{x}_j : d(\mathbf{x}_j, \mathbf{v}_i) = \min_k(d(\mathbf{x}_j, \mathbf{v}_k))\} \,.$$

5. If the $\mathbf{v}_i$ have not stabilized, go to 3.

The 'error' in the clustering is given by the sum of square distances of the data points to their allocated exemplar

$$E = \sum_{i=1}^{K} \sum_{\mathbf{x}_j \in V_i} d^2(\mathbf{x}_j, \mathbf{v}_i) \,. \tag{9.52}$$

It is straightforward to show that the algorithm monotonically decreases this quantity (so it must converge).

K-means is exceptionally widely used as it is effective and simple. Minimizing the square error can be made computationally efficient and works well for compact hyperspherical clusters. When Mahalanobis distance is used, K-means forms hyper-elliptical clusters.

Determining a good value for k automatically is a widely considered problem. A popular heuristic approach is to consider when the overall cost reduction by adding another cluster appears to benefit little: the graph of optimal E (equation 9.52) against K characteristically adopts an L-shape, and the location of the elbow of the L is a good choice for K. One approach locates the position of this plot that gives the best straight line fit to the left and right of each candidate K [Salvador and Chan, 2004]. A better theoretically founded approach considers incrementally increasing K by splitting the cluster which gives the optimal increase in the Bayesian Information Criterion—informally, splitting the 'sparsest' cluster—and then rerunning the algorithm [Pelleg and Moore, 2000]. Further answers to these and many related questions can be found in [Romesburg, 2004].

K-means is one of a family of algorithms that see wide use: similar others include the *ISODATA* cluster analysis method [Kaufman and Rousseeuw, 1990], the *mean shift* algorithm described in Section 7.1, *fuzzy* k-*means* (or *fuzzy* c-*means*) in which cluster membership is 'fuzzy' (see Section 9.7), *Kohonen networks* described in Section 9.3.2, *Hopfield networks* described in Section 9.3.3, and *Gaussian Mixture Models* described in Section 10.13. Note that statistical pattern recognition and cluster analysis can be combined—for instance, the minimum distance classifier can be taught using cluster analysis methods.

9.3 Neural nets

Neural nets have seen widespread use for some decades and represent a tool of great value in various areas generally regarded as 'difficult', particularly speech and visual pattern recognition.

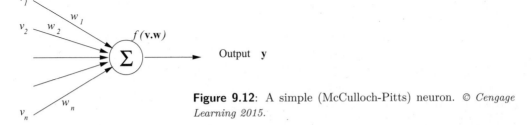

Figure 9.12: A simple (McCulloch-Pitts) neuron. © *Cengage Learning 2015.*

Most neural approaches are based on combinations of elementary processors (neurons), each of which takes a number of inputs and generates a single output. Associated with each input is a weight, and the output (in most cases) is then a function of the weighted sum of inputs; this output function may be discrete or continuous, depending on the variety of network in use. A simple neuron is shown in Figure 9.12—this model is derived from pioneering work on neural simulation conducted over 70 years ago [McCulloch and Pitts, 1943]. The inputs are denoted by $v_1, v_2, \ldots,$ and the weights by $w_1, w_2,$ $\ldots$; the total input to the neuron is then

$$x = \sum_{i=1}^{n} v_i\, w_i \tag{9.53}$$

or, more generally

$$x = \sum_{i=1}^{n} v_i\, w_i - \theta\,, \tag{9.54}$$

where θ is a threshold associated with this neuron. Also associated with the neuron is a **transfer function** $f(x)$ which provides the output; common examples are

$$f(x) = \begin{cases} 0 & \text{if } x \leq 0 \\ 1 & \text{if } x > 0 \end{cases}, \tag{9.55}$$

$$f(x) = \frac{1}{1 + e^{-x}}. \tag{9.56}$$

[Rosenblatt, 1962].

The general idea of collections (networks) of these neurons is that they are interconnected (so the output of one becomes the input of another, or others)—this idea mimics the high level of interconnection of elementary neurons found in brains, which is thought to explain the damage resistance and recall capabilities of humans. Such an interconnection may then take some number of external inputs and deliver up some (possibly different) number of external outputs—see Figure 9.13. What lies between then specifies the network: This may mean a large number of heavily interconnected neurons, or some highly structured (e.g., layered) interconnection, or, pathologically, nothing (so that inputs are connected straight to outputs).

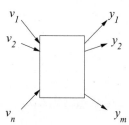

Figure 9.13: A neural network as a vector associator. © *Cengage Learning 2015.*

There are many uses to which such a structure may be put; the general task being performed is vector association. Examples may be:

- Classification: If the output vector (m-dimensional) is binary and contains only a single one, the position of the one classifies the input pattern into one of m categories.

- Auto-association: Some uses of neural networks cause them to re-generate the input pattern at the outputs (so $m = n$ and $v_i = y_i$); the purpose of this may be to derive a more compact vector representation from within the network internals.

- General association: At their most interesting, the vectors **v** and **y** represent patterns in different domains, and the network is forming a correspondence between them. For example, the inputs may represent a stream of written text and the outputs phonemes, making the network a speech generator [Sejnowski and Rosenberg, 1987].

Here we give only a brief overview to show the main principles of neural nets and their connections to conventional statistical pattern recognition. We do not discussed many alternative neural net techniques, methods, and implementations. Many further references may be found in a host of published papers and various introductory texts.

9.3.1   Feed-forward networks

Early neural networks involved no 'internals' (so the box in Figure 9.13 was empty); these *perceptrons* had a training algorithm developed which was shown to converge *if a solution to the problem at hands exists* [Minsky, 1988]; unfortunately, this proved very restrictive, requiring that the classification being performed be linearly separable This restriction was overcome by widely used **back-propagation** algorithm [Rumelhart and McClelland, 1986], which trains strictly layered networks in which it is assumed that at least one layer exists between input and output (it fact, it can be shown that two such 'hidden' layers always suffice [Kolmogorov, 1963; Hecht-Nielsen, 1987]). Such a network is shown in Figure 9.14, and is an example of a **feed-forward** network: data are admitted at the inputs and travel in one direction toward the outputs, at which the 'answer' may be read.

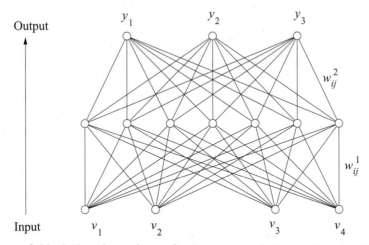

Figure 9.14: A three-layered neural net structure. © *Cengage Learning 2015.*

Such networks are 'taught' from a known training set. Back-propagation proceeds by comparing the output of the network to that expected, and computing an error measure based on sum of square differences. This is then minimized using gradient descent by altering the weights of the network. Denoting a member of the training set by $\mathbf{v}^i$, the actual outputs by $\mathbf{y}^i$, and the *desired* outputs by ω^i, the error is

$$E = \sum_i \sum_j (y_j^i - \omega_j^i)^2$$

and the algorithm performs the iterative updates

$$w_{ij}(k+1) = w_{ij}(k) - \epsilon \frac{\partial E}{\partial w_{ij}} \qquad (9.57)$$

until 'good' performance is seen.

The literature on back-propagation is large and thorough, and we present here a summary of the algorithm only.

Algorithm 9.6: Back-propagation learning

1. Assign small random numbers to the weights w_{ij}, and set $k = 0$.

2. Input a pattern $\mathbf{v}$ from the training set and evaluate the neural net output $\mathbf{y}$.

3. If $\mathbf{y}$ does not match the required output vector ω, adjust the weights

$$w_{ij}(k+1) = w_{ij}(k) + \epsilon \delta_j z_i(k) , \qquad (9.58)$$

where ϵ is called the **learning constant** or **learning rate**, $z_i(k)$ is the output of the node i, k is the iteration number, δ_j is an error associated with the node j in the adjacent upper level

$$\delta_j = \begin{cases} y_j(1 - y_j)(\omega_j - y_j) & \text{for output node } j , \\ z_j(1 - z_j) \sum_l \delta_l w_{jl} & \text{for hidden node } j . \end{cases} \qquad (9.59)$$

4. Go to step 2 and fetch the next input pattern.

5. Increment k, and repeat steps 2 to 4 until each training pattern outputs a suitably good approximation to that expected. Each circuit of this loop is termed an **epoch**.

The convergence process can be very slow, and there is an extensive literature on speeding the algorithm (see, for example, [Haykin, 1998]). The best known of these techniques is the introduction of **momentum**, which accelerates convergence across plateaus of the cost surface, and controls behavior in steep ravines. This approach rewrites equation (9.57) as

$$\Delta w_{ij} = \epsilon \frac{\partial E}{\partial w_{ij}}$$

and updates it to

$$\Delta w_{ij} := \epsilon \frac{\partial E}{\partial w_{ij}} + \epsilon \Delta w_{ij} ,$$

which updates equation (9.58) to

$$w_{ij}(k+1) = w_{ij}(k) + \epsilon \delta_j z_i(k) + \alpha \big(w_{ij}(k) - w_{ij}(k-1) \big) ; \qquad (9.60)$$

α is called the **momentum constant** and is chosen to be between 0 and 1, having the effect of contributing a proportion of the update of the previous iteration into the current one. Thus, in areas of very low gradient, some movement continues.

9.3.2 Unsupervised learning

A different class of networks are self-teaching—that is, they do not depend on the net being exposed to a a training set with known information about classes, but are able to self-organize themselves to recognize patterns automatically. Various types of networks exist under this general heading, of which the best known are Kohonen feature maps.

Kohonen maps take as input n-dimensional data vectors and generate an n-dimensional output that, within the domain of the problem at hand, 'best represents' the particular input given. More precisely, the network has a layer of neurons, each of which is connected to all n input vector components, each neuron calculates its input (equation 9.53), and that with the largest input is regarded as the 'winner'; the n weights associated with the input arcs to this node then represent the output. Figure 9.15 illustrates this. The weights are updated using a learning algorithm that finds the data structure for itself (i.e., no prior classification is needed or indeed known). It may be clear that such a network is performing the role of clustering—similar inputs generate the same output.

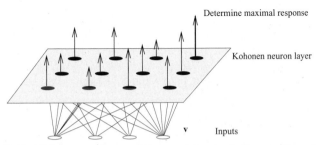

Figure 9.15: Kohonen self-organizing neural net. © *Cengage Learning 2015*.

The theory underlying Kohonen networks is derived from the operation of biological neurons, which are known to exist in locally 2D layers and in which neural responses are known to cluster. The derivation of the algorithm may be found in various standard texts [Kohonen, 1995] but may be summarized as follows.

Algorithm 9.7: Unsupervised learning of the Kohonen feature map

1. Assign random numbers with a small variance around the average values of the input feature vector elements to the weights w_{ij}.

2. Collect a sample of vectors $V = \{\mathbf{v}\}$ from the set to be analyzed.

3. Select a new vector $\mathbf{v} \in V$, and determine the neuron with the biggest input:
$$j^* = \operatorname*{argmax}_{j} \sum_{i} w_{ij}\, v_i .$$

4. For all neurons n_j within a neighborhood of radius r of n_{j^*}, perform the weight update with step size $\alpha > 0$ (learning rate)
$$w_{ij} := w_{ij} + \alpha\,(v_i - w_{ij}) . \tag{9.61}$$

5. Go to step 3.

6. Reduce r and α, and go to step 3.

Several other varieties of self-teaching net exist, of which the best known is perhaps ART (Adaptive Resonance Theory) [Carpenter and Grossberg, 1987]. More specialized texts provide ample detail.

9.3.3   Hopfield neural nets

Hopfield nets are used mostly in optimization problems [Hopfield and Tank, 1986]; however, it is possible to represent recognition as an optimization task—find the maximum similarity between a pattern $\mathbf{x}$ and one of the existing exemplars $\mathbf{v}$.

In the Hopfield neural model, the network does not have designated inputs and outputs, but rather the current configuration represents its state. The neurons, which are fully interconnected, have discrete (0/1 or -1/1) outputs, calculated from equation (9.55). Weights between neurons do not evolve (learn), but are computed from a set of known exemplars at initialization

$$w_{ij} = \sum_r \left(v_i^r v_j^r \right) , \quad i \neq j , \tag{9.62}$$

where w_{ij} is the interconnection weight between nodes i and j; and v_i^r is the ith element of the rth exemplar; $w_{ii} = 0$ for any i.

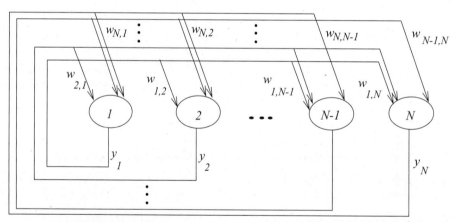

Figure 9.16: Hopfield recurrent neural net. © *Cengage Learning 2015*.

The Hopfield net acts as an associative memory where the exemplars are stored; its architecture is shown in Figure 9.16. When used for recognition, the feature vector to be classified enters the net in the form of initial values of node outputs. The Hopfield net then recurrently iterates using existing interconnections with fixed weights until a stable state is found—that such a state is reached can be proved under certain conditions (for which equation 9.62 is sufficient). The resulting stable state should be equal to the values of the exemplar that is closest to the processed feature vector in the Hamming metric sense. Supposing these class exemplars $\mathbf{v}^r$ are known, the recognition algorithm is as follows.

> **Algorithm 9.8: Recognition using a Hopfield net**
>
> 1. Based on existing exemplars $\mathbf{v}^i$ of r classes, compute the interconnection weights w_{ij} (equation 9.62).
>
> 2. Apply an unknown feature vector $\mathbf{x}$ as initial outputs $\mathbf{y}(0)$ of the net.
>
> 3. Iterate until the net converges (output $\mathbf{y}$ does not change):
>
> $$y_j(k+1) = f \sum_{i=1}^{N} w_{ij}\, y_i(k)\,. \qquad (9.63)$$

The final output vector $\mathbf{y}$ represents the exemplar of the class into which the processed feature vector $\mathbf{x}$ is classified. In other words, a Hopfield neural net transforms a non-ideal representation of an object (fuzzy, noisy, incomplete, etc.) to the ideal exemplar representation. The transformation of a noisy binary image of characters to a clear letter is one vision-related application.

The Hopfield neural net converges by seeking a minimum of a particular function—this is usually a *local* minimum, which may mean that the correct exemplar (the *global* minimum) is not found. Moreover, the number of local minima grows rapidly with the number of exemplars stored in the associative network. It can be shown that the minimum number of nodes N required is about seven times the number of memories M to be stored (this is known as the $0.15N \geq M$ rule) [McEliece et al., 1987], causing a rapid increase in the number of necessary nodes.

9.4 Syntactic pattern recognition

Quantitative description of objects using numeric parameters (the feature vector) is used in statistical pattern recognition, while **qualitative** descriptions are characteristic of syntactic pattern recognition. The object structure is contained in the syntactic description. If feature description is not able to represent the complexity of an object, or when an object can be represented as a hierarchical structure consisting of simpler parts, syntactic object description is appropriate. The elementary properties of the objects are called **primitives**: Section 8.2.4 covered the syntactic description of object borders using border primitives, these primitives representing parts of borders with a specific shape). Graphical or relational descriptions of objects where primitives represent subregions of specific shape is another example (see Sections 8.3.3 to 8.3.5). After each primitive has been assigned a symbol, relations between primitives in the object are described, and a **relational structure** results (Chapters 4 and 8). As in statistical recognition, the design of description primitives and their relation is not algorithmic. It is based on an analysis of the problem, designer experience, and abilities. However, there are some basic principles:

1. The number of primitive types should be small.

2. The primitives chosen must be able to form an appropriate object representation.

3. Primitives should be easily segmentable from the image.

4. Primitives should be easily recognizable using some statistical pattern recognition method.

5. Primitives should correspond with significant natural elements of the object (image) structure being described.

For example, if technical drawings are described, primitives are line and curve segments, binary relations describe relations such as *to be adjacent, to be left of, to be above,* etc. This description structure can be compared with the structure of a natural language. The text consists of sentences, sentences consist of words, words are constructed by concatenation of letters. Letters are considered primitives in this example; the set of all letters is called the **alphabet**. The set of all words in the alphabet that can be used to describe objects from one class (the set of all feasible descriptions) is named the **description language** and represents descriptions of all objects in the specific class. In addition, a **grammar** represents a set of rules that must be followed when words of the specific language are constructed from letters (of the alphabet). These definitions will be considered in more detail in Section 9.4.1.

Assume that the object is appropriately described by some primitives and their relations. Moreover, assume that the grammar is known for each class that generates descriptions of all objects of the specified class. Syntactic recognition decides whether the description word is or is not syntactically correct according to the particular class grammars, meaning that each class consists only of objects whose syntactic description can be generated by the particular grammar. Syntactic recognition is a process that looks for the grammar that can generate the syntactic word that describes an object.

Each relational structure with multiple relations can be transformed to a relational structure with at most binary relations; the image object is then represented by a **graph** which is **planar** if relations with adjacent regions only are considered. A graphical description is very natural, especially in the description of segmented images—examples were given in Section 8.3. Each planar graph can be represented either by a graph grammar or by a sequence of symbols (chain, word, etc.) over an alphabet. Sequential representation is not always advantageous in image object recognition because the valuable correspondence between the syntactic description and the object may be lost. Nevertheless, work with chain grammars is more straightforward and understandable, and all the main features of more complex grammars are included in chain grammars. Therefore, we will discuss principally sequential syntactic descriptions and chain grammars. More precise and detailed discussion of grammars, languages, and syntactic recognition methods can be found in [Fu, 1974, 1982].

Algorithm 9.9: Syntactic recognition

1. Learning: Based on the problem analysis, define the primitives and their possible relations.

2. Construct a description grammar for each class of objects using either hand analysis of syntactic descriptions or automated grammar inference (see Section 9.4.3).

3. Recognition: For each object, extract its primitives first; recognize the primitives' classes and describe the relations between them. Construct a description word representing an object.

4. Based on the results of the syntactic analysis of the description word, classify an object into that class for which its grammar (constructed in step 2) can generate the description word.

It can be seen that the main difference between statistical and syntactic recognition is in the learning process. Grammar construction can rarely be algorithmic using today's approaches, requiring significant human interaction. It is usually found that the more complex the primitives are, the simpler is the grammar, and the simpler and faster is the syntactic analysis. More complex description primitives on the other hand make step 3 of the algorithm more difficult and more time consuming; also, primitive extraction and evaluation of relations may not be simple.

9.4.1 Grammars and languages

Assuming that the primitives have been successfully extracted, all the inter-primitive relations can then be described syntactically as n-ary relations; these relations form structures (chains, trees, graphs) called **words** that represent the object or the pattern. Each pattern is therefore described by a word. Primitive classes can be understood as letters from the alphabet of symbols called **terminal symbols**. Let the alphabet of terminal symbols be V_t.

The set of patterns from a particular class corresponds to a set of words. This set of words is called the **formal language** and is described by a **grammar**. The grammar is a mathematical model of a generator of syntactically correct words (words from the particular language); it is a quadruple

$$G = [V_n, V_t, P, S], \tag{9.64}$$

where V_n and V_t are disjoint alphabets, elements of V_n are called **non-terminal symbols**, and elements of V_t are terminal symbols. Define V^* to be the set of all empty or non-empty words built from the terminal and/or non-terminal symbols. The symbol S is the grammar axiom or the *start* symbol. The set P is a non-empty finite subset of the set $V^* \times V^*$; elements of P are called the substitution rules. The set of all words that can be generated by the grammar G is called the **language** $L(G)$. Grammars that generate the same language are called **equivalent**.

A simple example will illustrate this terminology. Let the words generated by the grammar be squares of arbitrary size with sides parallel to the co-ordinate axes, and let the squares be represented by the Freeman chain code of the border in 4-connectivity (see Section 8.2.1). There are four terminal symbols (primitives) of the grammar in this case, $V_t = \{0, 1, 2, 3\}$. Let the non-terminal symbols be $V_n = \{s, a, b, c, d\}$. Note that the terminal symbols correspond to natural primitives of the 4-connectivity Freeman code; the non-terminal symbols were chosen from an infinite set of feasible symbols. The set of substitution rules P demonstrates how the start symbol $S = s$ can be transformed to words corresponding to the Freeman chain code description of squares:

$$P : (1)\ s \qquad\qquad \rightarrow \quad abcd\,, \tag{9.65}$$

$$(2)\ aAbBcCdD \quad \rightarrow \quad a1Ab2Bc3Cd0D\,, \tag{9.66}$$

$$(3)\ aAbBcCdD \quad \rightarrow \quad ABCD\,, \tag{9.67}$$

where A (B, C, D, respectively) is a variable representing any chain (including an empty one) consisting only of terminal symbols 1 $(2, 3, 0)$. Rule 3 stops the word generating process. For example, a square with a side length $l = 2$ with the Freeman chain description 11223300 is generated by the following sequence of substitution rules (see Figure 9.17)

$$s \rightarrow^1 abcd \rightarrow^2 a1b2c3d0 \rightarrow^2 a11b22c33d00 \rightarrow^3 11223300\,,$$

where the arrow superscript refers to the appropriate substitution rule. The simple analysis of generated words shows that the language generated consists only of Freeman chain code representations of squares with sides parallel to the plane co-ordinates.

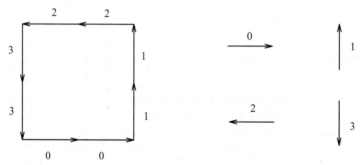

Figure 9.17: Square shape description. © *Cengage Learning 2015.*

Grammars can be divided into four main groups ordered from the general to the specific [Chomsky, 1966]:

1. Type 0—**General Grammars**
   There are no limitations for the substitution rules.

2. Type 1—**Context-Sensitive Grammars**
   Substitution rules can be of the form

$$W_1 \alpha W_2 \rightarrow W_1 U W_2\,, \tag{9.68}$$

   which can contain the substitution rule $S \rightarrow e$, where e is an empty word; words W_1, W_2, U consist of elements of V^*, $U \neq e$, $\alpha \in V_n$. This means that the non-terminal symbols can be substituted by the word U in the context of words W_1 and W_2.

3. Type 2—**Context-Free Grammars**
   Substitution rules have the form

$$\alpha \rightarrow U\,, \tag{9.69}$$

   where $U \in V^*$, $U \neq e$, $\alpha \in V_n$. Grammars can contain the rule $S \rightarrow e$. This means that the non-terminal symbol can be substituted by a word U independently of the context of α.

4. Type 3—**Regular Grammars**

The substitution rules of regular grammars are of the form

$$\alpha \rightarrow x\,\beta \qquad \text{or} \qquad \alpha \rightarrow x\,, \tag{9.70}$$

where $\alpha, \beta \in V_n$, $x \in V_t$. The substitution rule $S \rightarrow e$ may be included.

All the grammars discussed so far have been **non-deterministic**. The same left-hand side might appear in several substitution rules with different right-hand sides, and no rule exists that specifies which rule should be chosen. A non-deterministic grammar generates a language in which no words are 'preferred'. If it is advantageous to generate some words (those more probable) more often than others, substitution rules can be accompanied by numbers (for instance, by probabilities) that specify how often the substitution rule should be applied. If the substitution rules are accompanied by probabilities, the grammar is called **stochastic**. If the accompanying numbers do not satisfy the properties of probability (unit sum of probabilities for all rules with the same left-hand side), the grammar is called **fuzzy** [Zimmermann et al., 1984].

Note that the evaluation of the frequency with which each substitution rule should be used can substantially increase the efficiency of syntactic analysis in the recognition stage [Fu, 1974].

9.4.2 Syntactic analysis, syntactic classifier

If appropriate grammars exist that can be used for representation of all patterns in their classes, the last step is to design a syntactic classifier which assigns the pattern (the word) to an appropriate class. It is obvious that the simplest way is to construct a separate grammar for each class; an unknown pattern x enters a parallel structure of blocks that can decide if $x \in L(G_j)$, where $j = 1, 2, \ldots R$ and R is the number of classes; $L(G_j)$ is the language generated by the jth grammar. If the jth block's decision is positive, the pattern is accepted as a pattern from the jth class and the classifier assigns the pattern to the class j. Note that generally more than one grammar can accept a pattern as belonging to its class.

The decision of whether or not the word can be generated by a particular grammar is made during **syntactic analysis**. Moreover, syntactic analysis can construct the pattern derivation tree which can represent the structural information about the pattern.

If a language is finite (and of a reasonable size), the syntactic classifier can search for a match between the word being analyzed and all the words of the language. Another simple syntactic classifier can be based on comparisons of the chain word descriptions with typical representatives of classes comparing primitive type presence only. This method is very fast and easily implemented, though it does not produce reliable results since the syntactic information is not used at all. However, impossible classes can be rejected in this step, which can speed up the syntactic analysis process.

Syntactic analysis is based on efforts to construct the tested pattern by the application of some appropriate sequence of substitution rules to the start symbol. If the substitution process is successful, the analysis process stops and the tested pattern can be generated by the grammar. The pattern can be classified into the class represented by the grammar. If the substitution process is unsuccessful, the pattern is not accepted as representing an object of this class.

If the class description grammar is regular (type 3), syntactic analysis is very simple. The grammar can be substituted with a finite non-deterministic automaton and it is easy to decide if the pattern word is accepted or rejected by the automaton [Fu, 1982]. If the grammar is context free (type 2), the syntactic analysis is more difficult. Nevertheless, it can be designed using stack automata.

Generally, which process of pattern word construction is chosen is not important; the transformation process can be done in top-down or bottom-up manner.

A top-down process begins with the start symbol and substitution rules are applied in the appropriate way to obtain the same pattern word as that under analysis. The final goal of syntactic analysis is to generate the same word as the analyzed word; every partial substitution creates a set of subgoals, just as new branches are created in the generation tree. Effort is always devoted to fulfill the current subgoal. If the analysis is not successful in fulfilling the subgoal, it indicates an incorrect choice of the substitution rule somewhere in the previous substitutions, and back-tracking is invoked to get back to the nearest higher tree level (closer to the root), and to pick another applicable rule. The process of rule applications and back-tracking is repeated until the required pattern word results. If the whole generating process ends unsuccessfully, the grammar does not generate the word, and the analyzed pattern does not belong to the class.

This top-down process is a series of expansions starting with the start symbol $\hat{S}$. A bottom-up process starts with the analyzed word, which is **reduced** by applying reverse substitutions, the final goal being to reduce the word to the start symbol S. The main principle of bottom-up analysis is to detect subwords in the analyzed word that match the pattern on the right-hand side of some substitution rule, then the reduction process substitutes the former right-hand side with the left-hand side of the rule in the analyzed word. The bottom-up method follows no subgoals; all the effort is devoted to obtaining a reduced and simplified word pattern until the start symbol is obtained. Again, if the process is not successful, the grammar does not generate the analyzed word.

The pure top-down approach is not very efficient, since too many incorrect paths are generated. The number of misleading paths can be decreased by application of consistency tests. For example, if the word starts with a non-terminal symbol I, only rules with the right-hand side starting with I should be considered. Many more consistency tests can be designed that take advantage of prior knowledge. This approach is also called **tree pruning** (Figure 9.18) [Nilsson, 1982].

Tree pruning is often used if an exhaustive search cannot be completed because the search effort would exceed any reasonable bounds. Note that pruning can mean that the final solution is not optimal or may not be found at all (especially if tree search is used to find the best path through the graph, Section 6.2.4). This depends on the quality of the a priori information that is applied during the pruning process.

There are two main principles for recovery from following a wrong path. The first one is represented by the back-tracking mechanism already mentioned, meaning that the generation of words returns to the nearest point in the tree where another substitution rule can be applied which has not yet been applied. This approach requires the ability to re-construct the former appearances of generated subwords and/or remove some branches of the derivation tree completely.

The second approach does not include back-tracking. All possible combinations of the substitution rules are applied in parallel and several generation trees are constructed simultaneously. If any tree succeeds in generating the analyzed word, the generation process ends. If any tree generation ends with a non-successful word, this tree is abandoned.

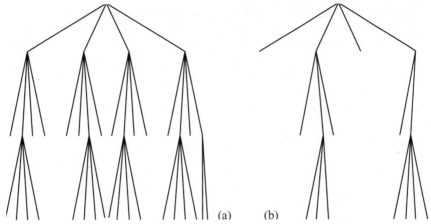

(a)   (b)

Figure 9.18: Tree pruning. (a) Original tree. (b) Pruning decreases size of the searched tree. © *Cengage Learning 2015.*

The latter approach uses more brute force, but the algorithm is simplified by avoiding back-tracking.

It is difficult to compare the efficiency of these two and the choice depends on the application; Bottom-up analysis is more efficient for some grammars, and top-down is more efficient for others. As a general observation, the majority of syntactic analyzers which produce all generated words is based on the top-down principle. This approach is appropriate for most grammars but is usually less efficient.

Another approach to syntactic analysis uses example relational structures of classes. The syntactic analysis consists of matching the relational structure that represents the analyzed object with the example relational structure. The main goal is to find an **isomorphism** of both relational structures. These methods can be applied to n-ary relational structures as well. Relational structure matching is a perspective approach to syntactic recognition, a perspective way of image understanding (see Section 9.5). A simple example of relational structure matching is shown in Figure 9.19. A detailed description of relational structure matching approaches can be found in [Barrow and Popplestone, 1971; Ballard and Brown, 1982; Baird, 1984].

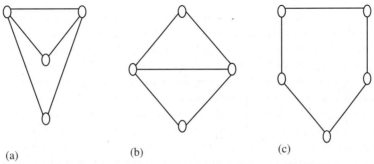

(a)   (b)   (c)

Figure 9.19: Matching relational structures: (a) and (b) match assuming nodes and relations of the same type; (c) does not match either (a) or (b). © *Cengage Learning 2015.*

9.4.3 Syntactic classifier learning, grammar inference

To model a language of any class of patterns as closely as possible, the grammar rules should be extracted from a training set of example words. This process of grammar construction from examples is known as **grammar inference**, the essence of which can be seen in Figure 9.20.

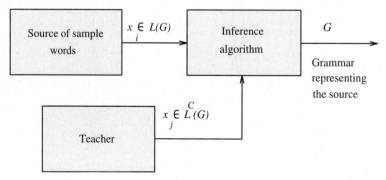

Figure 9.20: Grammar inference. © *Cengage Learning 2015.*

The source of words generates finite example words consisting of the terminal symbols. Assume that these examples include structural features that should be represented by a grammar G which will serve as a model of this source. All the words that can be generated by the source are included in the language $L(G)$, and the words that cannot be generated by the source represent a residuum of this set $L^C(G)$. This information enters the inference algorithm whose goal is to find and describe the grammar G. Words that are included in the language $L(G)$ can be acquired simply from the source of examples. However, the elements of $L^C(G)$ must be presented by a teacher that has additional information about the grammar properties [Barrero, 1991].

Note that the number of example words generated by the source is finite and it is therefore not sufficient to define the possibly infinite language $L(G)$ unambiguously. Any finite set of examples can be represented by an infinite set of languages, making it impossible to identify unambiguously the grammar that generated the examples. Grammar inference is expected to construct the grammar that describes the training set of examples, plus another set of words that in some sense have the same structure as the examples.

The inference methods can be divided into two groups, based on **enumeration** and **induction**. Enumeration detects the grammar G from the finite set M of grammars that can generate the entire training set of examples or its main part. The difficulty is in the definition of the set M of grammars and in the procedure to search for the grammar G. Induction-based methods start with the analysis of words from the training set; the substitution rules are derived from these examples using patterns of similar words.

There is no general method for grammar inference that constructs a grammar from a training set. Existing methods can be used to infer regular and context-free grammars, and may furthermore be successful in some other special cases. Even if simple grammars are considered, the inferred grammar usually generates a language that is much larger than the minimum language that can be used for appropriate representation of the class. This property of grammar inference is extremely unsuitable for syntactic analysis because of the computational complexity. Therefore, the main role in syntactic analyzer learning is still left to a human analyst, and the grammar construction is based on heuristics, intuition, experience, and prior information about the problem.

If the recognition is based on sample relational structures, the main problem is in its automated construction. The conventional method for the sample relational structure construction is described in [Winston, 1975], where the relational descriptions of objects from the training set are used. The training set consists of examples and counter-examples. The counter-examples should be chosen to have only one typical difference in comparison with a pattern that is a representative of the class.

9.5 Recognition as graph matching

Graphs with weighted nodes and weighted arcs often appear in image descriptions using relational structures. Graph comparisons can tell us whether the reality represented by an image matches prior knowledge incorporated into graphical models. Figure 9.21 shows a typical graph matching task.

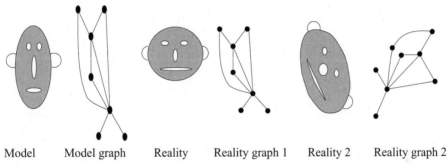

| Model | Model graph | Reality | Reality graph 1 | Reality 2 | Reality graph 2 |

Figure 9.21: Graph matching problem. © *Cengage Learning 2015.*

If the problem is to find an object (represented by a model graph) in a graphical representation of the image, the model must match a subgraph in the image graph exactly. An exact match of graphs is called graph **isomorphism**—for example, the graphs in Figure 9.21 are isomorphic.

Graph isomorphism and subgraph isomorphism evaluation is a classical problem in graph theory and is important from both practical and theoretical points of view. Graph theory and algorithms have an extensive literature (for example, [Harary, 1969; McHugh, 1990; Tucker, 1995; Bollobas, 2002]), The problem is actually more complex in reality, since the requirement of an exact match is very often too strict in recognition problems.

Because of imprecise object descriptions, image noise, overlapping objects, lighting conditions, etc., the object graph usually does not match the model graph exactly. Graph matching is a difficult problem, and evaluation of graph **similarity** is not any easier–an important problem is to design a metric which determines how similar two graphs are.

9.5.1 Isomorphism of graphs and subgraphs

Graph isomorphism problems can be divided into three main classes [Harary, 1969; Ballard and Brown, 1982].

1. **Graph isomorphism.** Given two graphs $G_1 = (V_1, E_1)$ and $G_2 = (V_2, E_2)$, find a *one-to-one* and *onto* mapping (an isomorphism) f between V_1 and V_2 such that for each edge of E_1 connecting any pair of nodes $v, v' \in V_1$, there is an edge of E_2 connecting $f(v)$ and $f(v')$; further, if $f(v)$ and $f(v')$ are connected by an edge in G_2, v and v' are connected in G_1.

2. **Subgraph isomorphism.** Find an isomorphism between a graph G_1 and subgraphs of another graph G_2. This problem is more difficult than the previous one.

3. **Double subgraph isomorphism.** Find all isomorphisms between subgraphs of a graph G_1 and subgraphs of another graph G_2. This problem is of the same order of difficulty as number 2.

It is known that the subgraph and double subgraph isomorphism problems are NP-complete (using known algorithms, solution time is proportional to an exponential function of input length)—it is still not known whether the graph isomorphism problem is NP-complete. Non-deterministic algorithms for graph isomorphism that use heuristics and look for suboptimal solutions give a solution in polynomial time in both graph and subgraph isomorphism testing. Isomorphism testing is computationally expensive for both weighted and unweighted graphs.

Node and arc weights can simplify isomorphism testing. More precisely, the weights may make disproof of isomorphism easier. Isomorphic weighted graphs have the same number of nodes and arcs with the same weight. An isomorphism test of two weighted graphs $G_1 = (V_1, E_1)$ and $G_2 = (V_2, E_2)$ can be based on partitioning the node sets V_1 and V_2 in a consistent manner looking for inconsistencies in the resulting set partitions—the goal is to achieve a one-to-one correspondence between nodes from sets V_1 and V_2. The algorithm consists of repeated node set partitioning steps, and the necessary conditions of isomorphism are tested after each step (the same number of nodes of equivalent properties in corresponding sets of both graphs). The node set partitioning may, for example, be based on the following properties:

- Node attributes (weights).

- The number of adjacent nodes (connectivity).

- The number of edges of a node (node degree).

- Types of edges of a node.

- The number of edges leading from a node back to itself (node order).

- The attributes of adjacent nodes.

After new subsets are generated based on one of these criteria, the cardinalities of corresponding subsets of nodes in graphs G_1 and G_2 are tested; see Figure 9.22a. Obviously, if v_{1i} is in several subsets V_{1j}, then the corresponding node v_{2i} must also be in the corresponding subsets V_{2j}, or the isomorphism is disproved

$$v_{2i} \in \bigcap_{j | v_{1i} \in V_{1j}} V_{2j} \,. \tag{9.71}$$

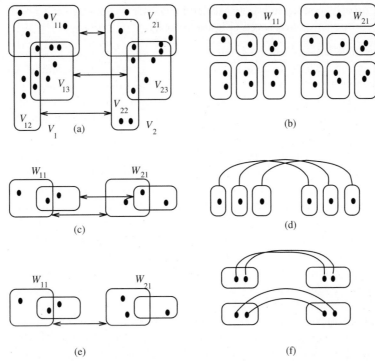

Figure 9.22: Graph isomorphism. (a) Testing cardinality in corresponding subsets. (b) Partitioning node subsets. (c) Generating new subsets. (d) Subset isomorphism found. (e) Graph isomorphism disproof. (f) Situation when arbitrary search is necessary. © *Cengage Learning 2015.*

If all the generated subsets satisfy the necessary conditions of isomorphism in step i, the subsets are split into new sets of nodes W_{1n}, W_{2n} (Figure 9.22b)

$$W_{1i} \bigcap W_{1j} = \emptyset \quad \text{for } i \neq j \,,$$
$$W_{2i} \bigcap W_{2j} = \emptyset \quad \text{for } i \neq j \,. \tag{9.72}$$

Clearly, if $V_{1j} = V_{2j}$ and if $v_{1i} \notin V_{1k}$, then $v_{2i} \in V_{2k}^C$, where V^C is the set complement. Therefore, by equation (9.71), corresponding elements v_{1i}, v_{2i} of W_{1n}, W_{2n} must satisfy

$$v_{2i} \in \left\{ \bigcap_{\{j \mid v_{1i} \in W_{1j}\}} W_{2j} \right\} \bigcap \left\{ \bigcap_{\{(k \mid v_{1i} \notin W_{1k}) \wedge (W_{1k} = W_{2k})\}} W_{2k}^C \right\} . \tag{9.73}$$

The cardinality of all the corresponding sets W_{1n}, W_{2n} is tested to disprove the graph isomorphism.

The same process is repeated in the following steps, applying different criteria for node subset generation. Note that new subsets are generated independently in W_{1i}, W_{2i} (Figure 9.22c).

The process is repeated unless one of three cases occurs:

1. All the corresponding sets W_{1i}, W_{2i} contain one node each. The isomorphism is found (Figure 9.22d).

2. The cardinality condition is not satisfied in at least one of the corresponding subsets. The isomorphism is disproved (Figure 9.22e).

3. No more new subsets can be generated before one of the previous cases occurs. In that situation, either the node set partitioning criteria are not sufficient to establish an isomorphism, or more than one isomorphism is possible. In this case, systematic arbitrary assignment of nodes that have more than one possible corresponding node and cardinality testing after each assignment may provide a solution (Figure 9.22f).

The last part of the process, based on systematic assignment of possibly corresponding nodes and isomorphism testing after each assignment, may be based on back-tracking principles. Note that the back-tracking approach can be used from the very beginning but it is more efficient to start the test using all available prior information about the graphs. The back-tracking process is applied if more than one potential correspondence between nodes is encountered. Back-tracking tests for directed graph isomorphism and a recursive algorithm are given in [Ballard and Brown, 1982] together with accompanying hints for improving efficiency.

Algorithm 9.10: Graph isomorphism

1. Take two graphs $G_1 = (V_1, E_1), G_2 = (V_2, E_2)$.

2. Use a node property criterion to generate subsets V_{1i}, V_{2i} of the node sets V_1 and V_2. Test whether the cardinality conditions hold for corresponding subsets. If not, the isomorphism is disproved.

3. Partition the subsets V_{1i}, V_{2i} into subsets W_{1j}, W_{2j} satisfying the conditions given in equation (9.72) (no two subsets W_{1j} or W_{2j} contain the same node). Test whether the cardinality conditions hold for all the corresponding subsets W_{1j}, W_{2j}. If not, the isomorphism is disproved.

4. Repeat steps 2 and 3 using another node property criterion in all subsets W_{1j}, W_{2j} generated so far. Stop if one of the three above-mentioned situations occurs.

5. Based on the situation that stopped the repetition process, the isomorphism either was proved, disproved, or some additional procedures (such as back-tracking) must be applied to complete the proof or disproof.

A classic approach to subgraph isomorphism uses a brute force enumeration process, described as a depth-first tree search algorithm [Ullmann, 1976]. As a way of improving efficiency, a refinement procedure is entered after each node is searched in the tree—the procedure reduces the number of node successors, which yields a shorter execution time. An alternative approach transforms the graph problem into a linear programming problem [Zdrahal, 1981].

The double subgraph isomorphism problem can be translated into a subgraph isomorphism problem using the **clique**—a complete (totally connected) subgraph—approach. A clique is said to be maximal if no other clique properly includes it. Note that a graph may have more than one maximal clique; however, it is often important to find the largest maximal clique: this is a well-known problem in graph theory. An example algorithm for finding all cliques of an undirected graph can be found in [Bron and Kerbosch, 1973]. The maximal clique $G_{\text{clique}} = (V_{\text{clique}}, E_{\text{clique}})$ of the graph $G = (V, E)$ can be found as follows [Niemann, 1990].

Algorithm 9.11: Maximal clique location

1. Take an arbitrary node $v_j \in V$; construct a subset $V_{\text{clique}} = \{v_j\}$.

2. In the set V_{clique}^C search for a node v_k that is connected with all nodes in V_{clique}. Add the node v_k to a set V_{clique}.

3. Repeat step 2 as long as new nodes v_k can be found.

4. If no new node v_k can be found, V_{clique} represents the node set of the maximal clique subgraph G_{clique} (the maximal clique that contains the node v_j).

To find the largest maximal clique, an additional maximizing search is necessary. Other clique-finding algorithms are discussed in [Ballard and Brown, 1982; Yang et al., 1989].

The search for isomorphism of two subgraphs (the double subgraph isomorphism) is transformed to a clique search using the **assignment graph** [Ambler, 1975]. A pair (v_1, v_2), $v_1 \in V_1$, $v_2 \in V_2$ is called an **assignment** if the nodes v_1 and v_2 have the same node property descriptions, and two assignments (v_1, v_2) and (v_1', v_2') are **compatible** if (in addition) all relations between v_1 and v_1' also hold for v_2 and v_2' (graph arcs between v_1, v_1' and v_2, v_2' must have the same weight, including the no-edge case). The set of assignments defines the set of nodes V_a of the assignment graph G_a. Two nodes in V_a (two assignments) are connected by an arc in the assignment graph G_a if these two nodes are compatible. The search for the maximum matching subgraphs of graphs G_1 and G_2 is a search for the maximum totally connected subgraph in G_a (the maximum totally compatible subset of assignments).

The maximum totally connected subgraph is a maximal clique, and the maximal clique-finding algorithm can be applied to solve this problem.

9.5.2 Similarity of graphs

Perfect matches are unlikely in reality, and the foregoing approaches are not able to distinguish between a small mismatch of two very similar graphs and the case when the graphs are not similar at all. If graph similarity is sought, the main stress is given to the ability to quantify the similarity. Having three graphs G_1, G_2, G_3, the question as to which two are more similar is a natural one [Buckley, 1990].

The similarity of two strings (chains) can be based on the **Levenshtein distance**, which is defined as the smallest number of deletions, insertions, and substitutions necessary to convert one string into the other [Schlesinger and Hlaváč, 2002]. Transformations of string elements can be assigned a specific transition cost to make the computed similarity (distance) more flexible and more sensitive. This principle can be applied to graph similarity as well. A set of feasible transformations of nodes and arcs (insertion, deletion, substitution, relabeling) is defined, and these transformations are accompanied by

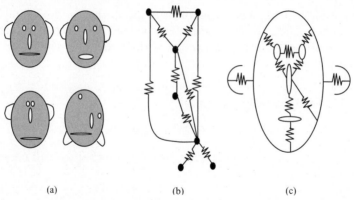

(a)   (b)   (c)

Figure 9.23: Templates and springs principle. (a) Different objects having the same description graphs. (b), (c) Nodes (templates) connected by springs, graph nodes may represent other graphs in finer resolution. © *Cengage Learning 2015.*

transition costs. Any sequence of transformations is assigned a combination of single step costs (like the sum of individual costs). The set of transformations that has the minimum cost and transforms one graph to another graph defines a distance between them [Niemann, 1990].

Note that similarity can be searched for in hierarchical graph structures. The graphs consist of a number of subgraphs in which isomorphism (or similarity) has already been proved. The next step is to detect, describe, and evaluate relations between these subgraphs (Figure 9.23, cf. Figure 9.21).

To explain the principles, a physical analogy of templates and springs [Fischler and Elschlager, 1973] is usually considered. The templates (subgraphs) are connected by springs (relations between subgraphs). The quality of the match of two graphs relates to the quality of the local fit (in corresponding templates) and to the amount of energy used to stretch the springs to match one graph onto the second (reference) graph. To make the graph similarity measure more flexible, extra costs may be added for missing parts of the graph as well as for some extra ones. The spring energy penalty may be made highly non-linear, better to reflect the descriptive character in particular applications.

9.6   Optimization techniques in recognition

Optimization is very flexible. In image recognition and understanding, the best image representation is sought, or the best match between image and model is required, or the best image understanding is the goal. Whenever 'the best' is considered, some objective function of *goodness* must be available, implying that an optimization technique can be applied which looks for the maximum ... for *the best*.

A function optimization problem is defined by some finite domain D and a function $f : D \to R$, R being the set of real numbers; optimization seeks the *best* value in D under f. The 'best' is understood as finding a value $\mathbf{x} \in D$ yielding either the minimum or the maximum of the function f:

$$f_{\min}(\mathbf{x}) = \min_{\mathbf{x} \in D} f(\mathbf{x}), \qquad\qquad f_{\max}(\mathbf{x}) = \max_{\mathbf{x} \in D} f(\mathbf{x}). \qquad (9.74)$$

The function f is called the **objective** function. Optimization methods for seeking maxima and minima are logically equivalent, and optimization techniques can be equally useful if either a maximum or minimum is required.

No optimization algorithm can guarantee finding a good solution to a problem if the objective function does not reflect the *goodness* of the solution. Therefore, the design of the objective function is a key factor in the performance of any optimization algorithm.

Most conventional approaches to optimization use calculus-based methods which can be compared to climbing a hill gradient of the objective function gives the steepest direction to climb. The main limitation of calculus-based methods is their local behavior; the search can easily end in a local maximum, and the global maximum can be missed (see Figure 9.24).

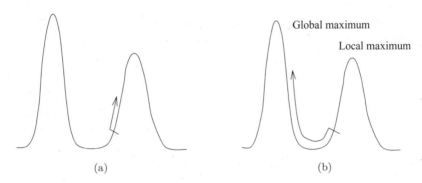

Figure 9.24: Limitations of hill climbing methods. © *Cengage Learning 2015.*

Several methods improve the probability of finding the global maximum; to start the hill climbing at several points in the search space, to apply enumerative searches such as dynamic programming, to apply random searches, etc. Among these possibilities are genetic algorithms and simulated annealing.

9.6.1 Genetic algorithms

Genetic algorithms (GA) use natural evolution mechanisms to search for the maximum of an objective function [Goldberg, 1989; Mitchell, 1998; Haupt and Haupt, 2004]. GAs do not guarantee that the global optimum will be found, but empirical results from many applications show that the final solution is usually very close to it. This is very important in image understanding applications, as will be seen in the next chapter. There are almost always several consistent (feasible) solutions that are locally optimal in image understanding, or matching, and only one of those possible solutions is the best one represented by the global maximum. The opportunity to find a (near) global optimum is very valuable in these tasks.

GAs differ substantially from other optimization methods in the following ways [Goldberg, 1989].

1. GAs work with a coding of the parameter set, not the parameters themselves. They require the natural parameter set of the problem to be coded as a finite-length string over some finite alphabet. This implies that any optimization problem representation must be transformed to a string representation; binary strings are

often used. The design of the problem representation as a string is an important part of the method.

2. GAs search from a population of points, not a single point. The population of solutions that is processed in each step is large, meaning that the search for the optimum is driven from many places in the search space simultaneously. This gives a better chance of finding the global optimum.

3. GAs use the objective function directly, not derivatives or other auxiliary knowledge. The search for new, better solutions depends on the values of the evaluation function only. Note that, as in other recognition methods, GAs find the (near) global optimum of the evaluation function but there is no guarantee at all that the evaluation function is relevant to the problem. The evaluation function describes the *goodness* of the particular string. The value of the evaluation function is called **fitness** in GAs.

4. GAs use probabilistic transition rules, not deterministic rules. Rules of transition from the current population of strings to a new and better population of strings are based on the natural idea of supporting good strings with higher fitness and removing poor strings with lower fitness. The best strings representing the best solutions are allowed to survive the evolution process with a higher probability.

   The survival of the fittest and the death of poor code strings is achieved by applying three basic operations: **reproduction, crossover**, and **mutation**.

The population of strings represents all the strings that are being processed in the current step of the GA. The sequence of reproduction, crossover, and mutation generates a new population of strings from the previous population.

Reproduction

The reproduction operator is responsible for the survival of the fittest and for the death of others based on a probabilistic treatment.

The mechanism copies strings with highest fitness into the next generation of strings. The selection process is usually probabilistic, the probability that a string is reproduced into the new population being given by its relative fitness in the current population—this is their mechanism of survival. The lower the fitness of the string, the lower the chances for survival. This process results in a set of strings where some strings of higher fitness may be copied more than once into the next population. The total number of strings in the population usually remains unchanged, and the average fitness of the new generation is higher than it was before.

Crossover

There are many variations of crossover. The basic idea is to 'mate' newly reproduced strings at random, randomly choosing a position for the border of each pair of strings, and to produce new strings by swapping all characters between the beginning of the string pairs and the border position; see Figure 9.25.

There is a probability parameter representing the number of pairs which will be processed by crossover, so not all newly reproduced strings are subject to it. It may be performed such that the best reproduced strings are kept in an unchanged form.

Crossover together with reproduction represent the main power of GAs. However, there is one more idea in the crossover operation: Blocks of characters can be detected in strings that have locally correct structure even if the string as a whole does not represent a good solution. These blocks of characters in strings are called **schemata**: they are substrings that can represent building blocks of the string, and can be understood as the local pattern of characters. Clearly, if schemata can be manipulated as locally correct blocks, the optimal solution can be located faster than if all the characters are handled independently. In every generation of n strings, about n^3 schemata are processed. This is called the **implicit parallelism** of genetic algorithms [Goldberg, 1989].

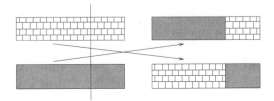

Figure 9.25: Principle of crossover. Two strings before (left) and after the crossover (right). © *Cengage Learning 2015.*

Mutation

Mutation plays only a secondary role in GAs. Its principle is randomly to change one character of some string of the population from time to time—it might, for example, take place approximately once per thousand bit transfers The main reason for mutation is the fact that some local configurations of characters in strings of the population can be totally lost as a result of reproduction and crossover—mutation protects GAs against such irrecoverable loss of good solution features.

Population convergence in GAs is a serious question. For practical purposes this question becomes one of when to stop generating new string populations. A common and practically proven criterion recommends that the population-generating process be stopped when the maximum achieved fitness in the population has not improved substantially through several previous generations.

The starting population can be generated at random, assuming the alphabet of characters and the desired length of strings are known. Nevertheless, as always, if some prior knowledge about the solution is available (the probable local patterns of characters, the probable percentages of characters in strings, etc.), then it is advantageous to use this information to make the starting population as fit as possible. The better the starting population, the easier and faster the search for the optimum.

Algorithm 9.12: Genetic algorithm

1. Create a starting population of code strings, and find the value of their objective functions.

2. Probabilistically reproduce high fitness strings in the new population, remove poor fitness strings (reproduction).

3. Construct new strings combining reproduced code strings from the previous population (crossover).

4. From time to time, change one character of some string at random (mutation).

5. Order code strings of the current population according to the value of their objective function (fitness).

6. If the maximum achieved string fitness does not increase over several steps, stop—otherwise return to step 2. The desired optimum is represented by the current string of maximum fitness.

See Section 10.10.2 for an example of the algorithm use for image analysis. A more detailed and precise description of genetic algorithms can be found in [Goldberg, 1989; Rawlins, 1991; Mitchell, 1996]. Many examples and descriptions of related techniques are included there as well, such as knowledge implementation into mutation and crossover, GA learning systems, hybrid techniques that combine good properties of conventional hill climbing searches and GAs, etc.

9.6.2 Simulated annealing

Simulated annealing [Kirkpatrick et al., 1983] represents another group of robust optimization methods. Similarly to GAs, simulated annealing searches for an extremum of an objective function (cost function) that represents the fitness of some complex system. Searching for a *minimum* is considered in this section because it simplifies the energy-related metaphor with the natural behavior of matter. Simulated annealing combines two basic optimization principles, **divide and conquer** and **iterative improvement** (hill climbing). This combination avoids getting stuck in local optima. It has as a basis a strong connection with statistical mechanics or thermodynamics, and multi-variate or combinatorial optimization. Simulated annealing may be suitable for NP-complete optimization problems; it does not guarantee that the global optimum is found, but the solution is usually near-optimal.

To explain the principle of simulated annealing, imagine a sugar bowl filled with cube sugar [Cerny, 1985]. Usually, some cubes do not fit and the lid cannot be closed. From experience, everybody knows that shaking the bowl will result in compaction of the cubes and the lid will close properly. In other words, considering the number of cubes that can be inside the bowl as an evaluation function, shaking the bowl results in a near-maximal solution. The degree of shaking is a parameter of this optimization process and corresponds to the heating and cooling process as described below.

Simulated annealing consists of downhill iteration steps combined with occasional uphill steps that make it possible to escape from local minima. The physical model of the process starts with heating matter until it melts; then the resulting liquid is cooled down slowly to keep a quasi-equilibrium. The cooling algorithm [Metropolis et al., 1953] consists of repeated random displacements (state changes) of atoms in the matter, and the energy change ΔE is evaluated after each state change. If $\Delta E \leq 0$ (lower energy), the state change is accepted, and the new state is used as the starting state of the next step. If $\Delta E > 0$, the state is accepted with probability

$$P(\Delta E) = \exp\left(\frac{-\Delta E}{k_B T}\right) . \tag{9.75}$$

To apply this physical model to an optimization problem, the temperature parameter T must be decreased in a controlled manner during optimization. It will be clear that at high values of T, changes that increase energy will be probable, but they become less likely as T declines.

Algorithm 9.13: Simulated annealing optimization

1. Let $\mathbf{x}$ be a vector of optimization parameters; compute the value of the objective function $J(\mathbf{x})$. Initialize T.

2. Perturb $\mathbf{x}$ slightly, creating $\mathbf{x}_{\text{new}}$, and compute the new value of the optimization function $J(\mathbf{x}_{\text{new}})$.

3. Generate a random number $r \in (0, 1)$. If

$$r < \exp\left(\frac{-\left[J(\mathbf{x}_{\text{new}}) - J(\mathbf{x})\right]}{k_B T}\right) \tag{9.76}$$

then assign $\mathbf{x} = \mathbf{x}_{\text{new}}$ and $J(\mathbf{x}) = J(\mathbf{x}_{\text{new}})$.

4. Repeat steps 2 and 3 some number of times determined by the cooling schedule.

5. Decrease T according to the cooling schedule, and go to 2.

6. When the cooling schedule is finished, $\mathbf{x}$ represents the solution of the optimization problem.

The sequence of temperatures and number of iterations n_T at each temperature is called the **cooling (or annealing) schedule**. Large values of n_T and small decrements of T yield low final values of the optimization function (the solution is close to the global minimum) but require long computation time. (Remember the sugar bowl example: the shaking is much stronger at the beginning and gradually decreases for the best results). Smaller values of n_T and large decrements in T proceed faster, but the results may not be close to the global minimum. The schedule must be chosen to give a solution close to the minimum without wasting too much computation time, but there is no known practically applicable way to design an optimal annealing schedule, although some general guidelines exist and appropriate parameters can be found for particular problems.

The annealing algorithm is easy to implement, and has been applied to many optimization problems, including pattern recognition, graph partitioning. It has been demonstrated to be of great value, although examples of problems do exist in which it performs less well than standard algorithms and other heuristics. In the computer vision area, applications include stereo correspondence [Barnard, 1987], boundary detection [Geman et al., 1990], texture segmentation [Bouman and Liu, 1991], and edge detection [Tan et al., 1992]. Implementation details and annealing algorithm properties together with an extensive list of references can be found in [van Laarhoven and Aarts, 1987; Otten and van Ginneken, 1989].

9.7 Fuzzy systems

Fuzzy systems are capable of representing diverse, non-exact, uncertain, and inaccurate knowledge or information. They use qualifiers that are very close to the human way of expressing knowledge, such as bright, medium dark, dark, etc. They can represent complex knowledge, and knowledge from contradictory sources. They are based on fuzzy logic, which represents a powerful approach to decision making [Zadeh, 1965; Zimmermann et al., 1984; Kosko, 1992; Cox, 1994; Haykin, 1998; Kecman, 2001].

9.7.1 Fuzzy sets and fuzzy membership functions

When humans describe objects, they often use imprecise descriptors such as *bright, large, rounded, elongated,* etc. For instance, fair-weather clouds may be described as small, medium dark or bright, somewhat rounded regions; thunderstorm clouds may be described as dark or very dark, large regions—people are quite comfortable with such descriptions. However, if the task is to recognize clouds from photographs of the sky automatically by using pattern recognition approaches, it becomes obvious that *crisp* boundaries (discrimination functions) must be drawn that separate the cloud classes. Decisions about boundaries may be quite arbitrary—a decision that a region R_1 characterized by average gray-level g, roundness r and size s represents a thunderstorm cloud, while R_2 characterized by average gray-level $g + 1$, the same roundness r, and size s does not. It may be more appropriate to consider a region R_1 as belonging to the set of fair-weather clouds with some *degree of membership* and belonging to the set of thunderstorm clouds with another degree of membership. Similarly, another region R_2 might belong to both cloud sets with some other degrees of membership. Fuzzy logic facilitates simultaneous membership of regions in different fuzzy sets. Figures 9.26a,b demonstrate the difference between the crisp and fuzzy sets representing the average gray-level of the cloud regions.

A **fuzzy set** S in a fuzzy space X is a set of ordered pairs

$$S = \left\{ (x, \mu_S(x)) | x \in X \right\}, \tag{9.77}$$

where $\mu_S(x)$ represents the grade of membership of x in S. The range of the membership function is a subset of non-negative real numbers whose supremum is finite. For convenience, a supremum of 1 is often used, $\sup_{x \in X} \mu_S(x) = 1$. Fuzzy sets are often denoted solely by the membership function.

The description of DARK regions presented in Figure 9.26b is a classic example of a fuzzy set and illustrates the properties of fuzzy spaces. The **domain** of the fuzzy set is depicted along the x axis and ranges from black to white (0–255), and the degree of membership $\mu(x)$ is along the vertical axis. The membership is between zero (no membership) and one (complete membership). Thus, a white region with an average gray-level of 255 has zero membership in the DARK fuzzy set, while the black region (average gray-level $= 0$) has complete membership. As shown in Figure 9.26b, the membership function may be linear, but a variety of other curves may also be used (Figure 9.26c,d).

Consider average gray-levels of fair-weather and thunderstorm clouds; Figure 9.27 shows possible membership functions associated with the fuzzy sets DARK, MEDIUM DARK, BRIGHT. As the figure shows, a region with a specific average gray-level g may belong to several fuzzy sets simultaneously. Thus, the memberships $\mu_{\text{DARK}}(g)$,

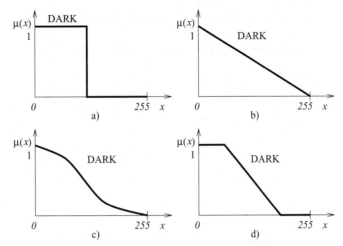

Figure 9.26: Crisp and fuzzy sets representing cloud regions of the same size and roundness, varying average gray-level g. (a) Crisp set showing the Boolean nature of the DARK set. (b) Fuzzy set DARK. (c), (d) Other possible membership functions associated with the fuzzy set DARK. © *Cengage Learning 2015.*

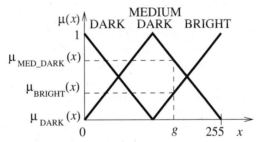

Figure 9.27: Membership functions associated with fuzzy sets DARK, MEDIUM DARK, and BRIGHT. Note that several membership values may be associated with a specific average gray-level g. © *Cengage Learning 2015.*

$\mu_{\text{MEDIUM DARK}}(g)$, $\mu_{\text{BRIGHT}}(g)$ represent the fuzziness of the description since they assess the degree of certainty about the membership of the region in the particular fuzzy set. The maximum membership value associated with any fuzzy set is called the **height** of the fuzzy set.

In fuzzy system design, normalized versions of membership functions are used. The **minimum normal form** requires at least one element of the fuzzy set domain to have a membership value of one, and the **maximum normal form** is such minimum normal forms for which at least one element of the domain has a membership value of zero.

In fuzzy reasoning systems, membership functions are usually generated in the minimum normal form; there is a wide range of possible fuzzy membership functions, such as linear, sigmoid, beta curve, triangular curve, trapezoidal curve, shouldered curve, arbitrary curve ... [Cox, 1994].

Shapes of fuzzy membership functions can be modified using **fuzzy set hedges**, which can intensify, dilute, form a complement, narrowly or broadly approximate the membership of the fuzzy set elements. Zero or more hedges and the associated fuzzy set constitute a single semantic entity called a **linguistic variable**. Suppose $\mu_{\text{DARK}}(x)$ represents the membership function of the fuzzy set DARK; then the intensified fuzzy set VERY DARK may have the membership function (Figure 9.28a)

$$\mu_{\text{VERY DARK}}(x) = \mu^2_{\text{DARK}}(x)\,. \tag{9.78}$$

Similarly, a diluting hedge creating a fuzzy set SOMEWHAT DARK may have a membership function (Figure 9.28b)

$$\mu_{\text{SOMEWHAT DARK}}(x) = \sqrt{\mu_{\text{DARK}}(x)}\,. \tag{9.79}$$

Multiple hedges can be applied to a single fuzzy membership function and a fuzzy set VERY VERY DARK can be created as

$$\mu_{\text{VERY VERY DARK}}(x) = \mu^2_{\text{DARK}}(x) \cdot \mu^2_{\text{DARK}}(x) = \mu^4_{\text{DARK}}(x)\,. \tag{9.80}$$

There are no underlying theoretically solid reasons for these hedge formulae, but they have the merit of success in practice—they simply 'seem to work' [Cox, 1994].

9.7.2 Fuzzy set operators

It is unusual that a recognition problem be solved using a single fuzzy set and an associated single membership function. Therefore, tools must be created to combine fuzzy sets, and to determine membership functions of such combinations. In conventional logic, membership functions are either zero or one (Figure 9.26) and for any class set S, a rule of non-contradiction holds: an intersection of a set S with its complement S^c is an empty set

$$S \cap S^c = \emptyset\,. \tag{9.81}$$

Clearly, this rule does not hold in fuzzy logic, since domain elements may belong to fuzzy sets and their complements simultaneously. There are three basic **Zadeh operators** on fuzzy sets: **fuzzy intersection**, **fuzzy union**, and **fuzzy complement**. Let $\mu_A(x)$ and $\mu_B(y)$ be two membership functions associated with two fuzzy sets A and B with domains X and Y. Then the intersection, union, and complement are pointwise defined for all $x \in X, y \in Y$ (note that other definitions also exist) as

$$\begin{aligned}
\text{Intersection } A \cap B : \quad & \mu_{A \cap B}(x,y) = \min\big(\mu_A(x), \mu_B(y)\big)\,, \\
\text{Union } A \cup B : \quad & \mu_{A \cup B}(x,y) = \max\big(\mu_A(x), \mu_B(y)\big)\,, \\
\text{Complement } A^c : \quad & \mu_{A^c}(x) = 1 - \mu_A(x)\,.
\end{aligned} \tag{9.82}$$

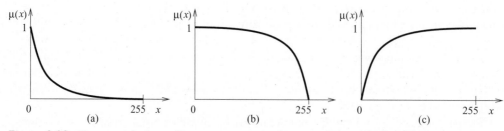

Figure 9.28: Fuzzy set hedges. Fuzzy set DARK is shown in Figure 9.26b. (a) Fuzzy set VERY DARK. (b) Fuzzy set SOMEWHAT DARK. (c) Fuzzy set NOT VERY DARK. © *Cengage Learning 2015.*

Note that fuzzy set operators may be combined with hedges and new fuzzy sets may be constructed; e.g., a fuzzy set NOT VERY DARK (see Figure 9.28) could be constructed as NOT (VERY (DARK))

$$\mu_{\text{NOT VERY DARK}}(x) = 1 - \mu_{\text{DARK}}^2(x) \,.$$

9.7.3 Fuzzy reasoning

In fuzzy reasoning, information carried in individual fuzzy sets is combined to make a decision. The functional relationship determining the degree of membership in related fuzzy membership functions is called the **method of composition** and results in the definition of a **fuzzy solution space**. To arrive at the decision, a **de-fuzzification** (decomposition) process determines a functional relationship between the fuzzy solution space and the decision. Processes of composition and de-fuzzification form the basis of fuzzy reasoning (Figure 9.29), which is performed in the context of a **fuzzy system model** that consists of control, solution, and working data variables; fuzzy sets; hedges; fuzzy rules; and a control mechanism. Fuzzy models use a series of propositions called fuzzy rules. Unconditional fuzzy rules are of the form

$$x \text{ is } A \tag{9.83}$$

and conditional fuzzy rules have the form

$$\text{if } x \text{ is } A \text{ then } w \text{ is } B \,, \tag{9.84}$$

where A and B are linguistic variables and x and w represent scalars from their respective domains. The degree of membership associated with an unconditional fuzzy rule is simply $\mu_A(x)$. Unconditional fuzzy propositions are used either to restrict the solution space or to define a default solution space. Since these rules are unconditional, they are applied directly to the solution space by applying fuzzy set operators.

Considering conditional fuzzy rules, there are several approaches to arrive at the decision. **Monotonic fuzzy reasoning** is the simplest approach that can produce a solution directly without composition and de-fuzzification. Suppose x represent a scalar gray-level describing darkness of a cloud, and w the severity of a thunderstorm. The knowledge of thunderstorm severity may be given by the fuzzy rule

$$\text{if } x \text{ is DARK then } w \text{ is SEVERE} \,. \tag{9.85}$$

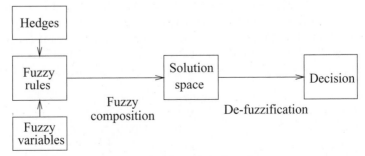

Figure 9.29: Fuzzy reasoning—composition and de-fuzzification. © *Cengage Learning 2015.*

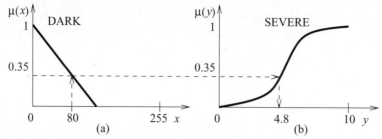

Figure 9.30: Monotonic fuzzy reasoning based on a single fuzzy rule: If the gray-level of the cloud is DARK, then the thunderstorm will be SEVERE. © *Cengage Learning 2015.*

The algorithm for monotonic fuzzy reasoning is shown in Figure 9.30. Based on determination of the cloud gray-level (x=80 in our case), the membership value $\mu_{DARK}(80) = 0.35$ is determined. This value is used to represent the membership value $\mu_{SEVERE}(w) = \mu_{DARK}(x)$ and the decision is made about the expected severity of the thunderstorm; in our case severity $w = 4.8$ on a scale between 0 and 10. This approach may also be applied to complex predicates of the form

$$\text{if } (x \text{ is } A) \bullet (y \text{ is } B) \bullet \ldots \bullet (u \text{ is } F) \text{ then } w \text{ is } Z \,, \tag{9.86}$$

where $\bullet$ represents the conjunctive AND or disjunctive OR operations. Fuzzy intersection and union operators can be used to combine the complex predicates; AND corresponds to fuzzy intersection and OR corresponds to fuzzy union. While the monotonic approach shows the fundamental concept of fuzzy reasoning, it can only be used for a monotonic single fuzzy variable controlled by a single fuzzy rule (possibly with a complex predicate). As the complexity of the predicate proposition increases, the validity of the decision tends to decrease.

Fuzzy composition

Knowledge related to the decision-making process is usually contained in more than one fuzzy rule. A large number of fuzzy rules may take part in the decision-making process and all fuzzy rules are fired in parallel during that process. Clearly, not all fuzzy rules contribute equally to the final solution, and rules that have no degree of truth in their premises do not contribute to the outcome at all. Several composition mechanisms facilitate rule combination.

The most frequently used approach is called the **min–max rule**; a sequence of minimizations and maximizations is applied. First, the minimum of the predicate truth (**correlation minimum**) $\mu_{A_i}(x)$ is used to restrict the consequent fuzzy membership function $\mu_{B_i}(w)$. Let the rules be in the form specified in equation (9.84), and let i represent the ith rule. Then, the consequent fuzzy membership functions B_i are updated in a pointwise fashion and the fuzzy membership functions B_i^+ are formed (Figure 9.31).

$$\mu_{B_i^+}(w) = \min\left(\mu_{B_i}(w), \mu_{A_i}(x)\right) . \tag{9.87}$$

Second, the pointwise maxima of these minimized fuzzy sets form the solution fuzzy membership function

$$\mu_S(w) = \max_i \left(\mu_{B_i^+}(w)\right) . \tag{9.88}$$

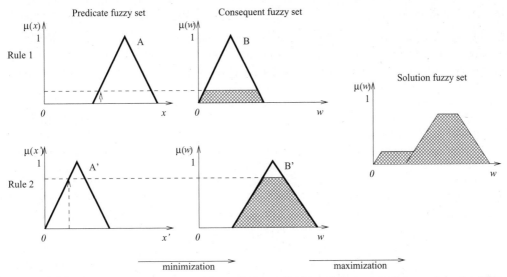

Figure 9.31: Fuzzy min–max composition using correlation minimum. © *Cengage Learning 2015*.

Figure 9.31 demonstrates the min–max composition process; again, complex predicates may be considered.

The correlation minimum described above is the most common approach to performing the first step of the min–max composition. An alternative approach called **correlation product** scales the original consequent fuzzy membership functions instead of truncating them. While correlation minimum is computationally less demanding and easier to de-fuzzify, correlation product represents in many ways a better method of minimization, since the original shape of the fuzzy set is retained (Figure 9.32).

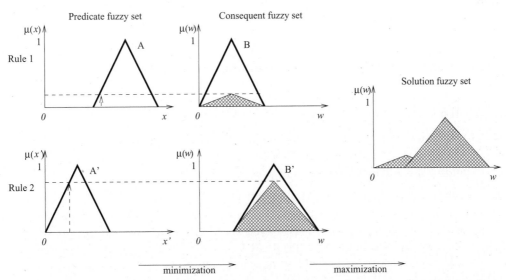

Figure 9.32: Fuzzy min–max composition using correlation product. © *Cengage Learning 2015*.

De-fuzzification

Fuzzy composition produces a single solution fuzzy membership function for each solution variable. To find the actual crisp solution that will be used for decision making, it is necessary to find a vector of scalar values (one value for each solution variable) that best represents the information contained in the solution fuzzy sets. This process is performed independently for each solution variable and is called de-fuzzification. Two de-fuzzification methods, called **composite moments** and **composite maximum**, are commonly used; many other varieties exist.

Composite moments look for the centroid c of the solution fuzzy membership function —Figure 9.33a shows how the centroid method converts the solution fuzzy membership function into a crisp solution variable c. Composite maximum identifies the domain point with the highest membership value in the solution fuzzy membership function. If this point is ambiguous (on a plateau or if there are two or more equal global maxima), the center of the plateau provides the crisp solution c' (Figure 9.33b). The composite moments approach produces a result that is sensitive to all the rules, while solutions determined using the composite maximum method are sensitive to the membership function produced by the single rule that has the highest predicate truth. While composite moments are used mostly in control applications, recognition applications usually use the composite maximum.

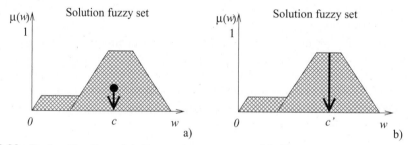

Figure 9.33: De-fuzzification. (a) Composite moments. (b) Composite maximum. © *Cengage Learning 2015.*

9.7.4 Fuzzy system design and training

Algorithm 9.14: Fuzzy system design

1. Design functional and operational characteristics of the system—determine the system inputs, basic processing approaches, and system outputs. In object recognition, the inputs are patterns and the output represents the decision.

2. Define fuzzy sets by decomposing each input and output variable of the fuzzy system into a set of fuzzy membership functions. The number of fuzzy membership functions associated with each variable depends on the task at hand: typically, an odd number between three and nine is created for each variable. It is recommended that neighboring functions overlap by 10–50%, and that the sum of the membership values of the overlap are less than one.

3. Convert problem-specific knowledge into the fuzzy *if–then* rules that represent a fuzzy associative memory. The number of designed rules is related to the number of input variables. For N variables each of which is divided into M fuzzy membership functions, M^N rules are required to cover all possible input combinations.

4. Perform fuzzy composition and de-fuzzification as described in Section 9.7.3.

5. Using a training set, determine the system's performance. If behavior does not meet the requirements, modify the set descriptions and/or rules and/or the composition and/or de-fuzzification approaches. The speed and success of this fine-tuning step depend on the problem complexity, the designer's level of understanding of the problem, and the level of the designer's experience.

As can be seen from steps 3 and 5 of this algorithm, the design of fuzzy rules may be a tedious and time-consuming process if the rules are to be designed from human experts, as has been typical in most existing applications. Several approaches have been reported that generate fuzzy *if–then* rules automatically using a training set as the source of knowledge and/or for automated adjusting membership functions of fuzzy sets [Ishibuchi et al., 1992, 1995; Abe and Lan, 1995; Homaifar and McCormick, 1995]. Some of the approaches use neural networks or genetic algorithms to control the learning process.

Many applications of fuzzy systems exist in pattern recognition and image processing. In the field of pattern recognition, fuzzy logic has been used for supervised and non-supervised recognition, sequential learning, fuzzy decision theoretic and syntactic classifiers, feature extraction, etc. In image processing and vision, fuzzy logic has been applied to image quality assessment, edge detection, image segmentation, color image segmentation, etc. Extensive work has been done in developing fuzzy geometry approaches [Rosenfeld, 1979, 1985]. Application of fuzzy logic to image segmentation was discussed in Section 7.4. Three-dimensional fuzzy-logic-based analysis of airway trees extracted from X-ray CT image data showed improved performance compared to crisp-rule-based methods [Park et al., 1998]. Use of fuzzy cost functions in optimal graph based image analysis (Section 7.7) was reported in [Haeker et al., 2007; Garvin et al., 2009].

9.8 Boosting in pattern recognition

It is rare that a single classifier will solve a problem completely, or indeed 'well enough'; recognizing this, it is common to combine a number of independent classifiers to improve overall performance. Often, these individual classifiers may be very weak (or **base**) in isolation (that is, in a two-class problem, a classifier may perform little better than 50%). We might train up a number of these simple classifiers, each time working with a different subset of the training examples, and somehow combine this collection of classifiers. This approach to achieving improved performance of any given learning algorithm is called **boosting**. The final combination of weak classifiers in a single classification rule that is much more accurate than any of the constituent rules.

The specifics of this general approach let the weak classifiers function sequentially and place the most weight on 'difficult' training examples, i.e., those that were misclassified in the previous round(s). To combine the weak rules in a single strong rule, a weighted majority vote of the weak classifier outputs is an obvious strategy. Boosting is then capable of producing very accurate classifications by combining classifications which are only moderately accurate. **AdaBoost** is the best known of these approaches and is widely used [Freund and Schapire, 1997].

Consider a pattern space X, a training set T of n patterns $\mathbf{x}_i$, their corresponding class identifiers ω_i, and assume two-class classification ($\omega_i \in \{-1, 1\}$)

$$T = \{(\mathbf{x}_1, \omega_1), \ldots (\mathbf{x}_n, \omega_n)\} \ .$$

Suppose we have a supervised learning algorithm W: given a training set T it will deliver a classifier $C_T = W(T)$. The AdaBoost algorithm can then be summarized as Algorithm 9.15 [Schapire, 2002]. Weak classifiers C_k are applied to the training set in which the importance of correctly classifying the individual examples varies step by step, and in each step k is specified by a set of weights $D_k(i)$, so that $\sum_{i=1}^{m} D_k(i) = 1$. Initially, the weights are uniform but at step $k+1$, the weights of examples incorrectly classified in step k are increased (in a relative sense). Consequently, the weak classifier W_{k+1} concentrates on the difficult examples misclassified in the previous round(s).

Algorithm 9.15: AdaBoost

1. Set $D_1(j) = \frac{1}{n}$, $j = 1, \ldots, n$, $i = 1$, and choose K.

2. Sample T_i from T according to D_i, and train $C_i = W(T_i)$.

3. Determine the *error* ϵ_i in C_i. Set $\alpha_i = \frac{1}{2} \log \left(\frac{1-\epsilon_i}{\epsilon_i} \right)$.

4. For all j, set $D_{i+1}(j) = D_i(j)e^{-\alpha_i}$ if C_i classifies $\mathbf{x}_j$ correctly, and $D_{i+1}(j) = D_i(j)e^{\alpha_i}$ otherwise. Renormalize the D_{i+1}.

5. Increment i and go to 2 until $i = K$.

6. Use the classifier

$$C(\mathbf{x}) = sign \left(\sum_{i=1}^{T} \alpha_i C_i(\mathbf{x}) \right) \ . \tag{9.89}$$

At step 3, the error is calculated as the probability of the classifier being wrong, *with respect to its training population*:

$$\epsilon_i = \sum_{j:C_i(\mathbf{x}_j) \neq \omega_j} D_i(j) \ .$$

It is assumed that W delivers better than random, so $\epsilon < 0.5$ and hence $\alpha > 0$. α_i serves two purposes:

- It underlies the adjustment to D_i. These increase for 'difficult' instances and decrease for 'easy' ones.

- It weights the final classifier sum.

Writing $\epsilon_i = \frac{1}{2} - \gamma_i$, then γ measures how much better the classifier is than random (so $\gamma > 0$). It can be shown [Freund and Schapire, 1997] that the final classifier C has an error rate less than

$$\prod_i 2\sqrt{\epsilon_i(1 - \epsilon_i)} \leq \exp\left(-2\sum_i \gamma_i^2\right) .$$

Most problems are not binary: patterns may belong to one of a number of classes. More generally, a pattern may belong to *several* of a number of classes. For example, classifying documents as *news, politics, sport, entertainment,* ..., a given item may belong to more than one category. Adaboost can be adapted to these more general problems.

Algorithm 9.16: AdaBoost-MH

1. Take $T = \{(\mathbf{x}_1, A_1), \ldots (\mathbf{x}_n, A_n)\}$, $A_j \subset Y = [1, k]$. Set $D_1(j, l) = \frac{1}{nk}$ for $j = 1, \ldots, n$, $l = 1, \ldots, k$, and choose K.

2. Sample T_i from T according to D_i, and train $C_i = W(T_i)$. The sign of $C_i(\mathbf{x}, j)$ indicates whether label j attaches to $\mathbf{x}$ or not.

3. Determine α_i.

4. **Update:** set $D_{i+1}(j, l) = D_i(j, l)e^{-\alpha_i C_i(\mathbf{x}_j, l)}$ if C_i classifies $\mathbf{x}_j$ correctly, and $D_{i+1}(j) = D_i(j)e^{\alpha_i C_i(\mathbf{x}_j, l)}$ otherwise.

5. Renormalize the $D_{i+1}(j, l)$.

6. Increment i and go to 2 until $i = K$.

7. Use

$$C(\mathbf{x}, l) = sign\left(\sum_{i=1}^{T} \alpha_i C_i(\mathbf{x}, l)\right) . \tag{9.90}$$

In addition to an ability to learn from examples, the ability to generalize and thus correctly classify previously unseen patterns is of basic importance. Theoretical considerations suggest that Adaboost may be prone to over-fitting, but experimental results show that typically it does not overfit, even when run for thousands of rounds. More interestingly, it was observed that AdaBoost sometimes continues to drive down the classification error long after the training error had already reached zero (see Figure 9.34). The error decrease can be associated with an increase in the *margin* that was introduced in association with SVMs (Section 9.2.5), which explicitly maximizes the minimum margin. In boosting, the margin is a number from the interval [-1,1] that is positive only if the strong classifier correctly classifies the pattern. The magnitude of the margin corresponds to the level of confidence in the classification.

Many modifications of AdaBoost exist. Incorporating a priori knowledge in the boosting scheme is introduced in [Rochery et al., 2002]. AdaBoost has the ability to identify *outliers* which are inherently difficult to classify; to deal with a possible decrease in AdaBoost's performance when a large number of outliers exists, *Gentle AdaBoost* and *BrownBoost* were introduced in [Friedman et al., 2000; Freund, 2001], in which the outliers' influence is less pronounced.

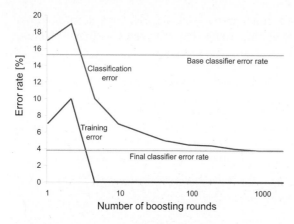

Figure 9.34: AdaBoost: training and testing error rate curves plotted against the number of boosting rounds. Note that testing error keeps decreasing long after training error has already reached zero. This is associated with a continuing increase in the margin that increases the overall classification confidence with additional rounds of boosting. © *Cengage Learning 2015*.

A very well known application of the boosting approach is the Viola-Jones face detector, explained in detail in Section 10.7. This in turn can be exploited as a pedestrian detector in video, described in Section 16.4.

In AdaBoost, the weak classifiers are frequently statistical in nature, but there is no special requirement on them. For example, rule-based classifiers may be considered. The individual weak classifiers do not even have to be of the same kind. This flexibility further increases the general character of boosting strategies when applied to pattern recognition problems.

9.9   Random forests

Random forests are a classification approach that is especially well suited for problems with many classes when large datasets are available for training [Breiman, 2001]. That they naturally deal with more than two classes, provide probabilistic outputs, offer excellent unseen data generalization, and are inherently parallel are all very intriguing characteristics of this approach [Criminisi and Shotton, 2013].

Here, we give a general overview of the underlying methodology, and a description of their use in image understanding is given in Section 10.8. Their treatment here is relatively brief, but many focused research articles devoted to them are easy to locate, starting with seminal publications [Breiman et al., 1984; Ho and Ohnishi, 1995]. The work of Quinlan offered an approach called the C4.5 algorithm to train decision trees optimally [Quinlan, 1993]. The concept of a single decision tree was extended to multiple such trees in a randomized fashion, forming random forests. Some aspects of random forests resemble the boosting strategy described in Section 9.8 since weak classifiers are associated with individual tree nodes and the entire forest yields a strong classification decision. This presentation is primarily based on [Criminisi et al., 2011], in which discussion of recent developments and additional implementation details can be found.

Random forests are used for two main decision making tasks: *classification* and *regression*. In classification (e.g., when classifying images into categories denoting types of captured scenes – beach, road, person, etc.), the decision-making output is a class label. In non-linear regression (e.g., predicting severity of flu season from – possibly multi-dimensional – social network data), the outcome is a continuous numeric value.

A *decision tree* consists of internal (or split) nodes and terminal (or leaf) nodes (see Figure 9.35). Arriving image patterns are evaluated in respective nodes of the tree and – based on the pattern properties—are passed to either left or right child nodes. Leafs L store the statistics of the patterns that arrived at a particular node during training. When a decision tree $\mathcal{T}_t$ is used for classification, the stored statistical information contains the probability of each class ω_r, $r \in 1, ..., R$ or $p_t(\omega_r|L)$. If used for regression, the statistical information contains a distribution over the continuous parameter that is being estimated. For a combined *classification–regression* task (Section 10.8), both kinds of statistics are collected. A random forest $\mathcal{T}$ then consists of a set of T such trees and each tree $\mathcal{T}_t$, $t \in \{1, ..., T\}$, is trained on a randomly sampled subset of the training data. It has been shown that ensembles of slightly different trees (differences resulting, e.g., from training on random training subsets) produce much higher accuracy and better noise insensitivity compared to single trees when applied to previously unseen data, demonstrating excellent generalization capabilities.

Once a decision tree is trained, predefined binary tests are associated with each internal node and unseen data patterns are passed from the tree root to one of the leaf nodes. The exact path is decided based on the outcome of the internal-node tests, each of which determines whether the data pattern is passed to one or the other child node. The process of binary decisions is repeated until the data pattern reaches a leaf node. Each of the leaf nodes contains a *predictor*, i.e., a classifier or a regressor, which associates the pattern with a desired output (classification label, regression value). If a forest of many trees is employed, the individual tree leaf predictors are combined to form a single prediction. In this sense, the decision-making process based on the node-associated binary predictors is fully deterministic.

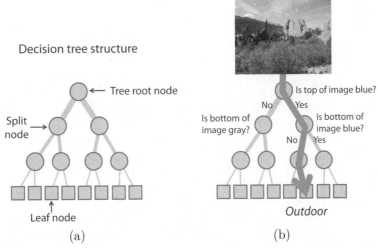

Figure 9.35: Decision tree. (a) Decision trees contain one root node, internal or split nodes (circles), and terminal or leaf nodes (squares). (b) A pattern arrives at the root and is sequentially passed to one of two children of each split node according to the node-based split function until it reaches a leaf node. Each leaf node is associated with a probability of a specific decision, for example associating a pattern with a class label. *Based on [Criminisi et al., 2011]. A color version of this figure may be seen in the color inset—Plate 16.*

9.9.1   Random forest training

The decision-making capabilities of the individual tree nodes will depend on the predefined binary tests associated with each internal node and on the leaf predictors. The
parameters of the binary tests can be either expert-designed or result from training. Let
S_i denote the subset of training data reaching node i, and S_i^L and S_i^R denote subsets
of training data reaching the left or right child nodes of node i, respectively. Since the
decisions at each node are binary, we have:

$$S_i = S_i^L \cup S_i^R \,, \qquad S_i^L \cap S_i^R = \emptyset \,. \tag{9.91}$$

The training process constructs a decision tree for which parameters of each binary test
were chosen to minimize some objective function. To stop construction of tree children at
a certain node of a certain branch, tree-growth stopping criteria are applied. If the forest
contains T trees, each tree $\mathcal{T}_t$ is trained independently of the others using a randomly
selected subset of the training set per tree.

Take a 4-class classification problem, in which the same number of 2D patterns belong
to each class (Figure 9.36). Comparing two of many ways in which the feature space may
be split—say, using a half-way horizontal or half-way vertical split line—it can be seen

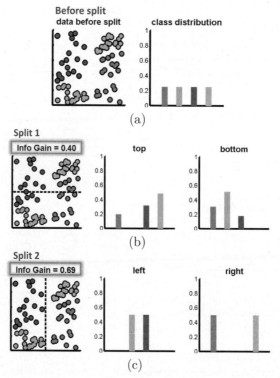

Figure 9.36: Information gain resulting from a split. (a) Class distributions prior to the split.
(b) Distributions after a horizontal split. (c) Distributions after a vertical split. Note that both
yield more homogeneous subsets and that the entropy of both subsets is decreases as a result of
these splits. *Based on [Criminisi et al., 2011]. A color version of this figure may be seen in the color
inset—Plate 17.*

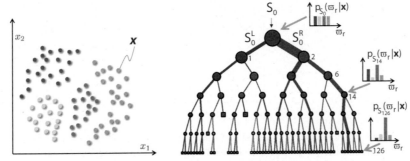

Figure 9.37: Tree training. Distribution of two-dimensional feature patterns in the feature space is reflected by the class distribution at the root-node level. Here class labels are color-coded and each class includes an identical number of patterns. As a result of training, binary decision functions associated with each split node are optimized—note the increased selectivity of class distributions at nodes more distant from the root (reflecting decreasing entropy). Relative numbers of training patterns passing through individual tree branches are depicted by their thickness. The branch colors correspond to the distribution of class labels. *Based on [Criminisi et al., 2011]. A color version of this figure may be seen in the color inset—Plate 18.*

that both yield more homogeneous subsets (higher similarity of subset-member patterns) and result in a lower entropy of the subsets (Section 2.3.3) than was the case prior to the splits. The change in entropy (equation 2.7), called the *information gain I*, is

$$I = H(S) - \sum_{i \in \{1,2\}} \frac{|S^i|}{|S|} H(S^i) \,. \tag{9.92}$$

Clearly the vertical split in Figure 9.36 separates the classes much better than the horizontal split and this observation is reflected in the differences in the information gain. The parameters of the internal-node binary decision elements can be set so that the information gain achieved on the training set by each split is maximized. Forest training is based on this paradigm.

As shown in Figure 9.37, the binary *split function* associated with a node j

$$h(\mathbf{x}, \theta_j) \in \{0, 1\} \tag{9.93}$$

directs the patterns $\mathbf{x}$ arriving at node j to either the left or the right child (0 or 1 decision). These node-associated split functions play the role of weak classifiers (see also Section 9.8). The weak learner at node j is characterized by parameters $\theta_j = (\phi_j, \psi_j, \tau_j)$ defining the feature selection function ϕ (specifying which features from the full feature set are used in the split function associated with node j), data separation function ψ (which hypersurface type is used to split the data, e.g., axis-aligned hyperplane, oblique hyperplane, general surface, etc.—see Figure 9.38), and threshold τ driving the binary decision.

Parameters θ_j must be optimized for all tree nodes j during training, yielding optimized parameters θ_j^*. One way to optimize the split function parameters is to maximize the information gain objective function

$$\theta_j^* = \operatorname*{argmax}_{\theta_j} I_j \,, \tag{9.94}$$

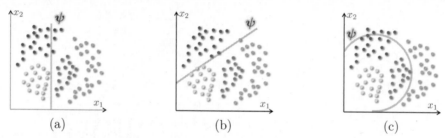

Figure 9.38: Weak learners can use a variety of binary discrimination functions. (a) Axis-aligned hyperplane. (b) General hyperplane. (c) General hypersurface. *Based on [Criminisi et al., 2011]. A color version of this figure may be seen in the color inset—Plate 19.*

where $I_j = I(S_j, S_j^L, S_j^R, \theta_j)$ and S_j, S_j^L, S_j^R represent training data before and after the left/right split at node j.

The decision tree is constructed during the training and a *stopping criterion* is needed for each tree node to determine whether child-nodes should be formed, or tree-branch construction terminated. Meaningful criteria include: defining a maximum allowed tree depth D (this is very popular); or allowing the node to form child nodes only if a pre-specified minimum information gain is achieved by a split during training; or not allowing child-node construction if a node is not on a frequented data path, i.e., if a node processes less than a pre-defined number of training patterns.

After training, tree leaf nodes contain information that will be used during the decision making process. If the goal is *classification*, each leaf node L stores the empirical distribution over the classes associated with a training subset that has reached that particular leaf node. Considering R classes, a probabilistic predictor model for pattern $\mathbf{x}$ and tree $\mathcal{T}_t$ is

$$p_t(\omega_r|\mathbf{x}), \text{ where } r \in \{1, ..., R\}. \tag{9.95}$$

If a **regression** task is considered, the output is a continuous variable. The leaf predictor model yields a posterior over the desired continuous variable.

A forest $\mathcal{T}$ consists of T trees that are randomly different from each other. The randomness is introduced during training, for example by employing a random subset of the training data for each tree of the forest (so called *bagging*), using randomized node optimization, or other approaches.

9.9.2 Random forest decision making

The behavior of the random forest decision process depends on the number T of trees forming the forest, the maximum allowed tree depth D, parameters of the randomness, choice of the weak learner model, objective function used for tree training, and of course the choice of features representing the underlying data.

The training described above is performed independently for each tree and may be performed in parallel. When using a forest consisting of T trees, the testing-set pattern $\mathbf{x}$ is simultaneously provided to all T roots of T trained trees and the tree-level processing can also be performed in parallel until the pattern reaches the tree leaves, each of which is providing a leaf-specific prediction. All tree predictions must be combined to form a single forest prediction that represents the forest output. The forest prediction can be obtained in several ways, for example by averaging all tree predictions or multiplying the

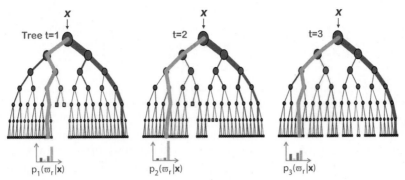

Figure 9.39: Decision making process using classification random forests—the same unseen pattern **x** arrives simultaneously at the roots of all trees forming the forest. At each node at which the pattern arrives, a test optimized during training is employed to direct the pattern to one of the two children. Due to the random character of training, each tree of the forest includes different split functions and the same pattern follows a different path through the tree nodes until a leaf is reached. Once the leaf is reached in each tree, the tree-specific class posteriors $p_t(\omega_r|\mathbf{x})$ are averaged (or multiplied) to yield a forest posterior $p(\omega_r|\mathbf{x})$. Note that there is one and only one path how a specific pattern **x** passes through the tree during decision making. Consequently, the probability $p_t(\omega_r|\mathbf{x})$, while linked to a single leaf node, represents the posterior associated with the entire tree. *Based on [Criminisi et al., 2011]. A color version of this figure may be seen in the color inset—Plate 20.*

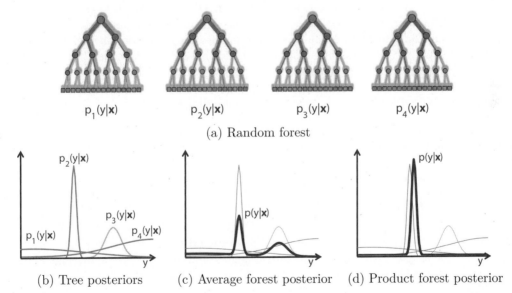

Figure 9.40: Random forest ensemble model for predicting continuous variable y. (a) Random forest consisting of 4 trees. (b) Posteriors of individual trees $p_t(y|\mathbf{x})$. (c) Forest posterior resulting from average-based ensemble model. (d) Forest posterior resulting from multiplication-based ensemble model. Note the strongest influence of the more informative trees on the forest posterior. *Based on [Criminisi et al., 2011]. A color version of this figure may be seen in the color inset—Plate 21.*

tree outputs together:

$$p(\omega_r|\mathbf{x}) = \frac{1}{T}\sum_{t=1}^{T} p_t(\omega_r|\mathbf{x}) \qquad \text{or} \qquad p(\omega_r|\mathbf{x}) = \frac{1}{Z}\prod_{t=1}^{T} p_t(\omega_r|\mathbf{x}) \, , \qquad (9.96)$$

where $1/Z$ provides probabilistic normalization.

Tree **ensemble models** combine contributions from many trees into a single forest-level output. Figure 9.39 depicts outputs from three randomly trained decision trees used for a classification task, these outputs are combined according to equation (9.96). Figure 9.40 shows how prediction outputs from multiple trees $(T = 4)$ can be combined for a regression-task random forest. Let the posterior outputs representing prediction of the desired continuous variable y for all four individual trees for pattern $\mathbf{x}$ be $p_t(y|\mathbf{x})$, $t \in \{1, .., 4\}$. Figure 9.40c shows the forest output obtained via averaging of individual tree outputs, and Figure 9.40d gives the output obtained by multiplying tree outputs. In both panels, the forest output benefits from combining the outputs and is influenced more strongly by the more confident portions of the individual tree outputs. Individual tree contributions may be noisy and averaging many tree posteriors decreases noise sensitivity. Understandably, product-based ensemble models are more sensitive to noise.

9.9.3 Random forest extensions

Random forest approaches have been shown highly applicable to supervised, unsupervised, and semi-supervised learning as well as for manifold learning using manifold forests. Discussion of such extensions and description of the effect of random forest parameters on their performance, accuracy, and generalization can be found in [Criminisi et al., 2011; Criminisi and Shotton, 2013]. The same publications also contain useful comparisons with support vector machines (Section 9.2.5), boosting approaches (Section 9.8), RANSAC (Section 10.3), and Gaussian mixture models/expectation-maximization (Section 10.13). Section 10.8 gives several practical examples demonstrating how random forests can be used for image analysis and understanding tasks.

9.10   Summary

- **Object recognition, pattern recognition**

    - Pattern recognition is used for region and object **classification**, and represents an important building block of complex machine vision processes.

    - No recognition is possible without **knowledge**. Knowledge about objects being processed, and hierarchically higher and more general knowledge about object classes is required.

- **Knowledge representation**

    - Descriptions and features

    - Grammars and languages

    - Predicate logic

- Production rules
- Fuzzy logic
- Semantic nets
- Frames, scripts

- **Statistical pattern recognition**

    - **Object recognition** is based on assigning classes to objects, using a **classifier**. The number of classes is usually known beforehand, and typically can be derived from the problem specification.

    - The classifier will use **patterns** sensed from the object to take decisions.

    - Nearest neighbor classifiers are straightforward to understand and widely used. They are expensive to use for high-dimensional or large datasets, and have been improved via K-D trees and approximation approaches.

    - For statistical pattern recognition, a **quantitative** description of objects using elementary numerical descriptions—**features**—is used. The set of possible patterns forms a **pattern space** or **feature space**. The **classes** form clusters in this space, which can be separated by **discrimination hyper-surfaces**.

    - A **statistical classifier** is a device with n inputs and 1 output. Each input is given by one of n features measured from an object to be classified. An R-class classifier generates one of R symbols ω_r, the **class identifiers**.

    - Classification parameters are determined from a **training set** of examples during **classifier learning**. Two common learning strategies are **probability density estimation** and **direct loss minimization**.

    - **Support vector machine** training is based on maximization of **margin** between two classes; non-linear classification is facilitated by the **kernel trick**. Multi-class classification is achieved by combining multiple 2-class classifiers.

    - **Cluster analysis** is one of many methods that do not need training sets for learning. It divides the set of patterns into subsets (clusters) based on mutual similarity of subset elements.

- **Neural nets**

    - Most neural approaches are based on combinations of elementary processors (**neurons**), each of which takes a number of inputs and generates a single output. Each input has a weight, and output is a function of the weighted sum of inputs.

    - **Feed-forward** networks are common in pattern recognition problems. Training uses a set of examples and is often based on **back-propagation**.

    - **Self-organizing** networks do not require a training set to cluster the patterns.

    - **Hopfield** networks do not have designated inputs and outputs; rather, the current configuration represents the state. The network acts as an associative memory where *exemplars* are stored.

- **Syntactic pattern recognition**

  – Syntactic pattern recognition uses a **qualitative** description of objects. Elementary properties of objects are called **primitives**. **Relational structures** are used to describe relations between the object primitives.

  – The set of all primitives is called the **alphabet**. The set of all words in the alphabet that can describe objects from one class is called the **description language**. A **grammar** is a set of rules that must be followed when words of the specific language are constructed from the alphabet.

  – Grammar construction usually requires significant human interaction. In simple cases, an automated process called **grammar inference** can be applied.

  – The recognition decision of whether or not the word can be generated by a particular grammar is made during **syntactic analysis**.

- **Recognition as graph matching**

  – Matching of a model and an object graph description can be used for recognition. An exact match of graphs is called graph **isomorphism**. Determination of graph isomorphism is computationally expensive.

  – In the real world, the object graph usually does not match the model graph exactly—isomorphisms cannot assess the level of mismatch. **Graph similarity** may identify objects represented by similar graphs.

- **Optimization techniques in recognition**

  – Optimization problems seek minimization or maximization of an **objective function**. Design of the objective function is a key factor in performance.

  – Most conventional approaches to optimization use calculus-based **hill climbing** methods. Search can easily end in local rather than global extrema.

  – **Genetic algorithms** use natural evolution mechanisms (*'survival of the fittest'*) to search for the maximum. Potential solutions are represented as strings. Genetic algorithms search from a population of potential solutions, not a single solution. The sequence of **reproduction**, **crossover**, and **mutation** generates a new population of strings from the previous population. The fittest string represents the final solution.

  – **Simulated annealing** combines two basic optimization principles, **divide and conquer** and **iterative improvement** (hill climbing). This combination avoids getting stuck in local optima.

- **Fuzzy systems**

  – Fuzzy systems are capable of representing diverse, non-exact, uncertain, and inaccurate knowledge or information. They use qualifiers that are very close to the human way of expressing knowledge.

  – Fuzzy reasoning is performed in the context of a **fuzzy system model** that consists of control, solution, and working data variables; fuzzy sets; hedges; fuzzy rules; and a control mechanism.

- **Fuzzy sets** represent properties of fuzzy spaces. **Membership functions** represent the fuzziness of the description and assess the degree of certainty about the membership of an element in the particular fuzzy set. Shape of fuzzy membership functions can be modified using **fuzzy set hedges**. A hedge and its fuzzy set constitute a single semantic entity called a **linguistic variable**.

- **Fuzzy** *if–then* **rules** represent fuzzy associative memory in which knowledge is stored.

- In fuzzy reasoning, information carried in individual fuzzy sets is combined to make a decision. The functional relationship determining the degree of membership in related fuzzy regions is called the **method of composition** and results in definition of a **fuzzy solution space**. To arrive at the decision, **de-fuzzification** is performed. Processes of composition and de-fuzzification form the basis of fuzzy reasoning.

- **Boosting**

  - Boosting achieves an improved classification performance by combining classification outcomes of a (large) number of 'weak' classifiers of moderate performance.

  - A single complex classification rule is replaced with a number of simple rules, which may perform only slightly better than random selection. Boosting is capable of producing very accurate classifications by combining outcomes of only moderately accurate classifiers.

  - AdaBoost is a widely used boosting algorithm, in which weak classifiers are sequentially trained on the training set, with each next classifier being trained on a differently weighted set of training patterns. Weighting is set according to the difficulty of classifying individual patterns, assessed according to the classification outcomes in previous steps.

  - The outcomes of all weak classifiers are combined to form a final strong classifier. The combination is based on a weighted majority vote.

  - There are no other requirements on the weak classifier selection than that they need to provide a better than random classification performance.

- **Random Forests**

  - Random forests are especially well suited for **problems with many classes** when **large datasets** are available for training.

  - Random forests are used for two main decision making tasks: **classification** and **regression**.

  - In **classification**, the decision-making output is a class label.

  - In **non-linear regression**, the outcome is a continuous numeric value.

  - Each tree of a forest can be trained in parallel. Once trained, predefined binary tests are associated with each internal node and previously unseen data patterns are passed from the tree root to a leaf nodes based on the outcome of the internal-node tests.

- A **random forest** consists of a set of decision trees, each of which may be trained on a randomly sampled subset of the training data.

- **Ensembles** of slightly different trees produce much higher accuracy and better noise insensitivity compared to single trees when employed for decision making.

9.11 Exercises

Short-answer questions

S9.1 Define the *syntax* and *semantics* of knowledge representation.

S9.2 Describe the following knowledge representations, giving for each one at least one example that is different from examples given in the text: *Descriptions* (features), *Grammars, Predicate logic, Production rules, Fuzzy logic, Semantic nets, Frames (scripts)*.

S9.3 Define the following terms: *Pattern, Class, Classifier, Feature space*.

S9.4 Define the terms: *Class identifier, Decision rule, Discrimination function*.

S9.5 Explain the main concepts and derive a mathematical representation of the discrimination functions for:

(a) A minimum distance classifier

(b) A minimum error classifier

S9.6 What is a training set? How is it designed? What influences its desired size?

S9.7 Explain the principle of a Support Vector Machine (SVM) classifier.

S9.8 Explain why learning should be inductive and sequential.

S9.9 Describe the conceptual differences between supervised and unsupervised learning.

S9.10 Draw schematic diagrams of a feed-forward and Hopfield neural networks. Discuss their major architectural differences.

S9.11 For what is the back-propagation algorithm used? Explain its main steps.

S9.12 What is the reason for including the momentum constant in back-propagation learning?

S9.13 Explain the functionality of Kohonen neural networks. How can they be used for unsupervised pattern recognition?

S9.14 Explain how Hopfield networks can be used for pattern recognition.

S9.15 Define the following terms: *Primitive, Alphabet, Description language, Grammar*.

S9.16 Describe the main steps of syntactic pattern recognition.

S9.17 Give a formal definition of a grammar.

S9.18 When are two grammars equivalent?

S9.19 What is grammar inference? Give its block diagram.

S9.20 Formally define: *A graph, Graph isomorphism, Subgraph isomorphism, Double subgraph isomorphism*.

S9.21 Define Levenshtein distance. Explain its application to assessing string similarity.

S9.22 Explain why hill-climbing optimization approaches may converge to local instead of global optima.

S9.23 Explain the concept and functionality of genetic algorithm optimization. What are the roles of reproduction, crossover, and mutation in genetic algorithms?

S9.24 Explain the concept of optimization based on simulated annealing. What is the annealing schedule?

S9.25 List the advantages and disadvantages of genetic algorithms and simulated annealing compared to optimization approaches based on derivatives.

S9.26 Define the terms:

(a) Fuzzy set

(b) Fuzzy membership function

(c) Minimum normal form of a fuzzy membership function

(d) Maximum normal form of a fuzzy membership function

(e) Fuzzy system

(f) Domain of a fuzzy set

(g) Hedge

(h) Linguistic variable

S9.27 Use Zadeh's definitions to define formally: *Fuzzy intersection, Fuzzy union, Fuzzy complement.*

S9.28 Explain fuzzy reasoning based on composition and de-fuzzification. Draw a block diagram of fuzzy reasoning.

S9.29 Explain the rationale behind using weak classifiers in the Adaboost training and classification process.

S9.30 The training process in boosting is sequential. Why is increasing weight placed on the training examples that were misclassified in the previous steps?

S9.31 Provide a flowchart outlining the training process for a single tree of depth $D = 3$ from a random forest. Using the flowchart, identify a path that a hypothetical single training pattern follows and describe how this training pattern contributes to the training process.

S9.32 Give an example of deriving a random forest posterior from posteriors of at least 3 individual trees:

(a) Using average-based ensemble model.

(b) Using multiplication-based ensemble model.

Problems

Create the following training and testing sets of feature vectors to use in some of the Problems that follow.

TRAIN1:

ω_i	ω_1	ω_1	ω_1	ω_1	ω_1	ω_2	ω_2	ω_2	ω_2	ω_2
x_1	2	4	3	3	4	10	9	8	9	10
x_2	3	2	3	2	3	7	6	6	7	6

TEST1:

ω_i	ω_1	ω_1	ω_1	ω_1	ω_1	ω_2	ω_2	ω_2	ω_2	ω_2
x_1	3	6	5	5	6	13	12	11	11	13
x_2	5	3	4	3	5	10	8	8	9	8

TRAIN2:

ω_i	ω_1	ω_1	ω_1	ω_1	ω_1	ω_2	ω_2	ω_2	ω_2	ω_2
x_1	2	6	-2	7	5	-2	-6	2	-4	-5
x_2	400	360	520	-80	180	-200	-200	-400	-600	-400

ω_i	ω_3	ω_3	ω_3	ω_3	ω_3
x_1	-10	-8	-15	-12	-14
x_2	200	140	100	50	300

TEST2:

ω_i	ω_1	ω_1	ω_1	ω_1	ω_1	ω_2	ω_2	ω_2	ω_2	ω_2
x_1	4	8	-3	9	6	-1	-4	3	-2	-3
x_2	600	540	780	-120	270	-250	-250	-470	-690	-470

ω_i	ω_3	ω_3	ω_3	ω_3	ω_3
x_1	-15	-13	-6	-17	-16
x_2	230	170	130	80	450

P9.1 Let a minimum distance classifier be used to recognize two-dimensional patterns from three classes K_1, K_2, K_3. The training set consists of five patterns from each class:

$$K_1 := \left\{ \begin{pmatrix} 0 \\ 6 \end{pmatrix}, \begin{pmatrix} 1 \\ 6 \end{pmatrix}, \begin{pmatrix} 2 \\ 6 \end{pmatrix}, \begin{pmatrix} 1 \\ 5 \end{pmatrix}, \begin{pmatrix} 1 \\ 7 \end{pmatrix} \right\},$$

$$K_2 := \left\{ \begin{pmatrix} 4 \\ 1 \end{pmatrix}, \begin{pmatrix} 5 \\ 1 \end{pmatrix}, \begin{pmatrix} 6 \\ 1 \end{pmatrix}, \begin{pmatrix} 5 \\ 0 \end{pmatrix}, \begin{pmatrix} 5 \\ 2 \end{pmatrix} \right\},$$

$$K_3 := \left\{ \begin{pmatrix} 8 \\ 6 \end{pmatrix}, \begin{pmatrix} 9 \\ 6 \end{pmatrix}, \begin{pmatrix} 10 \\ 6 \end{pmatrix}, \begin{pmatrix} 9 \\ 5 \end{pmatrix}, \begin{pmatrix} 9 \\ 7 \end{pmatrix} \right\}.$$

Determine (sketch) the discrimination functions in the two-dimensional feature space.

P9.2 Use some software to generate data from two or more Gaussian distributions: these could be 1D but it is more interesting to use 2D or higher dimension. Use these data to define training and test sets for 'leave one out' testing of an NN of kNN classifier. Summarize the results for various selections of Gaussians and values of k.

P9.3 Let a minimum error classifier be used to recognize two-dimensional patterns from two classes, each having a normal distribution $N(\boldsymbol{\mu}_r, \boldsymbol{\Psi}_r)$:

$$\boldsymbol{\mu}_1 = \begin{pmatrix} 2 \\ 5 \end{pmatrix}, \quad \boldsymbol{\Psi}_1 = \begin{pmatrix} 1 & 0 \\ 0 & 1 \end{pmatrix}, \quad \boldsymbol{\mu}_2 = \begin{pmatrix} 4 \\ 3 \end{pmatrix}, \quad \boldsymbol{\Psi}_2 = \begin{pmatrix} 1 & 0 \\ 0 & 1 \end{pmatrix}.$$

Assume unit loss functions and equal a priori probabilities of classes $P(\omega_1) = P(\omega_2) = 0.5$. Determine (sketch) the discrimination function in the two-dimensional feature space.

P9.4 Repeat Problem P9.3 considering modified parameters of the normal distributions:

$$\mu_1 = \begin{pmatrix} 2 \\ 5 \end{pmatrix}, \quad \Psi_1 = \begin{pmatrix} 1 & 0 \\ 0 & 3 \end{pmatrix}, \quad \mu_2 = \begin{pmatrix} 4 \\ 3 \end{pmatrix}, \quad \Psi_2 = \begin{pmatrix} 1 & 0 \\ 0 & 3 \end{pmatrix}.$$

P9.5 Repeat Problem P9.4 with $P(\omega_1) = P$, $P(\omega_2) = (1 - P)$. Show how the discrimination function locations in the two-dimensional feature space change as a function of P.

P9.6 Consider the training set specified in Problem P9.1. Assume that the three pattern classes have normal distributions and that a priori probabilities of classes are equal $P(\omega_1) = P(\omega_2) = P(\omega_3) = 1/3$. Determine (sketch) the discrimination functions of the minimum error classifier in the two-dimensional feature space. Discuss under what circumstances the discrimination functions of a minimum distance classifier are identical to discrimination functions of the minimum error classifier if both were trained using the same training set.

P9.7 Develop a program for training and classification using the minimum distance classifier. Assess classification correctness.

   (a) Train and test using data sets TRAIN1 and TEST1.

   (b) Train and test using data sets TRAIN2 and TEST2.

P9.8 Develop a program for training and classification using the minimum error classifier, considering unit loss functions. Assume the training data have normal distribution. Assess classification correctness.

   (a) Train and test using data sets TRAIN1 and TEST1.

   (b) Train and test using data sets TRAIN2 and TEST2.

P9.9 Develop a program for cluster analysis using the k-means approach. Vary the initialization of cluster starting points and explore its influence on clustering results. Vary the number of classes and discuss the results.

   (a) Use a combined data set TRAIN1 and TEST1.

   (b) Use a combined data set TRAIN2 and TEST2.

P9.10 Create a training set and a testing set of feature vectors using the shape description program developed in Problem P8.13 to determine shape feature vectors. Use simple shapes (e.g., triangles, squares, rectangles, circles, etc.) of different sizes. Select up to five discriminative features to form the feature vectors of analyzed shapes. The training as well as the testing sets should consist of at least 10 patterns from each class. The training and testing sets will be used in the experiments below.

P9.11 Apply the program developed in Problem P9.7 to the training and testing sets created in Problem P9.10. Assess classification correctness.

P9.12 Apply the program developed in Problem P9.8 to the training and testing sets created in Problem P9.10. Assume normal distributions, and that you have a sufficient number to determine representative dispersion matrices and mean values from the training set. Assess classification correctness in the testing set. Compare with the performance of the minimum distance classifier used in Problem P9.11.

P9.13 Apply the program developed in Problem P9.9 to the testing set created in Problem P9.10. First, assume that the number of classes is known. Assess clustering correctness and compare it with that of the supervised methods used in Problems P9.11 and P9.12. Then, vary the initialization of cluster starting points and explore the influence on clustering results.

P9.14 Download a program that performs back-propagation learning and classification (there are many to be found). Train and test a three-layer feed-forward neural network using artificial data from a two-dimensional feature space representing patterns from at least three separable classes.

P9.15 Apply the program of Problem P9.14 to the testing set created in Problem P9.10. Assess classification correctness and compare it with that of the statistical classification methods assessed in Problems P9.11 and P9.12.

P9.16 Choice of width of layers is often a problem. Repeat Problems P9.14 and P9.15, paying attention to the size of the hidden layer. Draw some conclusions about network performance and training time as the size of this layer varies.

P9.17 Implement Algorithm 9.7. For some datasets devised by you, or extracted from some known application, run the algorithm. Compare its performance for different sizes and topologies of output layer, and various choices of parameters.

P9.18 Implement a Hopfield network. Train it on digitized patterns of the digits 0–9; study its performance at pattern recall (e.g., of noisy examples of digits) for various resolutions of the patterns.

P9.19 Design a grammar G that can generate a language $L(G)$ of equilateral triangles of any size; primitives with $0°$, $60°$, and $120°$ orientation form the set of terminal symbols $V_t = \{a, b, c\}$.

P9.20 Design three different grammars producing the language $L(G) = \{ab^n\}$ for $n = 1, 2, \ldots$.

P9.21 Design a grammar that generates all characters P or d of the following properties:

- Character P is represented by a square with an edge length equal to one; a vertical line is attached to the bottom left corner of the square and may have any length.

- Character d is represented by a square with an edge length equal to one; a vertical line is attached to the top right corner of the square and may have any length.

Obviously, there are infinitely many such characters. Use the following set of terminal symbols $V_t = \{N, W, S, E\}$; terminal symbols correspond to directions of the chain code – north, west, south, east. Design your set of non-terminal symbols, using a start symbol s. Validate your grammar design on examples. Show all steps in generating at least two P and two d characters.

P9.22 Using Algorithm 9.10 prove or disprove isomorphism of the graphs shown in Figure 9.41.

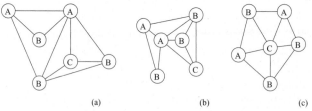

(a) (b) (c)

Figure 9.41: Problem P9.22. © *Cengage Learning 2015.*

P9.23 Determine the Levenshtein distance for the following string pairs:

(a) $S_1 = abadcdefacde$ $S_2 = abadddefacde$

(b) $S_1 = abadcdefacde$ $S_3 = abadefaccde$

(c) $S_1 = abadcdefacde$ $S_4 = cbadcacdae$

P9.24 Using genetic algorithm optimization, determine the maximum of the following function (this function has several local maxima; its visualization is available in, e.g., Matlab by typing **peaks**, see Figure 9.42):

$$z(x, y) = \quad 3(1 - x)^2 \exp\left[-x^2 - (y + 1)^2\right] - 10[(x/5) - x^3 - y^5] \exp\left[-x^2 - y^2\right]$$
$$-(1/3) \exp\left[-(x + 1)^2 - y^2\right]$$

Locate or develop a program for genetic algorithm-based optimization following Algorithm 9.12. Design the code string as consisting of n bits for the x value and n bits for the y value, the value of $z(x, y)$ represents the string fitness. Limit your search space to $x \in (-4, 4)$ and $y \in (-4, 4)$. Explore the role of the starting population, population size S, mutation rate M, and string bit length $2n$ on the speed of convergence and solution accuracy. For several values of S, M, n, plot the function values of maximum string fitness, average population fitness, and minimum string fitness as a function of the generation number.

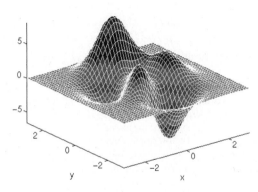

Figure 9.42: Problem P9.24. © *Cengage Learning 2015.*

P9.25 Using the definition of the fuzzy set SEVERE as given in Figure 9.30b, sketch the following fuzzy membership functions:

(a) VERY_SEVERE

(b) SOMEWHAT_SEVERE

(c) SOMEWHAT_NOT_SEVERE

P9.26 Using the fuzzy sets DARK and BRIGHT as given in Figure 9.27, sketch the single fuzzy membership function (NOT_VERY_DARK AND NOT_VERY_BRIGHT).

P9.27 Considering the fuzzy sets A and B given in Figure 9.43, derive intersection, union, and complement of the two fuzzy sets.

P9.28 Use the composite moments and composite maximum approaches to de-fuzzification to find the representative value of the fuzzy set provided in Figure 9.44.

P9.29 Flash flood represents a potential danger in many areas, and its prediction is an important part of meteorological forecasting. Clearly, the following conditions increase the flood danger:

(a) Rain amount in the past three days.

(b) Water saturation of soil.

(c) The rainfall expected in the next 24 hours.

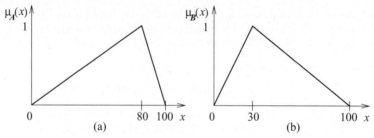

(a)   (b)

Figure 9.43: Problem P9.27. © *Cengage Learning 2015*.

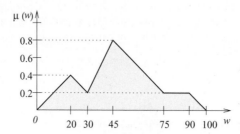

Figure 9.44: Problem P9.28. © *Cengage Learning 2015*.

Assuming the specified information is available, design a fuzzy logic system to determine the expected flood danger within the next 24 hours.

P9.30 Develop a program implementation of the fuzzy logic system designed in Problem P9.29. Explore, how different membership function shapes, and fuzzy logic composition and decomposition methods, influence the achieved results.

P9.31 Using any of the previously developed classifiers as the learning algorithm W, implement Algorithm 9.15 (AdaBoost); train/test this on datasets from earlier Problems, or on publicly available training/testing datasets with 2 classes. Compare AdaBoost performance with that of the other classification approaches.

P9.32 Using any of the previously developed classifiers to serve as the learning algorithm W, implement Algorithm 9.16 (AdaBoost-MH) and train/test on one of the many publicly available training/testing datasets with more than 2 classes. Compare AdaBoost-MH performance with that of the other classification approaches.

P9.33 Repeat Problem P9.32 using the random forest approach.

P9.34 Formulate and solve a practical pattern recognition problem using available open-source packages (e.g., [Weka 3 Team, 2013; R Software Team, 2013]).

P9.35 Make yourself familiar with solved problems and **Matlab** implementations of selected algorithms provided in the corresponding chapter of the **Matlab Companion** to this text [Svoboda et al., 2008]. The **Matlab Companion** homepage http://visionbook.felk.cvut.cz offers images used in the problems, and well-commented **Matlab** code is provided for educational purposes.

P9.36 Use the **Matlab Companion** [Svoboda et al., 2008] to develop solutions to additional exercises and practical problems provided there. Implement your solutions using **Matlab** or other suitable programming languages.

9.12   References

Abe S. and Lan M. A method for fuzzy rules extraction directly from numerical data and its application to pattern classification. *IEEE Transactions on Fuzzy Systems*, 3(2):129–139, 1995.

Aizerman A., Braverman E. M., and Rozoner L. I. Theoretical foundations of the potential function method in pattern recognition learning. *Automation and Remote Control*, 25: 821–837, 1964.

Ambler A. P. H. A versatile system for computer controlled assembly. *Artificial Intelligence*, 6 (2):129–156, 1975.

Baird H. S. *Model-Based Image Matching Using Location*. MIT Press, Cambridge, MA, 1984.

Ballard D. H. and Brown C. M. *Computer Vision*. Prentice-Hall, Englewood Cliffs, NJ, 1982.

Barnard S. T. Stereo matching by hierarchical microcanonical annealing. *Perception*, 1:832, 1987.

Barrero A. Inference of tree grammars using negative samples. *Pattern Recognition*, 24(1):1–8, 1991.

Barrow H. G. and Popplestone R. J. Relational descriptions in picture processing. *Machine Intelligence*, 6, 1971.

Beis J. and Lowe D. Shape indexing using approximate nearest-neighbour search in high-dimensional spaces. In *Proceedings of the Conference on Computer Vision and Pattern Recognition CVPR*, pages 1000–1006, Puerto Rico, 1997.

Bishop C. M. *Pattern Recognition and Machine Learning*. Springer, 2006.

Bollobas B. *Modern Graph Theory*. Springer, Berlin, 2002.

Boser B. E., Guyon I. M., and Vapnik V. N. A training algorithm for optimal margin classifiers. In *5th Annual ACM Workshop on COLT*, pages 144–152, Pittsburgh PA, 1992. ACM Press.

Bouman C. and Liu B. Multiple resolution segmentation of textured images. *IEEE Transactions on Pattern Analysis and Machine Intelligence*, 13(2):99–113, 1991.

Brachman R. and Levesque H. *Knowledge Representation and Reasoning*. Morgan Kaufmann, San Francisco, CA, 2004.

Breiman L., Friedman J., Olshen R., and Stone C. *Classification and Regression Trees*. Chapman & Hall, New York, 1984.

Breiman L. Random forests. In *Machine Learning*, pages 5–32, 2001.

Bron C. and Kerbosch J. Finding all cliques of an undirected graph. *Communications of the ACM*, 16(9):575–577, 1973.

Buckley F. *Distance in Graphs*. Addison-Wesley, Redwood City, CA, 1990.

Burges C. J. C. A tutorial on support vector machines for pattern recognition. *Data Mining and Knowledge Discovery*, 2:121–167, 1998.

Carpenter G. A. and Grossberg S. ART2: Self organization of stable category recognition codes for analog input patterns. *Applied Optics*, 26:4919–4930, 1987.

Cerny V. Thermodynamical approach to the travelling salesman problem: An efficient simulation algorithm. *Journal of Optimization Theory and Applications*, 45:41–51, 1985.

Chomsky N. *Syntactic Structures*. Mouton, Hague, 6th edition, 1966.

Cox E. *The Fuzzy Systems Handbook*. AP Professional, Cambridge, England, 1994.

Criminisi A. and Shotton J. *Decision Forests for Computer Vision and Medical Image Analysis*. Springer Verlag, London, 2013.

Criminisi A., Shotton J., and Konukoglu E. Decision forests for classification, regression, density estimation, manifold learning and semi-supervised learning. Technical Report MSR-TR-2011-114, Microsoft Research, Ltd., Cambridge, UK, 2011.

Devijver P. A. and Kittler J. *Pattern Recognition: A Statistical Approach*. Prentice-Hall, Englewood Cliffs, NJ, 1982.

Duda R. O. and Hart P. E. *Pattern Classification and Scene Analysis*. Wiley, New York, 1973.

Duda R. O., Hart P. E., and Stork D. G. *Pattern Classification*. Wiley, New York, 2nd edition, 2000.

Everitt B. S., Landau S., and Leese M. *Cluster Analysis*. Hodder Arnold, 4th edition, 2001.

Fischler M. A. and Elschlager R. A. The representation and matching of pictorial structures. *IEEE Transactions on Computers*, C-22(1):67–92, 1973.

Freund Y. An adaptive version of the boost by majority algorithm. *Machine Learning*, 43:293–318, 2001.

Freund Y. and Schapire R. E. A decision-theoretic generalization of on-line learning and an application to boosting. *Journal of Computer and System Sciences*, 55:119–139, 1997.

Friedman J., Hastie T., and Tibshirani R. Additive logistic regression: A statistical view of boosting. *The Annals of Statistics*, 38:337–374, 2000.

Friedman J. H., Bentley J. L., and Finkel R. A. An algorithm for finding best matches in logarithmic expected time. *ACM Transactions on Mathematical Software*, 3(3):209–226, 1977.

Fu K. S. *Syntactic Methods in Pattern Recognition*. Academic Press, New York, 1974.

Fu K. S. *Syntactic Pattern Recognition and Applications*. Prentice-Hall, Englewood Cliffs, NJ, 1982.

Garvin M. K., Abramoff M. D., Wu X., Russell S. R., Burns T. L., and Sonka M. Automated 3-D intraretinal layer segmentation of macular spectral-domain optical coherence tomography images. *IEEE Trans. Med. Imag.*, 28:1436–1447, 2009.

Geman D., Geman S., Graffigne C., and Dong P. Boundary detection by constrained optimisation. *IEEE Transactions on Pattern Analysis and Machine Intelligence*, 12(7):609–628, 1990.

Goldberg D. E. *Genetic Algorithms in Search, Optimization, and Machine Learning*. Addison-Wesley, Reading, MA, 1989.

Haeker M., Wu X., Abramoff M. D., Kardon R., and Sonka M. Incorporation of regional information in optimal 3-D graph search with application for intraretinal layer segmentation of optical coherence tomography images. In *Information Processing in Medical Imaging (IPMI)*, volume 4584 of *Lecture Notes in Computer Science*, pages 607–618. Springer, 2007.

Harary F. *Graph Theory*. Addison-Wesley, Reading, MA, 1969.

Haupt R. L. and Haupt S. E. *Practical genetic algorithms*. John Wiley & Sons, Inc., New York, NY, 2004.

Haykin S. *Fuzzy Sets and Fuzzy Logic: Theory and Applications*. Prentice Hall, New York, 2nd edition, 1998.

Hearst M. Trends and controversies: support vector machines. *IEEE Intelligent Systems*, 13:18–28, 1998.

Hecht-Nielson R. Kolmogorov's mapping neural network existence theorem. In *Proceedings of the First IEEE International Conference on Neural Networks*, volume 3, pages 11–14, San Diego, 1987. IEEE.

Ho K. H. L. and Ohnishi N. FEDGE—fuzzy edge detection by fuzzy categorization and classification of edges. In *Fuzzy Logic in Artificial Intelligence. Towards Intelligent Systems. IJCAI '95 Workshop. Selected Papers*, pages 182–196, 1995.

Homaifar A. and McCormick E. Simultaneous design of membership functions and rule sets for fuzzy controllers using genetic algorithms. *IEEE Transactions on Fuzzy Systems*, 3(2): 129–139, 1995.

Hopfield J. J. and Tank D. W. Computing with neural circuits: A model. *Science*, 233:625–633, 1986.

Ishibuchi H., Nozaki K., and Tanaka H. Distributed representation of fuzzy rules and its application to pattern classification. *Fuzzy Sets and Systems*, 52:21–32, 1992.

Ishibuchi H., Nozaki K., Yamamoto N., and Tanaka H. Selecting fuzzy if-then rules for classification problems using genetic algorithms. *IEEE Transactions on Fuzzy Systems*, 3:260–270, 1995.

Johnson R. A. and Wichern D. W. *Applied Multivariate Statistical Analysis*. Prentice-Hall, Englewood Cliffs, NJ, 2nd edition, 1990.

Kaufman L. and Rousseeuw P. J. *Finding Groups in Data: An Introduction to Cluster Analysis*. Wiley, New York, 1990.

Kecman V. *Learning and Soft Computing: Support Vector Machines, Neural Networks, and Fuzzy Logic Models*. MIT Press, Cambridge, MA, 2001.

Kirkpatrick S., Gelatt C. D., and Vecchi M. P. Optimization by simulated annealing. *Science*, 220:671–680, 1983.

Kohonen T. *Self-organizing Maps*. Springer Verlag, Berlin; New York, 1995.

Kolmogorov A. N. On the representation of continuous functions of many variables by superposition of continuous functions of one variable and addition. *Doklady Akademii Nauk SSSR*, 144:679–681, 1963. (AMS Translation, 28, 55-59).

Kosko B. *Neural Networks and Fuzzy Systems*. Prentice-Hall, Englewood Cliffs, NJ, 1992.

Leopold E. and Kindermann J. Text categorization with support vector machines. How to represent texts in input space? *Machine Learning*, 46(1-3):423–444, January 2002.

Li Y., Bontcheva K., and Cunningham H. Adapting SVM for data sparseness and imbalance: A case study in information extraction. *Natural Language Engineering*, 15(2):241–271, 2009.

McCulloch W. S. and Pitts W. A logical calculus of ideas immanent in nervous activity. *Bulletin of Mathematical Biophysics*, 5:115–133, 1943.

McEliece R. J., Posner E. C., Rodemich E. R., and Venkatesh S. S. The capacity of the Hopfield associative memory. *IEEE Transactions on Information Theory*, 33:461, 1987.

McHugh J. A. *Algorithmic Graph Theory*. Prentice-Hall, Englewood Cliffs, NJ, 1990.

Metropolis N., Rosenbluth A. W., Rosenbluth M. N., Teller A. H., and Teller E. Equation of state calculation by fast computing machines. *Journal of Chemical Physics*, 21:1087–1092, 1953.

Michalski R. S., Carbonell J. G., and Mitchell T. M. *Machine Learning I, II*. Morgan Kaufmann Publishers, Los Altos, CA, 1983.

Minsky M. L. *Perceptrons: An Introduction to Computational Geometry*. MIT Press, Cambridge, MA, 2nd edition, 1988.

Mitchell M. *An Introduction to Genetic Algorithms*. MIT Press, Cambridge, MA, 1996.

Mitchell M. *An Introduction to Genetic Algorithms*. MIT Press, Cambridge, MA, 1998.

More J. J. and Toraldo G. On the solution of large quadratic programming problems with bound constraints. *SIAM J. Optimization*, 1:93–113, 1993.

Muja M. and Lowe D. G. Fast approximate nearest neighbors with automatic algorithm configuration. In *VISAPP (1)*, pages 331–340, 2009.

Niemann H. *Pattern Analysis and Understanding*. Springer Verlag, Berlin–New York–Tokyo, 2nd edition, 1990.

Nilsson N. J. *Principles of Artificial Intelligence*. Springer Verlag, Berlin, 1982.

Otten R. H. and van Ginneken L. P. *The Annealing Algorithm*. Kluwer, Norwell, MA, 1989.

Park W., Hoffman E. A., and Sonka M. Segmentation of intrathoracic airway trees: A fuzzy logic approach. *IEEE Transactions on Medical Imaging*, 17:489–497, 1998.

Pelleg D. and Moore A. X-means: Extending K-means with efficient estimation of the number of clusters. In *Proceedings of the Seventeenth International Conference on Machine Learning*, pages 727–734, San Francisco, 2000. Morgan Kaufmann.

Pudil P., Novovicova J., and Kittler J. Floating search methods in feature selection. *Pattern Recognition Letters*, 15:1119–1125, 1994.

Quinlan J. R. *C4.5: Programs for machine learning*. Morgan Kaufmann Publishers Inc., San Francisco, CA, USA, 1993.

R Development Core Team. *R: A Language and Environment for Statistical Computing*. R Foundation for Statistical Computing, Vienna, Austria, 2008. URL http://www.R-project.org. ISBN 3-900051-07-0.

R Software Team. The Comprehensive R Archive Network. http://cran.r-project.org/, http://cran.r-project.org/web/packages/e1071/index.html, 2013.

Rao C. R. *Linear Statistical Inference and Its Application*. Wiley, New York, 1965.

Rawlins G. J. E. *Foundations of Genetic Algorithms*. Morgan Kaufmann, San Mateo, CA, 1991.

Reichgelt H. *Knowledge Representation: An AI Perspective*. Ablex, Norwood, NJ, 1991.

Rochery M., Schapire R., Rahim M., Gupta N., Riccardi G., Bangalore S., Alshawi H., and Douglas S. Combining prior knowledge and boosting for call classification in spoken language dialogue. In *International Conference on Accoustics, Speech and Signal Processing*, 2002.

Romesburg C. *Cluster Analysis for Researchers*. Lulu.com, 2004.

Rosenblatt R. *Principles of Neurodynamics*. Spartan Books, Washington, DC, 1962.

Rosenfeld A. Fuzzy digital topology. *Information Control*, 40:76–87, 1979.

Rosenfeld A. The perimeter of a fuzzy set. *Pattern Recognition*, 18:125–130, 1985.

Rumelhart D. and McClelland J. *Parallel Distributed Processing*. MIT Press, Cambridge, MA, 1986.

Salvador S. and Chan P. Determining the number of clusters/segments in hierarchical clustering/segmentation algorithms. In *Proceedings of the 16th IEEE Conference on Tools with Artificial Intelligence, ICTAI-2004*, pages 576–584, Los Alamitos, CA, USA, 2004. IEEE Computer Society.

Schapire R. E. The boosting approach to machine learning: An overview. In *Proc. MSRI Workshop on Nonlinear Estimation and Classification*, 2002.

Schlesinger M. I. and Hlaváč V. *Ten lectures on statistical and structural pattern recognition*, volume 24 of *Computational Imaging and Vision*. Kluwer Academic Publishers, Dordrecht, The Netherlands, 2002.

Schoelkopf B. SVMs - a practical consequence of learning theory (part of Hearst, M.A., Trends and controversies: support vector machines). *IEEE Intelligent Systems*, 13:18–21, 1998.

Sejnowski T. J. and Rosenberg C. R. Parallel systems that learn to pronounce English text. *Complex Systems*, 1:145–168, 1987.

Sharples M., Hogg D., Hutchinson C., Torrance S., and Young D. *Computers and Thought, A Practical Introduction to Artificial Intelligence*. MIT Press, Cambridge, MA, 1989.

Sklansky J. *Pattern Classifiers and Trainable Machines*. Springer Verlag, New York, 1981.

Sowa J. F. *Knowledge Representation: Logical, Philosophical, and Computational Foundations: Logical, Philosophical, and Computational Foundations*. Course Technology - Thomson, 1999.

Svoboda T., Kybic J., and Hlavac V. *Image Processing, Analysis, and Machine Vision: A MATLAB Companion*. Thomson Engineering, 2008.

Tan H. K., Gelfand S. B., and Delp E. J. A cost minimization approach to edge detection using simulated annealing. *IEEE Transactions on Pattern Analysis and Machine Intelligence*, 14 (1), 1992.

Tucker A. *Applied Combinatorics*. Wiley, New York, 3rd edition, 1995.

Ullmann J. R. An algorithm for subgraph isomorphism. *Journal of the Association for Computing Machinery*, 23(1):31–42, 1976.

van Laarhoven P. J. M. and Aarts E. H. L. *Simulated Annealing: Theory and Applications*. Kluwer and Dordrecht, Norwell, MA, 1987.

Wechsler H. *Computational Vision*. Academic Press, London–San Diego, 1990.

Weka 3 Team. Weka 3: Data Mining Software in Java. http://www.cs.waikato.ac.nz/ml/weka/, 2013.

Winston P. H., editor. *The Psychology of Computer Vision*. McGraw-Hill, New York, 1975.

Winston P. H. *Artificial Intelligence*. Addison-Wesley, Reading, MA, 2nd edition, 1984.

Yang B., Snyder W. E., and Bilbro G. L. Matching oversegmented 3D images to models using association graphs. *Image and Vision Computing*, 7(2):135–143, 1989.

Young T. Y. and Calvert T. W. *Classification, Estimation, and Pattern Recognition*. American Elsevier, New York–London–Amsterdam, 1974.

Zadeh L. A. Fuzzy sets. *Information and Control*, 8:338–353, 1965.

Zdrahal Z. A structural method of scene analysis. In *7th International Joint Conference on Artificial Intelligence*, Vancouver, Canada, pages 680–682, 1981.

Zimmermann H. J., Zadeh L. A., and Gaines B. R. *Fuzzy Sets and Decision Analysis*. North Holland, Amsterdam–New York, 1984.

Chapter 10

Image understanding

Image understanding requires mutual interaction of processing steps. Earlier chapters have presented the necessary building blocks for image understanding, and now an internal image model must be built that represents the machine vision system's concept about the image of the world.

Consider a typical human approach: We are well prepared to do image processing, analysis, and understanding, but despite this, it may sometimes be difficult to recognize what is seen if what to expect is not known. If a microscopic image of some tissue is presented to an observer who has never had a chance to study tissue structure or morphology, identification of diseased tissue may be impossible. Similarly it can be very hard to understand an aerial or satellite image of some urban area, even if the data correspond to a city with which the observer is familiar. Further, we can require the observer to watch the scene on a 'per part' basis—like using a telescope; this is an approach similar to a machine vision system's abilities. If a human observer solves the problem of orientation in such a scene, a first step may be to try to locate some known object. The observer constructs an image model of the city starting with the object believed to be recognized. Consider an aerial city view of Prague (Figure 10.1), and suppose our observer sees two Gothic towers. They may be the towers of Prague castle, of the Vysehrad castle, or of some other Gothic church. Perhaps the first hypothesis is that the towers belong to the Vysehrad castle; a model of Vysehrad consists of the adjacent park, closely located river, etc. The observer attempts to verify the hypothesis with the model: Does the model match the reality? If it matches, the hypothesis is supported. If it does not, the hypothesis is weakened and finally rejected, and the observer constructs a new hypothesis describing the scene, builds another model, and again tries to verify it. Two main forms of knowledge are used when the internal model is constructed—the general knowledge of placement of streets, houses, parks, etc., in cities, and specific knowledge of the order of specific houses, streets, rivers, etc., in the specific city.

A machine vision system can be asked to solve similar problems. The main difference between a human observer and an artificial vision system is in a lack of widely applicable, general, and modifiable knowledge of the real world in the latter. Machine vision systems construct internal models of the scene, verify them, and update them,

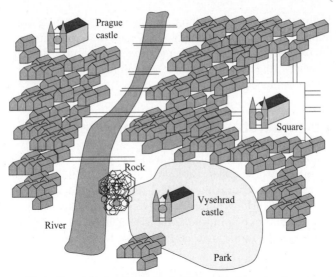

Figure 10.1: Simulated orientation problem. © *Cengage Learning 2015.*

and an appropriate sequence of processing steps must be performed to fulfill the given task. If the internal model matches the reality, image understanding is achieved. On the other hand, the example described above showed that existence of an image model is a prerequisite for perception; there is no inconsistency in this. The image representation has an incremental character; new data or perceptions are compared with an existing model, and are used for model modification. Image data interpretation is not explicitly dependent on image data alone. The variations in starting models, as well as differences in previous experience, cause the data to be interpreted differently, even if always consistently with the constructed model; any final interpretation can be considered correct if just a match between a model and image data is evaluated.

Machine vision consists of lower and upper processing levels, and image understanding is the highest processing level in this classification. The main task is to define control strategies that ensure an appropriate sequence of processing steps. Moreover, a machine vision system must be able to deal with a large number of interpretations that are hypothetical and ambiguous. Generally viewed, the organization of the system consists of a weak hierarchical structure of image models.

Despite decades of work, the image understanding process remains an open area of computer vision and is under continued investigation. Image understanding is one of the most complex challenges of AI, and to cover it in detail, it would be necessary to discuss relatively independent branches of AI—knowledge representation, relational structures, semantic networks, general matching, inference, production systems, problem solving, planning, control, feedback, and learning from experience, a difficult and not fully understood area. These areas are used and described in various AI references both elementary and advanced, and their application to computer vision is an active area of research. Nevertheless, to cover these topics in detail exceeds the frame of this book; therefore, we present here an overview of basic image understanding control strategies and describe contextual and semantic methods of image understanding as well as other popular, established techniques for statistical modeling of shape and appearance, hidden Markov models, Bayesian networks, expectation–maximization approaches, and boosted cascade methods for image understanding. Image understanding control is a crucial problem in machine vision, and the control strategies described give a better rationale for the application of various methods of image processing, object description, and recognition described earlier. At the same time, it explains why the specific AI methods are incorporated in image understanding processes.

10.1 Image understanding control strategies

Image understanding requires the cooperation of complex information processing tasks and appropriate control of these tasks. Biological systems include a very complicated and complex control strategy incorporating parallel processing, dynamic sensing subsystem allocation, behavior modifications, interrupt-driven shifts of attention, etc. As in other AI problems, the main goal of computer vision is to achieve machine behavior similar to that of biological systems by applying technically available procedures.

10.1.1 Parallel and serial processing control

Both parallel and serial approaches can be applied to image processing, although sometimes it is not obvious which steps should be processed in parallel and which serially. Parallel processing makes several computations simultaneously (e.g., several image parts can be processed simultaneously), and an extremely important consideration is the synchronization of processing actions—that is, the decision of when, or if, the processing should wait for other processing steps to be completed [Ghosh and Harrison, 1990; Prasanna Kumar, 1991; Hwang and Wang, 1994].

Operations are always sequential in serial processing. A serial control strategy is natural for conventional von Neumann computer architectures, and the large numbers of operations that biological organisms process in parallel often cannot be done serially at the required speed. Pyramid image representations, and corresponding pyramid processor architectures, resulted from speed requirements (including implementation of cognitive processes in lower processing levels, etc.). Parallel computers have become generally available, and despite substantial difficulties with their programming, the parallel processing option is now a reality. The feasibility of parallel processing implementation of various approaches and algorithms has been mentioned throughout this book, and it has been made clear that almost all low-level image processing can be done in parallel. However, high-level processing using higher levels of abstraction is usually serial in essence. There is an obvious comparison with the human strategy of solving complex sensing problems: A human always concentrates on a single topic during later phases of vision, even if the early steps are done in parallel.

10.1.2 Hierarchical control

Image information is stored in different representations during processing. There is one crucial question related to processing control: Should the processing be controlled by the image data information or by higher-level knowledge? These different approaches can be described as follows.

1. **Control by image data (bottom-up control):** Processing proceeds from the raster image to segmented image, to region (object) description, and to recognition.

2. **Model-based control (top-down control):** A set of assumptions and expected properties is constructed from applicable knowledge. The satisfaction of those properties is tested in image representations at different processing levels in a top-down direction, down to the original image data. The image understanding is an internal model verification, and the model is either accepted or rejected.

The two basic control strategies do not differ in the types of operation applied, but do differ in the sequence of their application, in the application either to all image data or just to selected image data, etc. The control mechanism chosen is not only a route to the processing goal, it influences the whole control strategy. Neither top-down nor bottom-up control strategies can explain the vision process or solve complex vision sensing problems in their standard forms. However, their appropriate combination can yield a more flexible and powerful vision control strategy.

10.1.3 Bottom-up control

A general bottom-up algorithm is:

Algorithm 10.1: Bottom-up control

1. Pre-processing: Transform the raster image to highlight information that may be useful in further processing steps. Appropriate transformations are applied throughout the image.

2. Segmentation: Detect and segment image regions that can correspond to real objects or object parts.

3. Understanding: If region descriptions were not used in step 2, determine an appropriate description for regions. Compare detected objects with real objects that are present in the solution domain (i.e., using pattern recognition techniques).

It is clear that bottom-up control strategies are based on the construction of data structures for the processing steps that follow. Note that each algorithm step can consist of several substeps; however, the image representation remains unchanged in the substeps. Bottom-up control is advantageous if a simple and efficient processing method is available that is independent of the image data content. Bottom-up control yields good results if unambiguous data are processed and if the processing gives reliable and precise representations for later processing steps. The recognition of well-illuminated objects in robotic applications is an example—in this case, bottom-up control results in fast and reliable processing. If input data are of low quality, bottom-up control can yield good results only if data unreliability causes only a limited number of insubstantial errors in each processing step. This implies that the main image understanding role must be played by a control strategy that is not only a concatenation of processing operations in the bottom-up direction, but that also uses an internal model goal specifications, planning, and complex cognitive processes.

A good example of a bottom-up control strategy is Marr's image understanding approach [Marr, 1982]. Processing begins with a two-dimensional intensity image and tries to achieve three-dimensional image understanding through a sequence of intermediate image representations. Marr's understanding strategy is based on a pure bottom-up data flow using only very general assumptions about the objects to be identified—a more detailed description of this approach is given in Section 11.1.1.

10.1.4 Model-based control

There is no general form of top-down control corresponding to Algorithm 10.1. The main top-down control principle is the construction of an internal model and its verification, meaning that the main principle is **goal-oriented processing**. Goals at higher processing levels are split into subgoals at lower levels, which are split again into subgoals etc., until the subgoals can be either accepted or rejected directly.

An example will illustrate this principle. Imagine that you are in a large hotel, and your spouse parked your white Volkswagen Beetle somewhere in the large parking lot in front of the hotel. You are trying to find your car, looking from the hotel room window. The first-level goal is to find the parking lot. A subgoal might be to detect all white cars in the parking lot and to decide which of those white cars are Volkswagen Beetles. All the given goals can be fulfilled by looking from the window and using general models (general knowledge) of cars, colors, and Beetles.

If all the former goals are fulfilled, the last goal is to decide if a particular white Volkswagen Beetle really is your car and not some other one; to satisfy this goal, specific knowledge of your car is necessary. You have to know what makes your car special—the differences between your car and others. If the test of specific properties is successful, the car is accepted as yours; the model you built for your white Beetle is accepted, the car is located, and the search is over. If the test of specific properties is not successful, you have to resume testing at some higher level, for instance, to detect another as yet untested white Volkswagen Beetle.

The general mechanism of top-down control is hypothesis generation and its testing. The internal model generator predicts what a specific part of the model must look like in lower image representations. The image understanding process consists of sequential hypothesis generation and testing. The internal model is updated during the processing according to the results of the hypothesis tests. Hypothesis testing relies on a (relatively small) amount of information acquired from lower representation levels, and the processing control is based on the fact that only necessary image processing is required to test each hypothesis. The model-based control strategy (top-down, **hypothesize and verify**) seems to be a way of solving computer vision tasks by avoiding brute-force processing; at the same time, it does not mean that parallel processing should not be applied whenever possible.

Unsurprisingly, real-world models play a substantial role in model vision. Many approaches presented throughout this book may be considered either models of a part of an image or object models. However, to represent a variety of real-world domains, to be able to model complex image objects, their physical properties must be included in the representation. This is especially true in modeling natural objects—human faces together with their mimics are a good example. Physical modeling is another branch of computer vision and image understanding [Kanade and Ikeuchi, 1991] in which four main techniques appear: reflection models for vision, relations between shape and reflection, statistical and stochastic modeling, and modeling deformable shapes (*elastics in vision*). Clearly, all these techniques may significantly increase the knowledge available in the image understanding process. From the point of view of the context being discussed here, deformable models of non-rigid objects seem to widen substantially the rank of feasible applications. Sections 10.4 and 10.5 discuss the application of deformable statistical models to representation and analysis of 2D, 3D, and 4D image data.

10.1.5 Combined control

Combined control mechanisms that use both data- and model-driven control strategies are widely used in vision applications, and usually give better results than any separately applied, basic control strategies. Higher-level information is used to make the lower-level processing easier, but alone is insufficient to solve the task. Seeking cars in aerial or satellite image data is a good example; data-driven control is necessary to find the cars, but at the same time, higher-level knowledge can be used to simplify the problem since cars appear as rectangular objects of specific size, and the highest probability of their appearance is on roads.

An illustrative example is a robust combined control approach to automated coronary border detection, where X-ray images are acquired after injecting a radio-opaque dye into the arteries of a human heart. A successful bottom-up algorithm using a graph search approach is given in Section 6.2.4, Figure 6.24.

Unfortunately, bottom-up graph search often fails in more complicated or low-quality images, in the presence of closely parallel, branching, or overlapping vessels. Image data representing such a case are shown in Figure 10.2 together with the result of the bottom-up graph search (the same method that worked so well for a single-vessel case). To achieve reliable border detection in difficult images, a hybrid control strategy was designed combining bottom-up and top-down control steps; the following principles are incorporated in the process.

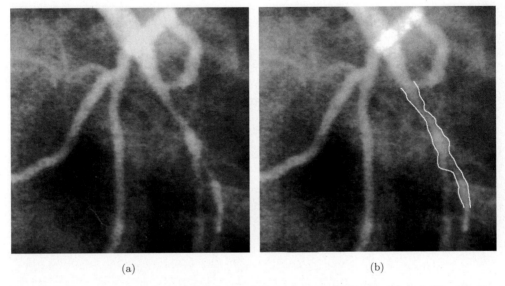

(a)   (b)

Figure 10.2: Coronary angiogram. (a) Original X-ray image. (b) Borders detected by a bottom-up graph search approach. Note the incorrect border at the bifurcation. © *Cengage Learning 2015.*

1. **Model-based approach:** The model favors symmetric left and right borders as those most typical in coronary imagery.

2. **Hypothesize and verify approach:** Based on multi-resolution processing, the approximate vessel border is detected at low resolution (which is faster) and precision is increased at full resolution.

3. **A priori knowledge:** Knowledge about directions of edges forming the vessel border is used to modify a graph search cost function.

4. **Multi-stage approach:** Models of different strength are applied throughout the processing.

The method searches for left and right coronary borders simultaneously, performing a three-dimensional graph search and the border symmetry model is thus incorporated in the search process—see Sections 6.2.4, 7.5.1. The model guides the search in regions of poor data, and where the image data have an acceptable quality, the search is guided by the image data.

A frequent problem of model-based control strategies is that the model control necessary in some parts of the image is too strong in other parts (the symmetry requirements of the model have a larger influence on the final border than a non-symmetric reality), corrupting the border detection results. This is the rationale for a multi-stage approach where a strong model is applied at low resolution, and a weaker model leaves enough freedom for the search to be guided predominantly by image data at full-resolution, thereby achieving higher overall accuracy. Nevertheless, the low-resolution coronary borders detected by cooperation with the model guarantee that the full-resolution search will not get lost—the low-resolution border is used as a model border in the full-resolution search.

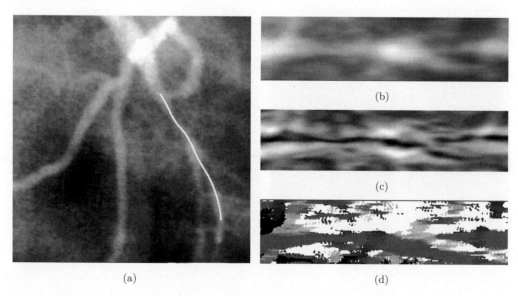

Figure 10.3: Steps of coronary border detection (I). (a) Centerline definition. (b) Straightened image data. (c) Edge detection. (d) Edge direction detection. © *Cengage Learning 2015*.

Algorithm 10.2: Coronary border detection—a combined control strategy

1. *(top-down)* Detect a vessel centerline in interaction with an operator (show which vessel is to be processed), and straighten the vessel image, Figure 10.3a,b.

2. *(bottom-up)* Detect image edges in full resolution, Figure 10.3c.

3. *(bottom-up)* Detect local edge directions in the straightened intensity image, Figure 10.3d.

4. *(top-down)* Modify the cost matrix using a priori knowledge about edge directions and the directional edge image, Figure 10.4a.

5. *(bottom-up)* Construct a low-resolution image and a low-resolution cost matrix.

6. *(top-down)* Search for the low-resolution pair of approximate borders using the vessel symmetry model Figure 10.4b.

7. *(top-down)* Find an accurate position of the full-resolution border using the low-resolution border as a model to guide the full-resolution search, Figure 10.4c. The symmetry model is much weaker than in the low-resolution search.

8. *(bottom-up)* Transform straightened image results to the original image, Figure 10.4d.

9. *(top-down)* Evaluate the coronary disease severity.

Results of this strategy applied to coronary vessel data are given in Figure 10.5.

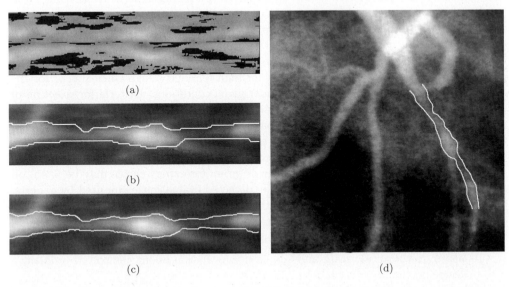

(a)

(b)

(c)   (d)

Figure 10.4: Steps of coronary border detection (II). (a) Modified cost function—cost increases in non-probable border locations image areas, where edge direction does not support location of the border. (b) Approximate coronary borders acquired in low resolution. (c) Precise full-resolution border in straightened image. (d) Full-resolution coronary borders in original image. © *Cengage Learning 2015.*

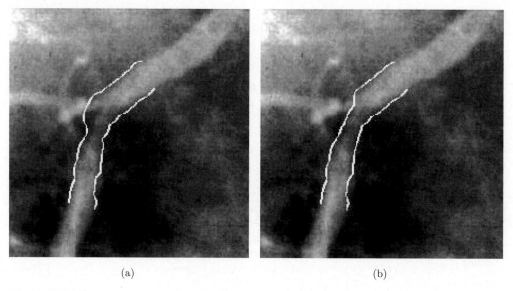

(a)   (b)

Figure 10.5: Coronary border detection. (a) Bottom-up graph search approach follows borders of the vessel branch. (b) Combined control graph search strategy follows coronary borders correctly. © *Cengage Learning 2015*.

10.1.6   Non-hierarchical control

There is always an upper and a lower level in hierarchical control. Conversely, non-hierarchical control can be seen as a cooperation of competing experts at the same level.

Non-hierarchical control can be applied to problems that can be separated into a number of subproblems, each of which requires some expertise: the order in which the expertise should be deployed is not fixed. The basic idea of non-hierarchical control is to ask for assistance from the expert that can help most to obtain the final solution. The chosen expert may be known, for instance, for high reliability, high efficiency, or for the ability to provide the most information under given conditions. Criteria for selection of an expert from the set may differ; one possibility is to let the experts calculate their own abilities to contribute to the solution in particular cases—the choice is based on these local and individual evaluations. Another option is to assign a fixed evaluation to each expert beforehand and help is then requested from the expert with the highest evaluation under given conditions [Ambler, 1975]. The criterion for expert choice may be based on some appropriate combination of empirically detected evaluations computed by experts, and evaluations dependent on the actual state of the problem solution.

Algorithm 10.3: Non-hierarchical control

1. Based on the actual state and acquired information about the solved problem, decide on the best action, and execute it.

2. Use the results of the last action to increase the amount of acquired information about the problem.

3. If the goals of the task are met, stop. Otherwise, return to step 1.

The blackboard principle is useful for handling non-hierarchical control of competing experts. Imagine a classroom full of experts; if any of them wants to share knowledge or observations with others, a note is made on the blackboard, so all others can see the results and use them. The blackboard is a specific data structure that can be accessed by all the experts and has been used in a variety of vision systems (e.g., VISIONS [Hanson and Riseman, 1978], COBIUS [Kuan et al., 1989]). It usually includes a mechanism that retrieves specialized subsystems which can immediately affect the standard control. These subsystems are very powerful and are called **daemons**—the blackboard must include a mechanism that synchronizes the daemon activity. Programming with daemons is not easy, and the design of daemon behavior is based on general knowledge of the problem domain. Therefore, the programmer can never be absolutely sure if the daemon procedure based on some specific property will be activated or not; moreover, there is no guarantee that the daemon will be activated in the correct way. To limit the uncertainty of daemon behavior, the following additional rules are usually added.

- The blackboard represents a continuously updated part of the internal model that corresponds to image data.

- The blackboard includes a set of rules that specify which daemon subsystem should be used in specific cases.

The blackboard is sometimes called the **short-term memory**—it contains information about interpretation of the image. The **long-term memory**, the knowledge base, consists of more general information that is valid for (almost) all representations of the problems to be solved [Hanson and Riseman, 1978].

In a system for the analysis of complex aerial photographs [Nagao and Matsuyama, 1980], all the information about a specific image is stored in the blackboard (segmented region properties and their relations). The blackboard can activate 13 subsystems of region detection, all of which communicate with the blackboard in a standard way, and the only way the subsystems can communicate with each other is via the blackboard. The data structure depends on the application; in this particular case, the structure takes advantage of a priori global knowledge of the domain such as the physical size of pixels, the direction of the sun, etc. Additionally, the blackboard maintains a property table in which observations on image regions are stored, together with information about the region class (resulting from recognition). An integral part of the blackboard is represented by the symbolic region image that provides information about relations between regions.

The primary aim of the blackboard system is to identify places of interest in the image that should be processed with higher accuracy, to locate places with a high probability of a target region being present. Approximate region borders are found first, based on a fast computation of just a few basic characteristics—saving computational time and making the detailed analysis easier. The control process follows the production system principle [Nilsson, 1982], using the information that comes from the region detection subsystems via the blackboard. The blackboard serves as a place where all the conflicts between region labeling are solved (one region can be marked by two or more region detection subsystems at the same time and it is necessary to decide which label is the best). Furthermore, labeling errors are detected in the blackboard, and are corrected using back-tracking principles. An interesting approach in which single or multiple 'robots' acting as intelligent agents work autonomously and may cooperate to achieve a common image analysis goal was reported in [Behloul et al., 2001; Ferrarini et al., 2005]. A multi-agent segmentation approach was presented in [Bovenkamp et al., 2004].

The principal image understanding control strategies have been presented here—it was noted that a wide variety of knowledge representation techniques, object description methods, and processing strategies must co-exist in any image understanding system. The role of knowledge and control is reviewed in [Rao and Jain, 1988] within the context of image and speech understanding systems such as ACRONYM [Brooks et al., 1979], HEARSAY [Lesser et al., 1975], and VISIONS [Hanson and Riseman, 1978]. Image understanding approaches following a bottom-up control strategy and allowing the use of semantic networks can be found in [Puliti and Tascini, 1993], and knowledge-based composition of image interpretation processes is discussed in [Jurie and Gallice, 1995; Gong and Kulikowski, 1995]. Bayesian belief networks and their use in image interpretation are considered in Section 10.11.3. Machine learning strategies for image understanding are discussed critically in [Kodratoff and Moscatelli, 1994]. Further, neural networks and fuzzy logic are increasingly considered suitable vehicles for image interpretation [Zheng, 1995; Udupa and Samarasekera, 1996].

10.2   SIFT: Scale invariant feature transform

Reliable object recognition is a popular vision goal, with widespread applications. In simple scenarios with known objects and carefully controlled pose and illumination, template matching approaches (Section 6.4) can be seen to work, but this is implausible in real-world problems: normally objects are subject to some scale, pose and illumination variation, and may well be subject to partial occlusion. A popular and successful answer to this more general problem is **SIFT**—the Scale Invariant Feature Transform [Lowe, 2004]—which extracts *stable* points from images and attaches to them robust features, a small subset of which, with geometric coherence, suffice to confirm a re-identification of objects in other images.

SIFT proceeds in three phases: key location detection to identify 'interest points', feature extraction to characterize them, and matching of feature vectors between models and images.

Key location detection

'Key locations' of an image are points within it that we might reasonably expect to appear in further images of the same object or scene—corners are an obvious example. In an image I_0 they are determined as maxima or minima of a DoG filter (Section 5.3.3) applied at all pixels of an image pyramid. The bottom of the pyramid is the original image, to which Gaussian filters with $\sigma = \sqrt{2}$ and $\sigma = 2$ are applied to give images A_0 and B_0 respectively. $A_0 - B_0$ is then a DoG filter with ratio $\sqrt{2}$. The next layer of the pyramid is formed by re-sampling B_0 with a pixel spacing of 1.5. (These operations are efficient: the Gaussians can be separated into 1D convolutions, and the 1.5 reduction is simple to implement).

Local extrema are determined in 3×3 windows at levels of this pyramid. If such an extremum is also greater/smaller than elements of the 3×3 windows at the corresponding positions above and below, then the pixel is maximal/minimal in three dimensions and is tagged as a key location—note that the central pyramid layer of the extremum captures the *scale* at which the pixel is 'key'. It delivers very stable points repeatedly (although see the original reference for an improved approach that filters out low contrast or unfavorably placed points).

Feature extraction

Given the key locations, we seek to derive a reliable feature vector to describe its immediate locality—this needs to take account of local edge directions and strengths. Firstly, a canonical direction is associated with each one. A very simple edge detector determines an edge direction R_i and magnitude M_i at each pixel of the images A_i, and small magnitudes are neglected. A Gaussian weighted window with σ three times that of the current scale is created, with the weights multiplying the thresholded magnitudes. A 36-bin histogram of directions R relative to the key location edge direction is accumulated with respect to these weights, and the canonical direction is then defined by the dominant peak in this histogram. If the histogram has competing peaks, they are all accepted by duplicating the keypoint with multiple orientations. Experiment suggests that this approach delivers stable keys and directions in the presence of noise, contrast and brightness distortion, and affine projection. A 500×500 image typically generates over 1000 such points.

An 8×8 window around the point has its edge magnitude and orientation values blurred, and a 4×4 array of 8-wide edge orientation histograms is compiled. Histogram contributions are the edge magnitudes weighted by a Gaussian centered at the key location. We now have a 128-dimensional vector: this is normalized to compensate for contrast variation; very large elements are neglected (and the vector renormalized) to compensate for a variety of common lighting change effects.

Matching

Suppose now we have a set of sample, or model, images each represented by some number of 128-dimensional vectors as described above. We may seek their appearance, or partial appearance, in a test image which has also generated a set of vectors. For each test vector, we locate its nearest neighbor in the union of sample vectors: of course, it may represent noise or some feature not in the training set—matches are rejected if the ratio between the distances to nearest and next-nearest neighbors is greater than some threshold (0.8 is reported as good), and this successfully rejects a high proportion of spurious matches. Nearest-neighbor location is obviously a computational load, and much effort has been devoted to efficient approaches to this general problem. An efficient modification of the K-D tree algorithm [Beis and Lowe, 1997] (see Section 9.2.2) can be employed. Any putative match gives a candidate location, scale and orientation of the model.

A Hough-like voting procedure (see Section 6.2.6) with wide bins—the original paper uses 30° for orientation, 2 for scale and 0.25 of model dimension for location—then collects multiple identifications of candidates. These Hough-like bins are sorted on occupancy and each candidate subjected to a verification. Each match provides a model point (x, y) and an image point (u, v). In many real-world circumstances it is reasonable to assume the image gives an *approximately* affine transform of the model, and so

$$\begin{bmatrix} u \\ v \end{bmatrix} = \begin{bmatrix} m_1 & m_2 \\ m_3 & m_4 \end{bmatrix} \begin{bmatrix} x \\ y \end{bmatrix} + \begin{bmatrix} t_x \\ t_y \end{bmatrix} . \tag{10.1}$$

Each match provides 2 equations for 6 unknowns, so provided the bin has a population of 3 or more this can be solved; with more than 3 it is overdetermined and a least-squared error solution can be found. The solution can be checked against observed matches; outliers are rejected and the transform recomputed—the match is rejected if this reduces the number of candidate matches to less than 3.

In summary, the algorithm can be outlined as follows:

Algorithm 10.4: Scale Invariant Feature Transform—SIFT

1. For an image I_0, derive A_0, B_0 by convolving with Gaussians of $\sigma = \sqrt{2}, 2$ respectively.

2. Keep a DoG filter of I_0 as $A_0 - B_0$.

3. Build an image pyramid by letting I_{i+1} be a 1.5 re-sampling of B_i.

4. Locate pyramid positions at which the DoG is extremal horizontally, and at layers above and below. These are **key locations**.

5. For each key location (at level i) determine a canonical direction as the maximum of a binned direction histogram, with respect to a suitably weighted window of edge magnitudes of A_i.

6. Describe each key location by a 128-dimensional vector which characterizes intensity magnitude and direction in a 8×8 neighborhood.

7. Matching: Determine plausible 128-dimensional matches between model and image as efficiently as possible. Accumulate candidate instances of the model in the image in a Hough-like manner. Test candidates and reject outliers. Retain populous candidates as matches.

SIFT proves extraordinarily robust: the requirement for no more than three matches to define a usable transform permits very significant occlusion since many more than 3 key points are customarily available. Matches can also usually be found through very significant distortion due to perspective projection and illumination changes.

An example of SIFT is shown in Figure 10.6[1]. Here, the model image of a book (235×173) is shown top left, and the 241 SIFT key locations at bottom left, where the arrow lengths indicate scale and orientation. A 473×455 scene including an occluded occurrence of the model is shown with 6 point matches—five of these are correct while one (from the 'I' to the 'A') is wrong: the Hough phase would reconcile these to one correct match. This is a challenging example as the occlusion masks most of the keypoints, the viewpoint has changed, the lighting on the glossy cover is significantly different and the matching criterion is strong. Less challenging examples generate many more, mostly correct, point matches. (Another example may be seen in Section 10.3.)

SIFT generated much research and a rich literature: It is an early example of a class of such detectors that derive their power from successful spatial descriptions local to interest

---

[1] This example was generated with publicly available software from http://www.cs.ubc.ca/~lowe/keypoints, with grateful acknowledgment to D. Lowe from the University of British Columbia for permission.

Figure 10.6: Left: A model (top), and its SIFT key locations (bottom); the arrows indicate orientation (in their direction) and scale (in their length). Right: location by SIFT of 6 point matches in a challenging image, 5 of which are correct. *Courtesy of J. Liddington.*

points that are robust to deformations of many kinds. Many adaptions, refinements and improvements can be found which variously improve on point detection, robustness, or seek to reduce the computational load of the matching phase. The Harris detector was introduced in Section 5.3.10 but this proves inferior to SIFT and its successors. Ke and Sukthankar have further improved SIFT as reported in [Ke and Sukthankar, 2004]. A widely used alternative to SIFT is SURF—Speeded Up Robust Features [Bay et al., 2006]; this uses a similar strategy but exhibits far better performance as it exploits integral images (see Section 4.2.1) which obviate the need for building a pyramid; further, the feature vector derived is shorter, and faster to build.

A useful comprehensive review of these techniques that considers their history, context and applicability may be found in [Tuytelaars and Mikolajczyk, 2007].

10.3 RANSAC: Fitting via random sample consensus

Suppose we are presented with some data that we know to be linearly related—it is reasonable and customary to derive the linear relationship by some least-squares approach, minimizing the sum of square residuals. Usually this is done by deriving an expression for this sum, differentiating it with respect to the parameters of the linear fit, equating to zero, and solving for the parameters. This approach extends straightforwardly to many models other than linear.

In the (likely) event that the data are imperfect, the resulting model will also be imperfect. Often this does not matter—if the noise in the data is in some sense well behaved, it may be that the resulting model is best-possible in some statistical sense. On the other hand, if there are serious outliers in the data, it is possible that the derived model is seriously distorted.

Recognizing this possibility, we can try to identify the outliers as the data points with greatest residuals with respect to the fitted model. These can be excluded, and the model recomputed. This superficially attractive idea is often used and in many circumstances may have help; on the other hand it makes assumptions about the nature of the data that may be invalid. This is because errors are characteristically of two kinds:

- Measurement errors: an observation from an image, or a parameter derived from such an observation, is not quite correct. It is common for these errors to be relatively small with (approximately) zero mean, and often normally distributed.

- Classification errors: these occur when something is mis-identified. Such errors are often (relatively) gross and there is no reason to expect them overall to have zero mean.

Errors of the second kind might distort the model so much that the remedial approach worsens rather than improves matters. This is well illustrated in a simple 2D case shown in Figure 10.7 [Fischler and Bolles, 1981].

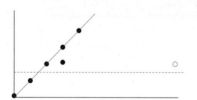

Figure 10.7: Influence of an outlier in least squares line fitting. With 6 valid data points and 1 gross outlier (white), the best line is shown in solid. Least squares, followed by discarding the worst outlier, reaches the dotted line after 3 discards [Fischler and Bolles, 1981]. © *Cengage Learning 2015.*

Underlying the least-squares approach is an assumption that using as much data as possible will have a beneficial smoothing effect. As discussed, there are many circumstances where this is false, and the opposite approach of using as little as possible may be better. In the case of seeking a linear fit, two points are sufficient to define a line: let us select two points at random from the data set and hypothesize that the line joining them is the correct model. We can test the model by asking how many of the remaining data points are in some sense 'close' to the guess—these are call **consensus** points. If there is a significant number of these, then recomputing the guess based on the consensus set will improve the model without us ever having to deal with the outliers.

This informally describes the **random sample consensus**—or RANSAC—algorithm [Fischler and Bolles, 1981]. More formally, this is:

Algorithm 10.5: Random sample consensus for model fitting—RANSAC

1. Suppose we have n data points $X = \{\mathbf{x}_1, \mathbf{x}_1, \ldots, \mathbf{x}_n\}$ to which we hope to fit a model determined by (at least) m points ($m \leq n$, so for a line, $m = 2$).

2. Set an iteration counter $k = 1$.

3. Choose at random m items from X and compute a model.

4. For some tolerance ϵ, determine how many elements of X are within ϵ of the derived model. If this number exceeds a threshold t, recompute the model over this consensus set (probably via least-squares, or some variant), and halt.

5. Set $k = k + 1$. If $k < K$, for some predetermined K, go to 3. Otherwise accept the model with the biggest consensus set so far, or fail.

There are many obvious possible enhancements to this simple presentation. Simplest is to observe that the random selection at step 3 may often be improved with foreknowledge of the data or its properties—that is, we may know that some data points may be more likely to fit a correct model than others.

The algorithm depends on a choice of three parameters:

- ϵ, the acceptable deviation from a good model. It is rare that this can be determined in any analytical sense. Empirically, we might fit a model to m points, measure the deviations, and set ϵ to be some number of standard deviations above the mean such error.

- t, the size of consensus set deemed to be 'enough'. This parameter actually serves two purposes simultaneously—it represents 'enough' data points to confirm a putative model, and 'enough' data points to refine the guess to the final best estimate. The first point here is not easy to specify, but $t - m > 5$ has been suggested [Fischler and Bolles, 1981]; on the other hand, the second requirement has been thoroughly studied in the literature—see, for example, [Sorenson, 1970].

- K, how many times to run the algorithm in search of a satisfactory fit. It has been argued [Fischler and Bolles, 1981] that we can compute the expected number of trials needed to select a subset of m 'good' data points. A simple statistical argument (see the original reference) gives this as w^{-m}, where w is the probability of a randomly selected datum being within ϵ of the model. The standard deviation of this estimate is also of the order of w^{-m}, and so $K = 2w^{-m}$ or $K = 3w^{-m}$ are argued to be reasonable choices. Of course, this requires some reasoning for at least a rough estimate of w.

RANSAC represents a paradigm change in model fitting: 'start small and grow' is an opposite approach to least-squares and related techniques that expect to average out deviations. RANSAC has proved to be a very fertile and reliable technique, particularly in many aspects of vision, and it has benefited from many improvements and applications in the quarter-century since its development [Zisserman, 2006]. Just one of these that has attracted significant popular attention is part of a suite—*Autostitch*—that knits partially-overlapping digital images together into panoramas [Brown and Lowe, 2003].

Autostitch proceeds by identifying 'interest points' (for example, corners) in images, and representing them as feature vectors that capture very local intensity properties. (These points are identified using SIFT, described in Section 10.2.) Efficient techniques

(a)

(b)

(c)

(d)

Figure 10.8: Use of RANSAC in panoramic stitching (the original images are, of course, in color): (a) An image pair that overlaps. (b) Each dot represents an 'interest point', whose vector matches a point in the other image. (c) The illustrated dots are the RANSAC 'inliers'; they conform to the hypothesis of the best-performing candidate homography that is tried. (d) Prior to smoothing, the resulting overlap. *Courtesy of D. Lowe, M. Brown, University of British Columbia.*

are deployed to locate probable matches for vectors in other images—when a pair of images has a significant number of such probable matches, it is a candidate for overlap.

If two images overlap, the 'difference' between them is characterized by three possible rotations of the camera (with respect to the three Cartesian axes), and a change in focal length: that is, four parameters. We seek a **homography** that captures this; a problem is that the set of possible matches determined initially is populated with a large number of false hits that will be very significant outliers from the correct homography. RANSAC is applied to the 'significant' number of matches with $m = 4$ to derive the best possible parameter set. Further processing at this point verifies the quality of the match, an overall resolution of camera geometry, and some sophisticated intensity filtering to obliterate the borders at physical overlaps.

The resulting algorithm is exceptionally robust and fast; it can resolve multiple panoramas and identify rogue images (that is, they are not part of the panorama set). The quality of the final image blend is strikingly good[2]. Figure 10.8 illustrates just a part of its progress on a single image pair—the Figure does not illustrate the selection of the particular pair as likely overlaps, nor does it show the final intensity smoothing that conceals the 'join'.

While Autostitch is not an image understanding method *per se*, it is easy to understand and a good illustration of the RANSAC method, and represents a general model fitting algorithm directly applicable to many image understanding tasks.

10.4 Point distribution models

The **point distribution model** (PDM) is a powerful shape description technique that is used in locating new instances of such shapes in other images [Cootes et al., 1992]. It is most useful for describing features that have well understood 'general' shape, but which cannot be easily described by a rigid model (that is, particular instances are subject to variation). Examples which have been the successful subject of applications of this approach include electrical resistors, faces, and bones within the hand; each of these exhibits properties of 'shape' that a human can comprehend and describe easily, but which do not permit rigid model-based description. The PDM has seen enormous application in a short time.

Figure 10.9: A contour representing a hand, with possible landmark points marked. © *Cengage Learning 2015*.

---

[2]Autostitch is freely available in demonstration form at http://www.cs.ubc.ca/~mbrown/autostitch/autostitch.html.

The PDM approach assumes the existence of a set of M examples (a training set) from which to derive a statistical description of the shape and its variation. In our context, we take this to mean some number of instances of the shape represented by a boundary (a sequence of pixel co-ordinates). In addition, some number N of **landmark** points is selected on each boundary; these points are chosen to correspond to a feature of the underlying object—for example (see Figure 10.9), if the shape represents a hand, we might choose 27 points that include the fingertips, points that 'divide' the fingers, and some suitable number of intermediates.

It is clear that if the hands so represented are in 'about the same place', so will the N landmark points be. Variations in the positions of these points would then be attributable to natural variation between individuals. We may expect, though, that these differences will be 'small' measured on the scale of the overall shape. The PDM approach allows us to model these 'small' differences (and, indeed, to identify which are truly small, and which are more significant).

Aligning the training data

In order to develop this idea, it is necessary first to align all the training shapes in an approximate sense (otherwise comparisons are not 'like with like'). This is done by selecting for each example a suitable translation, scaling, and rotation to ensure that they all correspond as closely as possible—informally, the transformations are chosen to reduce (in a least-squares sense) the difference between an aligned shape and a 'mean' shape derived from the whole set. Specifically, suppose we wish to align just two shapes—each of these is described by a vector of N co-ordinate pairs:

$$\mathbf{x}^1 = (x_1^1, y_1^1, x_2^1, y_2^1, \ldots, x_N^1, y_N^1)^T \,,$$
$$\mathbf{x}^2 = (x_1^2, y_1^2, x_2^2, y_2^2, \ldots, x_N^2, y_N^2)^T \,.$$

A transformation $\mathcal{T}$ of $\mathbf{x}^2$ composed of a translation (t_x, t_y), rotation θ, and scaling s may be represented by a matrix R applied to $\mathbf{x}^2$ using standard techniques,

$$\mathcal{T}(\mathbf{x}^2) = R \begin{bmatrix} x_i^2 \\ y_i^2 \end{bmatrix} + \begin{bmatrix} t_x \\ t_y \end{bmatrix} = \begin{bmatrix} x_i^2 s \cos\theta - y_i^2 s \sin\theta \\ x_i^2 s \sin\theta + y_i^2 s \cos\theta \end{bmatrix} + \begin{bmatrix} t_x \\ t_y \end{bmatrix}$$

and the 'best' such may be found by minimizing the expression

$$E = \left[\mathbf{x}^1 - R\mathbf{x}^2 - (t_x, t_y)^T \right]^T \left[\mathbf{x}^1 - R\mathbf{x}^2 - (t_x, t_y)^T \right] . \tag{10.2}$$

This minimization is a routine application of a least-squares approach [Cootes et al., 1992]—partial derivatives of E are calculated with respect to the unknowns (θ, s, t_x, and t_y) and set to zero, leaving simultaneous linear equations to solve.

This general idea is used to co-align all M shapes using the following algorithm.

Algorithm 10.6: Approximate alignment of similar training shapes

1. In a pairwise fashion, rotate, scale, and align each $\mathbf{x}^i$ with $\mathbf{x}^1$, for $i = 2, 3, \ldots, M$ to give the set $\{\mathbf{x}^1, \hat{\mathbf{x}}^2, \hat{\mathbf{x}}^3, \ldots, \hat{\mathbf{x}}^M\}$.

2. Calculate the mean of the transformed shapes (the details of this procedure are outlined in Section 10.4).

3. Rotate, scale, and align the mean shape to align to $\mathbf{x}^1$.

4. Rotate, scale, and align $\hat{\mathbf{x}}^2, \hat{\mathbf{x}}^3, \ldots, \hat{\mathbf{x}}^M$ to match to the adjusted mean.

5. If the mean has not converged, go to step 2.

Step 3 of this algorithm is necessary because otherwise it is ill-conditioned (unconstrained); without doing this, convergence will not occur. Final convergence may be tested by examining the differences involved in realigning the shapes to the mean.

This approach assumes that each of the landmark points is of equal significance, but that may not be the case. If for some reason one of them moves around the shape less than others, it has a desirable stability that we might wish to exploit during the alignment. This can be done by introducing a (diagonal) weight matrix W into equation (10.2):

$$E = \left[\mathbf{x}^1 - R\mathbf{x}^2 - (t_x, t_y)^T\right]^T W \left[\mathbf{x}^1 - R\mathbf{x}^2 - (t_x, t_y)^T\right] . \quad (10.3)$$

The elements of W indicate the relative 'stability' of each of the landmarks, by which a high number indicates high stability (so counts for more in the error computation), and a low number the opposite. There are various ways of measuring this; one [Cootes et al., 1992] is to compute for each shape the distance between landmarks k and l, and to let V_{kl} be the variance in these distances. A high variance indicates high mobility, and so setting the weight for the kth point to

$$w_k = \frac{1}{\sum_{l=1}^{N} V_{kl}}$$

has the desired weighting effect.

Deriving the model

The alignment provides M (mutually aligned) boundaries $\hat{\mathbf{x}}^1, \hat{\mathbf{x}}^2, \ldots, \hat{\mathbf{x}}^M$, and we proceed to determine the mean such, $\bar{\mathbf{x}}$. Each shape is given by N co-ordinate pairs,

$$\hat{\mathbf{x}}^i = \left[\hat{x}_1^i, \hat{y}_1^i, \hat{x}_2^i, \hat{y}_2^i, \ldots, \hat{x}_N^i, \hat{y}_N^i\right]^T$$

and so the mean shape is given by

$$\bar{\mathbf{x}} = \left[\bar{x}_1, \bar{y}_1, \bar{x}_2, \bar{y}_2, \ldots, \bar{x}_N, \bar{y}_N\right] ,$$

where

$$\bar{x}_j = \frac{1}{M} \sum_{i=1}^{M} \hat{x}_j^i \quad \text{and} \quad \bar{y}_j = \frac{1}{M} \sum_{i=1}^{M} \hat{y}_j^i .$$

Knowledge of this mean allows explicit measurement of the variation and co-variation exhibited by each landmark and landmark pair; we can write

$$\delta\mathbf{x}^i = \hat{\mathbf{x}}^i - \bar{\mathbf{x}} .$$

Doing this for each training vector, we can calculate the $2N \times 2N$ covariance matrix

$$S = \frac{1}{M} \sum_{i=1}^{M} \delta \mathbf{x}^i \left(\delta \mathbf{x}^i \right)^T .$$

This matrix has some particularly useful properties. If we imagine the aligned training set plotted in $2N$ dimensions, it will exhibit variation more in some directions than others (these directions will not, of course, in general align with the co-ordinate axes)—these variations are important properties of the shape we are describing. What these directions are, and their (relative) importance, may be derived from an eigen-decomposition of S—that is, solving the equation

$$S \mathbf{p}_i = \lambda_i \mathbf{p}_i . \tag{10.4}$$

Section 3.2.10 describes how principal components analysis may be derived from eigen-analysis, and explains how we might now find a lower-dimensional approximation of $\mathbf{x}$. The eigen-vectors of S will provide a basis, meaning that we can represent any vector $\mathbf{x}$ as a linear combination of the $2N$ different $\mathbf{p}^i$. If we write

$$P = \left[\mathbf{p}^1 \mathbf{p}^2 \mathbf{p}^3 \dots \mathbf{p}^{2N} \right] ,$$

then for any vector $\mathbf{x}$ a vector $\mathbf{b}$ exists such that

$$\mathbf{x} = \bar{\mathbf{x}} + P \mathbf{b} ,$$

where the components of $\mathbf{b}$ indicate how much variation is exhibited with respect to each of the eigenvectors.

If the eigen-vectors are ordered on eigen-value (high first), then eigenvectors of lower index describe most of the changes in the training set: we may expect that the contributions from $\mathbf{p}^{2N}$, $\mathbf{p}^{2N-1}$, ..., to play a small role in describing how far 'valid' shapes deviate from $\bar{\mathbf{x}}$. Therefore, if we write

$$P_t = \left[\mathbf{p}^1 \mathbf{p}^2 \mathbf{p}^3 \dots \mathbf{p}^t \right] ,$$
$$\mathbf{b}_t = \left[b_1, b_2, \dots, b_t \right]^T , \tag{10.5}$$

then the approximation

$$\mathbf{x} \approx \bar{\mathbf{x}} + P_t \mathbf{b}_t \tag{10.6}$$

will be good for sufficiently high $t \leq 2N$, if $\mathbf{x}$ is a valid shape with respect to the training set. This permits a dimensional compression of the representation—if there is a lot of structure in the data, t will be low (relative to $2N$) and good shape description will be possible very compactly by representing the shape as $\mathbf{b}_t$ rather than $\mathbf{x}$. One approach to this is to calculate λ_{total}, the sum of the λ_i, and choose t such that

$$\sum_{i=1}^{t} \lambda_i \geq \alpha \lambda_{\text{total}} \qquad 0 \leq \alpha \leq 1 .$$

The choice of α here will govern how much of the variation seen in the training set can be recaptured by the compacted model.

Further, it can be shown that the variance of b_i over the training set will be the associated eigenvalue λ_i; accordingly, for 'well-behaved' shapes we might expect

$$-3\sqrt{\lambda_i} \leq b_i \leq 3\sqrt{\lambda_i}$$

—that is, most of the population is within 3σ of the mean. This allows us to generate, from knowledge of P and λ_i, plausible shapes that are not part of the training set.

Example—metacarpal analysis

We can illustrate this theory with an example taken from automatic hand X-ray analysis. The finger bones (metacarpals) have characteristic long, thin shape with bulges near the ends—precise shape differs from individual to individual, and as an individual ages. Scrutiny of bone shape is of great value in diagnosing bone aging disorders and is widely used by pediatricians [Tanner et al., 1983].

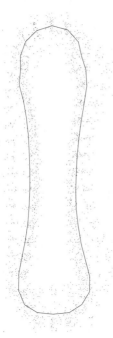

Index i	$\lambda_i/\lambda_{\text{total}}$ [%]	Cumulative total
1	63.3	63.3
2	10.8	74.1
3	9.5	83.6
4	3.4	87.1
5	2.9	90.0
6	2.5	92.5
7	1.7	94.2
8	1.2	95.4
9	0.7	96.1
10	0.6	96.7
11	0.5	97.2
12	0.4	97.6
13	0.3	97.9
14	0.3	98.2
15	0.3	98.5
16	0.2	98.7

Figure 10.10: Metacarpal PDM: Dots mark the observed landmark positions, and line denotes the mean shape. *Courtesy of N. D. Efford, School of Computing, University of Leeds.*

Table 10.1: Relative contributions to total data variance for the first 16 principal components. *Based on data from N. D. Efford, School of Computing, University of Leeds.*

From a collection of X-rays, 40 landmarks (so vectors are 80-dimensional) were picked out by hand on a number (approximately 50) of segmented metacarpals. Figure 10.10 illustrates (after alignment, as described in Section 10.4) the mean shape, together with the actual positions of the landmark points from the entire data set.

Following the procedure outlined in Section 10.4, the covariance matrix and its eigenvectors associated with the variation are extracted; the relative contribution of the most

Figure 10.11: The first mode of variation. Left to right: $-2.5\sqrt{\lambda_1}$, mean shape, $2.5\sqrt{\lambda_1}$. *Courtesy of N. D. Efford, School of Computing, University of Leeds.*

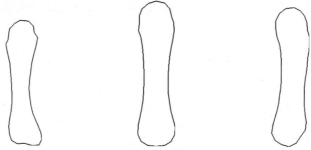

Figure 10.12: The third mode of variation. Left to right: $-2.5\sqrt{\lambda_3}$, mean shape, $2.5\sqrt{\lambda_3}$. *Courtesy of N. D. Efford, School of Computing, University of Leeds.*

influential components is illustrated in Table 10.1. From this we see that more than 95% of the shape variation is captured by the first eight modes of variation. Figure 10.11 illustrates the effect of varying the first mode of the mean shape by up to $2.5\sqrt{\lambda_1}$. This mode, which accounts for more than 60% of the variation seen in the data, captures the (asymmetric) thickening and thinning of bones (relative to their length), which is an obvious characteristic of maturity. In this example, it is clear that 2.5 is an unlikely factor for $\sqrt{\lambda_1}$, since the resulting shapes are too extreme—thus we may expect b_1 to be smaller in magnitude for this application.

Figure 10.12 similarly illustrates extremes of the third mode. The shape change here is somewhat subtler; part of what is captured is a bending (in banana fashion) of the bone. Both extremes have a plausible 'bone-like' look about them.

Fitting models to data

A strength of this approach is that it permits plausible shapes to be fitted to new data. Given an image in which we wish to locate an instance of a modeled shape (specifically, given an edge map of the image, so having information about where boundaries are most likely to lie), we require to know:

- The mean shape $\bar{\mathbf{x}}$.
- The transformation matrix P_t.
- The particular shape parameter vector $\mathbf{b}_t$.
- The particular pose (translation, rotation and scale).

Here, $\bar{\mathbf{x}}$ and P_t are known from the model construction. The identification of $\mathbf{b}_t$ and the pose is an optimization problem—locate the parameters that best fit the data at hand, subject to certain constraints. These constraints would include the known limits on reasonable values for the components of $\mathbf{b}_t$, and might also include domain knowledge about plausible positions for the object to constrain the pose. In the metacarpal example (Section 10.4), this would include knowledge that a bone lies within the hand silhouette, is aligned with the finger and is of a known approximate size.

This approach may be used successfully with a number of well-known optimization algorithms, some of which are described in Section 9.6. It is likely, however, that convergence would be slow. An alternative, quicker approach [Cootes and Taylor, 1992] is to use the PDM as the basis of an active shape model (ASM) (sometimes referred to as a 'smart snake'—snakes, which represent a different approach to boundary fitting, are described in Section 7.2). Here, we iterate toward the best fit by examining an approximate fit, locating improved positions for the landmark points, then recalculating pose and parameters.

Algorithm 10.7: Fitting an ASM

1. Initialize an approximate fit to image data; this may be done in any suitable way but is likely to depend on geometric constraints provided by the application, together with crude image properties. This gives in local (model) co-ordinates a shape description
$$\hat{\mathbf{x}} = (x_1, y_1, x_2, y_2, \ldots, x_N, y_N) \, .$$

2. At each landmark point, inspect the boundary normal close to the boundary, and locate the pixel of highest intensity gradient; mark this as the best target position to which to move this landmark point. This is illustrated in Figure 10.13. If there is no clear new target, the landmark is left where it is.

   We derive thereby a desired displacement vector.

3. Adjust the pose parameters to provide the best fit to the target points of the current landmarks.

   There are various ways of doing this, but Algorithm 10.6 provides one approach; a quicker approximation, which is adequate since the iteration will seek out a good solution in time, is given in [Cootes and Taylor, 1992].

4. Determine the displacement vector $\delta\widetilde{\mathbf{x}}$ that adjusts the model in the new pose to the target points (details follow the end of the algorithm).

5. Determine the model adjustment $\delta\mathbf{b}_t$ that best approximates $\delta\widetilde{\mathbf{x}}$. From equation (10.6) we have
$$\widetilde{\mathbf{x}} \approx \bar{\mathbf{x}} + P_t\,\mathbf{b}_t$$
and we seek $\delta\mathbf{b}_t$ such that
$$\widetilde{\mathbf{x}} + \delta\widetilde{\mathbf{x}} = \bar{\mathbf{x}} + P_t(\mathbf{b}_t + \delta\mathbf{b}_t) \, .$$

   Hence
$$\delta\widetilde{\mathbf{x}} \approx P_t\,\delta\mathbf{b}_t \, .$$

With the properties of eigen-matrices, we can deduce

$$\delta \mathbf{b}_t = P_t^T \, \delta \widetilde{\mathbf{x}}$$

as the best approximation. Note that since the modes of variation $t+1$, $t+2$, ..., are discounted, this is necessarily only an approximation. Note also that we can at this stage prevent components of the vector $\mathbf{b}_t$ from growing in magnitude beyond any limits we may set by limiting them as we see appropriate—that is, should this equation generate a component deemed to be too large in magnitude, it would be set to the appropriate limit. Thus the re-fitted model will (probably) not match the targets precisely.

6. Iterate from step 2 until changes become negligible.

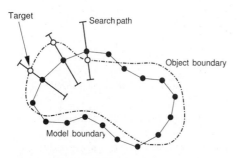

Figure 10.13: Searching an approximate model fit for target points to which landmarks may move. *Courtesy of N. D. Efford, School of Computing, University of Leeds.*

Step 2 assumes that a suitable target can be found, which may not always be true. If there is none, the landmark can be left where it is, and the model constraints will eventually pull it into a reasonable position. Alternatively, outlier landmarks can be automatically identified and replaced with model landmarks [Duta and Sonka, 1998]. There is also the option of locating targets by more sophisticated means than simple intensity gradient measurements.

Step 4 requires a calculation for $\delta \widetilde{\mathbf{x}}$. To perform this, note that we commence with a vector $\widetilde{\mathbf{x}}$ (in the 'local' frame), which is updated by a pose matrix and translation to provide $\mathbf{x}$ in the image frame,

$$\mathbf{x} = M(\theta, s)\widetilde{\mathbf{x}} + (t_x, t_y) \,,$$

where

$$M = M(\theta, s) = \begin{bmatrix} s\cos\theta & -s\sin\theta \\ s\sin\theta & s\cos\theta \end{bmatrix} \,.$$

New pose parameters $t_x + \delta t_x$, $t_y + \delta t_y$, $\theta + \delta\theta$, $s(1+\delta s)$ (from step 3) and a displacement $\delta \mathbf{x}$ (from step 2) have been calculated, giving the equation

$$\mathbf{x} + \delta \mathbf{x} = M\big(\theta + \delta\theta, s(1+\delta s)\big)(\widetilde{\mathbf{x}} + \delta\widetilde{\mathbf{x}}) + (t_x + \delta t_x, t_y + \delta t_y) \,.$$

Since

$$M^{-1}(\theta, s) = M(-\theta, s^{-1}) \,,$$

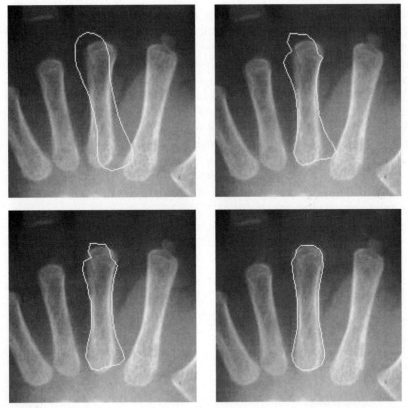

Figure 10.14: Fitting an ASM to a metacarpal; various stages of convergence—initialization, 3, 6, and 10 iterations. *Courtesy of N. D. Efford, School of Computing, University of Leeds.*

we obtain

$$\delta\widetilde{\mathbf{x}} = M\Big(-(\theta+\delta\theta), \big[s(1+\delta s)\big]^{-1}\Big)\big[M(\theta,s)\widetilde{\mathbf{x}} + \delta\mathbf{x} - (\delta t_x, \delta t_y)\big] - \widetilde{\mathbf{x}}\,.$$

This adjustment is 'raw' in the sense that it takes no account of the model; the next algorithm step compensates for this. Figure 10.14 illustrates Algorithm 10.7 where we see an initialization and the position of the model after 3, 6, and 10 iterations as a metacarpal is located. Note that the model locates the correct position despite the proximity of strong boundaries that could distract it—this does not occur because the shape of the boundary is tightly bound in.

An example of the application of these algorithms is given as part of Section 16.5.1.

Extensions

The literature on PDMs and ASMs is very extensive—the technique lends itself to a very wide range of problems, but has some drawbacks. The placing of the landmark points for construction of the training set is clearly very labor intensive, and in some applications it is error prone. Automatic placing of these points has been addressed [Duta et al., 1999; Davies et al., 2002a; Frangi et al., 2002]. Another approach to the same task is described in Section 16.5.1.

Efficiency of the approach has also been enhanced by the common idea of a multi-resolution attack [Cootes et al., 1994]. Using a coarse-to-fine strategy can produce benefits in both quality of final fit and reduction of computational load.

As presented, the approach is strictly linear in the sense that control points may only move along a straight line (albeit with respect to directions of maximum variation); non-linear effects are produced by combining contributions from different modes. Aside from being imperfect, this results in a representation that is not as compact as it might be if the non-linear aspects were explicitly modeled. This problem has been addressed in two ways: [Sozou et al., 1994] introduces the **Polynomial Regression** PDM, which assumes dependence between the modes, with minor modes being polynomial combinations of major ones; and Heap [Heap and Hogg, 1996] extends the linear model by permitting polar relationships between modes, thereby efficiently capturing the ability of (parts of) objects to rotate around one another.

A methodology for the construction of three-dimensional statistical shape models of the heart has been developed [Frangi et al., 2002]. Non-rigid registration was employed for the automated establishment of landmark correspondences across populations of healthy

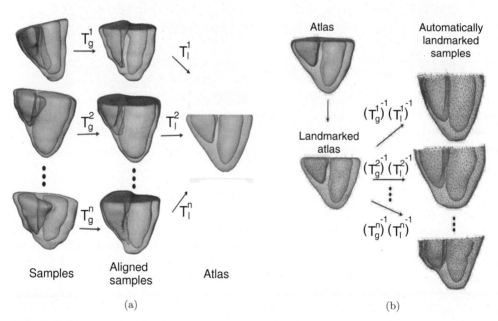

(a) (b)

Figure 10.15: Automated landmark definition–landmarking of cardiac ventricles in 3D. (a) Global and local transforms brings each sample shape to the atlas co-ordinate system. The global transforms T_g align the objects, e.g., by aligning long axes and fitting them in a common bounding box. Local transforms T_l are employed to achieve exact alignment of all samples with an 'atlas' shape. The atlas object is selected from existing samples to be most similar to all other samples. (b) Landmarks are identified on the atlas object—possibly in a random fashion, possibly as atlas object points of some specific properties, e.g., corners, inflexion points, ridges, etc. Landmarks defined in the atlas space are propagated to each of the original object samples using a sequence of inverted local and global transforms T_g^{-1} and T_l^{-1}. Using this approach, automated landmarking can be achieved. © *Cengage Learning 2015*.

and diseased hearts. The general layout of the method is to align all the images of the training set to an atlas that can be interpreted as a 'mean' shape. Once all the necessary transformations are obtained, they are inverted and used to propagate any number of arbitrarily sampled landmarks onto the atlas, to the co-ordinate system of each subject (Figure 10.15, see also [Zhang et al., 2010]). In this way, while it is still necessary to manually define the segmentation of each training image, we are relieved from manual landmark definition for establishing point correspondences across the training set. Further details of the method can be found in [Lelieveldt et al., 2006; Zhang et al., 2010]. Figure 10.16a illustrates a 3D ASM segmentation algorithm, see [van Assen et al., 2003]. The approach works in volumetric image data as well as in sparse data solely consisting of a limited number of image planes with differing orientations (Figure 10.16b).

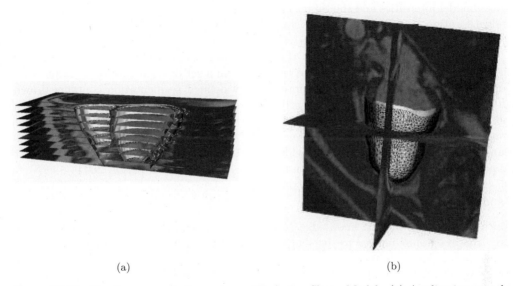

(a)   (b)

Figure 10.16: Cardiac segmentation using a 3D Active Shape Model. (a) Application to volumetric cardiac magnetic resonance data. In this case, a volumetric 3D model is fitted to volumetric image data in a fully 3D fashion. (b) Application to 3 sparse, arbitrarily oriented magnetic resonance image planes. In this example, a volumetric image data set is not available and is approximated by a set of (usually) perpendicular image planes in which image data exist. A fully three-dimensional model is fitted in the three image planes. *N. Paragios, Y. Chen, O. Faugeras, Handbook of Mathematical Models in Computer Vision, Springer, 2006.*

An ASM-based approach has been embedded in the internal energy term of an elastically deformable model [Kaus et al., 2004]. Manually segmented training samples are expressed as binary volumes and point correspondence is achieved by fitting a template mesh with a fixed point topology to each binary training sample. Multi-surface coupling is realized by integrating connecting vertices between interacting surfaces and adding a connection term to the internal energy. In addition, a spatially varying feature model is adopted for each landmark. Statistical shape constraints are imposed on the allowed elastic mesh deformations, while allowing for some flexibility to deviate from the trained shapes to facilitate untrained shape variability.

10.5 Active appearance models

The Active Appearance Model (AAM) combines modeling of shape and its variability with modeling of image appearance and its variability [Cootes et al., 1999, 2001]. AAMs are an extension of PDMs with a statistical intensity model of a complete image patch, as opposed to merely scanning image properties along lines near the landmarks as in ASM matching. An AAM is built by warping the training shapes to the average shape. Obviously, this requires a consistent mesh node localization in all shapes of the training set. After intensity normalization to zero mean and unit variance, the intensity average and principal components are computed. A subsequent combined PCA on the shape and intensity model parameters yields a set of components that simultaneously capture shape and texture variability.

AAM segmentation is based on minimizing a criterion expressing the difference between model intensities and the target image. This enables a rapid search for the correct model location during the matching stage. The sum of square differences between the model-generated patch and the underlying image is one simple such criterion.

A major advantage of AAMs is that the object shape and the underlying image appearance are derived via automated training from a set of segmentation examples. As for ASMs, AAMs are trained using interactively defined segmentation contours drawn in the original image data. Consequently, they are able to capture associations between observer preferences and the underlying image evidence, making them highly suitable for modeling expert observer behavior. Another advantage is the fact that multiple objects can be modeled in their spatial embedding. Detailed treatment of 2D AAMs and their application to image segmentation can be found in [Cootes and Taylor, 2004].

Modeling image appearance

With ASMs, only limited knowledge about image appearance is accommodated, usually from a scanline normal to the shape; for each landmark point an intensity model is generated analogous to the generation of the shape models. These local appearance models serve to generate proposed boundary locations during the ASM localization search. Clearly, only local appearance is modeled.

AAMs, however, describe the image appearance and the shape in an integral shape-appearance representation of an image patch [Cootes and Taylor, 2004]. In the equations below, the subscript s corresponds to shape parameters while the subscript g represents appearance or gray-level parameters. An AAM is constructed in the following manner.

Algorithm 10.8: AAM construction

1. Compute an ASM and approximate each shape sample as a linear combination of eigenvectors, where $\mathbf{b}_s = P_s^T (\mathbf{x} - \bar{\mathbf{x}})$ represents the sample shape parameters (equation 10.4).

2. Warp each image to the mean shape using linear or non-linear image interpolation.

3. Normalize each image to the average intensity and unit variance $\bar{\mathbf{g}}$.

4. Perform PCA on the normalized intensity images.

5. Express each intensity sample as a linear combination of eigenvectors, where $\mathbf{b}_g = P_g^T(\mathbf{g} - \bar{\mathbf{g}})$ represents the sample gray-level parameters.

6. Concatenate the shape coefficient vectors $\mathbf{b}_s$ and gray-level intensity coefficient vectors $\mathbf{b}_g$ in the following manner

$$\mathbf{b} = \begin{bmatrix} W\,\mathbf{b}_s \\ \mathbf{b}_g \end{bmatrix} = \begin{bmatrix} W\,P_s^T(\mathbf{x} - \bar{\mathbf{x}}) \\ P_g^T(\mathbf{g} - \bar{\mathbf{g}}) \end{bmatrix}, \tag{10.7}$$

where W is a diagonal weighting matrix that relates the different units of shape and gray-level intensity coefficients.

7. Apply PCA to the sample set of all $\mathbf{b}$ vectors, yielding the model

$$\mathbf{b} = Q\mathbf{c}, \tag{10.8}$$

where Q is a matrix consisting of eigenvectors (from equation 10.7) and $\mathbf{c}$ are resulting model coefficients characterizing how the model instance differs from the mean shape and mean appearance. In other words, with the zero vector $\mathbf{c} = 0$, the modeled instance corresponds to the mean shape and appearance.

Figure 10.17 gives an example of an appearance model built from multiple images of facial expressions. The figure shows the mean appearance from the set of face images as well as the model changes along one of the modes of shape and gray-level appearance.

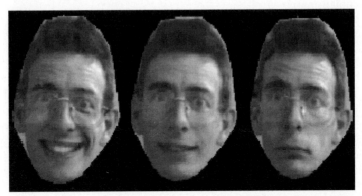

Figure 10.17: Appearance model of Dr. Tim Cootes. The middle panel shows mean shape and appearance, left and right panels show shape and appearance resulting from varying parameter **c** along one of the modes of combined shape and gray-level appearance (equation 10.8). *Courtesy of T. Cootes, University of Manchester, UK.*

AAM segmentation

Matching an appearance model to a target image involves finding an affine or similarity transformation, global intensity parameters, and appearance coefficients that minimize the root-mean-square (RMS) difference between the appearance model instance and the target image. The method described by Cootes [Cootes and Taylor, 2004] suggests using a gradient descent method that relates model coefficients with the difference between a synthesized model image and the target image.

Let $\mathbf{t}$ represent the parameters of transformation T, and $\mathbf{u}$ the global intensity parameters. As outlined above, shape $\mathbf{x}$ is derived in the target image from the appearance coefficients $\mathbf{c}$ and the transformation coefficients $\mathbf{t}$. The gray-level intensity vector $\mathbf{g}_s = T\mathbf{u}^{-1}(g_{im})$ in the target image spanned by the shape $\mathbf{x}$ is extracted using image warping; $\mathbf{g}_{im}$ represents the image patch warped from the target image to the mean shape. The model gray-level intensity vector $\mathbf{g}_m$ is derived from the appearance coefficients $\mathbf{c}$ and is later modified by the global intensity parameters $\mathbf{u}$.

Using a first order Taylor expansion on a set of known model parameters, matrix $\mathbf{R}$ is derived as described below. The Taylor expansion replaced the reduced-rank multivariate linear regression used in early AAM research since it is easier to implement, faster to calculate, requires substantially less memory, and produces comparable or better results [Cootes et al., 2001; Stegmann, 2004]. Using a set of training images, the parameters $\mathbf{c}$, $\mathbf{t}$, and $\mathbf{u}$ are randomly perturbed thus creating a residual $\mathbf{r}$ by calculating the difference between $\mathbf{g}_s$ and $\mathbf{g}_m$. For best results, the random displacement should be constrained to a relatively small range. The residual vector $\mathbf{r}$ is parameterized by $\mathbf{p}$ as:

$$\mathbf{r}(\mathbf{p}) = \mathbf{g}_s(\mathbf{p}) - \mathbf{g}_m(\mathbf{p})\,, \tag{10.9}$$

where $\mathbf{p}^T = (\mathbf{c}^T|\mathbf{t}^T|\mathbf{u}^T)$. From the displacements and difference images, a least-square solution to the first-order Taylor expansion at $\widetilde{\mathbf{p}}$ located in the proximity to the optimal parameter vector is

$$\mathbf{r}(\widetilde{\mathbf{p}} + \delta\mathbf{p}) \approx \mathbf{r}(\widetilde{\mathbf{p}}) + \frac{\partial\mathbf{r}(\widetilde{\mathbf{p}})}{\partial\mathbf{p}}\delta\mathbf{p}\,, \tag{10.10}$$

where the Jacobian matrix is

$$\frac{\partial\mathbf{r}(\widetilde{\mathbf{p}})}{\partial\mathbf{p}} = \frac{\partial\mathbf{r}}{\partial\mathbf{p}} = \begin{bmatrix} \frac{\partial\mathbf{r}_1}{\partial\mathbf{p}_1} & & \frac{\partial\mathbf{r}_1}{\partial\mathbf{p}_M} \\ & \ddots & \\ \frac{\partial\mathbf{r}_N}{\partial\mathbf{p}_1} & & \frac{\partial\mathbf{r}_N}{\partial\mathbf{p}_M} \end{bmatrix}\,, \tag{10.11}$$

and M is the number of model parameters, N is the number of components of the residual vector $\mathbf{r}$. Here, $\widetilde{\mathbf{p}}$ represents the estimate of parameter vector $\mathbf{p}$ and $\mathbf{p}^*$ is its optimal value. The parameter update is used to iteratively drive the vector of residuals to zero, eventually yielding the optimal parameter configuration. The optimal value of the update parameter is

$$\delta\mathbf{p} = \underset{\delta\mathbf{p}}{\arg\min} \|\mathbf{r}(\widetilde{\mathbf{p}} + \delta\mathbf{p})\|^2\,. \tag{10.12}$$

Aiming at $\|\mathbf{r}(\widetilde{\mathbf{p}} + \delta\mathbf{p})\|^2 = 0$, the desired update parameters can be obtained as the least-square solution of the Taylor expansion:

$$\delta\mathbf{p} = -\left(\frac{\partial\mathbf{r}^T}{\partial\mathbf{p}}\frac{\partial\mathbf{r}}{\partial\mathbf{p}}\right)^{-1}\frac{\partial\mathbf{r}^T}{\partial\mathbf{p}}\mathbf{r}(\widetilde{\mathbf{p}}) = -\mathbf{R}\mathbf{r}(\widetilde{\mathbf{p}})\,. \tag{10.13}$$

This is equivalent to finding the gradient of the image difference objective function. While it may seem that the Jacobian matrix shall be recalculated for each $\widetilde{\mathbf{p}}$, which would be computationally expensive, the following approximation can be used since AAMs operate on a standardized reference frame

$$\frac{\partial\mathbf{r}(\widetilde{\mathbf{p}})}{\partial\mathbf{p}} \approx \frac{\partial\mathbf{r}(\mathbf{p}^*)}{\partial\mathbf{p}}\,. \tag{10.14}$$

As a further simplification, the right hand side of this equation is considered constant for all training examples. Consequently, the matrix $\mathbf{R}$ is considered fixed and is estimated only once using numerical differentiation on the training set of P examples. Residuals at varying displacements are measured and combined with kernel w to smooth them. For k^{th} perturbation of parameter $\mathbf{e}_j$, the jth column of the Jacobian can be estimated as

$$\widetilde{\frac{\partial \mathbf{r}}{\partial p_j}} = \frac{1}{P} \sum_i^P \sum_k w(\delta p_{jk}) \frac{\mathbf{r}(\mathbf{p}_i^* + \delta p_{jk}\mathbf{e}_j) - \mathbf{r}(\mathbf{p}_i^* - \delta p_{jk}\mathbf{e}_j)}{2\,\delta p_{jk}} \tag{10.15}$$

and the kernel $w(\cdot)$ can be Gaussian [Cootes et al., 2001] or uniform [Stegmann, 2004]. This permits the pre-computation of $\mathbf{R}$ and is used in all AAM-based segmentations[3]. The corresponding model correction steps can be computed as

$$\delta\mathbf{p} = -\mathbf{R}(\mathbf{g}_s - \mathbf{g}_m) \tag{10.16}$$

and the AAM matching can be accomplished as follows:

Algorithm 10.9: Active appearance model matching

1. Place an appearance model roughly on the object of interest using the parameters $\mathbf{c}$, $\mathbf{t}$, and $\mathbf{u}$ and compute the difference image $\mathbf{g}_s - \mathbf{g}_m$.

2. Compute the RMS of the difference image, $E(\mathbf{r}) = \|\mathbf{r}\|^2$.

3. Compute model corrections $\delta\mathbf{p}$ as derived above from the residual (equation 10.16).

4. Set $k = 1$.

5. Compute new model parameters as $\mathbf{c} := \mathbf{c} - k\delta\mathbf{c}$, $\mathbf{t} := \mathbf{t} - k\delta\mathbf{t}$, and $\mathbf{u} := \mathbf{u} - k\delta\mathbf{u}$.

6. Based on these new parameters, recompute $\mathbf{g}_s - \mathbf{g}_m$ and recalculate the RMS.

7. If the RMS is less than E, accept these parameters and go to step 3.

8. Else set k to 1.5, 0.5, 0.25, etc. and go to step 5. Repeat steps 5–8 until the error cannot be reduced any further.

Figure 10.18 gives an example of AAM-based segmentation of cardiac ventricles in a 2D magnetic resonance image. In cardiac segmentation, the initial position of the model is determined by approximate identification of the left-ventricular position using a Hough transform for circles (Section 6.2.6).

AAMs are highly suited to robustly locating objects but are better suited for matching object appearance than for accurate delineation of object boundaries since the algorithm tends to produce plausible solutions, but borders may be imprecise. This is because it is optimized on global appearance and is thus less sensitive to local structures and boundary information commonly used in other segmentation algorithms (Figures 10.19a,b).

---

[3] A research-only version of the AAM code can be found at http://www.isbe.man.ac.uk/~bim/software/am_tools_doc/index.html

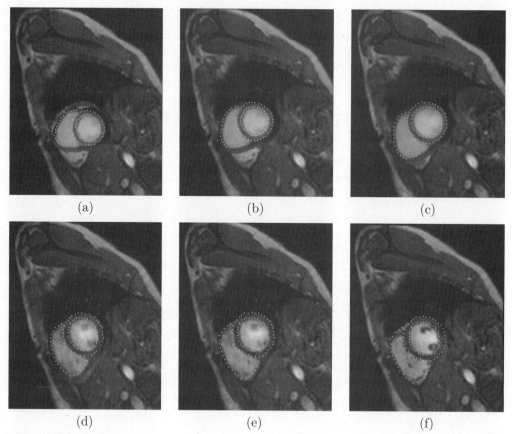

(a)   (b)   (c)

(d)   (e)   (f)

Figure 10.18: Cardiac image segmentation using AAM matching. (a) The process starts by positioning an average AAM in proximity to the target location. (b-e) Steps of the process in which differences between model and underlying image are minimized. Model position, orientation, shape, and appearance are gradually changing—note the change of model appearance from almost uniformly gray average model appearance at the beginning of the process to a close match, e.g., exhibiting papillary muscles (the dark spots inside of the circular left-ventricular blood pool) in the left ventricle. (f) Final location of the model defines segmentation borders superimposed over original data. © *Cengage Learning 2015*.

ASMs tend to find local structures fairly well; they typically match a shape-only model onto a target image based upon the edges or edge patterns normal to the shape borders. Their strength originates from a direct association between edge profiles and shape borders. However, they are very sensitive to initial placement and do not take advantage of the overall gray level appearance information.

Not surprisingly, combining ASM and AAM matching in a hybrid fashion during the final stages of optimization improves segmentation with respect to the accuracy of object boundary placement (Figure 10.19c). After conducting AAM matching to convergence, ASM and AAM matching are performed independently of each other and the resulting parameters are combined after each iteration. This is done by extracting the shape model $\mathbf{b}_s$ from the AAM, performing a best fit using only the shape model and the pose parameters $\mathbf{t}$ and then transforming the refined shape model back into the AAM. At the

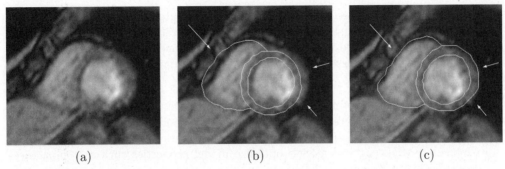

(a)   (b)   (c)

Figure 10.19: Comparison of 2D conventional AAM and multistage hybrid ASM/AAM segmentation of left and right ventricles in a cardiac short-axis MR image. (a) Original image. (b) Conventional AAM segmentation demonstrating good gray level appearance fit but locally poor border positioning accuracy (arrows). (c) Hybrid ASM/AAM approach result shows substantial improvement in border detection positioning. *S. C. Mitchell, B. P. F. Lelieveldt, R. J. van der Geest, H. G. Bosch, J. H. C. Reiber, and M. Sonka, "Multistage hybrid active appearance model matching: segmentation of left and right ventricles in cardiac MR images," IEEE Transactions on Medical Imaging, 20(5):415-423, May 2001.*

same time, AAM refinement is applied to the image yielding its own set of coefficients for shape and pose. The two sets of shape and pose coefficients are combined using a weighted average. Details of this multistage hybrid AAM image segmentation can be found in [Mitchell et al., 2001].

AAMs in higher-dimensional data

Initially, most PDM, ASM and AAM techniques were applied to 2D modeling and matching problems. Since many imaging modalities deliver 3D or 4D (dynamic 3D) image data, extensions to higher dimensions are desirable. Point correspondence is critical to achieving extension of PDMs to three and more dimensions; landmarks must be placed in a consistent way over a large database of training shapes, otherwise an incorrect parameterization of the object class results. The same landmarking approaches can be used for ASM and AAM modeling. In the 2D case, the most straightforward definition of point correspondence is by identifying evenly spaced sampling points between characteristic landmarks on a boundary, although this may lead to a suboptimal sampling. In the 3D case, the problem of defining a unique sampling of 3D surfaces is more complex, and far from trivial. Three main approaches to establishing 3D point correspondence can be distinguished:

- Correspondence by parameterization: this has mainly been applied to relatively simple geometries that can be described using a spherical or cylindrical co-ordinate system, in combination with a few well-defined landmarks to fix the co-ordinate frame. Applying this co-ordinate definition on all the samples yields parametrically corresponding landmarks [Mitchell et al., 2002].

- Correspondence by registration or fitting by mapping a 3D surface tessellation of one sample to all other samples. For instance, a 3D deformable surface may be matched to binary segmentations of new samples [Lorenz and Krahnstover, 2000].

By projecting the tessellation of the matched template to the new sample, correspondence for the new sample is achieved. Alternatively, non-rigid volumetric registration can be applied to define dense correspondences between training samples (see Figure 10.15). These approaches have the advantage of handling topologically more complex shapes.

- Correspondence by optimal encoding: a Minimum Description Length (MDL) criterion can be used to evaluate the quality of correspondence in terms of the ability to encode the whole training set for a given landmark distribution [Davies et al., 2002a,b]. MDL encoded models optimize model properties such as compactness and specificity [Stegmann, 2004].

2D + time AAMs

An extension to 2D + time modeling has been proposed in [Bosch et al., 2002; van der Geest et al., 2004], where the temporal dimension is encoded into the model. In addition to spatial correspondence, time correspondence is obtained by defining 'landmark time frames.' Shapes are interpolated to a fixed number of frames using nearest neighbor interpolation. This time correspondence allows the shape and intensity vectors to be simply concatenated over the whole sequence and treated as 2D images; the 2D AAM machinery described earlier can be applied unaltered. Although this is not strictly a fully 3D model, the segmentation is performed on all frames simultaneously, yielding time-continuous results. This approach has been applied to echocardiographic image sequences [Bosch et al., 2002] and slice-based cardiac MR image sequences [van der Geest et al., 2004].

3D AAMs: Modeling volume appearance

As discussed earlier, ASMs are updated using local intensity models in the vicinity of the landmarks. For AAMs, a complete intensity volume is modeled along with the shape. Model fitting is based on matching the model and the target image [Mitchell et al., 2002].

To create such an appearance model of a full volume, all the sample volumes are warped to the average shape to eliminate shape variation and yield voxel-wise correspondence across all the training samples. The voxel intensities can be represented as a shape-free vector of intensity values. Warping an image $\mathbf{I}$ to a new image $\mathbf{I}'$ involves creating a function which maps control points $\mathbf{x}_i$ to $\mathbf{x}'_i$ as well as the intermediate points. For the 2D case, either piecewise affine warping or thin-plate spline warping is adequate and landmark points are used to construct the shape area as a set of triangles.

In 3D models, piecewise affine warping may be extended to tetrahedra represented by corners, $\mathbf{x}_1, \mathbf{x}_2, \mathbf{x}_3, \mathbf{x}_4$. Any point within the tetrahedron is represented as $\mathbf{x} = \alpha \mathbf{x}_1 + \beta \mathbf{x}_2 + \gamma \mathbf{x}_3 + \delta \mathbf{x}_4$. In the general case, creating a tetrahedral representation of volume is solved using a 3D Delaunay triangulation algorithm. Because all volumes are warped to the average, barycentric co-ordinates, $\alpha, \beta, \gamma, \delta$ are precomputed for each fixed voxel point eliminating the time consuming process of searching for the enclosing tetrahedron for each voxel point during the matching.

After the warping phase, shape-free intensity vectors are normalized to an average intensity of zero and an average variance of one as described above. PCA is then applied to the shape-free intensity vectors to create an intensity model. In agreement with the AAM principle, shape information and intensity information are combined into a single

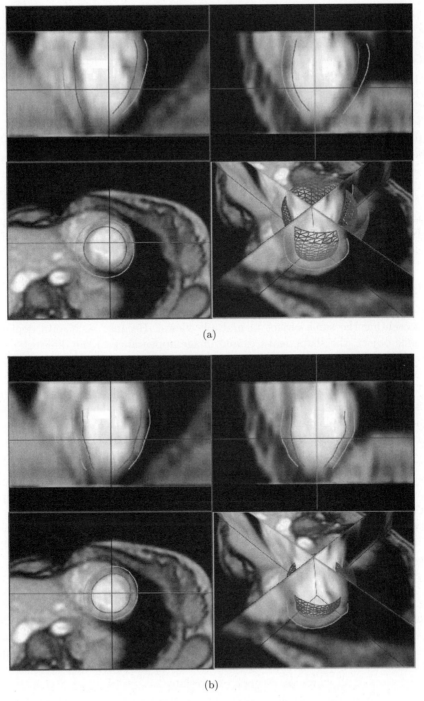

(a)

(b)

Figure 10.20: 3D AAM matching process. (a) The initial position of the model in the volumetric data set. (b) Final match result. The straight lines show the position of frames in the other two cutting planes.   *Handbook of Mathematical Models in Computer Vision, "3D active shape and appearance models in cardiac image analysis," 2006, pp. 471-486, B. Lelieveldt, A. Frangi, S. Mitchell, H. van Assen, S. Ordas, J. Reiber, and M. Sonka. A color version of this figure may be seen in the color inset—Plate 22.*

active appearance model. Lastly, another PCA is applied to the coefficients of the shape and intensity models to form a combined appearance model [Cootes et al., 2001].

Model matching in 3D is performed in the same way as AAM matching in 2D, i.e., an objective function describing a level of agreement between the model's shape and appearance, and its position on the target image is minimized. As in 2D, gradient descent optimization requires the partial derivatives of the error function defined by the intensity of the target and synthesized model volumes. While it is not possible to create such a function analytically, these derivatives may be approximated using a fixed matrix computed by randomly perturbing model coefficients for a set of known training images and observing the resulting difference in error images (as before, the random perturbations should be reasonably constrained) [Cootes et al., 2001]. Figure 10.20 demonstrates the model matching process from the initial model position to the final fit. The matching performance of 3D AAMs can be improved by augmenting the model with ASM-like scan line profiles that increase the model context awareness and lock-in range [Stegmann, 2004]. In addition to decreased computation time, an exhaustive search of several model initializations is facilitated, further improving the initialization robustness.

Multi-view AAMs

In some situations, the available image data consist of several mutually interrelated images representing the same object in multiple views. Because such data depict views of the same object, the shape features and image appearance in the different views are highly correlated. Multi-view AAMs capture the coherence and correlation between them. Model training and matching are performed on multiple (2D) views simultaneously, combining information from all views to yield a segmentation. The multi-view model is constructed by aligning training shapes for different views separately, and concatenating the aligned shape vectors $\mathbf{x}_i$ for each of the N views. A shape vector for N views is defined as

$$\mathbf{x} = (\mathbf{x}_1^T, \mathbf{x}_2^T, \mathbf{x}_3^T, \ldots) \,. \tag{10.17}$$

By applying PCA on the sample covariance matrix of the combined shapes, a shape model is computed for all frames simultaneously. The principal model components represent shape variations, which are intrinsically coupled for all views. The same applies to the intensity model. An image patch is warped on the average shape for view i and sampled into an intensity vector $\mathbf{g}_i$, the intensity vectors for each single frame are normalized to zero mean and unit variance, and concatenated

$$\mathbf{g} = (\mathbf{g}_1^T, \mathbf{g}_2^T, \mathbf{g}_3^T, \ldots) \,. \tag{10.18}$$

Analogously to the other AAMs, PCA is applied to the sample covariance matrices of the concatenated intensity sample vectors. Subsequently, each training sample is expressed as a set of shape and appearance coefficients. A combined model is computed from the combined shape–intensity sample vectors. In the combined model, the shapes and appearances of all views are strongly interrelated.

As in all AAMs, estimation of the gradient matrices for computing parameter updates during the image matching is performed by applying perturbations on the model, pose, and texture parameters, and measuring their effect on the residuals. Because of the correlations between views in the model, a disturbance in an individual model parameter yields residuals in all views simultaneously. The pose parameters, however, are perturbed

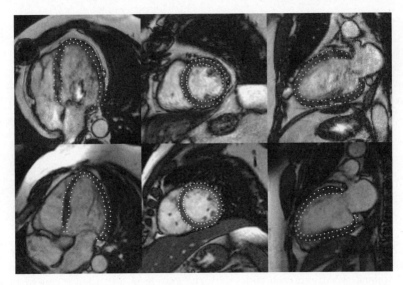

Figure 10.21: Multi-view AAM detected contours (white dotted lines) for two patients (top and bottom row) in a 4-chamber (left), short-axis (middle) and 2-chamber view (right). *Handbook of Mathematical Models in Computer Vision, "3D active shape and appearance models in cardiac image analysis," 2006, pp. 471-486, B. Lelieveldt, A. Frangi, S. Mitchell, H. van Assen, S. Ordas, J. Reiber, and M. Sonka.*

for each view separately. The model is trained to accommodate for trivial differences in object pose in each view, whereas the shape and intensity gradients are correlated for all views. In the matching procedure, the pose transformation for each view is also applied separately and the model coefficients intrinsically influence multiple frames at once. The permitted shape and intensity deformations are coupled for all frames, while the pose parameter vectors are optimized independently for each view.

Multi-view AAMs have been successfully applied to segmentation of long-axis cardiac MR views and left-ventricular angiograms [Oost et al., 2003, 2006]. Figure 10.21 provides examples of matching results for combined long- and short-axis cardiac MR scans.

Extensions

ASMs and AAMs see many successful applications in face recognition and modeling [Bettinger and Cootes, 2004; Cristinacce et al., 2004] as well as in medical image analysis. Extending the basic 2D approach to 3D and 4D segmentation is an important challenge; the definition of point correspondence is the most critical issue [Twining et al., 2006; Kittipanyangam and Cootes, 2006; Cootes and Taylor, 2006].

ASMs are matched to image data by locally updating the model according to image information in the vicinity of the landmarks. The main challenges for extending ASMs to 3D lie in generating update points using a robust classifier (preferably modality and training independent). In addition, the use of an intermediary mesh combined with local mesh updates enables application to sparse, arbitrarily oriented image planes, which is not possible with AAMs due to the requirement of a densely sampled intensity volume. For AAMs, the main extension to higher dimensions lies in defining a robust volume tessellation in 3D. Extensions to 2D + time, 3D + time and multiple views mainly rely

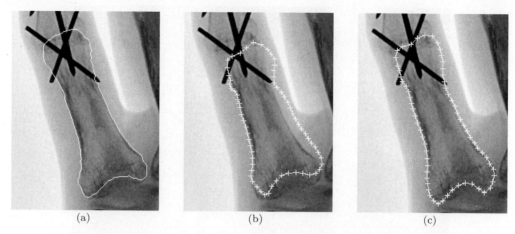

        (a)   (b)   (c)

Figure 10.22: Robust AAM segmentation of proximal phalanx X-ray image with implants. (a) Manually determined bone contours. (b) Result of AAM segmentation—landmarks marked by '+'. (c) Robust AAM approach copes with the gray level disturbance caused by implants and provides acceptable segmentation. *Information Processing in Medical Imaging, "Robust active appearance model matching," 2005, pp. 114-125, R. Beichel, H. Bischof, F. Leberl, and M. Sonka.*

on concatenating shape and intensity vectors for multiple time instances or geometric views.

    A major advantage, as well as limitation, of ASM and AAM approaches is associated with their reliance on a balanced and representative training set. When the number of training samples is limited, or when presented with non-representative cases, the shape models may over-constrain segmentation results towards the model. One solution lies in applying a constraint relaxation when the model is close to its final solution [Kaus et al., 2004]. Another approach was proposed in [Beichel et al., 2005] to cope with gross disturbances of objects in the analyzed data with no assumptions with respect to the kind of gray-value disturbance and the expected magnitude of residuals during matching (Figure 10.22). The method consists of two main stages. First, initial residuals are analyzed by means of a mean shift based mode detection step (Section 7.1). Second, an objective function is utilized for the selection of a mode combination without gross outliers. An increase of segmentation robustness was achieved showing that the method tolerated up to 50% area consisting of outlier information.

    The parameters of the matched ASMs or AAMs can be used for image understanding. For example in medical applications, computer-aided diagnosis of the functional status of a specific organ can frequently provide diagnostic information that may be difficult or impossible to obtain otherwise. The ability of 2D + time AAMs to automatically classify wall motion abnormalities from echocardiograms, a task known to be difficult for human experts and suffering from a large inter-observer variability, was demonstrated in [Bosch et al., 2005]. When the global assessment of object status from the parameters of the AAM or ASM is not sufficient a more localized analysis may be required. In this case, independent component analysis may be employed instead of the more conventional PCA to identify local object properties and deviations from the normal pattern [Suinesiaputra et al., 2004].

10.6 Pattern recognition methods in image understanding

Pattern recognition methods (Chapter 9) appear frequently in image understanding—classification-based segmentation of multi-spectral images (satellite images, magnetic resonance medical images, etc.) is a typical example.

10.6.1 Classification-based segmentation

The basic idea of classification-based segmentation is the same as that of statistical pattern recognition. Consider a magnetic resonance image (MRI) of the brain, and suppose the problem is to find areas of white matter, gray matter, and cerebro-spinal fluid (WM, GM, CSF). Suppose the image data is available in two image modalities of multi-spin-echo images as *T2*-weighted and *PD*-weighted images (see Figure 10.23). As can be seen, neither single image can be used to detect the required areas reliably.

Gray-level values of pixels in particular image channels, their combinations, local texture features, etc., may be considered elements of a feature vector, one of which is assigned to each pixel. If an MR brain image is considered, four features, $PD, T2, PD - T2$, $PD \times T2$ may be used to construct the vector; subsequent classification-based understanding may be supervised or unsupervised.

If supervised methods are used for classification, a priori knowledge is applied to form a training set (see Figure 10.24a); classifier learning based on this training set was described in Section 9.2.4. In the image understanding stage, feature vectors derived from local multi-spectral image values of image pixels are presented to the classifier, which assigns a label to each pixel of the image. Image understanding is then achieved by pixel labeling; labels assigned to the MR brain image pixels can be seen in Figure 10.24b. Thus the understanding process segments a multi-spectral image into regions of known labels; in this case areas of white matter, gray matter, and cerebro-spinal fluid.

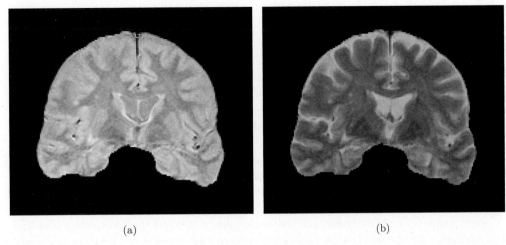

(a)   (b)

Figure 10.23: Magnetic resonance multi-spin-echo images. (a) *PD*-weighted. (b) *T2*-weighted. *Courtesy of N. Andreasen, G. Cohen, The University of Iowa.*

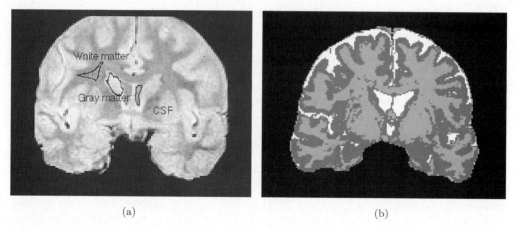

Figure 10.24: MR brain image labeling. (a) Training set construction. (b) Result of supervised classification labeling. *Courtesy of J. Parkkinen, University of Kuopio, G. Cohen, N. Andreasen, The University of Iowa.*

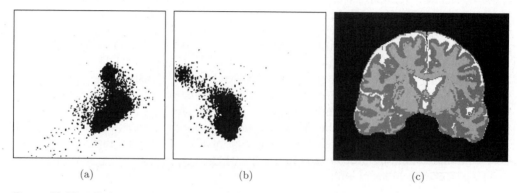

Figure 10.25: MR brain image labeling. (a) Clusters in feature space, (PD, $T2$) plane. (b) Clusters in feature space, ($PD, PD \times T2$) plane. (c) Result of unsupervised classification labeling. *Courtesy of J. Parkkinen, University of Kuopio, G. Cohen, N. Andreasen, The University of Iowa.*

Training set construction, and therefore human interaction, is necessary for supervised classification methods, but if unsupervised classification is used, this is avoided (see Section 9.2.6). As a result, the clusters and pixel labels do not have a one-to-one correspondence with the class meaning. This implies the image is segmented, but labels are not available to support image understanding. Fortunately, a priori information can often be used to assign appropriate labels to the clusters without direct human interaction. In the case of MR brain images, cerebro-spinal fluid is known always to form the brightest cluster, and gray matter to form the darkest cluster in *T2* pixel values; based on this information, clusters can be assigned appropriate labels. Cluster formation in feature space and results of unsupervised labeling are shown in Figure 10.25.

In the supervised classification of MR brain images, a Bayes minimum error classifier was applied, and the ISODATA method of cluster analysis was used for unsupervised labeling. Validation of results demonstrated high accuracy; further, both supervised and the unsupervised methods give almost identical results [Gerig et al., 1992]. Many other segmentation approaches use local and global image features and some of them utilize graph partitioning and data clustering [Wu and Leahy, 1993; Comaniciu and Meer, 1997].

10.6.2 Contextual image classification

The method presented above works well with non-noisy data, and if the spectral properties determine classes sufficiently well. If noise or substantial variations in in-class pixel properties are present, the resulting image segmentation may have many small (often one-pixel) regions, which are misclassified. Several standard approaches can be applied to avoid this misclassification, which is very common in classification-based labeling. All of them use contextual information to some extent [Kittler and Foglein, 1984a].

- We might apply a post-processing filter to a labeled image: small or single-pixel regions then disappear as the most probable label from a local neighborhood is assigned to them. This works well if the small regions are caused by noise. Unfortunately, they may result from true regions with different properties in the original multi-spectral image, and in this case such filtering would worsen labeling results. Post-processing filters are widely used in remote sensing applications (see Figure 10.26).

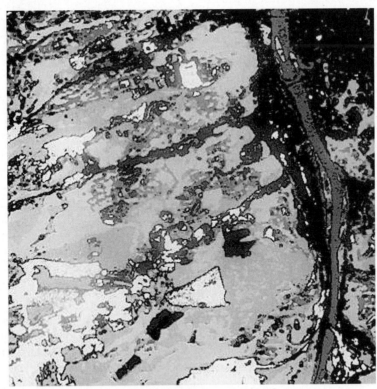

Figure 10.26: Remotely sensed data of Prague, Landsat Thematic Mapper. Unsupervised classification, post-processing filter applied: White—no vegetation (note the sport stadium), different shades of gray vegetation types and urban areas (shall be shown as different colors). *Courtesy of V. Cervenka, K. Charvat, Geodetic Institute Prague.*

- Pixel labels resulting from pixel classification in a given neighborhood can be used to form a new feature vector for each pixel, and a second-stage classifier based on the new feature vectors assigns final pixel labels. The contextual information is incorporated into the labeling process of the second-stage classifier learning [Wharton, 1982].

- Context may also be introduced in earlier stages, merging pixels into homogeneous regions and classifying these regions (see Chapter 6).

- Another contextual pre-processing approach is based on acquiring pixel feature descriptions from a pixel neighborhood. Mean values, variances, texture description, etc., may be added to (or may replace) original spectral data. This approach is very common in textured image recognition (see Chapter 15).

- Spectral and spatial information may be combined in the same stage of the classification process [Kittler and Foglein, 1984a,b; Kittler and Pairman, 1985]. The label assigned to each image pixel depends not only on multi-spectral gray-level properties of the particular pixel but also considers the context in the pixel neighborhood.

This section will discuss the last approach.

Contextual classification of image data is based on the Bayes minimum error classifier (Section 9.2.3, equation 9.17). For each pixel $\mathbf{x}_0$, a vector consisting of (possibly multi-spectral) values $f(\mathbf{x}_i)$ of pixels in a specified neighborhood $N(\mathbf{x}_0)$ is used as a feature representation of the pixel $\mathbf{x}_0$. Each pixel is represented by the vector

$$\boldsymbol{\xi} = \left(f(\mathbf{x}_0), f(\mathbf{x}_1), \ldots, f(\mathbf{x}_k) \right) , \tag{10.19}$$

where

$$\mathbf{x}_i \in N(\mathbf{x}_0) \quad i = 0, \ldots, k .$$

Some more vectors are defined which will be used later. Let labels (classification) of pixels in the neighborhood $N(\mathbf{x}_0)$ be represented by a vector (see Figure 10.27)

$$\boldsymbol{\eta} = (\theta_0, \theta_1, \ldots, \theta_k) , \tag{10.20}$$

where

$$\theta_i \in \{\omega_1, \omega_2, \ldots, \omega_R\}$$

and ω_s denotes the assigned class. Further, let the labels in the neighborhood excluding the pixel $\mathbf{x}_0$ be represented by a vector

$$\tilde{\boldsymbol{\eta}} = (\theta_1, \theta_2, \ldots, \theta_k) . \tag{10.21}$$

Theoretically, there may be no limitation on the neighborhood size, but the majority of contextual information is believed to be present in a small neighborhood of the pixel $\mathbf{x}_0$. Therefore, a 3×3 neighborhood in 4- or 8-connectivity is usually considered appropriate (see Figure 10.27) (computational demands increase exponentially with growth of neighborhood size).

A conventional minimum error classification method assigns a pixel $\mathbf{x}_0$ to a class ω_r if the probability of $\mathbf{x}_0$ being from the class ω_r is the highest of all possible classification probabilities (as given in equation 9.17):

$$\theta_0 = \omega_r \quad \text{if} \quad P\left(\omega_r | f(\mathbf{x}_0)\right) = \max_{s=1,\ldots,R} P\left(\omega_s | f(\mathbf{x}_0)\right) . \tag{10.22}$$

(a)   (b)

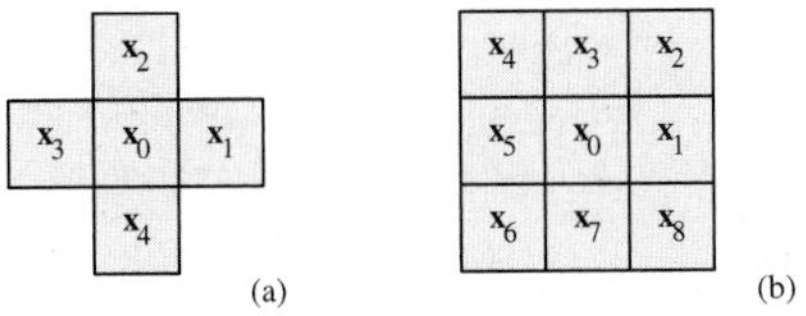

Figure 10.27: Pixel neighborhoods and indexing schemes used in contextual image classification. (a) 4-neighborhood. (b) 8-neighborhood. *© Cengage Learning 2015.*

A contextual classification scheme uses the feature vector $\boldsymbol{\xi}$ instead of $\mathbf{x}_0$, and the decision rule remains similar:

$$\theta_0 = \omega_r \quad \text{if} \quad P(\omega_r|\boldsymbol{\xi}) = \max_{s=1,\dots,R} P(\omega_s|\boldsymbol{\xi}) \,. \tag{10.23}$$

The a posteriori probability $P(\omega_s|\boldsymbol{\xi})$ can be computed using the Bayes formula

$$P(\omega_s|\boldsymbol{\xi}) = \frac{p(\boldsymbol{\xi}|\omega_s)P(\omega_s)}{p(\boldsymbol{\xi})} \,. \tag{10.24}$$

Note that each image pixel is classified using a corresponding vector $\boldsymbol{\xi}$ from its neighborhood, and so there are as many vectors $\boldsymbol{\xi}$ as there are pixels in the image. Many accompanying details, and a formal proof that contextual information increases classification reliability, are given in [Kittler and Foglein, 1984a]. The basic contextual classification algorithm can be summarized as follows.

Algorithm 10.10: Contextual image classification

1. For each image pixel, determine a feature vector $\boldsymbol{\xi}$ (equation 10.19).

2. From the training set, determine parameters of probability distributions $p(\boldsymbol{\xi}|\omega_s)$ and $P(\omega_s)$.

3. Compute maximum a posteriori probabilities $P(\omega_r|\boldsymbol{\xi})$ and label (classify) all pixels in the image according to equation (10.23). An image classification results.

A substantial limitation in considering larger contextual neighborhoods is exponential growth of computational demands with increasing neighborhood size. **Recursive contextual classification** overcomes these difficulties [Kittler and Foglein, 1984a,b; Kittler and Pairman, 1985]. The main trick of this method is in propagating contextual information through the image although the computation is still kept in small neighborhoods. Spectral and neighborhood pixel labeling information are both used in classification. Therefore, context from a distant neighborhood can propagate to the labeling θ_0 of the pixel $\mathbf{x}_0$; this is illustrated in Figure 10.28.

The vector $\tilde{\boldsymbol{\eta}}$ of labels in the neighborhood may further improve the contextual representation. Clearly, if the information contained in the spectral data in the neighborhood is unreliable (e.g., based on spectral data, the pixel $\mathbf{x}_0$ may be classified into a number of classes with similar probabilities), the information about labels in the neighborhood may increase confidence in one of those classes. If a majority of surrounding pixels are labeled as members of a class ω_i, the confidence that the pixel $\mathbf{x}_0$ should also be labeled ω_i increases.

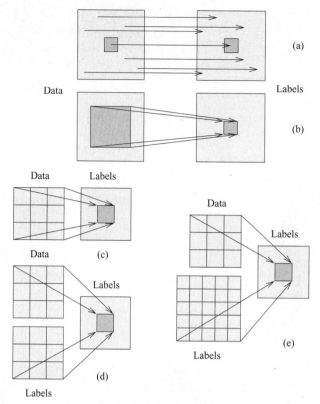

Figure 10.28: Principles of contextual classification. (a) Conventional non-contextual method. (b) Contextual method. (c) Recursive contextual method—step 1 of Algorithm 10.11. (d) First application of step 2. (e) Second application of step 2. © *Cengage Learning 2015.*

More complex dependencies may be found in the training set—for instance, imagine a thin striped noisy image. Considering labels in the neighborhood of the pixel $\mathbf{x}_0$, the decision rule becomes

$$\theta_0 = \omega_r \quad \text{if} \quad P(\omega_r|\boldsymbol{\xi}, \tilde{\boldsymbol{\eta}}) = \max_{s=1,\ldots,R} P(\omega_s|\boldsymbol{\xi}, \tilde{\boldsymbol{\eta}}) \, . \tag{10.25}$$

After several applications of the Bayes formula [Kittler and Pairman, 1985], the decision rule transforms into

$$\theta_0 = \omega_r \quad \text{if} \quad p(\boldsymbol{\xi}|\boldsymbol{\eta}_r)\, P(\omega_r|\tilde{\boldsymbol{\eta}}) = \max_{s=1,\ldots,R} p(\boldsymbol{\xi}|\boldsymbol{\eta}_s)\, P(\omega_s|\tilde{\boldsymbol{\eta}}) \, , \tag{10.26}$$

where $\boldsymbol{\eta}_r$ is a vector $\boldsymbol{\eta}$ with $\theta_0 = \omega_r$. Assuming necessary probability distribution parameters were determined in the learning process, the recursive contextual classification algorithm is:

Algorithm 10.11: Recursive contextual image classification

1. Determine an initial image pixel labeling using the non-contextual classification scheme, equation (10.22).

2. Update labels in each image pixel $\mathbf{x}_0$, applying the current label vectors $\boldsymbol{\eta}$, $\tilde{\boldsymbol{\eta}}$, and local spectral vector $\boldsymbol{\xi}$ to the decision rule equation (10.26).

3. Terminate if labels of all pixels in the image are stable; otherwise repeat 2.

Only a general outline of contextual classification methods has been given; for more details, discussion of convergence, other techniques, and specific algorithms, see [Kittler and Foglein, 1984a,b; Kittler and Pairman, 1985; Watanabe and Suzuki, 1989; Zhang et al., 1990]. A comparison of contextual classifiers is given in [Mohn et al., 1987; Watanabe and Suzuki, 1988], and a parallel implementation is described in [Tilton, 1987]. Contextual classification of textures based on the context of feature vectors is described in [Fung et al., 1990], and the application of neural networks to contextual image segmentation is given in [Toulson and Boyce, 1992].

A crucial idea is incorporated in the algorithm of recursive contextual image classification that will be seen several times in this chapter; this is information propagation from distant image locations without the necessity for expensive consideration of context in large neighborhoods. This approach is frequently used in image understanding.

10.6.3 Histograms of oriented gradients—HOG

A feature extraction chain that describes local object appearance and shape by constructing histograms of local intensity gradients has demonstrated great power [Dalal and Triggs, 2005]. It takes relatively coarse spatial context into consideration and employs a classifier to detect objects of interest. Locally normalized **histograms of oriented gradients** or **HOGs** build on earlier concepts like edge-oriented histograms [Freeman and Roth, 1995] and SIFT descriptors (Section 10.2) and utilize a classifier for object localization and recognition: linear SVMs (Section 9.2.5) were used in the original application, a very successful upright human detector [Dalal and Triggs, 2005]. The HOG description/recognition chain is shown in Figure 10.29.

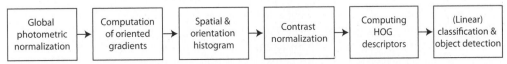

Figure 10.29: HOG-description chain for object detection and localization. The image window that is subjected to HOG description is covered by overlapping blocks, in which HOG features are computed and subsequently sent to a classifier. © *Cengage Learning 2015.*

An image region (**window**) is divided into smaller subregions (**cells**) and a local 1D histogram of gradient directions or edge orientations is constructed over all pixels of the cell. Configurations of several cells form **blocks** (Figure 10.30). As such, a specific configuration of adjacent image pixels forms a *cell*; a specific configuration of cells forms a *block*, and a number of blocks (possibly overlapping) can be used to cover the image *window* using a specific block/overlap grid. Therefore, defining the pixel/cell/block configurations and the block/window grid is part of the implementation.

As can be seen in Figure 10.29, contrast normalization is employed to gain insensitivity to illumination, shadowing, and other photometric transformations. Combined

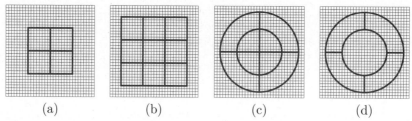

Figure 10.30: Examples of rectangular and circular blocks of cells that may be used in HOG descriptors. (a-d) The small squares corresponds to image pixels, each outlined area of pixels depicts a cell, and the respective configurations of cells give examples of block definitions. © *Cengage Learning 2015*.

histogram entries from an overlapping dense grid of local HOG descriptors form the final HOG description feature vector associated with the window. This feature vector is used for classification. The resulting HOG representation captures edge/gradient structure corresponding to the underlying local shape with controllable insensitivity to rotation and translation.

When analyzing the performance and behavior of HOG descriptors in the pedestrian detection task [Dalal and Triggs, 2005] (Figure 10.31), they outperformed Haar-wavelet (Section 3.2.7), SIFT (Section 10.2), and shape-context [Belongie et al., 2001] approaches.

Algorithm 10.12: HOG object detection and localization (Figure 10.29)

1. **Determination of window, cell, block sizes/shapes and overlap.** Based on the image detection task at hand, the size and shape of the image window must be determined (64×128 windows were used for pedestrian detection as shown in Figure 10.31; a sufficient margin around the object of interest should be included in the window—a 16-pixel margin was appropriate in the pedestrian detection case).

   Local information is binned in relatively small cells consisting of adjacent pixels, and the size and shape of the cells must be determined. Cells consisting of 6×6 to 8×8 pixels (6–8 pixel width corresponds to the width of a human limb) and organized in rectangular 2×2 or 3×3 blocks of cells were used in the pedestrian detection case. Alternatively, rectangular or circular blocks (of cells) may be defined. Figure 10.30 shows an example of rectangular and circular block options, among the many possible block designs. Rectangular cells are primarily used to construct the blocks due to their computational efficiency. Additionally, the block features are computed for overlapping blocks and therefore, a grid must be designed to determine parameters of the overlap.

2. **Photometric normalization.** Global image data normalization and gamma correction is performed over the entire image. Use of color (multi-band) image data is recommended when applicable and independent channel-specific gamma correction is recommended in that case.

3. **Computation of oriented gradients.** 1D or 2D directional gradient detectors with different levels of image smoothing can be used (higher-D gradient detectors are foreseeable in volumetric or higher-dimensional images). Most (if not

all) implementations employ a centered local 1D gradient detector [-1, 0, 1] with no smoothing ($\sigma = 0$, it was also reported to work best in the pedestrian detection case). The 1D gradient detectors are applied vertically and horizontally, equation (5.34) provides gradient direction. In color images, separate channel–specific image gradients can be computed and the largest-norm channel-specific gradient used.

4. **Spatial and orientation binning—constructing the histogram.** For each pixel of the analyzed cell, its gradient orientation is used to increment the respective histogram bin in proportion to the gradient magnitude. To gain invariance to minor orientation differences, these histogram bin contributions are linearly or bilinearly interpolated between the neighboring bin centers—each gradient direction thus contributes to several neighboring bins with interpolated weights. Histogram bins are evenly spaced over the $[0^o, 180^o)$ interval when working with unsigned gradients or over $[0^o, 360^o)$ when gradient orientation is used in addition to direction. Dense directional binning is important. 20° increments, leading to 9 bins, were shown to give good results in the pedestrian detection case when unsigned gradients were used—20° is quite small when dealing with edge direction differences. Signed gradients were shown appropriate in other applications.

5. **Contrast normalization:** To deal with positionally-varying gradient strengths due to illumination changes and foreground–background contrast differences, locally-sensed contrast must be normalized. Normalization is performed in blocks and each block is contrast-normalized separately (see equations 10.27–10.29 below, Figure 10.32, and [Dalal and Triggs, 2005; Dalal, 2006] for details). Even if individual blocks overlap, each (overlapping) block is normalized independently.

6. **Forming the final HOG descriptor.** A vector of components of normalized responses from each cell forming the block, and combined for all (overlapping) blocks in the detection window forms the final descriptor. The HOG descriptor is therefore associated with the entire window. The overlap of blocks allows local image information from individual cells to contribute to several block-based feature vectors, each of them subjected to a block-specific normalization, Figure 10.32e.

7. **Classification:** The HOG description vector is used for training and recognition employing any of the available feature-based classifier, working well with efficient linear classifiers—linear support vector machines performed very well for the pedestrian detection/localization task [Dalal and Triggs, 2005], Figure 10.32f,g.

8. **Object detection.** The detection window is moved across the image and the HOG description vector is obtained for all positions and scales. Non-maximum suppression (Section 5.3.5, Algorithm 6.4) is used for object detection and localization in the multi-scale image pyramid. PASCAL overlap non-maximal suppression is widely used and is (virtually) parameter-free [Everingham et al., 2010].

Figure 10.31: Example images used for HOG-based pedestrian detection/localization. © *2005 IEEE. Reprinted, with permission, from N. Dalal and B. Triggs, "Histograms of oriented gradients for human detection," Conference on Computer Vision and Pattern Recognition, pp. 886-893, 2005. A color version of this figure may be seen in the color inset—Plate 23.*

A number of contrast normalization schemes can be employed to construct HOG description features. If $\boldsymbol{\xi}$ is the non-normalized vector of histogram features, let $\|\boldsymbol{\xi}\|_k$ be its k-norm, $k = 1, 2$, and let ϵ be a small positive constant. The following normalization schemes were proposed and tested in [Dalal and Triggs, 2005; Dalal, 2006].

- **L2 norm**:

$$\boldsymbol{\xi} \to \frac{\boldsymbol{\xi}}{\sqrt{\|\boldsymbol{\xi}\|_2^2 + \epsilon^2}} \, . \tag{10.27}$$

- **L2-Hys norm**—L2 norm subjected to clipping, thus limiting the maximum to a pre-specified value—0.2 was shown to be appropriate—followed by an additional step of re-normalizing as in [Lowe, 2004].

- **L1 norm**:

$$\boldsymbol{\xi} \to \frac{\boldsymbol{\xi}}{\|\boldsymbol{\xi}\|_1 + \epsilon} \, . \tag{10.28}$$

- **L1-sqrt norm**—L1 norm followed by square root, thus effectively treating the descriptor vector as probability distributions:

$$\boldsymbol{\xi} \to \sqrt{\frac{\boldsymbol{\xi}}{\|\boldsymbol{\xi}\|_1 + \epsilon}} \, . \tag{10.29}$$

All four presented contrast normalization schemes markedly improve overall performance when compared to no normalization, but the simple L1 norm was least successful. Low sensitivity to the value of ϵ was observed.

The use of HOG descriptors has increased substantially since their introduction in [Dalal and Triggs, 2005; Dalal, 2006] and this approach is the most popular and successful person-detection approach in existence today. It has been adapted with some success to detect humans in difficult or unusual poses [Johnson and Everingham, 2011]. A number of other applications exist including human face detection, deer detection in thermal camera images to reduce animal–vehicle collisions, 3D extension to detect regions of interest in medical images, database image retrieval using hand-drawn shape sketches, and similar. There are several notable findings associated with the HOG descriptors. First, highly local gradients and their orientations, derived from non-smoothed images at fine scales, thus representing local abrupt edges, outperform features derived from smoothed image information. Second, the gradient orientation should be sampled quite

| (a) | (b) | (c) | (d) | (e) | (f) | (g) |

Figure 10.32: Example of HOG features when used for pedestrian detection. The detector is mostly responding to the pedestrian body contours (e.g., head, shoulders, feet). (a) Average gradient magnitude image constructed from all training samples. (b) Maximum positive weights of the SVM classifier, shown associated with individual blocks (larger and overlapping blocks, positioned at their center pixel). (c) Maximum negative weights of the SVM classifier. (d) Example test image window. (e) Rectangular HOG block descriptors from window (d). (f,g) Rectangular HOG block descriptors from window (d) weighted by positive (f) and negative (g) SVM weights. The linear SVM classifier correctly identifies window (d) as depicting a pedestrian. © *2005 IEEE. Reprinted, with permission, from N. Dalal and B. Triggs, "Histograms of oriented gradients for human detection," Conference on Computer Vision and Pattern Recognition, pp. 886-893, 2005. A color version of this figure may be seen in the color inset—Plate 24.*

finely. Third, spatial smoothing—applied after the local edge detection and performed at small blocks—can be relatively coarse. Fourth, local contrast normalization is essential for good performance and multiple independent local contrast normalizations can be combined in the overall descriptor—offering information redundancy that improves performance.

10.7 Boosted cascades of classifiers

The need for rapid face detection in a variety of images has motivated the development of a framework that is applicable to general object detection and object tracking tasks [Viola and Jones, 2001]. A key to its efficiency is use of the integral image described in Section 4.2.1 which is simple to calculate, and provides a very rich source of easily retrieved image information—the number of features that can be calculated far exceeds the number of image pixels. Learning based on AdaBoost (Section 9.8) selects a small number of well distinguishing features and yields a set of efficient classifiers: feature selection is performed using a modified AdaBoost algorithm in which the weak classifiers can only depend on a single feature [Tieu and Viola, 2004]. The classifiers are then ordered in a cascade sequence starting with simple and fast classifiers used for quickly rejecting object-detection hypotheses, to employing more complex and therefore more powerful but slower classifiers that however are applied only to the remaining hypotheses. This focus-of-attention approach is similar to the strategy we discussed in Section 6.4 where template matching was introduced and the need to quickly reject unlikely candidate locations was discussed. This strategy dramatically improves object detection speed.

The large number of features makes it likely that only a small proportion of them will be useful as classifiers: this small set can be selected using the AdaBoost algorithm.

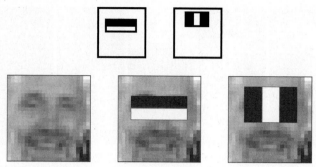

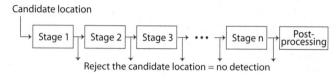

Figure 10.33: The first two classifiers that the algorithm finds used by the Viola Jones algorithm selected by Adaboost (first row). *Based on [Viola and Jones, 2001].* In the second row, an example of the algorithm in use.

Candidate location
→ Stage 1 → Stage 2 → Stage 3 → • • • → Stage n → Post-processing

Reject the candidate location = no detection

Figure 10.34: Detection cascade applied to each analyzed location–image subwindow. Early-stage simple classifiers reject less likely locations while maintaining a very low false negative rate. Later-stage more complex classifiers eliminate more and more false positives, while still set not to reject true positives. © *Cengage Learning 2015.*

In summary, 24×24 windows are processed using integral images; rectangles within the window are partitioned into 2, 3 or 4, and the partition is used as the basis of a simple difference measure. At each Adaboost iteration the best such is selected from the huge number available. For each selected feature, the weak learner finds an optimal threshold minimizing the number of misclassified examples from the training set. Each weak classifier is thus based on a single feature f_j and a threshold t_j

$$h_j(\mathbf{x}) = \quad 1 \quad \text{if} \quad p_j f_j(\mathbf{x}) < p_j t_j \ ,$$
$$\qquad\quad = -1 \quad \text{otherwise,} \tag{10.30}$$

where p_j is a polarity indicating the direction of the inequality sign and $\mathbf{x}$ is an image subwindow on which the individual rectangle features f_j are calculated. While no single feature will perform the overall classification task with low error, the sequential character of feature selection means that the features picked first have a relatively high classification success on their respective training sets (perhaps between 70% and 90%). Classifiers trained in later rounds on the remaining more difficult examples yield classification correctness of 50–60%. Algorithm 10.13 summarizes the process (cf. Algorithm 9.15).

Algorithm 10.13: Classifier generation for Viola-Jones face detection

1. Take a labeled data set of images $T = (I_1, \omega_1), (I_2, \omega_2), \ldots, (I_n, \omega_n)\}$ where $\omega_i \in \{-1, +1\}$ indicates the absence or presence of a face. Initialize weights $w_{1,j} = \frac{1}{2m}$ or $\frac{1}{2l}$ as ω_j is negative or positive respectively for $j = 1 \ldots n$, and m, l are the numbers of negatives and positives respectively. Set k=1.

2. Normalize the array $w_{k,j}$ to produce a probability distribution.

3. For each rectangular feature r_i train a classifier h_i and evaluate its error with respect to the weights. Choose the best performing, h_k, with error e_k.

4. Set

$$w_{k+1,j} = w_{k,j}\beta_k^{\delta_j}$$

where $\beta_k = \frac{e_k}{1-e_k}$ and $\delta_j = \{0,1\}$ as I_j is classified {incorrectly, correctly}.

5. Increment k and go to 2 until $k = K$, for some pre-determined limit K.

6. Use the classifier

$$h(I) = 1 \quad \text{if} \sum_{k=1}^{K} \alpha_k h_k(I) \geq \frac{1}{2}\sum_{k=1}^{K}\alpha_k, \tag{10.31}$$
$$= 0 \quad \text{otherwise}$$

where $\alpha_k = -\log(\beta_k)$.

Figure 10.35: Some of the training face images used in the face detection system based on the boosted cascade of classifiers. *Courtesy of P. Viola, Microsoft Live Labs and M. Jones, Mitsubishi Electric Research Labs. © 2001 IEEE. Reprinted, with permission, from P. Viola and M. Jones, "Rapid object detection using a boosted cascade of simple features," Proc. CVPR, pp. 511-518, IEEE, 2001.*

The first two classifiers that the algorithm finds are shown in Figure 10.33: the first corresponds to the frequent case when the eye region is darker than that of the nose and cheeks. The second exploits the fact that the eyes are usually darker compared to the bridge of the nose between them. The combination of the integral image approach and small number of very simple classifiers makes the overall algorithm exceptionally fast.

Once the most distinguishing features have been identified, a cascade of classifiers is built to both decrease processing time and increase performance. The early-stage simple classifiers are set so that their false negative rates (number of missed detections) is close to zero—of course, this results in an increase in the false positive rate (number of detections not corresponding to true objects). However, the simpler early stage classifiers are used to quickly reject the majority of candidate locations (subwindows in which features are computed). The increasingly complex classifiers are employed in the locations that remain unrejected. Ultimately, the remaining non-rejected locations are marked as the locations of identified objects.

Figure 10.34 shows this cascade of classifiers, a degenerate decision tree. For each location, classifier $n+1$ is only called if the classifier n has not rejected it. The classifiers in all individual stages are trained using AdaBoost and adjusted to minimize false negatives. In the case of face detection, a powerful first stage classifier can be constructed from the two features of Figure 10.33—this detects 100% of face objects with about 40% false positives. The later-stage classifiers have increasingly higher false-positive rates–but since they are only applied to the subset of high-likelihood locations, the likelihood of invoking these classifiers decreases with increased depth in the decision tree. The additional stages in the classifier cascade are added until overall requirements on detection performance are met. As can be expected, since the features are evaluated at multiple scales and the subwindows are allowed to overlap, there may be multiple detections for each detected object, coming from the overlapping subwindows. Such multiple detections must be post-processed to yield a single final detection per identified location in the image.

In detecting faces, the complete system [Viola and Jones, 2001] consisted of 38 stages and used over 6,000 features. Despite these large numbers, the system only required

(a)   (b)

Figure 10.36: Example results of face detection using boosted cascade classifiers. Each detection is identified by an overlaying rectangle. *Courtesy of P. Viola, Microsoft Live Labs and M. Jones, Mitsubishi Electric Research Labs. © 2001 IEEE. Reprinted, with permission, from P. Viola and M. Jones, "Rapid object detection using a boosted cascade of simple features," Proc. CVPR, pp. 511-518, IEEE, 2001.*

about 10 feature evaluations per subwindow. As such, it was achieving high detection speed on average even when tested on a difficult data set with 75 million subwindows and over 500 faces present in the image data. Figure 10.35 shows examples of the training face images, and Figure 10.36 shows face detection results obtained by the system—so successful has it become that it is widely applied in consumer digital cameras [Zhang and Zhang, 2010]. While a face detection problem was used to demonstrate the method, the approach itself is general and can be used for a variety of object detection and recognition tasks: Section 16.4 illustrates an important example.

10.8 Image understanding using random forests

Section 9.9 presented the main concepts of random forest classification and regression, and here we will focus on their use for image analysis and understanding for multi-class object detection that simultaneously uses the classification and regression capabilities. Random forests require large training datasets to be available and their generalization capabilities are not suited for small training datasets. All other things being equal, the size of the training dataset is the single most important parameter influencing random forest performance. A highly successful commercial use of random forests can be found in the Microsoft Kinect for XBox, in which they were trained on 900,000 examples of depth image data to recognize 31 separate human body parts of a human being in virtually any position and orientation. While such massive training requires substantial time to complete, and training a random forest consisting of merely three trees to a depth of 20 required one full day using a 1000 node cluster [Shotton et al., 2011], the body part detection runs at a frame rate of 200 frames per second on current commercial 2013 CPU/GPU hardware taking advantage of the natural parallelization of the recognition process. In this section specifics of employing random forests for image analysis and understanding as well as several examples are presented [Gall et al., 2012; Criminisi et al., 2011; Criminisi and Shotton, 2013; Shotton et al., 2011].

Compared to the general random forest method, use for image analysis has a number of specifics. Here, the classification capability of random forests will be used for object recognition and the regression capability will predict the object location. Recall that random forests are well suited for problems that require distinguishing among many object classes. First, the image is divided into patches of pre-determined size. To provide an image-based training set, each object of class ω_i is outlined by its bounding box and image patches falling within the bounding box are associated with a respective *class label*. For a patch to 'fall within' the box, either the entire patch or its center must be inside of the bounding box. Clearly, not requiring the entire patch to be located inside the object box permits better sampling of the object boundary information and is especially useful for tight bounding boxes. The remaining non-object patches of the image form background and are associated with a *background* label—of course, no bounding boxes are used to outline background. Patches may but do not have to be densely sampled: for each patch, a set of features is calculated—low-level features such as color, gradients, Gabor filter indices, and similar are frequently used since they can be computed efficiently. Alternatively, SIFT or SURF sparse features (Section 10.2) can be employed.

To inject randomness to the process, each tree $\mathcal{T}_t$ of the forest uses a randomly selected subset A_t of image patches for training. If an image patch is associated with an object label, an additional piece of information may be associated with each patch—for

Figure 10.37: Detection and localization of cars in outdoor scenes. Image patches associated with the 'car' class are shown in red, and those denoting background are shown in blue. Green vectors connect centers of individual non-background patches with a car-object reference point. *With kind permission from Springer Science+Business Media: Outdoor and Large-Scale Real-World Scene Analysis, "An introduction to random forests for multi-class object detection," 2012, pp. 243-263, J. Gall, N. Razavi, and L. Gool. A color version of this figure may be seen in the color inset—Plate 25.*

example, the distance from and orientation to a reference point of the training object may be associated with each training patch. This reference point may be class-specific or a center of the bounding box may be used for simplicity. It may become intuitively clear that recognizing an object patch as belonging to a specific object class and determining distance from and direction to its reference point may help recognize (classification) as well as locate (regression) the object in the recognition stage. Even at this early stage of description, the reader may notice a similarity with the Hough transform in which individual image features (usually edges) contribute to identification of an object instance in the accumulator space (Section 6.2.6). The exact definition of the reference point is of secondary importance as long as it is defined consistently across all training samples.

Since scale considerations are addressed during the recognition stage, image patches are all of the same size. In a number of applications, a patch size of 16×16 was shown appropriate for images that have been previously scaled so that the length of the bounding box outlining the object is about 100 pixels [Gall and Lempitsky, 2009]. Figure 10.37 shows examples of object and background image patches that are sized according to these recommendations. The tree-specific training set A_t consists of a set of patches P_i, which hold image, patch class information, and its relative location:

$$P_i = [\mathbf{I}_i, \omega_i, \mathbf{d}_i],\qquad(10.32)$$

where $\mathbf{I}_i$ holds the patch image information (e.g., as a set of calculated features), ω_i is the patch class label, and $\mathbf{d}_i$ is an offset vector from the patch center to the reference point. Since background patches are not associated with any reference point, a pseudo-offset of $\mathbf{d}_i = 0$ is used.

Each tree is trained in parallel as described in Section 9.9. Class probability and class-specific distribution of training patches need to be learned from the training set and associated with each leaf L from the set of all leaves, forming leaf-specific prediction models.

The leaf-specific class probability $p(\omega_r|L)$ can be derived from A^L_{t,ω_r}—the number of patches of class ω_r that arrive at leaf L of tree $\mathcal{T}_t$ after training, normalized to account for uneven distribution of classes in the training set of patches:

$$p(\omega_r|L) = \frac{|A^L_{t,\omega_r}| \cdot b_{t,\omega_r}}{\sum_{r=1,\dots,R}(|A^L_{t,\omega_r}| \cdot b_{t,\omega_r})},\qquad(10.33)$$

$$b_{t,\omega_r} = \frac{|A_t|}{|A_{t,\omega_r}|} , \qquad (10.34)$$

where A_t is the entire set used to train tree $\mathcal{T}_t$ and A_{t,ω_r} is a set of all patches in A_t belonging to class ω_r and R is the number of classes.

The class-specific spatial distribution of patches $p(\mathbf{d}|\omega_r, L)$ is derived from the offsets $\mathbf{d} \in D_{\omega_r}^L$ of all patches A_{t,ω_r}^L, where $D_{\omega_r}^L$ is the set of offsets associated with patches of class ω_r reaching node L. Figure 10.38 shows examples of leaf-specific statistics of trees for detection of cars in images from Figure 10.37.

In the detection stage, patches are densely sampled on previously unseen images and evaluated in each node of each tree forming the forest, starting at their roots to be sent to

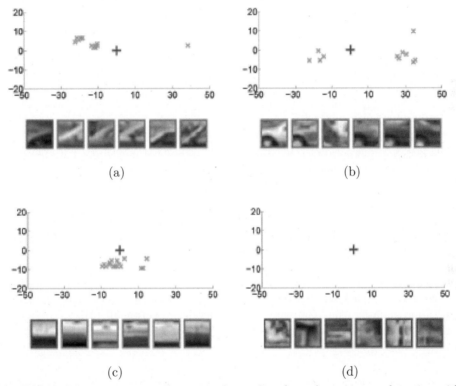

Figure 10.38: Information contained in several samples of tree leaves in car detection with a random forest (see Figure 10.37). Probabilities $p(\omega_r|L)$ that patches reach a specific tree leaf L are stored for each leaf and result from the relative numbers of positive (red) and negative (blue) examples that reach the leaf during training. The end-points of all offset vectors $\mathbf{d}$ are shown as green crosses for all positive examples (all negative examples have $\mathbf{d} = 0$). (a,c) The distribution of vectors $\mathbf{d}$ is frequently multimodal, showing correspondence of the positive patches with multiple object parts. (b) The wheel patches may be associated with either the front or the rear wheels. (d) The tree leaf associated with this panel only contains negative patches. © 2011 IEEE. Reprinted, with permission, from Gall, J., Yao, A., Razavi, N., Van Gool, L., Lempitsky, V., "Hough forests for object detection, tracking, and action recognition," IEEE Trans. Pattern Anal. Machine Intell, vol. 33, pp. 2188-2202, IEEE, 2011. A color version of this figure may be seen in the color inset—Plate 26.

one of the two child nodes until they reach a tree leaf. That way, each patch $P(\mathbf{y})$, where $\mathbf{y}$ denotes patch image location, eventually ends up in one of the tree leaves $L_t(\mathbf{y})$ per tree $\mathcal{T}_t$. To detect and localize an object in the image, contributions from multiple patches are considered and the patch configuration needs to point to a sufficiently consistent reference point $\mathbf{x}$, which then represents the location of the identified object. For this purpose, probabilities of object-class-and-location hypotheses $h_t(\omega_r, \mathbf{x}, s)$ need to be computed for each tree $\mathcal{T}_t$, each class ω_r, each reference point location $\mathbf{x}$, and each object scaling factor s.

For any patch located at $\mathbf{y}$, the single-tree probability that a patch $P(\mathbf{y})$ is associated with an object labeled ω_r at reference point $\mathbf{x}$ is calculated as [Gall et al., 2011]:

$$p(h_t(\omega_r, \mathbf{x}, s)|L_t(\mathbf{y})) = p(\mathbf{d}(\mathbf{x}, \mathbf{y}, s)|\omega_r, L_t(\mathbf{y}))p(\omega_r|L_t(\mathbf{y})) , \qquad (10.35)$$

where

$$\mathbf{d}(\mathbf{x}, \mathbf{y}, s) = \frac{s_u(\mathbf{y} - \mathbf{x})}{s} . \qquad (10.36)$$

Here, s_u represents the unit size of the training-object bounding box that is known from training. Similarly, probabilities $p(\mathbf{d}(\mathbf{x}, \mathbf{y}, s)|\omega_r, L_t(\mathbf{y}))$ and $p(\omega_r|L_t(\mathbf{y}))$ are known from training as explained above (see also equation 10.33). Note that distribution $p(h_t(\omega_r, \mathbf{x}, s)|L_t(\mathbf{y}))$ combines both the classification and regression aspects of the object detection and localization task.

As suggested earlier, a voting approach can be employed to approximate the distributions $p(\mathbf{d}(\mathbf{x}, \mathbf{y}, s)|\omega_r, L_t(\mathbf{y}))$. Let the distance vectors $\mathbf{d}$ associated with class ω_r and patch locations $\mathbf{y}$ that reached leaf L_t in tree $\mathcal{T}_t$ form a set $D_{\omega_r}^{L_t(\mathbf{y})}$. Then, equation (10.35) can be rewritten as

$$p(h_t(\omega_r, \mathbf{x}, s)|L_t(\mathbf{y})) = \frac{1}{|D_{\omega_r}^{L_t(\mathbf{y})}|} \left(\sum_{\mathbf{d} \in D_{\omega_r}^{L_t(\mathbf{y})}} \delta_{\mathbf{d}} \cdot \left(\frac{s_u(\mathbf{y} - \mathbf{x})}{s} \right) \right) p(\omega_r|L_t(\mathbf{y})) , \qquad (10.37)$$

where δ is a Dirac delta function. Equations (10.35–10.37) give the probabilities for a single tree. Figure 10.39 further demonstrates the approach. Alternatively, distributions can be approximated using Gaussian mixture models (Section 10.13).

Using an across-tree averaging approach (Section 9.9.2), a forest-based probability can be obtained

$$p(h(\omega_r, \mathbf{x}, s)|P(\mathbf{y})) = \frac{1}{T} \sum_t p(h_t(\omega_r, \mathbf{x}, s)|L_t(\mathbf{y})) . \qquad (10.38)$$

Using this forest-level probability, distribution over all patches and all trees results from accumulation

$$p(h(\omega_r, \mathbf{x}, s)|\mathbf{I}) = \frac{1}{|\mathcal{Y}|} \sum_{\mathbf{y} \in \mathcal{Y}} p(h_t(\omega_r, \mathbf{x}, s)|P(\mathbf{y})) , \qquad (10.39)$$

where $\mathbf{I}$ refers to the entire image and $\mathcal{Y}$ is the set of all patch locations $\mathbf{y}$. Applied to the image of Figure 10.39a at one scale, this equation yields a single strong mode shown in Figure 10.39c. Processing an image at multiple scales is demonstrated in Figure 10.40. To detect an object of scale s considering that the training objects were all scaled to a training size of s_u, each image needs to be scaled at s_u/s. Therefore, if all images

(a)   (b)   (c)   (d)

Figure 10.39: Pedestrian detection and localization using a random forest. (a) Three kinds of image patches are shown—head patch (red), foot patch (blue), background patch (green) (arrows). (b) Weighted votes of pedestrian's position, color coded with respect to which patch class contributes to a specific reference point location (equation 10.37). While the head patch class forms a single strong mode of possible reference point location (red), the foot patch class obtains similar responses from the left and right feet (blue), subsequently forming a two-mode response. A weak set of green responses (green arrow) with no clear mode(s) is associated with background patches. Here, the low probability of a background class to belong to the pedestrian object contributes to the low weights and overall weak response from background. (c) Accumulation of votes from all patches (equation 10.39 employed at one scale s)—a single strong mode emerges. (d) Pedestrian detection shown as a bounding box derived from the detected location of the reference point. © *2011 IEEE. Reprinted, with permission, from Gall, J., Yao, A., Razavi, N., Van Gool, L., Lempitsky, V., "Hough forests for object detection, tracking, and action recognition," IEEE Trans. Pattern Anal. Machine Intell, vol. 33, pp. 2188-2202, IEEE, 2011. A color version of this figure may be seen in the color inset—Plate 27.*

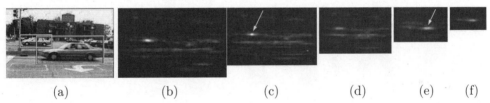

(a)   (b)   (c)   (d)   (e)   (f)

Figure 10.40: Objects are detected at multiple scales. (a) Two cars are marked in the original image, each located at a different distance from the observer. (b–f) Cars can be detected at multiple scales and locations by searching for modal maxima in the joint scale–location space. The larger car produces modal responses in panels (b–d) with a maximal modal peak associated with scale shown in panel (c). Similarly, the smaller car shows modal responses in panels (e–f) with a maximum shown in panel (e). *With kind permission from Springer Science+Business Media: Outdoor and Large-Scale Real-World Scene Analysis, "An introduction to random forests for multi-class object detection," 2012, pp. 243-263, J. Gall, N. Razavi, and L. Gool. A color version of this figure may be seen in the color inset—Plate 28.*

are scaled at all feasible scaling levels prior to being analyzed, the training-introduced scaling is already accounted for (equation 10.36) and object detection via identification of strong modes of equation (10.39) can be efficiently accomplished by employing mean shift mode detection (Section 7.1).

Many applications have emerged that use the random forest approach. Figures 10.41–10.43 show body part detection/localization from depth image data used in Microsoft Kinect for XBox [Shotton et al., 2011]. In this application, depth images consisting of 640×480 pixels are acquired at 30 frames per second at a depth-resolution of a few centimeters (Figure 10.41). These images are used to identify $R = 31$ body parts to

Figure 10.41: Employing random forests in Microsoft Kinect for XBox. (a) Original depth image (640 × 480 pixels), brightness corresponds to depth. (b) Color-coded ground truth for 31 body parts. (c) Reference point **x**′ associated with a patch at location **x**. *A. Criminisi, J. Shotton, and E. Konukoglu, Decision Forests for Classfication, Regression, Density Estimation, Manifold Learning and Semi-Supervised Learning. Microsoft Research technical report TR-2011-114. © 2012 Microsoft Corporation. All rights reserved. A color version of this figure may be seen in the color inset—Plate 29.*

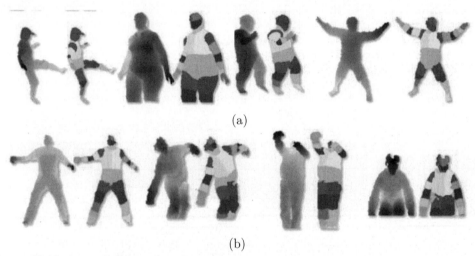

Figure 10.42: Examples of training and testing images with associated ground truth. (a) Training data consisted of a combination of real and synthetic depth datasets. (b) Real examples were used for testing. *© 2011 IEEE. Reprinted, with permission, from Shotton J., Fitzgibbon A., Cook M., Sharp T., Finocchio M., Moore R., Kipman A., and Blake A., "Real-time human pose recognition in parts from single depth images," Computer Vision and Pattern Recognition (CVPR), 2011 IEEE Conference, pp. 1297-1304, 2011. A color version of this figure may be seen in the color inset—Plate 30.*

which each image pixel belongs:

$$\omega_r \in \{\text{left/right hand, left/right shoulder, left/right elbow, neck, etc.}\}. \qquad (10.40)$$

Figure 10.42 shows examples of training and testing data.

Single-pixel image patches at location **x** are associated with depth-based features $f_{\mathbf{u},\mathbf{v}}(I, \mathbf{x})$

$$f_{\mathbf{u},\mathbf{v}}(I, \mathbf{x}) = d_I\left(\mathbf{x} \cdot \frac{\mathbf{u}}{d_I(\mathbf{x})}\right) - d_I\left(\mathbf{x} \cdot \frac{\mathbf{v}}{d_I(\mathbf{x})}\right), \qquad (10.41)$$

where $d_I(\mathbf{x})$ is depth at pixel **x** in image I, and **u** and **v** are two vectors representing two positional offsets with respect to **x**. These offsets therefore allow depth at **x** to be

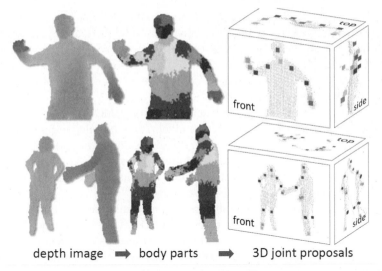

depth image ➡ body parts ➡ 3D joint proposals

Figure 10.43: Body parts are detected and localized in 3D. © *2011 IEEE. Reprinted, with permission, from Shotton J., Fitzgibbon A., Cook M., Sharp T., Finocchio M., Moore R., Kipman A., and Blake A., "Real-time human pose recognition in parts from single depth images," Computer Vision and Pattern Recognition (CVPR), 2011 IEEE Conference, pp. 1297-1304, 2011. A color version of this figure may be seen in the color inset—Plate 31.*

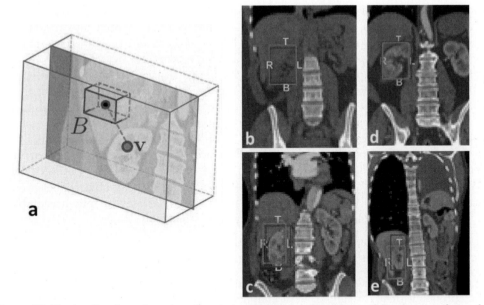

Figure 10.44: Application of random forests to 3D kidney detection and localization from abdominal X-ray CT images. (a) Distance vector between the center of a 3D patch and the reference point associated with a 3D kidney location is shown. (b–e) Example detections of kidneys show robustness of performance across subject-specific anatomical differences. Random-forest detections are shown in red while independent standard is in blue. *A. Criminisi, J. Shotton, and E. Konukoglu, Decision Forests for Classfication, Regression, Density Estimation, Manifold Learning and Semi-Supervised Learning. Microsoft Research technical report TR-2011-114. © 2012 Microsoft Corporation. All rights reserved. A color version of this figure may be seen in the color inset—Plate 31.*

simultaneously compared with depth at $\mathbf{x} + \mathbf{u}$ and depth at $\mathbf{x} + \mathbf{v}$, with $\mathbf{u}$ and $\mathbf{v}$ being parameters of this neighborhood depth comparison. The normalization factor $1/d_I(\mathbf{x})$ yields depth invariance of features and therefore 3D world coordinate invariance. These features together with pixel-based class information are used for training a random forest, which in the image analysis stage assigns one of the 32 labels to each image pixel (31 body part classes and background).

To obtain information about 3D positions of skeletal joints, the per-pixel information about body part labels must be pooled across pixels (for example) to find 3D centroids of all pixels with the same label. This approach however suffers from noise sensitivity and a mean-shift Gaussian-kernel weighted mode-finding approach was employed in the Kinect. Figure 10.43 demonstrates how three-dimensional information about the perceived body pose and location is provided by the described process.

Random forests are also finding applications in medical imaging. For example, whole-body segmentation of anatomical structures from 3D CT or MR image data and automatic detection of presence/absence of individual structures has been reported in [Criminisi et al., 2010]. Figure 10.44 demonstrates robustness of 3D kidney detection across subjects with natural anatomic variations.

10.9   Scene labeling and constraint propagation

Context plays a significant role in image understanding; the previous section considered context present in pixel data configurations, and this section considers **semantic** labeling of regions and objects. Assume that an image has been segmented into regions that correspond to objects or other entities, and let the objects and their interrelationships be described by a region adjacency graph and/or a semantic net (see Sections 4.2.3 and 9.1). Object properties are described by unary relations, and interrelationships between objects are described by binary (or n-ary) relations. Scene labeling then assigns a label (a meaning) to each image object to achieve an appropriate image interpretation.

The resulting interpretation should correspond with available scene knowledge. The labeling should be consistent, and if there is more than one interpretation should favor the most probable. Consistency means that no two objects of the image appear in an illegal configuration—e.g., an object labeled *house* in the middle of an object labeled *lake* will be considered inconsistent in most scenes. Conversely, an object labeled *house* surrounded by an object labeled *lawn* in the middle of a *lake* may be fully acceptable.

Two main approaches may be chosen to achieve this goal.

- **Discrete** labeling allows only one label to be assigned to each object in the final labeling. Effort is directed to achieving a consistent labeling all over the image.

- **Probabilistic** labeling allows multiple labels to co-exist in objects. Labels are probabilistically weighted, with a label confidence being assigned to each one.

The main difference is in interpretation robustness. Discrete labeling always either finds a consistent labeling or detects the impossibility of assigning consistent labels. Often, as a result of imperfect segmentation, discrete labeling fails to find a consistent interpretation even if only a small number of local inconsistencies is detected. Probabilistic labeling always gives an interpretation result together with a measure of confidence in the interpretation. Even if the result may be locally inconsistent, it often gives a better interpretation than a consistent and possibly unlikely interpretation resulting from a discrete labeling. Note that discrete labeling may be considered a special case of probabilistic labeling with one label probability always being 1 and all the others being 0 for each object.

The scene labeling problem is specified by:

- A set of objects R_i, $i = 1, \ldots, N$.

- A finite set of labels Ω_i for each object R_i (without loss of generality, the same set of labels will be considered for each object; $\Omega_i = \Omega_j$ for any $i, j \in [1, \ldots, N]$).

- A finite set of relations between objects.

- A compatibility function (reflecting constraints) between interacting objects.

To solve the labeling problem considering direct interaction of all objects in an image is computationally very expensive and approaches to solving labeling problems are usually based on **constraint propagation**. This means that local constraints result in local consistencies (local optima), and by applying an iterative scheme the local consistencies adjust to global consistencies (global optima) in the whole image.

Many types of relaxation exist, some, such as simulated annealing (Section 9.6.2), and stochastic relaxation [Geman and Geman, 1984] are used in statistical physics. Others, such as **relaxation labeling**, are typical in image understanding. To provide a better understanding of the idea, discrete relaxation is considered first.

10.9.1 Discrete relaxation

Consider the scene shown in Figure 10.45a. Six objects are present in the scene, including the background. Let the labels be *background (B), window (W), table (T), drawer (D), phone (P)*, and let the unary properties of object interpretations be (the example is meant to be illustrative only):

- A window is rectangular.

- A table is rectangular.

- A drawer is rectangular.

Let the binary constraints be:

- A window is located above a table.

- A phone is above a table.

- A drawer is inside a table.

- Background is adjacent to the image border.

Given these constraints, the labeling in Figure 10.45b is inconsistent. Discrete relaxation assigns all existing labels to each object and iteratively removes labels which may not be assigned to an object without violating the constraints. A possible relaxation sequence is shown in Figure 10.46.

At the beginning (Figure 10.46a), all labels are assigned to each object, and for each object all its labels are tested for consistency. Therefore, the label B can immediately be

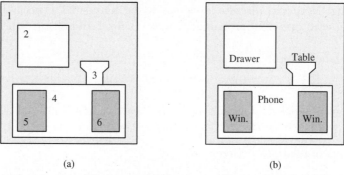

Figure 10.45: Scene labeling. (a) Scene example. (b) Inconsistent labeling. © *Cengage Learning 2015.*

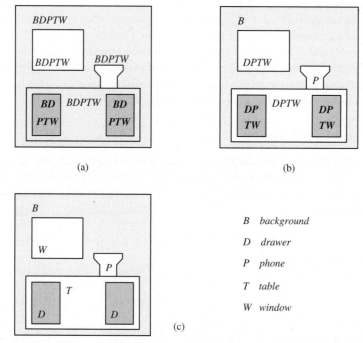

Figure 10.46: Discrete relaxation. (a) All labels assigned to each object. (b) Locally inconsistent labels are removed. (c) Final consistent labeling. © *Cengage Learning 2015.*

removed as inconsistent in objects 2, 3, 4, 5, and 6. Similarly, object 3 is not rectangular, therefore it violates the unary relation that must hold for T, W, D, etc.

The final consistent labeling is given in Figure 10.46c; note the mechanism of constraint propagation. The distant relations between objects may influence labeling in distant locations of the scene after several steps, making it possible to achieve a global labeling consistency of the scene interpretation although all the label-removing operations are local.

Algorithm 10.14: Discrete relaxation

1. Assign all possible labels to each object, considering the unary constraints.

2. Repeat steps 3–5 until global consistency is achieved or is found to be impossible.

3. Choose one object to update its labels.

4. Modify (delete inconsistent) labels of the chosen object by considering relations with other interacting objects.

5. If any object has no label, stop—a consistent labeling was not found.

The algorithm may be implemented in parallel with one difference: step 4 disappears as all objects are treated in parallel.

For a more detailed survey of discrete relaxation techniques, their properties, and technical difficulties that limit their applicability, see [Hancock and Kittler, 1990]. Although discrete relaxation is naturally parallel, a study of the complexity of discrete relaxation given in [Kasif, 1990] shows that a parallel solution is unlikely to improve known sequential solutions much.

10.9.2   Probabilistic relaxation

Constraints are a typical tool in image understanding. Discrete relaxation results in an unambiguous labeling; in a majority of real situations, however, it represents an over-simplified approach to image data understanding—it cannot cope with incomplete or imprecise segmentation. Using semantics and knowledge, image understanding is supposed to solve segmentation problems which cannot be solved by bottom-up interpretation approaches. Probabilistic relaxation may overcome the problems of missing objects or extra regions in the scene, but it results in an ambiguous image interpretation which is often inconsistent. It has been noted that a locally inconsistent but very probable (global) interpretation may be more valuable than a consistent but unlikely interpretation (e.g., a non-rectangular window located far above the table would be considered a phone in our example; this labeling would be consistent, even if very unlikely—see Figure 10.47).

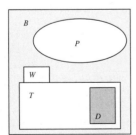

Figure 10.47: Consistent but unlikely labeling. © *Cengage Learning 2015*.

Consider the relaxation problem as specified above (regions R_i and sets of labels Ω_i) and, in addition, let each object R_i be described by a set of unary properties X_i. Similarly to discrete relaxation, object labeling depends on the object properties and on a measure of compatibility of the potential object labels with the labeling of other, directly interacting objects. All the image objects may be considered directly interacting, and a general form of the algorithm will be given assuming this. Nevertheless, only adjacent objects are usually considered to interact directly, to reduce computational demands of the relaxation. However, as before, more distant objects still interact with each other as a result of the constraint propagation. A region adjacency graph is usually used to store the adjacency information.

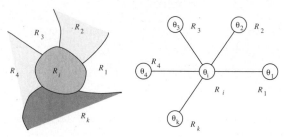

Figure 10.48: Local configuration of objects in an image—part of a region adjacency graph. © *Cengage Learning 2015.*

Consider the local configuration of objects given in Figure 10.48; let the objects R_j be labeled by θ_j; $\theta_j \in \Omega$; $\Omega = \{\omega_1, \omega_2, \ldots, \omega_R\}$. Confidence in the label θ_i of an object R_i depends on the configuration of labels of directly interacting objects. Let $r(\theta_i = \omega_k, \theta_j = \omega_l)$ represent the value of a compatibility function for two interacting objects R_i and R_j with labels θ_i and θ_j (the probability that two objects with labels θ_i and θ_j appear in a specific relation). The relaxation algorithm [Rosenfeld et al., 1976] is iterative and its goal is to achieve the locally best consistency in the entire image. The **support** q_j^s for a label θ_i of the object R_i resulting from the binary relation with the object R_j at the sth step of the iteration process is

$$q_j^s(\theta_i = \omega_k) = \sum_{l=1}^{R} r(\theta_i = \omega_k, \theta_j = \omega_l)\, P^s(\theta_j = \omega_l)\,, \tag{10.42}$$

where $P^s(\theta_j = \omega_l)$ is the probability that region R_j should be labeled ω_l. The support Q^s for the same label θ_i of the same object R_i resulting from all N directly interacting objects R_j and their labels θ_j at the sth step is

$$Q^s(\theta_i = \omega_k) = \sum_{j=1}^{N} c_{ij} q_j^s(\theta_i = \omega_k)$$
$$= \sum_{j=1}^{N} c_{ij} \sum_{l=1}^{R} r(\theta_i = \omega_k, \theta_j = \omega_l)\, P^s(\theta_j = \omega_l)\,, \tag{10.43}$$

where c_{ij} are positive weights satisfying $\sum_{j=1}^{N} c_{ij} = 1$. The coefficients c_{ij} represent the strength of interaction between objects R_i and R_j. Originally [Rosenfeld et al., 1976], an updating formula was given which specified the new probability of a label θ_i according to the previous probability $P^s(\theta_i = \omega_k)$ and probabilities of labels of interacting objects,

$$P^{s+1}(\theta_i = \omega_k) = \frac{1}{K} P^s(\theta_i = \omega_k)\, Q^s(\theta_i = \omega_k)\,, \tag{10.44}$$

where K is a normalizing constant

$$K = \sum_{l=1}^{R} P^s(\theta_i = \omega_l) \, Q^s(\theta_i = \omega_l) \,. \tag{10.45}$$

This form of the algorithm is usually referred to as a **non-linear relaxation scheme**. A **linear scheme** looks for probabilities such as

$$P(\theta_i = \omega_k) = Q(\theta_i = \omega_k) \quad \text{for all } i, k \tag{10.46}$$

with a non-contextual probability

$$P^0(\theta_i = \omega_k) = P(\theta_i = \omega_k | X_i) \tag{10.47}$$

being used only to start the relaxation process [Elfving and Eklundh, 1982].

Relaxation can also be treated as an optimization problem, the goal being maximization of the global confidence in the labeling [Hummel and Zucker, 1983]. The global objective function is

$$F = \sum_{k=1}^{R} \sum_{i=1}^{N} P(\theta_i = \omega_k) \sum_{j=1}^{N} c_{ij} \sum_{l=1}^{R} r(\theta_i = \omega_k, \theta_j = \omega_l) \, P(\theta_j = \omega_l) \tag{10.48}$$

subject to the constraint that the solution satisfies

$$\sum_{k=1}^{R} P(\theta_i = \omega_k) = 1 \quad \text{for any } i, \qquad P(\theta_i = \omega_k) \geq 0 \quad \text{for any } i, k \,. \tag{10.49}$$

Optimization approaches to relaxation can be generalized to allow n-ary relations among objects. A projected gradient ascent method [Hummel and Zucker, 1983] may be used to optimize equation (10.48), and an efficient version of this updating principle is introduced in [Parent and Zucker, 1989].

Convergence is an important property of iterative algorithms; as far as relaxation is concerned, convergence problems have not yet been satisfactorily solved. Although convergence of a discrete relaxation scheme can always be achieved by an appropriate design of the label updating scheme (e.g., to remove the inconsistent labels), convergence of more complex schemes where labels may be added, or of probabilistic relaxation, often cannot be guaranteed mathematically. Despite this fact, the relaxation approach may still be quite useful. Relaxation algorithms remain one of the cornerstones of the high-level vision understanding processes.

Relaxation algorithms are naturally parallel, since label updating may be done on all objects at the same time. Many parallel implementations exist, and parallel relaxation does not differ in essence from the serial version. A general version is:

Algorithm 10.15: Probabilistic relaxation

1. Define conditional probabilities of interpretations (labels) for all objects R_i in the image (e.g., using equation 10.47).

2. Repeat steps 3 and 4 until the best scene interpretation (a maximum of the objective function F) is reached.

3. Compute the objective function F (equation 10.48), which represents the quality of the scene labeling.

4. Update probabilities of object interpretations (labels) to increase the value of the objective function F.

Parallel implementations of relaxation algorithms can be found in [Kamada et al., 1988; Zen et al., 1990].

A problem with relaxation is that labeling can improve rapidly during early iterations, followed by a degradation which may be very severe. The reason is that the search for the global optimum over the image may cause highly non-optimal local labeling. A possible treatment that allows spatial consistency to be developed while avoiding labeling degradation is based on decreasing the neighborhood influence with the iteration count [Lee et al., 1989]. For a survey and an extensive list of references, see [Kittler and Illingworth, 1985; Kittler and Foglein, 1986; Kittler and Hancock, 1989]. A compact theoretical basis for probabilistic relaxation and close relations to the contextual classification schemes is given in [Kittler, 1987]. Improvements of algorithms for probabilistic relaxation can be found in [Lu and Chung, 1994; Christmas et al., 1996; Pelillo and Fanelli, 1997].

10.9.3   Searching interpretation trees

Relaxation is not the only way to solve discrete labeling problems, and classical methods of **interpretation tree** searching may be applied. A tree has as many levels as there are objects present in the scene; nodes are assigned all possible labels, and a depth-first search based on back-tracking is applied. Starting with a label assigned to the first object node (tree root), a consistent label is assigned to the second object node, to the third, etc. If a consistent label cannot be assigned, a back-tracking mechanism changes the label of the closest node at the higher level. All label changes are done in a systematic way.

An interpretation tree search tests all possible labellings, and therefore computational inefficiency is common, especially if an appropriate tree pruning algorithm is not available. An efficient method for searching interpretation trees was introduced in [Grimson and Lozano-Perez, 1987]. The search is heuristically guided towards a *good* interpretation based on a *quality of match* that is based on constraints and may thus reflect feasibility of the interpretation. Clearly, an infeasible interpretation makes all interpretations represented down the tree infeasible also. To represent the possibility of discarding the evaluated patch, an additional interpretation tree branch is added to each node. The general strategy is based on a depth-first approach in which the search is for the *best* interpretation. However, the search for the best solution can be very time consuming.

There have been many attempts to improve on the basic idea of the Grimson Lozano-Perez algorithm—a useful summary may be found in [Fisher, 1994]. Typically, correct interpretations are determined early on, and considerable time is spent by attempts to improve them further. Thus, a *cut-off* threshold is used to discontinue the search for an interpretation when the cut-off threshold is exceeded. This approach was found to be highly significant in improving the search times without adversely affecting the search results [Grimson and Lozano-Perez, 1987; Grimson, 1990]. [Fisher, 1993] divides a model into a tree of progressively smaller submodels which are combined to produce an overall match, while [Fletcher et al., 1996] uses a coarse-to-fine approach to describing features of surfaces to be matched (in this case, 3D data derived from MR head scans).

Yet another approach has demonstrated practical applicability for assessing similarity of medical images for database retrieval. Here, Voronoi diagrams representing arrangement of regions in an image (Section 4.2.3) were used together with a tree-based metric representing Voronoi diagram similarity [Tagare et al., 1995]. The approach presented in Section 10.7 is a very widely used example of a fast and efficient use of a classifier cascade organized in a decision tree [Viola and Jones, 2001; Viola et al., 2003].

10.10 Semantic image segmentation and understanding

This section presents a higher-level extension of region growing methods which were discussed in Section 6.3. It is presented here since it includes image region interpretation and may result in image understanding, and assumes an understanding of region growing, object description, minimum error classification, contextual classification, image understanding strategies, etc.

Algorithms already discussed in Section 6.3 merge regions on the basis of general heuristics using local properties of regions, and may be considered syntactic information-based methods. Conversely, semantic information representing higher-level knowledge was included in [Feldman and Yakimovsky, 1974] for the first time. It is intuitively clear that including more information, especially information about assumed region interpretation, can have a beneficial effect on the merging process, and it is also clear that context and criteria for global optimization of region interpretation consistency will also play an important role. Further, the approaches described here serve as examples of incorporating context, semantics, applying relaxation methods to propagate constraints, and show how the global consistency function may be optimized—for applications, see also [Cabello et al., 1990; Strat and Fischler, 1991].

The first issue in semantic region growing is the representation of image regions and their interrelationships, for which we use the region adjacency graph, introduced in Section 4.2.3. An artificial region may surround the image in order to treat all regions consistently. A dual graph can be constructed from the region adjacency graph in which nodes correspond to intersecting points of boundary segments of different regions and

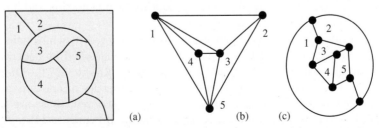

Figure 10.49: Region adjacency graphs. (a) Segmented image. (b) Region adjacency graph. (c) Dual graph. © *Cengage Learning 2015*.

arcs correspond to boundary segments. An example of a region adjacency graph and its dual is shown in Figure 10.49. Each time two regions are merged, both graphs change— the following algorithm [Ballard and Brown, 1982] describes how to update the region adjacency graph and its dual after merging two regions R_i and R_j.

Algorithm 10.16: Updating a region adjacency graph and dual to merge two regions

1. *Region adjacency graph*

   (a) Add all nonexistent arcs connecting region R_i and all regions adjacent to R_j.

   (b) Remove the node R_j and all its arcs from the graph.

2. *Dual graph*

   (a) Remove all arcs corresponding to the boundaries between regions R_i, R_j.

   (b) For each node associated with these arcs:

   - If the number of arcs associated with the node is equal to 2, remove this node and combine the arcs into a single one.
   - If the number of arcs associated with the node is larger than 2, update the labels of arcs that corresponded to parts of borders of region R_j to reflect the new region label R_i.

The region adjacency graph is one in which costs are associated with both nodes and arcs, implying that an update of these costs must be included in the given algorithm as node costs change due to the connecting two regions R_i and R_j.

10.10.1 Semantic region growing

Consider remotely sensed photographs, in which regions can be defined with interpretations such as *field, road, forest, town*, etc. It then makes sense to merge adjacent regions with the same interpretation into a single region. The problem is that the interpretation of regions is not known and the region description may give unreliable interpretations. In such a situation, it is natural to incorporate context into the region merging using a priori knowledge about relations (unary, binary) among adjacent regions, and then to apply constraint propagation to achieve globally optimal segmentation and interpretation throughout the image.

A region merging segmentation scheme is now considered in which semantic information is used in later steps, with the early steps being controlled by general heuristics similar to those given in Section 6.3 [Feldman and Yakimovsky, 1974]. Only after the preliminary heuristics have terminated are semantic properties of existing regions evaluated, and further region merging is either allowed or restricted; these are steps 4 and 6 of the algorithm. The same notation is used as in the previous section: A region R_i has properties X_i, its possible labels are denoted $\theta_i \in \{\omega_1, \ldots, \omega_R\}$, and $P(\theta_i = \omega_k)$ represents the probability that the interpretation of the region R_i is ω_k.

Algorithm 10.17: Semantic region merging

1. Initialize a segmentation with many small regions.

2. Merge all adjacent regions that have at least one weak edge on their common boundary.

3. For preset constants c_1 and c_2, and threshold T_1, merge neighboring regions R_i and R_j if $S_{ij} \leq T_1$, where

$$S_{ij} = \frac{c_1 + a_{ij}}{c_2 + a_{ij}} \qquad a_{ij} = \frac{(\text{area}_i)^{1/2} + (\text{area}_j)^{1/2}}{\text{perimeter}_i \ \ \text{perimeter}_j}. \qquad (10.50)$$

4. For all adjacent regions R_i and R_j, compute the conditional probability P that their mutual border B_{ij} separates them into two regions of the same interpretation ($\theta_i = \theta_j$), equation (10.53). Merge regions R_i and R_j if P is larger than a threshold T_2. If no two regions can be so merged, continue with step 5.

5. For each region R_i, compute the initial conditional probabilities

$$P(\theta_i = \omega_k | X_i) \quad k = 1, \ldots, R. \qquad (10.51)$$

6. Repeat this step until all regions are labeled as *final*. Find a *non-final* region with the highest confidence C_i in its interpretation (equation 10.55); label the region with this interpretation and mark it as *final*. For each *non-final* region R_j and each of its possible interpretations $\omega_k, k = 1, \ldots, R$, update the probabilities of its interpretations according to equation (10.56).

The first three steps of the algorithm do not differ in essence from Algorithm 6.17, but the final two steps, where semantic information has been incorporated, are very different and represent a variation of a serial relaxation algorithm combined with a depth-first interpretation tree search. The goal is to maximize an objective function

$$F = \prod_{i,j=1,\ldots,R} P\big(B_{ij} \text{ is between } \theta_i, \theta_j | X(B_{ij})\big) \prod_{i=1,\ldots,R} P(\theta_i | X_i) \prod_{j=1,\ldots,R} P(\theta_j | X_j) \quad (10.52)$$

for a given image partition.

The probability that a border B_{ij} between two regions R_i and R_j is a false one must be found in step 4. This probability P can be found as a ratio of conditional probabilities; let P_t denote the probability that the boundary should remain, and P_f denote the probability that the boundary is false (i.e., should be removed and the regions should be merged), and $X(B_{ij})$ denote properties of the boundary B_{ij}: then

$$P = \frac{P_f}{P_t + P_f}, \qquad (10.53)$$

where

$$P_f = \sum_{k=1}^{R} P\big[\theta_i = \theta_j | X(B_{ij})\big] P(\theta_i = \omega_k | X_i) P(\theta_j = \omega_k | X_j),$$

$$P_t = \sum_{k=1}^{R} \sum_{l=1; k \neq l}^{R} P\big[\theta_i = \omega_k \text{ and } \theta_j = \omega_l | X(B_{ij})\big]\, P(\theta_i = \omega_k | X_i)\, P(\theta_j = \omega_l | X_j)\,. \quad (10.54)$$

The confidence C_i of interpretation of the region R_i (step 6) can be found as follows: let θ_i^1, θ_i^2 represent the two most probable interpretations of region R_i. Then

$$C_i = \frac{P(\theta_i^1 | X_i)}{P(\theta_i^2 | X_i)}\,. \quad (10.55)$$

After assigning the final interpretation θ_f to a region R_f, interpretation probabilities of all its neighbors R_j (with *non-final* labels) are updated to maximize the objective function (10.52):

$$P_{\text{new}}(\theta_j) = P_{\text{old}}(\theta_j)\, P\big(B_{fj} \text{ is between regions labeled } \theta_f, \theta_j | X(B_{fj})\big)\,. \quad (10.56)$$

The computation of these conditional probabilities is costly in time, and it is customary to precompute them and refer to table values during processing. This table will have been constructed with suitable sampling.

It should be understood that appropriate models of the interrelationship between region interpretations, the collection of conditional probabilities, and methods of confidence evaluation must be specified to implement this approach.

10.10.2 Genetic image interpretation

The previous section described an early semantic region growing method, which is still conceptually up to date. However, there is a fundamental problem in the region growing segmentation approach—the results are sensitive to the split/merge order (see Section 6.3). The conventional approach usually results in an under-segmented or an over-segmented image. It is practically impossible to stop the region growing process with a high confidence that there are neither too many nor too few regions in the image.

A method [Pavlidis and Liow, 1990] was mentioned in Section 6.3.3 in which region growing always resulted in an over-segmented image and post-processing steps were used to remove false boundaries. A similar approach of removing false over-segmented regions can be found in a conceptually very different knowledge-based morphological region growing algorithm based on watersheds for graphs [Vincent and Soille, 1991]. Further, conventional region growing approaches are based on evaluation of homogeneity criteria and the goal is either to split a non-homogeneous region or to merge two regions, which may form a homogeneous region. Remember that the result is sensitive to the merging order; therefore, even if a merge results in a homogeneous region, it may not be optimal. In addition, there is no mechanism for seeking the optimal merges. Consequently, the semantic approach to segmentation and interpretation starts with an over-segmented image in which some merges are not best possible. The semantic process then tries to locate the maximum of some objective function by grouping regions which may already be incorrect and is therefore trying to obtain an optimal image interpretation from partially processed data where some significant information has already been lost. Further, conventional semantic region growing merges regions in an interpretation level only and does not evaluate properties of newly merged regions. It often ends in a local optimum of region labeling; the global optimum is not found because of the character of the optimization. Unreliable image segmentation and interpretation of complex images results.

The **genetic** image interpretation method solves these basic problems in the following manner.

- Both region merging and splitting is allowed; no merge or split is ever final, a better segmentation is looked for even if the current segmentation is already good.

- Semantics and higher-level knowledge are incorporated into the main segmentation process, not applied as post-processing after the main segmentation steps are over.

- Semantics are included in an objective evaluation function (that is similar to conventional semantic-based segmentation).

- In contrast to conventional semantic region growing, any merged region is considered a contiguous region in the semantic objective function evaluation, and all its properties are measured.

- The method does not seek local maxima; its search is likely to yield an image segmentation and interpretation specified by a (near) global maximum of an objective function.

The genetic image interpretation method is based on a *hypothesize and verify* principle (Section 10.1.4). An objective function (similar to the objective functions used in previous sections) which evaluates the quality of a segmentation and interpretation is optimized by a genetic algorithm (presented in Section 9.6.1). The method is initialized with an over-segmented image called a **primary segmentation**, in which starting regions are called **primary regions**. Primary regions are repeatedly merged into current regions during the segmentation process. The genetic algorithm is responsible for generating new populations of feasible image segmentation and interpretation hypotheses.

An important property of genetic algorithms is that the whole population of segmentations is tested in a single processing step, in which better segmentations survive and others die (see Section 9.6.1). If the objective function suggests that some merge of image regions was a good merge, it is allowed to survive into the next generation (the code string describing that particular segmentation survives), while bad region merges are removed (their description code strings die).

The **primary region adjacency graph** is the adjacency graph describing the primary image segmentation. The **specific region adjacency graph** represents an image after the merging of all adjacent regions of the same interpretation into a single region (collapsing the primary region adjacency graph). The genetic algorithm requires any member of the processed population to be represented by a code string. Each primary region corresponds to one element in the code string; this correspondence is made once at the beginning of the segmentation/interpretation process. A region interpretation is given by the current code string in which each primary region of the image corresponds uniquely to some specific position. Each feasible image segmentation defined by a generated code string (segmentation hypothesis) corresponds to a unique specific region adjacency graph. The specific region adjacency graphs serve as tools for evaluating objective segmentation functions. The specific region adjacency graph for each segmentation is constructed by collapsing a primary region adjacency graph.

Design of a segmentation optimization function (the fitness function in genetic algorithms) is crucial. The genetic algorithm is responsible for finding an optimum of the objective function, which must really represent segmentation optimality. To achieve this, the function must be based on properties of image regions and on relations between the regions—a priori knowledge about the desired segmentation must be included in the optimization criterion.

An applicable objective function may be similar to that given in equation (10.48), keeping in mind that the number of regions N is not constant since it depends on the segmentation hypothesis.

The conventional approach evaluates image segmentation and interpretation confidences of all possible region interpretations. Based on the region interpretations and their confidences, the confidences of neighboring interpretations are updated, some being supported and others becoming less probable. This conventional method can easily end at a consistent but suboptimal image segmentation and interpretation. In the genetic approach, the algorithm is fully responsible for generating new and increasingly better hypotheses about image segmentation. Only these hypothetical segmentations are evaluated by the objective function (based on a corresponding specific region adjacency graph). Another significant difference is in the region property computation—as mentioned earlier, a region consisting of several primary regions is treated as a single region in the property computation process which gives a more appropriate region description.

Optimization criteria consist of three parts. Using the same notation as earlier, the objective function consists of:

- A confidence in interpretation θ_i of region R_i according to region properties X_i

$$C(\theta_i|X_i) = P(\theta_i|X_i) \,. \tag{10.57}$$

- A confidence in interpretation θ_i of region R_i according to the interpretations θ_j of its neighbors R_j

$$C(\theta_i) = \frac{C(\theta_i|X_i) \sum_{j=1}^{N_A} \left[r(\theta_i, \theta_j) C(\theta_j|X_j) \right]}{N_A} \,, \tag{10.58}$$

where $r(\theta_i, \theta_j)$ represents the value of a compatibility function of two adjacent objects R_i and R_j with labels θ_i and θ_j, N_A is the number of regions adjacent to the region R_i (confidences C replace the probabilities P used in previous sections because they do not satisfy necessary conditions for probabilities; however, the intuitive meaning of interpretation confidences and interpretation probabilities remains unchanged).

- An evaluation of interpretation confidences in the whole image

$$C_{\text{image}} = \frac{\sum_{i=1}^{N_R} C(\theta_i)}{N_R} \tag{10.59}$$

or

$$C'_{\text{image}} = \sum_{i=1}^{N_R} \left(\frac{C(\theta_i)}{N_R} \right)^2 \,, \tag{10.60}$$

where $C(\theta_i)$ is computed from equation (10.58) and N_R is the number of regions in the corresponding specific region adjacency graph.

The genetic algorithm attempts to optimize the objective function C_{image}, which represents the confidence in the current segmentation and interpretation hypothesis.

As presented, the segmentation optimization function is based on both unary properties of hypothesized regions and on binary relations between these regions and their interpretations. A priori knowledge about the characteristics of processed images is used in evaluation of the local region confidences $C(\theta_i|X_i)$, and the compatibility function $r(\theta_i, \theta_j)$ represents the confidence that two regions with their interpretations can be present in an image in the existing configuration.

Algorithm 10.18: Genetic image segmentation and interpretation

1. Initialize the segmentation into primary regions, and define a correspondence between each region and the related position of its label in the code strings generated by a genetic algorithm.

2. Construct a primary region adjacency graph.

3. Pick the starting population of code strings at random. If a priori information is available that can help to define the starting population, use it.

4. *Genetic optimization.* Collapse a region adjacency graph for each code string of the current population (Algorithm 10.16). Using the current region adjacency graphs, compute the value of the optimization segmentation function for each code string from the population.

5. If the maximum of the optimization criterion does not increase significantly in several consecutive steps, go to step 7.

6. Let the genetic algorithm generate a new population of segmentation and interpretation hypotheses. Go to step 4.

7. The code string with the maximum confidence (the best segmentation hypothesis) represents the final image segmentation and interpretation.

A simple example

Consider an image of a ball on a lawn (see Figure 10.50). Let the interpretation labeling be B for *ball* and L for *lawn*, and let the higher-level knowledge be: *There is a circular ball in the image* and *the ball is inside the green lawn region*. In reality, some more a priori knowledge would be added even in this simple example, but this knowledge is sufficient for our purposes. The knowledge must be stored in appropriate data structures.

- Unary condition: Let the confidence that a region is a *ball* be based on its compactness (see Section 8.3.1),

$$C(\theta_i = B|X_i) = \text{compactness}(R_i) \qquad (10.61)$$

and let the confidence that a region is *lawn* be based on its greenness,

$$C(\theta_i = L|X_i) = \text{greenness}(R_i) . \qquad (10.62)$$

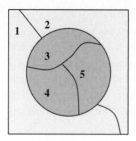

Figure 10.50: A simulated scene 'ball on the lawn'. © *Cengage Learning 2015*.

Let the confidences for regions forming a perfect ball or lawn be equal to one

$$C(B|\text{circular}) = 1 \qquad C(L|\text{green}) = 1 \,.$$

- Binary condition: Let the confidence that one region is positioned inside the other be given by a compatibility function

$$r(B \text{ is inside } L) = 1 \qquad\qquad (10.63)$$

and let the confidences of all other positional combinations be equal to zero.

The unary condition says that the more compact a region is, the better its circularity, and the higher the confidence that its interpretation is a ball. The binary condition is very strict and claims that a ball can only be completely surrounded by a lawn.

Suppose the primary image segmentation consists of five primary regions $R_1, \ldots, R_5$ (see Figure 10.50); the primary region adjacency graph and its dual are in shown in Figure 10.49. Let the region numbers correspond to the position of region labels in code strings which are generated by the genetic algorithm as segmentation hypotheses and assume, for simplicity, that the starting population of segmentation hypotheses consists of just two strings (in any practical application the starting population would be

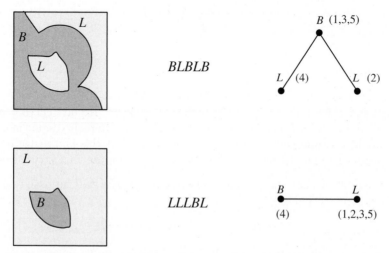

Figure 10.51: Starting hypotheses about segmentation and interpretation: interpretation, corresponding code strings, and corresponding region adjacency graphs. © *Cengage Learning 2015*.

significantly larger). Let the starting population be picked at random:

$$BLBLB$$
$$LLLBL$$

—this represents segmentation hypotheses as shown in Figure 10.51. After a random crossover between second and third positions, the population is as follows; confidences reflect the circularity of the region labeled *ball* and the positioning of the region labeled *ball* inside the *lawn* region—the confidence computation is based on equation (10.59):

$$BL|BLB \quad C_{\text{image}} = 0.00$$
$$LL|LBL \quad C_{\text{image}} = 0.12$$
$$LLBLB \quad C_{\text{image}} = 0.20$$
$$BLLBL \quad C_{\text{image}} = 0.00$$

The second and the third segmentation hypotheses are the best ones, so they are reproduced and another crossover is applied; the first and the fourth code strings die (see Figure 10.52):

$$LLL|BL \quad C_{\text{image}} = 0.12$$
$$LLB|LB \quad C_{\text{image}} = 0.20$$
$$LLLLB \quad C_{\text{image}} = 0.14$$
$$LLBBL \quad C_{\text{image}} = 0.18$$

After one more crossover,

$$LLBL|B \quad C_{\text{image}} = 0.20$$
$$LLBB|L \quad C_{\text{image}} = 0.18$$
$$LLBLL \quad C_{\text{image}} = 0.10$$
$$LLBBB \quad C_{\text{image}} = 1.00$$

The code string (segmentation hypothesis) $LLBBB$ has a high (the highest achievable) confidence. If the genetic algorithm continues generating hypotheses, the confidence of the best hypothesis will not be any better and so it stops. The optimum segmentation/interpretation is shown in Figure 10.53.

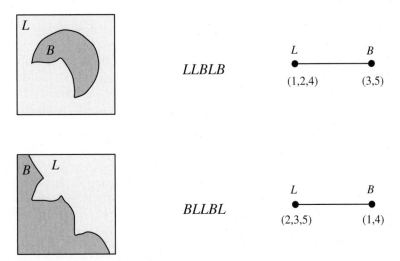

Figure 10.52: Hypotheses about segmentation and interpretation: interpretations, corresponding code strings, and corresponding region adjacency graphs. © *Cengage Learning 2015*.

Figure 10.53: Optimal segmentation and interpretation: interpretation, corresponding code string, and region adjacency graph. © *Cengage Learning 2015.*

Brain segmentation example

The previous example illustrated only the basic principles: practical applications require more complex a priori knowledge, the genetic algorithm has to work with larger string populations, the primary image segmentation has more regions, and the optimum solution is not found in three steps. Nevertheless, the principles remain the same, and interpretation of human magnetic resonance brain images [Sonka et al., 1996] is given here as such a complex example.

The genetic image interpretation method was trained on two-dimensional MR images depicting anatomically corresponding slices of the human brain. Knowledge about the unary properties of the specified neuroanatomic structures and about the binary properties between the structure pairs was acquired from manually traced contours in a training set of brain images (Figure 10.55a).

As has been apparent from the definition of the global objective function C_{image} [equation (10.59)], the unary properties of individual regions, hypothesized interpretations of the regions, and binary relationships between regions contribute to the computation of the confidence C_{image}.

In our case, the unary region confidences $C(\theta_i|X_i)$ and the compatibility functions $r(\theta_i, \theta_j)$ were calculated based on the brain anatomy and MR image acquisition parameters. The following approach to the confidence calculations was used in the brain interpretation task [Sonka et al., 1996]:

Unary confidences: The unary confidence of a region was calculated by matching the region's shape and other characteristic properties with corresponding properties representing the hypothesized interpretation (i.e., matching with the a priori knowledge).

Let the set of properties of region R_i be $X_i = \{x_{i1}, x_{i2}, \dots, x_{iN}\}$. Matching was done for each characteristic of the region $\{x_{ij}\}$, and the unary confidence $C(\theta_i|X_i)$ was calculated as follows:

$$C(\theta_i|X_i) = P(x_{i1}) \, P(x_{i2}) \, \dots \, P(x_{iN}) \, . \tag{10.64}$$

The feature confidences $P(x_{ik})$ were calculated by using the piecewise linear function shown in Figure 10.54. For example, let x_{ik} be the area of region R_i in the specific RAG and let R_i be labeled θ_i. According to a priori knowledge, assume that an object labeled θ_i has an area y_{ik}. Then

$$P(x_{ik}) = \begin{cases} 1.0 - \big(0.95 \, |x_{ik} - y_{ik}|\big)/L & : \quad |x_{ik} - y_{ik}| < L \, , \\ 0.05 & : \quad \text{otherwise.} \end{cases}$$

The limit L depends on the strength of the a priori knowledge for each particular feature.

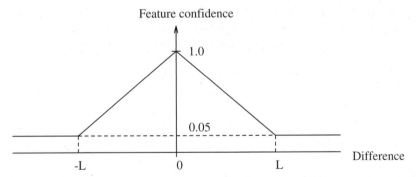

Figure 10.54: Piecewise linear function for calculating unary confidences. L is a limit which depends on the a priori knowledge. © *Cengage Learning 2015.*

Binary confidences: Binary confidences were defined between two regions based on their interrelationships.

The value of the compatibility function $r(\theta_i, \theta_j)$ was assigned to be in the range $[0,1]$, depending on the strength of the a priori knowledge about the expected configuration of regions R_i and R_j. For example, if a region R_i, labeled θ_i, is known always to be inside region R_j, labeled θ_j, then $r(\theta_i$ is_inside $\theta_j) = 1$ and $r(\theta_j$ is_outside $\theta_i) = 1$, whereas $r(\theta_j$ is_inside $\theta_i) = 0$ and $r(\theta_i$ is_outside $\theta_j) = 0$. Thus, low binary confidences serve to penalize infeasible configurations of pairs of regions.

Similarly to the calculation of the unary confidence, the compatibility function was calculated as follows:

$$r(\theta_i, \theta_j) = r(\theta_{ij1})\, r(\theta_{ij2}) \ \ldots\ r(\theta_{ijN})\,. \tag{10.65}$$

Here, $r(\theta_{ijk})$ is a binary relation (example: larger than/smaller than) between regions labeled θ_i and θ_j.

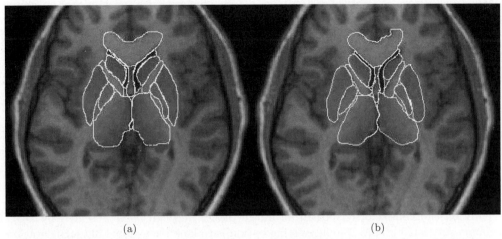

(a)   (b)

Figure 10.55: Automated segmentation and interpretation of MR brain images. (a) Observer-defined borders of the neuroanatomic structures correspond closely with (b) computer-defined borders. © *Cengage Learning 2015.*

After the objective function C_{image} was designed using a number of brain images from the training set, the genetic brain image interpretation method was applied to test images. For illustration, the primary region adjacency graph typically consisted of approximately 400 regions; a population of 20 strings and a mutation rate $\mu = 1/string\_length$ were used during the optimization. The method was applied to a test set of MR brain images and offered good image interpretation performance (Figure 10.55).

Semantic image understanding

Conventional semantic region growing methods start with a non-semantic phase and use semantic post-processing to assign labels to regions. Based on the segmentation achieved in the region growing phases, the labeling process is trying to find a consistent set of interpretations for regions. The genetic image interpretation approach functions in a quite different way.

First, there are no separate phases. The semantics are incorporated into the segmentation/interpretation process. Second, segmentation hypotheses are generated first, and the optimization function is used only for evaluation of hypotheses. Third, a genetic algorithm is responsible for generating segmentation hypotheses in an efficient way.

The method can be based on any properties of region description and on any relations between regions. The basic idea of generating segmentation hypotheses solves one of the problems of split-and-merge region growing—the sensitivity to the order of region growing. The only way to re-segment an image in a conventional region growing approach if the semantic post-processing does not provide a successful segmentation is to apply feedback control to change region growing parameters in a particular image part. There is no guarantee that a global segmentation optimum will be obtained even after several feedback re-segmentation steps.

In the genetic image interpretation approach, no region merging is ever final. Natural and constant feedback is contained in the genetic interpretation method because it is part of the general genetic algorithm—this gives a good chance that a (near) global optimum segmentation/interpretation will be found in a single processing stage.

Note that none of the methods presented in this chapter can guarantee a correct segmentation—all approaches try to achieve optimality according to the chosen optimization function. Therefore, a priori knowledge is essential to designing a good optimization function. A priori knowledge is often included in the form of heuristics, and moreover, may affect the choice of the starting population of segmentation hypotheses, which can affect computational efficiency.

An important property of the genetic image understanding method is the possibility of parallel implementation. Similarly to relaxation, this method is also naturally parallel. Moreover, there is a straightforward generalization leading to a genetic image segmentation and interpretation in three dimensions. Considering a set of image planes forming a three-dimensional image (such as MR or CT images), a primary segmentation can consist of regions in all image planes and can be represented by a 3D primary relational graph. The interesting option is to look for a global 3D segmentation and interpretation optimum using 3D properties of generated 3D regions in a single complex processing stage. In such an application, the parallel implementation would be a necessity.

10.11   Hidden Markov models

It is often possible when attempting image understanding to model the patterns being observed as a transitionary system. Sometimes these are transitions in time, but they may also be transitions through another pattern; for example, the patterns of individual characters when connected in particular orders represent another pattern that is a word. If the transitions are well understood, and we know the system state at a certain instant, they can be used to assist in determining the state at a subsequent point. This is a well-known idea, and one of the simplest examples is the **Markov model**.

A Markov model assumes a system may occupy one of a finite number of states $X_1, X_2, X_3, \ldots, X_n$ at times $t_1, t_2, \ldots$, and that the probability of occupying a state is determined solely by recent history. More specifically, a first-order Markov model assumes these probabilities depend only on the preceding state; thus a matrix $A = a_{ij}$ will exist in which

$$a_{ij} = P(\text{system is in state } j \mid \text{system was in state } i) . \tag{10.66}$$

Thus $0 \le a_{ij} \le 1$ and $\sum_{j=1}^{n} a_{ij} = 1$ for all $1 \le i \le n$. The important point is that these parameters are time independent—the a_{ij} do not vary with t. A second-order model makes similar assumptions about probabilities depending on the last two states, and the idea generalizes obviously to order-k models for $k = 3, 4, \ldots$

A trivial example might be to model weather forecasting: suppose that the weather on a given day may be *sunny* (1), *cloudy* (2), or *rainy* (3) and that the day's weather depends probabilistically on the preceding day's weather *only*. We might be able to derive a matrix A,

$$A = \begin{array}{c} \text{sun} \\ \text{cloud} \\ \text{rain} \end{array} \begin{bmatrix} 0.50 & 0.375 & 0.125 \\ 0.25 & 0.125 & 0.625 \\ 0.25 & 0.375 & 0.375 \end{bmatrix}, \tag{10.67}$$

so the probability of rain after a sunny day is 0.125, the probability of cloud after a rainy day is 0.375, and so on.

In many practical applications, the states are not directly observable, and instead we observe a different set of states $Y_1, \ldots, Y_m$ (where possibly $n \ne m$), where we can only guess the exact state of the system from the probabilities

$$b_{kj} = P(Y_k \text{ observed} \mid \text{system is in state } j) ,$$

so $0 \le b_{kj} \le 1$ and $\sum_{k=1}^{m} b_{kj} = 1$. The $n \times m$ matrix B that is so defined is also time independent; that is, the observation probabilities do not depend on anything except the current state, and in particular not on how that state was achieved, or when.

Extending the weather example, it is widely believed that the moistness of a piece of seaweed is an indicator of weather; if we conjecture four states, *dry* (1), *dryish* (2), *damp* (3) or *soggy* (4), and that the actual weather is probabilistically connected to the seaweed state, we might derive a matrix such as

$$B = \begin{array}{c} \text{dry} \\ \text{dryish} \\ \text{damp} \\ \text{soggy} \end{array} \begin{bmatrix} 0.60 & 0.25 & 0.05 \\ 0.20 & 0.25 & 0.10 \\ 0.15 & 0.25 & 0.35 \\ 0.05 & 0.25 & 0.50 \end{bmatrix}, \tag{10.68}$$

so the probability of observing dry seaweed when the weather is sunny is 0.6, the probability of observing damp seaweed when the weather is cloudy is 0.25, and so on.

A first-order **hidden Markov model (HMM)** $\lambda = (\pi, A, B)$ is specified by the matrices A and B together with an n-dimensional vector π to describe the probabilities of the state at time $t = 1$. The time-independent constraints are quite strict and in many cases unrealistic, but HMMs have seen significant practical application. In particular, they are successful in the area of speech processing [Rabiner, 1989], wherein the A matrix might represent the probability of a particular phoneme following another phoneme, and the B matrix refers to a feature measurement of a spoken phoneme (the Fourier spectrum, for example). It is recognized here that the fuzziness of speech means we cannot be certain which feature will be generated by which phoneme. The same ideas have seen wide application in optical character recognition (OCR) (for example, [Agazzi and Kuo, 1993],) and related areas, where the A matrix might refer to letter successor probabilities, and again the B matrix is a probabilistic description of which features are generated by which letters.

A HMM poses three questions:

Evaluation: Given a model and a sequence of observations, what is the probability that the model actually generated those observations? If two different models are available, $\lambda_1 = (\pi_1, A_1, B_1)$ and $\lambda_2 = (\pi_2, A_2, B_2)$, this question indicates which one better describes some given observations. For example, if we have two such models, together with a known weather sequence and a known sequence of seaweed observations, which model, λ_1 or λ_2, is the best description of the data?

Decoding: Given a model $\lambda = (\pi, A, B)$ and a sequence of observations, what is the most likely underlying state sequence? For pattern analysis, this is the most interesting question, since it permits an optimal estimate of what is happening on the basis of a sequence of feature measurements. For example, if we have a model and a sequence of seaweed observations, what is most likely to have been the underlying weather sequence?

Learning: Given knowledge of the set $X_1, X_2, X_3, \ldots, X_n$ and a sequence of observations, what are the best parameters π, A, B if the system is indeed a HMM? For example, given a known weather sequence and a known sequence of seaweed observations, what model parameters best describe them?

HMM evaluation

To determine the probability that a particular model generated an observed sequence, it is straightforward to evaluate all possible hidden state sequences, calculate their probabilities, and multiply by the probability that the sequence in question generated the observations in hand. If

$$Y^k = (Y_{k_1}, Y_{k_2}, \ldots, Y_{k_T})$$

is a T long sequence of observations, and

$$X^i = (X_{i_1}, X_{i_2}, \ldots, X_{i_T})$$

is a state sequence, we require

$$P(Y^k) = \sum_{X^i} P(Y^k|X^i)\, P(X^i)\,.$$

This quantity is given by summing over all possible sequences X^i, and for each such, determining the probability of the given observations; these probabilities are available from the B matrix, while the transition probabilities of X^i are available from the A matrix. Thus

$$P(Y^k) = \sum_{X^i} \pi(i_1) b_{k_1 i_1} \prod_{j=2}^{T} a_{i_{j-1} i_j} b_{k_j i_j}\,.$$

Exhaustive evaluation over the X^i is possible since π, A, B are all available, but the load is exponential in T and clearly not in general computationally realistic. The assumptions of the model, however, permit a short cut by defining a recursive definition of partial, or intermediate, probabilities. Suppose

$$\alpha_t(j) = P(\text{state } X_j \text{ at time } t) \quad 1 < t < T\,.$$

Since t is strictly between 1 and T, so this is an intermediate probability. Time independence allows us to write immediately

$$\alpha_{t+1}(j) = \sum_{i=1}^{n} \big[\alpha_t(i) a_{ij}\big] b_{k_{t+1} j} \qquad (10.69)$$

since a_{ij} represents the probability of moving to state j and $b_{jk_{t+1}}$ is the probability of observing what we do at this time. Thus α is defined recursively; it may be initialized from our knowledge of the initial states,

$$\alpha_1(j) = \pi(j) b_{k_1 j}\,.$$

At time T, the individual quantities $\alpha_T(j)$ give the probability of the observed sequence occurring, and with the actual (hidden) system terminating state being X_j. Therefore the total probability of the model generating the observed sequence Y_k is

$$P(Y^k) = \sum_{j=1}^{n} \alpha_T(j)\,.$$

The recursive definition permits the calculation of this quantity in 'synchronous steps' without the need for exhaustively evaluating all sequences X^i individually. Any number of models $\lambda_1 = (\pi_1, A_1, B_1)$, λ_2, λ_3, ... can be subjected to this *forward algorithm* [Baum and Eagon, 1963], and we would adopt the one with the maximal probability of causing the sequence observed:

$$\max_i \big[P(Y^k|\lambda_i)\big]\,.$$

In particular, in OCR word recognition the individual patterns may be features extracted from characters or groups of characters, and an individual model may represent an individual word. We would determine which word was most likely to have generated an observed feature sequence.

HMM decoding

Given that a particular model (π, A, B) generated an observation sequence of length T, $Y^k = (Y_{k_1}, \ldots, Y_{k_T})$, it is often not obvious what precise states the system passed through, $X^i = (X_{i_1}, \ldots, X_{i_T})$, and we therefore need an algorithm that will determine the most probable (or optimal in some sense) X^i given Y^k.

A simple approach might be to start at time $t = 1$ and ask what the most probable X_{i_1} would be, given the observation Y_{k_1}. Formally,

$$
\begin{aligned}
i_t &= \operatorname*{argmax}_{j} \left[P(X_j | Y_{k_t}) \right] \\
&= \operatorname*{argmax}_{j} \left[P(Y_{k_t} | X_j) P(X_j) \right] \\
&= \operatorname*{argmax}_{j} \left[b_{k_t j} P(X_j) \right],
\end{aligned}
\tag{10.70}
$$

which may be calculated given the probabilities of the X_j (or, more likely, some estimate thereof). This approach will generate an answer, but in the event of one or more observations being poor, a wrong decision may be taken for some t. It also has the possibility of generating illegal sequences (for example, a transition for which $a_{ij} = 0$). This frequently occurs in observation of noisy patterns, where an isolated best guess for a pattern may not be the same as the best guess taken in the context of a stream of patterns.

We do not decide on the value of i_t during the examination of the tth observation, but instead record how likely it is that a particular state *might* be reached, and if it were to be correct, which state was likely to have been its predecessor. Then at column T, a decision can be taken about the final state X_T based on the entire history, which is fed back to the earlier stages—this is the **Viterbi algorithm** [Viterbi, 1967]. The approach is similar to that developed for dynamic programming (Section 6.2.5); we reconstruct the system evolution by imagining an $N \times T$ lattice of states; at time t we occupy one of the N possible X_i in the tth column. States in neighboring columns are connected by transition probabilities from the A matrix, but our view of this lattice (see Figure 10.56,

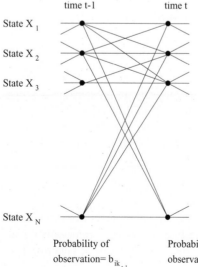

State X_1

State X_2

State X_3

time t-1   time t

State X_N

Probability of
observation= $b_{ik_{t-1}}$

Probability of
observation= b_{ik_t}

Figure 10.56: Part of a Markov model lattice. © *Cengage Learning 2015.*

cf. Figure 6.27) is attenuated by the observation probabilities B. The task is to find the route from the first to the Tth column of maximal probability, given the observation set.

Formally, we set

$$\delta_1(i) = \pi(i)b_{k_1 i} ,\tag{10.71}$$

$$\delta_t(i) = \max_j \left[\delta_{t-1}(j)a_{ji}b_{k_t i}\right] ,\tag{10.72}$$

$$\phi_t(i) = \operatorname*{argmax}_j \left[\delta_{t-1}(j)a_{ji}\right] ,\tag{10.73}$$

$$i_T = \operatorname*{argmax}_i \left[\delta_T(i)\right] ,\tag{10.74}$$

$$i_t = \phi_{t+1}(i_{t+1}) , \quad t = T-1,\ldots,1 .\tag{10.75}$$

Here, equation (10.71) initializes the first lattice column, combining the π vector with the first observation. Equation (10.72) is a recursion relation to define the subsequent column from the predecessor, the transition probabilities, and the observation; this gives the ith element of the tth column, and informally is the probability of the 'most likely' way of being in that position, given events at time $t-1$. Equation (10.73) is a back pointer, indicating where one is most likely to have come from at time $t-1$ if currently in state i at time t (see Figure 10.57). Equation (10.74) indicates what the most likely state is at time T, given the preceding $T-1$ states and the observations. equation (10.75) traces the back pointers through the lattice, initializing from the most likely final state.

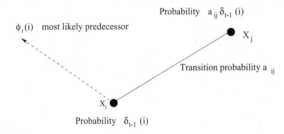

Figure 10.57: A close-up of the HMM lattice; moving from state i at time $t-1$ to state j at time t. © *Cengage Learning 2015.*

A simple example will illustrate this, considering the weather transition probabilities (equation 10.67) and the seaweed observation probabilities (equation 10.68), we might conjecture, without prior information, that the weather states on any given start day have equal probabilities, so $\pi = (\frac{1}{3}, \frac{1}{3}, \frac{1}{3})$. Suppose now we imagine a weather observer in a closed, locked room with a piece of seaweed—if on four consecutive days the seaweed is *dry, dryish, soggy, soggy*, the observer wishes to calculate the most likely sequence of weather states that have caused these observations. Starting with the observation *dry*, the first column of probabilities becomes (equation 10.71);

$$P(\text{dry observation and sunny weather}) = \delta_1(1) = 0.333 \times 0.6 = 0.2 ,$$
$$P(\text{dry observation and cloudy weather}) = \delta_1(2) = 0.333 \times 0.25 = 0.0833 ,\tag{10.76}$$
$$P(\text{dry observation and rainy weather}) = \delta_1(3) = 0.333 \times 0.05 = 0.0167 .$$

As expected, the *sunny* state is most probable. Now reasoning about the second day, $\delta_2(1)$ gives the probability of observing *dryish* seaweed on a *sunny* day, given the preceding day's information. For each of the three possible preceding states, we calculate the explicit probability and select the largest (equation 10.72);

P(day 1 is sunny *and* day 2 is sunny and seaweed is dryish)
$$= 0.2 \times 0.5 \times 0.2 = 0.02 \,,$$

P(day 1 is cloudy *and* day 2 is sunny and seaweed is dryish)
$$= 0.0833 \times 0.25 \times 0.2 = 0.00417 \,,$$

P(day 1 is rainy *and* day 2 is sunny and seaweed is dryish)
$$= 0.0167 \times 0.25 \times 0.2 = 0.000833 \,.$$

(10.77)

Thus the most probable way of reaching the *sunny* state on day 2 is from day 1 being sunny too; accordingly, we record $\delta_2(1) = 0.02$ and store the back pointer $\phi_2(1) = 1$ (equation 10.73). In a similar way, we find $\delta_2(2) = 0.0188$, $\phi_2(2) = 1$ and $\delta_2(3) = 0.00521$, $\phi_2(3) = 2$.

Probabilities δ and back pointers may be computed similarly for the third and fourth days; we discover $\delta_4(1) = 0.00007$, $\delta_4(2) = 0.00055$, $\delta_4(3) = 0.0011$—thus the most probable final state *given all preceding information*, is rainy. We select this (equation 10.74), and follow the ϕ back pointers of most probable predecessors to determine the optimal sequence (equation 10.75). In this case, it is *sunny, sunny, rainy, rainy*, which accords well with expectation given the model.

HMM learning

The task of learning the best model to fit a given observation sequence is the hardest of the three associated with HMMs, but an estimate (often suboptimal) can be made. An initial model is guessed, and this is refined to give a higher probability of providing the observations in hand via the *forward-backward* or **Baum-Welch** algorithm. This is essentially a gradient descent of an error measure of the current best model, and is a special case of the EM (expectation-maximization) algorithm considered in Section 10.13.

10.11.1 Applications

Early uses of the HMM approach were predominantly in speech recognition, where it is not hard to see how a different model may be used to represent each word, how features may be extracted, and how the global view of the Viterbi algorithm would be necessary to recognize phoneme sequences correctly through noise and garble [Rabiner, 1989; Huang et al., 1990]. HMMs are actively used in commercial speech recognizers [Green, 1995]. Wider applications in natural language processing have also been seen.

The same ideas translate naturally into the related language recognition domain of OCR and handwriting recognition. One use has been to let the underlying state sequence be grammatical tags, while the observations are features derived from segmented words in printed and handwritten text; the patterns of English grammar restrict which words may follow which others; this reduction of the size of candidate sets assists enormously in recognition. Similarly, HMMs lend themselves to analysis of letter sequences in text [Kundu et al., 1989], where transition probabilities are derived empirically from letter frequencies and patterns and the observation probabilities are the output of an OCR system—these are derived from a range of pattern features such as those described in Chapter 8. This system is seen to improve in performance when a second-order Markov model is deployed.

At a lower level, HMMs can be used to recognize individual characters. This may be done by skeletonizing characters and considering the sequence of stroke primitives to be a Markov process [Vlontzos and Kung, 1992]. Alternatively, vertical and horizontal projections (see Section 8.3.1) of binarized character images may be considered [Elms and Illingworth, 1994]. Observed through noise, a Fourier transform of the projections is derived as a feature vector, and a HMM for each possible character is trained using the Baum-Welch algorithm. Unknown characters are then identified by determining the best scoring model for features derived from an unseen image.

HMMs have found favor in analysis of visual sequences. Recognition of sign language from video has proved possible [Schlenzig et al., 1994; Brashear et al., 2003], and Markov models have significant success in describing transitions between submodels generated by PDMs (see Section 10.4) [Heap, 1998]. HMMs have also been applied successfully to lip and face tracking in real time [Oliver et al., 1997], and lip reading [Harvey et al., 1997]. The full range of applications (both inside and outside the area of computer vision) is very long—the power of the model and its analysis techniques far outweigh the problems associated with the inadequacy of its assumptions. This is particularly seen to be the case when it is combined with some of the other techniques we have described, such as PCA to reduce dimensionality with a noise removal effect.

10.11.2 Coupled HMMs

The HMM approach has proved enormously popular because it is straightforward to understand and implement, and maps so successfully onto a wide range of applications. The power of the model and its analysis techniques far outweigh the problems associated with the inadequacy of its assumptions in assuming a time independent model, and first-order behavior. This is particularly seen to be the case when it is combined with some of the other techniques we have described, such as PCA to reduce dimensionality with a noise removal effect.

Nevertheless, the obvious limitations of a simple HMM make it natural to extend the idea to compensate for its weaknesses. One way is to invest it with more memory, which may be done by building a model based on a second (or higher) order assumption, the current state then depending probabilistically on some number of predecessors. It is easy to see how this might be expected to improve performance; see, for example, [Kundu et al., 1989].

An alternative approach that has proved powerful is to recognize that more than one thing may be happening at once: an obvious example in speech recognition might be the audio input of the sound signal, and the video input of mouth and lip movements. Either or both of these might be used as the basis of a HMM for speech recognition, but if we also consider that the audio and sound features will be interdependent, we can see that two co-operating, or **coupled**, HMMs might be constructed. It is then a short step to extend the idea to any number of coupled models.

This idea was first deployed on visual interpretation of T'ai Chi [Brand et al., 1997], wherein features might be extracted from the motion of both arms, the movement of which is neither independent not wholly dependent. Formally, suppose we have two HMMs with associated parameters:

- HMM_1: with hidden states $X_1, X_2, \ldots X_{n_1}$ and observed states $Y_1, Y_2, \ldots Y_{m_1}$, initial probabilities $\pi(i)$, $i = 1, 2, \ldots, n_1$ and observation probabilities B^1.

- HMM_2: with hidden states $G_1, G_2, \ldots G_{n_2}$ and observed states $H_1, H_2, \ldots H_{m_2}$, initial probabilities $\mu(i)$, $i = 1, 2, \ldots, n_2$ and observation probabilities B^2.

The assumption now is that the transitions between the X and G states are probabilistically related; thus, instead of equation (10.66), we will define matrices A^1 and A^2:

$$A^1_{(ij)k} = P(HMM_1 \text{ is in state } k \mid HMM_1 \text{ was in state } i \text{ and } HMM_2 \text{ was in state } j)$$

(and $A^2_{(ij)k}$ similarly). These matrices are the basis of the coupling. This is illustrated in Figure 10.58.

The Viterbi algorithm may now be constructed similarly to before. If we observe sequences $(Y_{k_1}, \ldots, Y_{k_T})$ and $(H_{l_1}, \ldots, H_{l_T})$ then analogous to equations (10.71–10.74), we have:

$$\delta_1(i, j) = \pi(i)\, \mu(j)\, b^1_{k_1 i}\, b^2_{l_1 j} \tag{10.78}$$

$$\delta_t(i, j) = \max_{k,l} \left[\delta_{t-1}(k, l)\, a^1_{(kl)i}\, b^1_{k_t i}\, a^2_{(kl)j}\, b^2_{l_t j} \right] \tag{10.79}$$

$$\phi_t(i, j) = \operatorname*{argmax}_{k,l} \left[\delta_{t-1}(k, l)\, a^1_{(kl)i}\, a^2_{(kl)j} \right] \tag{10.80}$$

$$(i_T, j_T) = \operatorname*{argmax}_{i,j} \left[\delta_T(i, j) \right] \tag{10.81}$$

with the 'best' estimates of coupled states at times $T - 1, T - 2, \ldots, 1$ being computed through the back pointers given by equation (10.80).

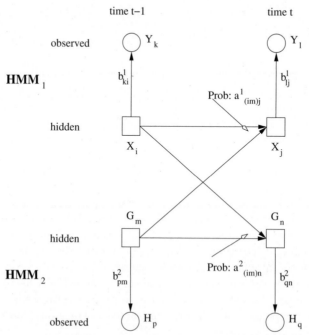

Figure 10.58: Part of a CHMM lattice at times $(t - 1)$ and t: transitions between X_i and X_j [HMM_1], and between G_m and G_n [HMM_2], are illustrated. It is assumed that the observed states are Y_k, Y_l, H_p, H_q. © *Cengage Learning 2015*.

It should be clear that this approach lends itself to the coupling of an arbitrary number of HMMs, with equations very similar to equations (10.78–10.81) emerging. The training [forward-backward] algorithm extends to the coupled case without difficulty.

The coupled HMM has proved a particularly rich development of the basic idea, and there are many uses of it to be found in the literature; a review of many techniques that includes coupled HMMs is given in [Buxton, 2002].

10.11.3 Bayesian belief networks

The example of weather forecasting introduced on page 543 is useful, but very limited. It is easy to imagine a more informed system in which, say, observed temperature also gives a clue to the weather. In turn, the weather might inform (probabilistically) your decision on whether to go to work by cycle or bus; this decision might also be influenced by your current health, your evening plans, etc. Figure 10.59 illustrates this richer example which might clearly be extended as far as we wish.

We assume in constructing networks of this kind that each node (seaweed state, temperature etc.) represents a random variable; the arrows represent causal influence which is probabilistic. In the case that all the variables are discrete, this implies a probability matrix—if there is an arrow from node A to node B, these probabilities provide the matrix $Pr(B|A)$. In applications of interest, some of these states will be observable and some hidden, in exactly the way we saw with HMMs. Such networks are termed **Bayesian belief networks** [BBNs]; it should be clear that HMMs are a (very small) special case of BBNs.

In considering such networks, we might assume that we know the connecting probability matrices, and we know the 'root' probabilities. Given some observations (of the observable states) what we seek is the posterior probability distribution of the hidden states.

The study of BBNs, like HMMs, is far from specific to computer vision—see [Pearl, 1987] for an authoritative early introduction—and full coverage of them here is not appropriate. It is sufficient to note that for tree structured networks (such as Figure 10.59), it is straightforward to consider nodes as being children (or grandchildren) of some nodes, and parents (or grandparents) of the others. Some of these (grand-)parents and (grand-)children are observable, and some not.

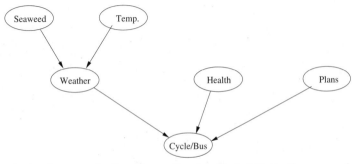

Figure 10.59: A simple example Bayesian network. Probabilistically, seaweed and temperature inform a judgment on the weather; simultaneously, mode of transport is probabilistically informed by weather, state of health and social plans. © *Cengage Learning 2015.*

Consider a node X: in the notation of [Pearl, 1987] we denote the observable evidence as e. e_X^- is that part of the observable evidence consequent on X (that can be reached following arrows rooted at X), and e_X^+ is the remaining observable part evidence. Bayesian reasoning permits the derivation of two probability vectors:

- The diagnostic support vector $\lambda(X)$, the probability of observing a consequent state as we do, given a particular value of X:

$$\lambda(X) = Pr(e_X^-|X = x_i) \,.$$

- The causal support vector $\pi(X)$: the probability of a particular value of X given an observed 'causing' state:

$$\pi(X) = Pr(X = x_i|e_X^+) \,.$$

Propagation theory permits an elegant derivation of these quantities, and thence the posterior probability distribution of all nodes.

It is easy to see how such structures might lend themselves to a relaxation approach (see Section 10.9), and there is a similarity in the structure of the problems these two ideas attack, and the ideas used: solutions evolve as the result of local operations (that might be parallelized) and evolve to some overall, if not global, solution. It has been recognized for some time that relaxation can be very slow in large problems[4] and Bayesian networks are faster (in terms of number of iterations) [Weiss, 1997].

The generic nature of the Bayesian network approach has made it applicable across AI; the interested reader is recommended to consult specialist texts [Pearl, 1987]; a useful review which considers vision application is [Buxton, 2002]. Frey provides a good account and comparative study of the advances made in vision applications involving combinatorial analysis of interacting scene elements [Frey and Jojic, 2005].

A successful example of such networks in the vision domain is the recognition of 'plays' in video transcriptions of American football: the game consists of tightly rehearsed offensive plays which an experienced observer has no difficulty in recognizing from video. A system has been built [Intille and Bobick, 2001] that takes trajectories of the players involved (offensive and defensive), and determines the probabilities of having 'seen' one of a number of pre-compiled plays—the success rate of the most probable play being the correct one is high. Clearly, what is described here is above a vision system in its level of reasoning, but it is easy to see how it might exploit the output of a tracker (see Section 16.5).

The system proceeds with a number of small networks, with approximately 20 nodes each. An example is a *catchpass* network that, for a specific player, will determine the probability of various outcomes, given the trajectory data—such outcomes might be the interception of the trajectories of another player and the ball. These (probabilistic) decisions are taken on the basis of a number of (hidden) 'belief' nodes, examples of which include *passthrown*.

---

[4]The drawbacks of relaxation were recognized long ago by Marr [Marr, 1982], where it is argued that such a slow process is inadequate to explain operation of the human brain.

10.12 Markov random fields

The concepts of Markov and Hidden Markov Models lead very naturally to the **Markov Random Field** or **MRF**. An MRF is defined by

- A set of nodes $V = v_1, \ldots, v_n$.

- A set of random variables $w_1, \ldots, w_n$ associated with each node.

- A set of undirected edges E connecting some pairs of nodes. Thus each node v_i has defined a set of neighbors N_i to which it is directly connected.

The key constraint is that the probability of the state of the ith random variable depends only on the states of the immediate neighbors of v_i:

$$P(w_i | \{w_j\}_{j \neq i}) = P(w_i | \{w_j\}_{j \in N_i}) . \qquad (10.82)$$

The similarity with the Markov condition (equation 10.66) may be clear—only strictly local states have influence, but at the same time the *indirect* influence of a node's state may be far reaching. This is attractive as it allows a relatively simple model to describe complex global behavior, and allows efficient (and often easily parallelizable) algorithms to be developed.

The graph structures so defined turn out to have widespread applications in imaging: very often the nodes correspond to pixels and edges would correspond to, e.g., 4-connectivity, but that is not essential. We shall present examples shortly (and have already seen one in Section 7.6).

Equation (10.82) constrains $P(w)$ to have some particular properties: in particular the Hammersley Clifford theorem [Besag, 1974] states that identification of the cliques (maximal complete subgraphs—see Section 9.5.1) $C_1, \ldots C_k$ of the graph defined by (V, E) permit the probability of $\mathbf{w} = (w_1, \ldots w_n)$ to be written as

$$P(\mathbf{w}) = \frac{1}{Z} \prod_{i=i}^{k} \phi_i(\mathbf{w}_{C_i}) , \qquad (10.83)$$

where the ϕ_i are potential functions and $\mathbf{w}_{C_i}$ represents the probabilities of the cliques' configurations. Thus the probability of the global state can be derived from knowledge of the behavior of the cliques defined by the neighborhood relation. If this is derived from the 4-connected pixel grid, the cliques are given simply by neighboring pixel pairs (vertical and horizontal), allowing a model to be built from the most local of constraints.

Equivalently, equation (10.83) may be written

$$P(\mathbf{w}) = \frac{1}{Z} \exp \left(- \sum_{i=i}^{k} \psi_i(\mathbf{w}_{C_i}) \right) ,$$

where the ψ_i are usually interpreted as energy or cost functions. The function Z is called the **partition function** and serves as a normalizing constant:

$$Z = \sum_{\mathbf{w}} P(\mathbf{w}) .$$

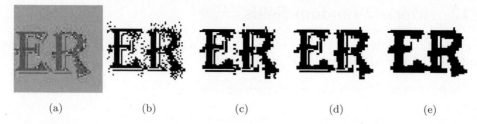

(a)   (b)   (c)   (d)   (e)

Figure 10.60: A noisy binary segmentation (b) of image (a) (taken from Figure 6.5) and three MRF improvements with progressively stronger smoothing. The *smoothness* to *data* ratio in the energy calculation is: (c) 1:1, (d) 1.5:1, (e) 2:1. The trade-off is clear—while the noise in the rightmost image is all but removed, the smoothing has also removed some detail of the original. © *Cengage Learning 2015.*

Naturally, we seek to maximize the expression of equation (10.83), and correspondingly to minimize the associated energy (or cost) $E(\mathbf{w})$:

$$E = \sum_{i=i}^{k} \psi_i(\mathbf{w}_{C_i}) \,. \tag{10.84}$$

This is a convenient formulation as a wide range of vision related problems can be formulated as an energy/cost minimization of the form

$$E = E_{data} + E_{smoothness} \,, \tag{10.85}$$

where the first term minimizes the difference between the model and the observed image, and the second imposes model constraints, usually implying 'smoothness in most places'.

A simple example, and its representation as an MRF, will illustrate: suppose we wish to 'clean' a binary segmentation (e.g., after thresholding in noise)—see Figure 10.60. Suppose the input image is f and the processed output g: then crudely setting $\delta(x,y) = |x - y|$, the data term

$$E_{data}(i,j) = \alpha\delta(f(i,j),g(i,j))$$

and smoothness term

$$E_{smoothness} = \beta(\delta(g(i,j),g(i+1,j)) + \delta(g(i,j),g(i,j+1))) \,,$$

when E is minimized, would encourage coherent regions that best match the input. The constants α, β (or more properly their ratio) control the relative influence of smoothness against faithfulness to input. (This two-state system is often referred to as an *Ising* model.)

Exactly how the expression of equation (10.84) is minimized leads to one of the more powerful features of MRFs; clearly we could initialize some solution and hope to iterate with some form of gradient descent, or perhaps use simulated annealing (Section 9.6.2), or any other optimization approach available. It transpires, however, that such approaches often fail to reach good solutions, and the *graph cut* approach already introduced in Section 7.6 proves far more powerful [Boykov et al., 2001a]. Extensive work exists on the efficient and optimal way of conducting this minimization that has resulted in the MRF formulation being one of the most popular techniques in vision.

Analogously to HMMs, the MRF is acting as a statistical *prior*; the optimal **w** states are the maximum a posteriori (MAP) estimate of the system, given the model and particular input. If the model has parameters ω, and the input data (perhaps an image) are **x**, we seek

$$\max_{\mathbf{w}} P(\mathbf{w}|\mathbf{x}, \omega) \propto P(\mathbf{x}|\mathbf{w}, \omega) P(\mathbf{w}|\omega) \tag{10.86}$$

(by Bayes Rule). The product on the right, when we consider log-probabilities as above, becomes a sum of a data term (representing the probability of observing **x** given **w**) and a 'smoothness' term (representing the probability of **w** given the model).

10.12.1 Applications to images and vision

The power and popularity of MRFs come from the number of applications that can be couched as energy minimizations of the form in equation (10.85). In addition to the simple case of binary segmentation described, well known examples include:

- *Multi-label segmentation* in which the input is a noisy segmentation into N regions, and the MRF imposes smoothness much as above to improve region boundaries. Measures of data energy/cost and smoothness may be as already described, but the graph construction, and the convergence algorithm, are more complex [Boykov et al., 2001b]. The prior segmentation need not necessarily be the product of any of the ideas we have seen hitherto, and could be abstracted from any features of the image. Figure 10.61 shows an example [Dee et al., 2012].

- More general *denoising* is amenable to a similar approach, as is interpolation of missing data values.

- *Stereo disparity* (described in detail in Section 11.6.1) can be extracted this way [Birchfield and Tomasi, 1999; Sun et al., 2003]. The disparity map (array of disparities) will be smooth almost everywhere, and the data cost will be derived from the intensity difference between putatively associated pixels in the two input images.

In addition to a wide range of other, perhaps less expected, applications, for example the removal of ink-bleed in archaic documents [Huang et al., 2008], or image synthesis [Kwatra et al., 2003].

The use of MRFs has spawned a wide literature: it was primarily developed in the late 1990s onward [Boykov et al., 2001a] and freely downloadable software implementations with very accessible interfaces are available (notably from the original developers at http://www.csd.uwo.ca/~olga/code.html [Boykov et al., 2001b; Boykov and Kolmogorov, 2004; Kolmogorov and Zabih, 2004], or from http://pub.ist.ac.at/~vnk/software.html). Books (and chapters in books) that cover this important area thoroughly are also available, for example [Boykov and Veksler, 2006; Blake et al., 2011; Prince, 2012]; these texts cover issues such as the critically important choice of energy functions, conditions under which graph-cuts will be guaranteed to locate a global energy minimum, and discussions of the various algorithms available to find the optimal cut.

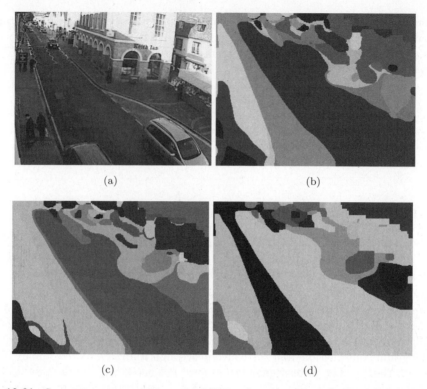

(a) (b)

(c) (d)

Figure 10.61: Semantic segmentation using MRFs: A video sequence is analyzed for regions of 'similar behaviour'—predominant traffic direction or pedestrian activities [Dee et al., 2012]. Movement patterns are detected and processed to deliver directional and speed clusters. (a) A traffic scene–one frame from a training sequence, (b) A description of activity within the traffic image sequence, characterizing motion, speed and direction. This imperfect segmentation is improved with an MRF. (c) Smoothness enforced with a ratio of 1:20 between *smoothness* and *data* requirements, (d) Again, with a ratio of 1:1. As more smoothness is enforced, smaller regions are lost.   *Courtesy of H. M. Dee, The University of Aberystwyth. A color version of this figure may be seen in the color inset—Plate 32.*

10.13 Gaussian mixture models and expectation–maximization

Suppose we have implemented a tracking system of a domestic, urban or traffic scene that delivers *trajectories* (perhaps the locus of the centroid of regions representing moving objects): Section 16.5 describes how this might be done. Such data are very noisy and hard to interpret and a common starting point is to locate areas of the image of 'geographical importance'—perhaps doorways or apertures at which objects appear or disappear, or maybe areas in which moving objects are stationary for some time. Figure 10.62a illustrates the nature of the problem.

It is easy, given the trajectory information (x_t, y_t), automatically to mark points in the image at which such events occur; this will result in clusters of marks around the areas on interest. At this stage, we might deploy something like the K-means approach (Algorithm 9.5) to 'locate' and record these areas, but this would be over-simplistic:

K-means returns a single point to represent a cluster, whereas geographical areas are spatially extended. In scenes such as parking lots, or domestic rooms, entrances and exits occupy a space bigger than the moving agents, and should be represented by a suitable area: of course, vehicles, people and animals are more inclined to use the 'center' of such apertures (see Figure 10.62b), and the representation should reflect this. This problem is usually solved by fitting a collection of multi-dimensional Gaussians (in this case 2D) to the data—a **Gaussian mixture model** (GMM).

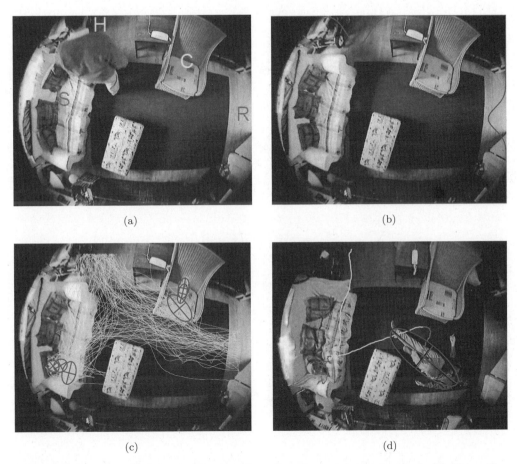

(a)

(b)

(c)

(d)

Figure 10.62: Analyzing the output of tracking data from a domestic scene. (a) The ceiling mounted camera surveys a scene in which people may enter or exit from two places: H and R. The application is interested in 'normal' stationary behavior by individuals in the scene: this would be on the sofa S or chair C. (b) Two 1D Gaussians—one at the top, the other on the right—capture the entry and exit points to the room. (c) Six 2D Gaussians capture positions of inactivity. Note the trajectory information from which the data are derived. (d) Unusual (unmodeled) behavior will be detected if trajectories halt in unmodeled positions. *Courtesy of S. J. McKenna, University of Dundee. With kind permission from Springer Science+Business Media: Pattern Analysis and Applications, Volume 7, Issue 4, 2004, pp 386-401, Stephen J. McKenna, figures 1, 12, 6 and 13, Copyright © 2005, Springer-Verlag London Limited. A color version of this figure may be seen in the color inset—Plate 33.*

Formally, suppose we are presented with N items of n-dimensional data $X=\{\mathbf{x}_1,\mathbf{x}_2,\ldots,\mathbf{x}_n\}$; in the case of scene geography modeling, $n = 2$ typically, but this is not a condition of the approach. We seek K Gaussian distributions $\Gamma_1,\Gamma_2,\ldots,\Gamma_K$ that best represent X, where Γ_i is normal with mean $\boldsymbol{\mu}_k$ and covariance Σ_k

$$\Gamma_k = N(\boldsymbol{\mu}_k, \Sigma_k)$$

together with K corresponding contribution weights π_k, $\sum_{k=1}^{K} \pi_k = 1$ such that

$$p(\mathbf{x}_j) = \sum_{k=1}^{K} \pi_k p(\mathbf{x}_j|\Gamma_k)$$

—the probability density function that is the weighted sum of the Γ_k. The problem is, given X, what are optimal values of π_k, $\boldsymbol{\mu}_k$, Σ_k?

To answer this, note if we know which of the distributions Γ_k generated a sample $\mathbf{x}_j$ we can reason about its probability

$$p(\mathbf{x}_j|\Gamma_k) = \frac{1}{(2\pi)^{\frac{n}{2}}|\Sigma_k|^{\frac{1}{2}}} \exp\left(-\frac{1}{2}(\mathbf{x}_j - \boldsymbol{\mu}_k)^T \Sigma_k^{-1}(\mathbf{x}_j - \boldsymbol{\mu}_k)\right)$$

and hence

$$p(\mathbf{x}_j) = \sum_{k=1}^{K} \frac{\pi_k}{(2\pi)^{\frac{n}{2}}|\Sigma_k|^{\frac{1}{2}}} \exp\left(-\frac{1}{2}(\mathbf{x}_j - \boldsymbol{\mu}_k)^T \Sigma_k^{-1}(\mathbf{x}_j - \boldsymbol{\mu}_k)\right)$$

—summing the weighted contributions of all the Γ_k. Now assuming the realizations of $\mathbf{x}$ to be independent

$$p(X) = \prod_{j=1}^{N} p(\mathbf{x}_j)$$

$$= \prod_{j=1}^{N} \sum_{k=1}^{K} \frac{\pi_k}{(2\pi)^{n/2}|\Sigma_k|^{1/2}} \exp\left(-\frac{1}{2}(\mathbf{x}_j - \boldsymbol{\mu}_k)^T \Sigma_k^{-1}(\mathbf{x}_j - \boldsymbol{\mu}_k)\right) \qquad (10.87)$$

$$L(X) = \log\left(p(X)\right)$$

$$= \sum_{j=1}^{N} \log\left(\sum_{k=1}^{K} \frac{\pi_k}{(2\pi)^{n/2}|\Sigma_k|^{1/2}} \exp\left(-\frac{1}{2}(\mathbf{x}_j - \boldsymbol{\mu}_k)^T \Sigma_k^{-1}(\mathbf{x}_j - \boldsymbol{\mu}_k)\right)\right) \qquad (10.88)$$

—and we seek choices for the model parameters π_k,Γ_k that maximize equation (10.87) (or, equivalently, the log-likelihood L, equation 10.88).

Performing this optimization is clearly non-trivial, but may be done–at high cost—by any one of a number of established techniques. A simpler alternative to these exists as the **expectation-maximization** (EM) algorithm that identifies a local maximum, usually of reasonable quality. EM proceeds iteratively: at each stage it estimates the influence of each Gaussian on each data sample (expectation), and then refines the estimates of the Gaussian parameters (maximization):

- If we have (an estimate of) $\boldsymbol{\mu}_k$ and Σ_k, $k = 1, \ldots, K$, we can compute the probability of the kth Gaussian being responsible for $\mathbf{x}_j$ as

$$p_{jk} = \frac{\pi_k p(\mathbf{x}_j | \Gamma_k)}{\sum_{i=1}^{K} \pi_i p(\mathbf{x}_j | \Gamma_i)} \tag{10.89}$$

—that is, the ratio of the probability of $\mathbf{x}_j$ given Γ_k to the overall probability of $\mathbf{x}_j$ (regardless of the generating Gaussian), suitably weighted by the *current* π_i.

- We can then define

$$\pi_k^{\text{new}} = \frac{1}{N} \sum_{j=1}^{N} p_{jk} \tag{10.90}$$

—that is, the mean p_{jk} over the data set.

Correspondingly, now we can estimate improved values of $\boldsymbol{\mu}_k$ and Σ_k:

$$\boldsymbol{\mu}_k^{\text{new}} = \frac{\sum_{j=1}^{N} p_{jk} \mathbf{x}_j}{\sum_{j=1}^{N} p_{jk}}, \tag{10.91}$$

$$\Sigma_k^{\text{new}} = \frac{\sum_{j=1}^{N} p_{jk}(\mathbf{x}_j - \boldsymbol{\mu}_k^{\text{new}})(\mathbf{x}_j - \boldsymbol{\mu}_k^{\text{new}})^T}{\sum_{j=1}^{N} p_{jk}}. \tag{10.92}$$

Formally, the algorithm is thus:

Algorithm 10.19: Gaussian mixture parameters via expectation-maximization

1. Select the target number of Gaussians K (how to make this selection is discussed further below).

2. Initialize K Gaussians: an easy way of doing this is to run K-means (Algorithm 9.5) on X and set $\boldsymbol{\mu}_k$ and Σ_k from the clusters so determined. K-means itself is susceptible to initialization, and alternatives are to choose points randomly from the dataset, or to select randomly from within the data bounding (hyper-)box.

   The weights π_k may, in the absence of any other information, be initialized to be uniform $\pi_k = 1/K$.

3. **Expectation**: Calculate for each data point $\mathbf{x}_j$ the p_{jk} from the known $\boldsymbol{\mu}_k$, Σ_k: equation (10.89).

4. **Maximization**: Update the Gaussian parameters: equations (10.90–10.92).

5. Iterate from (3) until convergence (or until the parameters of the Γ_k change negligibly).

The basis of this algorithm is far from new (see [Dempster et al., 1977]): under reasonable conditions it can be shown that no iteration decreases the likelihood given in equation (10.88), and therefore must converge.

Similarly to K-means, the algorithm does not assist in making the choice of K. An ad hoc approach to this is to start with a high number of Gaussians, let the algorithm converge, and then progressively remove those with low weights. Better founded approaches take an information theoretic view, and construct a cost function which is the negation of the log-likelihood (equation 10.88) augmented by some term measuring the information content of the model (suitably scaled) in an effort to seek the 'shortest model that does the job properly'. A full consideration of this problem is given by Roberts et al. [Roberts et al., 1998] where several techniques are considered. A successful example is captured by the principle of **minimum description length** which combines equation (10.88) with a count of the number of free parameters of the model M. M is comprised of the K covariance matrices (which are symmetric), the K means, and the K weights, subtracting 1 since the weights sum to 1:

$$M = K\frac{n(n+1)}{2} + Kn + (K-1)$$
$$= \frac{1}{2}Kn^2 + \frac{3}{2}Kn + (K-1).$$

Then the description length, to be minimized, is

$$C = -L(X) + \frac{1}{2}M \log N. \tag{10.93}$$

The first term measures the number of *nats*[5] needed to encode X, and the second the number needed to encode the model to suitable precision. A more elaborate, but costly, approach [Figueiredo and Jain, 2002] successfully minimizes a cost function over K and the model parameters simultaneously, which has the effect of solving problems caused by multiple-initialization and singular Gaussians discussed below.

Returning to the introductory example and considering data from surveying the scene in Figure 10.62a, we can use GMMs in two different ways [McKenna and Nait-Charif, 2004]:

1. Entry and exit points: in this application, these may be considered as 1-dimensional features by projecting trajectory starts and ends to an encompassing 1D contour (at simplest, the image boundary). Figure 10.62b illustrates the result—it is determined that two Gaussians fit the 1D projection best and they are plotted.

2. Positions of inactivity: this is a 2D problem with trajectory pauses being the input. Figure 10.62c illustrates the result—6 Gaussians cover the positions of individuals stopping in the room. (A refinement to the algorithm reduced this to the obvious two.)

Figures 10.62b and 10.62c illustrate some results. (The foregoing is a simplification of what is actually performed; see the original work for a full exposition [McKenna and Nait-Charif, 2004] in which an improvement on the parameter updates of equations (10.90–10.92) is used, and entry/exit points are also considered in 2D.) Figure 10.62d illustrates an application of these data—an individual has entered the room and become

---

[5] 'Bits' measure information content with respect to base-2 logarithms, and nats do the same job with respect to natural logarithms: 1 bit $= \log 2$ nats.

inactive (fallen) in an unexpected position, which would be detected as not being close to one of the modeled positions.

EM has seen very widespread application across computer vision and more widely in AI generally—below we present its specific application to HMMs (see Section 10.11)—but the generality of the approach provides wide opportunity for its exploitation. Just one example is in marrying difficult 3D voxel segmentation to the atlas[6] approach popular in medical applications [Pohl et al., 2006]. Traditionally, the atlas is registered to the image, after which segmentation is performed using the registration as a *prior*—here, the registration is conducted simultaneously and automatically with the segmentation. This reduces inaccuracies that are due to (over-)committing to the registration. Informally, at an iteration of the algorithm, a voxel segmentation into various tissue types is assumed: these have–from the atlas—known intensity distributions that provide an *expectation* which is best-matched to the observed image, from which the *maximization* step then refines the segmentation.

There are two problems with the algorithm in its simple form as described here. Firstly, it is not guaranteed to reach a global optimum, and it is customary to run it several times with different initializations and seek the 'best' result. Secondly, in areas of data sparseness it can develop singularities (that is, Gaussians surround single isolated data points) and is prey to over-specificity (as noted, Figueiredo and Jain address both these issues [Figueiredo and Jain, 2002]). The latter problem has been more straight-forwardly addressed by modifying the maximization step of the algorithm to make the Gaussians more 'fuzzy' [Cootes and Taylor, 1997]. Specifically, equation (10.92) is modified to become

$$\Sigma_k^{\text{new}} = \frac{\sum_{j=1}^{N} p_{jk} \left[(\mathbf{x}_j - \boldsymbol{\mu}_k^{\text{new}})(\mathbf{x}_j - \boldsymbol{\mu}_k^{\text{new}})^T + T_j \right]}{\sum_{j=1}^{N} p_{jk}},$$

where T_j is the covariance of a Gaussian distribution centered on (and peculiar to) the jth data point. The T_j are chosen to be broader in sparser areas; the p.d.f. of the jth Gaussian is given by

$$\frac{1}{(h\,\lambda_j)^n} V\left(\frac{\mathbf{x} - \mathbf{x}_j}{h\,\lambda_j}\right),$$

where V is a Gaussian with covariance equal to that of the data points, n is the data dimension, and

$$h = \left(\frac{4}{2n+1}\right)^{1/(n+4)}.$$

The 'fuzziness' is introduced by the factor λ_j: to determine this we construct a mixture of equal Gaussians centered at each data point;

$$p(\mathbf{x}) = \frac{1}{N} \sum_{j=1}^{N} \frac{1}{h^n} V\left(\frac{\mathbf{x} - \mathbf{x}_j}{h}\right),$$

set g as its geometric mean, and then

$$\lambda_j = \sqrt{\frac{p(\mathbf{x}_j)}{g}}.$$

---

[6] *Atlases* are a reference list of (usually) images that represent particular stages of a condition—clinicians will match a particular case to the 'closest' one in the atlas, giving an 'objective' measure.

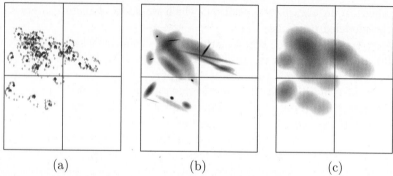

$$(a) \qquad\qquad (b) \qquad\qquad (c)$$

Figure 10.63: Building Gaussian mixture models. (a) Raw data; this is a 2D projection of an abstract, high-dimensional representation of the history of pose-changes of moving cattle [Magee, 2001]. (b) Standard EM algorithm: note the 'tight and crisp' distributions. (c) Modified EM algorithm—the Gaussians are much 'fuzzier'. *Courtesy of D. R. Magee, University of Leeds.*

This rather non-intuitive procedure is well explained by Magee [Magee, 2001] and further underlying theory may be found in [Silverman, 1986]. Figure 10.63 illustrates the effect that this adjustment to EM has when used to build GMMs.

Notice, importantly, that the EM algorithm is general—it does not depend upon the underlying model being a mixture of *Gaussians*, and in many presentations (in particular the original) this assumption is not made. At its most abstract, EM is presented as:

Algorithm 10.20: Expectation-maximization (a generalization of Algorithm 10.19)

1. Assume we are given a set of data X determined by a model which is governed by some parameters $\boldsymbol{\lambda}$. We wish to determine the maximum likelihood estimate of $\boldsymbol{\lambda}$ given X:

$$\boldsymbol{\lambda}^* = \underset{\boldsymbol{\lambda}}{\operatorname{argmax}} \left[L(X; \boldsymbol{\lambda}) \right] .$$

2. Determine *sufficient statistics* necessary for estimating $\boldsymbol{\lambda}$. 'Sufficient statistics' are functions of the data that convey all that is relevant in the estimation of the parameters[7]. (In the GMM case, p_{jk} in equation (10.89) was the sufficient statistic.)

3. Initialize $\boldsymbol{\lambda} = \boldsymbol{\lambda}^0$.

4. Expectation: Compute the sufficient statistics from the data, assuming $\boldsymbol{\lambda}^t$.

5. Maximization: Determine a maximum-likelihood estimate of $\boldsymbol{\lambda}^{(t+1)}$ from the sufficient statistics.

6. Iterate until convergence from (4).

---

[7]For example: if a distribution is known to be normal, and the variance is known to be σ^2, the mean of a sample X is a sufficient statistic for estimating the mean of the distribution μ. Knowing any more about the sample (in particular, the precise data) does not improve the statistician's estimate of μ.

A particular instance of use of EM is the Baum-Welch algorithm used for training HMMs—see page 548. Adopting the notation defined there, suppose we are given a 'guess' at the HMM parameters A, B and π (at initialization, this might even be random). Recall the definition of equation (10.69):

$$\alpha_t(j) = P(Y_{k_1}, Y_{k_2}, \ldots, Y_{k_t}, \text{and state } X_j \text{ at time } t | A, B, \pi),$$

$$\alpha_{t+1}(j) = \sum_{i=1}^{n} [\alpha_t(i) \, a_{ij}] b_{k_{t+1}j},$$

α is the *forward* parameter, telling us the probability of the observation sequence from time 1 to t culminating in state j at time t, given the model. Correspondingly, there is a *backward* parameter giving the probability of the succeeding observations originating from being in state j at time t:

$$\beta_t(j) = P(Y_{k_{t+1}}, Y_{k_{t+2}}, \ldots, Y_{k_T}, \text{and state } X_j \text{ at time } t | A, B, \pi),$$

$$\beta_t(j) = \sum_{i=1}^{n} [\beta_{t+1}(i) \, a_{ij}] b_{k_{t+1}j},$$

and $\beta_T(j) = 1$. Then the probability of the observation sequence and being in state j at time t, given the model, is

$$P(Y^k, X_{i_t} = X_j | A, B, \pi) = \alpha_t(j) \beta_t(j)$$

and so the probability of the sequence, given the model, is (for any t)

$$P(Y^k | A, B, \pi) = \sum_{j=1}^{n} \alpha_t(j) \beta_t(j) \,.$$

Now the overall probability of being in state j at time t, given the observation sequence and the model, is defined as $\gamma_t(j)$, and may be determined by

$$\gamma_t(j) = \frac{\alpha_t(j) \beta_t(j)}{\sum_{j=1}^{n} \alpha_t(j) \beta_t(j)} \tag{10.94}$$

and the probability of being in state r at time t and state s at time $(t+1)$ is defined as $\xi_t(r, s)$, and may be determined by

$$\xi_t(r, s) = \frac{\alpha_t(r) \, a_{rs} \, \beta_{t+1}(s) \, b_{k_{t+1}s}}{\sum_{p=1}^{n} \sum_{q=1}^{n} \alpha_t(p) \, a_{pq} \, \beta_{t+1}(q) \, b_{k_{t+1}q}}, \tag{10.95}$$

γ and ξ (and implicitly, α and β) are our sufficient statistics—they tell us all we need to know to update [improve] the current estimates of A, B and π:

$$\pi_j^{\text{new}} = \gamma_1(j), \tag{10.96}$$

$$a_{ij}^{\text{new}} = \frac{\sum_{t=1}^{T-1} \xi_t(i, j)}{\sum_{t=1}^{T-1} \gamma_t(i)}, \tag{10.97}$$

$$b_{ij}^{\text{new}} = \frac{\sum_{t=1, Y_{k_t} = Y_i}^{T} \gamma_t(j)}{\sum_{t=1}^{T} \gamma_t(j)} \,. \tag{10.98}$$

Equation (10.96) re-approximates π_j as the current best estimate of the probability of being in state j at $t = 1$; equation (10.97) re-approximates a_{ij} as the current best estimate of the probability of moving from state i to state j; and equation (10.98) re-approximates b_{ij} as the current best estimate of the probability of observing i from hidden state j.

Thus we have:

Algorithm 10.21: Baum-Welch training for HMMs (the forward-backward algorithm)

1. Initialize A, B, π using whatever foreknowledge is to hand; if there is none, randomize them.

2. Compute the quantities α, β, from the known observations and the current A, B, π, and thence γ and ξ—equations (10.94) and (10.95).

3. Re-estimate A, B, π from equations (10.96–10.98).

4. Iterate from (2) until convergence.

10.14 Summary

- **Image understanding**

  - Machine vision consists of **lower** and **upper processing levels**, and image understanding is the highest processing level in this classification.

  - The main **computer vision goal** is to achieve machine behavior similar to that of biological systems by applying technically available procedures.

- Image understanding **control strategies**

  - **Parallel** and **serial** processing control.

    * Parallel processing makes several computations simultaneously.
    * Serial processing operations are sequential.
    * Almost all low-level image processing can be done in parallel. High-level processing using higher levels of abstraction is usually serial in essence.

  - **Hierarchical** control

    * **Control by image data (bottom-up control)**: Processing proceeds from raster to segmented image, to region (object) description, and to recognition.
    * **Model-based control (top-down control)**: A set of assumptions and expected properties is constructed from applicable knowledge. Satisfaction of those properties is tested in image representations at different processing levels in a top-down direction, down to original image data. The image understanding is an internal model verification, and the model is either accepted or rejected.
    * **Combined** control uses both data- and model-driven control strategies.

- **Non-hierarchical** control does not distinguish between upper and lower processing levels; non-hierarchical control can be seen as a cooperation of competing experts at the same level (often) using the **blackboard** principle. The blackboard is a shared data structure that can be accessed by multiple experts.

- **Scale invariant feature transform—SIFT**

  - SIFT allows detection of known image feature configurations (points) in view-transformed image data.

  - SIFT extracts *stable* points from images and attaches to them **robust features**, a small subset of which, with **geometric coherence**, suffice to confirm a re-identification of objects in other images.

  - SIFT works in three phases: key location detection, feature extraction, and matching.

  - SIFT only requires three point matches to define a usable transform and is very robust and popular.

- **Model fitting via random sample consensus—RANSAC**

  - Traditional approaches to model fitting are frequently based on least squares approaches, minimizing the sum of square residuals.

  - If data are imperfect, the outliers may negatively affect the model.

  - RANSAC starts with a simple model based on a small subsample of the available data, then uses remaining data points to identify consensus and outlier points. The outliers are removed and the model recomputed.

  - RANSAC represents a paradigm change in model fitting: 'start small and grow' is an opposite approach to least-squares and related techniques that expect to average out deviations.

- **Point distribution models (PDMs)**

  - A PDM is a shape description technique applicable to locating new instances of related shapes in other images. It is most useful for describing features that have well-understood 'general' shape, but which cannot be easily described by a rigid model due to shape variability.

  - The PDM approach requires the existence of a training set of examples (often shape landmarks), from which to derive a statistical description of the shape and its variation.

  - PDMs describe the **modes of variation**—directions of maximum variation are ordered so that it is known where the variation in the model is most likely to occur. Most of the shape variations are usually captured in a small number of modes of variation.

- **Active appearance models (AAMs)**

  - An AAM combines modeling of shape and its variability with modeling of image appearance and its variability.

- – Separate PCA steps are employed to model shape and intensity variations in the training set.
- – A combined PCA on the shape and intensity model parameters yields a set of components that simultaneously capture shape and texture variability.
- – AAMs are an extension of PDMs with an added statistical intensity model of the image patch texture.
- – The AAM approach requires the existence of a training set of examples (image patches with identified object boundaries), from which to derive a statistical description of the shape, intensity, and their combined variation.

- **Pattern recognition** in image understanding

  - – Supervised or unsupervised pattern recognition methods may be used for pixel classification. In the image understanding stage, feature vectors derived from local multi-spectral image values of image pixels are presented to the classifier, which assigns a label to each pixel of the image. Image understanding is then achieved by pixel labeling.
  - – The resulting labeled image may have many small regions, which may be misclassified. **Context-based post-processing** approaches can be applied to avoid this misclassification.
  - – Local object appearance and shape can be described by **histograms of oriented features** (**HOGs**). Objects can be detected and localized in images via (linear) classification of the obtained feature vectors.

- **Boosted cascade of classifiers**

  - – The boosted cascade of classifiers uses a focus-of-attention paradigm.
  - – A large set of simple features is computed and a small set of best features is identified using AdaBoost.
  - – In the next stage, the classifiers are ordered in a cascade sequence starting with simple and therefore fast classifiers used for quickly rejecting object-detection hypotheses, to employing more complex and therefore more powerful but slower classifiers that are applied only to the remaining, not-yet rejected hypotheses.

- **Image understanding using random forests**

  - – Random forest image analysis divides images into **patches** of pre-determined size.
  - – An **image-based training set** consists of image patches found inside object-outlining bounding boxes. Object patches hold **class labels**; non-object patches are considered **background**.
  - – Joint **classification–regression** is used for **simultaneous object detection and localization**.
  - – **Scale** considerations are addressed during the recognition stage, therefore image patches are all of the same size.
  - – A highly successful commercial use of random forests can be found in Microsoft Kinect for XBox.

- **Scene labeling, constraint propagation**

  - **Discrete** labeling allows only one label to be assigned to each object in a final labeling. Effort is directed to achieving a consistent labeling throughout the image. Discrete labeling always finds either a consistent labeling or detects the impossibility of assigning consistent labels to the scene.

  - **Probabilistic** labeling allows multiple labels to co-exist in objects. Labels are weighted probabilistically, with a label confidence being assigned to each object label. Probabilistic labeling always gives an interpretation result together with a measure of confidence in the interpretation.

  - The **constraint propagation** principle facilitates local consistencies adjusting to global consistencies (global optima) in the whole image.

  - Object labeling depends on the **object properties** and on a **measure of compatibility** of the potential object labels with the labeling of other directly interacting objects. Distant objects still interact with each other due to constraint propagation.

  - When **searching interpretation trees**, tree nodes are assigned all possible labels, and a depth-first search based on back-tracking is applied. An interpretation tree search tests all possible labelings.

- **Semantic image segmentation and understanding**

  - **Semantic region growing** techniques incorporate context into the region merging using a priori knowledge about relations among adjacent regions, and then to apply constraint propagation to achieve globally optimal segmentation and interpretation throughout the image.

  - **Genetic image interpretation** is based on a **hypothesize and verify** principle. An objective function which evaluates the quality of a segmentation and interpretation is optimized by a genetic algorithm that is responsible for generating new populations of image segmentation and interpretation hypotheses to be tested.

- **Hidden Markov models**

  - When attempting image understanding, patterns being observed may be modeled as a **transitionary system**. If the transitions are well understood, and the system state is known at a certain instant, transitions can be used to assist in determining the state at a subsequent point. **Markov models** represent one of the simplest examples of this idea

  - **Hidden Markov models** pose three questions: **evaluation**, **decoding**, and **learning**.

  - The **Viterbi algorithm** can be used to reconstruct the system evolution from possibly inaccurate observations.

  - The simple HMM approach lends itself to various elaborations: *coupled* HMMs in which two (or more) HMMs probabilistically cooperate have been successful.

- **Bayesian belief networks**

  - Networks of hidden and visible activity may be connected by Markovian probabilistic relationships.

  - If these networks are circuit-free, efficient algorithms permit the calculation of posterior probabilities given the priors.

  - BBNs are a generic technique that are proving popular in assisting in reasoning in a wide range of computer vision systems.

- **Markov random fields**

  - Markov random fields are probabilistic network structures that generalize the Markov principle of local influence.

  - Theory allows their behavior to be characterized by that of cliques within the network. If the network is a grid, this means immediate neighbors only: this is very useful if the grid is a pixel array.

  - The theory maps onto a wide range of vision problems where a prior assumption is interpreted in the context of an image observation. The probabilistically most likely interpretation can be generated by an MRF.

  - There is a tradeoff between the strength of the prior and the influence of the observation.

  - Maximizing the likelihood of an MRF is frequently achieved with a very efficient graph-cut approach.

  - Applications of this theory in vision are many.

GMMs and EM

  - Gaussian mixture models provide an analytically accessible representation of many aspects of real-world scenes.

  - The Expectation-Maximization (EM) algorithm will determine the parameters of a Gaussian mixture (but maybe not optimally).

  - EM is in fact a general iterative procedure for seeking the unknown parameters of some descriptive model.

  - Another special case of EM is in the training of HMMs with the Baum-Welch algorithm.

10.15   Exercises

Short-answer questions

S10.1 Explain how human vision differs from computer vision. Why is the problem of image understanding so difficult when every small child "knows how to do it"?

S10.2 Explain with examples the differences between lower and upper processing levels.

S10.3 Explain the main ideas of the following image understanding control strategies; if possible, provide a block diagram. Specify their primary applicability within the image understanding process.

    (a) Serial control

    (b) Parallel control

    (c) Bottom-up control

    (d) Top-down control

    (e) Combined control

    (f) Non-hierarchical blackboard control

S10.4 What is conflict resolution? When is it needed?

S10.5 What is the difference between short-term and long-term memory?

S10.6 Give a real-world example of an image understanding application (other than those in the text) in which each of *bottom-up*, *top-down* and *combined control* strategies may be used.

S10.7 Summarize the *key location*, *feature extraction* and *matching* phases of SIFT.

S10.8 Take a linear 2D data set: add noise to selected data points until a least-squares fit fails to come close to 'correct' (many easily available packages will do this). What can you say about the perturbations you have made to achieve this?

S10.9 What kind of information can be represented by point distribution models?

S10.10 Explain the process of determining the modes of variation represented by point distribution models.

S10.11 Considering information provided in Table 10.1, how many principal components must be used in the point distribution model to leave less than 5% variation unexplained?

S10.12 What is the main difference between the PDM and AAM?

S10.13 List and explain all steps needed for

    (a) AAM training and

    (b) AAM-based segmentation

S10.14 Give the most obvious example of how statistical pattern recognition can be used in classification/labeling of multi-spectral satellite image data.

S10.15 Give the essential rationale why a boosted cascade of classifiers is an efficient approach to object detection.

S10.16 Considering AdaBoost, when and why do you stop boosting rounds?

S10.17 Explain principles of the joint classification–regression process when using random forests for object detection and localization.

S10.18 Explain the main strategy of discrete labeling. Give a real-world example of image interpretation to which discrete labeling can be applied, providing details.

S10.19 Explain why discrete relaxation is a special case of probabilistic relaxation.

S10.20 Explain the principle of genetic image segmentation and interpretation. Why are primary and specific adjacency graphs used?

S10.21 Name some shortcomings of conventional image segmentation based on region growing, and on semantic region growing. Does genetic image segmentation and interpretation solve these shortcomings? Which ones and how?

S10.22 Define an order-k Markov model.

S10.23 Define an order-k Hidden Markov model.

S10.24 Define in the context of HMMs:

- Evaluation
- Decoding
- Learning

S10.25 Cite with illustration some problems in which equation (10.85) well describes a vision related problem.

S10.26 Generate and plot some mixtures of 2, 3 and 4 1D Gaussians. Demonstrate to yourself that recapturing the original parameters from observations of the mixture would be difficult.

Problems

P10.1 Find an implementation of SIFT (one is mentioned in the text) and run it on an object of your choice. Determine what perturbations to lighting, or occlusion, are required to defeat its matching.

P10.2 Locate online an implementation of RANSAC. Take an image and shift it in an arbitrary direction. Detect interest points (perhaps by downloading a Harris detector, or similar), and use RANSAC to determine the shift. Experiment with the effect on execution time of number of points. Subject points independently to increasing noise and draw conclusions about robustness.

P10.3 Develop a function for shape alignment as described in Algorithm 10.6. Test its functionality using a variety of artificial shapes.

P10.4 Obtain a database of examples of some non-rigid shape (these may be synthetic). Choose some suitable number of landmark points and determine their 'best' placing on your dataset (if you are able to describe and develop an *automatic* placer, do so). Align all your examples using the program developed in Problem P10.3.

P10.5 Using the function written in Problem P10.3, develop a program determining mean shape and all modes of variation of a set of shapes. Apply the program to five sets consisting of at least 10 shapes each. Give the results in a form of a table similar to Table 10.1.

P10.6 Implement Algorithm 10.7, and test it on some instances of your shape that do not appear in the training dataset. How good is the fitting algorithm? Is it possible to characterize any errors made? If so, how might they be circumvented?

P10.7 Give an example of how statistical pattern recognition can be used in classification of multi-spectral satellite image data. Specify possible features, classes, training set, testing set, type of classifier, and post-processing steps.

P10.8 Implement a classifier-based image interpretation system to recognize objects of different colors in RGB color images. First, test the system using artificial color images. Next, test the system's performance in color images digitized from a scanner or a color TV camera. If the system's performance in digitized color images is unsatisfactory, implement some form of contextual post-processing. Discuss the improvements achieved.

P10.9 Considering the recursive contextual classification approach, after how many recursive steps will image information at (x, y) location (53,145) influence the labeling at location (45,130)?

P10.10 Implement the method for contextual image classification as given in Algorithm 10.10. Test in artificial and real-world images.

P10.11 Implement the method for recursive contextual image classification given in Algorithm 10.11. Test in artificial and real-world images.

P10.12 Using your implementation (developed in Problem P9.31 or P9.32) or one of the publicly available implementations of boosted cascades of classifier, develop a program for training and detection/localization of cars in outdoor scenes similar to those of Figure 10.37.

P10.13 Using your implementation (developed in Problem P9.33) or one of the publicly available implementations of random forests, develop a program for training and detection/localization of cars in outdoor scenes similar to those of Figure 10.37.

P10.14 Compare performance of the boosted cascade of classifiers and random forest approaches developed in Problems P10.12 and P10.13.

P10.15 Develop a program for image interpretation using discrete relaxation as described in Algorithm 10.14. Design a complete set of unary and binary properties needed to interpret scenes similar to that given in Figure 10.45. Test in computer-generated images that do and do not belong to the set of office scenes described.

P10.16 Develop a program for region adjacency graph construction from a segmented and labeled image.

P10.17 Using the program developed in Problem P10.16, create a program for region adjacency graph updating after two or more regions are merged.

P10.18 Explain why the objective function given in the following equation

$$F = \sum_{k=1}^{R} \sum_{i=1}^{N} P(\theta_i = \omega_k) \sum_{j=1}^{N} c_{ij} \sum_{l=1}^{R} r(\theta_i = \omega_k, \theta_j = \omega_l) P(\theta_j = \omega_l) \qquad (10.99)$$

subject to the constraint that the solution satisfies

$$\sum_{k=1}^{R} P(\theta_i = \omega_k) = 1 \quad \text{for any } i, \qquad P(\theta_i = \omega_k) > 0 \quad \text{for any } i, k \qquad (10.100)$$

is appropriate for image interpretation.

Explain what each of the terms represents, and how it contributes to image interpretation.

P10.19 Considering the 'ball on the lawn' example (Figure 10.50), sketch a specific region adjacency graph for the image segmentation and interpretation hypotheses represented by the following genetic strings: (a) LLBLB, (b) LLBBL, (c) BLLLB.

P10.20 Sketch a detailed block diagram of the genetic image interpretation method discussed in Section 10.10.2. How is the genetic algorithm used for generating segmentation and interpretation hypotheses?

P10.21 Determine, either from literature or empirically, the transition probabilities of the characters of English text (it will help to considers only letters and spaces, not case and punctuation). Define some feature measurements (simple ones may be based on bay and lake counts—see Section 2.3.1). Thereby construct a first-order HMM for letter transitions.

Use your model to decode a symbol stream (many HMM toolkits are available online). Where does it make mistakes? If possible, refine your feature set to improve the performance.

P10.22 Find an implementation of graph-cuts to optimize MRFs, and repeat the experiment shown in the text with a binary image segmented after noise is added. Evaluate the segmentation for various values of the smoothness/data trade-off. This could be done, knowing ground truth, using solutions developed to Problems P6.15 and P6.16.

P10.23 Implement (or locate an implementation of) EM for Gaussian Mixture Models. Create a data set of known mixture and run the implementation

    (a) For various numbers (correct and incorrect) of Gaussians;

    (b) For various degrees of noise added to the data;

    (c) For various initializations (e.g., via K-means).

P10.24 Make yourself familiar with solved problems and **Matlab** implementations of selected algorithms provided in the corresponding chapter of the **Matlab Companion** to this text [Svoboda et al., 2008]. The **Matlab Companion** homepage http://visionbook.felk.cvut.cz offers images used in the problems, and well-commented **Matlab** code is provided for educational purposes.

P10.25 Use the **Matlab Companion** [Svoboda et al., 2008] to develop solutions to additional exercises and practical problems provided there. Implement your solutions using **Matlab** or other suitable programming languages.

10.16 References

Agazzi O. E. and Kuo S. Hidden markov model based optical character recognition in the present of deterministic transformations. *Pattern Recognition*, 26(12):1813–1826, 1993.

Ambler A. P. H. A versatile system for computer controlled assembly. *Artificial Intelligence*, 6 (2):129–156, 1975.

Ballard D. H. and Brown C. M. *Computer Vision*. Prentice-Hall, Englewood Cliffs, NJ, 1982.

Baum L. E. and Eagon J. An inequality with applications to statistical prediction for functions of Markov processes and to a model for ecology. *Bulletin of the American Mathematical Society*, 73:360–363, 1963.

Bay H., Ess A., Tuytelaars T., and Van Gool L. Speeded-Up Robust Features (SURF). *Computer Vision Image Understanding*, 110(3):346–359, 2006.

Behloul F., Lelieveldt B. P. F., van der Geest R. J., and Reiber J. H. C. A virtual exploring robot for adaptive left ventricle contour detection in cardiac MR images. In *Medical Image Computing and Computer-Assisted Intervention-MICCAI*, pages 2287–2288, Berlin, 2001. Springer.

Beichel R., Bischof H., Leberl F., and Sonka M. Robust active appearance models and their application to medical image analysis. *IEEE Transactions on Medical Imaging*, 24:1151–1169, 2005.

Beis J. and Lowe D. Shape indexing using approximate nearest-neighbour search in high-dimensional spaces. In *Proceedings of the Conference on Computer Vision and Pattern Recognition CVPR*, pages 1000–1006, Puerto Rico, 1997.

Belongie S., Malik J., and Puzicha J. Matching shapes. In *Proceedings of 8th INternational Conference on Computer Vision, ICCV 2001*, pages 454–461, Vancouver, Canada, 2001. IEEE.

Besag J. Spatial Interaction and the Statistical Analysis of Lattice Systems. *Journal of the Royal Statistical Society. Series B (Methodological)*, 36(2):192–293, 1974. URL http://www.jstor.org/stable/2984812.

Bettinger F. and Cootes T. F. A model of facial behaviour. In *Proc. Int. Conf on Face and Gesture Recognition*, pages 123–128, 2004.

Birchfield S. and Tomasi C. Multiway cut for stereo and motion with slanted surfaces. In *Proceedings of the Seventh International Conference on Computer Vision (ICCV)*, pages 489–495, September 1999.

Blake A., Kohli P., and Rother C., editors. *Markov Random Fields for Vision and Image Processing*. MIT Press, 2011.

Bosch J. G., Mitchell S. C., Lelieveldt B. P. F., Nijland F., Kamp O., Sonka M., and Reiber J. H. C. Automatic segmentation of echocardiographic sequences by active appearance models. *IEEE Transactions on Medical Imaging*, 21:1374–1383, 2002.

Bosch J. G., Nijland F., Mitchell S. C., Lelieveldt B. P. F., Kamp O., Reiber J. H. C., and Sonka M. Computer-aided diagnosis via model-based shape analysis: Automated classification of wall motion abnormalities in echocardiograms. *Academic Radiology*, 12:358–367, 2005.

Bovenkamp E. G. P., Dijkstra J., Bosch J. G., and Reiber J. H. C. Multi-agent segmentation of IVUS images. *Pattern Recognition*, 37:647–663, 2004.

Boykov Y. and Veksler O. Graph cuts in vision and graphics: Theories and applications. In Paragios N., Chen Y., and Faugeras O., editors, *Handbook of Mathematical Models in Computer Vision*, pages 79–96. Springer, New York, 2006.

Boykov Y. and Kolmogorov V. An experimental comparison of min-cut/max-flow algorithms for energy minimization in vision. *IEEE Transactions on Pattern Analysis and Machine Intelligence*, 26(9):1124–1137., 2004.

Boykov Y., Veksler O., and Zabih R. Fast approximate energy minimization via graph cuts. *IEEE Transactions on Pattern Analysis and Machine Intelligence*, 23(11):1222–1239, 2001a.

Boykov Y., Veksler O., and Zabih R. Efficient approximate energy minimization via graph cuts. *IEEE Transactions on Pattern Analysis and Machine Intelligence*, 20(12):1222–1239, 2001b.

Brand M., Oliver N., and Pentland A. P. Coupled hidden Markov models for complex action recognition. In *Proceedings of the IEEE conference on Computer Vision and Pattern Recognition*, pages 994–999, Washington, DC, USA, 1997. IEEE Computer Society.

Brashear H., Starner T., Lukowicz P., and Junker H. Using multiple sensors for mobile sign language recognition. In *Proceedings of the 7th IEEE International Symposium on Wearable Computers*, pages 45–52, White Plains, NY, USA, 2003. IEEE Computer Society.

Brooks R. A., Greiner R., and Binford T. O. The ACRONYM model-based vision system. In *Proceedings of the International Joint Conference on Artificial Intelligence, IJCAI-6*, Tokyo, Japan, pages 105–113, 1979.

Brown M. and Lowe D. Recognising panoramas. In *CVPR '03: Computer Society Conference on Computer Vision and Pattern Recognition*, Madison, WI. IEEE Computer Society, 2003.

Buxton H. Learning and understanding dynamic scene activity. In Pece A., Wu Y. N., and Larsen R., editors, *Proceedings of the First International Workshop on Generative-Model-Based Vision, ECCV 2002*, Copenhagen, Denmark, 2002. Univ. of Copenhagen.

Cabello D., Delgado A., Carreira M. J., Mira J., Moreno-Diaz R., Munoz J. A., and Candela S. On knowledge-based medical image understanding. *Cybernetics and Systems*, 21(2-3):277–289, 1990.

Christmas W. J., Kittler J., and Petrou M. Labelling 2-D geometric primitives using probabilistic relaxation: reducing the computational requirements. *Electronics Letters*, 32:312–314, 1996.

Comaniciu D. and Meer P. Robust analysis of feature spaces: Color image segmentation. In *Proc. IEEE Conf. on Computer Vision and Pattern Recognition*, pages 750–755. IEEE, 1997.

Cootes T. and Taylor C. A mixture model for representing shape variation. In Clark A., editor, *Proceedings of the British Machine Vision Conference*, Colchester, UK, pages 110–119. BMVA Press, 1997.

Cootes T. F. and Taylor C. J. An algorithm for tuning an active appearance model to new data. In *Proc. British Machine Vision Conference*, pages 919–928, 2006.

Cootes T. F. and Taylor C. J. Statistical models of appearance for computer vision. Technical Report http://www.isbe.man.ac.uk/~bim/Models/app_models.pdf, Imaging Science and Biomedical Engineering, University of Manchester, U.K., 2004.

Cootes T. F. and Taylor C. J. Active shape models—'smart snakes'. In Hogg D. C. and Boyle R. D., editors, *Proceedings of the British Machine Vision Conference*, Leeds, UK, pages 266–275, London, 1992. Springer Verlag.

Cootes T. F., Taylor C. J., Cooper D. H., and Graham J. Training models of shape from sets of examples. In Hogg D. C. and Boyle R. D., editors, *Proceedings of the British Machine Vision Conference*, Leeds, UK, pages 9–18, London, 1992. Springer Verlag.

Cootes T. F., Taylor C. J., and Lanitis A. Active shape models: Evaluation of a multi-resolution method for improving image search. In Hancock E., editor, *Proceedings of the British Machine Vision Conference*, York, UK, volume 1, pages 327–336. BMVA Press, 1994.

Cootes T. F., Beeston C., Edwards G. J., and Taylor C. J. A unified framework for atlas matching using active appearance models. In Kuba A. and Samal M., editors, *Information Processing in Medical Imaging*, Lecture Notes in Computer Science, pages 322–333, Berlin, 1999. Springer Verlag.

Cootes T. F., Edwards G. J., and Taylor C. J. Active appearance models. *IEEE Transactions on Pattern Analysis and Machine Intelligence*, 23:681–685, 2001.

Criminisi A. and Shotton J. *Decision Forests for Computer Vision and Medical Image Analysis*. Springer Verlag, London, 2013.

Criminisi A., Shotton J., and Konukoglu E. Decision forests for classification, regression, density estimation, manifold learning and semi-supervised learning. Technical Report MSR-TR-2011-114, Microsoft Research, Ltd., Cambridge, UK, 2011.

Criminisi A., Shotton J., Robertson D., and Konukoglu E. Regression forests for efficient anatomy detection and localization in CT studies. In *MICCAI 2010 Workshop MCV*, volume LNCS 6533, pages 106–117. Springer Verlag, 2010.

Cristinacce D., Cootes T. F., and Scott I. A multistage approach to facial feature detection. In *Proc. British Machine Vision Conference, Vol. 1*, pages 277–286, 2004.

Dalal N. *Finding people in images and videos*. Ph.D. thesis, Institut National Polytechnique de Grenoble, July 2006. URL http://lear.inrialpes.fr/pubs/2006/Dal06.

Dalal N. and Triggs B. Histograms of oriented gradients for human detection. In *International Conference on Computer Vision & Pattern Recognition*, pages 886–893. IEEE, 2005.

Davies R. H., Twining C. J., Cootes T. F., Waterton J. C., and Taylor C. J. A minimum description length approach to statistical shape modeling. *IEEE Transactions on Medical Imaging*, 21(5):525–537, 2002a.

Davies R. H., Twining C. J., Cootes T. F., Waterton J. C., and Taylor C. J. 3D statistical shape models using direct optimisation of description length. In *Proc. European Conference on Computer Vision (ECCV)*, pages 3–21, 2002b.

Dee H. M., Hogg D. C., and Cohn A. G. Building semantic scene models from unconstrained video. *Computer Vision and Image Understanding*, 116(3):446–456, 2012.

Dempster A., Laird M., and Rubin D. Maximum likelihood from incomplete data via the EM algorithm. *Journal of the Royal Statistical Society, Series B*, 39(1):1–38, 1977.

Duta N. and Sonka M. Segmentation and interpretation of MR brain images: An improved active shape model. *IEEE Transactions on Medical Imaging*, 17:1049–1062, 1998.

Duta N., Sonka M., and Jain A. K. Learning shape models from examples using automatic shape clustering and Procrustes analysis. In *Information Processing in Medical Imaging*, pages 370–375, Berlin, 1999. Springer.

Elfving T. and Eklundh J. O. Some properties of stochastic labeling procedures. *Computer Graphics and Image Processing*, 20:158–170, 1982.

Elms A. J. and Illingworth J. Combining HMMs for the recognition of noisy printed characters. In Hancock E., editor, *Proceedings of the British Machine Vision Conference,* York, UK, volume 2, pages 185–194. BMVA Press, 1994.

Everingham M., Van Gool L., Williams C. K. I., Winn J., and Zisserman A. The PASCAL visual object classes (VOC) challenge. *International Journal of Computer Vision*, 88:303–338, 2010.

Feldman J. A. and Yakimovsky Y. Decision theory and artificial intelligence: A semantic–based region analyzer. *Artificial Intelligence*, 5:349–371, 1974.

Ferrarini L., Olofsen H., Reiber J. H. C., and Admiraal-Behloul F. A neurofuzzy controller for 3D virtual centered navigation in medical images of tubular structures. In *International Conference on Artificial Neural Networks–ICANN*, pages 371–376, Berlin, 2005. Springer – LNCS 3697.

Figueiredo M. and Jain A. Unsupervised learning of finite mixture models. *IEEE Transactions on Pattern Analysis and Machine Intelligence*, 24(3):381–396, 2002.

Fischler M. A. and Bolles R. C. Random sample consensus: A paradigm for model fitting with applications to image analysis and automated cartography. *Communications of the ACM*, 24(6):381–395, 1981.

Fisher R. B. Hierarchical matching beats the non-wildcard and interpretation tree model matching algorithms. In Illingworth J., editor, *Proceedings of the British Machine Vision Conference,* Surrey, UK, volume 1, pages 589–598. BMVA Press, 1993.

Fisher R. B. Performance comparison of ten variations of the interpretation tree matching algorithm. In Eklundh J. O., editor, *3rd European Conference on Computer Vision,* Stockholm, Sweden, volume 1, pages 507–512, Berlin, 1994. Springer Verlag.

Fletcher S., Bulpitt A., and Hogg D. Global alignment of MR images using a scale based hierarchical model. In Buxton B. and Cipolla R., editors, *4th European Conference on Computer Vision,* Cambridge, England, volume 2, pages 283–292, Berlin, 1996. Springer Verlag.

Frangi A., Rueckert D., Schnabel J., and Niessen W. Automatic construction of multiple-object three-dimensional statistical shape models: Application to cardiac modeling. *IEEE Transactions on Medical Imaging*, 21(9):1151–66, 2002.

Freeman W. T. and Roth M. Orientation histograms for hand gesture recognition. In *International Workshop on Automatic Face- and Gesture-Recognition*, pages 296–301, Zurich, Switzerland, 1995. IEEE.

Frey B. and Jojic N. A comparison of algorithms for inference and learning in probabilistic graphical models. *IEEE Transactions on Pattern Analysis and Machine Intelligence*, 27(9): 1392–1416, 2005.

Fung P. W., Grebbin G., and Attikiouzel Y. Contextual classification and segmentation of textured images. In *Proceedings of the 1990 International Conference on Acoustics, Speech, and Signal Processing—ICASSP 90,* Albuquerque, NM, pages 2329–2332, Piscataway, NJ, 1990. IEEE.

Gall J. and Lempitsky V. Class-specific hough forests for object detection. In *Computer Vision and Pattern Recognition, 2009. CVPR 2009. IEEE Conference on*, pages 1022–1029, 2009.

Gall J., Yao A., Razavi N., Van Gool L., and Lempitsky V. Hough forests for object detection, tracking, and action recognition. *Pattern Analysis and Machine Intelligence, IEEE Transactions on*, 33(11):2188–2202, 2011.

Gall J., Razavi N., and Gool L. An introduction to random forests for multi-class object detection. In Dellaert F., Frahm J.-M., Pollefeys M., Leal-Taixe L., and Rosenhahn B., editors, *Outdoor and Large-Scale Real-World Scene Analysis*, volume 7474 of *Lecture Notes in Computer Science*, pages 243–263. Springer Berlin Heidelberg, 2012.

Geman S. and Geman D. Stochastic relaxation, Gibbs distributions, and the Bayesian restoration of images. *IEEE Transactions on Pattern Analysis and Machine Intelligence*, 6(6): 721–741, 1984.

Gerig G., Martin J., Kikinis R., Kubler O., Shenton M., and Jolesz F. A. Unsupervised tissue type segmentation of 3D dual-echo MR head data. *Image and Vision Computing*, 10(6): 349–360, 1992.

Ghosh J. and Harrison C. G., editors. *Parallel Architectures for Image Processing*, Santa Clara, CA, Bellingham, WA, 1990. SPIE.

Gong L. and Kulikowski C. A. Composition of image analysis processes through object-centered hierarchical planning. *IEEE Transactions on Pattern Analysis and Machine Intelligence*, 17:997–1009, 1995.

Green T. A word in your ear. *Personal Computer World*, pages 354–370, 1995.

Grimson W. E. L. *Object Recognition by Computer: The Role of Geometric Constraints*. MIT Press, Cambridge, MA, 1990.

Grimson W. E. L. and Lozano-Perez T. Localizing overlapping parts by searching the interpretation tree. *IEEE Transactions on Pattern Analysis and Machine Intelligence*, 9(4): 469–482, 1987.

Hancock E. R. and Kittler J. Discrete relaxation. *Pattern Recognition*, 23(7):711–733, 1990.

Hanson A. R. and Riseman E. M. VISIONS—a computer system for interpreting scenes. In Hanson A. R. and Riseman E. M., editors, *Computer Vision Systems*, pages 303–333. Academic Press, New York, 1978.

Harvey R., Matthews I., Bangham J. A., and Cox S. Lip reading from scale-space measurements. In *Computer Vision and Pattern Recognition*, pages 582–587, Los Alamitos, CA, 1997. IEEE Computer Society.

Heap A. J. Wormholes in shape space: Tracking through discontinuous changes in shape. In Ahuja N., editor, *International Conference on Computer Vision*, Bombay, India, pages 344–349, Bombay, 1998. Narosa.

Heap A. J. and Hogg D. C. Extending the Point Distribution Model using polar coordinates. *Image and Vision Computing*, 14(8):589–600, 1996.

Huang X. D., Akiri Y., and Jack M. A. *Hidden Markov Models for Speech Recognition*. Edinburgh University Press, Edinburgh, Scotland, 1990.

Huang Y., Brown M. S., and Xu D. A framework for reducing ink-bleed in old documents. In *Proceedings of the IEEE International Conference on Computer Vision and Pattern Recognition*, 2008.

Hummel R. A. and Zucker S. W. On the foundation of relaxation labeling proceses. *IEEE Transactions on Pattern Analysis and Machine Intelligence*, 5(3):259–288, 1983.

Hwang S. Y. and Wang T. P. The design and implementation of a distributed image understanding system. *Journal of Systems Integration*, 4:107–125, 1994.

Intille S. and Bobick A. Recognizing planned multi-person action. *Computer Vision and Image Understanding*, 3:414–445, 2001.

Johnson S. and Everingham M. Learning effective human pose estimation from inaccurate annotation. In *IEEE Conference on Computer Vision and Pattern Recognition, CVPR 11*, pages 1465–1472, Los Alamitos, CA, USA, 2011. IEEE Computer Society.

Jurie F. and Gallice J. A recognition network model-based approach to dynamic image understanding. *Annals of Mathematics and Artificial Intelligence*, 13:317–345, 1995.

Kamada M., Toraichi K., Mori R., Yamamoto K., and Yamada H. Parallel architecture for relaxation operations. *Pattern Recognition*, 21(2):175–181, 1988.

Kanade T. and Ikeuchi K. Special issue on physical modeling in computer vision. *IEEE Transactions on Pattern Analysis and Machine Intelligence*, 13:609–742, 1991.

Kasif S. On the parallel complexity of discrete relaxation in constraint satisfaction networks. *Artificial Intelligence*, 45(3):275–286, 1990.

Kaus M., von Berg J., Weese J., Niessen W., and Pekar V. Automated segmentation of the left ventricle in cardiac. *Medical Image Analysis*, 8(3):245–254, 2004.

Ke Y. and Sukthankar R. PCA-SIFT: A more distinctive representation for local image descriptors. In *Proceedings of CVPR*, pages 506–513, 2004.

Kittipanyangam P. and Cootes T. F. The effect of texture representations on AAM performance. In *Proc. International Conference on Pattern Recognition*, pages 328–331, 2006.

Kittler J. Relaxation labelling. In *Pattern Recognition Theory and Applications*, pages 99–108. Springer Verlag, Berlin–New York–Tokyo, 1987.

Kittler J. and Foglein J. Contextual classification of multispectral pixel data. *Image and Vision Computing*, 2(1):13–29, 1984a.

Kittler J. and Foglein J. Contextual decision rules for objects in lattice configuration. In *7th International Conference on Pattern Recognition*, Montreal, Canada, pages 270–272, Piscataway, NJ, 1984b. IEEE.

Kittler J. and Foglein J. On compatibility and support functions in probabilistic relaxation. *Computer Vision, Graphics, and Image Processing*, 34:257–267, 1986.

Kittler J. and Hancock E. R. Combining evidence in probabilistic relaxation. *International Journal on Pattern Recognition and Artificial Intelligence*, 3:29–52, 1989.

Kittler J. and Illingworth J. Relaxation labelling algorithms—a review. *Image and Vision Computing*, 3(4):206–216, 1985.

Kittler J. and Pairman D. Contextual pattern recognition applied to cloud detection and identification. *IEEE Transactions on Geoscience and Remote Sensing*, 23(6):855–863, 1985.

Kodratoff Y. and Moscatelli S. Machine learning for object recognition and scene analysis. *International Journal of Pattern Recognition and Artificial Intelligence*, 8:259–304, 1994.

Kolmogorov V. and Zabih R. What energy functions can be minimized via graph cuts? *IEEE Transactions on Pattern Analysis and Machine Intelligence*, 26(2):147–159, 2004.

Kuan D., Shariat H., and Dutta K. Constraint-based image understanding system for aerial imagery interpretation. In *Proceedings of the Annual AI Systems in Government Conference*, Washington, DC, pages 141–147, 1989.

Kundu A., He Y., and Bahi P. Recognition of handwritten word: First and second order HMM based approach. *Pattern Recognition*, 22(3):283–297, 1989.

Kwatra V., Schödl A., Essa I., Turk G., and Bobick A. Graphcut textures: Image and video synthesis using graph cuts. *ACM Transactions on Graphics*, 22(3):277–286, 2003.

Lee D., Papageorgiou A., and Wasilkowski G. W. Computing optical flow. In *Proceedings, Workshop on Visual Motion*, Irvine, CA, pages 99–106, Piscataway, NJ, 1989. IEEE.

Lelieveldt B. P. F., Frangi A., Mitchell S., Assen H. v, Ordas S., Reiber J. H. C., and Sonka M. 3D active shape and appearance models in cardiac image analysis. In *Handbook of Mathematical Models in Computer Vision*, pages 471–486, Berlin, 2006. Springer.

Lesser V. R., Fennell R. D., Erman L. D., and Reddy D. R. Organisation of the HEARSAY II speech understanding system. *IEEE Transactions on Acoustics, Speech and Signal Processing*, 23(1):11–24, 1975.

Lorenz C. and Krahnstover N. Generation of point-based 3D statistical shape models for anatomical objects. *Computer Vision and Image Understanding*, 77(2):175–191, 2000.

Lowe D. G. Distinctive image features from scale-invariant keypoints. *International Journal of Computer Vision*, 60(2):91–110, 2004.

Lu C. S. and Chung P. C. Fuzzy-based probabilistic relaxation for textured image segmentation. In *Proceedings of the International Conference on Fuzzy Systems*, pages 77–82. IEEE, 1994.

Magee D. R. *Machine Vision Techniques for the Evaluation of Animal Behaviour*. Ph.D. thesis, University of Leeds, 2001. pages 91-93.

Marr D. *Vision—A Computational Investigation into the Human Representation and Processing of Visual Information*. Freeman, San Francisco, 1982.

McKenna S. J. and Nait-Charif H. Summarising contextual activity and detecting unusual inactivity in a supportive home environment. *Pattern Analysis and Applications*, 7(4):386–401, 2004.

Mitchell S. C., Bosch J. G., Lelieveldt B. P. F., van der Geest R. J., Reiber J. H. C., and Sonka M. 3-D Active Appearance Models: Segmentation of cardiac MR and ultrasound images. *IEEE Transactions on Medical Imaging*, 21:1167–1178, 2002.

Mitchell S., Lelieveldt B., van der Geest R., Bosch H., Reiber J., and Sonka M. Multistage hybrid active appearance model matching: Segmentation of left and right ventricles in cardiac MR images. *IEEE Trans. Med. Imag.*, 20:415–423, 2001.

Mohn E., Hjort N. L., and Storvik G. O. Simulation study of some contextual classification methods for remotely sensed data. *IEEE Transactions on Geoscience and Remote Sensing*, 25(6):796–804, 1987.

Nagao M. and Matsuyama T. *A Structural Analysis of Complex Aerial Photographs*. Plenum Press, New York, 1980.

Nilsson N. J. *Principles of Artificial Intelligence*. Springer Verlag, Berlin, 1982.

Oliver N., Pentland A. P., and Berard F. LAFTER: Lips and face real time tracker. In *Computer Vision and Pattern Recognition*, pages 123–129, Los Alamitos, CA, 1997. IEEE Computer Society.

Oost C. R., Lelieveldt B. P. F., Uzumcu M., Lamb H. J., Reiber J. H. C., and Sonka M. Multi-view active appearance models: Application to X-ray LV angiography and cardiac MRI. In Taylor C. and J.A. N., editors, *Information Processing in Medical Imaging*, volume 2732 of *Lecture Notes in Computer Science*, pages 234–245, Berlin, 2003. Springer Verlag.

Oost E., Koning G., Sonka M., Oemrawsingh P. V., Reiber J. H. C., and Lelieveldt B. P. F. Automated contour detection in x-ray left ventricular angiograms using multiview active appearance models and dynamic programming. *IEEE Transactions on Medical Imaging*, 25:1158–1171, 2006.

Parent P. and Zucker S. W. Radial projection: An efficient update rule for relaxation labeling. *IEEE Transactions on Pattern Analysis and Machine Intelligence*, 11(8):886–889, 1989.

Pavlidis T. and Liow Y. Integrating region growing and edge detection. *IEEE Transactions on Pattern Analysis and Machine Intelligence*, 12(3):225–233, 1990.

Pearl J. *Probabalistic reasoning in intelligent systems*. Morgan Kaufmann, San Mateo, CA, 1987.

Pelillo M. and Fanelli A. M. Autoassociative learning in relaxation labeling networks. *Pattern Recognition Letters*, 18:3–12, 1997.

Pohl K. M., Fisher J., Grimson W. E. L., Kikinis R., and Wells W. M. A bayesian model for joint segmentation and registration. *Neuroimage*, 31:228–239, 2006.

Prasanna Kumar V. K. *Parallel Architectures and Algorithms for Image Understanding*. Academic Press, Boston, 1991.

Prince S. J. D. *Computer Vision: Models, Learning, and Inference*. Cambridge University Press, New York, NY, USA, 2012.

Puliti P. and Tascini G. Knowledge-based approach to image interpretation. *Image and Vision Computing*, 11:122–128, 1993.

Rabiner L. R. A tutorial on Hidden Markov Models and selected applications in speech recognition. *Proceedings of the IEEE*, 77(2):257–286, 1989.

Rao A. R. and Jain R. Knowledge representation and control in computer vision systems. *IEEE Expert*, 3(1):64–79, 1988.

Roberts S. J., Husmeier D., Rezek I., and Penny W. D. Bayesian approaches to Gaussian mixture modeling. *IEEE Transactions on Pattern Analysis and Machine Intelligence*, 20 (11):1133–1142, 1998.

Rosenfeld A., Hummel R. A., and Zucker S. W. Scene labelling by relaxation operations. *IEEE Transactions on Systems, Man and Cybernetics*, 6:420–433, 1976.

Schlenzig J., Hunter E., and Jain R. Recursive identification of gesture inputers using HMMs. In *Proceedings of the 2nd Annual Conference on Computer Vision*, Sarasota, FL, pages 187–194, New York, 1994. IEEE Computer Society Press.

Shotton J., Fitzgibbon A., Cook M., Sharp T., Finocchio M., Moore R., Kipman A., and Blake A. Real-time human pose recognition in parts from single depth images. In *Computer Vision and Pattern Recognition (CVPR), 2011 IEEE Conference on*, pages 1297–1304, 2011.

Silverman B. M. *Density Estimation for Statistics and Data Analysis*. Chapman and Hall, New York, 1986.

Sonka M., Tadikonda S. K., and Collins S. M. Knowledge-based interpretation of MR brain images. *IEEE Transactions on Medical Imaging*, 15:443–452, 1996.

Sorenson H. W. Least-squares estimation: from Gauss to Kalman. *IEEE Spectrum*, pages 7–12, 1970.

Sozou P. D., Cootes T. F., Taylor C. J., and Di-Mauro A. C. A non-linear generalization of PDMs using polynomial regression. In Hancock E., editor, *Proceedings of the British Machine Vision Conference*, York, UK, volume 2, pages 397–406. BMVA Press, 1994.

Stegmann M. B. *Generative Interpretation of Medical Images*. Ph.D. thesis, Informatics and Mathematical Modeling Institute, Technical University of Denmark, 2004.

Strat T. M. and Fischler M. A. Context-based vision: Recognizing objects using information from both 2D and 3D imagery. *IEEE Transactions on Pattern Analysis and Machine Intelligence*, 13(10):1050–1065, 1991.

Suinesiaputra A., Frangi A. F., Uzumcu M., Reiber J. H. C., and Lelieveldt B. P. F. Extraction of myocardial contractility patterns from short-axes MR images using independent component analysis. In *Computer Vision and Mathematical Methods in Medical and Biomedical Image Analysis*, pages 75–86, Berlin, 2004. Springer.

Sun J., Zheng N., and Shum H.-Y. Stereo matching using belief propagation. *IEEE Transactions on Pattern Analysis and Machine Intelligence*, 25(7):787–800, 2003.

Svoboda T., Kybic J., and Hlavac V. *Image Processing, Analysis, and Machine Vision: A MATLAB Companion*. Thomson Engineering, 2008.

Tagare H. D., Vos F. M., Jaffe C. C., and Duncan J. S. Arrangement: A spatial relation between parts for evaluating similarity of tomographic sections. *IEEE Transactions on Pattern Analysis and Machine Intelligence*, 17:880–893, 1995.

Tanner J. M., Whitehouse R. H., Cameron N., Marshall W. A., Healy M. J. R., and Goldstein H. *Assessment of Skeletal Maturity and Prediction of Adult Height*. Academic Press, London, 1983.

Tieu K. and Viola P. Boosting image retrieval. *International Journal of Computer Vision*, 56: 781–796, 2004.

Tilton J. C. Contextual classification on the massively parallel processor. In *Frontiers of Massively Parallel Scientific Computation*, Greenbelt, MD, pages 171–181, Washington, DC, 1987. NASA.

Toulson D. L. and Boyce J. F. Segmentation of MR images using neural nets. *Image and Vision Computing*, 10(5):324–328, 1992.

Tuytelaars T. and Mikolajczyk K. Local invariant descriptors: a survey. *Foundations and Trends in Computer Graphics and Vision*, 3(3):177–280, 2007.

Twining C. J., Cootes T. F., Marsland S., Petrovic V. S., Schestowitz R. S., and Taylor C. Information-theoretic unification of groupwise non-rigid registration and model building. In *Proc. Medical Image Understanding and Analysis, Vol. 2*, pages 226–230, 2006.

Udupa J. K. and Samarasekera S. Fuzzy connectedness and object definition: Theory, algorithms, and applications in image segmentation. *Graphical Models and Image Processing*, 58:246–261, 1996.

van Assen H., Danilouchkine M. G., Behloul F., Lamb H. J., van der Geest R. J., Reiber J. H. C., and Lelieveldt B. P. F. Cardiac LV segmentation using a 3D active shape model driven by fuzzy inference. In *Proc. MICCAI*, volume 2878 of *Lecture Notes in Computer Science*, pages 535–540. Springer Verlag, Berlin, 2003.

van der Geest R. J., Lelieveldt B. P. F., Angelie E., Danilouchkine M., Sonka M., and Reiber J. H. C. Evaluation of a new method for automated detection of left ventricular contours in time series of magnetic resonance images using an active appearance motion model. *Journal of Cardiovascular Magnetic Resonance*, 6(3):609–617, 2004.

Vincent L. and Soille P. Watersheds in digital spaces: An efficient algorithm based on immersion simulations. *IEEE Transactions on Pattern Analysis and Machine Intelligence*, 13(6):583–598, 1991.

Viola P. and Jones M. Rapid object detection using a boosted cascade of simple features. In *Proceedings IEEE Conf. on Computer Vision and Pattern Recognition*, pages 511–518, Kauai, Hawaii, 2001. IEEE.

Viola P., Jones M., and Snow D. Detecting pedestrians using patterns of motion and appearance. In *Proc. Int. Conf. Computer Vision*, pages 734–741, Nice, France, 2003.

Viterbi A. J. Convolutional codes and their performance in communication systems. *IEEE Transactions on Communications Technology*, 13(2):260–269, 1967.

Vlontzos J. A. and Kung S. Y. HMMs for character recognition. *IEEE Transactions on Image Processing*, IP-1(4):539–543, 1992.

Watanabe T. and Suzuki H. An experimental evaluation of classifiers using spatial context for multispectral images. *Systems and Computers in Japan*, 19(4):33–47, 1988.

Watanabe T. and Suzuki H. Compound decision theory and adaptive classification for multi-spectral image data. *Systems and Computers in Japan*, 20(8):37–47, 1989.

Weiss Y. Interpreting images by propagating Bayesian beliefs. In Mozer M. C., Jordan M. I., and Petsche T., editors, *Advances in Neural Information Processing Systems*, volume 9, page 908. The MIT Press, 1997.

Wharton S. A contextual classification method for recognising land use patterns in high resolution remotely sensed data. *Pattern Recognition*, 15:317–324, 1982.

Wu Z. and Leahy R. An optimal graph theoretic approach to data clustering: Theory and its application to image segmentation. *IEEE Transactions on Pattern Analysis and Machine Intelligence*, 15:1101–1113, 1993.

Zen C., Lin S. Y., and Chen Y. Y. Parallel architecture for probabilistic relaxation operation on images. *Pattern Recognition*, 23(6):637–645, 1990.

Zhang C. and Zhang Z. A survey of recent advances in face detection. Technical Report MSR-TR-2010-66, Microsoft, June 2010.

Zhang H., Wahle A., Johnson R., Scholz T., and Sonka M. 4-d cardiac mr image analysis: Left and right ventricular morphology and function. *Medical Imaging, IEEE Transactions on*, 29:350–364, 2010.

Zhang M. C., Haralick R. M., and Campbell J. B. Multispectral image context classification using stochastic relaxation. *IEEE Transactions on Systems, Man and Cybernetics*, 20(1): 128–140, 1990.

Zheng Y. J. Feature extraction and image segmentation using self-organizing networks. *Machine Vision and Applications*, 8:262–274, 1995.

Zisserman A., editor. *Workshop on 25 Years of RANSAC (In conjunction with CVPR'06)*. New York, NY, 2006.

Chapter **11**

3D geometry, correspondence, 3D from intensities

A number of image analysis techniques aiming at 2D images have been presented in earlier chapters. What has been overlooked hitherto is the observation that the best vision system, our own, and so far unbeatable by machines, is geared to deal with the 3D world. In this chapter we shall start to fill the gap; we shall concentrate on intermediate-level vision tasks in which 3D scene properties are inferred from 2D image representations. Methods for extracting 3D information and interpreting 3D scenes will be presented.

There are many serious reasons why 3D vision using intensity images as input is regarded as difficult.

- The imaging system of a camera and the human eye performs perspective projection, which leads to considerable loss of information. All points along a line pointing from the optical center towards a scene point are projected to a single image point. We are interested in the inverse task that aims to derive 3D coordinates from image measurements—this task is under-constrained, and some additional information must be added to solve it unambiguously.

- The relationship between image intensity and the 3D geometry of the corresponding scene point is very complicated. Intensity depends on surface reflectivity parameters, orientation, type and position of illuminants, and the position of the viewer. Attempting to learn 3D geometry—surface orientation and depth—is another ill-conditioned task.

- Mutual occlusion of objects in the scene, and even self-occlusion of one object, further complicates the vision task.

- Noise in images, and the high time complexity of many algorithms, contributes further to the problem, although this is not specific to 3D vision.

The chapter is organized as follows: in Section 11.1, we shall consider various 3D vision paradigms, and Marr's theory of 3D vision from the late 1970s will be explained in more detail; albeit dated, this is still the most generally accepted paradigm. From 11.2 onward we explain geometrical issues that constitute mathematical machinery needed to solve 3D vision tasks. Section 11.7 tackles the relationship between image intensities and 3D shape of the corresponding scene point given by its surface normal.

11.1 3D vision tasks

No unified theory of 3D vision is available; different research groups may have different understandings of the task. Several 3D vision tasks and related paradigms illustrate the variety of opinions:

- Marr [Marr, 1982] defines 3D vision as '*From an image (or a series of images) of a scene, derive an accurate three-dimensional geometric description of the scene and quantitatively determine the properties of the object in the scene*'. Here, 3D vision is formulated as a 3D object reconstruction task, i.e., description of the 3D shape in a coordinate system independent of the viewer. One rigid object, whose separation from the background is straightforward, is assumed, and control of the process is strictly bottom-up from an intensity image through intermediate representations. Treating 3D vision as scene recovery seems reasonable. If vision cues give us a precise representation of a 3D scene then many visual tasks—for example, navigation of an autonomous vehicle, parts inspection, or object recognition —may be carried out. The recovery paradigm needs to know the relation between an image and the corresponding 3D world, and thus image formation needs to be described.

- Aloimonos and Shulman [Aloimonos and Shulman, 1989] see the central problem of computer vision as: '*. . . from one or the sequence of images of a moving or stationary object or scene taken by a monocular or polynocular moving or stationary observer, to* understand *the object or the scene and its three-dimensional properties*'. Here, it is the concept *understand* that makes this approach to computer vision different. If only a little a priori knowledge is available, as in human vision, then understanding is complicated. This might be seen as one limiting case; the other extreme in the complexity spectrum is, e.g., a simple object matching problem in which there are only several known possible interpretations.

- Wechsler [Wechsler, 1990] stresses the control principle of the process, stating that '*the visual system casts most visual tasks as minimization problems and solves them using distributed computation and enforcing nonaccidental, natural constraints*'. Computer vision is seen as a parallel distributed representation, plus parallel distributed processing, plus active perception. The understanding is carried in the 'perception—control—action' cycle.

- Aloimonos [Aloimonos, 1993] asks what principles might enable us to understand the vision systems of living organisms, and then to equip machines with visual capabilities. There are several of related questions:

  - *Empirical questions—What is?*— determine how existing visual systems are designed.

- *Normative questions—What should be?—* determine characteristics of either natural or ideal vision systems that would be desirable.

- *Theoretical questions—What could be?—* questions about mechanisms that could exist in intelligent visual systems.

System theory [Klir, 1991] provides a general framework that allows us understand complex phenomena using the machinery of mathematics. Objects and their properties need to be characterized, and a formal mathematical model is typically used for this abstraction. The model is specified by a relatively small number of parameters, which are typically estimated from the (image) data.

This methodology allows us to describe the same object using qualitatively different models (e.g., algebraic or differential equations) when varying resolution is used during observation. Studying changes of models with respect to several resolutions may give deeper insights into the problem.

An attempt to create a computer-based vision system comprises three intertwined problems:

1. **Feature observability in images.** We need to determine whether task-relevant information will be present in the primary image data.

2. **Representation.** This problem is related to the choice of model for the observed world, at various levels of interpretation complexity.

3. **Interpretation.** This problem tackles the semantics of the data—in other words, how are data mapped to the (real) world. The task is to make certain information explicit from a mathematical model storing it in an implicit form.

Two main approaches to artificial vision, according to the flow of information and the amount of a priori knowledge, are typically considered (see Chapter 10).

1. **Reconstruction, bottom-up.** The aim is to reconstruct the 3D shape of the object from an image or set of images, which might be either intensity or range images (distance from the observer). One extreme is given by Marr's theory [Marr, 1982], which is strictly bottom-up with very little a priori knowledge about the objects needed. Some, more practical, approaches aim to create a 3D model from real objects using range images [Flynn and Jain, 1991, 1992; Soucy and Laurendeau, 1992; Bowyer, 1992].

2. **Recognition, top-down, model-based vision.** The a priori knowledge about the objects is expressed by means of the models of the objects, where 3D models are of particular interest [Brooks et al., 1979; Goad, 1986; Besl and Jain, 1985; Farshid and Aggarwal, 1993]. Recognition based on CAD models is of practical importance [Newman et al., 1993]. Additional constraints embedded in the model make under-determined vision tasks possible in many cases.

Some authors propose object recognition systems in which 3D models are avoided. The **priming-based** (geons) approach is based on the idea that 3D shapes can be inferred directly from 2D drawings [Biederman, 1987]—the qualitative features are called **geons**. This mimics the human recognition process in which constituents of a single object (geons) and their spatial arrangement are pointers to a human memory.

The **alignment of 2D views** is another option—lines or points in 2D views can be used for aligning different 2D views. The correspondence of points, lines, or other features must be established first. A linear combination of views has been used [Ullman and Basri, 1991] for recognition, and various issues related to image-based scene representations in which a collection of images with established correspondences is stored instead of a 3D model is considered in [Beymer and Poggio, 1996]. How this approach can be used for displaying a 3D scene from any viewpoint is considered in [Werner et al., 1995].

11.1.1 Marr's theory

Marr was a pioneer in the study of computer vision whose influence has been, and continues to be, considerable despite his early death. He was critical of earlier work that, while successful in limited domains or image classes, was either empirical or unduly restrictive of the images with which it could deal. He proposed a more abstract and theoretical approach that permitted work to be put into a larger context. Restricting himself to the 3D interpretation of single, static scenes, Marr proposed that a computer vision system was just an example of an information processing device that could be understood at three levels:

1. **Computational theory**. The theory describes what the device is supposed to do—what information it provides from other information provided as input. It should also describe the logic of the strategy that performs this task.

2. **Representation and algorithm**. These address precisely how the computation may be carried out—in particular, information representations and algorithms to manipulate them.

3. **Implementation**. The physical realization of the algorithm—specifically, programs and hardware.

It is stressed that it is important to be clear about which level is being addressed in attempting to solve or understand a particular problem. Marr illustrates this by noting that the effect of an after-image (induced by staring at a light bulb) is a physical effect, while the mental confusion provoked by the well-known Necker cube illusion (see Figure 11.1) appears to be at a different theoretical level entirely.

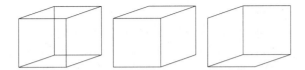

Figure 11.1: The Necker cube, and its two possible interpretations. © *Cengage Learning 2015.*

The point is then made that the lynchpin of success is addressing the theory rather than algorithms or implementation—any number of edge detectors may be developed, each one specific to particular problems, but we would be no nearer any general understanding of how edge detection should or might be achieved. Marr remarks that the complexity of the vision task dictates a sequence of steps refining descriptions of the geometry of visible surfaces. Having derived some such description, it is then necessary to remove the dependence on the vantage point and to transform the description into an **object-centered** one. The requirement, then, is to move from pixels to surface delineation, then to surface characteristic description (orientation), then to a full 3D description. These transformations are effected by moving from the 2D image to a **primal sketch**, then to a **2.5D sketch**, and thence to a **full 3D representation**.

The primal sketch

The primal sketch aims to capture, in as general a way as possible, the significant intensity changes in an image. Hitherto, such changes have been referred to as 'edges', but Marr makes the observation that this word implies a physical meaning that cannot be inferred at this stage. The first stage is to locate these changes at a range of scales (see Section 5.3.4)—informally, a range of blurring filters are passed across the image, after which second-order zero-crossings (see Section 5.3.2) are located for each scale of blur [Marr and Hildreth, 1980]. The blurring recommended is a standard Gaussian filter, see equation (5.47), while the zero-crossings are located with a Laplacian operator, see equation (5.35). The various blurring filters isolate features of particular scales; then zero-crossing evidence in the same locality at many scales provides strong evidence of a genuine physical feature in the scene.

To complete the primal sketch, these zero-crossings are grouped, according to their location and orientations, to provide information about tokens in the image (edges, bars, and blobs) that may help provide later information about (3D) orientation of scene surfaces. The grouping phase, paying attention to the evidence from various scales, extracts tokens that are likely to represent surfaces in the real world.

It is of interest to note that there is strong evidence for the existence of the various components used to build the primal sketch in the human visual system—we too engage in detection of features at various scales, the location of sharp intensity changes, and their subsequent grouping into tokens.

The 2.5D sketch

The 2.5D sketch reconstructs the relative distances from the viewer of surfaces detected in the scene, and may be called a **depth map**. Observe that the output of this phase uses as input features detected in the preceding one, but that in itself it does not give us a 3D reconstruction. In this sense it is midway between 2D and 3D representations, and in particular, nothing can be said about the 'other side' of any objects in view. Instead, it may be the derivation of a surface normal associated with each likely surface detected in the primal sketch, and there may be an implicit improvement in the quality of this information.

There are various routes to the 2.5D sketch, but their common thread is the continuation of the bottom-up approach in that they do not exploit any knowledge about scene contents, but rather employ additional clues such as knowledge about the nature of lighting or motion effects, and are thus generally applicable and not domain specific. The main approaches are known as **'shape from X'** techniques, and are described in Section 12.1. At the conclusion of this phase, the representation is still in viewer-centered coordinates.

The 3D representation

At this stage the Marr paradigm overlaps with top-down, model-based approaches. It is required to take the evidence derived so far and identify objects within it. This can only be achieved with some knowledge about what 'objects' are, and, consequently, some means of describing them. The important point is that this is a transition to an object-centered coordinate system, allowing object descriptions to be viewer independent.

This is the most difficult phase and successful implementation is remote, especially compared to the success seen with the derivation of the primal and 2.5D sketches—specifying what is required, however, has been very successful in guiding computer vision research since the paradigm was formulated. Unlike earlier stages, there is little physiological guidance that can be used to design algorithms since this level of human vision is not well understood. Marr observes that the target coordinate system(s) should be modular in the sense that each 'object' should be treated differently, rather than employing one global coordinate system (usually viewer centered). This prevents having to consider the orientation of model components with respect to the whole. It is further observed that a set of **volumetric** primitives is likely to be of value in representing models (in contrast to surface-based descriptions). Representations based on an object's 'natural' axes, derived from symmetries, or the orientation of stick features, are likely to be of greater use.

The Marr paradigm advocates a set of relatively independent modules; the low-level modules aim to recover a meaningful description of the input intensity image, the middle-level modules use different cues such as intensity changes, contours, texture, motion to recover shape, or location in space. It was shown later [Bertero et al., 1988; Aloimonos and Rosenfeld, 1994] that most low-level and middle-level tasks are ill-posed, with no unique solution; one popular way to make the task well-posed is **regularization** [Tichonov and Arsenin, 1977; Poggio et al., 1985]. A constraint requiring continuity and smoothness of the solution is often added.

11.1.2   Other vision paradigms: Active and purposive vision

When consistent geometric information has to be explicitly modeled (as for manipulation of the object), an object-centered coordinate system is appropriate. It is not certain that Marr's attempt to create object-centered coordinates is confirmed in biological vision; for example, Koenderink shows that the global human visual space is viewer centered and non-Euclidean [Koenderink, 1990]. For small objects, the existence of an object-centered reference frame has not been confirmed in psychological studies.

Two schools try to explain the vision mechanism:

- The first and older one tries to use explicit metric information in the early stages of the visual task (lines, curvatures, normals, etc.). Geometry is typically extracted in a bottom-up fashion without any information about the purpose of this representation. The output is a geometric model.

- The second and younger school does not extract metric (geometric) information from visual data until needed for a specific task. Data are collected in a systematic way to ensure that all the object's features are present in the data, but may remain uninterpreted until a specific task is involved. A database or collection of intrinsic images (or views) is the model.

Many traditional computer vision systems and theories capture data with cameras with fixed characteristics. The same holds for traditional theories; e.g., Marr's observer is static. Some researchers advocate **active perception** [Bajcsy, 1988; Landy et al., 1996] and purposive vision [Aloimonos, 1993]: in an active vision system, the characteristics of the data acquisition are dynamically controlled by the scene interpretation—many visual tasks tend to be simpler if the observer is active and controls its visual sensors. Controlled eye (or camera) movement is an example, where if there are not enough data to interpret the scene the camera can look at it from another viewpoint. In other words, active vision is intelligent data acquisition controlled by the measured, partially interpreted scene parameters and their errors from the scene. Active vision is an area of much current research.

The active approach can make most ill-posed vision tasks tractable. To provide an overview, we summarize how an active observer can change ill-posed tasks to well-posed ones—see Table 11.1 [Aloimonos and Rosenfeld, 1994].

Task	Passive observer	Active observer
Shape from shading	Ill-posed. Regularization helps but a unique solution is not guaranteed due to non-linearities.	Well-posed. Stable. Unique solution. Linear equations.
Shape from contour	Ill-posed. Regularization solution not formulated yet. Solution exists only for very special cases.	Well-posed. Unique solution for monocular or binocular observer.
Shape from texture	Ill-posed. Assumptions about texture needed.	Well-posed without assumptions.
Structure from motion	Well-posed but unstable.	Well-posed and stable. Quadratic constraints. simple solution.

Table 11.1: Active vision makes vision tasks well-posed. © *Cengage Learning 2015*.

It has been generally accepted in the vision community that accurate shape recovery from intensity images is difficult. The Marr paradigm is a nice theoretic framework, but unfortunately does not lead to successful vision applications performing, e.g., recognition and navigation tasks.

There is no established theory that provides a mathematical (computational) model explaining the 'understanding' aspects of human vision; an account is given in [Ullman, 1996]. Two developments towards a new vision theory are:

- **Qualitative vision**, which looks for a qualitative description of objects or scenes [Aloimonos, 1994]. The motivation is not to represent geometry that is not needed for qualitative (non-geometric) tasks or decisions. Further, qualitative information is more invariant to various unwanted transformations (e.g., slightly differing viewpoints) or noise than a quantitative one. Qualitativeness (or invariance) enables interpretation of observed events at several levels of complexity. Note that the human eye does not give precise measurements either; a vision algorithm should look for qualities in images, e.g., convex and concave surface patches in range data [Besl and Jain, 1988].

- The **purposive vision** paradigm, which may help to come up with simpler solutions [Aloimonos, 1992]. The key question is to identify the goal of the task, the motivation being to ease it by making explicit just that piece of information that is needed. Collision avoidance for autonomous vehicle navigation is an example where precise shape description is not needed. The approach may be heterogeneous, and a qualitative answer may be sufficient in some cases. The paradigm does not yet have a solid theoretical basis, but the study of biological vision is a rich source of inspiration. This shift of research attention resulted in many successful vision applications where no precise geometric description is necessary. Examples are collision avoidance, autonomous vehicle navigation, object tracking, etc. [Howarth, 1994; Buxton and Howarth, 1995; Fernyhough, 1997].

There are other vision tasks that need complete geometric 3D models, for example, to create a 3D CAD model from a real object, say, a clay model created by a human designer. Other applications are in virtual reality systems where interaction among real and virtual objects is needed. Some object recognition tasks use full 3D models as well.

11.2 Basics of projective geometry

Computer vision has seen rapid development and maturation of **multiple view geometry**, which deals with mathematics of relations between

- 3D points in the scene (and, more generally, lines and other simple geometric objects),

- their camera projections, and

- relations among multiple camera projections of a 3D scene.

The area developed from **photogrammetry**, which measures 3D distances from photographs. Photogrammetrical methods typically assume special and expensive cameras precisely calibrated in advance, and points in images measured manually and with high precision. It also addresses a rather limited class of tasks. In contrast, multiple view geometry in 3D computer vision aims at using common, off-the-shelf cameras that are partially calibrated, or not at all, at dealing with large inaccuracies in image measurements, and at automatic algorithms. Recent developments permit full automation of tasks such as 3D reconstruction of points and cameras from an unknown video sequence [http://www.2d3.com] or automated reconstruction from a large number of very different views of a 3D scene [Cornelius et al., 2004]. Multiple view geometry has been surveyed in several books [Faugeras, 1993; Hartley and Zisserman, 2003; Ma et al., 2004]

The mathematical vehicle for multiple view geometry is **projective geometry**. The basic sensor that provides computer vision with information about the surrounding 3D world is a camera capturing either still images or videos. Here, stressing the geometric aspect, we will explain how to use 2D image information for automated measurement of the 3D world, where measurements of 3D coordinates of points or distances from 2D images are of importance. We require to study **perspective projection** (called also central projection), which describes image formation by a pinhole camera or a thin lens. Parallel lines in the world do not remain parallel in a perspective image—consider, for

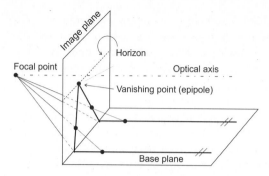

Figure 11.2: Perspective projection of parallel lines. © *Cengage Learning 2015.*

example, a view along a railway or into a long corridor. Figure 11.2 illustrates this, where also some commonly used terms are introduced.

Italian renaissance painters knew how to draw perspective images by the 15th century; their knowledge probably came from the Arabic scholar Alhazen's (Ibn al-Haytham) 'Book of Optics', which was written around the AD1000. A drawing by the German painter Dürer from illustrates practical knowledge of the perspective projection known to painters—Figure 11.3 materializes the notion of a projection ray.

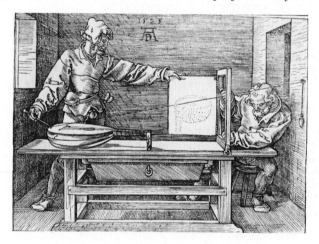

Figure 11.3: Man drawing a lute, year 1525. *Albrecht Dürer (1471-1528).*

11.2.1 Points and hyperplanes in projective space

We begin with a concise introduction to basic notation and the definitions of projective space [Semple and Kneebone, 1963; Mohr, 1993]. Consider $(d + 1)$-dimensional linear space without its origin $\mathcal{R}^{d+1} - \left\{ [0, \ldots, 0]^\top \right\}$, and define an equivalence relation

$$[x_1, \ldots, x_{d+1}]^\top \simeq [x'_1, \ldots, x'_{d+1}]^\top ,$$
$$\text{iff } \exists \alpha \neq 0 : [x_1, \ldots, x_{d+1}]^\top = \alpha [x'_1, \ldots, x'_{d+1}]^\top . \tag{11.1}$$

This means that two vectors in $\mathcal{R}^{d+1}$ are equivalent if they are the same up to a non-zero scale. The **projective space** $\mathcal{P}^d$ is the quotient space of this equivalence relation. It can be imagined as the set of all lines in $\mathcal{R}^{d+1}$ passing through the origin.

A point in $\mathcal{P}^d$ corresponds to an infinite set of parallel vectors in $\mathcal{R}^{d+1}$ and is uniquely given by any single such vector in $\mathcal{R}^{d+1}$. Such a vector is called the **homogeneous** (also projective) representative of the point in $\mathcal{P}^d$. A homogeneous vector represents the same point as any vector that differs by a non-zero scale. This scale is often chosen such that the vector has the number 1 in the rightmost position, e.g., $[x'_1, \ldots, x'_d, 1]^\top$. We will denote homogeneous vectors in bold, e.g., $\mathbf{x}$.

We are more accustomed to ordinary Cartesian coordinates of points (often called non-homogeneous coordinates). These are coordinates of points in the d-dimensional Euclidean space $\mathcal{R}^d$ occupying the plane with equation $x_{d+1} = 1$ in $\mathcal{R}^{d+1}$. The mapping from non-homogeneous vectors in $\mathcal{R}^d$ into $\mathcal{P}^d$ is given by

$$[x_1, \ldots, x_d]^\top \to [x_1, \ldots, x_d, 1]^\top . \tag{11.2}$$

The points $[x_1, \ldots, x_d, 0]^\top$ do not have an Euclidean counterpart, but represent points at infinity in a particular direction. Consider $[x_1, \ldots, x_d, 0]^\top$ as a limiting case of $[x_1, \ldots, x_d, \alpha]^\top$ that is projectively equivalent to $[x_1/\alpha, \ldots, x_d/\alpha, 1]^\top$, and assume that $\alpha \to 0$. This corresponds to a point in $\mathcal{R}^d$ going to infinity in the direction of the radius vector $[x_1/\alpha, \ldots, x_d/\alpha] \in \mathcal{R}^d$.

We also introduce **homogeneous coordinates** of hyperplanes in $\mathcal{P}^d$. A hyperplane in $\mathcal{P}^d$ is represented by the $(d+1)$-vector $\mathbf{a} = [a_1, \ldots, a_{d+1}]^\top$ such that all points $\mathbf{x}$ lying on the hyperplane satisfy $\mathbf{a}^\top \mathbf{x} = 0$ (where $\mathbf{a}^\top \mathbf{x}$ denotes the scalar product). Considering the points in the form $\mathbf{x} = [x_1, \ldots, x_d, 1]^\top$ yields the familiar formula $a_1 x_1 + \cdots + a_d x_d + a_{d+1} = 0$.

It follows that the hyperplane defined by d distinct points represented by vectors $\mathbf{x}_1, \ldots, \mathbf{x}_d$ lying on it is represented by a vector $\mathbf{a}$ orthogonal to vectors $\mathbf{x}_1, \ldots, \mathbf{x}_d$. This vector $\mathbf{a}$ can be computed, e.g., by SVD (see Section 3.2.9). Symmetrically, the point of intersection of d distinct hyperplanes $\mathbf{a}_1, \ldots, \mathbf{a}_d$ is the vector $\mathbf{x}$ orthogonal to them.

There are two particular cases of interest in computer vision:

1. **The projective plane** $\mathcal{P}^2$. We will denote points in $\mathcal{P}^2$ by $\mathbf{u} = [u, v, w]^\top$, lines (hyperplanes) in $\mathcal{P}^2$ by $\mathbf{l}$.

   In $\mathcal{P}^2$, we can use the cross-product for the join and intersection formulas: the line passing through two points $\mathbf{x}$ and $\mathbf{y}$ is represented by $\mathbf{l} = \mathbf{x} \times \mathbf{y}$ and the point of intersection of two lines $\mathbf{l}$ and $\mathbf{m}$ is $\mathbf{x} = \mathbf{l} \times \mathbf{m}$.

2. **The projective 3-space** $\mathcal{P}^3$. We will denote points in $\mathcal{P}^3$ by $\mathbf{X} = [X, Y, Z, W]^T$.

   In $\mathcal{P}^3$, hyperplanes become planes and one more entity occurs that has no counterpart in the projective plane: a 3D line. The elegant homogeneous representation by 4-vectors, available for points and planes in $\mathcal{P}^3$, does not exist for lines. A 3D line can be represented either by a pair of points lying on it but this representation is not unique, or by a (Grassmann-)Plücker matrix [Hartley and Zisserman, 2003].

Figure 11.4 shows graphically how to think of the projective space $\mathcal{P}^2$ as lines in $\mathcal{R}^3$ is illustrative. The plane π has the equation $x_3 = 1$. A line in $\mathcal{R}^3$ corresponds to a single point in $\mathcal{P}^2$. The plane in $\mathcal{R}^3$ passing through the origin $\mathbf{O}$ corresponds to a line in $\mathcal{P}^2$.

The apparent symmetry between points and hyperplanes in the projective space is formalized by the concept of **duality**: any true theorem about points and hyperplanes in $\mathcal{P}^d$ remains true if the words 'point', 'hyperplane', 'lies on', 'passes through' are respectively replaced with the words 'hyperplane', 'point', 'passes through', 'lies on'.

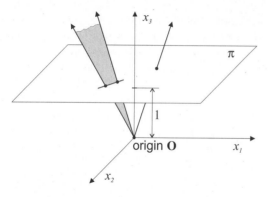

Figure 11.4: Pictorial illustration of the projective space $\mathcal{P}^2$. Points and lines in $\mathcal{P}^2$ are represented by rays and planes, respectively, which pass through the origin in the Euclidean space $\mathcal{R}^3$. © *Cengage Learning 2015.*

11.2.2 Homography

A **homography**, also known as **collineation** or **projective transformation**, is any mapping $\mathcal{P}^d \to \mathcal{P}^d$ that is linear in the embedding space $\mathcal{R}^{d+1}$. That is, a homography is given up to unknown scale and written as

$$\mathbf{u}' \simeq H\,\mathbf{u}\,, \tag{11.3}$$

where H is a $(d+1) \times (d+1)$ matrix. The transformation maps any triplet of collinear points to a triplet of collinear points (hence one of its names—collineation). If H is non-singular then distinct points are mapped to distinct points. An example of an image mapped by a 2D homography is in Figure 11.5.

(a)

(b)

Figure 11.5: Image (b) is a projective transformation of image (a). © *Cengage Learning 2015.*

The projective transformation of hyperplanes has a different form than that of points. It can be derived from the fact that if the original point $\mathbf{u}$ and a hyperplane $\mathbf{a}$ are incident, $\mathbf{a}^\top\mathbf{u} = 0$. They have to remain incident after the transformation too, $\mathbf{a}'^\top\mathbf{u}' = 0$. Using equation (11.3), we obtain that $\mathbf{a}' \simeq H^{-\top}\mathbf{a}$, where $H^{-\top}$ denotes the transposed inverse of H.

In computer vision, there are two simple cases where homography arises. First, projections of a planar scene by a pinhole camera are related by a 2D homography. This can be used to rectify images of planar scenes (e.g., building facades) to frontoparallel view. Second, the relation between two images of a 3D scene (planar or non-planar) by two pinhole cameras sharing a single center of projection is a 2D homography. This can be used for stitching panoramic images from photographs (see Section 10.3).

To become familiar with homogeneous notation, it is instructive to show in detail how the non-homogeneous 2D point $[u, v]^\top$ (e.g., a point in an image) is actually mapped to the non-homogeneous image point $[u', v']^\top$ by H using equation (11.3). With the components and the scale written explicitly, the equation reads

$$
\alpha \begin{bmatrix} u' \\ v' \\ 1 \end{bmatrix} = \begin{bmatrix} h_{11} & h_{12} & h_{13} \\ h_{21} & h_{22} & h_{23} \\ h_{31} & h_{32} & h_{33} \end{bmatrix} \begin{bmatrix} u \\ v \\ 1 \end{bmatrix}. \tag{11.4}
$$

Writing 1 in the third coordinate of $\mathbf{u}'$, we tacitly assume that $\mathbf{u}'$ is not a point at infinity, that is, $\alpha \neq 0$. To compute $[u', v']^\top$, we need to eliminate the scale α. This yields the expression

$$
u' = \frac{h_{11}u + h_{12}v + h_{13}}{h_{31}u + h_{32}v + h_{33}}, \qquad v' = \frac{h_{21}u + h_{22}v + h_{23}}{h_{31}u + h_{32}v + h_{33}},
$$

familiar to people who do not use homogeneous coordinates. Note that compared to this, expression (11.3) is simpler, linear, and can handle the case when $\mathbf{u}'$ is a point at infinity. These are the practical advantages of homogeneous coordinates.

Subgroups of homographies

Besides collinearity and closely related tangency, another well-known invariant of the projective transformation is the cross-ratio on a line (see Section 8.2.7). The group of projective transformations contains important subgroups: affine, similarity, and metric (also called Euclidean) transformations (Table 11.2). The subgroups are given by imposing constraints on the form of H. Besides cross-ratio, they have additional invariants.

Any homography can be uniquely decomposed as $H = H_P H_A H_S$, where

$$
H_P = \begin{bmatrix} I & \mathbf{0} \\ \mathbf{a}^\top & b \end{bmatrix}, \quad H_A = \begin{bmatrix} K & \mathbf{0} \\ \mathbf{0}^\top & 1 \end{bmatrix}, \quad H_S = \begin{bmatrix} R & -R\mathbf{t} \\ \mathbf{0}^\top & 1 \end{bmatrix}, \tag{11.5}
$$

and the matrix K is upper triangular. Matrices of the form of H_S represent Euclidean transformations. Matrices $H_A H_S$ represent affine transformations; thus matrices H_A represent the 'purely affine' subgroup of affine transformations, i.e., what is left of the affine group after removing from it (more exactly, factorizing it by) the Euclidean group. Matrices $H_P H_A H_S$ represent the whole group of projective transformations; thus matrices H_P represent the 'purely projective' subgroup of the projective transformation.

In the decomposition, the only non-trivial step is decomposing a general matrix A into the product of an upper triangular matrix K and a **rotation matrix** R: a rotation matrix is orthonormal ($R^\top R = I$) and non-reflecting ($\det R = 1$). This can be done by RQ-decomposition (analogous to QR decomposition [Press et al., 1992; Golub and Loan, 1989]). We will encounter such decomposition again in Section 11.3.3.

Name	Constraints on H	2D example	Invariants
projective	$\det H \neq 0$		collinearity tangency cross ratio
affine	$H = \begin{bmatrix} A & \mathbf{t} \\ \mathbf{0}^\top & 1 \end{bmatrix}$ $\det A \neq 0$		projective invariants + parallelism + length ratio on parallels + area ration + linear combinations of vectors centroid
similarity	$H = \begin{bmatrix} sR & -R\mathbf{t} \\ \mathbf{0}^\top & 1 \end{bmatrix}$ $R^\top R = I$ $\det R = 1$ $s > 0$		affine invariants + angles + ratio of lengths
metric (Euclidean, isometric)	$H = \begin{bmatrix} R & -R\mathbf{t} \\ \mathbf{0}^\top & 1 \end{bmatrix}$ $R^\top R = I$ $\det R = 1$		similarity invariants + length + area (volume)
identity	$H = I$		trivial case everything is invariant

Table 11.2: Subgroups of the (non-singular) projective transformation often met in computer vision. © *Cengage Learning 2015.*

11.2.3 Estimating homography from point correspondences

A frequent task in 3D computer vision is to compute the homography from (point) correspondences. By **correspondences**, we mean a set $\{(\mathbf{u}_i, \mathbf{u}'_i)\}_{i=1}^m$ of ordered pairs of points such that each pair corresponds in the transformation. The correspondences may be entered manually, or perhaps computed by an algorithm.

To compute H, we need to solve the homogeneous system of linear equations

$$\alpha_i \mathbf{u}'_i = H \mathbf{u}_i, \quad i = 1, \ldots, m \tag{11.6}$$

for H and the scales α_i. This system has $m(d+1)$ equations and $m+(d+1)^2-1$ unknowns; there are m of the α_i, $(d+1)^2$ components of H, while -1 suffices to determine H only up to an overall scale factor. Thus we see that $m = d+2$ correspondences are needed to determine H uniquely (up to scale).

Sometimes the correspondences form a **degenerate configuration** meaning that H may not be given uniquely even if $m \geq d+2$. A configuration is non-degenerate if no d points of $\mathbf{u}_i$ lie in a single hyperplane and no d points of $\mathbf{u}'_i$ lie in a single hyperplane.

When more than $d+2$ correspondences are available, the system (11.6) has no solution in general because of noise in measuring the correspondences. Thus, the easy task of solving a linear system becomes the more difficult one of **optimal estimation** of parameters of a parametric model. Here, we no longer solve equation (11.6), but rather minimize a suitable criterion, derived from statistical considerations.

The estimation methods that will be described here are not restricted to homography; they are generic methods applicable without conceptual changes to several other tasks in 3D computer vision. These include camera resectioning (Section 11.3.3), triangulation (Section 11.4.1), estimation of the fundamental matrix (Section 11.5.4) or the trifocal tensor (Section 11.6).

Maximum likelihood estimation

The statistically optimal approach is the **maximum likelihood** (ML) estimation. Consider the case $d = 2$—estimating homography from two images, such as in Figure 11.5. We assume that the non-homogeneous image points are random variables with normal distributions independent in each component, mean values $[\hat{u}_i, \hat{v}_i]^\top$ and $[\hat{u}'_i, \hat{v}'_i]^\top$, respectively, and equal variance. This assumption usually leads to good results in practice. It can be shown that ML estimation leads to minimizing the reprojection error in the least squares sense. That is, we need to solve the following constrained minimization task over $9 + 2m$ variables

$$\min_{H, u_i, v_i} \sum_{i=1}^{m} \left[(u_i - \hat{u}_i)^2 + (v_i - \hat{v}_i)^2 + \left(\frac{[u_i, v_i, 1]\mathbf{h}_1}{[u_i, v_i, 1]\mathbf{h}_3} - \hat{u}'_i \right)^2 + \left(\frac{[u_i, v_i, 1]\mathbf{h}_2}{[u_i, v_i, 1]\mathbf{h}_3} - \hat{v}'_i \right)^2 \right].$$
(11.7)

Here, $\mathbf{h}_i$ denotes the i-th row of matrix H, that is, $\mathbf{h}_1^\top \mathbf{u}/\mathbf{h}_3^\top \mathbf{u}$ and $\mathbf{h}_2^\top \mathbf{u}/\mathbf{h}_3^\top \mathbf{u}$ are the non-homogeneous coordinates of a point $\mathbf{u}$ mapped by H given by equation (11.4). The objective function being minimized is the reprojection error.

This task is non-linear and non-convex and typically has multiple local minima. A good (but in general not global) local minimum can be computed in two steps. First, an initial estimate is computed by solving a statistically non-optimal but much simpler minimization problem with a single local minimum. Second, the nearest local minimum of the optimal ML problem is computed by a local minimization algorithm. For this, the non-linear least squares Levenberg-Marquardt algorithm [Press et al., 1992] is the standard.

Linear estimation

To find a good initial but statistically non-optimal estimate, we solve the system of equations (11.6) by a method used in solving overdetermined linear systems in linear algebra known as **minimizing the algebraic distance**. It is also called the Direct

Linear Transformation [Hartley and Zisserman, 2003] or just a **linear estimation**. It often gives satisfactory results even without being followed by a non-linear method.

We represent the points in homogeneous coordinates, $\mathbf{u} = [u, v, w]^\top$. Rearranging (11.6) into a form suitable for solution can be done by manipulating components manually. However, we use two tricks, which permit the formulas to remain in matrix form.

First, to eliminate α from $\alpha\mathbf{u}' = H\mathbf{u}$, we multiply the equation from the left by a matrix, $G(\mathbf{u}')$, whose rows are orthogonal to $\mathbf{u}'$. This makes the left-hand side vanish because $G(\mathbf{u}')\mathbf{u}' = \mathbf{0}$ and we obtain $G(\mathbf{u}')H\mathbf{u} = \mathbf{0}$. If the image points have the form $w' = 1$ (i.e., $[u', v', 1]^\top$), this matrix can be chosen as

$$ G(\mathbf{u}) = G\big([u, v, 1]^\top\big) = \begin{bmatrix} 1 & 0 & -u \\ 0 & 1 & -v \end{bmatrix} = [I \,|\, -\mathbf{u}] \,. $$

This choice is not suitable if some image points have $w' = 0$ because then $G(\mathbf{u}')$ becomes singular if $u' = v'$. This can happen if the points are not directly measured in the image but computed indirectly (e.g., vanishing points) and therefore some of them can be at infinity. The choice that works in the general situation is $G(\mathbf{u}) = S(\mathbf{u})$, where

$$ S(\mathbf{u}) = S\big([u, v, w]^\top\big) = \begin{bmatrix} 0 & -w & v \\ w & 0 & -u \\ -v & u & 0 \end{bmatrix} \tag{11.8} $$

the **cross-product matrix**, which has the property that $S(\mathbf{u})\mathbf{u}' = \mathbf{u} \times \mathbf{u}'$ for any $\mathbf{u}$ and $\mathbf{u}'$.

Second, to re-arrange the equation $G(\mathbf{u}')H\mathbf{u} = \mathbf{0}$ such that the unknowns are rightmost in the product, we use the identity $AB\mathbf{c} = (\mathbf{c}^\top \otimes A)\mathbf{b}$ [Lütkepohl, 1996] where $\mathbf{b}$ is the vector constructed from the entries of matrix B stacked in column-first order and $\otimes$ is the Kronecker product of matrices. Applying this yields

$$ G(\mathbf{u}')H\mathbf{u} = \big[\mathbf{u}^\top \otimes G(\mathbf{u}')\big]\mathbf{h} = \mathbf{0} \,, $$

where $\mathbf{h}$ denotes the 9-vector $[h_{11}, h_{21}, \ldots, h_{23}, h_{33}]^\top$ of the entries of H. For $G(\mathbf{u}') = S(\mathbf{u}')$, in components this reads

$$ \begin{bmatrix} 0 & -uw' & uv' & 0 & -vw' & vv' & 0 & -ww' & wv' \\ uw' & 0 & -uu' & vw' & 0 & -vu' & ww' & 0 & -wu' \\ -uv' & uu' & 0 & -vv' & vu' & 0 & -wv' & wu' & 0 \end{bmatrix} \mathbf{h} = \begin{bmatrix} 0 \\ 0 \\ 0 \end{bmatrix} . $$

Considering all m correspondences yields

$$ \begin{bmatrix} \mathbf{u}_1^\top \otimes G(\mathbf{u}_1') \\ \mathbf{u}_2^\top \otimes G(\mathbf{u}_2') \\ \cdots \\ \mathbf{u}_m^\top \otimes G(\mathbf{u}_m') \end{bmatrix} \mathbf{h} = \mathbf{0} \,. \tag{11.9} $$

Denoting the left-hand $3m \times 9$ matrix by W, this reads $W\mathbf{h} = \mathbf{0}$. This system is overdetermined and has no solution in general. Singular Value Decomposition (SVD) can compute a vector $\mathbf{h}$ that minimizes $\|W\mathbf{h}\|$ subject to $\|\mathbf{h}\| = 1$, see Section 3.2.9.

In detail, $\mathbf{h}$ is the column of matrix V in the SVD decomposition $W = UDV^\top$ associated with the smallest singular value. Alternatively, we can compute $\mathbf{h}$ as the eigenvector of $W^\top W$ associated with the smallest eigenvalue; this is reported to be numerically slightly less accurate than SVD but has the advantage that matrix $W^\top W$ is only 9×9 while W is $3m \times 9$. Both ways work equally well in practice.

To get a meaningful result, components of vectors $\mathbf{u}_i$ and $\mathbf{u}'_i$ must not have very different magnitudes. This is not the case when, e.g., $\mathbf{u}_1 = [500, 500, 1]^\top$. This is not a matter of numerical precision; rather, similar magnitudes ensure that the minimum obtained by minimizing algebraic distance is reasonably near to the solution of (11.7). Similar magnitudes can be ensured by a kind of **preconditioning** known in numerical mathematics; in computer vision, it is often called **normalization** [Hartley, 1997]. Instead of (11.6), we solve the equation system $\bar{\mathbf{u}}'_i \simeq \bar{H}\,\bar{\mathbf{u}}_i$ where we substituted $\bar{\mathbf{u}}_i = H_{\mathrm{pre}}\,\mathbf{u}_i$ and $\bar{\mathbf{u}}'_i = H'_{\mathrm{pre}}\,\mathbf{u}'_i$. The homography H is then recovered as $H = H'^{-1}_{\mathrm{pre}}\,\bar{H}H_{\mathrm{pre}}$. The preconditioning homographies H_{pre} and H'_{pre} are chosen such that the components of $\bar{\mathbf{u}}_i$ and $\bar{\mathbf{u}}'_i$ have similar magnitudes. Assuming that the original points have the form $[u, v, 1]^\top$, a suitable choice is the anisotropic scaling and translation

$$\bar{H} = \begin{bmatrix} a & 0 & c \\ 0 & b & d \\ 0 & 0 & 1 \end{bmatrix},$$

where a, b, c, d are such that the mean of the preconditioned points $\bar{\mathbf{u}} = [\bar{u}, \bar{v}, 1]^\top$ is 0 and their variance is 1.

Note the difference between the size of the optimization problem (11.7) arising from maximum likelihood estimation, and the linear problem (11.9). While the former has $9 + 2m$ variables, the latter has only 9 variables: for large m, there is a difference in computation costs. However, equation (11.7) provides the optimal approach and is used in practice. There are approximations allowing the reduction of computation but still stay close to optimality, such as the Sampson distance [Hartley and Zisserman, 2003].

Robust estimation

Usually, we have assumed that correspondences are corrupted by additive Gaussian noise. If they contain gross errors, e.g., **mismatches** (see Figure 11.6), this statistical model is no longer correct and many methods may provide completely meaningless results. In this case, algorithms such as RANSAC (Section 10.3) may be deployed.

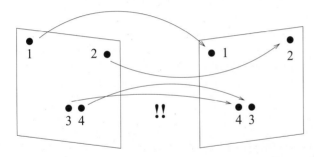

Figure 11.6: A mismatch in correspondences. © *Cengage Learning 2015.*

11.3   A single perspective camera

11.3.1   Camera model

Consider the case of one camera with a thin lens (considered from the point of view of geometric optics in Section 3.4.2). This pinhole model is an approximation suitable for many computer vision applications—the camera performs a central projection, the geometry of which is depicted in Figure 11.7. The plane π stretching horizontally is the **image plane** to which the real world projects. The vertical dot-and-dash line is the **optical axis**. The lens is positioned perpendicularly to the optical axis at the **focal point C** (also called the **optical center** or the **center of projection**). The focal length f is a parameter of the lens.

For clarity, we will adopt notation in which image points will be denoted by lower-case bold letters either in Euclidean (non-homogeneous) coordinates $\mathbf{u} = [u, v]^\top$ or by homogeneous coordinates $\mathbf{u} = [u, v, w]^\top$ (possibly with subscripts to distinguish different coordinate systems). All 3D scene points will be denoted by upper-case letters either in Euclidean coordinates $\mathbf{X} = [X, Y, Z]^\top$ or by homogeneous coordinates $\mathbf{X} = [X, Y, Z, W]^\top$ (possibly with subscripts).

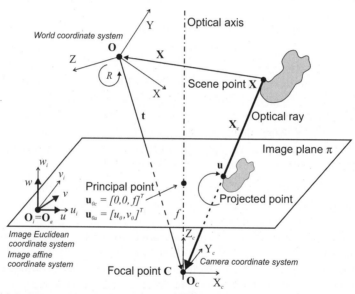

Figure 11.7: The geometry of a linear perspective camera. © *Cengage Learning 2015.*

The camera performs a linear transformation from the 3D projective space $\mathcal{P}^3$ to the 2D projective space $\mathcal{P}^2$. The projection is carried by an optical ray reflected from a scene point $\mathbf{X}$ (top right in Figure 11.7) or originating from a light source. The optical ray passes through the optical center $\mathbf{C}$ and hits the image plane at the projected point $\mathbf{u}$.

Further explanation requires four coordinate systems:

1. The **world Euclidean coordinate system** has its origin at the point $\mathbf{O}$. Points $\mathbf{X}, \mathbf{u}$ are expressed in the world coordinate system.

2. The **camera Euclidean coordinate system** (subscript $_c$) has the focal point $\mathbf{C} \equiv \mathbf{O}_c$ as its origin. The coordinate axis Z_c is aligned with the optical axis and its direction is from the focal point $\mathbf{C}$ towards the image plane. There is a unique relation between the world and the camera coordinate system given by the Euclidean transformation consisting of a translation $\mathbf{t}$ and a rotation R.

3. The **image Euclidean coordinate system** (subscript $_i$) has axes aligned with the camera coordinate system. The coordinate axes u_i, v_i, w_i are collinear with the coordinate axes X_c, Y_c, Z_c, respectively. Axes u_i and v_i lie in the image plane.

4. The **image affine coordinate system** (subscript $_a$) has coordinate axes u, v, w, and origin $\mathbf{O}_a$ coincident with the origin of the image Euclidean coordinate system $\mathbf{O}_i$. The coordinate axes u, w are aligned with the coordinate axes u_i, w_i, but the axis v may have a different orientation to the axis v_i.

   The reason for introducing the image affine coordinate system is the fact that pixels can exhibit shear, usually due to a misaligned photosensitive chip in the camera. In addition, coordinate axes can be scaled differently.

The projective transformation in the general case can be factorized into three simpler transformations which correspond to three transitions between these four different coordinate systems.

The first transformation (between 1 and 2 above) constitutes transition from the (arbitrary) world coordinate system $(\mathbf{O};\ X, Y, Z)$ to the camera centered coordinate system $(\mathbf{O}_c;\ X_c, Y_c, Z_c)$. The world coordinate system can be aligned with the camera coordinate system by translating the origin $\mathbf{O}$ to $\mathbf{O}_c$ by the vector $\mathbf{t}$ and by rotating the coordinate axes by the rotation matrix R. The transformation of point $\mathbf{X}$ to point $\mathbf{X}_c$ expressed in non-homogeneous coordinates is

$$\mathbf{X}_c = R\left(\mathbf{X} - \mathbf{t}\right). \tag{11.10}$$

The rotation matrix R expresses three elementary rotations of the coordinate axes—rotations along the axes X, Y, and Z. The translation vector $\mathbf{t}$ gives three elements of the translation of the origin of the world coordinate system with respect to the camera coordinate system. Thus there are six extrinsic camera parameters, three rotations and three translations.

Parameters R and $\mathbf{t}$ are called **extrinsic camera calibration parameters**.

Now we would like to express equation (11.10) in homogeneous coordinates. We already know from equation (11.5) that this can be done by a subgroup of homographies H_S

$$\mathbf{X}_c = \begin{bmatrix} R & -R\,\mathbf{t} \\ \mathbf{0}^\top & 1 \end{bmatrix} \mathbf{X}. \tag{11.11}$$

The second transformation (between 2 and 3 above) projects the 3D scene point $\mathbf{X}_c$ expressed in the camera centered coordinate system $(\mathbf{O}_c;\ X_c, Y_c, Z_c)$ to the point $\mathbf{u}_i$ in the image plane π expressed in the image coordinate system $(\mathbf{O}_i;\ u_i, v_i, w_i)$.

The $\mathcal{R}^3 \to \mathcal{R}^2$ projection in non-homogeneous coordinates gives two equations non-linear in Z_c

$$u_i = \frac{X_c\, f}{Z_c}, \qquad v_i = \frac{Y_c\, f}{Z_c}, \tag{11.12}$$

where f is the focal length. If the projection given by equation (11.12) is embedded in the projective space then the projection $\mathcal{P}^3 \to \mathcal{P}^2$ writes linearly in homogeneous coordinates as

$$\mathbf{u}_i \simeq \begin{bmatrix} f & 0 & 0 & 0 \\ 0 & f & 0 & 0 \\ 0 & 0 & 1 & 0 \end{bmatrix} \mathbf{X}_c \, . \tag{11.13}$$

A camera with the special focal length $f = 1$ (sometimes called a **camera with normalized image plane** [Forsyth and Ponce, 2003]) would yield the simpler equation

$$\mathbf{u}_i \simeq \begin{bmatrix} 1 & 0 & 0 & 0 \\ 0 & 1 & 0 & 0 \\ 0 & 0 & 1 & 0 \end{bmatrix} \mathbf{X}_c \, . \tag{11.14}$$

The third transformation (between 3 and 4 above) maps the image Euclidean coordinate system to the image affine coordinate system. It is of advantage to gather all parameters intrinsic to a camera (the focal length f is one of them) into a 3×3 matrix K called the **intrinsic calibration matrix**. K is upper triangular and expresses the mapping $\mathcal{P}^2 \to \mathcal{P}^2$ which is a special case of the affine transformation. This special case is also called an affine transformation factorized by rotations. It can be performed within the image plane, see Figure 11.7. This $\mathcal{P}^2 \to \mathcal{P}^2$ transformation is

$$\mathbf{u} \simeq K\mathbf{u}_i = \begin{bmatrix} f & s & -u_0 \\ 0 & g & -v_0 \\ 0 & 0 & 1 \end{bmatrix} \mathbf{u}_i \, . \tag{11.15}$$

The intrinsic calibration matrix parameters are as follows: f gives the scaling along the u axis and g gives scaling along the v axis. Often, both values are equal to the focal length, $f = g$. s gives the degree of shear of the coordinate axes in the image plane. It is assumed that the v axis of the image affine coordinate system is co-incident with the v_i axis of the image Euclidean coordinate system. The value s shows how far the u axis is slanted in the direction of axis v. The shear parameter s is introduced in practice to cope with distortions caused by, e.g., placing a photosensitive chip off-perpendicular to the optical axis during camera assembly.

Now we are ready to specify a pin-hole camera projection in full generality. We already know that it is a linear transformation from the 3D projective space $\mathcal{P}^3$ to the 2D projective space $\mathcal{P}^2$. The transformation is the product of the three factors derived above, given by equations (11.11), (11.14) and (11.15):

$$\mathbf{u} \simeq K \begin{bmatrix} 1 & 0 & 0 & 0 \\ 0 & 1 & 0 & 0 \\ 0 & 0 & 1 & 0 \end{bmatrix} \begin{bmatrix} R & -R\mathbf{t} \\ \mathbf{0}^\top & 1 \end{bmatrix} \mathbf{X} \, . \tag{11.16}$$

The product of the second and the third factors exhibits a useful internal structure; we can rewrite equation (11.16) as

$$\mathbf{u} \simeq K \begin{bmatrix} 1 & 0 & 0 & 0 \\ 0 & 1 & 0 & 0 \\ 0 & 0 & 1 & 0 \end{bmatrix} \begin{bmatrix} R & -R\mathbf{t} \\ \mathbf{0}^\top & 1 \end{bmatrix} \mathbf{X} = K \left[R \mid -R\mathbf{t} \right] \mathbf{X} = M \mathbf{X} \, . \tag{11.17}$$

If we express the scene point in homogeneous coordinates, we can write the perspective projection in a linear form using a single 3×4 matrix M, called the **projection matrix** (or camera matrix). The leftmost 3×3 submatrix of M describes a rotation and the rightmost column a translation. The delimiter | denotes that the matrix is composed of two submatrices. Observe that M contains all intrinsic and extrinsic parameters because

$$M = K\left[R \mid -R\mathbf{t}\right]. \tag{11.18}$$

These parameters can be obtained by decomposing M to K, R, and $\mathbf{t}$—this decomposition is unique. Denoting $M = [A \mid \mathbf{b}]$, we have $A = KR$ and $\mathbf{b} = -A\mathbf{t}$. Clearly, $\mathbf{t} = -A^{-1}\mathbf{b}$. Decomposing $A = KR$ where K is upper triangular and R is rotation can be done by RQ-decomposition, similar to the better known QR-decomposition [Press et al., 1992; Golub and Loan, 1989] (see Section 11.2.2).

11.3.2 Projection and back-projection in homogeneous coordinates

Equation (11.17) gives an important result: in homogeneous coordinates, the projection of a scene point $\mathbf{X}$ to an image point $\mathbf{u}$ by a camera is given by a simple linear mapping

$$\mathbf{u} \simeq M\mathbf{X}. \tag{11.19}$$

Note that this formula is similar to homography mapping, equation (11.3). However, for homography the matrix H was square and in general non-singular, thus the mapping was one-to-one. Here, M is non-square and thus the mapping is many-to-one: indeed, all scene points on a ray project to a single image point.

There is a single scene point that has no image in the camera, the center of projection $\mathbf{C}$; it has the property that $M\mathbf{C} = \mathbf{0}$. This permits recovery from M by, e.g., SVD: $\mathbf{C}$ is a vector orthogonal to the rows of M, or, in other words, the intersection of the planes given by these rows (Section 11.2.1). Clearly, this determines $\mathbf{C}$ uniquely up to scale.

Equation (11.17) also permits the derivation of simple expressions for back-projection of points and lines by camera M. By back-projection, we mean computation of the 3D scene entity that projects to a given image entity by M.

Given a homogeneous image point $\mathbf{u}$, we want to find its pre-image in the scene. This pre-image is not given uniquely; rather, all points on a scene ray will project to $\mathbf{u}$. One point on this ray is the projection center $\mathbf{C}$. Another point on the ray can be obtained from $\mathbf{u} = M\mathbf{X}$ as

$$\mathbf{X} = M^{+}\mathbf{u}. \tag{11.20}$$

Here, $M^{+} = M^{\top}(MM^{\top})^{-1}$ denotes **pseudoinverse**, being the generalization of inversion for non-square matrices. It has the property $MM^{+} = I$.

Given an image line $\mathbf{l}$ in homogeneous coordinates (Section 11.2.1), we want to find its pre-image in the scene. The solution is again not unique: a whole scene plane $\mathbf{a}$ will project to $\mathbf{l}$. A scene point $\mathbf{X}$ lying in $\mathbf{a}$ satisfies $\mathbf{a}^{\top}\mathbf{X} = 0$ and its projection is $\mathbf{u} = M\mathbf{X}$. This projection has to lie on $\mathbf{l}$, which yields $\mathbf{l}^{\top}\mathbf{u} = \mathbf{l}^{\top}M\mathbf{X} = 0$. It follows that

$$\mathbf{a} = M^{\top}\mathbf{l}. \tag{11.21}$$

This plane contains the projection center, $\mathbf{a}^{\top}\mathbf{C} = 0$.

11.3.3   Camera calibration from a known scene

Here we shall explain how to compute the camera projection matrix M from a set of image-scene point correspondences, i.e., from a set $\{(\mathbf{u}_i, \mathbf{X}_i)\}_{i=1}^m$ where $\mathbf{u}_i$ are homogeneous 3-vectors representing image points and $\mathbf{X}_i$ are homogeneous 4-vectors representing scene points.

The situation is similar to the estimation of homography, described in Section 11.2.3. We need to solve the homogeneous linear system

$$\alpha_i\, \mathbf{u}_i' = M\, \mathbf{X}_i, \quad i = 1, \ldots, m \tag{11.22}$$

for M and α_i. M is determined up to a scale, hence it has only 11 free parameters. It is left as an exercise to show that this system is under-determined for $m = 5$ and over-determined for $m = 6$. Thus, at least 6 (sometimes we say $5\frac{1}{2}$) correspondences are needed to compute M, although similarly to computation of homography, there are degenerate configurations from which M cannot be computed uniquely even if $m \geq 6$. The degenerate configurations are more complex than for homography ([Hartley, 1997; Hartley and Zisserman, 2003].

Linear estimation of M by minimizing the algebraic distance is entirely analogous to that for homography. Multiplying equation $\mathbf{u} \simeq M\mathbf{X}$ by $S(\mathbf{u})$ from the left makes the left-hand side vanish, yielding $\mathbf{0} = S(\mathbf{u})M\mathbf{X}$. Re-arranging this equation yields $[\mathbf{X}^\top \otimes S(\mathbf{u})]\mathbf{m} = \mathbf{0}$, where $\mathbf{m} = [m_{11}, m_{21}, \ldots, m_{24}, m_{34}]^\top$ and $\otimes$ is the Kronecker product. Considering all m correspondences yields the system

$$\begin{bmatrix} \mathbf{X}_1^\top \otimes S(\mathbf{u}_1) \\ \cdots \\ \mathbf{X}_m^\top \otimes S(\mathbf{u}_m) \end{bmatrix} \mathbf{m} = W\mathbf{m} = \mathbf{0}\,.$$

We minimize the algebraic distance $\|W\mathbf{m}\|$ subject to $\|\mathbf{m}\| = 1$ by SVD. A preconditioning, ensuring that the components of vectors $\mathbf{u}_i$ and $\mathbf{X}_i$ have similar magnitudes, is necessary. Optionally, one can decompose M to extrinsic and intrinsic parameters, as given by equation (11.18).

Having obtained a good initial estimate by the linear method, we may proceed to compute a maximum likelihood estimate by the non-linear least squares method. One has to be careful here to specify an appropriate noise model for scene points; this depends on the particular scenario in which the camera calibration is used.

In practice, the computer vision community make heavy use of a well-established and widely implemented algorithm due to Tsai [Tsai, 1986]. This recaptures from known scene points a pinhole camera as described, but permits also recapture of a parameter describing radial lens distortion (see Section 3.4.3). Many implementations of this are freely available online.

11.4   Scene reconstruction from multiple views

Here, we will consider how to compute 3D scene points from projections in several cameras. This task is easy if image points *and* camera matrices are given. Then one has to compute only the 3D scene points—this is described in Section 11.4.1. If the camera matrices are unknown, the task is to find the 3D points and the matrices; this is considerably more difficult, being in fact the central task of multiple view geometry.

11.4.1 Triangulation

Assume that the camera matrix M and the image points $\mathbf{u}$ are given and we want to compute the scene point $\mathbf{X}$. We denote different images by superscript j. Assume that n views are available, so that we want to solve the linear homogeneous system

$$\alpha^j \mathbf{u}^j = M^j \mathbf{X}, \quad j = 1, \ldots, n. \tag{11.23}$$

This is also known as **triangulation**; the name comes from photogrammetry where the process was originally interpreted in terms of similar triangles.

The task is relatively simple because equations (11.23) are linear in the unknowns. It is very similar to homography estimation (Section 11.2.3) and to camera calibration from a known scene (Section 11.3.3).

Geometrically, triangulation consists of finding the common intersection of n rays given by back-projection of the image points by the cameras. If there were no noise in measuring $\mathbf{u}^j$ and determining M^j then these rays would intersect in a single point and the system of equations (11.23) would have a single solution. In reality, the rays would be non-intersecting (skew) and the (overdetermined) system (11.23) would have no solution.

We might compute $\mathbf{X}$ as the scene point closest to all of the skew rays; for $n = 2$ cameras, this would reduce to finding the middle point of the shortest line segment between the two rays. However, this is statistically non-optimal. The correct approach is maximum likelihood estimation (see Section 11.2.2), leading to minimizing the reprojection error. Denoting by $[\hat{u}^j, \hat{v}^j]^\top$ the image points in non-homogeneous coordinates, we solve the optimization problem

$$\min_{\mathbf{X}} \sum_{j=1}^{m} \left[\left(\frac{\mathbf{m}_1^{j\top} \mathbf{X}}{\mathbf{m}_3^{j\top} \mathbf{X}} - \hat{u}^j \right)^2 + \left(\frac{\mathbf{m}_2^{j\top} \mathbf{X}}{\mathbf{m}_3^{j\top} \mathbf{X}} - \hat{v}^j \right)^2 \right], \tag{11.24}$$

where $\mathbf{m}_i^j$ denotes the i-th row of camera matrix M^j. This formulation assumes that only the image points are corrupted by noise and the camera matrices are not.

This non-convex optimization problem is known to have multiple local minima and is intractable in general, though a closed-form solution is known for the simplest case of $m = 2$ cameras [Hartley, 1997]. We solve it by first finding an initial estimate by a linear method and then using non-linear least squares.

To formulate the linear method, multiply equation $\mathbf{u} \simeq M\mathbf{X}$ by $S(\mathbf{u})$ from the left, yielding $\mathbf{0} = S(\mathbf{u})M\mathbf{X}$. Considering all n cameras, we obtain the system

$$\begin{bmatrix} S(\mathbf{u}^1)M^1 \\ \cdots \\ S(\mathbf{u}^n)M^n \end{bmatrix} \mathbf{X} = W\mathbf{X} = \mathbf{0}, \tag{11.25}$$

solved by minimizing the algebraic distance by SVD.

Preconditioning, ensuring that the components of $\mathbf{u}^j$ and M^j do not have very different magnitudes, is necessary. Sometimes, it suffices to replace $\mathbf{u} \simeq M\mathbf{X}$ with $\bar{\mathbf{u}} \simeq \bar{M}\mathbf{X}$ where $\bar{\mathbf{u}} = H_{\text{pre}}\mathbf{u}$ and $\bar{M} = H_{\text{pre}}M$. Here, H_{pre} is obtained as described in Section 11.2.3. However, sometimes this does not remove some large differences in entries of M. Then, we need to substitute $\bar{M} = H_{\text{pre}}MT_{\text{pre}}$, where T_{pre} is a suitable 4×4 matrix representing a 3D homography. In these cases, no single known method for determining T_{pre} and H_{pre} seems to be good in all situations and preconditioning is still a kind of art.

Note on 3D line reconstruction

Sometimes, we need to reconstruct geometric entities other than points. To reconstruct a 3D line from its projections $\mathbf{l}^j$ in the cameras M^j, recall from equation (11.21) that the back-projection of line $\mathbf{l}$ is the 3D plane with homogeneous coordinates $\mathbf{a} = M^\top \mathbf{l}$. With noise-free measurements, these planes should have a single line in common. We represent this line by two points $\mathbf{X}$ and $\mathbf{Y}$ lying on it, thus satisfying $\mathbf{a}^\top [\mathbf{X} \mid \mathbf{Y}] = [0, 0]$. To ensure that the two points are distinct, we require $\mathbf{X}^\top \mathbf{Y} = 0$. The intersection is obtained by solving the system

$$W[\mathbf{X} \mid \mathbf{Y}] = \begin{bmatrix} (\mathbf{l}^1)^\top M^1 \\ \cdots \\ (\mathbf{l}^n)^\top M^n \end{bmatrix} [\mathbf{X} \mid \mathbf{Y}] = \mathbf{0} , \qquad \mathbf{X}^\top \mathbf{Y} = 0 .$$

Let $W = U D V^\top$ be the SVD decomposition of W. The points $\mathbf{X}$ and $\mathbf{Y}$ are obtained as the two columns of V associated with the two smallest singular values.

This linear method can be followed by a maximum likelihood estimation. To reflect where noise enters the process correctly, a good criterion is to minimize the image reprojection error from the **end points** of the measured image line segments. The preconditioning is necessary because it ensures that components of $\mathbf{l}^j$ and M^j have similar magnitudes.

11.4.2   Projective reconstruction

Suppose there are m scene points $\mathbf{X}_i$ ($i = 1, \ldots, m$), (distinguished by subscripts), and m cameras M^j ($j = 1, \ldots, m$) (distinguished by superscripts). The scene points project to the camera images as

$$\alpha_i^j \mathbf{u}_i^j = M^j \mathbf{X}_i , \quad i = 1, \ldots, m , \quad j = 1, \ldots, n , \tag{11.26}$$

where we denote the i-th image point in the j-th image by both the subscript and the superscript, $\mathbf{u}_i^j$.

Consider the task when both scene points $\mathbf{X}_i$ and camera matrices M^j are unknown and to be computed from the known image points $\mathbf{u}_i^j$. Unlike triangulation (Section 11.4.1), the equation system (11.26) is non-linear in the unknowns and there is no obvious way of solving it. One typically wants to solve it given a redundant set of image points, to be resilient to noise. Thus, the problem given in equation (11.26) is overdetermined which makes it even harder.

The problem is solved in two steps:

1. Enumerate an initial and not very accurate estimate of the camera matrices M^j is computed from image points $\mathbf{u}_i^j$. This is done by estimating the coefficients of the **matching constraints** by solving a system of linear equations and then computing the camera matrices M^j from these coefficients. This translation of a non-linear system to a linear one inevitably ignores some non-linear relations among components of M^j. The matching constraints are derived in general in Section 11.4.3 for any number of views and in further detail in Sections 11.5 and 11.6 for two and three views.

2. A by-product of this process is also usually an initial estimate of the scene points $\mathbf{X}_i$. Then M^j and $\mathbf{X}_i$ are computed accurately using maximal-likelihood estimation (bundle adjustment), described in Section 11.4.4.

Projective ambiguity

Without solving the problem given in equation (11.26), something about the uniqueness of its solution can easily be derived. Let M^j and $\mathbf{X}_i$ be a solution to equation (11.26) and let T be an arbitrary non-singular 3×4 matrix. Then cameras $M'^j = M^j\, T^{-1}$ and scene points $\mathbf{X}'_i = T\, \mathbf{X}_i$ are also a solution because

$$M'^j\, \mathbf{X}'_i = M^j\, T^{-1}\, T\, \mathbf{X}_i = M^j\, \mathbf{X}_i \,. \tag{11.27}$$

Since multiplying by T means transforming by a 3D projective transformation, this result can be interpreted that we cannot recover the true cameras and 3D points more accurately than up to an overall 3D projective transformation. Any particular solution $\{M'^j, \mathbf{X}'_i\}$, satisfying equations (11.26) (or, a process of computing it) is called the (3D) **projective reconstruction**.

To clarify the meaning of 'ambiguity up to a transformation G', this assumes that there exists an unknown **true reconstruction** $\{M^j, \mathbf{X}_i\}$ and that our reconstruction, $\{M'^j, \mathbf{X}'_i\}$ differs from it by an unknown transformation from a certain group G of transformations. This means that we know something about the true scene and the true cameras but not everything. In the case of projective ambiguity, we know that if some points among $\mathbf{X}'_i$ are e.g. collinear, the corresponding true points among $\mathbf{X}_i$ were also collinear. However, a distance, an angle or a volume computed in the projective reconstruction is different in general from the true ones because these are not invariant to projective transformations, as discussed in Section 11.2.2.

It is always possible to choose T such that the first camera matrix has the simple form

$$M^1 = [I \mid \mathbf{0}] = \begin{bmatrix} 1 & 0 & 0 & 0 \\ 0 & 1 & 0 & 0 \\ 0 & 0 & 1 & 0 \end{bmatrix} .$$

This simplification is often convenient in derivations. In detail, we claim that for an arbitrary camera matrix M there exists a 3D homography T such that $MT^{-1} = [I \mid \mathbf{0}]$. We show that T can be chosen as

$$T = \begin{bmatrix} M \\ \mathbf{a}^\top \end{bmatrix} ,$$

where $\mathbf{a}$ is any 4-vector such that T has full rank. We can conveniently choose $\mathbf{a}$ to satisfy $M\mathbf{a} = \mathbf{0}$, i.e., $\mathbf{a}$ represents the projection center. Then $M = [I \mid \mathbf{0}]\, T$, which verifies the claim.

11.4.3 Matching constraints

Matching constraints are relations satisfied by collections of corresponding image points in n views. They have the property that a multilinear function of homogeneous image coordinates must vanish; the coefficients of these functions form **multiview tensors**. Examples of multilinear tensors are fundamental matrices and the trifocal tensor to be described shortly.

Let $\mathbf{u}^j$ be points in images $j = 1, \ldots, n$ with camera matrices M^j. The matching constraints require that there is a single scene point $\mathbf{X}$ that projects into $\mathbf{u}^j$, that is, $\mathbf{u}^j \sim M^j \mathbf{X}$ for all j. We saw in equation (11.23) that this can be expressed by the homogeneous matrix equation (11.25).

Note that the rows of $S(\mathbf{u})$ represent three image lines passing through $\mathbf{u}$, the first two lines being finite and the last one at infinity. By equation (11.21), the rows of the matrix $S(\mathbf{u})M$ represent three scene planes intersecting in the ray back-projected from $\mathbf{u}$ by camera M. Thus, the rows of matrix W in equation (11.25) represent scene planes that have the point $\mathbf{X}$ in common.

Equation (11.25) has a solution only if W is rank-deficient, that is, all its 4×4 subdeterminants vanish. This means that any four of the $3n \times 4$ scene planes represented by the rows of W have a point in common. We will denote these four planes by $\mathbf{a}$, $\mathbf{b}$, $\mathbf{c}$, $\mathbf{d}$. Choosing different quadruples $\mathbf{a}$, $\mathbf{b}$, $\mathbf{c}$, $\mathbf{d}$ yields different matching constraints. It turns out that they are all multilinear, although some only after dividing by a common factor.

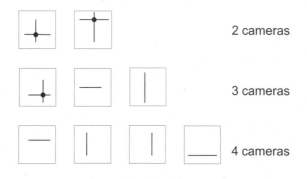

2 cameras

3 cameras

4 cameras

Figure 11.8: Geometric interpretation of bilinear, trilinear, and quadrilinear constraint in terms of four scene planes. © *Cengage Learning 2015*.

Two views. Any quadruple $\mathbf{a}$, $\mathbf{b}$, $\mathbf{c}$, $\mathbf{d}$ contains planes back-projected from at least two different views. Let these views be $j = 1, 2$ without loss of generality. The case when $\mathbf{a}$, $\mathbf{b}$, $\mathbf{c}$ are from view 1 and $\mathbf{d}$ is from view 2 is of no interest because these four planes always have a point in common. Therefore, let $\mathbf{a}$, $\mathbf{b}$ be from view 1 and $\mathbf{c}$, $\mathbf{d}$ from view 2, as shown in the top row of Figure 11.8 (lines at infinity are omitted). There are $3^2 = 9$ quadruples with this property. Each of the 9 corresponding determinants is divisible by a bilinear monomial. After division, all these determinants turn out to be equal, yielding a single **bilinear constraint**. This is widely known as the **epipolar constraint**, which will be discussed in detail in Section 11.5.1.

Three views. Let $\mathbf{a}$, $\mathbf{b}$ be from view 1, $\mathbf{c}$ from view 2, and $\mathbf{d}$ from view 3, as shown in the middle row of Figure 11.8. There are $3^3 = 27$ such choices. Each of the corresponding 27 determinants is divisible by a linear monomial. After division, we obtain only 9 different determinants. These provide 9 **trilinear constraints**.

We could also choose $\mathbf{c} = (M^2)^T \mathbf{l}^2$ and $\mathbf{d} = (M^3)^T \mathbf{l}^3$, where $\mathbf{l}^2$ and $\mathbf{l}^3$ are any image lines in views 2 and 3, not considering image points $\mathbf{u}^2$ and $\mathbf{u}^3$. This yields a single trilinear point-line-line constraint. In fact, this is the geometric essence of the trilinear constraint. The three-view constraints will be discussed in Section 11.6.

Four views. Let $\mathbf{a}$, $\mathbf{b}$, $\mathbf{c}$, $\mathbf{d}$ be from views 1, 2, 3, 4, respectively. There are $3^4 = 81$ such choices, yielding 81 **quadrilinear constraints**.

Again, we could consider four general image lines $l^1, \ldots, l^4$ instead of the image points $\mathbf{u}^1, \ldots, \mathbf{u}^4$, yielding a single quadrilinear constraint on four image lines. This is the geometrical essence of the quadrilinear constraint. Note that the constraint does not require that there is a scene line that projects to these image lines; rather, that there is a scene point whose projections lie on the image lines. We will not discuss four-view constraints further.

Five and more views. Matching constraints on five or more views are just the union of the sets of constraints on less than five views.

The usefulness of matching constraints lies mainly in the fact that their coefficients can be estimated from image correspondences. Indeed, corresponding image points (or lines) provide linear constraints on these coefficients.

11.4.4   Bundle adjustment

When computing a projective reconstruction from image correspondences, i.e., solving the system (11.26) for $\mathbf{X}_i$ and M^j, usually more than the minimal number of correspondences are available. Then the system (11.26) has no solution in general and we have to minimize the reprojection error, similarly to estimating homography (Section 11.2.3):

$$
\min_{\mathbf{X}_i, M^j} \sum_{i=1}^{m} \sum_{j=1}^{n} \left[\left(\frac{\mathbf{m}_1^j \mathbf{X}_i}{\mathbf{m}_3^j \mathbf{X}_i} - \hat{\mathbf{u}}_i^j \right)^2 + \left(\frac{\mathbf{m}_2^j \mathbf{X}_i}{\mathbf{m}_3^j \mathbf{X}_i} - \hat{\mathbf{u}}_i^j \right)^2 \right] , \quad i = 1, \ldots, m; \; j = 1, \ldots, n .
$$

(11.28)

To solve this problem, we first find an initial estimate by a linear method and then use non-linear least squares (the Levenberg-Marquardt algorithm). The non-linear least squares specialized for this task is known from photogrammetry as **bundle adjustment**. This term is, slightly informally, used also for non-linear least squares algorithms solving other tasks in multiple view geometry, e.g., homography estimation or triangulation.

Non-linear least squares may seem computationally prohibitive for many points and many cameras. However, implementations using sparse matrices [Triggs et al., 2000; Hartley and Zisserman, 2003] increase efficiency significantly, especially when coupled with modern hardware.

There is no single best method for computing a projective reconstruction from correspondences in many images, and the method to use depends heavily on the data. A different method should be used for an image sequence from a videocamera (when displacements between neighboring frames are small) [Fitzgibbon and Zisserman, 1998] than for a less organized set of images [Cornelius et al., 2004] when we do not know anything about camera locations beforehand.

An approach suitable for a videosequence is as follows. We start with projective reconstruction from two images done by estimating the fundamental matrix, decomposing to camera matrices (Section 11.5) and computing 3D points by triangulation (Section 11.4.1), followed by bundle adjustment. Then, the third camera matrix is computed by resectioning (Section 11.3.3) from the already reconstructed 3D points and the corresponding image points in the third image, again followed by bundle adjustment. This last step is repeated for all subsequent frames.

11.4.5   Upgrading the projective reconstruction, self-calibration

The overall projective ambiguity given by equation (11.27) is inherent: we cannot remove it without having additional knowledge. However, having suitable additional knowledge about the true scene and/or true cameras can provide constraints that narrow the class of the unknown transformations between our and true reconstruction.

There are several kinds of additional knowledge, permitting the projective ambiguity to be refined to an affine, similarity, or Euclidean one. Methods that use additional knowledge to compute a similarity reconstruction instead of mere projective one are also known as **self-calibration** because this is in fact equivalent to finding intrinsic camera parameters (introduced in Section 11.3.1). Self-calibration methods can be divided into two groups: constraints on the cameras and constraints on the scene. They often lead to non-linear problems, each of which requires a different algorithm. We do not discuss these in detail beyond a taxonomy (refer to [Hartley, 1997] for detail). Examples of constraints on the cameras are:

- Constraints on camera intrinsic parameters in the calibration matrix K (see Section 11.3.1):

  - The calibration matrix K is known for each camera. In this case, the scene can be reconstructed up to an overall scaling plus a four-fold ambiguity. This will be described in Section 11.5.2.

  - The intrinsic camera calibration matrices K are unknown and different for each camera but have a restricted form with zero skew (rectangular pixels)

    $$K = \begin{bmatrix} f & 0 & -u_0 \\ 0 & g & -v_0 \\ 0 & 0 & 1 \end{bmatrix} . \tag{11.29}$$

    It is known that this can reduce the ambiguity to a mere similarity when three or more views are available [Pollefeys et al., 1998; Hartley, 1997]. The algorithm becomes much easier when we further restrict K by $f = g$ (square pixels) and $u_0 = v_0 = 0$ (the principal point in the image center). These restrictions are, at least approximately, valid for real cameras. The method works reasonably well in practice.

  - The camera calibration matrices K containing intrinsic parameters are unknown but the same for each camera. In theory, this permits restricting the ambiguity to a similarity transformation [Maybank and Faugeras, 1992] via the Kruppa equations. However, the resulting polynomial equation system is so unstable and difficult to solve that the method is not used in practice.

- Constraints on camera extrinsic parameters R and $\mathbf{t}$ (i.e., the relative motion of the cameras):

  - Both rotation R and translation $\mathbf{t}$ are known [Horaud et al., 1995].

  - Only rotation R is known [Hartley, 1994].

  - Only translation $\mathbf{t}$ is known. The linear solution is due to [Pajdla and Hlaváč, 1995].

In Section 11.2.2, we listed some invariants of subgroups of the projective transformation. The scene constraints can often be understood as specifying a sufficient number of appropriate invariants in the scene, which permits the recovery of the corresponding transformation group. Examples of constraints on the scene are:

- At simplest, to specify 3D coordinates of at least five scene points (no four of them coplanar) which can be identified in the images. Denoting these five points by $\mathbf{X}_i$ and the reconstructed ones by $\mathbf{X}_i'$ for $i = 1, \ldots, 5$, we can compute T from equation system $\mathbf{X}_i' \simeq T\mathbf{X}_i$, as described in Section 11.2.3.

- Affine invariants may suffice to restrict the ambiguity from a projective transformation to an affine one. This is equivalent to computing a special scene plane in $\mathcal{P}^3$, the **plane at infinity**, on which all parallel lines and planes intersect. Thus, we can specify certain length ratios on lines or that certain lines are parallel in the scene.

- Similarity or metric invariants may suffice to restrict projective or affine ambiguity to a similarity or metric one. This is equivalent to computing a special (complex) conic lying at the plane at infinity, called the **absolute conic**. Specifying an appropriate set of angles or distances can suffice for this.

  In particular, in a man-made environment we can use **vanishing points**, which are images of points at infinity specifying (usually three, one vertical and two horizontal) mutually orthogonal directions in the scene.

Camera and scene constraints, such as described in this section, can be incorporated into bundle adjustment (Section 11.4.4).

11.5 Two cameras, stereopsis

To the uneducated observer, the most obvious difference between the human visual system and most of the material presented in earlier chapters of this book is that we have two eyes and therefore (a priori, at any rate) twice as much input as a single image. From Victorian times, the use of two slightly different views to provide an illusion of 3D has been common, culminating in the '3D movies' of the 1950s. Conversely, we might hope that a 3D scene, if presenting two different views to two eyes, might permit the recapture of depth information when the information therein is combined with some knowledge of the sensor geometry (eye locations).

Stereo vision has enormous importance. It has provoked a great deal of research into computer vision systems with two inputs that exploit the knowledge of their own relative geometry to derive depth information from the two views they receive.

Calibration of one camera and knowledge of the coordinates of one image point allows us to determine a ray in space uniquely. If two calibrated cameras observe the same scene point $\mathbf{X}$, its 3D coordinates can be computed as the intersection of two such rays (Section 11.4.1). This is the basic principle of **stereo vision** that typically consists of three steps:

- Camera calibration.
- Establishing point correspondences between pairs of points from the left and the right images.
- Reconstruction of 3D coordinates of the points in the scene.

In this section, we will denote mathematical entities related to the first image without a prime and the same entity related to the second image with prime. E.g., $\mathbf{u}$ and $\mathbf{u}'$.

11.5.1   Epipolar geometry; fundamental matrix

The geometry of a system with two cameras is shown in Figure 11.9. The line connecting optical centers $\mathbf{C}$ and $\mathbf{C}'$ is the **baseline**. The baseline intersects the image planes in the **epipoles** $\mathbf{e}$ and $\mathbf{e}'$. Alternatively, an epipole is the image of the projection center of one camera in the other camera, $\mathbf{e} = M\mathbf{C}'$ and $\mathbf{e}' = M'\mathbf{C}$.

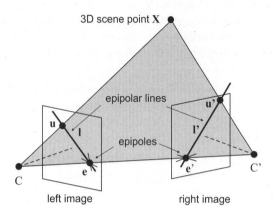

Figure 11.9: Geometry of two cameras. © *Cengage Learning 2015*.

Any scene point $\mathbf{X}$ observed by the two cameras and the two corresponding rays from optical centers $\mathbf{C}$, $\mathbf{C}'$ define an **epipolar plane**. This plane intersects the image planes in the **epipolar lines** (or just epipolars) $\mathbf{l}$ and $\mathbf{l}'$. Alternatively, an epipolar line is the projection of the ray in one camera into the other camera. All epipolar lines intersect in the epipole.

Let $\mathbf{u}$, $\mathbf{u}'$ be the projections of a scene point $\mathbf{X}$ in the first and second camera, respectively. The ray $\mathbf{CX}$ represents all possible positions of $\mathbf{X}$ for the first image and is seen as the epipolar line $\mathbf{l}'$ in the second image. The point $\mathbf{u}'$ in the second image that corresponds to $\mathbf{u}$ must thus lie on the epipolar line $\mathbf{l}'$ in the second image, $\mathbf{l}'^{\top}\mathbf{u}' = 0$. The situation is of course entirely symmetrical, we have also $\mathbf{l}^{\top}\mathbf{u} = 0$. The fact that the positions of two corresponding image points is not arbitrary is known as the **epipolar constraint**.

Recall that the ray from the first camera given by back-projected image point $\mathbf{u}$ passes through $\mathbf{C}$ and through the point $\mathbf{X} = M^{+}\mathbf{u}$, as stated by equation (11.20) in Section 11.3.2. The epipolar line $\mathbf{l}'$ is the projection of this ray in the second image, that is, it passes through image points $M'\mathbf{C} = \mathbf{e}'$ and $M'M^{+}\mathbf{u}$. Thus

$$\mathbf{l}' = \mathbf{e}' \times (M'M^{+}\mathbf{u}) = S(\mathbf{e}')\, M'M^{+}\mathbf{u}\,,$$

where we replaced the cross-product $\times$ with the cross-product matrix, defined by equation (11.8). We can see that the epipolar line $\mathbf{l}'$ is a linear mapping of the corresponding image point $\mathbf{u}$. Denoting the matrix representing this linear mapping by

$$F = S(\mathbf{e}')\, M'M^{+}\,, \tag{11.30}$$

we can write simply

$$\mathbf{l}' = F\mathbf{u}\,. \tag{11.31}$$

If we want a constraint on corresponding points in two images, we use $\mathbf{l}'^{\top}\mathbf{u}' = 0$, which yields

$$\mathbf{u}'^{\top} F \mathbf{u} = 0 \,. \tag{11.32}$$

This is the **epipolar constraint** in algebraic form [Longuet-Higgins, 1981], which had been known to photogrammetrists from the end of the 19th century. Matrix F is called the **fundamental matrix**—a slightly misleading name widely used for historical reasons; more appropriate names like **bifocal matrix** are used by some of the computer vision community.

Transposing equation (11.32) shows that if the cameras are interchanged then the fundamental matrix is replaced by its transpose.

Since M and M' have full rank in equation (11.30) and $S(\mathbf{e}')$ has rank 2, it follows that F has rank 2. A linear mapping that maps points to lines is called a (projective) **correlation**. A (projective) correlation is a collineation from a projective space onto its dual space, taking points to hyperplanes and preserving incidence. In our case, the (projective) correlation given by equation (11.31) is singular, meaning that non-collinear points map to lines with a common intersection. Since $\mathbf{e}'S(\mathbf{e}') = \mathbf{0}$, equation (11.30) implies $\mathbf{e}'^{\top} F = \mathbf{0}^{\top}$. By interchanging the images, we obtain the symmetrical relation $F\mathbf{e} = \mathbf{0}$. Thus, the epipoles are the left and right null vectors of F.

The fundamental matrix is a very important quantity in multiple view geometry. It captures all information that can be obtained about a camera pair from correspondences only.

Fundamental matrix from camera matrices in a restricted form

Equation (11.30) is an expression for computing F from two arbitrary camera matrices M and M'. Sometimes, however, the camera matrices have a restricted form. There are two following important cases in which this restricted form simplifies the expression (11.30).

First, the camera matrices have the form

$$M = [I \mid \mathbf{0}] \,, \qquad M' = [\tilde{M}' \mid \mathbf{e}'] \,. \tag{11.33}$$

To justify this form, recall from Section 11.4.2 that due to projective ambiguity, the first camera matrix can always be chosen as $M = [I \mid \mathbf{0}]$. Since the first projection center $\mathbf{C}$ satisfies $M\mathbf{C} = \mathbf{0}$, it lies in the origin, $\mathbf{C} = [0, 0, 0, 1]^{\top}$. Since the second camera matrix M' satisfies $M'\mathbf{C} = \mathbf{e}'$, its last column is necessarily the second epipole, as given by equation (11.33). Substituting into equation (11.30) and using $M^+ = [I \mid \mathbf{0}]^{\top}$ yields

$$F = S(\mathbf{e}') \, \tilde{M}' \,. \tag{11.34}$$

Second, the camera matrices have the form

$$M = K[I \mid \mathbf{0}] \,, \qquad M' = K'[R \mid -R\mathbf{t}] \,. \tag{11.35}$$

This describes calibrated cameras with intrinsic camera parameters in calibration matrices K and K' and the relative motion given by rotation R and translation $\mathbf{t}$. Noting that

$$M^+ = \begin{bmatrix} K^{-1} \\ \mathbf{0}^{\top} \end{bmatrix} \,, \qquad \mathbf{C} = \begin{bmatrix} \mathbf{0} \\ 1 \end{bmatrix} \,, \tag{11.36}$$

we have $F = S(M'\mathbf{C})\, M'M^+ = S(-K'R\mathbf{t})\, K'R\,K^{-1}$. Using that $S(H\mathbf{u}) \simeq H^{-T}S(\mathbf{u})\, H^{-1}$, which holds for any $\mathbf{u}$ and non-singular H, we obtain

$$F = K'^{-\top}R\,S(\mathbf{t})\,K^{-1}\,. \tag{11.37}$$

11.5.2   Relative motion of the camera; essential matrix

If the camera matrices have the form given in equation (11.35) and if intrinsic parameters given by calibration matrices K and K' are known then we can compensate for the affine transformation given by K, K'. Recall that several coordinate systems were introduced for single camera projection in Section 11.3.1 and Figure 11.7. The camera Euclidean coordinate system is denoted by subscript $_i$ and our measured points $\mathbf{u}_i$ live in it. The affine image coordinates are without any subscript. Following this convention, we have

$$\mathbf{u} = K^{-1}\mathbf{u}_i\,, \qquad \mathbf{u}' = (K')^{-1}\mathbf{u}'_i\,. \tag{11.38}$$

Using equation (11.37), the epipolar constraint according to equation (11.32) written for $\mathbf{u}_i$ and $\mathbf{u}'_i$ reads

$$\mathbf{u}'^{\top}_i E\,\mathbf{u}_i = 0\,, \tag{11.39}$$

where the matrix

$$E = R\,S(\mathbf{t}) \tag{11.40}$$

is known as the **essential matrix**.

The epipolar constraint in the form $\mathbf{u}'^{\top}_i R\,S(\mathbf{t})\,\mathbf{u}_i = 0$ has a simple geometrical meaning. Vectors $\mathbf{u}_i$ and $\mathbf{u}'_i$ can be seen either as homogeneous 2D points in the image affine coordinate system or, equivalently, as non-homogeneous 3D points in the camera Euclidean system. The epipolar constraint says that 3-vectors $\mathbf{u}_i$, $R^{-1}\mathbf{u}'_i$ and $\mathbf{t}$ are coplanar. This is indeed true because they all lie in the epipolar plane, provided that $\mathbf{u}'_i$ has been transformed into the same system as $\mathbf{u}_i$ and $\mathbf{t}$ by rotation R. Recall that three 3-vectors $\mathbf{a}$, $\mathbf{b}$, $\mathbf{c}$ are coplanar if and only if $\det[\mathbf{a}, \mathbf{b}, \mathbf{c}] = \mathbf{a}^{\top}(\mathbf{b} \times \mathbf{c}) = 0$.

The essential matrix has rank two. This means that exactly two of its singular values are non-zero. Unlike the fundamental matrix, the essential matrix satisfies an additional constraint that these two singular values are equal. This is because the singular values of a matrix are invariant to an orthonormal transformation of the matrix; thus, in the SVD decomposition $E = UDV^{\top}$ we have

$$D = \begin{bmatrix} \sigma & 0 & 0 \\ 0 & \sigma & 0 \\ 0 & 0 & 0 \end{bmatrix} = \mathrm{diag}[\sigma, \sigma, 0]\,. \tag{11.41}$$

Decomposing the essential matrix into rotation and translation

The essential matrix E captures information about the **relative motion** of the second camera with respect to the first, described by a translation $\mathbf{t}$ and rotation R. Given camera calibration matrices K and K', this relative motion can be computed from image correspondences as follows: estimate the fundamental matrix F from the correspondences (Section 11.5.4), compute $E = K'^{\top}F\,K$, and decompose E to $\mathbf{t}$ and R. Optionally, we can reconstruct 3D points from the image correspondences by triangulation (Section 11.4.1).

It remains to show how to decompose E into $\mathbf{t}$ and R. If the essential matrix E is determined only up to an unknown scale (which is indeed the case if it is estimated from image correspondences) then we see from equation (11.40) that the scale of $\mathbf{t}$ is unknown too. That means we can reconstruct the cameras and the scene points only up to an overall similarity transformation.

Denote

$$\bar{\mathbf{t}} = \begin{bmatrix} 0 \\ 0 \\ 1 \end{bmatrix}, \qquad \bar{R} = \begin{bmatrix} 0 & 1 & 0 \\ -1 & 0 & 0 \\ 0 & 0 & 1 \end{bmatrix}.$$

Note that $\bar{R}$ is a rotation matrix and that $\bar{R} S(\bar{\mathbf{t}}) = -\bar{R}^\top S(\bar{\mathbf{t}}) = \text{diag}[1,1,0]$. Let $E \simeq U \, \text{diag}[1,1,0] V^\top$ be the SVD decomposition of E. The translation can be computed from

$$S(\mathbf{t}) = V \, S(\bar{\mathbf{t}}) \, V^\top.$$

The rotation is not given uniquely, we have

$$R = U \bar{R} V^\top \quad \text{or} \quad R = U \bar{R}^\top V^\top.$$

We easily verify that $RS(\mathbf{t}) \simeq U \, \text{diag}[1,1,0] V^\top \simeq E$. The proof that there is no other decomposition can be found in [Hartley, 1992, 1997].

The scale ambiguity of $\mathbf{t}$ includes also the sign of $\mathbf{t}$. Altogether, we have four qualitatively different relative motions, given by two-fold rotation and two-fold translation ambiguity.

11.5.3 Decomposing the fundamental matrix to camera matrices

In Section 11.4.2, we proposed to find a particular solution to the projective reconstruction problem given by equation (11.26) from two images; that is, to find camera matrices and scene points that project to given image points. This can be done by estimating the fundamental matrix from the image points, decomposing it to two camera matrices, and then computing the scene points by triangulation (Section 11.4.1).

Here we describe how to decompose F to two camera matrices M and M' consistent with it. We know from Section 11.4.2 that due to projective ambiguity, the first matrix can be chosen as $M = [I \mid \mathbf{0}]$ without loss of generality. It remains to determine M'.

Recall that a matrix S is skew-symmetric if it satisfies $S + S^\top = 0$. Any matrix S that satisfies $\mathbf{X}^\top S \mathbf{X} = 0$ for every $\mathbf{X}$ is skew-symmetric: to see this, write the product in components as

$$\mathbf{X}^\top S \mathbf{X} = \sum_i s_{ii} X_i^2 + \sum_{i<j} (s_{ij} + s_{ji}) X_i X_j = 0,$$

where s_{ij} are the entries of S. This holds for all $\mathbf{X}$ only if s_{ii} and $s_{ij} + s_{ji}$ are always zero.

Substituting $\mathbf{u} = M\mathbf{X}$ and $\mathbf{u}' = M'\mathbf{X}$ to $\mathbf{u}'^\top F \mathbf{u} = 0$ yields

$$(M'\mathbf{X})^\top F (M\mathbf{X}) = \mathbf{X}^\top M'^\top F M \mathbf{X} = 0,$$

which holds for any non-zero 4-vector $\mathbf{X}$. It follows that the matrix $M'^\top FM$ is skew-symmetric. Denote $M' = [\tilde{M}' \mid \mathbf{b}']$, where $\tilde{M}'$ contains the first three columns of M' and $\mathbf{b}'$ is the last column of M'. We have

$$M'^\top F M = \begin{bmatrix} \tilde{M}'^\top \\ \mathbf{b}'^\top \end{bmatrix} F [I \mid \mathbf{0}] = \begin{bmatrix} \tilde{M}'^\top F & \mathbf{0} \\ \mathbf{b}'^\top F & 0 \end{bmatrix}.$$

Since the right-most matrix has to be skew-symmetric, $\tilde{M}'^{\top}F$ has to be skew-symmetric and $\mathbf{b}'^{\top}F$ has to vanish. The latter implies that $\mathbf{b}'$ is the second epipole, $\mathbf{e}'$; this has already been shown when justifying equation (11.33).

It is easy to see that if $\tilde{M}' = SF$ where S is an arbitrary skew-symmetric 3×3 matrix, $\tilde{M}'^{\top}F$ is skew-symmetric too. Just write $\tilde{M}'^{\top}F = -F^{\top}SF$ and verify that $(F^{\top}SF) + (F^{\top}SF)^{\top} = 0$. Conveniently, we can choose $S = S(\mathbf{e}')$.

To summarize, the camera matrices consistent with a fundamental matrix F can be chosen as

$$M = [I \mid \mathbf{0}], \qquad M' = [S(\mathbf{e}')\,F \mid \mathbf{e}']. \tag{11.42}$$

Note that even if the first camera matrix is fixed to $M = [I \mid \mathbf{0}]$, the second matrix M' is not determined uniquely by F because we have freedom in choosing S.

11.5.4 Estimating the fundamental matrix from point correspondences

Epipolar geometry has seven degrees of freedom [Mohr, 1993]. The epipoles $\mathbf{e}$, $\mathbf{e}'$ in the image have two coordinates each (giving 4 degrees of freedom), while another three come from the mapping of any three epipolar lines in the first image to the second. Alternatively, we note that the nine components of F are given up to an overall scale and we have another constraint $\det F = 0$, yielding again $9 - 1 - 1 = 7$ free parameters.

The correspondence of seven points in left and right images allows the computation of the fundamental matrix F using a non-linear algorithm [Faugeras et al., 1992], known as the **seven-point algorithm**. If eight points are available, the solution becomes linear and is known as the **eight-point algorithm**. Unlike the seven-point one, the eight-point algorithm can straightforwardly be extended for more than eight points.

Eight-point algorithm

Given $m \geq 8$ point pairs $(\mathbf{u}_i, \mathbf{u}'_i)$ in homogeneous coordinates, we solve the system

$$\mathbf{u}'^{\top}_i F\,\mathbf{u}_i = \mathbf{0}, \quad i = 1, \ldots, m.$$

This problem is very similar to homography estimation. As in Section 11.2.3, we use the identity

$$\mathbf{u}'^{\top}F\,\mathbf{u} = [\mathbf{u}^{\top} \otimes \mathbf{u}'^{\top}]\mathbf{f} = \begin{bmatrix} uu' & uv' & uw' & vu' & vv' & vw' & wu' & wv' & ww' \end{bmatrix}\mathbf{f} = \mathbf{0},$$

where $\mathbf{f} = [f_{11}, f_{21}, \ldots, f_{23}, f_{33}]^{\top}$ and $\otimes$ is the Kronecker product. Considering all m correspondences, we obtain

$$\begin{bmatrix} \mathbf{u}^{\top}_1 \otimes \mathbf{u}'^{\top}_1 \\ \cdots \\ \mathbf{u}^{\top}_m \otimes \mathbf{u}'^{\top}_m \end{bmatrix} \mathbf{f} = W\mathbf{f} = \mathbf{0}. \tag{11.43}$$

For eight correspondences in a non-degenerate configuration, this system has a single solution (up to scale). For more correspondences, it can be solved by minimizing algebraic distance and in both cases, we can obtain the solution by SVD. The image points have to be preconditioned, as described in Section 11.2.3.

The fundamental matrix F computed by the eight-point algorithm will be non-singular in general, so will not be a valid fundamental matrix. We can find a matrix $\tilde{F}$ of rank 2 that is nearest to F with respect to the Frobenius norm: decompose $F = UDV^\top$ by SVD; set the smallest singular value in the diagonal matrix D to zero, giving a new diagonal matrix $\tilde{D}$ with only two entries non-zero; compose back as $\tilde{F} = U\tilde{D}V^\top$.

Seven-point algorithm

If only $m = 7$ points are available, the solution of the system of equations (11.43) will be a two-dimensional linear subspace of $\mathcal{R}^9$, rather than a one-dimensional linear subspace as for $m = 8$. That is, there will be two vectors $\mathbf{f}$ and $\mathbf{f}'$ satisfying $W\mathbf{f} = W\mathbf{f}' = \mathbf{0}$. SVD yields these two mutually orthonormal vectors.

The idea of the seven-point algorithm is to find the points in this subspace satisfying the constraint $\det F = 0$. That is, we look for a scalar λ such that

$$\det[\lambda F + (1 - \lambda)F'] = 0 \,.$$

This cubic equation has three solutions in general, two of which can be complex. It follows that the seven-point algorithm can have one, two, or three different solutions for F.

If six or seven points are related by a homography, there is an infinite space of solutions for F. In other words, this is a degenerate configuration for computing F [Hartley and Zisserman, 2003].

Maximum likelihood estimation

The maximum likelihood estimation is similar to that of homography, however, here we have a slightly different constraint on correspondences and the additional constraint $\det F = 0$. Let $[\hat{u}_i, \hat{v}_i]^\top$ and $[\hat{u}'_i, \hat{v}'_i]^\top$ be the image points in non-homogeneous coordinates. Then we are solving the optimization problem

$$\min_{F, u_i, v_i, u'_i, v'_i} \sum_{i=1}^{m} \left[(u_i - \hat{u}_i)^2 + (v_i - \hat{v}_i)^2 + (u'_i - \hat{u}'_i)^2 + (v'_i - \hat{v}'_i)^2 \right], \quad i = 1, \dots, m \,,$$

$$[u'_i, v'_i, 1]F[u_i, v_i, 1]^\top = 0, \quad \det F = 0 \,.$$

$$(11.44)$$

A frequently used alternative is first to decompose F into camera matrices, reconstruct scene points by triangulation (Section 11.4.1), and then use the full bundle adjustment (Section 11.4.4). It is not an obstacle that the optimization is done over more variables than in the optimization problem specified by equation (11.44).

11.5.5 Rectified configuration of two cameras

The epipolar constraint reduces the dimensionality of the search space for a correspondence between $\mathbf{u}$ and $\mathbf{u}'$ in the right image from 2D to 1D.

A special arrangement of the stereo camera rig is called the **rectified configuration**; the terms 'canonical configuration', or 'rectilinear camera rig' are also used. Image planes coincide and the line $\mathbf{CC}'$ is parallel to them. This sends epipoles to infinity. In addition, epipolar lines coincide with image rows, see Figure 11.10. It is also assumed that the intrinsic calibration parameters of both cameras are the same. For this configuration, the computation is slightly simpler; it is often used when stereo correspondence

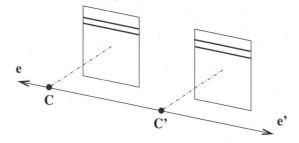

Figure 11.10: The rectified stereo configuration where the epipolar lines are parallel in the image, and epipoles move to infinity. © *Cengage Learning 2015.*

is to be determined by a human operator who will find matching points linewise to be easier. A similar conclusion holds for computer programs too; it is easier to move along horizontal lines (rasters) than along general lines. The geometric transformation that changes a general camera configuration with non-parallel epipolar lines to the canonical one is called **image rectification**.

Considering a rectified configuration, we shall see how to recover depth. The optical axes are parallel, which leads to the notion of **disparity** that is often used in stereo literature. A simple diagram demonstrates how we proceed. In Figure 11.11, we have a bird's-eye view of two cameras with parallel optical axes separated by a baseline distance $b = 2h$. The images both cameras provide, together with one point $\mathbf{X}$ with coordinates $(x, y, z)^\top$ in the scene, show this point's projection onto left ($\mathbf{u}$) and right ($\mathbf{u}'$) images. The coordinates in Figure 11.11 have the z axis representing distance from the cameras (at which $z = 0$) and the x axis representing 'horizontal' distance (the y coordinate, into the page, does not appear). The value $x = 0$ will be the position midway between the cameras; each camera image will have a local coordinate system which for the sake of convenience we measure from the center of the respective images—that is, a simple translation from the global x coordinate. Values u, u', v, v' give the coordinates within the local coordinate frame for the left, right camera, respectively; as the measurement is taken in the same height (row), $v = v'$.

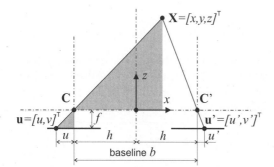

Figure 11.11: Elementary stereo geometry in the rectified configuration. The depth z of the point $\mathbf{X}$ in 3D scene can be calculated from the disparity $d = u' - u$. Values of u, u' are measured at the same height, i.e., $v = v'$. © *Cengage Learning 2015.*

It is clear that there is a **disparity** d between u and u' as a result of the different camera positions (that is $d = u - u'$, $d < 0$); we can use elementary geometry to deduce the depth z coordinate of $\mathbf{X}$.

Note that $\mathbf{u}$, $\mathbf{C}$ and $\mathbf{C}$, $\mathbf{X}$ are the hypotenuses of similar right-angled triangles (shown in gray in Figure 11.11). Noting further that h and the focal length f are (positive) numbers, z is a positive coordinate and x, u, u' are coordinates that may be positive or negative, we can then write

$$\frac{u}{f} = -\frac{h+x}{z}, \qquad \frac{u'}{f} = \frac{h-x}{z}. \tag{11.45}$$

Eliminating x from these equations gives $z\,(u'-u) = 2hf$ and hence

$$z = \frac{2hf}{u'-u} = \frac{bf}{u'-u} = \frac{bf}{d}. \tag{11.46}$$

Notice in this equation that $d = u' - u$ is the detected disparity in the observations of $\mathbf{X}$. If $(u'-u) \to 0$, then $z \to \infty$. Zero disparity indicates that the point is (effectively) at an infinite distance from the viewer—distant 3D points have a small disparity. Relative error in depth z is large for small disparity, and a wide baseline reduces the relative error in z.

The remaining two coordinates of the 3D point $\mathbf{X}$ can be calculated as

$$x = \frac{-b\,(u+u')}{2\,d}, \qquad y = \frac{b\,v}{d}. \tag{11.47}$$

11.5.6 Computing rectification

We have seen that stereo geometry implies that corresponding points can be sought in 1D space along epipolar lines. We have also mentioned that a rectified pair of cameras eases the search for stereo correspondences. It is possible to apply a special case of geometric transformation (except in degenerate cases) called **image rectification** to images captured by a stereo rig with non-parallel optical axes, resulting in a new set of images with parallel epipolar lines.

Left camera values will be identified by the subscript $_L$ and right camera values by the subscript $_R$. Let the superscript * denote values after rectification. The rectification procedure consists of two steps in which matrices K_L, K_R are intrinsic camera calibration matrices of left and right cameras, respectively.

1. Finding a pair of rectifying homographies H_L, H_R for left, right image, respectively such that corresponding epipolar lines are equivalent and parallel to image rows.

2. Warping images and modifying camera projection matrices. Images are warped using homographies H_L, H_R and the camera projection matrices modified as $M_L^* = H_L M_L$ and $M_R^* = H_R M_R$.

Cameras are rectified by homographies

$$\begin{aligned} M_L^* &= H_L M_L = H_L K_L R_L [I \mid -\mathbf{C_L}], \\ M_R^* &= H_R M_R = H_R K_R R_R [I \mid -\mathbf{C_R}]. \end{aligned} \tag{11.48}$$

Let $\mathbf{e}_L$, $\mathbf{e}_R$ be epipoles in the left, right images. Analogously let $\mathbf{l}_L$, $\mathbf{l}_R$ be epipolar lines and $\mathbf{u}_L$ and $\mathbf{u}_R$ be the projections of a scene point to image planes. Let F^* be the fundamental matrix corresponding to rectified images and $\lambda \neq 0$. The necessary condition for rectification which makes epipolar lines coincident with rows in both images is

$$\begin{aligned} \mathbf{l}_R^* = \mathbf{e}_R^* \times \mathbf{u}_R^* &= \lambda F^* \mathbf{u}_L^*, \\ [1,0,0]^\top \times [u',v,1]^\top = [1,0,0]^\top \times [u+d,v,1]^\top &= \lambda F^* [u,v,1]^\top, \end{aligned} \tag{11.49}$$

where

$$F^* \simeq \begin{bmatrix} 0 & 0 & 0 \\ 0 & 0 & 1 \\ 0 & -1 & 0 \end{bmatrix}. \tag{11.50}$$

The rectifying homographies are not unique. Two instances of rectification are shown in Figure 11.12. The interesting question is which of the many possible rectifications is the best, which we will discuss shortly.

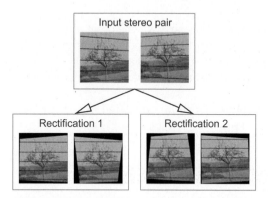

Figure 11.12: Two instances of many possible rectifications. *Courtesy of R. Šára and M. Matoušek, Czech Technical University, Prague.*

Algorithm 11.1: Image rectification

1. *Epipoles are translated to infinity in both images.*

   Let $\mathbf{e}_L = [e_1, e_2, 1]^\top$ be the epipole in the left image and $e_1^2 + e_2^2 \neq 0$. This epipole is mapped to $\mathbf{e}^* \simeq [1, 0, 0]^\top$ as the rotation of the epipole $\mathbf{e}_L$ to the axis u and the projection

   $$\hat{H}_L \simeq \begin{bmatrix} e_1 & e_2 & 0 \\ -e_2 & e_1 & 0 \\ -e_1 & -e_2 & e_1^2 + e_2^2 \end{bmatrix}. \tag{11.51}$$

2. *Epipolar lines are unified to get a pair of elementary rectifying homographies.*

   Since $\mathbf{e}_R^* = [1, 0, 0]^\top$ is both left and right null space of $\hat{F}$, the modified fundamental matrix becomes

   $$\hat{F} \simeq \begin{bmatrix} 0 & 0 & 0 \\ 0 & \alpha & \beta \\ 0 & \gamma & \delta \end{bmatrix} \tag{11.52}$$

   and elementary rectifying homographies $\bar{H}_L$, $\bar{H}_R$ are chosen to make $\alpha = \delta = 0$ and $\beta = -\gamma$.

   $$\bar{H}_L = H_S \hat{H}_L, \quad \bar{H}_R = \hat{H}_R, \quad \text{where } H_S = \begin{bmatrix} \alpha\delta - \beta\gamma & 0 & 0 \\ 0 & -\gamma & -\delta \\ 0 & \alpha & \beta \end{bmatrix}. \tag{11.53}$$

   Then

   $$F^* = \left(\hat{H}_R\right)^{-\top} F \left(H_S \hat{H}_L\right)^{-1}. \tag{11.54}$$

3. *A pair of optimal homographies is selected from the class preserving the fundamental matrix F^*.*

Let $\bar{H}_L$, $\bar{H}_R$ be elementary rectifying homographies (or some other rectifying homographies). Homographies H_L, H_R are also rectifying homographies provided they obey equation $H_R F^* H_L^\top = \lambda F^*$, $\lambda \neq 0$, which guarantees that images are kept rectified.

The internal structure of H_L, H_R permits us to understand the meaning of free parameters in the class of rectifying homographies

$$H_L = \begin{bmatrix} l_1 & l_2 & l_3 \\ 0 & s & u_0 \\ 0 & q & 1 \end{bmatrix} \bar{H}_L , \qquad H_R = \begin{bmatrix} r_1 & r_2 & r_3 \\ 0 & s & u_0 \\ 0 & q & 1 \end{bmatrix} \bar{H}_R , \qquad (11.55)$$

where $s \neq 0$ is a common vertical scale; u_0 is a common vertical shift; l_1, r_1 are left and right skews; l_2, r_2 are left and right horizontal scales; l_1, r_1 are left and right horizontal shifts and q is common perspective distortion.

This third step is necessary because elementary homographies may yield severely distorted images.

The algorithms differ by the way free parameters are selected. One approach minimizes residual image distortion [Loop and Zhang, 1999; Gluckman and Nayar, 2001]. Another approach takes into account how much the underlying data change using frequency spectrum analysis and minimizing image information loss [Matoušek et al., 2004].

11.6   Three cameras and trifocal tensor

Section 11.5 was devoted to the matching constraints between two views which manifest in epipolar geometry. We saw in Section 11.4.3 that matching constraints exist also amongst three and four views. This section describes the one for three views. Its form is that a set of trilinear functions of image coordinates must vanish.

We follow the derivation of the trifocal tensor from [Hartley and Zisserman, 2003]. The constraint among three views receives its simplest form as a formula that computes line $\mathbf{l}$ in the first view from a given line $\mathbf{l}'$ in the second view and a given line $\mathbf{l}''$ in the third view. The geometrical meaning of this construction is simple: back project the lines $\mathbf{l}'$ and $\mathbf{l}''$ to scene planes, find a common scene line of these planes, and project this line into the first view (see Figure 11.13).

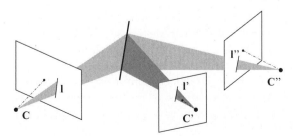

Figure 11.13: Illustration of the matching constraint among three views. Cameras have centers $\mathbf{C}$, $\mathbf{C}'$, $\mathbf{C}''$ and appropriate image planes. A line in 3D projects into lines $\mathbf{l}$, $\mathbf{l}'$, $\mathbf{l}''$. *© Cengage Learning 2015.*

Let the three views have camera matrices M, M' and M''. Due to projective ambiguity described in Section 11.4.2, we can choose $M = [I \mid \mathbf{0}]$ without loss of generality. Then, using the result from expression (11.33), we have

$$M = [I \mid \mathbf{0}], \qquad M' = [\tilde{M}' \mid \mathbf{e}'], \qquad M'' = [\tilde{M}'' \mid \mathbf{e}''],$$

where the epipole $\mathbf{e}'$ and $\mathbf{e}''$ is the projection of the first camera center, $\mathbf{C} = [0, 0, 0, 1]^\top$, in the second and third camera, respectively.

To satisfy the constraint, the scene planes

$$\mathbf{a} = M^\top \mathbf{l} = \begin{bmatrix} \mathbf{l} \\ 0 \end{bmatrix}, \qquad \mathbf{a}' = M'^\top \mathbf{l}' = \begin{bmatrix} \tilde{M}'^\top \mathbf{l}' \\ \mathbf{e}'^\top \mathbf{l}' \end{bmatrix}, \qquad \mathbf{a}'' = M''^\top \mathbf{l}'' = \begin{bmatrix} \tilde{M}''^\top \mathbf{l}'' \\ \mathbf{e}''^\top \mathbf{l}'' \end{bmatrix}, \quad (11.56)$$

back-projected from the image lines as given by equation (11.21), have a scene line in common. This happens only if the vectors in equation (11.56) are linearly dependent, that is, $\mathbf{a} = \lambda' \mathbf{a}' + \lambda'' \mathbf{a}''$ for some scalars λ' and λ''. Applying this to the fourth coordinates of the vectors in equation (11.56) yields $\lambda' \mathbf{e}'^\top \mathbf{l}' = -\lambda'' \mathbf{e}''^\top \mathbf{l}''$. Substituting to the first three coordinates of the vectors in equation (11.56) yields

$$\mathbf{l} \simeq (\mathbf{e}''^\top \mathbf{l}'') \tilde{M}'^\top \mathbf{l}' - (\mathbf{e}'^\top \mathbf{l}') \tilde{M}''^\top \mathbf{l}'' = (\mathbf{l}''^\top \mathbf{e}'') \tilde{M}'^\top \mathbf{l}' - (\mathbf{l}'^\top \mathbf{e}') \tilde{M}''^\top \mathbf{l}'' .$$

The expression can be further re-arranged to

$$\mathbf{l} \simeq [\mathbf{l}'^\top T_1 \mathbf{l}'', \ \mathbf{l}'^\top T_3 \mathbf{l}'', \ \mathbf{l}'^\top T_3 \mathbf{l}'']^\top , \qquad (11.57)$$

where we have denoted

$$T_i = \mathbf{m}'_i \mathbf{e}''^\top - \mathbf{m}''_i \mathbf{e}'^\top , \quad i = 1, 2, 3 \qquad (11.58)$$

and $\tilde{M}' = [\mathbf{m}'_1 \mid \mathbf{m}'_2 \mid \mathbf{m}'_2]$, $\tilde{M}'' = [\mathbf{m}''_1 \mid \mathbf{m}''_2 \mid \mathbf{m}''_2]$. The three 3×3 matrices T_i can be seen as slices of the $3 \times 3 \times 3$ **trifocal tensor**.

Expression (11.57) is bilinear in the coordinates of image lines and describes how to compute the image line in the first view given lines in the other two views. In Section 11.4.3, we derived that there is a single trilinear function involving point $\mathbf{u}$ in the first image, line $\mathbf{l}'$ and line $\mathbf{l}''$ that vanishes if there exists a scene point projecting to these. It follows from the incidence relation $\mathbf{l}^\top \mathbf{u} = 0$

$$[\mathbf{l}'^\top T_1 \mathbf{l}'', \ \mathbf{l}'^\top T_3 \mathbf{l}'', \ \mathbf{l}'^\top T_3 \mathbf{l}''] \mathbf{u} = 0 . \qquad (11.59)$$

The nine point-point-point matching constraints among image points $\mathbf{u}$, $\mathbf{u}'$ and $\mathbf{u}''$ in, respectively, the first, second and third view can be obtained by substituting any row of matrix $S(\mathbf{u}')$ for $\mathbf{l}'$ and any row of $S(\mathbf{u}'')$ for $\mathbf{l}''$.

The trifocal tensor $\{T_1, T_2, T_3\}$ has $3^3 = 27$ parameters but is defined only up to an overall scale, yielding 26 parameters. However, these parameters satisfy 8 non-linear relations, yielding only 18 free parameters. While we will not discuss these non-linear relations, note that for two views we only had a single non-linear relation, $\det F = 0$.

Given multiple correspondences in three views, the trifocal tensor can be estimated by solving the (possibly overdetermined) system of equations (11.57) or (11.59), which is linear in the components of the tensor. Here, preconditioning described in Section 11.2.3 is essential.

If the trifocal tensor is known then the projection matrices corresponding to individual cameras can be computed from the tensor. The trifocal tensor expresses relation between images and is independent of the particular 3D projection transform. This implies that the projection matrices corresponding to cameras can be computed up to a projective ambiguity. The algorithm for decomposing the trifocal tensor into three projection matrices can be found in [Hartley and Zisserman, 2003].

11.6.1 Stereo correspondence algorithms

We have seen in Section 11.5.1 that much can be learned about the geometry of a 3D scene if it is known which point from one image corresponds to a point in a second image. The solution of this **correspondence problem** is a key step in any photogrammetric, stereo vision, or motion analysis task. Here we describe how the same point can be found in two images if the same scene is observed from two different viewpoints. Of course, it is assumed that two images overlap and thus the corresponding points are sought in this overlapping area.

Some methods are based on the assumption that images constitute a linear (vector) space (e.g., eigenimages or linear interpolation in images [Werner et al., 1995; Ullman and Basri, 1991]); this linearity assumption is not valid for images in general [Beymer and Poggio, 1996], but some authors have overlooked this fact. The structure of a vector space assumes that the ith component of one vector must refer to the ith component of another; this assumes that the correspondence problem has been solved.

Automatic solution of the correspondence problem is an evergreen computer vision topic, and the pessimistic conclusion is that it is not soluble in the general case at all. The trouble is that the problem is inherently ambiguous. Imagine an extreme case, e.g., a scene containing a white, nontextured, flat object; its image constitutes a large region with uniform brightness. When corresponding points are sought in left and right images of the flat object there are not any features that could distinguish them. Another unavoidable difficulty in searching for corresponding points is the **self-occlusion** problem, which occurs in images of non-convex objects. Some points that are visible by the left camera are not visible by the right camera and vice versa (Figure 11.14).

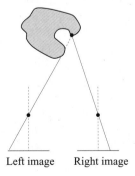

Left image   Right image

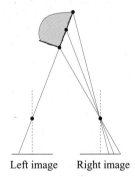

Left image   Right image

Figure 11.14: Self-occlusion makes search for some corresponding points impossible. © *Cengage Learning 2015*.

Figure 11.15: Exception from the uniqueness constraint. © *Cengage Learning 2015*.

Fortunately, uniform intensity and self-occlusion are rare, or at least uncommon, in scenes of practical interest. Establishing correspondence between projections of the same point in different views is based on finding image characteristics that are similar in both views, and the local similarity is calculated.

The inherent ambiguity of the correspondence problem can in practical cases be reduced using several constraints. Some of these follow from the geometry of the image capturing process, some from photometric properties of a scene, and some from prevailing object properties in our natural world. A vast number of different stereo correspondence algorithms have been proposed. We will give here only a concise taxonomy of approaches to finding correspondence—not all the constraints are used in all of them [Klette et al., 1996].

The first group of constraints depends mainly on the geometry and the photometry of the image capturing process.

Epipolar constraint: This says that the corresponding point can only lie on the epipolar line in the second image. This reduces the potential 2D search space into 1D. The epipolar constraint was explained in detail in Section 11.5.

Uniqueness constraint: This states that, in most cases, a pixel from the first image can correspond to at most one pixel in the second image. The exception arises when two or more points lie on one ray coming from the first camera and can be seen as separate points from the second. This case, which arises in the same way as self-occlusion, is illustrated in Figure 11.15.

Symmetry constraint: If the left and right images are interchanged then the same set of matched pairs of points has to be obtained.

Photometric compatibility constraint: This states that intensities of a point in the first and second images are likely to differ only a little. They are unlikely to be exactly the same due to the mutual angle between the light source, surface normal, and viewer differing, but the difference will typically be small and the views will not differ much. Practically, this constraint is very natural to image-capturing conditions. The advantage is that intensities in the left image can be transformed into intensities in the right image using very simple transformations.

Geometric similarity constraints: These build on the observation that geometric characteristics of the features found in the first and second images do not differ much (e.g., length or orientation of the line segment, region, or contour).

The second group of constraints exploits some common properties of objects in typical scenes.

Disparity smoothness constraint: This claims that disparity changes slowly almost everywhere in the image. Assume two scene points $\mathbf{p}$ and $\mathbf{q}$ are close to each other, and denote the projection of $\mathbf{p}$ into the left image as $\mathbf{p}_L$ and into the right image as $\mathbf{p}_R$, and $\mathbf{q}$ similarly. If we assume that the correspondence between $\mathbf{p}_L$ and $\mathbf{p}_R$ has been established, then the quantity

$$\left| \, |\mathbf{p}_L - \mathbf{p}_R| - |\mathbf{q}_L - \mathbf{q}_R| \, \right|$$

(the absolute disparity difference) should be small.

Feature compatibility constraint: This places a restriction on the origin of matched points. Points can match only if they have the same physical origin—for example, object surface discontinuity, border of a shadow cast by some objects, occluding boundary or specularity boundary. Notice that edges in an image caused by specularity or self-occlusion cannot be used to solve the correspondence problem, as they move with changing viewpoint. On the other hand, self-occlusion caused by abrupt discontinuity of the surface can be identified—see Figure 11.16.

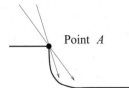

Figure 11.16: Self-occlusion due to abrupt surface discontinuity can be detected. © *Cengage Learning 2015*.

Disparity search range: This constrains the lengths of the search in artificial methods that seek correspondence.

Disparity gradient limit: This constraint originates from psycho-physical experiments in which it is demonstrated that the human vision system can only fuse stereo images if the disparity change per pixel is smaller than some limit. The constraint is a weak version of the disparity smoothness constraint.

Ordering constraint: This says that for surfaces of similar depth, corresponding feature points typically lie in the same order on the epipolar line (Figure 11.17a). If there is a narrow object much closer to the camera than its background, the order can be changed (Figure 11.17b). It is easy to demonstrate violation of this ordering constraint: hold two forefingers vertically, almost aligned but at different depths in front of your eyes. Closing the left eye and then the right eyes interchanges the left/right order of the fingers. The ordering constraint is violated only rarely in practice.

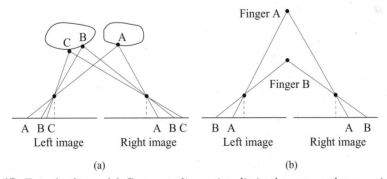

Figure 11.17: Epipolar lines. (a) Corresponding points lie in the same order on epipolar lines. (b) This rule does not hold if there is a big discontinuity in depths. © *Cengage Learning 2015*.

All these constraints have been of use in one or more existing stereo correspondence algorithms; we present here a taxonomy of such algorithms. From the historical point of view, correspondence algorithms for stereopsis were and still are driven by two main paradigms:

1. Low-level, correlation-based, bottom-up methods.

2. High-level, feature-based, top-down methods.

Initially, it was believed that higher-level features such as corners and straight line segments should be automatically identified, and then matched. This was a natural development from photogrammetry, which has been using feature points identified by human operators since the beginning of the twentieth century.

Psychological experiments with **random dot stereograms** performed by Julesz [Julesz, 1990] generated a new view: these experiments show that humans do not need to create monocular features before binocular depth perception can take place. A random dot stereogram is created in the following way: a left image is entirely random, and the right image is created from it in a consistent way such that some part of it is shifted according to disparity of the desired stereo effect. The viewer must glare at the random dot stereogram from a distance of about 20 centimeters. Such 'random dot stereograms' have been widely published under the name '3D images' in many popular magazines.

Correlation-based block matching

Correlation-based correspondence algorithms use the assumption that pixels in correspondence have very similar intensities. The intensity of an individual pixel does not give sufficient information, as there are typically many potential candidates with similar intensity and thus intensities of several neighboring pixels are considered. Typically, a 5×5 or 7×7 or 3×9 window may be used. These methods are sometimes called **area-based stereo**. Larger search windows yield higher discriminability.

We shall illustrate the approach with a simple algorithm called **block matching** [Klette et al., 1996]. Assuming the canonical stereo setup with parallel optical axes of both cameras, the basic idea of the algorithm is that all pixels in the window (called a block) have the same disparity, meaning that one and only one disparity is computed for each block. One of the images, say the left, is tiled into blocks, and a search for correspondence in the right image is conducted for each of these in the right image. The measure of similarity between blocks can be, e.g., the mean square error of the intensity, and the disparity is accepted for the position where the mean square error is minimal. Maximal change of position is limited by the disparity limit constraint. The mean square error can have more than one minimum, and in this case an additional constraint is used to cope with ambiguity.

The result does not obey the symmetry constraint, ordering constraint and gradient limit constraint because the result is not a one-to-one matching.

Another relevant approach is that of Nishihara [Nishihara, 1984], who observes that an algorithm attempting to correlate individual pixels (by, e.g., matching zero-crossings [Marr and Poggio, 1979]) is inclined towards poor performance when noise causes the detected location of such features to be unreliable. Nishihara notes that the sign (and magnitude) of an edge detector response is likely to be a much more stable property to match than the edge or feature locations, and devises an algorithm that simultaneously exploits a scale-space matching attack.

The approach is to match large patches at a large scale, and then refine the quality of the match by reducing the scale, using the coarser information to initialize the finer-grained match. An edge response is generated at each pixel of both images at a large scale (see Section 5.3.4), and then a large area of the left (represented by, say, its central pixel) is correlated with a large area of the right. This can be done quickly and efficiently by using the fact that the correlation function peaks very sharply at the correct position of a match, and so a small number of tests permits an ascent to a maximum of a correlation measure. This coarse area match may then be iteratively refined to any desired resolution, using the knowledge from the coarser scale as a clue to the correct disparity at a given position. At any stage of the algorithm, therefore, the surfaces in view are modeled as square prisms of varying height; the area of the squares may be reduced by performing the algorithm at a finer scale—for tasks such as obstacle avoidance it is possible that only coarse scale information is necessary, and there will be a consequent gain in efficiency.

Any stereo matching algorithm can be boosted by casting random-dot light patterns on the scene to provide patterns to match even in areas of the scene that are texturally uniform. The resulting system has been demonstrated in use in robot guidance and bin-picking applications, and has been implemented robustly in real time.

Feature-based stereo correspondence

Feature-based correspondence methods use interest points. Characteristically, these are pixels on edges, lines, corners, etc., and correspondence is sought according to properties of such features as, e.g., orientation along edges, or lengths of line segments. The advantages of feature-based methods over intensity-based correlation are:

- Feature-based methods are less ambiguous since the number of potential candidates for correspondence is smaller.

- The resulting correspondence is less dependent on photometric variations in images.

- Disparities can be computed with higher precision; features can be sought in the image to subpixel precision.

We present one early example of a feature-based correspondence method—the **PMF algorithm**, named after its inventors [Pollard et al., 1985]. It proceeds by assuming that a set of feature points has been extracted from each image by some interest operator. The output is a correspondence between pairs of such points. In order to do this, three constraints are applied: the epipolar constraint, the uniqueness constraint, and the disparity gradient limit constraint.

The first two constraints are common to all such algorithms—the third, however, of stipulating a disparity gradient limit, was its novelty. The **disparity gradient** measures the relative disparity of two pairs of matching points.

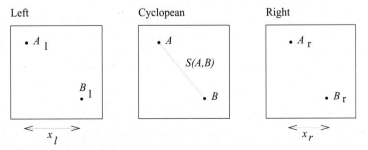

Figure 11.18: Definition of the disparity gradient. © *Cengage Learning 2015.*

Suppose (Figure 11.18) that a point A (B) in 3D appears as $A_l = (a_{xl}, a_y)$ $(B_l = (b_{xl}, b_y))$ in the left image and $A_r = (a_{xr}, a_y)$ $(B_r = (b_{xr}, b_y))$ in the right (the epipolar constraint requires the y coordinates to be equal); the **cyclopean** image is defined as that given by their average coordinates

$$A_c = \left(\frac{a_{xl} + a_{xr}}{2}, a_y \right) , \tag{11.60}$$

$$B_c = \left(\frac{b_{xl} + b_{xr}}{2}, b_y \right) \tag{11.61}$$

and their **cyclopean separation** S is given by their distance apart in this image

$$
\begin{aligned}
S(A, B) &= \sqrt{ \left[\left(\frac{a_{xl} + a_{xr}}{2} \right) - \left(\frac{b_{xl} + b_{xr}}{2} \right) \right]^2 + (a_y - b_y)^2 } \\
&= \sqrt{ \frac{1}{4} \left[(a_{xl} - b_{xl}) + (a_{xr} - b_{xr}) \right]^2 + (a_y - b_y)^2 } \\
&= \sqrt{ \frac{1}{4} (x_l + x_r)^2 + (a_y - b_y)^2 } .
\end{aligned}
\tag{11.62}
$$

The difference in disparity between the matches of A and B is

$$
\begin{aligned}
D(A, B) &= (a_{xl} - a_{xr}) - (b_{xl} - b_{xr}) \\
&= (a_{xl} - b_{xl}) - (a_{xr} - b_{xr}) \\
&= x_l - x_r .
\end{aligned}
\tag{11.63}
$$

The disparity gradient of the pair of matches is then given by the ratio of the disparity difference to the cyclopean separation:

$$
\begin{aligned}
\Gamma(A, B) &= \frac{D(A, B)}{S(A, B)} \\
&= \frac{x_l - x_r}{\sqrt{ \frac{1}{4} (x_l + x_r)^2 + (a_y - b_y)^2 }} .
\end{aligned}
\tag{11.64}
$$

Given these definitions, the constraint exploited is that, in practice, the disparity gradient Γ can be expected to be limited; in fact, it is unlikely to exceed 1. This means that very small differences in disparity are not acceptable if the corresponding points are extremely close to each other in 3D—this seems an intuitively reasonable observation, and it is supported by physical evidence [Pollard et al., 1985]. A solution to the correspondence problem is then extracted by a relaxation process in which all possible matches are scored according to whether they are supported by other (possible) matches that do not violate the stipulated disparity gradient limit. High-scoring matches are regarded as correct, permitting firmer evidence to be extracted about subsequent matches.

Algorithm 11.2: PMF stereo correspondence

1. Extract features to match in left and right images. These may be, for example, edge pixels.

2. For each feature in the left (say) image, consider its possible matches in the right; these are defined by the appropriate epipolar line.

3. For each such match, increment its likelihood score according to the number of other possible matches found that do not violate the chosen disparity gradient limit.

4. Any match which is highest scoring for both the pixels composing it is now regarded as correct. Using the uniqueness constraint, these pixels are removed from all other considerations.

5. Return to step 2 and re-compute the scores taking account of the definite match derived.

6. Terminate when all possible matches have been extracted.

Note here that the epipolar constraint is used in step 2 to limit to one dimension the possible matches of a pixel, and the uniqueness constraint is used in step 4 to ensure that a particular pixel is never used more than once in the calculation of a gradient.

The scoring mechanism has to take account of the fact that the more remote two (possible) matches are, the more likely they are to satisfy the disparity gradient limit. This is catered for by:

- Considering only matches that are 'close' to the one being scored. In practice it is typically adequate to consider only those inside a circle of radius equal to 7 pixels, centered at the matching pixels (although this number depends on the precise geometry and scene in hand).

- Weighting the score by the reciprocal of its distance from the match being scored. Thus more remote pairs, which are more likely to satisfy the limit by chance, count for less.

This algorithm has been demonstrated to work successfully. It is also attractive because it lends itself to parallel implementation and could be extremely fast on suitable hardware. It has a drawback (along with a number of similar algorithms) in that horizontal line segments are hard to match; they often move across adjacent rasters and, with parallel camera geometry, any point on one such line can match any point on the corresponding line in the other image.

Since PMF was developed many other algorithms of varying complexity have been proposed. Two computationally efficient and simple to implement algorithms utilize either optimization techniques called dynamic programming [Gimel'farb, 1999] or confidently stable matching [Sara, 2002]. An extensive list of stereo matching algorithm is maintained at http://cat.middlebury.edu/stereo/.

11.6.2 Active acquisition of range images

It is extremely difficult to extract 3D shape information from intensity images of real scenes directly. Another approach—'shape from shading'—will be explained in Section 11.7.1.

One way to circumvent these problems is to measure distances from the viewer to points on surfaces in the 3D scene explicitly; such measurements are called **geometric signals**, i.e., a collection of 3D points in a known coordinate system. If the surface relief is measured from a single viewpoint, it is called a **range image** or a **depth map**. Such explicit 3D information, being closer to the geometric model that is sought, makes geometry recovery easier.[1]

Two steps are needed to obtain geometric information from a range image:

1. The range image must be captured; this procedure is discussed in this section.

2. Geometric information must be extracted. Features are sought and compared to a selected 3D model. The selection of features and geometric models leads to one of the most fundamental problems in computer vision: how to represent a solid shape [Koenderink, 1990].

The term **active sensor** refers to a sensor that uses and controls its own images—the term 'active' means that the sensor uses and controls electromagnetic energy, or more specifically illumination, for measuring a distance between scene surfaces and the 'observer'. An active sensor should not be confused with the active perception strategy, where the sensing subject plans how to look at objects from different views.

RADAR (RAdio Detecting And Ranging) and **LIDAR** (LIght Detecting And Ranging) in one measurement yield the distance between the sensor and a particular point in a scene. The sensor is mounted on an assembly that allows movement around two angles, azimuth Θ and tilt Φ, corresponding to spherical coordinates. The distance is proportional to the time interval between the emission of energy and the echo reflected from the measured scene object—the elapsed time intervals are very short, so very high precision is required. For this reason, the phase difference between emitted and received signals is often used.

RADAR emits electromagnetic waves in meter, centimeter, or millimeter wavelength bands. Aside from military use, it is frequently used for navigation of autonomous guided vehicles.

LIDAR often uses laser as a source of a focused light beam. The higher the power of the laser, the stronger is the reflected signal and the more precise the measured range. If LIDAR is required to work in an environment together with humans, then the energy has an upper limit, due to potential harm to the unprotected eye. Another factor that influences LIDAR safety is the diameter of the laser beam: if it is to be safe, it should not be focused too much. LIDARs have trouble when the object surface is almost tangential to the beam, as very little energy reflects back to the sensor in this case. Measurements of specular surfaces are not very accurate, as they scatter the reflected light; while transparent objects (obviously) cannot be measured with optical lasers. The advantage of LIDAR is a wide range of measured distances, from a tenth of a millimeter to several kilometers; the accuracy of the measured range is typically around 0.01 millimeter. LIDAR provides one range in an instant. If a whole range image is to be captured, the measurement takes several tenths of a seconds as the whole scene is scanned.

Another principle of active range imaging is **structured light triangulation**, where we employ a geometric arrangement similar to that used for stereo vision, with optical

---

[1]There are techniques that measure full 3D information directly, such as mechanical coordinate-measuring machines (considered in Chapter 12) or computer tomography.

axes. One camera is replaced by an illuminant that yields a light plane perpendicular to the epipolars; the image-capturing camera is at a fixed distance from the illuminant. Since there is only one significantly bright point on each image line, the correspondence problem that makes passive stereo so problematic is avoided, although there will still be problems with self-occlusion in the scene. Distance from the observer can easily be calculated as in Figure 11.11. To capture a whole-range image, the rod with camera and illuminant should be made to move mechanically relative to the scene, and the trace of the laser should gradually illuminate all points to be measured. The conduct of the movement, together with the processing of several hundred images (i.e., one image for each distinct position of the laser-stripe) takes some time, typically from a couple of seconds to about a minute. Faster laser stripe range finders find a bright point corresponding to the intersection of a current image line using special-purpose electronics.

Figure 11.19 shows a view of such a scanner together with a target object (a wooden toy—a rabbit). The image seen by the camera with the distinct bright laser stripe is in Figure 11.20a, and the resulting range image is shown in Figure 11.20b.

Figure 11.19: Laser plane range finder. The camera is on the left side, the laser diode on the bottom. *Courtesy of T. Pajdla, Czech Technical University, Prague.*

In some applications, a range image is required in an instant, typically meaning one TV frame; this is especially useful for capturing range images of moving objects, e.g., moving humans (see Section 10.8). One possibility is to illuminate the scene by several stripes at once and code them; Figure 11.21a shows a human hand lit by a binary cyclic code pattern such that the local configuration of squares in the image allows to us to decode which stripe it is. In this case, the pattern with coded stripes is projected from a 36×24 mm slide using a standard slide projector. The resulting range image does not provide as many samples as in the case of a moving laser stripe—in our case only 64×80, see Figure 11.21b.

It is possible to acquire a dense range sample as in the laser stripe case in one TV frame; individual stripes can be encoded using spectral colors and the image captured by a color TV camera [Smutný, 1993].

There are other technologies available. One is sonar, which uses ultrasonic waves as an energy source. Sonars are used in robot navigation for close-range measurements,

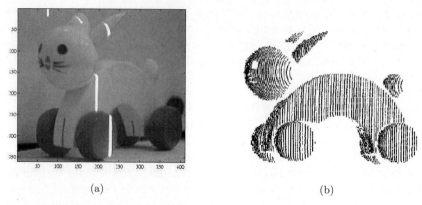

(a)   (b)

Figure 11.20: Measurement using a laser-stripe range finder. (a) The image seen by a camera with a bright laser stripe. (b) Reconstructed range image displayed as a point cloud. *Courtesy of T. Pajdla, Czech Technical University, Prague.*

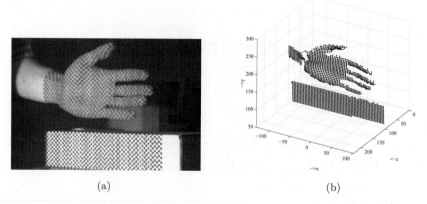

(a)   (b)

Figure 11.21: Binary-coded range finder. (a) The captured image of a hand. (b) Reconstructed surface. *Courtesy of T. Pajdla, Czech Technical University, Prague.*

but a disadvantage is that measurements are typically very noisy. The second principle is Moiré interferometry [Klette et al., 1996], in which two periodic patterns, typically stripes, are projected on the scene. Due to interference, the object is covered by a system of closed, non-intersecting curves, each of which lies in a plane of constant distance from the viewer. Distance measurements obtained are only relative, and absolute distances are unavailable. The properties of Moiré curves are very similar to height contours on maps.

11.7   3D information from radiometric measurements

We have argued several times in this book that the image formation from the radiometric point of view is well understood (Section 3.4.4). We have also explained that the inverse task in which the input is the intensity image and the output is 3D properties of a surface in the scene is ill-posed and extremely difficult to solve in most cases. Instead of solving it, a side-step is taken and objects in the image are segmented using some semantic information, but not directly the image formation physics. Nevertheless, there are special situations in which the inverse task to image formation has a solution. The first approach is **shape from shading**, and the second one **photometric stereo**.

11.7.1   Shape from shading

The human brain makes use of clues from shadows and shading in general. Not only do detected shadows give a clear indication of where occluding edges are, and the possible orientation of their neighboring surfaces, but general shading properties are of great value in deducing depth. A fine example of this is a photograph of a face; from a straight-on, 2D representation, our brains make good guesses about the probable lighting model, and then deductions about the 3D nature of the face—for example, deep eye sockets and protuberant noses or lips are often recognizable without difficulty.

Recall that the intensity of a particular pixel depends on the light source(s), surface reflectance properties, and local surface orientation expressed by a surface normal **n**. The aim of shape from shading is to extract information about normals of surfaces in view solely on the basis of an intensity image. If simplifying assumptions are made about illumination, surface reflectance properties, and surface smoothness, the shape from shading task has proven to be solvable. The first computer-vision related formulation comes from Horn [Horn, 1970, 1975]. Techniques similar to shape from shading were earlier proposed independently in photoclinometry [Rindfleisch, 1966], when astrogeologists wanted to measure steepness of slopes on planets in the solar system from intensity images observed by terrestrial telescopes.

Incremental propagation from surface points of known height

The oldest, and easiest to explain, method develops a solution along a space curve. This is also called the characteristic strip method.

We can begin to analyze the problem of global shape extraction from shading information when the reflectance function and the lighting model are both known perfectly [Horn, 1990]. Even given these constraints, it should be clear that the mapping 'surface orientation to brightness' is many-to-one, since many orientations can produce the same point intensity. Acknowledging this, a particular brightness can be produced by an infinite number of orientations that can be plotted as a (continuous) closed curve in gradient space. An example for the simple case of a light source directly adjacent to the viewer, incident on a matte surface, is shown in Figure 11.22—two points lying on the same curve (circles in this case) indicate two different orientations that will reflect light of the same intensity, thereby producing the same pixel gray-level.

The original formulation [Horn, 1970] to the general shape from shading task assumes a Lambertian surface, one distant point light source, a distant observer, and no interreflections in the scene. The proposed method is based on the notion of a **characteristic strip**: suppose that we have already calculated coordinates of a surface point $[x, y, z]^T$ and we want to propagate the solution along an infinitesimal step on the surface, e.g., taking small steps δx and δy, then calculating the change in height δz. This can be done if the components of the surface gradient p, q are known. For compactness we use an index notation, and express $p = \delta z / \delta x$ as z_x, and $\delta^2 x / \delta x^2$ as z_{xx}. The infinitesimal change of height is

$$\delta z = p \, \delta x + q \, \delta y \,. \tag{11.65}$$

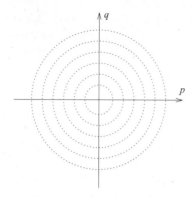

Figure 11.22: Reflectance map for a matte surface—the light source is adjacent to the viewer. © *Cengage Learning 2015*.

The surface is followed stepwise, with values of p, q being traced along with x, y, z. Changes in p, q are calculated using second derivatives of height $r=z_{xx}$, $s=z_{xy}=z_{yx}$, $t=z_{yy}$

$$\delta p = r\,\delta x + s\,\delta y \quad\text{and}\quad \delta q = s\,\delta x + t\,\delta y\,. \tag{11.66}$$

Consider now the image irradiance equation $E(x,y) = R(p,q)$, equation (3.96), and differentiate with respect to x, y to obtain the brightness gradient

$$E_x = r\,R_p + s\,R_q \quad\text{and}\quad E_y = s\,R_p + t\,R_q\,. \tag{11.67}$$

The direction of the step δx, δy can be chosen arbitrarily

$$\delta x = R_p\,\xi \quad\text{and}\quad \delta y = R_q\,\xi\,. \tag{11.68}$$

The parameter ξ changes along particular solution curves. Moreover, the orientation of the surface along this curve is known; thus it is called a characteristic strip.

We can now express changes of gradient δp, δq as dependent on gradient image intensities, which is the crucial trick. A set of ordinary differential equations can be generated by considering equations (11.66) and (11.67); dot denotes differentiation with respect to ξ

$$\dot{x} = R_p\,, \qquad \dot{y} = R_q\,, \qquad \dot{z} = p\,R_p + q\,R_q\,, \qquad \dot{p} = E_x\,, \qquad \dot{q} = E_y\,. \tag{11.69}$$

There are points on the surface for which the surface orientation is known in advance, and these provide boundary conditions during normal vector calculations. These are

- Points of a surface **occluding boundary**; an occluding boundary is a curve on the surface due to the surface rolling away from the viewer, i.e., the set of points for which the local tangent plane coincides with the direction towards the viewer. The surface normal at such a boundary can be uniquely determined (up to a sign), as it is parallel to the image plane and perpendicular to the direction towards the viewer. This normal information can be propagated into the recovered surface patch from the occluding boundary. Although the occlusion boundary uniquely constrains surface orientation, it does not constrain the solution sufficiently to recover depth uniquely [Oliensis, 1991].

- Singular points in the image; we have seen that at most surface points gradient is not fully constrained by image intensities. Suppose that the reflectance function

$R(p, q)$ has a global maximum, so $R(p, q) < R(p_0, q_0)$ for all $[p, q] \neq p_0, q_0$. This maximum corresponds to singular points in the image

$$E(x_0, y_0) = R(p_0, q_0) . \tag{11.70}$$

Here, the surface normal is parallel to the direction towards the light source. Singular points are in general sources and sinks of characteristic stripes.

Direct implementation of this method does not yield particularly good results, due to numerical instability of independent integrations along the stripes [Horn, 1990].

Global optimization methods

These methods are formulated as a variational task in which the whole image plays a role in the chosen functional. Results obtained are in general better than those generated by incremental methods.

We already know that under the simplifying conditions for recovery of surface normals from intensities (stated in Section 3.4.5), the image irradiance equation (3.96) relates image irradiance E and surface reflection R as

$$E(x, y) = R\big(p(x, y), q(x, y)\big) . \tag{11.71}$$

The task is to find the surface height $z(x, y)$ given the image $E(x, y)$ and reflectance map $R(p, q)$.

Now, presented with an intensity image, a locus of possible orientations for each pixel can be located in gradient space, immediately reducing the number of possible interpretations of the scene. Of course, at this stage, a pixel may be part of any surface lying on the gradient space contour; to determine which, another constraint needs to be deployed. The key to deciding which point on the contour is correct is to note that 'almost everywhere' 3D surfaces are smooth, in the sense that neighboring pixels are very likely to represent orientations whose gradient space positions are also very close. This additional constraint allows a relaxation process to determine a best-fit (minimum-cost) solution to the problem. The details of the procedure are very similar to those used to extract optical flow, and are discussed more fully in Section 16.2.1, but may be summarized as follows.

Algorithm 11.3: Reconstructing shape from shading

1. For each pixel (x_i, y_i), select an initial guess to orientation $p^0(x_i, y_i)$, $q^0(x_i, y_i)$. The subscript i addresses image pixels.

2. Apply two constraints:

   (a) The observed intensity $f(x_i, y_i)$ should be close to that predicted by the reflectance map $R(p(x_i, y_i), q(x_i, y_i))$ derived from foreknowledge of the lighting and surface properties.

   (b) Functions p and q vary smoothly—therefore their gradients $(\nabla p)^2$ and $(\nabla q)^2$ should be small.

3. Minimize the energy E

$$E = \sum_i \left(f(x_i, y_i) - R\big(p(x_i, y_i), q(x_i, y_i)\big) \right)^2 + \lambda \iint_\Omega (\nabla p)^2 + (\nabla q)^2 \, \mathrm{d}x \, \mathrm{d}y. \quad (11.72)$$

The first term of equation (11.72) is the intensity 'knowledge'. The second term is integrated along the whole (continuous) domain Ω. After discretization, the minimization is solved using the conjugate gradient descent method [Szeliski, 1990].

The significant work in this area is due to Horn [Horn, 1975] and Ikeuchi [Ikeuchi and Horn, 1981] and pre-dated the publication of Marr's theory, being complete in the form presented here by 1980. Shape from shading, as implemented by machine vision systems, is often not as reliable as other 'shape from' techniques, since it is so easy to confuse with reflections, or for it to fail through poorly modeled reflectance functions. This observation serves to reinforce the point that the human recognition system is very powerful, since in deploying elaborate knowledge it does not suffer these drawbacks.

Local shading analysis

Local shading analysis methods use just a small neighborhood of the current point on the surface, and seek a direct relation between the differential surface structure and the local structure of the corresponding intensity image. The surface is considered as a set of small neighborhoods, each defined in some local neighborhood of one of its points. Only an estimate of local surface orientation is available, not information about the height of a particular surface point.

The main advantage of local shading analysis is that it provides surface-related information to higher-level vision algorithms from a single monocular-intensity image without any need to reconstruct the surface in explicit depth form [Sara, 1995]. This is possible because the intensity image is closely related to local surface orientation. The surface normal and the shape operator ('curvature matrix') form a natural shape model that can be recovered from an intensity image by local computations except it is not usually possible to recover the signs of principal surface curvatures which result in a four-fold convex/concave/elliptic/hyperbolic ambiguity. This approach is, of course, much faster than the solution propagation or global variational methods but it does not provide local information on convexity and ellipticity of the surface.

The fundamental contribution to local shading analysis comes from Pentland [Pentland, 1984]; an overview can be found in [Pentland and Bichsel, 1994]. In addition, Šára [Sara, 1994] demonstrates:

1. Local surface orientation up to a sign and Gaussian curvature sign can be determined uniquely at occlusion boundaries. Further, orientation on a self-shadowing boundary can also be determined uniquely; self-shadowing contours are thus a rich source of unambiguous information about the surface.

2. The differential properties of isophotes (curves of constant image intensity) are closely related to the properties of the underlying surface. Isophotes are projections of curves of constant slant from the light direction if the surface reflectance is space invariant, or the illuminant is located at the vantage point.

11.7.2   Photometric stereo

Photometric stereo is a method that recovers surface orientation unambiguously, assuming a known reflectance function [Woodham, 1980]. Consider a particular Lambertian surface with varying albedo ρ. The key idea of photometric stereo is to look at the surface from one fixed viewing direction while changing the direction of incident illumination. Assume we have three or more such images of the Lambertian surface; then the surface normals can be uniquely determined based on the shading variations in the observed images if we know the illuminants' positions.

The lines of constant reflectance on the surface correspond to lines of constant irradiation E in the image (called also isophotes). The local surface orientation $\mathbf{n} = [-p, -q, 1]$ is constrained along a second-order curve in the reflectance map. For different illumination directions, the observed reflectance map $R(p, q)$ changes. This provides an additional constraint on possible surface orientation that is another second-order polynomial. Two views corresponding to two distinct illumination directions are not enough to determine the surface orientation $[-p, -q, 1]$ uniquely, and a third view is needed to derive a unique solution. If more than three distinct illuminations are at hand, an over-determined set of equations can be solved.

A practical setup for image capture consists of one camera and K point illumination sources, $K \geq 3$, with known intensities and illumination directions $L_1, \ldots, L_K$. Only one light source is active at any one time. The setup should be photometrically calibrated to take into account light source intensities, particular camera gain, and offset; such a calibration is described in [Haralick and Shapiro, 1993]. After photometric calibration, the images give K estimates of image irradiance $E_i(x, y)$; $i = 1, \ldots, K$.

If not all light is reflected from a surface, then albedo ρ, $0 \leq \rho \leq 1$, occurs in the image irradiance as shown in equation (3.94). For a Lambertian surface the image irradiance equation simplifies to

$$E(x, y) = \rho \, R(p, q) \,. \tag{11.73}$$

Recall equation (3.93) (called the cosine law), showing that the reflectance map of a Lambertian surface is given by the dot product of the surface normal $\mathbf{n}$ and the direction of the incident light L_i. If the surface reflectance map is substituted into equation (11.73), we get K image irradiance equations

$$E_i(x, y) = \rho \, L_i^\top \, \mathbf{n} \,, \quad i = 1, \ldots, K \,. \tag{11.74}$$

For each point x, y in the image we get a vector of image irradiances $\mathbf{E} = [E_1, \ldots, E_K]^\top$. The light directions can be written in the form of a $K \times 3$ matrix

$$L = \begin{bmatrix} L_1^\top \\ \vdots \\ L_K^\top \end{bmatrix} \,. \tag{11.75}$$

At each image point, the system of image irradiance equations can be written as

$$\mathbf{E} = \rho \, L \, \mathbf{n} \,. \tag{11.76}$$

The matrix L does not depend on the pixel position in the image, and we can thus derive a vector representing simultaneously surface albedo and a local surface orientation.

If we have three light sources, $K = 3$, we can derive a solution by inverting the regular matrix L

$$\rho \, \mathbf{n} = L^{-1} \, \mathbf{E} \tag{11.77}$$

and the unit normal is

$$\mathbf{n} = \frac{L^{-1} \, \mathbf{E}}{\|L^{-1} \, \mathbf{E}\|} \, . \tag{11.78}$$

For more than three light sources, the pseudo-inverse of a rectangular matrix is determined to get a solution in the least-square sense

$$\mathbf{n} = \frac{(L^{\top} L)^{-1} \, L^{\top} \, \mathbf{E}}{\|(L^{\top} L)^{-1} \, L^{\top} \, \mathbf{E}\|} \, . \tag{11.79}$$

Note that the pseudo-inversion or inversion in equation (11.78) must be repeated for each image pixel x, y to derive an estimate of the corresponding normal.

It has been shown how to position the lights to obtain photometric stereo results with minimal error [Drbohlav and Chantler, 2005a], and how to calibrate lights in the case that the only information available are positions of highlights in images [Drbohlav and Chantler, 2005b].

11.8 Summary

- 3D vision aims at inferring 3D information from 2D scenes, a task with embedded geometric and radiometric difficulties. The geometric problem is that a single image does not provide enough information about 3D structures, and the radiometric problem is the complexity of the physical process of intensity image creation. This process is complex, and typically not all input parameters are known precisely.

- **3D vision tasks**

  - There are several approaches to 3D vision, which may be categorized as **bottom-up** (or reconstruction) or **top-down** (model-based vision).

  - *Marr's theory*, formulated in the late 1970s, is an example of the bottom-up approach. The aim is to reconstruct qualitative and quantitative 3D geometric descriptions from one or more intensity images under very weak assumptions about objects in the scene.

  - Four representations are ordered in bottom-up fashion: (1) input intensity image(s); (2) primal sketch, representing significant edges in the image in viewer-centered coordinates; (3) 2.5D sketch, representing depth from the observer and local orientation of the surface; and (4) 3D representation, representing object geometry in coordinates related to the objects themselves.

  - The 2.5D sketch is derived from the primal sketch by a variety of techniques called shape from X.

  - 3D representations are very hard to obtain; this step has not been solved in the general case.

  - More recent perception paradigms such as active, purposive, and qualitative vision try to provide a computational model explaining the 'understanding' aspects of vision.

– None has yet led to direct practical applications, but many partial techniques (such as shape from X) are widely used in practice.

- **3D vision, its geometry**

  – 3D perspective geometry is the basic mathematical tool for 3D vision as it explains a pinhole camera.
  – Lines parallel in the 3D world do not project as parallel lines in 2D images.
  – The case of the single-perspective camera permits careful study of calibration of intrinsic and extrinsic camera parameters.
  – Two-perspective cameras constitute stereopsis and allow depth measurements in 3D scenes.
  – Epipolar geometry teaches us that the search for corresponding points is inherently one-dimensional. This can be expressed algebraically using the fundamental matrix.
  – This tool has several applications, such as image rectification, ego-motion estimation from calibrated cameras measurements, 3D Euclidean reconstruction from two fully calibrated cameras, 3D similarity reconstruction from two cameras with only intrinsic calibration parameters known, and 3D projective reconstruction from two uncalibrated cameras.
  – There is a trilinear relation among views of three cameras that is expressed algebraically using a trifocal tensor.
  – The application of the trilinear relation is in epipolar transfer; if two images are known, together with the trifocal tensor, the third perspective image can be computed.
  – The correspondence problem is core to 3D vision; various passive and active techniques to solve it exist.

- **Radiometry and 3D vision**

  – Radiometry informs us about the physics of image formation.
  – If position of illuminants, type, surface reflectance and viewer position are known, something can be learned about depth and scene surface orientation from one intensity image.
  – This task is called shape from shading.
  – The task is ambiguous and numerically unstable. Shape from shading can be understood in the simple case of Lambertian surfaces.
  – There is a practical method that uses one camera and three known illuminants; selective illumination provides three intensity images.
  – Photometric stereo allows a measure of orientation of surfaces.

11.9 Exercises

Short-answer questions

S11.1 Explain the difference between a bottom-up approach (object reconstruction) to 3D vision as opposed to top-down (model-based).

S11.2 Explain the basic idea of active vision, and give some examples of how this approach eases vision tasks.

S11.3 Give examples of perspective images from everyday life. Where do parallel lines in the world not correspond to parallel ones in images?

S11.4 What are the intrinsic and extrinsic calibration parameters of a single-perspective camera? How are they estimated from known scenes?

S11.5 Do zoom lenses typically have worse geometric distortion compared to fixed-focal-length lenses? Is the difference significant?

S11.6 What is the main contribution of epipolar geometry in stereopsis?

S11.7 Where are epipoles in the case of two cameras with parallel optical axes (the *canonical* configuration for stereopsis)?

S11.8 What is the difference between the fundamental and essential matrices in stereopsis?

S11.9 How are mismatches in correspondences treated in stereopsis?

S11.10 What are the applications of epipolar geometry in computer vision?

S11.11 Explain the principle, advantages, and applications of a trilinear relation among three cameras. What is epipolar transfer?

S11.12 Why cannot we get depth if the camera does not translate?

S11.13 Why cannot we get a correct panorama if the camera does translate?

S11.14 Stereo correspondence algorithms are typically lost if the left and right images have large regions of uniform brightness. How can depth acquisition still be made possible?

S11.15 Active range finders (e.g., with a laser plane) suffer from occlusions; some points are not visible by the camera and some are not lit. What are the ways of dealing with this problem?

S11.16 What is Moiré interferometry? Does it give absolute depth?

S11.17 Why is the relation between pixel intensity on one side and surface orientation, surface reflectance, illuminant types and position, and viewer position on the other side difficult?

S11.18 Under which circumstances can the surface orientation be derived from intensity changes in an image?

Problems

P11.1 This problem relates to Marr's theory, in particular the representation scheme called primal sketch (see Section 11.1.1).

Capture an intensity image (e.g., of an office scene), and run an advanced edge detector (such as Canny's or similar) on it. Threshold the magnitude of the image gradient.

Answer the following questions in an essay: Are the lines which you get the primal sketch? Would it be possible to derive a 2.5D sketch directly from it? How? Discuss what more would you need in the primal sketch. What about multiple scales?

P11.2 Explain the notion of homogeneous co-ordinates. Is projective transformation linear if expressed in homogeneous co-ordinates? Why are homogeneous co-ordinates often used in robotics to express the kinematics of a manipulating arm? (Hint: Express rotation and translation of an object in 3D space using homogeneous co-ordinates.)

P11.3 Take a camera with an off-the-shelf lens. Design and perform an experiment to find the intrinsic calibration parameters of it. Design and use an appropriate calibration object (for example, a grid like structure printed by laser printer on paper; you might capture it at different heights by placing it on a box of known height). Discuss the precision of your results. Is the pinhole model of your camera appropriate? (Hint: Look at distortions of a grid as in Figure 3.34.)

P11.4 Consider the case of two cameras (stereopsis) with baseline $2h$. A scene point lies on the optical axis at depth d from the baseline. Assume that the precision of pixel position measurement x in the image plane is given by dispersion σ^2. Derive a formula showing the dependence of the precision of depth measurement against dispersion. (Hint: Differentiate d according to x.)

P11.5 Conduct an experiment with stereo correspondences. For simplicity, capture a pair of stereo images using cameras in canonical configuration (epipolar lines correspond to lines in images), and cut corresponding lines from both images. Visualize the brightness profiles in those lines (for example, using Matlab). First, try to find correspondences in brightness manually. Second, decide if correlation-based or feature-based stereo techniques are more suitable for your case. Program it and test on your profiles.

P11.6 Conduct a laboratory experiment with photometric stereo. You will need one camera and three light sources. Take some opaque object and measure its surface orientation using photometric stereo (see Section 11.7.2).

P11.7 Make yourself familiar with solved problems and **Matlab** implementations of selected algorithms provided in the corresponding chapter of the **Matlab Companion** to this text [Svoboda et al., 2008]. The **Matlab Companion** homepage http://visionbook.felk.cvut.cz offers images used in the problems, and well-commented **Matlab** code is provided for educational purposes.

P11.8 Use the **Matlab Companion** [Svoboda et al., 2008] to develop solutions to additional exercises and practical problems provided there. Implement your solutions using **Matlab** or other suitable programming languages.

11.10 References

Aloimonos Y., editor. *Active Perception*. Lawrence Erlbaum Associates, Hillsdale, NJ, 1993.

Aloimonos Y. What I have learned. *CVGIP: Image Understanding*, 60(1):74–85, 1994.

Aloimonos Y. and Rosenfeld A. Principles of computer vision. In Young T. Y., editor, *Handbook of Pattern Recognition and Image Processing: Computer Vision*, pages 1–15, San Diego, 1994. Academic Press.

Aloimonos Y. and Shulman D. *Integration of Visual Modules—An Extension of the Marr Paradigm*. Academic Press, New York, 1989.

Aloimonos Y., editor. Special issue on purposive and qualitative active vision. *CVGIP B: Image Understanding*, 56, 1992.

Bajcsy R. Active perception. *Proceedings of the IEEE*, 76(8):996–1005, 1988.

Bertero M., Poggio T., and Torre V. Ill-posed problems in early vision. *IEEE Proceedings*, 76: 869–889, 1988.

Besl P. J. and Jain R. *Surfaces in range image understanding*. Springer Verlag, New York, 1988.

Besl P. J. and Jain R. C. Three-dimensional object recognition. *ACM Computing Surveys*, 17 (1):75–145, 1985.

Beymer D. and Poggio T. Image representations for visual learning. *Science*, 272:1905–1909, 1996.

Biederman I. Recognition by components: A theory of human image understanding. *Psychological Review*, 94(2):115–147, 1987.

Bowyer K. W. Special issue on directions in CAD-based vision. *CVGIP – Image Understanding*, 55:107–218, 1992.

Brooks R. A., Greiner R., and Binford T. O. The ACRONYM model-based vision system. In *Proceedings of the International Joint Conference on Artificial Intelligence, IJCAI-6*, Tokyo, Japan, pages 105–113, 1979.

Buxton H. and Howarth R. J. Spatial and temporal reasoning in the generation of dynamic scene representations. In Rodriguez R. V., editor, *Proceedings of Spatial and Temporal Reasoning*, pages 107–115, Montreal, Canada, 1995. IJCAI-95.

Cornelius H., Šára R., Martinec D., Pajdla T., Chum O., and Matas J. Towards complete free-form reconstruction of complex 3D scenes from an unordered set of uncalibrated images. In Comaniciu D., Mester R., and Kanatani K., editors, *Proceedings of the ECCV Workshop Statistical Methods in Video Processing*, pages 1–12, Heidelberg, Germany, 2004. Springer-Verlag.

Drbohlav O. and Chantler M. On optimal light configurations in photometric stereo. In *Proceedings of the 10th IEEE International Conference on Computer Vision*, volume II, pages 1707–1712, Beijing, China, 2005a. IEEE Computer Society.

Drbohlav O. and Chantler M. Can two specular pixels calibrate photometric stereo? In *Proceedings of the 10th IEEE International Conference on Computer Vision*, volume II, pages 1850–1857, Beijing, China, 2005b. IEEE Computer Society.

Farshid A. and Aggarwal J. K. Model-based object recognition in dense range images—a review. *ACM Computing Surveys*, 25(1):5–43, 1993.

Faugeras O. D. *Three-Dimensional Computer Vision: A Geometric Viewpoint*. MIT Press, Cambridge, MA, 1993.

Faugeras O. D., Luong Q. T., and Maybank S. J. Camera self-calibration: Theory and experiments. In *2nd European Conference on Computer Vision*, Santa Margherita Ligure, Italy, pages 321–333, Heidelberg, Germany, 1992. Springer Verlag.

Fernyhough J. F. *Generation of qualitative spatio-temporal representations from visual input*. Ph.D. thesis, School of Computer Studies, University of Leeds, Leeds, UK, 1997.

Fitzgibbon A. W. and Zisserman A. Automatic camera recovery for closed or open image sequences. In *Proceedings of the European Conference on Computer Vision*, volume LNCS 1406, pages 311–326, Heidelberg, Germany, 1998. Springer Verlag.

Flynn P. J. and Jain A. K. CAD-based computer vision: From CAD models to relational graphs. *IEEE Transaction on Pattern Analysis and Machine Intelligence*, 13(2):114–132, 1991.

Flynn P. J. and Jain A. K. 3D object recognition using invariant feature indexing of interpretation tables. *CVGIP – Image Understanding*, 55(2):119–129, 1992.

Forsyth D. and Ponce J. *Computer Vision: A Modern Approach*. Prentice Hall, New York, NY, 2003.

Gimel'farb G. *Handbook of Computer Vision and Applications*, volume 2, Signal processing and pattern recognition, chapter Stereo terrain reconstruction by dynamic programming, pages 505–530. Academic Press, San Diego, California, USA, 1999.

Gluckman J. and Nayar S. K. Rectifying transformations that minimize resampling effects. In Kasturi R. and Medioni G., editors, *Proceedings of the IEEE Computer Society Conference on Computer Vision and Pattern Recognition*, volume 1, pages 111–117. IEEE Computer Society, 2001.

Goad C. Fast 3D model-based vision. In Pentland A. P., editor, *From Pixels to Predicates*, pages 371–374. Ablex, Norwood, NJ, 1986.

Golub G. H. and Loan C. F. V. *Matrix Computations*. Johns Hopkins University Press, Baltimore, MD, 2nd edition, 1989.

Haralick R. M. and Shapiro L. G. *Computer and Robot Vision, Volume II.* Addison-Wesley, Reading, MA, 1993.

Hartley R. I. Estimation of relative camera positions for uncalibrated cameras. In *2nd European Conference on Computer Vision,* Santa Margherita Ligure, Italy, pages 579–587, Heidelberg, 1992. Springer Verlag.

Hartley R. I. Self-calibration from multiple views with a rotating camera. In Eklundh J. O., editor, *3rd European Conference on Computer Vision,* Stockholm, Sweden, pages A:471–478, Berlin, 1994. Springer Verlag.

Hartley R. I. In defense of the eight-point algorithm. *IEEE Transactions on Pattern Analysis and Machine Intelligence,* 19(6):580–593, 1997.

Hartley R. I. and Zisserman A. *Multiple view geometry in computer vision.* Cambridge University, Cambridge, 2nd edition, 2003.

Horaud R., Mohr R., Dornaika F., and Boufama B. The advantage of mounting a camera onto a robot arm. In *Proceedings of the Europe-China Workshop on Geometrical Modelling and Invariants for Computer Vision,* Xian, China, pages 206–213, 1995.

Horn B. K. P. Shape from shading. In Winston P. H., editor, *The Psychology of Computer Vision.* McGraw-Hill, New York, 1975.

Horn B. K. P. Height and gradient from shading. *International Journal of Computer Vision,* 5 (1):37–75, 1990.

Horn B. K. P. *Shape from shading: A method for obtaining the shape of a smooth opaque sobject from one view.* Ph.D. thesis, Department of Electrical Engineering, MIT, Cambridge, MA, 1970.

Howarth R. J. *Spatial representation and control for a surveillance system.* Ph.D. thesis, Department of Computer Science, Queen Mary and Westfield College, Univerity of London, UK, 1994.

Ikeuchi K. and Horn B. K. P. Numerical shape from shading and occluding boundaries. *Artificial Intelligence,* 17:141–184, 1981.

Julesz B. Binocular depth perception of computer-generated patterns. *Bell Systems Technical Journal,* 39, 1990.

Klette R., Koschan A., and Schlüns K. *Computer Vision—Räumliche Information aus digitalen Bildern.* Friedr. Vieweg & Sohn, Braunschweig, 1996.

Klir G. J. *Facets of System Science.* Plenum Press, New York, 1991.

Koenderink J. J. *Solid Shape.* MIT Press, Cambridge, MA, 1990.

Landy M. S., Maloney L. T., and Pavel M., editors. *Exploratory Vision: The Active Eye.* Springer Series in Perception Engineering. Springer Verlag, New York, 1996.

Longuet-Higgins H. C. A computer algorithm for reconstruction a scene from two projections. *Nature,* 293(10):133–135, 1981.

Loop C. and Zhang Z. Computing rectifying homographies for stereo vision. In *Proceedings of the IEEE Conference on Computer Vision and Pattern Recognition,* volume 1, pages 125–131. IEEE Computer Society, 1999.

Lütkepohl H. *Handbook of Matrices.* John Wiley & Sons, Chichester, England, 1996.

Ma Y., Soatto S., Košecká J., and Sastry S. S. *An invitation to 3-D vision : from images to geometric models.* Interdisciplinary applied mathematic. Springer, New York, 2004.

Marr D. *Vision—A Computational Investigation into the Human Representation and Processing of Visual Information.* Freeman, San Francisco, 1982.

Marr D. and Hildreth E. Theory of edge detection. *Proceedings of the Royal Society*, B 207: 187–217, 1980.

Marr D. and Poggio T. A. A computational theory of human stereo vision. *Proceedings of the Royal Society*, B 207:301–328, 1979.

Matoušek M., Šára R., and Hlaváč V. Data-optimal rectification for fast and accurate stereo-vision. In Zhang D. and Pan Z., editors, *Proceedings of the Third International Conference on Image and Graphics*, pages 212–215, Los Alamitos, USA, 2004. IEEE Computer Society.

Maybank S. J. and Faugeras O. D. A theory of self-calibration of a moving camera. *International Journal of Computer Vision*, 8(2):123–151, 1992.

Mohr R. Projective geometry and computer vision. In Chen C. H., Pau L. F., and Wang P. S. P., editors, *Handbook of Pattern Recognition and Computer Vision*, chapter 2.4, pages 369–393. World Scientific, Singapore, 1993.

Newman T. S., Flynn P. J., and Jain A. K. Model-based classification of quadric surfaces. *CVGIP: Image Understanding*, 58(2):235–249, 1993.

Nishihara H. K. Practical real-time imaging stereo matcher. *Optical Engineering*, 23(5):536–545, 1984.

Oliensis J. Shape from shading as a partially well-constrained problem. *Computer Vision, Graphics, and Image Processing: Image Understanding*, 54(2):163–183, 1991.

Pajdla T. and Hlaváč V. Camera calibration and Euclidean reconstruction from known translations. Presented at the workshop *Computer Vision and Applied Geometry,,* 1995.

Pentland A. P. Local shading analysis. *IEEE Transactions on Pattern Analysis and Machine Intelligence*, 6(2):170–187, 1984.

Pentland A. P. and Bichsel M. Extracting shape from shading. In Young T. Y., editor, *Handbook of Pattern Recognition and Image Processing: Computer Vision*, pages 161–183, San Diego, 1994. Academic Press.

Poggio T., Torre V., and Koch C. Computational vision and regularization theory. *Nature*, 317: 314–319, 1985.

Pollard S. B., Mayhew J. E. W., and Frisby J. P. PMF: A stereo correspondence algorithm using a disparity gradient limit. *Perception*, 14:449–470, 1985.

Pollefeys M., Koch R., and VanGool L. Self-calibration and metric reconstruction in spite of varying and unknown internal camera parameters. In *Proceedings of the International Conference on Computer Vision*, pages 90–95, New Delhi, India, 1998. IEEE Computer Society, Narosa Publishing House.

Press W. H., , Teukolsky S. A., Vetterling W. T., and Flannery B. P. *Numerical Recipes in C*. Cambridge University Press, Cambridge, England, 2nd edition, 1992.

Rindfleisch T. Photometric method form lunar topography. *Photogrammetric Engineering*, 32 (2):262–267, 1966.

Sara R. *Local shading analysis via isophotes properties*. Ph.D. thesis, Department of System Sciences, Johannes Kepler University Linz, 1994.

Sara R. Finding the largest unambiguous component of stereo matching. In Heyden A., Sparr G., Nielsen M., and Johansen P., editors, *Proceedings 7th European Conference on Computer Vision*, volume 3 of *Lecture Notes in Computer Science 2352*, pages 900–914, Berlin, Germany, May 2002. Springer.

Sara R. Isophotes: The key to tractable local shading analysis. In Hlavac V. and Sara R., editors, *International Conference on Computer Analysis of Images and Patterns,* Prague, Czech Republic, pages 416–423, Heidelberg, 1995. Springer Verlag.

Semple J. G. and Kneebone G. T. *Algebraic Projective Geometry.* Oxford University Press, London, 1963.

Smutný V. Analysis of rainbow range finder errors. In Hlaváč V. and Pajdla T., editors, *1st Czech Pattern Recognition Workshop*, pages 59–66. Czech Pattern Recognition Society, CTU, Prague, 1993.

Soucy M. and Laurendeau D. Surface modeling from dynamic integration of multiple range views. In *11th International Conference on Pattern Recognition,* The Hague, volume I, pages 449–452, Piscataway, NJ, 1992. IEEE.

Svoboda T., Kybic J., and Hlavac V. *Image Processing, Analysis, and Machine Vision: A MATLAB Companion.* Thomson Engineering, 2008.

Szeliski R. Fast surface interpolation using hierarchical basis functions. *Transactions on Pattern Analysis and Machine Intelligence*, 12(6):513–528, June 1990.

Tichonov A. N. and Arsenin V. Y. *Solution of ill-posed problems.* Winston and Wiley, Washington, DC, 1977.

Triggs B., McLauchlan P., Hartley R., and Fitzgibbon A. Bundle adjustment – A modern synthesis. In Triggs W., Zisserman A., and Szeliski R., editors, *Vision Algorithms: Theory and Practice*, volume 1883 of *LNCS*, pages 298–375. Springer Verlag, 2000.

Tsai R. Y. An efficient and accurate camera calibration technique for 3D machine vision. In *CVPR '86: Computer Society Conference on Computer Vision and Pattern Recognition,* Miami Beach, FL, pages 364–374, 1986.

Ullman S. *High-Level Vision: Object Recognition and Visual Cognition.* MIT Press, Cambridge, MA, 1996.

Ullman S. and Basri R. Recognition by linear combination of models. *IEEE Transactions on Pattern Analysis and Machine Intelligence*, 13(10):992–1005, 1991.

Wechsler H. *Computational Vision.* Academic Press, London–San Diego, 1990.

Werner T., Hersch R. D., and Hlaváč V. Rendering real-world objects using view interpolation. In *5th International Conference on Computer Vision,* Boston, USA, pages 957–962. IEEE Computer Society, 1995.

Woodham R. J. Photometric method for determining surface orientation from multiple images. *Optical Engineering*, 19:139–144, 1980.

Chapter 12

Use of 3D vision

In earlier (and later) chapters, we present a constructive approach to various aspects of image processing and vision that should allow readers to reproduce ideas and build systems of their own. Most of this chapter is somewhat different; 3D vision solves complex tasks having no settled and simple theory, and here we step aside and provide an overview of selected approaches, task formulations, applications and current research. We hope thereby that the reader will learn what the current state of 3D vision is; it is possible that the material herein will be at the limit of the abilities of the vision novice, but may form a useful primer for master's or Ph.D. courses.

12.1 Shape from X

Shape from X is a generic name for techniques that aim to extract shape from intensity images and other cues such as focus. Some of these methods estimate local surface orientation (e.g., surface normal) rather than absolute depth. If, in addition to this local knowledge, the depth of some particular point is known, the absolute depth of all other points can be computed by integrating the surface normals along a curve on a surface [Horn, 1986]. Several topics belonging to this category of methods have already been mentioned, i.e., *shape from stereo* (Sections 11.5, 11.6.1), *shape from shading* (Section 11.7.1), and *photometric stereo* (Section 11.7.2).

12.1.1 Shape from motion

Motion is a primary property exploited by human observers of the 3D world. The real world we see is dynamic in many respects, and the relative movement of objects in view, their translation and rotation relative to the observer, the motion of the observer relative to other static and moving objects all provide very strong clues to shape and depth—consider how just moving your head from side to side provides rich information from parallax effects. It should therefore come as no surprise to learn that attempts at shape extraction are able to make use of motion. Motion, and particularly lower-level algorithms associated with its analysis, is considered in detail in Chapter 16, and in this section study is restricted to shape extraction alone.

A study of human analysis of motion is instructive and was conducted comprehensively in a computational context by Ullman [Ullman, 1979]. Exactly how we make deductions from moving scenes is far from clear, and several theories have come and gone in efforts to understand this matter—in particular, **Gestaltist** theories. Gestalt psychology was a revolutionary psychological paradigm proposed in Germany in the early twentieth century ('Gestalt' means 'shape' or 'form' in German). It claims that more complicated mental processes cannot be simply composed from the simpler ones, and questioned the causality of events. Its suggestion that groupings of observations are of primary importance was disproved, notably by an experiment of Ullman's. On a computer screen, he simulated two coaxial cylinders of different radii rotating about their common axis in opposite directions. The view is perpendicular to the common axis; the cylinders were not drawn, but only randomly placed dots on their surfaces. Thus what is seen (on a per-point basis) is a large number of dots moving from left to right or right to left, at varying speeds. Exactly what speed and direction depends upon which cylinder surface a dot belongs to, and at what point of rotation it is—in fact, each individual dot executes simple harmonic motion about a point that is on a line that is the projection onto the image of the axis. The striking conclusion is that the human observer is in no doubt about the nature of the scene, despite the absence of surface clues and the complete absence of structure in any single frame from the sequence.

What we exploit are particular **constraints that assist in resolving the non-uniqueness of the interpretation** of a sequence of frames as a moving 3D scene. In fact, motion may be presented to us as widely spaced (in time) discrete frames, or as (pseudo-)continuous—that is, so many frames that changes between a given pair are imperceptible. We shall examine each case separately, each time using Ullman's observation that the extraction of 3D information from moving scenes can be done as a two-phase process:

1. **Finding correspondences** or calculating the nature of the flow is a lower-level phase that operates on pixel arrays.

2. The **shape extraction** phase follows as a separate, higher-level process. This phase is examined here.

It is worth noting that researchers are not unanimous in the view that these two phases should be held separate, and approaches exist that are different from those discussed here [Negahdaripour and Horn, 1985].

Note that one approach to the analysis of motion is superficially similar to that of stereo vision—images that are relatively widely separated in time are taken, and correspondences between visible features made. The solution to this correspondence problem is considered in detail in Chapter 16 and Section 11.6.1. It is worth remarking here that resemblance to the stereo correspondence problem is deceptive since the scene may well contain any number of independently moving objects, which could mean that correlations may be strictly local. Two images are not of the same scene, but (more probably) of the same objects in different relative positions.

Searching for correspondence in motion analysis may be easier than when attempting it in stereo imaging. It is often possible to capture a dense sequence of images (i.e., the time separation between neighboring frames is small so that corresponding features are very close, and the search for them almost trivial). Moreover, the position of the feature in the next frame can be predicted by estimating its trajectory using techniques similar to those of control theory. The Kalman filter and Condensation approaches (see Section 16.6.1) are common.

Rigidity, and the structure from motion theorem

For now, suppose that the correspondence problem has been solved, and that it remains to extract some shape information—that is, given that a collection of points has been identified in two different views, how might they be interpreted as 3D objects? As might be expected, the large number of possible interpretations is resolved by deploying a constraint; Ullman's success in this area was based on the psycho-physical observation that the human visual system seems to assume that objects are *rigid*. This rigidity constraint prompted the proof of an elegant **structure from motion theorem** saying that *three orthographic projections of four non-co-planar points have a unique 3D interpretation as belonging to one rigid body*. We shall proceed to outline the proof of this theorem, which is constructive and therefore permits the extraction of the appropriate geometry, given point correspondences in three frames from a motion sequence. In use, the theorem allows samples of four points to be taken from an image sequence—*if* they belong to the same (rigid) body, an interpretation is generated, but if they do not, the probability of there being a chance rigid interpretation turns out to be negligibly small, meaning that the algorithm is self-verifying in the sense that it generates only answers that are 'correct'. Thus if there are N points in the correspondence, we might test all selections of 4 points for rigid interpretation; some of these will be invalid, and others will group according to the rigid object to which they belong.

The theorem proof involves a re-phrasing of the problem to permit its definition as the solution of an equivalent problem in 3D geometry. Given three orthographic views of four points that have a rigid interpretation, the correspondence allows them to be labeled as O, A, B, and C in each image. First note that the body's motion may be decomposed into translational and rotational movement; the former gives the movement of a fixed point with respect to the observer, and the latter relative rotation of the body (for example, about the chosen fixed point). **Translational movement**, as far as it is recognizable, is easy to identify. All that can be resolved is movement perpendicular to the projection, and this is given by the translation (in 2D) of an arbitrarily chosen point, say O. Observe that motion parallel to the projection cannot be identified.

It remains to identify **rotational motion**; to do this we can assume that O is a fixed point, and seek to identify an interpretation of A, B and C as belonging to the same rigid body as O. Accordingly, we transform the problem to that of knowing three pairs of (2D) co-ordinates for A, B, and C with respect to a common origin O, each a different orthographic projection; what is now required is the (3D) directions of the projections.

Formally, suppose we have in 3D an origin O and three vectors $\mathbf{a}$, $\mathbf{b}$, and $\mathbf{c}$ corresponding to A, B, and C; given projections of $\mathbf{a}$, $\mathbf{b}$, and $\mathbf{c}$ onto three planes Π_1, Π_2, and Π_3 of unknown orientation, we require to reconstruct the 3D geometry of $\mathbf{a}$, $\mathbf{b}$, and $\mathbf{c}$. Now let the co-ordinate system of the plane Π_i be defined by vectors $\mathbf{x}_i$ and $\mathbf{y}_i$; that is, $\mathbf{x}_i$ and $\mathbf{y}_i$ are orthogonal 3D unit vectors lying in the plane Π_i. With respect to these systems, suppose that on plane Π_i the points' projections have co-ordinates (a_{xi}, a_{yi}), (b_{xi}, b_{yi}), (c_{xi}, c_{yi})—these nine pairs are the input to the algorithm. Finally, let $\mathbf{u}_{ij}$ be a unit vector lying on the line defined by the intersection of planes Π_i and Π_j.

Elementary co-ordinate geometry gives

$$a_{xi} = \mathbf{a}\,\mathbf{x}_i\,, \qquad a_{yi} = \mathbf{a}\,\mathbf{y}_i\,,$$
$$b_{xi} = \mathbf{b}\,\mathbf{x}_i\,, \qquad b_{yi} = \mathbf{b}\,\mathbf{y}_i\,, \tag{12.1}$$
$$c_{xi} = \mathbf{c}\,\mathbf{x}_i\,, \qquad c_{yi} = \mathbf{c}\,\mathbf{y}_i\,.$$

Further, since $\mathbf{u}_{ij}$ lies on both Π_i and Π_j, there must exist scalars $\alpha_{ij}, \beta_{ij}, \gamma_{ij}, \delta_{ij}$ such that

$$\alpha_{ij}^2 + \beta_{ij}^2 = 1\,, \qquad \gamma_{ij}^2 + \delta_{ij}^2 = 1\,, \tag{12.2}$$

and

$$\mathbf{u}_{ij} = \alpha_{ij}\,\mathbf{x}_i + \beta_{ij}\,\mathbf{y}_i\,,$$
$$\mathbf{u}_{ij} = \gamma_{ij}\,\mathbf{x}_j + \delta_{ij}\,\mathbf{y}_j\,, \tag{12.3}$$

and hence

$$\alpha_{ij}\,\mathbf{x}_i + \beta_{ij}\,\mathbf{y}_i = \gamma_{ij}\,\mathbf{x}_j + \delta_{ij}\,\mathbf{y}_j\,. \tag{12.4}$$

We can take the scalar product of this equation with each of $\mathbf{a}$, $\mathbf{b}$, and $\mathbf{c}$, and using equation (12.1) see that

$$\alpha_{ij}\,a_{xi} + \beta_{ij}\,a_{yi} = \gamma_{ij}\,a_{xj} + \delta_{ij}\,a_{yj}\,,$$
$$\alpha_{ij}\,b_{xi} + \beta_{ij}\,b_{yi} = \gamma_{ij}\,b_{xj} + \delta_{ij}\,b_{yj}\,, \tag{12.5}$$
$$\alpha_{ij}\,c_{xi} + \beta_{ij}\,c_{yi} = \gamma_{ij}\,c_{xj} + \delta_{ij}\,c_{yj}$$

—thus we have relations between unknowns $(\alpha, \beta, \gamma, \delta)$ in terms of known quantities $(a_x, a_y, \text{etc.})$.

It is easy to show that the equations (12.5) are linearly independent (this is where the fact that O, A, B, and C are not co-planar is used). Therefore, using the constraint of equation (12.2), it is possible to solve for $\alpha_{ij}, \beta_{ij}, \gamma_{ij}, \delta_{ij}$—in fact, there are two possible solutions that differ in sign only.

This (findable) solution is important, as it means that we are able to express the vectors $\mathbf{u}_{ij}$ in terms of the co-ordinate basis vectors $\mathbf{x}_i$, $\mathbf{y}_i$, $\mathbf{x}_j$, and $\mathbf{y}_j$. To see why this is important, picture the three planes in 3D—they intersect at the common origin O and therefore define a tetrahedron; what interests us is the *relative* angles between the planes, and if the geometry of the tetrahedron can be recaptured, these angles are available. Note, though, that knowledge of $\alpha_{ij}, \beta_{ij}, \gamma_{ij}, \delta_{ij}$ allows calculation of the distances

$$d_1 = |\mathbf{u}_{12} - \mathbf{u}_{13}|\,,$$
$$d_2 = |\mathbf{u}_{12} - \mathbf{u}_{23}|\,, \tag{12.6}$$
$$d_3 = |\mathbf{u}_{13} - \mathbf{u}_{23}|\,.$$

For example

$$\mathbf{u}_{12} - \mathbf{u}_{13} = (\alpha_{12}\,\mathbf{x}_1 + \beta_{12}\,\mathbf{y}_1) - (\alpha_{13}\,\mathbf{x}_1 + \beta_{13}\,\mathbf{y}_1)$$
$$= (\alpha_{12} - \alpha_{13})\mathbf{x}_1 + (\beta_{12} - \beta_{13})\mathbf{y}_1\,, \tag{12.7}$$

and hence

$$d_1 = (\alpha_{12} - \alpha_{13})^2 + (\beta_{12} - \beta_{13})^2\,. \tag{12.8}$$

since $\mathbf{x}_1$ and $\mathbf{y}_1$ are orthogonal. Now the tetrahedron formed by the three intersecting planes is defined by the origin O and a triangular base—we might consider the base given by the three points at unit distance from the origin. By construction, this triangle has sides d_1, d_2, d_3, and we can thus reconstruct the required tetrahedron.

Determining the 3D structure is now possible by noting that a particular point lies at the intersection of the normals to any two of the planes drawn from the projections of the point concerned.

There is a complication in the proof not discussed here that occurs when one of the d_i is zero, and the tetrahedron is degenerate. It is possible to resolve this problem without difficulty [Ullman, 1979].

It is worth noting that Ullman's result is the best possible in the sense that unique reconstruction of a rigid body cannot be guaranteed with fewer than three projections of four points, or with three projections of fewer than four points. It should also be remembered that the result refers to *orthographic* projection when in general image projections are *perspective* (of which, of course, the orthographic projection is a special case). This turns out not to be a problem since a similar result is available for the perspective projection [Ullman, 1979]. In fact this is not necessary, since it is possible to approximate neighborhoods within a perspective projection by a number of different orthographic projections; thus in such a neighborhood, the theorem as outlined is valid. Interestingly, there seems to be evidence that the human visual system uses this sort of orthographic approximation in extracting shape information from motion.

This result is of particular value in **active vision** applications [Blake and Yuille, 1992; Aloimonos, 1993] such as a robot arm having a camera mounted upon it; when such a system finds itself unable to 'see' particular objects of interest, the arm will move for a different view, which will then need reconciling with earlier ones.

Shape from optical flow

The motion presented to human observers is not that considered in the previous section, but rather is continuous—the scene in view varies smoothly. The approach of considering widely spaced (in time) views is therefore a simplification, and it is natural to ask how to treat the limiting case of separate frames being temporally very close to each other—it is well known that, in fact, the human eye perceives continuous motion from relatively few frames per second (as illustrated by cinema film). Clearly the approach of making correspondences is no longer any use since corresponding points will be separated by infinitesimally small distances—it is the apparent velocity (direction and speed) of pixels that is of interest in the study of continuous motion. In a continuous sequence, we are therefore interested in the apparent movement of each pixel (x, y) which is given by the **optical flow field** $(dx/dt, dy/dt)$. In Chapter 16, optical flow is considered at length and an algorithm is described for its extraction from observation of changes in the intensity function (gray-levels); accordingly, in this section it is assumed that the flow field is available, and we ask how it may be used to extract shape in the form of surface orientation (in fact, optical flow is useful for deducing a number of motion properties, such as the nature of the translational or rotational movement—these points are considered in Chapter 16).

Determining shape from optical flow is mathematically non-trivial, and here an early simplification of the subject is presented as an illustration [Clocksin, 1980]. The simplification is in two parts:

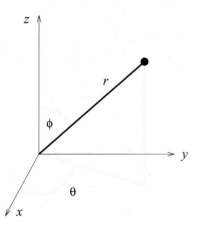

Figure 12.1: Definition of spherical polar co-ordinates. © *Cengage Learning 2015.*

- Motion is due to the observer travelling in a straight line through a static landscape. Without loss of generality, suppose the motion is in the direction of the z axis of a viewer-centered co-ordinate system (i.e., the observer is positioned at the origin).

- Rather than being projected onto a 2D plane, the image is seen on the surface of a unit sphere, centered at the observer (a 'spherical retina'). Points in 3D are represented in spherical polar rather than Cartesian co-ordinates—spherical polar co-ordinates (r, θ, φ) (see Figure 12.1) are related to (x, y, z) by the equations

$$r^2 = x^2 + y^2 + z^2 \,, \tag{12.9}$$

$$y = x \tan \theta \,, \tag{12.10}$$

$$z = r \cos \varphi \,. \tag{12.11}$$

Since the image is spherical, we can specify co-ordinates as (θ, φ) pairs rather than (x, y) as usual, and the optical flow is then $(\mathrm{d}\theta/\mathrm{d}t, \mathrm{d}\varphi/\mathrm{d}t)$. Supposing the observer's speed to be v (in the direction of the z axis), the motion of points in 3D is given by

$$\frac{\mathrm{d}x}{\mathrm{d}t} = 0 \,, \qquad \frac{\mathrm{d}y}{\mathrm{d}t} = 0 \,, \qquad \frac{\mathrm{d}z}{\mathrm{d}t} = -v \,. \tag{12.12}$$

Differentiating equation (12.9) with respect to t gives

$$2r \frac{\mathrm{d}r}{\mathrm{d}t} = 2x \frac{\mathrm{d}x}{\mathrm{d}t} + 2y \frac{\mathrm{d}y}{\mathrm{d}t} + 2z \frac{\mathrm{d}z}{\mathrm{d}t}$$

$$= -2vz \,,$$

$$\frac{\mathrm{d}r}{\mathrm{d}t} = -\frac{vz}{r} \tag{12.13}$$

$$= -v \cos \varphi \,.$$

Differentiating equation (12.10) with respect to t gives

$$\frac{\mathrm{d}y}{\mathrm{d}t} = \tan \theta \frac{\mathrm{d}x}{\mathrm{d}t} + x \sec^2 \theta \frac{\mathrm{d}\theta}{\mathrm{d}t} \,,$$

$$0 = 0 + x \sec^2 \theta \frac{\mathrm{d}\theta}{\mathrm{d}t} \,, \tag{12.14}$$

and hence

$$\frac{d\theta}{dt} = 0 \,.$$

(12.15)

Differentiating equation (12.11) with respect to t gives

$$\frac{dz}{dt} = \cos\varphi \, \frac{dr}{dt} - r\sin\varphi \, \frac{d\varphi}{dt}$$

and hence, by equations (12.12) and (12.13)

$$-v = -v\cos^2\varphi - r\sin\varphi \, \frac{d\varphi}{dt}$$

and so

$$\frac{d\varphi}{dt} = \frac{v(1 - \cos^2\varphi)}{r\sin\varphi} = \frac{v\sin\varphi}{r} \,.$$

(12.16)

Equations (12.15) and (12.16) are important. The former says that, for this particular motion, the rate of change of θ is zero (θ is constant). More interestingly, the latter says that given the optical flow $d\varphi/dt$, then the distance r of a 3D point from the observer can be recaptured up to a scale factor v. In particular, if v is known, then r, and a complete depth map, can be deduced from the optical flow. The depth map allows a reconstruction of the 3D scene and hence characteristics of surfaces (smoothly varying areas of r) and of edges (discontinuities in r) will be available.

In the case that v is not known, it turns out that surface information is still available directly from the flow. In particular, suppose a point P lies on a smooth surface, which at P may be specified by the direction of a normal vector $\mathbf{n}$. Such a direction may be specified by two angles α and β, where α is the angle between $\mathbf{n}$ and a plane Π_1 defined by P and the z axis, and β is the angle between $\mathbf{n}$ and a plane Π_2 which passes through P and the origin and is perpendicular to Π_1. Intuitively, it is clear that the rate of change of r with respect to θ and φ provides information about the direction of $\mathbf{n}$. Moderately straightforward co-ordinate geometry gives the relations

$$\tan\alpha = \frac{1}{r} \frac{\partial r}{\partial\varphi} \,, \qquad \tan\beta = \frac{1}{r} \frac{\partial r}{\partial\theta} \,.$$

(12.17)

These equations depend upon a knowledge of r (the depth map), but it is possible to combine them with equation (12.16) to overcome this. For convenience, write $d\varphi/dt = \dot\varphi$; then, by equation (12.16)

$$r = \frac{v\sin\varphi}{\dot\varphi}$$

(12.18)

and so

$$\frac{\partial r}{\partial\varphi} = v \, \frac{\dot\varphi\cos\varphi - \sin\varphi(\partial\dot\varphi/\partial\varphi)}{\dot\varphi^2} \,,$$

$$\frac{\partial r}{\partial\theta} = -v \, \frac{\sin\varphi(\partial\dot\varphi/\partial\theta)}{\dot\varphi^2} \,.$$

(12.19)

Substituting (12.18) and (12.19) into equations (12.17) gives

$$\tan\alpha = \cot\varphi - \frac{1}{\dot\varphi} \frac{\partial\dot\varphi}{\partial\varphi} \,,$$

$$\tan\beta = \frac{1}{\dot\varphi} \frac{\partial\dot\varphi}{\partial\theta} \,.$$

(12.20)

Thus, given the flow $\dot{\varphi}$ (which we assume), the angles α and β are immediately available, regardless of S and without any need to determine the depth map given by r.

The original reference [Clocksin, 1980] provides full information on this derivation, and proceeds to describe how edge information may also be extracted from knowledge of the flow. It also includes some interesting discussion of psycho-physical considerations of human motion perception in the context of a computational theory.

12.1.2   Shape from texture

A further property of which there is clear psycho-physical evidence of human use to extract depth is texture [Marr, 1982]. To appreciate this, it is only necessary to consider a regularly patterned object viewed in 3D. Two effects would be apparent: The angle at which the surface is seen would cause a (perspective) distortion of the **texture primitive** (**texel**), and the relative size of the primitives would vary according to distance from the observer. Simple examples, shown in Figure 12.2, are sufficient to illustrate this. Much use can be made of texture in computer vision at various levels of abstraction, and Chapter 15 examines them in some detail. Here we look briefly at the use of textural properties to assist in the extraction of shape [Bajcsy and Lieberman, 1976; Kanatani and Chou, 1989].

Figure 12.2: A simple texture pattern in 3D. The left side shows a vanishing brick wall and the right the shape of a body perceived from texture changes. © *Cengage Learning 2015*.

Considering a textured surface patterned with identical texels which have been recovered by lower-level processing, note that with respect to a viewer it has three properties at any point projected onto a retinal image: distance from the observer, **slant**; the angle at which the surface is sloping away from the viewer (the angle between the surface normal and the line of sight); and **tilt**, the direction in which the slant takes place. Attempts to re-capture some of this information is based on the **texture gradient**—that is, the direction of maximum rate of change of the perceived size of the texels, and a scalar measurement of this rate. One approach [Bajcsy and Lieberman, 1976] assumes a uniform texel size.

If the texture is particularly simple, the shape of the perceived texels will reveal surface orientation information. For example, if a plane is marked with identical circles, they will be seen in an image as ellipses (see Figure 12.3). The eccentricity of the ellipses provides information about the slant, while the orientation of the ellipse axes indicates the tilt [Stevens, 1979]. There is evidence to suggest [Stevens, 1979] that the human viewer

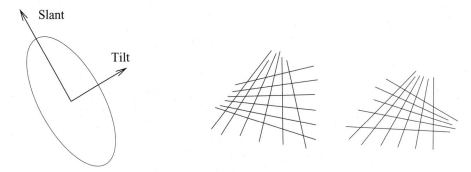

Figure 12.3: Slant and tilt are revealed by texel properties. © *Cengage Learning 2015.*

Figure 12.4: Tilt affects the appearance of texture. © *Cengage Learning 2015.*

uses texture gradient as a primary clue in the extraction of tilt and relative distance, but that slant is inferred by processing based on estimates of the other two parameters. Tilt is indicated by the direction of the texture gradient (see Figure 12.4), while the apparent size of objects decreases as the reciprocal of their distance from the viewer.

Large-scale texture effects can provide information about large-scale scene geometry; in particular, strong linear effects will indicate 'vanishing points' that may be joined to give the scene horizon. Note that it is not necessary in fact for the image to contain large numbers of long straight lines for this conclusion to be available, since often such lines can be inferred by a number of segments whose co-linearity may be deduced by, for example, a Hough transform. Such co-linearity may well be a property of urban scenes in which rectangular objects, some large, can predominate.

Texture has many interpretations and there is a correspondingly large number of attempts to exploit it in shape extraction—a useful grounding may be found in [Witkin, 1981]. A multiple-scale approach was used in [Blostein and Ahuja, 1989], while [Aloi-monos and Swain, 1985] give an interesting approach in which 'shape from texture' is shown to be equivalent to 'shape from shading', thereby allowing the use of established results in surface parameter extraction from shading. Texture is usually used as an additional or complementary feature, augmenting another, stronger clue in shape extraction.

12.1.3   Other shape from X techniques

Shape from focus/de-focus techniques are based on the fact that lenses have finite depth of field, and only objects at the correct distance are in focus; others are blurred in proportion to their distance. Two main approaches can be distinguished:

Shape from focus   measures depth in one location in an active manner; this technique is used in 3D measuring machines in mechanical engineering. The object to be measured is fixed on a motorized table that moves along x, y, z axes. A small portion of the surface is observed by a camera through a microscopic lens, and if the surface patch in view (given by a small image window) is in focus, then the image has the maximal number of high frequencies; this qualitative information about focus serves as feedback to the z-axis servo-motor. The image is put into focus and x, y, z co-ordinates read from the motorized table. If the depth of all points in the image are to be measured, a large number of images is captured by displacing the sensor in small increments from the scene, and the image of maximum focus is detected for each image point [Krotkov, 1987; Nayar and Nakagawa, 1994].

Shape from de-focus typically estimates depth using two input images captured at different depths. The relative depth of the whole scene can be reconstructed from image blur. The image is modeled as a convolution of the image with a proper point spread function (see Section 3.1.2); the function is either known from capturing setup parameters or estimated, for example by observing a sharp depth step in the image. The depth reconstruction, which is an ill-posed problem [Pentland, 1987], is performed by local frequency analysis. Depth from de-focus shares an inherent problem with shape from stereo and shape from motion, in that it requires the scene to be covered by a fine texture. A real-time (30Hz) depth from de-focus sensor has been built [Nayar et al., 1996]: The device uses active illumination by texture and analyzes relative blur in two images captured at two different depths. The derivation of the illumination pattern and depth estimation is posed as an optimization problem in the Fourier domain.

Shape from vergence uses two cameras fixed on a common rod. Using two servo-mechanisms, the cameras can change the direction of their optical axes (verge) in the plane containing a line segment joining their optical centers. Such devices are called **stereo heads**; see Figure 12.5. The aim of shape from vergence is to ease the correspondence problem for estimating depth [Krotkov and Bajcsy, 1993]; vergence is used to align individual feature points in both left and right images.

Shape from contour aims to describe a 3D shape from contours seen from one or more view directions. Objects with smooth bounding surfaces are quite difficult to analyze.

Following terminology given in [Ullman, 1996], assume the object is observed from some view point. The set of all points on the object surface where surface normal is perpendicular to the observer's visual ray is called a **rim** [Koenderink, 1990]. Note that

Figure 12.5: An example of a stereo head.
© *Cengage Learning 2015.*

in general the rim is not a planar curve. Assuming orthographic projection, the rim points generate a **silhouette** of an object in the image. Silhouettes can be easily and reliably captured if back-light illumination is used, although there is possible complication in the special case in which two distinct rim points project to a single image point.

The most general approach considers contours as silhouettes plus images of the salient curves on the surface, e.g., those corresponding to surface curvature discontinuities. The latter are often found using an edge detector from an intensity image. The trouble is that this process is often not robust enough; the simpler—and more common—approach explores silhouettes as contours. In Figure 12.6, silhouette and surface discontinuity are shown on an image of an apricot.

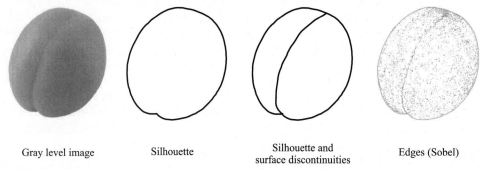

Gray level image   Silhouette   Silhouette and   Edges (Sobel)
                                               surface discontinuities

Figure 12.6: Apricot; contour as silhouette or as silhouette plus surface discontinuities, insufficient result of Sobel edge detector © *Cengage Learning 2015*.

The inherent difficulty in *shape from contour* comes from the loss of information in projecting 3D to 2D. We know that this projection is not invertible—this is illustrated in Figure 12.7, in which both a sphere and an ellipsoid project to the same ellipse. Humans are surprisingly successful at perceiving clear 3D shapes from contours, and it seems that tremendous background knowledge is used to assist. Understanding this human ability is one of the major challenges for computer vision. Contours are used as constraints on the shape they represent, and the aim is to reduce the number of possible interpretations. A fuller coverage of these approaches is in [Nevatia et al., 1994].

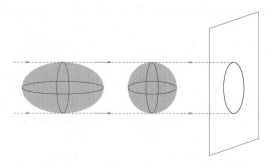

Figure 12.7: Ambiguity of the shape from contour task. © *Cengage Learning 2015*.

12.2 Full 3D objects

12.2.1 3D objects, models, and related issues

The notion of a **3D object** allows us to consider a 3D volume as a part of the entire 3D world. This volume has a particular interpretation (semantics, purpose) for the task in hand. Such an approach accords with the way general systems theory [Klir, 1991] treats complex phenomena, in which objects are separated from uninteresting background. Thus far, we have treated geometric (Section 11.2) and radiometric (Section 3.4.4) techniques that provide intermediate 3D cues, and it was implicitly assumed that such cues help to understand the nature of a 3D object.

Shape is another informal concept that humans typically connect with a 3D object. Recall the understanding we have when thinking of the shape of a mountain, or a vase or a cup. Computer vision aims at scientific methods for 3D object description, but there are no mathematical tools yet available to express shape in its general sense. The reader interested in abstract aspects of shape might consult texts on the shapes of solid objects [Koenderink, 1990]. Here, however, we shall not consider 3D shape issues in their full abstract sense. Instead, the simple geometrical approach treating parts of 3D objects locally as simple volumetric or surface primitives is used. Curvilinear surfaces with no restriction on surface shape are called **free-form surfaces**.

Roughly speaking, the 3D vision task distinguishes two classes of approach:

1. **Reconstruction** of the 3D object model or representation from real-world measurements with the aim of estimating a continuous function representing the surface.

2. **Recognition** of an instance of a 3D object in the scene. It is assumed that object classes are known in advance, and that they are represented by a suitable 3D model.

The reconstruction and recognition tasks use different representations of 3D objects. Recognition may use approaches that distinguish well between distinct classes, but do not characterize an object as a whole.

Humans meet and recognize often **deformable objects** that change their shape [Terzopoulos et al., 1988; Terzopoulos and Fleischer, 1988], an advanced topic that is too large to consider in this book.

Computer vision as well as computer graphics use **3D models** to encapsulate the shape of an 3D object. 3D models serve in computer graphics to generate detailed surface descriptions used to render realistic 2D images. In computer vision, the model is used either for reconstruction (copying, displaying an object from a different viewpoint, modifying an object slightly during animation) or for recognition purposes, where features are used that distinguish objects from different classes. There are two main classes of models: volumetric and surface. **Volumetric models** represent the 'inside' of a 3D object explicitly, while **surface models** use only object surfaces, as most vision-based measuring techniques can only see the surface of a non-transparent solid.

3D models make a transition towards an *object-centered* co-ordinate system, allowing object descriptions to be viewer independent. This is the most difficult phase within Marr's paradigm. Successful implementation is remote, especially compared to the success seen with the derivation of the primal and 2.5D sketches. Unlike earlier stages, there is little physiological guidance that can be used to design algorithms, since this level of human vision is not well understood. Marr observes that the target co-ordinate system(s) should be modular in the sense that each 'object' should be treated differently, rather than employing one global co-ordinate system—this prevents having to consider the orientation of model components with respect to the whole. Representations based on an object's 'natural' axes, derived from symmetries, or the orientation of stick features, are likely to be of greater use.

3D models of objects are common in other areas besides computer vision, notably computer-aided design (CAD) and computer graphics, where image synthesis is required —that is, an exact (2D) pictorial representation of some modeled 3D object. Use of an object representation which matches the representation generated by CAD systems has been an active research area for years, with substantial promise for industrial model-based vision. Progress in this area is presented in [Bowyer, 1992], with papers devoted to CAD-based models applied to pose estimation [Kriegman, 1992; Ponce et al., 1992; Seales and Dyer, 1992], 3D specular object recognition [Sato et al., 1992], and invariant feature extraction from range data [Flynn and Jain, 1992].

Various representation schemes exist, with different properties. A representation is called **complete** if two different objects cannot correspond to the same model, so a particular model is unambiguous. A representation is called **unique** if an object cannot correspond to two different models. Most 3D representation methods sacrifice either the completeness or the uniqueness property. Commercial CAD systems frequently sacrifice uniqueness; different design methodologies may produce the same object. Some solid modelers maintain multiple representations of objects in order to offer flexibility in design.

Due to self-occlusion of objects and to triangulation-based measuring methods, most vision-based measuring sensors inherently produce only partial 3D descriptions of objects. A fusion of several such measurements from different viewpoints is needed to obtain the shape of an object entirely. An ideal 3D sensor would provide a set of 3D uniformly sampled points on the surface together with their relation to neighboring points.

12.2.2   Line labeling

Early attempts to develop 3D vision systems tried to reconstruct a full 3D representation from a single, fully segmented view of a scene. The step between the dimensions was made by assuming that all objects in the scene had planar faces (see Figure 12.8), and that three faces met at each vertex. A perfect segmentation then provides straight-edged regions, and in general three of these will meet at a vertex. The idea was that this constraint was sufficient to permit a single 2D view to permit unambiguous reconstruction of a polyhedron. For obvious reasons, this is sometimes called a **blocks world** approach.

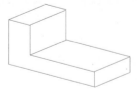

Figure 12.8: An example blocks world object. © *Cengage Learning 2015.*

The approach is clearly unrealistic for two reasons: First, the requirement for a perfect segmentation is unlikely to be met except in the most contrived situations; it is assumed that all edges are found, they are all linked into complete straight boundaries, and spurious evidence is filtered out. Second, there is a very limited number of circumstances in which objects do consist strictly of planar faces. It is perhaps possible that industrial applications exist where both conditions might be met by constraining the objects, and providing lighting of a quality that permits full segmentation.

The idea was pioneered some time ago by Roberts [Roberts, 1965], who made significant progress, especially considering the time at which the work was done. Independently, other researchers built on these ideas to develop what is now a very well known **line labeling** algorithm [Clowes, 1971; Huffman, 1971]. Mindful of the limitations of the blocks world approach, research into 3D vision has left these ideas behind and they are now of historical interest only. What follows is an overview of how line labeling works, but it is instructive in that first, it illustrates how the 3D reconstruction task may be naively approached, and second, it is good example of **constraint propagation** (see Chapter 10) in action. The algorithm rests on observing that, since each 3D vertex is a meeting of exactly three planar faces, only four types of junction may appear in any 2D scene (see Figure 12.9). In the 3D world, an edge may be concave or convex, and in its 2D projection the three faces meeting at a vertex may be visible or occluded. These finite possibilities permit an exhaustive listing of interpretations of a 2D vertex as a 3D vertex—there are in fact 22 of them [Clowes, 1971].

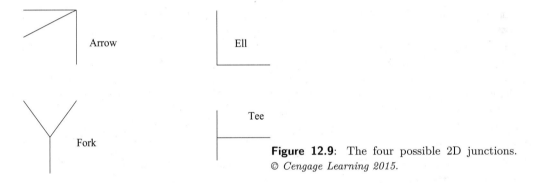

Figure 12.9: The four possible 2D junctions. © *Cengage Learning 2015.*

The problem now reduces to deriving a mutually consistent set of vertex labels; this may be done by employing constraints such as an edge interpretation (convex or concave) being the same at both ends, and that circumnavigating a region provides a coherent 3D surface interpretation. At a high level, the algorithm is as follows.

Algorithm 12.1: Line labeling

1. Extract a complete and accurate segmentation of the 2D scene projection into polygons.

2. Determine the set of possible 3D interpretations for each 2D vertex from a precomputed exhaustive list.

3. Determine 'edge-wise' coherent labellings of vertices by enforcing either concave or convex interpretations to each end of an edge.

4. Deduce an overall interpretation by requiring a circumnavigation of a region to have a coherent 3D interpretation.

Line labeling is able to detect 'impossible' objects such as that shown in Figure 12.10a, since it would not pass the final stage of the informally described algorithm; it would not, however, register Figure 12.10b, which defies a 3D interpretation along its upper front horizontal edge, as impossible. It is also unable, in the simple form described, to cope with 'accidental' junctions which are the meeting of four or more lines (caused by chance occlusion), although these could be analyzed as special cases.

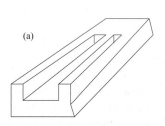
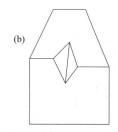

(a)

(b)

Figure 12.10: Impossible blocks world figures. © *Cengage Learning 2015.*

This simple approach received a lot of attention, and was extended to consider solids whose vertices may have more than three faces meeting at a vertex (such as square-based pyramids), and scenes in which regions might represent shadows of solids [Waltz, 1975]. Interestingly, while the number of possible junction interpretations increases enormously, the constraint satisfaction that is required for admissible candidate interpretations prevents the resulting algorithms becoming unworkable. More recent attempts at line label interpretations may be found in [Sugihara, 1986; Malik and Maydan, 1989; Shomar and Young, 1994]. In general, however, line labeling exists as an interesting historical idea. It is clear that its results are limited, and fraught with problems in overcoming 'special cases'.

12.2.3 Volumetric representation, direct measurements

An object is placed in some reference co-ordinate system and its volume is subdivided into small volume elements called **voxels**—it is usual for these to be cubes. The most straightforward representation of voxel-based volumetric models is the **3D occupancy grid**, which is implemented as a 3D Boolean array. Each voxel is indexed by its x, y, z co-ordinates; if the object is present in a particular space location the voxel has value 1, and otherwise 0. Creating such a voxel-based model is an instance of discretization with similar rules to those for 2D images; for example, the Shannon sampling theorem (see Section 3.2.5) applies. An example of a voxelized toroid is shown in Figure 12.11. One way of obtaining a voxel-based volumetric model is to synthesize it using a geometric modeler, i.e., a computer graphics program. This permits composite objects to be assembled from some number of basic solids such as cubes, cylinders, and spheres.

Another possibility is the case in which a volumetric model is to be created from an existing real object. A simple measuring technique has been used in mechanical engineering for a long time. The object is fixed to a **measuring machine**, and an absolute co-ordinate system is attached to it. Points on the object surface are touched by a **measuring needle** which provides 3D co-ordinates; see Figure 12.12. The precision depends on the machine and the size of the objects, typically ±5 micrometers.

In simpler machines, navigation of the needle on the surface is performed by a human operator; x, y, z co-ordinates are recorded automatically. Such a surface representation can easily be converted it into volumetric representation.

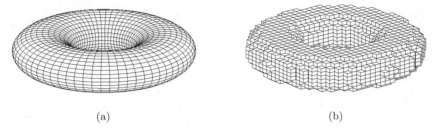

(a)   (b)

Figure 12.11: Voxelization (discretization) in 3D. (a) Continuous surface. (b) Voxelized image consisting of cubes of the same size. © *Cengage Learning 2015*.

Figure 12.12: An example of a fully motorized 3D measuring machine. Manufacturer, Mitutoyo, Inc., Japan. © *Cengage Learning 2015*.

Besides precision testing in machining or other mechanical engineering applications, this measuring technology may be used if the object is first created from clay by a designer. If computer-aided design (CAD) is to be brought into play, the 3D co-ordinates of the object are needed. An example is the automotive industry, where a clay model of a car body may be created at the scale 1:1. Actually only one half of the model is produced, as the car body is largely symmetric along the elongated axis. Such a model is measured on the 3D point measuring machine; as there are many points to be measured, the probe navigates semi-automatically. The points are organized into strips that cover the whole surface, and the probe has a proximity sensor that automatically stops on the surface or near to it. The probe is either a needle equipped with a force sensor or a laser probe performing the same measurement but stopping at a fixed and precise distance from the surface, e.g., 3 millimeters.

Another 3D measurement technique, **computed tomography**, looks inside the object and thus yields more detailed information than the binary occupancy grid discussed so far. Tomography yields a mass density in a 2D planar slice of the object. If 3D volumetric information is required, such slices are stacked on top of one another. The resulting 3D sample space consists of voxels, the values of which are mass densities addressed by the x, y, x co-ordinates. Computed tomography is used widely in medical imaging.

12.2.4   Volumetric modeling strategies

Constructive Solid Geometry

The principal idea of Constructive Solid Geometry (CSG), which has found some success is to construct 3D bodies from a selection of solid primitives. Popularly, these primitives are a cuboid, a cylinder, a sphere, a cone, and a 'half-space'—the cylinder and cone are considered to be infinite. They are scaled, positioned, and combined by union, intersection, and difference; thus a finite cone is formed by intersecting an infinite cone with an appropriately positioned half-space. A CSG model is stored as a tree, with leaf nodes representing the primitive solid and edges enforcing precedence among the set theoretical operations. The versatility of such a simply stated scheme is surprising. CSG models define properties such as object volume unambiguously, but suffer the drawback of being non-unique. For example, the solid illustrated in Figure 12.13—a mug—may be formed by the union of the cylinder with a hole and a handle. The cylinder with the hole is obtained from a full cylinder by subtracting (in the set sense) a smaller cylinder. It is not easy to model 'natural' shapes (a human head, for instance) with CSG. A more serious drawback is that it is not straightforward to recover surfaces given a CSG description; such a procedure is computationally very expensive.

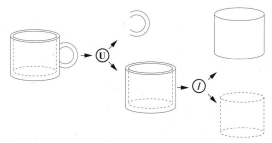

Figure 12.13: CSG representation of a 3D object—a mug. © *Cengage Learning 2015*.

Super-quadrics

Super-quadrics are geometric bodies that can be understood as a generalization of basic quadric solids, introduced in computer graphics [Barr, 1981]. Super-ellipsoids are instances of super-quadrics used in computer vision.

The implicit equation for a super-ellipsoid is

$$\left[\left(\frac{x}{a_1}\right)^{(2/\varepsilon_{\text{vert}})} + \left(\frac{y}{a_2}\right)^{(2/\varepsilon_{\text{vert}})}\right]^{(\varepsilon_{\text{hori}}/\varepsilon_{\text{vert}})} + \left(\frac{z}{a_3}\right)^{(2/\varepsilon_{\text{vert}})} = 1\,, \qquad (12.21)$$

where a_1, a_2, and a_3 define the super-quadric size in the x, y, and z directions, respectively. $\varepsilon_{\text{vert}}$ is the squareness parameter in the latitude plane and $\varepsilon_{\text{hori}}$ is the squareness parameter in the longitude plane. The squareness values used in respective planes are 0 (i.e., square) $\leq \varepsilon \leq 2$ (i.e., deltoid), as only those are convex bodies. If squareness parameters are greater than 2, the body changes to a cross-like shape. Figure 12.14 illustrates how squareness parameters influence super-ellipsoid shape.

Super-quadric fitting to range images is described in [Solina and Bajcsy, 1990; Leonardis et al., 1997], and the construction of full 3D model range images taken from several views using super-quadrics is shown in [Jaklič, 1997]. Super-quadric volumetric primitives can be deformed by bending, twisting, and tapering, and Boolean combinations of simple entities can be used to represent more complicated shapes [Terzopoulos and Metaxas, 1991].

Squareness	$\varepsilon_{\text{hori}}=0.1$	$\varepsilon_{\text{hori}}=1.0$	$\varepsilon_{\text{hori}}=1.9$
$\varepsilon_{\text{vert}}=0.1$			
$\varepsilon_{\text{vert}}=1.0$			
$\varepsilon_{\text{vert}}=1.9$			

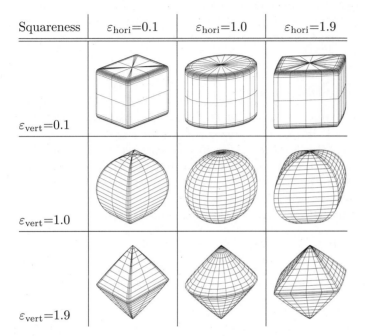

Figure 12.14: Super-ellipses. © *Cengage Learning 2015.*

Generalized cylinders

Generalized cylinders, or **generalized cones**, are often also called **sweep representations**. Recall that a cylinder may be defined as the surface swept out by a circle whose center is traveling along a straight line (spine) normal to the circle's plane. We can generalize this idea in a number of ways—we may permit any closed curve to be 'pulled along' any line in 3-space. We may even permit the closed curve to adjust as it travels in accordance with some function, so a cone is defined by a circle whose radius changes linearly with distance traveled, moving along a straight line. Further, the closed curve section need not contain the spine. Usually it is assumed that the curve is perpendicular to the spine curve at each point. In some cases this constraint is released. Figure 12.15 illustrates two simple generalized cylinders.

These generalized cones turn out to be very good at representing some classes of solid body [Binford, 1971; Soroka and Bajcsy, 1978]. The advantage of symmetrical

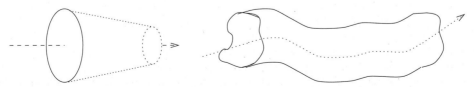

Figure 12.15: Solids represented as generalized cylinders. © *Cengage Learning 2015.*

volumetric primitives, such as generalized cylinders and super-quadrics, is their ability to capture common symmetries and represent certain shapes with few parameters. They are, however, ill-suited for modeling many natural objects that do not have the set of regularities incorporated into the primitives. An influential early vision system called ACRONYM [Brooks et al., 1979] used generalized cones as its modeling scheme.

There is a modification of the sweep representation called a **skeleton representation**, which stores only the spines of the objects [Besl and Jain, 1985].

12.2.5 Surface modeling strategies

A solid object can be represented by surfaces bounding it; such a description can vary from simple triangular patches to visually appealing structures such as non-uniform rational B-splines (NURBS) popular in geometric modeling. Computer vision solves two main problems with surfaces: First, reconstruction creates surface description from sparse depth measurements that are typically corrupted by outliers; second, segmentation aims to classify surface or surface patches into surface types.

Boundary representations (B-reps) can be viewed conceptually as a triple:

- A set of surfaces of the object.

- A set of space curves representing intersections between the surfaces.

- A graph describing the surface connectivity.

B-reps are an appealing and intuitively natural way of representing 3D bodies in that they consist of an explicit list of the bodies' faces. In the simplest case, 'faces' are taken to be planar, so bodies are always **polyhedral**, and we are dealing the whole time with piecewise planar surfaces. A useful side effect of this scheme is that properties such as surface area and solid volume are well defined. The simplest B-rep scheme would model everything with the simplest possible 2D polygon, the triangle. By taking small enough primitives quite satisfactory representations of complex objects can be achieved, and it is an obvious generalization to consider polygons with more edges than three.

Triangulation of irregular data points (e.g., a 3D point cloud obtained from a range scanner) is an example of an interpolation method. The best-known technique is called **Delaunay triangulation**, which can be defined in two, three, or more space dimensions. Delaunay triangulation is dual to the Voronoi diagram. We assume that the Euclidean distance between data points is known; then points that are closer to each other than to other points are connected. Let $d(P, Q)$ be the Euclidean distance between points P and Q, and S be the set of points $S=\{M_1, \ldots, M_n\}$. A Voronoi diagram on the set S is a set of convex polyhedra that covers the whole space. The polyhedron V_i consists of all points that are closer to the point M_i than to other points of S

$$V_i = \left\{ p; \ d(p, M_i) \leq d(p, M_j) \text{ for all } j = 1, 2, \ldots, n \right\}. \tag{12.22}$$

An algorithm to compute Delaunay triangulation can be found in [Preparata and Shamos, 1985]. A problem with Delaunay triangulation is that it triangulates the convex hull of the point set; constrained Delaunay triangulation [Faugeras, 1993] can be a solution.

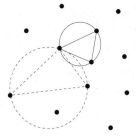

Figure 12.16: 2D Delaunay triangulation. The solid triangle belongs to the Delaunay triangulation but the dotted one does not, as its circumcircle contains an additional point. © *Cengage Learning 2015.*

We shall illustrate the idea of Delaunay triangulation on the simplest case of a 2D planar point set (see Figure 12.16). The task is to find triangles that cover all data points in such a way that the circumcircle of any one triangle contains only the three points that are vertices of that particular triangle. The triangulation has the following properties:

- The boundary of the set of points covered by triangles corresponds to the convex hull of the point set.

- The incremental algorithm constructing a triangulation of N points has expected time complexity $\mathcal{O}(N \log N)$ [Gubais et al., 1992].

- The 2D Delaunay triangulation algorithm provides a unique solution if no more than three points lie on one circle.

A drawback with polyhedral or triangulated B-reps is that the concept of 'face' may not be well defined. A face should have no 'dangling' edges, and the union of a body's faces should be its boundary. Unfortunately, the real world is not cooperative, and many (simple) bodies exist in which face boundaries are not well defined.

The next step in generalizing descriptions of surface patches is the **quadric surface model**. Quadric surfaces are defined using second-degree polynomials in three co-ordinates x, y, z. In implicit form, the equation has up to 10 coefficients and represents hyperboloids, ellipsoids, paraboloids, and cylinders

$$\sum_{i,j,k=0\ldots2} a_{ijk}\, x^i\, y^j\, z^k = 0\,. \tag{12.23}$$

More complicated objects may be created from quadric surface patches. **Parametric bi-cubic surfaces** defined by bivariate cubic polynomials are used in CAD systems; the commonly used Bézier surfaces fall into this category. These surfaces have the advantage that surface patches can be smoothly joined along the intersection curves, and undesirable curvature discontinuity artifacts are thus avoided. Such an approach permits much greater flexibility in the description, but it becomes important to restrict the number of possible face edges in order to limit the complexity of the computations involved.

12.2.6 Registering surface patches and their fusion to get a full 3D model

A **range image** represents distance measurements from an observer to an object; it yields a partial 3D description of the surface from one view only. It may be visualized as a fresco made by a sculptor—shape information from different views, e.g., from the other side of the object, is not available. Techniques for range image acquisition have been mentioned in Section 11.6.2.

Several range images are needed to capture the whole surface of an object. Each image yields a point cloud in the co-ordinates related to the range sensor, and successive images are taken in such a way that neighboring views overlap slightly, providing information for later fusion of partial range measurements into one global, object-centered, co-ordinate system.

A fusion of partial surface descriptions into global, object-centered co-ordinates implies known geometric transformations between the object and the sensor. The process depends on the data representing one view, e.g., from simple point clouds, triangulated surfaces, to parametric models as quadric patches.

Range image registration finds a rigid geometric transformation between two range images of the same object captured from two different viewpoints. The recovery can be based either on explicit knowledge of sensor positions, e.g., if it is held in a precise robot arm, or on geometric features measured from the overlapped parts of range data. Typically, both sources of information are used; an initial estimate of the appropriate geometric transformation can be provided by image feature correspondence, range image sensor data, an object manipulation device, or in many cases by a human operator.

This reconstruction task has been approached by several research groups, and many partial solutions have been proposed, e.g., [Hoppe et al., 1992; Higuchi et al., 1995; Uray, 1997]. We present here one of the possible approaches to the task. The method automates the construction of a 3D model of a 3D free-form object from a set of range images as follows.

1. The object is placed on a turntable and a **set of range images from different viewpoints is measured** by a structured-light (laser-plane) range finder.

2. A triangulated surface is constructed over the range images.

3. Large data sets are reduced by **decimation** of triangular meshes in each view.

4. Surfaces are registered into a common object-centered co-ordinate system and outliers in measurements are removed.

5. A full 3D model of the object is reconstructed by a surface fusion process.

Measurement from a laser-plane range finder provides a natural connectivity relation of points along stripes. Their parameterization allows easy construction of a 4-connected mesh following parametric curves just by connecting points found in the neighboring rows of the image and the points in neighboring scans with the same image row co-ordinate. The parameterization obtained of the measured surface is shown in Figure 12.17. The assumption of surface continuity is implemented as a restriction on the distance of neighboring points; only neighbors closer than a pre-defined ε are considered to lie on one surface next to each other. Points with no close neighbors are assumed to be outliers and are removed from data.

A 4-connected mesh cannot represent all objects; e.g., a sphere cannot be covered by a four-sided polygon. By splitting each polygon by an edge, a **triangulation** of the surface, which is able to represent any surface, is easily obtained. A polygon may be split two ways; it is preferable to choose the shortest edge because this results in triangles with larger inner angles.

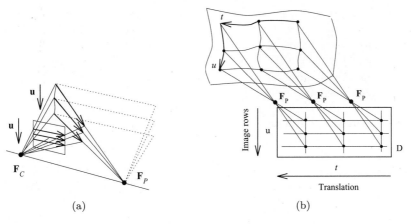

(a)   (b)

Figure 12.17: Surface parameterization is composed from the projected laser ray and translation. © *Cengage Learning 2015.*

Often, we wish to reduce the number of triangles representing the surface in areas where curvature is low [Soucy and Laurendeau, 1996]. Data reduction is particularly useful for the registration of neighboring views, since it has worst-case complexity $\mathcal{O}(N^2)$ in the number of points. We formulate the task as a search for the best approximation of a triangulated surface by another triangulated surface that is close to the vertices of the original mesh [Hoppe et al., 1992]. For instance, we might look for the closest triangulated surface with maximally n triangles, or we might want simultaneously to minimize n and a residual error to get a consensus between the precision and space costs using the minimum description length principle (MDL) [Rissanen, 1989]. The surface triangulation procedure and node decimation is demonstrated on the synthetic pattern in Figures 12.18 and 12.19. Decimation of a triangulated surface from a real range image is shown in Figure 12.20.

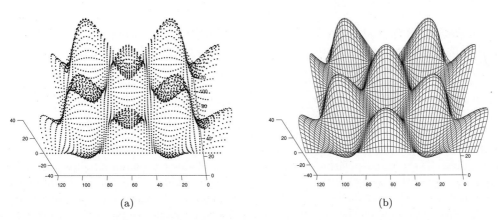

(a)   (b)

Figure 12.18: Surface construction and its decimation on a synthetic sinusoidal pattern. (a) Point cloud. (b) 4-connected mesh. *Courtesy of T. Pajdla, D. Večerka, Czech Technical University, Prague.*

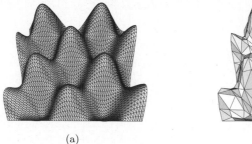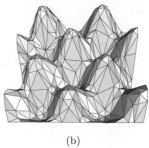

(a)   (b)

Figure 12.19: Surface construction and its decimation on a synthetic sinusoidal pattern. (a) Triangulated surface. (b) Surface after decimation of a number of triangles. *Courtesy of T. Pajdla, D. Večerka, Czech Technical University, Prague.*

Figure 12.20: Triangular mesh decimation for one rangeview of a real object—a small ceramic sculpture of an elephant. *Courtesy of T. Pajdla, P. Krsek, Czech Technical University, Prague.*

Integration of partial shape descriptions attempts to get known geometric transformations among the views in order to register them and express them in a common co-ordinate system. Precise alignment of the data can be done automatically by gradient minimization, provided good starting transformations are available. In some cases, matching based on invariant features detected on the visual surfaces can be used [Pajdla and Van Gool, 1995], but no method able to cope with a large variety of surfaces has yet been developed.

Figure 12.21 shows approximate manual surface registration, with the help of user interaction. The mutual position of two surfaces is defined by aligning three pairs of matching points; the user selects a few point pairs (the minimum is three) on the surfaces. The approximate registration is obtained by moving one of the surfaces so that the sum of squared distances between the matching point pairs is minimal. An interactive program, Geomview (authored by the Geometry Center, University of Minnesota), for 3D surface viewing and manipulation, was used to let the user do the registration. Figures 12.22–12.23 illustrate this procedure.

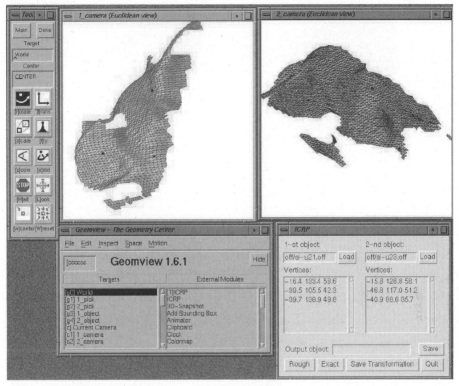

Figure 12.21: Manual registration of surfaces in Geomview. © *Cengage Learning 2015*.

When two partially overlapping surface patches are roughly registered, automatic refinement of the registration follows. It is assumed that two partially overlapping surfaces P and X related by a global transformation are available. In our case, all transformations are subgroups of a projective group in $\mathcal{P}^3$. Surface registration looks for the best Euclidean transformation T that overlays P and X. T is found by minimization of

$$e = \min_{T} \rho\big(P, T(X)\big) , \tag{12.24}$$

where ρ is a cost function evaluating the quality of match of two surfaces. In Euclidean geometry, it might be the distance between the points on a surface.

The **iterative closest point algorithm** (ICP) [Besl and McKay, 1992] solves the registration automatically provided a good initial estimate of T is available. The algorithm assumes that one of the surfaces is a subset of the second, meaning that only one surface can contain points without correspondence to the second surface. ICP is an iterative optimization procedure that looks for the geometric transformation of one surface to best match the second. It is likely that the cost function will be non-convex, and so there is a consequent danger of falling into local minima—thus a good initial estimate is needed.

We present here a modification of the ICP algorithm which is able to register partial corresponding surfaces. This approach uses the idea of reciprocal points [Pajdla and Van Gool, 1995] to eliminate points without correspondence. Assume point **p** is on the surface P and that y is the closest point on the surface X. The closest point on the

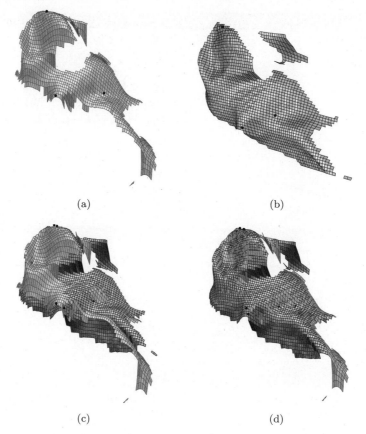

(a)   (b)

(c)   (d)

Figure 12.22: The process of registration. (a) Three points on the first surface. (b) Three points on the second surface. (c) Surfaces after rough registration. (d) After exact registration. *Courtesy of T. Pajdla, D. Večerka, Czech Technical University. A color version of this figure may be seen in the color inset—Plate 34.*

surface P to $\mathbf{y}$ is the point $\mathbf{r}$ (see Figure 12.24). Points $\mathbf{p}$, satisfying the condition that the distance is less then ϵ, are called ϵ-reciprocal—only these points are registered. Let P_ϵ denote the set of ϵ-reciprocal points on the surface P; then the iterative closest reciprocal point algorithm (ICRP) algorithm is as follows.

Algorithm 12.2: Iterative closest reciprocal points

1. Initialize $k = 0$ and $P_0 = P$.

2. Find closest points Y_k for P_k and X .

3. Find reciprocal points $P_{\epsilon 0}$ and $Y_{\epsilon k}$.

4. Compute the mean square distance d_k between $P_{\epsilon k}$ and $Y_{\epsilon k}$.

5. Compute the transformation T between $Y_{\epsilon k}$ and $P_{\epsilon 0}$ in the least-squares sense.

6. Apply the transformation T: $P_{k+1} = T(P_0)$.

7. Compute the mean square distance $d_{k'}$ between $P_{\epsilon k+1}$ and $Y_{\epsilon k}$.

8. Terminate if the difference $d_k - d_{k'}$ is below a preset threshold or if the maximal number of iterations is exceeded; otherwise go to step 2.

Figure 12.23: The process of registration: rendered result. *Courtesy of T. Pajdla, D. Večerka, Czech Technical University, Prague.*

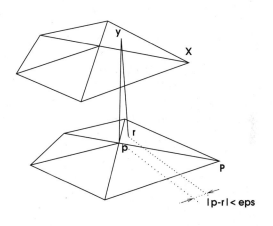

Figure 12.24: The notion of the closest point of the surface for introducing reciprocal points into the ICP algorithm. © Cengage Learning 2015.

When visual surfaces are properly registered, **surface integration** follows. All partial measurements will have been registered and can be expressed in one object-centered co-ordinate system, and constitute a global point. A problem is that the 3D object representation was created from overlapping surface patches corresponding to several views; these patches were integrated following one traversal around the object. All measurements are corrupted by some noise, and this noise is propagated from one surface patch to the other. The important issue is to have approximately the same error when joining the first and last patches. To ensure that the global error is minimal, registered surface points should be rearranged during the surface integration to maintain global consistency.

The next task is to create an analytic shape description of the object's surface by approximation, using some implicit or explicit formulae; commonly, this is not done for the whole object but just for parts of it. A multi-scale local noise model may be used [Šára and Bajcsy, 1998]: an uncertainty ellipsoid (called a fish scale) is used to integrate local information of the point cloud on the surface into a global shape description. The fish scales can be created at multiple resolutions, and their overlap and consistency is explored when creating a 3D shape model.

12.3   2D view-based representations of a 3D scene

12.3.1   Viewing space

Most 3D objects or scenes representations discussed hitherto have been **object-centered** —another option is to use **viewer-centered** representations, where the set of possible appearances of a 3D object is stored as a collection of 2D images. The trouble is that there is potentially an infinite number of possible viewpoints that induce an infinite number of object appearances. To cope with the huge number of viewpoints and appearances it is necessary to sample a viewpoint space and group together similar neighboring views. The original motivation was the recognition of polyhedral objects, which was later generalized to view-based recognition of curved objects [Ullman and Basri, 1991; Beymer and Poggio, 1996].

Consider two models of the viewing space as a representation of possible views on the object or scene. The general model of the viewing space considers all points in a 3D space in which the 3D object is located at the origin. This viewpoint representation is needed if perspective projection is used. A simplified model is a **viewing sphere** model that is often used in the orthographic projection case. Then the object is enclosed by a unit sphere; a point on the sphere's surface gives a viewing direction. The surface can be densely discretized into view patches.

To simplify working with a viewing sphere it is often approximated by a regular polyhedron, of which the most common choice [Horn, 1986] is an icosahedron (with 20 equilateral triangular faces). Twenty viewing directions defined by the centers of the triangles are often not enough, in which case the faces are further regularly divided into four triangles in a recursive manner. This yields 80, 320, 1280, . . . viewing directions.

12.3.2   Multi-view representations and aspect graphs

Other representation methods attempt to combine all the viewpoint-specific models into a single data structure. One of them is the **characteristic view technique** [Chakravarty and Freeman, 1982], in which all possible 2D projections of the convex polyhedral object are grouped into a finite number of topologically equivalent classes. Different views within an equivalence class are related via linear transformations. This general-purpose representation specifies the 3D structure of the object. A similar approach is based on **aspect** [Koenderink and v Doorn, 1979], which is defined as the topological structure of singularities in a single view of an object—aspect has useful invariance properties. Most small changes in vantage point will not affect aspect, and such vantage points (that is, most) are referred to as **stable**. Then the set of stable vantage points yielding a given aspect is contiguous in space, and the space surrounding an object may be partitioned into

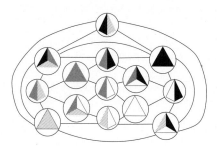

Figure 12.25: Aspect graph for the tetrahedron.
© *Cengage Learning 2015.*

subspaces from within which the same aspect is generated. An example of the aspect graph for the simplest regular polyhedron—a tetrahedron—is shown in Figure 12.25. Moving from one such subspace into another generates an **event**—a change in aspect; the event is said to connect the two aspects. It is now possible to construct an **aspect graph** with respect to this connectivity relationship in which nodes are aspects and edges are events. This aspect graph is sometimes referred to as the **visual potential** of the object, and paths through it represent orbits of an observer around the object.

12.4 3D reconstruction from an unorganized set of 2D views, and Structure from Motion

A collection of methods is presented in this section which extract the geometric structure of a scene from photographs and provide 3D coordinates of many points on surfaces constituting an (opaque) scene. The 'images to 3D-points' data pipeline provides a practical example of the underlying theory of 3D vision geometry introduced in Chapter 11.

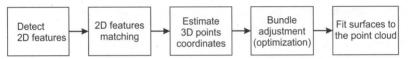

Figure 12.26: Structure from Motion pipeline. © *Cengage Learning 2015.*

Individual processing steps are arranged into a pipeline of methods/algorithms not requiring any human interaction. The input to the pipeline is an unorganized set of images which overlap in a sufficient number of image pairs, and the output is 3D information about object surfaces. The prerequisite is that there are enough views covering the scene to be reconstructed and that scene objects are sufficiently textured. Camera calibrations and viewer positions are estimated simultaneously with the 3D reconstruction—it is not required to know them in advance. The whole process is passive meaning that no extra energy is transmitted onto the scene. The Structure from Motion (SfM) pipeline is illustrated in Figure 12.26.

An example will illustrate: this uses the Hanau-Kesselstadt lion statue (worked by sculptor Christian Daniel Rauch (1777-1857) belonging to the baroque Palace Philippsruhe). The scene was covered by 57 color photos of resolution 2048×1536 pixels captured with an ordinary digital camera—the camera views are illustrated in Figure 12.27. The input images selection of the lion statue is shown in Figure 12.28. The cloud of 3D points in between the views illustrates the outcome of 3D reconstruction (explained in later paragraphs). Each view is represented by one pyramid; its vertex shows the center of projection of a particular camera and the pyramid base shows a particular image captured by this camera.

The (noncommercial) SfM WebService (http://ptak.felk.cvut.cz/sfmservice) was used for 3D reconstruction from 57 input images[1]. The processing follows the pipeline of Figure 12.26. Interest points and/or interest regions are detected in all input images using the Harris point detector (Section 5.3.10) and/or the Maximally Stable Extremal Regions

---

[1] The SfM WebService was developed by T. Pajdla and his team at the Czech Technical University in Prague. Registered users can submit sequences of images and use the service for 3D reconstruction

Figure 12.27: Visualization of locations from which the lion scene was photographed. *Courtesy of T. Pajdla, M. Jancosek, C. Albl, Czech Technical University in Prague.*

(MSER) detector (Section 5.3.11). Interest points or MSERs are described using SIFT (Section 10.2).

These descriptors are matched across images exploring the epipolar constraint. A robust RANSAC-based (Section 10.3) procedure is used for this purpose. An example of matches is shown in Figure 12.29.

A set of hundreds of thousands corresponding point pairs candidates serve as input to the algorithm, simultaneously reconstructing 3D points, estimating viewer location and estimating camera calibration parameters. Several different methods are at hand: standard ones [Mičušík and Pajdla, 2006], [Torii et al., 2009a], [Torii et al., 2009b], [Jancosek and Pajdla, 2011] as well as others based on minimal solvers approaching the issue from the algebraic geometry point of view [Kukelova et al., 2012], [Bujnak et al., 2012]. The outcome of 3D reconstruction is a dense 3D point cloud corresponding to detected interest points. Methods are capable of dealing with degenerate situations such as dominant planes, pure camera rotation (panoramas) and zooming. The bundle adjustment method (Section 11.4.4) is used to minimize the reprojection error in many views.

The outcome of the bundle adjustment is a refined cloud of 3D points, which are more consistent after all views are taken into account. The result for the lion statue is illustrated in Figure 12.30. Having the 3D point cloud, the last block of the pipeline

Figure 12.28: Fifteen of fifty seven input images of the lion statue. All fifty seven images are used for reconstruction. *Courtesy of T. Pajdla, M. Jancosek, C. Albl, Czech Technical University in Prague.*

Figure 12.29: Example of correspondences in a pair of images. *Courtesy of T. Pajdla, M. Jancosek, C. Albl, Czech Technical University in Prague.*

from Figure 12.26 comes into play. The 3D points have to be covered by a surface—this is usually done by triangulation covering 3D points by a triangular mesh as explained in Section 12.2.5. Figure 12.31 shows triangulated 3D points from Figure 12.30.

The triangular mesh for a different view on the lion statue is shown in Figure 12.32. The triangular mesh and the information about the color of each triangle in the scene was provided as input to a program permitting viewing of a 3D scene. In this particular case, the program was a VRML (Virtual Reality Modeling Language) viewer. The resulting textured triangular mesh from a view, which is similar to in Figure 12.32, is provided in

Figure 12.30: One view on the 3D point cloud. Each point is displayed in the color (here gray level) provided by input images. *Courtesy of T. Pajdla, M. Jancosek, C. Albl, Czech Technical University in Prague.*

Figure 12.31: The same view with a triangular mesh built on top of the point cloud from Figure 12.30. *Courtesy of T. Pajdla, M. Jancosek, C. Albl, Czech Technical University in Prague.*

Figure 12.32: Another view on the lion shown as triangular mesh. *Courtesy of T. Pajdla, M. Jancosek, C. Albl, Czech Technical University in Prague.*

Figure 12.33: The same view where the triangular mesh is colored (gray level here) by the appropriate color from input images. *Courtesy of T. Pajdla, M. Jancosek, C. Albl, Czech Technical University in Prague.*

Figure 12.33. The user of the viewer can, however, chose a different view and look at the scene from it.

This section has presented a specific system, but it may be noted that that commercial tools such as Street View from Google Inc., or Photosynth by Microsoft Labs and the University of Washington are based on methods explained in this section.

12.5 Reconstructing scene geometry

We have discussed 'formal' approaches to 3D reconstruction via matrices characteristic of the camera(s), and homographies: there exist in contrast a range of less formal techniques which—while lacking the precision we have exercised earlier—serve well in characterizing a scene in view. This is particularly useful in, for example, video sequences of urban scenes, where the objective is an understanding of qualitative behavior of traffic and pedestrians, rather than a precise interpretation of where an agent (some entity moving in the scene, perhaps a vehicle or a pedestrian) might be: to detect congestion or an unexpected event does not require information at the co-ordinate level. This sort of approach becomes more applicable with the prevalence of CCTV, and the widespread application of easily affordable webcams—an approximate knowledge of the groundplane permits an estimation of the speed (and velocity) of objects in motion. We might have discussed this topic in considering motion (Chapter 16), but it is equally well treated here.

A common thread in this approach is the identification of horizon 'vanishing points' and then to use established geometric techniques to obtain affine and metric rectification [Hartley and Zisserman, 2003]. Common scenes afford a wide range of opportunities to do this: examples include assuming constant piecewise linear movement [Bose and Grimson, 2003], parallel and orthogonal features of wheelbases [Zhang et al., 2008], assuming bounding boxes surround constant-height humans [Lv et al., 2006; Micusik and Pajdla, 2010], assuming constant road width in traffic scenes [Magee, 2004]. More elaborate approaches build on these approaches, for example by deploying information gain (entropy) arguments to maximize the power of interpretation [Breitenstein et al., 2008].

We will illustrate the idea with a recent application in which common assumptions cannot be exploited. Suppose we have a scene in which geometrical clues, and consistent motion, are unobservable—this is common in congestion where building features are not consistently visible, and individuals regularly occlude each other [Hales et al., 2013]. Street scenes or sports stadia are good examples, in which we would still seek knowledge of the ground geometry and analysis of movement in view.

Some definitions and plausible assumptions are:

- The ground is (effectively) planar. In fact, if it is piecewise planar, an elaboration of this approach would recapture each component.

- The plane is defined in the camera co-ordinate system by the equation $\mathbf{n} \cdot \mathbf{X} = d$ where d is the normal distance of the plane from the origin and $\mathbf{n}$ is the plane normal,

$$\mathbf{n} = \begin{pmatrix} a \\ b \\ c \end{pmatrix} = \begin{pmatrix} \sin\psi\sin\theta \\ \cos\psi\sin\theta \\ \cos\theta \end{pmatrix}$$

θ gives the angle of elevation and ψ the yaw.

- Assuming a perspective projection model of the camera (Figure 2.1), the back projection of an image point (x,y) onto the plane is then $\mathbf{X} = (X, Y, Z)$, where

$$\begin{aligned} X &= \alpha x Z \\ Y &= \alpha y Z \\ Z &= \frac{d}{\alpha a x + \alpha b y + c} \end{aligned} \qquad (12.25)$$

and α is the negative reciprocal of the camera focal length.

- We are only seeking to reconstruct up to scale, and can set $d = 1$. Further, it is reasonable to assume that the camera is positioned at a reasonable height above the scene.

- Individuals in the scene move at approximately constant speed. Different individuals may have different speeds, but we may expect them to be comparable.

- Individuals can be tracked over limited time periods—perhaps a small number of seconds—before they are lost by occlusion. These short image trajectories $(\mathbf{x}_1, \mathbf{x}_2, \ldots, \mathbf{x}_N)$ will be assumed to be linear segments of a 3D trajectory on the ground plane, sampled at regular time intervals.

The image segment $\mathbf{x}_{t-1}, \mathbf{x}_t$ then represents a distance L_t in 3D, where from equation (12.25)

$$L_t^2 = \alpha^2 \left(\frac{x_t}{\gamma_t} - \frac{x_{t-1}}{\gamma_{t-1}} \right)^2 + \alpha^2 \left(\frac{y_t}{\gamma_t} - \frac{y_{t-1}}{\gamma_{t-1}} \right)^2 + \left(\frac{1}{\gamma_t} - \frac{1}{\gamma_{t-1}} \right)^2 , \tag{12.26}$$

where

$$\gamma_t = \alpha x_t a + \alpha y_t b + c .$$

A particular trajectory T defines a set of such distances L^T: if our assumptions are correct, all elements of L^T are equal—thus the standard deviation of this set $\sigma(L^T)$ is of interest. Choices of α, θ, ψ that minimize this quantity may be regarded as a good match to the data. In fact, we wish to choose parameters to minimize this measure over all trajectories: since different objects may move at different speeds, we seek to minimize

$$E_1 = \sum_T \left(\frac{\sigma(L^T)}{\mu(L^T)} \right)^2 \tag{12.27}$$

—that is, normalizing the standard deviation by the mean length $\mu(L_T)$. Since we expect agents to move with comparable speed, we also seek to minimize the variance of means

$$E_2 = \sigma \left(\mu(L_T) \right) . \tag{12.28}$$

Recovery of the ground plane parameters thus becomes a minimization of $E_1 + \lambda E_2$ for some λ. It is not surprising that the problem space is complex, and common nonlinear minimization algorithms fall into poor solutions. On the other hand, a coarse-to-fine strategy of quantizing (α, θ, ψ) space generates much better solutions: the original reference has details [Hales et al., 2013].

In implementation, the popular KLT tracker (see Section 16.3.2) is used to deliver image trajectories: very short ones are discarded, and clusters of similar trajectories (perhaps coming from the same individual, or from agents moving collectively) are clustered. Empirically, it was discovered that setting the error-weight parameter to 1 delivered acceptable results. When benchmarked against well-known test-sets [CVPR, 2009], errors in θ and ψ rarely exceed 10° and are usually much less. Relative speeds deduced from solution parameters show greater plausibility than those recovered from other popular algorithms [Bose and Grimson, 2003]. Figure 12.34 illustrates one example.

This example shows how a sufficient quantity of vague information, with suitable reasoning, can deliver real-world information of value in the absence of formal calibration. Algorithms of this kind permit cheap consumer electronics to be deployed easily and to discover enough about what they are surveying to deliver useful 3D information. A very good and early grounding in this technique may be found in [Criminisi, 1999].

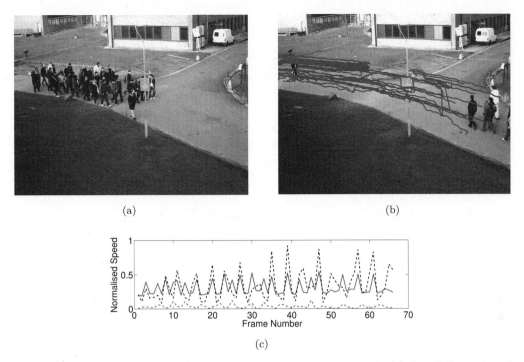

(a)

(b)

(c)

Figure 12.34: Use of scene geometry for people movement tracking. (a) A still from one of the PETS sequences [CVPR, 2009]. (b) From the same sequence—some KLT tracks overlaid. (c) Normalized speeds—ground truth in black and this algorithm in red (solid). For comparison, the green line is derived from [Bose and Grimson, 2003]. *Courtesy of I. Hales, University of Leeds. A color version of this figure may be seen in the color inset—Plate 35.*

12.6 Summary

- We have seen an overview of this topic: We have given a taxonomy of various 3D vision tasks, a summary of current approaches, formulated tasks, and shown some applications.

- **Shape from X**

  - Shape may be extracted from motion, optical flow, texture, focus/de-focus, vergence, and contour.

  - Each of these techniques may be used to derive a 2.5D sketch for Marr's vision theory; they are also of practical use on their own.

- **Full 3D objects**

  - Line labeling is an outmoded but accessible technique for reconstructing objects with planar faces.

  - Transitions to 3D objects need a co-ordinate system that is object centered.

  - 3D objects may be measured mechanically by computed tomography, by range-finders or by shape from motion techniques.

- Volumetric modeling strategies include constructive solid geometry, super-quadrics and generalized cylinders.

- Surface modeling strategies include boundary representations, triangulated surfaces, and quadric patches.

- **3D model-based vision**

  - To create a full 3D model from a set of range images, the surfaces must first be registered—rotations and translations should be found that match one surface to another.

  - Model-based vision uses a priori knowledge about an object to ease its recognition.

  - Techniques exist to locate curved objects from range images.

- **2D view-based representations of a 3D scene**

  - 2D view-based representations of 3D scenes may be achieved with multi-view representations.

  - It is possible to select a few stored reference images, and render any view from them.

  - Interpolation of views is not enough and view extrapolation is needed. This requires knowledge of geometry, and the view-based approach does not differ significantly from 3D geometry reconstruction.

  - It is possible to perform a 3D reconstruction from an unorganized set of 2D views. This approach has been used widely recently by, e.g., Google Street View.

- **Reconstructing scene geometry**

  - Large scale scene features such as plane parameters may be recaptured from properties of known objects such as straight lines and approximate size.

  - Well known geometric results identify vanishing points and ground orientation.

  - Similar approaches may well work even if large scale clues are unavailable.

12.7   Exercises

Short-answer questions

S12.1 For each of the following *shape from X* techniques, briefly describe the principle underlying it, explain how they can be of practical use, and give some examples.

- Motion
- Texture
- Focus
- Vergence
- Contour

S12.2 Give a counter-example in which apparent motion measured by an optical flow field does not correspond to actual motion of the 3D points. [Hint: Consider an opaque sphere, where (1) the sphere does not move and illumination changes; (2) the sphere rotates and the illumination is constant.]

S12.3 Fashion designers cheat the human ability to derive shape from texture. How do they do it?

S12.4 Give an example of a rim which is not a planar curve.

S12.5 Are there line drawings that do not correspond to physically plausible polyhedral objects? If yes, show an example.

S12.6 What was the contribution of image interpretation via line labeling to computer vision? Where else can it be used and why? (Hint: model-based 3D object recognition)

S12.7 Describe how to create a full 3D model of an object from range images taken from different views.

S12.8 Outline how a reconstruction of a 3D scene from unorganized set of 2D views may be acquired. What steps are needed?

Problems

P12.1 Conduct a laboratory experiment that establishes depth from focus. Take a fixed-focus lens with small depth of focus, and switch off the auto-focus feature of the lens if possible. Open the aperture as much as possible; mount the camera with the lens on a stand that can adjust the distance between the camera and the object.

Select a small window in the image that corresponds to a point in the scene from which the distance is measured. Devise an algorithm that assists in achieving the sharpest image. (Hint: The sharpest image has the most high frequencies; is there some method to find such an image that is simpler than the Fourier transform?)

Finally, the distance to the scene surface corresponding to the patch can be read from the mechanical scale on the stand.

P12.2 Most computer vision techniques measure co-ordinates of distinct points on a 3D object surface, e.g., those where correspondences were found; the result is a 3D point cloud. The human notion of shape is not of a point cloud. Elaborate on this problem, e.g., in the case of human face where 3D data are measured using stereopsis. How would you move from a point cloud to a surface? Is the surface the shape we seek? (Hint: Shape is treated from the geometer's point of view in [Koenderink, 1990]).

P12.3 Using a standard digital camera, take some shots of a 3D object of your choice and exercise the software at (http://ptak.felk.cvut.cz/sfmservice.

P12.4 Make yourself familiar with solved problems and **Matlab** implementations of selected algorithms provided in the corresponding chapter of the **Matlab Companion** to this text [Svoboda et al., 2008]. The **Matlab Companion** homepage http://visionbook.felk.cvut.cz offers images used in the problems, and well-commented **Matlab** code is provided for educational purposes.

P12.5 Use the **Matlab Companion** [Svoboda et al., 2008] to develop solutions to additional exercises and practical problems provided there. Implement your solutions using **Matlab** or other suitable programming languages.

12.8 References

Aloimonos J. and Swain M. J. Shape from texture. In *9th International Joint Conference on Artificial Intelligence,* Los Angeles, volume 2, pages 926–931, Los Altos, CA, 1985. Morgan Kaufmann Publishers.

Aloimonos Y., editor. *Active Perception.* Lawrence Erlbaum Associates, Hillsdale, NJ, 1993.

Bajcsy R. and Lieberman L. Texture gradient as a depth cue. *Computer Graphics and Image Processing,* 5:52–67, 1976.

Barr A. H. Superquadrics and angle-preserving transformations. *IEEE Computer Graphics and Applications,* 1(1):11–23, 1981.

Besl P. J. and Jain R. C. Three-dimensional object recognition. *ACM Computing Surveys,* 17 (1):75–145, 1985.

Besl P. J. and McKay N. D. A method for registration of 3-D shapes. *IEEE Transactions on Pattern Analysis and Machine Intelligence,* 14(2):239–256, 1992.

Beymer D. and Poggio T. Image representations for visual learning. *Science,* 272:1905–1909, 1996.

Binford T. O. Visual perception by computer. In *Proceedings of the IEEE Conference on Systems, Science and Cybernetics,* Miami, FL, 1971. IEEE.

Blake A. and Yuille A. *Active Vision.* MIT Press, Cambridge, MA, 1992.

Blostein D. and Ahuja N. Shape from texture: Integrating texture-element extraction and surface estimation. *IEEE Transactions on Pattern Analysis and Machine Intelligence,* 11: 1233–1251, 1989.

Bose B. and Grimson E. Ground plane rectification by tracking moving objects. In *IEEE International Workshop on Visual Surveillance and PETS,* 2003.

Bowyer K. W. Special issue on directions in CAD-based vision. *CVGIP – Image Understanding,* 55:107–218, 1992.

Breitenstein M. D., Sommerlade E., Leibe B., Gool L. J. V., and Reid I. Probabilistic parameter selection for learning scene structure from video. In Everingham M., Needham C. J., and Fraile R., editors, *Proceedings of the British Machine Vision Conference 2008, Leeds, September 2008,* pages 1–10. British Machine Vision Association, 2008.

Brooks R. A., Greiner R., and Binford T. O. The ACRONYM model-based vision system. In *Proceedings of the International Joint Conference on Artificial Intelligence, IJCAI-6,* Tokyo, Japan, pages 105–113, 1979.

Bujnak M., Kukelova Z., and Pajdla T. Efficient solutions to the absolute pose of cameras with unknown focal length and radial distortion by decomposition to planar and non-planar cases. *IPSJ Transactions on Computer Vision and Applications,* 4:78–86, May 2012. ISSN 1882-6695.

Chakravarty I. and Freeman H. Characteristic views as a basis for three-dimensional object recognition. *Proceedings of The Society for Photo-Optical Instrumentation Engineers Conference on Robot Vision,* 336:37–45, 1982.

Clocksin W. F. Perception of surface slant and edge labels from optical flow—a computational approach. *Perception,* 9:253–269, 1980.

Clowes M. B. On seeing things. *Artificial Intelligence,* 2(1):79–116, 1971.

Criminisi A. *Accurate Visual Metrology from Single and Multiple Uncalibrated Images.* Ph.D. thesis, University of Oxford, Dept. Engineering Science, 1999. D.Phil. thesis.

CVPR. PETS 2009 data set, 2009. http://www.cvg.rdg.ac.uk/PETS2009/a.html.

Faugeras O. D. *Three-Dimensional Computer Vision: A Geometric Viewpoint.* MIT Press, Cambridge, MA, 1993.

Flynn P. J. and Jain A. K. 3D object recognition using invariant feature indexing of interpretation tables. *CVGIP – Image Understanding*, 55(2):119–129, 1992.

Gubais L. J., Knuth D. E., and M S. Randomized incremental construction of Delunay and Voronoi diagrams. *Algorithmica*, 7:381–413, 1992.

Hales I., Hogg D., Ng K. C., and Boyle R. D. Automated ground-plane estimation for trajectory rectification. In *Proceedings of CAIP 2013, York UK*, volume II. Springer Verlag, LNCS 8048, 2013.

Hartley R. I. and Zisserman A. *Multiple view geometry in computer vision.* Cambridge University, Cambridge, 2nd edition, 2003.

Higuchi K., Hebert M., and Ikeuchi K. Building 3-D models from unregistered range images. *Graphics Models and Image Processing*, 57(4):313–333, 1995.

Hoppe H., DeRose T., Duchamp T., McDonald J., and Stuetzle W. Surface reconstruction from unorganized points. *Computer Graphics*, 26(2):71–78, 1992.

Horn B. K. P. *Robot Vision.* MIT Press, Cambridge, MA, 1986.

Huffman D. A. Impossible objects as nonsense sentences. In Metzler B. and Michie D. M., editors, *Machine Intelligence*, volume 6, pages 295–323. Edinburgh University Press, Edinburgh, 1971.

Jaklič A. *Construction of CAD models from Range Images.* Ph.D. thesis, Department of Computer and Information Science, University of Ljubljana, Ljubljana, Slovenia, 1997.

Jancosek M. and Pajdla T. Multi-view reconstruction preserving weakly-supported surfaces. In Felzenszwalb P., Forsyth D., and Fua P., editors, *CVPR 2011: Proceedings of the 2011 IEEE Computer Society Conference on Computer Vision and Pattern Recognition*, pages 3121–3128, New York, USA, June 2011. IEEE Computer Society, IEEE Computer Society. ISBN 978-1-4577-0393-5. doi: 10.1109/CVPR.2011.599569.

Kanatani K. and Chou T. C. Shape from texture: General principle. *Artificial Intelligence*, 38 (1):1–48, 1989.

Klir G. J. *Facets of System Science.* Plenum Press, New York, 1991.

Koenderink J. J. *Solid Shape.* MIT Press, Cambridge, MA, 1990.

Koenderink J. J. and Doorn A. J. v. Internal representation of solid shape with respect to vision. *Biological Cybernetics*, 32(4):211–216, 1979.

Kriegman D. J. Computing stable poses of piecewise smooth objects. *CVGIP – Image Understanding*, 55(2):109–118, 1992.

Krotkov E. P. Focusing. *International Journal of Computer Vision*, 1:223–237, 1987.

Krotkov E. P. and Bajcsy R. Active vision for reliable ranging: Cooperating focus, stereo, and vergence. *International Journal of Computer Vision*, 11(2):187–203, 1993.

Kukelova Z., Bujnak M., and Pajdla T. Polynomial eigenvalue solutions to minimal problems in computer vision. *IEEE Transactions on Pattern Analysis and Machine Intelligence*, 34 (7):1381–1393, July 2012. ISSN 0162-8828.

Leonardis A., Jaklič A., and Solina F. Superquadrics for segmenting and modeling range data. *IEEE Transactions on Pattern Analysis and Machine Intelligence*, 19(11):1289–1295, 1997.

Lv F., Zhao T., and Nevatia R. Camera calibration from video of a walking human. *IEEE Transactions on Pattern Analysis and Machine Intelligence*, 28(9), 2006.

Magee D. R. Tracking multiple vehicles using foreground, background and motion models. *Image and Vision Computing*, 22(2):143–155, 2004.

Malik J. and Maydan D. Recovering three-dimensional shape from a single image of curved object. *IEEE Transactions on Pattern Analysis and Machine Intelligence*, 11(6):555–566, 1989.

Marr D. *Vision—A Computational Investigation into the Human Representation and Processing of Visual Information*. Freeman, San Francisco, 1982.

Mičušík B. and Pajdla T. Structure from motion with wide circular field of view cameras. *IEEE Transactions on Pattern Analysis and Machine Intelligence*, 28(7):1135–1149, July 2006. ISSN 0162-8828.

Micusik B. and Pajdla T. Simultaneous surveillance camera calibration and foot-head homology estimation from human detections. In *Proceedings of the 2010 IEEE Conference on Computer Vision and Pattern Recognition*, pages 1562–1569, Los Alamitos, CA, USA, 2010. IEEE Computer Society.

Nayar S. K. and Nakagawa Y. Shape from focus. *IEEE Transactions on Pattern Analysis and Machine Intelligence*, 16(8):824–831, 1994.

Nayar S. K., Watanabe M., and Hoguchi M. Real-time focus range sensor. *IEEE Transactions on Pattern Analysis and Machine Intelligence*, 18(12):1186–1197, 1996.

Negahdaripour S. and Horn B. K. P. Determining 3D motion of planar objects from image brightness measurements. In *9th International Joint Conference on Artificial Intelligence*, Los Angeles, volume 2, pages 898–901, Los Altos, CA, 1985. Morgan Kaufmann Publishers.

Nevatia R., Zerroug M., and Ulupinar F. Recovery of three-dimensional shape of curved objects from a single image. In Young T. Y., editor, *Handbook of Pattern Recognition and Image Processing: Computer Vision*, pages 101–129, San Diego, CA, 1994. Academic Press.

Pajdla T. and Van Gool L. Matching of 3-D curves using semi-differential invariants. In *5th International Conference on Computer Vision*, Boston, USA, pages 390–395. IEEE Computer Society, 1995.

Pentland A. A new sense for depth of field. *IEEE Transactions on Pattern Analysis and Machine Intelligence*, 9(4):523–531, 1987.

Ponce J., Hoogs A., and Kriegman D. J. On using CAD models to compute the pose of curved 3d objects. *CVGIP – Image Understanding*, 55(2):184–197, 1992.

Preparata F. P. and Shamos M. I. *Computational Geometry—An Introduction*. Springer Verlag, Berlin, 1985.

Rissanen J. *Stochastic Complexity in Statistical Inquiry*. World Scientific, Series in Computer Science, IBM Almaden Research Center, San Jose, CA, 1989.

Roberts L. G. Machine perception of three-dimensional solids. In Tippett J. T., editor, *Optical and Electro-Optical Information Processing*, pages 159–197. MIT Press, Cambridge, MA, 1965.

Šára R. and Bajcsy R. Fish-scales: Representing fuzzy manifolds. In Chandran S. and Desai U., editors, *Proceedings of the 6th International Conference on Computer Vision (ICCV)*, pages 811–817, New Delhi, India, January 1998. IEEE Computer Society, Narosa Publishing House.

Sato K., Ikeuchi K., and Kanade T. Model based recognition of specular objects using sensor models. *CVGIP – Image Understanding*, 55(2):155–169, 1992.

Seales W. B. and Dyer C. R. Viewpoints from occluding contour. *CVGIP – Image Understanding*, 55(2):198–211, 1992.

Shomar W. J. and Young T. Y. Three-dimensional shape recovery from line drawings. In *Handbook of Pattern Recognition and Image Processing: Computer Vision*, volume 2, pages 53–100, San Diego, CA, 1994. Academic Press.

Solina F. and Bajcsy R. Recovery of parametric models from range images: The case for superquadrics with global deformations. *IEEE Transactions on Pattern Analysis and Machine Intelligence*, 12(2):131–147, 1990.

Soroka B. I. and Bajcsy R. K. A program for describing complex three dimensional objects using generalised cylinders. In *Proceedings of the Pattern Recognition and Image Processing Conference* Chicago, pages 331–339, New York, 1978. IEEE.

Soucy M. and Laurendeau D. Multiresolution surface modeling based on hierarchical triangulation. *Computer Vision and Image Understanding*, 63(1):1–14, 1996.

Stevens K. A. Representing and analyzing surface orientation. In Winston P. A. and Brown R. H., editors, *Artificial Intelligence: An MIT Persepctive*, volume 2. MIT Press, Cambridge, MA, 1979.

Sugihara K. *Machine Interpretation of Line Drawings*. MIT Press, Cambridge, MA, 1986.

Svoboda T., Kybic J., and Hlavac V. *Image Processing, Analysis, and Machine Vision: A MATLAB Companion*. Thomson Engineering, 2008.

Terzopoulos D. and Fleischer K. Deformable models. *The Visual Computer*, 4(6):306–331, 1988.

Terzopoulos D. and Metaxas D. Dynamic 3D models with local and global deformations: Deformable superquadrics. *IEEE Transactions on Pattern Analysis and Machine Intelligence*, 13(7):703–714, 1991.

Terzopoulos D., Witkin A., and Kass M. Constraints on deformable models: Recovering 3-D shape and nonrigid motion. *Artificial Intelligence*, 36:91–123, 1988.

Torii A., Havlena M., and Pajdla T. From google street view to 3d city models. In *OMNIVIS '09: 9th IEEE Workshop on Omnidirectional Vision, Camera Networks and Non-classical Cameras*, page 8, Los Alamitos, USA, Octorber 2009a. IEEE Computer Society Press. ISBN 978-1-4244-4441-0. CD-ROM.

Torii A., Havlena M., and Pajdla T. Omnidirectional image stabilization by computing camera trajectory. In Wada T., Huang F., and Lin S. Y., editors, *PSIVT '09: Advances in Image and Video Technology: Third Pacific Rim Symposium*, volume 5414 of *Lecture Notes in Computer Science*, pages 71–82, Berlin, Germany, January 2009b. Springer Verlag. ISBN 978-3-540-92956-7.

Ullman S. *The Interpretation of Visual Motion*. MIT Press, Cambridge, MA, 1979.

Ullman S. *High-Level Vision: Object Recognition and Visual Cognition*. MIT Press, Cambridge, MA, 1996.

Ullman S. and Basri R. Recognition by linear combination of models. *IEEE Transactions on Pattern Analysis and Machine Intelligence*, 13(10):992–1005, 1991.

Uray P. *From 3D point clouds to surface and volumes*. Ph.D. thesis, Technische Universitaet Graz, Austria, 1997.

Waltz D. L. Understanding line drawings of scenes with shadows. In Winston P. H., editor, *The Psychology of Computer Vision*, pages 19–91. McGraw-Hill, New York, 1975.

Witkin A. P. Recovering surface shape and orientation from texture. *Artificial Intelligence*, 17:17–45, 1981.

Zhang Z., Li M., Huang K., and Tan T. Robust automated ground plane rectification based on moving vehicles for traffic scene surveillance. In *Proceedings of the International Conference on Image Processing, ICIP 2008, October 12-15, 2008, San Diego, California, USA*, pages 1364–1367, 2008.

Chapter 13

Mathematical morphology

13.1 Basic morphological concepts

Mathematical morphology is a well-established area of image-analysis that stands separately from the mainstream. It is based on the algebra of non-linear operators operating on object shape and in many respects supersedes the linear algebraic system of convolution. It performs in many tasks—pre-processing, segmentation using object shape, and object quantification—better and more quickly than the standard approaches. There is a rich background literature: [Serra, 1982, 1987; Giardina and Dougherty, 1988; Dougherty, 1992; Heijmans, 1994].

Our approach is introductory [Haralick and Shapiro, 1992; Vincent, 1995; Soille, 2003]. Morphological tools are implemented in most image analysis packages, and we give the reader enough to apply them in a qualified way. Mathematical morphology is very often used in applications where shape of objects and speed is an issue—for example, analysis of microscopic images (in biology, material science, geology, and criminology), industrial inspection, optical character recognition, and document analysis.

The non-morphological approach to image processing is calculus-related, being based on the point-spread function concept and linear transformations such as convolution, and we have discussed image modeling and processing from this point of view in other chapters. Mathematical morphology uses tools of non-linear algebra and operates with point sets, their connectivity and shape. Morphological operations simplify images, and quantify and preserve the main shape characteristics of objects.

Morphological operations are used predominantly for the following purposes:

- Image pre-processing (noise filtering, shape simplification).

- Enhancing object structure (skeletonizing, thinning, thickening, convex hull,).

- Segmenting objects from the background.

- Quantitative description of objects (area, perimeter, projections,).

Mathematical morphology exploits point set properties, results of integral geometry, and topology. The initial assumption states that real images can be modeled using **point sets** of any dimension (e.g., N-dimensional Euclidean space); the Euclidean 2D space $\mathcal{E}^2$ and its system of subsets is a natural domain for planar shape description. Standard set algebra is used; **set difference** is defined by

$$X \setminus Y = X \cap Y^c. \tag{13.1}$$

Computer vision uses the digital counterpart of Euclidean space—sets of integer pairs ($\in \mathcal{Z}^2$) for binary image morphology or sets of integer triples ($\in \mathcal{Z}^3$) for gray-scale morphology or binary 3D morphology.

We begin by considering binary images that can be viewed as subsets of the 2D space of all integers, $\mathcal{Z}^2$. A point is represented by a pair of integers that give co-ordinates with respect to the two co-ordinate axes of the digital raster; the unit length of the raster equals the sampling period in each direction. We talk about a *discrete grid* if the neighborhood relation between points is well defined. This representation is suitable for both rectangular and hexagonal grids, but a rectangular grid is assumed hereafter.

A binary image can be treated as a 2D point set. Points belonging to objects in the image represent a set X—these points are pixels with value equal to one. Points of the complement set X^c correspond to the background with pixel values equal to zero. The origin (marked as a diagonal cross in our examples) has co-ordinates $(0,0)$, and co-ordinates of any point are interpreted as (x, y) in the common way used in mathematics. Figure 13.1 shows an example of such a set—points belonging to the object are denoted by small black squares. Any point x from a discrete image $X = \big\{ (1,0), (1,1), (1,2), (2,2), (0,3), (0,4) \big\}$ can be treated as a vector with respect to the origin $(0,0)$.

Figure 13.1: A point set example. © *Cengage Learning 2015.*

A **morphological transformation** Ψ is given by the relation of the image (point set X) with another small point set B called a **structuring element**. B is expressed with respect to a local origin $\mathcal{O}$ (called the representative point). Some typical structuring elements are shown in Figure 13.2. Figure 13.2c illustrates the possibility of the point $\mathcal{O}$ not being a member of the structuring element B.

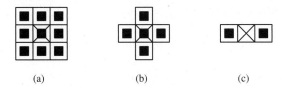

(a)   (b)   (c)

Figure 13.2: Typical structuring elements. © *Cengage Learning 2015.*

To apply the morphological transformation $\Psi(X)$ to the image X means that the structuring element B is moved systematically across the entire image. Assume that B is positioned at some point in the image; the pixel in the image corresponding to the representative point $\mathcal{O}$ of the structuring element is called the **current** pixel. The result of the relation (which can be either zero or one) between X and B in the current position is stored in the output image in the current image pixel position.

The **duality** of morphological operations is deduced from the existence of the set complement; for each morphological transformation $\Psi(X)$ there exists a dual transformation $\Psi^*(X)$:

$$\Psi(X) = \left(\Psi^*(X^c)\right)^c . \tag{13.2}$$

The **translation** of the point set X by the vector h is denoted by X_h; it is defined by

$$X_h = \left\{p \in \mathcal{E}^2 , \ p = x + h \text{ for some } x \in X\right\} . \tag{13.3}$$

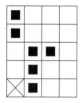   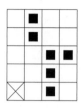

Figure 13.3: Translation by a vector.
© *Cengage Learning 2015.*

13.2 Four morphological principles

It is appropriate to restrict the set of possible morphological transformations in image analysis by imposing several constraints; we shall present here four morphological principles that express such constraints. A full understanding of these is not essential to a comprehension of what follows, and they may be taken for granted. A detailed explanation of these matters may be found in [Serra, 1982].

Humans have an intuitive understanding of *spatial structure*—the structure of the Alps versus an oak tree crown is perceived as different. Besides the need for objective descriptions of such objects, the scientist requires a quantitative description. Generalization is expected as well; the interest is not in a specific oak tree, but in the class of oaks.

The morphological approach with quantified results consists of two main steps: (a) geometrical transformation and (b) the actual measurement. [Serra, 1982] gives two examples. The first is from chemistry, where the task is to measure the surface area of some object. First, the initial body is reduced to its surface, e.g., by marking by some chemical matter. Second, the quantity of the marker needed to cover the surface is measured. Another example is from sieving analysis, often used in geology when the distribution of sizes of milled rocks is of interest. The milled product is passed through sieves with different sizes of holes from coarse to fine. The result is a sequence of subsets of milled product. For each sieve size some oversize particles remain on it after sieving, and these are measured.

A morphological operator is (by definition) composition of a mapping Ψ (or geometrical transformation) followed by a measure μ which is a mapping $Z \times \ldots \times Z \longrightarrow R$. The geometrically transformed set $\Psi(X)$ can be the boundary, oversized particles in sieving analysis, etc., and the measure $\mu[\Psi(X)]$ yields a number (weight, surface area, volume, etc.). The discussion here is simplified just to the transformation Ψ, but the axiomatics can be transposed to measures as well.

A morphological transformation is called **quantitative** if and only if it satisfies four basic principles [Serra, 1982].

- **Compatibility with translation**: Let the transformation Ψ depend on the position of the origin $\mathcal{O}$ of the co-ordinate system, and denote such a transformation by $\Psi_{\mathcal{O}}$. If all points are translated by the vector $-h$, it is expressed as Ψ_{-h}. The **compatibility with translation** principle is given by

$$\Psi_{\mathcal{O}}(X_h) = \big(\Psi_{-h}(X)\big)_h . \tag{13.4}$$

If Ψ does not depend on the position of the origin $\mathcal{O}$, then the compatibility with translation: principle reduces to invariance under translation

$$\Psi(X_h) = \big(\Psi(X)\big)_h . \tag{13.5}$$

- **Compatibility with change of scale**: Let λX represent the scaling of a point set X. This is equivalent to change of scale with respect to some origin. Let Ψ_{λ} denote a transformation that depends on the positive parameter λ (change of scale). **Compatibility with change of scale** is given by

$$\Psi_{\lambda}(X) = \lambda \, \Psi \left(\frac{1}{\lambda} X \right) . \tag{13.6}$$

If Ψ does not depend on the scale λ, then compatibility with change of scale reduces to invariance to change of scale

$$\Psi(\lambda X) = \lambda \, \Psi(X) . \tag{13.7}$$

- **Local knowledge**: The local knowledge principle considers the situation in which only a part of a larger structure can be examined—this is always the case in reality, due to the restricted size of the digital grid. The morphological transformation Ψ satisfies the **local knowledge principle** if for any bounded point set Z' in the transformation $\Psi(X)$ there exists a bounded set Z, knowledge of which is sufficient to provide Ψ. The local knowledge principle may be written symbolically as

$$\big(\Psi(X \cap Z)\big) \cap Z' = \Psi(X) \cap Z' . \tag{13.8}$$

- **Upper semi-continuity**: The upper semi-continuity principle says that the morphological transformation does not exhibit any abrupt changes. A precise explanation needs many concepts from topology and is given in [Serra, 1982].

13.3 Binary dilation and erosion

Sets of black and white pixels constitute a binary image. Assume that only black pixels are considered, and the others are treated as a background. The primary morphological operations are dilation and erosion, and from these two, more complex morphological operations such as opening, closing, and shape decomposition can be derived. We present them here using Minkowski's formalism [Haralick and Shapiro, 1992]. The Minkowski algebra is closer to the notions taught in standard mathematics courses (an alternative is Serra's formalism based on stereological concepts [Serra, 1982]).

13.3.1 Dilation

The morphological transformation **dilation** $\oplus$ combines two sets using vector addition (or Minkowski set addition, e.g., $(a, b) + (c, d) = (a + c, b + d)$). The dilation $X \oplus B$ is the point set of all possible vector additions of pairs of elements, one from each of the sets X and B

$$X \oplus B = \left\{ p \in \mathcal{E}^2 : p = x + b, \ x \in X \text{ and } b \in B \right\} . \tag{13.9}$$

Figure 13.4 illustrates an example of dilation:

$$X = \left\{ (1, 0), (1, 1), (1, 2), (2, 2), (0, 3), (0, 4) \right\} ,$$
$$B = \left\{ (0, 0), (1, 0) \right\} ,$$
$$X \oplus B = \left\{ (1, 0), (1, 1), (1, 2), (2, 2), (0, 3), (0, 4), (2, 0), (2, 1), (2, 2), (3, 2), (1, 3), (1, 4) \right\} .$$

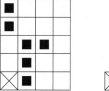

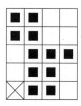

Figure 13.4: Dilation. © *Cengage Learning 2015.*

Figure 13.5 shows a 256×256 original image (the emblem of the Czech Technical University) on the left. A structuring element of size 3×3, see Figure 13.2a, is used. The result of dilation is shown on the right side of Figure 13.5. In this case the dilation is an *isotropic* expansion (it behaves the same way in all directions). This operation is also sometimes called *fill* or *grow*.

Figure 13.5: Dilation as isotropic expansion. © *Cengage Learning 2015.*

Dilation with an isotropic 3×3 structuring element might be described as a transformation which changes all background pixels neighboring the object to object pixels.

Dilation has several interesting properties that may ease its hardware or software implementation; we present some here without proof. The interested reader may consult [Serra, 1982] or the tutorial paper [Haralick et al., 1987].

The dilation operation is commutative

$$X \oplus B = B \oplus X \tag{13.10}$$

and is also associative

$$X \oplus (B \oplus D) = (X \oplus B) \oplus D . \tag{13.11}$$

Dilation may also be expressed as a union of shifted point sets

$$X \oplus B = \bigcup_{b \in B} X_b \tag{13.12}$$

and is invariant to translation

$$X_h \oplus B = (X \oplus B)_h . \tag{13.13}$$

Equations (13.12) and (13.13) show the importance of shifts in speeding up implementation of dilation, and this holds for implementations of binary morphology on serial computers in general. One processor word represents several pixels (e.g., 32 for a 32-bit processor), and shift or addition corresponds to a single instruction. Shifts may also be easily implemented as delays in a pipeline parallel processor.

Dilation is an **increasing** transformation:

$$\text{If } X \subseteq Y \text{ then } X \oplus B \subseteq Y \oplus B . \tag{13.14}$$

Dilation is used to fill small holes and narrow gulfs in objects. It increases the object size—if the original size needs to be preserved, then dilation is combined with erosion, described in the next section.

  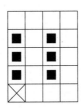

Figure 13.6: Dilation where the representative point is not a member of the structuring element. © *Cengage Learning 2015.*

Figure 13.6 illustrates the result of dilation if the representative point is not a member of the structuring element B; if this structuring element is used, the dilation result is substantially different from the input set. Notice that the connectivity of the original set has been lost.

13.3.2 Erosion

Erosion $\ominus$ combines two sets using vector subtraction of set elements and is the dual operator of dilation. Neither erosion nor dilation is an invertible transformation

$$X \ominus B = \left\{ p \in \mathcal{E}^2 : p + b \in X \text{ for every } b \in B \right\} . \tag{13.15}$$

This formula says that every point p from the image is tested; the result of the erosion is given by those points p for which all possible $p + b$ are in X. Figure 13.7 shows an example of the point set X eroded by the structuring element B:

$$X = \left\{ (1,0), (1,1), (1,2), (0,3), (1,3), (2,3), (3,3), (1,4) \right\} ,$$
$$B = \left\{ (0,0), (1,0) \right\} ,$$
$$X \ominus B = \left\{ (0,3), (1,3), (2,3) \right\} .$$

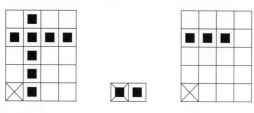

Figure 13.7: Erosion. © *Cengage Learning 2015.*

Figure 13.8: Erosion as isotropic shrink. © *Cengage Learning 2015.*

Figure 13.8 shows erosion by a 3×3 element (see Figure 13.2a) of the same original as Figure 13.5. Notice that single-pixel-wide lines disappear. Erosion with an isotropic structuring element is called **shrink** or **reduce** by some authors.

Basic morphological transformations can be used to find the contours of objects in an image very quickly. This can be achieved, for instance, by subtraction from the original picture of its eroded version—see Figure 13.9.

Figure 13.9: Contours obtained by subtraction of an eroded image from an original (left). © *Cengage Learning 2015.*

Erosion is used to simplify the structure of an object—objects or their parts with width equal to one will disappear. It might thus decompose complicated objects into several simpler ones.

There is an equivalent definition of erosion [Matheron, 1975]. Recall that B_p denotes B translated by p

$$X \ominus B = \left\{ p \in \mathcal{E}^2 : B_p \subseteq X \right\}. \tag{13.16}$$

The erosion might be interpreted by structuring element B sliding across the image X; then, if B translated by the vector p is contained in the image X, the point corresponding to the representative point of B belongs to the erosion $X \ominus B$.

An implementation of erosion might be simplified by noting that an image X eroded by the structuring element B can be expressed as an intersection of all translations of the image X by the vector[1] $-b \in B$

$$X \ominus B = \bigcap_{b \in B} X_{-b} \,. \tag{13.17}$$

If the representative point is a member of the structuring element, then erosion is an anti-extensive transformation; that is, if $(0,0) \in B$, then $X \ominus B \subseteq X$. Erosion is also translation invariant

$$X_h \ominus B = (X \ominus B)_h \,, \tag{13.18}$$
$$X \ominus B_h = (X \ominus B)_{-h} \,, \tag{13.19}$$

and, like dilation, is an increasing transformation:

$$\text{If } X \subseteq Y \text{ then } X \ominus B \subseteq Y \ominus B \,. \tag{13.20}$$

If B, D are structuring elements, and D is contained in B, then erosion by B is more aggressive than by D; that is, if $D \subseteq B$, then $X \ominus B \subseteq X \ominus D$. This property enables the ordering of erosions according to structuring elements of similar shape but different sizes.

Denote by $\check{B}$ the *symmetrical set* to B (also called the *transpose* [Serra, 1982] or *rational set* [Haralick et al., 1987]) with respect to the representative point $\mathcal{O}$

$$\check{B} = \{-b : b \in B\} \,. \tag{13.21}$$

For example

$$\begin{aligned} B &= \big\{(1,2),(2,3)\big\} \,, \\ \check{B} &= \big\{(-1,-2),(-2,-3)\big\} \,. \end{aligned} \tag{13.22}$$

We have already mentioned that erosion and dilation are dual transformations. Formally

$$(X \ominus Y)^C = X^C \oplus \check{Y} \,. \tag{13.23}$$

The differences between erosion and dilation are illustrated by the following properties. Erosion (in contrast to dilation) is not commutative

$$X \ominus B \neq B \ominus X \,. \tag{13.24}$$

The properties of erosion and intersection combined together are

$$\begin{aligned} (X \cap Y) \ominus B &= (X \ominus B) \cap (Y \ominus B) \,, \\ B \ominus (X \cap Y) &\supseteq (B \ominus X) \cup (B \ominus Y) \,. \end{aligned} \tag{13.25}$$

On the other hand, image intersection and dilation cannot be interchanged; the dilation of the intersection of two images is contained in the intersection of their dilations

$$(X \cap Y) \oplus B = B \oplus (X \cap Y) \subseteq (X \oplus B) \cap (Y \oplus B) \,. \tag{13.26}$$

---

[1]This definition of erosion, $\ominus$, differs from that used in [Serra, 1982]. There $\ominus$ denotes Minkowski subtraction, which is an intersection of all translations of the image by the vector $b \in B$. In our case the minus sign has been added. In our notation, if convex sets are used, the dilation of erosion (or the other way around) is identity.

The order of erosion may be interchanged with set union. This fact enables the structuring element to be decomposed into a union of simpler structuring elements

$$B \oplus (X \cup Y) = (X \cup Y) \oplus B = (X \oplus B) \cup (Y \oplus B) \,,$$

$$(X \cup Y) \ominus B \supseteq (X \ominus B) \cup (Y \ominus B) \,,$$
$$B \ominus (X \cup Y) = (X \ominus B) \cap (Y \ominus B) \,. \tag{13.27}$$

Successive dilation (respectively, erosion) of the image X first by the structuring element B and then by the structuring element D is equivalent to the dilation (erosion) of the image X by $B \oplus D$:

$$(X \oplus B) \oplus D = X \oplus (B \oplus D) \,,$$
$$(X \ominus B) \ominus D = X \ominus (B \oplus D) \,. \tag{13.28}$$

13.3.3   Hit-or-miss transformation

The hit-or-miss transformation is a morphological operator for finding local patterns of pixels, where *local* means the size of the structuring element. It is a variant of template matching that finds collections of pixels with certain shape properties (such as corners, or border points), and can also be used for thinning and thickening of objects (Section 13.5.3).

Operations described hitherto used a structuring element B, and we have tested points for their membership of X; we can also test whether some points do not belong to X. An operation may be denoted by a pair of disjoint sets $B = (B_1, B_2)$, called a **composite structuring element**. The **hit-or-miss** transformation $\otimes$ is defined as

$$X \otimes B = \left\{ x : \ B_1 \subset X \text{ and } B_2 \subset X^c \right\} \,. \tag{13.29}$$

This means that for a point x to be in the resulting set, two conditions must be fulfilled simultaneously. First the part B_1 of the composite structuring element that has its representative point at x must be contained in X, and second, the part B_2 of the composite structuring element must be contained in X^c.

The hit-or-miss transformation operates as a binary matching between an image X and the structuring element (B_1, B_2). It may be expressed using erosions and dilations as well

$$X \otimes B = (X \ominus B_1) \cap (X^c \ominus B_2) = (X \ominus B_1) \setminus (X \oplus \check{B}_2) \,. \tag{13.30}$$

13.3.4   Opening and closing

Erosion and dilation are not inverse transformations—if an image is eroded and then dilated, the original image is not re-obtained. Instead, the result is a simplified and less detailed version of the original image.

Erosion followed by dilation creates an important morphological transformation called **opening**. The opening of an image X by the structuring element B is denoted by $X \circ B$ and is defined as

$$X \circ B = (X \ominus B) \oplus B \,. \tag{13.31}$$

Dilation followed by erosion is called **closing**. The closing of an image X by the structuring element B is denoted by $X \bullet B$ and is defined as

$$X \bullet B = (X \oplus B) \ominus B \,. \tag{13.32}$$

If an image X is unchanged by opening with the structuring element B, it is called *open with respect to B*. Similarly, if an image X is unchanged by closing with B, it is called *closed with respect to B*.

Opening and closing with an isotropic structuring element is used to eliminate specific image details smaller than the structuring element—the global shape of the objects is not distorted. Closing connects objects that are close to each other, fills up small holes, and smooths the object outline by filling up narrow gulfs. Meanings of 'near', 'small', and 'narrow' are related to the size and the shape of the structuring element. Opening is illustrated in Figure 13.10, and closing in Figure 13.11.

Figure 13.10: Opening (original on the left). © *Cengage Learning 2015*.

Figure 13.11: Closing (original on the left). © *Cengage Learning 2015*.

Unlike dilation and erosion, opening and closing are invariant to translation of the structuring element. Equations (13.14) and (13.20) imply that both opening and closing are increasing transformations. Opening is anti-extensive ($X \circ B \subseteq X$) and closing is extensive ($X \subseteq X \bullet B$).

Opening and closing, like dilation and erosion, are dual transformations

$$(X \bullet B)^C = X^C \circ \breve{B} \,. \tag{13.33}$$

Iteratively used openings and closings are **idempotent**, meaning that reapplication of these transformations does not change the previous result. Formally:

$$X \circ B = (X \circ B) \circ B \,, \tag{13.34}$$

$$X \bullet B = (X \bullet B) \bullet B \,. \tag{13.35}$$

13.4   Gray-scale dilation and erosion

Binary morphological operations acting on binary images are easily extendible to gray-scale images using the 'min' and 'max' operations. Erosion (respectively, dilation) of an image is the operation of assigning to each pixel the minimum (maximum) value found over a neighborhood of the corresponding pixel in the input image. The structuring element is more rich than in the binary case, where it gave only the neighborhood. In the gray-scale case, the structuring element is a function of two variables that specifies the desired local gray-level property. The value of the structuring element is added (subtracted) when the maximum (or minimum) is calculated in the neighborhood.

This extension permits a *topographic view* of gray-scale images—the gray-level is interpreted as the height of a particular location of a hypothetical landscape: light and dark spots in the image correspond to landscape hills and hollows. This morphological approach permits the location of global image properties, i.e., to identify characteristic topographic features on images as valleys, mountain ridges (crests), and watersheds.

13.4.1   Top surface, umbra, and gray-scale dilation and erosion

Consider a point set A in n-dimensional Euclidean space, $A \subset \mathcal{E}^n$, and assume that the first $(n-1)$ co-ordinates of the set constitute a spatial domain and the nth co-ordinate corresponds to the value of a function or functions at a point ($n = 3$ for gray-scale images). This interpretation matches the topographic view for a 3D Euclidean space, where points are given by triples of co-ordinates; the first two co-ordinates locate the position in the 2D support set and the third co-ordinate gives the height.

The **top surface** of a set A is a function defined on the $(n-1)$-dimensional support. For each $(n-1)$-tuple, the top surface is the highest value of the last co-ordinate of A, as illustrated in Figure 13.12. If the space is Euclidean the highest value means supremum.

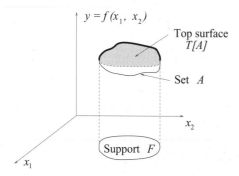

Figure 13.12: Top surface of the set A corresponds to maximal values of the function $f(x_1, x_2)$. © *Cengage Learning 2015.*

Let $A \subseteq \mathcal{E}^n$ and the support $F = \{x \in \mathcal{E}^{n-1}$ for some $y \in \mathcal{E}, (x,y) \in A\}$. The *top surface* of A, denoted by $T[A]$, is a mapping $F \to \mathcal{E}$ defined as

$$T[A](x) = \max \{y, \ (x,y) \in A\} . \tag{13.36}$$

An **umbra** is a region of complete shadow resulting from obstructing light by a non-transparent object. In mathematical morphology, the umbra of a function f is a set that consists of the top surface of f and everything below it; see Figure 13.13.

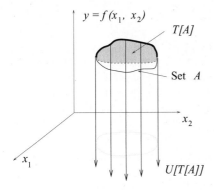

Figure 13.13: Umbra of the top surface of a set is the whole subspace below it. © *Cengage Learning 2015.*

Formally, let $F \subseteq \mathcal{E}^{n-1}$ and $f : F \to \mathcal{E}$. The *umbra* of f, denoted by $U[f]$, $U[f] \subseteq F \times \mathcal{E}$, is defined by

$$U[f] = \left\{ (x, y) \in F \times \mathcal{E}, \ y \leq f(x) \right\} . \tag{13.37}$$

We see that the umbra of an umbra of f is an umbra.

We can illustrate the top surface and umbra in the case of a simple 1D gray-scale image. Figure 13.14 illustrates a function f (which might be a top surface) and its umbra.

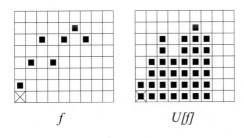

$$f \qquad\qquad U[f]$$

Figure 13.14: Example of a 1D function (left) and its umbra (right). © *Cengage Learning 2015.*

We can now define the gray-scale dilation of two functions as the top surface of the dilation of their umbras. Let $F, K \subseteq \mathcal{E}^{n-1}$ and $f : F \to \mathcal{E}$ and $k : K \to \mathcal{E}$. The *dilation* $\oplus$ of f by k, $f \oplus k : F \oplus K \to \mathcal{E}$ is defined by

$$f \oplus k = T\left\{ U[f] \oplus U[k] \right\} . \tag{13.38}$$

Notice here that $\oplus$ on the left-hand side is dilation in the *gray-scale* image domain, and $\oplus$ on the right-hand side is dilation in the *binary* image.

Similarly to binary dilation, one function, say f, represents an image, and the second, k, a small structuring element. Figure 13.15 shows a discretized function k that will play the role of the structuring element. Figure 13.16 shows the dilation of the umbra of f (from the example given in Figure 13.14) by the umbra of k.

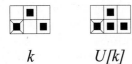

$$k \qquad\qquad U[k]$$

Figure 13.15: A structuring element: 1D function (left) and its umbra (right). © *Cengage Learning 2015.*

This definition explains what gray-scale dilation means, but does not give a reasonable algorithm for actual computations. We shall see that a computationally plausible

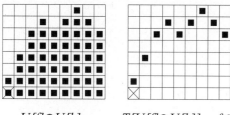

Figure 13.16: 1D example of gray-scale dilation. The umbras of the 1D function f and structuring element k are dilated first, $U[f] \oplus U[k]$. The top surface of this dilated set gives the result, $f \oplus k = T\big[U[f] \oplus U[k]\big]$. © *Cengage Learning 2015.*

way to calculate dilation can be obtained by taking the maximum of a set of sums:

$$(f \oplus k)(x) = \max\big\{f(x-z) + k(z),\ z \in K,\ x - z \in F\big\}. \tag{13.39}$$

The computational complexity is the same as for convolution in linear filtering, where a summation of products is performed.

The definition of **gray-scale erosion** is analogous to dilation. The gray-scale erosion of two functions (point sets):

1. Takes their umbras.

2. Erodes them using binary erosion.

3. Gives the result as the top surface.

Let $F, K \subseteq \mathcal{E}^{n-1}$ and $f : F \to \mathcal{E}$ and $k : K \to \mathcal{E}$. The *erosion* $\ominus$ of f by k, $f \ominus k : F \ominus K \to \mathcal{E}$ is defined by

$$f \ominus k = T\big\{U[f] \ominus U[k]\big\}. \tag{13.40}$$

Erosion is illustrated in Figure 13.17. To decrease computational complexity, the actual computations are performed in another way as the minimum of a set of differences (notice the similarity to correlation):

$$(f \ominus k)(x) = \min_{z \in K}\big\{f(x+z) - k(z)\big\}. \tag{13.41}$$

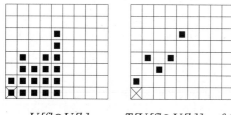

Figure 13.17: 1D example of gray-scale erosion. The umbras of 1D function f and structuring element k are eroded first, $U[f] \ominus U[k]$. The top surface of this eroded set gives the result, $f \ominus k = T\big[U[f] \ominus U[k]\big]$. © *Cengage Learning 2015.*

We illustrate morphological pre-processing on a microscopic image of cells corrupted by noise in Figure 13.18a; the aim is to reduce noise and locate individual cells. Figure 13.18b shows erosion of the original image, and Figure 13.18c illustrates dilation of the original image. A 3×3 structuring element was used in both cases—notice that the noise has been considerably reduced. The individual cells can be located by the reconstruction operation (to be explained in Section 13.5.4). The original image is used as a mask and the dilated image in Figure 13.18c is an input for reconstruction. The result is shown in image 13.18d, in which the black spots depict the cells.

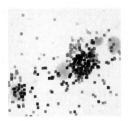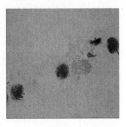

Figure 13.18: Morphological pre-processing: (a) cells in a microscopic image corrupted by noise; (b) erosion of original image, the noise is more prominent; (c) dilation of original image, the noise has disappeared; (d) reconstructed cells. *Courtesy of P. Kodl, Rockwell Automation Research Center, Prague.*

13.4.2 Umbra homeomorphism theorem, properties of erosion and dilation, opening and closing

The top surface always inverts the umbra operation; i.e., the top surface is a left inverse of the umbra, $T[U[f]] = f$. However, the umbra is not an inverse of the top surface. The strongest conclusion that can be deduced is that the umbra of the top surface of a point set A contains A (recall Figure 13.13).

The notion of top surface and umbra provides an intuitive relation between gray-scale and binary morphology. The **umbra homeomorphism theorem** states that the umbra operation is a homeomorphism from gray-scale morphology to binary morphology. Let $F, K \subseteq \mathcal{E}^{n-1}$, $f : F \to \mathcal{E}$, and $k : K \to \mathcal{E}$. Then [Haralick and Shapiro, 1992]:

$$
\begin{aligned}
\text{(a)} \quad & U[f \oplus k] = U[f] \oplus U[k]\,, \\
\text{(b)} \quad & U[f \ominus k] = U[f] \ominus U[k]\,.
\end{aligned}
\qquad (13.42)
$$

The umbra homeomorphism is used for deriving properties of gray-scale operations. The operation is expressed in terms of umbra and top surface, then transformed to binary sets using the umbra homeomorphism property, and finally transformed back using the definitions of gray-scale dilation and erosion. Using this idea, properties already known from binary morphology can be derived, e.g., commutativity of dilation, the chain rule that permits decomposition of large structural elements into successive operations with smaller ones, duality between erosion and dilation.

Gray-scale opening and closing is defined in the same way as in the binary morphology. **Gray-scale opening** is defined as $f \circ k = (f \ominus k) \oplus k$. Similarly, **gray-scale closing** $f \bullet k = (f \oplus k) \ominus k$. The *duality* between opening and closing is expressed as (recall that $\check{k}$ means the transpose, i.e., symmetric set with regards to origin of co-ordinates)

$$
-(f \circ k)(x) = \big((-f) \bullet \check{k}\big)(x)\,.
\qquad (13.43)
$$

There is a simple geometric interpretation of gray-scale opening [Haralick and Shapiro, 1992]. The opening of f by structuring element k can be interpreted as sliding k on the landscape f. The position of all highest points reached by some part of k during the slide gives the opening, and a similar interpretation exists for erosion.

Gray-scale opening and closing is often used in applications to extract parts of a gray-scale image with given shape and gray-scale structure.

13.4.3   Top hat transformation

The top hat transformation is used as a simple tool for segmenting objects in gray-scale images that differ in brightness from background, even when the background is of uneven gray-scale. The top hat transform is superseded by the watershed segmentation (to be described in Section 13.7.3) for more complicated backgrounds.

Assume a gray-level image X and a structuring element K. The residue of opening as compared to the original image $X \setminus (X \circ K)$ constitutes an operation called a *top hat transformation* [Meyer, 1978].

The top hat transformation is a good tool for extracting light objects (or, conversely, dark ones) on a dark (or light) but slowly changing background. Those parts of the image that cannot fit into structuring element K are removed by opening. Subtracting the opened image from the original provides an image where removed objects stand out clearly. The actual segmentation can be performed by simple thresholding. The concept is illustrated for the 1D case in Figure 13.19, where we can see the origin of the transformation name. If an image were a hat, the transformation would extract only the top of it, provided that the structuring element is larger than the hole in the hat.

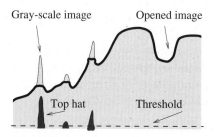

Figure **13.19**: The top hat transform permits the extraction of light objects from an uneven background. © *Cengage Learning 2015.*

Figure 13.20 provides an example from visual industrial inspection. A factory producing glass capillaries for mercury maximal thermometers had the following problem: The thin glass tube should be narrowed in one particular place to prevent mercury falling back when the temperature decreases from the maximal value. This is done by using

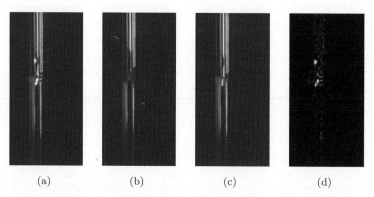

(a)   (b)   (c)   (d)

Figure **13.20**: An industrial example of gray-scale opening and top hat segmentation, i.e., image-based control of glass tube narrowing by gas flame. (a) Original image of the glass tube, 512×256 pixels. (b) Erosion by a one-pixel-wide vertical structuring element 20 pixels long. (c) Opening with the same element. (d) Final specular reflection segmentation by the top hat transformation. *Courtesy of V. Smutný, R. Šára, CTU Prague, P. Kodl, Rockwell Automation Research Center, Prague.*

a narrow gas flame and low pressure in the capillary. The capillary is illuminated by a collimated light beam—when the capillary wall collapses due to heat and low pressure, an instant specular reflection is observed and serves as a trigger to cover the gas flame. Originally the machine was controlled by a human operator who looked at the tube image projected optically on the screen; the gas flame was covered when the specular reflection was observed. This task had to be automated and the trigger signal learned from a digitized image. The specular reflection is detected by a morphological procedure.

13.5 Skeletons and object marking

13.5.1 Homotopic transformations

Topological properties are associated with continuity (Section 2.3.1), and mathematical morphology can be used to study such properties of objects in images. There is an interesting group among morphological transformations called **homotopic transformations** [Serra, 1982].

A transformation is homotopic if it does not change the continuity relation between regions and holes in the image. This relation is expressed by the homotopic tree; its root corresponds to the background of the image, first-level branches correspond to the objects (regions), second-level branches match holes within objects, etc. Figure 13.21

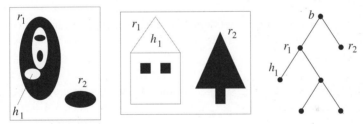

Figure 13.21: The same homotopic tree for two different images. © *Cengage Learning 2015*.

shows an example of two images having the same homotopic tree. On the left side are some biological cells and at center a house and a spruce tree. The tree's root b corresponds to the background, node r_1 matches the larger cell (the outline of the house), and node r_2 matches the smaller cell (the spruce tree). Node h_1 corresponds to the empty hole in the cell r_1 (the hole inside the roof of the house)—the other correspondences to nodes should now be clear. A transformation is homotopic if it does not change the homotopic tree.

13.5.2 Skeleton, medial axis, maximal ball

It is sometimes advantageous to convert an object to an archetypal stick figure called a **skeleton** (also considered in Section 8.3.4). We shall explain this in the context of 2D Euclidean space first, which is more illustrative than on the digital grid that we shall consider later.

The skeleton was introduced under the name **medial axis transform** [Blum, 1967] and illustrated on a 'grassfire' scenario: Assume a region (point set) $X \subset \mathcal{R}^2$: a grassfire is lit on the entire region boundary at the same instant, and propagates towards the region interior with constant speed. The skeleton $S(X)$ is the set of points where two or more firefronts meet; see Figure 13.22.

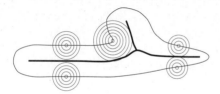

Figure 13.22: Skeleton as points where two or more firefronts of grassfire meet. © *Cengage Learning 2015.*

A more formal definition of skeleton is based on the concept of maximal ball. A **ball** $B(p, r)$ with center p and radius r, $r \geq 0$, is the set of points with distances d from the center less than or equal to r. The ball B included in a set X is said to be *maximal* if and only if there is no larger ball included in X that contains B, i.e., each ball B', $B \subseteq B' \subseteq X \implies B' = B$. Balls and maximal balls are illustrated in Figure 13.23.

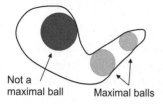

Not a
maximal ball   Maximal balls

Figure 13.23: Ball and two maximal balls in a Euclidean plane. © *Cengage Learning 2015.*

The distance metric d that is used depends on the grid and definition of connectivity. Unit balls in a plane (i.e., unit disks) are shown in Figure 13.24.

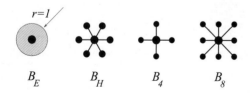

$r{=}1$

B_E B_H B_4 B_8

Figure 13.24: Unit-size disk for different distances, from left side: Euclidean distance, 6-, 4-, and 8-connectivity, respectively. © *Cengage Learning 2015.*

The plane $\mathcal{R}^2$ with the usual Euclidean distance gives the ball B_E. Three distances and balls are often defined in the discrete plane $\mathcal{Z}^2$. If a hexagonal grid and 6-connectivity is used, the hexagonal ball B_H is obtained. If the support is a square grid, two unit balls are possible: B_4 for 4-connectivity and B_8 for 8-connectivity.

The *skeleton by maximal balls* $S(X)$ of a set $X \subset \mathcal{Z}^2$ is the set of centers p of maximal balls

$$S(X) = \left\{ p \in X : \exists r \geq 0, \ B(p, r) \text{ is a maximal ball of } X \right\}.$$

This definition of skeleton has an intuitive meaning in the Euclidean plane. The skeleton of a disk reduces to its center, the skeleton of a stripe with rounded endings is a unit thickness line at its center, etc.

Figure 13.25 shows several objects together with their skeletons—a rectangle, two touching balls, and a ring. The properties of the (Euclidean) skeleton can be seen here—in particular, the skeleton of two adjacent circles consists of three distinct points instead of a straight line joining these two points, as might be intuitively expected.

The skeleton by maximal balls has two unfortunate properties in practical applications. First, it does not necessarily preserve the homotopy (connectivity) of the original

Figure 13.25: Skeletons of rectangle, two touching balls, and a ring. © *Cengage Learning 2015.*

set; and second, some of the skeleton lines may be wider than one pixel in the discrete plane. We shall see later that the skeleton is often substituted by sequential homotopic thinning that does not have these two properties.

Dilation can be used in any of the three discrete connectivities to create balls of varying radii. Let nB be the ball of radius n

$$n\,B = B \oplus B \oplus \ldots \oplus B\,. \tag{13.44}$$

The skeleton by maximal balls can be obtained as the union of the residues of opening of the set X at all scales [Serra, 1982]

$$S(X) = \bigcup_{n=0}^{\infty} \Big((X \ominus nB) \setminus (X \ominus nB) \circ B \Big)\,. \tag{13.45}$$

The trouble with this is that the resulting skeleton is completely disconnected and this property is not useful in many applications. Thus *homotopic skeletons* that preserve connectivity are often preferred (Section 13.5.3).

13.5.3 Thinning, thickening, and homotopic skeleton

One application of the hit-or-miss transformation (Section 13.3.3) is **thinning** and **thickening** of point sets. For an image X and a composite structuring element $B = (B_1, B_2)$ (notice that B here is not a ball), *thinning* is defined as

$$X \oslash B = X \setminus (X \otimes B) \tag{13.46}$$

and *thickening* is defined as

$$X \odot B = X \cup (X^c \otimes B)\,. \tag{13.47}$$

When thinning, a part of the boundary of the object is subtracted from it by the set difference operation. When thickening, a part of the boundary of the background is added to the object. Thinning and thickening are dual transformations

$$(X \odot B)^c = X^c \oslash B\,, \qquad B = (B_2, B_1)\,. \tag{13.48}$$

Thinning and thickening transformations are very often used sequentially. Let $\{B_{(1)}, B_{(2)}, B_{(3)}, \ldots, B_{(n)}\}$ denote a sequence of composite structuring elements $B_{(i)} = (B_{i_1}, B_{i_2})$. *Sequential thinning* can then be expressed as a sequence of n structuring elements for square rasters

$$X \oslash \{B_{(i)}\} = \Big(((X \oslash B_{(1)}) \oslash B_{(2)}) \ldots \oslash B_{(n)} \Big) \tag{13.49}$$

and *sequential thickening* as

$$X \odot \{B_{(i)}\} = \left(\left((X \odot B_{(1)}) \odot B_{(2)} \right) \dots \odot B_{(n)} \right). \tag{13.50}$$

There are several sequences of structuring elements $\{B_{(i)}\}$ that are useful in practice. Many of them are given by a permissible rotation of a structuring element in the appropriate digital raster (e.g., hexagonal, square, or octagonal). These sequences, sometimes called the **Golay alphabet** [Golay, 1969], are summarized for the hexagonal raster in [Serra, 1982]. We shall present 3×3 matrices for the first two rotations of the Golay alphabet for octagonal rasters, from which the other rotations can easily be derived.

A composite structuring element can be expressed by a single matrix only. A value of one in it means that this element belongs to B_1 (it is a subset of objects in the hit-or-miss transformation), and a value zero belongs to B_2 and is a subset of the background. An asterisk $*$ in the matrix denotes an element that is not used in the matching process, so its value is not significant.

Thinning and thickening sequential transformations converge to some image—the number of iterations needed depends on the objects in the image and the structuring element used. If two successive images in the sequence are identical, the thinning (or thickening) is stopped.

Sequential thinning by structuring element L

This thinning is quite important, as it serves as the homotopic substitute of the skeleton; the final image consists only of lines of width one and isolated points.

Figure 13.26: Sequential thinning using element L after five iterations. © *Cengage Learning 2015.*

Figure 13.27: Homotopic substitute of the skeleton (element L). © *Cengage Learning 2015.*

The structuring element L from the Golay alphabet is given by

$$L_1 = \begin{bmatrix} 0 & 0 & 0 \\ * & 1 & * \\ 1 & 1 & 1 \end{bmatrix}, \quad L_2 = \begin{bmatrix} * & 0 & 0 \\ 1 & 1 & 0 \\ * & 1 & * \end{bmatrix}, \quad \dots \tag{13.51}$$

(The other six elements are given by rotation.) Figure 13.26 shows the result of five iterations of thinning with L, and Figure 13.27 shows the homotopic substitute of the skeleton when idempotency was reached (in both cases, the original is shown on the left).

Sequential thinning by structuring element E

Assume that the homotopic substitute of the skeleton by element L has been found. The skeleton is usually jagged, because of sharp points on the outline of the object, but it is possible to 'smooth' it by sequential thinning by structuring element E. Using n iterations, several points (whose number depends on n) are removed from the ends of lines of width one (and isolated points as well). If thinning by element E is performed until the image does not change, then only closed contours remain.

Figure 13.28: Five iterations of sequential thinning by element E. © *Cengage Learning 2015.*

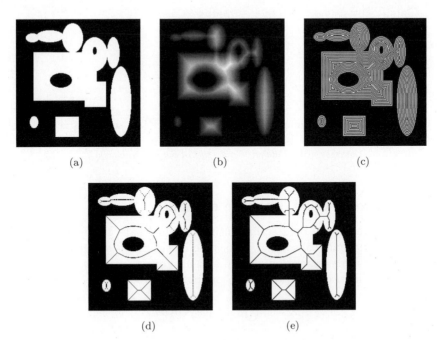

Figure 13.29: Performance of Vincent's quick skeleton by maximal balls algorithm. (a) Original binary image. (b) Distance function (to be explained later). (c) Distance function visualized by contouring. (d) Non-continuous skeleton by maximal balls. (e) Final skeleton. © *Cengage Learning 2015.*

The structuring element E from the Golay alphabet is given again by rotated masks,

$$E_1 = \begin{bmatrix} * & 1 & * \\ 0 & 1 & 0 \\ 0 & 0 & 0 \end{bmatrix} \,, \quad E_2 = \begin{bmatrix} 0 & * & * \\ 0 & 1 & 0 \\ 0 & 0 & 0 \end{bmatrix} \,, \quad \ldots \tag{13.52}$$

Figure 13.28 shows sequential thinning (five iterations) by the element E of the skeleton from Figure 13.27. Notice that lines have been shortened from their free ends.

There are three other elements M, D, C in the Golay alphabet [Golay, 1969] which are not much used in practice. Other morphological algorithms are used instead to find skeletons, convex hulls, and homotopic markers.

The computationally most efficient algorithm of which we are aware creates the connected skeleton as the minimal superset of the skeleton by maximal balls [Vincent, 1991]. Its performance is shown in Figure 13.29: homotopy is preserved.

The skeleton can be applied to native 3D images as well, e.g., in the analysis of computer tomography images. Figure 13.30 illustrates examples of thinning of 3D point sets; parallel algorithms are available [Ma and Sonka, 1996; Palagyi et al., 2006].

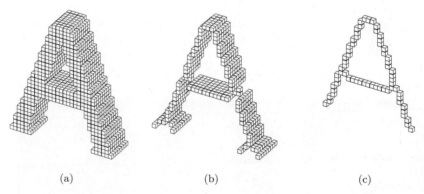

(a)   (b)   (c)

Figure 13.30: Morphological thinning in 3D. (a) Original 3D data set, a character A. (b) Thinning performed in one direction. (c) One voxel thick skeleton obtained by thinning image (b) in second direction. *Courtesy of K. Palagyi, University of Szeged, Hungary.*

13.5.4 Quench function, ultimate erosion

The binary point set X can be described using maximal balls B. Every point p of the skeleton $S(X)$ by maximal balls has an associated ball of radius $q_X(p)$; the term **quench function** is used for this association. An important property of $q_X(p)$ is that the quench function permits the reconstruction of the original set X completely as a union of its maximal balls B

$$X = \bigcup_{p \in S(X)} \left(p + q_X(p)B \right) . \tag{13.53}$$

This formula allows lossless compression of a binary image. Similar ideas are used for encoding documents in CCITT group 4 compression algorithms.

It is useful to distinguish several types of extrema, and use the analogy of a topographic view of images to make the explanation more intuitive. The *global maximum* is the pixel with highest value (lightest pixel, highest summit in the countryside); similarly, the *global minimum* corresponds to the deepest chasm in the countryside.

A pixel p of a gray-scale image is a *local maximum* if and only if for every neighboring pixel q of a pixel p, $I(p) \geq I(q)$. For example, the local maximum may mean that the landscape around is studied in a small neighborhood of the current position (neighborhood in morphology is defined by the structuring element). If no ascent is seen within the neighborhood, the pixel is at a local maximum.

The *regional maximum* M of a digital gray-scale image I is a connected set of pixels with an associated value h (plateau at altitude h), such that every neighboring pixel of M has strictly lower value than h. Topographically, regional extrema correspond to geographic summits and hollows. If M is a regional maximum of I and $p \in M$, then p is a local maximum, but the converse does not hold. Local and regional maxima are illustrated for the 1D case in Figure 13.31. The definition of various maxima allows us to analyze the quench function, which is also useful to define **ultimate erosion**, which is often used as a marker of convex objects in binary images. The ultimate erosion of a set X, denoted $\mathrm{Ult}(X)$, is the set of regional maxima of the quench function. The natural markers are centers of the largest maximal balls, but a problem arises if the objects are overlapping—here ultimate erosion comes into play. Consider first the simplest case, in which the set X consists of two overlapping disks (see Figure 13.32). The skeleton is a line segment between the centers. The associated quench function has regional maxima that are located at the disk centers in this particular example. These maxima are called ultimate erosion and can be used as markers of overlapping objects. Ultimate erosion provides a tool that extracts one marker per object of a given shape, even if objects overlap. The remaining trouble is that some objects are still multiply marked.

Consider a binary image, a set X, consisting of three rounded overlapping components of different size. When iteratively eroding the set by a unit-size ball, the set is shrunk, then separates, and finally disappears, as illustrated in Figure 13.33. During the successive erosions, the residuals of connected components (just before they disappear) are stored. Their union is the ultimate erosion of the original set X (Figure 13.34).

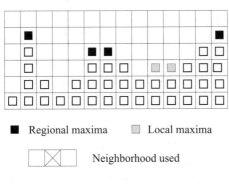

■ Regional maxima   ▨ Local maxima

⊠ Neighborhood used

Figure 13.31: 1D illustration of regional and local maxima. © *Cengage Learning 2015.*

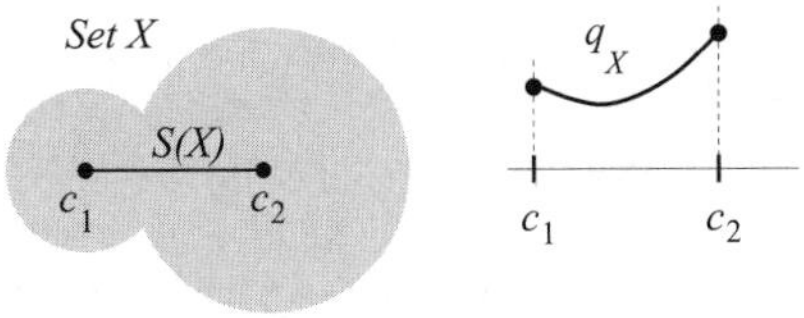

Figure 13.32: Skeleton of a set X, and associated quench function $q_X(p)$. Regional maxima give the ultimate erosion. © *Cengage Learning 2015.*

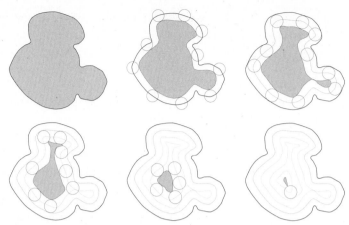

Figure 13.33: When successively eroded, components are separated from the rest and finally disappear from the image. The union of residua just before disappearance gives ultimate erosion. © *Cengage Learning 2015.*

13.5.5   Ultimate erosion and distance functions

We seek to present the ultimate erosion procedure formally, and introduce the **morphological reconstruction** operator for this purpose. Assume two sets A, B, $B \subseteq A$. The reconstruction $\rho_A(B)$ of the set A from set B is the union of connected components of A with non-empty intersection with B (see Figure 13.35—notice that set A consists of two components). Notice that B may typically consist of markers that permit the reconstruction of the required part of the set A. Markers point to the pixel or small region that belongs to the object. Markers are found either by a human operator (which is common, e.g. in biology) or can be found automatically. Morphological reconstruction will be discussed in detail in Section 13.5.7.

Figure 13.34: Ultimate erosion is the union of residual connected components before they disappear during erosions. © *Cengage Learning 2015.*

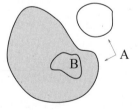

Figure 13.35: Reconstruction $\rho_A(B)$ (in gray) of the set A from B. Notice that set A may consist of more than one connected component. Note that only the portion of A that contains B is reconstructed while the other component of A that does not include B will disappear after reconstruction of A from B. © *Cengage Learning 2015.*

Let $\mathcal{N}$ be the set of integers. Ultimate erosion can be expressed by the formula

$$\text{Ult}(X) = \bigcup_{n \in \mathcal{N}} \Big((X \ominus nB) \setminus \rho_{X \ominus nB}\big(X \ominus (n+1)B \big) \Big) . \tag{13.54}$$

There is a computationally effective ultimate erosion algorithm that uses the distance function (which is the core of several other quick morphological algorithms, as we shall see). The **distance function** $\text{dist}_X(p)$ associated with each pixel p of the set X is the size of the first erosion of X that does not contain p, i.e.,

$$\forall p \in X , \quad \text{dist}_X(p) = \min \big\{ n \in \mathcal{N},\ p \text{ not in } (X \ominus nB) \big\} . \tag{13.55}$$

This behaves as one would expect: $\text{dist}_X(p)$ is the shortest distance between the pixel p and background X^C.

There are two direct applications of the distance function.

- The ultimate erosion of a set X corresponds to the union of the regional maxima of the distance function of X.

- The skeleton by maximal balls of a set X corresponds to the set of local maxima of the distance function of X.

The final concept to be introduced is **skeleton by influence zones**, often abbreviated *SKIZ*. Let X be composed of n connected components X_i, $i = 1, \ldots, n$. The influence zone $Z(X_i)$ consists of points which are closer to set X_i than to any other connected component of X:

$$Z(X_i) = \big\{ p \in \mathcal{Z}^2,\ \forall i \neq j,\ d(p, X_i) \leq d(p, X_j) \big\} . \tag{13.56}$$

The skeleton by influence zones denoted $\text{SKIZ}(X)$ is the set of boundaries of influence zones $\big\{ Z(X_i) \big\}$.

13.5.6 Geodesic transformations

Geodesic methods [Vincent, 1995] modify morphological transformations to operate only on some part of an image. For instance, if an object is to be reconstructed from a marker, say a nucleus of a cell, it is desirable to avoid growing from a marker outside the cell. Another important advantage of geodesic transformations is that the structuring element can vary at each pixel, according to the image.

The basic concept of geodesic methods in morphology is geodesic distance. The path between two points is constrained within some set. The term has its roots in an old discipline—geodesy—that measures distances on the Earth's surface. Suppose that a traveler seeks the distance between London and Tokyo—the shortest distance passes *through* the Earth, but obviously the geodesic distance that is of interest to the traveler is constrained to the Earth's surface.

The **geodesic distance** $d_X(x, y)$ is the shortest path between two points x, y which remains entirely contained in the set X. If there is no path connecting points x, y, we set $d_X(x, y) = +\infty$. Geodesic distance is illustrated in Figure 13.36.

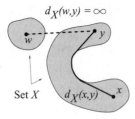

Figure 13.36: Geodesic distance $d_X(x,y)$.
© *Cengage Learning 2015.*

A **geodesic ball** is a ball constrained by some set X. The geodesic ball $B_X(p,n)$ of center $p \in X$ and radius n is defined as

$$B_X(p,n) = \{p' \in X, \; d_X(p,p') \leq n\} . \qquad (13.57)$$

The existence of a geodesic ball permits dilation or erosion only within some subset of the image; this leads to definitions of geodesic dilations and erosions of a subset Y of X.

The **geodesic dilation** $\delta_X^{(n)}$ of size n of a set Y inside the set X is defined as

$$\delta_X^{(n)}(Y) = \bigcup_{p \in Y} B_X(p,n) = \{p' \in X, \; \exists p \in Y, \; d_X(p,p') \leq n\} . \qquad (13.58)$$

Similarly the dual operation of **geodesic erosion** $\epsilon_X^{(n)}(Y)$ of size n of a set Y inside the set X can be written as

$$\epsilon_X^{(n)}(Y) = \{p \in Y, \; B_X(p,n) \subseteq Y\} = \{p \in Y, \; \forall p' \in X \setminus Y, \; d_X(p,p') > n\} . \qquad (13.59)$$

Geodesic dilation and erosion are illustrated in Figure 13.37.

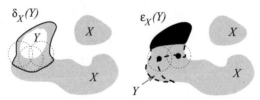

Figure 13.37: Geodesic dilation (left) and erosion (right) of the set Y inside the set X. © *Cengage Learning 2015.*

The outcome of a geodesic operation on a set $Y \subseteq X$ is always included within the set X. Regarding implementation, the simplest geodesic dilation of size 1 $(\delta_X^{(1)})$ of a set Y inside X is obtained as the intersection of the unit-size dilation of Y (with respect to the unit ball B) with the set X

$$\delta_X^{(1)} = (Y \oplus B) \cap X . \qquad (13.60)$$

Larger geodesic dilations are obtained by iteratively composing unit dilations n times

$$\delta_X^{(n)} = \underbrace{\delta_X^{(1)} \left(\delta_X^{(1)} \left(\delta_X^{(1)} \ldots (\delta_X^{(1)}) \right) \right)}_{n \; times} . \qquad (13.61)$$

The fast iterative way to calculate geodesic erosion is similar.

13.5.7 Morphological reconstruction

Assume that we want to reconstruct objects of a given shape from a binary image that was originally obtained by thresholding. All connected components in the input image constitute the set X. However, only some of the connected components were marked by markers that represent the set Y. This task and its desired result are shown in Figure 13.38.

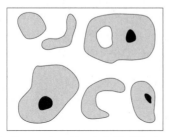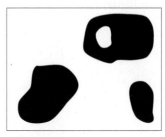

Figure 13.38: Reconstruction of X (X shown in light gray) from markers Y (black). The reconstructed result is shown in black on the right side. © *Cengage Learning 2015*.

Successive geodesic dilations of the set Y inside the set X enable the reconstruction of the connected components of X that were initially marked by Y. When dilating from the marker, it is impossible to intersect a connected component of X which did not initially contain a marker Y; such components disappear.

Geodesic dilations terminate when all connected components set X previously marked by Y are reconstructed, i.e., idempotency is reached:

$$\forall n > n_0, \ \delta_X^{(n)}(Y) = \delta_X^{(n_0)}(Y) \,. \tag{13.62}$$

This operation is called **reconstruction** and denoted by $\rho_X(Y)$. Formally,

$$\rho_X(Y) = \lim_{n \to \infty} \delta_X^{(n)}(Y) \,. \tag{13.63}$$

In some applications it is desirable that one connected component of X is marked by several markers Y. If it is not acceptable for the sets grown from various markers to become connected, the notion of influence zones can be generalized to **geodesic influence zones** of the connected components of set Y inside X. This is illustrated in Figure 13.39.

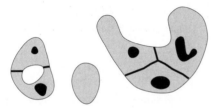

Figure 13.39: Geodesic influence zones. © *Cengage Learning 2015*.

We are now ready to generalize the reconstruction to gray-scale images; this requires the extension of geodesy to gray-scale images. The core of the extension is the statement (which is valid for discrete images) that any increasing transformation defined for binary images can be extended to gray-level images [Serra, 1982]. By this transformation we mean a transformation Ψ such that

$$\forall X, Y \subset \mathcal{Z}^2, \ Y \subseteq X \implies \Psi(Y) \subseteq \Psi(X) \,. \tag{13.64}$$

The generalization of transformation Ψ is achieved by viewing a gray-level image I as a stack of binary images obtained by successive thresholding—this is called the threshold decomposition of image I [Maragos and Ziff, 1990]. Let D_I be the domain of the image I, and the gray values of image I be in $\{0, 1, \ldots, N\}$. The thresholded images $T_k(I)$ are

$$T_k(I) = \left\{ p \in D_I, \ I(P) \geq k \right\}, \quad k = 0, \ldots, N \,. \tag{13.65}$$

The idea of threshold decomposition is illustrated in Figure 13.40.

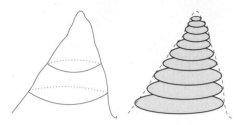

Figure 13.40: Threshold decomposition of a gray-scale image. © *Cengage Learning 2015.*

Threshold-decomposed images $T_k(I)$ obey the inclusion relation

$$\forall k \in [1, N], \ T_k(I) \subseteq T_{k-1}(I) \,. \tag{13.66}$$

Consider the increasing transformation Ψ applied to each threshold-decomposed image; their inclusion relationship is kept. The transformation Ψ can be extended to gray-scale images using the following **threshold decomposition principle**:

$$\forall p \in D_I, \ \Psi(I)(p) = \max \left\{ k \in [0, \ldots, N], \ p \in \Psi(T_k(I)) \right\} \,. \tag{13.67}$$

Returning to the reconstruction transformation, the binary geodesic reconstruction ρ is an increasing transformation, as it satisfies

$$Y_1 \subseteq Y_2, \ X_1 \subseteq X_2, \ Y_1 \subseteq X_1, \ Y_2 \subseteq X_2 \implies \rho_{X_1}(Y_1) \subseteq \rho_{X_2}(Y_2) \,. \tag{13.68}$$

We are ready to generalize binary reconstruction to **gray-level reconstruction** applying the threshold decomposition principle (equation 13.67). Let J, I be two gray-scale images defined on the same domain D, with gray-level values from the discrete interval $[0, 1, \ldots, N]$. If, for each pixel $p \in D$, $J(p) \leq I(p)$, the gray-scale reconstruction $\rho_I(J)$ of image I from image J is given by

$$\forall p \in D, \ \rho_I(J)(p) = \max \left\{ k \in [0, N], \ p \in \rho_{T_k}(T_K(J)) \right\} \,. \tag{13.69}$$

Recall that binary reconstruction grows those connected components of the mask which are marked. The gray-scale reconstruction extracts peaks of the mask I that are marked by J (see Figure 13.41).

The duality between dilation and erosion permits the expression of gray-scale reconstruction using erosion.

Figure 13.41: Gray-scale reconstruction of mask I from marker J. © *Cengage Learning 2015.*

13.6 Granulometry

Granulometry was introduced by stereologists (mathematicians attempting to understand 3D shape from cross sections)—the name comes from the Latin **granulum**, meaning grain. Matheron [Matheron, 1967] used it as a tool for studying porous materials, where the distribution of pore sizes was quantified by a sequence of openings of increasing size. Currently, granulometry is an important tool of mathematical morphology, particularly in material science and biology applications. The main advantage is that granulometry permits the extraction of shape information without a priori segmentation.

Consider first a sieving analysis analogy, where the input is a heap of stones (or granules) of different sizes—the task is to analyze how many stones in the heap fit into several size classes. Such a task is solved by sieving using several sieves with increasing sizes of holes in the mesh. The result of analysis is a discrete function; on its horizontal axis are increasing sizes of stones and on its vertical axis the numbers of stones of that size. In morphological granulometry, this function is called a **granulometric spectrum** or **granulometric curve**.

In binary morphology, the task is to calculate a granulometric curve where the independent variable is the size of objects in the image. The value of the granulometric curve is the number of objects of given size in the image. The most common approach is that sieves with increasing hole sizes (as in the example) are replaced by a sequence of openings with structural elements of increasing size.

Granulometry plays a very significant role in mathematical morphology, analogous to the role of frequency analysis in image processing or signal analysis. Frequency analysis expands a signal into a linear combination of harmonic signals of growing frequency. The frequency spectrum provides the contribution of individual harmonic signals—it is clear that the granulometric curve (spectrum) is analogous to a frequency spectrum.

Let $\Psi = (\psi_\lambda)$, $\lambda \geq 0$, be a family of transformations depending on a parameter λ. This family constitutes a **granulometry** if and only if the following properties of the transformation ψ hold:

$$
\begin{aligned}
\forall \lambda \geq 0 \quad & \psi_\lambda \text{ is increasing}, \\
& \psi_\lambda \text{ is anti-extensive}, \\
\forall \lambda \geq 0,\ \mu \geq 0 \quad & \psi_\lambda \psi_\mu = \psi_\mu \psi_\lambda = \psi_{\max(\lambda\mu)}\ .
\end{aligned}
\tag{13.70}
$$

The consequence of property (equation 13.70) is that for every $\lambda \geq 0$ the transformation ϕ_λ is idempotent. (ψ_λ), $\lambda \geq 0$ is a decreasing family of openings (more precisely, algebraic openings [Serra, 1982] that generalize the notion of opening presented earlier). It can be shown that for any convex structuring element B, the *family of openings* with respect to $\lambda B = \{\lambda b,\ b \in B\}$, $\lambda \geq 0$, constitutes a granulometry [Matheron, 1975].

Consider more intuitive granulometry acting on discrete binary images (i.e., sets). Here the granulometry is a sequence of openings ψ_n indexed by an integer $n \geq 0$—

each opening result is smaller than the previous one. Recall the analogy with sieving analysis; each opening, which corresponds to one sieve mesh size, removes from the image more than the previous one. Finally, the empty set is reached. Each sieving step is characterized by some measure $m(X)$ of the set (image) X (e.g., number of pixels in a 2D image, or volume in 3D). The rate at which the set is sieved characterizes the set. The pattern spectrum provides such a characteristic.

The **pattern spectrum**, also called *granulometric curve*, of a set X with respect to the granulometry $\Psi = \psi_n$, $n \geq 0$ is the mapping

$$PS_\Psi(X)(n) = m[\psi_n(X)] - m[\psi_{n-1}(X)], \quad \forall n > 0. \tag{13.71}$$

The sequence of openings $\Psi(X)$, $n \geq 0$ is a decreasing sequence of sets, i.e., $[\psi_0(X) \supseteq \psi_1(X) \supseteq \psi_2(X) \supseteq \dots]$. The granulometry and granulometric curve can be used.

Suppose that the granulometric analysis with family of openings needs to be computed for a binary input image. The binary input image is converted into a gray-level image using a granulometry function $G_\Psi(X)$, and the pattern spectrum PS_Ψ is calculated as a histogram of the granulometry function.

The *granulometry function* $G_\Psi(X)$ of a binary image X from granulometry $\Psi = (\psi_n)$, $n \geq 0$, maps each pixel $x \in X$ to the size of the first n such that $x \notin \psi_n(X)$:

$$x \in X, \ G_\Psi(X)(x) = \min\{n > 0, \ x \notin \psi_n(X)\}. \tag{13.72}$$

The pattern spectrum PS_Ψ of a binary image X for granulometry $\Psi = (\psi_n)$, $n \geq 0$, can be computed from the granulometry function $G_\Psi(X)$ as its histogram

$$\forall n > 0, \ PS_\Psi(X)(n) = \text{card}\{p, \ G_\Psi(X)(p) = n\}, \tag{13.73}$$

where 'card' denotes cardinality. An example of granulometry is given in Figure 13.42. The input binary image with circles of different radii is shown in Figure 13.42a; Figure 13.42b shows one of the openings with a square structuring element. Figure 13.42c

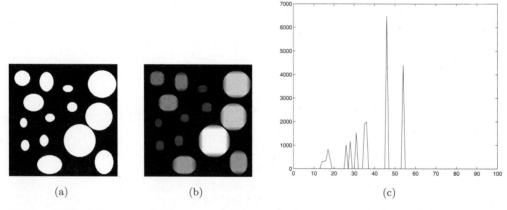

(a)   (b)   (c)

Figure 13.42: Example of binary granulometry performance. (a) Original binary image. (b) Maximal square probes inscribed—the initial probe size was 2×2 pixels. (c) Granulometric power spectrum as histogram of (b)—the horizontal axis gives the size of the object and the vertical axis the number of pixels in an object of given size. *Courtesy of P. Kodl, Rockwell Automation Research Center, Prague.*

illustrates the granulometric power spectrum. At a coarse scale, three most significant signals in the power spectrum indicate three prevalent sizes of object. The less significant signals on the left side are caused by the artifacts that occur due to discretization. The Euclidean circles have to be replaced by digital entities (squares).

Notice that granulometries extract size information without the need to identify (segment) each object a priori. In applications, this is used for shape description, feature extraction, texture classification, and removal of noise introduced by image borders.

Granulometric analysis was historically costly to perform but this is no longer the case. For binary images, the basic idea towards speed-up is to use linear structuring elements for openings and more complex 2D ones derived from it, such as cross, square, or diamond (see Figure 13.43). The next source of computational saving is the fact that some 2D structuring elements can be decomposed as Minkowski addition of two 1D structuring elements. For example, the square structuring element can be expressed as Minkowski addition of horizontal and vertical lines [Haralick et al., 1995; Vincent, 1995]. *Gray-scale granulometric analysis* permits the extraction of size information directly from gray-level images. The interested reader should consult [Vincent, 1994].

Figure 13.43: Structural elements used for fast binary granulometry are derived from line structuring elements, e.g., cross, square, and diamond. © *Cengage Learning 2015.*

13.7   Morphological segmentation and watersheds

13.7.1   Particle segmentation, marking, and watersheds

Segmentation usually means finding objects of interest in an image. Mathematical morphology helps mainly to segment images of texture or images of particles—here we consider **particle segmentation** in which the input image can be either binary or gray-scale. In the binary case, the task is to segment overlapping particles; in the gray-scale case, the segmentation is the same as object contour extraction [Vincent, 1995].

Morphological particle segmentation is performed in two basic steps: (1) location of particle markers, and (2) watersheds used for particle reconstruction. The latter is explained later in this section.

Marker extraction resembles human behavior when one is asked to indicate objects; the person just points to objects and does not outline boundaries. The **marker** of an object or set X is a set M that is included in X. Markers have the same homotopy as the set X, and are typically located in the central part of the object (particle).

A robust marker-finding technique will need to know the nature of the objects sought, and thus application-specific knowledge should be used. Often combinations of non-morphological and morphological approaches are used. Moreover, object marking is in many cases left to the user, who marks objects manually on the screen. Typically, software for analysis of microscopic images has user-friendly tools for manual or semi-automatic marking.

When objects are marked, they can be grown from the markers, e.g., using the watershed transformation (Section 13.7.3), which is motivated by the topographic view of images. Consider the analogy of a landscape and rain; water will find the swiftest descent path until it reaches some lake or sea. We know that lakes and seas correspond to regional minima. The landscape can be entirely partitioned into regions which attract water to a particular sea or lake—we call these **catchment basins**. These regions are influence zones of the regional minima in the image. **Watersheds** (or **watershed lines**) separate catchment basins. Watersheds and catchment basins are illustrated in Figure 13.44.

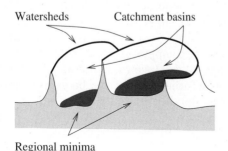

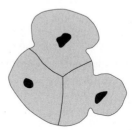

Figure 13.44: Illustration of catchment basins and watersheds in a 3D landscape view. © *Cengage Learning 2015*.

Figure 13.45: Segmentation by geodesic influence zones (SKIZ) need not lead to correct results. © *Cengage Learning 2015*.

13.7.2 Binary morphological segmentation

If the task is to find objects that differ in brightness from an uneven background, the top hat transformation (Section 13.5.4) is a simple solution. This approach finds peaks in the image function that differ from the local background: the gray-level shape of the peaks does not play any role, but the shape of the structuring element does. Watershed segmentation takes into account both sources of information and supersedes the top hat method.

Morphological segmentation in binary images aims to find regions corresponding to individual overlapping objects (typically particles), and most of the tools for performing this task have already been explained. Each particle is marked first—ultimate erosion may be used for this purpose (Section 13.5.4), or markers may be placed manually. The next task is to grow objects from the markers provided they are kept within the limits of the original set and parts of objects are not joined when they come close to each other.

The oldest technique for this purpose is called **conditional dilation**. Ordinary dilation is used for growing, and the result is constrained by two conditions: remain in the original set, and do not join particles.

Geodesic reconstruction (Section 13.5.7) is more sophisticated and performs much faster than conditional dilation. The structuring element adapts according to the neighborhood of the processed pixel.

Geodesic influence zones (Section 13.5.7) are sometimes used for segmenting particles. Figure 13.45 shows that the result can differ from our intuitive expectation.

The best solution is the **watershed transformation**; for the theoretical background and fast implementation techniques, see Section 13.7.3 and [Bleau et al., 1992; Vincent, 1993, 1995]. The original binary image is converted into gray-scale using the negative distance transform (equation 13.55). If a drop of water falls onto a topographic surface

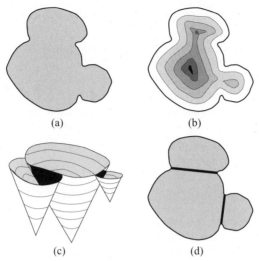

(a)   (b)

(c)   (d)

Figure 13.46: Segmentation of binary particles. (a) Input binary image. (b) Gray-scale image created from (a) using the −dist function. (c) Topographic notion of the catchment basin. (d) Correctly segmented particles using watersheds of image (b). © *Cengage Learning 2015*.

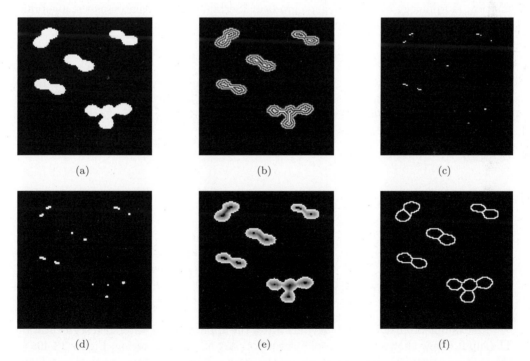

(a)   (b)   (c)

(d)   (e)   (f)

Figure 13.47: Particle segmentation by watersheds. (a) Original binary image. (b) Distance function visualized using contours. (c) Regional maxima of the distance function used as particle markers. (d) Dilated markers. (e) Inverse of the distance function with the markers superimposed. (f) Resulting contours of particles obtained by watershed segmentation. *Courtesy of P. Kodl, Rockwell Automation Research Center, Prague.*

of this image, it will follow the steepest slope towards a regional minimum. This idea is illustrated in Figure 13.46.

Application of watershed particle segmentation is shown in Figure 13.47. An image of a few touching particles is the input Figure 13.47a, and the distance function calculated from the background is visualized using contours in Figure 13.47b. Regional maxima of the distance function serve as markers of the individual particles (Figure 13.47c). The markers are dilated in Figure 13.47d. In preparation for watershed segmentation, the distance function is negated, and is shown together with the dilated markers in Figure 13.47e. The final result of particle separation is illustrated in Figure 13.47f, where particle contours are shown.

13.7.3   Gray-scale segmentation, watersheds

The markers and watersheds method can also be applied to gray-scale segmentation. Watersheds are also used as crest-line extractors in gray-scale images. The contour of a region in a gray-level image corresponds to points in the image where gray-levels change most quickly—this is analogous to edge-based segmentation considered in Chapter 6. The watershed transformation is applied to the gradient magnitude image in this case (see Figure 13.48). There is a simple approximation to the gradient image used in mathematical morphology called Beucher's gradient [Serra, 1982], calculated as the algebraic difference of unit-size dilation and unit-size erosion of the input image X

$$\operatorname{grad}(X) = (X \oplus B) - (X \ominus B). \tag{13.74}$$

The main problem with segmentation via gradient images without markers is over-segmentation (Figure 13.47c). Some techniques to limit this in watershed segmentation are given in [Vincent, 1993]. Watershed segmentation methods with markers do not suffer from over-segmentation, of course.

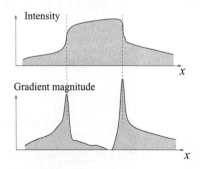

Figure 13.48: Segmentation in gray-scale images using gradient magnitude. © *Cengage Learning 2015*.

An example from ophthalmology illustrates the application of watershed segmentation. The input image shows a microscopic picture of part of a human retina, Figure 13.49a—the task is to segment individual cells on the retina. The markers/watershed paradigm was followed, with markers being found using a carefully tuned Gaussian filter (see Figure 13.49b). The final result with outlined contours of cells is in Figure 13.49c.

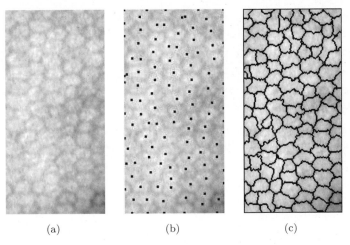

(a)   (b)   (c)

Figure 13.49: Watershed segmentation of a human retina image. (a) Original gray-scale image. (b) Dots are superimposed markers found by non-morphological methods. (c) Boundaries of retina cells found by watersheds from markers (b). *Courtesy of R. Šára, Czech Technical University, Prague and P. Kodl, Rockwell Automation Research Center Prague.*

13.8 Summary

- **Mathematical morphology**

  - Mathematical morphology stresses the role of *shape* in image pre-processing, segmentation, and object description. It leads to mathematically sound and fast algorithms.

  - The basic entity is a *point set*; it operates using transformations described using operators in a relatively simple *non-linear algebra*. It is a counterpart to traditional signal processing based on linear operators.

  - It is divided into *binary mathematical morphology* which operates on binary images, and *gray-level mathematical morphology* which acts on gray-level images.

- **Morphological operations**

  - Morphological operations are *relations of two sets*. One is an image and the second a small *structuring element* that systematically traverses the image. Its relation to the image in each position is stored in the output image.

  - Fundamental operations of mathematical morphology include *dilation* which expands objects and *erosion* which shrinks them. They are not invertible; their combination constitutes new operations—*opening* and *closing*.

  - Thin and elongated objects are often simplified using a *skeleton*—a line that is in 'the middle of the object'.

  - The *distance function* to the background constitutes a basis for many fast operations. *Ultimate erosion* is used to mark blob centers. There is an efficient reconstruction algorithm that grows the object from the marker to its original boundary.

    – *Geodesic transformations* allow changes to the structuring element during processing and thus provide more flexibility.

    – They provide quick and efficient segmentation algorithms: the *watershed transform* is one of the better ones. Boundaries of regions are influence zones of regional minima (i.e., seas and lakes in the landscape). Region boundaries are watershed lines between these seas and lakes.

    – Segmentation is often performed from interactively chosen *markers*, or from some automatic procedure that takes into account semantic properties of the image.

    – **Granulometry** is a quantitative tool for analyzing images with particles of different size (similar to sieving analysis). The result is a discrete *granulometric curve* (spectrum).

13.9 Exercises

Short-answer questions

S13.1 What is mathematical morphology?

S13.2 What is a structuring element? What is its role in mathematical morphology?

S13.3 Give the definition of erosion and dilation for binary images.

S13.4 Is erosion a commutative operation?

S13.5 What is the difference between the result of opening performed once and twice? What is idempotency?

S13.6 Gray-level dilation and erosion are a generalization of the same notions in binary images. Describe how they are done.

S13.7 What is the top hat transformation and when is it used? Sketch a 1D example of the image profile demonstrating the use of top hat transform, show the top-hat transform result.

S13.8 What is the skeleton by maximal balls? What does the skeleton of two touching filled circles look like?

S13.9 What does the homotopic skeleton of two touching balls look like?

S13.10 Explain the role of ultimate erosion for marking particles.

S13.11 What is a regional maximum?

S13.12 What is geodesic distance? How is it used in mathematical morphology?

S13.13 What is granulometry?

S13.14 Name three application areas in which granulometry analysis may be used.

S13.15 What is the relation between a granulometric curve (spectrum) and the Fourier spectrum?

S13.16 What is a watershed? How is it used for morphological segmentation?

Problems

P13.1 It is probably not going to be computationally efficient to re-implement morphological algorithms personally. There are many packages around that perform morphology fast—Matlab is just one example. Locate such software and exercise any or all of the algorithms described in this chapter.

P13.2 Prove that dilation is commutative and associative.

P13.3 Opening followed by closing can be used to remove salt and pepper noise from binary images. Explain the principle and discuss the shape and size of a structuring element suitable for this operation.

P13.4 Consider a one-dimensional gray-scale image (signal). Draw a picture that demonstrates that gray-scale dilation fills narrow bays in the image.

P13.5 Explain how the top hat transformation permits the segmentation of dark characters on a light background with varying intensity. Draw a picture of a one-dimensional cross section through the image.

P13.6 What is a homotopic transformation? Describe at least two algorithms for skeletonization. Do they produce a homotopic skeleton?

P13.7 What is the difference between thinning with the Golay structuring elements L (equation 13.51) and E (equation 13.52)?

P13.8 Explain the calculation steps of the skeleton by maximal balls in Figure 13.29.

P13.9 Explain the role of markers in morphological segmentation. Why would an attempt to perform watershed segmentation without markers lead to over-segmentation?

P13.10 Dilate the image given in Figure 13.50a with the structuring element given in Figure 13.50b.

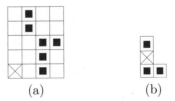

(a)   (b)

Figure 13.50: (a) Image to be processed. Assume that image data are undefined outside of the image domain. (b) Structuring element.
© *Cengage Learning 2015*.

P13.11 Using ultimate erosion, develop an approach for counting adjacent/touching objects in an image (like pebbles or coffee beans). Demonstrate robustness of your approach (or lack of) with respect to the initial segmentation of the objects (binarization). Apply the same approach to images of objects of increasing segmentation difficulty.

P13.12 Assuming that the approach developed in Problem P13.11 does not perform sufficiently well for some of the more difficult images, augment your method with other morphologic steps. Use *only* mathematical morphology operations to solve this problem.

P13.13 Use the markers obtained by ultimate erosion (Problems P13.11, P13.12) to segment the same images using watershed transformation.

P13.14 Modify the watershed algorithm so that objects and borders are segmented separately. (Hint: apart from extracting object markers, it is necessary to extract markers for borders.) Use *only* mathematical morphology operations to solve this problem.

P13.15 Make yourself familiar with solved problems and **Matlab** implementations of selected algorithms provided in the corresponding chapter of the **Matlab Companion** to this text [Svoboda et al., 2008]. The **Matlab Companion** homepage http://visionbook.felk.cvut.cz offers images used in the problems, and well-commented **Matlab** code is provided for educational purposes.

P13.16 Use the **Matlab Companion** [Svoboda et al., 2008] to develop solutions to additional exercises and practical problems provided there. Implement your solutions using **Matlab** or other suitable programming languages.

13.10   References

Bleau A., deGuise J., and LeBlanc R. A new set of fast algorithms for mathematical morphology II. Identification of topographic features on grayscale images. *CVGIP: Image Understanding*, 56(2):210–229, 1992.

Blum H. A transformation for extracting new descriptors of shape. In Wathen-Dunn W., editor, *Proceedings of the Symposium on Models for the Perception of Speech and Visual Form*, pages 362–380, Cambridge, MA, 1967. MIT Press.

Dougherty E. R. *An Introduction to Mathematical Morphology Processing*. SPIE Press, Bellingham, WA, 1992.

Giardina C. R. and Dougherty E. R. *Morphological Methods in Image and Signal Processing*. Prentice-Hall, Englewood Cliffs, NJ, 1988.

Golay M. J. E. Hexagonal parallel pattern transformation. *IEEE Transactions on Computers*, C–18:733–740, 1969.

Haralick R. M. and Shapiro L. G. *Computer and Robot Vision, Volume I*. Addison-Wesley, Reading, MA, 1992.

Haralick R. M., Stenberg S. R., and Zhuang X. Image analysis using mathematical morphology. *IEEE Transactions on Pattern Analysis and Machine Intelligence*, 9(4):532–550, 1987.

Haralick R. M., Katz P. L., and Dougherty E. R. Model-based morphology: The opening spectrum. *Graphical Models and Image Processing*, 57(1):1–12, 1995.

Heijmans H. J. *Morphological Image Operators*. Academic Press, Boston, 1994.

Ma C. M. and Sonka M. A fully parallel 3D thinning algorithm and its applications. *Computer Vision and Image Understanding*, 64:420–433, 1996.

Maragos P. and Ziff R. Threshold superposition in morphological image analysis. *IEEE Transactions on Pattern Analysis and Machine Intelligence*, 12(5), 1990.

Matheron G. *Eléments pour une theorie des milieux poreux* (in French). Masson, Paris, 1967.

Matheron G. *Random Sets and Integral Geometry*. Wiley, New York, 1975.

Meyer F. Contrast feature extraction. In Chermant J.-L., editor, *Quantitative Analysis of Microstructures in Material Science, Biology and Medicine*, Stuttgart, Germany, 1978. Riederer Verlag. Special issue of *Practical Metalography*.

Palagyi K., Tschirren J., Hoffman E. A., and Sonka M. Quantitative analysis of pulmonary airway tree structures. *Computers in Biology and Medicine*, 36:974–996, 2006.

Serra J. *Image Analysis and Mathematical Morphology*. Academic Press, London, 1982.

Serra J. Morphological optics. *Journal of Microscopy*, 145(1):1–22, 1987.

Soille P. *Morphological Image Analysis*. Springer-Verlag, Berlin, 2 edition, 2003.

Svoboda T., Kybic J., and Hlavac V. *Image Processing, Analysis, and Machine Vision: A MATLAB Companion.* Thomson Engineering, 2008.

Vincent L. Fast opening functions and morphological granulometries. In *Proceedings Image Algebra and Morphological Image Processing V*, pages 253–267, San Diego, CA, 1994. SPIE.

Vincent L. Morphological grayscale reconstruction in image analysis: Applications and efficient algorithms. *IEEE Transactions on Image Processing*, 2(2):176–201, 1993.

Vincent L. Efficient computation of various types of skeletons. In *Proceedings of the SPIE Symposium Medical Imaging,* San Jose, CA, volume 1445, Bellingham, WA, 1991. SPIE.

Vincent L. Lecture notes on granulometries, segmentation and morphological algorithms. In Wojciechowski K., editor, *Proceedings of the Summer School on Morphological Image and Signal Processing,* Zakopane, Poland, pages 119–216. Silesian Technical University, Gliwice, Poland, 1995.

Chapter 14

Image data compression

Image processing is often very difficult because of the large amounts of data used to represent an image. Technology permits ever-increasing image resolution (spatially and in gray-levels), and increasing numbers of spectral bands, and there is a consequent need to limit the resulting data volume. Examples of this problem are everywhere; raw video—whether high definition or not—represents many megabytes per second. Medical applications such as CT and MR are 3D (or 4D, if dynamic in time) and are likewise extremely data hungry. One possible approach to decreasing the necessary amount of storage is to work with compressed image data.

We have seen that segmentation techniques have the side effect of image compression; by removing all areas and features that are not of interest, and leaving only boundaries or region descriptors, the reduction in data quantity is considerable. However, from this sort of representation no image reconstruction (or only very limited reconstruction) to the original image is possible. Conversely, image compression algorithms aim to remove redundancy in data in a way which makes image reconstruction possible; this is sometimes called **information preserving compression**. Compression is the main goal of the algorithm—we aim to represent an image using fewer bits per pixel. It is necessary to find statistical properties of the image to design an appropriate compression transformation of the image; the more correlated the image data are, the more data items can be removed. In this chapter, we will discuss this group of methods which do not change image entropy or image information content; the literature on compression is compendious—just three useful references would be [Salomon, 2000; Sayood, 2000; Shukla and Prasad, 2011].

A general algorithm for data compression and image reconstruction is shown in a block diagram in Figure 14.1. The first step removes information redundancy caused by high correlation of image data—transform compressions, predictive compressions, and hybrid approaches are used. The second step is coding of transformed data using a code of fixed or variable-length. An advantage of variable-length codes is the possibility of coding more frequent data using shorter code words and therefore increasing compression efficiency, while an advantage of fixed length coding is a standard codeword length that offers easy handling and fast processing. Compressed data are decoded after transmission

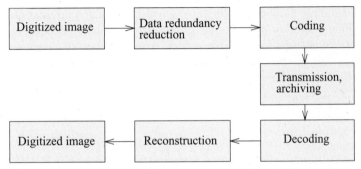

Figure 14.1: Data compression and image reconstruction. © *Cengage Learning 2015.*

or archiving and reconstructed. Note that no non-redundant image data may be lost in the data compression process—otherwise error-free reconstruction is impossible.

Data compression methods can be divided into two principal groups: information preserving—or **lossless**—compression permits error-free data reconstruction, while **lossy** compression methods do not preserve information completely. In image processing, a faithful reconstruction is often not necessary in practice and then the requirements are weaker, but the compression must not cause significant changes in an image. Data compression success in the reconstructed image is usually measured by the mean square error (MSE), signal-to-noise ratio etc., although these global error measures do not always reflect subjective image quality.

Compression design consists of two parts. Image data properties must be determined first; gray-level histograms, image entropy, various correlation functions, etc., often serve this purpose. The second part yields an appropriate compression technique with respect to measured image properties.

Data compression methods with loss of information are typical in image processing and therefore this group of methods is described in some detail. Although lossy compression techniques can give substantial image compression with very good quality reconstruction, there are considerations that may prohibit their use. For example, diagnosis in medical imaging is often based on visual image inspection, so no loss of information can be tolerated and information preserving techniques must be applied. Information preserving compression methods are mentioned briefly at the end of the chapter.

14.1   Image data properties

Information content of an image is an important property, of which *entropy* is a measure (Section 2.3.3). If an image has G gray-levels and the probability of gray-level k is $P(k)$ (see Section 3.3), then entropy H_e, not considering correlation of gray-levels, is defined as

$$H_e = - \sum_{k=0}^{G-1} P(k) \, \log_2 \left(P(k) \right) . \tag{14.1}$$

Information **redundancy** r is defined as

$$r = b - H_e , \tag{14.2}$$

where b is the smallest number of bits with which the image quantization levels can be represented. This definition of image information redundancy can be evaluated only if a good estimate of entropy is available, which is usually not so because the necessary statistical properties of the image are not known. Image data entropy however can be estimated from a gray-level histogram [Moik, 1980; Pratt, 1991]. Let $h(k)$ be the frequency of gray-level k in an image f, $0 \le k \le 2^b - 1$, and let the image size be $M \times N$. The probability of occurrence of gray-level k can be estimated as

$$\tilde{P}(k) = \frac{h(k)}{MN} \tag{14.3}$$

and the entropy can be estimated as

$$\tilde{H}_e = -\sum_{k=0}^{2^b-1} \tilde{P}(k) \log_2\left(\tilde{P}(k)\right). \tag{14.4}$$

The information redundancy estimate is $\tilde{r} = b - \tilde{H}_e$. The definition of the **compression ratio** K is then

$$K = \frac{b}{\tilde{H}_e}. \tag{14.5}$$

Note that a gray-level histogram gives an inaccurate estimate of entropy because of gray-level correlation. A more accurate estimate can be obtained from a histogram of the first gray-level differences.

Theoretical limits of possible image compression can be found using these formulae. For example, the entropy of satellite remote sensing data may be $\tilde{H}_e \in [4, 5]$, where image data are quantized into 256 gray-levels, or 8 bits per pixel. We can easily compute the information redundancy as $\tilde{r} \in [3, 4]$ bits. This implies that these data can be represented by an average data volume of 4–5 bits per pixel with no loss of information, and the compression ratio would be $K \in [1.6, 2]$.

14.2   Discrete image transforms in image data compression

Image data representation by coefficients of discrete image transforms (see Section 3.2) is the basic idea of this approach. The coefficients are ordered according to their importance, i.e., according to their contribution to the image information content, and the least important (low-contribution) coefficients are omitted. Coefficient importance can be judged, for instance, in correspondence to spatial or gray-level visualization abilities of the display; image correlation can then be avoided and data compression results.

The *Karhunen-Loève* transform is the foremost in removing correlated image data. This transform builds a set of non-correlated variables with decreasing variance. The variance of a variable is a measure of its information content; therefore, a compression strategy is based on considering only transform variables with high variance. More details about the Karhunen-Loève transform can be found in Section 3.2.10.

The Karhunen-Loève transform is computationally expensive, with a two-dimensional transform of an $M \times N$ image having computational complexity $\mathcal{O}(M^{\in}N^{\in})$. It is the

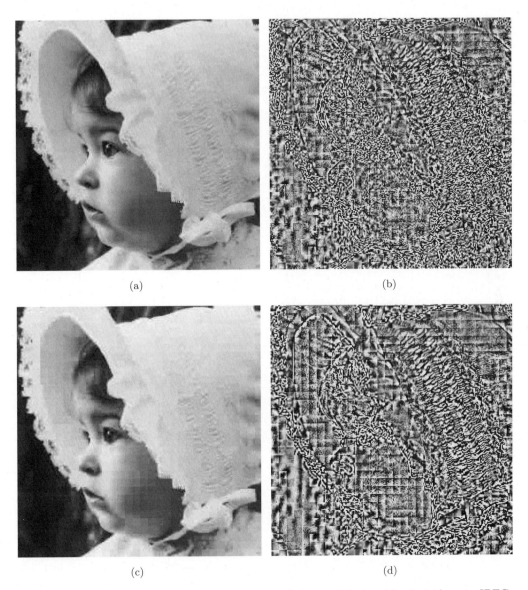

(a)

(b)

(c)

(d)

Figure 14.2: Discrete cosine image compression applied to subblocks of 8×8 pixels as in JPEG. (a) Reconstructed image, compression ratio $K = 6.2$. (b) difference image—differences between pixel values in the original and the reconstructed image ($K = 6.2$); the maximum difference is 56 gray-levels, mean squared reconstruction error MSE = 32.3 gray-levels (the image is histogram equalized for visualization purposes). (c) Reconstructed image, compression ratio $K = 10.5$. (d) Difference image—differences between pixel values in the original and the reconstructed image ($K = 10.5$); the maximum difference is 124 gray-levels, MSE = 70.5 gray-levels (the image is histogram equalized for visualization purposes). *Courtesy of A. Kruger, G. Prause, The University of Iowa.*

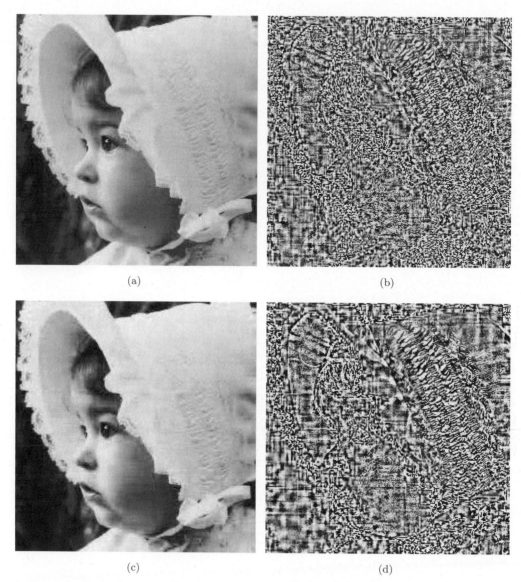

(a)

(b)

(c)

(d)

Figure 14.3: Wavelet image compression. (a) Reconstructed image, compression ratio $K = 6.2$. (b) Difference image—differences between pixel values in the original and the reconstructed image ($K = 6.2$); the maximum difference is 37 gray-levels, mean squared reconstruction error MSE = 32.0 gray-levels (the image is histogram equalized for visualization purposes). (c) Reconstructed image, compression ratio $K = 10.5$. (d) Difference image—differences between pixel values in the original and the reconstructed image ($K = 10.5$); the maximum difference is 79 gray-levels, MSE = 65.0 gray-levels (the image is histogram equalized for visualization purposes). *Courtesy of G. Prause and A. Kruger, The University of Iowa.*

only transform that guarantees non-correlated compressed data, and the resulting compression is optimal in the statistical sense. This makes the transform basis vectors image dependent, which also makes the transform difficult to apply for routine image compression. Therefore, it is often only used as a benchmark to evaluate other transforms. For example, one reason for the popularity of the discrete cosine transform DCT-II is that its performance approaches the Karhunen-Loève transform better than others.

Other discrete image transforms (Section 3.2) are computationally less demanding; fast algorithms of these transforms have computational complexity $\mathcal{O}(\mathcal{M}\mathcal{N}\log_{\in}(\mathcal{M}\mathcal{N}))$. Cosine, Fourier, Hadamard, Walsh, or binary transforms are all suitable for image data compression. If an image is compressed using discrete transforms, it is usually divided into, e.g., 16×16 pixel, subimages to speed up calculations, and then each subimage is transformed and processed separately. The same is true for image reconstruction, with each subimage being reconstructed and placed into the appropriate image position. This image segmentation into a grid of subimages does not consider any possible data redundancy caused by subimage correlation even if this correlation is the most serious source of redundancy. *Recursive block* coding [Farelle, 1990] is an approach to reducing inter-block redundancy and tiling effects (blockiness). The most popular image transform used for image compression is the discrete cosine transform with many modifications, and variations of wavelet transforms (Section 3.2.7).

Figure 14.2 illustrates the use of the discrete cosine transform. The DCT-II applied here provides good compression with low computational demands, the compression ratios being $K = 6.2$ and $K = 10.5$. The lower compression ratio was achieved after setting 90.0% of the transform coefficients to zero; the higher ratio after setting 94.9% of the coefficients to zero. Note that square blocks resulting from **DCT compression** and reconstruction decrease image quality for larger compression ratios. Consequently, **wavelet image compression** is of interest, since it can be efficiently applied to the entire image and thus the square artifacts are not present. Wavelet compression consists of the same steps as DCT compression, but the DCT is replaced by a wavelet transform followed by generally identical quantization and coding. Figure 14.3 shows the reconstructed image after wavelet compression with two different compression ratios, $K = 6.2$ and $K = 10.5$. The lower compression ratio (Figure 14.3a,b) was achieved after setting 89.4% of the transform coefficients to zero, the higher ratio (Figure 14.3a,b) resulted after setting 94.4% of the coefficients to zero. Note that no blocking artifacts exist.

While DCT compression is the basis for the widely used JPEG compression standard (Section 14.9.1), wavelet compression has become the basis for JPEG–2000 (Section 14.9.2).

14.3 Predictive compression methods

Predictive compressions use image information redundancy (correlation of data) to construct an estimate $\tilde{f}(i,j)$ of the gray-level value of an image element (i,j) from values of gray-levels in its neighborhood. In image parts where data are not correlated, the estimate $\tilde{f}$ will not match the original value. The differences between estimates and reality, which may be expected to be relatively small in absolute terms, are coded and transmitted (stored) together with prediction model parameters—the whole set now represents compressed image data. The gray value at location (i,j) is reconstructed from a

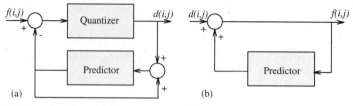

Figure 14.4: Differential pulse code modulation: (a) compression; (b) reconstruction. © *Cengage Learning 2015.*

computed estimate $\tilde{f}(i,j)$ and the stored difference $d(i,j)$

$$d(i,j) = \tilde{f}(i,j) - f(i,j) \,. \tag{14.6}$$

This method is called **differential pulse code modulation** (DPCM)—its block diagram is presented in Figure 14.4. Experiments show that a linear predictor of the third order is sufficient for estimation in a wide variety of images. If the image is processed line by line, the estimate $\tilde{f}$ can be computed as

$$\tilde{f}(i,j) = a_1 \, f(i,j-1) + a_2 \, f(i-1,j-1) + a_3 \, f(i-1,j) \,, \tag{14.7}$$

where a_1, a_2, a_3 are image prediction model parameters. These parameters are set to minimize the mean quadratic estimation error e

$$e = \mathcal{E}\left\{ \left(\tilde{f}(i,j) - f(i,j) \right)^2 \right\} \,, \tag{14.8}$$

and the solution, assuming f is a stationary random process with a zero mean, using a predictor of the third order, is

$$\begin{aligned}
a_1 \, R(0,0) + a_2 \, R(0,1) + a_3 \, R(1,1) &= R(1,0) \,, \\
a_1 \, R(0,1) + a_2 \, R(0,0) + a_3 \, R(1,0) &= R(1,1) \,, \\
a_1 \, R(1,1) + a_2 \, R(1,0) + a_3 \, R(0,0) &= R(0,1) \,,
\end{aligned} \tag{14.9}$$

where $R(m,n)$ is the autocorrelation function of the random process f (see Chapter 2). The image data autocorrelation function is usually of exponential form and the variance of differences $d(i,j)$ is usually smaller than the variance of the original values $f(i,j)$, since the differences $d(i,j)$ are not correlated. The (probable) relatively small magnitude of the differences $d(i,j)$ makes data compression possible.

Predictive compression algorithms are described in detail in [Rosenfeld and Kak, 1982; Netravali, 1988]. A second order predictive method with variable code length coding of the differences $d(i,j)$ produced the compressed images shown in Figure 14.5 achieving data compression ratios of $K = 3.8$ and $K = 6.2$. Note that horizontal lines and false contours resulting from the predictive compression and reconstruction decrease the image quality for larger compression ratios.

Many modifications of predictive compression methods can be found in the literature, some of them combining predictive compression with other coding schemes [Daut and Zhao, 1990; Zailu and Taxiao, 1990].

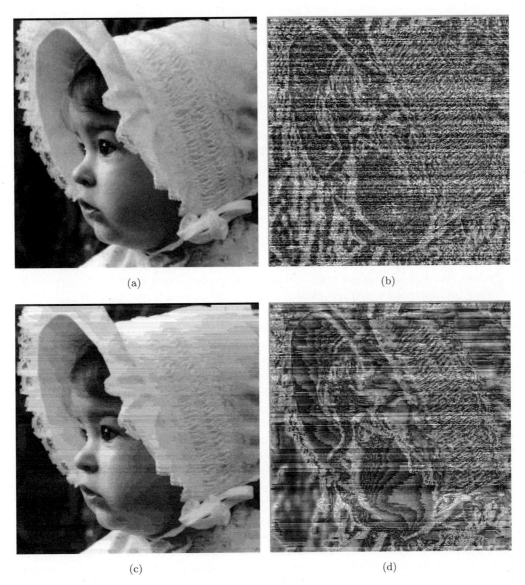

(a)

(b)

(c)

(d)

Figure 14.5: Predictive compression. (a) Reconstructed image, compression ratio $K = 3.8$. (b) Difference image—differences between pixel values in the original and the reconstructed image ($K = 3.8$); the maximum difference is 6 gray-levels (the image is histogram equalized for visualization purposes). (c) Reconstructed image, compression ratio $K = 6.2$. (d) Difference image—differences between pixel values in the original and the reconstructed image ($K = 6.2$); the maximum difference is 140 gray-levels (the image is histogram equalized for visualization purposes). *Courtesy of A. Kruger, The University of Iowa.*

14.4   Vector quantization

Dividing an image into small blocks and representing these blocks as vectors is another option [Gray, 1984; Chang et al., 1988; Netravali, 1988; Gersho and Gray, 1992]. The basic idea for this approach comes from information theory (Shannon's rate distortion theory), which states that better compression performance can always be achieved by coding vectors instead of scalars. Input data vectors are coded using unique codewords from a codeword dictionary, and instead of vectors, the vector codes are stored or transmitted. The codeword choice is based on the best similarity between the image block represented by a coded vector and the image blocks represented by codewords from the dictionary. The code dictionary (code book) is transmitted together with the coded data. The advantage of **vector quantization** is a simple receiver structure consisting of a look-up table, but a disadvantage is a complex coder. The coder complexity is not caused directly by the vector quantization principle; the method can be implemented in a reasonably simple way, but the coding will be very slow. To increase the processing speed, data structures such as K-D trees (see Section 9.2.2) and other special treatments are needed which increase the coder complexity. Further, the necessary statistical properties of images are usually not available. Therefore, the compression parameters must be based on an image training set and the appropriate code book may vary from image to image. As a result, images with statistical properties dissimilar from images in the training set may not be well represented by the code vectors in the look-up table. Furthermore, edge degradation may be more severe than with other techniques. To decrease the coder complexity, the coding process may be divided into several levels, two being typical. The coding process is hierarchical, using two or more code books according to the number of coding levels. However, the combination of a complex coder facilitating high compression ratios and a simple decoder may be advantageous in **asymmetric** applications when the image is compressed once and decompressed many times. Within such a scenario, the higher compression ratio gained by the more complex coder and/or more time-consuming compression algorithm does not matter as long as the decompression process is simple and fast. Multimedia encyclopedias and paperless publishing serve as good examples. On the other hand, in **symmetric** applications such as video conferencing, similar complexity of coding and decoding operations is required.

A modification that allows blocks of variable size is described in [Boxerman and Lee, 1990], where a segmentation algorithm is responsible for detecting appropriate image blocks. The block vector quantization approach may also be applied to compression of image sequences. Identifying and processing only blocks of the image that change noticeably between consecutive frames using vector quantization and DPCM is also possible. Hybrid DPCM combined with vector quantization of colored prediction errors is presented in [De Lameillieure and Bruyland, 1990].

14.5   Hierarchical and progressive compression methods

Multi-resolution pyramids may also be used for efficient hierarchical image compression. **Run length** codes (Section 4.2.2, Figure 4.4) identify long runs of the same value pixels, and store them as this value together with a word count. If the image is characterized by such long runs, this will significantly reduce storage requirements. A similar approach may be applied to image pyramids. A substantial reduction in bit volume can be obtained by merely representing a source as a pyramid [Rao and Pearlman, 1991], and even more significant reduction can be achieved for images with large areas of the same gray-level if a quadtree coding scheme is applied (see Section 4.3.2). An example is given in Figure 14.6, where the principle of quadtree image compression is presented. Large image areas of the same gray-level can be represented in higher-level quadtree nodes without the necessity of including lower-level nodes in the image representation [White, 1987]. Clearly, the compression ratio achieved is image dependent and a fine checkerboard image, for instance, will not be represented efficiently using quadtrees. Modifications of the basic method exist, some of them successfully applied to motion image compression [Strobach, 1990] or incorporating hybrid schemes [Park and Lee, 1991].

This compression approach affords the feasibility of progressive image transmission and the idea of smart compression.

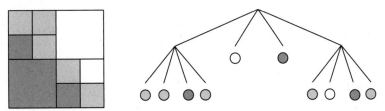

Figure 14.6: Quadtree image compression: original image and corresponding quadtree. © *Cengage Learning 2015.*

Progressive image transmission is based on the fact that transmitting all image data may not be necessary under some circumstances. Imagine a situation in which an operator is searching an image database looking for a particular image. If the transmission is based on a raster scanning order, all the data must be transmitted to view the whole image, but often it is not necessary to have the highest possible image quality to find the image for which the operator is looking. Images do not have to be displayed with the highest available resolution, and lower resolution may be sufficient to reject an image. This approach is commonly used by WWW image transmissions. In progressive transmission, the images are represented in a pyramid structure, the higher pyramid levels (lower resolution) being transmitted first. The number of pixels representing a lower-resolution image is substantially smaller and thus the user can decide from lower-resolution images whether further image refinement is needed. A standard M-pyramid (mean or matrix pyramid) consists of about one third more nodes than the number of image pixels. Several pyramid encoding schemes have been designed to decrease the necessary number of nodes in pyramid representation: reduced sum pyramids, difference pyramids, and reduced difference pyramids [Wang and Goldberg, 1989]. The reduced difference pyramid has the number of nodes exactly equal to the number of image pixels and can be used for a lossless progressive image transmission with some degree of compression. Using an appropriate interpolation method in the image reconstruction stage, reasonable image quality can be achieved at a bit rate of less than 0.1 bit/pixel and excellent quality at a bit rate of about 1.2 bits/pixel. Progressive image transmission is illustrated in Figure 3.11, where a sequence of four resolutions is presented. Considering a hypothetical progressive image transmission, a 1/8-resolution image is transmitted first (Figure 3.11d). Next, the image is transmitted and displayed in 1/4 resolution (Figure 3.11c), followed by 1/2 resolution (Figure 3.11b) and then full resolution (Figure 3.11a).

Smart compression is based on the properties of human visual sensors. The spatial resolution of the eye decreases significantly with increasing distance from the optical axis, so the eye only sees in high resolution in a very small area close to the point where it is focused. Similarly, as with image displays, where it does not make sense to display or even transmit an image in higher resolution than that of the display device, it is not necessary to display an image in full resolution in areas where the eyes are not focused. This is the principle of smart image compression. The main difficulty is in determining the areas of interest in the image on which the user will focus. When considering a smart progressive image transmission, the image is first transmitted in higher resolution in areas of interest—this improves the subjective rating of transmission speed as sensed by a user. The areas of interest may be obtained in a feedback control manner by tracking the user's eyes (assuming the communication channel is fast enough). The image point on which the user is focused may be used to increase resolution in that particular area so that the most important data are transmitted first. This smart image transmission and compression may be extremely useful if applied to dynamic image generators in driving or flight simulators, or to high-definition television.

14.6   Comparison of compression methods

The main goal of image compression is to minimize image data volume with no significant loss of information, and all basic image compression groups have advantages and disadvantages. Transform-based methods better preserve subjective image quality, and are less sensitive to statistical image property changes both inside a single image and between images. Prediction methods, on the other hand, can achieve higher compression ratios in a much less expensive way, tend to be much faster than transform-based or vector quantization compression schemes, and can easily be realized in hardware. If compressed images are transmitted, an important property is insensitivity to transmission channel noise. Transform-based techniques are significantly less sensitive to channel noise—if a transform coefficient is corrupted during transmission, the resulting image distortion is spread homogeneously through the image or image part and is not too disturbing. Erroneous transmission of a difference value in prediction compressions causes not only an error in a particular pixel, it influences values in the neighborhood because the predictor involved has a considerable visual effect in a reconstructed image. Vector quantization methods require a complex coder, their parameters are very sensitive to image data, and they blur image edges. The advantage is in a simple decoding scheme consisting of a look-up table only. Pyramid-based techniques have a natural compression ability, and are suitable for dynamic image compression and for progressive and smart transmission approaches.

Hybrid compression methods combine good properties of the various groups. A hybrid compression of three-dimensional image data (two spatial dimensions plus one spectral dimension) is a good example. A two-dimensional discrete transform (cosine, Hadamard, ...) is applied to each mono-spectral image followed by a predictive compression in the third dimension of spectral components. Hybrid methods combine the different dimensionalities of transform compressions and predictive compressions. As a general rule, at least a one-dimensional transform compression precedes predictive compression steps. In addition to combinations of transform and predictive approaches, predictive approaches are often combined with vector quantization.

14.7   Other techniques

Various other compression methods exist. If an image is quantized into a small number of gray-levels and has a small number of regions of the same gray-level, an effective compression method may be based on **coding region borders** [Wilkins and Wintz, 1971]. Image representation by its *low and high frequencies* is another method—reconstruction is a superposition of inverse transforms of low- and high-frequency components. The low-frequency image can be represented by a significantly smaller volume of data than the original, while the high-frequency image has significant image edges only and can be represented efficiently [Graham, 1967]. **Region growing** compression stores an algorithm for region growing from seed points, each region being represented by its seed point. If an image can be represented only by region seed points, significant compression is achieved.

Block truncation coding divides an image into small square blocks of pixels and each pixel value in a block is truncated to one bit by thresholding and moment preserving selection of binary levels [Delp and Mitchell, 1979; Rosenfeld and Kak, 1982; Kruger, 1992]. One bit value per pixel has to be transmitted, together with information describing how to recreate the moment preserving binary levels during reconstruction. This is fast and easy to implement. **Visual pattern image** coding is capable of high-quality compression with very good compression ratios (30:1) and is exceptionally fast [Silsbee et al., 1991].

Fractal image compression is another approach offering extremely high compression ratios and high-quality image reconstruction. Additionally, because fractals are infinitely magnifiable, fractal compression is resolution independent and so a single compressed image can be used efficiently for display in any resolution, including some higher than the original [Furht et al., 1995]. Breaking an image into pieces (fractals) and identifying self-similar ones is the principle of the approach [Barnsley and Hurd, 1993; Fisher, 1994]. First, the image is partitioned into non-overlapping domain regions of any size and shape that completely cover it. Then, larger range regions are defined that can overlap and need not cover the entire image. These range regions are geometrically transformed using affine transforms (Section 5.2.1) to match the domain regions. Then the set of affine coefficients together with information about the selection of domain regions represents the fractal image encoding. The fractally compressed images are stored and transmitted as recursive algorithms—sets of equations with instructions on how to reproduce the image. Clearly, this is compute demanding. However, decompression is simple and fast; domain regions are iteratively replaced with appropriately geometrically transformed range regions using the affine coefficients. Thus, fractal compression is another example of useful asymmetric compression-decompression scheme.

14.8   Coding

In addition to techniques designed explicitly to cope with 2D (or higher-dimensional) data, there is a wide range of well-known algorithms designed with serial data (e.g., simple text files) in mind. Very well known is **Huffman encoding**, which can provide optimal compression and error-free decompression [Rosenfeld and Kak, 1982]. The main idea of Huffman coding is to represent data by codes of variable length, with more frequent data being represented by shorter codes. Many modifications of the original algorithm

[Huffman, 1952] exist, with adaptive Huffman coding algorithms requiring only one pass over the data [Knuth, 1985; Vitter, 1987]. The **Lempel-Ziv** (or Lempel-Ziv-Welch, LZW) algorithm of **dictionary-based** coding [Ziv and Lempel, 1978; Nelson, 1989] has found wide favor as a standard compression algorithm. Here, data are represented by pointers referring to a dictionary of symbols.

These, and a number of similar techniques, are in widespread use for de-facto standard image representations which are popular for WWW image exchange. Of these, the *GIF* format (Graphics Interchange Format) is frequently used. GIF is designed for the encoding of RGB images (and the appropriate palette) with pixel depths between 1 and 8 bits. Blocks of data are encoded using the LZW algorithm. GIF has two main versions— 87a and 89a [Compuserve, 1989], the latter supporting the storing of text and graphics in the same file. Additionally, *TIFF* (Tagged Image File Format) is widely encountered. TIFF has gone through a number of versions to incorporate RGB color, compressed color (LZW), other color formats, and ultimately (in Version 6 [Aldus, 1992]), JPEG compression (see Section 14.9)—these versions all have backward compatibility. There are some recorded problems with the JPEG implementation, and TIFF has a reputation for being complex, although this is undeserved and it is a powerful programmer's tool.

14.9   JPEG and MPEG image compression

There is an increasing effort to achieve standardization in image compression. The Joint Photographic Experts Group (JPEG) has developed an international standard for general purpose, color, still image compression. As a logical extension of JPEG still image compression, the Motion Picture Experts Group (MPEG) standard was developed for full-motion video image sequences with applications to digital video distribution and high-definition television (HDTV) in mind.

14.9.1   JPEG—still image compression

The JPEG compression system is widely used in many application areas. Four compression modes are furnished:

- Sequential DCT-based compression.

- Progressive DCT-based compression.

- Sequential lossless predictive compression.

- Hierarchical lossy or lossless compression.

While the lossy compression modes were designed to achieve compression ratios around 15 with very good or excellent image quality, the quality deteriorates for higher compression ratios. A compression ratio between 2 and 3 is typically achieved in the lossless mode.

Sequential JPEG compression

Following Figure 14.1, sequential JPEG compression consists of a forward DCT transform, a quantizer, and an entropy encoder, while decompression starts with entropy decoding followed by dequantizing and inverse DCT.

In the compression stage, the unsigned image values from the interval $[0, 2^b - 1]$ are first shifted to cover the interval $[-2^{b-1}, 2^{b-1} - 1]$. The image is then divided into 8×8 blocks and each block is independently transformed into the frequency domain using the DCT-II transform (Section 3.2.6, equation 3.46). Many of the 64 DCT coefficients have zero or near-zero values in typical 8×8 blocks, which forms the basis for compression. The 64 coefficients are quantized using a quantization table $Q(u, v)$ of integers from 1 to 255 that is specified by the application to reduce the storage/transmission requirements of coefficients that contribute little or nothing to the image content. The following formula is used for quantization:

$$F_Q(u, v) = \text{round} \left(\frac{F(u, v)}{Q(u, v)} \right) . \tag{14.10}$$

After quantization, the DC coefficient $F(0, 0)$ is followed by the 63 AC coefficients that are ordered in a 2D matrix in a zigzag fashion according to increasing frequency. The DC coefficients are then encoded using predictive coding (Section 14.3), the rationale being that average gray-levels of adjacent 8×8 blocks (DC coefficients) tend to be similar.

The last step of the sequential JPEG compression algorithm is entropy encoding. Two approaches are specified by the JPEG standard. The baseline system uses simple Huffman coding, while the extended system uses arithmetic coding and is suitable for a wider range of applications.

Sequential JPEG decompression uses all the steps described above in the reverse order. After entropy decoding (Huffman or arithmetic), the symbols are converted into DCT coefficients and dequantized:

$$F_Q'(u, v) = F_Q(u, v) \, Q(u, v) , \tag{14.11}$$

where again, the $Q(u, v)$ are quantization coefficients from the quantization table that is transmitted together with the image data. Finally, the inverse DCT transform is performed according to equation (3.47) and the image gray values are shifted back to the interval $[0, 2^b - 1]$.

The JPEG compression algorithm can be extended to color or multi-spectral images with up to 256 spectral bands.

Progressive JPEG compression

The JPEG standard also facilitates progressive image transmission (Section 14.5). In the progressive mode, a sequence of scans is produced, each containing a coded subset of DCT coefficients. Thus, a buffer is needed at the output of the quantizer to store all DCT coefficients of the entire image. These coefficients are selectively encoded.

Three algorithms are defined as part of the JPEG progressive compression standard: **progressive spectral selection**, **progressive successive approximation**, and the **combined progressive algorithm**. In the progressive spectral selection approach, the DC coefficients are transmitted first, followed by groups of low-frequency and higher-frequency coefficients. In the progressive successive approximation, all DCT coefficients are sent first with lower precision, and their precision is increased as additional scans are transmitted. The combined progressive algorithm uses both of the above principles together.

Sequential lossless JPEG compression

The lossless mode of the JPEG compression uses a simple predictive compression algorithm and Huffman coding to encode the prediction differences (Section 14.3).

Hierarchical JPEG compression

Using the hierarchical JPEG mode, decoded images can be displayed either progressively or at different resolutions. An image pyramid is created and each lower-resolution image is used as a prediction for the next-higher level (Section 14.5). Sequential DCT, progressive DCT, or lossless modes can be used to encode the lower-resolution images.

In addition to still image JPEG compression, motion JPEG (MJPEG) compression exists that can be applied to real-time full motion applications. However, MPEG compression represents a more common standard and is described below.

14.9.2   JPEG–2000 compression

JPEG–2000 is an international standard for still image compression which overcomes some limitations of the original standard (Section 14.9.1). Despite the naming similarity, it is not an extension of JPEG—rather, it is a different, very powerful and flexible environment for image compression. Its flexibility allows compression of different types of still images (bi-level, gray-level, color, multi-band) with different characteristics (natural images, scientific, medical, military imagery, text, rendered graphics) within a unified system. It removes the need for different compression mechanisms for lossless and lossy compression by representing the lossless compression as a cohesive extension of lossy compression. This important paradigm shift compared to the JPEG standard permits the compression of image data in a lossless manner and—at a later time—a selective data removal to represent images in a lossy fashion while increasing the compression ratio. Note that this lossless and lossy behavior can be achieved from the same compressed image data source—this feature is called **quality scalability**. Another JPEG–2000 feature is the option of **resolution scalability**, which allows the extraction of lower resolution images from the same data source. Additionally, **spatial scalability** provides a tool to selectively reconstruct individually defined regions from the compressed image data source.

While the standard creates a unified image compression environment, it only specifies the decoder operations, bitstream syntax, and file format, effectively allowing for future improvements and innovations of the coding operation. For encoding, two primary paths and several options exist. A reversible component transform (RCT) is used with the 5×3 wavelet filter (Section 3.2.7) whenever lossless compression is desired. Decreased bit rates and increased compression ratios can be achieved by truncation during the quantization step–of course yielding a decrease in image quality.

For purely lossy coding, the YCbCr transform (shown here for RGB image data) transforms the RGB signal to the intensity component Y and two color components (C_b for blue and C_r for red) as follows:

$$Y = +0.299\,R + 0.587\,G + 0.114\,B\,,$$
$$C_b = -0.168736\,R - 0.331264\,G + 0.5\,B\,,$$
$$C_r = +0.5\,R - 0.418688\,G - 0.081312\,B\,. \tag{14.12}$$

After this, a 9×7 wavelet transform, and arbitrary quantization by division, is used in addition to truncation. Both of these main paths have several options for identification of the region of interest, coding options to trade complexity and performance, and choices about the amount of scalability in the bitstream.

For better understanding, the high-level coverage of the JPEG–2000 compression approach given below exploits the compression rather than the reconstruction path. More detailed information can be found in [Taubman and Marcellin, 2001; Colyer and Clark, 2003]. Figure 14.7 gives an overview of the JPEG–2000 compression approach; the main data path is shown in the bottom of the schematic diagram.

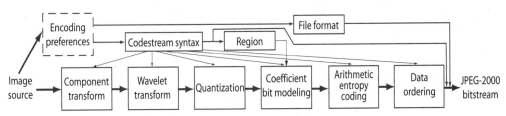

Figure 14.7: Schematic of JPEG–2000 data compression. © *Cengage Learning 2015.*

To start the compression, the image is divided into rectangular, non-overlapping tiles on a regular grid (border tiles may be sized as needed). Arbitrary tile sizes are allowed, up to using a single tile representing the entire image. The *component transform* block takes the original image data as input and decorrelates the image components of a multi-band image—typically the R,G,B channels of the color image. Decorrelation yields an improved compression performance and allows for visually relevant quantization. As described above, when using the lossless path, RCT is employed which maps integers to integers. When the lossy (irreversible) path is used the floating-point YCbCr transform is employed in the same way as it is used in the original color JPEG compression.

The *wavelet transform* is the heart of the JPEG–2000 compression and can be performed in two ways. Both of the wavelet transform options provide lower resolution and spatial decorrelation of the images. The 9×7 biorthogonal Daubechies filter provides the highest compression, while the Le Gall 5×3 filter is of a lower complexity and allows lossless compression. The advanced parts of the JPEG–2000 standard facilitate simultaneous use of multiple wavelets including user-defined wavelet transforms for which the coefficients are specified in the bitstream. One of the most obvious artifacts of the original JPEG compression is the blocky character of the reconstructed images due to the rectangular image blocks to which the DCT is applied. Since the wavelet compression can be applied to the entire image, which is converted into a series of wavelets, the blockiness may be completely removed. Even if the block-based wavelet transformation is employed, the blockiness is substantially decreased; smoother color toning and clearer edges result in locations of sharp changes of color.

The *quantization* step offers a trade-off between compression ratio and image quality. Similar to JPEG, the wavelet coefficients can be divided by a different value for each image subband. Some of the coded data can be discarded to increase the compression ratio. Many approaches exist this [Zeng et al., 2000]. The *context model* groups quantized wavelet coefficients according to their statistical similarity to increase the efficiency of their compression. Individual coefficient bitplanes are processed by one of three coding passes described in [Taubman et al., 2000]. The *binary arithmetic coder* provides lossless compression of each coding pass of quantized wavelet coefficients. Portions of the data output from the arithmetic coder form the compressed data *bitstream*. The coded data are collected into *packets*. Each packet has a compressed header allowing data to be accessed in almost any order, although some order requirements are maintained. Specific orderings facilitate several progressive compression options, e.g., according to the resulting image resolution, quality, location, or their combinations.

The *codestream syntax* prescribes marker segments, which determine the location of the coded data with respect to a given spatial image location, resolution, and quality. Any image-related data which are not directly needed to reconstruct the image are stored in the optional *file format* data. Data format information was included to avoid formation of non-standard proprietary formats as happened with the original JPEG standard. The file format begins with a unique signature, has a profile indicator, and repeats the width, height, and depth information from the codestream. The file format data may also contain a limited color specification, capture and display resolution, intellectual property rights information, and/or additional meta-data [Boliek et al., 2000].

The benefits of JPEG–2000 are wide [Gormish et al., 2000]. In web-based applications, it allows initial and quick display of a low resolution version of the image, say of a map. Later, any part of the map can be requested via the region of interest selection and the server would only provide the necessary additional data for that spatial region at the required resolution. Further, if the user requests a printout of that region, a higher resolution version that is matched to the printer resolution would be fetched over the network and, based on the gray-level or color printer capabilities, only grayscale or color information would be transferred. The selective transmission of only necessary data by the specific application is an inherent and intriguing feature of the JPEG–2000 standard.

Similarly, consider the common situation of storing high resolution digital photographs, and running out of storage space. With current compression approaches, one image must be deleted before we can store another. If photos are stored using JPEG–2000, it is possible incrementally decrease the quality of all stored images in order to make space for new ones.

JPEG–2000 is a much better compression tool than JPEG when high image quality is demanded, even when using lossy compression. For lossy compression, data has shown that JPEG–2000 can typically compress images 20–200% more than JPEG. Note that JPEG–2000 can handle up to 256 image channels while the original JPEG was, due to its common implementation, limited to only 3-channel color data. JPEG–2000 compression ratios of about 2.5 are typical for lossless compression. *Motion JPEG* (discussed in the previous section) is frequently used for editing production-quality video without the existence of an internationally accepted standard. JPEG–2000 includes standardized *Motion JPEG-2000* format.

For applications requiring either higher image quality or low bitrates, and if previously unavailable and newly included features are of interest, JPEG–2000 is the compression standard of choice. The original JPEG standard is not likely to disappear quickly. It will probably survive as a useful tool for lower complexity applications.

14.9.3   MPEG—full-motion video compression

Video and associated audio data can be compressed using *MPEG*. Using inter-frame compression, compression ratios of 200 can be achieved in full-motion, motion-intensive video applications maintaining reasonable quality. MPEG facilitates many features of the compressed video; random access, fast forward/reverse searches, reverse playback, audio-visual synchronization, robustness to error, editability, format flexibility, and cost trade-off [LeGall, 1991; Steinmetz, 1994]. Three standards are frequently cited:

- MPEG-1 for compression of low-resolution (320 × 240) full-motion video at rates of 1–1.5 Mb/s

- MPEG-2 for higher-resolution standards such as TV and HDTV at rates of 2–80 Mb/s

- MPEG-4 for small-frame full motion compression with slow refresh needs, rates of 9–40 kb/s for video telephony and interactive multimedia such as video conferencing

MPEG can be equally well used for both symmetric and asymmetric applications. Here, video compression will be described; a description of the audio compression that is also part of the standard can be found elsewhere [Pennebaker and Mitchell, 1993; Steinmetz, 1994].

The video data consist of a sequence of image frames. In the MPEG compression scheme, three frame types are defined: *intraframes I*; *predicted frames P*; and *forward, backward, or bi-directionally predicted or interpolated frames B*. Each frame type is coded using a different algorithm; Figure 14.8 shows how the frame types may be positioned in the sequence.

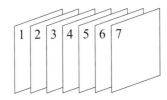

I B B P B B I......

Figure 14.8: MPEG image frames. © *Cengage Learning 2015.*

I-frames are self-contained and coded using a DCT-based compression method similar to JPEG. Thus, I-frames serve as random access frames in MPEG frame streams and consequently are compressed with the lowest compression ratios. P-frames are coded using forward predictive coding with reference to the previous I- or P-frame, and their compression ratio is substantially higher than that for I-frames. B-frames are coded using forward, backward, or bi-directional motion-compensated prediction or interpolation using two reference frames, closest past and future I- or P-frames, and offer the highest compression ratios.

Note that in the hypothetical MPEG stream shown in Figure 14.8, the frames must be transmitted in the following sequence (subscripts denote frame numbers): I_1–P_4–B_2–B_3–I_7–B_5–B_6– etc.; the frames B_2 and B_3 must be transmitted after frame P_4 to enable frame interpolation used for B-frame decompression. Clearly, the highest compression ratios can be achieved by incorporation of a large number of B-frames; if only I-frames are used, MJPEG compression results. The following sequence seems to be effective for a large number of applications [Steinmetz, 1994]

$$(I\,B\,B\,P\,B\,B\,P\,B\,B\,)(I\,B\,B\,P\,B\,B\,P\,B\,B\,)\ldots \qquad (14.13)$$

While coding the I-frames is straightforward, coding of P- and B-frames incorporates motion estimation (see also Chapter 16). For every 16×16 block of P- or B-frames, one motion vector is determined for P- and forward or backward predicted B-frames, two motion vectors are calculated for interpolated B-frames. The motion estimation technique is not specified in the MPEG standard, but block matching techniques are widely used, generally following the matching approaches presented in Section 6.4, equation (6.32) [Furht et al., 1995]. After the motion vectors are estimated, differences between the predicted and actual blocks are determined and represent the error terms which are encoded using DCT. As usually, entropy encoding is employed as the final step.

A specific MPEG-4 variant often referred to as *MP4* (MPEG-4 Part 14) is in widespread use, especially for streaming across the Internet. MP4 is a general container that is able to store video, audio, subtitles, stills etc.

14.10 Summary

- **Image data compression**

  - The main goal of image compression is to minimize image data volume with no significant loss of information.

  - Image compression algorithms aim to remove redundancy present in data (correlation of data) in a way which makes image reconstruction possible; this is *information preserving compression*.

  - A typical image *compression/decompression* sequence consists of data redundancy reduction, coding, transmission, decoding, and reconstruction.

  - Data compression methods can be divided into two principal groups:

    * *Information preserving—lossless*—compressions permit error-free data reconstruction.

    * *Lossy* compression methods do not preserve information completely.

- **Image data properties**

  - Information content of an image is an important property of which *entropy* is a measure.

  - Knowing image entropy, information *redundancy* can be determined.

- **Discrete image transforms in image data compression**

  - Image data are represented by *coefficients* of discrete image transforms. Transform coefficients are *ordered* according to their importance, i.e., according to their contribution to the image information contents. Low-contribution coefficients are omitted.

  - To remove correlated (redundant) image data, the *Karhunen-Loève* transform is the most effective.

  - *Cosine, Fourier, Hadamard, Walsh*, or *binary* transforms are all suitable for image data compression.

— Performance of the *discrete cosine transform DCT-II* approaches that of the Karhunen-Loève transform better than others. The DCT is usually applied to small image blocks (typically 8×8 pixels), yielding quality-decreasing blocking artifacts for larger compression ratios.

— Consequently, *wavelet image compression* is of interest because it does not generate square image compression artifacts.

- **Predictive compression methods**

  — Predictive compressions use image information redundancy to construct an estimate of gray-level values from values of gray-levels in the neighborhood.

  — *Differences* between estimates and reality, which are expected to be relatively small in absolute terms, are coded and transmitted together with prediction model parameters.

- **Vector quantization**

  — Vector quantization compression is based on dividing an image into small blocks and representing these blocks as *vectors*.

  — Input data vectors are coded using unique *codewords* from a *codeword dictionary*; instead of vectors, the vector codes are stored or transmitted.

  — The code dictionary (code book) is transmitted together with the coded data.

- **Hierarchical and progressive compression methods**

  — Substantial reduction in bit volume can be obtained by representing a source as a pyramid. More significant reduction can be achieved for images with large areas of the same gray-level in a quadtree coding scheme.

  — Hierarchical compression facilitates *progressive* and *smart* image transmission.

  — Progressive image transmission is based on the fact that transmitting all image data may not be necessary under some circumstances.

  — Smart compression is based on the properties of human visual sensors—it is not necessary to display an image in full resolution in areas where the user's eyes are not focused.

- **Comparison of compression methods**

  — Transform-based methods better preserve subjective image quality, and are less sensitive to statistical image property changes both inside a single image and between images.

  — Prediction methods can achieve larger compression ratios in a less expensive way, and tend to be faster than transform-based or vector quantization compression schemes.

  — Vector quantization methods require a complex coder, their parameters are very sensitive to image data, and they blur image edges. The advantage is in a simple decoding scheme consisting of a look-up table only.

- **Other techniques**

  - *Fractal image compression* offers extremely high compression ratios and high-quality image reconstruction. Breaking an image into pieces (fractals) and identifying self-similar ones is the main principle. Fractals are infinitely magnifiable, thus fractal compression is *resolution independent* and a single compressed image can be efficiently used for display in any image resolution.

- **Coding**

  - *Huffman encoding* can provide optimal compression and error-free decompression. The main idea of Huffman coding is to represent data by codes of variable length, with more frequent data being represented by shorter codes.

- **JPEG and MPEG image compression**

  - JPEG and JPEG-2000 represent international standards in image compression.
  - JPEG image compression was developed for general-purpose, color, still image compression. Four JPEG compression modes exist:
    * Sequential DCT-based compression
    * Progressive DCT-based compression
    * Sequential lossless predictive compression
    * Hierarchical lossy or lossless compression
  - JPEG-2000 is designed to overcome some JPEG limitations. Despite the naming similarity, it is different to JPEG.
  - JPEG-2000 is wavelet-transform based and offers a rich and flexible set of new functionalities in respect of quality, resolution, and spatial scalability.
  - JPEG-2000 typically outperforms JPEG compression in applications requiring either high quality image reconstruction or low bitrate compression.
  - The *MPEG standard* was developed for full-motion video image sequences.
  - Three standards are frequently cited:
    * MPEG-1 for compression of low-resolution full-motion video
    * MPEG-2 for higher-resolution standards
    * MPEG-4 for small-frame full-motion compression with slow refresh needs

14.11   Exercises

Short-answer questions

S14.1 Explain the difference between lossy and lossless image compression,

S14.2 Give definitions of:

(a) Image entropy

(b) Image redundancy

(c) Compression ratio

S14.3 How can image entropy be used to determine information redundancy?

S14.4 Draw a diagram of image compression/transmission/decompression – include all main steps.

S14.5 Explain the basic idea of image compression using discrete image transforms.

S14.6 Explain the basic idea of predictive image compression.

S14.7 Explain the basic idea of image compression based on vector quantization.

S14.8 What are symmetric and asymmetric image compression applications?

S14.9 Explain the concept of progressive image transmission and smart compression.

S14.10 Explain the basic idea of fractal image compression.

S14.11 What is the basic idea of Huffman coding?

S14.12 What kind of image data can be compressed using the JPEG and MPEG compression algorithms?

S14.13 What are the four compression modes available in the JPEG compression standard? Describe the algorithm employed in each of the four modes.

S14.14 What are the main differences between original JPEG and JPEG-2000 compression schemes?

S14.15 What image data are the three most frequently used MPEG standards applied to?

S14.16 Explain the roles of the **I-**, **P-**, **B-** frames in MPEG compression.

S14.17 MPEG compression – why are individual frames in an image sequence compressed using different approaches?

Problems

P14.1 Assume a gray-level image represented using 2 bits per pixel. The probabilities of the four gray-levels $\{0, 1, 2, 3\}$ are as follows: $P(0) = 0.1$, $P(1) = 0.3$, $P(2) = 0.5$, $P(3) = 0.1$.

    (a) Determine the image entropy.

    (b) Determine the information redundancy.

    (c) Determine the theoretically achievable lossless image compression ratio.

    (d) What is the minimum size of a 4-level 512×512 image after such lossless compression?

P14.2 Repeat Problem P14.1 considering a 4-level image in which all gray-levels are equally probable.

P14.3 Compare entropies of two 4-level images A and B;

    • A: $P(0) = 0.2$, $P(1) = 0.0$, $P(2) = 0.0$, $P(3) = 0.8$

    • B: $P(0) = 0.0$, $P(1) = 0.8$, $P(2) = 0.0$, $P(3) = 0.2$.

P14.4 Develop a program to compute an estimate of the achievable compression ratio of an image from its gray-level histogram.

P14.5 Compare image compression performance for several widely available algorithms. Using any image viewer capable of converting between different formats, compare the storage requirements of a variety of image formats such as PBM, GIF, TIFF–no compression, TIFF–LZW compression, JPEG at 50%, 25%, 15%, 5%. By re-opening the stored images, compare the image quality visually; do you see any blocking artifacts if JPEG compression was employed? Order the image formats/compression parameters according to their storage requirements. What can be concluded if you assess the image quality considering the storage requirements?

P14.6 Use your computer screen-grabbing tools to grab a portion of a text from a window. Store it in a gray-scale mode using GIF and JPEG (75%, 25%, and 5%). Compare the storage requirements and the resulting image quality.

P14.7 Develop a program for transform-based image compression by applying the Fourier transform to 8×8 blocks (use any 2D discrete Fourier transform implementation—they are easily downloadable). Compute a difference image between the reconstructed image and the original image. Determine the compression ratio and the maximum gray-level difference. Perform the compression in the following ways:

    (a) Retain 15% of the transform coefficients.

    (b) Retain 25% of the transform coefficients.

    (c) Retain 50% of the transform coefficients.

P14.8 Develop a program for DPCM image compression using a third-order predictor.

P14.9 GIF (lossless) and JPEG (lossy) compressed images are commonly used on the World Wide Web. Determine compression ratios of several GIF and JPEG compressed images; assume that original color images were represented using 24 bits per pixel and gray-scale images by 8 bits per pixel. Which compression scheme seems to provide consistently higher compression ratio? Can you determine by inspection which of the two compression approaches was used?

P14.10 MPEG compressed image sequences are commonly used on the World Wide Web. Determine compression ratios of several MPEG compressed sequences; assume that original color images were represented using 24 bits per pixel. (An MPEG viewer that provides information about the number of frames in the sequence will be needed.)

P14.11 Make yourself familiar with solved problems and **Matlab** implementations of selected algorithms provided in the corresponding chapter of the **Matlab Companion** to this text [Svoboda et al., 2008]. The **Matlab Companion** homepage http://visionbook.felk.cvut.cz offers images used in the problems, and well-commented **Matlab** code is provided for educational purposes.

P14.12 Use the **Matlab Companion** [Svoboda et al., 2008] to develop solutions to additional exercises and practical problems provided there. Implement your solutions using **Matlab** or other suitable programming languages.

14.12 References

Aldus. *TIFF Developer's Toolkit, Revision 6.0.* Aldus Corporation, Seattle, WA, 1992.

Barnsley M. and Hurd L. *Fractal Image Compression.* A K Peters Ltd., Wellesley, MA, 1993.

Boliek M., Houchin S., and Wu G. JPEG 2000 next generation image compression system: Features and syntax. In *Proceedings ICIP-2000, Vol. 2*, pages 45–48. IEEE, 2000.

Boxerman J. L. and Lee H. J. Variable block-sized vector quantization of grayscale images with unconstrained tiling. In *Visual Communications and Image Processing '90*, Lausanne, Switzerland, pages 847–858, Bellingham, WA, 1990. SPIE.

Chang C. Y., Kwok R., and Curlander J. C. Spatial compression of Seasat SAR images. *IEEE Transactions on Geoscience and Remote Sensing*, 26(5):673–685, 1988.

Colyer G. and Clark R. *Guide to the practical implementation of JPEG 2000 – PD 6777.* British Standards Institute, London, 2003.

Compuserve. *Graphics Interchange Format: Version 89a.* CompuServe Incorporated, Columbus, OH, 1989.

Daut D. G. and Zhao D. Improved DPCM algorithm for image data compression. In *Image Processing Algorithms and Techniques,* Santa Clara, CA, pages 199–210, Bellingham, WA, 1990. SPIE.

De Lameillieure J. and Bruyland I. Single stage 280 Mbps coding of HDTV using HDPCM with a vector quantizer based on masking functions. *Signal Processing: Image Communication,* 2(3):279–289, 1990.

Delp E. J. and Mitchell O. R. Image truncation using block truncation coding. *IEEE Transactions on Communications,* 27:1335–1342, 1979.

Farelle P. M. *Recursive Block Coding for Image Data Compression.* Springer Verlag, New York, 1990.

Fisher Y. *Fractal Compression: Theory and Applications to Digital Images.* Springer Verlag, Berlin, New York, 1994.

Furht B., Smoliar S. W., and Zhang H. *Video and Image Processing in Multimedia Systems.* Kluwer, Boston–Dordrecht–London, 1995.

Gersho A. and Gray R. M. *Vector Quantization and Signal Compression.* Kluwer, Norwell, MA, 1992.

Gormish M. J., Lee D., and Marcellin M. W. JPEG 2000: Overview, architecture, and applications. In *Proceedings ICIP-2000, Vol. 2,* pages 29–32, 2000.

Graham D. N. Image transmission by two–dimensional contour coding. *Proceedings IEEE,* 55: 336–346, 1967.

Gray R. M. Vector quantization. *IEEE ASSP Magazine,* 1(2):4–29, 1984.

Huffman D. A. A method for the construction of minimum-redundancy codes. *Proceedings of IRE,* 40(9):1098–1101, 1952.

Knuth D. E. Dynamic Huffman coding. *Journal of Algorithms,* 6:163–180, 1985.

Kruger A. Block truncation compression. *Dr Dobb's J Software Tools,* 17(4):48–55, 1992.

LeGall D. MPEG: A video compression standard for multimedia applications. *Communications of the ACM,* 34:45–68, 1991.

Moik J. G. *Digital Processing of Remotely Sensed Images.* NASA SP–431, Washington, DC, 1980.

Nelson M. R. LZW data compression. *Dr Dobb's J Software Tools,* 14, 1989.

Netravali A. N. *Digital Pictures: Representation and Compression.* Plenum Press, New York, 1988.

Park S. H. and Lee S. U. Pyramid image coder using classified transform vector quantization. *Signal Processing,* 22(1):25–42, 1991.

Pennebaker W. B. and Mitchell J. L. *JPEG Still Image Data Compression Standard.* Van Nostrand Reinhold, New York, 1993.

Pratt W. K. *Digital Image Processing.* Wiley, New York, 2nd edition, 1991.

Rao R. P. and Pearlman W. A. On entropy of pyramid structures. *IEEE Transactions on Information Theory,* 37(2):407–413, 1991.

Rosenfeld A. and Kak A. C. *Digital Picture Processing.* Academic Press, New York, 2nd edition, 1982.

Salomon D. *Data Compression: The Complete Reference.* Springer, 2 edition, 2000.

Sayood K. *Introduction to data compression.* Morgan Kaufmann Publishers, Burlington, USA, 2 edition, 2000.

Shukla K. K. and Prasad M. *Lossy Image Compression.* Springer, 2011.

Silsbee P., Bovik A. C., and Chen D. Visual pattern image sequencing coding. In *Visual Communications and Image Processing '90,* Lausanne, Switzerland, pages 532–543, Bellingham, WA, 1991. SPIE.

Steinmetz R. Data compression in multimedia computing—standards and systems, parts i and ii. *Journal of Multimedia Systems*, 1:166–172 and 187–204, 1994.

Strobach P. Tree-structured scene adaptive coder. *IEEE Transactions on Communications*, 38 (4):477–486, 1990.

Svoboda T., Kybic J., and Hlavac V. *Image Processing, Analysis, and Machine Vision: A MATLAB Companion.* Thomson Engineering, 2008.

Taubman D. S., Ordentlich E., Weinberger M., Seroussi G., Ueno I., and Ono F. Embedded block coding in JPEG 2000. In *Proceedings ICIP-2000, Vol. 2*, pages 33–36. IEEE, 2000.

Taubman D. S. and Marcellin M. W. *JPEG 2000: Image Compression Fundamentals, Standards and Practice.* Kluwer, Boston, MA, 2001.

Vitter J. S. Design and analysis of dynamic Huffman codes. *Journal of the ACM*, 34(4):825–845, 1987.

Wang L. and Goldberg M. Reduced-difference pyramid: A data structure for progressive image transmission. *Optical Engineering*, 28(7):708–716, 1989.

White R. G. Compressing image data with quadtrees. *Dr Dobb's J Software Tools*, 12(3):16–45, 1987.

Wilkins L. C. and Wintz P. A. Bibliography on data compression, picture properties and picture coding. *IEEE Transactions on Information Theory*, 17:180–199, 1971.

Zailu H. and Taxiao W. MDPCM picture coding. In *1990 IEEE International Symposium on Circuits and Systems,* New Orleans, LA, pages 3253–3255, Piscataway, NJ, 1990. IEEE.

Zeng W., Daly S., and Lei S. Visual optimization tools in JPEG 2000. In *Proceedings ICIP-2000, Vol. 2*, pages 37–40. IEEE, 2000.

Ziv J. and Lempel A. Compression of individual sequences via variable-rate coding. *IEEE Transactions on Information Theory*, 24(5):530–536, 1978.

Chapter 15

Texture

Texture refers to properties that represent the surface or structure of an object (in reflective or transmissive images, respectively); it is widely used, and perhaps intuitively obvious, but has no precise definition due to its wide variability. We might define texture as *something consisting of mutually related elements*; therefore we are considering a group of pixels and the texture described is highly dependent on the number considered [Haralick, 1979]. Examples are shown in Figure 15.1; dog fur, grass, river pebbles, cork, checkered textile, and knitted fabric.

Texture consists of texture **primitives** or texture **elements**, sometimes called **texels**. Primitives in grass and dog fur are represented by several pixels and correspond to a stalk or a pile; cork is built from primitives that are comparable in size with pixels. It is difficult, however, to define primitives for the checkered textile or fabric, which can be defined by at least two hierarchical levels. The first corresponds to textile checks or knitted stripes, and the second to the finer texture of the fabric or individual stitches. As we have seen in many other areas, this is a problem of **scale**; texture description is **scale dependent**.

The main aim of texture analysis is recognition and texture-based shape analysis. Textured properties of regions were referred to many times while considering image segmentation (Chapter 6), and derivation of shape from texture was discussed in Chapter 11. Texture is usually described as **fine**, **coarse**, **grained**, **smooth**, etc., implying that some more precise features must be defined to make machine recognition possible. Such features can be found in the texture **tone** and **structure** [Haralick, 1979]. Tone is based mostly on pixel intensity properties in the primitive, while structure is the spatial relationship between them.

Each pixel can be characterized by its location and tonal properties. A texture primitive is a contiguous set of pixels with some tonal and/or regional property, and can be described by its average intensity, maximum or minimum intensity, size, shape, etc. The spatial relationship of primitives can be random, or they may be pairwise dependent, or some number of primitives can be mutually dependent. Image texture is then described by the number and types of primitives and by their spatial relationship.

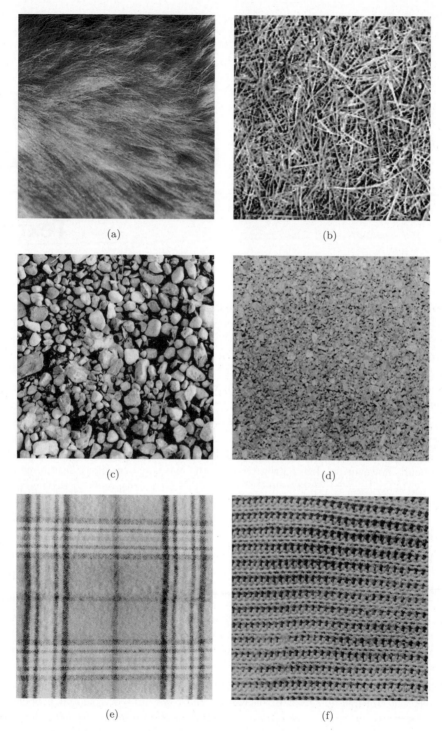

Figure 15.1: Textures. (a) Dog fur. (b) Grass. (c) River pebbles. (d) Cork. (e) Checkered textile. (f) Knitted fabric. © *Cengage Learning 2015.*

Figures 15.1a,b and 15.2a,b show that the same number and the same type of primitives do not necessarily give the same texture. Similarly, Figures 15.2a and 15.2c show that the same spatial relationship of primitives does not guarantee texture uniqueness, and therefore is not sufficient for description. Tone and structure are not independent; textures always display both even though one or the other usually dominates, and we usually speak about one or the other only. Tone can be understood as tonal properties of primitives, taking primitive spatial relationships into consideration. Structure refers to spatial relationships of primitives considering their tonal properties as well.

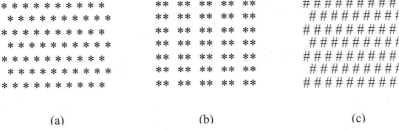

(a)   (b)   (c)

Figure 15.2: Artificial textures. © *Cengage Learning 2015*.

If the texture primitives are small and if the tonal differences between neighboring primitives are large, a **fine** texture results (Figures 15.1a,b and 15.1d). If the primitives are larger and consist of several pixels, a **coarse** texture results (Figures 15.1c and 15.1e). Again, this is a reason for using both tonal and structural properties in texture description. Note that the fine/coarse texture characteristic depends on scale.

Further, textures can be classified according to their strength—texture strength then influences the choice of description method. **Weak** textures have small spatial interactions between primitives, and can be adequately described by frequencies of primitive types appearing in some neighborhood. Because of this, many statistical properties are evaluated in the description of weak textures. In **strong** textures, the spatial interactions between primitives are somewhat regular. To describe strong textures, the frequency of occurrence of primitive pairs in some spatial relationship may be sufficient. Strong texture recognition is usually accompanied by an exact definition of primitives and their spatial relationships.

It remains to define a constant texture. One existing definition [Sklansky, 1978] suggests '*an image region has a constant texture if a set of its local properties in that region is constant, slowly changing, or approximately periodic*'. The set of local properties can be understood as primitive types and their spatial relationships. An important part of the definition is that the properties must be repeated inside the constant texture area. How many times must the properties be repeated? Assume that a large area of constant texture is available, and consider smaller and smaller parts of that texture, digitizing it at constant resolution as long as the texture character remains unchanged. Alternatively, consider larger and larger parts of the texture, digitizing it at constant raster, until details become blurred and the primitives finally disappear. We see that image resolution (scale) must be a consistent part of the description; if the resolution is appropriate, texture character does not change for any position in our window.

Two main texture description approaches exist—**statistical** and **syntactic** [Haralick, 1979]. Statistical methods are suitable if primitive sizes are comparable with pixel sizes. Syntactic and **hybrid** methods (combinations of statistical and syntactic) are more suitable for textures where primitives can be assigned a label—the primitive type—meaning that primitives can be described using a larger variety of properties than just tonal properties; for example, shape description. Instead of tone, brightness will be used more often in the following sections because it corresponds better to gray-level images.

Research on pre-attentive (early) vision [Julesz, 1981] shows that human ability to recognize texture quickly is based mostly on **textons**, which are elongated blobs (rectangles, ellipses, line segments, line ends, crossings, corners) that can be detected by pre-attentive vision, while the positional relationship between neighboring textons must be done slowly by an attentive vision subsystem. As a result of these investigations, methods based on texton detection and texton density computation were developed.

15.1   Statistical texture description

Statistical description methods describe each texture by a feature vector of properties which represents a point in a multi-dimensional feature space. The aim is to find a deterministic or probabilistic decision rule assigning a texture to some specific class (see Chapter 9).

15.1.1   Methods based on spatial frequencies

Measuring spatial frequencies is the basis of a large group of recognition methods. Textural character is in direct relation to the spatial size of the primitives; coarse textures are built from larger primitives, fine textures from smaller primitives. Fine textures are characterized by higher spatial frequencies, coarse textures by lower spatial frequencies.

One of many related spatial frequency methods evaluates the **auto-correlation function of a texture**. In an auto-correlation model, a single pixel is considered a texture primitive, and a primitive tone property is the gray-level. Texture spatial organization is described by the correlation coefficient that evaluates linear spatial relationships between primitives. If the texture primitives are relatively large, the auto-correlation function value decreases slowly with increasing distance, while it decreases rapidly if texture consists of small primitives. If primitives are placed periodically in a texture, the auto-correlation increases and decreases periodically with distance.

Texture can be described using the following algorithm.

Algorithm 15.1: Auto-correlation texture description

1. For an $M \times N$ image, evaluate auto-correlation coefficients for several different values of position difference p, q:

$$C_{ff}(p,q) = \frac{MN}{(M-p)(N-q)} \frac{\sum_{i=1}^{M-p} \sum_{j=1}^{N-q} f(i,j)f(i+p,j+q)}{\sum_{i=1}^{M} \sum_{j=1}^{N} f^2(i,j)} . \tag{15.1}$$

2. Alternatively, the auto-correlation function can be determined in the frequency domain from the image power spectrum [Castleman, 1996]:

$$C_{ff} = \mathcal{F}^{-1}\{|F|^2\} . \tag{15.2}$$

If the textures are circularly symmetric, the auto-correlation texture description can be computed as a function of the absolute position difference not considering direction—that is, a function of one variable.

Spatial frequencies can also be determined from an **optical image transform** (recall that the Fourier transform can be realized by a convex lens—see Section 3.2) [Shulman, 1970], a big advantage of which is that it may be computed in real time. The Fourier transform describes an image by its spatial frequencies; average values of energy in specific wedges and rings of the Fourier spectrum can be used as textural description features (see Figure 15.3). Features evaluated from rings reflect coarseness of the texture—high energy in large-radius rings is characteristic of fine textures (high frequencies), while high energy in small radii is characteristic of coarser ones Features evaluated from wedge slices of the Fourier transform image depend on directional properties—if a texture has many edges or lines in a direction ϕ, high energy will be present in a wedge in direction $\phi+\pi/2$.

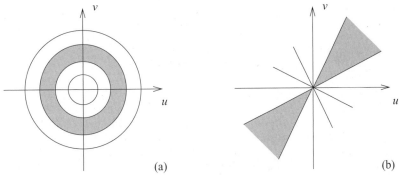

(a)   (b)

Figure 15.3: Partitioning of Fourier spectrum. (a) Ring filter. (b) Wedge filter reflecting the Fourier spectrum symmetry. © *Cengage Learning 2015*.

Similarly, a **discrete image transform** may be used. An image is usually divided into small $n \times n$ non-overlapping subimages, and the gray-levels of its pixels may be interpreted as an n^2-dimensional vector, and an image can be represented as a set of vectors. These vectors are transformed applying a Fourier, Hadamard, or other discrete image transform (Section 3.2). The new co-ordinate system's basis vectors are related to the spatial frequencies of the original image and can be used for texture description [Rosenfeld, 1976]. When description of noisy texture becomes necessary, the problem becomes more difficult. Liu and Jernigan extracted a set of 28 spatial frequency-domain features, and determined a subset insensitive to additive noise: dominant peak energy, power spectrum shape, entropy [Liu and Jernigan, 1990].

Many problems remain with spatial frequency methods—resulting descriptions are not invariant even to monotonic image gray-level transforms, and it can be shown [Weszka et al., 1976] that the frequency-based approach is less efficient than others. A joint spatial/spatial frequency approach is recommended; the Wigner distribution was shown to be useful in a variety of synthetic and Brodatz textures [Reed et al., 1990].

15.1.2   Co-occurrence matrices

Co-occurrence matrix methods are based on the repeated occurrence of some gray-level configuration in the texture; this configuration varies rapidly with distance in fine textures and slowly in coarse textures [Haralick et al., 1973]. Suppose the part of a textured image to be analyzed is an $M \times N$ rectangular window. An occurrence of some gray-level configuration may be described by a matrix of relative frequencies $P_{\phi,d}(a, b)$, describing how frequently two pixels with gray-levels a, b appear in the window separated by a distance d in direction ϕ. These matrices are symmetric if defined as given below. However, an asymmetric definition may be used, where matrix values are also dependent on the direction of co-occurrence. A co-occurrence matrix computation scheme was given in Algorithm 4.1.

Setting $D = (M \times N) \times (M \times N)$, non-normalized frequencies of co-occurrence as functions of angle and distance can be represented formally as

$$
\begin{aligned}
P_{0°,d}(a, b) &= \left| \left\{ [(k, l), (m, n)] \in D : \right. \right. \\
&\qquad \left. \left. k - m = 0, |l - n| = d, f(k, l) = a, f(m, n) = b \right\} \right|, \\
P_{45°,d}(a, b) &= \left| \left\{ [(k, l), (m, n)] \in D : \right. \right. \\
&\qquad \left. \left. (k - m = d, l - n = -d) \vee (k - m = -d, l - n = d), f(k, l) = a, f(m, n) = b \right\} \right|, \\
P_{90°,d}(a, b) &= \left| \left\{ [(k, l), (m, n)] \in D : \right. \right. \\
&\qquad \left. \left. |k - m| = d, l - n = 0, f(k, l) = a, f(m, n) = b \right\} \right|, \\
P_{135°,d}(a, b) &= \left| \left\{ [(k, l), (m, n)] \in D : \right. \right. \\
&\qquad \left. \left. (k - m = d, l - n = d) \vee (k - m = -d, l - n = -d), f(k, l) = a, f(m, n) = b \right\} \right|.
\end{aligned}
\tag{15.3}
$$

An example will illustrate for the distance $d = 1$. A 4×4 image with four gray-levels is given in Figure 15.4. The element $P_{0°,1}(0, 0)$ represents the number of times two pixels

$$
\begin{array}{cccc}
0 & 0 & 1 & 1 \\
0 & 0 & 1 & 1 \\
0 & 2 & 2 & 2 \\
2 & 2 & 3 & 3
\end{array}
$$

Figure 15.4: Gray-level image.
© Cengage Learning 2015.

with gray-levels 0 and 0 appear separated by distance 1 in direction $0°$; $P_{0°,1}(0, 0) = 4$ in this case. The element $P_{0°,1}(3, 2)$ represents the number of times two pixels with gray-levels 3 and 2 appear separated by distance 1 in direction $0°$; $P_{0°,1}(3, 2) = 1$. Note that $P_{0°,1}(2, 3) = 1$ due to matrix symmetry:

$$
P_{0°,1} = \begin{vmatrix}
4 & 2 & 1 & 0 \\
2 & 4 & 0 & 0 \\
1 & 0 & 6 & 1 \\
0 & 0 & 1 & 2
\end{vmatrix}, \qquad
P_{135°,1} = \begin{vmatrix}
2 & 1 & 3 & 0 \\
1 & 2 & 1 & 0 \\
3 & 1 & 0 & 2 \\
0 & 0 & 2 & 0
\end{vmatrix}.
$$

Texture classification can be based on criteria derived from the following co-occurrence matrices.

- **Energy**, or angular second moment (an image homogeneity measure—the more homogeneous the image, the larger the value)

$$\sum_{a,b} P_{\phi,d}^2(a,b) \, . \tag{15.4}$$

- **Entropy:**

$$-\sum_{a,b} P_{\phi,d}(a,b) \, \log_2 P_{\phi,d}(a,b) \, . \tag{15.5}$$

- **Maximum probability:**

$$\max_{a,b} P_{\phi,d}(a,b) \, . \tag{15.6}$$

- **Contrast** (a measure of local image variations; typically $\kappa = 2, \lambda = 1$):

$$\sum_{a,b} |a - b|^\kappa \, P_{\phi,d}^\lambda(a,b) \, . \tag{15.7}$$

- **Inverse difference moment:**

$$\sum_{a,b;a\neq b} \frac{P_{\phi,d}^\lambda(a,b)}{|a - b|^\kappa} \, . \tag{15.8}$$

- **Correlation** (a measure of image linearity, linear directional structures in direction ϕ result in large correlation values in this direction):

$$\frac{\sum_{a,b} \left[(ab) P_{\phi,d}(a,b) \right] - \mu_x \mu_y}{\sigma_x \sigma_y} \, , \tag{15.9}$$

where μ_x, μ_y are means and σ_x, σ_y are standard deviations

$$\mu_x = \sum_a a \sum_b P_{\phi,d}(a,b) \, , \qquad \sigma_x^2 = \sum_a (a - \mu_x)^2 \sum_b P_{\phi,d}(a,b) \, ,$$

$$\mu_y = \sum_b b \sum_a P_{\phi,d}(a,b) \, , \qquad \sigma_y^2 = \sum_b (b - \mu_y)^2 \sum_a P_{\phi,d}(a,b) \, .$$

Algorithm 15.2: Co-occurrence method of texture description

1. Construct co-occurrence matrices for given directions and given distances.

2. Compute texture feature vectors for four directions ϕ, different values of d, and the six characteristics. This results in many correlated features.

The co-occurrence method describes second-order image statistics and works well for a large variety of textures (see [Gotlieb and Kreyszig, 1990] for a survey of texture descriptors based on co-occurrence matrices). Good properties of the co-occurrence method are the description of spatial relations between tonal pixels, and invariance to monotonic gray-level transformations. On the other hand, it does not consider primitive shapes, and therefore cannot be recommended if the texture consists of large primitives. Memory requirements were once a disadvantage, although this is much less the case today. The number of gray-levels could be reduced to 32 or 64, decreasing co-occurrence matrix sizes, but loss of gray-level accuracy is a negative effect (although this loss is usually insignificant in practice). Likewise, the method is computationally expensive but this is not a significant constraint on modern hardware.

15.1.3   Edge frequency

Methods discussed so far describe texture by its spatial frequencies, but comparison of textural edge frequencies can be used as well. Edges can be detected either as micro-edges using small edge operator masks, or as macro-edges using large masks [Davis and Mitiche, 1980]—virtually any edge detector can be used (see Section 5.3.2). The distance-dependent texture description function $g(d)$ can be computed for any subimage f defined in a neighborhood N for variable distance d:

$$
\begin{aligned}
g(d) = \quad & \big|f(i,j) - f(i+d,j)\big| + \big|f(i,j) - f(i-d,j)\big| \\
+ & \big|f(i,j) - f(i,j+d)\big| + \big|f(i,j) - f(i,j-d)\big| \, .
\end{aligned}
\tag{15.10}
$$

The function $g(d)$ is similar to the negative auto-correlation function; its minimum (resp. maximum) corresponds to the maximum (minimum) of the auto-correlation function.

Algorithm 15.3: Edge-frequency texture description

1. Compute a gradient $g(d)$ for all pixels of the texture.

2. Evaluate texture features as average values of gradient in specified distances d.

Dimensionality of the texture description feature space is then given by the number of distance values d used to compute the edge gradient.

Several other texture properties may be derived from first-order and second-order statistics of edge distributions [Tomita and Tsuji, 1990].

- **Coarseness:** Edge density is a measure of coarseness. The finer the texture, the higher the number of edges present in the texture edge image.

- **Contrast:** High-contrast textures are characterized by large edge magnitudes.

- **Randomness:** This is measured as entropy of the edge magnitude histogram.

- **Directivity:** An approximate measure of directivity may be determined as entropy of the edge direction histogram. Directional textures have an even number of significant histogram peaks, directionless textures have a uniform edge direction histogram.

- **Linearity:** Texture linearity is indicated by co-occurrences of edge pairs with the same edge direction at constant distances, and edges are positioned in the edge direction (see Figure 15.5, edges a and b).

- **Periodicity:** Texture periodicity can be measured by co-occurrences of edge pairs of the same direction at constant distances in directions perpendicular to the edge direction (see Figure 15.5, edges a and c).

- **Size:** Texture size may be based on co-occurrences of edge pairs with opposite edge directions at constant distance in a direction perpendicular to the edge directions (see Figure 15.5, edges a and d).

Note that the first three measures are derived from first-order statistics, the last three from second-order statistics.

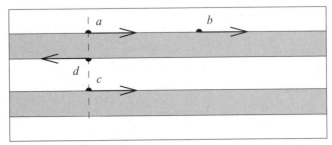

Figure 15.5: Texture linearity, periodicity, and size measures may be based on image edges. *Based on [Tomita and Tsuji, 1990].*

Many existing texture recognition methods are based on texture detection. The concepts of pre-attentive vision and textons have been mentioned, which are also based mostly on edge-related information. A zero-crossing operator was applied to edge-based texture description in [Perry and Lowe, 1989]; the method determines image regions of a constant texture, assuming no a priori knowledge about the image, texture types, or scale. Feature analysis is performed across multiple window sizes.

A slightly different approach to texture recognition may require detection of borders between homogeneous textured regions. A hierarchical algorithm for textured image segmentation is described in [Fan, 1989], and a two-stage contextual classification and segmentation of textures based on a coarse-to-fine principle of edge detection is given in [Fung et al., 1990]. Texture description and recognition in the presence of noise represents a difficult problem. A noise-tolerant texture classification approach based on a Canny-type edge detector is discussed in [Kjell and Wang, 1991] where texture is described using periodicity measures derived from noise-insensitive edge detection.

15.1.4   Primitive length (run length)

A large number of neighboring pixels of the same gray-level represents a coarse texture, pixels represents a fine texture, and the lengths of texture primitives in different directions can serve as a texture description [Galloway, 1975]. A **primitive** is a maximum contiguous set of constant-level pixels located in a line; these can then be described by gray-level, length, and direction. Texture description features can be based on computation of continuous probabilities of the length and gray-level of primitives in the texture.

Let $B(a, r)$ be the number of primitives of all directions having length r and gray-level a, M, N the image dimensions, and L the number of image gray-levels. Let N_r be the maximum primitive length in the image, and let K be the total number of runs

$$K = \sum_{a=1}^{L} \sum_{r=1}^{N_r} B(a,r) \,. \tag{15.11}$$

Then:

- **Short primitives emphasis:**

$$\frac{1}{K} \sum_{a=1}^{L} \sum_{r=1}^{N_r} \frac{B(a,r)}{r^2} \,. \tag{15.12}$$

- **Long primitives emphasis:**

$$\frac{1}{K} \sum_{a=1}^{L} \sum_{r=1}^{N_r} B(a,r)r^2 \,. \tag{15.13}$$

- **Gray-level uniformity:**

$$\frac{1}{K} \sum_{a=1}^{L} \left[\sum_{r=1}^{N_r} B(a,r) \right]^2 \,. \tag{15.14}$$

- **Primitive length uniformity:**

$$\frac{1}{K} \sum_{r=1}^{N_r} \left[\sum_{a=1}^{L} B(a,r) \right]^2 \,. \tag{15.15}$$

- **Primitive percentage:**

$$\frac{K}{\sum_{a=1}^{L} \sum_{r=1}^{N_r} r\, B(a,r)} = \frac{K}{MN} \,. \tag{15.16}$$

A general algorithm might then be the following.

Algorithm 15.4: Primitive-length texture description

1. Find primitives of all gray-levels, all lengths, and all directions.

2. Compute texture description features as given in equations (15.12–15.16). These features then provide a description vector.

15.1.5 Laws' texture energy measures

Laws' texture energy measures determine texture properties by assessing average gray-level, edges, spots, ripples, and waves [Laws, 1979; Wu et al., 1992]. They are derived from three simple vectors: $L_3 = (1, 2, 1)$ (averaging); $E_3 = (-1, 0, 1)$ (first difference, edges); and $S_3 = (-1, 2, -1)$ (second difference, spots). After convolution of these vectors with themselves and each other, five vectors result:

$$L_5 = (1, 4, 6, 4, 1),$$
$$E_5 = (-1, -2, 0, 2, 1),$$
$$S_5 = (-1, 0, 2, 0, -1),$$
$$R_5 = (1, -4, 6, -4, 1),$$
$$W_5 = (-1, 2, 0, -2, -1).$$

(15.17)

Mutual multiplying of these vectors, considering the first term as a column vector and the second term as a row vector, results in 5×5 Laws' masks. For example,

$$L_5^T \times S_5 = \begin{bmatrix} -1 & 0 & 2 & 0 & -1 \\ -4 & 0 & 8 & 0 & -4 \\ -6 & 0 & 12 & 0 & -6 \\ -4 & 0 & 8 & 0 & -4 \\ -1 & 0 & 2 & 0 & -1 \end{bmatrix}.$$

(15.18)

By convolving the masks with an image and calculating energy statistics, a feature vector is derived that can be used for texture description.

15.1.6 Local binary patterns—LBPs

Local binary pattern (LBP) approach were introduced by Ojala et al. [Ojala et al., 1996], motivated by three-valued texture units originally presented by Wang and He [Wang and He, 1990]. The main idea of the LBP approach—as its name reflects—is to locally threshold the brightness of a pixel's neighborhood at the center pixel gray level to form a binary pattern. The LBP description given here is based on [Ojala et al., 1996; Pietikainen et al., 2000; Ojala et al., 2001, 2002b].

The LBP operator is gray-scale invariant and is derived as follows: texture is described in a local neighborhood of a central pixel, the neighborhood consisting of P $(P > 1)$ equally spaced points on a circle of radius $R > 0$ centered at the center pixel. The texture is described as a joint distribution

$$T = t(g_c, g_0, g_1, ..., g_{P-1}),$$

(15.19)

where g_c is the gray level of the central pixel and $g_0, ..., g_{P-1}$ are gray values of the neighborhood pixels. Assuming the coordinates of G_c are (0,0), coordinates of the neighborhood pixels g_p are given by $[-R \sin(2\pi p/P), R \cos(2\pi p/P)]$. If a point does not fall exactly at the center of a pixel, its value is estimated by interpolation (Figure 15.6).

Using this texture representation, gray-scale invariance can be achieved using gray-level differences rather than brightness values:

$$T = t(g_c, g_0 - g_c, g_1 - g_c, ..., g_{P-1} - g_c).$$

(15.20)

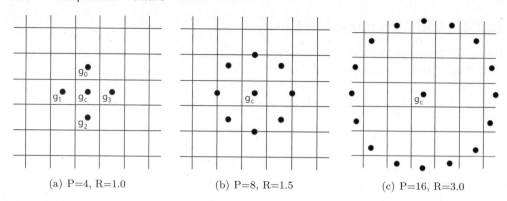

(a) P=4, R=1.0   (b) P=8, R=1.5   (c) P=16, R=3.0

Figure 15.6: Circularly symmetric neighborhoods for different values of P and R [Ojala et al., 2002b]. © *Cengage Learning 2015*.

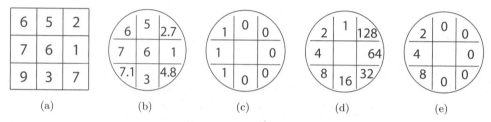

(a)   (b)   (c)   (d)   (e)

Figure 15.7: Binary texture description operator $LBP_{8,1}$. (a) Original gray values of a 3×3 image. (b) Gray-level interpolation achieves symmetric circular behavior. Linear interpolation was used for simplicity (Section 5.2.2). (c) Circular operator values after binarization, equations (15.23–15.24). (d) Directional weights. (e) Directional values associated with $LBP_{8,1}$—the resulting value of $LBP_{8,1} = 14$. If rotationally normalized, the weighting mask would rotate by one position counterclockwise, yielding $LBP_{8,1}^{ri} = 7$. © *Cengage Learning 2015*.

Assuming that brightness g_c is independent of the differences $g_p - g_c$ (not quite valid but close-enough to permit approximation), texture can be represented as:

$$T \approx l(g_c)t(g_0 - g_c, g_1 - g_c, ..., g_{P-1} - g_c), \tag{15.21}$$

where the image luminance is represented by $l(g_c)$ and the texture by the brightness differences between the central and neighboring pixels. Since image luminance itself does not contribute to texture properties, texture description can be based on differences only:

$$T \approx t(g_0 - g_c, g_1 - g_c, ..., g_{P-1} - g_c). \tag{15.22}$$

Texture description is given by calculating occurrences of neighborhood brightness patterns in a P-layer histogram, each layer corresponding to one of P direction for given value of R. Clearly, all differences are zero for a constant-brightness region, high in all directions for a spot located at g_c, and exhibit varying values along local image edges. This histogram can be used for texture discrimination.

This description is invariant to brightness shifts. To achieve invariance to brightness scaling, the absolute values of gray level differences may be replaced with their signs as shown in Figure 15.7a,b.

$$T \approx t(s(g_0 - g_c), s(g_1 - g_c), ..., s(g_{P-1} - g_c)), \tag{15.23}$$

where

$$
s(x) = \begin{cases} 1 & \text{for } x \geq 0 \\ 0 & \text{for } x < 0 \end{cases} . \tag{15.24}
$$

When the operator elements are ordered to form a circular chain with values of zero and one, then specific directions can be consistently weighted forming a scalar chain code descriptor. The chain code contributors can be summed over the entire circular neighborhood of P pixels as depicted on Figure 15.7c,d and the local texture pattern can be described by a single number for any specific (P, R) combination. Weights 2^p can be assigned in a circular fashion with p increasing for all P points:

$$
\text{LBP}_{P,R} = \sum_{p=0}^{P-1} s(g_p - g_c) 2^p . \tag{15.25}
$$

For a texture patch, these $\text{LBP}_{P,R}$ values can be used to form single- or multi-dimensional histograms or feature vectors, or can be further processed to become rotation and/or spatial scale invariant as described below.

When the image is rotated, image gray values travel around the circle, affecting the LBP values. To achieve rotational invariance it is natural to normalize the circular chain code in a way that minimizes the resulting LBP^{ri} value (Figure 15.7, see also Section 8.2.1):

$$
\text{LBP}_{P,R}^{ri} = \min_{i=0,1,\ldots,P-1} \{ ROR(\text{LBP}_{P,R}, i) \} , \tag{15.26}
$$

where $ROR(x, i)$ denotes a circular bitwise right shift on the P-bit number x i-times—or simply rotating the circular neighbor set clockwise so that the resulting LBP value is minimized (bitwise operation instructions for right (ROR) and left (ROL) circular shifts exist in Intel x86 instruction set). Patterns $\text{LBP}_{P,R}^{ri}$ can be used as feature detectors—for $\text{LBP}_{8,R}^{ri}$, 36 such feature detectors can be formed as shown in Figure 15.8. Pattern #0 would indicate a bright spot location, #8 a dark spot location or a flat area, #4 corresponds to straight edges, etc.

While the $\text{LBP}_{8,R}^{ri}$ features do not perform very well in real-world problems [Pietikainen et al., 2000], local binary patterns can be derived from them which start representing fundamental texture properties. Such derived LBP's are called **uniform patterns** due to having uniform circular structure with minimal spatial transitions. For $\text{LBP}_{8,R}^{ri}$, such uniform patterns are shown in the first row of Figure 15.8. The uniform patterns can be considered **microstructure templates** with the same interpretation as given above—#0 being a bright spot microtemplate, etc. Formally, a **uniformity measure** U can be introduced, reflecting the number of 0/1 (or 1/0) transitions. Note that all the uniform patterns have U values of 2 or less, while all other patterns have a U value of at least 4. Subsequently, a gray-scale and rotation invariant texture descriptor is defined as

$$
\text{LBP}_{P,R}^{riu2} = \begin{cases} \sum_{p=0}^{P-1} s(g_p - g_c) & \text{if } U(\text{LBP}_{P,R}) \leq 2 \\ P+1 & \text{otherwise} \end{cases} , \tag{15.27}
$$

where

$$
U(\text{LBP}_{P,R}) = |s(g_{P-1} - g_c) - s(g_0 - g_c)| + \sum_{p=1}^{P-1} |s(g_p - g_c) - s(g_{p-1} - g_c)| . \tag{15.28}
$$

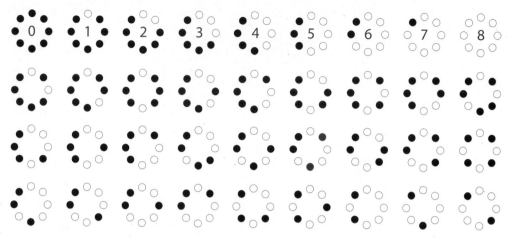

Figure 15.8: For example, when considering $P = 8$ and any value of R, 36 unique circularly symmetric feature detectors can be formed: black and white circles correspond to bit values of 0 and 1. The first row shows the 9 "uniform" patterns with their $\text{LBP}_{8,R}^{riu2}$ values given (equation 15.27). *Based on [Ojala et al., 2002b].*

Here, the superscript $riu2$ denotes rotational invariant uniform patterns with uniformity values of at most 2. Note that only P+2 patterns can exist: P+1 uniform patterns and one additional 'catch-all' pattern (Figure 15.8). Mapping from $\text{LBP}_{P,R}$ to $\text{LBP}_{P,R}^{riu2}$ is best implemented using a look-up table with 2^P elements.

Texture description is based on a histogram of $\text{LBP}_{P,R}^{riu2}$ operator outputs accumulated over a texture patch. The reason this approach works much better than using $\text{LBP}_{P,R}^{ri}$ features directly is associated with the overwhelmingly larger proportion of uniform patterns when collecting the microstructure templates. Due to their relatively low occurrence frequencies, statistical properties of 'non-uniform' patterns cannot be reliably estimated and resulting noisy estimates negatively influence texture discrimination. For example, when analyzing Brodatz textures, $\text{LBP}_{8,1}^{ri}$ features consist of 87% uniform and only 13% non-uniform patterns. Since only 9 uniform templates exist while three times as many (27) non-uniform templates can be formed, the frequency differences become even more striking. Similarly, the uniform/non-uniform frequency distributions are 67–33% for $\text{LBP}_{16,2}^{ri}$ and 50–50% for $\text{LBP}_{24,3}^{ri}$ on the same set of textures. These distributions seem quite stable across different texture discrimination problems [Ojala et al., 2002b].

The choice of P and R remains to be considered. Increasing P helps with overcoming the crudeness of angular quantization. Clearly, P and R are related in the sense that the radius must increase proportionally with denser angular sampling, or the number of non-redundant pixel values in the circular neighborhood will become a limiting factor (nine non-redundant pixels are available for $R = 1$). At the same time, if P is increased too much, the size 2^P of the look-up table will affect computational efficiency. Practical experiments limited P values to 24 [Ojala et al., 2002b], resulting in a 16MB look-up table, an easily manageable size. Additional aspects of rotation-invariant variance measure and multi-resolution analysis of textures are all discussed in [Ojala et al., 2002b].

When using LBP features and pattern histograms for texture classification, non-parametric statistical tests were employed to determine dissimilarity of the histogram description from all class-specific histograms of LBP features obtained during training.

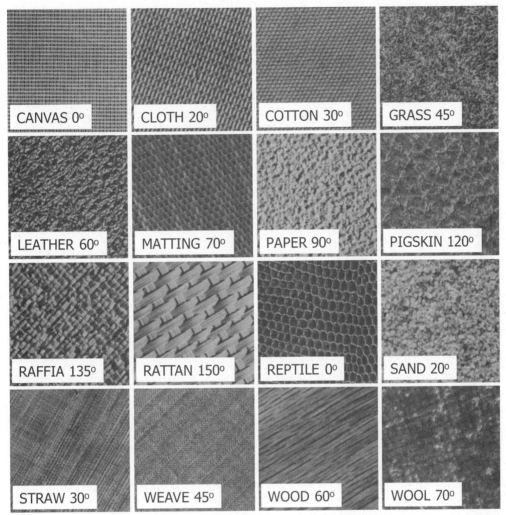

Figure 15.9: Samples of 16 Brodatz textures used for $\text{LBP}_{P,R}^{riu2}$ evaluation in [Ojala et al., 2002b]. Patches shown are 180×180 pixels and were rotated at different angles in addition to the angular rotations depicted in the figure. *Courtesy of M. Pietikainen, T. Ojala, Oulu University, Finland.*

The lowest (and perhaps below-minimum threshold) dissimilarity criterion identifies the most likely texture class the patch sample belongs to. This has an additional advantage of permitting an ordering of the most likely classifications according to their likelihood. Non-parametric statistical tests like chi-square or G (log-likelihood ratio) can be used to assess the goodness of fit.

When this approach was applied to classification of 16 Brodatz textures (Figure 15.9), the $\text{LBP}_{P,R}^{riu2}$ histograms, followed by goodness-of-fit analysis, outperformed wavelet transforms, Gabor transforms, and Gaussian Markov Random Field approaches while exhibiting the lowest computational complexity. Rotational invariance was demonstrated by training the LBP method in textures of single orientation and testing independent samples rotated using 6 different angles (Figure 15.9). $\text{LBP}_{8,1}^{riu2}$, $\text{LBP}_{16,2}^{riu2}$, and $\text{LBP}_{24,3}^{riu2}$ were used and 100% classification was achieved for some feature combinations including variance measures, compared with the second best 95.8% reported in [Porter and Cana-garajah, 1997], achieved using wavelets. Another set of experiments used 24 classes of natural textures acquired using a robotic arm-mounted camera at different angles and with varying controlled illumination. The LBP method demonstrated excellent performance. Test image data and the texture classification software test suite *OUTEX* can be accessed at http://www.outex.oulu.fi/ [Ojala et al., 2002a].

An interesting adaption of these ideas has constructed LBPs of gradient images to assist in face recognition [Vu et al., 2012]. The approach—in which gradient LBPs were supplemented by Gaussian mixture model (GMMs, Section 10.13) and support vector machines (SVMs, Section 9.2.5)—proves very fast and efficient, outperforming comparable techniques in performance as well.

An extension of LBPs called **local ternary patterns** or LTPs, takes advantage of creating a third pattern in equation (15.24) [Tan and Triggs, 2010]. LTPs allow three labels to form an insensitivity interval around the value of the central pixel:

$$s'(x) = \begin{cases} 1 & \text{for } x > t \\ 0 & \text{for } x \geq -t \text{ and } x \leq t \ , \\ -1 & \text{for } x < -t \end{cases} \qquad (15.29)$$

where t is an insensitivity threshold. Compared to LBPs, LTPs were found more discriminant and less sensitive to noise in uniform regions. Note however, that gray-level transform invariance is somewhat compromised.

15.1.7 Fractal texture description

Fractal-based texture analysis was introduced in [Pentland, 1984], where a correlation between texture coarseness and fractal dimension of a texture was demonstrated. A fractal is defined [Mandelbrot, 1982] as a set for which the Hausdorff-Besicovich dimension [Hausdorff, 1919; Besicovitch and Ursell, 1937] is strictly greater than the topological dimension; therefore, fractional dimension is the defining property. Fractal models typically relate a metric property such as line length or surface area to the elementary length or area used as a basis for determining the metric property—measuring coast length is a frequently used example [Pentland, 1984; Lundahl et al., 1986]. Suppose coastal length is determined by applying a 1-km-long ruler end-to-end to the coastline; the same procedure can be repeated with a 0.5-km ruler, and other shorter or longer rulers. It is easy to see that shortening the ruler will be associated with an increase in total length. Importantly, the relation between the ruler length and the measured coast length can be considered a measure of the coastline's geometric properties, e.g., its roughness. The functional relationship between the ruler size r and the measured length L can be expressed as

$$L = c\, r^{1-D} \ , \qquad (15.30)$$

where c is a scaling constant and D is the **fractal dimension** [Mandelbrot, 1982]. Fractal dimension has been shown to correlate well with the function's intuitive roughness.

While equation (15.30) can be applied directly to lines and surfaces, it is often more appropriate to consider the function as a stochastic process. One of the most important stochastic fractal models is the *fractional Brownian motion model* [Mandelbrot, 1982], which considers naturally rough surfaces as the end results of random walks. Importantly, intensity surfaces of textures can also be considered as resulting from random walks, and the fractional Brownian motion model can be applied to texture description.

Fractal description of textures is typically based on determination of fractal dimension and **lacunarity** to measure texture roughness and granularity from the image intensity function. The topological dimension of an image is equal to three—two spatial dimensions and the third representing the image intensity. Considering the topological dimension T_d, the fractal dimension D can be estimated from the Hurst coefficient H [Hurst, 1951; Mandelbrot, 1982] as

$$D = T_d - H .$$
(15.31)

For images $(T_d = 3)$, the Hurst parameter H or the fractal dimension D can be estimated from the relationship

$$E\left((\Delta f)^2\right) = c \left[(\Delta r)^H\right]^2 = c(\Delta r)^{6-2D} ,$$
(15.32)

where $E()$ is an expectation operator, $\Delta f = f(i,j) - f(k,l)$ is the intensity variation, c is a scaling constant, and $\Delta r = \|(i,j) - (k,l)\|$ is the spatial distance. A simpler way to estimate fractal dimension is to use the equation:

$$E\left(|\Delta f|\right) = \kappa(\Delta r)^{3-D} ,$$
(15.33)

where $\kappa = E\left(|\Delta f|\right)_{\Delta r=1}$. By taking logarithms and noting that $H = 3 - D$,

$$\log E\left(|\Delta f|\right) = \log \kappa + H \log(\Delta r) .$$
(15.34)

The parameter H can be obtained by using least-squares linear regression to estimate the slope of the curve of gray-level differences $gd(k)$ versus κ in log–log scales [Wu et al., 1992]. Considering an $M \times M$ image f,

$$gd(k) = \frac{1}{\mu} \left(\sum_{i=0}^{M-1} \sum_{j=0}^{M-k-1} |f(i,j) - f(i,j+k)| + \sum_{i=0}^{M-k-1} \sum_{j=0}^{M-1} |f(i,j) - f(i+k,j)| \right) ,$$
(15.35)

where $\mu = 2\,M(M - k - 1)$. The scale k varies from 1 to the maximum selected value s. Fractal dimension D is then derived from the value of the Hurst coefficient. The approximation error of the regression line fit should be determined to demonstrate that the texture is a fractal, and can thus be efficiently described using fractal measures. A small value of the fractal dimension D (large value of the parameter H) represents a fine texture, while large D (small H) corresponds to a coarse texture.

Single fractal dimension is not sufficient for description of natural textures. Lacunarity measures describe characteristics of textures of different visual appearance that have the same fractal dimension [Voss, 1986; Keller et al., 1989; Wu et al., 1992]. Given a fractal set A, let $P(m)$ represent the probability that there are m points within a box of size L centered about an arbitrary point of A. Let N be the number of possible points within the box, then $\sum_{m=1}^{N} P(m) = 1$ and the lacunarity λ is defined as

$$\lambda = \frac{M_2 - M^2}{M^2} ,$$
(15.36)

where

$$M = \sum_{m=1}^{N} m\, P(m)\,, \qquad\qquad M_2 = \sum_{m=1}^{N} m^2 P(m)\,. \qquad (15.37)$$

Lacunarity represents a second-order statistic and is small for fine textures and large for coarse ones.

A multi-resolution approach to fractal feature extraction was introduced in [Wu et al., 1992]. The multi-resolution feature vector MF that describes both texture roughness and lacunarity is defined as

$$MF = \left(H^{(m)}, H^{(m-1)}, \dots, H^{(m-n+1)} \right), \qquad (15.38)$$

where the parameters $H^{(k)}$ are estimated from pyramidal images $f^{(k)}$, where $f^{(m)}$ represents the full-resolution image of size $M = 2^m$, $f^{(m-1)}$ is the half-resolution image of size $M = 2^{m-1}$, etc., and n is the number of resolution levels considered. The multi-resolution feature vector MF can serve as a texture descriptor. Textures with identical fractal dimensions and different lacunarities can be distinguished, as was shown by classification of ultrasonic liver images in three classes—normal, hepatoma, and cirrhosis [Wu et al., 1992]. Practical considerations regarding calculation of fractal-based texture description features can be found in [Sarkar and Chaudhuri, 1994; Huang et al., 1994; Jin et al., 1995].

15.1.8   Multiscale texture description—wavelet domain approaches

Texture description is highly scale dependent. To decrease scale sensitivity, a texture may be described in multiple resolutions and an appropriate scale chosen to achieve maximal discrimination [Unser and Eden, 1989]. **Gabor transforms** and **wavelets** (Section 3.2.7) are well suited to multi-scale characterization [Coggins and Jain, 1985; Mallat, 1989; Bovik et al., 1990; Unser, 1995]. Both are multi-scale spatial—spatial frequency filtering approaches, which were in the past dominated by Gabor filters. Wavelets have been successfully applied to texture classification using pyramid- or tree-structured discrete wavelet transforms [Mallat, 1989; Chang and Kuo, 1993] (Section 3.2.7), typically outperforming conventional texture characterization approaches.

Unser showed that overcomplete **discrete wavelet frames** outperform standard critically sampled wavelet texture feature extraction [Unser, 1995]—what follows is based on this work. Considering a discrete version of the wavelet transform in l_2 (the space of square summable sequences [Rioul, 1993]) textures are described using orthogonal wavelet frames. First, consider the principle of this approach using a single-dimensional signal x. Take a prototype filter h satisfying

$$H(z)\,H(z^{-1}) + H(-z)\,H(-z^{-1}) = 1\,, \qquad (15.39)$$

where $H(z)$ is the z-transform of h [Oppenheim et al., 1999], and let the filter also be subjected to the lowpass constraint $H(z)|_{z=1} = 1$. A complementary high-pass filter g is then obtained by shift and modulation

$$G(z) = z\, H(-z^{-1})\,. \qquad (15.40)$$

Using these two prototypes, a sequence of filters of increasing width can be iteratively generated as follows:

$$H_{i+1}(z) = H(z^{2^i}) \, H_i(z) \,, \tag{15.41}$$

$$G_{i+1}(z) = G(z^{2^i}) \, H_i(z) \,, \tag{15.42}$$

for $i = 0, \ldots, I-1$, initialized with $H_0(z) = 1$. The filters represent perfect reconstruction filter banks, which are used for definition of the individual wavelets used below. In the signal domain, a two-scale relationship is obtained:

$$h_{i+1}(k) = [h]_{\uparrow 2^i} * h_i(k) \,,$$
$$g_{i+1}(k) = [g]_{\uparrow 2^i} * h_i(k) \,, \tag{15.43}$$

where $[.]_{\uparrow m}$ represents upsampling by a factor of m. In general, each iteration dilates the filters h_i and g_i by a factor of two; this sequence of filters is used to decompose the signal in subbands of approximately one octave each. Importantly, such filter sequences provide a full coverage of the frequency domain.

An orthogonal wavelet decomposition obtained by such a sequence of filters yields discrete normalized basis functions

$$\varphi_{i,l}(k) = 2^{i/2} \, h_i(k - 2^i l) \,, \tag{15.44}$$

$$\psi_{i,l}(k) = 2^{i/2} \, g_i(k - 2^i l) \,, \tag{15.45}$$

where i and l are scale and translation indices, respectively; the product $2^{i/2}$ is for inner product normalization. Consider a sequence of nested subspaces $l_2 \supset V_0 \supset V_1 \supset \ldots \supset V_I$. Here, $V_i = \text{span}\{\varphi_{i,l}\}_{l \in Z}$ is the approximation space at resolution i. Let subspaces W_i $(i = 1, \ldots, I)$ represent residue space at resolution i, defined as an orthogonal complement of V_i with respect to V_{i-1}, i.e., $V_{i-1} = V_i + W_i$ and $V_i \perp W_i$. The minimum l_2-norm approximation of x at scale i which corresponds to the orthogonal projection into V_i is given by

$$x_{(i)}(k) = \sum_{l \in Z} s_{(i)}(l) \, \varphi_{i,l} \,, \tag{15.46}$$

$$s_{(i)}(l) = \big\langle x(k), \varphi_{i,l}(k) \big\rangle_{l_2} \,, \tag{15.47}$$

where $\langle ., . \rangle$ represents the standard l_2 inner product and $\varphi_{i,0}(k) = 2^{i/2} h_i(k)$ is the discrete scaling function at resolution i. The residue (projection of x into W_i), is given by the complementary wavelet expansion

$$x_{(i-1)}(k) - x_{(i)}(k) = \sum_{l \in Z} d_{(i)}(l) \, \psi_{i,l} \,, \tag{15.48}$$

$$d_{(i)}(l) = \big\langle x(k), \psi_{i,l}(k) \big\rangle_{l_2} \,, \tag{15.49}$$

where $\psi_{i,0}(k) = 2^{i/2} g_i(k)$ is the discrete wavelet at scale i.

By combining the residues over all scales to a given depth I, a full discrete wavelet expansion of the signal is obtained

$$x(k) = \sum_{l \in Z} s_{(I)}(l) \, \varphi_{I,l} + \sum_{i=1}^{I} \sum_{l \in Z} d_{(i)}(l) \, \psi_{i,l} \,, \tag{15.50}$$

where d_i are wavelet coefficients and s_I are expansion coefficients of a coarser approximation $x_{(I)}$, see equation (15.46).

Importantly for texture analysis, equations (15.47) and (15.49) can be obtained by simple filtering and down-sampling, yielding

$$s_{(I)}(l) = 2^{I/2}[h_I^T * x]_{\downarrow 2^I}(l)\,,$$
$$d_{(i)}(l) = 2^{i/2}[g_i^T * x]_{\downarrow 2^i}(l)\,, \tag{15.51}$$

where $i = 1, \ldots, I$; $h^T(k) = h(-k)$; and $[.]_{\downarrow m}$ is down-sampling by a factor of m. An efficient algorithm based on direct filtering with a **filter bank** exists and is typically used for this purpose [Mallat, 1989].

The most frequently used discrete wavelet transform features for texture analysis are **wavelet energy signatures** [Chang and Kuo, 1993; Mojsilovic et al., 2000; Arivazhagan and Ganesan, 2003] and their second-order statistics [Van de Wouwer et al., 1999]. While the wavelet-based features can be used directly for texture description, this suffers from the lack of translation invariance which—as described earlier—is an important property in describing texture. One possibility to overcome this limitation is to compute the discrete wavelet transform for all possible shifts of the input signal, giving the following decomposition formulae:

$$s_I^{\text{DWF}}(k) = \left\langle h_I(k-l), x(k) \right\rangle_{l_2} = h_I^T * x(k)\,,$$
$$d_i^{\text{DWF}}(k) = \left\langle g_i(k-l), x(k) \right\rangle_{l_2} = g_i^T * x(k)\,, \tag{15.52}$$

where $i = 1, \ldots, I$ and DWF denotes a discrete wavelet frame representation to distinguish this equation from the earlier one (equation 15.51). Hereon, we will deal with this DWF representation without specifically using the superscript. Equation (15.52) represents a non-sampled version of equation (15.51). The wavelet frame coefficients can be used for translation-invariant texture description. Importantly, a simple reconstruction formula exists and both decomposition and reconstruction can be obtained using filter banks [Unser, 1995].

Practical implementation is based on the two-scale relationship given in equation (15.43) yielding a fast iterative decomposition algorithm

$$s_{i+1}(k) = [h]_{\uparrow 2^i} * s_i(k)\,,$$
$$d_{i+1}(k) = [g]_{\uparrow 2^i} * s_i(k)\,, \tag{15.53}$$

where $i = 0, \ldots, I$, with the initial condition $s_0 = x$ (Figure 15.10). A convolution with the basic filters h and g is repeated in each step, yielding an approach the complexity of which is identical in each step and proportional to the number of samples.

Extending the single-dimensional case described above to higher-dimensional signals (to allow its use for texture image analysis) calls for the use of a tensor product formulation [Mallat, 1989]. In a two-dimensional image, four distinct basis functions (four distinct filters) are defined corresponding to the different cross-products of the one-dimensional functions φ and ψ. The decomposition can therefore be obtained by successive one-dimensional processing along the rows and columns of an image. The output of the filter bank given in equation (15.52) can be rearranged in an N-component vector where N is the number of subbands

$$\mathbf{y}(k,l) = \left(y_i(k,l)\right)_{i=1,\ldots,N} = \left[s_I(k,l); \, d_I(k,l); \, \ldots; \, d_1(k,l)\right]^T\,. \tag{15.54}$$

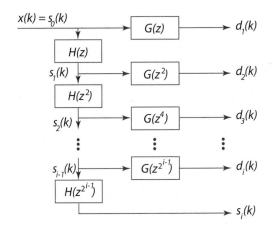

Figure 15.10: Fast iterative approach to discrete wavelet decomposition. © *Cengage Learning 2015.*

For a spatial coordinate pair (k, l), the resulting $\mathbf{y}(k, l)$ is a linear transformation of the input vector $\mathbf{x}(k, l)$, which is a block representation of the input image centered at (k, l). Applying the 2D separable wavelet transform with a depth I yields $N = 1 + 3I$ features.

The texture can consequently be described by the set of N first-order probability density functions $p(y_i)$, for $i = 1, \ldots, N$. Also, a more compact representation can be obtained by using a set of channel variance features

$$v_i = \text{var}\{y_i\} \tag{15.55}$$

(see [Unser, 1986] for justification of this approach). Needless to say, texture description capabilities of this methods depend on the appropriate choice of filter bank.

The channel variances v_i can be estimated from average sum of squares over a region of interest R of the analyzed texture

$$v_i = \frac{1}{N_R} \sum_{(k,l) \in R} y_i^2(k, l) \,, \tag{15.56}$$

where N_R is the number of pixels in region R. As mentioned above, the lowpass condition requires $H(z)|_{z=1} = 1$, which in turn yields $E\{y_1\} = E\{x\}$, and $E\{y_i\} = 0$ for $i = 1, \ldots, N$. It is therefore recommended to subtract $E\{x\}^2$ from the lowpass channel feature to obtain a better estimate of the variance.

If the discrete wavelet transform is employed, a smaller number of coefficients results due to subsampling. Nevertheless, the variance estimates can be obtained in the same manner. However, an adverse effect on texture classification performance can be observed due to a resulting increased variability of features.

An assessment of the performance of the wavelet domain multiscale approach described above is given in [Unser, 1995]. In experiments performed on 256×256 Brodatz textures [Brodatz, 1966], wavelet and filter bank decompositions were performed by global processing of the images. The performance was assessed in 64 (8×8) non-overlapping subregions sized 32×32 pixels in which the texture was described using independent feature vectors $\mathbf{v} = (v_1, \ldots, v_N)$ evaluated according to equation (15.56). Performance assessment demonstrated that the *discrete* wavelet frame approach always outperformed the *discrete* wavelet transform approach. It shows that true multi-resolution feature extraction with two or three levels ($I = 2, 3$) is preferable to local single-scale analysis.

The results also showed that even with $n = 0$, the DWF features performed very well. Importantly, the multiscale approach with 3 decompositions ($n = 3$) at 3 levels of scale ($I = 3$) and using 10 features outperformed (correctness of 99.2%) the single scale DWF approach ($n = 0$, $I = 1$) which used 4 features (correctness of 96.5%). This is notable since other comparison studies previously demonstrated that this DWF approach ($n = 0$, $I = 1$, equivalent to local linear transform using a 2×2 Hadamard transform [Unser, 1986]) typically outperforms most other statistical texture description methods including co-occurrence matrices, correlation, etc. and can thus be used as a reference method for single-scale analysis. The studies in [Unser, 1995] also compare performance of various orthogonal and non-orthogonal wavelet transforms.

Comparison of texture classification behavior of Gabor transforms and wavelets is given in [Vautrot et al., 1996]. If texture segmentation is required, a coarse-to-fine multi-resolution strategy may be used Approximate border positions between texture regions are detected first in a low-resolution image, accuracy being improved in higher resolutions using the low-level segmentation as a priori information. Wavelet-domain hidden Markov models (Section 10.11), and especially hidden Markov trees [Fan and Xia, 2003] are designed directly considering the intrinsic properties of wavelet transforms and combine the multiscale approach offered by wavelets with modeling of mutual statistical dependencies and non-Gaussian statistics frequently encountered in real-world texture analysis [Crouse et al., 1998].

15.1.9   Other statistical methods of texture description

there is a rich variety of other texture description techniques; we present here only the basic principles of the chief ones [Haralick, 1979; Ahuja and Rosenfeld, 1981; Davis et al., 1983; Derin and Elliot, 1987; Tomita and Tsuji, 1990].

The **mathematical morphology** approach looks for spatial repetitiveness of shapes in a binary image using structure primitives (see Chapter 13). If the structuring elements consist of a single pixel only, the resulting description is an autocorrelation function of the binary image. Using larger and more complex structuring elements, general correlation can be calculated—the element usually represents some simple shape, such as a square, a line, etc. When a binary textured image is eroded texture properties are present in the eroded image [Serra and Verchery, 1973]. One possibility for feature vector construction is to apply different structuring elements to the textured image and to count the number of pixels with unit value in the eroded images, each number forming one element of the feature vector. The morphological approach stresses the shape properties of texture primitives, but its applicability is limited due to the assumption of a binary textured image: gray-level mathematical morphology may help to solve this problem. Morphological texture description is often successful in granulated materials, which can be segmented by thresholding. Using a sequence of openings and counting the number of pixels after each step, a texture measure was derived in [Dougherty et al., 1989].

The **texture transform** represents another approach. Each texture type present in an image is transformed into a unique gray-level; the general idea is to construct an image g where the pixels $g(i, j)$ describe a texture in some neighborhood of the pixel $f(i, j)$ in the original textured image f. If micro-textures are analyzed, a small neighborhood of $f(i, j)$ must be used, and an appropriately larger neighborhood should be used for description of macro-textures. In addition, a priori knowledge can be used to guide the transformation and subsequent texture recognition and segmentation. Local texture orientation can also be used to transform a texture image into a feature image, after which supervised classification is applied to recognize textures.

Linear estimates of gray-levels in texture pixels can also be used for texture description. Pixel gray-levels are estimated from gray-levels in their neighborhood—this method is based on the **autoregression texture model**, where linear estimation parameters are used [Deguchi and Morishita, 1978]. Model parameters vary substantially in fine textures, but remain relatively unchanged in coarse textures. This model has been compared with second-order spatial statistics [Gagalowicz et al., 1988]; it was found that although the results were comparable, spatial statistics performed more quickly and reliably.

The **peak and valley** method [Mitchell et al., 1977; Ehrick and Foith, 1978] is based on detection of local extrema of the brightness function in vertical and horizontal scans of a texture image. Fine textures have a large number of small-sized local extrema, coarse textures are represented by a smaller number of larger-sized local extrema—higher peaks and deeper valleys.

The sequence of pixel gray-levels can be considered a **Markov chain** in which transition probabilities of an mth-order chain represent $(m+1)^{th}$-order statistics of textures [Pratt and Faugeras, 1978]. This approach may also be used for texture synthesis [Gagalowicz, 1979].

A more recent development is the **deterministic tourist walk** which uses a partially self-avoiding deterministic walk for texture analysis [Backes et al., 2010]. The method is inherently multi-scale and demonstrated good performance in comparison with Gabor and Fourier transforms, and co-occurrence matrix methods. Another scale-invariant approach using a novel family of texture description filters invariant to orientation, contrast, and scale and robust to local skew has been demonstrated [Mellor et al., 2008]. Successful application for image retrieval was based on χ-squared similarity measures applied to histograms built from local filter responses.

Many of the texture description features presented so far are interrelated; the Fourier power spectrum, the autoregression model, and autocorrelation functions represent the same subset of second-order statistics. The mathematical relationships between texture description methods are summarized in [Tomita and Tsuji, 1990], an experimental comparison of performance between several methods can be found in [Du Buf et al., 1990; Iversen and Lonnestad, 1994; Zhu and Goutte, 1995; Wang et al., 1996], and criteria for comparison are discussed in [Soh et al., 1991].

It has been shown that higher than second-order statistics contain little information that can be used for texture discrimination [Julesz and Caelli, 1979]. Nevertheless, identical second-order statistics do not guarantee identical textures; examples can be found in [Julesz and Bergen, 1987] together with a study of human texture perception. Texture-related research of the human visual system seems to bring useful results, and a texture analysis method based on studies of it was designed to emulate the process of texture feature extraction in each individual channel in the multi-channel spatial filtering model of perception [Rao, 1993].

15.2 Syntactic texture description methods

Syntactic and hybrid texture description methods are not as widely used as statistical approaches [Tomita et al., 1982]. **Syntactic** texture description is based on an analogy between the texture primitive spatial relations and the structure of a formal language.

Descriptions of textures from one class form a language that can be represented by its grammar, which is inferred from a training set of words of the language (from descriptions of textures in a training set)—during a learning phase, one grammar is constructed for each texture class present in the training set. The recognition process is then a syntactic analysis of the texture description word. The grammar that can be used to complete the syntactic analysis of the description word determines the texture class (see Section 9.4).

Purely syntactic texture description models are based on the idea that textures consist of primitives located in almost regular relationships. Primitive descriptions (discussed at the beginning of this chapter) and rules of primitive placement must be determined to describe a texture [Tsuji and Tomita, 1973; Lu and Fu, 1978]. One of the most efficient ways to describe the structure of primitive relationships is using a grammar which represents a rule for building a texture from primitives, by applying transformation rules to a limited set of symbols. Symbols represent the texture primitive types and transformation rules represent the spatial relations between primitives. In Chapter 9 it was noted that any grammar is a very strict formula, but textures of the real world are usually irregular, and structural errors, distortions, or even structural variations are frequent. This means that no strict rule can be used to describe a texture in reality. To make syntactic description of real textures possible, variable rules must be incorporated into the description grammars, and non-deterministic or stochastic grammars must be used (see Section 9.4 and [Fu, 1974]). Further, there is usually no single description grammar for a texture class, which might be described by an infinite number of different grammars using different symbols and different transformation rules, and different grammar types as well. Here, we will discuss chain grammars and graph grammars; other grammars suitable for texture description (tree, matrix) can be found in [Ballard and Brown, 1982; Fu, 1982; Vafaie and Bourbakis, 1988]. Another approach to texture description using generative principles is to use **fractals** [Mandelbrot, 1982; Barnsley, 1988].

15.2.1   Shape chain grammars

The simplest grammars that can be used for texture description are shape chain grammars (see Section 9.4). They generate textures beginning with a start symbol followed by application of transform rules, called **shape rules**—the process ends if no further transform rule can be applied. Texture synthesis consists of two steps: first, the transform rule is found, and then the rule must be geometrically adjusted to match the generated texture exactly (rules are more general; they may not include size, orientation, etc.).

Algorithm 15.5: Shape chain grammar texture synthesis

1. Start a synthesis process by applying some transform rule to the start symbol.

2. Find a part of a previously generated texture that matches the left side of some transform rule. This match must be an unambiguous correspondence between terminal and non-terminal symbols of the left-hand side of the chosen transform rule with terminal and non-terminal symbols of the part of the texture to which the rule is applied. If no such part of the texture can be found, stop.

3. Find an appropriate geometric transform that can be applied to the left-hand side of the chosen rule to match it to the considered texture part exactly.

4. Apply this transform to the right-hand side of the transform rule.

5. Substitute the specified part of the texture (the part that matches a geometrically transformed left-hand side of the chosen rule) with the geometrically transformed right-hand side of the chosen transform rule.

6. Continue with step 2.

We can demonstrate this algorithm on an example of hexagonal texture synthesis. Let V_n be a set of non-terminal symbols, V_t a set of terminal symbols, R a set of rules, S the start symbol (as in Section 9.4). The grammar [Ballard and Brown, 1982] is illustrated in Figure 15.11, which can then be used to generate hexagonal texture following Algorithm 15.5—note that the non-terminal symbol may appear in different rotations. Rotation of primitives here is represented by a small circle attached to one side of the primitive hexagon in Figure 15.11. Recognition of hexagonal textures is the proof that the texture can be generated by this grammar; the texture recognition uses syntactic analysis as described in Section 9.4. Note that according to the grammar of Figure 15.11, the texture shown in Figure 15.12a will be accepted, but that of Figure 15.12b will be rejected.

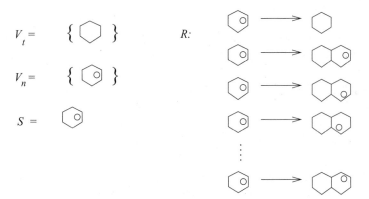

Figure 15.11: Grammar generating hexagonal textures. © *Cengage Learning 2015.*

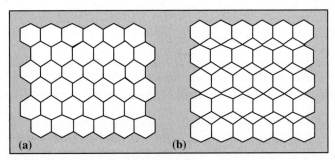

Figure 15.12: Hexagonal textures. (a) Accepted; (b) Rejected. © *Cengage Learning 2015.*

15.2.2   Graph grammars

Texture analysis is more common than texture synthesis in machine vision tasks (even if texture synthesis is generally more common, e.g., in computer graphics and computer games). The natural approach to texture recognition is to construct a planar graph of primitive layout and to use it in the recognition process. Primitive classes and primitive spatial relations must be known to construct such a graph; spatial relationships between texture primitives will then be reflected in the graph structure. Texture primitive classes will be coded in graph nodes, each primitive having a corresponding node in the graph, and two nodes will be connected by an arc if there is no other primitive in some specified neighborhood of these two primitives. The size of this neighborhood is the main influence on the complexity of the resulting planar graph—the larger the neighborhood, the smaller the number of arcs. Note that choosing the neighborhood too large may result in no arcs for some nodes (the same may be true for the neighborhood being too small). Characteristic properties of some graphs used practically (relative neighborhood graphs, Gabriel graphs, Voronoi diagrams) are described in [Urquhart, 1982; Ahuja, 1982; Tuceryan and Jain, 1990]. These graphs are undirected since the spatial neighborhood relation is symmetric, with weighted arcs and nodes. Each node is labeled with a primitive class to which it corresponds, and arcs are weighted by their length and direction.

The texture classification problem is then transformed into a graph recognition problem for which the following approaches may be used.

1. Simplify the texture description by decomposition of the planar graph into a set of chains (sequences of adjacent nodes), and apply the algorithms discussed in the previous section. The chain descriptions of textures can represent border primitives of closed regions, different graph paths, primitive neighborhood, etc. A training set is constructed from the decomposition of several texture description planar graphs for each texture class. Appropriate grammars are inferred which represent textures in the training sets. The presence of information noise is highly probable, so stochastic grammars should be used. Texture classification consists of the following steps.

   - A classified texture is represented by a planar graph.
   - The graph is decomposed into chains.
   - The description chains are presented for syntactic analysis.
   - A texture is classified into the class whose grammar accepts all the chains of the decomposed planar graph. If more than one grammar accepts the chains, the texture can be classified into the class whose grammar accepted the chains with the highest probability.

   The main advantage of this approach is its simplicity but a disadvantage is the impossibility of reconstructing the original planar graph from the chain decomposition —some some portion of the syntactic information is lost during decomposition.

2. Another class of planar graph description may be represented by a stochastic graph grammar or by an extended graph grammar for description of distorted textures. This approach is very difficult from both the implementational and algorithmic points of view; the main problem is in grammar inference.

3. The planar graphs can be compared directly using graph matching approaches. It is necessary to define a 'distance' between two graphs as a measure of their similarity; if such a distance is defined, standard methods used in statistical classifier learning can be used—exemplar computation, cluster analysis, etc.

The syntactic approach is valued for its ability to describe a texture character at several hierarchical levels. It permits a qualitative analysis of textures, for decomposition into descriptive substructures (primitive grouping), to incorporate texture descriptions into the whole description of image, scene, etc. From this point of view, it significantly exceeds the complexity of simple object classification. Not considering the implementation difficulties, the second approach from the list above is recommended; if a descriptive graph grammar is chosen appropriately, it can generate a class of graphs independently of their size. It can be used if a pattern is sought in an image at any hierarchical level. An example of a planar graph describing a texture is shown in Figure 15.13.

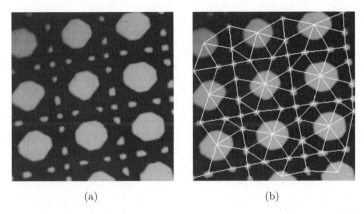

(a)   (b)

Figure 15.13: Planar graph describing a texture. (a) Texture primitives. (b) Planar graph overlaid. © *Cengage Learning 2015.*

15.2.3 Primitive grouping in hierarchical textures

Several levels of primitives can be detected in hierarchical textures—lower-level primitives form some specific pattern which can be considered a primitive at a higher description level (Figure 15.14). The process of detecting these primitive patterns (units) in a texture is called **primitive grouping**. Note that these units may form new patterns at an even higher description level. Therefore, the grouping process must be repeated until no new units can be formed.

Grouping makes a syntactic approach to texture segmentation possible, and plays the same role as local computation of texture features in statistical texture recognition. It has been claimed several times that different primitives and/or different spatial relationships represent different textures. Consider an example (Figure 15.15a) in which the primitives are the same (dots) and textures differ in the spatial relations between them. If a higher hierarchical level is considered, different primitives can be detected in both textures—the textures do not consist of the same primitive types any more (Figure 15.15b).

A primitive grouping algorithm is described in [Tomita and Tsuji, 1990].

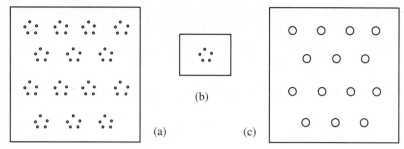

Figure 15.14: Hierarchical texture. (a) Texture. (b) A pattern formed from low-level primitives, this pattern can be considered a primitive in the higher level. (c) Higher-level texture. © *Cengage Learning 2015.*

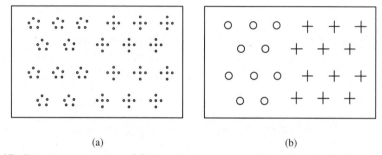

(a)   (b)

Figure 15.15: Primitive grouping. (a) Two textures, same primitives in the lowest description level. (b) The same two textures, different primitives in the higher description level. © *Cengage Learning 2015.*

Algorithm 15.6: Texture primitive grouping

1. Determine texture primitive properties and classify primitives into classes.

2. Find the nearest and the second nearest neighbor for each texture primitive. Using the primitive class and distances to the nearest two neighboring primitives d_1, d_2, classify low-level primitives into **new** classes, see Figure 15.16.

3. Primitives with the same **new** classification which are connected (close to each other), are linked together and form higher-level primitives, see Figure 15.16.

4. If any two resulting homogeneous regions of linked primitives overlap, let the overlapped part form a separate region, see Figure 15.17.

Regions formed from primitives of the lower level may be considered primitives in the higher level and the grouping process may be repeated for these new primitives. Nevertheless, sophisticated control of the grouping process is necessary to achieve meaningful results—it must be controlled from a high-level vision texture understanding subsystem. A recursive primitive grouping, which uses histograms of primitive properties and primitive spatial relations is presented in [Tomita and Tsuji, 1990] together with examples of syntactic-based texture segmentation results.

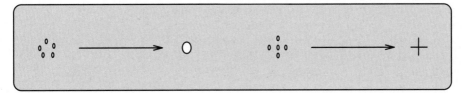

Figure 15.16: Primitive grouping—low-level primitive patterns are grouped into single primitives at a higher level. © *Cengage Learning 2015*.

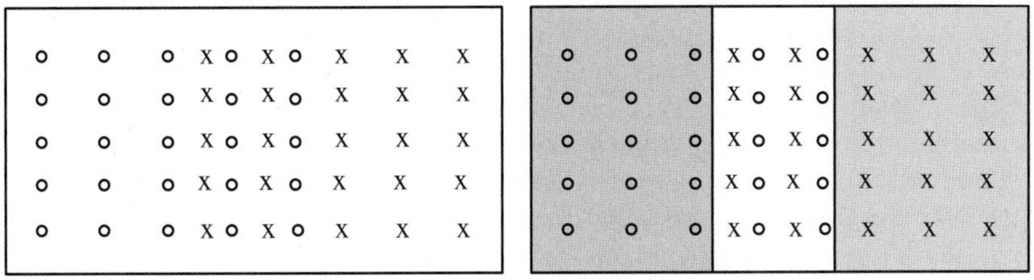

Figure 15.17: Overlap of homogeneous regions results in their splitting. © *Cengage Learning 2015*.

15.3 Hybrid texture description methods

Purely syntactic methods of texture description experience many difficulties with syntactic analyzer learning and with graph (or other complex) grammar inference, which is why purely they are not widely used. On the other hand, a precise definition of primitives brings many advantages and it is not wise to avoid it completely. Hybrid methods of texture description combine the statistical and syntactic approaches; they are partly syntactic because primitives are exactly defined, and partly statistical because spatial relations between primitives are based on probabilities [Conners and Harlow, 1980].

The hybrid approach to texture description distinguishes between weak and strong textures. The syntactic part of weak texture description divides an image into regions based on a tonal image property (e.g., constant gray-level regions) which are considered texture primitives. Primitives can be described by their shape, size, etc. The next step constructs histograms of sizes and shapes of all the texture primitives contained in the image. If the image can be segmented into two or more sets of homogeneous texture regions, the histogram is bi-modal and each primitive is typical of one texture pattern. This can be used for texture segmentation.

If the starting histogram does not have significant peaks, a complete segmentation cannot be achieved. The histogram-based segmentation can be repeated in each hitherto segmented homogeneous texture region. If any texture region consists of more than one primitive type, the method cannot be used and spatial relations between primitives must be computed. Some methods are discussed in [Haralick, 1979].

Description of strong textures is based on the spatial relations of texture primitives and two-directional interactions between primitives seem to carry most of the information. The simplest texture primitive is a pixel and its gray-level property, while the maximum contiguous set of pixels of constant gray-level is a more complicated texture primitive [Wang and Rosenfeld, 1981]. Such a primitive can be described by its size, elongatedness, orientation, average gray-level, etc. The texture description includes spatial relations between primitives based on distance and adjacency relations. Using more complex texture primitives brings more textural information. On the other hand, all the properties of single pixel primitives are immediately available without the necessity of being involved in extensive primitive property computations.

The hybrid multi-level texture description and classification method [Sonka, 1986] is based on primitive definition and spatial description of inter-primitive relations. The method considers both tone and structural properties and consists of several steps. Texture primitives are extracted first, and then described and classified. As a result of this stage, a classifier knows how to classify texture primitives. Known textures are then presented to the texture recognition system. Texture primitives are extracted from the image and the first-level classifier recognizes their classes. Based on recognized texture primitives, spatial relations between primitive classes are evaluated for each texture from the training set. Spatial relations between texture primitives are described by a feature vector used to adjust a second-level classifier. If the second-level classifier is set, the two-level learning process is over, and unknown textures can be presented to the texture recognition system. The primitives are classified by the first-level classifier, spatial primitive properties are computed and the second-level classifier assigns the texture to one of the texture classes. Some hybrid methods use Fourier descriptors for shape coding and a texture is modeled by a reduced set of joint probability distributions obtained by vector quantization. The LBP approach presented earlier in Section 15.1.6 is an inherently hybrid texture description approach—uniform patterns can be understood as texture primitives while estimating the distributions of these primitives (microtemplates) combines the structural and statistical image analysis [Ojala et al., 2002b].

15.4 Texture recognition method applications

Textures are very common in our world, and application possibilities are almost unlimited: estimated crop yields and localization of diseased forests from remotely sensed data, automatic diagnosis of lung diseases from X-ray images, recognition of cloud types from meteorological satellite data, detection of textile pattern imperfections, are just some examples of applications.

Classical applications of spatial frequency-based texture description methods include recognition of roads, road crossings, buildings, agricultural regions, and natural objects, or classification of trees into classes. An interesting proof of the role of textural information in outdoor object recognition was done by comparison of classification correctness if textural information was and was not used. Spectral information-based classification achieved 74% correctly classified objects, while adding textural information increased accuracy to 99% [Haralick, 1979]. Industrial applications of texture description and recognition are becoming more and more common. Examples can be found in almost all branches of industrial and biomedical activities—quality inspection in the motor or textile industries [Wood, 1990; Xie, 2008], workpiece surface monitoring, road surface skidding estimation, micro-electronics, remote sensing, mammography [Miller and Astley, 1992], MR brain imaging [Toulson and Boyce, 1992], pulmonary parenchyma characterization [Xu et al., 2006], three-dimensional texture analysis [Ip and Lam, 1995; Kovalev et al., 2001], content-based data retrieval from image databases, etc.

15.5   Summary

- **Texture**

  - Texture is widely used and intuitively obvious but has no precise definition due to its wide variability.
  - Texture consists of texture **primitives** (texture **elements**) called **texels**.
  - A texture primitive is a contiguous set of pixels with some tonal and/or regional property.
  - **Texture description** is based on **tone** and **structure**. Tone describes pixel intensity properties in the primitive, while structure reflects spatial relationships between primitives.
  - Texture description is **scale dependent**.
  - **Statistical** methods of texture description compute different texture properties and are suitable if texture primitive sizes are comparable with the pixel sizes.
  - **Syntactic** and **hybrid** methods (combination of statistical and syntactic) are more suitable for textures where primitives can be easily determined and their properties described.

- **Statistical texture description**

  - Statistical methods describe textures in a form suitable for statistical pattern recognition. Each texture is described by a feature vector of properties which represents a point in a multi-dimensional feature space.
  - Coarse textures are built from larger primitives, fine textures from smaller primitives. Textural character is in direct relation to the spatial size of the primitives.
  - Fine textures are characterized by higher spatial frequencies, coarse textures by lower spatial frequencies.
  - Measuring spatial frequencies is the basis of a large group of texture recognition methods:
    * Autocorrelation function of a texture
    * Optical image transform
    * Discrete image transform
  - Texture description may be based on repeated occurrence of some gray-level configuration in the texture; this configuration varies rapidly with distance in fine textures, slowly in coarse textures. **Co-occurrence matrices** represent such an approach.
  - **Edge frequency** approaches describe frequencies of edge appearances in texture.
  - In the **primitive length (run length)** approach, texture description features can be computed as continuous probabilities of the length and the gray-level of primitives in the texture.

- **Laws' texture measures** determine texture properties by assessing average gray-level, edges, spots, ripples, and waves in texture.

- **Local Binary Patterns (LBP)** identify local microstructure templates and estimate their distribution in the texture. Local neighborhoods are thresholded to binary patterns, histogram distributions of which are used for description.

- The **fractal** approach to texture description is based on correlation between texture coarseness and fractal dimension and texture granularity and lacunarity.

- **Wavelet** texture description

  * These are typically more efficient than other statistical methods.
  * Wavelet energy signatures or their second-order statistics are frequently used.
  * Standard wavelet approaches are not translation invariant.
  * Discrete wavelet frames introduce translational invariance and can be efficiently implemented using filter banks.
  * Wavelet-based hidden Markov models and hidden Markov trees incorporate independence between wavelet subbands for additional performance enhancement.

- Other statistical approaches exist:

  * Mathematical morphology
  * Texture transform

- Varieties of texture properties may be derived from **first-order** and **second-order statistics** of elementary measures such as co-occurrences, edge distributions, primitive lengths, etc.

- Higher order statistics contain little information that can be used for texture discrimination.

- **Syntactic and hybrid texture description**

  - Syntactic texture description is based on an analogy between texture primitive spatial relations and structure of a formal language.

  - Hybrid methods combine statistical and syntactic approaches; they are partly syntactic because primitives are exactly defined, and partly statistical because spatial relations between primitives are based on probabilities.

  - Purely syntactic texture description models utilize the idea that textures consist of primitives located in almost regular relationships. Primitive descriptions and rules of primitive placement must be determined to describe a texture.

  - Textures of the real world are usually irregular, with frequent structural errors, distortions, and/or structural variations causing strict grammars to be inapplicable. To make syntactic description of real textures possible, variable rules must be incorporated into the description grammars, and non-deterministic or stochastic grammars must be used.

- Syntactic texture description methods include:

    * **Shape chain grammars**, which are the simplest grammars that can be used for texture description. They generate textures beginning with a start symbol followed by application of **shape transform rules**.
    * **Graph grammars** construct a **planar graph of primitive layout**. Primitive classes and their spatial relations must be known to construct such a graph; spatial relationships between texture primitives are reflected in the graph structure. Texture classification is then transformed into a **graph recognition** problem.

- The syntactic approach is valued for its ability to describe a texture character at several **hierarchical levels**.

- **Primitive grouping** can be performed if lower-level primitives that form some specific pattern can be considered a primitive at a higher description level.

- Syntactic and hybrid texture description methods are not as widely used as statistical approaches.

15.6 Exercises

Short-answer questions

S15.1 What is a texel?

S15.2 Explain the difference between weak and strong textures.

S15.3 Explain the difference between fine and coarse textures.

S15.4 What is the role of scale in texture description?

S15.5 Specify the main texture description and recognition strategies employed in statistical, syntactic, and hybrid methods. For each of the three general approaches, describe the texture types for which the approach can be expected to perform well and for which it is not appropriate.

S15.6 Determine whether the following texture features exhibit relatively higher or lower values in fine textures compared to coarse textures:

  (a) Energy in a small-radius circle of the Fourier power spectrum (Figure 15.3a)

  (b) Average edge frequency feature (equation 15.10) for a small value of d

  (c) Short primitive emphasis

  (d) Long primitive emphasis

  (e) Fractal dimension

  (f) Lacunarity

S15.7 Name several texture description features that are well suited for characterization of directional textures.

S15.8 Explain why deterministic grammars are too restrictive for description of real-world textures.

S15.9 On a rectangular grid, sketch the geometric pattern of an $LBP_{4,4}$ texture description feature detector.

S15.10 What is the main reason for rotational invariance of $\text{LBP}^{ri}_{P,R}$ texture descriptor compared to $\text{LBP}_{P,R}$?

S15.11 Explain why use of LTPs as opposed to LBPs for texture description compromises gray-level transform invariance.

S15.12 Define fractal dimension and lacunarity, explain how these measures can be used for texture description.

S15.13 Define a stochastic grammar. How is it useful for texture description?

S15.14 Explain the rationale for primitive grouping. What are its advantages? To which textures is this approach applicable? How can it be used for texture description?

S15.15 Suggest some application areas in which texture description and recognition can be used.

Problems

P15.1 Using the World Wide Web, find several images of dissimilar homogeneous textures (Brodatz textures [Brodatz, 1966] from a Web-based database may be a good choice)

1. Create your personal database TD1 from these images of at least 5 texture type ranging gradually from fine to coarse.

2. Create a texture database TD2 of three dissimilar texture classes with at least ten images belonging to each class.

3. Create a database TD3 of at least three homogeneous directional textures (use preferably several images from each class) and rotate each at 9 random angles – this will form a database of 10 directional images for each texture.

These three databases will be used in some of the experiments below.

P15.2 Implement Fourier transform based descriptors.

P15.3 Determine the co-occurrence matrices $P_{0°,2}$, $P_{45°,2}$, and $P_{90°,3}$ for the image in Figure 15.4.

P15.4 Determine the average edge frequency function (equation 15.10) for $d \in \{1, 2, 3, 4, 5\}$ for a 30×30 checkerboard image with 3×3 binary checkers (values of 0 and 1, 0-level checker in the upper left corner).

P15.5 For a 30×30 checkerboard image with 3×3 binary checkers (values of 0 and 1, 0-level checker in the upper left corner) and a 30×30 image with vertical binary 3-pixel-wide stripes (0-level stripe along the left image edge), determine the following non-directional texture descriptors:

(a) Short primitives emphasis

(b) Long primitives emphasis

(c) Gray-level uniformity

(d) Primitive length uniformity

(e) Primitive percentage

P15.6 Repeat Problem P15.5 with modified texture descriptors that consider directionality of primitives.

P15.7 Develop functions for computing the following texture features in an image of a given size:

    (a) Co-occurrence descriptors

    (b) Average edge frequency

    (c) Primitive length descriptors

    (d) Laws' energy descriptors

    (e) $LBP_{P,R}^{riu2}$ descriptors

    (f) Fractal texture descriptors

P15.8 For five highly dissimilar textures ranging from fine to coarse selected from your database TD1 (Problem P15.1) and using the functions developed in Problem P15.7, determine:

    (a) Co-occurrence features specified by equations (15.4–15.9)

    (b) Average edge frequency

for four distinct values of d (e.g., $d = 1, 3, 5, 7$; note that you may select other values of d according to the scale of your textures). Select three texture descriptors to determine what can be concluded from inspection of the relationship between the texture descriptors and the value of d in each texture. Further, what can be concluded for the relationship between texture coarseness and the values of individual texture descriptors?

P15.9 For five highly dissimilar textures ranging from fine to coarse selected from your database TD1 (Problem P15.1) and using the functions developed in Problem P15.7, determine:

    (a) Primitive length features specified by equations (15.12)–(15.16)

    (b) Laws' energy features

    (c) $LBP_{P,R}^{riu2}$ features

    (d) Fractal-based texture features—fractal dimension and lacunarity

What can be concluded for the relationship between texture coarseness and the values of individual texture descriptors?

P15.10 Design a shape chain grammar that generates the texture shown in Figure 12.4. Show the first few steps of the generation process.

P15.11 Design a shape chain grammar that generates the texture shown in Figure 15.12b.

P15.12 Using your database of classes TD2 (Problem P15.1), develop a program for statistical texture description and recognition. Texture descriptors should reflect the discriminative properties of the three classes. Train a simple statistical classifier (Chapter 9) using half of the texture images from each class, and determine classification correctness using the remaining texture images.

P15.13 Using your database TD3 (Problem P15.1) of texture classes that include rotated images, develop a program for statistical texture description and recognition so that textures are recognized regardless of their orientation. Texture descriptors should reflect the discriminative properties of the three classes. Do not use LBP descriptors for this problem. Train a simple statistical classifier (Chapter 9) using half of the texture images from each class, and determine classification correctness using the remaining texture images.

P15.14 Repeat Problem P15.13 using LBP and LBP^{riu2} texture descriptors. Compare the performance of these two descriptors with each other as well as with results obtained in Problem P15.13

P15.15 Using the images from your databases TD1–TD3 (Problem P15.1) create several artificial images that contain three to five regions of different texture. Develop a texture classification program that performs texture recognition in rectangular windows. Using a moving window, the program should classify each window into one of the classes. Train the classifier in single-texture images using windows of the same size as is used in the classification phase. Assess image segmentation accuracy as the percentage of correctly classified image area.

P15.16 Make yourself familiar with solved problems and **Matlab** implementations of selected algorithms provided in the corresponding chapter of the **Matlab Companion** to this text [Svoboda et al., 2008]. The **Matlab Companion** homepage http://visionbook.felk.cvut.cz offers images used in the problems, and well-commented **Matlab** code is provided for educational purposes.

P15.17 Use the **Matlab Companion** [Svoboda et al., 2008] to develop solutions to additional exercises and practical problems provided there. Implement your solutions using **Matlab** or other suitable programming languages.

15.7   References

Ahuja N. Dot pattern processing using Voronoi neighborhood. *IEEE Transactions on Pattern Analysis and Machine Intelligence*, 4:336–343, 1982.

Ahuja N. and Rosenfeld A. Mosaic models for textures. *IEEE Transactions on Pattern Analysis and Machine Intelligence*, 3(1):1–11, 1981.

Arivazhagan S. and Ganesan L. Texture classification using wavelet transform. *Pattern Recogn. Lett.*, 24:1513–1521, 2003.

Backes A. R., Goncalves W. N., Martinez A. S., and Bruno O. M. Texture analysis and classification using deterministic tourist walk. *Pattern Recognition*, 43:686–694, 2010.

Ballard D. H. and Brown C. M. *Computer Vision*. Prentice-Hall, Englewood Cliffs, NJ, 1982.

Barnsley M. F. *Fractals Everywhere*. Academic Press, Boston, 1988.

Besicovitch A. S. and Ursell H. D. Sets of fractional dimensions (V): On dimensional numbers of some continuous curves. *Journal of the London Mathematical Society*, 12:18–25, 1937.

Bovik A. C., Clark M., and Geisler W. S. Multichannel texture analysis using localized spatial filters. *IEEE Transactions on Pattern Analysis and Machine Intelligence*, 12:55–73, 1990.

Brodatz P. *Textures: A Photographic Album for Artists and Designers*. Dover, Toronto, 1966.

Castleman K. R. *Digital Image Processing*. Prentice-Hall, Englewood Cliffs, NJ, 1996.

Chang T. and Kuo C. C. Texture analysis and classification with tree-structure wavelet transform. *IEEE Transactions on Image Processing*, 2:429–441, 1993.

Coggins J. M. and Jain A. K. A spatial filtering approach to texture analysis. *Pattern Recognition Letters*, 3:195–203, 1985.

Conners R. W. and Harlow C. A. Toward a structural textural analyser based on statistical methods. *Computer Graphics and Image Processing*, 12:224–256, 1980.

Crouse M. S., Nowak R. D., and Baraniuk R. G. Wavelet-based statistical signal processing using hidden Markov models. *IEEE Transactions on Signal Processing*, 46:886–902, 1998.

Davis L. S. and Mitiche A. Edge detection in textures. *Computer Graphics and Image Processing*, 12:25–39, 1980.

Davis L. S., Janos L., and Dunn S. M. Efficient recovery of shape from texture. *IEEE Transactions on Pattern Analysis and Machine Intelligence*, 5(5):485–492, 1983.

Deguchi K. and Morishita I. Texture characterization and texture-based partitioning using two-dimensional linear estimation. *IEEE Transactions on Computers*, 27:739–745, 1978.

Derin H. and Elliot H. Modelling and segmentation of noisy and textured images using Gibbs random fields. *IEEE Transactions on Pattern Analysis and Machine Intelligence*, 9(1): 39–55, 1987.

Dougherty E. R., Kraus E. J., and Pelz J. B. Image segmentation by local morphological granulometries. In *Proceedings of IGARSS '89 and Canadian Symposium on Remote Sensing*, Vancouver, Canada, pages 1220–1223, New York, 1989. IEEE.

Du Buf J. M. H., Kardan M., and Spann M. Texture feature performance for image segmentation. *Pattern Recognition*, 23(3–4):291–309, 1990.

Ehrick R. W. and Foith J. P. A view of texture topology and texture description. *Computer Graphics and Image Processing*, 8:174–202, 1978.

Fan G. and Xia X. G. Wavelet-based texture analysis and synthesis using hidden Markov models. *IEEE Trans. Circuits and Systems*, 50:106–120, 2003.

Fan Z. Edge-based hierarchical algorithm for textured image segmentation. In *International Conference on Acoustics, Speech, and Signal Processing*, Glasgow, Scotland, pages 1679–1682, Piscataway, NJ, 1989. IEEE.

Fu K. S. *Syntactic Methods in Pattern Recognition*. Academic Press, New York, 1974.

Fu K. S. *Syntactic Pattern Recognition and Applications*. Prentice-Hall, Englewood Cliffs, NJ, 1982.

Fung P. W., Grebbin G., and Attikiouzel Y. Contextual classification and segmentation of textured images. In *Proceedings of the 1990 International Conference on Acoustics, Speech, and Signal Processing—ICASSP 90*, Albuquerque, NM, pages 2329–2332, Piscataway, NJ, 1990. IEEE.

Gagalowicz A. Stochatic texture fields synthesis from a priori given second order statistics. In *Proceedings, Pattern Recognition and Image Processing*, Chicago, IL, pages 376–381, Piscataway, NJ, 1979. IEEE.

Gagalowicz A., Graffigne C., and Picard D. Texture boundary positioning. In *Proceedings of the 1988 IEEE International Conference on Systems, Man, and Cybernetics*, pages 16–19, Beijing/Shenyang, China, 1988. IEEE.

Galloway M. M. Texture classification using gray level run length. *Computer Graphics and Image Processing*, 4:172–179, 1975.

Gotlieb C. C. and Kreyszig H. E. Texture descriptors based on co-occurrence matrices. *Computer Vision, Graphics, and Image Processing*, 51(1):70–86, 1990.

Haralick R. M. Statistical and structural approaches to texture. *Proceedings IEEE*, 67(5): 786–804, 1979.

Haralick R. M., Shanmugam K., and Dinstein I. Textural features for image classification. *IEEE Transactions on Systems, Man and Cybernetics*, 3:610–621, 1973.

Hausdorff F. Dimension und ausseres Mass. *Mathematische Annalen*, 79:157–179, 1919.

Huang Q., Lorch J. R., and Dubes R. C. Can the fractal dimension of images be measured? *Pattern Recognition*, 27:339–349, 1994.

Hurst H. E. Long-term storage capacity of reservoirs. *Transactions of the American Society of Civil Engineers*, 116:770–808, 1951.

Ip H. H. S. and Lam S. W. C. Three-dimensional structural texture modeling and segmentation. *Pattern Recognition*, 28:1299–1319, 1995.

Iversen H. and Lonnestad T. An evaluation of stochastic models for analysis and synthesis of gray-scale texture. *Pattern Recognition Letters*, 15:575–585, 1994.

Jin X. C., Ong S. H., and Jayasooriah. A practical method for estimating fractal dimension. *Pattern Recognition Letters*, 16:457–464, 1995.

Julesz B. Textons, the elements of texture perception, and their interactions. *Nature*, 290: 91–97, 1981.

Julesz B. and Bergen J. R. Textons, the fundamental elements in preattentive vision and perception of textures. In *Readings in Computer Vision*, pages 243–256. Morgan Kaufmann Publishers, Los Altos, CA, 1987.

Julesz B. and Caelli T. On the limits of Fourier decompositions in visual texture perception. *Perception*, 8:69–73, 1979.

Keller J. M., Chen S., and Crownover R. M. Texture description and segmentation through fractal geometry. *Computer Vision, Graphics, and Image Processing*, 45(2):150–166, 1989.

Kjell B. P. and Wang P. Y. Noise-tolerant texture classification and image segmentation. In *Intelligent Robots and Computer Vision IX: Algorithms and Techniques*, Boston, pages 553–560, Bellingham, WA, 1991. SPIE.

Kovalev V. A., Kruggel F., Gertz H. J., and Cramon D. Y. v. Three-dimensional texture analysis of MRI brain datasets. *IEEE Transactions on Medical Imaging*, 20:424–433, 2001.

Laws K. I. Texture energy measures. In *DARPA Image Understanding Workshop*, Los Angeles, CA, pages 47–51, Los Altos, CA, 1979. DARPA.

Liu S. S. and Jernigan M. E. Texture analysis and discrimination in additive noise. *Computer Vision, Graphics, and Image Processing*, 49:52–67, 1990.

Lu S. Y. and Fu K. S. A syntactic approach to texture analysis. *Computer Graphics and Image Processing*, 7:303–330, 1978.

Lundahl T., Ohley W. J., Kay S. M., and Siffert R. Fractional Brownian motion: A maximum likelihood estimator and its application to image texture. *IEEE Transactions on Medical Imaging*, 5:152–161, 1986.

Mallat S. G. A theory of multiresolution signal decomposition: The wavelet representation. *IEEE Transactions on Pattern Analysis and Machine Intelligence*, 11(7):674–693, 1989.

Mandelbrot B. B. *The Fractal Geometry of Nature*. Freeman, New York, 1982.

Mellor M., Hong B. W., and Brady M. Locally rotation, contrast, and scale invariant descriptors for texture analysis. *IEEE Transactions on Pattern Analysis and Machine Intelligence*, 30: 52–61, 2008.

Miller P. and Astley S. Classification of breast tissue by texture analysis. *Image and Vision Computing*, 10(5):277–282, 1992.

Mitchell O. R., Myer C. R., and Boyne W. A max-min measure for image texture analysis. *IEEE Transactions on Computers*, 26:408–414, 1977.

Mojsilovic A., Popovic M. V., and Rackov D. M. On the selection of an optimal wavelet basis for texture charactrization. *IEEE Transactions on Image Processing*, 9:2043–2050, 2000.

Ojala T., Pietikainen M., and Harwood D. A comparative study of texture measures with classification based on feature distributions. *Pattern Recognition*, 29:51–59, 1996.

Ojala T., Valkealahti K., Oja E., and Pietikainen M. Texture discrimination with multi-dimensoinal distributions of signed gray level differences. *Pattern Recognition*, 34:727–739, 2001.

Ojala T., Maenpaa T., Pietikainen M., Viertola J., Kyllonen J., and Huovinen S. Outex - new framework for empirical evaluation of texture analysis algorithms. In *Proc. 16th International Conference on Pattern Recognition*, volume 1, pages 701–706, Quebec, Canada, 2002a.

Ojala T., Pietikainen M., and Maenpaa M. Multiresolution gray-scale and rotation invariant texture classification with locally binary patterns. *IEEE Transactions on Pattern Analysis and Machine Intelligence*, 24:971–987, 2002b.

Oppenheim A. V., Schafer R. W., and Buck J. R. *Discrete-Time Signal Processing*. Prentice Hall, New York, 2nd edition, 1999.

Pentland A. P. Fractal-based description of natural scenes. *IEEE Transactions on Pattern Analysis and Machine Intelligence*, 6:661–674, 1984.

Perry A. and Lowe D. G. Segmentation of non-random textures using zero-crossings. In *1989 IEEE International Conference on Systems, Man, and Cybernetics*, Cambridge, MA, pages 1051–1054, Piscataway, NJ, 1989. IEEE.

Pietikainen M., Ojala T., and Xu Z. Rotation-invariant texture classification using feature distributions. *Pattern Recognition*, 33:43–52, 2000.

Porter R. and Canagarajah N. Robust rotation-invariant texture classification: Wavelet, Gabor filter, and GMRF based schemes. *IEE Proc. Vision, Image, Signal Processing*, 144:180–188, 1997.

Pratt W. K. and Faugeras O. C. Development and evaluation of stochastic-based visual texture features. *IEEE Transactions on Systems, Man and Cybernetics*, 8:796–804, 1978.

Rao A. R. Identifying high level features of texture perception. *CVGIP – Graphical Models and Image Processing*, 55:218–233, 1993.

Reed T. R., Wechsler H., and Werman M. Texture segmentation using a diffusion region growing technique. *Pattern Recognition*, 23(9):953–960, 1990.

Rioul O. A discrete-time multiresolution theory. *IEEE Trans on Signal Proc.*, 41:2591–2606, 1993.

Rosenfeld A., editor. *Digital Picture Analysis*. Springer Verlag, Berlin, 1976.

Sarkar N. and Chaudhuri B. B. An efficient differential box-counting approach to compute fractal dimension of image. *IEEE Transactions on Systems, Man and Cybernetics*, 24:115–120, 1994.

Serra J. and Verchery G. Mathematical morphology applied to fibre composite materials. *Film Science Technology*, 6:141–158, 1973.

Shulman A. R. *Optical Data Processing*. Wiley, New York, 1970.

Sklansky J. Image segmentation and feature extraction. *IEEE Transactions on Systems, Man and Cybernetics*, 8(4):237–247, 1978.

Soh Y., Murthy S. N. J., and Huntsberger T. L. Development of criteria to compare model-based texture analysis methods. In *Intelligent Robots and Computer Vision IX: Algorithms and Techniques*, Boston, pages 561–573, Bellingham, WA, 1991. SPIE.

Sonka M. A new texture recognition method. *Computers and Artificial Intelligence*, 5(4):357–364, 1986.

Svoboda T., Kybic J., and Hlavac V. *Image Processing, Analysis, and Machine Vision: A MATLAB Companion*. Thomson Engineering, 2008.

Tan X. and Triggs B. Enhanced local texture feature sets for face recognition under difficult lighting conditions. *Image Processing, IEEE Transactions on*, 19:1635–1650, 2010.

Tomita F. and Tsuji S. *Computer Analysis of Visual Textures*. Kluwer, Norwell, MA, 1990.

Tomita F., Shirai Y., and Tsuji S. Description of textures by a structural analysis. *IEEE Transactions on Pattern Analysis and Machine Intelligence*, 4(2):183–191, 1982.

Toulson D. L. and Boyce J. F. Segmentation of MR images using neural nets. *Image and Vision Computing*, 10(5):324–328, 1992.

Tsuji S. and Tomita F. A structural analyser for a class of textures. *Computer Graphics and Image Processing*, 2:216–231, 1973.

Tuceryan M. and Jain A. K. Texture segmentation using Voronoi polygons. *IEEE Transactions on Pattern Analysis and Machine Intelligence*, 12(2):211–216, 1990.

Unser M. Local inear transforms for texture measurements. *Signal Processing*, 11:61–79, 1986.

Unser M. Texture classification and segmentation using wavelet frames. *IEEE Transactions on Image Processing*, 4:1549–1560, 1995.

Unser M. and Eden M. Multiresolution feature extraction and selection for texture segmentation. *IEEE Transactions on Pattern Analysis and Machine Intelligence*, 11(7):717–728, 1989.

Urquhart R. Graph theoretical clustering based on limited neighbourhood sets. *Pattern Recognition*, 15(3):173–187, 1982.

Vafaie H. and Bourbakis N. G. Tree grammar scheme for generation and recognition of simple texture paths in pictures. In *Third International Symposium on Intelligent Control 1988*, Arlington, VA, pages 201–206, Piscataway, NJ, 1988. IEEE.

Van de Wouwer G., Scheunders P., and Van Dyck D. Statistical texture characterization from wavelet representations. *IEEE Transactions on Image Processing*, 8:592–598, 1999.

Vautrot P., Bonnet N., and Herbin M. Comparative study of different spatial/spatial frequency methods for texture segmentation/classification. In *Proceedings of the IEEE International Conference on Image Processing*, Lausanne, Switzerland, pages III:145–148, Piscataway, NJ, 1996. IEEE.

Voss R. Random fractals: Characterization and measurement. In *Scaling Phenomena in Disordered Systems*. Plenum Press, New York, 1986.

Vu N.-S., Dee H. M., and Caplier A. Face recognition using the POEM descriptor. *Pattern Recognition*, 45(7):2478–2488, 2012.

Wang L. and He D. C. Texture classification using texture spectrum. *Pattern Recognition*, 23:905–910, 1990.

Wang S. and Rosenfeld A. A relative effectiveness of selected texture primitive. *IEEE Transactions on Systems, Man and Cybernetics*, 11:360–370, 1981.

Wang Z., Guerriero A., and Sario M. D. Comparison of several approaches for the segmentation of texture images. *Pattern Recognition Letters*, 17:509–521, 1996.

Weszka J. S., Dyer C., and Rosenfeld A. A comparative study of texture measures for terrain classification. *IEEE Transactions on Systems, Man and Cybernetics*, 6(4):269–285, 1976.

Wood E. J. Applying Fourier and associated transforms to pattern characterization in textiles. *Textile Research Journal*, 60(4):212–220, 1990.

Wu C. M., Chen Y. C., and Hsieh K. S. Texture features for classification of ultrasonic liver images. *IEEE Transactions on Medical Imaging*, 11:141–152, 1992.

Xie X. A review of recent advances in surface defect detection using texture analysis techniques. *Electronic Letters on Computer Vision and Image Analysis*, 7:1–22, 2008.

Xu Y., Sonka M., McLennan G., Guo J., and Hoffman E. MDCT-based 3-D texture classification of emphysema and early smoking related pathologies. *IEEE Transactions on Medical Imaging*, 25:464–475, 2006.

Zhu Y. M. and Goutte R. A comparison of bilinear space/spatial-frequency representations for texture discrimination. *Pattern Recognition Letters*, 16:1057–1068, 1995.

Chapter 16

Motion analysis

Increasing processing power and, especially, the wide deployment of surveillance technology have made automated study of motion desirable and possible. Detection and tracking of human faces, pedestrian or vehicular motion are now common applications; additionally, object-based video compression, driver assistance, autonomous vehicles, robot navigation, user interfaces, smart room tracking, etc. can be seen. We have already considered the extraction of 3D shape and relative depth from motion in Section 12.1.1.

The usual input to a motion analysis system is a temporal image sequence. A set of assumptions can help to solve motion analysis problems—as always, prior knowledge helps to decrease the complexity of analysis. Prior knowledge may include information about the camera motion—mobile or static—and information about the time interval between consecutive images, especially whether this interval was short enough for the sequence to represent continuous motion. This prior information helps in the choice of an appropriate motion analysis technique. As in other areas of machine vision, there is no foolproof technique in motion analysis, no general algorithm; furthermore, the techniques presented in this chapter work only if certain conditions are met. A very interesting aspect of motion analysis is research into visual sensing of living organisms that are extremely well adapted to motion analysis. The psycho-physiological and cognitive aspects of motion sensing can be studied in [Ullman, 1979; Watson and Ahumada, 1985; Koenderink, 1986; Gescheider, 1997; Beutel et al., 2000; Cummins and Cummins, 2000; Kaernbach et al., 2003].

There are three main groups of motion-related problems from the practical point of view:

1. **Motion detection** is the simplest problem. This registers any detected motion and is often used for security purposes. This group usually uses a single static camera.

2. **Moving object detection and location** represents another set of problems. A camera is usually in a static location and objects are moving in the scene, or the camera moves and objects are static. These problems are considerably more difficult in comparison with the first group. If only moving object detection is required

(note the difference between motion detection and moving object detection), the solution can be based on motion-based segmentation methods. Other more complex problems include the detection of a moving object, the detection of the trajectory of its motion, and the prediction of its future trajectory. Image object-matching techniques are often used to solve this task—typically, direct matching in image data, matching of object features, matching of specific representative object points (corners, etc.) in an image sequence, or representing moving objects as graphs and consequent matching of these graphs. Another variety of approaches will parameterize the 2D projections of objects in view and make predictions about their movement, which are used and reinforced later in the image sequence. Practical examples of methods from this group include cloud tracking from a sequence of satellite meteorological data, including cloud character and motion prediction, motion analysis for autonomous road vehicles, automatic satellite location by detecting specific points of interest on the Earth's surface, city traffic analysis, and many military applications. The most complex methods of this group work even if both camera and objects are moving.

3. The third group is related to the **derivation of 3D object properties** from a set of 2D projections acquired at different instants. Three-dimensional object description is covered in Chapter 11 and an excellent survey of motion-based recognition approaches is given in [Cedras and Shah, 1995]. Practical solutions to 3D scene reconstruction from live video is described in [Akbarzadeh et al., 2006]

Even though motion analysis is often called *dynamic image analysis*, it is sometimes based on a small number of consecutive images, maybe just two or three in a sequence. This is similar to an analysis of static images, and the motion is actually analyzed at a higher level, looking for *correspondence* between pairs of points of interest in sequential images. A two-dimensional representation of a (generally) three-dimensional motion is called a *motion field*, in which each point is assigned a *velocity vector* corresponding to the motion direction, velocity, and distance from an observer at an appropriate image location.

A different approach analyzes motion from *optical flow* computation (Section 16.2), where a very small time distance between consecutive images is required, with very marginal change between two consecutive images. Optical flow computation results in motion direction and motion velocity determination at (possibly all) image points. The immediate aim of optical flow-based image analysis is to determine a motion field. As will be discussed later, optical flow does not always correspond to the true motion field because illumination changes are reflected in the optical flow. Object motion parameters can be derived from computed optical flow vectors. In reality, estimates of optical flow or point correspondence are noisy, but, unfortunately, three-dimensional interpretation of motion is ill-conditioned and requires high precision of optical flow or point correspondence. To overcome these difficulties, approaches that are not based on optical flow or point correspondence are used, since if the intermediate step (optical flow, point correspondence) does not have to be computed, possible errors can be avoided. Estimates of general motion of multiple moving objects in an image sequence based on gray-level and image gradient without using any higher-level information such as corners or borders is introduced in [Wu and Kittler, 1990]. Motion field construction using steerable filters also falls into this category [Freeman and Adelson, 1991; Huang and Chen, 1995]. A conceptually similar approach is presented in Section 16.4, in which image-based and motion-based information are used simultaneously. By focusing on short-term motion patterns rather than on their tracking over extended periods of time, this approach does not require any complex intermediate representations. By analyzing temporal differences between shifted blocks of rectangle filters, it yields respectable performance in low quality small resolution images [Viola et al., 2003].

Motion field or *velocity field* computations represent a compromise technique; information similar to the optical flow is determined, but it is based on images acquired at intervals that are not short enough to ensure small changes due to motion. The velocity field can also be acquired if the number of images in a sequence is small.

Motion evaluation may or may not depend on object detection. An example of object-independent analysis is optical flow computation, whereas velocity field computation or differential methods search for points of interest or points of motion and represent object-dependent analysis. Object-dependent methods are usually based on searching for a correspondence between points of interest or between regions. One approach to motion analysis uses active contour models (snakes, discussed in Section 7.2). In motion analysis, the initial estimate necessary to start the snake energy minimization process is obtained from the detected position of the contour in the previous frame.

On the other hand, in situations when image-based information may be available to specifically characterize an object of interest, its usage is very helpful. Such information is used in kernel-based object detection and tracking as discussed in Section 16.5.2 [Comaniciu et al., 2000, 2003]. That method is based on spatially masking the target object with an isotropic kernel, followed by applying a smooth similarity function, which reduces the tracking problem to a maximum similarity search in the vicinity of the previous location. The similarity optimization is then efficiently performed using the mean shift algorithm (Section 7.1).

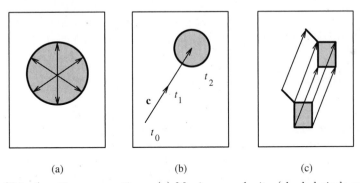

(a)   (b)   (c)

Figure 16.1: Object motion assumptions. (a) Maximum velocity (shaded circle represents area of possible object location). (b) Small acceleration (shaded circle represents area of possible object location at time t_2). (c) Common motion and mutual correspondence (rigid objects). © *Cengage Learning 2015*.

If motion analysis is based on detection of moving objects or object feature points, the following object motion assumptions can help to localize moving objects (Figure 16.1).

- **Maximum velocity**: Assume that a moving object is scanned at time intervals of dt. A possible position of a specific object point in an image is inside a circle with its center at the object point position in the previous frame and its radius $c_{max}\, dt$, where c_{max} is the assumed maximum velocity of the moving object.

- **Small acceleration**: The change of velocity in time dt is bounded by some constant.

- **Common motion** (similarity in motion): All the object points move in a similar way.

- **Mutual correspondence**: Rigid objects exhibit stable pattern points. Each point of an object corresponds to exactly one point in the next image in sequence and vice versa, although there are exceptions due to occlusion and object rotation.

To generalize, image motion analysis and especially object tracking combine two separate but interrelated components:

- localization and representation of the object of interest (target), a mainly bottom-up process that needs to overcome inherent changes in the appearance, orientation, illumination, and scale of the target;

- trajectory filtering and data association, a top-down process that considers object dynamics and uses various sources of a priori information, as well as generation and evaluation of motion hypotheses, frequently using motion models.

Needless to say, stress may be on one or the other component based on the nature of the motion application. For example, tracking aircraft on radar or video images would depend heavily on the motion models associated with the individual aircraft types. In contrast, tracking human faces in a crowded scene where abrupt and unpredictable motion is more likely will probably depend more on target representation than on motion models. Equally important is to distinguish between single and multiple target tracking and design methods accordingly: all of these are addressed in the following sections. With motion analysis and object tracking being one of the most advanced application areas of machine vision, it shall be no surprise that methods, approaches, and strategies described in previous chapters will frequently be referenced and used as pre-requisite knowledge.

16.1 Differential motion analysis methods

Simple subtraction of images acquired at different instants in time makes motion detection possible, assuming a stationary camera position and constant illumination. A *difference image* $d(i,j)$ is a binary image where non-zero values represent image areas with motion, that is, areas where there was a substantial difference between gray-levels in consecutive images f_1 and f_2:

$$d(i,j) = 0 \quad \text{if} \quad \left| f_1(i,j) - f_2(i,j) \right| \leq \varepsilon \,,$$
$$ = 1 \quad \text{otherwise,} \tag{16.1}$$

where ε is a small positive number. Figure 16.2 shows an example of motion detection using a difference image. The difference image can be based on more complex image features such as average gray-level in some neighborhood, local texture features, etc. It is clear that the motion of any object distinct from its background can be detected (considering motion detection represents motion registration only).

Let f_1 and f_2 be two consecutive images separated by a time interval. An element $d(i,j)$ of the difference image between images f_1 and f_2 may have a value one due to any one of the following reasons (Figure 16.2):

1. $f_1(i,j)$ is a pixel on a moving object,
   $f_2(i,j)$ is a pixel on the static background,
   (or vice versa).

2. $f_1(i,j)$ is a pixel on a moving object,
   $f_2(i,j)$ is a pixel on another moving object.

3. $f_1(i,j)$ is a pixel on a moving object,
   $f_2(i,j)$ is a pixel on a different part of the same moving object.

4. Noise, inaccuracies of stationary camera positioning, etc.

The system errors mentioned in the last item must be suppressed. The simplest solution is not to consider any regions of the difference image that are smaller than a specified threshold, although this may prevent slow motion and small object motions being detected. Further, results of this approach are highly dependent on an object–background contrast. On the other hand, we can be sure that all the resulting regions in the difference images result from motion. Section 16.5 considers these matters further.

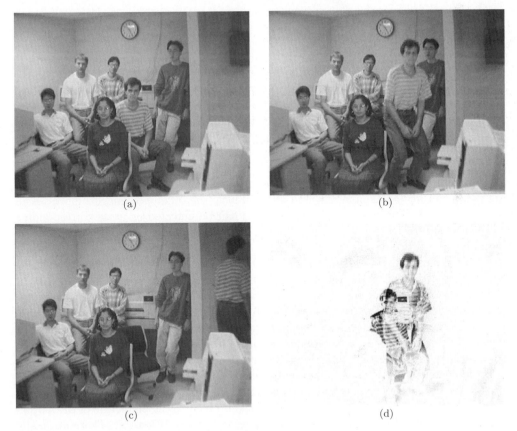

(a)

(b)

(c)

(d)

Figure 16.2: Motion detection. (a) First frame of the image sequence. (b) Frame 2 of the sequence. (c) Last frame (frame 5). (d) Differential motion image constructed from image frames 1 and 2 (inverted to improve visualization). © *M. Sonka 2015.*

Trajectories detected using differential image motion analysis may not reveal the direction of the motion. If direction is needed, construction of a *cumulative difference image* can solve this problem. Cumulative difference images contain information about motion direction and other time-related motion properties, and about slow motion and small object motion as well. The cumulative difference image d_{cum} is constructed from a sequence of n images, with the first image (f_1) being considered a reference image. Values of the cumulative difference image reflect how often (and by how much) the image gray-level was different from the gray-level of the reference image:

$$d_{cum}(i,j) = \sum_{k=1}^{n} a_k \left| f_1(i,j) - f_k(i,j) \right|,$$ (16.2)

a_k gives the *significance* of images in the sequence of n images; more recent images may be given greater weights to reflect the importance of current motion and to specify current object location. Figure 16.3 shows the cumulative difference image determined from the sequence of five image frames depicting motion analyzed in Figure 16.2.

Figure 16.3: Cumulative difference image determined from a sequence of five frames depicting motion analyzed in Figure 16.2 (inverted for improved visualization). © *Cengage Learning 2015.*

Suppose that an image of a static scene is available, and only stationary objects are present in it. If this image is used for reference, the difference image suppresses all motionless areas, and any motion in the scene can be detected as areas corresponding to the actual positions of the moving objects in the scene. Motion analysis can then be based on a sequence of difference images.

A problem with this approach may be the impossibility of getting an image of a static reference scene if the motion never ends; then a learning stage must construct the reference image. The most straightforward method is to superimpose moving image objects on non-moving image backgrounds from other images taken in a different phase of the motion. Which image parts should be superimposed can be judged from difference images, or the reference image can be constructed interactively (which can be allowed in the learning stage). Section 16.5.1 describes approaches to this problem.

Subsequent analysis usually determines motion trajectories; often only the centroid trajectory is needed. The task may be considerably simplified if objects can be segmented out of the first image of the sequence. A practical problem is the prediction of the motion trajectory if the object position in several previous images is known. There are many methods [Jain, 1981, 1984; Jain et al., 1995] that find other motion parameters from difference images—whether the object is approaching or receding, which object overlaps which, etc. Note that difference motion analysis methods give good examples of motion analysis principles and present a good introduction to the problem; unfortunately, difference images do not carry enough information to work reliably in reality. Some problems are common for most motion field detection approaches—consider just a simple example of a rectangular object moving parallel to the object boundary; differential motion analysis can only detect the motion of two sides of the rectangle (see Figures 16.4a,b). Similarly, an aperture problem may cause ambiguity of contained motion information— in the situation shown in Figure 16.4c, only part of an object boundary is visible and it is impossible to determine the motion completely. The arrows indicate three possibilities of motion, all yielding the same final position of the object boundary in the image. Differential motion analysis is often used in digital subtraction angiography, where vessel motion is estimated.

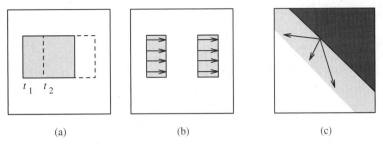

(a)   (b)   (c)

Figure 16.4: Problems of motion field construction. (a) Object position at times t_1 and t_2. (b) Motion field. (c) Aperture problem—ambiguous motion. © *Cengage Learning 2015.*

While the difference image carries information about presence of motion, characteristics of motion derived from it are not very reliable. The motion parameter estimation robustness can be improved if intensity characteristics of regions or groups of pixels in two image frames are compared. A conceptually straightforward approach to *robust motion detection* is to compare corresponding areas of the image. Such corresponding *superpixels* are usually formed by non-overlapping rectangular regions, the size of which can be derived from the camera aspect ratio. Then, the superpixels may be matched in the compared frames using correlation or likelihood approaches [Jain et al., 1995].

Detecting *moving edges* helps overcome several limitations of differential motion analysis methods. By combining spatial and temporal image gradients, differential analysis can be used reliably for detection of slow-moving edges as well as of weak edges that move with higher speed. Moving edges can be determined by logical AND operations of the spatial and temporal image edges [Jain et al., 1979]. The spatial edges can be identified by virtually any edge detector from the variety given in Section 5.3.2, the temporal gradient can be approximated using the difference image, and the logical AND can be implemented through multiplication. Then, the moving edge image $d_{\mathrm{med}}(i,j)$ can be determined as

$$d_{\mathrm{med}}(i,j) = S(i,j)\,D(i,j)\,, \qquad (16.3)$$

where $S(i,j)$ represents edge magnitudes determined in one of the two analyzed image frames and $D(i,j)$ is the absolute difference image. An example of a moving-edge image determined from the first and second frames of an image sequence (Figure 16.2) is given in Figure 16.5.

Figure 16.5: Moving-edge image determined from the first and second frames of the image sequence analyzed in Figure 16.2 (inverted for improved visualization). © *Cengage Learning 2015.*

16.2 Optical flow

Optical flow reflects image changes due to motion during a time interval dt, and the optical flow field is the velocity field that represents the three-dimensional motion of object points across a two-dimensional image [Kearney and Thompson, 1988]. Optical flow is an abstraction typical of the kind that computational methods try to achieve. Therefore, it should represent only those motion-related intensity changes in the image that are required in further processing, and all other changes reflected in the optical flow should be considered detection errors. For example, optical flow should not be sensitive to illumination changes and motion of unimportant objects (e.g., shadows). However, non-zero optical flow is detected if a fixed sphere is illuminated by a moving source, and a smooth sphere rotating under constant illumination provides no optical flow despite the rotational motion and the true non-zero motion field [Horn, 1986]. Of course, the aim is to determine an optical flow that corresponds closely with the true motion field. Optical flow computation is a necessary precondition of subsequent higher-level processing that can solve motion-related problems if a camera is stationary or moving; it provides tools to determine parameters of motion, relative distances of objects in the image, etc. A simulated example of two consecutive images and a corresponding optical flow image are shown in Figure 16.6.

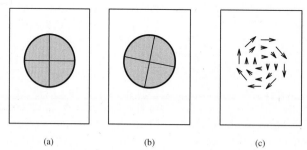

(a)   (b)   (c)

Figure 16.6: Optical flow. (a) Time t_1. (b) Time t_2. (c) Optical flow. © *Cengage Learning 2015.*

16.2.1 Optical flow computation

Optical flow computation is based on two assumptions:

  1. The observed brightness of any object point is constant over time.

2. Nearby points in the image plane move in a similar manner (the *velocity smoothness constraint*).

Suppose we have a continuous image; $f(x, y, t)$ refers to the gray-level of (x, y) at time t. Representing a dynamic image as a function of position and time permits it to be expressed as a Taylor series:

$$f(x + \mathrm{d}x, y + \mathrm{d}y, t + \mathrm{d}t) = f(x, y, t) + f_x \mathrm{d}x + f_y \mathrm{d}y + f_t \mathrm{d}t + O(\partial^2) , \qquad (16.4)$$

where f_x, f_y, f_t denote the partial derivatives of f. We can assume that the immediate neighborhood of (x, y) is translated some small distance $(\mathrm{d}x, \mathrm{d}y)$ during the interval $\mathrm{d}t$; that is, we can find $\mathrm{d}x, \mathrm{d}y, \mathrm{d}t$ such that

$$f(x + \mathrm{d}x, y + \mathrm{d}y, t + \mathrm{d}t) = f(x, y, t) . \qquad (16.5)$$

If $\mathrm{d}x, \mathrm{d}y, \mathrm{d}t$ are very small, the higher-order terms in equation (16.4) vanish and

$$-f_t = f_x \frac{\mathrm{d}x}{\mathrm{d}t} + f_y \frac{\mathrm{d}y}{\mathrm{d}t} . \qquad (16.6)$$

The goal is to compute the velocity

$$\mathbf{c} = \left(\frac{\mathrm{d}x}{\mathrm{d}t}, \frac{\mathrm{d}y}{\mathrm{d}t} \right) = (u, v) , \qquad (16.7)$$

f_x, f_y, f_t can be computed, or at least approximated, from $f(x, y, t)$. The motion velocity can then be estimated as

$$-f_t = f_x u + f_y v = \nabla f \, \mathbf{c} , \qquad (16.8)$$

where ∇f is a two-dimensional image gradient. It can be seen from equation (16.8) that the gray-level difference f_t at the same location of the image at times t and $t + \mathrm{d}t$ is a product of spatial gray-level difference and velocity in this location according to the observer.

Equation (16.8) does not specify the velocity vector completely; rather, it only provides the component in the direction of the brightest gradient (see Figure 16.4c). To solve the problem completely, a smoothness constraint is introduced; that is, the velocity vector field changes slowly in a given neighborhood. Full details of this approach may be found in [Horn and Schunk, 1981], but the approach reduces to minimizing the squared error quantity

$$E^2(x, y) = \left(f_x u + f_y v + f_t \right)^2 + \lambda \left(u_x^2 + u_y^2 + v_x^2 + v_y^2 \right) , \qquad (16.9)$$

where $u_x^2, u_y^2, v_x^2, v_y^2$ denote partial derivatives squared as error terms. The first term represents a solution to equation (16.8), the second term is the smoothness criterion, and λ is a Lagrange multiplier. Using standard techniques [Horn and Schunk, 1981], this reduces to solving the differential equations

$$\left(\lambda^2 + f_x^2 \right) u + f_x f_y v = \lambda^2 \, \bar{u} - f_x f_t , \qquad (16.10)$$

$$f_x f_y u + \left(\lambda^2 + f_y^2 \right) v = \lambda^2 \, \bar{v} - f_y f_t ,$$

where $\bar{u}, \bar{v}$ are mean values of the velocity in directions x and y in some neighborhood of (x, y). It can be shown that a solution to these equations is

$$u = \bar{u} - f_x \frac{P}{D}, \tag{16.11}$$

$$v = \bar{v} - f_y \frac{P}{D}, \tag{16.12}$$

where

$$P = f_x \bar{u} + f_y \bar{v} + f_t, \qquad D = \lambda^2 + f_x^2 + f_y^2. \tag{16.13}$$

Determination of the optical flow is then based on a Gauss-Seidel iteration method using pairs of (consecutive) dynamic images [Horn, 1986; Young, 1971].

Algorithm 16.1: Relaxation computation of optical flow from dynamic image pairs

1. Initialize velocity vectors $\mathbf{c}(i, j) = 0$ for all (i, j).

2. Let k denote the number of iterations. Compute values u^k, v^k for all pixels (i, j)

$$
\begin{aligned}
u^k(i, j) &= \bar{u}^{k-1}(i, j) - f_x(i, j) \frac{P(i, j)}{D(i, j)}, \\
v^k(i, j) &= \bar{v}^{k-1}(i, j) - f_y(i, j) \frac{P(i, j)}{D(i, j)}.
\end{aligned}
\tag{16.14}
$$

Partial derivatives f_x, f_y, f_t can be estimated from pairs of consecutive images.

3. Stop if

$$\sum_i \sum_j E^2(i, j) < \varepsilon,$$

where ε is the maximum permitted error; return to step 2 otherwise.

If more than two images are to be processed, efficiency may be increased by using the results of one iteration to initialize the current image pair in sequence.

Algorithm 16.2: Optical flow computation from an image sequence

1. Evaluate starting values of the optical flow $\mathbf{c}(i, j)$ for all points (i, j).

2. Let m be the sequence number of the currently processed image. For all pixels of the next image, evaluate

$$
\begin{aligned}
u^{m+1}(i, j) &= \bar{u}^m(i, j) - f_x(i, j) \frac{P(i, j)}{D(i, j)}, \\
v^{m+1}(i, j) &= \bar{v}^m(i, j) - f_y(i, j) \frac{P(i, j)}{D(i, j)}.
\end{aligned}
\tag{16.15}
$$

3. Repeat step 2 to process all images in the sequence.

Both these algorithms are naturally parallel. The iterations may be very slow, with a computational complexity $\mathcal{O}(n^p)$, where p is the order of the partial differential equation set (16.10). Experimentally, it is found that thousands of iterations are needed until convergence if a second-order smoothness criterion is applied [Glazer, 1984]. On the other hand, the first 10–20 iterations usually leave an error smaller than the required accuracy, and the rest of the iterative process is then very gradual.

If the differences dx, dy, dt are very small, all the higher-order terms vanish in the continuous derivative of equation (16.4). Unfortunately, in reality this is often not the case if subsequent images are not taken frequently enough. As a result, the higher-order terms do not vanish and an estimation error results if they are neglected. To decrease this error, the second-order terms may be considered in the Taylor series, and the problem becomes a minimization of an integral over a local neighborhood N [Nagel, 1987]:

$$\iint_N \left[f(x,y,t) - f(x_0,y_0,t_0) - f_x[x-u] - f_y[y-v] - \frac{1}{2}f_{xx}[x-u]^2 \right.$$
$$\left. - f_{xy}[x-u][y-v] - \frac{1}{2}f_{yy}[y-v]^2 \right]^2 dx\,dy. \quad (16.16)$$

This minimization is rather complex and may be simplified for image points that correspond to corners (Section 5.3.10). Let the co-ordinate system be aligned with the main curvature direction at (x_0, y_0); then $f_{xy} = 0$ and the only non-zero second-order derivatives are f_{xx} and f_{yy}. However, at least one of them must cross zero at (x_0, y_0) to get a maximum gradient: If, say, $f_{xx} = 0$, then $f_x \to$ max and $f_y = 0$. With these assumptions, equation (16.16) simplifies, and the following formula is minimized [Vega-Riveros and Jabbour, 1989]:

$$\sum_{x,y \in N} \left[f(x,y,t) - f(x_0,y_0,t_0) - f_x(x-u) - \frac{1}{2}f_{yy}(y-v)^2 \right]^2. \quad (16.17)$$

A conventional minimization approach of differentiating equation (16.17) with respect to u and v and equating to zero results in two equations in the velocity components u, v.

16.2.2 Global and local optical flow estimation

Optical flow computation will be in error to the extent that the constant brightness and velocity smoothness assumptions are violated—unfortunately, in real imagery, this is quite common. Typically, the optical flow changes dramatically in highly textured regions, around moving boundaries, depth discontinuities, etc. [Kearney and Thompson, 1988]. A significant advantage of global relaxation methods of optical flow computation is to find the smoothest velocity field consistent with the image data; as discussed in Section 10.9, an important property of relaxation methods is their ability to propagate local constraints globally. As a result, not only constraint information but also all optical flow estimation errors propagate across the solution. Therefore, even a small number of problem areas in the optical flow field may cause widespread errors and poor estimates.

Since global error propagation is the biggest problem of the global optical flow computation scheme, local optical flow estimation may be a better solution. The local estimate is based on the same brightness and smoothness assumptions, and the idea is to divide the image into small regions where the assumptions hold. This solves the error propagation problem but another arises—in regions where spatial gradients change slowly, the optical flow estimation becomes ill-conditioned because of lack of motion information, and it cannot be detected correctly. If a global method is applied to the same region, the information from neighboring image parts propagates and represents a basis for optical flow computation even if the local information was not sufficient by itself. The conclusion is that global sharing of information is beneficial in constraint sharing and detrimental with respect to error propagation [Kearney and Thompson, 1988].

One way to cope with the smoothness violation problem is to detect regions in which the smoothness constraints hold. Two heuristics for identifying neighboring constraint equations that differ substantially in their flow value were introduced in [Horn and Schunk, 1981]. The main problem is in selecting a threshold to decide which flow value

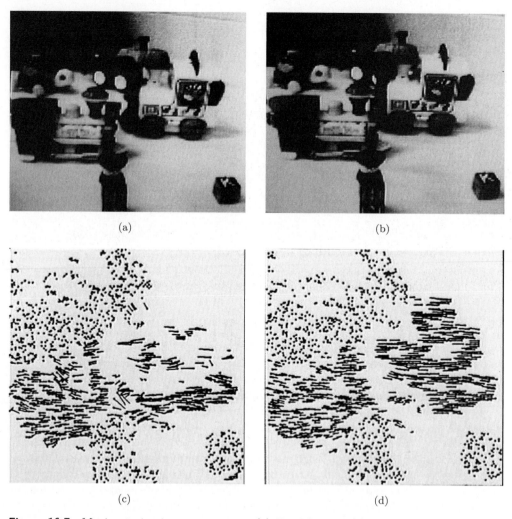

(a)   (b)

(c)   (d)

Figure 16.7: Moving trains image sequence. (a) First frame. (b) Last frame. (c) Optical flow detection—local optimization method. (d) Optical flow detection—method of continuous adaptation to errors. (Only 20% of vectors with moderate and high confidence shown.) *Courtesy of J. Kearney, The University of Iowa.*

difference should be considered substantial—if the threshold is set too low, many points are considered positioned along flow discontinuities, while if the threshold is too high, some points violating smoothness remain part of the computational net. The boundary between smooth subnets is not closed; paths between them remain, and the error propagation problem is not solved.

An approach of continuous adaptation to errors was introduced in [Kearney et al., 1987]. As with the basic global relaxation method, optical flow is determined iteratively by combining the local average flow vector with the gradient constraint equation. However, a confidence is assigned to each flow vector based on heuristic judgments of correctness, and the local average flow is computed as a weighted average by confidence. Thus, the propagation of error-free estimates is inhibited. Details of confidence estimation, smoothness violation detection, combining partial estimates, implementa-

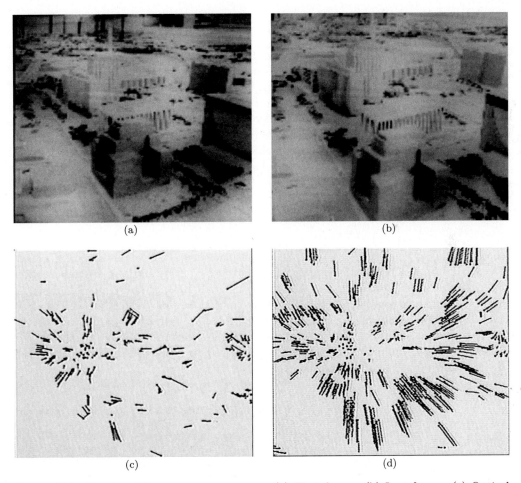

(a)

(b)

(c)

(d)

Figure 16.8: Simulated flyover image sequence. (a) First frame. (b) Last frame. (c) Optical flow detection—local optimization method. (d) Optical flow detection—method of continuous adaptation to errors. (Again, only 20% of vectors with moderate and high confidence shown.) *Courtesy of J. Kearney, The University of Iowa.*

tion details, and discussion of results are given in [Kearney et al., 1987; Kearney and Thompson, 1988].

Performance of the method is illustrated in Figures 16.7 and 16.8. The first image pair, shown in Figures 16.7a,b, contains a collection of toys, and the second pair of images (Figures 16.8a,b) simulates a view from an aircraft flying over a city. Optical flow resulting from a simple local optimization is shown in Figures 16.7c and 16.8c, and results of the global method of continuous adaptation to errors are given in Figures 16.7d and 16.8d. The optical flow improvement achieved by the latter method is clearly visible.

Comparison of the performance of many optical flow techniques is given in [Barron et al., 1994]—local differential approaches [Fleet and Jepson, 1990; Lucas and Kanade, 1981] were found to be most accurate and robust. Techniques using global smoothness constraints were found to produce visually attractive motion fields, but give an accuracy suitable only for qualitative use, insufficient for ego-motion computation and 3D structure from motion detection.

16.2.3   Combined local–global optical flow estimation

Variational methods of optical flow computation, e.g., the classical Horn–Schunck approach described above using Gauss-Seidel iterative solution method is known to produce good results and dense flow fields, but suffer from slow convergence, rendering it unsuitable for real-time applications [Weickert and Schnoerr, 2001]. Combining the global Horn–Schunck variational approach with a local least-square Lucas–Kanade method [Lucas and Kanade, 1981], the approach named **combined local–global (CLG) method** was introduced in [Bruhn et al., 2002] which offers real-time performance [Bruhn et al., 2005]. The CLG method computes the optical flow field $(u, v)^T$ in a rectangular image domain Ω by minimization of the functional

$$E(u, v) = \int_\Omega \left(w^T J_\rho(\nabla_3 f) w + \alpha(|\nabla u|^2 + |\nabla v|^2) \right) dx dy \,, \tag{16.18}$$

where $w(x, y) = (u(x, y), v(x, y), 1)^T$ is the displacement, ∇u is the spatial gradient of $(u_x, u_y)^T$, $\nabla_3 f$ is the spatio-temporal gradient $(f_x, f_y, f_t)^T$, and α is a regularization parameter. $J_\rho(\nabla_3 f)$ is the structure tensor [Bigun et al., 1991] given by $K_\rho * (\nabla_3 f \nabla_3 f^T)$, where $*$ denotes convolution and K_ρ is a Gaussian with standard deviation ρ. Equation (16.18) represents a pure Horn–Schunck method for $\rho \to 0$ and the pure Lucas–Kanade method for $\alpha \to 0$. When the parameters are set to combine both approaches, good properties of both are maintained, resulting in dense flow fields and robustness to noise.

The energy functional minimization can be obtained by solving the Euler–Lagrange equations

$$\alpha \Delta u - (J_{11}(\nabla_3 f)u) + J_{12}(\nabla_3 f)v + J_{13}(\nabla_3 f)) = 0 \,, \tag{16.19}$$

$$\alpha \Delta v - (J_{21}(\nabla_3 f)u) + J_{22}(\nabla_3 f)v + J_{23}(\nabla_3 f)) = 0 \,, \tag{16.20}$$

where Δ denotes the Laplacian; boundary conditions shall reflect that normal derivative vanishes at boundaries of Ω

$$\partial_n u = 0 \,, \partial_n v = 0 \,. \tag{16.21}$$

Numerical solving of the above Euler–Lagrange equations can be performed, e.g., using the traditional Gauss–Seidel iteration approach [Young, 1971], but this approach is not fast enough for real-time optical flow computation since after an initial stage of fast improvements by removing higher frequency error parts (via smoothing) it suffers from a slow process of achieving necessary accuracy since the available smoothing processes do not efficiently deal with the remaining low-frequency error components. Multigrid methods overcome the problem by using a coarse-to-fine hierarchy of equation systems delivering excellent error-reduction behavior [Briggs et al., 2000; Trottenberg et al., 2001]. Here, low frequencies on the finest grid reappear as higher frequencies on the coarser grids and can therefore be successfully removed. A two-orders of magnitude speed-up was reported by implementing the CLG method using a full multigrid method for solving the linear system of equations compared to commonly used variational techniques of optical flow computation [Bruhn et al., 2005].

16.2.4 Optical flow in motion analysis

Optical flow gives a description of motion and can be a valuable contribution to image interpretation even if no quantitative parameters are obtained from motion analysis. Optical flow can be used to study a large variety of motions—moving observer and static objects, static observer and moving objects, or both moving. Optical flow analysis does not result in motion trajectories as described in Section 16.1; instead, more general motion properties are detected that can significantly increase the reliability of complex dynamic image analysis [Thompson et al., 1985; Kearney et al., 1987; Aggarwal and Martin, 1988].

Motion, as it appears in dynamic images, is usually some combination of four basic elements:

- Translation at constant distance from the observer.
- Translation in depth relative to the observer.
- Rotation at constant distance about the view axis.
- Rotation of a planar object perpendicular to the view axis.

Optical-flow based motion analysis can recognize these basic elements by applying a few relatively simple operators to the flow. Motion form recognition is based on the following facts (Figure 16.9):

- Translation at constant distance is represented as a set of parallel motion vectors.
- Translation in depth forms a set of vectors having a common focus of expansion.
- Rotation at constant distance results in a set of concentric motion vectors.
- Rotation perpendicular to the view axis forms one or more sets of vectors starting from straight line segments.

Exact determination of rotation axes and translation trajectories can be computed, but with a significant increase in difficulty of analysis.

Consider translational motion: if the translation is not at constant depth, then optical flow vectors are not parallel, and their directions have a single **focus of expansion**

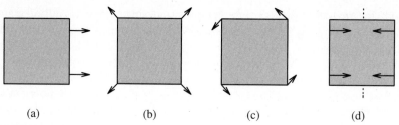

Figure 16.9: Motion form recognition. (a) Translation at constant distance. (b) Translation in depth. (c) Rotation at constant distance. (d) Planar object rotation perpendicular to the view axis. © *Cengage Learning 2015.*

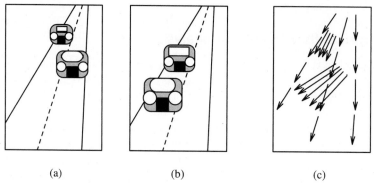

Figure 16.10: Focus of expansion. (a) Time t_1. (b) Time t_2. (c) Optical flow. © *Cengage Learning 2015.*

(FOE). If the translation is at constant depth, the FOE is at infinity. If several independently moving objects are present in the image, each motion has its own FOE—this is illustrated in Figure 16.10, where an observer moves in a car towards other approaching cars on the road.

Mutual velocity

The mutual velocity **c** of an observer and an object represented by an image point can be found in an optical flow representation. Let the mutual velocities in directions x, y, z be $c_x = u, c_y = v, c_z = w$, where z gives information about the depth (note that $z > 0$ for points in front of the image plane). To distinguish image co-ordinates from real-world co-ordinates in the following, let the image co-ordinates be x', y'. From perspective considerations, if (x_0, y_0, z_0) is the position of some point at time $t_0 = 0$, then the position of the same point at time t can, assuming unit focal distance of the optical system and constant velocity, be determined as follows:

$$(x', y') = \left(\frac{x_0 + ut}{z_0 + wt}, \frac{y_0 + vt}{z_0 + wt} \right) . \tag{16.22}$$

FOE determination

The FOE in a two-dimensional image can be determined from this equation. Let us assume motion directed towards an observer; as $t \to -\infty$, the motion can be traced back to the originating point at infinite distance from the observer. The motion towards an observer continues along straight lines and the originating point in the image plane is

$$\mathbf{x}'_{\text{FOE}} = \left(\frac{u}{w}, \frac{v}{w} \right) .$$ (16.23)

Note that the same equation can be used for $t \to \infty$ and motion in the opposite direction. Clearly, any change of motion direction results in changes of velocities u, v, w, and the FOE changes its location in the image [Jain, 1983].

Distance (depth) determination

Because of the presence of a z co-ordinate in equation (16.22), optical flow can be used to determine the current distance of a moving object from the observer's position. The distance information is contained indirectly in equation (16.22). Assuming points of the same rigid object and translational motion, at least one actual distance value must be known to evaluate the distance exactly. Let $D(t)$ be the distance of a point from the FOE, measured in a two-dimensional image, and let $V(t)$ be its velocity $\mathrm{d}D/\mathrm{d}t$. The relationship between these quantities and the optical flow parameters is then

$$\frac{D(t)}{V(t)} = \frac{z(t)}{w(t)} .$$ (16.24)

This formula is a basis for determination of distances between moving objects. Assuming an object moving towards the observer, the ratio z/w specifies the time at which an object moving at a constant velocity w crosses the image plane. Based on the knowledge of the distance of any single point in an image which is moving with a velocity w along the z axis, it is possible to compute the distances of any other point in the image that is moving with the same velocity w

$$z_2(t) = \frac{z_1(t) \, V_1(t) \, D_2(t)}{D_1(t) \, V_2(t)} ,$$ (16.25)

where $z_1(t)$ is the known distance and $z_2(t)$ is the unknown distance. Using the given formulae, relations between real-world co-ordinates x, y and image co-ordinates x', y' can be found related to the observer position and velocity:

$$x(t) = \frac{x'(t) \, w(t) \, D(t)}{V(t)} , \qquad y(t) = \frac{y'(t) \, w(t) \, D(t)}{V(t)} , \qquad z(t) = \frac{w(t) \, D(t)}{V(t)} .$$ (16.26)

Note that the above equations cover both the moving objects and the moving camera as long as the motion is along the camera optical axis. Situations in which motion is not realized along the optical axis are treated in [Jain et al., 1995].

Collision Prediction

A practical application is analysis of robot motion, where the optical flow approach is able to detect potential collisions with scene objects. Observer motion—as seen from optical flow representation—aims into the FOE of this motion; co-ordinates of this FOE are $(u/w, v/w)$. The origin of image co-ordinates (the imaging system focal point) proceeds in the direction $\mathbf{s} = (u/w, v/w, 1)$ and follows a path in real-world co-ordinates at each time instant defined as a straight line,

$$(x, y, z) = t\,\mathbf{s} = t\left(\frac{u}{w}, \frac{v}{w}, 1\right) , \tag{16.27}$$

where the parameter t represents time. The position of an observer $\mathbf{x}_{\text{obs}}$ when at its closest point of approach to some $\mathbf{x}$ in the real world is then

$$\mathbf{x}_{\text{obs}} = \frac{\mathbf{s}\,(\mathbf{s} \cdot \mathbf{x})}{\mathbf{s} \cdot \mathbf{s}} . \tag{16.28}$$

The smallest distance d_{min} between a point $\mathbf{x}$ and an observer during observer motion is

$$d_{\text{min}} = \sqrt{(\mathbf{x} \cdot \mathbf{x}) - \frac{(\mathbf{x} \cdot \mathbf{s})^2}{\mathbf{s} \cdot \mathbf{s}}} . \tag{16.29}$$

Thus, a circular-shaped observer with radius r will collide with objects if their smallest distance of approach $d_{\text{min}} < r$.

The analysis of motion, computation of FOE, depth, possible collisions, time to collision, etc., are all very practical problems. Interpretation of motion is discussed in [Subbarao, 1988], and motion analysis and computing range from an optical flow map is described in [Albus and Hong, 1990]. A comprehensive approach to motion parameter estimation from optical flow together with a comprehensive overview of existing techniques is given in [Hummel and Sundareswaran, 1993]. Ego-motion estimation from optical flow fields determined from multiple cameras is presented in [Tsao et al., 1997]. Obstacle detection by evaluation of optical flow is presented in [Enkelmann, 1991]. Edge-based obstacle detection derived from determined size changes is presented in [Ringach and Baram, 1994]. Time to collision computation from first-order derivatives of image flow is described in [Subbarao, 1990], where it is shown that higher-order derivatives, which are unreliable and computationally expensive, are not necessary. Computation of FOE does not have to be based on optical flow; the spatial gradient approach and a natural constraint that an object must be in front of the camera to be imaged are used in a direct method of locating FOE in [Negahdaripour and Ganesan, 1992].

16.3   Analysis based on correspondence of interest points

Optical flow can be applied only if the intervals between image acquisitions are very short. if they are not, motion detection based on correspondence of **interest points (feature points)** is an alternative. Detection of corresponding object points in subsequent images is a fundamental part of this method—if this correspondence is known, velocity fields can easily be constructed (this does not consider the hard problem of constructing a dense velocity field from a sparse-correspondence-point velocity field).

The first step of the method is to find significant points in all images of the sequence—points least similar to their surrounding representing object corners, borders, or any other characteristic features in an image that can be tracked over time. Point detection is followed by a matching procedure, which looks for correspondences between these points. The process results in a sparse velocity field construction.

16.3.1   Detection of interest points

There is a host of interest point detectors that have developed over the years—see Section 5.3.10: an early one is the *Moravec*; well-used alternatives are the Kitchen-Rosenfeld and Zuniga–Haralick operators. The *Harris* corner detector (described in Section 5.3.10) has proved very popular.

16.3.2   Lucas–Kanade point tracking

Suppose we have two images I_1 and I_2 of a dynamic scene that are separated in time by a short interval, implying that individual points will not have moved far. If a pixel (x, y) in I_1 moves to $(x + u, y + v)$ in I_2, we will be able to assume that u and v are 'small'; we will also assume that the pixel remains unaltered in appearance (intensity), so

$$I_2(x + u, y + v) - I_1(x, y) = 0 . \tag{16.30}$$

Since the displacement is small, we can make a linear approximation to $I_2(x+u, y+v)$ via a Taylor expansion:

$$I_2(x + u, y + v) \approx I_2(x, y) + \frac{\partial I_2}{\partial x} u + \frac{\partial I_2}{\partial y} v . \tag{16.31}$$

Combining equations (16.30) and (16.31) gives

$$(I_2(x, y) - I_1(x, y)) + \frac{\partial I_2}{\partial x} u + \frac{\partial I_2}{\partial y} v = 0 , \tag{16.32}$$

an equation connecting the temporal and spatial differences around (x, y), in which u and v are unknown, that is a restatement of equation (16.7).

Clearly we cannot solve for two unknowns from this single equation: but if we make the assumption that an immediate neighborhood of (x, y) behaves in the same manner, more equations can be derived. For example, if we assume that all of the 3×3 window centered at (x, y) moves (u, v) between frames, and does not change in intensity, then equation (16.32) provides nine linear equations for the two unknowns, and the system is now overdetermined. We can construct a 9×2 matrix A, each row of which is an estimate of $\frac{\partial I_2}{\partial x}$, $\frac{\partial I_2}{\partial y}$ at respective pixels, and a 9×1 vector $\mathbf{b}$, each component of which is the difference in intensities between I_1, I_2 at respective pixels:

$$A \begin{pmatrix} u \\ v \end{pmatrix} = \mathbf{b} .$$

A least-squares 'best' solution to this system is then available from

$$A^T A \begin{pmatrix} u \\ v \end{pmatrix} = A^T \mathbf{b} , \tag{16.33}$$

which is a 2×2 system, solvable if $A^T A$ is invertible.

Writing for brevity $I_x = \frac{\partial I_2}{\partial x}$ (and similar), we can see that

$$A^T A = \begin{pmatrix} \sum I_x I_x & \sum I_x I_y \\ \sum I_x I_y & \sum I_y I_y \end{pmatrix} ,$$

where the sum if taken over the small local neighborhood—the Harris matrix introduced as equation (5.73). As in the discussion there, this approach requires stability in $(A^T A)^{-1}$, which is provided by the two eigenvalues being 'not too small', and of comparable magnitude to each other. This will imply some structure (a corner, or similar feature) at the pixel in question, thereby avoiding the aperture problem described in Section 5.3.10. In practice, we might compute the minimum eigenvalue λ_m of $(A^T A)^{-1}$ at each pixel, select via some threshold those which are 'large enough', then retain pixels at which λ_m is locally maximal, and then retain all such pixels that are separated by some minimum distance.

The reasons that this approach might fail are a violation of its assumptions: maintaining local intensity, or significant local motion. The latter problem can often be addressed by an iterative approach: velocity estimates are made at pixels in I_1, which is then warped towards I_2, and the procedure is then repeated.

This approach to point tracking was first outlined in 1981 [Lucas and Kanade, 1981], and was developed with widespread impact into the *KLT tracker* [Shi and Tomasi, 1994] (which is freely available in many implementations on the WWW.) This work successfully uses the Lucas–Kanade approach to determine automatically in an image sequence points which are 'trackable' (so satisfy the criteria outlined above), and which have 'real' meaning in the scene. The key to this is recognizing that simple translation is not likely to be a good representation of motion in even small spatial windows, and that an affine model is likely to be much better—in the notation used above, we conjecture a 2×2 matrix D such that (x, y) in I_1 moves to

$$D \begin{pmatrix} x \\ y \end{pmatrix} + \begin{pmatrix} u \\ v \end{pmatrix}$$

in I_2. The pure translational model is still used for tracking frame-to-frame, but the affine model can be used to confirm that the feature being tracked is 'good'. D can be recaptured by a least-squares approach very similar to that used to solve for pure translation; then the dissimilarity (sum of square differences) between the original window and its [affine] transformed version can be considered. This successfully handles change of scale of features as camera distance changes, but will detect, for example, that a strong feature that is an accident of viewpoint (two strong boundaries crossing, but belonging to different scene features) is not a good candidate for tracking as viewpoint evolves.

Since its first publication, Lucas–Kanade flow computation, and associated trackers, have acquired huge popularity. A good survey of the algorithm's developments and generalizations may be found in [Baker and Matthews, 2004]. In its most general form to incrementally warp—not necessarily in an affine way—an image I to a template T, the algorithm may be summarized as:

Algorithm 16.3: General Lucas–Kanade tracking

1. Initialize a warp $\mathbf{W}(\mathbf{x}; \mathbf{p})$, determined by some parameters $\mathbf{p}$.

2. Warp I with $\mathbf{W}(\mathbf{x}; \mathbf{p})$ to $\hat{I}$, and determine the error $T - \hat{I}$.

3. Warp the gradient of I, ∇I with $\mathbf{W}(\mathbf{x}; \mathbf{p})$, and evaluate the Jacobian $\frac{\partial \mathbf{W}}{\partial \mathbf{p}}$. Compute the 'steepest descent' image $\nabla I \frac{\partial \mathbf{W}}{\partial \mathbf{p}}$, and the *Hessian* matrix

$$H = \sum_{\mathbf{x}} \left[\nabla I \frac{\partial \mathbf{W}}{\partial \mathbf{p}} \right]^T \left[\nabla I \frac{\partial \mathbf{W}}{\partial \mathbf{p}} \right].$$

4. Compute

$$\Delta \mathbf{p} = H^{-1} \sum_{\mathbf{x}} \left[\nabla I \frac{\partial \mathbf{W}}{\partial \mathbf{p}} \right]^T [T(\mathbf{x}) - \hat{I}].$$

5. Set

$$\mathbf{p} = \mathbf{p} + \Delta \mathbf{p}$$

and go to 2 until $\|\Delta \mathbf{p}\| < \epsilon$.

This is, as in the more elementary exposition given above, a least-squares minimization of an error measure, applied iteratively until convergence. The only constraint put on the warping function $\mathbf{W}$ is that it be differentiable with respect to its parameters $\mathbf{p}$. Baker and Matthews give a comprehensive discussion of convergence, efficiency and other issues [Baker and Matthews, 2004].[1]

An example of KLT tracking is given in Figure 16.11, where motion of 'good' points over 0.5 seconds is illustrated: these data were subsequently used as input to a system that built semantic models of scenes (here a Metro station) from unconstrained video [Dee et al., 2012].

Figure 16.11: KLT tracking applied to a video scene of a Metro station: the algorithm automatically determines trackable points that persist over the sequence. These 'tracklets' can be used subsequently to derive a semantic description of the scene. *Courtesy of H. M. Dee, The University of Aberystwyth. A color version of this figure may be seen in the color inset—Plate 36.*

16.3.3 Correspondence of interest points

Assuming that interest points have been located in all images of a sequence, a correspondence between points in consecutive images is sought. Many approaches may be applied

---

[1]There is an associated website http://www.ri.cmu.edu/projects/project_515.html providing a variety of Matlab source codes and test images.

to seek an optimal correspondence, and several possible solutions have been presented earlier (Chapters 9 and 11). The graph matching problem, stereo matching, and 'shape from X' problems treat essentially the same problem.

An early, probabilistic method [Thompson and Barnard, 1981] is a good example of the main ideas of this approach: the correspondence search process is iterative and begins with the detection of all potential correspondence pairs in consecutive images. A maximum velocity assumption can be used for potential correspondence detection, which decreases the number of possible correspondences, especially in large images. Each pair of corresponding points is assigned a number representing the probability of correspondence. These probabilities are then iteratively recomputed to get a globally optimum set of pairwise correspondences (the maximum probability of pairs in the whole image, equation 16.39) using another assumption: **common motion principle**. The process ends if each point of interest in a previous image corresponds with precisely one point of interest in the next **and**

- The global probability of correspondences between image point pairs is significantly higher than other potential correspondences.

- *Or* the global probability of correspondences of points is higher than a pre-selected threshold.

- *Or* the global probability of correspondences gives a maximum probability (optimum) of all possible correspondences (note that $n!$ possible correspondences exist for n pairs of interest points).

Let $A_1 = \{\mathbf{x}_m\}$ be the set of all interest points in the first image, and $A_2 = \{\mathbf{y}_n\}$ the interest points of the second image. Let $\mathbf{c}_{mn}$ be a vector connecting points $\mathbf{x}_m$ and $\mathbf{y}_n$ ($\mathbf{c}_{mn}$ is thus a velocity vector; $\mathbf{y}_n = \mathbf{x}_m + \mathbf{c}_{mn}$). Let the probability of correspondence of two points $\mathbf{x}_m$ and $\mathbf{y}_n$ be P_{mn}. Two points $\mathbf{x}_m$ and $\mathbf{y}_n$ can be considered potentially corresponding if their distance satisfies the assumption of maximum velocity

$$|\mathbf{x}_m - \mathbf{y}_n| \le c_{\max} , \qquad (16.34)$$

where $c_{\max}$ is the maximum distance a point may move in the time interval between two consecutive images. Two correspondences of points $\mathbf{x}_m \mathbf{y}_n$ and $\mathbf{x}_k \mathbf{y}_l$ are termed consistent if

$$|\mathbf{c}_{mn} - \mathbf{c}_{kl}| \le c_{\mathrm{dif}} , \qquad (16.35)$$

where c_{dif} is a preset constant derived from prior knowledge. Clearly, consistency of corresponding point pairs increases the probability that a correspondence pair is correct. This principle is applied in Algorithm 16.4 [Barnard and Thompson, 1980].

Algorithm 16.4: Velocity field computation from two consecutive images

1. Determine the interest points A_1 and A_2 in images f_1, f_2, and detect all potential correspondences between point pairs $\mathbf{x}_m \in A_1$ and $\mathbf{y}_n \in A_2$.

2. Construct a data structure in which potential correspondence information of all points $\mathbf{x}_m \in A_1$ with points $\mathbf{y}_n \in A_2$ is stored, as follows

$$\left[\mathbf{x}_m, (\mathbf{c}_{m1}, P_{m1}), (\mathbf{c}_{m2}, P_{m2}), \dots, (V^*, P^*) \right] . \qquad (16.36)$$

P_{mn} is the probability of correspondence of points $\mathbf{x}_m$ and $\mathbf{y}_n$, and V^* and P^* are special symbols indicating that no potential correspondence was found.

3. Initialize the probabilities P_{mn}^0 of correspondence based on local similarity—if two points correspond, their neighborhood should correspond as well:

$$P_{mn}^0 = \frac{1}{(1 + kw_{mn})} \, , \tag{16.37}$$

where k is a constant and

$$w_{mn} = \sum_{\Delta\mathbf{x}} \left[f_1(\mathbf{x}_m + \Delta\mathbf{x}) - f_2(\mathbf{y}_n + \Delta\mathbf{x}) \right]^2 , \tag{16.38}$$

$\Delta\mathbf{x}$ defines a (usually symmetric) neighborhood for match testing by ranging between some small negative and positive values.

4. Iteratively determine the probability of correspondence of a point $\mathbf{x}_m$ with points $\mathbf{y}_n$ as a weighted sum of probabilities of correspondence of all *consistent* pairs $\mathbf{x}_k\mathbf{y}_l$, where $\mathbf{x}_k$ are neighbors of $\mathbf{x}_m$ and the consistency of $\mathbf{x}_k\mathbf{y}_l$ is evaluated according to $\mathbf{x}_m, \mathbf{y}_n$. The *quality* q_{mn} of the correspondence pair is

$$q_{mn}^{(s-1)} = \sum_k \sum_l P_{kl}^{(s-1)} , \tag{16.39}$$

where s denotes an iteration step, k refers to all points $\mathbf{x}_k$ that are neighbors of $\mathbf{x}_m$, and l refers to all points $\mathbf{y}_l \in A_2$ that form pairs $\mathbf{x}_k\mathbf{y}_l$ consistent with $\mathbf{x}_m\mathbf{y}_n$.

5. Update the probabilities of correspondence for each point pair $\mathbf{x}_m, \mathbf{y}_n$

$$\hat{P}_{mn}^{(s)} = P_{mn}^{(s-1)} \left(a + bq_{mn}^{(s-1)} \right) , \tag{16.40}$$

where a and b are preset constants. Normalize

$$P_{mn}^s = \frac{\hat{P}_{mn}^s}{\sum_j \hat{P}_{mj}^s} \, . \tag{16.41}$$

6. Repeat steps 4 and 5 until the best correspondence $\mathbf{x}_m\mathbf{y}_n$ is found for all points $\mathbf{x}_m$.

7. Vectors $\mathbf{c}_{ij}$ of the correspondence form a velocity field of the analyzed motion.

The velocity field resulting from this algorithm applied to the image pairs given in Figures 16.7a,b and 16.8a,b are shown in Figure 16.12. Note that the results are much better for the train sequence; compare the flyover velocity field with the optical flow results given in Figure 16.8d.

Velocity fields can be applied in position prediction tasks as well as optical flow. A good example of interpretation of motion derived from detecting interest points is

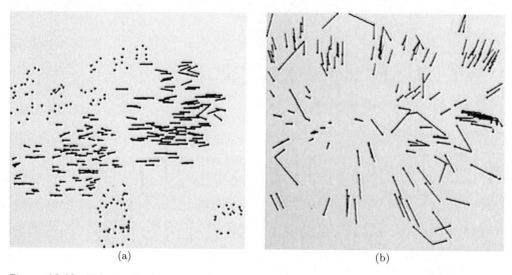

Figure 16.12: Velocity fields of the train sequence (left) and flyover (right) (original images shown in Figures 16.7a,b and 16.8a,b). *Courtesy of J. Kearney, The University of Iowa.*

given in [Scott, 1988]. Detection of moving objects from a moving camera using point correspondence in two orthographic views is discussed in [Thompson et al., 1993]. Fluid motion analysis using particle correspondence and dynamic programming is described in [Shapiro et al., 1995]. Two algorithms applicable to motion analysis in long monocular image sequences were introduced in [Hu and Ahuja, 1993].

Approaches that allow object registration without determination of explicit point correspondences exist. In [Fua and Leclerc, 1994], a method using full three-dimensional surface models is presented that may be used together with shape from motion analysis. An accurate and fast method for motion analysis that seeks correspondence of moving objects via a multi-resolution Hough transform is introduced in [Bober and Kittler, 1994].

16.4   Detection of specific motion patterns

In many cases, we are interested in detecting a specific class of motion, in which case some motion-specific information may be derived from a training set of examples and a classifier trained to distinguish between this and other phenomena that can be observed in the image sequences. The approach described below is motivated by detection of pedestrian motion but it can be applied to a variety of other applications.

Pedestrian motion detection and tracking are important tasks in surveillance applications. In non-pedestrian motion-related applications, training a target detector on a set of examples often yields an efficient detector with success shown for detecting cars, human faces, etc. Such detectors scan through an image looking for a match between the detector and the input image data. The candidate objects can then be tracked over time, further increasing the reliability of detection and the associated tracking. Several approaches are discussed below in Section 16.5. Many such methods first analyze the image-based information that is later processed using motion analysis techniques. These approaches require complex intermediate representations and perform matching, segmentation, alignment, registration, and motion analysis. Since the detection/tracking is carried out in an open loop, failures occurring in the earlier steps may affect the performance in the later stages.

While these approaches see useful performance in some applications, they are not very suitable for pedestrian motion detection and tracking due to the inherent variability of body pose and clothing. The task is made more difficult by the typically low resolution character of the analyzed images: surveillance cameras may depict pedestrians in image patches as small as 20×10 pixels, yet human motion patterns are easily distinguishable even in such low-resolution data. One such system assesses motion periodicity directly from the tracked images and analyzes long temporal sequences to reject candidates with inconsistent motion patterns [Cutler and Davis, 2000].

A substantially different approach was presented in [Viola et al., 2003], in which image-based and motion-based information are used simultaneously. This method focuses on detection of short-term motion patterns rather than on tracking over extended periods of time. This work is closely related to the object detection method described in Section 10.7 and uses the AdaBoost learning paradigm (Section 9.8). As in Section 10.7, pedestrian motion detection uses a small set of simple rectangle filters trained on a set of examples, and can be evaluated very efficiently at any scale (Section 4.2.1). To capture the motion pattern, the filters need to work with short temporal image sequences.

In general, motion can be detected by determination of temporal differences in corresponding image blocks. The size of such image blocks determines the analysis scale, and for multi-scale analysis, blocks of different sizes are considered. Clearly, optical flow (Section 16.2) is able to provide the necessary information. However, the relatively high computational demands of optical flow calculation is not well suited for multi-scale analysis. On the other hand, the computational efficiency of rectangular filters and their multi-scale capabilities are well suited to this task. Simply considering differences between scale-specific blocks in pairs of images over time can serve as an identifier of motion (Section 16.1). Additionally, motion direction can be derived from differences between shifted image blocks, one from the image frame acquired at time t, the other at time $t + \delta t$. Five such images were shown as highly relevant

$$
\begin{aligned}
\Delta &= \mathrm{abs}(I_t - I_{t+1})\,, \\
U &= \mathrm{abs}(I_t - I_{t+\delta t} \uparrow)\,, \\
D &= \mathrm{abs}(I_t - I_{t+\delta t} \downarrow)\,, \\
L &= \mathrm{abs}(I_t - I_{t+\delta t} \leftarrow)\,, \\
R &= \mathrm{abs}(I_t - I_{t+\delta t} \rightarrow)\,,
\end{aligned}
\tag{16.42}
$$

where the arrows represent the direction of the image shift. For example, $I_{t+1} \downarrow$ refers to an image frame $t + \delta t$ shifted down by ψ pixels with respect to the previous image frame I_t. Figure 16.13 shows examples of the Δ, U, D, L, R images.

Similarly, filters f_k measure the magnitude of motion.

$$
f_k = r_k(S)\,.
\tag{16.43}
$$

Several filter types can be designed. Filters

$$
f_i = r_i(\Delta) - r_i(S)
\tag{16.44}
$$

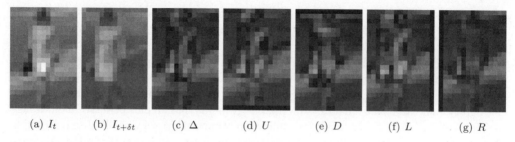

(a) I_t (b) $I_{t+\delta t}$ (c) Δ (d) U (e) D (f) L (g) R

Figure 16.13: Motion and appearance difference images derived according to equation (16.42). Image R has the lowest energy and as such, corresponds to the right-to-left direction of motion. © M. Sonka 2015.

reflect the likelihood that a particular region is moving in a tested direction $\uparrow, \downarrow, \leftarrow$, or $\rightarrow$. Here, S is one of the difference images $\{U, D, L, R\}$ and r_i is a single rectangle sum within the detection window.

Motion shear can be determined using filters

$$f_j = \phi_j(S) \, . \qquad (16.45)$$

Rectangle appearance filters f_m contribute to detecting image patterns of expected static image properties

$$f_m = \phi(I_t) \qquad (16.46)$$

from the first frame of the two-frame image sequence. As before, the filters $f_\bullet$ can be efficiently evaluated using the integral image representation described in Section 4.2.1.

Similarly to preceding work [Viola and Jones, 2001], the filters $f_\bullet$ can be of any size, aspect ratio, or position as long as they fit in the detection image block. As such, a large number of filters can be designed and a best subset of filters and a corresponding classifier must be designed to separate the moving objects with motion-specific properties from the rest of the image. The classifier C consists of a linear combination of the selected features and, after the AdaBoost training phase, reflects a thresholded sum of features

$$C(I_t, I_{t+\delta t}) = 1 \quad \text{if} \quad \sum_{s=1}^{N} F_s\left(I_t, I_{t+\delta t}\right) > \theta \, ,$$
$$= 0 \quad \text{otherwise.} \qquad (16.47)$$

The feature F_s is a thresholded image that outputs one of two possible values

$$F_s(I_t, I_{t+\delta t}) = \alpha \quad \text{if} \quad f_s(I_t, I_{t+\delta t}, \Delta, U, D, L, R) > t_s \, ,$$
$$= \beta \quad \text{otherwise,} \qquad (16.48)$$

where $t_s \in \mathcal{R}$ is a feature threshold and f_s is one of the filters $f_\bullet$. As before, the N features f_s are selected using AdaBoost from all possible filters, these being a function of one or more parameters $I_t, I_{t+\delta t}, \Delta, U, D, L,$ and/or R, respectively. The values of α, β, t_s, and θ are computed during the AdaBoost training process (Section 9.8). Each of the N rounds of AdaBoost chooses from the full set of motion and appearance features. As a result, a mix of features balancing the appearance and motion descriptors is selected.

To support multi-scale detection, the parameter ψ used for calculating the shifted images in directions $\uparrow, \downarrow, \leftarrow, \rightarrow$ must be defined with respect to the detection scale. Consequently, motion-invariant detection of object motion speed is achieved. This invariance can be obtained in the training process by scaling all training samples to a pre-determined base resolution (i.e., bounding block size with respect to pixel counts in x and y directions). In [Viola et al., 2003], a base resolution of 20×15 pixels was used. During analysis, multi-scale behavior is achieved by operating on image pyramids (Section 4.3.1), which are computed from the pyramidal representations of the analyzed image frames I_t^l and $I_{t+\delta t}^l$

$$\Delta^l = \text{abs}(I_t^l - I_{t+1}^l) \,,$$
$$U^l = \text{abs}(I_t^l - I_{t+\delta t}^l \uparrow) \,,$$
$$D^l = \text{abs}(I_t^l - I_{t+\delta t}^l \downarrow) \,,$$
$$L^l = \text{abs}(I_t^l - I_{t+\delta t}^l \leftarrow) \,,$$
$$R^l = \text{abs}(I_t^l - I_{t+\delta t}^l \rightarrow) \,,$$

(16.49)

where l denotes the pyramid level. Features are computed from the pyramidal representations in a scale-invariant fashion. In [Viola et al., 2003], a scale factor of 0.8 was used to generate successive pyramid levels all the way down to the pre-determined size of the base-resolution image block (20×15 pixels in the discussed case).

Once the features are selected, a boosted cascade of classifiers (Section 10.7, Algorithm 10.13 is used to increase the detection efficiency (see Figure 10.34). Simple classifiers with high detection rates and relatively high false positive rates are employed in the early stages of the boosted cascade, with more complex classifiers using larger numbers of features being used in later stages. Each stage of the cascade attempts to reduce both the detection and the false positive rates, obviously with a goal of reducing the false positive rate more rapidly than the detection rate.

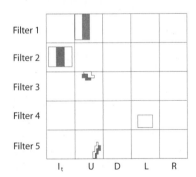

Figure 16.14: The first 5 features identified by the feature selection process for detecting walking pedestrians. Features reflect that pedestrians were centered in the training images, tend to be different from background, and four of them use the motion-difference images. *Based on [Viola et al., 2003].*

In the example application, a dynamic pedestrian detector was learned from sequences consisting of 2,000 frames. Each of the cascade classifiers was trained on 2,250 positive and 2,250 negative examples, each example consisting of two 20×15 image windows from two consecutive image frames ($\delta t = 1$). The positive examples were selected as scaled bounding boxes of the pedestrians, the negative examples did not include pedestrians. During the feature selection, 54,624 filters were considered, uniformly subsampled from a much larger set of all possible filters that can be defined on the 20×15 subwindow. Figure 16.14 shows the first 5 features learned. As further demonstrated

Figure 16.15: Results of pedestrian detection using dynamic pedestrian detector. *Courtesy of P. Viola, Microsoft Live Labs and M. Jones, Mitsubishi Electric Research Labs. © 2003 IEEE. Reprinted, with permission, from P. Viola, M. J. Jones, D. Snow, "Detecting Pedestrians Using Patterns of Motion and Appearance," Proceedings of the Ninth IEEE International Conference on Computer Vision (ICCV 2003), IEEE, 2003.*

in [Viola et al., 2003], the motion information was crucial for the achieved performance of the pedestrian detector, the dynamic pedestrian detector clearly outperformed the static pedestrian detector built using the generally identical boosted cascade of classifiers approach, but not using the motion-difference image information. Figure 16.15 shows several typical detection outcomes of the presented method.

16.5 Video tracking

Surveillance CCTV is becoming or has become ubiquitous in many countries. Recognizing that only a tiny percentage of this video is viewed 'live', this has generated enormous interest in computer vision algorithms that can monitor scenes automatically. While the application value (albeit sinister) of such work in monitoring the movements of people and traffic is obvious, there is a good number of related applications that might use the same algorithms and technology. Popular examples are in the agricultural domain for animal tracking, and sport, where successful real-time tracking is very lucrative, providing the potential for developments in training techniques: see, for example, [Intille and Bobick, 1995; Magee and Boyle, 2002; Needham and Boyle, 2001].

In fact, this area is very wide and provokes many deep and interesting problems both within and without vision. At simplest, we wish to take video signals, preferably in real-time, and determine activity of interest within them ('interest' here is obviously domain specific)—these are areas where computer vision can assist. The problem may become as complex as we wish by considering pan-tilt-zoom (PTZ) cameras, and cameras with overlapping fields of view. Thereafter, we may be interested in modeling and observing behavior (another very subjective word)—in municipal scenes we might wish to identify criminal behavior; in traffic scenes we might wish to identify congestion or accidents; in sports scenes we might wish to identify particular strategies.

Unsurprisingly, these issues are key in robotics where agents may monitor their progress and surroundings visually. This is a burgeoning research area that this book does not address, but key within it is the concept of **Simultaneous Localization and Mapping**, or **SLAM**. SLAM recognizes that robots may use 'maps' of their environment to aid navigation and obstacle avoidance, but that pre-compiled maps may well be inaccurate, or evolve, or indeed may not exist. Accordingly, the robot constructs a map as it moves. It will be clear that this is a problem of some depth, dependent on an understanding of the agent's kinematics, its models of what it may 'see' and its ability to re-recognize scenes from new viewpoints. It is often presented as a 'chicken and egg' issue—the robot cannot move securely without the map, but the map cannot be built until the robot has moved. In all probability, the robot will use a variety of sensors (in addition to visual) and so a full coverage is beyond this text—nevertheless, SLAM-based systems will use a number of the topics of this chapter as components. Just one example is robotic exploration of the sea-bed wreck of the Titanic, where multiple visual images often have small overlap, but the surveying vehicle's inertial sensors provide independent input to mapping [Eustice et al., 2005]. The interested reader is directed toward robotics literature, and any number of useful WWW-based tutorials.

In this section we shall outline how a video signal might be processed to deliver data on blobs (objects) moving in the scene. Conceptually a simple task, it proves very challenging in reality and has benefited enormously from theoretical work coupled with increasing processor power.

16.5.1   Background modeling

The obvious approach to monitoring video is to ask what is moving in the scene, which is most simply done by comparing what we see with an empty, background scene, and performing some sort of comparison or subtraction. A video represents a sequence of frames (images)—much the simplest approach to modeling background is to consider the first frame to *be* the background, and to subtract intensities pixel by pixel in all successors. Non-zero differences then represent movement; these may be thresholded (with varying degrees of sophistication) and grouped (perhaps using morphological approaches) to derive blobs that will be the objects moving in the scene (Section 16.1).

It is easy to see why this will not normally work. Such an approach detects every single movement, howsoever small—this would include wind shaking trees, and the tiniest camera movement. More subtly, changes in lighting of any degree would have catastrophic effects. We would only take this very simple approach in conditions under very strict control; an absolutely rigid camera with no environmental variation in lighting or shadow, and minimal or absent moving 'clutter'. These constraints obviously exclude most scenes of any real interest.

More reasonably, we might concede that 'background' is not constant and try to maintain a background frame dynamically. Success has been had with this approach by taking the mean or (more usually) median intensity at each pixel of the last K frames. This will have the effect, over a period K, of allowing a per-pixel update of lighting changes, although of course a slow moving object of uniform intensity might then become absorbed into background.

Algorithm 16.5: Background maintenance by median filtering

1. Initialize: Acquire K frames. At each pixel, determine the median intensity of these K. If the image sequence is in color, this is done for each of the R,G,B streams. The median represents the current background value.

2. Acquire frame $K+1$. Compute the difference between this frame and the current background at each pixel (a scalar for a gray image; a vector for RGB).

3. Threshold this difference to remove/reduce noise. Simple thresholds may be too crude at this point and there is scope for using, e.g., hysteresis (Algorithm 6.5).

4. Use some combination of blurring and morphological operations (Sections 13.3.1 and 13.3.2) to remove very small regions in the difference image, and to fill in 'holes' etc. in larger ones. Surviving regions represent the moving objects.

5. Update the median measurement, incorporating frame $K+1$ and discarding the current earliest measurement.

6. Return to (2) for the next frame.

Step 5 here is potentially very expensive, demanding the storage of the last K images and a per-pixel sort at each frame. An efficient short cut is available [McFarlane and Schofield, 1995]: only the current background is stored, and intensities are incremented by one if the current frame is brighter at the pixel, and decremented if it is darker. This trick converges the background onto an intensity for which half the updates are brighter and half darker—that is, the median.

This median filter approach to background maintenance is simple to understand and has been applied with some success. Figure 16.16 illustrates the result from a cheap, free-standing camera watching an unconstrained scene [Baumberg and Hogg, 1994a]. We will derive a large number of silhouettes that can be analyzed for shape—in this applica-

Figure 16.16: Left—a pedestrian scene; right—movement extracted from the scene by maintaining a median-filtered background. Post-processing has been applied to remove 'small' blobs and to tidy up the figure boundary. *Courtesy of A. M. Baumberg, University of Leeds.*

tion, each silhouette is characterized by a cubic B-spline (Section 8.2.5) determined by 40 boundary points (i.e., 80 parameters in 2D); these are then used to train a point distribution model (Section 10.4) which permits very efficient description of walking figures in 18 dimensions (the remaining 62 containing very little information).

Median-based background generation is straightforward and can be made to run fast. Nevertheless, it is limited in its application, being vulnerable to scenes in which there are many moving objects, or objects moving slowly. The choice of the interval length K in Algorithm 16.5.1, and the various parameters of difference thresholding and post-processing, make it sensitive. A more robust algorithm [Stauffer and Grimson, 1999] that compensates for these drawbacks is popularly used when the simple one fails.

The idea is to model each pixel independently, in each case as a mixture of Gaussians (see Section 10.13). Depending on local behavior, some of these Gaussians will represent background and some foreground: the algorithm provides a means of deciding which. This seemingly elaborate approach becomes necessary since:

- If each pixel were the result of a particular surface under invariant lighting, a single Gaussian would be sufficient to model its appearance under system noise.

- If the lighting were varying slowly over time, then a single adapting Gaussian would be sufficient.

In practice, multiple surfaces might well appear, and lighting conditions can change in a number of ways at a variety of rates.

Consider a particular pixel with intensity g_t at time t, $t = 1, 2, \ldots$ (we consider here the simple case of gray-scale images—the formal algorithm will be presented for RGB). The recent history of the process g_t will be modeled as K Gaussians, $N_k = N(\mu_k, \sigma_k^2)$ where $k = 1, \ldots, K$. We shall expect these Gaussians to evolve in time as the environment evolves, and objects come and go, so more properly we write

$$N_{kt} = N(\mu_{kt}, \sigma_{kt}^2) \quad k = 1, \ldots, K. \tag{16.50}$$

The choice of K is governed by issues of computational efficiency (remember this is being executed at each pixel), and values in the range 3–7 are commonly used. Obviously, $K > 2$; otherwise, the idea reduces to a simple foreground-background model—$K = 3$ permits two backgrounds and one foreground model.

Associated with each Gaussian is a weight ω_{kt} which also evolves in time. Then the probability of observing g_t is

$$P(g_t) = \sum_{k=1}^{K} \omega_{kt} \frac{1}{\sqrt{2\pi}} \exp\left(\frac{-(g_t - \mu_{kt})^2}{\sigma_{kt}^2}\right). \tag{16.51}$$

These weights are normalized to sum to 1.

As the process proceeds, we could in principle use the EM algorithm (see Section 10.13) to update the Gaussian parameters but this would prove very costly. Instead, the pixel is compared to each Gaussian: if it is within 2.5 standard deviations of the mean it is considered a 'match'; if there is more than one match, the best such is taken—this is a 'winner takes all' strategy. Now:

- If a match is found, for Gaussian l say, we set

$$\omega_{kt} = (1 - \alpha)\,\omega_{k(t-1)} \quad \text{for} \quad k \neq l\,,$$
$$= \omega_{k(t-1)} \qquad\quad \text{for} \quad k = l\,, \tag{16.52}$$

and then re-normalize the ω. α is a learning constant: $1/\alpha$ determines the speed at which parameters change. The parameters of the matched Gaussian are updated as

$$\mu_{lt} = (1 - \rho)\,\mu_{l(t-1)} + \rho\,g_t\,,$$
$$\sigma_{lt}^2 = (1 - \rho)\,\sigma_{l(t-1)}^2 + \rho\,(g_t - \mu_{lt})^2\,,$$

where

$$\rho = \alpha\,P(g_t|\mu_l, \sigma_l^2)\,.$$

- If a match is not found, the least popular Gaussian (lowest ω) is lost, and is replaced by a new one with mean g_t. It is assigned a high variance and low weight (relative to the other $K - 1$ distributions) at this stage. This is the mechanism whereby new objects are 'spotted', and gives them the opportunity, should they persist, of becoming part of the local background.

At this stage, the Gaussian most likely to have given the pixel its current intensity is known, and it remains to decide whether it is background or foreground. This is achieved via a constant T of the whole observation operation: it is assumed that in all frames, the proportion of background pixels always exceeds T. Then, the Gaussians are ordered on the expression ω_{kt}/σ_{kt}—a high value implies either a high weight, or a low variance (or both). Either of these conditions would encourage our belief that the pixel was background. Then the distributions $k = 1, \ldots B$ are considered to be background where

$$B = \underset{b}{\operatorname{argmin}} \left(\sum_{k=1}^{b} \omega_{kt} > T \right) \tag{16.53}$$

and thus a decision is given on the current pixel.

Formally, considering multi-dimensional pixels, the algorithm is:

Algorithm 16.6: Background maintenance by Gaussian mixtures

1. Initialize: Choose K the number of Gaussians and a learning constant α: values in the range 0.01–0.1 are commonly used. At each pixel, initialize K Gaussians $N_k = N(\boldsymbol{\mu}_k, \Sigma_k)$ with mean vector $\boldsymbol{\mu}_k$ and covariance matrix Σ_k, and corresponding weights ω_k. Since the algorithm will evolve this may safely be done crudely on the understanding that early measurements may be unreliable.

2. Acquire frame t, with intensity vector $\mathbf{x}_t$—probably this will be an RGB vector $\mathbf{x}_t = (r_t, g_t, b_t)$. Determine which Gaussians match this observation, and select the 'best' of these as l. In the 1D case, we would expect an observation to be within, say, 2.5σ of the mean. In the multi-dimensional case, a simplifying assumption is made for computational complexity reasons: the different components of the observation are taken to be independent and of equal variance σ_k^2, allowing a quick test for 'acceptability'.

3. *If a match is found as Gaussian l:*

   (a) Set the weights according to equation (16.52), and re-normalize.

(b) Set

$$\rho = \alpha \, N(\mathbf{x}_t | \boldsymbol{\mu}_l, \sigma_l)$$

and

$$\boldsymbol{\mu}_{lt} = (1 - \rho) \, \boldsymbol{\mu}_{l(t-1)} + \rho \, \mathbf{x}_t \,,$$
$$\sigma_{lt}^2 = (1 - \rho) \, \sigma_{l(t-1)}^2 + \rho \, (\mathbf{x}_t - \boldsymbol{\mu}_{lt})^T (\mathbf{x}_t - \boldsymbol{\mu}_{lt}) \,.$$

4. *If no Gaussian matched* $\mathbf{x}_t$: then determine $l = \underset{k}{\arg\min}(\omega_k)$ and delete N_l. Then set

$$\boldsymbol{\mu}_{lt} = \mathbf{x}_t \,,$$
$$\sigma_{lt}^2 = 2 \, \underset{k}{\max} \, \sigma_{k(t-1)}^2 \,,$$
$$\omega_{lt} = 0.5 \, \underset{k}{\min} \, \omega_{k(t-1)} \,.$$

(The algorithm is reasonably robust to these choices.)

5. Determine B as in equation (16.53), and thence from the current 'best match' Gaussian whether the pixel is likely to be foreground or background.

6. Use some combination of blurring and morphological dilations and erosions to remove very small regions in the difference image, and to fill in 'holes' etc. in larger ones. Surviving regions represent the moving objects in the scene.

7. Return to (2) for the next frame.

Figure 16.17 illustrates the evolving balance of Gaussians weights in a simple scene.

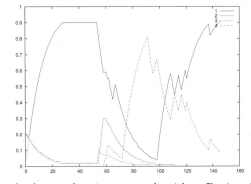

Figure 16.17: Progress of the Stauffer-Grimson background maintenance algorithm. During the sequence, the woman walks from right to left leading the horse; the indicated pixel (black dot, upper center) is background, is then obscured by her clothing and arm, and then the horse. The plot shows the weights of four Gaussians: at initialization the background, Gaussian 1, comes to dominate (capped here at weight 0.9). Other intensity patterns come and go (the horse is Gaussian 4), and at the end of the sequence the background resumes dominance. *Courtesy of B. S. Boyle, University of Leeds.*

This algorithm has proved very popular and has been the subject of many refinements: it is usefully and clearly considered from the point of view of implementation in [Power and Schoonees, 2002]. Particular useful enhancements are to allow α to start high (maybe 0.1) and reduce in time (perhaps to 0.01). Improvements to the Gaussian mixture models approach that simultaneously model multiple foregrounds have been very successfully demonstrated in tracking urban traffic scenes [Magee, 2004].

While other approaches exist (for example, the task may be performed using a PCA approach in which *eigen-backgrounds* are derived from a training set, and 'foreground' reveals itself as significant deviations from a mean image [Oliver et al., 1999]) most current implementations will use a variant of one of the algorithms presented here.

16.5.2   Kernel-based tracking

While background modeling may simplify object tracking, it can be more valuable not to require any specific background treatment: the requirement that only small changes occur between two consecutive frames is satisfied in most applications due to the high frame rate of video sequences. If this requirement is met, gradient-based object localization and tracking can be accomplished using a general correlation criterion [Bascle and Deriche, 1995] and considering illumination and geometry changes [Hager and Belhumeur, 1996]. An intriguing, highly efficient approach to real-time tracking was introduced in [Comaniciu et al., 2000]. Their method is based on spatially masking the target object with an isotropic kernel, followed by applying a smooth similarity function, which reduces the tracking problem to a maximum similarity search in the vicinity of the previous location. The similarity optimization is then efficiently performed using the mean shift algorithm (Section 7.1). An in-depth treatment of kernel-based object tracking is given in [Comaniciu et al., 2003].

First, the desired *target properties* must be determined—for example by estimating a probability density function q from image data. In real-world video tracking, working with color information is typical and information about the *color* distribution of the tracked object may be used to form a feature space. To track the target from frame to frame, the target model identified in the previous frame is first centered at the origin of a local coordinate system. The current-frame *target candidate* is then located at a position $\mathbf{y}$. The target candidate feature description can be characterized by a probability density function $p(\mathbf{y})$, which is estimated from the current image frame data. For computational efficiency, discrete probability density functions are employed; m-bin histograms are used as simple and frequently sufficient representations. As such, the target model $\hat{\mathbf{q}}$ and target candidate $\hat{\mathbf{p}}(\mathbf{y})$ probability density functions are defined as:

$$\hat{\mathbf{q}} = \{\hat{q}_u\} , \qquad \sum_{u=1}^{m} \hat{q}_u = 1 , \tag{16.54}$$

$$\hat{\mathbf{p}}(\mathbf{y}) = \{\hat{p}_u(\mathbf{y})\} , \qquad \sum_{u=1}^{m} \hat{p}_u = 1 , \tag{16.55}$$

where $u = 1, \ldots, m$. Let $\hat{\rho}(\mathbf{y})$ be a similarity function between $\hat{\mathbf{p}}$ and $\hat{\mathbf{q}}$

$$\hat{\rho}(\mathbf{y}) \equiv \rho[\hat{\mathbf{p}}(\mathbf{y}), \hat{\mathbf{q}}] . \tag{16.56}$$

For a tracking task, the similarity $\hat{\rho}(\mathbf{y})$ coincides with the likelihood that a tracked target already located in the previous frame is present at position $\mathbf{y}$ in the current frame.

Therefore, the local maxima of $\hat{\rho}(\mathbf{y})$ correspond to the presence of the target in the current frame of the analyzed image sequence.

There are many ways the similarity function can be defined. Clearly, using solely spectral information cannot provide a smooth similarity function since even closely adjacent locations may exhibit large variability. Consequently, hill-climbing optimization techniques are insufficient, and exhaustive (and thus expensive) optimization techniques do not allow efficient implementations. One of the main ideas to achieve regularization of the similarity function is spatially masking the object with an isotropic kernel [Comaniciu et al., 2000]. The feature-space description is then represented by the kernel weights and $\hat{\rho}(\mathbf{y})$ is a smooth function in $\mathbf{y}$.

The *target model* is derived from an elliptic region that is first normalized to a unit circle to remove the influence of the target scale. The target region, consisting of n pixels, is thus represented using *normalized* pixel coordinates $\{\mathbf{x}_i^*\}$; the normalization uses the center of the unit circle as the origin. This target region is registered with a convex and monotonically decreasing kernel K with a profile $k(x)$ such that

$$k(x) : [0, \infty] \to \mathcal{R} \quad \text{so that} \quad K(\mathbf{x}) = k\big(\|\mathbf{x}\|^2\big) . \tag{16.57}$$

Comaniciu at al. recommend using an Epanechnikov kernel (see Section 7.1 and equation 7.4). The kernel weights are in agreement with our understanding that pixels farther away from the center are less reliable due to possible occlusions, interference with background, or similar boundary effects. Recall that the image features are represented using an m-bin histogram. Each target model pixel at location $\mathbf{x}_i^*$ must be associated with the index $b(\mathbf{x}_i^*)$ of its bin in the quantized feature space using function $b : \mathcal{R}^2 \to \{1, \dots, m\}$. The probability $\hat{q}_u$ of the feature $u \in \{1, \dots, m\}$ is then computed as

$$\hat{q}_u = C \sum_{i=1}^{n} k\big(\|\mathbf{x}_i^*\|^2\big) \, \delta\Big(b(\mathbf{x}_i^*) - u\Big) , \tag{16.58}$$

where δ is the Kronecker delta function[2] and C is a normalization constant

$$C = \frac{1}{\sum_{i=1}^{n} k\big(\|\mathbf{x}_i^*\|^2\big)} . \tag{16.59}$$

The *target candidate* is represented by *normalized* pixel locations $\{\mathbf{x}_i\}$ for $i = 1, \dots, n_h$, centered at $\mathbf{y}$ in the current frame, where h denotes the bandwidth of kernel K with the same profile $k(x)$ that was used for the target model. Importantly, the normalization is inherited from the frame containing the target model. The bandwidth defines the scale of the target candidate, thus also determining the number of pixels in the current frame that need to be analyzed during the localization process. The probability $\hat{p}_u$ of feature $u \in \{1, \dots, m\}$ is

$$\hat{p}_u = C_h \sum_{i=1}^{n_h} k\left(\left\|\frac{\mathbf{y} - \mathbf{x}_i}{h}\right\|^2\right) \delta\Big(b(\mathbf{x}_i) - u\Big) \tag{16.60}$$

with the normalization constant

$$C_h = \frac{1}{\sum_{i=1}^{n_h} k\big(\|(\mathbf{y} - \mathbf{x}_i)/h\|^2\big)} . \tag{16.61}$$

---

[2]Kronecker delta: $\delta(l) = 1$ for $l = 0$; $\delta(l) = 0$ otherwise.

Since C_h does not depend on $\mathbf{y}$, it can be pre-calculated for the given kernels and bandwidths. The similarity function (equation 16.56) inherits the properties of the employed kernel K. Using a smooth differentiable kernel allows the similarity function optimization to use simple hill climbing techniques. Several applicable histogram similarity measures are compared in [Puzicha et al., 1999].

Naturally, the similarity function needs to be a *metric* to evaluate the *distance* between the target model and the respective candidates. The distance $d(\mathbf{y})$ between two distributions can be estimated using the Bhattacharyya coefficient assessing the similarity between $\mathbf{p}$ and $\mathbf{q}$ [Djouadi et al., 1990]:

$$d(\mathbf{y}) = \sqrt{1 - \rho\big[\hat{\mathbf{p}}(\mathbf{y}), \hat{\mathbf{q}}\big]} , \qquad (16.62)$$

where

$$\hat{\rho}(\mathbf{y}) \equiv \rho\big[\hat{\mathbf{p}}(\mathbf{y}), \hat{\mathbf{q}}\big] = \sum_{u=1}^{m} \sqrt{\hat{p}_u(\mathbf{y})\,\hat{q}_u} . \qquad (16.63)$$

To find the most likely location of the target in the current frame, the distance (equation 16.62) must be minimized and/or the Bhattacharyya coefficient (equation 16.63) maximized as a function of $\mathbf{y}$. The optimization starts from the target model position in the previous frame and—relying on the smoothness property of the similarity function—uses the gradient-based mean shift approach (Section 7.1). Clearly, the current-frame target position must be within the attraction area of the similarity function (defined by the bandwidth of the kernel) for the hill-climbing to be successful.

Individual tracking steps start in the current frame from the target model position $\mathbf{y}_0$ determined in the previous frame. The model itself is first estimated from the initial frame of the tracked sequence. Due to possible changes in appearance over time, a mechanism to update the target model must be available. To initialize each tracking step, the probability of the target candidate $\{\hat{p}_u(\hat{\mathbf{y}}_0)\}$ for $u = 1, \ldots, m$ is computed at location $\mathbf{y}_0$. A Taylor expansion around the values $\{\hat{p}_u(\hat{\mathbf{y}}_0)\}$ yields the following approximation of the Bhattacharyya coefficient (equation 16.63)

$$\rho\big[\hat{\mathbf{p}}(\mathbf{y}), \hat{\mathbf{q}}\big] \approx \frac{1}{2} \sum_{u=1}^{m} \sqrt{\hat{p}_u(\hat{\mathbf{y}}_0)\,\hat{q}_u} + \frac{1}{2} \sum_{u=1}^{m} \hat{p}_u(\mathbf{y})\sqrt{\frac{\hat{q}_u}{\hat{p}_u(\hat{\mathbf{y}}_0)}} . \qquad (16.64)$$

A reasonably close approximation results as long as the target candidate $\{\hat{p}_u(\hat{\mathbf{y}})\}$ does not change dramatically from the initial $\{\hat{p}_u(\hat{\mathbf{y}}_0)\}$ in subsequent frames. Note that the requirement of $\{\hat{p}_u(\hat{\mathbf{y}}_0)\} > 0$ (or greater than some small ϵ) is enforceable for all $u = 1, \ldots, m$ by excluding the violating features.

The tracking process optimizes the target candidate location as given in equation (16.60). By employing equation (16.64), the second right-hand side term of the following equation must be maximized with the first term being independent of $\mathbf{y}$

$$\rho\big[\hat{\mathbf{p}}(\mathbf{y}), \hat{\mathbf{q}}\big] \approx \frac{1}{2} \sum_{u=1}^{m} \sqrt{\hat{p}_u(\hat{\mathbf{y}}_0)\,\hat{q}_u} + \frac{C_h}{2} \sum_{u=1}^{n_h} w_i\, k\left(\left\|\frac{\mathbf{y} - \mathbf{x}_i}{h}\right\|^2\right) , \qquad (16.65)$$

where

$$w_i = \sum_{u=1}^{m} \sqrt{\frac{\hat{q}_u}{\hat{p}_u(\hat{\mathbf{y}}_0)}}\, \delta\big(b(\mathbf{x}_i) - u\big) . \qquad (16.66)$$

The second term that is maximized reflects a density estimate computed with kernel profile $k(x)$ at $\mathbf{y}$ in the current frame, weighted by w_i. Using a mean shift procedure, the maximum can be efficiently located in a recursive fashion starting from location $\hat{\mathbf{y}}_0$ as follows (see also Figure 7.1 and equation 7.12)

$$\hat{\mathbf{y}}_1 = \sum_{i=1}^{n_h} \mathbf{x}_i\, w_i\, g\left(\left\|\frac{\hat{\mathbf{y}}_0 - \mathbf{x}_i}{h}\right\|^2\right) \bigg/ \sum_{i=1}^{n_h} w_i\, g\left(\left\|\frac{\hat{\mathbf{y}}_0 - \mathbf{x}_i}{h}\right\|^2\right), \qquad (16.67)$$

where $g(x) = -k'(x)$ is differentiable for $x \in [0, \infty)$ except at a finite number of points.

Algorithm 16.7: Kernel-based object tracking

1. Assumptions: The target model $\{\hat{q}_u\}$ exists for all $u = 1, \ldots, m$. The tracked object location in the previous frame $\hat{\mathbf{y}}_0$ is known.

2. Using the previous frame target location $\hat{\mathbf{y}}_0$ as the initial location of the target candidate in the current frame, compute $\{\hat{p}_u(\hat{\mathbf{y}}_0)\}$ for $u = 1, \ldots, m$ and

$$\rho\left[\hat{\mathbf{p}}(\hat{\mathbf{y}}_0), \hat{\mathbf{q}}\right] = \sum_{u=1}^{m} \sqrt{\hat{p}_u(\hat{\mathbf{y}}_0)\hat{q}_u}\,.$$

3. Derive weights $\{w_i\}$ for $i = 1, \ldots, n_h$ according to equation (16.66).

4. Determine the new location of the target candidate according to equation (16.67).

5. Compute the new likelihood value $\{\hat{p}_u(\hat{\mathbf{y}}_1)\}$ for $u = 1, \ldots, m$ and determine

$$\rho\left[\hat{\mathbf{p}}(\hat{\mathbf{y}}_1), \hat{\mathbf{q}}\right] = \sum_{u=1}^{m} \sqrt{\hat{p}_u(\hat{\mathbf{y}}_1)\hat{q}_u}\,.$$

6. If the similarity between the new target region and the target model is less than that between the old target region and the model

$$\rho\left[\hat{\mathbf{p}}(\hat{\mathbf{y}}_1), \hat{\mathbf{q}}\right] < \rho\left[\hat{\mathbf{p}}(\hat{\mathbf{y}}_0), \hat{\mathbf{q}}\right]$$

perform the remainder of this step: move the target region half way between the new and old locations

$$\hat{\mathbf{y}}_1 := \frac{1}{2}\left(\hat{\mathbf{y}}_0 + \hat{\mathbf{y}}_1\right), \qquad (16.68)$$

and evaluate the similarity function in this new location

$$\rho\left[\hat{\mathbf{p}}(\hat{\mathbf{y}}_1), \hat{\mathbf{q}}\right].$$

Return to the beginning of this step.

7. If $\|\hat{\mathbf{y}}_1 - \hat{\mathbf{y}}_0\| < \epsilon$, stop. Otherwise, use the current target location as a start for the new iteration, i.e., $\hat{\mathbf{y}}_0 := \hat{\mathbf{y}}_1$, and continue with step 3.

The value of ϵ in step 7 is chosen so that the vectors $\hat{\mathbf{y}}_0$ and $\hat{\mathbf{y}}_1$ would be referencing the same pixel in the original image coordinates. Usually, the maximum number of iterations is also limited to satisfy real-time performance requirements. Note that step 6 is only included to avoid potential numerical problems of mean shift maximization, which is a rare event, and in practice this step may be omitted. Consequently, the calculation of the Bhattacharyya coefficient is avoided in steps 2 and 5, yielding an additional speed-up for such a modification. Then, the algorithm only performs the weight computations in step 3, derives the new position in step 4, and tests the kernel shift in step 7. In that case, the Bhattacharyya coefficient is only computed after the convergence to evaluate the similarity between the target model and the candidate.

To facilitate changes of scale, the bandwidth h of the kernel must be properly adjusted during the tracking process. Let h_{prev} be the bandwidth used in the previous frame. The best bandwidth h_{opt} for the current frame is determined by repeating the target localization algorithm for three values of h:

$$h = h_{\text{prev}}, \tag{16.69}$$

$$h = h_{\text{prev}} + \Delta h, \tag{16.70}$$

$$h = h_{\text{prev}} - \Delta h, \tag{16.71}$$

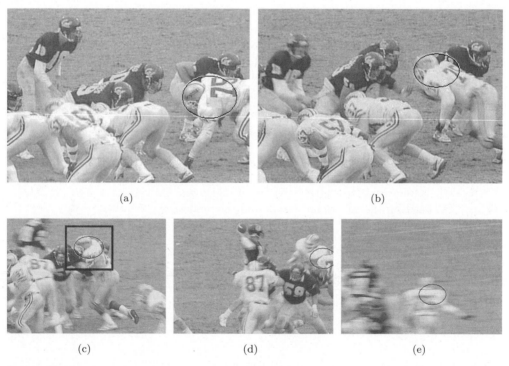

(a)   (b)

(c)   (d)   (e)

Figure 16.18: Kernel-based tracking of player #75: frames 30, 75, 105, 140, and 150 in a 154 long sequence. The tracker copes well with partial occlusion, camera motion, clutter, and blurring. Rectangular subwindow marked in panel (c) is used in Figure 16.19. *Courtesy of P. Meer, Rutgers University.* © *2003 IEEE. Reprinted, with permission, from D. Comaniciu, V. Ramesh, P. Meer, "Kernel-based object tracking," IEEE Trans. Pattern Anal. Machine Intell., vol. 25, pp. 564-575, 2003.*

with a 10% difference between the tested values being typical: $\Delta h = 0.1\, h_{\text{prev}}$. The best bandwidth is determined by the highest value of the Bhattacharyya coefficient. To avoid an overly sensitive modifications of the bandwidth, the new bandwidth is determined as

$$h_{\text{new}} = \gamma\, h_{\text{opt}} + (1 - \gamma)\, h_{\text{prev}} \,, \tag{16.72}$$

typically $\gamma = 0.1$ is used. Clearly, the optimal bandwidth value as a function of time carries potentially valuable information about the tracked object.

Figure 16.18 shows 5 351×240 pixel frames from a 154-frame sequence; the goal was to track movement of player number 75. Target initialization was performed manually by drawing an ellipse as shown in panel (a). The color space was quantized in $16 \times 16 \times 16$ bins, which served as features. Figure 16.19a shows the number of mean shift iterations as a function of the frame number—about 4 iterations were needed on average for frame-to-frame tracking. Values of the Bhattacharyya similarity coefficient corresponding to Figure 16.18c are shown in Figure 16.19b together with the start- and end-locations of the mean shift iterations. Additional examples can be found in [Comaniciu et al., 2000, 2003].

The tracking task shown in Figure 16.18 did not assume any motion model. As such, the tracker was well suited to the abrupt changes of motion direction and unpredictable camera view changes typical of a football game video. However, background modeling (Section 16.5.1) and motion models (Section 16.6) can be incorporated in the kernel-based trackers, see [Comaniciu et al., 2003] for details. It is also worth noting that the kernel based trackers can track multiple objects in parallel, simply by maintaining several target models and their iterative tracking. The number of simultaneously tracked objects is only limited by the available computational resources—so that the real-time behavior of the trackers is not compromised. For example, if a single-target tracker can track

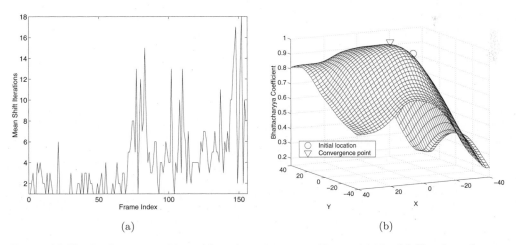

(a) (b)

Figure 16.19: Performance of kernel-based tracking—see Figure 16.18. (a) Number of mean shift iterations as a function of frame number. (b) Similarity surface depicting the values of the Bhattacharyya coefficient within the rectangle shown in Figure 16.18c. Start and end locations of the mean shift iterations are depicted to show the optimization process yielding the object tracking behavior. *Courtesy of P. Meer, Rutgers University. © 2003 IEEE. Reprinted, with permission, from D. Comaniciu, V. Ramesh, P. Meer, "Kernel-based object tracking," IEEE Trans. Pattern Anal. Machine Intell., vol. 25, pp. 564-575, 2003.*

objects at a frame rate of 250 frames per second, such a tracker can independently track 10 objects at a standard video frame rate of 25 fps.

16.5.3 Object path analysis

If there is only one object in the image sequence, the task can often be solved using approaches already described, but if there are many objects moving simultaneously and independently, more complex approaches are needed to incorporate individual object motion-based constraints. In such situations, motion assumptions/constraints described earlier should be examined (maximum velocity, small acceleration, common motion, mutual correspondence, smoothness of motion). Consequently, it is possible to formulate the notion of path coherence which implies that the motion of an object at any point in an image sequence will not change abruptly [Jain et al., 1995].

The **path coherence function** Φ represents a measure of agreement between the derived object trajectory and the motion constraints. Path coherence functions should follow four principles [Sethi and Jain, 1987; Jain et al., 1995]:

- The function value is always positive.

- The function reflects local absolute angular deviations of the trajectory.

- The function should respond equally to positive and negative velocity changes.

- The function should be normalized $\big[\Phi(\cdot) \in (0,1]\big]$.

Let the trajectory T_i of an object i be represented by a sequence of points in the projection plane

$$T_i = \left(X_i^1, X_i^2, \ldots, X_i^n\right),\tag{16.73}$$

where X_i^k represents a (three-dimensional) trajectory point in image k of the sequence (see Figure 16.20). Let $\mathbf{x}_i^k$ be the projection image co-ordinates associated with the point X_i^k. Then the trajectory can be expressed in vector form

$$T_i = \left(\mathbf{x}_i^1, \mathbf{x}_i^2, \ldots, \mathbf{x}_i^n\right).\tag{16.74}$$

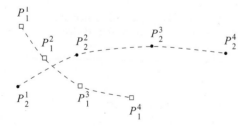

Figure 16.20: The trajectories of two objects moving simultaneously and independently. © *Cengage Learning 2015.*

Deviation function

Deviation in the path can be used to measure path coherence. Let d_i^k be the deviation in the path of the point i in the image k

$$d_i^k = \Phi\left(\overline{\mathbf{x}_i^{k-1}\,\mathbf{x}_i^k},\,\overline{\mathbf{x}_i^k\,\mathbf{x}_i^{k+1}}\right) \qquad \text{or} \qquad d_i^k = \Phi\left(X_i^{k-1}, X_i^k, X_i^{k+1}\right),\tag{16.75}$$

where $\overline{\mathbf{x}_i^{k-1}\,\mathbf{x}_i^k}$ represents the motion vector from point X_i^{k-1} to point X_i^k and Φ is the path coherence function. The deviation D_i of the entire trajectory of the object i is then

$$D_i = \sum_{k=2}^{n-1} d_i^k \,. \tag{16.76}$$

Similarly, for m trajectories of m moving objects in the image sequence, the overall trajectory deviation D can be determined as

$$D = \sum_{i=1}^{m} D_i \,. \tag{16.77}$$

With the overall trajectory deviation defined in this way, the multiple object trajectory tracking can be solved by minimizing the overall trajectory deviation D.

Path coherence function

It remains to define the path coherence function Φ. In agreement with motion assumptions, if the image acquisition frequency is high enough, the direction and velocity changes in consecutive images should be smooth. Then the path coherence function can be defined as

$$
\begin{aligned}
\Phi\big(P_i^{k-1}, P_i^k, P_i^{k+1}\big) &= w_1\left(1 - \cos\theta\right) + w_2\left(1 - 2\frac{\sqrt{s_k\,s_{k+1}}}{s_k + s_{k+1}}\right) \\
&= w_1\left(1 - \frac{\left|\overline{\mathbf{x}_i^{k-1}\,\mathbf{x}_i^k} \cdot \overline{\mathbf{x}_i^k\,\mathbf{x}_i^{k+1}}\right|}{\left\|\overline{\mathbf{x}_i^{k-1}\,\mathbf{x}_i^k}\right\| \left\|\overline{\mathbf{x}_i^k\,\mathbf{x}_i^{k+1}}\right\|}\right) + w_2\left(1 - 2\frac{\sqrt{\left\|\overline{\mathbf{x}_i^{k-1}\,\mathbf{x}_i^k}\right\| \left\|\overline{\mathbf{x}_i^k\,\mathbf{x}_i^{k+1}}\right\|}}{\left\|\overline{\mathbf{x}_i^{k-1}\,\mathbf{x}_i^k}\right\| \left\|\overline{\mathbf{x}_i^k\,\mathbf{x}_i^{k+1}}\right\|}\right), \quad (16.78)
\end{aligned}
$$

where the angle θ and distances s_k, s_{k+1} are given by Figure 16.21. The weights w_1, w_2 reflect the importance of direction coherence and velocity coherence.

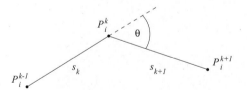

Figure 16.21: Path coherence function—definition of the angle θ and distances s_k, s_{k+1}. © Cengage Learning 2015.

Occlusion

When simultaneously tracking several objects with independent motion, object occlusion is almost guaranteed to occur. Consequently, some objects may partially or completely disappear in some image frames which can result in trajectory errors. If minimization of the overall trajectory deviation D (equation 16.77) is performed using the given path coherence function, it is assumed that the same number of objects (object points) is detected in each image and that the detected object points consistently represent the same objects (object points) in every image. Clearly, this is not the case if occlusion occurs.

To overcome this problem, additional local trajectory constraints must be considered and trajectories must be allowed to be incomplete if necessary. Incompleteness may reflect occlusion, appearance or disappearance of an object, or missing object points due to changed object aspect resulting from motion or simply due to poor object detection. Thus, additional motion assumptions that were not reflected in the definition of the path coherence function must be incorporated. An algorithm called the *greedy exchange* has been developed which finds the maximum set of complete or partially complete trajectories and minimizes the sum of local smoothness deviations for all identified trajectories. Local smoothness deviation is constrained not to exceed a preset maximum Φ_{max} and the displacement between any two successive trajectory points X_i^k, X_i^{k+1} must be less than a preset threshold d_{max}. To deal efficiently with incomplete trajectories, phantom points are introduced and used as substitutes for those which are missing. These hypothetical points allow each potential trajectory to be treated as complete and permit consistent

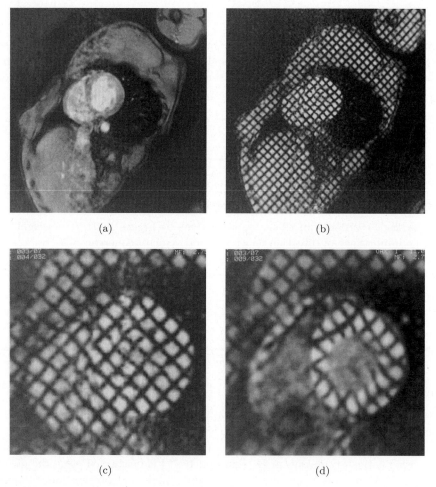

(a)   (b)

(c)   (d)

Figure 16.22: Magnetic resonance heart image. (a) Original chest image, diastole. (b) Chest image with magnetic resonance markers, diastole. (c) Image of the heart with markers, diastole. (d) Image with markers, systole. *Courtesy of D. Fisher, S. M. Collins, The University of Iowa.*

application of the optimization function. Details of the algorithm and example results can be found in [Sethi and Jain, 1987; Jain et al., 1995].

A conceptually similar method that minimizes a proximal uniformity cost function (reflecting the assumption that a small distance is usually traveled in a short time and a smooth trajectory is followed) was presented in [Rangarajan and Shah, 1991]. A two-stage algorithm exists, in which the first stage performs a forward search that extends trajectories up to the current frame and the second stage is a rule-based backward correcting algorithm that corrects wrong correspondences introduced in the last few frames.

Spatio-temporal approaches to analysis of image sequences with multiple independently moving objects represent another alternative to motion analysis. A minimum description length (MDL) approach to motion analysis of long image sequences has been developed: the method first constructs a family of motion models, each model corresponding to some meaningful motion type—translation, rotation, their combination, etc. Using the motion description length, the principle of progressive perception from extension in time, and optimal modeling of a limited period of observations, the objects in the image sequences are segmented to determine when objects change their type of motion or when a new part of an object appears. If the motion information in two consecutive frames is ambiguous, it is resolved by minimizing the motion description length in a long image sequence. Examples and applications for stationary and moving observers are given in [Gu et al., 1996].

A different method of interest-point correspondence and trajectory detection has been used in the analysis of cardiac wall motion from magnetic resonance images [Fisher et al., 1991], where rigid body motion assumptions could not be used since the human heart changes its shape over the cardiac cycle. Interest points were magnetically applied to the heart muscle using a special magnetic resonance pulse sequence known as SPAMM (spatial modulation of magnetization). This results in an image with a rectangular grid of markers, see Figure 16.22; heart motion is clearly visible on images if markers are applied. The first step of the motion analysis algorithm is a precise automatic detection

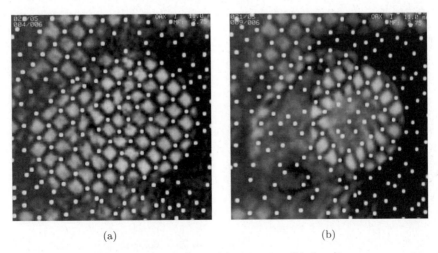

(a)   (b)

Figure 16.23: Detected position of markers. (a) Diastole. (b) Systole. *Courtesy of D. Fisher, S. M. Collins, The University of Iowa.*

of markers. Using a correlation technique (Section 6.4), the exact position of markers is determined (possibly at subpixel resolution), see Figure 16.23.

To track the marker locations, specific knowledge about small relative motion of marker positions in consecutive frames is used. Markers are considered as nodes of a two-dimensional graph, and dynamic programming (Section 6.2.5) is used to determine optimal trajectories. The optimality criterion is based on distance between markers in consecutive images, on the quality of marker detection, and on consistency of motion direction in consecutive images. Marker quality evaluation results from the marker detection correlation process. Successor nodes are determined by requiring that the trajectory length between successors be less than some specified constant. Identified and tracked markers are illustrated in Figure 16.24, and a velocity field is shown in Figure 16.25.

A survey of many other approaches to motion correspondence, trajectory parameterization, representation of relative motion and motion events, overview of useful region-based features, matching and classification approaches, and approaches to motion recognition including cyclic motion, lipreading, gesture interpretation, motion verb recognition, and temporal textures classification, is given in [Cedras and Shah, 1995].

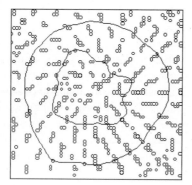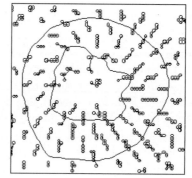

Figure 16.24: Velocity field. Identified markers (left) and tracked markers (right). Note that the dynamic programming has removed most of the spurious nodes that occur in the center of the cavity. *Courtesy of D. Fisher, S. M. Collins, The University of Iowa.*

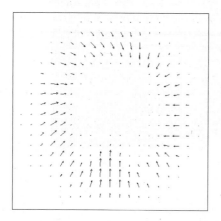

Figure 16.25: Velocity field derived from the information in Figure 16.24. *Courtesy of D. Fisher, S. M. Collins, The University of Iowa.*

16.6   Motion models to aid tracking

In fact, the tracking task represents an example of a very old and well-studied problem in control theory: the estimation of the state of a time-varying system via a sequence of noisy measurements. Here, the system states are the position, pose, etc. of the agents moving in the scene and the measurements are whatever feature vectors we choose to extract. This class of problem has been known since Gauss sought to determine the orbits of celestial bodies [Gauss, 1809], and it recurs in many fields of science and engineering.

Formally, we may have a model of an object in a scene that we see through noise; thus we *model* $\mathbf{x}$ and *observe* $\mathbf{z}$, where $\mathbf{x}$ and $\mathbf{z}$ are feature vectors, not necessarily of the same dimension. In the circumstance of observing through an image sequence, in particular motion, we may be able to use the models and observations in two ways.

- Multiple observations $\mathbf{z}_1, \mathbf{z}_2, \ldots$ should permit an improved estimate of the underlying model $\mathbf{x}$. It is possible that this model evolves in time, in which case $\mathbf{z}_k$ will give an estimate of $\mathbf{x}_k$; provided we have a clear understanding of how $\mathbf{x}_k$ changes with k, it should still be possible to use the $\mathbf{z}_k$ to estimate this more complex model.

- The estimate of $\mathbf{x}$ at time k may also provide a prediction for the observation $\mathbf{x}_{k+1}$, and thereby for $\mathbf{z}_{k+1}$.

This suggests a feedback mechanism, or predictor controller (Figure 16.26), whereby we observe $\mathbf{z}_k$, estimate $\mathbf{x}_k$, predict $\mathbf{x}_{k+1}$ thereby predict $\mathbf{z}_{k+1}$, observe $\mathbf{z}_{k+1}$ *taking advantage of the prediction*, and then update our estimate of $\mathbf{x}_{k+1}$. This approach is in widespread use in computer vision, particularly within real-time tracking applications. The most popular ways of doing it are via **Kalman filters** [Kalman, 1960] or **particle filters**, particularly the Condensation algorithm [Isard and Blake, 1998]. Another increasingly popular approach to aid object tracking is to employ hidden Markov models (see Section 10.11).

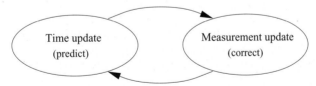

Figure 16.26: The predictor-corrector iterative cycle; the time update predicts events at the next step, and the measurement update adjusts estimates in the light of observation. © *Cengage Learning 2015*.

16.6.1   Kalman filters

For a particular class of model and observation, a classical approach delivers an optimal solution. The Kalman filter proceeds by assuming that the system is linear, that observations of it are linear functions of the underlying state, and that noise, both in the system and in measurement, is white and Gaussian (although slight variations and extensions of this model may be found in more specialized texts). In fact, the Kalman filter can be shown to provide a least-squares best estimate of system behavior—the model and observation estimates have minimal variance under the assumptions [Sorenson, 1970].

Formally[3], we have the model

$$\mathbf{x}_{k+1} = A_k \mathbf{x}_k + \mathbf{w}_k \,,$$
$$\mathbf{z}_k = H_k \mathbf{x}_k + \mathbf{v}_k \,. \tag{16.79}$$

The matrices A_k describe the evolution of the underlying model state, while $\mathbf{w}_k$ is zero mean Gaussian noise. We assume that $\mathbf{w}_k$ has covariance Q_k

$$Q_k = E[\mathbf{w}_k \, \mathbf{w}_k^T] \,,$$
$$(Q_k)_{ij} = E(w_k^i \, w_k^j) \,,$$

where w_k^i denotes the ith component of vector $\mathbf{w}_k$. The matrices H_k are the measurement matrices, describing how the observations are related to the model; $\mathbf{v}_k$ is another zero mean Gaussian noise factor, with covariance R_k.

Given $\mathbf{x}_{k-1}$ (or an estimate $\hat{\mathbf{x}}_{k-1}$) we can now compute from equation (16.79) an a priori estimate $\mathbf{x}_k = A_{k-1}\mathbf{x}_{k-1}$. Conventionally, this is referred to as $\hat{\mathbf{x}}_k^-$ to indicate (via ^) that it is an estimate, and (via $^-$) that it is 'before' observation. Correspondingly, we can define $\hat{\mathbf{x}}_k^+$ as the updated estimate computed 'after' observation—it is this computation that the Kalman filter provides. Of course, we will be expecting $\hat{\mathbf{x}}_k^+$ to be an improvement on $\hat{\mathbf{x}}_k^-$.

Associated with each estimate are errors

$$\mathbf{e}_k^- = \mathbf{x}_k - \hat{\mathbf{x}}_k^- \,,$$
$$\mathbf{e}_k^+ = \mathbf{x}_k - \hat{\mathbf{x}}_k^+ \,, \tag{16.80}$$

with corresponding covariances P_k^- and P_k^+. Note that these errors are caused by $\mathbf{w}_k$ and the error in the estimate.

The Kalman filter operates by examining the residual

$$\mathbf{z}_k - H_k \, \hat{\mathbf{x}}_k^-$$

to which $\mathbf{e}_k^-$ and the noise $\mathbf{v}_k$ contribute. In the absence of the noise, and if the estimate is perfect, this is zero. The approach is to seek a matrix K_k, the **Kalman gain** matrix, to update $\hat{\mathbf{x}}_k^-$ to $\hat{\mathbf{x}}_k^+$ in a least squares sense

$$\hat{\mathbf{x}}_k^+ = \hat{\mathbf{x}}_k^- + K_k \left(\mathbf{z}_k - H_k \hat{\mathbf{x}}_k^- \right) \,. \tag{16.81}$$

If we can derive K_k, then $\hat{\mathbf{x}}_k^-$ may be updated to $\hat{\mathbf{x}}_k^+$ (since the other terms of the equation are known) and the problem is solved.

Equations (16.80) and (16.81) give

$$\begin{aligned}
\mathbf{e}_k^+ &= \mathbf{x}_k - \hat{\mathbf{x}}_k^+ \\
&= \mathbf{x}_k - \left((I - K_k \, H_k) \, \hat{\mathbf{x}}_k^- - K_k \, \mathbf{z}_k \right) \\
&= \mathbf{x}_k - (I - K_k \, H_k) \, \hat{\mathbf{x}}_k^- - K_k \, (H_k \, \mathbf{x}_k + \mathbf{v}_k) \\
&= (I - K_k \, H_k) \, \mathbf{e}_k^- + K_k \, \mathbf{v}_k \,.
\end{aligned} \tag{16.82}$$

---

[3]The derivation that follows is non-trivial. For most readers, it may be sufficient to know that the assumptions of equation (16.79), and the results of equations (16.85)–(16.87) are sufficient to proceed to an implementation.

By definition

$$P_k^- = E\left[\mathbf{e}_k^- \mathbf{e}_k^{-T}\right],$$
$$P_k^+ = E\left[\mathbf{e}_k^+ \mathbf{e}_k^{+T}\right],$$
$$R_k = E\left[\mathbf{v}_k \mathbf{v}_k^T\right],$$

and independence of errors gives

$$E\left[\mathbf{e}_k^- \mathbf{v}_k^T\right] = E\left[\mathbf{v}_k \mathbf{e}_k^{-T}\right] = 0 \tag{16.83}$$

and so equation (16.82) leads to

$$P_k^+ = (I - K_k H_k) P_k^- (I - K_k H_k)^T + K_k R_k K_k^T . \tag{16.84}$$

K_k is now chosen to minimize the sum of the diagonal of P_k^+, trace(P_k^+), which is the sum of the posterior error variances—this is the 'least squares' aspect of the algorithm. This we do by taking the partial derivative of trace(P_k^+) with respect to K_k and equating to zero. It is known (see, for example, [Gelb, 1974]) that if B is a symmetric matrix then

$$\frac{\partial}{\partial A} \, \text{trace}(ABA^T) = 2AB$$

and so from equation (16.84)

$$-2 (I - K_k H_k) P_k^- H_k^T + 2 K_k R_k = 0$$

whence, solving for K_k,

$$K_k = P_k^- H_k^T (H_k P_k^- H_k^T + R_k)^{-1} \tag{16.85}$$

wherein

$$P_k^- = A_k P_{k-1}^+ A_k^T + Q_{k-1} . \tag{16.86}$$

Elementary manipulation also provides the relation

$$P_k^+ = (I - K_k H_k) P_k^- . \tag{16.87}$$

If the functions describing the underlying state and/or the measurements are non-linear, an Extended Kalman filter can be obtained by linearization while the posterior density is still considered Gaussian [Bar-Shalom and Fortmann, 1988]. Parameterization of the mean and covariance of a posteriori density was introduced in [Julier and Uhlmann, 1997] and is called an **Unscented Kalman filter**.

Examples

In its formulaic form, the Kalman filter is not intuitive: to illustrate it, consider a trivial example [Gelb, 1974]. Suppose we have a constant scalar x, observed through uncorrelated Gaussian noise of zero mean and variance r. In this case we have $A_k = I = 1$ and $H_k = I = 1$:

$$x_{k+1} = x_k ,$$
$$z_k = x_k + v_k ,$$

where v_k is normally distributed about 0 with variance r. Immediately, we see from equation (16.85) that

$$K_k = \frac{p_k^-}{p_k^- + r} \, . \tag{16.88}$$

We can deduce covariance relations from equations (16.86) and (16.87):

$$p_{k+1}^- = p_k^+ \, ,$$
$$p_{k+1}^+ = (1 - K_{k+1}) \, p_{k+1}^- = \left(\frac{r}{p_{k+1}^- + r} \right) p_{k+1}^- = p_k^+ \frac{r}{p_k^+ + r} \, . \tag{16.89}$$

Equation (16.89) provides a recurrence relation; writing $p_0 = p_0^+$, we can deduce

$$p_k^+ = \frac{r \, p_0}{k \, p_0 + r}$$

which, substituted into equation (16.88), gives

$$K_k = \frac{p_0}{r + k \, p_0}$$

and so, from equation (16.81),

$$\hat{x}_k^+ = \hat{x}_k^- + \frac{p_0}{r + k \, p_0} (z_k - \hat{x}_k^-) \, ,$$

which tells us the intuitively obvious—as k grows, new measurements provide less and less information.

More interestingly, consider the example introduced in Section 16.5.1 (page 816); recall that we have an 80D shape vector $\mathbf{x}$ (40 control points) which is reduced to an 18D representation via PCA:

$$\mathbf{x} = \bar{\mathbf{x}} + P \mathbf{b} \, ,$$

where $\mathbf{b}$ is the 18D vector derived from the PDM, and $\bar{\mathbf{x}}$ is the 'mean shape' (see Section 10.4). We note that a spline (object) appears in the scene after due translation, rotation, and scaling; if the current offset is (o_x, o_y), the scale is s and the rotation is θ, we may model the boundary by

$$Q = \begin{bmatrix} s \cos \theta & -s \sin \theta \\ s \sin \theta & s \cos \theta \end{bmatrix} \, , \tag{16.90}$$
$$\begin{bmatrix} X_i \\ Y_i \end{bmatrix} = Q \begin{bmatrix} x_i \\ y_i \end{bmatrix} + \begin{bmatrix} o_x \\ o_y \end{bmatrix} \, ,$$

where x_i, y_i are the 40 two-dimensional points defining the spline. Then if we write $\mathbf{o} = (o_x, o_y, o_x, o_y, \ldots, o_x, o_y,)$ (40 times), and

$$\mathcal{Q} = \begin{bmatrix} Q & \cdots & 0 \\ \vdots & \cdots & \vdots \\ 0 & \cdots & Q \end{bmatrix} \tag{16.91}$$

(an 80×80 matrix, which is 40 instances of the same 2×2 matrix), then the shape vector $\mathbf{X}$ is related to the state $\mathbf{b}$ by the equation

$$\mathbf{X} = Q \left(P \mathbf{b} + \bar{\mathbf{x}} \right) + \mathbf{o} \,. \tag{16.92}$$

When a new object is detected, it will not be clear what the best estimates of its scale, trajectory, or model parameters are, but given suitable assumptions we might initialize these parameters and then iterate them during successive frames using a Kalman filter to converge on a good estimate [Baumberg and Hogg, 1994b]. We suppose that the object to be initialized has bounding box given by lower left co-ordinates (x_l, y_l) and upper right (x_r, y_r), and that the mean height of figures in a training set is h_m. Rewriting equation (16.90) as

$$\begin{bmatrix} s\cos\theta & -s\sin\theta \\ s\sin\theta & s\cos\theta \end{bmatrix} = \begin{bmatrix} a_x & -a_y \\ a_y & a_x \end{bmatrix} \,,$$

we can then initialize the figure as the mean shape, $\hat{\mathbf{b}}^0 = \mathbf{0}$, and

$$\hat{a}_x^0 = \frac{y_r - y_l}{h_m} \,, \qquad\qquad \hat{a}_y^0 = 0 \,,$$

$$\hat{o}_x^0 = \frac{x_l + x_r}{2} \,, \qquad\qquad \hat{o}_y^0 = \frac{y_l + y_r}{2} \,,$$

so the figure is scaled to its bounding box, aligned vertically, with the origin at the center of the box.

A stochastic model for the shape will be more stable than an assumption of uniform change, so we assume

$$\mathbf{b}^k = \mathbf{b}^{k-1} + \mathbf{w}^{k-1} \,,$$

where $\mathbf{w}$ is a zero mean, normally distributed noise term, $w_i^k \sim N(0, \sigma_i)$. The eigen-analysis gives the variance of b_i over the training set as λ_i, and σ_i is initialized as $\sigma_i = \kappa \lambda_i$, where characteristically $\kappa = 0.05$—thus the shape estimate is allowed to vary within an ellipsoid that is a subset of that defined by the training set. (Recall that the eigen-decomposition assumes that $E(b_i \, b_j) = 0$.)

Then we will assume that:

1. The object is moving uniformly in 2D subject to additive noise

$$\frac{\mathrm{d}}{\mathrm{d}t} \begin{bmatrix} o_x \\ \dot{o}_x \end{bmatrix} = \begin{bmatrix} \dot{o}_x \\ 0 \end{bmatrix} + \begin{bmatrix} v_x \\ w_x \end{bmatrix} \,,$$

   for noise terms v_x and w_x (and similarly for o_y). This gives the frame update equation

$$\begin{bmatrix} o_x^{k+1} \\ \dot{o}_x^{k+1} \end{bmatrix} = \begin{bmatrix} 1 & \Delta t \\ 0 & \Delta t \end{bmatrix} \begin{bmatrix} o_x^k \\ \dot{o}_x^k \end{bmatrix} + \begin{bmatrix} v_x \\ w_x \end{bmatrix} \tag{16.93}$$

   (where Δt is the time step between frames). v_x and w_x are noise terms, with $v_x \sim N(0, q_v)$, $w_x \sim N(0, q_w)$.

2. The alignment parameters a_x, a_y are constant, subject to noise

$$\begin{bmatrix} a_x^{k+1} \\ a_y^{k+1} \end{bmatrix} = \begin{bmatrix} a_x^k \\ a_y^k \end{bmatrix} + \begin{bmatrix} w_{ax} \\ w_{ay} \end{bmatrix} \,, \tag{16.94}$$

   where $w_{ax}, w_{ay} \sim N(0, q_a)$.

The Kalman filter proceeds by estimating origin, alignment, and shape independently of each other. Given estimates of the parameters, we predict the next state $\hat{\mathbf{X}}^-$ from equation (16.92) and use this to make an observation from the image $\mathbf{z}$.

To update the x-origin co-ordinate we need to consider the state $(\hat{o}_x, \hat{o}_x)$. Many measurements of the origin are available from the expression

$$\mathbf{z} - \mathcal{Q}\left(P\,\hat{\mathbf{b}} + \overline{\mathbf{x}}\right).$$

These measurements, together with the update relation equation (16.93) and the noise variance properties, provide the necessary ingredients for the application of the filter, which can then be used to provide the best estimate of the origin in the next frame.

To update the alignment parameters with the observation $\mathbf{z}$, we use the measurement model

$$\mathbf{z} - \hat{\mathbf{o}} = H \begin{bmatrix} a_x \\ a_y \end{bmatrix},$$

where H is a $N \times 2$ measurement matrix defined by manipulation of equation (16.92). Again, updating estimates for the alignment is now a straightforward application of the theory.

Likewise, equation (16.92) provides a measurement model for the 18 shape parameters; it can be shown that each of these may be extracted independently of the others, permitting a model of the form

$$\mathbf{z} - \hat{\mathbf{X}} = \mathbf{h}_i\left(b_i - \hat{b}_i\right)$$

to be constructed, where $\mathbf{h}_i$ is an $N \times 1$ measurement matrix.

The Kalman filter is key to providing real-time performance in this application. Estimates of where the silhouette ought to be permit very localized search for edges in new frames, obviating the need for operations over the whole image. This operation is performed by determining the edge normal at the predicted position, and searching along it for the position of maximum contrast with the reference background. If no likely point is found (the contrast is low), 'no observation' is recorded and the associated predictions are not updated. This is particularly powerful since it permits the figure to suffer partial occlusion and still be tracked—this is illustrated by scenes with artificially introduced occlusion in Figure 16.27. This application is described in full detail, with various elaborations, in [Baumberg, 1995].

 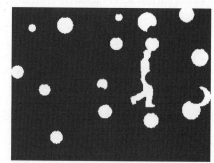

Figure 16.27: Tracking through occlusion. *Courtesy of A. M. Baumberg, University of Leeds.*

16.6.2 Particle filters

Kalman filters are an established piece of control theory and have proved very useful in aiding the tracking task. However, the underlying assumptions are limiting, and often restrict their use in real-world scenarios. Tracking through substantial noise and clutter in real-time (the requirement for many systems) is problematic: the assumption of local unimodal, Gaussian distributions is often invalid. Indeed, in many applications there will be no satisfactory approximation with an accessible mathematical representation. This has led to the application of a more general approach using **particle filters** in which systems are represented by sets of probabilistically derived samples that provide an empirical description of what is and is not 'likely'. Interestingly, this more general (and powerful) approach can be made to run satisfactorily in real-time, and has a more accessible analysis than the Kalman filter.

A particle filter approximates distributions by exploiting their temporal structure; in computer vision they were popularized mainly in the CONditional DENSity propagATION—**CONDENSATION**—algorithm [Isard and Blake, 1998], on which this presentation is based. Supposing a system to be in states $X_t = \{\mathbf{x}_1, \mathbf{x}_2, \ldots, \mathbf{x}_t\}$, where the subscript t denotes time, we may at time t have a probability density function telling us what $\mathbf{x}_t$ is likely to be. This will be represented by a set of **particles**—a set of sample states—whose occurrence will be governed by the p.d.f. As before, we will also have a sequence of observations $Z_t = \{\mathbf{z}_1, \mathbf{z}_2, \ldots, \mathbf{z}_t\}$ probabilistically related to the $\{\mathbf{x}_i\}$, and a Markovian assumption that $\mathbf{x}_t$ depends probabilistically on the preceding state $\mathbf{x}_{t-1}$, and that we can model this $P(\mathbf{x}_t|\mathbf{x}_{t-1})$. The important difference is that there is no constraint (in particular of linearity or Gaussian behavior) on any of these relations.

Condensation is an iterative procedure that maintains at each step a set of N samples $\mathbf{s}_i$ with associated weights π_i

$$S_t = \left\{ (\mathbf{s}_i, \pi_i) \right\}, \quad i = 1, 2, \ldots, N, \quad \sum_i \pi_i = 1,$$

$$= \left\{ (\mathbf{s}_{ti}, \pi_{ti}) \right\}. \tag{16.95}$$

Together, these samples and weights represent the probability density function of $\mathbf{x}_t$ given Z_t; this distribution is not expected to have a formulaic representation; in particular it may be multi-modal. The task is to derive S_t given S_{t-1}.

In order to generate N new samples and associated weights at time t, we select N times from S_{t-1} *taking account of the weights*, subject the sample to the Markov assumption (whatever it might be), and then re-weight the result in the light of the known observation $\mathbf{z}_t$. Formally:

Algorithm 16.8: Condensation (particle filtering)

1. Assume a weighted sample set at time $t - 1$ is known

$$S_{t-1} = \left\{ (\mathbf{s}_{(t-1)i}, \pi_{(t-1)i}) \right\}, \quad i = 1, 2, \ldots, N.$$

Set

$$c_0 = 0,$$
$$c_i = c_{i-1} + \pi_{(t-1)i}, \quad i = 1, 2, \ldots, N, \tag{16.96}$$

(the cumulative probabilities).

2. To determine the nth sample of S_t, select a random number in the range $[0,1]$, and determine $j = \operatorname{argmin}_i(c_i > r)$; we shall propagate sample j. This is called *importance sampling*, a sampling technique that weights towards the more probable.

3. *Prediction* (Figure 16.26): Use knowledge of the Markovian behavior of $\mathbf{x}_t$ to derive $\mathbf{s}_{tn}$. How precisely this is done depends upon the Markov relationship: in the Kalman case, we would have

$$\mathbf{s}_{tn} = A_{t-1}\mathbf{s}_{(t-1)j} + \mathbf{w}_{t-1}$$

for matrices A_{t-1} and noise $\mathbf{w}_{t-1}$, but this relationship is not constrained. Importantly, note that $\mathbf{s}_{(t-1)j}$ may well be selected more than once as we iterate from (2), but this propagation may be expected to generate different $\mathbf{s}_{tn}$ as a result of the noise.

4. *Correction* (Figure 16.26): Use the current observation $\mathbf{z}_t$ and knowledge of the observation probabilities to set

$$\pi_{tn} = p(\mathbf{z}_t|\mathbf{x}_t = \mathbf{s}_{tn})\,.$$

5. Iterate N times from (2).

6. Normalize $\{\pi_{ti}\}$ so that $\sum_i \pi_{ti} = 1$.

7. Our best estimate of $\mathbf{x}_t$ will now be

$$\mathbf{x}_t = \sum_{i=1}^{N} \pi_{ti}\,\mathbf{s}_{ti} \tag{16.97}$$

or, more generally for any moment

$$E\big[f(\mathbf{x}_t)\big] = \sum_{i=1}^{N} \pi_{ti}\,f(\mathbf{s}_{ti})\,.$$

This algorithm can model arbitrarily complex p.d.f.'s, allowing it to maintain an arbitrary number of hypotheses simultaneously. Eventually we might expect the data evolution to reduce this to a smaller number until a single one survives.

A simple example might illustrate: suppose we have a 1D process so x_t and z_t are just real numbers. Suppose at time t that x_t is subject to a known displacement v_t (perhaps v_t is constant, or x_t exhibits simple harmonic motion), corrupted by zero-mean normally distributed noise

$$x_{t+1} = x_t + v_t + \epsilon_t\,, \quad \epsilon_t \text{ distributed as } N(0, \sigma_1^2)$$

and further suppose that z_t is observed through some blur, such that z may be expected to be normally distributed about x with variance σ_2^2. Condensation would operate by initializing N 'guesses' at x_1, $S_1 = \{s_{11}, s_{12}, \ldots, s_{1N}\}$; in the absence of any other information the initial weights may be uniform.

Now S_2 is generated: select s_j from S_1 by importance sampling (whatever the values of π_{1i}), and set $s_{21} = s_j + v_1 + \epsilon$, where ϵ is drawn from $N(0, \sigma_1^2)$—repeat this N times to generate the particles for $t = 2$. Now set

$$\pi_{2i} = \exp\left(\frac{(s_{2i} - z_2)^2}{\sigma_2^2}\right)$$

then renormalize the π_{2i} and the iteration is complete. The best guess for x_2 is

$$\sum_{i=1}^{N} \pi_{2i} \, s_{2i} \; .$$

This example is trivial: in most applications, we would not expect $\mathbf{x}$ and $\mathbf{z}$ to belong to the same domain (as they do here): commonly, $\mathbf{x}$ might be a parameterized boundary (or part), while $\mathbf{z}$ might be a local pixel property, perhaps an intensity gradient [Isard and Blake, 1998]. $p(\mathbf{z}|\mathbf{x})$ will then measure the probability of the local observed pixel effects $\mathbf{z}$ given a certain parameter choice $\mathbf{x}$.

A more sophisticated example will illustrate better how this algorithm may be used in practice. Black and Jepson [Black and Jepson, 1998] consider the problem of recognizing gestures written on a whiteboard—this implies tracking the hand making the gesture and comparing its trajectory to a number of known models (there are nine, of varying complexity). A simplification of this application follows: one of these trajectories is a sequence of x, y velocities sampled uniformly in time;

$$\mathbf{m} = \big\{ (\dot{x}_0, \dot{y}_0), (\dot{x}_1, \dot{y}_1), \ldots (\dot{x}_N, \dot{y}_N) \big\} \; .$$

(For clarity, we will omit the dots henceforward.) These models may be built in a number of ways—perhaps derived from the mean of a training set.

An input to the system at any instant will be a *partial* (as yet incomplete) trace—to match it we require to know:

ϕ: The position (phase) within the model that aligns it with the current input; that is, how much of the model has been executed to date.

α: An amplitude scaling factor, indicating how much taller (or shorter) the input is with respect to the model.

ρ: A temporal scaling factor, indicating how much faster (or slower) the input is being provided with respect to the model.

A state of the system (which we will be propagating via Condensation) is then $\mathbf{s} = (\phi, \alpha, \rho)$: given an observed trajectory Z_t and a state $\mathbf{s}$, we can transform $Z_t = (\mathbf{z}_1, \mathbf{z}_2, \ldots, \mathbf{z}_t)$ to be a partial model. We will seek to match these observations to a recent time window w wide.

The probability of this observation, given the state $\mathbf{s}$, will be

$$P(\mathbf{z}_t|\mathbf{s}) = P(z_t^x|\mathbf{s}) \times P(z_t^y|\mathbf{s}) \, ,$$

where

$$P(z_t^x|\mathbf{s}) = \frac{1}{\sqrt{2\pi}\,\sigma_x} \exp\left(\frac{-\sum_{j=0}^{w-1}(z_{t-j}^x - \alpha\,m_{\phi-\rho j}^x)^2}{2\,\sigma_x(w-1)}\right)$$

and $P(z_t^y|\mathbf{s})$ similarly. σ_x and σ_y are estimates of the standard deviations of the relevant measurements.

1000 samples were initialized randomly with $\alpha \in [0.7, 1.3]$ and $\rho \in [0.7, 1.3]$. ϕ is initialized to be 'small' and the initial weights can be set to be uniformly $1/1000$. The Markovian relationships are

$$\phi_t = \phi_{t-1} + \rho_{t-1} + \epsilon_\phi\,, \quad \epsilon_\phi = N(0, \sigma_\phi)\,,$$
$$\alpha_t = \alpha_{t-1} + \epsilon_\alpha\,, \quad\quad \epsilon_\alpha = N(0, \sigma_\alpha)\,,$$
$$\rho_t = \rho_{t-1} + \epsilon_\rho\,, \quad\quad \epsilon_\rho = N(0, \sigma_\rho)\,;$$

$\sigma_\phi = \sigma_\alpha = \sigma_\rho = 0.1$ has been seen to work.

The Condensation algorithm has proved very popular in a number of examples—Figure 1.3 shows just one example. A number of enhancements have been developed: a particular issue has been the tracking of multiple objects, when the computational load of the algorithm starts to become prohibitive, and also independent trackers are prone to coalescing on the strongest evidence they find (the most evident object). Solutions to this problem have appeared as partitioned sampling [MacCormick and Blake, 1999]. Khan et al. [Khan et al., 2005] consider the interesting problem of tracking multiple objects that are interacting, using a Markov chain Monte Carlo [MCMC] approach, and this is enhanced by French [French, 2006] in modeling 'co-operative' agents, in this case flocking ducks. Interaction between the agents moving in the scene provides new information and constraints on the expected (relative) motion that can be used to advantage.

16.6.3   Semi-supervised tracking—TLD

The area of tracking has proved extremely fertile, both in application and in theoretical (and practical) depth. The appetite for real-time tracking is enormous and already the list of active areas is very long. For example, consider vision-based gesture recognition: this is an area in which techniques such as those discussed here are proving very fertile in assisting real-time interpretation of gesture by the user in unconstrained office scenes (that is, very cluttered); it should be easy to see how robust solutions to this problem would have very far-reaching effects on computer interfaces for users everywhere. (A snapshot of the state of this activity in 2006 is in [Gibet et al., 2006]).

While a number of powerful trackers have been developed, most are limited by problems surrounding training, appearance change and handling intermittent occlusion or disappearance. Any success implies the incorporation of a *detector* to spot the reappearance of an object, which in turn implies the pre-training of the detector. The detector would need adapt to object appearances not yet encountered, usually achieved by adaptive tracking—but if the tracker 'loses' the object, adaptive updates to the detector may worsen rather than improve matters.

Predator is a successful tracker designed to overcome these difficulties [Kalal et al., 2009] (from which this description is adapted) that simultaneously tracks, learns and detects: for this reason the framework is often referred to as **TLD**. Suppose we have an image sequence $I_0, I_1, \ldots$, and are given the bounding box B_0 of an object at time $t = 0$:

we seek the bounding boxes of the object $B_1, B_2, \ldots$ at subsequent times. The sequence B_t represents the trajectory of the object T_t—it is probable that we will describe the object in a feature space U, in which we will call the trajectory T_t^f. An unknown subset of $L^* \subset U$ represents all possible appearances of the object; at time $t = 0$ we know exactly one element $x_0 \in L^*$.

Now suppose a tracker is implemented (the Lucas-Kanade approach of Section 16.3.2 is usually used); for small values of t this will permit (probably) reasonable growth $L_1, L_2, \ldots$ toward L^*, but if the tracker loses accuracy then L_t will start to incorporate poor or wrong instances of the model.

At a general time t we will expect L_t to include some correct model instances L_t^c, and some incorrect ones L_t^e;

$$L_t = L_t^c \cup L_t^e, \;\; L_t^c \subset L^*, \;\; L_t^e \cap L^* = \emptyset$$

L_t is derived from L_{t-1} by two processes:

- Growing: the trajectory to date T_t^f is evaluated and the subset P that is considered to be positive identified; then we set $L_t = L_{t-1} \cup P$.

- Pruning: a subset N of L_{t-1} is estimated that contains incorrect instances of the model, and we set $L_t = L_{t-1} - N$.

The success or otherwise of this simple idea depends of course on the tracker, and the quality of the estimates of P and N.

The original implementation used the Lucas-Kanade tracker to estimate frame-to-frame bounding box movement and scale change, and represented the model by 15×15 intensity-normalized patches. We can then compute the normalized cross correlation between two patches as $NCC(x_i, x_j)$, and take the distance between them to be $d((x_i, x_j) = 1 - NCC(x_i, x_j)$. The distance of a patch x_i from L_t is defined as

$$d(x_i, L_t) = min_{x \in L_t} d(x_i, x).$$

The detector has exacting demands: it needs to be very fast, to learn fast, and to perform well on limited training data. Unlike other 'dynamic' algorithms that adapt to new instances and 'forget' older ones, it needs to retain all it has learned. The original approach used is a simplification of local binary patterns (Section 15.1.6) called a 2-bit binary classifier (2bitBP): each patch generates a number of such 2-bit responses and a random forest classifier is trained from them (see Section 9.9). These choices satisfy the requirements of the algorithm but are not critical to it.

Likewise, the precise implementation of growing and pruning need to be chosen. The first implementation did this by:

Growing: A threshold θ is chosen. If the distance of x_i to L_t is less than this threshold, *and* for some $j > i$, x_j is also less than θ to L_t, then all x_k, $i < k < j$ are added to the model. The reasoning is that if a tracker drifts off the model, it is unlikely to return; but if it does return, the deviation from the model is probably better explained by change in appearance of the tracked object.

Pruning: If the assumption is made that an object appears in the image at most once, then if the tracker and detector agree on object locations, all alternative detections are marked as false positives and pruned.

TLD is a framework or paradigm, and the choices itemized above pertain to the Predator instance (its first). At a high level, the algorithm is:

Algorithm 16.9: Tracking-Learning-Detection—TLD

1. Initialize a model with a correct instance x_0: $L_0 = x_0$. (This may be done by a user outlining a bounding box in the first frame of a sequence.)

2. At time t, track x_{t-1} into the current frame.

3. Detect all instances of L_{t-1} in the current frame.

4. Determine the positive examples P and grow, and determine the negative examples N and prune: $L_t = L_{t-1} \cup P - N$.

5. Set x_t to be the most confident patch: this may be the result of tracking or detection.

6. Set $t = t + 1$ and go to 2.

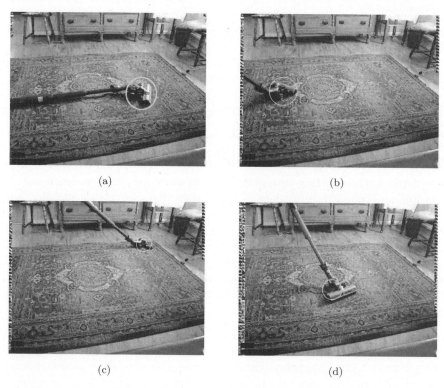

(a)   (b)

(c)   (d)

Figure 16.28: Predator: This simple example illustrates successful tracking of the head of a vacuum cleaner. (a) Initialization, done by hand; (b) Movement across a very challenging background (the rug), and change of pose; (c) Another change of pose and significant change of scale; (d) Further change of scale and significant change of pose—note only the leftmost part of the machine (that was originally visible) is being tracked. © *Cengage Learning 2015.*

The TLD resource page http://info.ee.surrey.ac.uk/Personal/Z.Kalal/tld.html contains a good account of this algorithm, together with demonstration software and data, and source codes. An example, produced with this software, is shown in Figure 16.28; illustrations of the tracker surviving occlusion and disappearance of targets may be viewed online. TLD has received close study since its development, together with formal justification of its behavior—see, for example, [Kalal et al., 2010, 2012].

16.7 Summary

- **Motion analysis**

    - Motion analysis is dealing with three main groups of motion-related problems:
        * Motion detection
        * Moving object detection and location
        * Derivation of 3D object properties

    - A two-dimensional representation of a (generally) three-dimensional motion is called a **motion field** wherein each point is assigned a **velocity vector** corresponding to the motion direction, velocity, and distance from an observer at an appropriate image location.

    - Motion analysis and object tracking combine two separate but interrelated components:
        * Localization and representation of the object of interest (target).
        * Trajectory filtering and data association.
        * One or the other may be more important based on the nature of the motion application.

    - **Optical flow** represents one approach to motion field construction, in which motion direction and motion velocity are determined at possibly all image points.

    - **Feature point correspondence** is another method for motion field construction. Velocity vectors are determined only for corresponding feature points.

    - Object **motion parameters** can be derived from computed motion field vectors.

    - **Motion assumptions** can help to localize moving objects. Frequently used assumptions include:
        * Maximum velocity
        * Small acceleration
        * Common motion
        * Mutual correspondence

- **Differential motion analysis**

    - Subtraction of images acquired at different instants in time makes motion detection possible, assuming a stationary camera position and constant illumination.

- There are many problems associated with this approach, and results of subtraction are highly dependent on an object–background contrast.

- A **cumulative difference image** improves performance of differential motion analysis. It provides information about motion direction and other time-related motion properties, and about slow motion and small object motion.

- Detecting **moving edges** helps further overcome the limitations of differential motion analysis methods. By combining the spatial and temporal image gradients, the differential analysis can be reliably used for detection of slow-moving edges as well as detection of weak edges that move with higher speed.

- **Optical flow**

  - Optical flow reflects the image changes due to motion during a time interval dt which must be short enough to guarantee small inter-frame motion changes.

  - The optical flow field is the velocity field that represents the three-dimensional motion of object points across a two-dimensional image.

  - Optical flow computation is based on two assumptions:
    * The observed brightness of any object point is constant over time.
    * Nearby points in the image plane move in a similar manner (the **velocity smoothness** constraint).

  - Optical flow computation will be in error if the constant brightness and velocity smoothness assumptions are violated. In real imagery, their violation is quite common. Typically, the optical flow changes dramatically in highly textured regions, around moving boundaries, at depth discontinuities, etc. Resulting errors propagate across the entire optical flow solution.

  - Global error propagation is the biggest problem of global optical flow computation schemes, and local optical flow estimation helps overcome the difficulties.

  - Optical flow analysis does not result in motion trajectories; instead, more general motion properties are detected that can significantly increase the reliability of complex motion analysis. Parameters that are detected include:
    * Mutual object velocity
    * Focus of expansion (FOE) determination
    * Distance (depth) determination
    * Collision prediction

- **Motion analysis based on correspondence of interest points**

  - This method finds significant points (**interest points, feature points**) in all images of the sequence—points least similar to their surroundings, representing object corners, borders, or any other characteristic features in an image that can be tracked over time.

  - The Lucas-Kanade tracker is widely used: it tracks robustly by solving a linear system, assuming local patches move similarly.

  - The KLT tracker uses the Lucas-Kanade approach to derive *automatically* points that are robust through an image [video] sequence.

    – Point detection is followed by a matching procedure, which looks for correspondences between these points in time.

    – The process results in a sparse velocity field.

    – Motion detection based on correspondence works even for relatively long interframe time intervals.

- **Detection of specific motion patterns**

    – Motion-specific information can be derived from training sets of examples. Distinguishing between different forms of motion and other phenomena can be achieved.

    – Image-based and short-term motion-based information are used simultaneously.

    – Motion detection uses a small set of simple rectangular filters that work at any scale; motion is detected by detecting temporal differences in corresponding image blocks. The small set of filters is selected from a large set of filters using the AdaBoost approach.

- **Video tracking**

    – Background modeling

        * Tracking in video is often based on some sort of subtraction of the current frame from a model of the background scene.

        * Naive approaches are subject to noise and subtle background evolution. Median filtering is the strongest such simple technique.

        * Much more robust approaches exist: prominent among them is to model each pixel as mixture of Gaussians. Parameter update is done in real time with heuristic approximation.

    – Kernel-based tracking

        * Gradient-based object localization and tracking can be accomplished using a general correlation criterion.

        * Kernel-based tracking is highly efficient and facilitates tracking in real time.

        * It is based on spatially masking the target object with an isotropic kernel, followed by applying a smooth similarity function, which reduces the tracking problem to a maximum similarity search in the vicinity of the previous location.

        * The similarity optimization is performed using the mean shift algorithm.

    – Object path analysis

        * If several independently moving objects are tracked, the solution methods often rely on motion constraints and minimize a **path coherence function** that represents a measure of agreement between the derived object trajectory and the motion constraints.

- **Motion models**

  - A predictor-corrector mechanism may be used to estimate object movement through observed noise, and then correct the prediction.

  - **Kalman filtering**

    * Kalman filtering is an approach that is frequently used in dynamic estimation and represents a powerful tool when used for motion analysis.

    * Kalman filtering requires the system to be linear, with observations of it to be linear functions of the underlying state. Noise, both in the system and in measurement, is assumed to be white and Gaussian.

    * While the assumptions are often unrealistic if applied to image sequences, they represent a convenient choice.

  - **Particle filtering**

    * The Kalman filter is widely implemented but has limiting assumptions. Particle filters overcome many of these.

    * Particle filter are based on a statistical sampling approach at each time step; the sample is adjusted on the basis of image observation.

    * The popular realization of a particle filter in vision is CONDENSATION.

  - **Track-learn-detect—TLD**

    * Most trackers are limited by pose changes, occlusion etc.

    * Many trackers will include a *detector* to (re-)discover objects on appearance in an image.

    * TLD tracks and detects simultaneously, and updates its learning of an object model dynamically too.

    * It operates at a range of scales, and usually builds on the Lucas-Kanade point tracker.

    * While tracking, the model absorbs new appearances, and prunes out those that are regarded as improbable.

16.8   Exercises

Short-answer questions

S16.1 Describe the differences between motion detection and moving-object detection.

S16.2 Name the object motion assumptions, and explain their rationale.

S16.3 Explain how cumulative difference images can be used in motion analysis.

S16.4 What is the aperture problem? What are its consequences? How can this problem be overcome?

S16.5 What are the two basic assumptions used for optical flow computation. Are the assumptions realistic? What problems arise if they are violated?

S16.6 Describe two approaches that increase optical flow computation robustness when the optical flow assumptions are not valid.

S16.7 Specify how optical flow can be used to determine:

(a) Mutual velocity of an observer and an object

(b) The focus of expansion

(c) Distance of a moving object from the observer

(d) Possible collision of the object with an observer and time to collision

S16.8 Explain the image frame rate requirements for motion analysis using optical flow and motion analysis based on correspondence of interest points.

S16.9 Explain the concept of motion analysis based on correspondence of interest points. Why is the correspondence problem difficult?

S16.10 Determine properties of a path coherence function and explain how it can be used for object tracking.

S16.11 Explain how occlusion may be handled in object tracking. Why are phantom points needed?

Problems

Using a static camera, create image sequences consisting of ten image frames depicting one, three, and five moving objects on a non-homogeneous background (the sequence used in Figure 16.2 illustrates an example). These image sequence(s) will be used in the problems below.

P16.1 Develop a program for motion detection in the sequences you have created. If the approach is based on differential image analysis, pay special attention to automated threshold determination.

P16.2 Develop a program for motion analysis using cumulative difference images. Determine the trajectory of the moving objects.

P16.3 Develop a program for motion analysis using moving edges, and apply it to your image sequences.

P16.4 At time $t_0 = 0$, a point object is located at real-world coordinates $x_0, y_0, z_0 = (30, 60, 10)$ and is moving with a constant speed $(u, v, w) = (-5, -10, -1)$ towards the observer. Assuming unit focal distance of the optical system:

(a) Determine the location of the object at the image co-ordinates (x', y') at time t_0.

(b) Determine the image co-ordinates of the focus of expansion.

(c) Determine the time of the object collision with the observer.

P16.5 Develop and test a function for detection of interest points.

P16.6 Develop a program for motion analysis using correspondence of interest points. Generate frame-to-frame velocity fields, not necessarily using the subsequent frames. Apply it to image sequences with one, three, and five moving objects and assess the results.

P16.7 Develop an image tracking program using path coherence, and use it to generate object motion trajectories.

P16.8 Implement the simple 1D example described after Algorithm 16.8 and run it with various parameter selections to observe Condensation in its simplest case.

P16.9 Download the TLD software from http://info.ee.surrey.ac.uk/Personal/Z.Kalal/tld.html and run it on a video selection of your own: discover how distorted or occluded the model may become before being lost.

P16.10 Make yourself familiar with solved problems and **Matlab** implementations of selected algorithms provided in the corresponding chapter of the **Matlab Companion** to this text [Svoboda et al., 2008]. The **Matlab Companion** homepage http://visionbook.felk.cvut.cz offers images used in the problems, and well-commented **Matlab** code is provided for educational purposes.

P16.11 Use the **Matlab Companion** [Svoboda et al., 2008] to develop solutions to additional exercises and practical problems provided there. Implement your solutions using **Matlab** or other suitable programming languages.

16.9 References

Aggarwal J. K. and Martin W. *Motion Understanding*. Kluwer, Boston, 1988.

Akbarzadeh A., Frahm J. M., Mordohai P., Clipp B., Engels C., Gallup D., Merrell P., Phelps M., Sinha S., Talton B., Wang L., Yang Q., Stewenius H., Yang R., Welch G., Towles H., Nister D., and Pollefeys M. Towards urban 3D reconstruction from video. In *Third International Symposium on 3D Data Processing, Visualization and Transmission (3DPVT)*, June 2006.

Albus J. S. and Hong T. H. Motion, depth, and image flow. In *Proceedings of the 1990 IEEE International Conference on Robotics and Automation,* Cincinnati, OH, pages 1161–1170, Los Alamitos, CA, 1990. IEEE.

Baker S. and Matthews I. Lucas-kanade 20 years on: A unifying framework. *International Journal of Computer Vision*, 56:221–255, 2004.

Bar-Shalom Y. and Fortmann T. *Tracking and Data Association.* Academic Press, New York NY, 1988.

Barnard S. T. and Thompson W. B. Disparity analysis of images. *IEEE Transactions on Pattern Analysis and Machine Intelligence*, 2(4):333–340, 1980.

Barron J. L., Fleet D. J., and Beauchemin S. S. Performance of optical flow techniques. *International Journal of Computer Vision*, 12:43–77, 1994.

Bascle B. and Deriche R. Region tracking through image sequences. In *Proc. 5th Int. Conf. on Computer Vision*, pages 302–307, Cambridge, MA, 1995.

Baumberg A. M. *Learning deformable models for tracking human motion.* Ph.D. thesis, School of Computer Studies, University of Leeds, Leeds, UK, 1995.

Baumberg A. M. and Hogg D. C. An efficient method of contour tracking using active shape models. In *Proceedings of the IEEE Workshop on Motion on Non-rigid and Articulated Objects*, pages 194–199, Texas, 1994a.

Baumberg A. M. and Hogg D. C. Learning flexible models from image sequences. In Eklundh J. O., editor, *3rd European Conference on Computer Vision*, Stockholm, Sweden, pages 299–308, Berlin, 1994b. Springer Verlag.

Beutel J., Kundel H. L., and Metter R. L. V. *Handbook of Medical Imaging, Volume 1. Physics and Psychophysics.* SPIE, Bellingham, WA, 2000.

Bigun J., Granlund G. H., and Wiklund J. Multidimensional orientation estimation with applications to texture analysis and optical flow. *IEEE Transactions on Pattern Analysis and Machine Intelligence*, 13:775–790, 1991.

Black M. J. and Jepson A. D. Recognizing temporal trajectories using the condensation algorithm. In Yachida M., editor, *Proceedings of the 3rd International Conference on Face and Gesture Recognition,* Nara, Japan, pages 16–21. IEEE Computer Society, 1998.

Bober M. and Kittler J. Estimation of complex multimodal motion: An approach based on robust statistics and Hough transform. *Image and Vision Computing*, 12:661–668, 1994.

Briggs W. L., Henson V. E., and McCormick S. F. *A Multigrid Tutorial*. SIAM, Philadelphia, PA, 2nd edition, 2000.

Bruhn A., Weickert J., Feddern C., Kohlberger T., and Schnoerr C. Combining advantages of local and global optic flow methods. In Gool L. v, editor, *Pattern Recognition - LNCS Vol. 2449*, pages 454–462, Berlin, 2002. Springer.

Bruhn A., Weickert J., Feddern C., Kohlberger T., and Schnoerr C. Variational optic flow computation in real-time. *IEEE Transactions on Image Processing*, 14:608–615, 2005.

Cedras C. and Shah M. Motion-based recognition: A survey. *Image and Vision Computing*, 13: 129–154, 1995.

Comaniciu D., Ramesh V., and Meer P. Real-time tracking of non-rigid objects using mean shift. In *Proc. IEEE Conf. on Computer Vision and Pattern Recognition, vol. II*, pages 142–149, Hilton Head Island, SC, 2000.

Comaniciu D., Ramesh V., and Meer P. Kernel-based object tracking. *IEEE Transactions on Pattern Analysis and Machine Intelligence*, 25:564–575, 2003.

Cummins D. D. and Cummins R. *Minds, Brains and Computers - The Foundations of Cognitive Science: An Anthology*. Blackwell Publishing, 2000.

Cutler R. and Davis L. Robust real-time periodic motion detection. *IEEE Transactions on Pattern Analysis and Machine Intelligence*, 22:781–796, 2000.

Dee H. M., Hogg D. C., and Cohn A. G. Building semantic scene models from unconstrained video. *Computer Vision and Image Understanding*, 116(3):446–456, 2012.

Djouadi A., Snorrason O., and Garber F. The quality of training-sample estimates of the Bhattacharyya coefficient. *IEEE Transactions on Pattern Analysis and Machine Intelligence*, 12:92–97, 1990.

Enkelmann W. Obstacle detection by evaluation of optical flow fields from image sequences. *Image and Vision Computing*, 9(3):160–168, 1991.

Eustice R., Singh H., Leonard J., Walter M., and Ballard R. Visually navigating the RMS Titanic with SLAM information filters. In *Proceedings of Robotics: Science and Systems*, Cambridge, USA, June 2005.

Fisher D. J., Ehrhardt J. C., and Collins S. M. Automated detection of noninvasive magnetic resonance markers. In *Computers in Cardiology,* Chicago, IL, pages 493–496, Los Alamitos, CA, 1991. IEEE.

Fleet D. J. and Jepson A. D. Computation of component image velocity from local phase information. *International Journal of Computer Vision*, 5:77–105, 1990.

Freeman W. T. and Adelson E. H. The design and use of steerable filters. *IEEE Transactions on Pattern Analysis and Machine Intelligence*, 13:891–906, 1991.

French A. P. *Visual Tracking: from an individual to groups of animals*. Ph.D. thesis, University of Nottingham, 2006.

Fua P. and Leclerc Y. G. Registration without correspondences. In *CVPR '94: Computer Society Conference on Computer Vision and Pattern Recognition,* Seattle, WA, pages 121–128, Los Alamitos, CA, 1994. IEEE.

Gauss K. F. *Theoria motus corporum coelestium in sectionibus conicis solem ambientium.* F Perthes and I H Besser, Hamburg, Germany, 1809.

Gelb A., editor. *Applied Optimal Estimation*. MIT Press, Cambridge, MA, 1974.

Gescheider G. A. *Psychophysics: The Fundamentals*. LEA, 3rd edition, 1997.

Gibet S., Courty N., and Kamp J., editors. *Gesture in Human-Computer Interaction and Simulation, 6th International Gesture Workshop, GW 2005, Berder Island, France, May 18-20, 2005, Revised Selected Papers*, volume 3881 of *LNCS*, 2006. Springer.

Glazer F. Multilevel relaxation in low level computer vision. In A R., editor, *Multiresolution Image Processing and Analysis*, pages 312–330. Springer Verlag, Berlin, 1984.

Gu H., Shirai Y., and Asada M. MDL-based segmentation and motion modeling in a long image sequence of scene with multiple independently moving objects. *IEEE Transactions on Pattern Analysis and Machine Intelligence*, 18:58–64, 1996.

Hager G. and Belhumeur P. Real-time tracking of image regions with changes in geometry and illumination. In *Proc. of IEEE Conf. on Computer Vision and Pattern Recognition*, pages 403–410, San Francisco, CA, 1996.

Horn B. K. P. *Robot Vision*. MIT Press, Cambridge, MA, 1986.

Horn B. K. P. and Schunk B. Determining optical flow. *Artificial Intelligence*, 17:185–204, 1981.

Hu X. and Ahuja N. Motion and structure estimation using long sequence motion models. *Image and Vision Computing*, 11:549–569, 1993.

Huang C. L. and Chen Y. T. Motion estimation method using a 3D steerable filter. *Image and Vision Computing*, 13:21–32, 1995.

Hummel R. and Sundareswaran. Motion parameter estimation from global flow field data. *IEEE Transactions on Pattern Analysis and Machine Intelligence*, 15:459–476, 1993.

Intille S. and Bobick A. Visual tracking using closed-worlds. In *5th International Conference on Computer Vision*, Boston, USA, pages 672–678, 1995.

Isard M. and Blake A. Condensation—conditional density propagation for visual tracking. *IJCV*, 29(1):5–28, 1998.

Jain R. Dynamic scene analysis using pixel–based processes. *Computer*, 14(8):12–18, 1981.

Jain R. Direct computation of the focus of expansion. *IEEE Transactions on Pattern Analysis and Machine Intelligence*, 5(1):58–64, 1983.

Jain R. Difference and accumulative difference pictures in dynamic scene analysis. *Image and Vision Computing*, 2(2):99–108, 1984.

Jain R., Martin W. N., and Aggarwal J. K. Segmentation through the detection of changes due to motion. *Computer Graphics and Image Processing*, 11:13–34, 1979.

Jain R., Kasturi R., and Schunck B. G. *Machine Vision*. McGraw-Hill, New York, 1995.

Julier S. and Uhlmann J. A new extension of the Kalman filter to nonlinear systems. In *Proceedings SPIE, Vol. 3068*, pages 182–193, Bellingham, WA, 1997. SPIE.

Kaernbach C., Schroger E., and Muller H. *Psychophysics Beyond Sensation: Laws and Invariants of Human Cognition*. LEA, 2003.

Kalal Z., Matas J., and Mikolajczyk K. Online learning of robust object detectors during unstable tracking. In *Proceedings of the IEEE On-line Learning for Computer Vision Workshop*, pages 1417–1424, 2009.

Kalal Z., Matas J., and Mikolajczyk K. P-n learning: Bootstrapping binary classifiers by structural constraints. In *CVPR*, pages 49–56, 2010.

Kalal Z., Mikolajczyk K., and Matas J. Tracking-learning-detection. *IEEE Trans. Pattern Anal. Mach. Intell.*, 34(7):1409–1422, 2012.

Kalman R. E. A new approach to linear filtering and prediction problems. *Transactions of the ASME—Journal of Basic Engineering*, 82:35–45, 1960.

Kearney J. K. and Thompson W. B. Bounding constraint propagation for optical flow estimation. In Aggarwal J. K. and Martin W., editors, *Motion Understanding*. Kluwer, Boston, 1988.

Kearney J. K., Thompson W. B., and Boley D. L. Optical flow estimation—an error analysis of gradient based methods with local optimization. *IEEE Transactions on Pattern Analysis and Machine Intelligence*, 9(2):229–244, 1987.

Khan Z., Balch T., and Dellaert F. Mcmc-based particle filtering for tracking a variable number of interacting targets. *IEEE Transactions on Pattern Analysis and Machine Intelligence*, 27(1):1805 – 1918, 2005.

Koenderink J. J. Optic flow. *Vision Research*, 26(1):161–180, 1986.

Lucas B. D. and Kanade T. An iterative image registration technique with an application to stereo vision. In *Proceedings of the 7th international joint conference on Artificial intelligence - Volume 2*, IJCAI'81, pages 674–679, San Francisco, CA, USA, 1981. Morgan Kaufmann Publishers Inc. URL http://dl.acm.org/citation.cfm?id=1623264.1623280.

MacCormick J. and Blake A. A probabilistic exclusion principle for tracking multiple objects. In *International Conference on Computer Vision,* Corfu, Greece, pages 572–578, 1999.

Magee D. R. Tracking multiple vehicles using foreground, background and motion models. *Image and Vision Computing*, 22(2):143–155, 2004.

Magee D. R. and Boyle R. D. Detecting Lameness using 'Re-sampling condensation' and 'Multi-stream Cyclic Hidden Markov Models'. *Image and Vision Computing*, 20(8):581–594, 2002.

McFarlane N. J. B. and Schofield C. P. Segmentation and tracking of piglets in images. *Machine Vision and Applications*, 8:187–193, 1995.

Nagel H. H. On the estimation of optical flow: Relations between different approaches and some new results. *Artificial Intelligence*, 33:299–324, 1987.

Needham C. J. and Boyle R. D. Tracking multiple sports players through occlusion, congestion and scale. In *Proc. British Machine Vision Conf.*, pages 93–102, 2001.

Negahdaripour S. and Ganesan V. Simple direct computation of the FOE with confidence measures. In *Proceedings, 1992 Computer Vision and Pattern Recognition,* Champaign, IL, pages 228–233, Los Alamitos, CA, 1992. IEEE.

Oliver N., Rosario B., and Pentland A. A Bayesian computer vision system for modeling human interactions. In Christensen H. I., editor, *Proceedings of ICVS99,* Gran Canaria, Spain, pages 255–272. Springer Verlag, 1999.

Power P. W. and Schoonees J. A. Understanding background mixture models for foreground segmentation. In Kenwright D., editor, *Proceedings, Imaging and Vision Computing New Zealand,* Auckland, NZ, 2002.

Puzicha J., Rubner Y., Tomasi C., and Buhmann J. Empirical evaluation of dissimilarity measures for color and texture. In *Proc. 7th Int. Conf. on Computer Vision*, pages 1165–1173, Kerkyra, Greece, 1999.

Rangarajan K. and Shah M. Establishing motion correspondence. *CVGIP – Image Understanding*, 54:56–73, 1991.

Ringach D. L. and Baram Y. A diffusion mechanism for obstacle detection from size-change information. *IEEE Transactions on Pattern Analysis and Machine Intelligence*, 16:76–80, 1994.

Scott G. L. *Local and Global Interpretation of Moving Images*. Pitman–Morgan Kaufmann, London–San Mateo, CA, 1988.

Sethi I. K. and Jain R. Finding trajectories of feature points in a monocular image sequence. *IEEE Transactions on Pattern Analysis and Machine Intelligence*, 9(1):56–73, 1987.

Shapiro V., Backalov I., and Kavardjikov V. Motion analysis via interframe point correspondence establishment. *Image and Vision Computing*, 13:111–118, 1995.

Shi J. and Tomasi C. Good features to track. *Computer Vision and Pattern Recognition*, pages 593–600, 1994.

Sorenson H. W. Least-squares estimation: from Gauss to Kalman. *IEEE Spectrum*, pages 7–12, 1970.

Stauffer C. and Grimson W. E. L. Adaptive background mixture models for real-time tracking. In *CVPR '99: Computer Society Conference on Computer Vision and Pattern Recognition*, Ft. Collins, USA, volume 2, pages 246–252, 1999.

Subbarao M. *Interpretation of Visual Motion: A Computational Study*. Pitman–Morgan Kaufmann, London–San Mateo, CA, 1988.

Subbarao M. Bounds on time-to-collision and rotational component from first-order derivatives of image flow. *Computer Vision, Graphics, and Image Processing*, 50(3):329–341, 1990.

Svoboda T., Kybic J., and Hlavac V. *Image Processing, Analysis, and Machine Vision: A MATLAB Companion*. Thomson Engineering, 2008.

Thompson W. B. and Barnard S. T. Lower level estimation and interpretation of visual motion. *Computer*, 14(8):20–28, 1981.

Thompson W. B., Mutch K. M., and Berzins V. A. Dynamic occlusion analysis in optical flow fields. *IEEE Transactions on Pattern Analysis and Machine Intelligence*, 7(4):374–383, 1985.

Thompson W. B., Lechleider P., and Stuck E. R. Detecting moving objects using the rigidity constraint. *IEEE Transactions on Pattern Analysis and Machine Intelligence*, 15:162–166, 1993.

Trottenberg U., Oosterlee C., and Schueller A. *Multigrid*. Academic Press, Dan Diego, CA, 2001.

Tsao A. T., Hung T. P., Fuh C. S., and Chen Y. S. Ego-motion estimation using optical flow fields observed from multiple cameras. In *Computer Vision and Pattern Recognition*, pages 457–462, Los Alamitos, CA, 1997. IEEE Computer Society.

Ullman S. *The Interpretation of Visual Motion*. MIT Press, Cambridge, MA, 1979.

Vega-Riveros J. F. and Jabbour K. Review of motion analysis techniques. *IEE Proceedings, Part I: Communications, Speech and Vision*, 136(6):397–404, 1989.

Viola P. and Jones M. Rapid object detection using a boosted cascade of simple features. In *Proceedings IEEE Conf. on Computer Vision and Pattern Recognition*, pages 511–518, Kauai, Hawaii, 2001. IEEE.

Viola P., Jones M., and Snow D. Detecting pedestrians using patterns of motion and appearance. In *Proc. Int. Conf. Computer Vision*, pages 734–741, Nice, France, 2003.

Watson A. B. and Ahumada A. J. Model of human-model sensing. *Journal of the Optical Society of America*, 2:322–342, 1985.

Weickert J. and Schnoerr C. A theoretical framework for convex regularizers in PDE-based computation of image motion. *International Journal of Computer Vision*, 45:245–264, 2001.

Wu S. F. and Kittler J. General motion estimation and segmentation. In *Visual Communications and Image Processing '90*, Lausanne, Switzerland, pages 1198–1209, Bellingham, WA, 1990. SPIE.

Young D. M. *Iterative Solution of Large Scale Linear Systems*. Academic Press, New York, NY, 1971.

Index

Symbols

2.5D sketch, 586–587, 655
2D co-ordinate system, 646
2D projection, 331, 332, 657, 670, 788
2D shape, 101, 329, 331
3D information, 329, 645
3D interpretation, 585, 646, 657, 658
3D model, 655
3D object, 655
3D representation, 13, 586, 656
3D shape, 101, 329, 332

A

A-algorithm, 197–204, 209
AAM, 492–502
aberrations, 86
accuracy, 241
ACRONYM, 474, 662
active appearance model, *see* AAM
active perception, 587
active sensor, 628
active shape model, *see* ASM
active vision, 648
acuity, 25
AdaBoost, 440–442, 513, 514, 516, 811–813
additive noise, 28
adjacency, 281
affinity, *see* fuzzy affinity
AGC, *see* automatic gain control
albedo, 94
aliasing, 63
anti-aliasing, 65
anti-extensive transformation, 691
aperture problem, 156, 793, 806
aperture stop, 84
arc (of a graph), 106

area, 103, 110, 337, 354–355, 358, 662, 684
area-based stereo, 624
ASM, 487–491
aspect, 670
aspect graph, 671
autocorrelation, 728
automatic gain control, 42
Autostitch, 479, 481

B

B-reps, 662
back-tracking, 208, 418, 424, 473, 530
background, 18
    uneven, 698
background modeling, 815, 820
ball, 700
    geodesic, 708
    maximal, 700
    unit, 700
balloon, 267
band-limited, 63
baseline, 610, 615
bay, 23
Bayes formula, 395, 504, 506–508
Bayesian belief networks, 551–552
bin-picking, 625
blackboard, 473
blocks world, 656
blooming, 41
blur
    atmospheric turbulence, 163
    Gaussian, 24, **140**, 145
    motion, 163
    smoothing, 125
    wrong focus, 163
body reflection, 31

boosting, 439–442, 513–517, 810–814
border, 21
    detection, **187**, 431
        optimal, **196–210**, 288, **295–303**
        simultaneous, 289
    extended, 193–195
    inner, 21, 191, 192
    inter-pixel, 193
    occlusion, 632
    outer, 21, 191–194
boundary, *see* border
BRDF, 93
brightness, **12**, 13, 90, 101, 118, 128, 358, 359, 506, 631, 750
    correction, 117
    interpolation, 123–124
    transformation, 117–120
brightness interpolation
    bi-cubic, 124
    linear, 124
    nearest neighbor, 123

C
C4.5, 442
CAD, 502
calculus, 133, 427, 684
calibration matrix, 600
camera, 11, 42, 101, 350, 353, 787, 788, 794
    analog, 42
    jitter, 42
Canny edge detector, 136, 144–147
canonical configuration, 615
CCD, 41
cellular complex, 19
center of gravity, 358, 371, 372
central limit theorem, 126
CFL condition, 280
chain, 104
    code, 104, 195, **336–339**, 344, 354
    Markov, 769
chamfering, 19, 235
Chan-Vese functional, 279
characteristic polynomial, 73
characteristic strip, 631
characteristic view, 670
class, 390

equivalence, 18
    identifier, 392
classification
    contextual, **505–509**, 530
        recursive, 507
classifier, 390, 417
    base, 439
    boosted
        cascade, 513–517, 810–814
    learning, 393, 396, **398–400**, 420
    linear, 392–393
    maximum likelihood, 395
    minimum distance, 393, 407
    minimum error, 395–400
    nearest neighbor, 393
    NN, 393
    non-linear, 392
    random forest, 442–448
        bagging, 446
        C4.5, 442
        classification, 442, 446
        decision making, 446
        ensemble model, 448
        information gain, 445
        manifold forest, 448
        manifold learning, 448
        predictor, 443
        regression, 442, 446
        semi-supervised forest, 448
        semi-supervised learning, 448
        stopping criterion, 446
        supervised learning, 448
        training, 444
        unsupervised learning, 448
    setting, 395, 397
    support vector machine, 400, 511
    syntactic, 417
    weak, 439, 513
clique, 424, 425
closing, 692–693
cluster analysis, 38, 406, 407
    fuzzy
        k-means, 407
    mean shift, 255, 261
CMOS, 41
CMY, 37
co-occurrence matrix, 102
co-ordinate system

object-based, 13, 655
polar, 336
rectangular, 335
tangential, 336, 337
COBIUS, 473
code
dictionary, 730, 734
Freeman, 104
leaf, 111
run length, 105
coding
Huffman, 733, 734
low and high frequencies, 733
region border, 733
collineation, 592
color
constancy, 39
gamut, 34
hue, 37
image, 30
L,u,v, 259
map, 38
metamer, 32
model, 33
palette, 734
perceived, 259
primary, 30
saturation, 37
secondary, 36
table, 38
value, 37
YIQ, 36
YUV, 37
combination
convex, 34
linear, 51
compatibility function, **525**, 536, 537
compression, 5, 7, 236, 722–740
application
asymmetric, 730, 739
symmetric, 730, 739
dictionary-based, 734
DPCM, **728**, 730
fractal, 733
hierarchical, 730–732
hybrid, 722, 730, 731, **732**
JPEG, 734–736
JPEG-2000, 736–738

Lempel-Ziv, 734
MJPEG, 736, 738, 739
MJPEG-2000, 738
motion JPEG, *see* MJPEG, compression
MPEG, 734, 738–740
predictive, 722, **727–728**, 732
progressive, 730–732
pyramid, 730
ratio, **724**, 727, 728, 731
region growing, 733
scalability
quality, 736
resolution, 736
spatial, 736
smart, 731, 732
transform, 722, **724**, 732
vector quantization, **730**, 732
wavelet, 727
computer aided diagnosis, 502
computer graphics, 13, 101, 346, 772
Condensation, 831, **837–840**
cone, 32
confidence, 507–539
configuration
canonical, 615
degenerate, 595
rectified, 615
conic, 351, 352
connected component labeling, 333
connectedness, *see* fuzzy connectedness
connectivity
eight, 19
four, 18
fuzzy, 280–288
problems, 19
constraint
propagation, **524–528**, 531, 532, 657
constructive solid geometry, 660
context, 178, 465, 469, **505–524**, 531, 532
contiguous
multiple, 18
simple, 18
contour
false, 15
partitioning, 344

contrast, **25**, 118, 157, 188, 232, 753, 754, 791
control strategy, 386, **465–474**
 bottom-up, 205, 385, **467–468**, 469, 471, 527
 combined, 469
 hierarchical, 466, 472
 model-based, 468, 470
 non-hierarchical, 472
 parallel, 466, 468
 serial, 466
 top-down, 467–469, 471
convex hull, 22, 684
convex region, 22
convolution, **51**, 123, 148, 149
 discrete, 52
 mask, 52, 125
 theorem, 59
coordinate system
 object-based, 587
corner, 156
 definition, 156
 detector, 147, 155, 156
  Harris, 157, 805
  Moravec, 157, 805
correction, gamma, 42
correlation, 80, 348, 722–724, 727
 projective, 611
correspondence, 121, 156, 621, 645, 646, 788–790, 804, 807–809, 829
 correlation-based, 624
 feature-based, 625
 landmark, 490, 497
 point, 490, 497
 problem, 156, 626, 645, 646
 time, 498
cost function, 197–204, 311
 automated design, 210
 edge based, 311–312
 Gibbs model, 296
 region based, 279, **312–313**
cost transform, 202, 210
covariance matrix, 75
crack edge, 21
criterion
 detection, 144
 localization, 144
 one response, 144

cross ratio, 350
crossover, 428–430
curvature, 337
 deformation, 274
 peak, 345
 primal sketch, 346
curve
 decomposition, 346
 detection, 212, 214–216, 218
 digital straight segment, 337, 343
 DSS, 337
 granulometric, 711
cyclopean image, 626
cyclopean separation, 626

D

data structure, 100
 hierarchical, 108
 relational, 107
 traditional, 101
de-fuzzification, 435, 438
 composite maximum, 438
 composite moments, 438
decimation, 664
decision rule, 392, 398
deficit of convexity, 23
deformable objects, 655
deformation
 constant, 274
 curvature, 274
degenerate configuration, 595
degradation, 163
 atmospheric turbulence, 163
 relative motion, 163
 wrong lens focus, 163
depth, 13, 651
 of field, 85
 of focus, 84
depth map, 586, 628, 650
diagram, Voronoi, 531
Dice evaluation, 237
difference of Gaussians, *see* DoG
diffusion, generalized, 269
dilation, 688–689
 conditional, 714
 geodesic, 708
 gray-scale, 694–697
Dirac distribution, 51

discrete convolution, 52
discrimination function, 392, 396
disparity, 555, 616, 626
    gradient, **625**, 626
    gradient limit, 625
distance, 17
    chessboard (D_8), 17
    city block (D_4), 17
    Euclidean (D_E), 17
    function, 19, 707, 717
    geodesic, 707
    Hausdorff, 238
    Levenshtein, 425
    Mahalanobis, 407
    Sampson, 597
    transform, 19
distribution function, 80
DoG, 141, 474
domain
    range, 260
    spatial, 260
DSS, 343
duality, 591
duality, morphological, 686
dyadic, 69
dynamic programming, 206–210
    intelligent scissors, 209, 268
    live lane, 210
    live wire, 209, 268

E
Ebbinghaus illusion, 26
edge, 5, 7, **21**, 586
    chain, 187, 205
    crack, 21, 191, 193, 222, 223
    detector, 431
    direction, 134
    magnitude, 134
    relaxation, **190–191**, 205
edge detector, 133–143, 585
    Canny, 144–147, 755
    facet model, 147
    in multi-spectral image, 148
    Kirsch, 139
    Laplace, 135, 137
    Marr-Hildreth, 139
    parametric, 136, 147
    Prewitt, 137
    Roberts, 137
    Sobel, 138
    zero-crossing, 139
effect, blooming, 41
eigen-image, 76
eigenvalues
    multiple, 73
elastics, 468
EM, *see* expectation-maximization
entropy, **24**, 722–724, 754
    condition, 279
epipolar
    constraint, 606, 610, 611, **622**
    line, 610, 627
    plane, 610
epipolar constraint, 627
epipole, 610
equation
    irradiance, 95
erosion, 689–692
    geodesic, 708
    gray-scale, 694–697
    ultimate, 705
essential matrix, 612
estimation
    density, 255, 262
        gradient, 257
        mode, 258
    non-parametric, 257
estimator
    multivariate density, 256
Euler-Poincaré characteristic, 355
event (aspect), 671
exemplar, 393, 406, 412, 413
expansion
    isotropic, 688
expectation-maximization, 183, 548,
    556–564, 817

F
face detection, 442, 513, 514, 516
facet, 147
fast marching, 278
feature, 386
    cascade
        boosted, 513
    discriminativity, 397
    informativity, 397

simple, 513
space, 255, 391
  color, 259
synthesis, 146
vector, 386
feedback, 6, 188, 732
fill, morphological, 688
filter, 116–165
  bank, 765–767
  Gaussian, 586
  median, 130–132, 816
  particle, *see* particle filter
  separable, 127
filtering
  averaging, 125
  band-pass, 149, 150
  discontinuity preserving, 255
  discontinuity-preserving, 261
  high-pass, 149, 150
  inverse, 163
  Kalman, 162
  low-pass, 149
  mean shift, 255, 261
  median, 130
  Wiener, 164
fitness function, 535
focal point, 83, 598
Forward algorithm, 545
fractal, 348, 770
  dimension, 337, 762
frame, 390
free-form surface, 655
Freeman code, 104
Fresnel lens, 85
Frobenius norm, 615
front propagation, 273
function
  autocorrelation, 80
  autocovariance, 80
  continuous, 11
  cross correlation, 80, 841
  cross covariance, 80
  digital, 11
  Dirac, 51
  discrete, 11
  distance, 19, 707
  distribution, 80
  fitness, 535

kernel, 403
level set, 276
partition, 553
point spread, 53
quench (morphology), 704
speed, 274
functional
  Chan-Vese, 279
  Mumford-Shah, 279
fundamental matrix, 610
fuzzy
  adjacency, 281
  affinity, 281
  complement, 434
  composition, 435
    min–max, 436
  connectedness, 282
    absolute, 288
    hard-adjacency, 281
    map, 282
  connectivity, 280–288
    2-object, 286
    absolute, 282, 286
    iterative, 286
    multiple-object, 286
    relative, 286
    scale-based, 286
  correlation
    minimum, 436
    product, 437
  intersection, 434
  logic, 281, 388, 432–439
  membership function
    maximum normal form, 433
    minimum normal form, 433
  reasoning
    monotonic, 435
  set, 432
    hedge, 433
  space, 432
  system, 432–439
    model, 435
  union, 434

G
gamma correction, 42
gamut, 34
ganglion cell, 143

Gaussian filter, 140, 141, 586
Gaussian mixture models, 407, **556–564**, 762, 817–820
Gaussian noise, 28
generalized cylinders, 661
genetic algorithm, 427–430, 439, 535–542
genus, 355
geodesic transformation, 707
Geographical Information Systems, 111
geometric signals, 628
geometric transformation, 120–124
Gestaltist theory, 645
GIF, 734
GIS, 111
Golay alphabet, 702
gradient descent, 409, 494, 500, 548, 634
gradient operator, 125, 133–143
    approximated by differences, 135
    Kirsch, 139
    Laplace, 137
    Prewitt, 137
    Roberts, 137
    Sobel, 138
gradient space, 92
gradient vector flow, *see* snake
grammar, **387**, 414–420, 770–773
    context-free, 416
    context-sensitive, 416
    fuzzy, 417
    general, 416
    inference, 414, **420–421**
    non-deterministic, 417
    regular, 417
    stochastic, 417
granulometry (morphological), 711
graph, **106**, 193, 197, 206, 235, 353, 365, 387, 414, 418, 421–426
    arc, 106
    assignment, 425
    constraint
        hard, 296, 300, 303, 311, 317
        soft, 296, 311, 317
        surface separation, 309
    construction, 306
    geometric, 303
    graph cuts, 295–303
        seeds, 296

isomorphism, 421–426
    labeled, 389
    maximum flow, 295–303
        augmenting path, 298
        push-relabel, 298
        residual graph, 298
    minimum closed set, 310
    minimum s-t cut, **295–317**
    neighborhood, 372
    node, 106
    region, 365, 370
    region adjacency, 106, 112, 179, 223, 225, 372, 528, 531, 532, 535–538
    search, **196–203**, 209, **295–317**, 469, 470
        advanced approaches, 288
        heuristic, **199–205**, 209
        LOGISMOS, 303–317
        three-dimensional, 289
    similarity, 421, 425, 426
    weighted, 106, 193, 197, 421, 422
graph cut, 554
gray-scale transformation, 117
greedy exchange algorithm, 828
grid, 14
    hexagonal, 15
    square, 15
groundplane, 675
group, 349, 352
    Lie, 349
    plane-projective, 349
grow, morphological, 688
GVF, *see* snake

H
hanging togetherness, 281
Hausdorff distance, *see* distance, Hausdorff
HEARSAY, 474
heuristic, 199, 201, 204, 209, 222, 232, 531, 532, 542
hidden Markov model, **543–551**, 561, 831
    Baum-Welch algorithm, 548, 549, 563, 564
    coupled, 549–551
    decoding, 544, 546–548

evaluation, 544–545
forward algorithm, 545
Forward-Backward algorithm, 548, 563, 564
learning, 544, 548
second order, 549
Viterbi algorithm, 546, 548
hidden Markov tree, 768
histogram, **23**, 179, 181–183, 186, 221, 723, 724
bimodal, 182
cumulative, 119
equalization, 37, 118–120
multi-modal, 182
smoothed, 186
transformation, 183
histograms of oriented gradients, *see* HOG
hit-or-miss transformation, 692
HOG, 509
hole, 18
homogeneity, 220, 221, 224–232
homogeneous coordinates, 591
homography, 481, 592
homotopic substitute (of skeleton), 702, 703
homotopic transformation, 699
horizon, 652, 675
Hough transform, 210–217
HSV, 37
hue, 37
human visual system, 586
hypothesis, 468, 535–542
hypothesize and verify, 345, 373, **468**, 470, 535
hysteresis, 146, 188

I

ICP algorithm, 667
illumination, 90
image
binary, 102
co-ordinates, 13
color, 30
compression, *see* compression
cyclopean, 626
databases, 236
difference, 790–793
digitization, 14–16
dynamic, 14
element, 15, 281
function, 11
iconic, 101
indexed, 38
integral, 103, 513, 514, 812
interpretation, 465, 542
irradiance equation, 95
multispectral, 32
palette, 38
plane, 598
pre-processing, 116–165
pseudo-color, 38
quality, 27
reconstruction, 722–728, 731
rectification, 616, 617
registration, 156, 233, 561, 664
representation, 5
scale-space, 144, 345
segmented, 101
sharpening, 5, 135
skew, 122
static, 13
understanding, 8, **464–542**
random forest, 517–524
imaging modalities, 12
implementation, in Marr's theory, 585
importance sampling, 838
impossible objects, 658
impulse
Dirac, 51
limited, 64
increasing transformation, 689, 691
inference, 465
information entropy, 24
integral image, *see* image, integral
intelligent scissors, 209, 268
intensity image, 12, 13, 116, 139, 467, 633
interest point, 155, 156, 625
interpretation
genetic, 534, 535
tree, 530
interval tree, 144, 345
invariants, 332, 349, 350, 352
moment, 359
scalar, 350

inverse filtering, 163
inverse transformation, 692
irradiance, 4, 42, 90
    equation, 632
    spectral, 93
Ising model, 554
ISODATA, 407, 504
isotropic, 140, 151, 158, 690, 693, 789,
        820, 821, 845
isotropic expansion, 688
iteration
    Gauss-Seidel, 796, 800
    multigrid, 801

J
Jacobian determinant, 122
jitter, 42
Jordan block, 73
just-enough-interaction, 313

K
K-D tree, 394, 475, 730
K-means, **406**, 556, 559, 560
Kalman filter, 162, 831–837
    extended, 833
    unscented, 833
Kalman gain matrix, 832
kernel, 403
    bandwidth, 257
    Epanechnikov, 256, 257
    normal, 256
    polynomial
        homogeneous, 403
        non-homogeneous, 403
    radial basis function, 403
        Gaussian, 403
    trick, 403
Kinect, 517
knowledge, 6, 8, **386–390**, 428, 430
    a priori, 187, 188, 196, 211, 219, 225,
        331, 470, 473, 503, 532, 536,
        540
    base, 386–388
    procedural, 388
    representation, 386–390, 465

L
label, 333–335, 473, 503–509, 524–530,
        532, 533, 536–538

collision, 333, 335
labeling, 333, 354, 473, 504, 505, 507,
        508, **524–542**
    consistent, 524, 526
    discrete, **525**, 530
    probabilistic, 524, **527**
    semantic, 524
lacunarity, 763
Lagrange multipliers, 795
lake, 23
Lambertian surface, 94
landmarking, 490, 497
landmarks, 373
language, 414–420
Laplacian, 135, 586
Laplacian of Gaussian, 140
learning, **397–406**, 410, 415, 420, 430
    from experience, 465
    unsupervised, 406
least squares, 477
leave K out testing, 397
leave one out testing, 397
length
    focal, 84
lens
    Fresnel, 85
    telecentric, 85
    thick, 85
    thin, 83
level sets, 273–280
    fast marching, 278
    front propagation, 273
    narrow band, 278
LIDAR, 628
light, 117, 143
    source, 13, 631, 632
line
    finding, 155
    labeling, 656–658
    thinning, 155
linear combination, 51
linear system, 53
linearity, 50
linearly separable, 391
linguistic
    variable, 388, 434, 435
live lane, 210
live wire, 209, 268

local shading analysis, 634
location of interest, 155
LOGISMOS, 303–317
Lucas–Kanade point tracking, 234, 800, 805–807, 841
luminance, 37
luminous efficacy, 89
luminous flux, 89

M

magnification, 84
map
    cumulative edge, 146
    depth, 651
    edge, 486
    fuzzy connectedness, 282
    reflectance, 94, 633
    region, 106
marker, 713
Markov assumption, 837
Markov chain, 769
Markov model, 543
Markov Random Fields, *see* MRF
Marr (David), 8, 585
Marr's theory, 139, 467, 585–587, 656
Marr-Hildreth edge detector, 136, 139, 145
matching, 232–236, 426, 427, 465, 474–477
    chamfer, 235
    graphs, 421
    relational structures, 419
    subgraphs, 425
mathematical morphology, 369
matrix, 101
    calibration, 600
    co-occurrence, 102
    covariance, 75
    essential, 612
    fundamental, 610
    Jacobian, 494
    projection, 601
maximal ball, 700
MCMC, 840
MDL, 665, 829
mean shift, 255–262, 407
    basin of attraction, 258, 262
medial axis, 370

median, 130
memory
    long-term, 473
    short-term, 473
metric, 17, 822
Mexican hat, 141
Minkowski algebra, 688
model, 178, 203, 204, 217, 220, 464, 465, **467–473**, 534
    3D, 655
    active contour, **263–273**, 789
        geodesic, 273–280
        geometric, 273–280
        level set, 273–280
    deformable, 263, 273
        geometric, 273–280
        parametric, 273
    facet, 147, 155, 157
    quadric surface, 663
    surface, 655
    volumetric, 655, 658
Moiré interferometry, 630
moment
    invariant, 359
        affine, 359
    statistical, 57, 110
Moravec detector, 805
morphological transformation, 686
    quantitative, 687
morphology, 684–716, 768
mother wavelet, 67
motion, 644, 787–843
    analysis, 787–843
        correspondence of interest points, 788, 789, **804–829**
        differential, 789–793
    assumptions, 789, 826, 829
    continuous, 648
    correspondence of interest points, 830
    cyclic, 830
    description length, 829
    events, 830
    features, 830
    field, 788
    gesture interpretation, 830
    lipreading, 830
    path analysis, 826–830

path coherence, 826
    deviation, 826
    function, 826, 827
recognition, 830
relative, 830
rotational, 646, 648, 794
trajectory
    parameterization, 830
translational, 646, 648, 801, 803
verb recognition, 830
motion tracking, 814
MP4, 740
MRF, 295, 553–555, 761
multi-view representation, 670
multiple contiguous, 18
Mumford-Shah functional, 279
mutation, 428–430

N

nats, 560
nearest neighbor, *see* classifier, NN
Necker cube, 585
neighbor, 17
neural nets, 407–413, 439
    adaptive resonance theory, 412
    back-propagation, 409–410
    epoch, 410
    feed-forward nets, 409–410
    gradient descent, 409
    Hopfield, 407, **412–413**
    Kohonen networks, 407, **411–412**
    momentum, 410
    transfer function, 408
    unsupervised learning, 411–412
NN classifier, *see* classifier, NN
node (of a graph), 106
noise, 5, 7, 28, 330, 336, 339, 354, 359, 360, 369, 505
    additive, 28
    Gaussian, 28, 831, 832
    impulse, 30
    multiplicative, 30
    quantization, 30
    salt-and-pepper, 30
    white, 28, 831
non-maximal suppression, 145, 188
norm
    L2, 512

L2-Hys, 512
NTSC, 14
NURBS, 662

O

object, 18
    coloring, 333
    connected component labeling, 333
    description, 391
        formal, 391
        qualitative, 391, 413
        quantitative, 391, 413
        relational, 413
    identification, 333–335
    impossible, 658
    labeling, 333, 354
    recognition, 385–431, 474
    reconstruction, 329, 330
objective function, 529, 530, 533–537
occlusion, 330, 342, 373, 658, 790, 836
occupancy grid, 658
OCR, 7, 233, 329, 355, 544, 545, 548
octrees, 111
opening, 692–693
operator
    morphological, 686
    Zadeh, 434
optical axis, 598
optical center, 598
optical flow, 633, 648, 788, **794–804**, 809
    computation, 788, 789
    field, 648
    global and local estimation, 797
    method
        CLG, 800
        combined local-global, 800
        least square, 800
        variational, 800
    real-time, 800
optimization, 206, 207, 235, 397, 400, 412, **426–431**, 487
orthographic
    projection, 13, 646, 648
    view, 646
OUTEX, 762
over-fitting, 400, 441

P

PAL, 14
palette, 38, 734
parallel implementation, 8, 102, 108, 195, 217, 466, 509, 527, 529, 542, 627, 689, 797
particle filter, 831, **837–840**
partition function, 553
path, 17
    simple, 195
pattern, 391
    space, 391
    vector, 391
pattern recognition, 385–421
    capacity, 401
    statistical, 390, 413, 414
    syntactic, 413–421
PCA, *see* principal component analysis
PDM, **481–491**, 817
    alignment, 482
    covariance matrix, 484, 485
    eigen-decomposition, 484
    landmark, **482**, 483, 485, 487–489
    polar, 490
    polynomial regression, 490
perception, 25, 27, 465, 769
    human, 15, 25, 651
    visual, 25
perceptron, 409
perimeter, 193, 222, 223, 332, 337, 684
perspective
    projection, *see* projection, perspective, 648
photo-emission, 40
photometry, 89
photosensitive, 40
picture element, 15
pixel, 15
    adjacency, 17
    hexagonal, 15
planning, 465
point
    focal, 83
    of interest, 155
    principal, 83
    representative, 685
    sampling, 14
    sets (morphological), 685

simple, 368
    vanishing, 609, 675
point distribution model, *see* PDM
polynomial
    characteristic, 73
post-processing, 505, 534, 535, 542
power spectrum, 31, 81
pre-processing, 116–165, 467, 506
    classification, 116
    local, 125
precision, 241
predicate logic, 387, 389
predictor-controller, 831
primal sketch, 586–587, 655
    curvature, 346
primitive
    texture, 651
    volumetric, 587
principal component analysis, 74, 820
principal point, 83
principle
    superposition, 51
    uncertainty, 57
probability, 80
    density, 80, 398
        estimation, 398
    distribution, 80
problem
    aperture, 156
production
    rules, 387
    system, 387, 388, 465, 473
projection, 77, 355, 646, 648, 684
    histogram, 355
    orthographic, 13, 646, 648
    parallel, 13
    perspective, 12, 13, 589, 648
projection matrix, 600
projective reconstruction, 605
projective transformation, 592
PROLOG, 387
propagation theory, 552
pseudo-color, 38, 120
purposive vision, 589
pyramid, **108**, 225–227, 466, 730, 731
    equivalent window, 111
    irregular, 112
    Laplacian, 112

M-pyramid, 108
matrix, 108
reduction factor, 111
reduction window, 111
regular, 111
T-pyramid, 108
tree, 108

Q
quadric surface model, 663
quadtree, **109**, 225, 232, 335, 337, 354, 372, 731
qualitative vision, 588
quantization, 15
vector, 38
quench function, 704

R
R-table, 216
RADAR, 628
radial distortion, 88
radiance, 4, 90, 92
spectral, 93
radiant flux, 89
radiometry, 89
random dot stereograms, 624
random forest, 442–448, 517–524, 841
random sample consensus, *see* RANSAC
range image, 628, 663
RANSAC, 477–481
receptive field, 143
reconstruction
morphological, 706, 709
projective, 605
rectification, 616, 617
rectified configuration, 615
rectilinear cameras, 615
reduce, 690
redundancy, 24, 79, 125
information, 722–727
reflectance, 13, 92
coefficient, 94
function, 94
map, 94
surface, 92
reflectance function, 631
reflection
body, 31

surface, 31
region, **17**, 19
concavity tree, 364
convex, 22
decomposition, 353, **370–371**
growing, 179
identification, 333–335
skeleton, 348, 353, 365, 367, 369–371
region adjacency graph, 106
region adjacency graph , 112
region map, 106
regional extreme, 705
registration, *see* image, registration
relation
neighborhood, 102
spatial, 102
relational structure, 389, 413, 419, 421, 465
relaxation, 190, **525–530**, 533, 542, 552, 626, 633, 796, 797, 799
discrete, 525, 527
probabilistic, 527, 529
remote sensing, 120, 186, 187, 505, 532, 724
representation, 585
3D, 586
complete, 656
geometric, 101
iconic image, 101
intermediate, 13, 100
level of, 100
multi-view, 670
relational model, 101
segmented image, 101
skeleton, 662
unique, 656
reproducibility, 241
reproduction, 428, 429
resolution
radiometric, 14
spatial, 8, 14
spectral, 14
temporal, 8
time, 14
restoration, 162–165
deterministic, 162
geometric mean filtering, 165
inverse filtering, 163

power spectrum equalization, 165
stochastic, 162
Wiener filtering, 164
retina
cone, 32
rod, 32
rigidity constraint, 646
rim, 653
rod, 32
rotating mask, 129
rotational movement, 646, 648, 794
run length coding, **105**, 334, 372, 730

S
sampling, 14–15, 62–65
importance, 838
interval, 62
point, 14
saturation, 37
scale, 143–147, 312, 330, 586, 747–749, 755, 764
Scale Invariant Feature Transform, *see* SIFT
scale-space, 143, 330, 345, 346, 369, 374, 624
segmentation, 7, 178–232, 467
border detection, 197–204, 217
border tracing, 191–196, 208
extended, 193–195
inner, 191, 192
outer, 191–194
classification-based, 503–506
complete, 7, 178, 179, 218
dynamic programming, 206–210
edge thresholding, 188
edge-based, 179, **187–219**, 232
evaluation, 236–241
border positioning errors, 238–239
mutual overlap, 237–238
STAPLE, 241
supervised, 237–239
unsupervised, 240–241
fuzzy connectivity, 280–288
global, 179
Hough transform, 210–217
generalized, 215, 217
match-based, 235

mean shift, 255–262
morphological, 713
multi-thresholding, 182
partial, 7, 178, 187, 188, 218
region construction
from borders, 218
from partial borders, 219
region growing, 179, 220–232, 531, 534, 542
color image, 220
merging, 193, 221–224
over-growing, 232
semantic, 531–534
split-and-merge, 225
splitting, 222, 224, 225
under-growing, 232
region-based, 179, 195, 220–229
semantic, 531
region growing, 532–534
texture, 431
thresholding, **179–187**, 219, 223, 225
minimum error, 183
multi-spectral, 186
Otsu, 183, 184
p-tile, 181, 188
tree, 225, 227
watersheds, 229, 534
self-occlusion, 621
semantic net, 389, 465, 524
semantics, 4, 386, 389, 527, 531, 535, 542
sensor
CCD, 41
photo-emission, 40
photosensitive, 40
separable
linearly, 391
separable filter, 127
set difference, 685
shading, 631
Shannon sampling theorem, 14, 63
shape, 329–373, 655
class, 330, 373
description
area, 337, 342, **354–355**, 356–358, 371
bending energy, 339
border length, 337, 339

chord distribution, 340
compactness, 193, 353, **357**, 537
contour-based, 330, 332, **335–353**
convex hull, 360, 361, 364
cross ratio, 350
curvature, 332, **337**, 343–348, 370
direction, 353, **357**
eccentricity, 356
elongatedness, 330, 353, **356**, 357, 369
Euler's number, 355
external, 330, 332
Fourier descriptors, 339, **341–342**
graph, 353, **365**
height, 355
internal, 330, 332
invariants, 349, 350, 352
moments, 342, 348, 357, **358–360**, 371
moments, area-based, 360
moments, contour-based, 360
perimeter, 193, 222, 223, 332, **337**
polygonal, **343–345**, 346, 371
projection-invariant, 331, 349
projections, 355
rectangularity, 353, **357**
region concavity tree, 364
region-based, 330, 332, 348, **353–373**
run length, 334, 372
segment sequence, 339, **343**
signature, 339
sphericity, 357
spline, **346–348**, 817
statistical, 330, 353
syntactic, 329, 330, 344, 371
width, 355
primitive, 370
shape from
contour, 653
de-focus, 653
focus, 652
motion, 644–651
optical flow, 648

shading, 631–634, 652
stereo, 621–627
texture, 651–652
vergence, 653
X, 586, 644
sharpening, 135
shrink, 690
SIFT, 474–477, 479
key location, 474
sifting, 51
signal, 11
signal-to-noise ratio, 29
silhouette, 654
simple contiguous, 18
simulated annealing, 430, 431
Simultaneous Localization and Mapping, *see* SLAM
singular point, 633
singular value decomposition, 73, 148
skeleton, 348, 353, 365, 367, 369–371, 662, 684, 699–702
by influence zones, 707
by maximal balls, 700
skew, 122
SKIZ, skeleton by influence zones, 707
SLAM, 815
slant, 651
smart snake, 487
smoothing, 125–127
averaging, 125
averaging according to inverse gradient, 129
averaging with limited data validity, 128
edge preserving, 125
Gaussian, 345
non-linear mean filter, 133
order statistics, 132
rank filtering, 132
rotating mask, 129
snake, 218, **263–273**, 789
B-snakes, 268
finite difference, 268
finite element, 268
Fourier, 268
gradient vector flow, 268–272
growing, 266
GVF, 268–272

Hermite polynomial, 268
united, 268
SNR, 29
spatial angle, 90
spatial element, 281
spectral
BRDF, 93
density, 81
irradiance, 93
radiance, 93
spectrophotometer, 31
spectrum, 81
frequency, 150, 151, 711
granulometric, 711
power, 31
spel, *see* spatial element
spline, 264
STAPLE, 241
state space search, 222
stereo
correspondence, 431, 645
photometric, 635
vision, 233, 609, 645
stereopsis, 609
STFT—short time FT, 58
stochastic process, 79–81
stationary, 81
uncorrelated, 80
structure from motion theorem, 646
structured light, 628
structuring element (morphological), 685
sufficient statistics, 562
super-quadrics, 660
supergrid, 193, 222, 223
superposition principle, 51
support vector, 400, 402
support vector machine, 392, 400–405,
762
kernel function, 403
margin, 400, 441
surface
coupled, 303
detection, 288
multiple, 308, 310, 311
optimal, 303, 317
single, 306, 308
free-form, 655
reflection, 31

SVD, *see* singular value decomposition
SVM, *see* support vector machine
sweep representations, 661
symbol
non-terminal, 415
terminal, 415
syntactic analysis, **415–420**, 770–772
syntax, 4, 386
system approach, 143
system theory, 584

T
telecentric lens, 85
template matching, 233–236, 474, 513
tensor
multiview, 605
terahertz, 1, 7
test set, 397
texel, 651, 652, 747
texton, 750, 755
texture, 178, 179, 181, 187, 221, 431,
503, 506, 509, 651, **747–
776**, 830
Brodatz, 751, 760, 761, 767
coarse, 747, 749–752, 755, 769
description
auto-correlation, 750
autocorrelation, 769
autoregression model, 769
chain grammar, 770
co-occurrence, 752, 753
discrete transform, 751
edge frequency, 754
fractal, 762, 770
grammar, 770
graph grammar, 772, 773, 775
hybrid, 749, 769, 775–776
Laws' energy measures, 757
morphology, 768
multiscale, 764–768
optical transform, 751
peak and valley, 769
primitive grouping, 773
primitive length, 755
run length, 755
shape rules, 770
statistical, 749–769, 773, 775
syntactic, 749, 769–775

texture properties, 754
texture transform, 768
wavelet frames, 764–768
wavelets, 761, 764–768
deterministic tourist walk, 769
element, 747
fine, 747, 749–752, 755, 769
gradient, 651, 652
hierarchical, 773
LBP, 757–762, 776
    uniform, 759
local ternary patterns, 762
measure
    uniformity, 759
primitive, 219, 651, **747**, 749, 769,
    770, 772, 774, 775
segmentation, 755, 768, 773–775
strong, 749, 775
structure, 747, 749
synthesis, 770, 771
template
    microstructure, 759
tone, 747, 749, 776
weak, 749, 775
theory, computational, 585
thickening, 684, 701–702
    sequential, 702
thin lens, 83
thinning, 353, 365–367, 369, 684, 701–
    702
    sequential, 701
threshold, 179
    optimal, 183
    Otsu, 183, 184
    selection, 179, 181
        optimal, 183
thresholding, 118, 282, 554
    adaptive, 179
    optimal, 183
    with hysteresis, 146
TIFF, 734
tilt, 651
tolerance interval, 343
top surface (morphological), 694
top-down approach, 418, 419, 467, 468
topology, 22
    discrete, 19
tracking, 814

kernel, 820–826
mean shift, 820–826
Predator, 840, 842
semi-supervised, 840–843
TLD, 840–843
training set, 393, **396–397**, 398, 400,
    406, 410, 420, 421, 482, 503,
    508
transformation
    affine, 122
    anti-extensive, 691
    bilinear, 121
    binary, 727
    brightness correction, 117
    cosine, 727, 732
    discrete wavelet, 69
    distance, 19, 369
    fast wavelet, 69
    Fourier, 14, 19, 53–64, 77, 125, 135,
        148–150, 152, 163, 164, 234,
        330, 341, 342, 549, 727, 751
        inverse, 59
    Gabor, 761, 764
    geodesic, 707
    geometric, 120–124
        brightness interpolation, 123
        change of scale, 122
        pixel co-ordinate, 121
        rotation, 122
        skewing, 122
    gray-scale, 117–120
        histogram equalization, 118–120
        logarithmic, 120
        pseudo-color, 120
        thresholding, 118
    Haar, 68
    Hadamard, 79, 727, 732
    Hadamard-Haar, 78
    hat, 124, 141
    homotopic, 699
    Hotelling, 74
    Hough, 78, **210–217**, 348, 652
    increasing, 689, 691
    inverse, 692
    Karhunen-Loève, 74, 724
    morphological, 686
    Paley, 78
    pixel brightness, 117–120

pixel co-ordinate, 121
projective, 592
Radon, 77–78, 211, 355
recursive block coding, 727
reversible component, 736
rubber sheet, 22
sine, 78
Slant-Haar, 78
symmetric axis, 369
top hat, 698
Walsh, 78, 727
wavelet, 66, 764
z, 764
translation, morphological, 686
translational movement, 646, 648, 801, 803
transmission
progressive, 731, 732
smart, 732
tree
decision, 443
interval, 345
pruning, 202, 418
triangulation, 603
trichromacy, 32
trifocal tensor, 620

U
ultimate erosion, 705
umbra (morphological), 694
uncertainty principle, 57
unit ball, 700
unsharp masking, 135
unsupervised learning, 406
upper semi-continuity, 687

V
vanishing point, 609, 652, 675
vector quantization, 38
velocity
field, 789
computation, 808
smoothness constraint, 795, 797
vector, 788
vergence, 653
vertex, 656
view
topographic (morphology), 694

viewing space, 670
viewing sphere, 670
viewpoint, 13
vignetting, 91
vision
active, 648
stereo, 233, 609, 645
view-based, 670
VISIONS, 473, 474
visual
potential, 671
system human, 25, 586, 609, 646, 648, 732, 769
Viterbi algorithm, 206, 546, 548
volumetric model, 658
volumetric primitives, 587
voxel, **15**, 185, 658

W
watersheds, 229, 714
wavelet, 66, 67, 764–768
energy
signature, 766
frames, 764–768
discrete, 764
mother, 67
packet, 72
weighted graph, 106
white balancing, 40
white noise, 28
Wiener filtering, 164

X
XBox, 517
Kinect, 517

Z
Zadeh operators, 434
zero-crossing, 136, **139**, 145, 345, 586, 624, 755
Zuniga–Haralick operator, 157, 805